mar·ket·ing

Marketing is the activity, set of institutions, and processes for creating, *capturing,* communicating, delivering, and exchanging offerings that have value for customers, clients, partners, and society at large.

The definition of marketing, established by the American Marketing Association, October 2007.

Marketing

Fifth Edition

Dhruv Grewal, PhD
Babson College

Michael Levy, PhD
Babson College

MARKETING, FIFTH EDITION

Published by McGraw-Hill Education, 2 Penn Plaza, New York, NY 10121. Copyright © 2016 by McGraw-Hill Education. All rights reserved. Printed in the United States of America. Previous edition © 2014, 2012, 2010, and 2008. No part of this publication may be reproduced or distributed in any form or by any means, or stored in a database or retrieval system, without the prior written consent of McGraw-Hill Education, including, but not limited to, in any network or other electronic storage or transmission, or broadcast for distance learning.

Some ancillaries, including electronic and print components, may not be available to customers outside the United States.

This book is printed on acid-free paper.

2 3 4 5 6 7 8 9 0 DOR/DOR 1 0 9 8 7 6 5

ISBN   978-0-07-772902-8
MHID   0-07-772902-1

Senior Vice President, Products & Markets: *Kurt L. Strand*
Vice President, General Manager, Products & Markets: *Michael Ryan*
Vice President, Content Design & Delivery: *Kimberly Meriwether David*
Managing Director: *Susan Gouijnstook*
Brand Managers: *Sankha Basu* and *Kim Leistner*
Director, Product Development: *Meghan Campbell*
Lead Product Developer: *Kelly Delso*
Digital Product Analyst: *Kerry Shanahan*
Director, Content Design & Delivery: *Terri Schiesl*
Program Manager: *Mary Conzachi*
Content Project Managers: *Christine Vaughan, Danielle Clement*, and *Judy David*
Buyer: *Carol A. Bielski*
Design: *Matt Diamond*
Content Licensing Specialist: *Keri Johnson*
Cover Image: *Shutterstock © amalia19*
Compositor: *Aptara®, Inc.*
Typeface: *10/12 Palatino LT Std*
Printer: *R. R. Donnelley*

Section/chapter opener coffee image: *Jonelle Weaver/Getty Images*

All credits appearing on page or at the end of the book are considered to be an extension of the copyright page.

Library of Congress Cataloging-in-Publication Data

Grewal, Dhruv.
    Marketing / Dhruv Grewal, PhD, Babson College, Michael Levy, PhD, Babson
    College.—Fifth Edition.
      pages cm
    ISBN 978-0-07-772902-8 (alk. paper)—ISBN 0-07-772902-1 (alk. paper)
    1. Marketing. I. Levy, Michael, 1950- II. Title.
HF5415.G675 2016
658.8—dc23

                              2014046046

www.mhhe.com

To our families for their never-ending support.

To my wife Diana; and my children, Lauren and Alex;
and my uncle and aunt, Anji and Jeet Seth.

—Dhruv Grewal

To my wife, Marcia, and daughter, Eva.

—Michael Levy

about the authors

Dhruv Grewal

Dhruv Grewal, PhD (Virginia Tech), is the Toyota Chair in Commerce and Electronic Business and a professor of marketing at Babson College. He is listed in The World's Most Influential Scientific Minds, Thompson Reuters 2014 (only eight from the marketing field and 95 from economics and business are listed). He was awarded the 2013 university-wide Distinguished Graduate Alumnus from his alma mater, Virginia Tech, the 2012 Lifetime Achievement Award in Pricing (AMA Retailing & Pricing SIG), the 2010 Lifetime Achievement Award in Retailing (AMA Retailing SIG), the 2010 AMS Cutco/Vector Distinguished Educator Award, the 2010 Lifetime Achievement Award in Retailing (AMA Retailing SIG), and in 2005 the Lifetime Achievement in Behavioral Pricing Award (Fordham University, November 2005). He is a Distinguished Fellow of the Academy of Marketing Science. He was ranked first in the marketing field in terms of publications in the top-six marketing journals during the 1991–1998 period and again for the 2000–2007 period. He ranked eighth in terms of publications in JM and JMR during the 2009–2013 period and ranked seventh in terms of publications in *Journal of Public Policy & Marketing* for the period 1992–2001. He was also ranked first in terms of publications and third in citations for pricing research for the time period 1980–2010 in 20 marketing and business publications. He has served as VP, research and conferences, American Marketing Association Academic Council (1999–2001), and as VP, development for the Academy of Marketing Science (2000–2002). He was co-editor of *Journal of Retailing* from 2001 to 2007. He co-chaired the 1993 Academy of Marketing Science Conference, the 1998 Winter American Marketing Association Conference, the 2001 AMA doctoral consortium, the American Marketing Association 2006 Summer Educators Conference, the 2011 DMEF research summit, and the 2012 and 2015 AMA/ACRA Retailing Conference.

Professor Grewal has published over 120 articles in journals such as the *Journal of Retailing, Journal of Marketing, Journal of Consumer Research, Journal of Marketing Research, Journal of Consumer Psychology, Journal of Applier Psychology,* and *Journal of the Academy of Marketing Science,* as well as other journals. He currently serves on numerous editorial review boards, such as the *Journal of Retailing, Journal of Marketing, Journal of Consumer Psychology, Journal of the Academy of Marketing Science, Academy of Marketing Science Review, Journal of Interactive Marketing, Journal of Business Research,* and *Journal of Public Policy & Marketing.* He has over 21,000 citations based on Google scholar.

He has won a number of awards for his teaching: 2005 Sherwin-Williams Distinguished Teaching Award, Society for Marketing Advances; 2003 American Marketing Association Award for Innovative Excellence in Marketing Education; 1999 Academy of Marketing Science Great Teachers in Marketing Award; Executive MBA Teaching Excellence Award (1998); School of Business Teaching Excellence Awards (1993, 1999); and Virginia Tech Certificate of Recognition for Outstanding Teaching (1989). He has won numerous awards for his research: William R. Davidson JR Best Paper Awards 2010 and 2012, Luis W. Stern Award 2011 (AMA IO Sig), William R. Davidson Journal of Retailing Honorable Mention Awards 2010 and 2011, Babson College Faculty Scholarship Award (2010), University of Miami School of Business Research Excellence Award for the years 1991, 1995, 1996, and 1998, Best Services Paper Award (AMA Services SIG 2002), Stanley C. Hollander Best Retailing Paper (AMS 2002 and 2008) and M. Wayne DeLozier Best Conference Paper (AMS 2002 and 2008). He also received Best Reviewer Awards (*Journal of Retailing* 2008, *Journal of Marketing* 2014) and a Distinguished Service Award (*Journal of Retailing* 2009).

Professor Grewal has taught executive seminars and courses and/or worked on research projects with numerous firms, such as Dell, ExxonMobil, IRI, Radio Shack, Telcordia, Khimetriks, Profit-Logic, McKinsey, Ericsson, Motorola, Nextel, FP&L, Lucent, Sabre, Goodyear Tire & Rubber Company, Sherwin-Williams and Asahi. He has delivered seminars in the United States, Europe, Latin America, and Asia. He has also served as an expert witness or worked as a consultant on numerous legal cases.

Michael Levy

Michael Levy, PhD (Ohio State University), is the Charles Clarke Reynolds Professor of Marketing and director of the Retail Supply Chain Institute at Babson College. He received his PhD in business administration from The Ohio State University and his undergraduate and MS degrees in business administration from the University of Colorado at Boulder. He taught at Southern Methodist University before joining the faculty as professor and chair of the marketing department at the University of Miami.

Professor Levy was recognized for 25 years of dedicated service to the editorial review board of the *Journal of Retailing* in 2011. He won the McGraw-Hill Corporate Achievement Award for Grewal–Levy *Marketing 2e* with Connect in the category of excellence in content and analytics (2010); Revision of the Year for *Marketing 2e* (Grewal–Levy) from McGraw-Hill/Irwin (2010); the Babson Faculty Scholarship Award (2009); and the Distinguished Service Award, *Journal of Retailing* (2009) (at winter AMA). He was rated as one of the best researchers in marketing in a survey published in *Marketing Educator* (Summer 1997). He has developed a strong stream of research in retailing, business logistics, financial retailing strategy, pricing, and sales management. He has published over 50 articles in leading marketing and logistics journals, including the *Journal of Retailing, Journal of Marketing, Journal of the Academy of Marketing Science,* and *Journal of Marketing Research.* He has served on the editorial review boards of the *Journal of Retailing, Journal of the Academy of Marketing Science, International Journal of Physical Distribution and Materials Management, International Journal of Business Logistics, ECR Journal, European Business Review,* and has been on the editorial advisory boards of *European Retail Research* and the *European Business Review.* He is co-author of *Retailing Management,* 9e (2014), the best-selling college-level retailing text in the world. Professor Levy was co-editor of the *Journal of Retailing* from 2001 to 2007. He co-chaired the 1993 Academy of Marketing Science conference and the 2006 summer AMA conference.

Professor Levy has worked in retailing and related disciplines throughout his professional life. Prior to his academic career, he worked for several retailers and a housewares distributor in Colorado. He has performed research projects with many retailers and retail technology firms, including Accenture, Federated Department Stores, Khimetrics (SAP), Mervyn's, Neiman Marcus, ProfitLogic (Oracle), Zale Corporation, and numerous law firms.

New to the Fifth Edition

Some exciting new additions to the Fifth Edition!

Chapter 1, Overview of Marketing, starts with a discussion of Starbucks' success and the role of marketing in it. There is a new Superior Service box on how the Sol Wave House is incorporating twitter to enhance customers' experience there. A new Social and Mobile Marketing box that discusses how companies are partnering with social media sites such as Twitter and Facebook appears in this chapter. There is a new Adding Value on new innovations in the "smart" market. Also, a new Ethical and Societal Dilemma box on how firms are using the location technology in smartphones has been added. Finally, we conclude with a new case study highlighting Starbucks' growth strategy, a nice tie-back to the opener and the cover concept.

CHAPTER 1

OVERVIEW OF MARKETING

LEARNING OBJECTIVES

LO1 Define the role of marketing in organizations.

LO2 Describe how marketers create value for a product or service.

LO3 Understand why marketing is important both within and outside the firm.

Showing a remarkable flair for understatement, the CEO of Starbucks, Howard Schultz, recently admitted, "We have a lot going on."¹ Let's think about all the things Starbucks is doing at the moment, in its attempt to market itself as an appealing product and service provider for all its customers, both current and potential.

Its ubiquitous stores—from the long-standing locations in U.S. cities and towns to international expansion into a vast range of new nations—are easy to locate and visit. A recent count showed that the chain maintains more than 20,000 stores, spanning 62 countries.² By making sure its stores, with their familiar siren logo, are easy to find, Starbucks guarantees that most people can readily find a place to get their coffee fix. For the vast majority of buyers,

an addictive Salted Caramel Mocha, or just a grea[...] black coffee, is convenient to find and very familia[...]

Starbucks vigorously competes with the [...] McDonald's, Dunkin' Donuts, and independent [...] houses. Not too long ago, McDonald's was no[...] competitor in the coffee market because all it s[...] plain coffee. But when it started promoting its [...] Starbucks was quick to respond, to make sure it [...] the lead. Starbucks' "coffee war" with Dunkin' D[...] famous in the areas in which they compete head[...] although each chain has its geographic stron[...] Dunkin' in the East and Starbucks in the West.³ [...] dent coffeehouses and smaller regional chains, [...] many as being more hip and less commercial, also[...] ually nip at Starbucks' heels.

Starbucks continues to innovate and expand with a variety of products, making them available in various locations beyond its own stores. Unsatisfied with dominating just the coffee market, it added Tazo teas to its product line early in its history; more recently it purchased the Teavana chain of tea stores.⁴ In addition, it purchased the Evolution Fresh line of fresh juices, sells bags of its own brand of ground coffee and whole beans, as well as coffee-flavored ice cream in not only its own stores but also in grocery stores. But the expansion is not limited to beverages. For example, Starbucks' latest

collaboration with Danone, the yogurt company, is developing a new line of dairy products called Evolution Fresh to sell in various outlets.⁵

There are plenty of jokes about how Starbucks manages to charge upwards of $5 for a jolt of caffeine, but a quick glance at its marketing methods and strategies helps explain why it can do so. The products it sells are appealing to customers and fulfill their needs; they taste good, are available readily and conveniently, and offer the benefit of helping them wake up to start their day (or stay awake for a long night of studying). Thus the exchange of money for

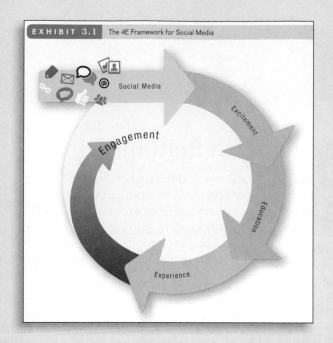

EXHIBIT 3.1 The 4E Framework for Social Media

Social Media

Excitement

Engagement

Education

Experience

Chapter 2, Developing Marketing Strategies and a Marketing Plan, begins with a comparison between Nike vs. adidas that weaves throughout the chapter. We introduce a new Adding Value box highlighting how online retail meets brick and mortar: Tesco's HomePlus virtual stores. There is a new Ethical and Societal Dilemma addressing the safety concerns for factory workers in the garment industry. Finally, a new case study highlighting the yogurt wars—Pinkberry versus Red Mango—closes this chapter.

Chapter 3, Social and Mobile Marketing, starts by highlighting the success Gatorade has experienced with its innovative Social Media Mission Control Center. We introduce a new 4E framework visual in Exhibit 3.1. There is a new Social and Mobile Marketing box on how Lexus and Jimmy Fallon launched an original campaign that engaged viewers via social media. Exhibit 3.2 uses new examples to illustrate different social media campaigns. We introduced a description of Instagram in the Media-Sharing Sites section. The Going Mobile and Social section was redesigned to describe the seven primary motivations for mobile app usage (Exhibit 3.4) and the different App pricing models. A new Exhibit 3.5 illustrates Apple App Store revenue by app category pricing models. We conclude this chapter with a new case study: Images, Sales, Brands: How Red Bull Uses Various Social Media Techniques to Achieve All Its Objectives.

We start **Chapter 4,** Marketing Ethics, by highlighting ethical concerns with computer cookies used by marketers to track customers' web activity. Exhibit 4.5 highlights the CRS programs for 10 major companies. We end the chapter with a new case study examining the ethical concerns related to new technologies designed for young children.

Social & Mobile Marketing **3.1**   Late-Night Laughs to Order[i]

Social media appear to have brought us full circle. In the early days of television, nearly all the advertisements were live. Then taping became the main method. But as recent technologies have made it easy for viewers to speed past or completely skip the advertising messages, some marketers are revisiting the idea of live advertising. This isn't the same old notion though. By recombining an idea from broadcast media with new functionalities enabled by social media, marketers seek to ensure that viewers are not only interested in the new content but even might determine it.

A Lexus-sponsored program, "It's Your Move After Dark," ran on *Late Night with Jimmy Fallon* over the course of four weeks. During the first commercial break on each Thursday's show, a Lexus advertisement prominently displayed a hashtag. By linking to it, viewers could submit their ideas for commercials. Then in a later advertising break during the same show, an improvisational comedy troupe acted out the chosen ideas. The acting troupes—Fun Young Guys, Magnet Theater Touring Company, MB's Dream and Stone Cold Fox—were all from New York, well known for their comedy. In actuality, their performances took place under the Brooklyn Bridge, adding to the vibrancy and reality of the setting.

To appeal to the widest audience of Fallon fans possible, separate advertisements were chosen and enacted for the East and West Coast broadcasts. The submissions came through a wide variety of media channels, including Facebook, Twitter, and Tumblr. Such ready access, real-time

In an innovative campaign, Jimmy Fallon viewers could submit ideas for Lexus commercials via Twitter and see an improvised version later in the night on the show.

interactivity, and potential influence—together with the promise of funny, totally new advertising content and perhaps even a live, on-air goof—promised that Fallon's youthful, edgy audience wanted to tune in to the commercials, as much as they did to the show.

The advertisements are not the only way Fallon has relied on social media to connect with his audience of course. He has nearly 10 million Twitter followers, and on a regular basis he challenges them to post the funniest, silliest, or craziest responses to topics he provides, such as "#howigotfired," "#whydonttheymakethat," and "#awkwarddate." The best contributions are highlighted on Fallon's Twitter feed but also might make it onto the network broadcast, as he reads out his favorite bits. That is, the consumers of his content also provide some of that content.

On the flip side, content from the traditional television channel constantly makes it onto social media sites. Excerpts from Fallon's shows are some of the most popular YouTube videos, including a skit in which President Barack Obama "slow jams" the news, a sing-along with Carly Rae Jepson and the Roots of "Call Me Maybe" using found materials as instruments, and of course, any skits featuring his pal Justin Timberlake.

As Fallon moves from *Late Night* to the *Tonight Show,* he promises that such tactics and antics will continue. As long as he keeps his viewers excited and willing to contribute and engage with him, his social media dominance appears likely to persist, regardless of what time he appears on people's televisions.

Chapter 5, Analyzing the Marketing Environment, begins with a discussion of a how hotels are responding to new customer needs—for example, by offering increasingly extensive accommodations for pets. A new Social and Mobile Marketing box discusses the discrepancies between where marketers are devoting their media budget and what types of media Millennials actually interact with. A new Adding Value box pertaining to how marketers successfully and unsuccessfully use gender-based marketing strategies has been added. There is also a new Adding Value box discussing a recent trend in grocery stores to have in-house dietitians highlight healthy food options. A new Ethical and Social Dilemma box pertaining to the use of palm oil in General Mills' products has been added. A new Social & Mobile Marketing box on the 2014 Consumer Electronics Show (CES) is also presented.

Chapter 6, Consumer Behavior, begins with discussing Google Glasses and other wearable technologies. The following new boxes are added: Ethical and Societal Dilemma on how Google is punishing companies that use questionable techniques to improve their search engine optimization; Social and Mobile Marketing on the new health-related apps; Superior Service on the success of H-E-B supermarkets; and another new Social and Mobile Marketing box on how Sephora implements cross-channel marketing.

Chapter 7, Business-to-Business Marketing, starts with an interesting discussion on how 3D printing could potentially change B2B marketing. A new Superior Service on applications of IBM's Watson computer was added. The chapter ends with a new case study on how Levi Strauss & Co. buys materials to manufacture jeans.

Chapter 8, Global Marketing, has a new opener highlighting Coca-Cola's efforts to expand its market share in India. The Choosing a Global Marketing Strategy section has been restructured around the three primary strategies companies employ. New boxes include an Ethical and Societal Dilemma about how Chinese regulations have changed car-buying trends; a Social and Mobile Marketing box that compares and contrasts Facebook's strategies for entering Brazil and China; an Adding Value box examining Starbucks' entrance into the Indian market; another Adding Value box contrasting Ford's and Chevy's strategies to bring their American muscle cars into the global market; and a Superior Service describing the success of Alibaba. Finally, there is a new case study at the conclusion of this chapter that highlights the globalization of McDonald's.

Chapter 9, Segmentation, Marketing, and Positioning, opens with how Netflix targeted different segments in regards to its new original shows. New boxes include a Social and Mobile Marketing box highlighting Facebook's struggle to remain relevant while gaining popularity among an older audience; a Superior Service on how

CHAPTER 8

GLOBAL MARKETING

LEARNING OBJECTIVES

LO1 Describe the components of a country market assessment.

LO2 Understand the marketing opportunities in BRIC countries.

LO3 Identify the various market entry strategies.

LO4 Highlight the similarities and differences between a domestic marketing strategy and a global marketing strategy.

Reviewing the tumultuous history and modern operations of Coca-Cola in India is like taking a quick survey of global marketing issues. From early failures to notable impacts on local regulations to joint efforts to growth efforts, the story of how this global brand has sought to make its mark in this developing nation is instructive.

When Coke first thought to move into India in the 1970s, it confronted a critical cultural difference between its home base and this foreign market. India was officially closed to foreign investment at the time, which meant that to enter, Coke would have to find an equal, Indian partner. Such a joint venture partnership would have required it to share its famously protected, secret formula

for making its carbonated beverage. It was totally unwilling to do so, thus it left for more than 20 years.

But as many developing nations have, India liberalized its economy, opening it to more foreign investments and offering more opportunities for foreign companies to enter. Accordingly, Coca-Cola came back in the mid-1990s,[1] but only a few years after its primary rival Pepsi had established a strong base there. To ensure its competitiveness and expand its coverage of the Indian consumer market, Coke bought four local soda brands from the Indian company Parle, so that it gained about 60 percent of the market, far outpacing Pepsi's 30 percent. Yet Coke itself is not the most popular carbonated drink. That distinction belongs to Thums Up, one of the Indian brands Coca-Cola purchased.[2]

Thus, Coke still faces some critical problems in the Indian market. In particular, people just don't drink that much Coke. Whereas the average global consumer drinks 92 bottles of Coke each year, the average

How the World Buys Its Coke
2011 per capita consumption of 8-ounce servings of Coke beverages in select countries

U.S. 403
Mexico 728
France 149
Brazil 230
India 12
South Africa 247
Russia 73
China 38

Source: Coca-Cola

Coke is a top global brand. However, its typical customer in India only buys 12 bottles per year, compared to 728 in Mexico, making India a country with enormous growth potential.

airline companies are using the data they collect to improve customer experiences; an Ethical and Societal Dilemma box discussing the ethical issues regarding loyalty programs; an Adding Value examining the cancellation of the show *Longmire*; and another new Adding Value box discussing *Self* magazine's repositioning strategy.

Chapter 10, Marketing Research, begins with a discussion about the marketing research Disney undertakes to better serve its customers. The Internal Secondary Data section now includes information regarding big data. There are several new boxes including a Superior Service examining the pros and cons of McDonald's extending its breakfast hours; a Social and Mobile Marketing highlighting the difficulties Nielsen is facing because of new trends in television watching behavior; another Superior Service illustrating the accuracy of Google Analytics in regard to the success of movies; and a new Ethical and Societal Dilemma discussing the ethical concerns surrounding the use of mannequins equipped with recording tools.

Chapter 11, Product, Branding, and Packaging Decisions, begins with a new opener on Red Bull's branding strategy. A new Ethical and Societal Dilemma box about Coca-Cola's promise to stop advertising to children has been added. This chapter also includes a new Adding Value box regarding American Airlines' rebranding strategy.

Chapter 12, Developing New Products, begins with another discussion of the applications of 3D printing, this time in regard to the development of innovative new products across various industries. The chapter concludes with a new case study analyzing the launch of Google Glass.

Chapter 13, Services: The Intangible Products, includes an opening vignette that describes how companies like Samsung and Seamless food delivery service are using Twitter to provide excellent customer service. A new Social and Mobile Marketing box discusses how American Express connects its customers with deals via its Twitter account and TripAdvisor.

Chapter 14, Pricing Concepts for Establishing Value, describes pricing concepts using new examples from Procter & Gamble (opening vignette) and Disney and Universal theme parks (Superior Service box). The influence of the Internet and economic factors on pricing are now integrated throughout the chapter and book. The chapter ends with a new case study on Planet Fitness.

Chapter 15, Strategic Pricing Methods, opens with an examination of McDonald's unsuccessful launch of its Mighty Wing product line and the general effect that McDonald's has on market prices. New examples in this chapter include an Adding Value box describing how various companies are changing the meaning of value options to refer to the benefits they offer; another Adding Value box discussing Walmart's expansion into the organic food market; and a new Ethical and Societal Dilemma box highlighting instances of price fixing in the candy industry.

McDonald's announced plans to introduce chicken wings for a limited time, between September and November. It also released projections that it would sell approximately 250 million orders. Even before the McDonald's Mighty Wings appeared on any menus, prices jumped, based mainly on predictions.

Of course, in anticipation of its menu addition, McDonald's also started stockpiling its inventory of wings.

It did so in grand fashion, purchasing approximately 50 million pounds of wings, which left other wing joints struggling to find supply of wings and chicken producers searching for buyers for the other parts of their chickens. Accordingly, the price changes have been dramatic in the wholesale market, up from approximately $0.90 per pound to just over $2.00. The McDonald's effect is not limited to wings, either. Since the fast-food giant added

Chapter 16, Supply Chain and Channel Management, opens with a new vignette highlighting how exceptional channel and supply chain management has contributed to Amazon's success. The different bases of channel power are illustrated in a new exhibit. There is a new Superior Service box about the different strategies Amazon and Walmart are using to win the same-day grocery delivery market.

Chapter 17, Retailing and Omnichannel Marketing, begins with a discussion of how the implementation of omnichannel marketing has aided the success of H&M's flagship Times Square location. Other new examples include a Superior Service box about Trader Joe's; an Adding Value box highlighting the myWeeklyAd service offered to CVS ExtraCare members; and a Social and Mobile Marketing box detailing how Home Depot is improving customer experiences with modern technology.

Chapter 18, Integrated Marketing Communications, discusses the concepts that are important to consider regarding integrated marketing communications (IMC). A new Adding Value box appears highlighting the unique aspects of Jeep's celebrity endorsement strategy. There is a new Social and Mobile Marketing box examining how Google is using a combination of nostalgia and modern technology to promote various companies including Coca-Cola. Finally, there is a new case study accentuating Volvo's IMC strategy.

Chapter 19, Advertising, Public Relations, and Sales Promotions, starts with examinations of Chipotle's "Food with Integrity" and "Cultivating Thought" campaigns. There is a new Social and Mobile Marketing box on Twitter's advertising formats and future plans.

Chapter 20, Personal Selling and Sales Management, begins with a description of how the Boeing Companies' personal selling approach has engaged clients and made Boeing the top-ranking airline manufacturer. The chapter includes two new boxes, a Superior Service box on the cloud-based CRM system provided by Salseforce.com, and an Ethical & Societal Dilemma box analyzing the implications of realtors becoming reality TV stars.

Greater Learning

Across the country, instructors and students continue to raise an important question: How can courses further support students throughout the learning process to shape future business leaders? While there is no one solution, we see the impact of new learning technologies and innovative study tools that not only fully engage students in course material but also inform instructors of the students' skill and comprehension levels. Interactive learning tools, including those offered through McGraw-Hill Connect, are being implemented to increase teaching effectiveness and learning efficiency in thousands of colleges and universities. By facilitating a stronger connection with the course and incorporating the latest technologies—such as McGraw-Hill LearnSmart, an adaptive learning program—these tools enable students to succeed in their college careers, which will ultimately increase the percentage of students completing their postsecondary degrees and create the business leaders of the future.

McGraw-Hill Connect

McGraw-Hill *Connect*® is the leading online assignment and assessment solution that connects students with the tools and resources they need to achieve success while providing instructors with tools to quickly pick content and assignments according to the learning objectives they want to emphasize.

Connect improves student learning and retention by adapting to the individual student, reinforcing concepts with engaging presentations and activities that prepare students for class, help them master concepts, and review for exams.

Grade Distribution

Without LearnSmart	With LearnSmart
A 19.3%	A 30.5%
B 38.6%	B 33.5%
C 28.0%	C 22.6%

58% more A's with LearnSmart

Student Retention Rate

Without LearnSmart: 31% Dropout Rate

With LearnSmart: 20% Dropout Rate

35% fewer dropouts with LearnSmart

SmartBook

Fueled by LearnSmart, SmartBook is the first and only adaptive reading experience available today. SmartBook personalizes content for each student in a continuously adapting reading experience. Reading is no longer a passive and linear experience, but an engaging and dynamic one where students are more likely to master and retain important concepts, coming to class better prepared.

LearnSmart

LearnSmart is the most widely used and intelligent adaptive learning resource. It is proven to strengthen memory recall, improve course retention, and boost grades by distinguishing between what students know and what they don't know and honing in on the concepts that they are most likely to forget. LearnSmart continuously adapts to each student's needs by building an individual learning path. As a result, students study smarter and retain more knowledge.

SmartBook Achieve

Accelerate student success with SmartBook Achieve™—the first and only adaptive study experience that pinpoints individual student knowledge gaps and provides targeted, interactive help at the moment of need.

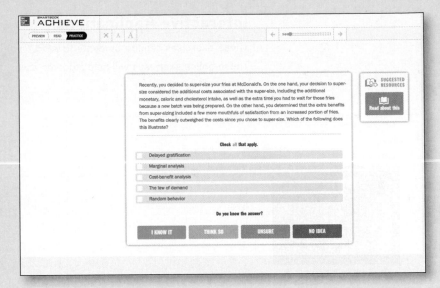

Interactive Presentations

Interactive Presentations within Connect are designed to reinforce learning by offering a visual presentation of the Learning Goals highlighted in every chapter of the text. Interactive Presentations are engaging, online, professional presentations (fully Section 508 compliant) covering the same core concepts directly from the chapter, while offering additional examples and graphics. Interactive Presentations teach students Learning Goals in a multimedia format, bringing the course and the book to life. Interactive Presentations are a great prep tool for students—when the students are better prepared, they are more engaged and better able to participate in class.

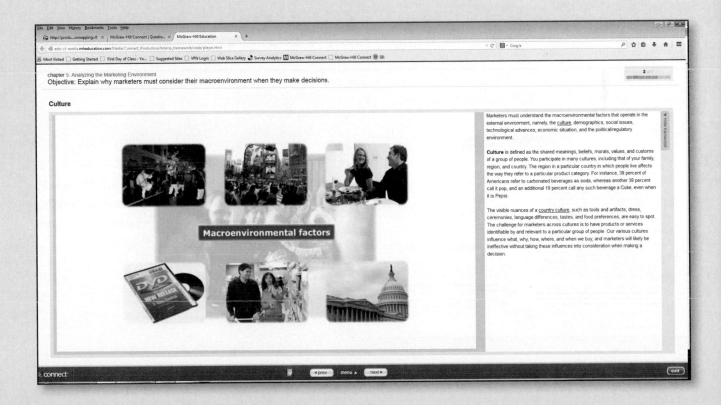

Interactive Applications

These exercises require students to APPLY what they have learned in a real-world scenario. These online exercises will help students assess their understanding of the concepts.

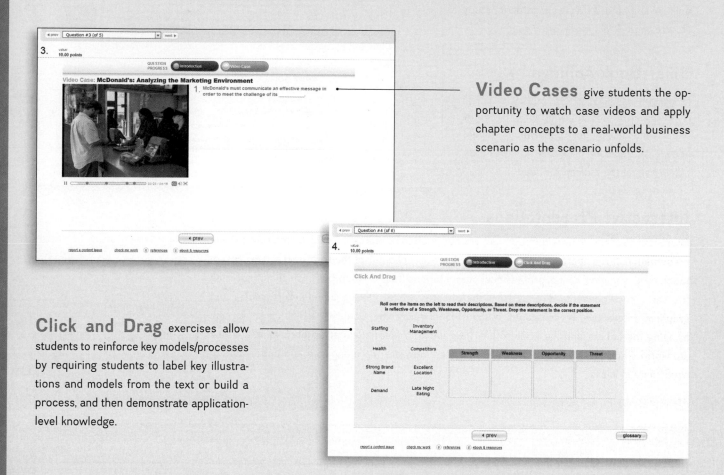

Video Cases give students the opportunity to watch case videos and apply chapter concepts to a real-world business scenario as the scenario unfolds.

Click and Drag exercises allow students to reinforce key models/processes by requiring students to label key illustrations and models from the text or build a process, and then demonstrate application-level knowledge.

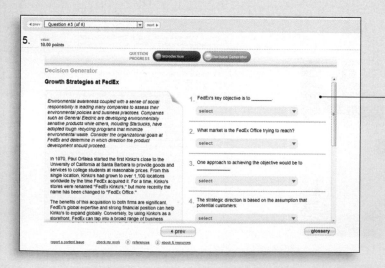

Decision Generators require students to make real business decisions based on specific real-world scenarios and cases.

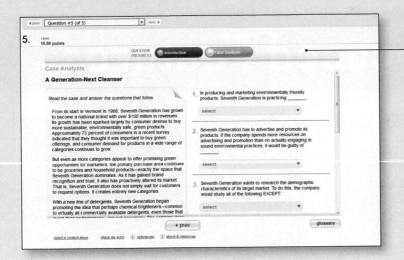

Case Analyses encourage students to read a case and answer closed-ended questions to demonstrate critical-thinking skills.

Integrated E-Book

- A web-optimized e-book is seamlessly integrated within Connect.

- Students can access Interactive Presentations gain a greater understanding of core concepts through animated videos provided in the margins of the eBook. These 3-minute iSeeit! videos apply concepts through tangible scenarios.

- Students can highlight and take notes to learn course material.

- The integrated e-book provides students with a cost-saving alternative to the traditional Textbook.

Marketer's Showdown

Nine cases focusing on up-to-the-minute issues in the music, automotive, and soft drink industries are designed to allow students to analyze the marketing problem, choose a proposed solution, and then watch their proposal debated by marketing professionals. After the debate, students have the opportunity to change their plan or stick to their guns, then see the outcome of their decisions.

Student-Focused Features

Chapter-Opening Vignettes focusing on well-known companies draw students into a discussion about some of the challenges these companies face.

how many couples are using Disney for their honeymoon. In turn, it can distribute its attractions according to its target market: plenty of rides for kids, as well as romantic sites for couples to enjoy the weather and their time alone.

A more recent initiative takes Disney to the cutting edge of market research. Its massive new system, spanning all its parks and hotel properties, relies on a wristband, called My Magic+. The wristband represents hotel guests' room key and credit card, so simply by swiping it they can access their rooms or charge their poolside lunch to their room account. For day visitors to the parks, the bands enable them to check in for rides, make dinner reservations,

Check Yourself questions positioned throughout the chapter after key points allow students to stop and think about what they have learned.

CHECK YOURSELF

1. What are some consumer-oriented pricing tactics?
2. What are some B2B-oriented pricing tactics?

Real-World Examples are used to illustrate concepts throughout the text. The authors give students the opportunity to think about how concepts are used in their everyday life. This is shown through various boxed elements:

- **Adding Value**—illustrate how companies add value not only in providing products and services, but also in making contributions to society.

- **Ethical and Societal Dilemmas**—emphasize the role of marketing in society.

- **Social and Mobile Marketing**—discuss how social media are used in marketing products.

- **Superior Service**—highlight the emerging role of the service industry.

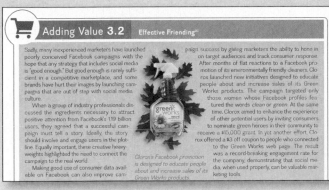

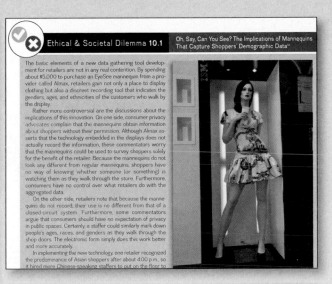

End-of-Chapter Materials include summary sections organized by chapter learning objective, designed to revisit and reinforce key concepts. Key Terms include definitions and page references for the chapter, and a master list of key terms with definitions can be found at the back of the text. Marketing Applications ask students to consider what they have learned in the chapter to answer essay-style questions. Quiz Yourself questions allow students to test their knowledge by answering chapter-specific questions and checking their skill level against the answer key provided in the back of the text. Net Savvy activities encourage students to go to the web to research and/or write about a particular company or current practices. End-of-chapter cases are designed to help students develop analytical, critical-thinking, and technology skills.

Marketing Applications Each chapter concludes with 8 to 11 Marketing Applications. These essay-style questions determine whether students have grasped the concepts covered in each chapter by asking them to apply what they have learned to marketing scenarios that are relevant to their lives.

Instructor Resources

Connect offers instructors auto-gradable material in an effort to facilitate learning and to save time.

INSIGHT

Student Progress Tracking *Connect* keeps instructors informed about how each student, section, and class is performing, allowing for more productive use of lecture and office hours. The progress tracking function enables instructors to:

- View scored work immediately and track individual or group performance with assignment and grade reports.

- Access an instant view of student or class performance relative to learning objectives.

- Collect data and generate reports required by many accreditation organizations, such as AACSB.

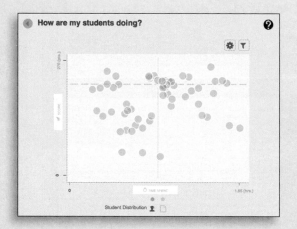

Connect's Instructor Library

Connect's Instructor Library serves as a one-stop, secure site for essential course materials, allowing you to save prep time before class. Resources found in the library include:

- Instructor's Manual
- Connect Instructor's Manual
- PowerPoint Presentations
- TestBank/EZ Test
- Monthly Newsletters
- Videos
- Video Guide

Instructor's Manual: The authors have carefully reviewed all resources provided in the Instructor's Manual to ensure cohesion with the text. It includes everything an instructor needs to prepare a lecture, including lecture outlines, discussion questions, and teaching notes. PowerPoint® slides offer material from the text, as well as expanded coverage to supplement discussion.

Test Bank and EZ Test Online: The Test Bank and Computerized Test Bank offer multiple-choice, true/false, short answer, essay, and application questions.

Video

Chapter-specific videos are provided to complement each chapter of the text. Eight of the 20 videos have been updated to include interesting companies that students will identify with such as Dunkin' Donuts, adidias, and Dannon.

Video Guide

The Video Guide offers additional teaching notes to accompany the chapter videos and provides discussion questions.

Connect Instructor's Manual

This Instructor's Manual offers instructor what they need to set up Connect for their courses. It explains everything from how to get started to suggestions of what to assign and ideas about assigning credit. This tool was developed by instructors who have used and continue to use Connect successfully in their course. This Instructor's Manual can be found in Connect, on the Instructor's Resource CD, and on the OLC.

Newsletter

The authors provide a monthly newsletter containing articles, videos, and podcasts about current topics related to marketing. Every article is supported with discussion questions to assist in bringing relevant topics into the classroom. Faculty and students are encouraged to visit www.grewallevymarketing.com to read articles, post comments, and search for specific content according to topic or chapter.

The newsletter is also available to instructors within the Connect Library and is provided in Word and PowerPoint® formats.

Teaching Options and Solutions

Blackboard® Partnership

McGraw-Hill Education and Blackboard have teamed up to simplify your life. Now you and your students can access Connect and Create right from within your Blackboard course—all with one single sign-on. The gradebooks are seamless, so when a student completes an integrated Connect assignment, the grade for that assignment automatically (and instantly) feeds your Blackboard grade center. Learn more at **www.domorenow.com.**

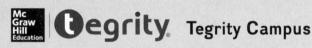

Create

Instructors can now tailor their teaching resources to match the way they teach! With McGraw-Hill Create, www.mcgrawhillcreate.com, instructors can easily rearrange chapters, combine material from other content sources, and quickly upload and integrate their own content, like course syllabi or teaching notes. Find the right content in Create by searching through thousands of leading McGraw-Hill textbooks. Arrange the material to fit your teaching style. Order a Create book and receive a complimentary print review copy in three to five business days or a complimentary electronic review copy via e-mail within one hour. Go to **www. mcgrawhillcreate.com** today and register.

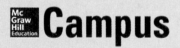

Tegrity Campus

Tegrity makes class time available 24/7 by automatically capturing every lecture in a searchable format for students to review when they study and complete assignments. With a simple one-click start-and-stop process, you capture all computer screens and corresponding audio. Students can replay any part of any class with easy-to-use browser-based viewing on a PC or Mac. Educators know that the more students can see, hear, and experience class resources, the better they learn. In fact, studies prove it. With patented Tegrity "search anything" technology, students instantly recall key class moments for replay online or on iPods and mobile devices. Instructors can help turn all their students' study time into learning moments immediately supported by their lecture. To learn more about Tegrity, watch a two-minute Flash demo at **http:// tegritycampus.mhhe.com.**

McGraw-Hill Campus™

McGraw-Hill Campus is a new one-stop teaching and learning experience available to users of any learning management system. This institutional service allows faculty and students to enjoy single sign-on (SSO) access to all McGraw-Hill Higher Education materials, including the award-winning McGraw-Hill Connect platform, from directly within the institution's website. With McGraw-Hill Campus, faculty receive instant access to teaching materials (e.g., eTextbooks, test banks, PowerPoint slides, animations, learning objects, etc.), allowing them to browse, search, and use any instructor ancillary content in our vast library at no additional cost to instructor or students.

Course Design and Delivery

In addition, students enjoy SSO access to a variety of free content (e.g., quizzes, flash cards, narrated presentations, etc.) and subscription-based products (e.g., McGraw-Hill Connect). With McGraw-Hill Campus enabled, faculty and students will never need to create another account to access McGraw-Hill products and services. Learn more at **www.mhcampus.com.**

Assurance of Learning Ready

Many educational institutions today focus on the notion of assurance of learning, an important element of some accreditation standards. *Marketing* is designed specifically to support instructors' assurance of learning initiatives with a simple yet powerful solution. Each test bank question for *Marketing* maps to a specific chapter learning objective listed in the text. Instructors can use our test bank software, EZ Test and EZ Test Online to easily query for learning objectives that directly relate to the learning outcomes for their course. Instructors can then use the reporting features of EZ Test to aggregate student results in similar fashion, making the collection and presentation of assurance of learning data simple and easy.

AACSB Tagging

McGraw-Hill Education is a proud corporate member of AACSB International. Understanding the importance and value of AACSB accreditation, *Marketing* recognizes the curricula guidelines detailed in the AACSB standards for business accreditation by connecting selected questions in the text and the test bank to the six general knowledge and skill guidelines in the AACSB standards. The statements contained in *Marketing* are provided only as a guide for the users of this textbook. The AACSB leaves content coverage and assessment within the purview of individual schools, the mission of the school, and the faculty. While the *Marketing* teaching package makes no claim of any specific AACSB qualification or evaluation, we have within *Marketing* labeled selected questions according to the six general knowledge and skills areas.

McGraw-Hill Customer Experience Group Contact Information

At McGraw-Hill Education, we understand that getting the most from new technology can be challenging. That's why our services don't stop after you purchase our products. You can e-mail our Product Specialists 24 hours a day to get product training online. Or you can search our knowledge bank of Frequently Asked Questions on our support website. For Customer Support, call **800-331-5094** or visit **www.mhhe.com/support.** One of our Technical Support Analysts will be able to assist you in a timely fashion.

acknowledgments

We would like to acknowledge the considerable contributions of Elisabeth Nevins Caswell, Scott Motyka (Northeastern University), and Jenny Esdale (Babson College). Kate Woodworth, and Laurie Covens for their help throughout the development of this edition of *Marketing*.

We wish to express our sincere appreciation to Leroy Robinson of University of Houston–Clear Lake for preparing the Instructor's Manual and the PowerPoint slides, and Kelly Luchtman for the video production. The support, expertise, and occasional coercion from our executive editor Sankha Basu and product developer Kelly Delso are greatly appreciated. The book would also never have come together without the editorial and production staff at McGraw-Hill Education Christine Vaughan, lead content project manager; Matt Diamond, designer; Keri Johnson, lead content licensing specialist; Danielle Clement, content project manager; and Carol Bielski, senior buyer.

Our colleagues in industry have been invaluable in providing us with case, video, advertising, and photo materials.

Over the years, we have had the opportunity to work with many talented and insightful colleagues. We have benefited from our research and discussions with them. Some of these colleagues are: Anne L. Roggeveen, Victoria Crittenden, Ross Petty, Danna Greenberg, Kate McKone-Sweet, Bala Iyer, Nancy Dlott (Babson College); Ruth Bolton, Steve Brown, and Terry Bristol (Arizona State University); Ramon Avila (Ball State University); Krista Hill, Bridgewater State University; Joan Lindsey-Mullikin and Norm Borin (Cal Poly, San Luis Obispo); Keith Coulter, Clark University; Larry D. Compeau (Clarkson University); Don Lehmann and Keith L. Wilcox (Columbia); Praveen Kopalle, Scott Neslin, and Kusum Ailawadi (Dartmouth); Rajneesh Suri (Drexel); Rajesh Chandrashekaran (Fairleigh Dickinson University); Gopal Iyer and Tamara Mangleburg (Florida Atlantic University); Anthony Miyazaki and Walfried Lassar (Florida International University); Hooman Estelami (Fordham University); William Dodds (Ft. Lewis College); Ronnie Goodstein (Georgetown); V. Kumar (Georgia State University); Jean-Charles Chebat (HEC Montreal); Namwoon Kim (Hong Kong Polytechnic University); K. Sivakumar (Lehigh University); Ko de Ruyter, Martin Wetzels, and Dominik Mahr (Maastricht University); Maria Elena Vazquez Lira, Monterrey Tec, and Scott Motyka (Northeastern University); Douglas M. Lambert and Walter Zinn (Ohio State University); Lauren S. Beitelspacher (Portland State University); Nancy M. Puccinelli (Oxford University); Lauren S. Beitelspacher (Portland State University); Wagner Kamakura (Rice); Dinesh Gauri, Syracuse University; Thomas Rudolph (St. Gallen University); Jens Nordfält (Stockholm School of Economics); Zhen Zhu (Suffolk University); Venkatesh Shankar, Mark Houston, and Manjit Yadav (Texas A&M); Julie Baker and William Cron (Texas Christian University); Rodney C. Runyan, Texas State University, Adam Rapp, and Kristy Reynolds (University of Alabama); Yu Ma, (University of Alberta); Merrie Brucks and Ajith Kumar (University of Arizona); Cheryl Nikata (University of Illinois, Chicago); David Hardesty (University of Kentucky); Arun Sharma, A. Parasuraman, R. Krishnan, Howard Marmorstein, Anuj Mehrotra, and Michael Tsiros (all from University of Miami); A. C. Samli (University of North Florida); Rajiv Dant (University of Oklahoma); Monika Kukar Kinney and Kent Monroe (University of Richmond); Abhijit Guha (University of South Carolina); Valerie Folkes (University of Southern California); Jeanne S. Munger (University of Southern Maine); Robert Peterson (University of Texas at Austin); Carolyn Costley (University of Waikato); Rob Palmatier (University of Washington); Jerry Gotlieb (University of Western Kentucky);

Abhijit Biswas, and Sujay Dutta (Wayne State University); M. Joseph Sirgy, Julie Ozanne, and Ed Fern (Virginia Tech).

We would like to thank the following instructors for providing feedback to shape the fifth edition. A special thank you to:

Wendi L. Achey
Northampton Community College

Ebru Ulusoy Akgun
University of Maine

Audrey Ashton-Savage
Peter T. Paul College of Business and Economics, University of New Hampshire

Nisreen Bahnan
Salem State University

Linda Jane Coleman
Salem State University

Kevin Joseph Cumiskey
Eastern Kentucky University

Laura Dix
Ferris State University

Kim Donahue
Indiana University, Kelley School of Business Indianapolis

Jerome Gafford
University of North Alabama

James Gorman
Houson University of Alabama

Daniel E. Hallock
University of North Alabama

Dana L. E. Harrison
East Tennessee State University

Reba Heberlein
Madison Area Technical College

Tarique Hossain
California State Polytechnic University

Elizabeth Jane
Wilson Suffolk University

Mayuresh M. Kelkar
Salem State University

Todd Korol
Monroe Community College

Kathleen A. Krentler
San Diego State University

Jamie Lambert
Ohio University

Marilyn Lavin
University of Wisconsin-Whitewater

Patricia Marco
Madison College

Mary Christene Martin
Fort Hays State University

Carolyn A. Massiah
University of Central Florida

Maria McConnell
Lorain County Community College

Joyce L. Meyer
The University of Alabama

Susan Myrden
University of Maine

Steve Noll
Madison Area Technical College

Matthew O'Hern
University of Oregon

David Terry Paul
The Ohio State University

Frank Allen Philpot
George Mason University

Lori A. Radulovich
Baldwin Wallace University

Jean Marc Rejaud
Fashion Institute of Technology

Harper Andrew Roehm, Jr.
University of North Carolina–Greensboro

Donald Shemwell
East Tennessee State University

John Striebich
Monroe Community College

Robert Scott Taylor
Moberly Area Community College

Steven A. Taylor
Illinois State University

Deborah Utter
Boston University

For their contributions to previous editions of *Marketing,* we gratefully acknowledge:

Wendi Achey
Northampton Community College

Praveen Aggarwal
University of Minnesota, Duluth

Maria Aria
Camden County College

Dennis Arnett
Texas Tech University

Gerard Athaide
Loyola College of Maryland

Timothy W. Aurand
Northern Illinois University

Laurie Babin
University of Louisiana at Monroe

Ainsworth Bailey
University of Toledo

Aysen Bakir
Illinois State University

Joyce Banjac
Myers University

Harvey Bauman
Lees McRae College

Oleta Beard
University of Washington

Sandy Becker
Rutgers Business School

Hannah Bell-Lombardo
Bryant University

Ellen Benowitz
Mercer County Community College

Gary Benton
Western Kentucky University

Joseph Ben-Ur
University of Houston at Victoria

Patricia Bernson
County College of Morris

Harriette Bettis-Outland
University of West Florida

Parimal Bhagat
Indiana University of Pennsylvania

Amit Bhatnagar
University of Wisconsin, Milwaukee

Jan Bingen
Little Priest Tribal College

John Bishop
University of South Alabama–Mobile

Nancy Bloom
Nassau Community College

Claire Bolfing
James Madison University

Karen Bowman
University of California

Tom Boyd
California State University–Fullerton

Nancy Boykin
Tarleton State University

Cathy Brenan
Northland Community and Technical College

Martin Bressler
Houston Baptist University

Claudia Bridges
California State University

Glen H. Brodowsky
California State University, San Marcos

Greg Broekemier
University of Nebraska Kearney

Gary Brunswick
Northern Michigan University

Alan J. Bush
University of Memphis

John Buzza
Monmouth University

Linda Calderone
SUNY, Farmingdale

Nathaniel Calloway
University of Maryland, University College

Rae Caloura
Johnson & Wales University

Michaelle Cameron
St. Edwards University

Catherine Campbell
University of Maryland

Carlos Castillo
University of Minnesota, Duluth

Eve Caudill
Winona State University

Carmina Cavazos
University of Saint Thomas

Lindell Chew
Linn University of Missouri

Dorene Ciletti
Duquesne University

Melissa Clark
University of North Alabama

Terry Clark
Southern Illinois University–Carbondale

Joyce Claterbos
University of Kansas

Gloria Cockerell
Collin County College

Paul Cohen
Florida Atlantic University

Mark E. Collins
University of Tennessee

Clare Comm
University of Massachusetts, Lowell

Sherry Cook
Southwest Missouri State University

Stan Cort
Case Western Reserve University

Keith Cox
University of Houston

Ian Cross
Bentley College

Geoffrey Crosslin
Kalamazoo Valley Community College

Brent Cunningham
Jacksonville State University

Clayton L. Daughtrey
Metropolitan State College of Denver

Charlene Davis
Trinity University

Joseph DeFilippe
Suffolk County Community College

George Deitz
University of Memphis

Kathleen DeNisco
Erie Community College

Tilokie Depoo
Monroe College

Monique Doll
Macomb Community College

Kimberly Donahue
Indiana University–Purdue University at Indianapolis

Jim D'Orazio
Cleveland State University

Michael Dore
University of Oregon

James Downing
University of Illinois–Chicago

Michael Drafke
College of DuPage

Leon Dube
Texas A&M University

Colleen Dunn
Bucks County Community College

John Eaton
Arizona State University–Tempe

Kellie Emrich
Cuyahoga Community College

Nancy Evans
New River Community College

Keith Fabes
Berkeley College

Tina Facca
John Carroll University

Joyce Fairchild
Northern Virginia Community College

David J. Faulds
University of Louisville

Larry Feick
University of Pittsburgh

Karen Flaherty
Oklahoma State University–Stillwater

Leisa Flynn
Florida State University

William Foxx
Auburn University

Alan Friedenthal
Kingsborough Community College

Douglas Friedman
Penn State University

Stanley Garfunkel
Queensborough Community College

S. J. Garner
Eastern Kentucky University

David Gerth
Nashville State Community College

Peggy Gilbert
Missouri State University

Kelly Gillerlain
Tidewater Community College

George Goerner
Mohawk Valley Community College

Jana Goodrich
Penn State Behrend

Robin Grambling
University of Texas at El Paso

Kimberly D. Grantham
University of Georgia

James I. Gray
Florida Atlantic University

Kelly Gredone
Bucks County Community College

Tom Greene
Eastern Washington University

Michael Greenwood
Mount Wachusett Community College

Barbara Gross
California State University–Northridge

David Grossman
Florida Southern College

Hugh Guffey
Auburn University

Reetika Gupta
Lehigh University

John Hafer
University of Nebraska at Omaha

Allan Hall
Western Kentucky University

Joan Hall
Macomb Community College

Clark Hallpike
Elgin Community College

James E. Hansen
University of Akron

Don Hanson
Bryant University

Jeffrey Harper
Texas Tech University

Dorothy Harpool
Wichita State University

Lynn Harris
Shippensburg University

Linda Hefferin
Elgin Community College

Charlane Held
Onondaga Community College

Lewis Hershey
Fayetteville State University

Jonathan Hibbard
Boston University

Tom Hickman
Loyola University

Robbie Hillsman
University of Tennessee–Martin

Nathan Himelstein
Essex County College

Adrienne Hinds
Northern Virginia Community College at Annandale

John Hobbs
University of Oklahoma

Don Hoffer
Miami University

Craig Hollingshead
Texas A&M University, Kingsville

Donna Hope
Nassau Community College

Ronald Hoverstad
University of the Pacific

Kris Hovespian
Ashland University

James Hunt
University of North Carolina Wilmington

Shane Hunt
Arkansas State University

Julie Huntley
Oral Roberts University

Sean Jasso
University of California–Riverside

Carol Johanek
Washington University, St. Louis

Doug Johansen
University of North Florida

Candy Johnson
Holyoke Community College

Maria Johnson
Macomb Commity College, Clinton Township

Keith Jones
North Carolina A&T University

Janice Karlen
CUNY–Laguardia Community College

Eric J. Karson
Villanova University

Rajiv Kashyap
William Paterson University

Josette Katz
Atlantic Cape Community College

Garland Keesling
Towson University

Imran Khan
University of South Alabama–Mobile

Todd Korol
Monroe Community College

Dennis Lee Kovach
Community College of Allegheny County

Dmitri Kuksov
Washington University–St Louis

Jeff Kulick
George Mason University

Michelle Kunz
Morehead State University

Ann T. Kuzma
Minnesota State University, Mankato

John Kuzma
Minnesota State University at Mankato

Sandie Lakin
Hesser College

Timothy Landry
University of Oklahoma

Don Larson
Ohio State University

Felicia Lassk
Northeastern University

J. Ford Laumer
Auburn University

Marilyn Lavin
University of Wisconsin, Whitewater

Kenneth Lawrence
New Jersey IT

Freddy Lee
California State University, Los Angeles

Rebecca Legleiter
Tulsa CC Southeast Campus

Hillary Leonard
University of Rhode Island

Natasha Lindsey
University of North Alabama

Guy Lochiatto
Massachusetts Bay Community College

Paul Londrigan
Mott Community College

Terry Lowe
Heartland Community College

Dolly Loyd
University of Southern Mississippi

Harold Lucius
Rowan University

Alicia Lupinacci
Tarrant Community College

Stanley Madden
Baylor University

Lynda Maddox
George Washington University

Moutusi Maity
University of Wisconsin, Whitewater

Cesar Maloles
California State University, East Bay

Karl Mann
Tennessee Tech University

Cathy Martin
University of Akron

Melissa Martin
George Mason University

Carolyn Massiah
University of Central Florida

Tamara Masters
Brigham Young University

Erika Matulich
University of Tampa

Bob Mayer
Mesa State College

Nancy McClure
University of Central Oklahoma

Maria McConnnell
Lorain County Community College

Dennis Menezes
University of Louisville, Louisville

Mohan Menon
University of South Alabama

Michelle Meyer
Joliet Junior College

Ivor Mitchell
University of Nevada Reno

Mark Mitchell
University of South Carolina

Steven Moff
Pennsylvania College of Technology

Rex Moody
University of Colorado

Rex Moody
Central Washington University at Ellensburg

Melissa Moore
Mississippi State University

Linda Morable
Richland College

Farrokh Moshiri
University of California–Riverside

Dorothy Mulcahy
Bridgewater State College

James Munch
Wright State University–Dayton

Brian Murray
Jefferson Community College

Suzanne Murray
Piedmont Technical College

James E. Murrow
Drury University

Noreen Nackenson
Nassau Community College

Sandra Blake Neis
Borough of Manhattan Community College

John Newbold
Sam Houston State University

Keith Niedermeier
University of Pennsylvania

Martin Nunlee
Syracuse University

Hudson Nwakanma
Florida A & M University

Lois Olson
San Diego State University

Beng Ong
California State University, Fresno

Daniel Onyeagba
Argosy University, Atlanta

Karen Overton
Houston Community College

Deborah L. Owens
University of Akron

Esther Page-Wood
Western Michigan University

Richard Pascarelli
Adelphi University

Terry Paul
Ohio State University, Columbus

Michael Pearson
Loyola University

Jerry Peerbolte
University of Arkansas–Fort Smith

Glenn Perser
Houston Community College

Diane Persky
Yeshiva University

Susan Peters
California State Polytechnic University at Pomona

Renee Pfeifer-Luckett
University of Wisconsin at Whitewater

Frank Alan Philpot
George Mason University

Gary Pieske
Minnesota State Community and Technical College

Jeff Podoshen
Temple University

Carmen Powers
Monroe Community College

Mike Preis
University of Illinois–Champaign

Susan Price
California Polytechnic State University

Lori Radulovich
Baldwin-Wallace College

Bruce Ramsey
Franklin University

Rosemary Ramsey
Wright State University

Srikumar Rao
Long Island University

Kristen Regine
Johnston & Wales University

Joseph Reihing
Nassau Community College

William Rice
California State University–Fresno

Patricia Richards
Westchester Community College

Eric Rios
Eastern University

Ann Renee Root
Florida Atlantic University

Janet Robinson
Mount St. Mary's College

Tom Rossi
Broome Community College

Heidi Rottier
Bradley University

Juanita Roxas
California State Polytechnic University

Donald Roy
Middle Tennessee State University

Linda Salisbury
Boston College

Nick Sarantakes
Austin Community College

Shikhar Sarin
Boise State University

Carl Saxby
University of Southern Indiana

Diana Scales
Tennessee State University

Dwight Scherban
Central Connecticut State University

James Schindler
Columbia Southern University

Jeffrey Schmidt
University of Oklahoma–Norman

Laura Shallow
St. Xavier University

Dan Sherrell
University of Memphis

Philip Shum
William Paterson University

Lisa Simon
California Polytechnic State University, San Luis Obispo

Rob Simon
University of Nebraska–Lincoln

Erin Sims
Devry University at Pomona

Lauren Ruth Skinner
University of Alabama at Birmingham

Karen Smith
Columbia Southern University

Lois J. Smith
University of Wisconsin

Julie Z. Sneath
University of South Alabama

Brent Sorenson
University of Minnesota–Crookston

James Spiers
Arizona State University–Tempe

Geoffrey Stewart
University of Louisiana

John Striebich
Monroe Community College

Randy Stuart
Kennesaw State University

James Swanson
Kishwaukee College

James Swartz
California State Polytechnic University

Robert R. Tangsrud, Jr.
University of North Dakota

Steve Taylor
Illinois State University

Sue Taylor
Southwestern Illinois College

Sharon Thach
Tennessee State University

Mary Tharp
University of Texas at San Antonio

Frank Tobolski
Lake in the Hills

Louis A. Tucci
College of New Jersey

Sue Umashankar
University of Arizona

Deborah Utter
Boston University

Ven Venkatesan
University of Rhode Island at Kingston

Bronis Verhage
Georgia State University

Deirdre Verne
Westchester Community College

Steve Vitucci
Tarleton University Central Texas

Keith Wade
Webber International University

Suzanne Walchli
University of the Pacific

Wakiuru Wamwara-Mbugua
Wright State University–Dayton

Bryan Watkins
Dominican University, Priory Campus

Ron Weir
East Tennessee State University

Ludmilla Wells
Florida Gulf Coast University

Thomas Whipple
Cleveland State University

Tom Whitman
Mary Washington College

Kathleen Williamson
University of Houston–Clear Lake

Phillip Wilson
Midwestern State University

Doug Witt
Brigham Young University

Kim Wong
Albuquerque Tech Institute

Letty Workman
Utah Valley University

Courtney Worsham
University of South Carolina

Brent Wren
University of Alabama–Huntsville

Alex Wu
California State University–Long Beach

Joseph Yasaian
McIntosh College

Poh-Lin Yeoh
Bentley College

Paschalina Ziamou
Bernard M. Baruch College

We would like to thank all the professors who were instrumental in guiding our
revision of not only the text, but also Connect and other ancillary materials

Ivan Abel
St. John's University

Wendi Achey
Northampton Community College

Praveen Aggarwal
University of Minnesota, Duluth

Keanon Alderson
California Baptist University

Rosalyn Amaro
Florida State College at Jacksonville

Maria Aria
Camden County College

Jill S. Attaway
Illinois State University

Michelle Barnhart
Oregon State University

Robert Belenger
Bristol Community College

Tom Bilyeu
Southwestern Illinois College

Mark Blake
York College of Pennsylvania

Maurice Bode
Delgado Community College

Jean M. Brown
*University of Alabama in
Huntsville*

Gary Brunswick
Northern Michigan University

Desislava Budeva
Ramapo College of New Jersey

Melissa Burnett
Missouri State University

Susan Carder
Northern Arizona University

Ella Carter
Bowie State University

Debi Cartwright
Truman State University

Haozhe Chen
East Carolina University

Angeline Close
The University of Texas at Ausin

Kathleen Ferris-Costa
Bridgewater State University

Kevin Coulson
Emporia State University

Brent Cunningham
Jacksonville State University

Beth Deinert
Southeast Community College

David DiRusso
Millersville University

Michael Dotson
Appalachian State University

Colleen Dunn
Bucks County Community College

Diane Edmondson
Middle Tennessee State University

Burcak Ertimur
Fairleigh Dickinson University

David J. Faulds
University of Louisville

Amy Feest
Tunxis Community College

Troy A. Festervand
Middle Tennessee State University

Paul Fombelle
Northeastern University

John Fraedrich
*Southern Illinois University–
Carbondale*

Theresa E. Frame
Horry Georgetown Technical College

Sheila Fry
Champlain College

Jerome Gafford
Univeristy of North Alabama

Tao (Tony) Gao
Northeastern University

Lance Gentry
Colorado State University–Pueblo

Nabarun Ghose
The University of Findlay

Connie Golden
Lakeland Community College

Lisa Goolsby
Southern Adventist University

Deborah M. Gray
Central Michigan University

Susan Greer
Horry-Georgetown Technical College

Cynthia Grether
Delta College

Mike Griffith
Lone Star College–Kingwood

Barbara Gross
California State University, Northridge

Chiquan Guo
*The University of Texas–Pan
American*

Jamey Halleck
Marshall University

Richard Hanna
Northeastern University

David Eric Hansen
Texas Southern University

Jeffrey Harper
Texas Tech University

Perry Hidalgo
Gwinnett Technical College

Diane Holtzman
*Richard Stockton College of
New Jersey*

Monica Hodis
St. John Fisher College

Donna Hope
Nassau Community College

Gorman Houston
University of Alabama

Erika Hovland
Temple University

Vince Howe
*University of North Carolina,
Wilmington*

Miriam Huddleston
Harford Community College

James B. Hunt
*University of North Carolina,
Wilmington*

Eva Hyatt
Appalachian State University

Roxanne Jackson
Vance-Granville Community College

Grace Jebakumari Johnson
University of Wisconsin–Milwaukee

Victoria Jones
*University of North Carolina,
Wilmington*

Sungwoo Jung
Columbus State University

Vishal Kashyap
Xavier University

Mark Kay
Montclair State University

Sylvia Keyes
Bridgewater State University

Tina Kiesler
California State University, Northridge

Brian Kinard
University of North Carolina, Wilmington

John Kinnett
Columbus State University

Peter Knight
University of Wisconsin, Parkside

Michael W. Kroff
Montana State University

Ann T. Kuzma
Minnesota State University, Mankato

Theodore Labay
Bishop State Community College

Donald W. Larson
The Ohio State University

James R. Lashley
Bowie State University

E. Scott Lathrop
*Whitman School of Management,
Syracuse University*

Debra Laverie
Texas Tech University

Cary LeBlanc
Assumption College

David M. Lee
Sam Houston State University

Andrea Licari
St. John's University

Junsang Lim
Virginia State University

Bryan D. Little
Marshall University

Ruth Lumb
*Minnesota State University,
Moorhead*

Guy Lochiatto
MassBay Community College

Anne Weidemanis Magi
University of South Florida

Datha Damron-Martinez
Truman State University

David Matthews
*SUNY Adirondack (Adirondack
Community College)*

Fredric Mayerson
Kingsborough Community College

Myke McMullen
Long Beach Community College

Rajiv Mehta
New Jersey Institute of Technology

Sanjay S. Mehta
Sam Houston State University

Jeffrey Meier
Fox Valley Technical College

Michael Mejza
University of Nevada, Las Vegas

Robert Meyer
Parkland College

Elizabeth Miller
Boston College

Iris Mohr
St. John's University

Josefer Montes
Walla Walla University

Dorothy J. Mulcahy
Bridgewater State University

Jay Mulki
Northestern University–Boston

Benjamin Muller
Portland Community College

Gergana Nenkov
Boston College

John Newbold
Sam Houston State University

Hudson Nwakanma
Florida A&M University

Matt O'Hern
University of Oregon

Richard B. Osborn
York College of Pennsylvania

Rodney Oudan
Worcester State University

Lauren Paisley
Genesee Community College

Mahatapa Palit
*Borough of Manhattan Community
College*

Janet Parish
Texas A&M University

Raymond A. Parkins, Jr.
Florida State College at Jacksonville

Ed Petkus
Ramapo College of New Jersey

Julie M. Pharr
Tennessee Tech University

Rajani Ganesh Pillai
North Dakota State University

Sampath Ranganathan
University of Wisconsin–Green Bay

Mohammed Rawwas
University of Northern Iowa

Virginia Reilly
Ocean County College

John E. Robbins
Winthrop University

Ann R. Root
Florida Atlantic University

Robert Rouwenhorst
University of Iowa

Donald P. Roy
Middle Tennessee State University

Alberto Rubio-Sanchez
University of the Incarnate Word

Catherine Ruggieri
St. John's University, New York

Doreen Sams
Georgia College & State University

Robin Schallie
Fox Valley Technical College

Douglas Scott
State College of Florida

Christine Seel
Delaware Valley College

Daaim Shabazz
Florida A&M University

Abhay Shah
Colorado State University–Pueblo

Rick Shannon
Western Kentucky University

Kenneth Shaw
*State University of New York,
Oswego*

Robert Simon
University of Nebraska–Lincoln

Peter D. Simonson
North Dakota State University

David Smith
Bemidji State University

Dennis Spector
Naugatuck Valley Community College

Vernon R. Stauble
San Bernardino Valley College

Susan Steiz
Norwalk Community College

Geoffrey Stewart
University of Louisiana

Karen L. Stewart
Richard Stockton College of New Jersey

Susan Stone
Shippensburg University of Pennsylvania

Ray Stroup, Jr.
University of Louisiana at Lafayette

James Swenson
Minnesota State University, Moorhead

Steven Taylor
Illinois State University

Ramendra Thakur
University of Louisiana–Lafayette

Norman Thiel
Walla Walla University

Dennis Tootelian
California State University, Sacramento

Philip Trocchia
University of South Florida, St. Petersburg

Sven Tuzovic
Pacific Lutheran University

Leo Vasquez
San Bernardino Valley College,
San Bernardino

Franck Vigneron
California State University Northridge

Doug Wilson
University of Oregon–Lundquist
College of Business

Roger Wilson
Fairmont State University

Doug Witt
Brigham Young University

Mike Wittmann
The University of Southern Mississippi

Van R. Wood
Virginia Commonwealth University

Jefrey R. Woodall
York College of Pennsylvania

Kim Wong
Central New Mexico Community College

Ashley Wright
Spartanburg Community College

Elle Wu
Louisiana State University

Charles Wyckoff
Riverside Community College

Ge Xiao
Wilkes University

Jim Zemanek
East Carolina University

Lin Zhang
Truman State University

We express our thanks to all faculty who have contributed to the development of digital learning content:

Lauren Spinner Beitelspacher
University of Alabama, Birmingham

Barbara Black
University of Miami

Donna Haeger,
Monroe Community College

Todd Korol
Monroe Community College

Melissa Martin
George Mason University

Leroy Robinson
University of Houston, Clear Lake

John Striebech
Monroe Community College

Lois Olson
San Diego State University

A special thank you to Steven A. Taylor of Illinois State University, Elizabeth Jane Wilson of Suffolk University, Kevin Bertotti of iTVk, and Becky and Patrick of We Write Good for their efforts in authoring and producing the iSee it! videos in Connect.

We'd also like to thank the team at Hurix—Sumesh Yoganath, Namrata Gunjal, and Ashwin Srivastav—for their contributions, as well as Sue Sullivan of Editors, Inc.

brief contents

table of contents

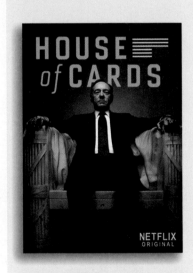

12 DEVELOPING NEW PRODUCTS   370

13 SERVICES: THE INTANGIBLE PRODUCT   406

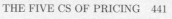

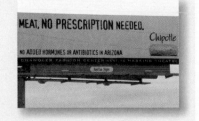

connect interactive assignment guide

This text is supported by interactive assignments that help reinforce and assess learning. In order to access these assignments, you need to have purchased Connect. The following guide provides you with a quick reference for locating the interactive assignments offered for each chapter.

SECTION 1: ASSESSING THE MARKETPLACE

1 Overview of Marketing

Interactive Assignment 1.1: Zipcar: Creating Value in the Marketplace **LOs: 01-01, 01-02, 01-03**

Interactive Assignment 1.2: The Marketing Mix: Travel Goods and Services **LO: 01-01**

Interactive Assignment 1.3: Jeans **LOs: 01-01, 01-02**

Interactive Assignment 1.4: Value: The Bottled Water Industry **LOs: 01-01, 01-02**

Interactive Assignment 1.5: Pinkberry versus Red Mango **LOs: 01-01, 01-02**

Interactive Assignment 1.6: Introduction to Marketing—Red Mango **LOs: 01-01, 01-02**

Interactive Assignment 1.8: Value Creation through the Marketing Mix **LO: 01-02**

2 Developing Marketing Strategies and a Marketing Plan

Interactive Assignment 2.1: The Walt Disney Company and the Strategic Marketing Planning Process **LOs: 02-02, 02-03, 02-04, 02-05**

Interactive Assignment 2.2: Staples: Implementing the Marketing Mix **LO: 02-05**

Interactive Assignment 2.3: Home Shopping Network **LOs: 02-01, 02-04, 02-05**

Interactive Assignment 2.4: SWOT Analysis—Domino's Pizza **LO: 02-02**

Interactive Assignment 2.8: Growth Strategies at FedEx **LO: 02-07**

Interactive Assignment 2.9: The Netflix Rollercoaster: How a Strategy Can Fail **LOs: 02-01, 02-02, 02-05, 02-06, 02-07**

Interactive Assignment 2.10: The Marketing Plan **LO: 02-02**

3 Social and Mobile Marketing

Interactive Assignment 3.1: Dell: Successfully Using Social Media **LOs: 03-01, 03-02, 03-04**

Interactive Assignment 3.1: Types of Social Media **LOs: 03-02, 03-03**

Interactive Assignment 3.2: Social Media: GE Healthymagination **LOs: 03-01, 03-02, 03-04**

Interactive Assignment 3.3: Social Media Metrics **LO: 03-04**

4 Marketing Ethics

Interactive Assignment 4.1: Integrating Ethics into Marketing Strategy **LOs: 04-03, 04-04**

Interactive Assignment 4.2: Newman's Own Organics: Ethics and Social Responsibility **LOs: 04-02, 04-04**

Interactive Assignment 4.3: Whose Side Are You On? Ethics in Marketing Practice **LOs: 04-01, 04-03, 04-04**

Interactive Assignment 4.4: Ethics: Icebreaker **LOs: 04-02, 04-04, 04-05**

Interactive Assignment 4.6: Ethical Marketing **LO: 04-04**

5 Analyzing the Marketing Environment

Interactive Assignment 5.1: Understanding Demographic Segmentation **LOs: 05-02, 05-03**

Interactive Assignment 5.2: Dole Analyzes the Environment **LOs: 05-02, 05-04**

Interactive Assignment 5.3: McDonald's: Analyzing the Marketing Environment **LOs: 05-02, 05-04**

ASSESSING THE MARKETPLACE

Section One, Assessing the Marketplace, contains five chapters. Following an introduction to marketing in Chapter 1, Chapter 2 focuses on how a firm develops its marketing strategy and a marketing plan. A central theme of that chapter is how firms can effectively create, capture, deliver, and communicate value to their customers. Chapter 3 is devoted to understanding how one can develop social and mobile marketing strategies. Chapter 4 focuses attention on marketing ethics. An ethical decision framework is developed and presented, and the key ethical concepts are linked back to the marketing plan introduced in Chapter 2. Finally, Chapter 5, Analyzing the Marketing Environment, focuses on how marketers can systematically uncover and evaluate opportunities.

CHAPTER 1

OVERVIEW OF MARKETING

LEARNING OBJECTIVES

LO1 Define the role of marketing in organizations.

LO2 Describe how marketers create value for a product or service.

LO3 Understand why marketing is important both within and outside the firm.

Showing a remarkable flair for understatement, the CEO of Starbucks, Howard Schultz, recently admitted, "We have a lot going on."[1] Let's think about all the things Starbucks is doing at the moment, in its attempt to market itself as an appealing product and service provider for all its customers, both current and potential.

Its ubiquitous stores—from the long-standing locations in U.S. cities and towns to international expansion into a vast range of new nations—are easy to locate and visit. A recent count showed that the chain maintains more than 20,000 stores, spanning 62 countries.[2] By making sure its stores, with their familiar siren logo, are easy to find, Starbucks guarantees that most people can readily find a place to get their coffee fix. For the vast majority of buyers,

an addictive Salted Caramel Mocha, or just a great cup of black coffee, is convenient to find and very familiar.

Starbucks vigorously competes with the likes of McDonald's, Dunkin' Donuts, and independent coffeehouses. Not too long ago, McDonald's was not a true competitor in the coffee market because all it sold was plain coffee. But when it started promoting its McCafés, Starbucks was quick to respond, to make sure it stayed in the lead. Starbucks' "coffee war" with Dunkin' Donuts is famous in the areas in which they compete head-to-head, although each chain has its geographic strongholds—Dunkin' in the East and Starbucks in the West.[3] Independent coffeehouses and smaller regional chains, seen by many as being more hip and less commercial, also continually nip at Starbucks' heels.

Starbucks continues to innovate and expand with a variety of products, making them available in various locations beyond its own stores. Unsatisfied with dominating just the coffee market, it added Tazo teas to its product line early in its history; more recently it purchased the Teavana chain of tea stores.[4] In addition, it purchased the Evolution Fresh line of fresh juices, sells bags of its own brand of ground coffee and whole beans, as well as coffee-flavored ice cream in not only its own stores but also in grocery stores. But the expansion is not limited to beverages. For example, Starbucks' latest

collaboration with Danone, the yogurt company, is developing a new line of dairy products called Evolution Fresh to sell in various outlets.[5]

There are plenty of jokes about how Starbucks manages to charge upwards of $5 for a jolt of caffeine, but a quick glance at its marketing methods and strategies helps explain why it can do so. The products it sells are appealing to customers and fulfill their needs: they taste good, are available readily and conveniently, and offer the benefit of helping them wake up to start their day (or stay awake for a long night of studying). Thus the exchange of money for coffee—or tea or juice or yogurt or a nice pastry—they regard as a good value, despite the relatively high cost. The lines outside the doors of many Starbucks locations at 8:00 a.m. demonstrate this perceived value.

Starbucks also connects with fans through social marketing channels, including its popular My Starbucks Idea site. The site is an innovative approach designed to develop new products. Customers share ideas about everything "Starbucks," from store designs to new drink recipes. They can also join one of the many discussions in the customer forums. Additionally, the site connects customers to its Twitter and Facebook sites, and also links people to its mobile phone applications (apps) that they can use to pay for drinks or other products in Starbucks stores.

It's a lot to be going on, indeed. But by adopting the principles and methods of marketing that this textbook covers, Starbucks has created a market that it continues to dominate, bringing benefits to the company and its shareholders, as well as to consumers.

LO1 Define the role of marketing in organizations.

WHAT IS MARKETING?

Unlike other subjects you may have studied, marketing already is very familiar to you. You start your day by agreeing to do the dishes in exchange for a freshly made cup of coffee. Then you fill up your car with gas. You attend a class that you have chosen and paid for. After class, you pick up lunch (and maybe a frozen dessert) at the cafeteria, which you eat while reading a book on your iPad. Then you leave campus to have your hair cut and take in a movie. On your bus ride back to school, you pass the time by buying a few songs from Apple's iTunes. In each case, you have acted as the buyer and made a decision about whether you should part with your time and/or money to receive a particular product or service. If, after you return home, you decide to sell some clothes you don't wear much anymore on eBay, you have become a seller. In each of these transactions, you were engaged in marketing.

The American Marketing Association states that "marketing is the activity, set of institutions, and processes for creating, *capturing*, communicating, delivering, and exchanging offerings that have value for customers, clients, partners, and society at large."[6] What does this definition really mean? Good marketing is not a random activity; it requires thoughtful planning with an emphasis on the ethical implications of any of those decisions on society in general. Firms develop a marketing plan (Chapter 2) that specifies the marketing activities for a specific period of time. The marketing plan also is broken

EXHIBIT 1.1   Core Aspects of Marketing

- Marketing helps create value.
- Marketing is about satisfying customer needs and wants.
- Marketing entails an exchange.
- Marketing requires product, price, place, and promotion decisions.
- Marketing can be performed by both individuals and organizations.
- Marketing affects various stakeholders.

Marketing

down into various components—how the product or service will be conceived or designed, how much it should cost, where and how it will be promoted, and how it will get to the consumer. In any exchange, the parties to the transaction should be satisfied. In our previous example, you should be satisfied or even delighted with the song you downloaded, and Apple should be satisfied with the amount of money it received from you. Thus, the core aspects of marketing are found in Exhibit 1.1. Let's see how these core aspects look in practice.

Marketing Is about Satisfying Customer Needs and Wants

Understanding the marketplace, and especially consumer needs and wants, is fundamental to marketing success. In the broadest terms, the marketplace refers to the world of trade. More narrowly, however, the marketplace can be segmented or divided into groups of people who are pertinent to an organization for particular reasons. For example, the marketplace for soft drinks may include most people in the world, but as Pepsi and Coke battle each other worldwide, they divide the global population into a host of categories: men versus women, calorie-conscious or not, people who prefer carbonated versus noncarbonated drinks, and multiple categories of flavor preferences, among others.[7] If you manufacture a beverage with zero calories, you want to know for which marketplace segments your product is most relevant, then make sure that you build a marketing strategy that targets those groups. Certain diet- and health-conscious customers may prefer Diet Coke or Diet Pepsi; others may opt for bottled water products like Dasani or Aquafina.

Although marketers would prefer to sell their products and services to everyone, it is not practical to do so. Because marketing costs money, good marketers carefully seek out potential customers who have both an interest in the product

Coke and Pepsi have divided the world into two camps: Coke-lovers and Pepsi-lovers. Which are you?

What type of customer would buy a $120,000 hybrid car?

and an ability to buy it. For example, most people need some form of transportation, and many people probably would like to own the new hybrid from Lexus. Starting at more than $120,000, the Lexus LS 600h L is one of the most sophisticated hybrid cars on the market. But Lexus is not actually interested in everyone who wants an LS 600h L, because not everyone can afford to spend that much on a car. Instead, Lexus defines its viable target market as those consumers who want and can afford such a product.[8] Although not all companies focus on such a specific, and wealthy, target, all marketers are interested in finding the buyers who are most likely to be interested in their offerings.

Marketing Entails an Exchange

Marketing is about an *exchange*—the trade of things of value between the buyer and the seller so that each is better off as a result. As depicted in Exhibit 1.2, sellers provide products or services, then communicate and facilitate the delivery of their offering to consumers. Buyers complete the exchange by giving money and information to the seller. Suppose you learn about a new Katy Perry album by

EXHIBIT 1.2   Exchange: The Underpinning of Seller–Buyer Relationships

Communications and delivery

Goods/services producers (sellers)

Money and information

Customers/ consumers (buyers)

hearing one of her songs on Sirius XM Satellite Radio. The same day, a friend tweets on her Twitter account that she loves the new album, and you visit the Katy Perry Facebook fan page, which is full of recommendations. From there, you click into the iTunes Store, where you can purchase the song you heard, multiple songs, or the entire new album. You begin with the song you heard, which you continue to love after hearing it several times. Therefore, you go back to iTunes and take advantage of its offer to complete the album by downloading the rest of the songs to your iTunes library. Your billing information is already in the company's system, so you do not have to enter your credit card number or other information. Furthermore, iTunes creates a record of your purchase, which it uses, together with your other purchase trends, to create personalized recommendations of other albums or songs that you might like. Thus, Apple uses the valuable information you provide to facilitate future exchanges and solidify its relationship with you.

You can exchange your money on the iTunes store for the latest Katy Perry album.

Marketing Requires Product, Price, Place, and Promotion Decisions

Marketing traditionally has been divided into a set of four interrelated decisions and consequent actions known as the marketing mix, or four Ps: product, price, place, and promotion (as defined in Exhibit 1.3).[9] The four Ps comprise the controllable set of decisions or activities that the firm uses to respond to the wants of its target markets. But what does each of these activities in the marketing mix entail?

Product: Creating Value Although marketing is a multifaceted function, its fundamental purpose is to create value by developing a variety of offerings, including goods, services, and ideas, to satisfy customer needs.[10] Take, for example, a cup of coffee. At one time, people in the United States made a pot of coffee at home or picked up a cup on the run from a McDonald's or Dunkin' Donuts. Because Starbucks and competitive firms realize customers have needs beyond just buying a cup of joe, they are offering their customers a variety of options. This variety includes lattes, cappuccinos, macchiatos, Frappuccino, hot chocolate, smoothies, teas, bottled juices, Refreshers, and regular brewed coffee, providing customers with interesting choices for which they are willing to pay a premium. The experience of watching the coffee being made by a barista in a setting that often resembles a quaint café in Florence, Italy, adds to the perceived value of the product, and to the price!

Goods are items that you can physically touch. Nike shoes, Pepsi-Cola, a Frappuccino, Kraft cheese, Tide, an iPad, and countless other

EXHIBIT 1.3 The Marketing Mix

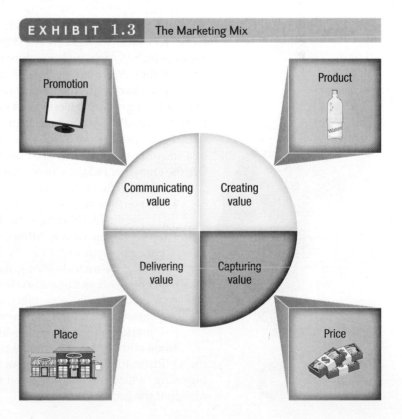

Marketers have transformed coffee from a simple morning drink into an entire experience that adds value for the customer.

products are examples of goods. As we describe at the start of Chapter 2, Nike primarily makes shoes but also adds value to its products by, for example, offering custom designs under its Nike ID brand that increase their fashionable appeal and enlisting popular celebrities such as Rafael Nadal to add their names to the designs.

Unlike goods, services are intangible customer benefits that are produced by people or machines and cannot be separated from the producer. When people buy tickets—whether for airline travel, a sporting event, or the theater—they are paying not for the physical ticket stub but of course for the experience they gain. For people who like to drink their coffee in a cozy, warm setting, Starbucks offers an experience that feels like home but encourages social interaction. Hotels, insurance agencies, and spas similarly provide services. Getting money from your bank, whether through an ATM or from a teller, is another example of using a service. In this case, cash machines usually add value to the banking experience because they are conveniently located, fast, and easy to use.

Many offerings in the market combine goods and services.[11] When you go to an optical center, you get your eyes examined (a service) and purchase new contact lenses (a good). If you attend a Bruno Mars concert, you can be enthralled by the world-class performance. To remember the event, you might want to pick up a shirt or a souvenir from the concert. With these tangible goods, you can relive and remember the enjoyment of the experience over and over again.

Hotels are well known for combining products (e.g., beds, sheets, televisions) with services (e.g., concierge, spas) to appeal to consumers. As Superior Service 1.1 shows, some hotels are at the cutting edge of service, coming up with innovative, unique ideas to help give customers the best experience they can, one that fits their needs and desires.

Ideas include thoughts, opinions, and philosophies; intellectual concepts such as these also can be marketed. Groups promoting bicycle safety go to schools, give talks, and sponsor bike helmet poster contests for the members of their primary market—children. Then their secondary target market segment, parents and siblings, gets involved through their interactions with the young contest participants. The exchange of value occurs when the children listen to the sponsors' presentation and wear their helmets while bicycling, which means they have adopted, or become "purchasers," of the safety idea that the group marketed.

Rafael Nadal plays tennis in Nike shoes.

Superior Service 1.1 | A Hotel to Get Away from It All—and Expand Your Twitter Feed[i]

In a world in which texting injuries—such as the accidents that happen when people hit a lamppost because they are looking down at their phones while walking—are increasingly common, a vacation without the distraction of modern technology might not be practical or appealing. Whereas once people might have dreamed of a vacation on a desert island, where no one could reach them, today many young travelers seek a destination that recognizes and facilitates their interactions through social media.

On the beautiful island of Majorca, Spain, the Sol Wave House is trying to do just that for Twitter users. The staff includes a Twitter concierge, whose job is to follow and respond to tweets by guests who might want information about places to party that night or need to have food delivered poolside. The interactions all rely on the hotel's proprietary app and Wi-Fi network that only registered guests can access.

Once they do, they can stay in contact with not only the Twitter concierge but also the cute potential date lounging a couple of deck chairs down on the pool deck. A tweet with a hashtag like "#chair10" alerts the person sitting in that chair to the user's interest. Alternatively, guests can just wait for the Twitter concierge to announce what time the next social gathering will be taking place. Beyond these immediate interactions, the hotel's entire décor is focused on Twitter users. Mirrors in the rooms feature funny moustaches and other decorations to enable guests to take and post funny selfies.

According to the hotel's vice president for global branding, "In our business, rooms are rooms and suites are suites, but in the end it's always about what you are doing to deliver an

Need information from the concierge on best place to dine? At the Sol Wave House it's only a tweet away.

experience to a customer." Thus competitive hotels promise similar experiences, such as the Ushuaia Ibiza Beach Hotel, where sensors placed throughout the grounds of the resort allow guests to update their Facebook statuses instantaneously.

On the other end of the spectrum, a growing number of hotels promise a "digital detox," such that they prohibit the use of phones or other technology in certain zones throughout their grounds. At the Quincy Hotel in Washington, guests who agree to lock their phones in the hotel's safe for their stay receive a gift certificate to a local bookstore.

Price: Capturing Value Everything has a price, although it doesn't always have to be monetary. Price, therefore, is everything the buyer gives up—money, time, and/or energy—in exchange for the product.[12] Marketers must determine the price of a product carefully on the basis of the potential buyer's belief about its value. For example, United Airlines can take you from New York to Denver. The price you pay for that service depends on how far in advance you book the ticket, the time of year, and whether you want to fly coach or business class. If you value the convenience of buying your ticket at the last minute for a ski trip between Christmas and New Year's Day and you want to fly business class, you can expect to pay four or five times as much as you would for the cheapest available ticket. That is, you have traded off a lower price for convenience. For marketers, the key to determining prices is figuring out how much customers are willing to pay so that they are satisfied with the purchase and the seller achieves a reasonable profit.

Place: Delivering the Value Proposition The third P, place, represents all the activities necessary to get the product to the right customer when that customer wants it. For Starbucks, that means expanding its storefronts constantly and proactively, so that it is easy for caffeine junkies to find their fix. Creative locations, such as kiosks at the baggage claim in airports or

When you attend a Bruno Mars concert you are paying for a service.

small booths in grocery stores, represent the chain's effort to improve its offering on this dimension of the marketing mix.

Place more commonly deals specifically with retailing and marketing channel management, also known as *supply chain management. Supply chain management* is the set of approaches and techniques that firms employ to efficiently and effectively integrate their suppliers, manufacturers, warehouses, stores, and other firms involved in the transaction (e.g., transportation companies) into a seamless value chain in which merchandise is produced and distributed in the right quantities, to the right locations, and at the right time, while minimizing systemwide costs and satisfying the service levels required by the customers. Many marketing students initially overlook the importance of marketing channel management, because a lot of these activities are behind the scenes. But without a strong and efficient marketing channel system, merchandise isn't available when customers want it. Then customers are disappointed, and sales and profits suffer.

Promotion: Communicating the Value Proposition Even the best products and services will go unsold if marketers cannot communicate their value to customers. Promotion is communication by a marketer that informs, persuades, and reminds potential buyers about a product or service to influence their opinions and elicit a response. Promotion generally can enhance a product's or service's value. When the publisher of the well-known Babar books wanted to celebrate the 80th anniversary of the series, it initiated a $100,000 campaign. Working in collaboration with toy and bookstores, the campaign did not just suggest people buy the books and read about an elephant king. Instead, it embraced a sense of nostalgia and evoked a simpler time, in which grandparents might read pleasant stories to their grandchildren.[13]

Such collaborative promotions can be especially effective tactics for marketers, particularly if they can team up with a popular sport, as Social and Mobile Marketing 1.1 details.

Marketing Can Be Performed by Both Individuals and Organizations

Imagine how complicated the world would be if you had to buy everything you consumed directly from producers or manufacturers. You would have to go from farm to farm buying your food and then from manufacturer to manufacturer to purchase the table, plates, and utensils you needed to eat that food. Fortunately, marketing intermediaries, such as retailers, accumulate merchandise from producers in large amounts and then sell it to you in smaller amounts. The process by which businesses sell to consumers is known as B2C (business-to-consumer) marketing, whereas the process of selling merchandise or services from one business to another is called B2B (business-to-business) marketing. With the advent of various Internet auction sites (e.g., eBay) and social media, consumers have started marketing their products and services to other consumers. This third category, in which consumers sell to other consumers, is C2C (consumer-to-consumer) marketing. These marketing transactions are illustrated in Exhibit 1.4.

EXHIBIT 1.4	Marketing Can Be Performed by Both Individuals and Organizations

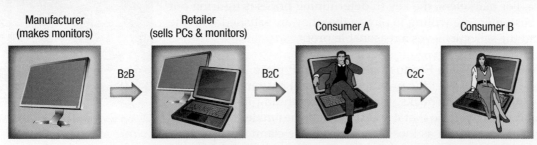

Manufacturer (makes monitors)		Retailer (sells PCs & monitors)		Consumer A		Consumer B
	B2B		B2C		C2C	

Social & Mobile Marketing 1.1   Snacks, Teams, Players, and Promotions[ii]

Sponsorships of sports teams are nothing new. Firms have been naming stadiums, providing gear, and calling themselves the "official product of" popular sporting events and teams for years. But such promotions can take on new life and new facets when they bring the power of social media marketing to bear on their campaigns.

Take the example of Mondelēz International and its latest deal in conjunction with various soccer teams and players. The company maintains such well-known brands as Chips Ahoy! and Oreo cookies, Wheat Thins and Ritz crackers, Cadbury candies, and Sour Patch Kids Stride gum. Thus its product assortment is quite strongly geared toward children and families.

Recent trends suggest that more children today play soccer (17.1 percent of them play at least once a year) than other sports such as baseball (13.4 percent), football (4.5 percent), or hockey (1.1 percent). Mondelēz was quick to make the connection and entered into a sponsorship agreement that made it the official snack brand of the U.S. men's and women's national soccer teams. Furthermore, it signed individual sponsorship deals with some stars of the sport, such as Alex Morgan, Omar Gonzalez, and Clint Dempsey.

Despite this popularity among children and their infamous soccer moms, soccer still struggles in television ratings compared with other sports. Accordingly, the promotional campaigns associated with the sponsorship have very little to do with television. Instead, the focus is on in-store and social media efforts.

In conjunction with its sponsorship of U.S. soccer, Mondelēz has entered into a partnership with Twitter to increase its advertising spending at the site. In return, Twitter will share its real-time marketing expertise, offer customized marketing research findings, and host various training programs for the packaged-goods company.

This effort represents a continuation of Mondelez's already strong social media presence. For example, Oreo has nearly 35 million followers on Facebook. It also won praise for its quick thinking during the power outage at Super Bowl XLVII, when it immediately tweeted, "You can still dunk in the dark." By linking a snack that appeals to children with a sport they love, Mondelēz vastly increases the chances that moms will bring the tasty cookies for a postgame celebration with the little league team.

Mondelēz is the official snack brand for the U.S. men's and women's national soccer teams. To appeal to its young target market, it uses social media instead of television. Pictured here, wearing a Sour Patch Kids T-shirt, is U.S. soccer star Alex Morgan giving a "high five."

Individuals can also undertake activities to market themselves. When you apply for a job, for instance, the research you do about the firm, the résumé and cover letter you submit with your application, and the way you dress for an interview and conduct yourself during it are all forms of marketing activities. Accountants, lawyers, financial planners, physicians, and other professional service providers also constantly market their services one way or another.

"Milk Life" replaced the famous "Got Milk" campaign in 2014, but the ads still create a high level of awareness for the milk industry.

Marketing Affects Various Stakeholders

Most people think of marketing as a way to facilitate the sale of products or services to customers or clients. But marketing can also affect several other stakeholders (e.g., supply chain partners, society at large). Partners in the supply chain include wholesalers, retailers, or other intermediaries such as transportation or warehousing companies. All of these entities are involved in marketing to one another. Manufacturers sell merchandise to retailers, but the retailers often have to convince manufacturers to sell to them. After many years of not being able to purchase products from Ralph Lauren because it sells below the manufacturers' suggested retail price (MSRP), TJX Companies, Inc., operators of Marshall's and TJMaxx, among others, is now Ralph Lauren's largest customer.[14]

Marketing also can aim to benefit an entire industry or society at large. The dairy industry's Milk Processor Education Program (MilkPEP) used a very successful, award-winning campaign with its slogan "Got Milk?" aimed at different target segments. This campaign has not only created high levels of awareness about the benefits of drinking milk but also increased milk consumption in various target segments, perhaps in response to the use of various celebrities, from Dwayne "the Rock" Johnson and Victor Cruz to Miranda Lambert and Nina Dobrev. In 2014, "milk life" replaced the famous "Got Milk" campaign, but the latest ads continue to create a high level of awareness for the milk industry. The campaigns benefit the entire dairy industry and promote the health benefits of drinking milk to society at large.

Marketing Helps Create Value

Marketing didn't get to its current prominence among individuals, corporations, and society at large overnight.[15] To understand how marketing has evolved into its present-day, integral business function of creating value, let's look for a moment at some of the milestones in marketing's short history (see Exhibit 1.5).

EXHIBIT 1.5 Marketing Evolution: Production, Sales, Marketing, and Value

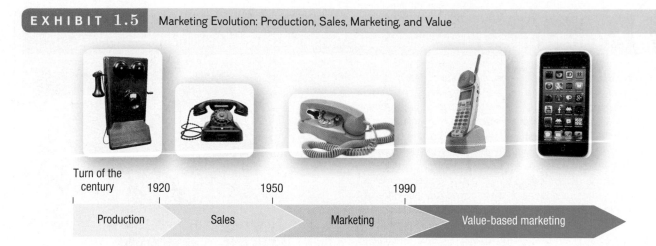

Turn of the century | 1920 | 1950 | 1990

Production ▶ Sales ▶ Marketing ▶ Value-based marketing

Production-Oriented Era Around the turn of the 20th century, most firms were production oriented and believed that a good product would sell itself. Henry Ford, the founder of Ford Motor Company, once famously remarked, "Customers can have any color they want so long as it's black." Manufacturers were concerned with product innovation, not with satisfying the needs of individual consumers, and retail stores typically were considered places to hold the merchandise until a consumer wanted it.

Sales-Oriented Era Between 1920 and 1950, production and distribution techniques became more sophisticated and the Great Depression and World War II conditioned customers to consume less or manufacture items themselves, so they planted victory gardens instead of buying produce. As a result, manufacturers had the capacity to produce more than customers really wanted or were able to buy. Firms found an answer to their overproduction in becoming sales oriented: they depended on heavy doses of personal selling and advertising.

Market-Oriented Era After World War II, soldiers returned home, got new jobs, and started families. At the same time, manufacturers turned from focusing on the war effort toward making consumer products. Suburban communities, featuring cars in every garage, sprouted up around the country, and the new suburban fixture, the shopping center, began to replace cities' central business districts as the hub of retail activity and a place to just hang out. Some products, once in limited supply because of World War II, became plentiful. And the United States entered a buyers' market—the customer became king! When consumers again had choices, they were able to make purchasing decisions on the basis of factors such as quality, convenience, and price. Manufacturers and retailers thus began to focus on what consumers wanted and needed before they designed, made, or attempted to sell their products and services. It was during this period that firms discovered marketing.

Value-Based Marketing Era Most successful firms today are market oriented.[16] That means they generally have transcended a production or selling orientation and attempt to discover and satisfy their customers' needs and wants. Before the turn of the 21st century, better marketing firms recognized that there was more to good marketing than simply discovering and providing what consumers wanted and needed; to compete successfully, they would have to give their customers greater value than their competitors did. (The importance of value is appropriately incorporated into the AMA definition of marketing discussed earlier.)

Value reflects the relationship of benefits to costs, or what you *get* for what you *give*.[17] In a marketing context, customers seek a fair return in goods and/or services for their hard-earned money and scarce time. They want products or services that meet their specific needs or wants *and* that are offered at a price that they believe is a good value. A good value, however, doesn't necessarily mean the product or service is inexpensive. If it did, luxury goods manufacturers like

Gucci provides value to its target customers.

Adding Value 1.1   Smartphone? Try Smart Glasses, Smart Monitors, Smart . . .[iii]

It may be hard to imagine, but just a few short years ago the idea of being able to talk to someone while away from home was a massive added value. Then the value added became being able check e-mail on a phone. Such offerings seem incredibly basic today. Obviously, the "smart" market is a dynamic and rapidly changing one in which the definition of what constitutes value also changes constantly.

Some of the most modern smart gadgets seek to make it easier for people to engage in their day-to-day activities. An app by Mercedes-Benz allows car owners to unlock their doors or open the trunk with their phones. Alternatively, an external device, Hone, attaches to key chains and allows smartphone users to activate a visual and audio signal so that they can find their car keys wherever they left them (e.g., in the freezer, tucked in a drawer).

For exercise fans, the Nike Fit band calculates steps taken, calories burned, and time spent exercising, then syncs the information gathered from the wristband with a mobile app that combines all the information in one place. The UP band, by Jawbone, tracks all this information, as well as sleep times and food intake. Thus it can tell users how long they took to fall asleep and how many hours of deep sleep they actually got. Then it promises to summarize this information in "Insights," which suggest recommendations based on individual trends. If a person sleeps poorly after snacking late in the day, UP will recommend no more eating after 8:00 p.m., for example. For even more adventurous exercisers, the Crash Sensor, a device made to mount onto a bicycle helmet, alerts emergency contacts if a crash occurs and provides coordinates so that emergency crews can find a hiker lost in the wilderness.

Other smart tools are a little more forward thinking, moving us into a future world in which connecting to anyone, anywhere doesn't even require our thumbs. Perhaps the most widely talked about version is Google Glass, the technology that puts the web in the corner of users' vision and allows them to connect, using only eye movement. This revolutionary innovation appears likely to change virtually everything (pun intended). However, its rollout has been slow thus far and the

Smartphones and related connected devices/apps, such as Google Glass, are revolutionizing the marketplace.

company has sought to avoid moving smartphone apps to Glass. So Google has created guidelines for developing "Glassware": keep the information concise, keep alerts relevant, make tasks easy, and make information provision timely.

Nearly as ubiquitous as the chatter about the device are the concerns about it. Critics have questioned how Google Glass might alter social interactions, cause accidents by people focused on the web rather than where they are walking, and even rewire our cognitive capacities. The promise of Google Glass is so intriguing, though, that consumers are lining up to pay around $1,500 for the potential to mess with their brain matter.

Porsche or Gucci would go out of business. There are customers willing to pay asking prices for all types of goods at all price levels because to those individuals, what they get for what they give is a good value.

A creative way to provide value to customers is to engage in **value cocreation**.[18] In this case, customers can act as collaborators to create the product or service. When clients work with their investment advisers, they cocreate their investment portfolios; when Nike allows customers to custom design their sneakers, they are cocreating. Adding Value 1.1 examines how companies are adding value to smartphones by developing smart accessories.

In the next section, we explore the notion of value-based marketing further. Specifically, we look at various options for attracting customers by providing them with better value than the competition does. Then we discuss how firms compete on the basis of value. Finally, we examine how firms transform the value concept into their value-driven activities.

How Do Marketing Firms Become More Value Driven?

LO2 Describe how marketers create value for a product or service.

Firms become value driven by focusing on four activities. First, they share information about their customers and competitors across their own organization and with other firms that help them get the product or service to the marketplace, such as manufacturers and transportation companies. Second, they strive to balance their customers' benefits and costs. Third, they concentrate on building relationships with customers. Fourth, they need to take advantage of new technologies and connect with their customers using social and mobile media.

Sharing Information In a value-based, market-oriented firm, marketers share information about customers and competitors (see Chapter 9 on marketing research) and integrate it across the firm's various departments. The fashion designers for J. Crew, for instance, collect purchase information and research customer trends to determine what their customers will want to wear in the next few weeks; simultaneously, the logisticians—those persons in charge of getting the merchandise to the stores—use the same purchase history to forecast sales and allocate appropriate merchandise to individual stores. Sharing and coordinating such information represents a critical success factor for any firm. Imagine what might happen if J. Crew's advertising department were to plan a special promotion but not share its sales projections with those people in charge of creating the merchandise or getting it to stores.

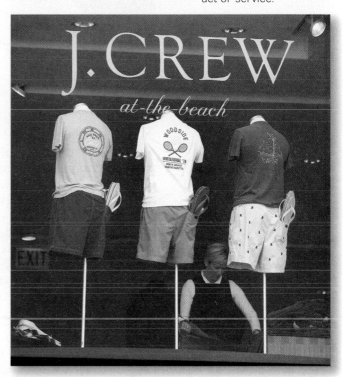

Collecting and sharing information among departments at J.Crew is important for its success.

Balancing Benefits with Costs Value-oriented marketers constantly measure the benefits that customers perceive against the cost of their offerings. They use available customer data to find opportunities to satisfy their customers' needs better, keep down costs, and develop long-term loyalties. For example, IKEA does not have highly paid salespeople to sell its furniture, but its simple designs mean customers can easily choose a product and assemble it themselves.

Building Relationships with Customers During the past couple of decades, marketers have begun to develop a *relational orientation* as they have realized

Furniture retailer IKEA focuses on what its customers value—low prices and great design.

Apple makes its new products compatible with existing ones to maintain a long-term relationship with its customers.

that they need to think about their customers in terms of relationships rather than transactions.[19] To build relationships, firms focus on the lifetime profitability of the relationship, not how much money is made during each transaction. Thus, Apple makes its innovations compatible with existing products to encourage consumers to maintain a long-term relationship with the company across all their electronic needs.

This relationship approach uses a process known as customer relationship management (CRM), a business philosophy and set of strategies, programs, and systems that focus on identifying and building loyalty among the firm's most valued customers.[20] Firms that employ CRM systematically collect information about their customers' needs and then use that information to target their best customers with the products, services, and special promotions that appear most important to them.

Marketers connect with customers by using social and mobile media.

Connecting with Customers Using Social and Mobile Media
Marketers are steadily embracing new technologies, such as social and mobile media, to allow them to connect better with their customers and thereby serve their needs more effectively. Businesses take social and mobile media seriously, including these advanced tools in the development of their marketing strategies. In turn, 93 percent of marketers assert that they use social media tools for their businesses.[21] That's largely because approximately 4.2 billion people link to some social media sites through their mobile devices.[22]

Yet even with this astounding penetration, only 10 percent of the world's population uses Facebook—which means 90 percent still has not signed up. The United States and United Kingdom may be approaching saturation, but there is still huge growth potential for social networks. Before users can sign up for Facebook, though, they need access to high-speed Internet.[23] Other countries continue to experience higher Facebook growth rates as they gain greater Internet access, and as Facebook becomes available in more languages (around 70 currently). The global average Internet penetration rate hovers below 40 percent, with massive populations in Africa and Asia still limited in their access.[24]

Beyond social media sites, online travel agencies such as Expedia, Travelocity, Orbitz, Priceline, and Kayak have become the first place that users go to book travel arrangements. According

Make travel arrangements online either through Facebook or your mobile app and check-in is a breeze.

to the U.S. Travel Association, in addition to asking friends and relying on their own experience, 10 percent of travelers turned to destination websites, 9 percent relied on websites run by specific providers, another 5 percent used social networking, and 4 percent of them depended on their mobile devices to plan their trips.[25] Customers who book hotels using travel agencies become loyal to the agency that gives them the lowest prices, rather than to any particular hotel brand. So hotels are using social media and mobile applications to lure customers back to their specific brands by engaging in conversations with them on Facebook and allowing fans of the page to book their hotel reservations through Facebook. Some hotel chains have mobile applications that allow customers to make changes to their reservations, shift check-in and check-out times, and add amenities or services to their stays. The hotels know a lot about their customers because they collect information about their previous visits, including the type of room they stayed in, their preferences (from pillows to drinks consumed from the minibar), and the type of room service they prefer.

Several restaurant chains are exploiting location-based social media applications, such as Happy Cow Vegin Out, Yelp, Food spotting, in Bloom, and Alfred.[26] By using location-based apps on mobile phones, customers can find restaurants that cater to their specific dietary requirements (such as Happy Cow, which identifies nearby vegetarian restaurants) or find well-rated (by Yelp users) restaurants nearby. The result is that users are driving the way brands and stores are interacting with social media. Location-based services are thus appealing, though they also may create some concerns, as Ethical and Societal Dilemma 1.1 describes.

Buffalo Wild Wings suggests that its diners check in to its locations using their phones. The target customers for this chain are young and tech savvy, and with its in-house games and sports broadcasts, Buffalo Wild Wings is uniquely situated to encourage customers to connect and bring their friends along. It offers contests and encourages frequent visits to win. Customers can earn free chicken wings or soft drinks within their first three visits. Other contests encourage patrons to upload photos of the crowd's reaction to a big play. Moreover, customers can develop their own challenges from their bar stools. Approximately 10,000 people participated in 33,000 challenges, and 5,000 rewards were given out in the first week of Buffalo Wild Wings' contests by using location-based applications.[27]

Ethical & Societal Dilemma 1.1   Beckoning Consumers with the iBeacon[iv]

When iPad and iPhone owners updated their systems to iOS 7, they also transformed their devices into a new type of communication channel, whether they realized it or not. Specifically, the latest operating system update installed iBeacon software onto their mobile devices.

The iBeacon software works as a location service, such that transmitters can send messages to any user with an iPhone or iPad that has been updated to iOS 7. Apple soon announced that it already had installed transmitters into all of its U.S. stores. When Apple fans visit the stores, the iBeacon location service will push notifications to them based on their specific location. A shopper who pauses by the updated MacBook Air might receive a message on her phone about its battery life or compatibility with her phone. Another consumer who breezes past the phones could receive a reminder that he is eligible for an upgrade.

This application is notable; it indicates that Apple has jumped ahead of its competitors in devising and implementing hyper-targeted, micro-location-based marketing. For its retail stores, the software reveals not just whether a potential customer is in the same town or near the parking lot, but also whether a shopper is literally standing near the accessory display.

This rollout in the Apple stores appears to be just the tip of the iceberg. Recent model iPhones and iPads can not only receive messages using the iBeacon software but also be easily configured to serve as a transmitter of iBeacon messages. This means that virtually every retailer that invests in an iPad can use the software similar to the way Apple uses it: pushing notifications to shoppers who are already in the store, locating them precisely, and learning exactly how they move through the store. One estimate suggests that there are approximately 200 million potential iBeacon transmitters already in circulation—even before the functionality has gained widespread acclaim.

For Apple, the competitive advantage appears nearly insurmountable because when users updated to iOS 7, they also

This Estimote Beacon enables Apple users to opt-in to receive micro-location-based messages in physical locations, helping them find products, deals, and more information about their surroundings.

opted in to the iBeacon application, agreeing to accept the micro-location-based push notifications. Other stores will need to get consumers to agree to receive similar messages. For big retailers such as Walmart, it might not be hard; they can simply include the software in their regular apps that consumers already may have downloaded.

Furthermore, Apple has essentially blazed the trail for this latest innovation for retail. Combining its dominance in the tablet market, popularity in the mobile phone market, and first-mover advantages in the location service market, it appears that the iBeacon is set to become the standard.

But even if Apple has thought ahead about how to make sure users adopt the iBeacon, it might not have considered all the implications for users' privacy. Are companies responsible for making sure their customers know their identity and location are being revealed to marketers all the time? Or are customers the ones responsible for opting out of such location-based services?

CHECK YOURSELF

1. Does providing a good value mean selling at a low price?
2. How are marketers connecting with customers through social and mobile media?

 LO3 Understand why marketing is important both within and outside the firm.

WHY IS MARKETING IMPORTANT?

Marketing once was only an afterthought to production. Early marketing philosophy went something like this: "We've made it; now how do we get rid of it?" However, marketing not only has shifted its focus dramatically, it also has evolved into a major business function that crosses all areas of a firm or organization, as illustrated in Exhibit 1.6. Marketing advises production about how much of the company's product to make and then tells logistics when to ship it. It creates

EXHIBIT 1.6 Importance of Marketing

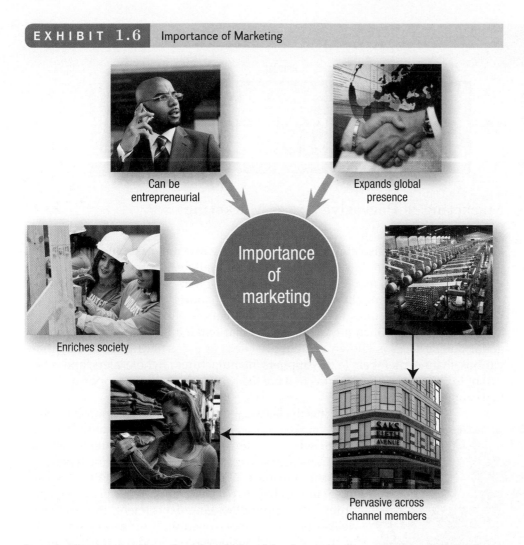

Can be entrepreneurial

Expands global presence

Importance of marketing

Enriches society

Pervasive across channel members

long-lasting, mutually valuable relationships between the company and the firms from which it buys.[28] It identifies those elements that local customers value and makes it possible for the firm to expand globally. Marketing has had a significant impact on consumers as well. Without marketing, it would be difficult for any of us to learn about new products and services. Understanding marketing can even help you find a job after you finish school.

Marketing Expands Firms' Global Presence

A generation ago Coca-Cola was available in many nations, but Levi's and most other U.S. brands weren't. Blue jeans were primarily an American product—made in the United States for the U.S. market. But today most jeans, including those of Levi Strauss & Co., are made in places other than the United States and are available nearly everywhere. Thanks to MTV and other global entertainment venues, cheap foreign travel, and the Internet, you share many of your consumption behaviors with college students in countries all over the globe. The best fashions, music, and even food trends disseminate rapidly around the world. Take a look at your next shopping bag. Whatever it contains, you will find goods from many countries—produce from Mexico, jeans from Japan, electronics from Korea. Global manufacturers and retailers continue to make inroads into the U.S. market. The Dutch grocery store giant Ahold is among the top five grocery store chains in the United States, though you may never have heard of it because it operates under names such as Stop & Shop, GIANT, and Peapod in the United States.[29] As marketing helps expand firms' global presence, it also enhances global career opportunities for marketing professionals.

EXHIBIT 1.7   Supply Chain

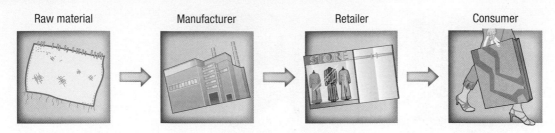

| Raw material | Manufacturer | Retailer | Consumer |

Marketing Is Pervasive across Marketing Channel Members

Firms do not work in isolation. Manufacturers buy raw materials and components from suppliers, which they sell to wholesalers, retailers, or other businesses after they have turned the materials into products (see Exhibit 1.7). Every time materials or products are bought or sold, they are transported to a different location, which sometimes requires that they be stored in a warehouse operated by yet another organization. Such a group of firms that make and deliver a given set of goods and services is known as a supply chain or a marketing channel. All the various channel members (e.g., suppliers, manufacturers, wholesalers, and retailers) of the supply chain are firms that are likely to provide career opportunities to marketing professionals.

You may soon be receiving your Amazon orders on Sunday.

Effectively managing supply chain relationships often has a marked impact on a firm's ability to satisfy the consumer, which results in increased profitability for all parties. Consider the recently announced agreement between Amazon and the U.S. Postal Service (USPS) to expand their supply chain to provide Sunday delivery of Amazon orders. In a groundbreaking experiment, the USPS will deliver packages emblazoned with Amazon's smile logo to customers and businesses on Sundays, the first time it has assigned delivery drivers to work on that day. Neither of the USPS's main competitors, UPS and FedEx, offer Sunday delivery. For Amazon, the deal provides a stellar competitive benefit: Buyers can plan on receiving items they order every day of the week. The deal appears particularly appealing to Amazon's Prime customers, who pay an annual fee to guarantee two-day delivery. For a shopper browsing Amazon on Friday, it means receiving all purchases within those two days, instead of having to discount Sunday and wait for Monday for the delivery.[30]

Marketing Enriches Society

Should marketing focus on factors other than financial profitability, like good corporate citizenry? Many of America's best-known corporations seem to think so because they have undertaken various marketing activities, such as developing greener products, making healthier food options and safer products in this direction, and improving their supply chains to reduce their carbon footprint. At a more macro level, firms are making socially responsible activities an integral component of everything they do.

Socially responsible firms recognize that including a strong social orientation in business is a sound strategy that is in both its own and its customers' best interest. It shows the consumer marketplace that the firm will be around for the long run and can be trusted with the marketplace's business. In a volatile market, investors view firms that operate with high levels of corporate responsibility and ethics as safe investments. Similarly, firms have come to realize that good corporate citizenship through socially responsible actions should be a priority because it will help their bottom line in the long run.[31]

Marketing Can Be Entrepreneurial

Whereas marketing plays a major role in the success of large corporations, it also is at the center of the successes of numerous new ventures initiated by **entrepreneurs,** or people who organize, operate, and assume the risk of a business venture.[32] Key to the success of many such entrepreneurs is that they launch ventures that aim to satisfy unfilled needs. Some examples of successful ventures (and their founders) that understood their customers and added value include:

When you think of Oprah Winfrey, think big: Harpo Productions, Inc.; O, The Oprah Magazine; O at Home magazine; Harpo Films; the OWN television network; not to mention her philanthropic work with the Oprah Winfrey Foundation.

- Ben & Jerry's (Ben Cohen and Jerry Greenfield)
- Birchbox (Hayley Barna and Katia Beauchamp)
- Amazon (Jeff Bezos)
- Netflix (Reed Hastings)
- OWN (Oprah Winfrey)

An extraordinary entrepreneur and marketer, Oprah Winfrey was a self-made billionaire before she turned 50 years of age. Winfrey went from being the youngest person and first African American woman to anchor news at WTVF-TV in Nashville, Tennessee, to being only the third woman in history to head her own production studio. Under the Oprah banner are a variety of successful endeavors, including Harpo Films, Oprah's Book Club, Oprah.com, the Oxygen television network, and the Oprah Winfrey Network (OWN). In addition to producing two of the highest rated talk shows ever on television, *The Oprah Winfrey Show* and *Dr. Phil,* Harpo Studios has produced films such as *Beloved* and *Tuesdays with Morrie.* Oprah's philanthropic contributions are vast and varied. Through the Oprah Winfrey Foundation and Oprah's Angel Network, people worldwide have raised more than $80 million for scholarships, schools, women's shelters, and youth centers.[33] Although her signature televised talk show has ended, her influence persists.

Great and distinguished entrepreneurs have visions of how certain combinations of products and services can satisfy unfilled needs.[34] They find and understand a marketing opportunity (i.e., the unfilled need), conduct a thorough examination of the marketplace, and develop and communicate the value of their product and services to potential consumers.

CHECK YOURSELF

1. List five functions that illustrate the importance of marketing.
2. A firm doing the right thing emphasizes the importance of marketing to _____.

Reviewing Learning Objectives

 Define the role of marketing in organizations.

Marketing is the activity, set of institutions, and processes for creating, capturing, communicating, delivering, and exchanging offerings that have value for customers, clients, partners, and society at large. Marketing strives to *create value* in many ways. If marketers are to succeed, their customers must believe that the firm's products and services are valuable; that is, they are worth more to the customers than they cost. Another important and closely related marketing role is to capture value of a product or service based on potential buyers' beliefs about its value. Marketers also enhance the value of products and services through various forms of *communication*, such as advertising and personal selling. Through communications, marketers educate and inform customers about the benefits of their products and services and thereby increase their perceived value. Marketers facilitate the *delivery of value* by making sure the right products and services are available when, where, and in the quantities their customers want. Better marketers are not concerned about just one transaction with their customers. They recognize the value of loyal customers and strive to develop *long-term relationships* with them.

 Describe how marketers create value for a product or service.

Value represents the relationship of benefits to costs. Firms can improve their value by increasing benefits, reducing costs, or both. The best firms integrate a value orientation into everything they do. If an activity doesn't increase benefits or reduce costs, it probably shouldn't occur. Firms become value driven by finding out as much as they can about their customers and those customers' needs and wants. They share this information with their partners, both up and down the marketing channel, so the entire chain collectively can focus on the customer. The key to true value-based marketing is the ability to design products and services that achieve precisely the right balance between benefits and costs. Value-based marketers aren't necessarily worried about how much money they will make on the next sale. Instead, they are concerned with developing a lasting relationship with their customers so those customers return again and again.

 Understand why marketing is important both within and outside the firm.

Successful firms integrate marketing throughout their organizations so that marketing activities coordinate with other functional areas such as product design, production, logistics, and human resources, enabling them to get the right product to the right customers at the right time. Marketing helps facilitate the smooth flow of goods through the supply chain, all the way from raw materials to the consumer. From a personal perspective, the marketing function facilitates your buying process and can support your career goals. Marketing also can be important for society through its embrace of solid, ethical business practices. Firms "do the right thing" when they sponsor charitable events, seek to reduce environmental impacts, and avoid unethical practices; such efforts endear the firm to customers. Finally, marketing is a cornerstone of entrepreneurialism. Not only have many great companies been founded by outstanding marketers, but an entrepreneurial spirit pervades the marketing decisions of firms of all sizes.

Key Terms   ■LEARNSMART·

- B2B (business-to-business) marketing, 10
- B2C (business-to-consumer) marketing, 10
- consumer-to-consumer C2C (consumer-to-consumer) marketing, 10
- customer relationship management (CRM), 16

- entrepreneur, 21
- exchange, 6
- goods, 7
- ideas, 8
- marketing, 4
- marketing channel, 20
- marketing mix (four Ps), 7

- marketing plan, 4
- relational orientation, 15
- service, 8
- supply chain, 20
- value, 13
- value cocreation, 14

Marketing Applications

1. Do you know the difference between needs and wants? When companies that sell coffee develop their marketing strategy, do they concentrate on satisfying their customers' needs or wants? What about a utility company, such as the local power company? A humanitarian agency, such as Doctors without Borders?

2. People can apply marketing principles to finding a job. If the person looking for a job is the product, describe the other three Ps.

3. What is the difference between a good and a service? When you buy a music subscription on Pandora, are you buying a good or a service? Would your answer be different if you bought an MP3 album on Amazon?

4. One of your friends was recently watching TV and saw an advertisement that she liked. She said, "Wow that was great marketing!" Was the ad, in fact, marketing?

5. Using the four Ps, discuss how the Apple iBeacon will create value for customers.

6. Columbia Sportswear sells a men's fleece vest for $36 and an Omni-Heat Jacket for $1,200. Is Columbia Sportswear providing the target markets for these products with a good value? Explain your answer.

7. Assume you have been hired into the marketing department of a major consumer products manufacturer, such as Nike. You are having lunch with some new colleagues in other departments—finance, manufacturing, and logistics. They are arguing that the company could save millions of dollars if it just got rid of the marketing department. Develop an argument that would persuade them otherwise.

8. Why do marketers like Apple find it important to embrace societal needs and ethical business practices? Provide an example of a societal need or ethical business practice that Apple is addressing.

Quiz Yourself

1. Melanie works for a small computer software company. Her boss is constantly improving the company's products but neglects customers, billing, and promoting of the company. Her boss is probably stuck in the _____ era.
   a. production-oriented
   b. sales-oriented
   c. market-oriented
   d. value-based marketing
   e. retailing-oriented

2. In delivering value, marketing firms attempt to find the most desirable balance between:

   a. the need for value and the perception of value
   b. explicit versus implicit value
   c. the need to provide benefits to customers and the desire to keep down costs
   d. the desire to satisfy customers and the need to keep customers from running the company
   e. the need for product improvement and the need for advertising

   (Answers to these two questions can be found on page 651.)

Net Savvy

1. Visit Apple (www.apple.com). What value does Apple provide customers? What are the advantages to using Apple to buy music or to rent or buy videos?

2. Go to Facebook.com and click on "About" at the bottom of the page, then click on the About tab. What is Facebook's mission? How could a marketer use Facebook, and what other social media tools could they use? What are the drawbacks a marketer might face when using Facebook to communicate with their customers?

3. Visit Mondelēz International's website (www.mondelezinternational.com), then click on the "Brand Family" link. In what major categories does Mondelēz have brands? Can you identify related categories in which the company should compete?

Chapter Case Study

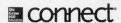

A STARBUCKS JUGGERNAUT

Recall the quote from Howard Schultz, CEO of Starbucks, that we cited in the opening vignette to this chapter: "We have a lot going on." As this chapter has sought to demonstrate, good marketing requires that its practitioners always have a lot happening. Marketing demands concentration and creativity, close attention and open-mindedness, as well as careful analysis and the courage to take risks. Schultz recently offered another quote that summarizes these demands quite effectively: "We cannot be content with the status quo," he said. "Any business today that embraces the status quo as an operating principle is going to be on a death march."[35]

Starbucks' march seems to be in the opposite direction. In particular, its net revenues and stock prices have risen continuously since 2009.[36] Thus, for 2012 its global revenues reached a record-setting $13.3 billion. Its stock price recently reached more than $74 per share.[37]

International Expansions

Part of the reason for these increased sales has been Starbucks' continued pursuit of growth and expansion. Along with finding new locations in its home market of the United States, recent international expansions have spread the brand to Turkey, India, and Norway. In 2014 it plans to enter Colombia. Accordingly, the number of stores worldwide has grown to more than 20,000, demonstrating its consistent commitment to keep getting better, rather than resting on its laurels (or tea leaves).

Such expansions require a little flexibility, though, to make sure the marketing plan matches the market. In the United States, Starbucks actively avoids any franchise agreements. It wants to own all its stores to ensure consistency and quality. But that strict preference has not worked well in Europe, where it discovered it needed some help to access smaller markets. Although still a small segment of its total stores, nine franchisees in the United Kingdom now own 45 Starbucks stores.[38] Furthermore, in nations with strict laws regarding foreign ownership of business, such as India and China, Starbucks has agreed to enter into joint venture partnerships, to make sure it can access these massive and growing markets.

Yet Starbucks is also all too aware of the damage done in the mid-2000s, when it expanded so rapidly and indiscriminately that customers starting rejecting the chain as too ubiquitous—too much, everywhere they turned. The company slumped during that period, suffering from a weakened reputation, negative press, and consumer complaints about quality.

Starbucks has quickly spread across the globe, including to this location in China.

Product Innovation

Growth for the corporation also comes about through expanding into new product lines. The purchase of Teavana for $620 million represents its efforts to do for tea what it already has done for coffee—turn it into a pleasurable, happy experience that people can treat themselves to on a daily basis. Its Teavana stores have more than 100 flavors on hand, including nontraditional names such as Slimful Chocolate Decadence Oolong, Cococaramel Sea Salt, Yunnan Golden Pu-Erh, and Spice of Life.[39]

Of course, this is not to suggest that Starbucks has never erred in its marketing decisions. Even the best marketers are prone to stumble sometimes. When Starbucks sought to expand its line of breakfast foods, consumers responded with a widespread "eh." The offerings, such as egg sandwiches, were bland and unappealing and they often took too long to prepare, especially for busy baristas during the morning rush.

But part of the success of the chain is its ability to learn from its mistakes. When Starbucks purchased La Boulange Café and Bakery for $100 million, it tasked the chain's founder, Pascal Rigo, with laying out a specific plan for adding to the pastries in its display cases. Rigo had multiple tasks to complete before his croissants and muffins would make it into Starbucks. He had to find a way to fit freezers into every single Starbucks store (not an easy task in tiny shops, where space is at a premium). He had to define a training plan to help baristas learn how and when to suggest and sell the pastries. And he needed to identify or create local bakeries that could be trusted to make the products consistently and on time and supply them to each store.[40]

These tasks were part of the marketing plan; without establishing a good supply, Starbucks would not allow the foods into its well-designed, appealing stores. But by paying attention to the detail and thinking creatively, Rigo and Starbucks found a way to make La Boulange pastries an appealing addition to Starbucks stores.

Promotion Innovations

Starbucks is leveraging the promotion P as well by developing thoughtful campaigns that reflect currency and the image and corporate personality that it wishes to portray. In the fall of 2013, responding to growing concern over a potential shutdown of the federal government due to political gridlock, Starbucks launched a promotional campaign that helped assuage customers' fears (if only slightly) by giving them a free cup of coffee. Starbucks' "Come Together" campaign offered a reward for showing kindness to a stranger by giving a free coffee to any customer who bought a cup for someone else in line.[41]

Pricing

From its inception, Starbucks has charged premium (say "high") prices. With relatively few specialty coffeehouses in the United States at the time, it stood out as being unique in many markets. Most Americans had never tasted freshly ground espresso, let alone cappuccinos or lattes. They certainly hadn't experienced the warm, inviting, and relaxing atmosphere in which they could sit and visit with friends or do some reading or work. The personalized exchange customers had with a barista was also unusual.

Even after it experienced intense competition from McDonald's, Dunkin'Donuts, and independent coffeehouses; rapid expansion both in the United States and internationally; and a back to its roots change of strategy that reflects quality products and superior service, it still commands a premium price. Moving into the future, Starbucks is counting on the increased use of payment via smartphone apps, prepaid cards, and credit cards to take away some of the sting of its relatively high prices. Where price increases used to be very obvious when you had to count out the dollars, using a prepaid card makes customers less sensitive to the premium prices.[42]

Improvements to the Supply Chain

As the La Boulange example shows, Starbucks has learned the importance of a consistent supply of products. The supply chain is critical to any good marketing effort, another lesson that Starbucks seemingly has learned the hard way. When it first chose to distribute ground coffee and beans through grocery stores, it turned to an existing consumer packaged-goods company, Kraft, for help. The partnership was not successful and ultimately fell apart.

In particular, Starbucks alleged that Kraft was not doing enough to market and promote its branded goods. In demonstrating its ability to pay attention to changes in its situation, Starbucks also contended that the partnership was limiting its marketing capacities. For example, the agreement required that it produce only single-serve coffee pods that fit Kraft's Tassimo system. Thus, Starbucks could not compete with other providers for the segment of consumers who had purchased other systems, such as Keurig.[43]

By securing greater control over its distribution, Starbucks also can more rapidly and effectively implement new strategies for its consumer packaged-goods business. This sector is a strong focus for Starbucks, which hopes to sell more packaged goods through additional channels, such as hotels and restaurants, as well as grocery stores. However, terminating the agreement opened up Starbucks to a lawsuit, brought by Kraft, that accused it of failing to meet the terms of their partnership contract.

These features of Starbucks' strategy highlight how marketing can lead to success. But they also demonstrate that the coffee chain's success was not predestined or guaranteed. In its marketing, Starbucks has made plenty of missteps before, and it's likely it will do so again. The goal, for Starbucks and for any great marketer, is to make sure that the value for customers is sufficient to overcome any stumbles, and then to work harder to avoid them.

Questions

1. Visit the Starbucks website and list some other ways, beyond those listed in the case, that it tries to create and provide value with and for customers.

2. What sorts of expansions seem most likely to benefit Starbucks in the future? Which seem riskiest?

3. How can Starbucks ensure that it continues to meet customers' expectations and needs? List some specific ways.

4. Visit the Starbucks website and identify its latest promotion. How does this promotion help create value for the customer and, ultimately, Starbucks?

5. Why can Starbucks charge so much for a latte when they are less expensive at chains like Dunkin' Donuts?

Endnotes

1. Stephanie Strom, "Starbucks Plans to Move Beyond Beans," *The New York Times*, October 8. 2013.

2. Starbucks, "Starbucks Company Profile," http://globalassets.starbucks.com/assets/9a6616b98dc64271ac8c910fbee47884.pdf.

3. Alvin Chang and Matt Carroll, "Split Country: Dunkin' vs. Starbucks," *Boston Globe/Boston.com* (n.d.).

4. Alexandra Wolfe, "Howard Schultz: What Next, Starbucks?," *The Wall Street Journal*, September 27, 2013; Susan Berfield, "Starbucks Starts Throwing a Very Big Tea Party," *Bloomberg Businessweek*, October 25, 2013.

5. Stephanie Strom, "Want a Yogurt with That Vente Latte? Starbucks and Danone to Join Forces," *The New York Times*, July 23, 2013.

6. The American Marketing Association, http://www.marketingpower.com. We added the word in italics. Discussions of the latest revision of the AMA's marketing definition are widespread. See Gregory T. Gundlach and William L. Wilkie, "AMA's New Definition of Marketing: Perspective and Commentary on the 2007 Revision," *Journal of Public Policy & Marketing* 28, no. 2 (2008), pp. 259–64; see also the fall 2007 issue of the *Journal of Public Policy & Marketing* 26, no. 2, which contains eight different perspectives on the new definition.

7. Mike Esterl, "Coke Tailors Its Soda Sizes," *The Wall Street Journal*, September 19, 2011, http://online.wsj.com; Natalie Zmuda, "Diet Coke Blasts Past Pepsi," *Advertising Age*, March 17, 2011, http://adage.com; Natalie Zmuda, "Can Pepsi's Big Marketing Shake-Up Bring Back Fizz to Its Beverage Brands?" *Advertising Age*, June 20, 2011.

8. http://www.lexus.com.

9. The idea of the four Ps was conceptualized by E. Jerome McCarthy, *Basic Marketing: A Managerial Approach* (Homewood, IL: Richard D. Irwin, 1960).

10. Raphael Thomadsen, "Seeking an Expanding Competitor: How Product Line Expansion Can Increase All Firms' Profits," *Journal of Marketing Research* 49 (June 2012), pp. 349–60.

11. Wolfgang Ulaga and Werner Reinartz, "Hybrid Offerings: How Manufacturing Firms Combine Goods and Services Successfully," *Journal of Marketing* 75 (November 2011), pp. 5–23.

12. Anja Lambrecht and Catherine Tucker, "Paying with Money or Effort: Pricing When Customers Anticipate Hassle," *Journal of Marketing Research* 49 (February 2012), pp. 66–82.

13. Stuart Elliot, "A New Coronation for the King of Elephants," *The New York Times*, November 13, 2012.

14. Personal communication, Trang Connelly, TJX Companies, Inc., September 2013.

15. Peter C. Verhoef et al., "A Cross-National Investigation into the Marketing Department's Influence within the Firm: Toward Initial

Empirical Generalizations," *Journal of International Marketing* 19 (September 2011), pp. 59–86.

16. George S. Day, "Aligning the Organization with the Market," *Marketing Science Institute* 5, no. 3 (2005), pp. 3–20.

17. Kimmy Wa Chan, Chi Kin (Bennett) Yim, and Simon S. K. Lam, "Is Customer Participation in Value Creation a Double-Edged Sword? Evidence from Professional Financial Services across Cultures," *Journal of Marketing* 74, no. 3 (May 2010); Dhruv Grewal, Kent B. Monroe, and R. Krishnan, "The Effects of Price Comparison Advertising on Buyers' Perceptions of Acquisition Value and Transaction Value," *Journal of Marketing* 62 (April 1998), pp. 46–60.

18. Anne L. Roggeveen, Michael Tsiros, and Dhruv Grewal, "Understanding the Co-Creation Effect: When Does Collaborating with Customers Provide a Lift to Service Recovery?" *Journal of the Academy of Marketing Science* 40, no. 6 (2012), pp. 771–90; Sigurd Troye and Magne Supphellen, "Consumer Participation in Coproduction: 'I Made It Myself' Effects on Consumers' Sensory Perceptions and Evaluations of Outcome and Input Product," *Journal of Marketing* 76 (March 2012), pp. 33–46.

19. Anita Luo and V. Kumar, "Recovering Hidden Buyer-Seller Relationship States to Measure the Return on Marketing Investment in Business-to-Business Markets," *Journal of Marketing Research* 50, no. 1 (2013), pp. 143–60; V. Kumar and Denish Shah, "Can Marketing Lift Stock Prices?," *Sloan Management Review* 52, no. 4 (2011), pp. 24–26; V. Kumar et al., "Is Market Orientation a Source of Sustainable Competitive Advantage or Simply the Cost of Competing?" *Journal of Marketing* 75 (January 2011), pp. 16–30; Stephen A. Samaha, Robert W. Palmatier, and Rajiv P. Dant, "Poisoning Relationships: Perceived Unfairness in Channels of Distribution," *Journal of Marketing* 75 (May 2011), pp. 99–117.

20. Luo and Kumar, "Recovering Hidden Buyer-Seller Relationship States"; V. Kumar, Denish Shah, and Rajkumar Venkatesan, "Managing Retailer Profitability—One Customer at a Time!" *Journal of Retailing* 82, no. 4 (2006), pp. 277–94.

21. Belle Beth Cooper, "10 Surprising Social Media Statistics That Will Make You Rethink Your Social Strategy," *Fast Company*, http://www.fastcompany.com.

22. Harsh Ajmera, "Social Media Facts, Figures, and Statistics 2013," *Digital Insights*, http://blog.digitalinsights.in.

23. http://thenextweb.com.

24. "World Internet Penetration Rates," *Internet World Stats*, http://www.internetworldstats.com.

25. U.S. Travel Association, "Travel Facts and Statistics," http://www.ustravel.org.

26. "5 Apps for Searching Nearby Restaurants," *The RecApp*, April 23, 2012, http://www.therecapp.com.

27. Ibid.

28. Raji Srinivasan, Gary L. Lilien, and Shrihari Sridhar, "Should Firms Spend More on Research and Development and Advertising During Recessions?" *Journal of Marketing* 75 (May 2011), pp. 49–65.

29. http://www.ahold.com.

30. Ron Nixon, "Postal Service to Make Sunday Deliveries for Amazon," *The New York Times*, November 11, 2013.

31. Philip Kotler, "Reinventing Marketing to Manage the Environmental Imperative," *Journal of Marketing* 75 (July 2011), pp. 132–35; Katherine White, Rhiannon MacDonnell, and John H. Ellard, "Belief in a Just World: Consumer Intentions and Behaviors toward Ethical Products," *Journal of Marketing* 76 (January 2012), pp. 103–18.

32. http://dictionary.reference.com/search?q=Entrepreneurship.

33. http://www.oprah.com; "Oprah Winfrey," http://en.wikipedia.org/wiki/Oprah_Winfrey.

34. For a series of contributions about how entrepreneurs contribute to society, see the special section on social entrepreneurship in *Journal of Public Policy & Marketing*, 31 (Spring 2012).

35. Wolfe, "Howard Schultz: What Next, Starbucks?"

36. Starbucks, "Fiscal Year 2012 Annual Report," http://investor.starbucks.com.

37. Wolfe, "Howard Schultz: What Next, Starbucks?"

38. Julie Jargon, "Starbucks Tries Franchising to Perk Up Europe Business," *The Wall Street Journal*, November 29, 2013.

39. Berfield, "Starbucks Starts Throwing a Very Big Tea Party."

40. Strom, "Starbucks Aims to Move Beyond Beans."

41. "Free Coffee in Starbucks' 'Come Together' Promo," *USA Today*, October 10, 2013.

42. Jeff Sommer, "Dear Starbucks: A Penny for Your Thoughts," *The New York Times*, January 14, 2012.

43. Venessa Wong, "Starbucks' $2.7 Billion Decision to 'Control Its Own Destiny,'" *Bloomberg Businessweek*, November 13, 2013.

i. Stephanie Rosenbloom, "A Hotel Room with 140 Characters," *The New York Times*, October 3, 2013.

ii. Andrew Adam Newman, "Snacks for Soccer Stars, and Their Fans," *The New York Times*, October 8, 2013; Warc, "Mondelez in Twitter Tie-Up," *Warc.com*, September 13, 2013, http://www.warc.com; Angela Watercutter, "How Oreo Won the Marketing Super Bowl with a Timely Blackout Ad on Twitter," *Wired*, February 4, 2013, http://www.wired.com.

iii. Alvaris Falcon, "20 Gadgets That Make Your Smartphone Even Smarter," *Hongkiat.com*, http://www.hongkiat.com/; David Pogue, "2 Wristbands Keep Tabs on Fitness," *The New York Times*, November 14, 2012, http://www.nytimes.com; Clare Cain Miller, "New Apps Arrive on Google Glass," *The New York Times*, May 16, 2013, http://bits.blogs.nytimes.com; Daniel J. Simons and Christopher F. Chabris, "Is Google Glass Dangerous?," *The New York Times*, May 24, 2013, http://www.nytimes.com.

iv. Matthew Panzarino, "The Open Secret of iBeacon: Apple Could Have 250M Potential Units in the Wild by 2014," *TechCrunch*, December 7, 2013, http://techcrunch.com; Zach Miners, "Apple Tracks Shoppers in Iits Stores with Nationwide iBeacon Rollout," *InfoWorld*, December 9, 2013, http://www.infoworld.com.

Credits

CHAPTER 2

DEVELOPING MARKETING STRATEGIES AND A MARKETING PLAN

LEARNING OBJECTIVES

LO1 Define a marketing strategy.

LO2 Describe the elements of a marketing plan.

LO3 Analyze a marketing situation using SWOT analyses.

LO4 Describe how a firm chooses which consumer group(s) to pursue with its marketing efforts.

LO5 Outline the implementation of the marketing mix as a means to increase customer value.

LO6 Summarize portfolio analysis and its use to evaluate marketing performance.

LO7 Describe how firms grow their business.

EXPECTATIONS.

For world-class athletes, the drive to improve is never-ending: They constantly train to run faster, hit harder, complete more flips in the air. Victory is hard won but gratifying, and remaining at the top demands constant vigilance.

And so it is for Nike, a company dedicated to providing both top athletes and their casual counterparts all the tools they need to compete at their highest levels. Nike's marketing strategy rests on several key points and concepts that spread throughout the company and influence everything it does. In particular, it constantly seeks to improve its own performance through innovation and in-depth analyses of its competitors. Sounds a little like the Olympics, doesn't it?

Created by runners in Oregon, Nike began in the early 1970s as an American company, focused mainly on the American market.[1] Its first running shoes featured a then-innovative design with a waffle-patterned sole. The customers were mainly elite runners, determined to find

the lightest shoe they could. But as *Forrest Gump* recounted, running also was gaining popularity among casual athletes, and just like Forrest, many members of this community sported Nikes on their feet.

By 1984 the company had gone public, and it had found Michael Jordan. Thus the entire market—and the very concept of sponsorship—changed forever. The Air Jordan line of basketball shoes turned Nike into a massive success, with broad appeal to sports fans of virtually all ages and profiles. Nike continues to affiliate with high-profile, elite basketball players, including 48 NBA All-Stars such as Dwayne Wade, Kobe Bryant, and LeBron James.[2]

Waffle-soled shoes and athletic partnerships sparked the notion of innovative ideas as the keys to victory. The company persists in introducing new and exciting concepts, at a rapid pace rarely matched by other firms. For example, Nike's partnership with Apple allows runners with the Nike+ Sensor inserted in their shoes to program their iPhones or iPods to play a collection of songs that matches their distance or time goals.[3] The sensor also keeps track of their speed and distance, and Nike saves the data and provides platforms for social interactions among runners in the same area.

Going a step further down the tech road, Nike also has introduced the FuelBand, a flexible wrist monitor that keeps track of how much a person moves during the day. Even the most chair-bound office worker can determine if she has reached her goal of 10,000 steps per day by taking the stairs to go to lunch. The simple interface turns red if movement is insufficient and green when the goal is in reach. Nike also provides a means for users to share the Nike Fuel points they have earned throughout the day online. With these moves, "Nike has transformed itself into a digital force," a role that improves its competitiveness across its various product lines.[4]

Alongside its digitally oriented strategy, Nike demonstrates its innovation in another modern realm: creative sustainability. By paying attention to its broader environment, Nike recognized that it needed to be more environmentally conscious, for three main reasons. First, when resources become scarcer, competition for them increases, which means higher costs. Second, rising energy costs means Nike's production costs would rise even further. Third, if it could divorce its own growth from reliance on such scarce resources, Nike realized that it would not be limited in its expansion.[5]

For example, it has changed the production process for its clothing lines to make it more environmentally efficient. Traditional fabric dyeing processes would use around 150 liters of water to process 1 kilogram of fabric. With its new Color Dry system, Nike not only eliminates water completely from the dyeing process but also reduces the chemicals needed and minimizes the amount of dye that gets wasted. Nike estimates that it reduces energy consumption by 63 percent.[6]

For shoes, it also has completely revamped its manufacturing process. To create the Flyknit Racer, Nike came up with not just a new shoe but an entirely new production method. Rather than stitching together pieces of prefabricated material to make the shoe's upper, the Flyknit process knits together polyester yarn. Thus each shoe uses only as much material as is required, can be adjusted regularly (i.e., micro engineered) to improve fit or durability, and comes in at nearly an ounce lighter than competitive running shoes.

These strategies clearly have been working. Nike's annual revenues and profits both have increased by approximately 60 percent in the past decade.[7] Profits for 2013 also were a remarkable 22 percent higher than the previous year, largely due to the company's strategic focus on innovation.[8] Furthermore, its market share continues to increase, outpacing both the average growth of the market and its competitors' rates of growth.[9]

The significance of such stellar performance is not lost on some of the brand's most famous customers. Serena Williams—who has worn the company's products for years but who is also a clothing entrepreneur in her own right—notes that observing Nike has helped her realize "I'm not disrupting my brand enough. I need to do it more. Nike always tries to improve. They never say, 'I'm No. 1, and I'm happy.' They always say, 'How can we get better?' Beyond a company, beyond entrepreneurship, you can really take that attitude in your life, like, I want to be a great mother, or a great student, or a great doctor. What can I do to be better?"[10]

The Nike FuelBand allows athletes to track their workouts seamlessly.

In this chapter, we start by discussing a *marketing strategy,* which outlines the specific actions a firm intends to implement to appeal to potential customers. Then we discuss how to do a *marketing plan,* which provides a blueprint for implementing the marketing strategy. The chapter concludes with a discussion of strategies firms use to grow. Appendix 2A explains how to write a marketing plan and provides an annotated example.

WHAT IS A MARKETING STRATEGY?

LO1 Define a marketing strategy.

A marketing strategy identifies (1) a firm's target market(s), (2) a related marketing mix (its four Ps), and (3) the bases on which the firm plans to build a sustainable competitive advantage. A sustainable competitive advantage is an advantage over the competition that is not easily copied and can be maintained over a long period of time. A competitive advantage acts like a wall that the firm has built around its position in a market. This wall makes it hard for outside competitors to contact customers inside—otherwise known as the marketer's target market. Of course, if the marketer has built a wall around an attractive market, competitors will attempt to break down the wall. Over time, advantages will erode because of these competitive forces, but by building high, thick walls, marketers can sustain their advantage, minimize competitive pressure, and boost profits for a longer time. Thus, establishing a sustainable competitive advantage is key to long-term financial performance.

For Nike, its thickest wall is the result of its solid foundation of innovation, which has produced a strong brand and a loyal customer base. Customers know the Nike swoosh well and consider the brand as a first option when they need running, basketball, or even just casual athletic shoes. This appeal reflects Nike's careful targeting and marketing mix implementation. In terms of the four Ps, Nike is constantly trying to come up with new versions of its relatively basic products, namely, shoes and related apparel. To sell these varied products, it relies on multiple channels: online, in dedicated Nike stores and superstores, and through independent retailers such as Foot Locker. Its pricing spans a broad range, from lower end, simpler options for casual shoes to the most expensive, technically sophisticated, highly reputed lines associated with big-name athletes. And these popular athletes are central to its promotion efforts. Nike remains dominant in most athletic fields, and it feels confident about expanding further.

Foot Locker is one of many independent retailers that carry Nike shoes.

There are four macro, or overarching, strategies that focus on aspects of the marketing mix to create and deliver value and to develop sustainable competitive advantages, as we depict in Exhibit 2.1:[11]

- **Customer excellence:** Focuses on retaining loyal customers and excellent customer service.

- **Operational excellence:** Achieved through efficient operations and excellent supply chain and human resource management.

- **Product excellence:** Having products with high perceived value and effective branding and positioning.

- **Locational excellence:** Having a good physical location and Internet presence.

Customer Excellence

Customer excellence is achieved when a firm develops value-based strategies for retaining loyal customers and provides outstanding customer service.

Retaining Loyal Customers Sometimes the methods a firm uses to maintain a sustainable competitive advantage help attract and maintain loyal customers. For instance, having a strong brand, unique merchandise, and superior customer service all help solidify a loyal customer base. In addition, having loyal customers is, in and of itself, an important method of sustaining an advantage over competitors.

EXHIBIT 2.1   Macro Strategies for Developing Customer Value

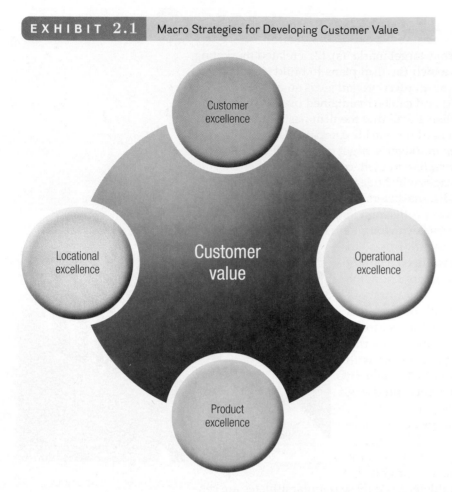

EXHIBIT 2.1   Macro Strategies for Developing Customer Value

Loyalty is more than simply preferring to purchase from one firm instead of another.[12] It means that customers are reluctant to patronize competitive firms. Loyal customers buy Nike apparel for all their sporting and casual endeavors, even if adidas goes on sale or opens a new store right around the corner from their house.

More and more firms realize the value of achieving customer excellence through focusing their strategy on retaining loyal customers. Nike doesn't think in terms of selling a single pair of fashionable shoes for $100; instead, it focuses on satisfying the customer who buys track shoes for herself, Cole Haan dress shoes for her spouse, soccer shoes for her daughter, and basketball shoes for her son. Conservatively, she might buy five pairs of shoes every year for 20 years. She is not a $100 customer; combining all purchases for her family over the years, she is at least a $10,000 shoe customer—and that doesn't even count the shorts, shirts, and socks she adds to her purchases. Viewing customers with a lifetime value perspective, rather than on a transaction-by-transaction basis, is key to modern customer retention programs.[13] We will examine how the lifetime value of a customer is calculated in Chapter 10, Appendix 10A.

One way to build customer loyalty is to provide your target market something unique. For example, when *Self* magazine recognized that its target markets of millennial female readers were interested in fashion as well as fitness, it sought to become a provider of content related to both topics.[14] In addition to expanding the editorial content published in the magazine, *Self* has applied its brand to other products, such as yoga mats and a dramatic romance movie, that also appeal to its target market.

Another method of achieving customer loyalty creates an emotional attachment through loyalty programs. These loyalty programs, which constitute part of an overall customer relationship management (CRM) program, prevail in many industries, from airlines to hotels to movie theaters to retail stores. With such programs, firms can identify members through the loyalty card or membership information the consumer provides when he or she makes a purchase. Using that purchase information, analysts determine which types of merchandise certain groups of customers are buying and thereby tailor their offering to better meet the needs of their loyal customers. For instance, by analyzing their databases, banks develop profiles of customers who have defected in the past and use that information to identify customers who may defect in the future. Once it identifies these customers, the firm can implement special retention programs to keep them.

Providing Outstanding Customer Service Marketers also may build sustainable competitive advantage by offering excellent customer service,[15] though consistency in this area can prove difficult. Customer service is provided by employees, and invariably, humans are less consistent than machines. Firms that offer good customer service must instill its importance in their employees over a long period of time so that it becomes part of the organizational culture.

Disney offers excellent examples of both of these types of customer excellence. First, Disney's My Magic system enables visitors to swipe their Magic Band wristbands to make purchases, open their hotel room door, get dinner reservations, or check in for rides, throughout the park and its grounds. The system also enables Disney to collect a remarkable amount of information about what each guest is doing, at virtually every moment of his or her visit to its theme parks.[16]

Disney's employees and cast members provide the highest level of customer service.

Second, its customer service is virtually unparalleled. Visitors to Disney parks are greeted by "assertively friendly" staff who have been extensively trained to find ways to provide better service. The training includes information about how to recognize the signs that a visitor is lost, so the Disney employee can offer help locating a destination. It also highlights the need to communicate frequently and collaboratively about every aspect of the park, so a custodian at one end of the Magic Kingdom likely knows what time a restaurant on the other side opens.[17]

Although it may take considerable time and effort to build such a reputation for customer service, once a marketer has earned a good service reputation, it can sustain this advantage for a long time because a competitor is hard pressed to develop a comparable reputation. Superior Service 2.1 describes the superb customer service at Singapore Airlines.

Operational Excellence

Firms achieve operational excellence, the second way to achieve a sustainable competitive advantage, through their efficient operations, excellent supply chain management, and strong relationships with their suppliers.

All marketers strive for efficient operations to get their customers the merchandise they want, when they want it, in the required quantities, and at a lower delivered cost than that of their competitors. By so doing, they ensure good value to their customers, earn profitability for themselves, and satisfy their customers' needs. In addition, efficient operations enable firms either to provide their consumers with lower-priced merchandise or, even if their prices are not lower than those of the competition, to use the additional margin they earn to attract customers away from competitors by offering even better service, merchandise assortments, or visual presentations.

Firms achieve efficiencies by developing sophisticated distribution and information systems as well as strong relationships with vendors. Like customer relationships, vendor relations must be developed over the long term and generally cannot be easily offset by a competitor.[18] Furthermore, firms with strong relationships may gain exclusive rights to (1) sell merchandise in a particular region, (2) obtain special terms of purchase that are not available to competitors, or (3) receive popular merchandise that may be in short supply.

You are likely aware of, and perhaps have taken advantage of, Amazon's Prime shipping program, offering free two-day shipping on all orders for $99 a year. Perhaps you have paid for overnight delivery with Amazon, or if you live in one of the 11 cities in the United States that offer it, you may have paid for same-day shipping. With attractive shipping options like these, how are other online retailers able to compete? One innovative solution is being offered by eBay. Understanding that many customers want products quickly, the eBay Now service

Superior Service 2.1 | Customer Service at Singapore Airlines[i]

As many U.S.-based airlines continue to compete based on providing low-cost options, Singapore Airlines maintains its industry-leading levels of customer satisfaction on its international flights. This dedication earns the airline not only awards, such as being named the best economy-class airline in the world, but also customer loyalty. The airline's commitment to excellence has been an important part of its brand strategy since the company's inception.

In its early days, Singapore Airlines faced stiff competition. So the airline elected to position itself as a leader in technology, innovation, quality, and customer service. Over the ensuing decades, it has remained committed to that strategy, introducing such customer-friendly services as hot meals, free alcoholic and nonalcoholic drinks, scented hot towels, video-on-demand for all travelers, and personal entertainment systems. When other airlines imitate its ideas, Singapore Airlines develops new ones, such as a centralized, all-in-one business panel with in-seat power supply and USB ports; a 15.4-inch LCD screen in its video systems; and a seat that folds out fully to a flat bed for business class.

Being innovative is critical, but as one recent flier noted, "What really helps the airline stand apart is not the seats or the food or even the entertainment (though it has all that), but the service." The airline's cabin crew consists of both men and women, though they are referred to as Singapore Girl—an iconic image of the company that was created in 1972 and still persists. The women dress in a signature sarong, created by a French haute-couture designer. All crew members receive rigorous training to ensure they maintain a peaceful and elegant cabin ambiance and caring service.

Staying ahead of the competition requires continual investment in innovation, a price Singapore Airlines is willing to pay to earn the significant rewards, in the form of a loyal and motivated staff and return customers. To remain competitive, the airline's financial structure accommodates innovation without passing any exorbitant costs on to consumers. With that kind of business sense, it's no wonder Singapore Airlines remains profitable even as other airlines struggle to survive.

Singapore Airlines superior service includes a centralized, all-in-one business panel with in-seat power supply and USB ports; a 15.4-inch LCD screen in its video systems; and a seat that folds out fully to a flat bed for business class. Most important, however, is the superior service provided by flight attendants.

offers a personal buyer that will not only purchase the product you want locally, but deliver the product in "about an hour"! Operational excellence is required for eBay to execute this program effectively. Not only does it need to have the technology to coordinate the personal buyers, but it needs to have an effective human resources hiring program that selects and trains employees capable of going the extra mile to please its customers.[19]

Product Excellence

Product excellence, the third way to achieve a sustainable competitive advantage, occurs by providing products with high perceived value and effective branding and positioning. Some firms have difficulty developing a competitive advantage through their merchandise and service offerings, especially if competitors can deliver similar products or services easily. However, others have been able to

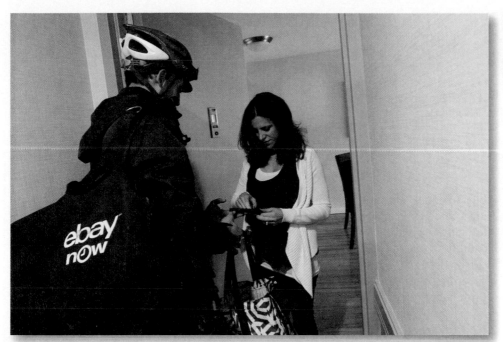

Is two days too long to wait for delivery? With eBay's Now service you can get your product the same day.

maintain their sustainable competitive advantage by investing in their brand itself; positioning their product or service using a clear, distinctive brand image; and constantly reinforcing that image through their merchandise, service, and promotion. For instance, *Bloomberg Businessweek*'s top global brands—such as Coca-Cola, IBM, Microsoft, Google, GE, McDonald's, Intel, Apple, Disney, and Samsung—are all leaders in their respective industries, at least in part because they have strong brands and a clear position in the marketplace.[20]

Locational Excellence

Locational excellence is particularly important for retailers and service providers. Many say "The three most important things in retailing are location, location, location." For example, most people will not walk or drive very far when looking to buy a cup of coffee. A competitive advantage based on location is sustainable because it is not easily duplicated. For example, McDonald's has developed a strong competitive advantage with its location selection. The high density of stores it has established in some markets makes it very difficult for a competitor to enter that market and find good locations. After all, if McDonald's has a store on the corner of a busy intersection, no other competitor can take that location, and will instead have to settle for a less-worthy spot.

Multiple Sources of Advantage

In most cases, a single strategy, such as low prices or excellent service, is not sufficient to build a sustainable competitive advantage. Firms require multiple approaches to build a "wall" around their position that stands as high as possible.

Southwest Airlines consistently has positioned itself as a carrier that provides good service at a good value—customers get to their destination on time for a reasonable price without having to pay extra for checked luggage. At the same time, its customers know not to have extraordinary expectations, unlike those they might develop when they purchase a ticket from Singapore Airlines. They don't expect food service or seat assignments. But they do expect—and even more important, get—on-time flights that are reasonably priced. By developing its unique capabilities in several areas, Southwest has built a very high wall around its position as the value player in the airline industry, which has resulted in a huge cadre of loyal customers.

LO2 Describe the elements of a marketing plan.

THE MARKETING PLAN

Effective marketing doesn't just happen. Firms like Nike carefully plan their marketing strategies to react to changes in the environment, the competition, and their customers by creating a marketing plan. A marketing plan is a written document composed of an analysis of the current marketing situation, opportunities and threats for the firm, marketing objectives and strategy specified in terms of the four Ps, action programs, and projected or pro-forma income (and other financial) statements.[21] The three major phases of the marketing plan are planning, implementation, and control.[22]

Although most people do not have a written plan that outlines what they are planning to accomplish in the next year, and how they expect to do it, firms do need such a document. It is important that everyone involved in implementing the plan knows what the overall objectives for the firm are and how they are going to be met. Other stakeholders, such as investors and potential investors, also want to know what the firm plans to do. A written marketing plan provides a reference point for evaluating whether or not the firm has met its objectives.

A marketing plan entails five steps, depicted in Exhibit 2.2. In Step 1 of the planning phase, marketing executives, in conjunction with other top managers,

EXHIBIT 2.2   The Marketing Plan

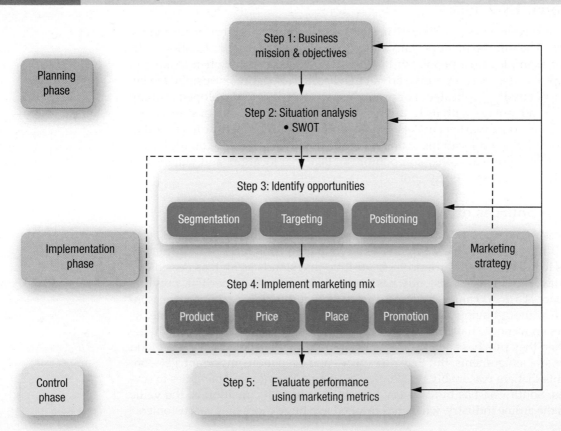

define the mission and/or vision of the business. For the second step, they evaluate the situation by assessing how various players, both in and outside the organization, affect the firm's potential for success. In the implementation phase, marketing managers identify and evaluate different opportunities by engaging in a process known as segmentation, targeting, and positioning (STP) (Step 3). They then are responsible for implementing the marketing mix using the four Ps (Step 4). Finally, the control phase entails evaluating the performance of the marketing strategy using marketing metrics and taking any necessary corrective actions (Step 5).

As indicated in Exhibit 2.2, it is not always necessary to go through the entire process for every evaluation (Step 5). For instance, a firm could evaluate its performance in Step 5, then go directly to Step 2 to conduct a situation audit without redefining its overall mission.

We first discuss each step involved in developing a marketing plan. Then we consider ways of analyzing a marketing situation, as well as identifying and evaluating marketing opportunities. We also examine some specific strategies marketers use to grow a business. Finally, we consider how the implementation of the marketing mix increases customer value. A sample marketing plan is provided in Appendix 2A, following this chapter.

Step 1: Define the Business Mission

The mission statement, a broad description of a firm's objectives and the scope of activities it plans to undertake,[23] attempts to answer two main questions: What type of business are we? What do we need to do to accomplish our goals and objectives? These fundamental business questions must be answered at the highest corporate levels before marketing executives can get involved. Most firms want to maximize stockholders' wealth by increasing the value of the firms' stock and paying dividends.[24] Let's look at Nike and adidas as examples:

- **Nike's Mission Statement:** "To bring inspiration and innovation to every athlete* in the world," and then with its asterisk, defines an athlete by quoting one of its founders: "If you have a body, you are an athlete."[25]

- **adidas's Mission Statement:** "The adidas group strives to be the global leader in the sporting goods industry with brands built on a passion for sport and a sporting lifestyle."[26]

For both of these firms, marketing is primarily responsible for enhancing the value of the company's offering for its customers and other constituents, whether in pursuit of a profit or not. Another key goal or objective often embedded in a mission statement relates to how the firm is building its sustainable competitive advantage.

Both Nike's and adidas's ads reflect their mission statements. Nike's ads (left) consistently inspire athletes to excel; adidas's ads (right) emphasize passion for sports.

Teach For America helps
provide education to all kids.

LO3 Analyze a marketing
situation using SWOT
analyses.

However, owners of small, privately held firms frequently have other objectives, such as achieving a specific level of income and avoiding risks. Nonprofit organizations like Teach For America instead have nonmonetary objectives:

- **Teach For America's Mission Statement:** "To build the movement to eliminate educational inequity by enlisting our nation's most promising future leaders in the effort."[27]

Nike's strengths include its innovative product tradition. It was the first to introduce the Nike+ iPod, a sensor that when inserted into shoes gives the runner instant feedback on factors such as running time, distance, pace, and calories burned.

Step 2: Conduct a Situation Analysis

After developing its mission, a firm would perform a situation analysis using a SWOT analysis that assesses both the internal environment with regard to its **S**trengths and **W**eaknesses and the external environment in terms of its **O**pportunities and **T**hreats. In addition, it should assess the opportunities and uncertainties of the marketplace due to changes in **C**ultural, **D**emographic, **S**ocial, **T**echnological, **E**conomic, and **P**olitical forces (CDSTEP). These factors are discussed in more detail in Chapter 4. With this information, firms can anticipate and interpret change, so they can allocate appropriate resources.

Consider how Nike might conduct a SWOT analysis, as outlined in Exhibit 2.3. We focus on Nike here, but we also recognize that its marketing managers might find it helpful to perform parallel analyses for competitors, such as adidas. Because a company's strengths (Exhibit 2.3, upper left) refer to the positive internal attributes of the firm, in this example we might include Nike's great brand recognition and the visibility of the celebrities who wear its products. Furthermore, its introductions of the Nike+ iPod, FuelBand, and Flyknit were the first of their kind, continuing the innovative tradition that has marked Nike since it first came up with waffle-soled running shoes. Its name recognition makes consumers more likely to try out these innovations when they appear on the market—especially when they see their favorite athlete wearing similar apparel on the court or in the field.

Yet every firm has its weaknesses, and Nike is no exception. Weaknesses (Exhibit 2.3, upper right) are negative attributes of the firm. Nike relies heavily—perhaps even too heavily—on its athletic shoe lines, especially for running and basketball. It also aligns itself closely with the athletes that serve as its brand ambassadors, highlighting them as "heroes." But on multiple occasions these athletes have become embroiled in scandals that are embarrassing and potentially damaging to the brand. Furthermore, in response to the popular emergence of other shoe options, such as "toning" and "barefoot" models, Nike has largely suggested they are fads that will not last, stressing instead its traditional athletic shoe models and innovating new forms.[28]

Keke Palmer is wearing her Nikes at a Nickelodeon event.

Opportunities (Exhibit 2.3, lower left) pertain to positive aspects of the external environment. Among Nike's opportunities, it appears determined to pursue dominance in other, sometimes niche, sports markets. Although not the official sponsor of the 2014 Sochi Winter Olympics, Nike took advantage of the opportunity to build a strong connection with the games. It launched a "Play Russian" campaign in Russia that featured Russian Olympic hopefuls (Adelina Sotnikova and Alexander Ovechkin, among others) and implied the country's harsh winters were the perfect conditioning for winter athletes.[29]

Another notable opportunity for Nike is growth in global markets. It sells products in 170 countries worldwide through independent distributors, Nike stores, the website, and licenses.[30] It aims to expand further, and it has devoted

EXHIBIT 2.3		Examples of Elements in a SWOT Analysis	
		Environment	Evaluation
		Positive	*Negative*
Nike	**Internal**	**Strengths** Strong brand Strong celebrity endorsers Innovative products	**Weakness** Overreliance on footwear Scandals involving celebrity endorsers
	External	**Opportunity** Emerging countries Other fashion segments	**Threats** Cheaper imports Imitation products Retail becoming price competitive
adidas	**Internal**	**Strengths** Strong brand Portfolio of brands Strong global presence	**Weakness** Management of numerous brands
	External	**Opportunity** Emerging countries	**Threats** Cheaper imports Imitation products Recessionary forces

significant resources to improving its prominence among European football players and fans.[31]

Finally, threats (Exhibit 2.3, lower right) represent the negative aspects of the company's external environment. For example, its widespread market dominance makes Nike the primary target for all its competitors,[32] from adidas to New Balance to Li Ning, China's largest shoemaker. All of these firms want to take market share from Nike, which means it must constantly be a little bit on the defensive. Furthermore, as Nike itself acknowledges: "Our products face intense competition. . . . Failure to maintain our reputation and brand image could negatively impact our business. . . . If we are unable to anticipate consumer preferences and develop new products, we may not be able to maintain or increase our net revenues and profits."[33]

LO4 Describe how a firm chooses which consumer group(s) to pursue with its marketing efforts.

Step 3: Identify and Evaluate Opportunities Using STP (Segmentation, Targeting, and Positioning)

After completing the situation audit, the next step is to identify and evaluate opportunities for increasing sales and profits using segmentation, targeting, and positioning (STP). With STP, the firm first divides the marketplace into subgroups or segments, determines which of those segments it should pursue or target, and finally decides how it should position its products and services to best meet the needs of those chosen targets (more details on the STP process can be found in Chapter 8).

Segmentation Many types of customers appear in any market, and most firms cannot satisfy everyone's needs. For instance, among Internet users some do research online, some shop, some look for entertainment, and many do all three. Each of these groups might be a market segment consisting of consumers who respond similarly to a firm's marketing efforts. The process of dividing the market into groups of customers with different needs, wants, or characteristics—who therefore might appreciate products or services geared especially for them—is called market segmentation.

Let's look at Hertz, the car rental company. The example in Exhibit 2.4 reveals some of the segments that Hertz targets. With the Adrenaline Collection, Hertz offers up the Chevrolet Camaro or Corvette, the Ford Mustang, and Dodge's Challenger, seeking to appeal to thrill seekers and gear heads on vacation. Its Prestige Collection features various Cadillac and Mercedes models, targeting business customers and families who prefer a luxurious ride. With its Green collection of cars such as the Toyota Prius and Ford Fusion, and even some electric vehicle options in selected locations, Hertz appeals to environmentally conscious customers. It also offers commercial vans for service customers.[34] Thus, Hertz uses a variety of demographics—gender, age, income, interests—to identify customers who might want the Prestige, Green, and Adrenaline collections, but it also applies psychological or behavioral factors, such as a need to move possessions across town, to identify likely consumers of its commercial vans.

EXHIBIT 2.4 Hertz Market Segmentation Illustration

	Segment 1	Segment 2	Segment 3	Segment 4	Segment 5
Segments	Single thrill seekers and gear heads on vacation	Business customers and families who prefer a luxurious ride	Environmentally conscious customers	Families	Commercial customers
	Adrenaline collection	Prestige Collection	Green Collection	SUV/Changeover/4x4	Commercial Van/Truck
Cars Offered	Corvette ZHZ	Infiniti QX56	Toyota Prius	Toyota Rav 4	
	Chevrolet Camaro	Cadillac Escalade	Ford Fusion	Ford Explorer	Ford Cargo Van

Hertz targets several markets. Its "Fun Collection" (left) appeals to single people and couples wanting to have fun; while its "Prestige Collection" (right) appeals to its business customers and families who prefer a luxurious ride.

Targeting After a firm has identified the various market segments it might pursue, it evaluates each segment's attractiveness and decides which to pursue using a process known as target marketing **or** targeting. For example, Hertz realizes that its primary appeal for the SUV/Miniva/4x4 collection centers on young families, so the bulk of its marketing efforts for this business is directed toward that group.

Soft drink manufacturers also divide their massive markets into submarkets or segments. Coca-Cola, for instance, makes several different types of Coke, including regular, Coke II, and Cherry Coke. Among its diet colas, it targets Coke Zero to men and Diet Coke to women because men prefer not to be associated with diets. It also markets Sprite to those who don't like dark colas, Fruitopia and Minute Maid for more health-conscious consumers, and Dasani bottled water for purists.

Positioning Finally, when the firm decides which segments to pursue, it must determine how it wants to be positioned within those segments. Market positioning involves the process of defining the marketing mix variables so that target customers have a clear, distinctive, desirable understanding of what the product does or represents in comparison with competing products. Hertz positions itself as a quality car (and truck) rental company that is the first choice for each of its target segments. In its marketing communications it stresses that customers will get peace of mind when they rent from Hertz, the market leader in the car rental business, and be able to enjoy their journey (e.g., leisure consumers) and reduce travel time (e.g., business consumers).[35]

To segment the coffee drinker market, Starbucks uses a variety of methods, including geography (e.g., college campuses versus shopping/business districts) and benefits (e.g., drinkers of caffeinated versus decaffeinated products). After

Social & Mobile Marketing 2.1   Truly Mobile Pizza[ii]

The pizza delivery business has always been mobile in one sense, but Pizza Hut is making sure that it spreads into mobile commerce as well. This first-mover introduced its mobile website in 2007, an iPhone application in 2009, and apps for the iPad, Android, and Windows Mobile 7 in 2010. By 2013, it had partnered with Microsoft to become the first restaurant to offer orders through Xbox 360 consoles.

The decision to go mobile was based on a few insights that Pizza Hut gleaned from its market research. In particular, if it did not offer mobile access quickly, its competitors might be the first to do so in the competitive pizza delivery market. The Pizza Hut app lets customers order food through a user-friendly experience, but it also makes sure to identify the closest store locations for delivery or pickup service to further emphasize convenience.

Without much information to identify the consumers who would use the app, Pizza Hut anticipated more orders from college-age men, who do not like to cook and want their food on demand, but also are not willing to stop a video game to take the time to order food through more traditional channels. The assumption seemed reasonable—but it also was dead wrong. Further market research, based on the introduction of the app, has shown that there are just as many pizza connoisseurs 55 years and older with iPhones as there are 13- to 24-year-olds ordering the pies.

Pizza Hut's mobile app makes ordering pizza a piece of cake.

determining which of those segments represent effective targets, Starbucks positions itself as a firm that develops a variety of products that match the wants and needs of the different market segments—espresso drinks, coffees, teas, bottled drinks, pastries, and cooler foods.

After identifying its target segments, a firm must evaluate each of its strategic opportunities. A method of examining which segments to pursue is described in the Growth Strategies section later in the chapter. Firms typically are most successful when they focus on opportunities that build on their strengths relative to those of their competition. In Step 4 of the marketing plan, the firm implements its marketing mix and allocates resources to different products and services.

For example, Pizza Hut decided to jump on changing consumer desires for rapid access to its offering by constantly expanding its mobile applications, but it also found its positioning as a convenient option appealing to more markets than it even expected, as Social and Mobile Marketing 2.1 reveals.

Step 4: Implement Marketing Mix and Allocate Resources

LO5 Outline the implementation of the marketing mix as a means to increase customer value.

When the firm has identified and evaluated different growth opportunities by performing an STP analysis, the real action begins. It has decided what to do, how to do it, and how many resources should be allocated to it. In the fourth step of the planning process, marketers implement the actual marketing mix—product, price, promotion, and place—for each product and service on the basis of what they believe their target markets will value. At the same time, marketers make important decisions about how they will allocate their scarce resources to their various products and services.

Product and Value Creation Products These products include services and constitute the first of the four Ps. Because the key to the success of any marketing program is the creation of value, firms attempt to develop products and services that customers perceive as valuable enough to buy. Dyson fans and fan heaters draw in and redirect surrounding air without potentially dangerous or fast-spinning blades or visible heating elements. Although more expensive than conventional fans and space heaters, these sculpturally beautiful appliances are perceived by consumers to be a valuable alternative to products that haven't significantly changed since the early 1900s.

Price and Value Capture Recall that the second element of the marketing mix is price. As part of the exchange process, a firm provides a product or a service, or some combination thereof, and in return, it gets money. Value-based marketing requires that firms charge a price that customers perceive as giving them a good value for the product they receive. Clearly, it is important for a firm to have a clear focus in terms of what products to sell, where to buy them, and what methods to use in selling them. But pricing is the only activity that actually brings in money and therefore influences revenues. If a price is set too high, it will not generate much volume. If a price is set too low, it may result in lower-than-optimal margins and profits. Therefore, price should be based on the value that the customer perceives. Dyson fans can retail for $150 or more while conventional fans retail for

Dyson creates value with its innovative products (left). It can therefore charge significantly more than the price of conventional fans (right).

Airfoil section creates negative pressure

Viscous shearing draws air in

Surrounding air drawn into airflow

High-speed jet

Discover more at dyson.com/fans

dyson air multiplier
No blades. No buffeting.

around $25. Customers can decide what they want from their fan and choose the one at the price they prefer.

Place and Value Delivery For the third P, place, the firm must be able, after it has created value through a product and/or service, to make the product or service readily accessible when and where the customer wants it. Recently, Tesco took an innovative step along these lines when it opened HomePlus virtual stores in several South Korean subway stations. The virtual stores in subway stations look like grocery stores—except that they are just LCD screens! The virtual markets allow customers to shop with their smartphones; their items will be delivered to their doorstep.[36] Adding Value 2.1 takes a look at how these innovations deliver great value—along with groceries.

Promotion and Value Communication Integrated marketing communications (IMC) represents the promotion P of the four Ps. It encompasses a variety of communication disciplines—advertising, personal selling, sales promotion, public relations, direct marketing, and online marketing including social media—in combination to provide clarity, consistency, and maximum communicative impact.[37] Using the various disciplines of its IMC program, marketers communicate a *value proposition,* which is the unique value that a product or service provides to its customers and how it is better than and different from those of competitors, to their customers.

A creative promotion paired the creative savvy of Disney with the vast reach of the Home Shopping Network (HSN) to invent a 24-hour, nonstop block of programming on HSN in advance of the opening of the 2013 film *Oz: The Great and Powerful.* A massive *Oz*-themed hot-air balloon made a stop at HSN's headquarters before it flew on to make an appearance at the Daytona 500. On HSN's website, customers could purchase *Oz* merchandise, watch exclusive making-of-the-movie videos, take a quiz to determine which witch they most represent, and click a link to buy tickets to a local showing of the movie. Disney provided HSN employees with early screenings of the film as well, to make sure they were well informed about the stories behind the merchandise they would be selling.[38] The *Oz* promotion was effective because it not only was unique and got people talking, but the hot-air balloon tied in directly with the movie and, more importantly, created a sense of whimsy and magic—which exemplified the movie's value proposition.

Step 5: Evaluate Performance Using Marketing Metrics

The final step in the planning process includes evaluating the results of the strategy and implementation program using marketing metrics. A metric is a measuring system that quantifies a trend, dynamic, or characteristic. Metrics are used to explain why things happened and also project the future. They make it possible to compare results across regions, strategic business units (SBUs), product lines, and time periods. The firm can determine why it achieved or did not achieve its performance goals with the help of these metrics. Understanding the causes of the performance, regardless of whether that performance exceeded, met, or fell below the firm's goals, enables firms to make appropriate adjustments.

Typically, managers begin by reviewing the implementation programs, and their analysis may indicate that the strategy (or even the mission statement) needs to be reconsidered. Problems can arise both when firms successfully implement poor strategies and when they poorly implement good strategies.

Who Is Accountable for Performance? At each level of an organization, the business unit and its manager should be held accountable only for the revenues, expenses, and profits that they can control. Thus, expenses that affect several levels of the organization (such as the labor and capital expenses associated with operating a corporate headquarters) shouldn't be arbitrarily assigned to lower levels. In the case of a store, for example, it may be appropriate to evaluate performance objectives based on sales, sales associate productivity, and energy costs. If the corporate

Adding Value 2.1   Online Retail Meets Bricks and Mortar: Tesco's HomePlus Virtual Stores[iii]

South Korea is known for its tech innovations, introduced by highly creative companies and embraced by a forward-thinking consumer public. But the top app in this tech-savvy nation isn't associated with some space-age fantasy. Instead, it pertains to a seemingly perpetual, distinctly old-fashioned task: grocery shopping.

The international retailer Tesco chose Korea as the site to open its HomePlus virtual stores back in 2011. In subway stations, virtual stores began appearing on LCD screens. Shoppers on their way to or from work could scan the barcodes or QR codes for the items they wanted to purchase with their smartphones. The virtual stores are laid out in a grid, similar to a brick-and-mortar store, which helped shoppers feel familiar with the radically new approach. Furthermore, the app allows them to schedule home delivery, such that fresh produce, food for their pets, replenished cleaning supplies, and maybe even dinner for themselves can be waiting on their doorstep when they get home.

The remarkable success of this app has prompted Tesco to expand the placement of HomePlus stores to bus depots and other commuter routes. Within about six months of the introduction, nearly 1 million consumers had downloaded and used the HomePlus app.

Despite the success and popularity of HomePlus, Tesco continues to keep its physical stores open, with no plans to eliminate them. Two main features demand this dual approach. First, Korea is somewhat unique in terms of its significant embrace and acceptance of virtual tools and high-tech options. In many other countries, including Tesco's UK home market, and in rural areas where access to public spaces like bus stops is just as challenging as getting to the local store, acceptance may be less widespread. Even in Korea, consumers tend to use HomePlus for dry goods but still like to be able to touch and feel vegetables and fruit before buying them.

Second, for many people, shopping is an enjoyable pastime that gets them out of their houses or offices for a brief time. Noting this persistent preference, Tesco is seeking to integrate virtual offerings more effectively into some of its stores. For example, it is considering plans to add interactive tablets in its in-store cafés. Customers could take a break, have a cup of tea, and type in a few ingredients that sound appealing to them. The tablets then might produce recipes that match the ingredients, along with a map showing the customers where to find each needed item.

The Home Plus Virtual Stores have created a whole new way of providing the third P, place, and value delivery.

Promotional discounts is one way General Mills is trying to save the cereal industry.

office lowers prices to get rid of merchandise and therefore profits suffer, then it's not fair to assess a store manager's performance based on the resulting decline in store profit.

Performance evaluations are used to pinpoint problem areas. Reasons performance may be above or below planned levels must be examined. If a manager's performance is below planned levels, was it because the sales force didn't do an adequate job, because the economy took a downward turn, because competition successfully implemented a new strategy, or because the managers involved in setting the objectives aren't very good at making estimates? The manager should be held accountable only in the case of the inadequate sales force job or setting inappropriate forecasts.

When it appears that actual performance is going to be below the plan because of circumstances beyond the manager's control, the firm can still take action to minimize the harm. For example, the cereal industry has been beset by a wealth of setbacks due to trends in the wider consumer environment. People seek to cut carbohydrates out of their diets, but cereal is mostly carbs. Many consumers are recognizing their allergies to gluten, but many cereals include wheat as a main ingredient. In response, the largest cereal maker General Mills (GM) has called on its competitors to step up their marketing efforts to save the industry. Leading the way, it increased its advertising budget by 7 percent and initiated promotional discounts on some of its most popular cereal brands, including Cheerios.[39]

In remarkable cases such as this, marketing managers must ask themselves several relevant questions: How quickly were plans adjusted? How rapidly and appropriately were pricing and promotional policies modified? In short, did I react to salvage an adverse situation, or did my reactions worsen the situation?

Performance Objectives and Metrics Many factors contribute to a firm's overall performance, which makes it hard to find a single metric to evaluate performance.[40] One approach is to compare a firm's performance over time or to competing firms, using common financial metrics such as sales and profits. Another method of assessing performance is to view the firm's products or services as a portfolio. Depending on the firm's relative performance, the profits from some products or services are used to fuel growth for others.

With its extensive data, Google claims that it can use a combination of metrics to predict the performance of a major motion picture, up to a month prior to the date it opens in theaters. Using search volume for the movie title in combination with several other metrics, such as the season and whether the movie is a sequel, Google promises a 94 percent accurate prediction of box office performance. Other proprietary metrics include the volume of clicks on search ads. If, for example, one movie prompted 20,000 more paid clicks than another film, it will bring in approximately $7.5 million more in revenues during its opening weekend. Beyond the implications for opening weekend, Google asserts that weekday searches in the weeks leading up to the release offer better predictors of continued revenues. That is, if a film fan searches for a movie title on a Tuesday, she or he is more likely to hold off on seeing the movie, rather than rushing out during opening weekend.[41]

Financial Performance Metrics Some commonly used metrics to assess performance include revenues, or sales, and profits. For instance, sales are a global measure of a firm's activity level. However, a manager could easily increase sales by lowering prices, but the profit realized on that merchandise (gross margin) would suffer as a result. An attempt to maximize one metric may therefore lower another. Thus, managers must understand how their actions affect multiple performance metrics. It's usually unwise to use only one metric because it rarely tells the whole story. Furthermore, as Ethical and Societal Dilemma 2.1 details, focusing too much on financial metrics could be deadly, especially if it means ignoring measures reflecting labor safety.

Ethical & Societal Dilemma **2.1**   Lowering Costs—But at What Cost?[iv]

When observers assess flexible, global, rapid supply chains, they tend to rely on financial metrics and focus on the benefits: Effective supply chains help multinational retailers get the merchandise that customers want on the shelves when they want it, usually at much lower production costs. In turn, they lower prices for customers. As a result, the firm enjoys higher profits by selling more of a product that cost it less to produce. Such supply chains also encourage the sort of innovation that induces the fast-changing fashion industry or makes the average lifecycle of consumer electronics products run less than eight months, which can be good for economies overall, as people buy more stuff more frequently.

But flexible, global, rapid supply chains also require suppliers to find ways to work faster and more efficiently, even if that sometimes means putting workers' health, safety, and even lives at risk. In April 2013 the Rana Plaza in Bangladesh collapsed, killing more than 1,100 garment workers—the deadliest disaster in the history of an industry that has never been known for great working conditions.

It might be easy to assume that the terrible events are evidence simply of poor oversight in Bangladesh, where a fire in November 2012 also killed more than 100 factory workers. But some of the companies that had outsourced their manufacturing to Rana Plaza had corporate codes in place, mandating safe working conditions. They also checked some of the factories for their compliance with the codes. The remarkable news is that at least two of the factories that were located in Rana Plaza passed recent safety audits—when they clearly were unsafe.

For international firms, this situation is unsettling. If they implement corporate codes of conduct for their suppliers, then use predetermined metrics to monitor those suppliers, and yet still face controversy, what further steps can they take to protect the people who make the products they sell? One option is to work more closely with suppliers, rather than just auditing them. Big multinationals also could simply pay for safety improvements in their factories all over the world.

Another argument suggests that changing safety standards ultimately will require government intervention, because an efficient supply chain will never prioritize costly preventative moves to increase worker safety. Performance metrics almost automatically prioritize the financial side. To shift the focus to worker safety in Bangladesh, for example, the central government announced a cooperative effort with the International Labour Organization to enforce labor standards.

Ultimately, the responsibility may be the consumers'. As long as buyers demand low-priced products rather than responsible supply chains, that's what they will get.

The garment factory collapse in Bangladesh was a great tragedy that forced international firms to improve working conditions.

EXHIBIT 2.5	Performance Metrics: Nike vs. adidas			
		2012	2013	% Change
Nike	Net Sales	$23.3B	$25.3B	8.60%
	Net Profit	$ 2.2B	$ 2.5B	13.60%
	Net Profit/Net Sales	9.40%	9.90%	5.30%
Adidas	Net Sales	$ 19.2B	$18.7B	−2.60%
	Net Profit	$675.9M	$ 1.0B	47.90%
	Net Profit/Net Sales	3.50%	5.30%	51.40%

In addition to assessing the absolute level of sales and profits, a firm may wish to measure the relative level of sales and profits. For example, a relative metric of sales or profits is its increase or decrease over the prior year. In addition, a firm may compare its growth in sales or profits relative to other benchmark companies (e.g., Coke may compare itself to Pepsi).

The metrics used to evaluate a firm vary depending on (1) the level of the organization at which the decision is made and (2) the resources the manager controls. For example, while the top executives of a firm have control over all of the firm's resources and resulting expenses, a regional sales manager has control over only the sales and expenses generated by his or her salespeople.

Let's look at Nike's sales revenue and profits (after taxes) and compare them with those of adidas (Exhibit 2.5).

LO6 Summarize portfolio analysis and its use to evaluate marketing performance.

Portfolio Analysis In portfolio analysis, management evaluates the firm's various products and businesses—its "portfolio"—and allocates resources according to which products are expected to be the most profitable for the firm in the future. Portfolio analysis is typically performed at the strategic business unit (SBU) or product line level of the firm, though managers also can use it to analyze brands or even individual items. An SBU is a division of the firm itself that can be managed and operated somewhat independently from other divisions and may have a different mission or objectives. For example, Goodyear is one of the largest tire firms in the world, selling its products on six continents in over 180 countries and with sales of approximately $21 billion. Its four SBUs are organized by geography: North American; Europe, Middle East, African; Latin American; and Asia Pacific.[42]

A product line, in contrast, is a group of products that consumers may use together or perceive as similar in some way. One line of product for Goodyear could be car, van, sport-utility vehicle (SUV), and light truck while another line could be high-performance tires or aviation tires.

One of the most popular portfolio analysis methods, developed by the Boston Consulting Group (BCG), requires that firms classify all their products or services into a two-by-two matrix, as depicted in Exhibit 2.6.[43] The circles represent brands, and their sizes are in direct proportion to the brands' annual sales. The horizontal axis represents the relative market share.

In general, market share is the percentage of a market accounted for by a specific entity,[44] and is used to establish the product's strength in a particular market. It

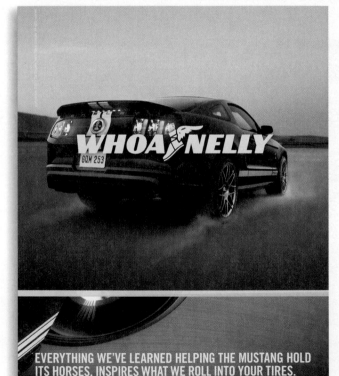

EVERYTHING WE'VE LEARNED HELPING THE MUSTANG HOLD ITS HORSES, INSPIRES WHAT WE ROLL INTO YOUR TIRES.

EAGLE® F1 ULTRA-HIGH PERFORMANCE STOPPING POWER.   **GOODYEAR** MORE DRIVEN

Goodyear, one of the largest tire firms in the word, organizes its strategic business units by geography. This ad for high-performance tires, one of Goodyear's many product lines, was designed for its North American SBU.

EXHIBIT 2.6 Boston Consulting Group Matrix

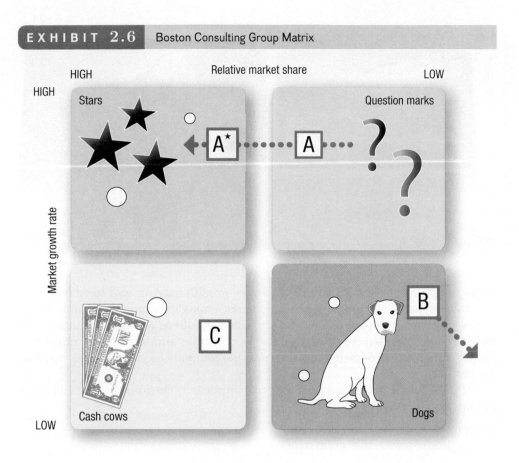

is usually discussed in units, revenue, or sales. A special type of market share metric, relative market share, is used in this application because it provides managers with a product's relative strength, compared with that of the largest firm in the industry.[45] The vertical axis is the market growth rate, or the annual rate of growth of the specific market in which the product competes. Market growth rate thus measures how attractive a particular market is. Each quadrant has been named on the basis of the amount of resources it generates for and requires from the firm.

Stars Stars (upper left quadrant) occur in high-growth markets and are high market share products. That is, stars often require a heavy resource investment in such things as promotions and new production facilities to fuel their rapid growth. As their market growth slows, stars will migrate from heavy users of resources to heavy generators of resources and become cash cows.

Cash Cows Cash cows (lower left quadrant) are in low-growth markets but are high market share products. Because these products have already received heavy investments to develop their high market share, they have excess resources that can be spun off to those products that need it. For example, the firm may decide to use the excess resources generated by Brand C to fund products in the question mark quadrant.

Question Marks Question marks (upper right quadrant) appear in high-growth markets but have relatively low market shares; thus, they are often the most managerially intensive products in that they require significant resources to maintain and potentially increase their market share. Managers must decide whether to infuse question marks with resources generated by the cash cows, so that they can become stars, or withdraw resources and eventually phase out the products. Brand A, for instance, is currently a question mark, but by infusing it with resources, the firm hopes to turn it into a star.

In which Boston Consulting quadrant do these two products fit?

Dogs Dogs (lower right quadrant) are in low-growth markets and have relatively low market shares. Although they may generate enough resources to sustain themselves, dogs are not destined for "stardom" and should be phased out unless they are needed to complement or boost the sales of another product or for competitive purposes. In the case depicted in Exhibit 2.6, the company has decided to stop making Brand B.

Now let's look at Apple and some of its products.[46] The four that we will focus our attention on are:

- iPhone
- iPod
- iMac Desktop
- iPad

Let's consider each of these products and place them into the BCG matrix based on the data. The iPhone has clearly been the star, with growth rates nearing 90 percent in some years. By selling so many phones so rapidly, while also introducing new models at a steady clip, it remains atop the smartphone market. And its sales have persistently increased, from approximately $46 million in 2011 to $78 million in 2012 to $91 million in 2013.[47]

The iPod tells a different story. With a staggering absolute market share consistently above 75 percent, its relative market share is 100 percent, and with more than 300 million iPods sold in a little over 10 years, it definitely has been an important product for Apple. Unfortunately, the MP3 market is contracting and during the last quarter of 2013, sales of iPods slowed to their lowest level since their introduction in 2005. Combine the lack of growth with a large relative market share and it is likely that the iPod is a cash cow for Apple.[48]

Although popular with graphic designers, the growth rate of the Mac Desktop has slowed enough that it has even declined in some recent quarters. Given that it also has a small relative market share in the desktop market, the iMac can be tentatively classified as a dog. Should Apple get rid of the iMac? For at least two reasons, this is probably a bad idea. First, it risks alienating graphic designers and other Apple loyalists who depend on the iMac. Because these customers may also enjoy other Apple products, their dissention may adversely affect sales of these other products. Second, discontinuing the iMac would leave a gaping hole in its portfolio and would therefore hurt its brand image as a computer company.

Then we have the iPad, with an incredible sales growth rate from 2010 to 2011 of 333 percent, and sales of approximately 55 million units as of early 2012. Looking at 2011 as a whole, the iPad captured 66.6 percent of the tablet market (two out of every three tablets sold were iPads). But by the end of 2011 its absolute market share had dropped to 57 percent. Then in 2013, growth was a mere

Like the Dalai Lama, Apple approaches the world by thinking differently.

3 percent.[49] Where on the BCG matrix would you classify the iPad? Does its continued excellent market enter it into the star category? Or is the erosion of its growth enough to make it a question mark?

Although quite useful for conceptualizing the relative performance of products or services and using this information to allocate resources, the BCG approach, and others like it, is often difficult to implement in practice. In particular, it is difficult to measure both relative market share and industry growth. Furthermore, other measures easily could serve as substitutes to represent a product's competitive position and the market's relative attractiveness. Another issue for marketers is the potential self-fulfilling prophecy of placing a product or service into a quadrant. As we have shown in our Apple iPad example, whether it is classified as a star or a question mark has profound implications on how it is treated and supported within the firm. Question marks require more marketing and production support.

Because of these limitations, many firms have tempered their use of matrix approaches to achieve a more balanced approach to evaluating products and services and allocating their resources. Instead of assigning allocation decisions to the top levels of the organization, many firms start at lower management levels and employ checks and balances to force managers at each level of the organizational hierarchy to negotiate with those above and below them to reach their final decisions.

Strategic Planning Is Not Sequential

The planning process in Exhibit 2.2 suggests that managers follow a set sequence when they make strategic decisions. Namely, after they've defined the business mission, they perform the situation analysis, identify strategic opportunities, evaluate alternatives, set objectives, allocate resources, develop the implementation plan, and, finally, evaluate their performance and make adjustments. But actual planning processes can move back and forth among these steps. For example, a situation analysis may uncover a logical alternative, even though this alternative might not be included in the mission statement, which would mean that the mission statement would need to be revised. The development of the implementation plan also might reveal that insufficient resources have been allocated to a particular product for it to achieve its objective. In that case, the firm would need to either change the objective or increase the resources; alternatively, the marketer might consider not investing in the product at all.

Now that we have gone through the steps of the marketing plan, let's look at some growth strategies that have been responsible for making many marketing firms successful.

CHECK YOURSELF

1. What are the five steps in creating a marketing plan?
2. What tool helps a marketer conduct a situation analysis?
3. What is STP?
4. What do the four quadrants of the portfolio analysis represent?

LO7 Describe how firms grow their business.

GROWTH STRATEGIES

Firms consider pursuing various market segments as part of their overall growth strategies, which may include the four major strategies in Exhibit 2.7.[50] The rows distinguish those opportunities a firm possesses in its current markets from those it has in new markets, whereas the columns distinguish between the firm's current marketing offering and that of a new opportunity. Let's consider each of them in detail.

Market Penetration

A **market penetration strategy** employs the existing marketing mix and focuses the firm's efforts on existing customers. Such a growth strategy might be achieved by attracting new consumers to the firm's current target market or encouraging current customers to patronize the firm more often or buy more merchandise on each visit. A market penetration strategy generally requires greater marketing efforts, such as increased advertising and additional sales and promotions, or intensified distribution efforts in geographic areas in which the product or service already is sold.

To penetrate its target market, TV network MTV found that it needed new ways to engage its viewers. The young audience to which MTV traditionally appeals consists of text-messaging, video-gaming multitaskers who no longer accept plain video programming on their televisions. Thus, the network is working hard to develop additional strategies and outlets to retain viewers, as well as to encourage them to spend more time interacting with its content. MTV discovered that interactions with the audience through alternative channels increase ratings for its shows. Therefore, in addition to producing and airing reality shows such as *America's*

EXHIBIT 2.7   Markets/Products and Services Strategies

PRODUCTS AND SERVICES

	Current	New
Current (MARKETS)	Market penetration	Product development
New	Market development	Diversification

To increase market penetration with its young target audience, MTV produces reality shows like "America's Best Dance Crew."

Best Dance Crew and *Jersey Shore*, MTV has partnered with video game producer Yoostar to offer "Yoostar on MTV" for Xbox 360. The game provides a massive library of constantly updated shows, music videos, and recordings of live events. Using the green screen technology contained in the game, fans of these shows can insert themselves into scenes they've already seen their more famous teen peers undergo. Of course, the game also allows them to upload their completed performance to Facebook, Twitter, or a Yoostar dedicated website.[51] On MTV's website, dedicated forums, blogs, and activities for each show also encourage viewers to connect with characters in their shows. Not only can viewers talk about the characters as if they were friends, but they can buy the products they wear and download the music played during the show.[52]

Market Development

A market development strategy employs the existing marketing offering to reach new market segments, whether domestic or international. Domestically, MTV pursues a market development strategy by targeting older customers who were MTV viewers in their youth, but are now attracted to Music Television shows that are reminiscent of their teenage years. On the other hand, international expansion generally is riskier than domestic expansion because firms must deal with differences in government regulations, cultural traditions, supply chains, and language. However, many U.S. firms, including MTV, enjoy a competitive advantage in global markets—such as Mexico, Latin America, Europe, China, and Japan—because, especially among young people, U.S. culture is widely emulated for consumer products.

For example, because of rising prosperity worldwide and rapidly increasing access to cable television that offers U.S. programming, fashion trends from the United States have spread to young people in emerging countries. Since its founding in 1981, MTV has expanded well beyond the United States, with niche sites in nearly 50 countries, including the United Kingdom, Japan, Brazil, Pakistan, and Slovakia. It is available in 562 million households in 161 countries and 33 languages.[53] The global MTV generation prefers soft drinks to tea, athletic shoes to sandals, french fries to rice, and credit cards to cash. To achieve such growth, MTV leveraged its existing media content but also delivers culturally relevant content using local DJs and show formats.

MTV's Real World Las Vegas cast members: Heather Marter, Dustin Zito, Naomi Defensor, and Real World Cancun cast member, Jasmine Reynaud.

Shows such as Made are one of MTV's attempts to diversify its offerings.

Product Development

The third growth strategy option, a product development strategy, offers a new product or service to a firm's current target market. Consider MTV's dynamic lineup: The network constantly develops new pilots and show concepts to increase the amount of time viewers can spend watching MTV. For example, each iteration of *16 and Pregnant* and the follow-up *Teen Mom* series, each version of *The Real World* reality series, and new series such as *Hard Times with RJ Berger* and *Catfish* all represent new programs designed to attract and retain existing viewers. Along with its new TV series, MTV develops new online products to engage consumers through more than 25 niche blogs, as well as a website that it uses to dominate a greater share of viewers' minds and time. These various MTV-branded niche sites pertain to social, political, and environmental issues that appeal to different segments in its target market. The sites further encourage viewers to get involved in real-world issues (not *The Real World* issues) through mobile technologies. By visiting the sites, MTV promises that consumers can share mobile content, educate themselves, and take action on important issues.[54]

Diversification

A diversification strategy, the last of the growth strategies from Exhibit 2.7, introduces a new product or service to a market segment that currently is not served. Diversification opportunities may be either related or unrelated. In a related diversification opportunity, the current target market and/or marketing mix shares something in common with the new opportunity.[55] In other words, the firm might be able to purchase from existing vendors, use the same distribution and/or management information system, or advertise in the same newspapers to target markets that are similar to their current consumers. MTV has pursued a related diversification by introducing TV series that focus on more positive social messages, instead of on wealth, celebrities, and excessive youth culture (e.g., *The Hills*, *My Super Sweet 16*). In series such as *I Used to Be Fat* and *Made*, recognizable and seemingly familiar teens still appeal to viewers and provide a healthy dose of drama. However, the plotlines of these shows focus on how people overcome adversity or struggle with everyday challenges to attain some level of happiness.[56]

In contrast, in an unrelated diversification, the new business lacks any common elements with the present business. Unrelated diversifications do not capitalize on either core strengths associated with markets or with products. Thus, they would be viewed as very risky. For instance, if Nike ventured into the child day care service industry, it would be an unrelated diversification because it is so different from its core business and therefore very risky.

CHECK YOURSELF

1. What are the four growth strategies?
2. What type of strategy is growing the business from existing customers?
3. Which strategy is the riskiest?

Reviewing Learning Objectives

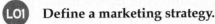

LO1 Define a marketing strategy.

A marketing strategy identifies (1) a firm's target markets(s), (2) a related marketing mix (four Ps), and (3) the bases on which the firm plans to build a sustainable competitive advantage. Firms use four macro strategies to build their sustainable competitive advantage. Customer excellence focuses on retaining loyal customers and excellent customer service. Operational excellence is achieved through efficient operations and excellent supply chain and human resource management. Product excellence entails having products with high perceived value and effective branding and positioning. Finally, locational excellence entails having a good physical location and Internet presence.

LO2 Describe the elements of a marketing plan.

A marketing plan is composed of an analysis of the current marketing situation, its objectives, the strategy for the four Ps, and appropriate financial statements. A marketing plan represents the output of a three-phase process: planning, implementation, and control. The planning phase requires that managers define the firm's mission and vision and assess the firm's current situation. It helps answer the questions, "What business are we in now, and what do we intend to be in the future?" In the second phase, implementation, the firm specifies, in more operational terms, how it plans to implement its mission and vision. Specifically, to which customer groups does it wish to direct its marketing efforts, and how does it use its marketing mix to provide good value? Finally, in the control phase, the firm must evaluate its performance using appropriate metrics to determine what worked, what didn't, and how performance can be improved in the future.

LO3 Analyze a marketing situation using SWOT analyses.

SWOT stands for strengths, weaknesses, opportunities, and threats. A SWOT analysis occurs during the second step in the strategic planning process, the situation analysis. By analyzing what the firm is good at (its strengths), where it could improve (its weaknesses), where in the marketplace it might excel (its opportunities), and what is happening in the marketplace that could harm the firm (its threats), managers can assess their firm's situation accurately and plan its strategy accordingly.

LO4 Describe how a firm chooses which consumer group(s) to pursue with its marketing efforts.

Once a firm identifies different marketing opportunities, it must determine which are the best to pursue. To accomplish this task, marketers go through a segmentation, targeting, and positioning (STP) process. Firms segment various markets by dividing the total market into those groups of customers with different needs, wants, or characteristics who therefore might appreciate products or services geared especially toward them. After identifying the different segments, the firm goes after, or targets, certain groups on the basis of the firm's perceived ability to satisfy the needs of those groups better than competitors and do so profitably. To complete the STP process, firms position their products or services according to the marketing mix variables so that target customers have a clear, distinctive, and desirable understanding of what the product or service does or represents relative to competing products or services.

Outline the implementation of the marketing mix as a means to increase customer value.

The marketing mix consists of the four Ps—product, price, promotion, and place—and each P contributes to customer value. To provide value, the firm must offer a mix of products and services at prices their target markets will view as indicating good value. Thus, firms make trade-offs between the first two Ps, product and price, to give customers the best value. The third P, promotion, informs customers and helps them form a positive image about the firm and its products and services. The last P, place, adds value by getting the appropriate products and services to customers when they want them and in the quantities they need.

 Summarize portfolio analysis and its use to evaluate marketing performance.

Portfolio analysis is a management tool used to evaluate the firm's various products and businesses—its "portfolio"—and allocate resources according to which products are expected to be the most profitable for the firm in the future. A popular portfolio analysis tool developed by the Boston Consulting Group classifies all products into four categories. The first, stars, are in high-growth markets and have high market shares. The second, cash cows, are in low-growth markets but have high market share. These products generate excess resources that can be spun off to products that need them. The third category, question marks, are in high-growth markets but have relatively low market shares. These products often utilize the excess resources generated by the cash cows. The final category, dogs, are in low-growth markets and have relatively low market shares. These products are often phased out.

 Describe how firms grow their business.

Firms use four basic growth strategies: market penetration, market development, product development, and diversification. A market penetration strategy directs the firm's efforts toward existing customers and uses the present marketing mix. In other words, it attempts to get current customers to buy more. In a market development strategy, the firm uses its current marketing mix to appeal to new market segments, as might occur in international expansion. A product development growth strategy involves offering a new product or service to the firm's current target market. Finally, a diversification strategy takes place when a firm introduces a new product or service to a new customer segment. Sometimes a diversification strategy relates to the firm's current business, such as when a women's clothing manufacturer starts making and selling men's clothes, but a riskier strategy is when a firm diversifies into a completely unrelated business.

Key Terms

- control phase, 37
- customer excellence, 31
- diversification strategy, 54
- implementation phase, 37
- integrated marketing communications (IMC), 44
- locational excellence, 35
- market development strategy, 53
- market growth rate, 49
- market penetration strategy, 52
- market positioning, 41
- market segment, 40
- market segmentation, 40
- market share, 48
- marketing plan, 36
- marketing strategy, 31
- metric, 44
- mission statement, 37
- operational excellence, 33
- planning phase, 36
- product development strategy, 54
- product excellence, 34
- product line, 48
- related diversification, 54
- relative market share, 49
- segmentation, targeting, and positioning (STP), 40
- situation analysis, 38
- strategic business unit (SBU), 48
- sustainable competitive advantage, 31
- SWOT analysis, 38
- target marketing/targeting, 41
- unrelated diversification, 54

Marketing Applications

1. How have Nike and adidas created sustainable competitive advantages for themselves?

2. Perform a SWOT analysis for the company that made your favorite shoes.

3. How does adidas segment its market? Describe the primary target markets for adidas. How does it position its various offerings so that it appeals to these different target markets?

4. How does Hertz add value for business customers through the implementation of the four Ps?

5. Dyson successfully sells its fans and heaters for $150 to $400, whereas most conventional fans sell for around $25. Explain what is the value it creates and how this affects the price it can charge.

6. Of the four growth strategies described in the chapter, which is the riskiest? Which is the easiest to implement? Why?

7. Choose three companies. You believe the first builds customer value through product excellence, the second through operational excellence, and the third through customer excellence. Justify your answer.

8. You are in the job market and have received offers from three very different firms. Develop a marketing plan to help market yourself to prospective employers.

Quiz Yourself

1. Even when large discount retailers enter a market, a few small, local retailers survive and prosper. These small retailers have probably developed a(n) _____ that allows them to survive.
   a. advertising campaign
   b. plan to evaluate results
   c. sustainable competitive advantage
   d. set of performance metrics
   e. SWOT analysis

2. Many of today's college graduates will make their livings providing goods and services to Baby Boomers, the large group of Americans born in the period after World War II. Baby Boomers are a _____ market segment.
   a. psychological
   b. behavioral
   c. social
   d. product-based
   e. demographic

   (Answers to these two questions can be found on page 651.)

Toolkit SWOT Analysis

Assume you are a marketing analyst for a major company and are trying to conduct a situation analysis using SWOT analysis. Please use the toolkit provided in your instructor's Connect course and complete the SWOT grids for each company using the appropriate items.

Net Savvy

1. The mission statement for Quaker Oats cites its origins as "inspired by the power and wholesome goodness of the amazing oat." Frito-Lay looks a little more to the present, citing its mission "To be the world's favorite snack and always within arm's reach." These different perspectives also reflect the quite different positioning adopted by each company. Visit the websites of each manufacturer and review the descriptions of the company, its mission, and its values. Do you believe these two disparate mission statements reflect what the firms do and how they are portrayed in the media? Justify your answer.

2. More and more firms seem to be entering the dating service industry. Visit http://www.eharmony.com and tour the website to find the types of activities and methods such companies use to help match compatible couples. Then visit http://www.match.com and do the same. What are the similarities and differences of these two online dating services? Pick one and perform a SWOT analysis for it.

3. Black and Decker (http://www.blackanddecker.com) and DeWalt (http://www.dewalt.com) are owned by the same parent company, and both sell similar products. Visit each of their wesites and identify what markets each brand targets. Next, discuss how the two companies use the marketing mix differently to target these unique target markets.

Chapter Case Study

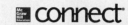

THE GREAT YOGURT BATTLE

Let's think about the options available for your frozen dessert indulgence: ice cream, frozen custard, gelato, frozen yogurt, sherbet, sorbet, water ice, single-serving desserts such as Popsicles, milkshakes, and blended treats that combine frozen dairy products with bits of cookies or candies.[57] In addition to their wide variety of flavors, they also come in reduced-fat, soy, organic, fair-trade, probiotic, nutrition-enhanced, and gluten-free versions. Faced with all these choices and options, how is a brand to make its mark?

This case focuses particularly on sales of frozen yogurt—a relatively small, but growing, part of the $25 billion frozen dessert market. Its growth trends have spawned intense competition among existing frozen yogurt shops, as well as inspired new brands to set up shop. Specifically, the modern U.S. market features approximately 1,500 shops, maintained by 268 different companies. These firms are projected to earn $800 million in revenue this year.[58]

To build and maintain a loyal customer base, each frozen yogurt brand seeks to distinguish itself from its competitors by offering products, services, and ambiance that are so appealing that customers shun competitors. Since it opened in 2005, for example, Pinkberry has attracted loyal fans devoted to its tart-flavored yogurt, which contains probiotics and promises to aid digestion. Stores offer a limited number of exotic flavors, many of which are seasonal, and a wide array of high-end toppings.[59] The minimalism in the flavor choices is part of the company's brand image, as reflected in the stark, bright store layouts. That is, this popular new chain offers consistency across its products and its store images, even as it promises that customers can eat healthy, low-fat, hormone-free milk products and still indulge in unusual yogurt flavors and interesting toppings.[60]

In contrast, the more traditional dessert idea offered by TCBY allows consumers to help themselves to yogurt flavors like cake batter, red velvet cake, and peanut butter, and then pile on candy, cookies, fruit, sauces, and sprinkles.[61] Because the stores calculate the costs of each dessert by weight rather than by serving size, customers feel free to create towering frozen creations that they might have felt awkward ordering. It also results in a higher per-serving cost.[62]

Originating in South Korea, Red Mango started opening the doors on its U.S. stores in 2007. It purposefully seeks locations in college towns, reasoning that students tend to be more health conscious and thus would be attracted to its all-natural, gluten-free, low-fat options.[63] In keeping with its goal of

RASPBERRY CHEESECAKE
all-natural • nonfat • probiotic

How does Red Mango add value for its customers?

appealing mainly to students and young consumers, it also promotes its cold coffee options. The stores themselves encourage lingering, with comfortable seating and even large-screen televisions in some stores.

These chains and their smaller competitors also are adding new product lines to leverage the exploding popularity of Greek-style yogurt. Adding desserts based on the newly introduced (at least in the United States) style has expanded the market dramatically. Yet analysts argue that there is still plenty of room for growth. The United States eats far less yogurt per capita than most European nations, for example.[64] In contrast, other observers caution that frozen yogurt is just one more dessert fad, rather like cupcake shops, that will reach a peak and then fade away relatively soon.

On grocery store shelves, the brands see room to grow. Sales of frozen yogurt products jumped by 74 percent in a recent two-year period. In that same span of time, sales of ice cream products grew by a mere 3.9 percent.[65]

As these examples show, newcomers must constantly try to find a foothold in the market. Already established businesses must grow and change their product offerings and corporate citizenry to keep pace with customer needs and tastes. Pinkberry stresses health and style; TCBY gives customers more choices and more control over portions; Red Mango targets young college consumers.

Questions

1. Perform a SWOT analysis for each of the companies mentioned in this case study. How are the results similar? How do they differ?

2. Which growth strategies seem most likely for each of the companies mentioned in this case? Why?

3. What sorts of marketing metrics would be most helpful for a brand manager of a frozen yogurt chain?

Endnotes

1. "About Nike Inc.," http://nikeinc.com.

2. Bob Young, "No NBA? Let the Shoe Wars Begin," *Arizona Republic*, October 16, 2011, http://www.azcentral.com.

3. "Nike+ iPod," http://www.apple.com.

4. Austin Carr, "Nike: The Number 1 Most Innovative Company of 2013," *Fast Company*, February 11, 2013.

5. Don Blair, "Case Study: Nike CFO Don Blair Reveals Strategy for Profit Growth," *CFOGlobalHQ*, October 30, 2013, http://www.cfoglobalhq.com.

6. Nike, "Nike.Inc Unveils ColorDry Technology and High-Tech Facility to Eliminate Water and Chemicals in Dyeing," December 2, 2013, http://nikeinc.com.

7. Ibid.

8. Blair, "Case Study: Nike CFO Don Blair Reveals Strategy for Profit Growth."

9. Trefis Team, "Why Nike Will Outpace the Sports Apparel Market's Growth," *Forbes.com*, May 13, 2013, http://www.forbes.com.

10. Carr, "Nike: The Number 1 Most Innovative Company of 2013."

11. Michael Treacy and Fred Wiersema, *The Disciplines of Market Leaders* (Reading, MA: Addison-Wesley, 1995). Treacy and Wiersema suggest the first three strategies. We suggest the fourth—locational excellence.

12. V. Kumar et al., "Establishing Profitable Customer Loyalty for Multinational Companies in the Emerging Economies: A Conceptual Framework," *Journal of International Marketing* 21 (March 2013), pp. 57–80; Yuping Liu-Thompkins and Leona Tam, "Not All Repeat Customers Are the Same: Designing Effective Cross-Selling Promotion on the Basis of Attitudinal Loyalty and Habit," *Journal of Marketing* 77 (September 2013), pp. 21–36.

13. Melea Press and Eric J. Arnould, "How Does Organizational Identification Form? A Consumer Behavior Perspective," *Journal of Consumer Research* 38 (December 2011), pp. 650–66.

14. Tanzina Vega, "Self Magazine Refocuses for a Younger Audience," *The New York Times*, February 10, 2013.

15. Valarie A. Zeithaml, Mary Jo Bitner, and Dwayne D. Gremler, *Services Marketing: Integrating Customer Focus across the Firm*, 5th ed. (Burr Ridge, IL: McGraw-Irwin, 2009).

16. Brooks Barnes, "At Disney Parks, a Bracelet Meant to Build Loyalty (and Sales)," *The New York Times*, January 7, 2013.

17. Carmine Gallo, "Customer Service the Disney Way," *Forbes*, April 14, 2011.

18. Diane M. Martin and John W. Schouten, "Consumption-Driven Market Emergence," *Journal of Consumer Research* 40 (February 2014), pp. 855–70. Also see articles in special issue edited by John T. Mentzer and Greg Gundlach, "Exploring the Relationship between Marketing and Supply Chain Management: Introduction to the Special Issue," *Journal of the Academy of Marketing Science* 38, no. 1 (2010), pp. 1–4.

19. Hilary Stout, "In War for Same-Day Delivery, Racing Madly to Go Last Mile," *The New York Times,* November 23, 2013, http://www.nytimes.com.

20. http://www.interbrand.com.

21. "Marketing Plan," *American Marketing Association Dictionary,* http://www.marketingpower.com.

22. Donald Lehman and Russell Winer, *Analysis for Marketing Planning,* 7th ed. (Burr Ridge, IL: McGraw-Hill/Irwin, 2008).

23. Nancy J. Sirianni et al., "Branded Service Encounters: Strategically Aligning Employee Behavior with the Brand Positioning," *Journal of Marketing* 77 (November 2013), pp. 108–23; Andrew Campbell, "Mission Statements," *Long Range Planning* 30 (1997), pp. 931–33.

24. Gene R. Laczniak and Patrick E. Murphy, "Stakeholder Theory and Marketing: Moving from a Firm-Centric to a Societal Perspective," *Journal of Public Policy & Marketing* 31 (Fall 2012), pp. 284–92; Alfred Rappaport, *Creating Shareholder Value: The New Standard for Business Performance* (New York: Wiley, 1988).

25. http://help-us.nike.com.

26. "Corporate Mission Statement," *adidas Group,* http://adidas-group.corporate-publications.com.

27. "Mission Statement," *Teach For America,* http://www.teachforamerica.org.

28. Matt Townsend, "As Nike Scoffs, Toning Shoes Gain Traction," *Bloomberg Businessweek,* June 7–13, 2010, pp. 22–24.

29. Sebastian Joseph, "Nike Exploits Winter Olympics Interest with 'Play Russian' Campaign," *Marketing Week,* November 29, 2013, http://www.marketingweek.co.uk.

30. Nike, 10-K report, July 20, 2010.

31. Russel Parsons, "Nike Beating Official Sponsor adidas in World Cup Stakes," *Marketing Week,* June 24, 2010, p. 7.

32. Eric Siemans, "New Balance TV Spots Target Nike," *Portland Business Journal,* March 7, 2011, http://www.bizjournals.com.

33. Nike, 10-K report, July 19, 2013.

34. https://www.hertz.com/rentacar/productsandservices/productsandservicesRegions.do.

35. https://images.hertz.com/pdfs/VMVWeb.pdf; http://www.adweek.com/aw/content_display/creative/new-campaigns/e3i21cea1586dd4edf5d50f9a17e7f18bf3.

36. Sandy Smith, "Category Killing, Korea Style," *Stores,* October 2011.

37. Terence A. Shimp, *Advertising Promotion and Other Aspects of Integrated Marketing Communication,* 8th ed. (Mason, OH: South-Western, 2008); T. Duncan and C. Caywood, "The Concept, Process, and Evolution of Integrated Marketing Communication," in *Integrated Communication: Synergy of Persuasive Voices,* ed. E. Thorson and J. Moore (Mahwah, NJ: Erlbaum, 1996); see also various issues of the *Journal of Integrated Marketing Communications,* http://jimc.medill.northwestern.edu.

38. Susan Thurston, "Movie Buzz for HSN," *Tampa Bay Times,* February 23, 2013.

39. Annie Gasparro, "In the Low-Carb Age, Does Cereal Have a Future?" *The Wall Street Journal,* September 19, 2013.

40. Ofer Mintz and Imran S. Currim "What Drives Managerial Use of Marketing and Financial Metrics and Does Metric Use Affect Performance of Marketing-Mix Activities?" *Journal of Marketing* 77 (March 2013), pp. 17–40.

41. Kirsten Acuna, "Google Says It Can Predict Which Films Will Be Huge Box Office Hits," *Business Insider,* June 6, 2013.

42. Goodyear, 10-K, February 12, 2013.

43. This discussion is adapted from Roger A. Kerin, Steven W. Hartley, and William Rudelius, *Marketing,* 10th ed. (Burr Ridge, IL: McGraw-Hill/Irwin, 2011).

44. P. Farris et al., *Marketing Metrics: 50+ Metrics Every Executive Should Master* (Upper Saddle River, NJ: Pearson, 2006), p. 17.

45. Relative market share = Brand's market share ÷ Largest competitor's market share. If, for instance, there are only two products in a market, A and B, and product B has 90 percent market share, then A's relative market share is 10 ÷ 90 = 11.1 percent. If, on the other hand, B only has 50 percent market share, then A's relative market share is 10 ÷ 50 = 20 percent. Ibid., p. 19.

46. Apple Inc., "Form 10-K 2011 Annual Report," October 30, 2013.

47. Ibid.

48. Sherilynn Macale, "Apple Has Sold 300M iPods, Currently Holds 78% of the Music Player Market," *The Next Web,* October 4, 2011, http://thenextweb.com; Chris Smith, "iPad Tablet Market Share Down to 57 Percent," *Techradar.com,* February 16, 2012, http://www.techradar.com; Ken Yeung, "Apple Sold 4.6M Macs and 3.49M iPods in Q4 FY2013," *The Next Web,* October 28, 2013, http://thenextweb.com.

49. Joe Wilcox, "iPad Market Share Plunged 20 Percent in Q4 2010," *BetaNews,* February 2011, http://betanews.com; Mohit Agrawal, "Tablets OS Market Share," *Telecom Circle,* October 7, 2011, http://www.telecomcircle.com; Apple, "Apple Reports Fourth Quarter Results," October 28, 2013, http://www.apple.com.

50. Roger Kerin, Vijay Mahajan, and P. Rajan Varadarajan, *Contemporary Perspectives on Strategic Market Planning* (Boston: Allyn & Bacon, 1991), chapter 6; Susan Mudambi, "A Topology of Strategic Choice in Marketing," *International Journal of Market & Distribution Management* (1994), pp. 22–25.

51. http://www.gamestop.com/xbox-360/movies-tv/yoostar-onmtv/91616.

52. http://www.mtv.com/shows/teen_mom/season_3/series.jhtml.

53. http://www.viacom.com/ourbrands/globalreach/Pages/default.aspx.

54. http://www.stayteen.org/; http://www.mtv.com/mobile/.

55. A. A. Thompson et al., *Crafting and Executing Strategy,* 18th ed. (New York: McGraw-Hill /Irwin, 2012).

56. http://www.mtv.com/shows/made/series.jhtml; Tim Arango, "Make Room, Cynics; MTV Wants to Do Some Good," *The New York Times,* April 18, 2009; Robert Seidman, "MTV Continues to Diversify Slate with New Scripted Comedies 'The Hard Times of RJ Berger' and 'Warren the Ape,'" *tvbythenumbers.com,* January 15, 2010.

57. Packaged Facts, "Ice Cream and Frozen Desserts in the U.S.: Markets and Opportunities in Retail and Foodservice," January 2010.

58. Lawrence Delevigne, "What Private Equity Loves about the Booming Frozen Yogurt Trend," *CNBC.com,* October 13, 2013, http://www.cnbc.com/id/101103927.

59. Yolanda Santosa, "The Making of Pinkberry," *Brand Packaging,* November 2, 2011, http://www.brandpackaging.com.

60. "FAQ," http://www.pinkberry.com/faq.html.

61. "Menu_Nutrition," http://tcby.com.

62. Jaime Levy Pessin, "Yogurt Chains Give Power to the People," *The Wall Street Journal,* August 22, 2011.

63. IBIS World, "Frozen Yogurt Stores in the US Industry Market Research Report," November 12, 2013, http://www.prweb.com.

64. Packaged Facts, "The Yogurt Market and Yogurt Innovation: Greek Yogurt and Beyond," March 29, 2013.

65. "Frozen Yogurt Growth Freezing Out Ice Cream," *Progressive Grocer*, September 18, 2013.

i. Jennifer Polland, "Singapore Airlines Really Does Have the Best Economy Seats in the World," *Business Insider*, March 8, 2013; "Singapore Airlines Tops Survey for Best Service," *The New York Times*, http://community.nytimes.com; Singapore Airlines, http://www.singaporeair.com; Matt O'Sullivan, "Singapore Airlines and Air New Zealand Forge New Alliance," *The Sydney Morning Herald*, January 16, 2014; "Singapore Girls: You're a Great Way to Fly," http://www.singaporeair.com.

ii. Peter Johnston, "Share of the Mobile Pie," *Stores*, October 2011; Brad Tuttle, "Hungry and Lazy Customers Rejoice! It's Getting Even Easier to Order Food," *Time*, April 25, 2013.

iii. Ibid.; Tesco, "Tesco HomePlus Expands Number of Virtual Stores," news release, February 7, 2012, http://www.tescoplc.com; Andy Potts, "The Emporium Strikes Back," *The Economist*, July 13, 2013, http://www.economist.com.

iv. James Surowiecki, "After Rana Plaza," *The New Yorker*, May 20, 2013.

Credits

WRITING A MARKETING PLAN

Have a plan. Follow the plan, and you'll be surprised how successful you can be. Most people don't have a plan. That's why it's easy to beat most folks.

—Paul "Bear" Bryant, football coach, University of Alabama

WHY WRITE A MARKETING PLAN?[1]

As a student, you likely plan out much in your life—where to meet for dinner, how much time to spend studying for exams, which courses to take next semester, how to get home for winter break, and so on. Plans enable us to figure out where we want to go and how we might get there.

For a firm, the goal is not much different. Any company that wants to succeed (which means any firm whatsoever) needs to plan for a variety of contingencies, and marketing represents one of the most significant. A marketing plan—which we defined in Chapter 2 as a written document composed of an analysis of the current marketing situation, opportunities and threats for the firm,

marketing objectives and strategy specified in terms of the four Ps, action programs, and projected or pro forma income (and other financial) statements—enables marketing personnel and the firm as a whole to understand their own actions, the market in which they operate, their future direction, and the means to obtain support for new initiatives.[2]

Because these elements—internal activities, external environments, goals, and forms of support—differ for every firm, the marketing plan is different for each firm as well. However, several guidelines apply to marketing plans in general; this appendix summarizes those points and offers an annotated example.

MARKETING PLAN VERSUS BUSINESS PLAN

Of course, firms consider more than marketing when they make plans and therefore commonly develop business plans as well. Yet as this book highlights, marketing constitutes such an important element of business that business plans and marketing plans coincide in many ways.[3] Both marketing and business plans generally encompass

1. Executive summary.
2. Company overview.
3. Objectives or goals, usually according to strategic plan and focus.
4. Situation analysis.
5. Customer segmentation, target marketing, and positioning analysis.
6. Marketing strategy.
7. Financial projections.
8. Implementation plan.
9. Evaluation and control metrics.
10. Appendix

However, a business plan also includes details about R&D and operations, and both may feature details about other key topics, depending on the focus of the company and the plan.

STRUCTURE OF A MARKETING PLAN

This section briefly describes each of the elements of a marketing plan.[4]

Executive Summary

The executive summary essentially tells the reader why he or she is reading this marketing plan—what changes require consideration, what new products need discussion, and so forth—and suggests possible actions to take in response to the information the plan contains.

Company Overview

In this section, the plan provides a brief description of the company, including perhaps its mission statement, background, and competitive advantages.

Objectives/Goals

This section offers more specifics about why readers are reading the marketing plan. What does the company want to achieve, both overall and with this particular marketing plan?

Situation Analysis

Recall from Chapter 2 that a situation analysis generally relies on SWOT considerations; therefore, this section describes the strengths, weaknesses, opportunities, and threats facing the company.

STP Analysis

The analysis proceeds by assessing the market in which the company functions, the products it currently offers or plans to offer in the future, and the characteristics of current or potential customers.

Marketing Strategy

The marketing strategy may be very specific, especially if the plan pertains to, for example, a stable product in a familiar market, or it may be somewhat open to varied possibilities, such as when the firm plans to enter a new market with an innovative product.

Financial Projections

On the basis of the knowledge already obtained, the marketing plan should provide possible developments and returns on the marketing investments outlined in the marketing strategy.

Implementation Plan

This portion of the marketing plan includes the timing of promotional activities, when monitoring will take place, and how expansions likely will proceed.

Evaluation and Control Metrics

The firm must have a means of assessing the marketing plan's recommendations; the marketing plan therefore must indicate the methods for undertaking this assessment, whether quantitatively or qualitatively.

Appendix

The final section(s) offers additional information that might be of benefit, such as a list of key personnel, data limitations that may influence the findings, and suggestions of the plan, relevant legislation, and so forth.

INFORMATION SOURCES[5]

When writing a marketing plan, you likely can turn to a variety of your firm's in-house information sources, including annual reports, previous marketing plans, published mission statements, and so on. In addition, various sources offer suggestions and examples that may provide you with direction and ideas. A reference librarian can help you find many of these sources, which likely are available through your university's library system.

- Knowthis.com—"a knowledge source for marketing" http://www.knowthis.com/tutorials/principles-of-marketing/how-to-write-a-marketing-plan/21.htm.
- Encyclopedia of American Industries—introduces industry structure; arranged by SIC and NAICS codes.
- Standard & Poor's NetAdvantage—surveys of more than 50 industries, with financial data about companies in each industry.
- Investext Plus—brokerage house reports.
- IBISWorld—market research on thousands of industries; classified by NAICS code.
- Statistical Abstract of the United States—a vast variety of statistics on a wealth of topics.
- U.S. Bureau of the Census—detailed statistical data gathered every 10 years on all aspects of the U.S. population.
- County Business Patterns: U.S. Bureau of the Census—payroll and employee numbers for most NAICS codes.
- Consumer Expenditure Study: U.S. Bureau of Labor Statistics—income and expenditures by household, classified by various demographics.

- LifeStyle Market Analyst—lifestyle information about geographic areas, lifestyle interest groups, and age and income groups.

- Mediamark Reporter—information about demographics, lifestyles, product and brand usage, and advertising media preferences.

- Scarborough Arbitron—local market consumer information for various media in 75 local markets for consumer retail shopping behavior, product consumption, media usage, lifestyle behavior, and demographics.

- Simmons Study of Media and Markets—products and consumer characteristics; various media audiences and their characteristics.

- Sourcebook America—demographic data, including population, spending potential index, income, race, and *Tapestry* data, presented by state, county, DMA, and zip code, as well as business data by county and zip code.

- Rand McNally Commercial Atlas and Marketing Guide—maps and tables showing demographic, industrial, transportation, railroad, airline, and hospital data.

- "Survey of Buying Power," Sales and Marketing Management—current state, county, city, and town estimates of population by age, retail sales by store group, effective buying income, and buying power index.

- Annual & 10-K reports from *Thomson One Banker*, *Edgar*, and *LexisNexis*—business descriptions, product listings, distribution channels, possible impact of regulations and lawsuits, and discussions of strategic issues.

- MarketResearch.com Academic—market research reports on a variety of consumer products.

- Mintel Reports Database—market research reports focusing on consumer products, lifestyles, retailing, and international travel industry.

LINGUISTIC AND VISUAL SUGGESTIONS

Again, recall that all marketing plans differ because all firms differ. However, just as rules exist that dictate what makes for good writing, some rules or guidelines apply to all well-written marketing plans.

- Maintain a professional attitude in the writing and presentation.

- Keep descriptions and summaries concise. Get to the point.

- Use standard, edited English.

- Proofread the entire plan multiple times to catch grammatical, spelling, or other such errors that could dampen the professionalism of the writing.

- Adopt a businesslike tone; avoid flowery or jargon-filled writing.

- Employ direct, rather than passive, and present, rather than past, tense whenever possible (e.g., "We plan to achieve 30 percent growth in two years" rather than "The plan was that 30 percent growth would be achieved by the firm within two years").

- Be positive.

- Avoid meaningless superlatives (e.g., "Our goal is tremendous growth").

- Be specific; use quantitative information whenever possible.

- Insert graphics to convey important concepts succinctly, including photos, graphs, illustrations, and charts.

- Avoid using so many visual elements that they clutter the plan.

- Lay out the plan clearly and logically.

- Organize sections logically, using multiple levels of headings, distinguished clearly by font differences (e.g., bold for first-level heads, italics for second-level heads).

- Consider the use of bullet points or numbered lists to emphasize important points.

- Exploit modern technology (e.g., graphics software, page layout software, laser printers) to ensure the plan looks professional.

- Adopt an appropriate font to make the text easy to read and visually appealing—avoid using anything smaller than 10-point font at a minimum.

- Avoid unusual or decorative fonts; stick with a common serif type to make the text easy to read.

- Consider binding the report with an attractive cover and clear title page.

- Generally, aim for a plan that consists of 15–30 pages.

Endnotes

1. This appendix was written by Tom Chevalier, Britt Hackmann, and Elisabeth Nevins Caswell, in conjunction with the textbook authors (Dhruv Grewal and Michael Levy) as the basis of class discussion, rather than to illustrate either effective or ineffective marketing practice.

2. http://www.knowthis.com (accessed May 16, 2008); see also "Marketing Plan Online," http://www.quickmba.com (accessed May 16, 2008); "Marketing Plan," http://www.businessplans.org (accessed May 18, 2008).

3. Roger Kerin, Steven Hartley, and William Rudelius, Marketing (New York: McGraw-Hill/Irwin, 2008), p. 53.

4. Ibid., p. 54; http://www.knowthis.com (accessed May 16, 2008).

5. This listing of sources largely comes from the Babson College Library Guide, http://www3.babson.edu, May 12, 2008 (accessed May 15, 2008). Special thanks to Nancy Dlott.

6. This marketing plan presents an abbreviated version of the actual plan for PeopleAhead. Some information has been changed to maintain confidentiality.

7. Publishers' and Advertising Directors' Conference, September 21, 2005.

8. Mintel International Group, "Online Recruitment–US," January 1, 2005, http://www.marketresearch.com (accessed September 1, 2005).

9. Corzen Inc., May 1, 2004, http://www.wantedtech.com (accessed May 17, 2004).

10. Mintel International Group, "Online Recruitment–US."

PEOPLEAHEAD MARKETING PLAN ILLUSTRATION[6]

PeopleAhead Marketing Plan: Condensed

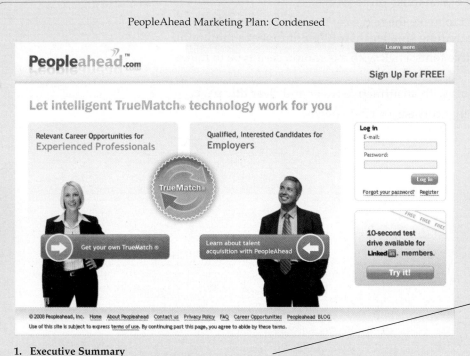

1. Executive Summary

PeopleAhead focuses on career advancement done right. Instead of making the job search a one-time event, PeopleAhead provides a platform for people to find, advance, and develop their careers by sharing career goals, discussing professional development plans, and socializing with other professionals.

PeopleAhead culminates the career advancement experience with its proprietary TrueMatch® technology, which identifies synergies between the companies hiring talent (employers) and PeopleAhead members (job candidates) who wish to be hired. By anonymously presenting only prequalified career opportunities to members, who confirm their interest and recommend others, PeopleAhead transforms the ineffective online hiring process into a highly efficient career-matching system. PeopleAhead was founded by Carlos Larracilla and Tom Chevalier to improve people's lives by helping them achieve their career aspirations. The vision for PeopleAhead was conceived of in January 2006, with a notion that personality alignment is critical to matching the right people with the right career opportunities. Since then, the idea has grown and morphed into a company that matches the right person with the right career opportunity by aligning personality, competencies, experience, and interests.

Tom and Carlos combine human resources, system development, and sales experience to deliver a groundbreaking, TrueMatch®-branded talent matching network that makes it easier for people to achieve their career aspirations and improves the way companies identify individuals who will be able to contribute to their long-term success. The organizational chart of PeopleAhead is available in Appendix A.

Instead of using separate "Executive Summary" and "Company Overview" sections, this marketing plan begins with a general overview that includes both aspects and answers the key questions: "What type of business are we?" and "What do we need to do to accomplish our objectives?" (see Chapter 2).

As this plan does, a marketing plan should start with a positive, upbeat assessment of what the company does and what it hopes to continue doing.

Note the personalization of the company founders, which may help readers feel connected to the company.

2. Strategic Objectives

2.1. Mission

PeopleAhead's mission is to help individuals with career advancement and improve the human capital in companies. The site will act as a networking platform for professionals and career matching as opposed to job and resume-posting searches.

The paragraph provides a general outline of the firm's objectives; the bulleted list offers more specific goals, and the subsequent sections go into more detail about the various factors that may influence these objectives.

2.2. Goals:

- Use brand-matching technology: TrueMatch®
- Build critical mass of users.
- Drive traffic to the Web site through marketing blitzes.
- Utilize word-of-mouth advertising from satisfied users.

2.3. Business Summary

- **Business customers:** This group provides PeopleAhead's revenues. Customers purchase contact information about the Top Ten PROfiles gleaned from the individual member base that have been sorted and ranked by the TrueMatch® technology. PeopleAhead will focus on small and medium businesses (see Market Segmentation section), because these entities are underserved by large competitors in the online recruitment market, and because research shows that this demographic has a less efficient recruitment process that would benefit most readily from PeopleAhead's services. Within this segment, customers include HR managers who are responsible for the sourcing of candidates, functional area managers who require new talent for their team, and executives whose business objectives rely on human capital and efficiency of operations.

By referring to another section, the plan makes clear where it is heading and enables readers to cross-reference the information.

- **Individual members:** This group does not pay for services but is the main source of data points for PeopleAhead's TrueMatch® system. PeopleAhead will focus on building a base of individual members who range from recent graduates to individuals with 5–7 years of continuous employment. Ideal members are those who are currently employed or will be graduating within nine months and are "poised" to make a career change. These individuals can utilize the services to the fullest extent and are valuable candidates for business customers.

The plan acknowledges both a general, potential target market and the ideal targets.

2.4. Competitive Advantage

- **TrueMatch® offers a branded technology,** marketed to both business customers and individual candidates for its "black box" value proposition, which establishes PeopleAhead as the category leader for recruitment-matching software. This technology provides a point of differentiation from competitors, which may have technically similar matching software but constantly need to reinforce their marketing messages with explanations of their value proposition.

As Chapter 2 suggests, the plan notes PeopleAhead's sustainable competitive advantage as part of its overall mission statement.

- **For individual candidates,** PeopleAhead will be the favored career advancement platform online, where individuals enthusiastically create a history and have connections (invited friends, coworkers, and mentors) in place that will make PeopleAhead a staple among their favorite Web sites. PeopleAhead delivers True-Match® career opportunities, professional development plans that let people establish a professional record, and valuable career advancement tools, including automatic position feedback, "recommend-a-friend," and team-based career networking.

- **For business customers,** PeopleAhead makes online sourcing and qualification of candidates quick and efficient by prequalifying potential candidates, seeking recommendations for hard-to-find individuals, and delivering only the Top 10 most highly qualified candidates who have preconfirmed interest in the available position. PeopleAhead will be the most effective candidate-company matching platform available in the market, delivering prequalified, preconfirmed candidates.

In discussing both the external market and the internal advantages of PeopleAhead, the plan carefully distinguishes between individual job candidates and businesses, thus differentiating the focus and objectives according to this segmentation.

3. Situation Analysis—Online Recruitment

Online recruitment is the system whereby companies use the Web to locate and qualify prospective candidates for available positions. The methods employed by online recruitment service providers to serve this market range from resume aggregation to assessment test application to linking strategies. However, the common underlying objective is to locate candidates who would not be found by traditional recruitment methods and use computing power to qualify candidates quickly and with more accuracy than would be possible manually.

3.1. Industry Analysis

Large online recruitment Web sites make this a tedious process by requiring companies to search through many resumes manually to find the right candidate. Other sites solicit recommendations for positions. However, resumes are often "enhanced," such that almost all candidates appear qualified, and information found in the resume or provided through a recommendation is simply not sufficient to make an educated hiring decision. Companies need more information and intelligent tools that make this screening process more accurate.

3.1.1. Market Size:

The market size for both member segments in 2005 was as follows:

Figures provide a visually attractive break in the text and summarize a lot of information in an easy-to-read format.

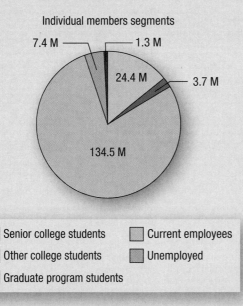

Individual members segments

7.4 M — 1.3 M

24.4 M — 3.7 M

134.5 M

- ■ Senior college students
- □ Other college students
- ■ Graduate program students
- ■ Current employees
- ■ Unemployed

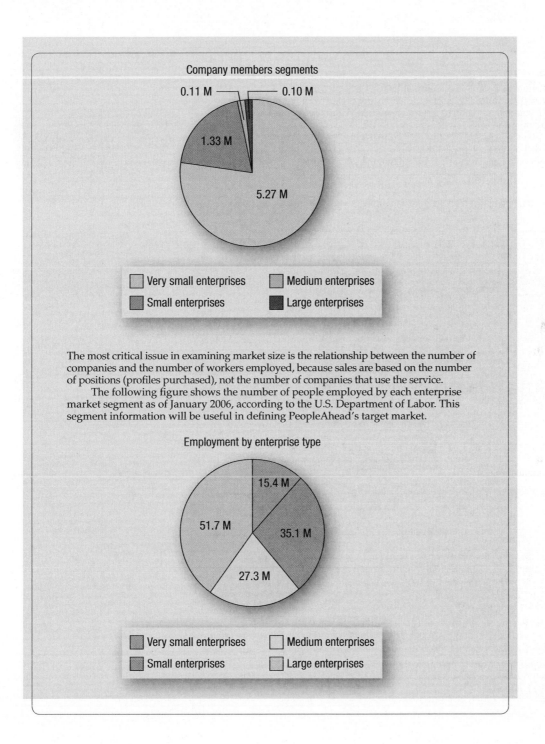

Company members segments

The most critical issue in examining market size is the relationship between the number of companies and the number of workers employed, because sales are based on the number of positions (profiles purchased), not the number of companies that use the service.

The following figure shows the number of people employed by each enterprise market segment as of January 2006, according to the U.S. Department of Labor. This segment information will be useful in defining PeopleAhead's target market.

Employment by enterprise type

3.1.2. Market Growth

PeopleAhead will operate in the online recruitment market. The growth of this industry is subject to two primary constraints: U.S. economic health and online recruitment advertisement adoption rates. Understanding these constraints will help identify PeopleAhead's opportunity. General indicators suggest the U.S. economy (GDP) will grow at an average annual rate of 4% for the next decade.[7] Online recruitment advertising is expected to grow by 35% per year to reach $7.6 billion by 2010.[8] Not only is the market expanding, but it is exhibiting rapid adoption by new entities, as the following graph shows.[9]

> Another visually attractive graph summarizes complicated information easily. The use of high-quality color can add a professional feel to a marketing plan.

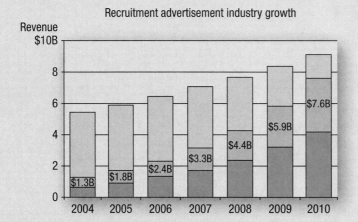

Recruitment advertisement industry growth

Legend:
- ☐ Total recruitment advertisement
- ☐ Total online recruitment market
- ■ Main competitors: Monster, CareerBuilder, and Yahoo/HotJobs

3.1.3. Market Needs

- **The right person for the right position:** The right employee for one company or position is not the same for all others. Not only must companies locate intelligent individuals with relevant experience, but they also prefer people who are aligned with the position requirements in terms of personality, competencies, and fit with the company culture.

- **Prescreening qualification tools:** Increasing the number of candidates through online recruitment can be advantageous, but it can also be a hindrance. When sourcing candidates, recruiters need tools that help them qualify applicants.

- **Time savings:** Companies need to complete the online sourcing and qualification of candidates quickly. Leaving positions unfilled can cause critical performance gaps to emerge within the company.

3.1.4. Market Trends

The methods by which online recruitment service providers deliver candidates has been undergoing a migration from resume aggregation and search services like Monster and CareerBuilder to new Web 2.0 methodologies that include passive recruitment, "meta tagging," and social networking.

The underlying objective of these Web 2.0 services is to allow individuals to remain on a few, trusted Web sites while enabling companies to access those individuals for financial purposes. In parallel, the focus is moving from aggregation of unique visitors toward engaging existing users more intensively. Internet users are growing familiar with sites that encourage socializing, collaborating, and distributing private information online to help improve network benefits and need to be engaged to maintain contact.

3.2. SWOT Analysis

	Positive	Negative
Internal	**STRENGTHS** • Industry best practices: The networking model used by PeopleAhead draws on the industry accepted best practices contact protocols drawn from multiple industries, including online feedback, recruitment, and social networking and offline professional networking. TrueMatch® software aligns business objectives with appropriate candidates. • Team expertise: The combined talents of the founders include human resources, system development, sales, and marketing. • Web development expertise: PeopleAhead has partnered with an award-winning European software development provider. This company provides quality usually reserved for high-budget projects, at terms that are favorable for a start-up company.	**WEAKNESSES** • Absence of industry "influentials": As a start-up, PeopleAhead does not currently have resources to attract influential industry managers. • Inability to guarantee critical mass: As is true of many Internet companies, the business must solve the "chicken and egg" puzzle to build critical mass. • Verifying efficiency of matching capabilities: In theory, the system has an absolute guarantee of effectivity; computations make decisions rather than humans. However, the matching capabilities must be verified as accurate to gain widespread acceptance. • Broad target market: Because PeopleAhead is targeting a wide range of businesses, the product being developed has not been "customized" ideally for each segment.
External	**OPPORTUNITIES** • Service gap: Recruiters are not pleased with current online recruitment vendors. • Industry gap: Job turnover is every 3.5 years per person. • Demand for productive candidates. • Online recruitment advertising: Growing by 35% per year, to reach $7.6 billion by 2010.[10]	**THREATS** • Convergence: Existing competitors may form strategic alliances and establish powerful positions before PeopleAhead can establish itself. • Inability to protect model: Very little intellectual property created by Web sites is protected by law. Although PeopleAhead will pursue

(continued)

Before engaging in a firm-specific SWOT analysis (see Chapter 2), this marketing plan assesses the external market environment further and thus establishes a basis for the subsequent SWOT analysis.

Using a table and bullet points, the plan summarizes a lot of information succinctly and clearly.

Note that the analysis uses outside sources to support its claims.

External	OPPORTUNITIES	THREATS
	• Fragmented business models: Online recruitment is fragmented by recruitment methodology: active (people who need jobs), passive (people who are not looking but would move if enticed), poised (people unsatisfied with jobs they have), and network (finding people of interest based on who or what they know).	aggressive IP protection strategies, the model could be copied or mimicked by competitors. • Inadequate differentiation: Inability to explain our differentiation would relegate PeopleAhead to (unfair) comparisons with competitors. Without differentiation, People-Ahead will not be able to create scale through network effects.

3.3. Competition

Most online recruitment Web sites compete in the active recruitment market, including Monster, CareerBuilder, and Yahoo/HotJobs. The pervasive segment includes job seekers who actively look for jobs, post their resumes, and search for jobs on company Web sites. Most active recruiters offer free services to users and charge companies on a fee basis. Companies can post jobs and search for candidate resumes in the database (average fee for local searches is $500 and nationwide is $1,000). In this first-generation online recruitment business model, competitors face the challenge to make the process more user-friendly and reduce the effort required to make these sites deliver results.

> If PeopleAhead chooses to adopt a competitor-based pricing strategy (see Chapter 13), detailed information about how other recruitment firms work will be mandatory.

• **Monster:** Monster.com is the sixteenth most visited Web site in the United States, with more than 43 million professionals in its viewer base. Monster earns revenue from job postings, access to its resume database, and advertisements on Web sites of partner companies.

> Information about competitors' revenues, customers, growth, and so forth often is available publicly through a variety of sources.

• **Careerbuilder:** Careerbuilder.com has experienced 75% growth for the past five years. This job post/resume search company uses its media ownership to attract passive candidates from partner Web sites. It achieves growth through affiliate partnerships that host job searches on affiliated Web pages, such as Google, MSN, AOL, *USA Today,* Earthlink, BellSouth, and CNN. Job posting is the primary activity, sold together with or separately from resume searches.

• **Passive recruitment:** The second generation of online recruitment locates candidates who are not necessarily looking for jobs but who could be convinced to move to a new position if the right opportunity was presented. The most recognized competitors in this category include Jobster, LinkedIn, and H3 (Appendix B).

> For information that may not belong in the main text, an appendix offers an effective means to provide detail without distracting readers.

3.4. Company Analysis

PeopleAhead's mission is simple: improve people's lives through career advancement. PeopleAhead recognizes that career advancement means many things to many people and provides a fresh perspective on career networking that is flexible yet powerful:

> This section offers the "product" component of the market/product/customer analysis. Because People-Ahead's product is mostly a service (see Chapter 12), it focuses on some intangible features of its offering.

• **Users are not alone:** Finding a job is not easy. Why search solo? PeopleAhead unites groups of friends, coworkers, and mentors to create natural, team-based career discovery.

• **Job posting is not natural:** People spend countless hours searching job listings and posting resumes, only to be overlooked because their writing style or resume format does not match an overburdened recruiter's preference. Good people, not resumes, make great companies. PeopleAhead's TrueMatch technology matches the right people with the right position. No posting, no applying—just good, quality matches.

- **Professionals being professionals:** There is a place online for social networking, pet networking, and music networking. So why is there no outlet for career networking online—the activity that consumes the majority of our professional lives? PeopleA-head is a place where professionals share their experiences, achievements, and objectives with other professionals that care and can be found by employers who value their professionalism.

The last—and some would say most important—piece of the analysis puzzle: customers.

3.5. Customer Analysis

PeopleAhead's R&D efforts show that the impetus to improve recruitment effectivity is pervasive and that unmet needs revolve around a few core issues: the ability to find qualified talent, establishing a fit between the candidate and the company culture, verifying the candidate's career progression, and working quickly and cost effectively. The following customer characteristics represent ideal attributes that align with PeopleAhead's service offering. This information might be used in conjunction with the Marketing Strategy.

3.5.1. Business Customer

- **Industry:** Because companies that value human capital are more likely to take a chance on a start-up that promotes professional development, the broadly defined professional services industry, including insurance, banking, and consulting, is the primary focus.
- **Functional area:** PeopleAhead's system identifies "people" people, so positions that require human interaction are more aligned with system capabilities than those with stringent skill requirements, sets such as programming or accounting.
- **Size:** Large businesses (>1000 employees) have high volume requirements and demand vendors with proven track records; small businesses (<25 employees) hire fewer people and may not justify acquisition costs. PeopleAhead aligns best with medium-sized customers.
- **Hiring need:** PeopleAhead serves two types of searches very well: those with too many applicants and those with too few applicants. By drawing applicants that most systems overlook and delivering only the most qualified applicants, the system assures the right candidate is identified quickly.

Although the introduction to this appendix and the plan's organization suggest that analyses of competitors, products, and customers are separate, as this plan shows, a firm usually cannot address one without considering the other. Here, in the "customer" section, the plan notes what its competitors fail to do and therefore why it offers a more valuable service.

3.5.2. Individual Member

- **Background:** People who value professional development and are familiar with computer networking technologies; most are likely college educated, motivated by career success, and aware of their professional competencies/deficiencies.
- **Situation:** Members should have a professional development plan to share with others who can help them achieve their objectives—likely people who are inquisitive about their professional future and not content with their current situation. The common industry terminology for this group of people is "poised candidates."
- **Outlook:** Proactive people who research, plan, self-educate, and talk about their career. Probably the clearest example of proactivity is a student who devotes time, effort, and financial resources toward career advancement.

Understanding a target customer is not just about numbers. PeopleAhead tries to consider what customers think and feel when searching for jobs too.

4. Marketing Strategy

4.1. Market Segmentation

4.1.1. Business Customers

- **Small enterprises.** Businesses with 10–99 employees. Companies with fewer than 10 employees are categorized as "Very Small Enterprises" and will not be a primary target market.
- **Medium enterprises.** Businesses with 100–1,000 employees.

4.1.2. Individual Members

- **Senior college students.** Students in the process of searching for a first career.
- **Graduate program students.** Mid-career candidates searching for new career opportunities, such as internships, part-time during enrollment, or full-time after graduation.
- **Current employees.** Persons who are currently employed but are poised to locate better career opportunities.
- **Unemployed.** Persons searching for jobs not included in previous segments.

4.2. Target Market

PeopleAhead plans to focus resources on small to medium enterprises (SMEs) in the New England metro market, including Boston, Providence, Hartford, Stamford, Norwalk, Worcester, and Springfield. Online recruitment companies compete for national recruitment spending, but most job seekers are locally based, so market penetration is possible by covering a single geographical location. By maintaining this focus, PeopleAhead will be better equipped to build a critical mass of users that represent the job-seeking population and thus improve both users' and customers' experience, customer service, and the use of financial resources.

4.3. User Positioning

To the proactive professional, PeopleAhead is career advancement done right—providing a platform to discover, plan, and advance careers by uniting friends, coworkers, and mentors with companies searching for the right talent.

5. Marketing Mix

5.1. Products/Services Offered

The first planned offering is **group profiling;** users self-associate with groups to share development plans. Access to groupings is permission based and similar to social networking. Members will be able to share professional experiences with people they know. Group profiling may prompt "voyeur" networking, such that members join to view the profiles of the people they know.

PeopleAhead will then open **group profiling to business customers,** who will be granted access to groups of members to target people they want to hire.

The next added feature will be **user feedback** on professional development plans. PeopleAhead will track data from successful member profile matches to provide feedback for members who have not been matched successfully.

The plan continues with the same segmentation throughout. Here the plan discusses targeting and what makes each segment attractive.

By already identifying key markets in the previous section, the plan provides a foundation for a more specific targeting statement in this section.

The final step in the STP process: Positioning for the segmented, targeted market.

PeopleAhead's mission

Given its own section in this plan, a discussion of the marketing mix constitutes a key element of the strategic planning process (see Chapter 2).

According to well-known marketing concepts, the marketing mix consists of the four Ps: product (service here), price, place (distribution here), and promotion.

The product (service) offering must establish the value for consumers: Why should they expend effort or resources to obtain the offering?

5.2. Price

In addition to a basic pricing schedule, PeopleAhead will offer bulk pricing and contract pricing to business customers to satisfy unique customer needs. The pricing model is expected to remain constant, but customer feedback will be analyzed to ensure alignment with their requirements.

Continuing the new customer acquisition plan, PeopleAhead will encourage new trials by offering promotional pricing to new customers.

5.3. Distribution

- **PeopleAhead Challenge:** The PeopleAhead Challenge will act as a primary user acquisition strategy. Selection will be focused on successful target segments demanded by customers.
- **Direct sales:** Direct customer contact is the preferred method of communication during the first six months. Telesales is the anticipated eventual sales model, due to reduced costs and quicker customer sales cycle, but it limits intimacy between the customer and PeopleAhead. During the initial stages, intimacy and excellent customer service are more highly desired than reduced cost, and direct sales achieves that objective.
- **Industry events:** Attendance at HR industry and recruitment events will supplement direct sales efforts.
- **Challenge groups:** Word-of-mouth distribution by PeopleAhead members.

5.4. Promotion

- **Public profiling:** When the product is ready, with proper precautions for protecting competitive advantages, PeopleAhead can increase its Web presence. Strategies include contributing articles to recruitment publishers, writing op/ed pieces, public profiling of the founders on Web sites like LinkedIn, Ziggs, and zoominfo, and blogging.
- **Blogger community testimonials:** Influential users of blogs will be invited to try the system and be granted "exclusive" access to the inner workings of the site. A subsequent linking blitz will put opinion pieces in front of recruiters, job seekers, and the investment community.
- **Strategic alliances:** PeopleAhead offers a product that complements the services offered by many large organizations. Partner opportunities exist with
  a. Universities, colleges, academic institutions
  b. Professional associations, clubs, industry affiliation groups
  c. Online associations, groups, blogs
  d. Professional services firms, outplacement firms, and executive search firms

Strategic alliances serve multiple purposes: They can help PeopleAhead increase public exposure, increase the user base, expand product offerings, and increase revenue opportunities. These benefits will be considered and partnerships proposed prior to the official launch. For strategic purposes, PeopleAhead prefers to focus on product development in the near term (3 months) and then reassess potential alliances after system efficacy has been proven.

Making the product (service) available where and when consumers want it may seem somewhat easier for PeopleAhead because of the vast development of the Internet; however, the firm still needs to consider how it can ensure people know where and how to access its offering.

The plan offers a specific time frame, which recognizes the potential need to make changes in the future, as the market dictates.

PeopleAhead.com
delivers:

▷Target marketing for hard-to-fill positions

▷Qualified & pre-confirmed candidates

▷Intelligent candidate ranking tools

▷Results

6. Financials

Start-up costs consist primarily of Web site design and development, legal representation (business formation, contract negotiation, and intellectual property protection), and general overhead. PeopleAhead projects start-up expenditures of $70,000 during inception, of which $30,000 has been funded by the founding team.

After the Web site launches, the cost structure will consist of sales agent salaries, general and administrative operating costs, and marketing. In the first year, marketing expenses are projected to be $6,250 per month. Monthly overhead likely will reach $24,750 and remain constant.

A. Projected Income Statement

Pro Forma Income Statement

	Year 1	Year 2	Year 3	Year 4	Year 5
Sales	**$56,453**	**$2,683,665**	**$8,170,655**	**$16,312,843**	**$30,921,013**
Gross Margin	$54,194	$2,316,318	$7,383,829	$14,780,329	$28,244,172
Gross Margin %	96.00%	86.31%	90.37%	90.61%	91.34%
Net Profit	**($156,906)**	**$717,403**	**$3,356,768**	**$7,035,155**	**$14,180,041**

The marketing plan needs to identify not only costs but also potential revenues to cover those costs.

Certain assumptions or marketing research form the basis for its estimation of start-up costs.

This section contains a lot of numbers in a small space; the graphs and tables help depict those numbers clearly and visually.

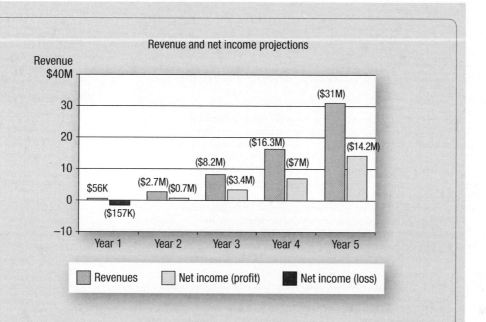

Revenue and net income projections

7. **Implementation Plan**

The launch of PeopleAhead will use a phased approach, beginning with building brand awareness. Brand awareness should be developed through the founders' visible presence at professional events, online searches, membership in professional associations, networking, and strategic alliances. This visibility will help gain investment capital.

7.1. Objective—Growth

- During the first six months of commercial availability, the primary objective is to expand both the user and customer base to maintain a 100:1 user to customer ratio.

  - **Business customers:** Sign 24 regular customers and 72 occasional customers. Execute 117 position matches.
  - **Individual members:** Convert 10,000 people to PeopleAhead members.

7.2. Marketing Objectives—Growth

- **PeopleAhead Challenge:** Pursue groups that were effective during beta trial and represent a cohesive set of profiles. Expand and refine the Challenge to reflect lessons learned.

- **Increase member networking activity:** Increase user numbers through networking initiated by existing members. Improve user experience to promote networking.

- **Increase profile completeness:** Increase user engagement with platform.

- **Generate traffic.**

- **Public relations campaign (PR):** Increase awareness of PeopleAhead brand through concentrated PR efforts directed at the target market of customers and users.

This plan divides the objectives into three categories: overall objective, marketing, and financial. Although this is a marketing plan, it must also include other aspects that influence marketing, such as financial status.

7.3. *Financial Objectives*

- **Efficient marketing expenditures:** 9,000 target users (10,000 year-end total − 1,000 during beta) × $5.00 target acquisition cost = $45,000 budget.
- **Revenue:** $482.50 per position × 117 positions = $56,452.50 revenue.

> By offering quantitative, direct goals, PeopleAhead ensures that it can measure its progress toward those goals.

7.4. *Key Success Factors:*

- **Economical marketing to relevant constituents:** PeopleAhead needs to establish communication (distribution) channels that pinpoint relevant constituents in a manner consistent with mission values. Limited by resources, chosen channels must aggregate many relevant eyes with free, minimal, or deferred costs involved.
- **Crafting of brand identity:** The contrast between PeopleAhead and competitors lies not only in product differentiation but also in the company's mission statement and delivery. One-time job search is available from thousands of online recruitment sources. Social networking has been covered from diverse angles, attracting many different audiences. The challenge is to associate www.PeopleAhead.com and TrueMatch technology with "career advancement done right." The goal is to become the only company that a person thinks of for long-term career discovery, advancement, and development.
- **Efficient value delivery:** The base of customers (both individual and business) needs to receive the proposed value in a timely manner, with consideration given to quality versus quantity of results, alignment with existing objectives, and overall experience with the PeopleAhead brand.
- **Critical mass of business customers and individual users:** The matching process requires that both customers and users exist in the system from the outset of commercialization. This need brings to the forefront the "chicken and egg" scenario; establishing either customers or users requires the other constituent to exist already. The exact number that constitutes "critical mass" ranges from 100 users per position to 10 users per position, depending on compatibility between each constituency.
- **System effectivity:** The ability of PeopleAhead's TrueMatch software to provide relevant candidate recommendations is critical. The effectiveness of the software depends on the algorithms that match users with positions and the networking protocol that initiates recommendations between users and the people they know. Proposing an inappropriate match could jeopardize the credibility of the system.
- **Intellectual property (IP) strategy:** PeopleAhead is engaged in two primary segments of online enterprise: online recruitment and social networking. Existing competitors have made many efforts to protect their methodologies through U.S. patents. However, precedent has not been established for the legal assertions made by these companies. As a result, PeopleAhead will assume an offensive IP strategy, consisting of diligent IP infringement review, patent application where appropriate, and aggressive trade secret protection of best practices.
- **Financial support:** The founders' investment is sufficient to form the business core and take delivery of PeopleAhead's Web site and software. Financial support will be required to fund operations, execute the IP strategy, and secure customers and users to meet financial targets. Without funding, PeopleAhead will not be able to proceed beyond the product development stage.
- **Sales process:** PeopleAhead's business model requires the acquisition of both business customers who have available positions and users who will be matched

with those positions. These two constituents may be reached through different sales processes without overlap.

8. Evaluation & Control

PeopleAhead will evaluate user profiles to identify sets of profiles that are valuable to new business customers, which will aid in the selection of subsequent target market customers.

8.1. Business Customers

Face-to-face meetings, phone conversations, and e-mail survey contacts with people from a range of industries, company sizes, and functional areas provide a means to (1) build relationships with prospective customers, (2) understand customer needs, and (3) ensure alignment between PeopleAhead's product and customers' recruitment preferences. A summary of the key findings is listed here:

- **Employee fit:** Will the applicant fit our corporate culture? Will the applicant fit with the team we're considering? Will the applicants' competencies fit with the position requirements?
- **Pay for performance:** Objections to recruitment services focus not on price (though it is a consideration) but rather on lack of performance.
- **Unqualified applicants:** Many people who want a job apply, whether they are qualified or not. Recruiters then must scan resumes and weed out unqualified applicants instead of getting to know the qualified applicants.
- **Hard costs vs. soft costs:** Most companies track the recruitment costs of hiring providers, but few measure the time costs of hiring, opportunity costs of hiring the wrong employee, or productivity costs of leaving a position unfilled. Recruitment performance must be easy to measure. Value selling is difficult in the human resources departments.
- **Valuable recommendations:** Most recruiters use online recruitment as a necessary but ineffective means of candidate sourcing, secondary to recommendations. Recommendations include the recommender's judgment of the candidate's fit with the available position.

8.2. Individual Members

Periodic surveys of various prospective users of online recruitment services indicate (1) current services, (2) methods that work well, and (3) biggest problems with online recruitment providers. The following is a qualitative summary of the key findings:

- **Willingness to try:** Careers are important to people; they are averse to spending time uploading resume information to online recruitment Web sites only because of the lack of perceived value. They will spend time when the career opportunities are perceived as valuable.
- **Frustration:** Job seekers are frustrated with available online recruitment providers. Networking is the favored method for career advancement.
- **Lack of differentiation:** Regardless of the qualifications a job seeker possesses, it is difficult to make them evident in a traditional resume.
- **Motivation shift over time:** Early professionals are motivated by financial rewards. Mid-career professionals recommend people because it helps the people they know. Late-career professionals hope to improve their own job search opportunities.

Appendix A. Organizational Chart of PeopleAhead

Appendix B. Competition: Passive Recruiters

> The evaluation section retains the segmentation scheme established previously between business customers and individual members.

> Additional useful information that might clutter the plan should appear in an appendix, but is not included in this illustration.

CHAPTER 3

SOCIAL AND MOBILE MARKETING

LEARNING OBJECTIVES

LO1 Describe the 4E framework of social media marketing.

LO2 Understand the types of social media.

LO3 Understand various motivations for using mobile applications and how they are priced.

LO4 Recognize and understand the three components of a social media strategy.

Social media have revolutionized how companies communicate with, listen to, and learn from customers. Their influence is far-reaching, whether firms are selling online or in stores, providing services or products, or dealing primarily with consumers or business customers. Modern listening and analysis tools (such as those provided by IBM or by Salesforce. com, a company that specializes in customer relationship management software and cloud computing) allow firms to identify salient, pertinent trends and customer input through social media.

Despite their potential importance, social media strategies remain haphazard, uncertain, and not particularly effective in many firms. Gatorade, however, offers a stellar example of a carefully designed plan for connecting effectively with customers, controlling social media

MISSION CONTROL

buzz, and responding to trends as they arise. Although Gatorade's basic marketing strategy continues to include famous athletic spokespersons, it constantly seeks new ways to use these superb athletes to help ensure consumers' connections with the brand.

Residing in the marketing department at its Gatorade's Chicago headquarters is its Social Media Mission Control Center, which hosts massive monitors that track social media referring to Gatorade and its competitors. One monitor stays on blog trends; another summarizes the topics and sentiments expressed in tweets, all in real time.[1]

One day not too long ago, social media chatter indicated consumers' highly favorable responses to a just-released commercial featuring a new song by rapper

David Banner. Gatorade worked immediately with Banner to develop the snippet into a full-length song, which it distributed within a day through its Facebook and Twitter sites. Mission Control also is responsible for connecting fans with athletes associated with Gatorade. During the Super Bowl, it hosted discussions through the Ustream social media site.[2]

According to Gatorade (and its owner, PepsiCo), Mission Control actually has six main missions: (1) monitor online discussions, (2) monitor the sports landscape, (3) engage in proactive social media outreach, (4) track media performance, (5) track brand attitudes, and (6) track sports trends and buzz. Through the insights it gathers from consumers, Gatorade can influence not only its marketing communications but also its products and brand.[3]

In addition to this innovative and unique Mission Control Center, Gatorade takes care of "old-school" social media too. Its Facebook page contains little explicit advertising for the brand. Instead, it posts provocative questions in an attempt to get fans to engage in conversations with the brand and one another. Its Twitter feed consists mainly of inspirational sayings and quotes. On YouTube, Gatorade offers easy access to some of its most famous commercials from over the years—ads that have taken on an iconic cult following, including old favorites describing how to "Be Like Mike" and more recent versions that challenge "Is It In You?"[4]

When consumers search for Gatorade on popular search engines, they also see page after page of company-sponsored results, rather than outside comments.[5] As this outcome reveals, Gatorade has done the preliminary work, through search engine optimization and brand building, to control most of what people see online. Although no company can prevent negative comments online (such as common complaints about Gatorade's taste), Gatorade has managed to ensure that those negative comments are hidden under a wave of positive, company-approved messages. Consumers must look harder to find the criticisms.

In this sense, Gatorade prepared itself for social media marketing well before any of these tools were readily available. Then, it leveraged its strong reputation and applied a proactive attitude toward social media to design its groundbreaking Social Media Mission Control Center. As a result, Gatorade accounts for an astounding 75 percent of the social buzz related to sports drinks.[6]

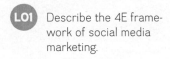

LO1 Describe the 4E framework of social media marketing.

THE 4E FRAMEWORK FOR SOCIAL MEDIA

As we will see throughout the book and as we saw in the chapter opener, social media are becoming integral components of any integrated marketing communications strategy. The term social media refers to content distributed through online and mobile technologies to facilitate interpersonal interactions. These media use various firms that offer services or tools to help consumers and firms build connections. Through these connections, marketers and customers share information of all forms—from their thoughts about products or images, to uploaded pictures, music, and videos.

The changes and advances in social, mobile, and online technologies have created a perfect storm, forcing firms to change how they communicate with their customers. Traditional ways to market their products using brick-and-mortar stores, traditional mass media (e.g., print, television, radio), and other sales promotional vehicles (e.g., mail, telemarketing) are no longer sufficient for many firms. The presence of social, mobile, and online marketing is steadily expanding relative to these more traditional forms of integrated marketing communications (IMC).

The changing role of traditional media, sales promotions, and retail, coupled with the new social, mobile, and online media, has led to a different way of thinking about the objectives of marketing communications using the 4E framework (see Exhibit 3.1):

- **E**xcite customers with relevant offers.
- **E**ducate them about the offering.
- Help them **e**xperience products, whether directly or indirectly.
- Give them an opportunity to **e**ngage with their social network.

| EXHIBIT 3.1 | The 4E Framework for Social Media |

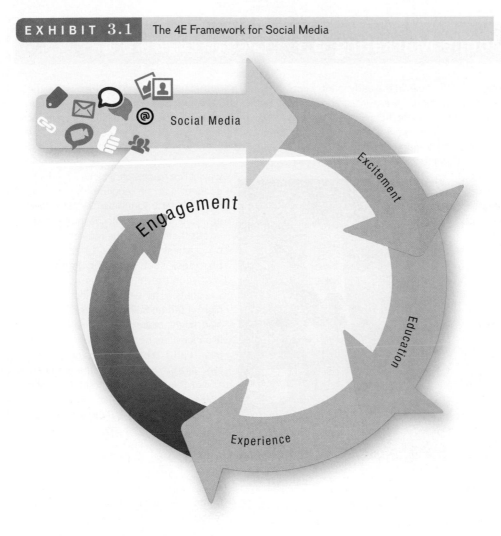

Social and Mobile Marketing 3.1 recounts how Jimmy Fallon got viewers more excited and engaged with his late-night talk show by leveraging the power of social media.

Excite the Customer

Marketers use many kinds of social media–related offers to excite customers, including mobile applications and games to get the customers excited about an idea, product, brand, or company. Firms actively use social networks such as Facebook, Pinterest, and Google+ to communicate deals that are likely to excite consumers, such as when the Minnesota Timberwolves encouraged Facebook fans to post a great shot of a dunk onto their Pinterest page for a chance to win tickets to a game.[7]

To excite customers, an offer must be relevant to its targeted customer. Relevancy can be achieved by providing personalized offers, which are determined through insights and information obtained from customer relationship management and/or loyalty programs. To obtain these insights and information, the firm might use online analytic tools such as Google analytics.

In some cases location-based software and applications help bring the offer to the customers when they are in the process of making a purchase decision. For instance, Staples may provide a loyal customer a relevant coupon based on previous purchases through his or her mobile phone, while the customer is in the store—a very relevant and hopefully exciting experience.

Social & Mobile Marketing 3.1   Late-Night Laughs to Order[i]

Social media appear to have brought us full circle. In the early days of television, nearly all the advertisements were live. Then taping became the main method. But as recent technologies have made it easy for viewers to speed past or completely skip the advertising messages, some marketers are revisiting the idea of live advertising. This isn't the same old notion though. By recombining an idea from broadcast media with new functionalities enabled by social media, marketers seek to ensure that viewers are not only interested in the new content but even might determine it.

A Lexus-sponsored program, "It's Your Move After Dark," ran on *Late Night with Jimmy Fallon* over the course of four weeks. During the first commercial break on each Thursday's show, a Lexus advertisement prominently displayed a hashtag. By linking to it, viewers could submit their ideas for commercials. Then in a later advertising break during the same show, an improvisational comedy troupe acted out the chosen ideas. The acting troupes—Fun Young Guys, Magnet Theater Touring Company, MB's Dream and Stone Cold Fox—were all from New York, well known for their comedy. In actuality, their performances took place under the Brooklyn Bridge, adding to the vibrancy and reality of the setting.

To appeal to the widest audience of Fallon fans possible, separate advertisements were chosen and enacted for the East and West Coast broadcasts. The submissions came through a wide variety of media channels, including Facebook, Twitter, and Tumblr. Such ready access, real-time

In an innovative campaign, Jimmy Fallon viewers could submit ideas for Lexus commercials via Twitter and see an improvised version later in the night on the show.

interactivity, and potential influence—together with the promise of funny, totally new advertising content and perhaps even a live, on-air goof—promised that Fallon's youthful, edgy audience wanted to tune in to the commercials, as much as they did to the show.

The advertisements are not the only way Fallon has relied on social media to connect with his audience of course. He has nearly 10 million Twitter followers, and on a regular basis he challenges them to post the funniest, silliest, or craziest responses to topics he provides, such as "#howigotfired," "#whydonttheymakethat," and "#awkwarddate." The best contributions are highlighted on Fallon's Twitter feed but also might make it onto the network broadcast, as he reads out his favorite bits. That is, the consumers of his content also provide some of that content.

On the flip side, content from the traditional television channel constantly makes it onto social media sites. Excerpts from Fallon's shows are some of the most popular YouTube videos, including a skit in which President Barack Obama "slow jams" the news, a sing-along with Carly Rae Jepson and the Roots of "Call Me Maybe" using found materials as instruments, and of course, any skits featuring his pal Justin Timberlake.

As Fallon moves from *Late Night* to the *Tonight Show,* he promises that such tactics and antics will continue. As long as he keeps his viewers excited and willing to contribute and engage with him, his social media dominance appears likely to persist, regardless of what time he appears on people's televisions.

Exhibit 3.2 highlights some illustrative and successful social media campaigns because they are exciting and relevant to their audiences.

Educate the Customer

An imperative of well-designed social media marketing offers is that they have a clear call to action to draw customers through their computers, tablets, and mobile devices into online websites or traditional retail stores. When potential customers arrive at the websites or stores, the marketer has a golden opportunity to educate them about its value proposition and communicate the offered benefits. Some of this information may be new, but in some cases, education is all about reminding people about what they already know. Therefore, by engaging in appropriate education, marketers are expanding the overlap of the benefits that they provide with the benefits that customers require. In this sense, the second E of the 4E framework constitutes a method to develop a sustainable competitive advantage. Several social media tools are critical in helping marketers educate their potential customers, such as blogs and blogging tools (e.g., WordPress and Twitter), HubSpot (all-in-one marketing software), YouTube, and Google+, as well as some lesser known options such as Roost or Schedulicity. Adding Value 3.1 highlights how HubSpot can be used to educate customers better.

Experience the Product or Service

Although most of the top videos on YouTube are funny, silly, or otherwise entertaining, the site's most useful contributions may be the vivid information it provides about a firm's goods and services—how they work, how to use them, and where they can be obtained. YouTube and similar sites can come relatively close to simulating real experiences. Such benefits are very common for products that have long been sold online—so much so that we might forget that it used to be difficult to assess these products before buying them. But today, consumers can download a chapter of a new book to their tablet before buying it. They can try out a software option for a month before buying it. They often can listen to a few seconds or even an entire song before purchasing from iTunes. The

The Minnesota Timberwolves excited Facebook fans by offering a chance to win tickets by posting pictures of a dunk to its Pinterest page.

EXHIBIT 3.2	Illustrative Social Media Campaigns

Campaign	Description
Justin Bieber's "Girlfriend"	To launch his new perfume, Girlfriend, Justin Bieber launched a $20 million social media campaign focusing on Twitter and Tumblr. He invited fans to help create a 60-second television commercial for the fragrance and post their entries on Tumblr. With over 22 million followers on Twitter and more than 44 million likes on Facebook, this was a great strategy for Bieber to access his young, hip fanbase.
Water Is Life "Hashtag Killer"	To drive awareness about serious developing world problems, nonprofit Water Is Life launched a "Hashtag Killer" campaign in which it took on the insensitive #firstworldproblems hashtag and Twitter meme. It began by creating a video on YouTube in which Haitians read tweets that had been tagged as "#firstworldproblems" such as a child sitting on a mound of dirt saying, "I hate when my leather seats aren't heated." Amazingly, Haitians engaged with the campaign themselves and offered consolation to people with tweets such as: "I'm sorry your leather seats weren't heated. . . . I hope your day gets better!" The campaign was a remarkable success—individuals donated over one million days of clean water.
"One Small Tweet"	After Neil Armstrong's death at age 82, the John F. Kennedy Library and Museum in New York launched a Twitter campaign, "One Small Tweet." The organization set up a website that re-created Armstrong's journey to the moon. For each tweet that included the hashtag "#onesmalltweet" the re-creation moved 100 miles closer to the moon.
"Nike Barbershop"	The "Nike Barbershop" campaign started with a commercial in which Mario Balotelli, striker for soccer club Milan, tells a barber he wants to be remembered. The commercial proceeds with a montage of hairstyles, and ends with Mario sporting a mohawk. But this is just the beginning—viewers could then download the Nike Barbershop app, make pictures of themselves with 10 different iconic soccer hairstyles, and share them with friends. The top posts were flown to one of the real Nike Barbershop physical locations in Buenos Aires, Madrid, Mexico City, Milan, or Paris to get the haircut for real. Finally, Nike created a popup Nike Barbershop in Warsaw for Europe's major soccer tournament.

Water is Life's "Hashtag Killer" campaign posted videos on YouTube of Haitians reading and responding to tweets to excite individuals to donate to their cause.

diffusion of such products has expanded to feature a wealth of new channels and media options.

For other offerings, such as services, social media again offer experience-based information that was not previously available unless consumers bought and tried the product or service. Need help choosing a new nail polish color or lipstick, or applying a new makeup trend? Check blogs such as Temptalia (http://www.temptalia.com), which offers both advice and tutorials. Relied too long on clip-on ties? Head over to Tie-a-Tie (http://www.tie-a-tie.net/) to find pictures, videos, and step-by-step instructions on how to manage a Windsor, Pratt, or bowtie knot, as well as advice on what to wear to an interview.

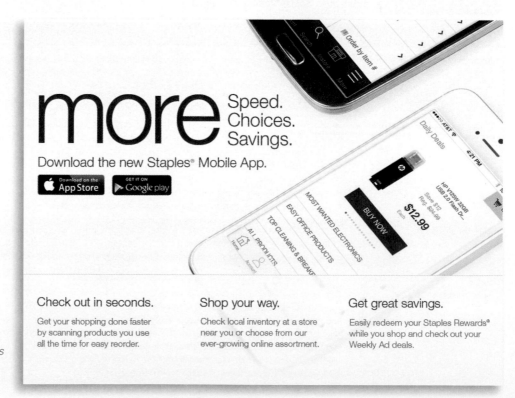

Staples excites its customers by giving them instant rewards through their mobile phone, while they are in the store.

Adding Value 3.1 Educating Customers Using HubSpot[ii]

Hy-Line Cruises is a ferry company with vessels for travel to and from Cape Cod and islands, deep-sea fishing trips, and sightseeing. While it had a strong Internet presence through its website, Facebook, and Twitter, it didn't know if its efforts were leading to increased sales. Using HubSpot's SEO (search engine optimization) and blogging tools, Hy-Line began to match its blogging content to the keywords and phrases its potential customers were using. Not only did the new blogging content contain information about ferry services, but it also made recommendations about where to eat and what to do once on the Cape and Islands. It also developed a free downloadable Insider's Guide for each destination, and kept track of—and through e-mail—thanked each potential customer. Compared to the previous year before it started using HubSpot's services, Hy-Line generated five times more cruise offers to Nantucket, and 17 times more Fall Daytrip Specials to Martha's Vineyard.

Hy-Line Cruises uses HubSpot to enhance its social media presence.

Home Depot has long been a source for do-it-yourselfers (DIYers). But if eager customers forget what the salesclerk said about installing a newly purchased water heater, they can check the retailer's website (http://www6.homedepot.com/how-to/index.html) to get detailed, in-depth instructions. They also will find a section that enables them to chat with other users who might have run into similar problems in their own installation projects.

Nikon's Digital Learning Center (see http://www.flickr.com/groups/nikondigitallearningcenter/; http://www.flickr.com/Nikon) provides Flickr members with "tutorials, practical photography tips and advice from Nikon photo professionals to assist them in taking the photos they've always dreamed of capturing."[8] Beyond just providing static photography tips that could be found in a book, Nikon created a two-way dialogue with customers, inviting professional photographers to provide instruction and host question-and-answer sessions, and encouraging users to post their own

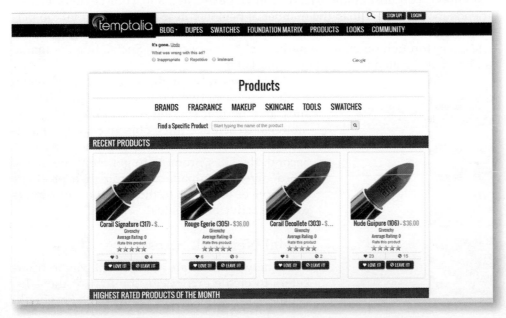

Need help choosing a new lipstick or applying a new makeup trend? Check blogs such as Temptalia.

photos. The more than 64,000 members of the learning center thus learn from others' experiences, even as they create their own.

Engage the Customer

In a sense, the first three Es set the stage for the last one: engaging the customer. With engagement comes action, the potential for a relationship, and possibly even loyalty and commitment. Through social media tools such as blogging and microblogging, customers actively engage with firms and their own social networks. Such engagement can be negative or positive. Positively engaged consumers tend to be more profitable consumers, purchasing 20 to 40 percent more than less engaged customers.[9]

But negative engagement has the potential to be even more damaging than positive engagement is beneficial. In the aftermath of Hurricane Sandy, for example, two different retailers, The Gap and American Apparel, each sought to promote online sales. American Apparel sent out an e-mail blast to customers on the East Coast, promising 20 percent off all online purchases, "in case you're bored during the storm." The Gap instead relied on Twitter, posting the notice, "Stay safe! We'll be doing lots of Gap.com shopping today. How about you?" In both cases, consumers reacted angrily and rapidly. On Twitter, thousands of them complained that the promotions exhibited "tackiness" and a lack of consideration for the very real threat facing people affected by the storm. The story also made it into mainstream media, prompting the retailers to issue apologies and explanations.[10]

CHECK YOURSELF

1. What are the 4 Es?
2. What social media elements work best for each of the 4 Es?

Next we'll look at the role of various social media tools in shaping the 4E framework for social media.

 **LO2** Understand the types of social media.

CATEGORIES OF SOCIAL MEDIA

Consider your own Facebook site. Are all your real-life friends your online friends too? Do you actually know all the friends registered on your online site? In all likelihood, you host online friends you've never met, and your circle of virtual friends may be larger than the number of people you see regularly or talk to personally. Accordingly, the audience for marketers could be bigger on social media sites than through other, more traditional forms of media. Such a huge potential audience has gotten the attention of marketers.

Marketers rely on the three types of social media: social networking sites, media-sharing sites, and thought-sharing sites (or blogs) (see Exhibit 3.3) to achieve three objectives. First, members promote themselves to gain more friends. Second, the sites promote to get more members. Third, outside companies promote their products and services to appeal to the potential consumers who are active on the sites.

Social Network Sites

Social network sites are an excellent way for marketers to create *excitement,* the first of the 4 Es. People can interact with friends (e.g., Facebook)

EXHIBIT 3.3   Types of Social Media

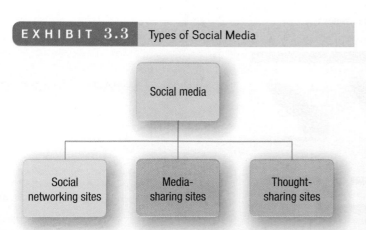

or business acquaintances (e.g., LinkedIn). Although the amount of time people spend on such sites varies, research indicates they are widely used, between one and four hours every day.[11]

Facebook On this well-known social network platform, more than 1.19 billion monthly active users give companies a forum for interacting with their fans. Thus Facebook not only assures individual users a way to connect with others, but also gives marketers the ability to target their audience carefully. Companies have access to the same features that regular users do, including a "wall" where they can post company updates, photos, and videos or participate in a discussion board. Through this form of free exposure, the company can post content and information regarding products, events, news, or promotions that might be exciting to their customers. Only the fans of its page generally have access to such information, so the company can specifically target its fans. Successful companies on Facebook attempt to excite their customers regularly. On the fan page for the discount clothing retailer Forever 21, for example,[12] when a fan clicks to indicate that he or she "likes" a certain post, the message gets relayed to a news feed. Then every friend of that user sees what he or she likes, creating an exciting and huge multiplier effect.

Fright is another form of excitement, which is what the movie studio responsible for *Devil's Due* sought to invoke with its highly controversial promotional campaign. A link from the horror movie's web page allowed users to connect to their personal Facebook pages and change their religious affiliation to "Satanism."[13] In return, it promised an "exclusive offering," namely, a 16-second trailer for the movie. In addition, the studio combined this relatively shocking option with videos of its "Devil Baby" stunt: A mock baby carriage, left on the street, pulled concerned passersby in, at which point an animatronic, horrible-looking doll popped up to scare the people.[14]

Display advertising with "Facebook ads" instead targets specific groups of people, according to their profile information, browsing histories, and other preferences. If online users reveal an interest in ski equipment or Burton snowboards, marketers can target both groups. Facebook offers a variation on more traditional forms of promotion, with the promise of more accurate targeting and segmentation. But being effective and relevant on Facebook is not simply a matter

Adding Value **3.2**   Effective Friending[iii]

Sadly, many inexperienced marketers have launched poorly conceived Facebook campaigns with the hope that any strategy that includes social media is "good enough." But good enough is rarely sufficient in a competitive marketplace, and some brands have hurt their images by launching campaigns that are out of step with social media culture.

When a group of industry professionals discussed the ingredients necessary to attract positive attention from Facebook's 1.19 billion users, they agreed that a successful campaign must tell a story. Ideally, the story should involve and engage users in the plotline. Equally important, these creative heavyweights highlighted the need to connect the campaign to the real world.

Making good use of consumer data available on Facebook can also improve cam-

Clorox's Facebook promotion is designed to educate people about and increase sales of its Green Works products.

paign success by giving marketers the ability to hone in on target audiences and track consumer response. After months of flat reactions to a Facebook promotion of its environmentally friendly cleaners, Clorox launched new initiatives designed to educate people about and increase sales of its Green Works products. The campaign targeted only those women whose Facebook profiles featured the words *clean* or *green*. At the same time, Clorox aimed to enhance the experience of other potential users by inviting consumers to nominate green heroes in their community to receive a $15,000 grant. In yet another effort, Clorox offered a $3 off coupon to people who connected to the Green Works web page. The result was a record-breaking engagement rate for the company, demonstrating that social media, when used properly, can be valuable marketing tools.

LinkedIn is an excellent place to begin your search for a marketing job.

of shifting an offline ad into social network sites, as Adding Value 3.2 recognizes.

LinkedIn A professional instead of casual or friendship-based site, LinkedIn allows users to share their professional lives. With more than 259 million users, it is a place where users can post their résumés, network with other professionals, and search for jobs.[15] It is *not* the place where you will see games such as Mafia Wars or FarmVille; instead, users post to question-and-answer forums, job search, and post personal intellectual property, such as presentations they have given.

The professional networking benefits of LinkedIn are particularly beneficial for small-business owners. More than 12 million of LinkedIn's users are small-business owners, making it an excellent resource for entrepreneurs to network with like-minded firms, identify the best vendors, or build brand reputation by participating in LinkedIn's professional association groups. With more than 150,000 company profiles on LinkedIn, it also offers a great place to prospect for new business customers and keep an eye on and get key information about competitors.[16]

Google+ With Google+, the company that essentially defined search engines sought to compete in the social media realm. Although it has attracted hundreds of millions of users, most analysts suggest it is not an effective competitor

Superior Service 3.1 | Social Network Helps Small Businesses Grow[iv]

Any small business, especially a new one, comes right up against the bottom line. A skeletal staff and tight budgets may make it tough to take on a new task, like social media management. Yet some small-business owners have found that social networks are an essential tool to reach customers and put their products on the map.

Specializing in luxury watches like Cartier and Rolex that sell for at least $4,000 each, Melrose Jewelers has used social networks to connect with its primary customer base: young, upwardly mobile consumers who are technologically savvy. Its social media activity, including Facebook (with 100,000 likes), a blog, and YouTube, increased sales by 71 percent the first year. One Facebook campaign, a personality quiz that helped customers decide which watch best suited

them, attracted $100,000 in sales. Facebook's customer testimonials also helped build credibility with older customers.

Negri Electronics, a high-end cell phone vendor, uses Google+ for customer communication. Google+ "circles" enable the owner to send specialized messages to each customer group. Google+ also has made web searching more social, because the +1 feature allows the owner to prioritize web pages for "circle" members. The owner of Mansfield Fine Furniture disagrees though. After six months in business he has about a dozen customers who have purchased his pieces, which range in price from $500 to $5,000 each. He finds Facebook yields a more robust customer response because Google+ is not yet widely used.

thus far. Even when users register, they do not engage closely with the site; Google+ accounted for a mere 2 percent of all social media shares.[17] In an apparent response to this lack of interest, Google recently sought to force closer engagement. For example, on YouTube (which Google purchased in 2006) users must provide a G+ account, as well as their real names, before they may post a comment. Rather than attracting more members, the move angered longtime active YouTube participants—so much so that more than 110,000 of them petitioned Google to rescind the requirement.[18]

Yet it would be risky to ignore Google+ completely. It offers several functions that other social networking sites do not. For example, its "Communities" feature lets people interested in similar topics form their own groups. Unlike Facebook, Google+'s Communities allow brands to join as members—for example, a paddle brand or seller of suntan lotion could easily interact with the members of a group devoted to paddleboarding. Moreover, with Google+'s unique "Hangouts" feature, brands can host discussions or focus groups, as well as post live product demonstrations.[19]

Superior Service 3.1 highlights how social network tools help small businesses expand by teaching their customers about what they can provide.

Media-Sharing Sites

The World Wide Web has the ability to connect people more easily and in more ways than have ever been possible before. Media-sharing sites explicitly rely on this capability to enable users to share content they have generated, from videos on YouTube to pictures on Flickr and so on. In terms of the 4E framework, companies use such sites to highlight how consumers can *experience* their goods or services, as well as encourage consumers to *engage* with the firm, its other social media outlets, and other consumers.

YouTube On this video-sharing social media platform with more than 1 billion unique monthly visitors, users upload, share, and view videos. This medium gives companies a chance to express themselves in a different way than they have in the past. YouTube videos also show up in Google searches, making it an appealing vehicle for retailers.[20] The site's demographics indicate visitors are affluent, of the age range most appealing to retailers, and racially reflective of the wider U.S. population.[21]

YouTube also provides an effective medium for hosting contests and posting instructional videos. The Home Depot attracts thousands of viewers with an array of videos detailing new products available in stores, as well as instructional do-it-yourself videos, like "How To Tips for Mowing Your Lawn" or "How To Repair a Toilet."[22] These videos maintain the core identity of the Home Depot brand while also adding value for consumers, who learn useful ways to improve their homes. Home Depot reinforces its brand image and makes itself more relevant to the consumer's life.

Companies can broadcast from their own channel, that is, a YouTube site that contains content relevant only to the company's own products.[23] For example, Home Shopping Network (HSN) offers consumers an interesting vehicle to utilize the 4E framework—*excite, educate, experience,* and *engage* using a multichannel strategy with its television channel as its central focus. As competition in this field has increased, HSN has added to its communication arsenal, an integrated social media component that inlcudes Facebook, Instragram, Twitter, and Pinterest, which are all integrated across each platform and into the live TV segment. But perhaps the most powerful tool it has added is its dedicated YouTube channel, which it exploits to reach target shoppers in an exciting way that maximizes the value of its media content. Products promoted on HSN are available on YouTube almost immediately after they appear on television. Then HSN marketers can use the information gathered from YouTube to target its direct mail campaigns. For example, it could send jewelry promotions to households that viewed the YouTube video clip for a necklace. Consumer responses get monitored 24/7 and measured against hourly sales goals. There's thus never a dull moment.

Instagram With Instagram, people who have downloaded the app (more than 100 million and counting) can take a photo of themselves or their surroundings.[24] The app enables them to add fun filters, such as causing the picture to look as if it were taken by an old Polaroid camera. Then they can upload the artistic creation to various social networking sites, including Twitter, Tumblr, or Facebook.

The name of this app evokes the founders' idea of its use: a sort of modern-day, immediate telegram.[25] It was effective enough that it attracted the attention of some of the most famous names in media sharing, including Justin Beiber, Kim Kardashian, and Tony Hawk—which increased its popularity even more. Recognizing the value of a mobile option, Facebook purchased Instagram in 2012. For the first time, the social media giant promised not to absorb its purchase, but to allow Instagram to continue functioning much as it had been all along.[26]

Instagram recently added video-sharing capabilities as well, though another app had beat it to that punch. Vine, which was purchased by Twitter in 2012, lets

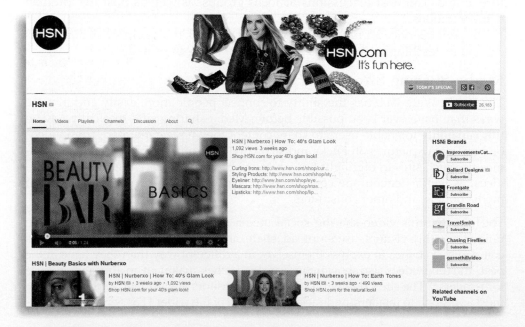

Products promoted on Home Shopping Network (HSN) are available on its dedicated YouTube channel almost immediately after they appear on television.

users capture and share 6-second videos. Advertisers already have embraced this option, finding that the short time limit appeals to consumers. People are ready to share a quick video, far more so than a longer commercial, which enhances the chances of a Vine marketing campaign going viral.[27]

Flickr and Other Photo Sites Whereas YouTube allows users to share videos, Flickr, Picasa, TwitPic, Photobucket, and Imgur allow them to share photos. They tend to be less popular as marketing tools, yet some innovative companies have found ways to engage with customers, such as by hosting picture posting competitions or using photos to communicate core tenets and values.[28]

The UK brand Innocent, known for selling pure 100 percent fruit smoothies, uses Flickr to communicate its quirky brand image. Its photo posting competitions, such as the Funny Shaped Fruit Competition (http://www.flickr.com/groups/funnyshapedfruit/), provide significant entertainment value. But it also uses Flickr for more serious purposes, such as to post photos related to its Big Knit charity promotion.

Thought-Sharing Sites

Thought-sharing sites consist of different types of blogs: corporate, professional, personal, and micro. In terms of the 4E framework, blogs are particularly effective at *educating* and *engaging* users, and in many cases enhance their *experience* with the products and services being discussed.

Blogs Originally confined to a journal or diary in a person's room, the blog (from "weblog") on the Internet has allowed us to make our thoughts open to the world through thought-sharing websites. For corporations, the comment section allows marketing managers to create a two-way dialogue directly with the end users. The wide availability of free blogging tools—which enables nontechnically oriented people to create their own blogs, such as WordPress, Blogger, and Typepad—have made blogging a very popular pastime. Companies have responded to this interest and now have several ways to include blogging in their social media marketing strategy. Blogs provide firms the opportunity to *educate* their customers about their offers and offerings by explaining their offerings, and to *engage* them by responding to their communications, both positive and negative. The reach that marketers have to their customer from blogs can be categorized by the level of control they offer.

Innocent uses Flickr to post photos for its Big Knit charity promotion.

Corporate blogs, which are created by the companies themselves, have the highest level of control because to a large degree, they can control the content posted on them. Of course, blogs also allow customers to respond to posts, so the content can never be completely controlled, but marketing managers have a good opportunity to pepper their blogs with the messages they wish their customers to see. The best corporate blogs illustrate the importance of engaging customers around the core brand tenets without being overly concerned with a hard sell.

The popular regional grocery store chain Wegmans (http://www.wegmans.com/blog/) blogs to generate loyalty and generate sales by sharing employees' ideas about entertaining, nutrition, and recipes. General Electric (http://www.gereports.com/) *educates* customers through its blog by telling entertaining stories geared at getting customers to realize it sells more than just light bulbs.[29] For Boeing (http://www.boeingblogs.com/randy/), the goal is to *engage* people, even though it produces items that regular consumers are unlikely to encounter or purchase directly. Therefore "Randy's Journal" features travel stories, fun pictures of planes being built, and promises of exciting new innovations from the company.

From a marketing perspective, professional blogs are those written by people who review and give recommendations on products and services. Marketers often offer free products or provide modest remuneration to top-rated professional bloggers, in the hopes of getting a good product review. Marketers have less control over

Wegmans' blog is designed to engage customers with healthy and nutritious recipes and interesting food-related ideas and stories.

professional bloggers than they do their own corporate blogs. But consumers seem to trust professional bloggers' reviews much more than corporate blogs and other more traditional media, like advertising. Such trust may be fleeting, however, as more consumers realize that professional bloggers are often compensated for positive reviews. "Mommy blogs," a particularly popular type of professional blog, feature advice and product recommendations from one mother to many others. The primary topics covered by these professional bloggers vary slightly but often focus on pertinent tips for saving money on groceries, getting peanut butter out of hair, or dealing with illness.[30]

Finally, **personal blogs** are written by people who receive no products or remuneration for their efforts. Thus, of the three types of blogs, marketers have the lowest level of control over this type. However, personal blogs are useful for monitoring what is going on in the marketplace and for responding to customer complaints or compliments.

Microblogs As the name implies, a **microblog** differs from a traditional blog in size—short sentences, short videos, or individual images. On the most popular microblogging site, Twitter, users are limited to 140-character messages. Twitter provides another option for companies to *educate* their customers by providing corporate and product information, and to *engage* them by providing a platform for two-way communications. Even companies that may have once resisted social media are now realizing that Twitter offers an important communications channel.

As much as Twitter can help build a firm's brand image, though, it can also tarnish it instantly. Firms have to watch out for hacked Twitter accounts or ill-considered tweets. Twitter can also act as an international, rapidly spread complaint forum.[31]

A central problem for companies is ownership of relevant Twitter handles and responsibility for outgoing Twitter communication. If Twitter control is shared by several people, the message usually gets muddled. But if only one or two people are in charge, the need to respond to the vast number of incoming tweets might become overwhelming. Therefore, different companies manage their Twitter strategies in various ways.

Whole Foods tries to develop a broader engagement with customers by interacting with its millions of followers. It instituted a weekly Twitter chat, for an hour every Thursday, during which Whole Foods representatives discuss topics such as holiday menu planning and healthy eating. Many Whole Foods stores also have their own Twitter accounts to answer questions directly related to their stores.

In contrast, Best Buy hires an army of specialists to manage its Twitter accounts: not just the main account @BestBuy, but also @BestBuy_Deals, @GeekSquad, and @BestBuyNews. The specialists who work Best Buy's help desk also will answer questions through Twitter, at @Twelpforce. Users who tweet the help desk receive an almost instant response from one of Best Buy's 3,000 employees who have signed up to participate on the task force, which further helps showcase the broad spectrum of expertise available through Best Buy.[32]

For small companies with limited marketing budgets, the use of tweeted promotional messages is particularly appealing. A local bakery tweeted, "Two new scones: Lemon Blueberry and Chorizo Cheddar!" and received responses from 400 Twitter followers—a huge captive audience for a local entity.

GOING MOBILE AND SOCIAL

LO3 Understand various motivations for using mobile applications and how they are priced.

Of the more than 100 million people who have smartphones in the United States, approximately half of them make purchases on these devices. Sixty-five percent of Americans own a smartphone and in 2013, 102 billion apps were downloaded creating a total revenue across app stores of close to $26 billion, even though 92 percent of apps downloaded are free. Mobile app downloads are expected to grow to 286 billion annually by 2017.[33] Thus, mobile marketing is significant and growing. Although there are a large number of people in every age group who own smartphones, the highest ownership is for young adults (79 percent, aged 18–24) and teens (70 percent, aged 13–17). Although we call smartphone apps "mobile" apps, they aren't always used by people "on the go"—people spend 68 percent of their time using smartphone apps from their home![34]

As Exhibit 3.4 illustrates, there are seven primary needs that apps meet. They include the need to find "me time," socialize, shop, accomplish, prepare, discover, and self-express. We will briefly discuss each of these needs, as well as popular apps that have been developed to attract customers with these needs. Finally, we

---

EXHIBIT 3.4 Seven Primary Motivations for Mobile App Usage

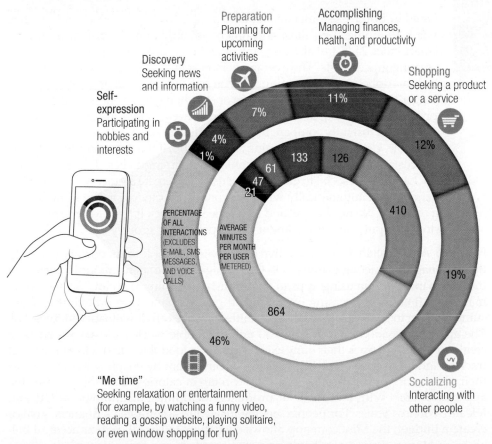

Source: "Vision Statement: How People Really Use Mobile," *Harvard Business Review*, January–February 2013, http://www.hbr.org.

With more than 500,000,000 downloads, Candy Crush Saga clearly fulfills for many people an important need for unproductive "Me Time."

Growing faster than Twitter and Facebook, Weixin has 300 million users, mainly in China, and allows people to send videos, photos, messages, web links, status updates and news to friends.

discuss the four types of pricing models for apps: ad-supported, freemium, paid apps, and paid apps with in-app purchases.

Need for Me Time Although we need to organize, accomplish, and socialize we also need to have time set aside just for us—to be unproductive. The most popular need is all about entertainment and relaxation. Not surprisingly, people spend the most amount of time each month seeking fun—about 46 percent of their smartphone time—by watching TV and movies, playing games, and reading.[35] Common apps for watching videos include Netflix, YouTube, and Hulu. For reading there's Kindle for adults and storybook apps like Nighty Night HD for children. The most popular game on the planet (as of 2014) is Candy Crush Saga. With more than 500 million downloads, it is a match-three game similar to Bejeweled in which players have to match colored candies in sets of three to complete different level objectives.

Need to Socialize Consumers want to stay connected with their friends and apps can help people achieve this goal. The average person spends about 19 percent of their smartphone time interacting with friends (and the rest of the world).[36] Although we are all familiar with Twitter and Facebook, a number of specialized apps to interact through different mediums exist as well. The app Vine allows users to share mini movies on Twitter; Skype allows people to place video calls; Tumblr and Pinterest focus on image sharing; and SnapChat sends pictures and videos that are automatically deleted a few seconds after opening. In China, the social networking app Weixin (pronounced way-SHEEN) allows users to send videos, photos, messages, web links, status updates, and news and has been released as WeChat in the United States. Weixin has had a faster adoption rate than either Facebook or Twitter, with more than 300 million users in only three years.[37]

Need to Shop Customers demand to be able to shop when and where they want. Shopping apps allow consumers not only to make purchases from a smartphone 24/7, but also do many other tasks such as comparing prices and creating grocery lists. The average person spends about 12 percent of his or her smartphone time shopping.[38] When out shopping, smartphone users no longer have to go from store to store or stop home to go online and compare prices. A process called showrooming enables customers to scan a product in a store and instantly compare the prices online to see whether a better deal is available. Using the showrooming Amazon app, if the Amazon price is better, the customer can buy the product online with a single click. The grocery app Out of Milk has brought social to grocery lists; users can create a grocery (or any other type) list and sync it automatically with everyone else's devices in the same household. Out of bread? No need to call and ask someone to pick it up next time he or she is at the store; just put it in the app and it will appear in the grocery list.

Need to Accomplish Consumers live busy lives and look to mobile apps to help them manage their activities and goals. On average, people spend about 11 percent of their smartphone time using apps to accomplish something (Exhibit 3.4), including managing finances, increasing overall health, and enhancing productivity.[39] Consumers trying to get in shape and live a healthy lifestyle can download MyFitnessPal. The app downloaded by more than 50 million people worldwide allows users to create a profile and track their daily exercise, create a food diary to track calories, and track weight loss. The app also adds a social component by enabling people to post their success at, for instance, keeping below a target calorie level. Additionally, the app can interact with a number of products, including FitBit, Jawbone UP, and iHealth Wireless Scales. For people seeking instead to accomplish a financial goal or create a budget, the Mint.com app allows customers to see all of their account balances and transactions across banks and credit cards in one convenient place.

Need to Prepare As our lives get busier and faster paced, the need to keep organized and make quick decisions continues to grow. Apps meet this need by helping us prepare and plan. Users spend about 7 percent of their smartphone time using apps like calendars, trip planners, and flight trackers.[40] Kayak, a free app on all major platforms, provides a convenient way for people to plan trips. Kayak allows users to find flights, hotels, and rental cars and compare prices across hundreds of travel sites to find the best deals. Once the trip is booked, travelers can get up-to-the-minute information on flight statuses, and if there is a problem with a flight, the app has the phone numbers for all major airlines. Cloud-based file storage apps like Dropbox and Google Drive allow customers to store files in the cloud and access them from any device. Finally, Business Calendar helps people plan their day with an interactive calendar that integrates multiple calendars (e.g., Google Calendar, Outlook Calendar) and allows users to link an event to people in their contacts list and put a daily agenda widget on their smartphone home screen.

MyFitnessPal fulfills the common need to accomplish weight loss.

Need to Discover Apps also help fulfill our need for information, to know what's going on around us, and to open our minds to new ideas. This need is met through news and weather apps, on which people spend about 4 percent of their smartphone time.[41] One of the most popular apps for news and information is Flipboard, a unique app that produces a full-screen magazine aggregating a number of news and entertainment sources based on user-defined topics such as top stories, entertainment, local news, and business news. The app also adds a social component by allowing the reader to send stories to friends or post on Facebook. Speaking of Facebook, in early 2014 Facebook launched Paper, an app designed to compete directly with Flipboard.

Need to Self-Express Finally, individuals have diverse interests and tastes, and as a result, have a need for apps that are tailored to their hobbies and passions. Surprisingly, the average person spends only about 1 percent of his or her smartphone time engaging in personal interests.[42] For the beginning astronomer, Google's SkyMap allows users to hold their smartphones up to the sky and, using GPS and compass data, the app shows them what they are looking at. Want to know how to use a badger brush while shaving? How about finding people who love balloon animals as much as you? TapaTalk aggregates tens of thousands of interest groups into a single app, making it easy to connect aficionados of just about any interest or hobby.

As you can see from this discussion, apps can meet several needs at once. Sharing an interesting story with friends via Flipboard can meet the needs of discovery and socialization. When a person looks at the latest 4K TVs sold on Amazon just for fun, she can be meeting three needs—me time, discovery, and shopping. Consider the person who purchases Chinese food via GrubHub's app on her ride on home; she's not only shopping, but she's also avoiding making dinner to get some extra me time. With this information in mind, apps (and advertising within those apps) can be designed and targeted in ways that better apply the 4 Es.

App Pricing Models

A key decision for firms producing apps is what to charge for them. There are four basic ways of generating revenue from apps—ad-supported apps, freemium apps, paid apps, and paid apps with in-app purchases.

Not only does Flipboard aggregate all of the news important to you in one place, its unique format gives the app the look and feel of a printed magazine.

Ad-supported apps are free to download, but place ads on the screen when using the program to generate revenue. Although there are many of these types of apps, the majority of app revenue is generated from the remaining three pricing models, discussed next.

Freemium apps are apps that are free to download but include **in-app purchases**. In-app purchases are when a game or app prompts or allows customers to make small "micropurchases" to enhance an app or game. Common examples include extra lives, bonus maps, in-game currency, a subscription, and unique character unlocks. In Candy Crush Saga, you get five lives to play in the game. When you lose a life, it takes 30 minutes in real-life time to get that life back. If you're playing a particularly hard level and lose all your lives in minutes, you'll have to wait two and a half hours to play again. This is where in-app purchases come in. For just $0.99, you can get all five lives back immediately so you can keep playing.[43] Candy Crush Saga is estimated to earn the developer between $623,000 and $850,000 *a day* in revenue from in-app purchases.[44]

The remaining two pricing models are paid apps and paid apps with in-app purchases. **Paid apps** charge the customer an up-front price to download the app ($0.99 is the most common), but offer full functionality once downloaded. Similar to the freemium model, **paid apps with in-app purchases** require the consumer to pay initially to download the app and then offer the ability to buy additional functionality.

Which is the best pricing model? Time will tell, but it appears that freemium apps may be the winner. As Exhibit 3.5 shows, free apps with in-app purchases make up the vast majority of revenue from Apple's App Store in 8 of 10 app categories. According to Distimo, a research firm specializing in the mobile app market, 71 percent of apps in Apple's App Store implement a freemium pricing model, and 92 percent of revenues from Apple's App Store and 98 percent from Google's Play App Store come from freemium pricing.[45]

EXHIBIT 3.5   Apple App Store Revenue by App Category Pricing Models

% of revenue generated in Apple's App Store from January through November 2013, by app category and pricing model

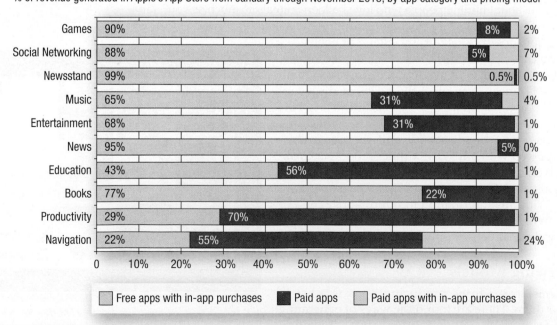

	Free apps with in-app purchases	Paid apps	Paid apps with in-app purchases
Games	90%	8%	2%
Social Networking	88%	5%	7%
Newsstand	99%	0.5%	0.5%
Music	65%	31%	4%
Entertainment	68%	31%	1%
News	95%	5%	0%
Education	43%	56%	1%
Books	77%	22%	1%
Productivity	29%	70%	1%
Navigation	22%	55%	24%

Source: Adapted from Christel Schoger, "2013 Year in Review," *Distimo Report,* December 2013, http://www.distimo.com.

CHECK YOURSELF

1. What are the seven types of customer motivations for using mobile apps?
2. What are the four options to price mobile apps?
3. What are some of the most popular types of mobile applications?

HOW DO FIRMS ENGAGE THEIR CUSTOMERS USING SOCIAL MEDIA?

 LO4 Recognize and understand the three components of a social media strategy.

Now that we have an understanding of the various social and mobile media that are at the firm's disposal, it is important to determine how firms should go about engaging customers through social and mobile media. The three-stage process found in Exhibit 3.6 involves *listening* to what customers have to say, **analyzing** the information available through various touch points, and finally implementing (or **doing**) social media tactics to excite customers.

Listen

From a market research point of view, companies can learn a lot about their customers by listening (and monitoring) what they say on their social networks, blogs, review sites, and so on. Customers appear willing to provide their opinions on just about anything including their interests and purchases—both their own and their friends'. Writing blogs and providing opinions via polls about such diverse topics as BOTOX treatments, ASICS running shoes, or a particular play of an NFL team during the playoffs all constitute new ways that customers communicate with one another—and with marketers who are paying attention.

Marketers can analyze the content found on sites like Facebook, Twitter, and online blogs and reviews to assess the favorableness or unfavorableness of the sentiments using a technique known as sentiment analysis. Sentiment analysis allows marketers to analyze data from these sources to collect consumer comments about companies and their products. The data are then analyzed to distill customer attitudes and preferences, including reactions to specific products and campaigns. Scouring millions of sites with sentiment analysis techniques provides new insights into what consumers really think. Companies plugged into this real-time information and these insights can become more nimble, allowing for numerous quick changes such as a product rollout, a new advertising campaign, or reactions to customer complaints.

Several companies specialize in monitoring social media.[46] For example, Salesforce.com offers sentiment analysis and then helps its clients such as GE,

EXHIBIT 3.6   Social Media Engagement Process

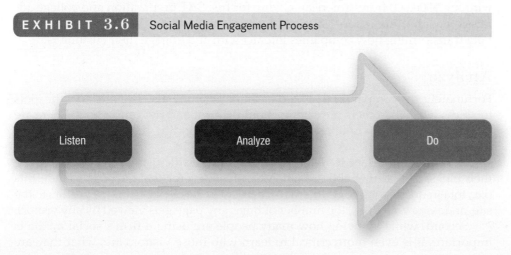

Listen   Analyze   Do

The NFL blog is one way fans communicate with each other during and after games.

Kodak, Microsoft, and PepsiCo engage with its customers.[47] Using sentiment analysis techniques, it processes a constant stream of online consumer opinion from blogs, Facebook, and other networking sites, including 90 million Twitter tweets a day. The Salesforce.com tools for managing consumer sentiment data allow companies to identify opinion trends that might warrant an online corporate response. For instance, Salesforce.com may identify negative consumer sentiment and then provide services to help the client respond. Reacting to attitudes uncovered in sentiment analysis allows companies to counteract negative opinions, maybe influence those perceptions, and perhaps win customer loyalty.[48]

As an example of how a firm like Salesforce.com can help its clients engage their customers, consider the nonprofit New York–based Let's Get Ready that helps low-income high school students get into college.[49] When it decided to compete for American Giving Awards funding, Let's Get Ready needed broader support. Salesforce.com helped the organization find web-based conversations among individuals and groups who might share its educational mission. It further helped Let's Get Ready reach out to potential supporters, share information about its work, and ask for votes. The campaign worked: Let's Get Ready placed second, winning $500,000 from American Giving for free SAT preparation and college admission counseling to motivated students. Sentiment analysis thus is fundamentally transforming how companies interact with and engage their customers.

Analyze

Fortunately, the companies that help facilitate listening also provide analytic tools to assess what customers are saying about the firm and its competitors. There are three main categories of analysis used for understanding data collected from social media.[50]

First, it is important to determine amount of traffic using their sites, visiting their blogs, or tweeting about them. Measures used for this purpose include hits (i.e., total requests for a page), visits to a particular site or page, unique visitors to the site, and page views (i.e., the number of times any page gets viewed by any visitor).

Second, while knowing how many people are using a firm's social media is important, it is even more critical to learn who those visitors are, what they are

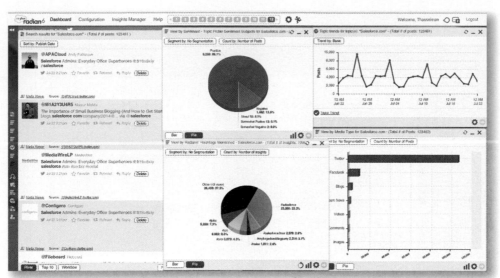

Salesforce.com's Radian6 website analyzes customer sentiment for its customers, which enables them to identify opinion trends that might warrant an online corporate response.

doing, and what engages and excites them. To analyze these factors, social media marketers use metrics such as the bounce rate, which refers to the percentage of times a visitor leaves the site almost immediately, such as after viewing only one page. Analyzing which pages are the most frequent entry and exit locations provides direction on how to make a website more effective. In addition, following visitors' click paths shows how users proceed through the information—not unlike how grocery stores try to track the way shoppers move through their aisles. A firm can use this information to provide users with an easier navigation experience through the site so they can more quickly find what they are looking for. The data analysis can also reveal conversion rates, a measure that indicates what percentage of visitors or potential customers act as the marketer hopes, whether by clicking, buying, or donating. Click paths and conversion rates can also reveal what users might have wanted, but did not find, at the site.

Third, some companies want to analyze data that come from other sites, such as measuring where people have come from to get to the company's site. Did they search through Google or Amazon? Did they receive a referral from a friend? Which keywords did they use to find the firm? Firms can use keyword analysis to determine what keywords people use to search on the Internet for their products and services. With this information, they can refine their websites by choosing keywords to use on their site that their customers use. Then they can assess the return on investment (ROI) made by improving the site. This would be done by calculating the incremental profit increase divided by the investment on the site improvement. For social media, it is more challenging to determine ROI than for more traditional marketing applications because the revenue generated by social media is often not directly related to the expenditure. So, instead of traditional ROI measures, firms often examine questions like: Does having more Twitter followers correlate with having higher sales? Do Facebook fans of the company's buy more than non-fans?[51]

These analyses require well-trained marketing managers, marketing analytic software, and perhaps some help with consulting specialists (e.g., IBM, SAS, PricewaterhouseCoopers). But almost everyone seems to be turning to Google Analytics these days because it offers a sophisticated, in-depth form of analysis, all for free. Not only does Google Analytics track the elements included in Exhibit 3.7, but it also is highly customizable.[52]

Do

Even the greatest analysis has little use if firms fail to implement what they have learned from analyzing their social and mobile media activity. That is, social media may be all about relationships, but ultimately, firms need to use

EXHIBIT 3.7 Analytics

Type of Analytic	How It's Used	Competitors Offering Similar Analytics
Content	Understand what's popular and what's not on a firm's website, including page load times and site navigation.	Adobe SiteCatalyst, Clickstream, Coremetrics, IBM SurfAid, Mtracking, VisiStat
Social	Track effectiveness of social media programs, including information on social media referred conversion rates and engagement metrics.	Facebook Insights, Twitter Web Analytics, Webtrends, HootSuite, TweetDeck
Mobile	Track website access from mobile devices, track which ads direct people to a firm's app, and understand what mobile platform performs best.	AppClix, Bango, Flurry, Localytics, Medialets, Webtrends
Conversion	Moving beyond page views and visitor counts, conversion analytics measures sales, downloads, video plays, or any other action important to a firm.	ClickTale, KeyMetric, Latitude
Advertising	Track the effectiveness of social, mobile, and search and display ads and divide ad effectiveness by device, platform, or type.	ad:tech, MediaMelon, MediaCloud, Metronome, Snoobi, Adomic

Source: http://www.google.com/analytics/features/index.html.

their connections to increase their business.[53] They might launch a new Facebook campaign, actively blog, or provide mobile offers.

What do you do when consumers get tired of the flavors of chips you offer? Instead of developing several new flavors and giving them to focus groups and test markets, in 2013 Lay's took to the Internet. It launched the "Do Us a Flavor" campaign in which customers could suggest new flavor combinations online. After 3.8 million submissions, expert chefs and actor Eva Longoria chose the three finalists: Cheesy Garlic Bread, Chicken & Waffles, and Sriracha. Each of these flavors were developed and sold in stores from February to May and customers were encouraged to try the new flavors and vote for their favorite one. After more than a million votes were tallied on Facebook, Karen Weber-Mendham was given $1 million or 1 percent of the 2013 net sales of her flavor (whichever was higher) for her Cheesy Garlic Bread flavor. The other two finalists received $50,000 each. This campaign was so successful that Lay's launched the contest in several other countries, including the UK, Australia, India, and South Africa, resulting in flavors such as Chili & Chocolate, Late Night Kabob, and Cajun Squirrel. To continue to engage its customers, Lay's launched the "Do Us a Flavor" contest in the United States again in 2014.[54]

To illustrate how firms might go about undertaking such campaigns, consider the steps involved in developing and implementing a Facebook marketing campaign (Exhibit 3.8).[55] These steps are not unlike the steps used in any integrated marketing communications (IMC) program. (See Chapter 18 for more details.) Assume a marketer was developing a Facebook marketing campaign for a new product that they have designed.

1. **Identify strategy and goals.** The firm has to determine exactly what it hopes to promote and achieve through its campaign. Does it want to increase awareness of the product? Is it hoping more potential customers might visit and "like" its Facebook page? Is its focus mainly on increasing sales of the product? Depending on what the company aims to achieve, it might focus on developing a Facebook page, creating a Facebook app, or hosting a Facebook event.

The Lay's Do Us a Flavor campaign effectively crowd-sourced product development.

EXHIBIT 3.8	How to Do a Social Media Marketing Campaign

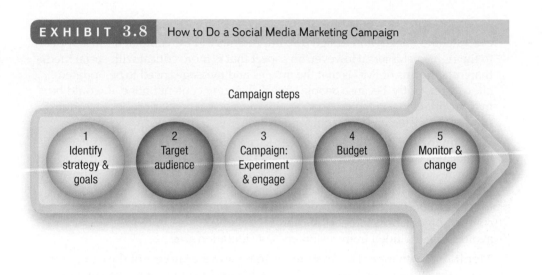

Campaign steps

1 Identify strategy & goals

2 Target audience

3 Campaign: Experiment & engage

4 Budget

5 Monitor & change

2. **Identify target audience.** The next step is to determine whom the firm is targeting. As Exhibit 3.9 shows, Facebook enables the firm to perform targeting that is based on location, language, education, gender, profession, age, relationship status, likes/dislikes, and friends or connections. The marketer's aim is to find a big enough audience to reach those who might adopt their product without being so big that they end up trying to appeal to someone way outside their target audience.

3. **Develop the campaign: Experiment and engage.** Now that the firm knows who it is targeting, the next step is to develop the communications, including the copy and images. Here again, the process is not very different from any other IMC

EXHIBIT 3.9	Example Facebook Targeting Choices

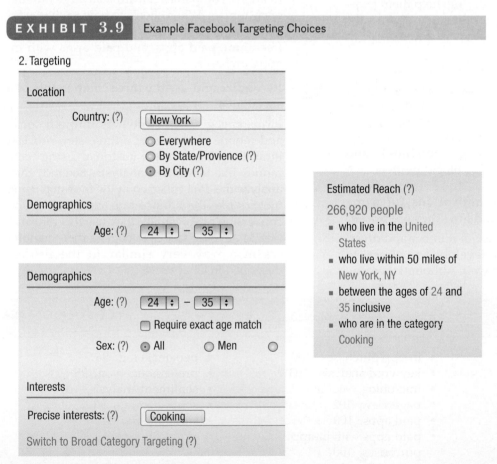

2. Targeting

Location

Country: (?) [New York]

○ Everywhere
○ By State/Provience (?)
◉ By City (?)

Demographics

Age: (?) [24 ⬍] – [35 ⬍]

Demographics

Age: (?) [24 ⬍] – [35 ⬍]

☐ Require exact age match

Sex: (?) ◉ All   ○ Men   ○

Interests

Precise interests: (?) [Cooking]

Switch to Broad Category Targeting (?)

Estimated Reach (?)

266,920 people

- who live in the United States
- who live within 50 miles of New York, NY
- between the ages of 24 and 35 inclusive
- who are in the category Cooking

Source: From http://www.facebook.com/business/ads/.

campaign. There should be a call to action that is clear and compelling. Strong, eye-catching images and designs are important. And the campaign must appeal to the right customers. However, an aspect that is more critical with social media than other forms of IMC is that the images and messages need to be updated almost constantly. Because people expect changing content online, it would be inappropriate to run the same campaign for several months, as the firm might if it was advertising on television, for example.

4. **Develop the budget.** Budgeting is key. Facebook allows advertisers to set a daily budget: Once their costs (usually per click) reach a certain level, the ad disappears for the rest of the day. Of course, this option can be risky if the firm is getting great feedback, and all of a sudden, a compelling ad disappears. Therefore, similar to the campaign content, budgets demand nearly constant review. For example, if a competitor lowers its price significantly, it might be necessary to follow suit to avoid being excluded from customers' consideration sets.

5. **Monitor and change.** The final step is to review the success of the campaign and make changes as necessary. Facebook's Ad Manager offers various metrics and reports, such as number of clicks on ads, audience demographics, and ad performance for specific time periods.

Reviewing Learning Objectives

LO1 Describe the 4E framework of social media marketing.

The 4E framework recognizes that marketers must **e**xcite customers with relevant offers; **e**ducate them about the offering; help them experience products, whether directly or indirectly; and give them an opportunity to **e**ngage.

LO2 Understand the types of social media.

Users of social media employ them to promote themselves or their products and services. They do so through three main categories: social networking sites (e.g., Facebook, LinkedIn), media-sharing sites (e.g., YouTube), and thought-sharing sites (e.g., blogs, Twitter).

LO3 Understand various motivations for using mobile applications and how they are priced.

As mobile users increase in number and diversity, the applications developed to appeal to them are spreading as well. Although there are well over a million apps, they meet seven basic customer motivations: for "me time," to socialize, shop, accomplish, prepare, discover, and self-express. By meeting a multiple of these motivations, companies can attract a large number of customers. When choosing how to charge for apps, firms have four options: ad-supported, freemium, paid apps, and paid apps with in-app purchases.

LO4 Recognize and use the three components of a social media strategy.

Firms engage with customers through social and mobile media using a three-step process. First, they listen to the customer using techniques like sentiment analysis. Second, they analyze the data collected in the first step using metrics like the bounce rate, click paths, and conversion rates. Finally, they use this information to develop tactics to engage their customers in a way very similar to the process described in Chapter 18.

Key Terms

- ad-supported apps, 100
- blog, 95
- bounce rate, 103
- click path, 103
- conversion rate, 103
- corporate blog, 95
- freemium apps, 100
- hit, 102

- in-app purchases, 100
- keyword analysis, 103
- microblog, 96
- page view, 102
- paid apps, 100
- paid apps with in-app purchases, 100

- personal blog, 96
- professional blog, 95
- sentiment analysis, 101
- showrooming, 98
- social media, 84

Marketing Applications

1. Evaluate Gatorade's social media strategy using the 4E framework.

2. Using the components of the 4E framework, outline how an entrepreneur marketing T-shirts can augment or enhance his or her marketing mix efforts.

3. Suppose an herbal tea company introduced a new product called mint-enhanced tea—mint and lemon herbal tea. How should it go about creating excitement using various social and mobile media tools?

4. If you were marketing a new running shoe, what sort of mobile applications might enhance your marketing efforts?

5. Assume you work for a large consumer packaged-goods firm that has discovered that its latest line of snack foods is moving very slowly off store shelves. Recommend a strategy for listening to what consumers are saying on blogs, review sites, and the firm's website. Describe how your strategy might provide insights into consumers' sentiments about the new product line.

6. As an intern for Dunkin' Donuts, you have been asked to develop a social media campaign for a new glazed muffin. The objective of the campaign is to increase awareness and trial of the new line of muffins. How would you go about putting together such a campaign?

7. You were just hired by a company that wants to produce apps that help people become healthier by exercising, eating well, and reducing stress. Which customer motivations would you recommend the company focus on? Describe the app you would design, the customer motivations it meets, and why your app is the right design for your potential customers.

8. The company loves the idea for the app you suggested in the previous question, but is concerned about how it will make money on the app. Suggest a pricing model for the app and discuss why this model will maximize profits.

Quiz Yourself

1. Suppose that Nike wanted to use Facebook to increase awareness of a new line of tennis shoes. Which of the following methods would allow Nike to specifically target Facebook users who have mentioned tennis in their profiles?

   a. Uploading a coupon to the Nike fan page.

   b. Encouraging Facebook users to "like" the Nike page so their friends will see this action.

   c. Placing a Facebook ad.

   d. Creating a Facebook tab allowing users to view the tennis clothing within Facebook.

   e. Placing a Facebook link on the Nike corporate website.

2. When a company that uses social media runs a contest online, it will measure its effectiveness in a variety of ways. One such measure is the conversion rate. The conversion rate for the contest promotion would be:

   a. the number of people who entered the contest.

   b. the number of people who entered the contest plus the number of people who visited the page describing the contest.

   c. the number of people who visited the page describing the contest.

   d. the percentage of visitors to the page describing the contest who entered the contest.

   e. the percentage of fans of the company's page who learned about the contest.

   (Answers to these two questions can be found on page 651.)

Net Savvy

1. Go to http://www.facebook.com/business and learn about how to build pages, ads, and sponsored stories and how to take advantage of mobile applications. What are some of the steps that Facebook suggests a person consider when marketing using ads?

2. Go to SalesForce.com Radian6's website (http://www.salesforcemarketingcloud.com/products/social-media-listening/) and check out its top case studies. How do these case studies provide insights into how listening and analytic systems can help firms improve their social media marketing?

3. Learn about Coca-Cola and Google's "Project Re: Brief" social media campaign on YouTube (http://www.youtube.com/watch?v=45Z-GevoYB8). Which of the 4E components does this campaign leverage?

4. A student who graduates with a marketing degree likely has a good foundation for jobs that utilize social media. Go to Monster.com and search for jobs in your area with the keyword "social media." Would you be interested in pursuing one or more of these positions? Why or why not?

Chapter Case Study

IMAGES, SALES, BRANDS: HOW RED BULL USES VARIOUS SOCIAL MEDIA TECHNIQUES TO ACHIEVE ALL ITS OBJECTIVES

It isn't as if the social media strategy adopted by Red Bull—the energy drink that "gives you wings"—is a trade secret. Granted, the private company has a policy that discourages employees from giving interviews. But its overall strategy is clear from its actions and their outcomes. The success it has accrued from this strategy therefore isn't a matter of doing things differently than anyone else. It's a function of doing them better.

To begin, Red Bull distinguishes its goals for leveraging social media contacts. Is it hoping for more brand exposure, or is it pursuing sales increases? Depending on its focus, it adopts distinct, appealing methods that are specific and unique to each social media platform. Then it implements these tactics consistently and comprehensively, to increase the chances that they will be widely shared and recognized.

Social Media for Name Recognition

When Felix Baumgartner (purposefully) fell to Earth from 127,852 feet up, it broke all sorts of records. His jump was from the highest height ever achieved by a human. During the 4-minute, 20-second freefall, he also reached greater speeds—up to Mach 1.25, faster than the speed of sound—than anyone else ever has. The event was a breakthrough on various levels. Baumgartner's pressure suit was the first version to be able to protect the human body in space but still enable maneuverability. To address the threat of ebullism (i.e., when liquid in the body evaporates due to high altitudes, causing a person's blood to literally boil), Baumgartner and his team derived new medical techniques with widespread applications. His parachute also adopted a new "reefed" design to reduce drifting, with clear implications for airdrops of materials and supplies.[56]

In reporting on all these remarkable feats, Baumgartner's name was mentioned frequently—though not as frequently as the project that sponsored his jump and all the technology that went into supporting it: the Red Bull Stratos project. Every official mention of the event included the full name, such that Red Bull Stratos often appeared as a single term. It was not just the Stratos project. It was the Red Bull Stratos project.

And what a project it was, leading to the creation of not just scientific advances but also a remarkable video. That video, taken from the camera mounted on Baumgartner's helmet, features vast, picturesque views of Earth and the sense of plummeting. Red Bull immediately made it available for people to check out at their leisure. But the real target—the people whom Red Bull hoped would be most engaged by the video and the stunt in general—were extreme sports fanatics. These folks willingly put their bodies at risk on a regular basis to perform some cool stunt to cause their friends to marvel. For them, there may be no better stunt than having some guy fall from space.[57] In full awareness of this appeal, Red Bull made sure that the video

Sponsored by Red Bull, Felix Baumgartner's jump reached speeds of Mach 1.25.

was prominent on its YouTube channel. On the day of the jump itself, approximately 8 million streamed the video live and in real time. Also on that day, the number of subscribers to Red Bull's YouTube channel increased by a remarkable 87,801.[58]

On Twitter, recognizing that 140 characters was not nearly enough to communicate the awesomeness of the stunt, it simply used hashtags and links to connect followers to the video, whether through YouTube or on a Red Bull site. Although Red Bull's main Twitter feed did not exhibit any notable differences, the dedicated Red Bull Stratos Twitter feed prompted more than 20,000 mentions in tweets by others on that day.

The Red Bull Stratos Facebook page featured several photos during and after the jump. Just one shot of a landed Baumgartner, still in his space suit and on his knees beside his reefed parachute, prompted more than 20,000 comments, more than 50,000 shares, and nearly half a million likes.[59]

Thus the example of the Red Bull Stratos project and its attendant coverage through social media suggests several things Red Bull did well. It knew its audience and its own goals, and it understood how different channels could help it attain those goals. To ensure that it appealed to the target audience, it engaged them in an exciting, never-before-tried, daredevil experience. Moreover, it shared the scientific lessons learned through the project, to give those who wanted it an education.

But it also spent a lot of money to get Baumgartner to space and back down again. And that meant that it needed to translate some of the brand awareness it developed into sales. Luckily for Red Bull, its social media strategy also has room for that effort.

Social Media for Performance

Red Bull does not just send athletes to space. It also sponsors them on the pitch, in the form of the New York Red Bull MLS team, which plays in Red Bull Arena in Harrison, New Jersey. In one recent game, the team's star forward Thierry Henry scored yet another goal. Afterward, he leaned, with his right arm up against the goal post and left hand on his hip. The pose, caught on camera, almost immediately became a Twitter meme as amateur photo editors placed him against a variety of backgrounds.[60]

The team was quick to move on this social media coup. It rapidly posted the photo to its website and encouraged fans to vote for it as their favorite shot of the season. Immediately above and below the encouragement to engage with the brand also appeared links that would allow fans to purchase tickets for a full season, half season, or individual games.[61]

Beyond these consumer-related uses of social and mobile media, Red Bulls' international sales efforts depend on "SoLoMo" (referring to social, location, and mobile) software. Users who download the Red Bull app receive alerts on their smartphones about in-store promotions as soon as they arrive at the retail site. If they also attend Red Bull events, such as a flugtag or BMX race, selected patrons even might receive a special invitation to come backstage to meet some of the stars of the show.

Each of Red Bull's mobile sales representatives is equipped with her or his own tablet computer, loaded with mobile software. Thus on visits to retail sites and vendors, the salespeople can provide the latest inventory information. They also present detailed analytics to show vendors how best to position their coolers of Red Bull products and how to line up the cans in the display case to encourage sales.[62]

Combining the Uses of Social Media

When you are as good at engaging and exciting people through social media as Red Bull is, the next step might be to make social media your main focus. Although the privately held company has not publicized any such plans, commentators suggest that it appears poised to transform itself into a media company that just happens to sell energy drinks.[63] The extent and amount of content it creates, featuring extreme sports and even sports it has created (ever hear of ice racing?), is similar in quality to sports videos produced by well-known networks. If Red Bull can convince networks to purchase its coverage of Shaun White on the half-pipe, it enters a new market. If Shaun White happens to be wearing a hat with the Red Bull logo, well then that's just an added bonus.

Such predictions actually resonate quite well with what Red Bull already does in social media. For example, though it maintains a plethora of Facebook pages and Twitter accounts for various events and locations, virtually none of them ever feature pictures of its drink product. Instead, they offer exciting in-sport shots or humorous images. Fans can—and do—comment, but Red Bull rarely responds. That may be because its primary goal is to establish an edgy, exciting image as a lifestyle brand, which it feels confident will translate into product sales.[64]

Questions

1. What social and mobile media tools is Red Bull using?
2. Evaluate Red Bull's social media marketing strategy using the 4E framework?
3. How should Red Bull assess the effectiveness of these campaigns? Describe how it should respond to insights gained by this assessment.

Endnotes

1. Adam Ostrow, "Inside Gatorade's Social Media Control Center," *Mashable.com,* June 15, 2010, http://mashable.com.

2. Ekaterina Walter, "How Top Brands Like Gatorade and the Super Bowl Use Social-Media Command Centers," *Fast Company,* June 22, 2012.

3. PepsiCo, "Gatorade Mission Control," YouTube, https://www.youtube.com.

4. Sarah McNew, "Social Media Breakdown: A Look at Gatorade's Social Media Marketing Efforts," *Social Toaster,* May 6, 2013, http://www.socialtoaster.com/blog-entry/social-media-breakdown-look-gatorades-social-media-marketing-efforts.

5. "Gatorade's Social Media Command Center?" *Hive Health Media,* May 17, 2013, http://www.hivehealthmedia.com/gatorades-social-media-command-center/.

6. Lisa Joy Rosner, "Gatorade Generates the Buzz, Pocari Sweat Heats Up in Love; NetBase Brand Passion Index Measures Social Data on Sports Drinks," *The Wall Street Journal,* July 10, 2013, http://online.wsj.com/article/PR-CO-20130710-906433.html.

7. Mike Gingerich, "4 Ways to Boost Your Facebook Engagement with Promotions," *Social Media Examiner,* January 8, 2013, http://www.socialmediaexaminer.com/boost-your-facebook-engagement-with-promotions/.

8. Nikon, press release, August 22, 2007, http://press.nikonusa.com/post/2007/08/22/nikons-new-digital-learning-center-on-flickr-provides-a-first-of-its-kind-interactive-experience-that-assists-everyday-people-in-taking-better-photos/.

9. Chris Barry et al., "Putting Social Media to Work," 2011, Bain & Co., http://www.bain.com/Images/BAIN_BRIEF_Putting_social_media_to_work.pdf.

10. Tim Nudd, "American Apparel, Gap Blasted for Hurricane Sandy Ad Fails," *Adweek,* October 30, 2012.

11. Coca-Cola Retailing Research Council and the Integer Group, "Social Networking Personas: A Look at Consumer and Shopper Mind Sets," in *Untangling the Social Web: Insights for Users, Brands, and Retailers,* March 2012, http://www.cokesolutions.com/BusinessSolutions/Studies/Untangling%20the%20Social%20Web_Part%203.pdf.

12. Forever 21 Facebook Fan Page, http://www.facebook.com/#!/Forever21?ref=ts.

13. John Squires, "Controversial Devil's Due Promotion Invites You to Convert to Satanism," *Fear.net,* January 7, 2014, http://www.fearnet.com/news/news-article/controversial-devils-due-promotional-campaign-invites-you-convert-satanism.

14. Scott Meslow, "Why Moviegoers Should Be Wary of 'Viral Video' Campaigns," *The Week,* January 14, 2014.

15. "LinkedIn Announces Fourth Quarter and 2011 Fiscal Year Financial Results," *LinkedIn,* February 9, 2012, http://press.linkedin.com/node/1104.

16. Guy Kawaski, "Ten Ways for Small Businesses to Use LinkedIn," *LinkedIn Blog,* April 12, 2010, http://blog.linkedin.com.

17. Joe Hindy, "The Latest Social Share Numbers Are In and Google+ Isn't Doing So Well," *AndroidAuthority.com,* July 19, 2013, http://www.androidauthority.com.

18. Violet Blue, "Forced Google Plus Integration on YouTube Backfires, Petition Hits 112,000," *ZDNet.com,* November 14, 2013, http://www.zdnet.com.

19. Dorie Clark, "Why You Should Be on Google Plus (Even Though No One Else Is)," *Forbes,* January 14, 2013.

20. Ross Blum, "Where Have All the Customers Gone?" p. 8.

21. "In The Know," YouTube, Fall 2009, http://www.gstatic.com/youtube/engagement/platform/autoplay/advertise/downloads/YouTube_InTheKnow.pdf.

22. The Home Depot Branded Channel, http://www.youtube.com/user/homedepot?blend=2&ob=4#p/a.

23. "Brand Channels," YouTube, http://www.gstatic.com/youtube/engagement/platform/autoplay/advertise/downloads/YouTube_BrandChannels.pdf.

24. "Instagram," *Wikipedia,* August 2, 2013, http://en.wikipedia.org/wiki/Instagram.

25. Somini Sengupta, Nicole Perlroth, and Jenna Wortham, "Behind Instagram's Success, Networking the Old Way," *The New York Times,* April 13, 2012, http://www.nytimes.com/2012/04/14/technology/instagram-founders-were-helped-by-bay-area-connections.html?pagewanted=all&_r=2&.

26. Shayndi Raice and Spencer E. Ante, "Insta-Rich: $1 Billion for Instagram," *The Wall Street Journal,* April 10, 2012, http://online.wsj.com/article/SB10001424052702303815404577333840377381670.html.

27. Finlo Rohrer, "Vine: Six Things People Have Learned about Six-Second Video in a Week," *BBC News Magazine,* January 31, 2013, http://www.bbc.co.uk/news/magazine-21267741.

28. "Brands on Flickr," *Supercollider,* July 12, 2008, http://geoff-northcott.com/blog/2008/07/brands-on-flickr/.

29. Mark W. Schaefer, "The 10 Best Corporate Blogs in the World," *BusinessGrow.com,* January 1, 2011, http://www.businessesgrow.com/2011/01/05/the-10-best-corporate-blogs-in-the-world/.

30. http://www.topmommyblogs.com/pages/todays_popular_blogs.html.

31. Elizabeth Holmes, "Tweeting without Fear," *The Wall Street Journal,* December 9, 2011.

32. Ibid.

33. "Gartner Says Mobile Apps Stores Will See Annual Downloads Reach 102 Billion in 2013," *Gartner,* September 19, 2013, http://www.gartner.com; "Ring the Bells: More Smartphones in Students' Hands Ahead of Back-to-School Season," *Nielsen Newswire,* October 29, 2013, http://www.nielsen.com.

34. "Seven Shades of Mobile," *AOL, BBDO, and InsightsNow! Report,* November 12, 2012, http://www.behaviorlens.com.

35. "Vision Statement: How People Really Use Mobile," *Harvard Business Review,* January–February 2013, http://www.hbr.org.

36. Ibid.

37. David Barboza, "A Popular Chinese Social Networking App Blazes Its Own Path," *The New York Times,* January 20, 2014.

38. "Vision Statement: How People Really Use Mobile."

39. Ibid.

40. Ibid.

41. Ibid.

42. Ibid.

43. Ashley Feinberg, "I Just Spent $236 on Candy Crush, Help," *Gizmodo,* August 7, 2013, http://www.gizmodo.com.

44. Stuart Dredge, "Candy Crush Saga: '70% of People on the Last Level Haven't Paid Anything,'" *The Guardian,* September 10, 2013, http://www.theguardian.com; "Candy Crush Saga Most Popular Game App on the Planet," *Metro,* January 30, 2014, http://www.metro.co.uk.

45. Josh Wolonick, "Here's How Big the In-App Purchases Market Is for Apple and Google," *Minyanville,* January 16, 2014, http://www.minyanville.com.

46. Katie Van Domelin, "Social Media Monitoring Tools—How to Pick the Right One," July 7, 2010, http://www.convinceandconvert.com/social-media-monitoring/social-media-monitoring-tools-how-to-pick-the-right-one/.

47. "New Salesforce.com Features Help to Scale 'Social' across the Enterprise," Salesforce.com website, November 12, 2011, http://www.Salesforce.com.com.

48. Salesforce.com website, http://www.Salesforce.com.com.

49. Let's Get Ready website, http://www.letsgetready.org.

50. Laura S. Quinn and Kyle Andrei, "A Few Good Web Analytics Tools," May 19, 2011, http://www.techsoup.org.

51. Christina Warren, "How to Measure Social Media ROI," October 27, 2009, http://mashable.com/2009/10/27/social-media-roi/.

52. "iNoobs: What Is Google Analytics?" http://inspiredm.com; http://www.google.com/analytics/features/index.html; http://www.advanced-web-metrics.com; Kevin Ryan, "What Can the Average Marketer Learn from Google Creative Lab?" *Advertising Age,* April 19, 2013.

53. Amy Porterfield, "3 Steps to an Effective Social Media Strategy," *Social Media Examiner,* March 1, 2012, http://www.socialmediaexaminer.com.

54. "Lay's Brand Names Cheesy Garlic Bread Flavored Potato Chips as 'Do Us a Flavor' Contest Winner; Creator Receives $1 Million or More in Grand Prize Winnings," *Pepsico,* May 7, 2013, http://www.pepsico.com; http://www.fritolays.com/lays/; Jenna Mullins, "The Submissions for New Lay's Chip Flavors Are Getting Out of Control (but We Love It)," *E! Online,* http://www.eonline.com/.

55. Andy Shaw, "How to Create a Facebook Ad Campaign," *Social Media Tips,* September 23, 2011, http://exploringsocialmedia.com/how-to-create-a-facebook-ad-campaign/.

56. Red Bull Stratos, "Scientific Data Review," http://www.redbullstratos.com.

57. Rick Mulready, "The Secret to Red Bull's Media Success Is There Is No Secret," November 6, 2013, http://rickmulready.com.

58. SocialBakers, "Red Bull Stratos on Social Media," http://www.socialbakers.com.

59. Ibid.

60. Jack Bell, "Red Bulls' Henry Strikes a Pose, and Starts a Trend," *The New York Times,* September 21, 2013.

61. http://www.newyorkredbulls.com/.

62. Clint Boulton, "Red Bull Eyes 'SoLoMo' Software to Grow Business," *The Wall Street Journal,* April 30, 2012.

63. *Wall Street Journal Live,* "Lunch Break: Interview with John Jurgensen," December 20, 2013, http://online.wsj.com.

64. David Moth, "How Red Bull Uses Facebook, Twitter, Pinterest, and Google+," *eConsultancy.com,* February 21, 2013, http://econsultancy.com.

i. Stuart Elliot, "Live Commercials Coming to 'Late Night,'" *The New York Times,* September 18, 2013; Jeanine Poggi, "Lexus to Air Live Ads, Fueled by Social Suggestions, during NBC's 'Late Night,'" *Advertising Age,* September 18, 2013; Chris Perry, "How Social Media Propelled Fallon's Tonight Show Takeover," *Forbes,* April 6, 2013; YouTube, "Late Night with Jimmy Fallon," http://www.youtube.com/user/latenight.

ii. http://www.hubspot.com/customers/hy-line-cruises.

iii. Ann-Christine Diaz, "Facebook 101: Is Your Brand Worth a Like?" *Ad Age Digital,* January 30, 2012; Emil Protalinski, "Facebook Passes 1.19 Billion Monthly Active Users, 874 Million Mobile Users, and 728 Million Daily Users," *The Next Web,* October 30, 2013, http://www.thenextweb.com; Pam Dyer, "Facebook Advertising Case Study: Clorox Green Works," http://www.pamorama.net/2011/02/26/facebook-advertising-case-study-clorox-green-works/.

iv. M. P. Mueller, "Small Businesses That Understand Social Media," *The New York Times,* July 11, 2011, http://blogs.nytimes.com; David H. Freedman, "Debating the Merits of Facebook and Google+," *The New York Times,* February 7, 2012, http://blogs.nytimes.com.

Credits

Opener: Anthony Shop & Social Driver, copyright 2013; p. 85: © Chris Ryan/OJO Images/Getty Images; p. 86: © NBC, Lloyd Bishop/AP Images; p. 87: © Genevieve Ross/AP Images ; p. 88(top): Courtesy WATERisLIFE; p. 88(bottom): Courtesy of Staples, Inc.; p. 89(top): © Oleg Albinsky/iStock/360/Getty Images RF; p. 89(bottom): Courtesy Temptalia.com; p. 91: © Weng lei - Imaginechina via AP Images; p.92(top): © Michelle Pemberton/Rapport Press/Newscom; p. 92(bottom): Courtesy LinkedIn; p. 93: © Dave M. Benett/Getty Images Entertainment/Getty Images; p. 94: Courtesy HSN, Inc.; p. 95: © John Boud/Alamy; p. 96: Courtesy Wegmans; p. 98(top): © Gabriel Bouys/AFP/Getty Images; p. 98(bottom): © Keepin sh - Imaginechina via AP Images; p. 99(top): Courtesy MyFitnessPal, Inc.; p. 99(bottom): © Alliance Images/Alamy; p. 102: Courtesy NFL Properties, LLC; p.103: © copyright salesforce.com, inc. Used with permission.; p. 104: © Richard Levine/Alamy; p. 108: © PRNewsFoto/PRNEWSWIRE/Red Bull Media House via AP Images.

MARKETING ETHICS

LO1 Identify the ethical values marketers should embrace.

LO2 Distinguish between ethics and social responsibility.

LO3 Identify the four steps in ethical decision making.

LO4 Describe how ethics can be integrated into a firm's marketing strategy.

LO5 Describe the ways in which corporate social responsibility programs help various stakeholders.

Imagine if every time you played Angry Birds or some other silly, fun game on your mobile phone, personally identifying information—such as your location, the other apps loaded on your phone, your gender, your age, your political leanings, your sexual orientation, and your buying habits—got sent to a massive data repository, accessible to various marketers and government agencies. Or don't just imagine it. Read about it in documents leaked by the infamous Edward Snowden.[1] Such information gathering is really nothing new, of course. When people access the web through their computers, they create cookies, or snippets of data that enable marketers to discern where a shopper starts the search process, how he or she proceeds, and where the online encounter ends—as well as what the shopper buys, or doesn't. A long history of arguments—even before the computer era—debated the acceptability of wiretaps on telephones, whether traditional or mobile, and whether governments had the right to gather specific information (e.g., recordings) or only metadata (e.g., general information about the number called, when, and for how long).

DOWNLOAD   PLAY NOW   WATCH

ANGRY BIRDS

iPhone iPad Android Kindle
Mac PC Windows Phone

DOWNLOAD

ANGRY BIRDS STAR WARS

iPhone iPad Android Kindle
Windows Phone 8 Mac PC
Windows 8

DOWNLOAD

BAD PIGGIES

iPhone iPad Android Kindle
Mac PC

DOWNLOAD

These debates are complex, in-depth, and serious. They also are becoming increasingly important for marketers as the marketing environment expands to include advanced technology and brand-new methods for collecting data. On one side, the marketing industry has sought to find solutions and self-regulation that would calm customers, avoid the imposition of stronger regulations, and still enable marketing firms to gain access to valuable information about consumer behaviors. But those attempts appear to have stalled, because the online marketing industry simply has not been able to agree about how to police itself. On the other side, legislation introduced by the U.S. Senate attempts to police these activities, mandating the provision of a do-not-track option that would allow computer users to opt-out, easily and quickly, from cookie implantations.[2]

Yet cookies might not be the real problem for much longer. In the growing movement away from computer interfaces and toward mobile commerce, marketers can turn to cutting-edge technologies to locate customers through their smartphones and other devices, determine their collective behaviors, and target them with incredibly specific advertisements. For example, a new venture called Drawbridge (founded by a former employee of Google's mobile advertising division) maintains partnerships with various advertising platforms and publishers, which create notifications of every visit a user makes to a website or app. These notifications in turn enter data analyses that rely on statistical modeling to determine which person is using which devices and link them together—as well as determine whether multiple users rely on the same device. Thus when a person downloads an app through her phone, then later visits a site that appeared in that app, the software enables advertisers to connect those devices as belonging to a single user. In turn, information from both devices gets integrated. The next day, if this user visits a travel site through her computer, she might receive an advertisement for rental cars through her phone. However, if her spouse visits a gaming site instead, Drawbridge knows that it is a different user and personalizes the advertising accordingly.[3]

Many consumers reject such tactics and issue increasing demands for privacy protections. Online browsers, such as Apple's Safari and Mozilla's Firefox, have introduced or are working on cookie-blocking technology, which might just prompt marketers to seek new ways to get around the blocks. Instead, noting the increasing sophistication of the technologies, some mobile service providers are asking for users' permission to track them. For example, Verizon promised coupons to consumers who agreed to let it share information about their mobile browsing behaviors with advertisers, and AT&T simply announced that it had begun selling aggregated consumer data to advertisers.

Denying that they are tracking users has proved unsuccessful, because it largely is not true. Microsoft faced great embarrassment recently: Just weeks after it initiated a publicity campaign that asserted that its consumers' privacy was its top priority, Snowden-related leaks showed that the U.S. National Security Administration had been tapping its records for half a decade.[4]

The scandal surrounding wiretapping by government agencies, especially in the United States and United Kingdom, adds another wrinkle to this discussion. A recent estimate by Forrester Research suggested that consumer fear and worry—sparked by the disclosure that spy agencies were collecting vast amounts of personal data from Internet and mobile service providers—would cost the cloud computing industry approximately $180 billion in lost revenues.[5]

The reason for marketers' insistence on using cookies and other tracking technologies, even in the face of customer discontent and legislative threats, is the outstanding value that the information collected can provide. Only by knowing how, when, and where people really browse online and through their mobile devices can marketers make sure that they target consumers accurately. These data also represent a major source of revenue for targeted advertising firms that sell consumer data to other advertisers, promising the most accurate information when it comes to selecting who will receive their marketing messages. But they also represent potentially serious intrusions into people's privacy. Thus marketers sit at the heart of modern, international discussions of the efficacy, ethicality, and effectiveness of technological snooping.

Which is the more important corporate objective: making a profit or obtaining, keeping, and protecting customers?[6] Although firms cannot stay in business without earning a profit, using profit as the sole guiding light for corporate action can lead to short-term decisions that cause the firm to lose customers in the long run. The balancing act may turn out to be the quest to place the company on the firmest footing possible.

This question leads into the primary ethical dilemma facing managers, that is, how to balance shareholder interests with the needs of society. In our opening example, consumers seek greater protections of their privacy, whereas marketers want access to more and better data about those individual consumers to be able to target them with appealing products, at the right time, in the right place, and at the right price—and thereby make more sales.

Other industries face similar ethical dilemmas and seek to find appropriate balances. Since the early 2000s, most processed foods (e.g., cereals, salad dressings) have contained ingredients made from plants whose DNA has been manipulated in a laboratory. To weather frosts better and produce a greater yield of crops, tomatoes are spliced with salmon genes, for example. Such genetically modified organisms, or GMOs, appear in a majority of the foods that U.S. consumers eat daily, yet most people remain unaware of their presence because the U.S. Food and Drug Administration does not require GMO food product labeling.[7] The ethical question for food manufacturers is whether they label their products as containing GMOs. On one hand, many consumers express a preference to know and worry about potential negative health effects (though no available scientific evidence has confirmed this threat). On the other hand, genetic modifications increase crop yields and lower production costs, and avoiding a GMO label could help companies sell more of their products. Most food manufacturers seem to be fighting GMO labeling. However, in 2014 General Mills decided to make some of its products, such as Cheerios, completely free of GMOs, and Whole Foods has committed to issuing labels on all GMO-containing foods it sells by 2018.[8]

Whole Foods has committed to issuing labels on all GMO-containing foods it sells by 2018.

As these examples show, sometimes the ethical dilemma has as much to do with defining our terms as with what the products contain. But even if the question seems to be one of terminology, if customers believe they can no longer trust a company or that the company is not acting responsibly, they will no longer support that company by purchasing its products or services or investing in its stock. For marketers, the firm's ability to build and maintain consumer trust by conducting ethical, transparent, clear transactions must be of paramount importance.

In this chapter, we start by examining what marketing ethics is and why behaving ethically is so important to successful marketing and to long-term profits. We then discuss how firms can create an ethical climate among employees and how their individual behavior can affect the ability of the firm to act ethically. To help you make ethical marketing decisions, we provide a framework for ethical decision making and then examine some ethical issues within the context of the marketing plan (from Chapter 2). Finally, in Appendix 4A we present some scenarios that highlight typical ethical challenges marketing managers often must face.

THE SCOPE OF MARKETING ETHICS

Business ethics refers to the moral or ethical dilemmas that might arise in a business setting. **Marketing ethics**, in contrast, examines those ethical problems that are specific to the domain of marketing. Firms' attempts to apply sound ethical principles must be a continuous and dynamic process.[9] The nearby cartoon illustrates the importance of making good ethical decisions. Because the marketing profession is often singled out among business disciplines as the root cause of a host of ethical lapses (e.g., unethical advertising, the promotion of shoddy products), anyone involved in marketing must recognize the ethical implications of his or her actions. These can involve societal issues, such as the sale of products or services that may damage the environment; global issues, such as the use of

child labor (see Chapter 8 as well); and individual consumer issues, such as deceptive advertising[10] or the marketing of dangerous products.[11] **Deceptive advertising** is a representation, omission, act, or practice in an advertisement that is likely to mislead consumers acting reasonably under the circumstances.

ETHICAL ISSUES ASSOCIATED WITH MARKETING DECISIONS

Unlike other business functions such as accounting or finance, people in marketing interact directly with the public. Because they are in the public eye, it should not be surprising that marketing and sales professionals sometimes rank poorly in ratings of the most trusted professions. In a recent Gallup survey, most professions were rated much higher than advertising or sales professions—lobbyists came in last, and members of Congress fared only slightly better, about the same as car salespeople[12] (see Exhibit 4.1.) For marketers, who depend on the long-term trust of their customers, this low ranking is very disappointing.

Yet there is some good news too.[13] Although many consumers remain highly skeptical of business, and especially of marketing, the marketing function interacts with a vast number of entities outside the firm on a regular basis. Therefore, it has a tremendous opportunity to build public trust. Creating an ethical climate that establishes the health and well-being of consumers as the firm's number one priority just makes good business sense.

| EXHIBIT 4.1 | Attitudes about Ethical Standards of Various Professions |

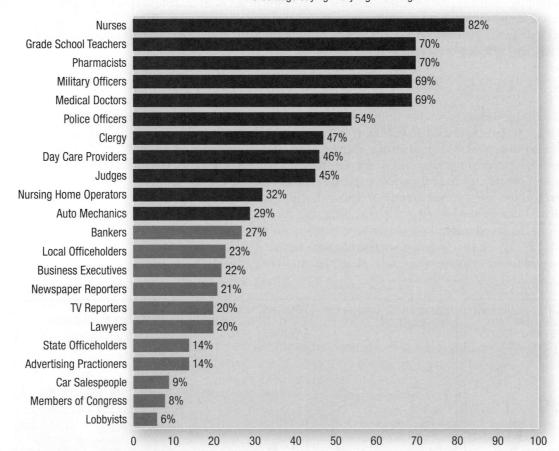

Percentage saying "very high" or "high"

Profession	Percentage
Nurses	82%
Grade School Teachers	70%
Pharmacists	70%
Military Officers	69%
Medical Doctors	69%
Police Officers	54%
Clergy	47%
Day Care Providers	46%
Judges	45%
Nursing Home Operators	32%
Auto Mechanics	29%
Bankers	27%
Local Officeholders	23%
Business Executives	22%
Newspaper Reporters	21%
TV Reporters	20%
Lawyers	20%
State Officeholders	14%
Advertising Practioners	14%
Car Salespeople	9%
Members of Congress	8%
Lobbyists	6%

Creating an Ethical Climate in the Workplace

The process of creating a strong ethical climate within a marketing firm (or in the marketing division of any firm) includes having a set of values that guides decision making and behavior such as Johnson & Johnson's credo. General Robert Wood Johnson wrote and published the first "credo" for Johnson & Johnson (J&J) in 1943[14]—a one-page document outlining the firm's commitments and responsibilities to its various stakeholders. The J&J credo can be summarized as follows:

> We believe our first responsibility is to doctors, nurses, patients, mothers, fathers, and all others who use our products and services. We are responsible to our employees. We must respect their dignity and recognize their merit. Compensation must be fair and adequate and working conditions clean, orderly, and safe. We are responsible to the communities in which we live and work and to the world community as well. Our final responsibility is to our stockholders. When we operate according to these principles, the stockholders should realize a fair return.

Today, J&J continues to follow this credo in its daily business practices, as was evidenced by the infamous Tylenol recall. In the 1980s, seven people taking Tylenol died of cyanide poisoning. Without worrying initially about whether the poison got into the products during production or on the shelf, J&J immediately and voluntarily withdrew all Tylenol from the market until it could ensure its products' safety.

Even more recently, J&J responded to new limits on acetaminophen dosages (the active ingredient in Tylenol) by reassuring consumers that they were safe—as long as they followed the dosage instructions on the packaging.[15] In advertising communications that touted Tylenol as "the safest brand of pain reliever you can choose," J&J also was careful to remind people that taking more than the recommended dosage could cause them serious liver damage.

Nurses and doctors are among the most trusted professionals.

But not all firms operate according to the principles in J&J's credo. For instance, Merck & Co. withdrew its highly successful drug Vioxx from the marketplace because of evidence that it increased the chance of heart attacks and strokes in patients taking the drug.[16] But the move came at least four years after studies found individuals using Vioxx had a greater number of cardiovascular problems than an older, established medication. Although Merck continued to monitor these ongoing studies, it did not act nor did it initiate new studies. In another pharmaceutical example, AstraZeneca, the maker of the schizophrenia drug Seroquel, faced sanctions and fines for misrepresenting the appropriate uses of the drug to medical practitioners. Eventually, AstraZeneca agreed to pay $520 million to settle the claims of its unethical, "off-label" marketing efforts.[17] Would Merck and AstraZeneca have performed more ethically had they been working with J&J's credo for ethical behavior?[18]

Johnson & Johnson, makers of Tylenol, continues to act in accordance with its original 1943 "credo" to be responsible to everyone who uses its products and services.

Everyone within a firm must share the same understanding of its ethical values and how they translate into the business activities of the firm. They also need to share a consistent language to discuss them. Once the values are understood, the firm must develop explicit rules and implicit understandings that govern all the firm's transactions. Top management must commit to establishing an ethical climate, and employees throughout the firm must be dedicated to that climate because the roots of ethical conflict often are the competing values of individuals. Each individual holds his or her own set of values, and sometimes those values result in inner turmoil or even conflicts between employees. For instance, a salesperson may believe that it is important to make a sale because her family depends on her for support, but at the same time, she may feel that the product she is selling is not appropriate for a

Adding Value 4.1   Walmart Wants to Be the Corporate "Good Guy"[i]

Walmart is known for its low prices and for driving its vendors nearly to tears to get them. Now it is pressuring its vendors to supply it with environmentally friendly merchandise with labels to prove it. In the future, merchandise sold at Walmart will have the environmental equivalent of nutrition labels, providing information on the product's carbon footprint, the amount of water and air pollution used to produce it, and other environmental issues. To measure how a vendor's products are doing, it has developed a sustainability index that simultaneously takes several issues into consideration. In particular, Walmart required its top 200 factories to cut their energy usage by 20 percent by 2012. Walmart achieved this amazing goal, reducing energy consumption by 2.168 kilowatt-hours, or the equivalent amount of energy that would be needed to power 1.46 million homes for a whole year.

It also has committed to buying more of the products it sells in its U.S. stores from U.S. suppliers, in an effort to address high unemployment rates. More directly, it has promised to hire up to 100,000 U.S. veterans, to help address the job challenges many soldiers face upon leaving the military.

Nor has Walmart limited its efforts to the United States. It has sought to increase food safety in China, where the relatively underdeveloped infrastructure can create the danger of contamination of fresh and packaged food products. Walmart created a fleet of customized vans, outfitted with the latest tools for conducting food safety inspections. The vans, staffed by trained specialists, deliver the "China Mobile Labs"

to 33 stores throughout Guangzhou, Dongguan, and Shenzhen and ensure the safety and quality of the products they sell.

To reduce the use of plastic bags, and thereby mitigate harm to the environment, Walmart has initiated several campaigns. In particular, plastic bag usage has dropped significantly throughout Asia—by 40 percent in Japan, 86 percent in China, and 90 percent in India.

Walmart has not always been touted as a good corporate citizen, though. In the 1990s, workers at some factories producing clothing for Walmart alleged they had been subjected to inhumane conditions. More recently, two governmental organizations accused Walmart of buying from 15 factories that engage in abuse and labor violations, including child labor, 19-hour shifts, and below-subsistence wages. It and other companies have also been accused of dumping hazardous waste in Oklahoma City.

So why is Walmart attempting to position itself as the retail industry's sustainability leader? The initiatives and related publicity position Walmart as a good corporate citizen and thereby enhance its image. But the retail giant expects its moves to be good for business as well. Its customers, especially younger consumers, are increasingly concerned about how the products they use affect the environment and the people who produce them. Furthermore, Walmart believes that many of these initiatives can help streamline its supply chain processes and therefore provide additional financial benefits to its suppliers and customers.

Why is Walmart attempting to position itself as the retail industry's sustainability leader?

particular customer. Once the rules are in place, there must be a system of controls that helps resolve such dilemmas and rewards appropriate behavior—that is, behavior consistent with the firm's values—and punishes inappropriate behavior. Adding Value 4.1 examines how Walmart is pushing to be a better corporate citizen on several fronts.

Like companies that develop and apply their ethical codes, many professions, including the marketing profession, also have their own codes of ethics that firms and individuals in the profession agree to abide by. The generally accepted code in marketing, developed by the American Marketing Association, flows from universal norms of conduct to the specific values to which marketers should aspire.[19] It indicates that the basic ethical values marketers should aspire to are honesty, responsibility, fairness, respect, openness, and citizenship. Each subarea within marketing, such as marketing research, advertising, pricing, and so forth, has its own code of ethics that deals with the specific issues that arise when conducting business in those areas.

Now let's examine the ethical role of the individuals within the firm and how individuals contribute to the firm's ethical climate.

The Influence of Personal Ethics

LO1 Identify the ethical values marketers should embrace.

Every firm is made up of individuals, each with his or her own needs and desires. Let's start by looking at why people may make *un*ethical decisions and how firms can establish a process for decision making that ensures they choose ethical alternatives instead.

Why People Act Unethically Every individual is a product of his or her culture, upbringing, genes, and various other influences. Yet people also continue to grow emotionally in their understanding of what is and is not ethical behavior. As a six-year-old child, you might have thought nothing of taking your brother's toy and bonking him on the head with it. As an adult, you probably have outgrown this behavior. But all of us vary in the way we view more complex situations, depending on our ethical understandings.

Consider product recalls of toys, for example. How can certain manufacturers engage in such egregious behavior as using lead paint on toys or including magnets that can be swallowed in toys marketed toward young children? What makes people take actions that create so much harm? Are all the individuals who contributed to that behavior just plain immoral? These simple questions have complex answers.

As another example, imagine that a brand manager for a car company discovers from conversations with a member of the development team that the hot new energy-efficient hybrid model that is set to go into full production shortly has a potentially dangerous design flaw. There are two options for the brand manager: delay production and remedy the design flaw, which pushes production off schedule, delays revenue, and may result in layoffs and loss of the manager's bonus; or stay on schedule, put the flawed design into production, achieve planned revenues and bonus, and hope it does not result in injuries to consumers and loss of revenue for the firm due to recalls later. This type of dilemma occurs nearly every day in thousands of business environments.

When asked in a survey whether they had seen any unethical behavior among their colleagues, chief marketing officers responded that they had observed employees participating in high-pressure, misleading, or deceptive sales tactics (45 percent); misrepresenting company earnings, sales, and/or revenues (35 percent); withholding or destroying information that could hurt company sales or image (32 percent); and conducting false or misleading advertising (31 percent).[20] Did all the marketers in these situations view their actions as unethical? Probably not. There may have been extenuating circumstances. In marketing, managers often face the choice of doing what is beneficial for them and possibly the firm in the short run and doing what is right and beneficial for the firm and society in the long run.

For instance, a manager might feel confident that earnings will increase in the next few months and therefore believe it benefits himself, his branch, and his employees to exaggerate current earnings just a little. Another manager might

What is the "real" price? Did the manager bring the T-shirts in at an artificially high level and then immediately mark them down?

feel considerable pressure to increase sales in a retail store, so she brings in some new merchandise, marks it at an artificially high price, and then immediately puts it on sale, deceiving consumers into thinking they are getting a good deal because they viewed the initial price as the real price. These decisions may have been justifiable at the time, but they have serious consequences for the company.

To avoid such dire consequences, the short-term goals of each employee must be aligned with the long-term goals of the firm. In our hybrid car example, the brand manager's short-term drive to receive a bonus conflicted with the firm's long-term aim of providing consumers with safe, reliable cars. To align personal and corporate goals, firms need to have a strong ethical climate, explicit rules for governing transactions including a code of ethics, and a system for rewarding and punishing inappropriate behavior.

In the next section, we add the concept of corporate social responsibility to our discussion of ethics.

 Distinguish between ethics and social responsibility.

Ethics and Corporate Social Responsibility

Although no single, established definition of the concept exists,[21] **corporate social responsibility (CSR)** generally entails voluntary actions taken by a company to address the ethical, social, and environmental impacts of its business operations and the concerns of its stakeholders. The AMA's definition refers to it as the serious consideration of "the impact of the company's actions and operating in a way that balances short-term profit needs with society's long-term needs, thus ensuring the company's survival in a healthy environment."[22] This notion goes beyond the individual ethics that we've discussed so far, but for a company to act in a socially responsible manner, the employees of the company must also first maintain high ethical standards and recognize how their individual decisions lead to optimal collective actions of the firm. Firms with strong ethical climates tend to be more socially responsible.

Dannon, which makes Activia yogurt products, is both ethical and socially responsible. It has an ethical commitment to make healthy food. It is socially responsible since it is involved in many activities and charities that help people.

However, it is important to distinguish between ethical business practices and corporate social responsibility programs. Ideally, firms should implement programs that are socially responsible, *and* its employees should act in an ethically responsible manner. (See Exhibit 4.2, upper left quadrant.) Dannon yogurt, for example, has long supported internal research into healthy eating, which supports its ethical commitment to bring "health food to as many people as possible."[23] It is also socially responsible, in that it donates food and money to the hunger-relief charity Feeding America, encourages employees to volunteer in their communities, holds annual Children's Day outreach programs, and reduces its environmental footprints.

Being socially responsible generally means going above and beyond the norms of corporate ethical behavior. For example, a firm's employees may conduct their activities in an ethically acceptable manner, but the firm may still not be considered socially responsible because its activities have little or no impact on anyone other than its closest stakeholders: its customers, employees, and stockholders (Exhibit 4.2, upper right quadrant).

EXHIBIT 4.2   Ethics versus Social Responsibility

Ethics versus Social Responsibility

	Socially Responsible	Socially Irresponsible
Ethical	Both ethical and socially responsible	Ethical firm not involved with the larger community
Unethical	Questionable firm practices, yet donates a lot to the community	Neither ethical nor socially responsible

Employees at some firms that are perceived as socially responsible can nevertheless take actions that are viewed as unethical (Exhibit 4.2, lower left quadrant). For instance, a firm might be considered socially responsible because it makes generous donations to charities but is simultaneously involved in questionable sales practices. Walmart was recently ranked as the worst-paying company by the National Employment Law Project, but even as it was underpaying its employees, it was donating more than $1 billion in cash and in-kind items to charitable causes.[24] Ethically, how do we characterize a firm that obtains its profits in part through questionable practices, then donates a large percentage of those profits to charity? The worst situation, of course, is when firms behave both unethically and in a socially unacceptable manner (Exhibit 4.2, lower right quadrant).

Investors more and more desire to invest in firms that are socially responsible, and consumers increasingly are purchasing services and products from these companies. They also may be willing to pay more if they can be assured the companies truly are ethical.[25] According to a recent poll conducted by *Time magazine,* even in economically constrained settings, 38 percent of U.S. consumers actively tried to purchase from companies they considered responsible. The magazine cites the rise of the "ethical consumer" and the evolution of the social contract "between many Americans and businesses about what goes into making the products we buy."[26]

With such ethical consumers making up more and more of the market, many large companies have recognized that they must be perceived as socially responsible by their stakeholders to earn their business. Other companies began their operations with such a commitment, as Adding Value 4.2 describes.

We cannot expect every member of a firm always to act ethically. However, a framework for ethical decision making can help move people to work toward common ethical goals.

Walmart employees protest low wages.

Adding Value 4.2   The Barefoot Entrepreneur[ii]

Blake Mycoskie doesn't just want his customers to buy his shoes; he wants to turn them into benefactors. In this innovative approach to marketing, his company, TOMS Shoes, does not just engage in charitable acts; the charitable acts are the company. There is no separating TOMS from the social responsibility it embraces.

Mycoskie started out manufacturing a revised version of a traditional Argentinean shoe called alpargatas and selling them to consumers outside their generally impoverished source nation. The combination of the comfortable shoes and the extreme poverty he observed led to a simple code: "You buy a pair of TOMS, and I give a pair to a child on your behalf. One for One." Thus, consumers who buy TOMS Shoes do so because they know that with their purchase, they help donate shoes to people in need. Their choices reflect their desire to make their money count for something.

As the company has grown, it also has added lines of vegan and recycled shoes. Most recently, it expanded into sunglasses, where the One for One philosophy dictates that for every pair sold, TOMS provides eye care, such as medicines, glasses, or surgery, to someone else in the world at risk of losing his or her sight.

But when it comes to procuring other products, finding a socially responsible seller that actively engages in tactics to benefit people and communities might remain challenging for individual shoppers. Therefore, Mycoskie determined that he would bring together sellers and vendors whose work benefited communities onto one online platform. Then shoppers could visit a single site, where they knew that each item they purchased had social, as well as consumption, benefits.

On the TOMS Marketplace website, visitors can search by product line (e.g., apparel, tech, accessories), by their preferred cause (e.g., education, job creation, water), by global region, or by brand. The approximately 200 different products benefit diverse causes: Buying a backpack from Stone + Cloth funds education initiatives in East Africa, whereas the purchase of handmade wooden headphones from LSTN means that the

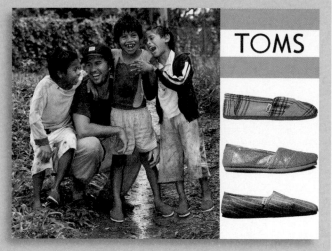

When you buy a pair of TOMS shoes, it gives a pair to a child in need.

company will help restore the hearing of a person with hearing impairment.

Although the TOMS model remains dedicated to a buy one, give one approach, the Marketplace does not require the same commitment from all its 30 or so sellers. Instead, Mycoskie reviews each provider to ensure it "had a mission of improving people's lives baked into its business model." Furthermore, TOMS purchases all the products on the site. In that sense, it functions like a wholesaler that not only procures supply but also takes responsibility for storing, warehousing, shipping, and other logistics.

Detractors argue that TOMS actually may do some harm, in that its provisions might reduce demand for locally produced products. But TOMS already has given away more than 1 million pairs of shoes, so consumers have bought at least that many—at an average price of $55 per pair. Clearly, the value they find in these cloth shoes goes well beyond the simple linen and canvas parts that go into making them.

LO3 Identify the four steps in ethical decision making.

A Framework for Ethical Decision Making

Exhibit 4.3 outlines a simple framework for ethical decision making. Let's consider each of the steps.

Step 1: Identify Issues The first step is to identify the issue. For illustrative purposes, we'll investigate the use (or misuse) of data collected from consumers by a marketing research firm. One of the issues that might arise is the way the data are collected. For instance, are the respondents told about the real purpose of the study? Another issue might be whether the results will be used in a way that might mislead or even harm the public, such as selling the information to a firm to use in soliciting the respondents.

Step 2: Gather Information and Identify Stakeholders In this step, the firm focuses on gathering facts that are important to the ethical issue, including all

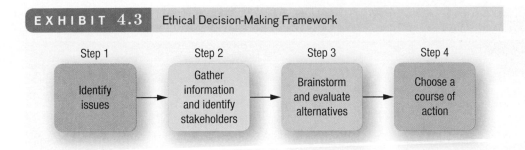

EXHIBIT 4.3 Ethical Decision-Making Framework

relevant legal information. To get a complete picture, the firm must identify all the individuals and groups that have a stake in how the issue is resolved.

Stakeholders typically include the firm's employees and retired employees, suppliers, the government, customer groups, stockholders, and members of the community in which the firm operates. Beyond these, many firms now also analyze the needs of the industry and the global community, as well as one-off stakeholders such as future generations and the natural environment itself. In describing its sustainability and transparency efforts, for example, the electronics firm Philips notes that it tries to communicate with and consider "anyone with an interest in Philips."[27]

Step 3: Brainstorm Alternatives After the marketing firm has identified the stakeholders and their issues and gathered the available data, all parties relevant to the decision should come together to brainstorm any alternative courses of action. In our example, these might include halting the market research project, making responses anonymous, instituting training on the AMA Code of Ethics for all researchers, and so forth. Management then reviews and refines these alternatives, leading to the final step.

Step 4: Choose a Course of Action The objective of this last step is to weigh the various alternatives and choose a course of action that generates the best solution for the stakeholders, using ethical practices. Management will rank the alternatives in order of preference, clearly establishing the advantages and disadvantages of each. It is also crucial to investigate any potential legal issues associated with each alternative. Of course, any illegal activity should be rejected immediately.

To choose the appropriate course of action, marketing managers will evaluate each alternative by using a process something like the sample ethical decision-making metric in Exhibit 4.4. The marketer's task here is to ensure that he or she has applied all relevant decision-making criteria and to assess his or her level of confidence that the decision being made meets those stated criteria. If the marketer isn't confident about the decision, he or she should reexamine the other alternatives. Using Exhibit 4.4, you can gauge your own ethical response. If your scores tend to be in the green area (1 and 2), then the situation is not an ethically troubling situation for you. If, in contrast, your scores tend to be in the red area (6 and 7), it is ethically troubling, and you know it. If your scores are scattered or in the yellow area, you need to step back and reflect on how you wish to proceed.

In using such an ethical metric or framework, decision makers must consider the relevant ethical issues, evaluate the alternatives, and then choose a course of action that will help them avoid serious ethical lapses.

Next, let's illustrate how the ethical decision-making metric in Exhibit 4.4 can be used to make ethical business decisions.

Myra Jansen, the head cook at Lincoln High School in Anytown, USA, has had enough. Reports showing that children rarely eat enough vegetables have combined with studies that indicate school kids have a limited amount of time to eat their lunches. The combination has led to increasing obesity rates and troublesome reports about the long-term effects. Myra has therefore decided that the Tater Tots and hotdogs are out. Vegetables and healthy proteins are in.

EXHIBIT 4.4	Ethical Decision-Making Metric

	Decision						
	Yes		Maybe			No	
Test	1	2	3	4	5	6	7
The Publicity Test Would I want to see this action that I'm about to take described on the front page of the local paper or in a national magazine?							
The Moral Mentor Test Would the person I admire the most engage in this activity?							
The Admired Observer Test Would I want the person I admire most to see me doing this?							
The Transparency Test Could I give a clear explanation for the action I'm contemplating, including an honest and transparent account of all my motives, that would satisfy a fair and dispassionate moral judge?							
The Person in the Mirror Test Will I be able to look at myself in the mirror and respect the person I see there?							
The Golden Rule Test Would I like to be on the receiving end of this action and all its potential consequences?							

Source: Adapted from *The Art of Achievement: Mastering the 7 Cs of Business and Life.* © 2002 by Tom Morris, published by Andrews McMeel Publishing LLC, an Andrews McMeel Universal company, Kansas City, Missouri.

The problem, of course, is getting the kids to eat raw vegetables, plant proteins, and lean meat. For many teenagers, recommending that they eat healthy food at lunch is akin to calling detention a play date. But Myra has a plan: She's going to reformulate various menu items using different ingredients and just never tell the students. Thus the regular hot dogs will be replaced with turkey or soy dogs. The Tater Tots will contain the more nutrient-dense sweet potatoes instead of the vitamin-deficient regular spuds they used to be made out of. She is convinced she can make such switches for most of the menu items, and none of the children need to know.

Most of the kitchen staff members are onboard with the idea and even have suggested other possible menu switches that would benefit the students by ensuring that they receive a well-balanced meal at school. School board members, when apprised of the idea, got very excited and praised Myra for her innovative thinking. But the community liaison for the school, whose job it is to communicate with parents and other members of the community, is not so sure. Salim Jones is nervous about how students will react when they learn that they have been deceived. He also has two small children of his own, one of whom has a severe wheat allergy. Thus the Joneses are extremely cautious about eating out, always asking for a detailed, specific list of ingredients for anything they order.

Using his training in ethical decision making, Salim sits down to evaluate his alternatives, beginning with identifying possible options available to the school district as well as the various stakeholders who might be affected by the decision. He comes up with the following list:

1. Switch out the food without telling students.

2. Leave menus as they are.

3. Switch out the food ingredients but also tell students exactly what is in each item in the cafeteria.

To make a clear recommendation to the board about what would be the best ethical choice, Salim decides to evaluate each alternative using a series of questions similar to those in Exhibit 4.4.

Question 1: Would I want to see this action described on the front page of the local paper? The school board's reaction caused Salim to think that the larger community would appreciate the effort to improve students' health. Thus, option 1 appears best for these stakeholders, and possibly for society, which may reduce the prevalence of obesity among these students. However, he shudders to think about how angry students might be if they learned they had been tricked. They also likely are accustomed to their menu as it is, and therefore, they would prefer option 2.

Question 2: Would the person I admire most engage in this activity, and would I want him or her to see me engage in this activity? For most of his life, Salim has held up Mahatma Gandhi as his ideal for how to act in the world. For Gandhi, truth was an absolute concept, not something that could be changed depending on the situation. Therefore, Salim believes Gandhi would strongly disapprove of option 1. However, Gandhi also worried about the ethics of eating and avoided food choices that had negative effects on society, so he might reject option 2 as well.

Question 3: Can I give a clear explanation for my action, including an honest account of my motives? In thinking about his children, Salim realizes that he is prioritizing their needs, more so than the needs of other children, such as those who struggle with weight issues. That is, he worries that his daughter might unknowingly be exposed to wheat in a school cafeteria, so he prefers option 3.

Question 4: Will I be able to look at myself in the mirror and respect what I see? By bringing up the ethics of this decision, even when it seems as if everyone else has agreed with it, Salim feels confident that he has taken the right first step. The option chosen is still important, but it is a group decision, and Salim thinks he is doing his part.

Question 5: Would I want to be on the receiving end of this action and its consequences? Salim struggles most with this question. He remembers the kind of junk foods he chose when he was in college and the 20 pounds he put on as a result. He wishes now that his parents had given him rules to follow about what to eat at school. But he also remembers how rebellious he was and knows that he probably would not have followed those rules. And at the same time, he hates the idea that someone could give him food to eat with falsified ingredients.

On the basis of this exercise, Salim decides that he wants to recommend option 3 to the school board. When he does so, Myra Jansen protests loudly: "This is ridiculous! I know better what kids should be eating, and I know too that some community liaison has no idea what they are willing to eat. You've got to trick them to get them to eat right." Another school board member agrees, noting, "They're just kids. They don't necessarily have the same rights as adults, so we are allowed to decide what's best for them. And hiding the healthy ingredients to get the kids to eat healthy foods is what's best."

So what does the school board decide?

CHECK YOURSELF

1. Identify the stages in the ethical decision-making framework.

LO4 Describe how ethics can be integrated into a firm's marketing strategy.

INTEGRATING ETHICS INTO MARKETING STRATEGY

Ethical decision making is not a simple process, though it can get easier as decision makers within the firm become accustomed to thinking about the ethical implications of their actions from a strategic perspective. In this section, we examine how ethical decision making can be integrated into the marketing plan introduced in Chapter 2. The questions vary at each stage of the strategic marketing planning process. For instance, in the planning stage, the firm will decide what level of commitment to its ethical policies and standards it is willing to declare publicly. In the implementation stage, the tone of the questions switches from "can we?" serve the market with the firm's products or services in an ethically responsible manner to "should we?" be engaging in particular marketing practices. The key task in the control phase is to ensure that all potential ethical issues raised during the planning process have been addressed and that all employees of the firm have acted ethically. Let's take a closer look at how ethics can be integrated at each stage of the strategic marketing planning process.

Planning Phase

Marketers can introduce ethics at the beginning of the planning process simply by including ethical statements in the firm's mission or vision statements (recall our discussion of various mission statements in Chapter 2). Johnson & Johnson has its credo; other firms use mission statements that include both ethical and social responsibility precepts for shaping the organization. For instance, the mission statement for natural skin care company Burt's Bees is to "create natural, Earth-friendly personal care products formulated to help you maximize your well-being and that of the world around you,"[28] which reflects not only what is good for its customers but for society in general.

For General Electric, the complexity of its organization and the wealth of ethical issues it faces necessitated an entire booklet, "The Spirit and the Letter." This booklet outlines not only a statement of integrity from the CEO and a code of conduct, but also detailed policies for dealing with everything from international competition laws to security and crisis management to insider trading. In addition, GE publishes an annual citizenship report to determine the scope of its impacts, "produced for the benefit of all stakeholders, including GE employees—the people whose actions define GE every day."[29]

During the planning stage, ethical mission statements can take on another role as a means to guide a firm's SWOT analysis. Newman's Own, for example, has what most would consider a simple but powerful purpose: The company would sell salad dressing (initially; it expanded later to many other product lines) and use the proceeds to benefit charities. This simple idea began in Paul Newman's basement, when he and a friend produced a batch of salad dressing to give as holiday gifts. When they also decided to check with a local grocer to see if it would be interested in the

Since 1982, Newman's Own has given over $400 million to charities like Newman's Hole in the Wall Gang camps for children with life-threatening diseases.

product, they found they could sell 10,000 bottles in two weeks. Thus Newman's Own, a nonprofit organization, quickly grew to include dozens of products. Today, Newman's Own and Newman's Own Organic products are sold in many countries around the world and include more than 100 varieties and dozens of lines, from coffee to popcorn to dog food. Profits from Newman's Own—over $400 million since 1982—have been donated to thousands of charities, especially Newman's Hole in the Wall Gang camps for children with life-threatening diseases.[30]

The unique mission of the company and the entrepreneurial flair of the founders made this nonprofit a smashing, ongoing success. Employees of Newman's Own have the great satisfaction of giving back to society, various charities benefit from the donations, and customers enjoy good food with a clear conscience.

Implementation Phase

In the implementation phase of the marketing strategy, when firms are identifying potential markets and ways to deliver the 4Ps to them, firms must consider several ethical issues. Sometimes a firm's choice of target market and how it pursues it can lead to charges of unethical behavior. For instance, to "like" Grey Poupon's Facebook page consumers would have to apply through their Facebook app. This app would then examine the customer's post history and decide whether the person had "good taste." If they had good taste, they could like the page; if not, then they were not allowed to be part of, as Grey Poupon put it, "the most discerning page on Facebook." Although it may sound fun, there are several privacy issues that made it unethical—users had to allow Grey Poupon to post on their timelines and Grey Poupon got access to their post history.[31] Marketing through social media has some particular ethical concerns associated with it, as Social and Mobile Marketing 4.1 shows.

Once the strategy is implemented, controls must be in place to be certain that the firm has actually done what it has set out to do. These activities take place in the next phase of the strategic marketing planning process.

Control Phase

During the control phase of the strategic marketing planning process, managers must be evaluated on their actions from an ethical perspective. Systems must be in place to check whether each potentially ethical issue raised in the planning process was actually successfully addressed. Systems used in the control phase must also react to change. The emergence of new technologies and new markets ensures that new ethical issues continually arise. In particular, people expect to be able to move normally in public spaces without their location being recorded for subsequent use.[32] Yet marketers regularly collect data on people's location through purchase transactions, and posts on social and mobile sites such as Facebook, Twitter, and Flickr. Additionally, several retailers' credit card systems have been violated resulting in the theft of consumer data of millions of people, the most egregious of which have been the estimated 110 million at Target and 1.1 million at Neiman Marcus at the end of 2013.[33] Although most experts blame the thefts on U.S.-based credit card companies' reticence to adopt a more secure type of credit card that is used in Europe and elsewhere, the retailers and their customers suffer the consequences.

Many firms have emergency response plans in place just in case they ever encounter a situation similar to the Tylenol tampering emergency or an industrial accident at a manufacturing plant. Ethics thus remains an ongoing crucial component of the strategic marketing planning process and should be incorporated into all the firm's decision making down the road.

CHECK YOURSELF

1. What ethical questions should a marketing manager consider at each stage of the marketing plan?

Social & Mobile Marketing 4.1   Who Tweeted Me to Buy a Ford Fiesta?[iii]

Auto manufacturers have long paid celebrities to be spokespeople for their lines of vehicles. But maybe customers really want to hear from people like themselves rather than a celebrity paid millions of dollars to promote a car. Although car companies can save a lot of money by paying normal people less than they pay celebrities, they do not want just anyone to promote their products. They want social media gurus or popular Twitter and blog figures with legions of followers.

Marketing campaigns by Lexus, Ford, and Land Rover all promote their products socially on the web. Ford recruited 100 people with strong online followings to test-drive the Ford Focus and then talk about their experiences online. Ford previously had been successful with its Ford Fiesta campaign, in which anyone who test drove the newly introduced car posted YouTube videos, Flickr photos, and Twitter tweets—adding up to more than 7 million views on YouTube and 4 million mentions on Twitter. As a result, over 130,000 people visited the Ford Fiesta website, 83 percent of whom had never owned a Ford before. The campaign certainly received a lot of attention, though the actual sales conversion has not been disclosed.

Influential online informants also can have negative influences though. Even if a firm pays a blogger or tweeter, no rule can force him or her to write positive reviews. But the likelihood is that a paid blogger will be more positive than an unpaid, disinterested reviewer. Thus the Federal Trade Commission (FTC) has created guidelines for blogging and tweeting, saying that those who post messages must disclose any compensation they may have received for talking about the product. They also must disclose if there is a connection, such as an employee–employer relationship, between the endorser and the marketer of the product that might affect how people evaluate the endorsement.

Ford Fiesta's social media campaign draws attention to its traditional media ads.

But such guidelines have little to say about the growing industry available for selling "fake clicks." Whether a thumbs-up on a YouTube video, following a Twitter account, or liking a Facebook page, a click can be bought for as little as half a cent per click. Want 250 Google+ shares? It'll cost you $12.95 from Buy Plus. For 1,000 followers on Instagram, just pay $12 to InstagramEngine.

Originally, these fake click companies designed software bots to generate fake clicks, but social media companies quickly caught on and blocked them. Now click farms have replaced the bots, such that actual people manually click, all day long, every day. These fake clicks are hard to differentiate from genuine user clicks, and the industry is exploding. An estimated $40 to $360 million was spent buying fraudulent Twitter followers, and more than 14.1 million Facebook accounts are fake.

L05 Describe the ways in which corporate social responsibility programs help various stakeholders.

CORPORATE SOCIAL RESPONSIBILITY

In 1906, Upton Sinclair published *The Jungle,* his novel exposing the horrific conditions in U.S. meatpacking plants, which prompted President Theodore Roosevelt and Congress to force meat companies to take responsibility for the safety of their products. The notion of societal marketing and corporate social responsibility has changed significantly since then, and recent decades have seen its prevalence increase rapidly. Today, companies are undertaking a wide range of corporate social responsibility initiatives, such as establishing corporate charitable foundations; supporting and associating with existing nonprofit groups; supporting minority activities; and following responsible marketing, sales, and production practices. Exhibit 4.5 provides several illustrations of the CSR programs undertaken by major firms.

For example, FedEx seeks social responsibility in several realms,[34] including:

- *Charitable donations.* Through its "Special Delivery" program, FedEx has donated its services to help various charitable organizations collect and then

EXHIBIT 4.5	Sampling of Major Companies' CSR Programs
Company	**Illustration of CSR Program**
Amazon.com	Developed nonprofit Simple Pay Donation system to help nonprofits raise money easily
BMW	Light Up Hope and BMW Children's Safety programs
Coca-Cola	Spent $102 million through The Coca-Cola Campaign focusing on water stewardship, healthy and active lifestyles, community recycling, and education
FedEx	Transported more than 67 planes worth of aid to disaster victims
General Electric	Ecomagination campaign, GE Volunteers Foundation
Google	Google.org funds for pro-profit entrepreneurship in Africa, Google China Social Innovation Cup for College Students
McDonald's	99 percent of fish come from MSC-fisheries, transitioning to sustainable food and packaging sources, Ronald McDonald House charities
Procter & Gamble	Live, Learn, and Thrive improves the lives of children worldwide.
Southwest Airlines	Employees donate volunteer hours to Ronald McDonald Houses throughout the U.S.
Starbucks	Develops ecologically friendly growing practices, LEED certified stores

Source: Adapted from http://money.cnn.com/magazines/fortune/most-admired/.

distribute more than 1 million pounds of food, nearly half a million toys, and a quarter of a million pieces of clothing. More than 90 truckloads, 67 planes, and 15 ocean liners also have carried relief supplies around the globe.

- *Diversity.* FedEx maintains formal groups to ensure it meets global diversity standards. For example, its Corporate Diversity Council develops and promotes diversity programs both within the company and throughout the communities in which FedEx operates. Six different affinity groups provide dedicated support to employees who are African American, Hispanic, Asian, women, LGBT, and dealing with cancer.

- *Fuel conservation.* In line with its stated goal to reduce its greenhouse gas emissions by 20 percent, FedEx is in the process of replacing both its jets and its delivery trucks with more efficient versions. For example, it operates the largest North American commercial fleet of hybrid vehicles, and its new wide-body planes can use a continuous approach on their descent, which reduces their fuel consumption.

- *Alternative energy sources.* Several of FedEx's domestic hub facilities already rely completely on solar power. It also is seeking to add more such facilities across the world.

Some economists and social commentators suggest that CSR is unnecessary and that the goal of any corporation in a capitalist economy is single and simple: make money.[35] The fallout from the recent global economic crisis seems to have pushed economists to repudiate this school of thought. But how does it benefit the company or its shareholders if a company worries about such unquantifiable issues as being a good citizen?

When companies embrace CSR, they appeal not only to their shareholders but also to their key stakeholders (Exhibit 4.6), including their own employees, consumers, the marketplace, and society at large. The insurance provider Aflac differentiates its goal "to be a profitable company" from its calling "to be an ethical partner to our stakeholders—one that plays by the rules and demonstrates leadership in the arena of business ethics."[36]

EXHIBIT 4.6 Key CSR Stakeholders

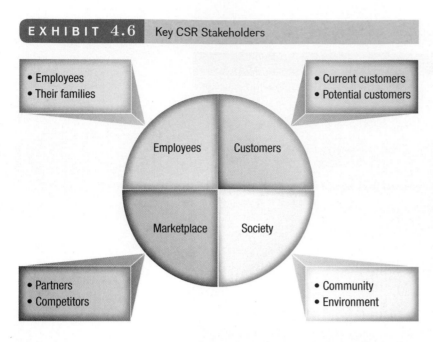

- Employees
- Their families

- Current customers
- Potential customers

Employees | Customers

Marketplace | Society

- Partners
- Competitors

- Community
- Environment

Let's consider each of these stakeholder categories to understand the meaning and effects of corporate social responsibility in the modern marketing arena as well as how CSR ultimately can benefit the firm that undertakes it.

Employees Perhaps the most basic corporate social responsibility to employees is to ensure a safe working environment, free of threats to their physical safety, health, or well-being. In some cases, this basic level of safety seems insufficient to achieve responsibility to workers. Aflac regards its pay-for-performance structure a key element of its responsibility to its employees, with the notion that everyone, from call center operators to the CEO, faces the same compensation standards. In this sense, it ensures equality of treatment and fairness in compensation. In doing so, Aflac earns a reputation as a good place to work and increases the number of people who apply for jobs there. These happy employees also should provide better service to customers, which in turn ensures better outcomes for the firm.

In addition to focusing on employees, more and more firms realize that happy employee families make happy and productive employees. Consequently, firms are focusing their efforts on outreach programs aimed at their employees' families.

Customers Especially as changes in the marketing environment emerge, firms must consider the effects on the customers who currently patronize them and future customers whom they are targeting. Corporate social responsibility programs must take such shifts and trends into account and react to them quickly. A few of the trends that are receiving the most attention include respecting and protecting privacy in an electronic world and ensuring the healthiness of products, especially those aimed at children, as we discuss in this chapter's case study. Moreover, CSR often increases consumer awareness of the firm, which can lead to better brand equity and sales in the long run.

Walt Disney's VoluntEAR program is one of the best CSR programs in the world.

GE is the industry leader in CSR with its ecomagination program.

Walt Disney often is praised for having one of the best CSR programs in the world. In one year, Disney gave more than $370 million to charity, and its employees donated 667,013 hours of their time through Disney's VoluntEAR program. Partnering with Give Kids the World, these employees renovated 88 vacation villas that the charitable organization offers to the families of children with life-threatening illnesses, so that they can take life-affirming vacations.[37]

Marketplace When one firm in the industry leads the way toward CSR, its partners and competitors often have no choice but to follow—or run the risk of not doing business or being left behind. To address issues such as global warming, water scarcity, and energy, GE uses a program it calls ecomagination, which encompasses a business strategy composed of four commitments: to double investments in clean research and development (R&D), increase revenues from ecomagination products, reduce greenhouse gas emissions, and inform the public about these issues.[38] When confronted with such initiatives, other energy companies are forced to make a decision: continue as they have been doing or adopt more responsible practices themselves. In either case, the initiating firm enjoys an advantage by gaining a reputation for being on the cutting edge of CSR efforts.

Society Firms expend considerable time and energy engaging in activities aimed at improving the overall community and the physical environment. According to a McKinsey & Co. survey, 95 percent of CEOs believe that society increasingly expects companies to take on public responsibilities.[39] That is, in a broad sense, companies cannot ignore societal demands for them to act responsibly. A firm that fails to do so causes damage to all the preceding stakeholders as well as to itself.

For example, reports that the artificial sweeteners in diet sodas might have ill effects, such as long-term weight gain and possible links to developing cancer, have led customers to alter their buying habits. Specifically, sales of diet soda have dropped 6.8 percent in a year, more than three times the decline in regular soda sales. Even though organizations such as the American Diabetic Association and the U.S. Food and Drug Administration have affirmed that diet sodas are safe, the broader shift in societal opinions demands that beverage companies seek new options. In particular, many companies are researching the potential use of stevia, a plant with naturally sweet properties, to replace the artificial versions.[40]

CHECK YOURSELF

1. How has corporate social responsibility evolved since the turn of the 21st century?
2. Provide examples of each of the stakeholders that firms should consider in their corporate social responsibility efforts.

Reviewing Learning Objectives

 Identify the ethical values marketers should embrace.

Being a part of an ethically responsible firm should be important to every employee, but it is particularly important to marketers because they interact most directly with customers and suppliers, which offers a multitude of ethical questions and opportunities. AMA's Code of Ethics indicates that the basic ethical values marketers should aspire to are honesty, responsibility, fairness, respect, openness, and citizenship.

Distinguish between ethics and social responsibility.

Individuals and firms can (and should) act ethically, but the outcome of their acts may not affect society in general. An ethical act may affect only the firm's immediate stakeholders, such as its employees, customers, and suppliers. To be socially responsible, a firm also must take actions that benefit the community in a larger sense, such as helping people who have been affected by a natural disaster like a hurricane.

 Identify the four steps in ethical decision making.

First, firms can include ethics and social responsibility in their corporate mission. Second, they should institute policies and procedures to ensure that everyone working for the firm is acting in an ethically responsible manner. Third, firms can model their ethical policies after a well-established code of ethics like the one provided by the American Marketing Association. Fourth, when making ethically sensitive decisions, firms can utilize a metric such as the ethical decision-making metric shown in Exhibit 4.4.

 Describe how ethics can be integrated into a firm's marketing strategy.

Ethical and socially responsible considerations should be integrated into the firm's mission statement, as long as top management follows through and commits to supporting a strong ethical climate within the organization. When considering their marketing strategy, firms should ask not only "can we implement a certain policy?" but also "should we do it?" Finally, in the control phase, marketers must determine whether they truly have acted in an ethical and socially responsible manner. If not, they should make changes to the marketing strategy.

 Describe the ways in which corporate social responsibility programs help various stakeholders.

To answer this question, we first have to identify the various stakeholders of a company, namely, customers, employees, the marketplace, and society. CSR benefits these stakeholders as follows:

- *Customers:* When companies adopt CSR, customers know that they can trust the firms to provide healthy, ethically acceptable products and services. Many customers also feel better about buying from a company that engages in responsible practices, which provides them with the additional value of feeling good about buying from that company.
- *Employees:* A firm committed to CSR likely treats its employees with decency and respect. For many employees (especially members of Generation Y), working for an

irresponsible firm would be antithetical to their own morals and values.

- *Marketplace:* An industry improves its practices, and avoids scandals, when it ensures that the participating firms act responsibly and appropriately in all areas.

- *Society:* This stakeholder is local, national, or global communities. The benefits of CSR in all cases are numerous—cleaner air and water, aid to the underprivileged, and healthier product options all can result from CSR by companies.

Key Terms

■ILEARNSMART

- business ethics, 115
- corporate social responsibility (CSR), 120
- deceptive advertising, 116
- ethical climate, 117
- marketing ethics, 115

Marketing Applications

1. Discuss why marketers use Internet cookies and the potential ethical issues this practice creates.

2. Why are marketers likely to be faced with more ethical dilemmas than members of other functional areas in business, such as finance, accounting, or real estate?

3. Develop an argument for why a cosmetics manufacturer should build and maintain an ethical climate.

4. A clothing company gives generously to charities and sponsors donation drives to help lower-income teen girls get reasonably priced prom dresses. It also locates its manufacturing plants in countries with few labor laws, such that it does not know if children are working in its factories, and works to prevent union activity among its employees in the United States. Evaluate this company from an ethical and social responsibility perspective.

5. Based on the evaluation you developed for question 4, provide responses to the ethical decision-making metric from Exhibit 4.4. Provide a rationale for your score for each question.

6. A company that makes granola and other "healthy" snacks has the following mission statement: "Our goal is to profitably sell good-tasting, healthy products and to better society." Although its products are organic, they also are relatively high in sugar and calories. The company gives a small portion of its profits to the United Way. Evaluate its mission statement.

7. A health inspector found some rodent droppings in one batch of granola made by the same company in question 6. What should the company do?

8. Choose a company that you believe is particularly socially responsible that is not discussed in this chapter. How do you justify your choice? What counterarguments might someone make to suggest that your chosen company is not responsible? Consider all key stakeholders in developing both sides of the argument.

Quiz Yourself

1. The Johnson & Johnson credo:
   a. was a response to the Tylenol incident
   b. proved ineffective when the company needed to act in the Tylenol crisis, which was a clear lesson to other companies to update similar documents
   c. was copied by all other pharmaceutical companies
   d. offers an extremely detailed description of potential problems for the company
   e. has guided the firm since it was written in the 1940s

2. When making decisions, managers often have to decide between doing what is beneficial for them (and possibly the firm) in the short run, and doing what is right and beneficial for the firm and

for society in the long run. To address this conflict, a firm must:

a. evaluate its quarterly profit statement from an ethics standpoint

b. state its long-term goals in general terms to not interfere with managers' short-term goals

c. always put society's needs ahead of the firm's needs

d. ensure that long-term goals are aligned with the short-term goals of each individual within the firm

e. do all of the above

(Answers to these two questions can be found on page 651.)

Net Savvy

1. Perhaps no subdiscipline of marketing receives more scrutiny regarding ethical compliance than direct marketing, a form of nonstore retailing in which customers are exposed to and purchase merchandise or services through an impersonal medium such as telephone, mail, or the Internet.[41] Ethical issues in direct marketing cover a broad spectrum because this means of selling is conducted through all forms of communication. The Direct Marketing Association (DMA) takes ethics very seriously and has numerous programs to ensure its member organizations comply with its Code of Ethics. Go to the website for the Direct Marketing Association

(http://www.the-dma.org/). Click on "Advocacy." List the different ways that the DMA is involved in assisting consumers and the industry to create a more ethical marketplace.

2. An increasing number of firms are stating their strong commitment to corporate social responsibility initiatives. The Corporate Social Responsibility Newswire Service keeps track of these various initiatives and posts stories on its website about what various corporations are doing. Go to http://www.csrwire.com/ and choose one story. Write a description of the corporation and the initiative.

Chapter Case Study

IS THERE AN APP FOR GOOD PARENTING?

If you've gone to a mall or family restaurant recently, it's likely that you have seen children playing games or watching videos on tablets. Whereas it used to be difficult to get children to behave in stores or at a restaurant, parents are finding that a tablet or smartphone can be an effective babysitter. Manufacturers have picked up on this trend and offer several tablets designed specifically for kids: Samsung has the Galaxy Tab 3 Kids Edition, LeapFrog sells the LeapPad2 PowerLearning Tablet, nabi provides the nabi XD and nabi 2, and ClickN offers the KIDS 7" tablet, to name just a few.

Producing and selling technology for kids has proven a profitable business. But when is it too much technology? The American Academy of Pediatrics and the Mayo Clinic both urge parents to not allow children younger than two years of age to interact with any device with a screen (television, computer, tablet), out of concern that it will have negative effects on children's brain development, including the threats of language delays and damage to their social, emotional, and cognitive skills.[42] Furthermore, research has shown that increased "screen time" (defined as the number of hours children spend interacting with any device with an electronic screen) leads to increased risks of obesity, irregular sleep, behavioral problems, and impaired academic performance.

Despite such warnings, companies continue to produce technology products geared toward younger and younger children.[43] One of the latest is Fisher-Price's Newborn-to-Toddler Apptivity Seat[44]—essentially a small chair for newborns, with a bar that hangs an iPad a few inches from the child's face. As might be expected, the introduction prompted a massive outcry from child advocacy groups, such as the Campaign for a Commercial-Free Childhood (CCFC), which filed complaints with the Federal Trade Commission about claims Fisher-Price has posted on its website, asserting that the chair in concert with a tablet actually helps babies' brain development.

Fisher-Price's response? It has added a "note to customers" on the product's web page. After suggesting that parents limit their children's screen time, it goes on to state, "we realize this type of technology in infant products isn't for everyone. That's why our Apptivity Seat is just one of more than a dozen baby seats we make, giving parents lots of choices with the options they prefer for their family's lifestyle."[45]

Nor is the company alone in its efforts. With the 2-in-1 iPotty, CTA Digital suggests that parents affix their tablet to their children's potty training seats. Then the children can play with an app or watch a video while learning how to use the potty—often a challenging task for both parents and their children. Since its introduction, the potty seat has been extremely popular, becoming one of the company's top-selling products.[46]

The offerings also do not stop at products. Mattel (the parent company of Fisher-Price) has developed a suite of iPad Apptivity apps, available for free to parents who buy the seat. The early development content shows high-contrast patterns, so babies' young eyes can follow them, and features soothing sounds of nature. For slightly older children, the app advances to introduce numbers and letters. Each visual presentation times out after 10 to 12 minutes.

On an even more advanced level, Netflix has expanded its line of self-produced content, beyond fan favorites such as *Arrested Development* or *Orange Is the New Black*, to include series for children.[47] By appealing to young consumers, Netflix hopes to increase the loyalty of the entire household, reasoning that parents are unlikely to cancel their subscription if Netflix is the only place kids can get the latest episodes of some of their favorite shows.

While parents may want devices that keep their children entertained, screen time at such a young age may be harmful to children's cognitive development.

For parents, innovative products for children can be a lifesaver: They keep kids entertained, help with potty training, and offer a convenient distraction. Moreover, many parents today already rely heavily on tablets and other screens for their own purposes, making it difficult for them to avoid screen time for their children. In this sense, companies are merely providing the products and services that parents, and their children, want.

Questions

1. Who benefits from products designed to give children and babies more screen time? Who is harmed?

2. Who has a greater ethical responsibility in relation to children and screen time: companies or parents? Present arguments for both sides.

3. What does Fisher-Price's "note to parents" on its website suggest about its corporate ethics policy?

Endnotes

1. James Glanz, Jeff Larson, and Andrew W. Lehren, "Spy Agencies Tap Data Streaming from Phone Apps," *The New York Times*, January 27, 2014.

2. John Bussey, "Taming the Spies of Web Advertising," *The Wall Street Journal*, August 8, 2013.

3. Claire Cain Miller and Somini Sengupta, "Selling Secrets of Phone Users to Advertisers," *The New York Times*, October 5, 2013.

4. Simon Dumenco, "Microsoft: 'Your Privacy Is Our Priority.' NSA: 'LOL!'" *Advertising Age*, June 7, 2013.

5. Matt Appuzo and Nicole Perlroth, "U.S. Relaxes Some Data Disclosure Rules," *The New York Times*, January 27, 2014.

6. Theodore Levitt, *Marketing Imagination* (Detroit, MI: Free Press, 1983).

7. Amy Harmon and Andrew Pollack, "Battle Brewing over Labeling of Genetically Modified Food," *The New York Times*, May 24, 2012.

8. Laura Parker, "The GMO Labeling Battle Is Heating Up—Here's Why," *National Geographic*, January 11, 2014; Stefanie Strom,

"Major Grocer to Label Foods with Gene-Modified Content," *The New York Times,* March 8, 2013.

9. For a detailed compilation of articles that are involved with ethical and societal issues, see Gregory T. Gundlach, Lauren G. Block, and William W. Wilkie, *Explorations of Marketing in Society* (Mason, OH: Thompson Higher Education, 2007); G. Svensson and G. Wood, "A Model of Business Ethics," *Journal of Business Ethics* 77, no. 3 (2007), pp. 303–22.

10. Christy Ashley and Hillary A. Leonard, "Betrayed by the Buzz? Covert Content and Consumer–Brand Relationships," *Journal of Public Policy & Marketing* 28, no. 2 (2009), pp. 212–20.

11. Elizabeth S. Moore and Victoria J. Rideout, "The Online Marketing of Food to Children: Is It Just Fun and Games?" *Journal of Public Policy & Marketing* 26, no. 2 (2007), pp. 202–20; Elizabeth S. Moore, "Perspectives on Food Marketing and Childhood Obesity: Introduction to the Special Section," *Journal of Public Policy & Marketing* 26, no. 2 (2007), pp. 157–61; Elizabeth S. Moore, "Food Marketing Goes Online: A Content Analysis of Websites for Children," in *Obesity in America: Development and Prevention,* vol. 2, ed. Hiram E. Fitzgerald and Vasiliki Mousouli (Westport, CT: Praeger, 2007), pp. 93–115; William L. Wilkie and Elizabeth S. Moore, "Marketing's Contributions to Society," *Journal of Marketing* 63 (Special Issue, 1999), pp. 198–219.

12. Gallup, "Honesty/Ethics in Professions," http://www.gallup.com.

13. http://www.workingvalues.com.

14. http://www.jnj.com.

15. Vanessa O'Connell and Shirley Wang, "J&J Acts Fast on Tylenol," *The Wall Street Journal,* July 9, 2009.

16. Erin Cavusgil, "Merck and Vioxx: An Examination of an Ethical Decision-Making Model," *Journal of Business Ethics* 76 (2007), pp. 451–61.

17. Jeanne Whalen, "AstraZeneca Sharpens Focus on Ethics," *The Wall Street Journal,* December 3, 2009, http://online.wsj.com; "AstraZeneca Weighs Response to UK Body on Ethics Code Breach," *The Wall Street Journal,* March 9, 2010, http://online.wsj.com.

18. For an interesting discussion of why pharmaceutical companies seem to have lost their ethical luster, see Matthew Herper, "Big Pharma: What Went Wrong?," http://www.forbes.com.

19. http://www.marketingpower.com/AboutAMA/Pages/Statement%20of%20Ethics.aspx.

20. http://www.cmomagazine.com. This survey was conducted in 2006; more recent reports suggest that 49 percent of respondents to a 2009 survey reported having seen ethical misconduct overall. See Ethics Resource Center, "2009 National Business Ethics Survey," http://www.ethics.org.

21. Alexander Dahlsrud lists 37 definitions! See "How Corporate Social Responsibility Is Defined," *Corporate Social Responsibility and Environmental Management* 15, no. 1 (January–February 2008), pp. 1–13.

22. "Social Responsibility," *AMA Dictionary of Marketing Terms,* http://www.marketingpower.com/_layouts/Dictionary.aspx?dLetter=S.

23. Christopher Marquis et al., "The Dannon Company: Marketing and Corporate Social Responsibility," *Harvard Business School Case 9-410-121,* April 1, 2010.

24. Rick Ungar, "Walmart Store Holding Thanksgiving Charity Food Drive—for Its Own Employees!" *Forbes,* November 18, 2013; http://foundation.walmart.com.

25. Michael Connor, "Survey: U.S. Consumers Willing to Pay for Corporate Responsibility," *Business Ethics,* March 29, 2010, http://business-ethics.com.

26. Richard Stengel, "Doing Well by Doing Good," *Time magazine,* September 10, 2009, http://www.time.com.

27. "2011 World's Most Ethical Companies," *Ethisphere,* http://ethisphere.com/2011-worlds-most-ethical-companies.

28. http://www.burtsbees.com.

29. General Electric, "Sustainable Growth: GE 2010 Citizenship Report," http://www.gecitizenship.com; General Electric, "The Spirit and the Letter," http://integrity.ge.com.

30. Interviews with Nell Newman and Peter Meehan, cofounders of Newman's Own Organic, 2007; http://www.newmansown.com/charity/ .

31. Ross Wilson, "The Best and Worst of Facebook 2012," *Ignite Social Media,* December 13, 2012, http://www.ignitesocialmedia.com.

32. Andrew J. Blumberg and Peter Eckerdsly, "On Locational Privacy, and How to Avoid Losing It Forever," *Electronic Frontier Foundation White Paper,* August 2009, http://www.eff.org.

33. Elizabeth A. Harris, Nicole Perlroth, and Nathaniel Popper, "Neiman Marcus Data Breach Worse Than First Said," *The New York Times,* January 23, 2014.

34. http://about.van.fedex.com/.

35. The most famous proponent of this view was Milton Friedman. See, for example, *Capitalism and Freedom* (Chicago: University of Chicago Press, 2002); or *Free to Choose: A Personal Statement* (Orlando, FL: Harcourt, 1990).

36. Dan Amos, "Aflac's Ethics in Action: Pay for Performance—Keep Stakeholders Informed," January 12, 2009, http://ethisphere.com.

37. https://thewaltdisneycompany.com/blog/infographic-disneys-charitable-giving-reaches-370-million-2013; http://disneyparks.disney.go.com/blog/galleries/2014/01/disney-cast-members-create-an-extreme-village-makeover-for-give-kids-the-world/#photo-5.

38. http://www.ge.com/news/our_viewpoints/energy_and_climate.html; "GE Launches New Ecomagination Healthcare Products, Opens Renewable Energy HQ," February 2, 2010, http://www.greenbiz.com.

39. D. B. Bielak, S. Bonini, and J. M. Oppenheim, "CEOs on Strategy and Social Issues," *McKinsey Quarterly,* 2007, http://www.mckinseyquarterly.com.

40. United Press International, "Diet Soda Sales: Flat Would Be Better," December 9, 2013, http://www.upi.com.

41. http://www.marketingpower.com/_layouts/Dictionary.aspx.

42. See http://www.mayoclinic.org/children-and-tv/art-20047952.

43. Cecilia Kang, "Infant iPad Seats Raise Concerns about Screen Time for Babies," *The Washington Post,* December 10, 2013.

44. http://www.fisher-price.com/img/product_shots/X7045-newborn-to-toddler-apptivity-seat-d-2.jpg.

45. http://www.fisher-price.com/en_US/brands/babygear/products/78030.

46. Kang, "Infant iPad Seats Raise Concerns about Screen Time for Babies."

47. "Dreamworks Animation to Create Netflix's First Original Kids' Show," *Advertising Age,* February 12, 2013.

i. "Walmart Energy Efficiency Program Achieves Energy Savings of 20% Across 210 Supplier Factories in China," *PR Newswire,* April 22, 2013; Jessica Wohl, "Walmart Announces $50 Billion Buy American Campaign," *The Huffington Post,* January 15, 2013; "Walmart Launches Major Initiative to Make Food Healthier and Healthier Food More Affordable," http://walmartstores.com; Stephanie Rosenbloom, "At Walmart, Labeling to Reflect Green Intent," *The New York Times,* July 16, 2009; Stephanie Rosenbloom, "Wal-Mart to Toughen Standards," *The New York Times,* October 22, 2008; Adam Aston, "Walmart: Making Its Suppliers Go Green," *BusinessWeek,* May 18, 2009.

ii. http://www.toms.com/our-movement; http://www.toms.com/corporate-info/; http://www.insightargentina.org; Andrew Adam Newman, " 'Buy One, Give One' Spirit Imbues an Online Store," *Los Angeles Times,* November 4, 2013; George Anderson, "Toms Offers a Different Way to Shop," *Retail Wire,* November 6, 2013; Christina Binkley, "Charity Gives Shoe Brand Extra Shine," *The Wall Street Journal,* April 1, 2010, http://online.wsj.com.

iii. "Market for Selling Fake Social Media Clicks Has Big Following," *Los Angeles Times,* January 6, 2014; Suzanne Vranica, "Tweeting to Sell Cars," *The Wall Street Journal,* November 14, 2010; http://business.ftc.gov; Gary Hoffman, "Selling Cars on Twitter," *AOL Autos,* August 10, 2010.

Credits

APPENDIX 4A

UNDERSTANDING ETHICS USING SCENARIOS

In this appendix, we present nine ethical scenarios designed to assist you in developing your skills at identifying ethical issues. There is no one right answer to the dilemmas below, just as there will be no correct answers to many of the ethical situations you will face throughout your career. Instead, these scenarios can help you develop your sensitivity toward ethical issues, as well as your ethical reasoning skills. As mentioned throughout the chapter, Exhibit 4.4 provides an ethical decision-making metric to assist you in evaluating the following and all such ethical dilemmas you may face.

Scenario 1: R.J. Reynolds: Promotions to the Youth Market

Tobacco giant R.J. Reynolds sent a set of coasters featuring its cigarette brands and recipes for mixed drinks with high alcohol content to young adults, via direct mail, on their 21st birthdays (the legal age for alcohol consumption). The alcohol brands in the recipes included Jack Daniels, Southern Comfort, and Finlandia Vodka. The reverse side of the coaster read, "Go 'til Daybreak, and Make Sure You're Sittin'." The campaign, called "Drinks on Us," clearly promoted abusive and excessive drinking. This campaign was eventually stopped because the cigarette company did not have permission to use the alcohol brands.

The FDA (Federal Drug Administration) has been given the authority to regulate tobacco, including banning certain products, limiting nicotine, and blocking labels such as "low tar" and "light" that could wrongly imply certain products are less harmful.[1] The law doesn't let the FDA ban nicotine or tobacco entirely. A committee has been formed to study several issues, including dissolvable tobacco products, product changes, and standards, and report back to the FDA. Of particular interest is the increase in the share of smokers using menthol cigarettes from 31 to almost 34 percent in four years, with more pronounced increases among young smokers. It also showed that among black smokers, 82.6 percent used menthol cigarettes, compared with 32.3 percent for Hispanic smokers and 23.8 percent for white smokers.[2] A ban on cigarettes with flavors such as clove, chocolate, or fruit took effect in 2009 because they are believed to appeal to youth.

After graduation, you have an offer to work in either marketing or sales at R.J. Reynolds, the tobacco company that sells many popular brands of cigarettes. The pay and benefits are very competitive. The job market is tight, and if you don't get a job right away, you will have to live with your parents. Should you take the job?

Scenario 2: Car Manufacturer Gives Bribes for Contracts

A car and truck manufacturer just found out that two of its overseas business units have been engaging in bribery over a ten-year period of time. The company paid $56 million in bribes to more than 20 countries to gain government contracts for their vehicles.[3] The company is now paying millions in criminal and civil charges because of its violation of the Foreign Corrupt Practices Act (FCPA), and it admits to earning more than $50 million in profits based on its corrupt transactions. The car company recorded the bribe payments as commissions, special discounts, or necessary payments. Should the manufacturer discontinue its operations with the countries that were unlawfully bribed to buy its cars? Are financial fines sufficient to repair the problem? How can companies be sure the commissions they earn are true commissions and not a bribe?

Scenario 3: Retailers Lack Ethical Guidelines

Renata has been working at Peavy's Bridal for less than a year now. Her sales figures have never been competitive with those of her coworkers, and the sales manager has called her in for several meetings to discuss her inability to close the sale. Things look desperate; in the last meeting, the sales manager told her that if she did not meet her quota next month, the company would likely have to fire her.

In considering how she might improve her methods and sales, Renata turned to another salesperson, namely, the one with the most experience in the store. Marilyn has been with Peavy's for nearly 30 years, and she virtually always gets the sale. But how?

"Let me tell you something sweetie," Marilyn tells her. "Every bride-to-be wants one thing: to look beautiful on her wedding day, so everyone gasps when they first see her. And hey, the husband is going to think she looks great. But let's be honest here—not everyone is all that beautiful. So you have to convince them that they look great in one, and only one, dress. And that dress had better be the most expensive one they try, or they won't believe you anyway! And then you have to show them how much better they look with a veil. And some shoes. And a tiara . . . you get the picture! I mean, they need all that stuff anyway, so why shouldn't we make them feel good while they're here and let them buy from us?"

Should she follow Marilyn's advice and save her job?

Scenario 4: Giving Credit Where Credit Isn't Due

A catalog retailer that carries home and children's items, such as children's furniture, clothing, and toys, was seeking a way to reach a new audience and stop the declining sales and revenue trends it was suffering. A market research firm hired by the cataloger identified a new but potentially risky market: lower-income single parents. The new market seemed attractive because of the large number of single parents, but most of these homes were severely constrained in terms of their monetary resources.

The research firm proposed that the cataloger offer a generous credit policy that would allow consumers to purchase up to $500 worth of merchandise on credit without a credit check, provided they signed up for direct payment of their credit account from a checking account. Because these were high-risk consumers, the credit accounts would carry extremely high interest rates. The research firm believed that even with losses, enough accounts would be paid off to make the venture extremely profitable for the catalog retailer.

Should the cataloger pursue this new strategy?

Scenario 5: The Jeweler's Tarnished Image

Sparkle Gem Jewelers, a family-owned and -operated costume jewelry manufacturing business, traditionally sold its products only to wholesalers. Recently however, Sparkle Gem was approached by the charismatic Barb Stephens, who convinced the owners to begin selling through a network of distributors she had organized. The distributors recruited individuals to host jewelry parties in their homes. Sparkle Gem's owners, the Billing family, has been thrilled with the revenue generated by these home parties and started making plans for the expansion of the distributor network.

However, Mrs. Billing just received a letter from a jewelry party customer, who expressed sympathy for her loss. Mrs. Billing was concerned and contacted the letter writer, who told her that Barb Stephens had come to the jewelry party at her church and told the story of Sparkle Gem. According to Stephens's story, Mrs. Billing was a young widow struggling to keep her business together after her husband had died on a missionary trip. The writer had purchased $200 worth of jewelry at the party and told Mrs. Billing that she hoped it helped. Mrs. Billing was stunned. She and her very-much-alive husband had just celebrated their 50th wedding anniversary.

What should Mrs. Billing do now?

Scenario 6: No Wonder It's So Good

Enjoy Cola is a new product produced by ABC Beverage and marketed with the slogan "Relax with Enjoy." Unlike other colas on the market, Enjoy does not contain caffeine and therefore is positioned as the perfect beverage to end the day or for a slow-paced weekend and as a means to help consumers relax and unwind. The market response has been tremendous, and sales of Enjoy have been growing rapidly, especially among women.

ABC Beverage decided not to list on the ingredients label that Enjoy contains a small amount of alcohol because it is not required to do so by the government unless the alcohol content is more than 1 percent.

Mia Rodriguez, the marketing director for Enjoy, only recently learned that Enjoy contains small amounts of alcohol and is troubled about ABC's failure to disclose this information on the ingredients list. She worries about the impact of this omission on consumers who have alcohol sensitivities or those who shouldn't be consuming alcohol, such as pregnant women and recovering alcoholics.

What should Rodriguez do? What would you do in her position?

Scenario 7: Bright Baby's Bright Idea

Bartok Manufacturing produces a line of infant toys under the Bright Baby brand label. The Consumer Product Safety Commission (CPSC) recently issued a recall order for the Bright Baby car seat gym, a very popular product. According to the CPSC, the gym contains small parts that present a choking hazard. The CEO of Bartok Manufacturing, Bill Bartok, called an executive meeting to determine the firm's strategy in response to the recall.

Mike Henderson, Bartok's CFO, stated that the recall could cost as much as $1 million in lost revenue from the Bright Baby line. Noting that there had been no deaths or injuries from the product, just the potential for injury, Henderson proposed that the remaining inventory of car seat gyms be sold in regions where there are no rules such as the CPSC's. Sue Tyler, the marketing director for Bartok, recommended that the product be repackaged and sold under a different brand name so that the Bright Baby name would not be associated with the product. Bartok, though a bit leery of the plan, agreed to go along with it to avoid the monetary losses.

What would you have recommended to the CEO?

Scenario 8: Money from Mailing Lists[4]

Sports Nostalgia Emporium sells autographed sports memorabilia online. Recently, the director of marketing, John Mangold, started using a mailing list he had purchased from Marketing Metrix, a marketing research firm that sells consumer information. Mangold relies on such purchased mailing lists to grow the company and sends printed catalogs to thousands of people each month. The mailing lists he gets from Marketing Metrix are much more effective than other mailing lists and generate almost twice as much revenue.

In a recent conversation with a sales representative from Marketing Metrix, Mangold discovered the reason its lists were so effective: Marketing Metrix tracks the online behavior of consumers and uses that information to create targeted lists. The mailing lists that Mangold has been using consist of consumers who visited the websites of Sports Nostalgia Emporium's competitors. Based on what he can discern, Mangold believes that these consumers are not aware that someone is collecting information about their online behavior, along with their names and addresses, and selling it to other firms.

Should Mangold continue to use the Marketing Metrix mailing list? If so, should he tell his new customers how he got their names and addresses? Do consumers need to give consent before firms can collect information about their behavior?

Scenario 9: The Blogging CEO[5]

David Burdick is the CEO of ACME Bubblegum, a successful public company. As one of the cofounders of the company, Burdick has enjoyed speaking and writing about the success of ACME Bubblegum for several years. Typically, he speaks at

conferences or directly to the press, but recently, he has been blogging about his firm anonymously. Specifically, he defended a recent advertising campaign that was unpopular among consumers and pointedly attacked one of ACME Bubblegum's competitors. Burdick deeply enjoys his anonymous blogging and believes that none of his readers actually know that he works for ACME Bubblegum.

Should Burdick be allowed to praise his company's performance anonymously online? Should he be allowed to attack his competitors without disclosing his relationship with the company? How would you feel if the CEO of a company at which you shopped was secretly writing criticisms of his or her competition? How would you feel if you knew a writer for your favorite blog was actually closely involved in a company that the blog community discussed?

Endnotes

1. Michael Felberbaum, "Panel to Examine Menthol Cigarettes' Impact," *Associated Press,* March 29, 2010.

2. Ibid., based on a study by the Substance Abuse and Mental Health Services Administration in November, 2009.

3. Department of Justice, Office of Public Affairs, "Daimler AG and Three Subsidiaries Resolve Foreign Corrupt Practices Act Investigation and Agree to Pay $93.6 Million in Criminal Penalties," press release, April 1, 2010; Michael Connor, "Daimler Agrees to Pay $185 Million to Settle Bribery Charges," *Business Ethics,* March 26, 2010, http://businessethics.com.

4. Emily Steel, "How Marketers Hone Their Aim Online," *The Wall Street Journal,* June 19, 2007, p. B6.

5. "Mr. Mackey's Offense," *The Wall Street Journal,* July 16, 2007, p. A12.

CHAPTER 5

ANALYZING THE MARKETING ENVIRONMENT

LEARNING OBJECTIVES

LO1 Outline how customers, the company, competitors, and corporate partners affect marketing strategy.

LO2 Explain why marketers must consider their macroenvironment when they make decisions.

LO3 Describe the differences among the various generational cohorts.

LO4 Identify various social trends that impact marketing.

Travelers needing a place to grab some shut-eye once knew exactly what to expect when they pulled off the highway to find a hotel chain: a basic room, acceptable bed, relatively Spartan shower, some generic landscape art, and, if they were lucky, a little slightly stale breakfast in the morning. Such expectations are no longer the norm, though, as the hotel industry continues to respond to changing customer needs by transforming itself into one of the most innovative sectors marketing its services today. Consider a few examples.

Recall from Superior Service 1.1 that we described a hotel in Majorca, Spain, that offers guests a Twitter

concierge to ensure they can remain easily and readily in contact throughout their vacation.[1] Following this trend, the UK Thomas Cook hotel chain has rolled out a new line of SunConnect resorts that feature, for example, a proprietary ConnectScout app that helps families on vacation schedule their Xbox game times and find geo-catching sites.[2]

For modern pet "parents," today's hotel offerings also reflect the increasing belief that pets—especially lovable, drooling, goofy dogs—are part of the family, with the same rights to luxury, comfort, and enjoyment as any human family member. Accordingly, they span a range as broad and varied as the different types of dogs they welcome. At luxury hotels, dogs might be welcomed with a treat bag containing a toy, water dish, and leash (all emblazoned with the hotel's logo, of course). Owners can request a Ritz-Carlton–branded dog bed to be put in their rooms, or rent a "puppy purse" to carry around their tiny pets.[3]

Beyond product comforts, dog-pertinent service options are remarkably extensive. Dog walkers are available to cover daily bathroom chores for busy travelers. Canine pedicures—or (sorry) "pet-icures"—trim and buff dogs' many nails. Some hotels even offer pet psychics, including one former marketing executive who switched career paths one night, after waking up to find her dog talking to her. The range of services is so extensive because people are so passionate about their pets. Marketing research reveals that pet owners seek out offers for their pets that match the offers they prefer for themselves. Thus a weekly visitor to the manicurist is far more likely to seek out someone to take care of her pet's nails too. Furthermore, rather than limiting their canine companions to leisure trips, increasing numbers of business travelers like to bring along a slobbery piece of home, in the form of their best canine friend. While they take business meetings and interact with clients, they can rest assured that their pooch will be shuttled between the hotel and a doggie daycare location, where it can interact with other dogs, for about $299 a day. One hotel chain estimates that approximately 100,000 pets (99 percent of them dogs) stay in its hotels each year.

These innovative approaches are just the tip of the proverbial iceberg, as the hotel industry actively seeks to speed up and expand its introduction of new products and services, often by testing them in a few locations to gather feedback from travelers. Only one Hyatt Regency has a soundproof conference room, which may improve teleconferencing capabilities for business guests. The AKA hotel in Beverly Hills may be the only one that maintains a small cinema, for private screenings. But if these concepts work well in one place, we can expect to see more of these rooms throughout the chains.[4]

LO1 Outline how customers, the company, competitors, and corporate partners affect marketing strategy.

A MARKETING ENVIRONMENT ANALYSIS FRAMEWORK

As the opening vignette illustrates, marketers continue to find changes in what their customers demand or expect and adapt their product and service offerings accordingly. By paying close attention to customer needs and continuously monitoring the business environment in which the company operates, a good marketer can identify potential opportunities.

Exhibit 5.1 illustrates factors that affect the marketing environment. The centerpiece, as always, is consumers. Consumers may be influenced directly by the immediate actions of the focal company, the company's competitors, or corporate partners that work with the firm to make and supply products and services to consumers. The firm, and therefore consumers indirectly, is influenced by the macroenvironment, which includes various impacts of culture, demographics, and social, technological, economic, and political/legal factors. We discuss each of these components in detail in this chapter and suggest how they might interrelate.

Because the consumer is the center of all marketing efforts, value-based marketing aims to provide greater value to consumers than competitors offer.

EXHIBIT 5.1   Understanding the Marketing Environment

146

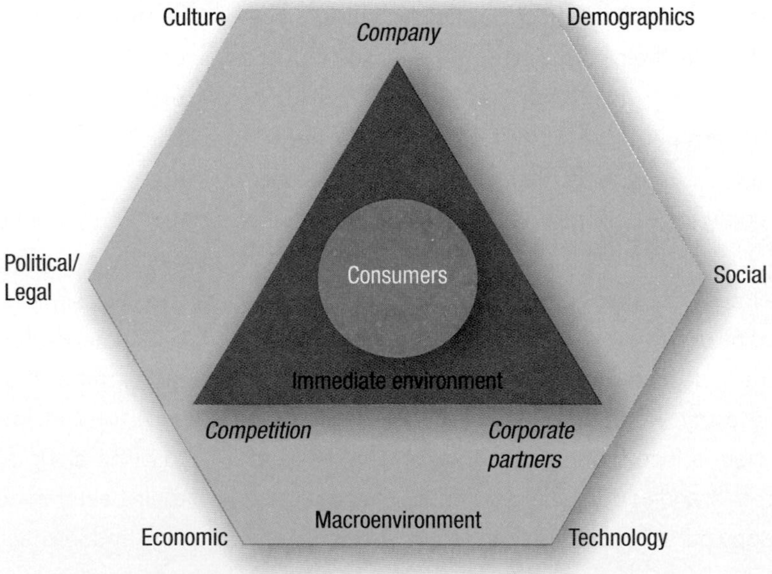

Therefore, the marketing firm must consider the entire business process, all from a consumer's point of view.[5] Consumers' needs and wants, as well as their ability to purchase, depend on a host of factors that change and evolve over time. Firms use various tools to keep track of competitors' activities and consumer trends, and they rely on various methods to communicate with their corporate partners. Furthermore, they monitor their macroenvironment to determine how such factors influence consumers and how they should respond to them. Sometimes, a firm can even anticipate trends.

THE IMMEDIATE ENVIRONMENT

Exhibit 5.2 illustrates the factors that affect consumers' immediate environment: the company's capabilities, competitors, and corporate partners.

Company Capabilities

In the immediate environment, the first factor that affects the consumer is the firm itself. Successful marketing firms focus on satisfying customer needs that match their core competencies. The primary strength of Corning is its ability to manufacture glass: The company initially made its name by producing the glass enclosure to encase Thomas Edison's lightbulb. But by successfully leveraging its core competency in glass manufacturing while also recognizing marketplace trends toward mobile devices, Corning shifted its focus. As a result, Corning is one of the leading producers of durable, scratch-resistant glass on the faces of smartphones and tablets. More than 1 billion mobile devices feature its Gorilla Glass.[6] Marketers can use analyses of their external environment, like the SWOT analysis described in Chapter 2, to categorize any opportunity as attractive or unattractive. If it appears attractive, they also need to assess it in terms of their existing competencies.

Competitors

Competition also significantly affects consumers in the immediate environment. It is therefore critical that marketers understand their firm's competitors, including their strengths, weaknesses, and likely reactions to the marketing activities that their own firm undertakes. Such questions can become very complicated when one parent

EXHIBIT 5.2   Understanding the Immediate Environment

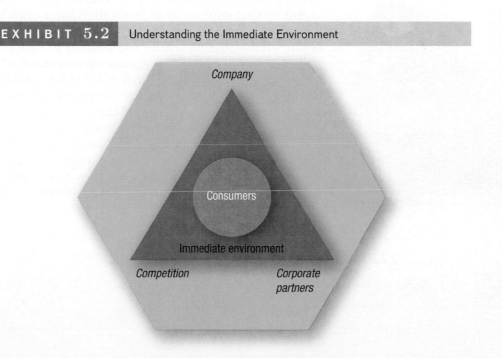

Gillette and Schick are actively engaged in fierce competition for the razor market.

company, such as Luxottica, owns several competing brands, such as Pearle Vision, LensCrafters, and Sunglass Hut. When Luxottica devotes more of its marketing budget to one "child," the others suffer. In one year in which advertising for LensCrafters reached $48.5 million but the budget for Pearle Vision was only $14 million, sales for the former jumped 8 percent but those of the latter fell by 3.3 percent.[7] At the same time, Luxottica must consider the moves of true competitors, especially as discount retailers such as Target, Walmart, and Sam's Club expand their optical services offerings.

Watching competitors is a constant effort—and often a serious battle—in many consumer goods categories. No one would want to get caught in the war between the two razor giants, Gillette Co. and Energizer USA, which makes Schick razors, as each manufacturer works to add ever more blades to its disposable razors.[8] Gillette accused Schick of engaging in false and misleading advertising when ads claimed that its Hydro razor would hydrate skin. Schick's parent company countered with the complaint that Gillette's Fusion ProGlide Razor ads attempt to deceive when they assert that the blades are "Gillette's thinnest blades ever." All these efforts represent the companies' recognition of what their closest competitor is doing, as well as their attempts to halt tactics they consider damaging. But at the same time, each razor company touts its benefits over its competitors because the ultimate goal, of course, is to appeal to consumers.

Corporate Partners

Few firms operate in isolation. For example, automobile manufacturers collaborate with suppliers of sheet metal, tire manufacturers, component part makers, unions, transport companies, and dealerships to produce and market their automobiles successfully. Parties that work with the focal firm are its corporate partners.

Consider an example that demonstrates the role these partners play and how they work with the firm to create a single, efficient manufacturing system. Unlike most outdoor clothing manufacturers that use synthetic nonrenewable materials, Nau makes modern urban+outdoor apparel from renewable sources such as sustainably harvested eucalyptus and recycled plastic bottles. It was founded by a team of entrepreneurs who left companies such as Nike and Patagonia. To develop clothing from sustainable materials that were rugged and beautiful, these founders

Nau works with its corporate partners to develop socially responsible outdoor (left) and urban (right) apparel.

turned to manufacturing partners around the world to develop new fabrics that are performance-driven and technical. One example of an innovative fabric used in Nau's jackets is a blend of recycled polyester and organic cotton that is coated and bonded to recycled polyester knit. The result is a water-resistant, breathable technical soft shell material that is ideal for outdoor activities. To complement the new fabrics, the company uses only organic cotton and wool from "happy sheep," provided by partners in the ranching industry that embrace animal-friendly practices. Not only does Nau represent the cutting edge of sustainability and green business; it also clearly demonstrates how "going green" can prompt companies to work more closely with their partners to innovate.[9]

CHECK YOURSELF

1. What are the components of the immediate environment?

MACROENVIRONMENTAL FACTORS

LO2 Explain why marketers must consider their macroenvironment when they make decisions.

In addition to understanding their customers, the company itself, their competition, and their corporate partners, marketers must understand the macroenvironmental factors that operate in the external environment, namely, the culture, demographics, social trends, technological advances, economic situation, and political/regulatory environment, or CDSTEP, as shown in Exhibit 5.3.

Culture

We broadly define culture as the shared meanings, beliefs, morals, values, and customs of a group of people.[10] Transmitted by words, literature, and institutions, culture is passed down from generation to generation and learned over time. You participate in many cultures: Your family has a cultural heritage, so perhaps your mealtime traditions include eating rugelach, a traditional Jewish pastry, or sharing corned beef and cabbage to celebrate your Irish ancestry on St. Patrick's Day. In addition, your school or workplace shares its own common culture. In a broader sense, you also participate in the cultural aspects of the town and country in which you live. The challenge for marketers is to have products or services identifiable by and relevant to a particular group of people. Our various cultures influence what, why, how, where, and when we buy. Two dimensions of culture that marketers must take into account as they develop their marketing strategies are the culture of the country and that of a region within a country.

Country Culture The visible nuances of a country's culture, such as artifacts, behavior, dress, symbols, physical settings, ceremonies, language differences, colors and tastes, and food preferences, are easy to spot. But the subtler aspects of country culture generally are trickier to identify and navigate. Sometimes the best answer is to establish a universal appeal within the specific identities of country culture. Apple and other global firms have successfully bridged the cultural gap by producing advertising that appeals to the same target market across countries. The pictures and copy are the same. The only thing that changes is the language.

Regional Culture The region in which people live in a particular country has its own regional culture that affects many aspects of people's life, including the way they might refer to a particular product category like soft drinks. In the soft drink market,

---

EXHIBIT 5.3 The Macroenvironment

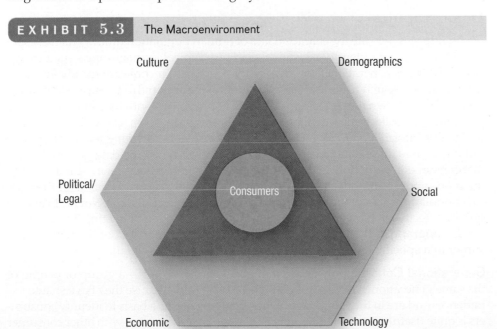

Some firms, like Apple, bridge the cultural gap by using the same advertising in different countries. Only the language is different, as illustrated by this billboard in Germany.

41 percent of Americans refer to carbonated beverages as "soda," whereas another 38 percent call them "pop," and an additional 15 percent call any such beverage a "Coke," even when it is Pepsi.[11] Eat lunch in Indiana and you'll have the best luck ordering a "pop" from the midwesterner who owns the restaurant, but if you then head to Atlanta for dinner, you'd better order your "Coke," regardless of the brand you prefer. Head to Massachusetts and the term is "soda," but if you move to Texas, you might be asked if you'd like a Dr Pepper—a generic term for carbonated beverages in the Lone Star state because it was first formulated there in 1885.[12] Imagine the difficulty these firms have in developing promotional materials that transcend these regional differences.

Demographics

Demographics indicate the characteristics of human populations and segments, especially those used to identify consumer markets. Typical demographics such as age (which includes generational cohorts), gender, race, and income are readily available from market research firms such as IRI (formerly SymphonyIRI Group). Many firms undertake their own market research as well. For example, with its ExtraCard loyalty program, CVS collects massive amounts of data about shoppers who visit all its stores. It uses this information to target offers for, say, cosmetics to young female shoppers. But it also uses these data to benefit its communities. When the data gathered show that consumers—especially elderly customers of the pharmacy chain—are not refilling their prescriptions at the expected rate, CVS proactively interacts with these at-risk populations to encourage adherence to their medical plans.[13] Not all firms are quite as effective in their efforts though, as Social and Mobile Marketing 5.1 describes.

Demographics thus provide an easily understood snapshot of the typical consumer in a specific target market, as the next few sections detail.

LO3 Describe the differences among the various generational cohorts.

Generational Cohorts Consumers in a *generational cohort*—a group of people of the same generation— have similar purchase behaviors because they have shared experiences and are in the same stage of life. Applying age as a basis to identify consumers is quite useful to marketers, as long as it is used in conjunction with other consumer characteristics. For example, most media are characterized by the consumers who use

Social & Mobile Marketing 5.1 — Understanding Connections, Both with and by Young Consumers[i]

For marketing executives, choices about where and how much to spend to appeal to consumers should depend mainly on a careful analysis of where those consumers are exposed to marketing messages. But when a generation gap appears between these two groups, advertising choices may reflect marketers' preferences more than consumers'.

A clear manifestation comes from advertising for beauty products. Previous generations of consumers often relied on insights and advice from big, glossy fashion magazines. Lush, expensive, two-page spreads, with glamorous shots of beauty products in use, seemed effective and appropriate. But Millennials who still read such magazines likely access them online and skip quickly over such long and intrusive ads, with little appreciation for the quality of the shot. Furthermore, recent research shows that such high-quality visual tactics used in print advertisements do not translate particularly well to online product sites. On retail websites, the pretty pictures are largely ineffective because shoppers seek concrete information about their purchase decisions.

According to Forrester Research, 91 percent of Millennials are active Internet users. To reach the web, 59 percent of them use smartphones, 35 percent rely on tablets, and 70 percent employ their laptops. Across these various uses, this younger generation of consumers spends an average of 25 hours online every week.

Their electronic media usage is not the only impressive number describing these consumers: The Millennial market encompasses approximately 105 million consumers, with annual buying power of about $200 billion. Yet even when they recognize and appreciate the size and opportunity that these consumers represent, many marketers—especially those who have reached executive positions after long careers—continue to devote the bulk of their media spending to channels that Millennials simply don't use that much anymore, such as magazines and television.

The main reason for this error might be a somewhat clichéd image of Baby Boomers, confused and overwhelmed by the new options created through technological advances. Faced with a wealth of choices, such as small independent blogs, content-generating sites, and aggregators, these marketing executives retreat to familiar ground. If they aren't sure what each type of site does, they can't determine which is the best option.

Even marketers who embrace technology channels for advertising exhibit a tendency to prefer well-established, widely known spaces, such as Facebook or Google. For young consumers who seek exciting, interactive media content, such options have little chances of success.

them.[14] Age groups can identify appropriate media in which firms should advertise, as discussed in Social and Mobile Marketing 5.1. Although there are many ways to cut the generational pie, we describe four major groups, as listed in Exhibit 5.4.

Members of Generation Z (Gen Z) are also known as Digital Natives because people in this group were born into a world that already was full of electronic gadgets and digital technologies such as the Internet and social networks.[15] These technologies are being developed and adopted at an unprecedented rate. Whereas it took 38 years for the radio to be adopted by 50 million people and 13 years for television, it only took 2 years for the same number of consumers to sign up for Facebook.

Members of Generation Y (Gen Y), also called Millennials, include more than 60 million people in the United States alone, born between 1977 and 2000. As the children of the Baby Boomers, this group is the biggest cohort since the original postwar World War II boom. It also varies the most in age, ranging from teenagers to adults who have their own families.[16]

The next group, Generation X (Gen X), includes people born between 1965 and 1976 and represents some 41 million Americans. Vastly unlike their Baby Boomer parents, Xers are the first generation of latchkey children (those who grew up in homes in which both parents worked), and 50 percent of them have divorced parents.

After World War II the birthrate in the United States rose sharply, resulting in a group known as the Baby Boomers, the 78 million Americans born between 1946 and 1964. Now

EXHIBIT 5.4	Generational			
Generational cohort	Gen Z	Gen Y	Gen X	Baby Boomers
Range of birth years	2001–2014	1977–2000	1965–1976	1946–1964
Age in 2014	0–13	14–37	38–49	50–68

Tweens are always connected.

that the oldest Boomers are collecting Social Security, it is clear that this cohort will be the largest population of 50-plus consumers the United States has ever seen.

Income Income distribution in the United States has grown more polarized—the highest-income groups are growing, whereas many middle- and lower-income groups' real purchasing power keeps declining. Although the trend of wealthy households outpacing both poor and middle classes is worldwide, it is particularly prominent in the United States. For 2013, the average weekly income of the richest 1 to 10 percent of the population was more than $1,917, the average (median) weekly income for the United States as a whole was $827, and the poorest 10 percent of the population earned less than $392 per week. Furthermore, the number of people who earn less than the poverty line ($23,550 for a family of four in 2013) continues to grow.[17] The wealthiest 1 percent control 34.6 percent of Americans' total net worth; the bottom 90 percent control only 26.9 percent in comparison.[18] The increase in wealthy families may be due to the maturing of the general population, the increase in dual-income households, and the higher overall level of education. It also may prompt some ethical concerns about the distribution of wealth. However, the broad range in incomes creates marketing opportunities at both the high and low ends of the market.

Although some marketers choose to target only affluent population segments, others have had great success delivering value to middle- and low-income earners. Consider, for example, the toys presented by the specialty retailer Hammacher Schlemmer (HS) versus the mass appeal of Walmart's toy sections. Toy buyers at Walmart are looking for inexpensive products; those at Hammacher Schlemmer go to great lengths to find unusual toys such as the Giant Gumball Machine which holds 14, 450 gumballs, pictured, or the Mind Controlled UFO.[19]

Education Studies show that higher levels of education lead to better jobs and higher incomes.[20] According to the U.S. Bureau of Labor Statistics, employment that requires a college or secondary degree accounts for nearly half of all projected job growth in the near future. Moreover, average annual earnings are higher for those with degrees than for those without. Those who did not graduate from high school have an average weekly salary of $468, high school grads earn $648, and those with a bachelor's degree earn $1,216.[21]

For some products, marketers can combine education level with other data such as occupation and income and obtain pretty accurate predictions of purchase behavior. For instance, a full-time college student with a part-time job may have relatively little personal income but will spend his or her disposable dollars differently than would a high school graduate who works in a factory and earns a similar income. Marketers need to be quite cognizant of the interaction among education, income, and occupation.

Gender Years ago gender roles appeared clear, but those male and female roles have been blurred. In particular, women today outperform men scholastically, earn higher grades on average, and graduate from both high school and college at greater rates. Perhaps unsurprisingly, recent studies also show that approximately 15 percent of married women in Western economies earn more than their husbands in the workplace.[22] These shifts in status, attitudes, and behaviors affect the way many firms need to design and promote their products and services. More firms are careful about gender neutrality in positioning their products and attempt to transcend gender boundaries, especially through increased interactions with their customers. On the basis of its research with men, for example, the children's stroller company Bugaboo International designed a high-tech, black-and-chrome contraption with dirt bike tires. Several other long-held assumptions about who buys what also are being challenged in today's marketing environment, as Adding Value 5.1 describes.

Hammacher Schlemmer's Giant Gumball Machine targets the affluent population segments.

Adding Value 5.1   Where Gender Matters—and Where It Doesn't[ii]

In the past, the demographic patterns seemed clear: Women bought personal care products, fragrances, women's clothing, and groceries. Men bought stereo equipment, video games, tires, and men's clothing—if they had to. But in modern-day marketing environments, virtually all of these easy classifications are being challenged by shoppers who have little time to waste with gender stereotypes. And marketers are quickly catching on.

For example, when Urban Outfitters was redesigning its website, it stumbled on what the web designers thought was a brilliant and simple change. They would personalize the site so that female visitors immediately were directed to dresses and blouses, while male visitors saw work shirts and tough-guy jeans. The response was quick—and negative. Female visitors complained that they were the ones buying most of the clothing for the men in their lives. And on top of that, they found the gender-biased marketing offensive.

At the same time, more and more men are in the market for grooming and personal care products. The suggested reasons are many. Maybe the modern generation simply is more accustomed to shopping for themselves. Or perhaps job seekers in a tight economy need any edge they can get, and feeling confident about their personal grooming as they head to interviews might tip the scales in their favor. Regardless of the reason, the conventional wisdom that personal care and fragrance sellers could market just to women has gone out the window.

Overall it appears that men and women have approximately equal influences on households' spending. In a recent survey, 85 percent of women and 84 percent of men agreed that they shared responsibility for shopping decisions.

Such equality of influence is not to say that women and men shop the same way though. As men take on more grocery shopping tasks—a role traditionally assigned to women—some grocery retailers are experimenting with ways to appeal to them. For example, men appear to hate to ask for help, so the stores need to be efficient and clearly laid out with good signage, rather than providing an abundance of customer service.

Best Buy similarly recognized that women are a massive market for electronics, smartphones, and mobile devices. But its stores tended to attract very few female shoppers. Therefore, its recent store design revisions aim to appeal to women with household appliance sections that look more like kitchens than like industrial shipyards and hand sanitizer dispensers placed next to the video game test consoles.

As gender roles shift, more grocery chains are gearing up to better meet the needs of their male customers.

The Hispanic market is so large in some areas of the United States that marketers develop entire marketing programs just to meet their needs.

The Hispanic market is so large in some areas of the United States that marketers develop entire marketing programs just to meet their needs.

Ethnicity[23] Because of immigration and increasing birthrates among various ethnic and racial groups, the United States continues to grow more diverse. Approximately 80 percent of all population growth in the next 20 years is expected to come from African American, Hispanic, and Asian communities. Minorities now represent approximately one-quarter of the population; by 2050 they will represent about 50 percent, and nearly 30 percent of the population will be Hispanic.[24] The United Nations also estimates that approximately 1 million people per year will emigrate from less developed nations to the United States over the next 40 years.[25] Many foreign-born Americans and recent immigrants tend to concentrate in a handful of metropolitan areas, such as New York, Los Angeles, San Francisco, and Chicago.

 LO4 Identify various social trends that impact marketing.

Among the different groups, Hispanic buying power is projected to reach $1.3 trillion in 2015, a cumulative increase of around 25 percent compared with 2010.[26] The 50 million Hispanic consumers in the United States have increasing influences on mainstream U.S. culture, as Superior Service 5.1 highlights. Many families have been in the United States for multiple generations, and the consumer behavior of these highly acculturated Hispanics differs little from that of other groups of Americans. For example, they use credit cards, are minimally influenced by advertising and product placements, exhibit greater sensitivity to in-store promotions, and are likely to shop online and from catalogs.

The United States is like a salad bowl, a mix made up of people from every corner of the world.

The census of 2010 counts 42 million African American U.S. households, who are more affluent and suburban than previous studies suggested. They also tend to be younger, such that 47 percent are between the ages of 18 and 49 years (i.e., a key age demographic for many marketers). The number of black households earning more than $75,000 has increased by 47 percent since 2005, and by 2015 trends indicate that a majority of black Americans will live in the suburbs.[27] For example, in the Atlanta metropolitan area the city lost 8 percent of its African American households, while the surrounding suburbs gained a remarkable 40 percent.[28] For this demographic segment, especially as it moves increasingly to the suburbs, Home Depot has developed particular

Superior Service 5.1 — Serving Up Cultural Preferences, One Slice at a Time[iii]

Food marketers like Kraft Foods and Anheuser-Busch are making their products and advertising more user-friendly for Hispanic consumers by adding Spanish translations to packaging and selling lime-infused beer. The Dallas-based pizza chain Pizza Patrón is going the opposite direction and adding English to its existing Spanish-language marketing materials. The shift comes in response to focus groups and surveys that indicated the chain was attracting younger and more multicultural customers.

When the first Pizza Patrón opened in 1986, it lured first-generation immigrants who tended to order in Spanish. Recognizing the opportunity to differentiate Pizza Patrón from other pizza chains, the company's founder focused on opening new stores in neighborhoods that were predominantly Hispanic, offered menu choices likely to appeal to Hispanics, used Spanish on menus and menu boards, and focused advertising on Spanish-speaking radio and television stations. The strategy resulted in a chain that has grown to 100 stores in 25 years, with projected revenues of more than $40 million.

Now the Pizza Patrón restaurants are serving the children of these early customers. These young diners, who frequently have purchasing power in the household because of their English language skills, are more fully integrated into American culture. According to a recent U.S. Census Bureau report, young Hispanics are the fastest-growing segment of the youth population in the United States, making them a valuable resource for Pizza Patrón. As a result, Pizza Patrón is shifting its marketing mix so that significantly more ads run in English-language media outlets. New stores will open in neighborhoods that are less heavily Hispanic, as well as in areas where Hispanics have moved.

Despite the appeal of this new audience, the chain doesn't want to run the risk of alienating its existing customer base. As a result, the restaurants will continue to offer food that appeals to its target clientele, including toppings like chorizo sausage and jalapeno peppers, churros, and lime-and-pepper-flavored chicken wings. While English is the primary language on menu boards and printed materials, these marketing tools will still contain Spanish. The store also plans new marketing efforts designed to appeal to its traditional clientele, including in-store displays relating to holidays traditionally celebrated by Hispanics and Spanish-language phrases that mean more to Hispanic customers than to those who simply translate the individual words.

---

appeals featuring national figures such as Tom Joyner and Steve Harvey.

Finally, Asian Americans make up only about 5.6 percent of the U.S. population, but they also represent the fastest-growing minority population, tend to earn more, have more schooling, and be more likely to be professionally employed or own a business.

Social Trends

Various social trends appear to be shaping consumer values in the United States and around the world, including a greater emphasis on health and wellness concerns, greener consumers, and privacy concerns.

Health and Wellness Concerns Health concerns, especially those pertaining to children, are prevalent, critical, and widespread. In the past 20 years, child obesity has doubled and teenage obesity tripled in the United States, leading to skyrocketing rates of high blood pressure, high cholesterol, early signs of heart disease, and type 2 diabetes among children. The U.S. Centers for Disease Control and Prevention (CDC) also estimates that approximately one-third of U.S. adults are obese, and the incidence of diabetes has reached 8.3 percent—with much higher rates for people still undiagnosed or classified as having prediabetes.[29] It is also increasing at alarming rates in other countries and among consumers who adopt more Western diets.

This Subway ad speaks directly to the issue of childhood obesity and responds to the new advertising guidelines adopted by marketers. The SUBWAY FRESH FIT FOR KIDS™ meal, which meets the American Heart Association criteria for a heart-healthy meal, provides a nutritional choice for customers wanting a quick service food alternative for their children.

Adding Value 5.2   Transforming Grocery Stores into Health Providers[iv]

Increasing numbers of supermarkets now feature a new type of employee who floats among aisles, offering advice and suggestions for shoppers. By keeping a registered dietitian on staff, various grocery chains seek to meet their customers' demands for more information about healthy choices, as well as expand their roles in their customers' lives.

Dietitians have long been members of grocery store corporations, but usually they sat in corporate offices and informed executives on product decisions. Moving down the supply chain and into stores, today's dietitian staff advise consumers directly about the products they see on the shelves of their local store. A parent whose child suffers severe food allergies can ask about safe options. A consumer struggling with weight can learn about the best options for reducing calories and fat. And environmentally conscious buyers can determine the difference between "all-natural" and "organic" (the former claim is unregulated; the latter means the product has passed a series of stringent tests).

The Food Marketing Institute recently determined that about one-third of grocery store chains—including Hy-Vee, Safeway, and Wegmans—have added dietitians at the retail level, whereas 86 percent keep one on staff at the corporate level. In addition, predictions suggest that the number of retail dietitians will double in coming years.

Much of the advice dietitians offer to shoppers in stores is free, though some stores also offer more extensive consultations for a fee. Furthermore, the stores use their recommendations

Grocery stores, including Coborn's, provide a NuVal ranking from 1 to 100 for each product. Higher scores reflect more nutritious food choices.

to promote certain products as "dietitians' picks," highlighted by shelf signs and promotions.

For example, Safeway's new "Simple Nutrition" program highlights 22 separate potential health benefits associated with the various products on its shelves. A third-party organization also has established a NuVal ranking system that assigns each product a nutrition value score, from 1 to 100. The scores reflect more than 30 criteria, such as cholesterol, sugar, and sodium levels, as well as the amount of calcium or protein provided.

The practice of yoga is growing as more consumers embrace a healthy lifestyle.

New advertising guidelines therefore require marketers to produce food in reasonably proportioned sizes. Advertised food items must provide basic nutrients, have less than 30 percent of their total calories from fat, and include no added sweeteners. The advertising also cannot be aired during children's programming, and companies cannot link unhealthy foods with cartoon and celebrity figures. For example, Burger King no longer uses SpongeBob SquarePants to promote burgers and fries.[30] Yet for many consumers, finding the healthiest options using existing labels and packaging continues to be a challenge. Some retailers offer services to help customers with such choices, as Adding Value 5.2 explains.

At the same time, consumers' interest in improving their health has opened up several new markets and niches focused on healthy living. For example, consumer spending on yoga classes, mats, and clothing has increased consistently in recent years.[31] Yoga studios actually combine multiple modern trends: As the economy sours, people face increasing stress, which they hope to reduce through yoga. In addition, yoga studios are relatively inexpensive to open and operate, so entrepreneurs and consumers appreciate the value for the money they offer. And of course, Americans remain consistently on the lookout for exercise mechanisms that can help them shed pounds and match media images of athletic prowess and beautiful bodies. Thus competition is growing in this industry, and some studios have begun to combine their basic yoga classes with additional offers to attract clients, such as food services, acupuncture, or massages.[32]

Ethical & Societal Dilemma 5.1   Green Cereal?[v]

At times it may seem that massive conglomerates are slow to change, but some companies are clearly learning some lessons when it comes to responsible sourcing. Just a few years ago, Nestlé suffered terrible consumer backlash when it agreed to purchase a small amount of palm oil (used in its chocolate candies) from a company that cleared rain forests to access the palms.

Wary of such reactions, General Mills (GM) quickly promised that all the palm oil used in any of its products and packaging would come from responsible, sustainable sources by 2015. Recent estimates suggest that such moves are achieving some success. The rate of Amazonian deforestation in 2012 was lower than at any other point since the Brazilian government started tracking this statistic in 1988. But neither GM nor any of its competitors in the consumer packaged-goods industry have reached the goal of complete sustainability quite yet.

Determined not to limit itself to palm oil, GM also committed to improving the trade conditions for vanilla farmers that supply the raw material for the traditional, favorite flavor of its Häagen-Dazs ice cream. With a two-year investment of $125 million in Madagascar, GM plans to train small vanilla farmers in sustainable methods that also increase crop quality, such as yield improvements and curing techniques. Ideally, these tactics also will enhance the earnings of local farmers and their communities.

Next, GM helped found—in collaboration with the U.S. Department of Agriculture (USDA) and Environmental Protection Agency (EPA)—the U.S. Food Waste Challenge. This initiative seeks not only to reduce the environmental impacts of waste collected in landfills but also to address spreading food insecurity concerns. By reducing the waste and loss of food products,

The demand for palm oil can often lead to rain forests, such as this one, being clear cut.

the collaborators hope to feed more people or at least use the edible remainders for productive uses such as animal feed.

These examples reflect GM's overall sustainability mission and efforts. It has released Global Responsibility Reports annually for more than 40 years. It also touts its efforts widely through its blog, press releases, and other communications. In this sense, GM runs the risk that skeptical consumers will come to believe it publicizes its good works to cover up bad behavior. But as the CEO of General Mills has readily acknowledged, "We're finding opportunities to collaborate with business, government and non-governmental organizations on important systemic solutions. While we're proud of our progress, we also know there is still much more to be done. We are committed to continued progress in these areas. Our business requires it and future generations depend on it."

Greener Consumers Green marketing involves a strategic effort by firms to supply customers with environmentally friendly merchandise.[33] Many consumers, concerned about everything from the purity of air and water to the safety of beef and salmon, believe that each person can make a difference in the environment. For example, nearly half of U.S. adults now recycle their soda bottles and newspapers, and European consumers are even more green. Germans are required by law to recycle bottles, and the European Union does not allow beef raised on artificial growth hormones to be imported.

Demand for green-oriented products has been a boon to the firms that supply them. Marketers encourage consumers to replace older versions of washing machines and dishwashers with water- and energy-saving models and to invest in phosphate-free laundry powder and mercury-free and rechargeable batteries. New markets emerge for recycled building products, packaging, paper goods, and even sweaters and sneakers as well as for more efficient appliances, lighting, and heating and cooling systems in homes and offices. Jumping on the green bandwagon, Frito-Lay's SunChips line of snack foods uses solar power at one of its eight production facilities to harness the sun's energy to produce its products.[34] Ethical and Societal Dilemma 5.1 examines some of the challenges companies face in making green products.

These green products and initiatives suggest a complicated business model. Are they good for business? Some green options are more expensive than traditional products and initiatives. Are consumers interested in or willing to pay the higher prices for green products? Are firms really interested in improving the environment? Or are they disingenuously marketing products or services as environmentally friendly, with the goal of gaining public approval and sales rather than actually improving the environment? This type of exploitation is common enough that it even has produced a new term: greenwashing. Consumers need to question whether a firm is spending significantly more money and time advertising being green and operating with consideration for the environment than actually spending these resources on environmentally sound practices.

Privacy Concerns More and more consumers worldwide sense a loss of privacy. At the same time that the Internet has created an explosion of accessibility to consumer information, improvements in computer storage facilities and the manipulation of information have led to more and better security and credit check services. Yet controversies still erupt, and some observers suggest hackers are just getting more effective. In 2013, for example, Target suffered a massive security breach that allowed hackers to steal credit and debit card information for 40 million customers, as well as personal information, including phone numbers and addresses, for another 70 million.[35]

Every time a consumer surfs the web and clicks on a site, online marketers can place "cookies" on that user's computer, showing them where he or she starts, proceeds, and ends the online encounter—as well as what he or she buys, and doesn't. For many consumers, such close access to their behaviors is an unacceptable invasion of privacy.

Realizing consumers are upset about this issue, the marketing industry as a whole has sought to find solutions and self-regulations that would calm customers, satisfy cautious regulators, and still enable marketing firms to gain access to invaluable information about consumer behaviors. Those attempts appear to have stalled. The online marketing industry simply has not been able to agree about how to police itself. It looks like it may be up to Congress to address this growing issue.[36]

Technological Advances

Technological advances have accelerated during the past decade, improving the value of both products and services. Consumers have constant access to the Internet everywhere through services such as Wi-Fi, Mobile Hotspots, 4G, and LTE. Smartphones using the iOS and Android systems allow for greater computing, data storage, and communication. Tablet computers, starting with the iPad, have extended mobile computing even further by offering a larger mobile interface in environments that traditionally have limited access.

These examples of advanced technology make consumers increasingly dependent on the help they receive from the providers of the technology. Thus Netflix suggests which movies we should watch, Pandora outlines the music we should listen to, and Amazon tells us what we should read.

Near field communication technology takes payments, coupons, and loyalty card data from customers as they walk by the scanner. The next broad wave of mobile applications is likely to expand the use of wireless payments, through applications such as Google Wallet, Master card's Easy Pay, and Isis Mobile Wallet, all of which enable customers' phones to serve as m-wallets.

From the firm's perspective, the technology called radio frequency identification device (RFID) enables it to track an item from the moment it was manufactured, through the distribution system, to the retail store, and into the hands of the final consumer. Because they are able to determine exactly how much of each product is at a given point in the supply chain, retailers can also communicate with their suppliers and collaboratively plan to meet their inventory needs.

Mobile devices enhance the customer's experience by making it easier to interact with the manufacturer or retailer or other customers, and they add a

Social & Mobile Marketing **5.2** The News from This Year's CES[vi]

Every year, the Consumer Electronics Show (CES) in Las Vegas gets bigger and more impressive, hosting the top names in technology and electronics and providing a harbinger of the things to come. The 2014 version was no exception. Some of the main trends emerging from the show are as follows:

1. *Conversational appliances inside connected homes.* Advances in technology promise that not only will our refrigerators tell us when the milk is getting low, but our washing machines will warn us that the rinse cycle is about to start. Bathroom scales will link to online sites to help dieters keep track of their progress. These smart appliances also will have specific recommendations and services for each member of the household, ensuring individual-level targeting.

2. *Really smart, really sharp, really big televisions.* It might seem as if this trend would be covered in the connected homes prediction, but it is so remarkable that it earned its own place on most lists. Televisions are getting bigger than ever, with improved 4K resolution (four times better than the HD televisions currently on the market). The LEDs are getting better too, with an organic version (OLED) that provides better contrast. Finally, the big screens are curving, such that even if viewers have a relatively small room and must sit close to the television, they can still enjoy the full peripheral view.

3. *Fitness, readily on hand.* For a trade show that stereotypically has appealed to tech geeks, fitness was a major theme at CES. The latest innovations make it far easier for consumers to track their exercise rates, times, and distances, then engage with others by uploading the data to shared sites. Enhancing this ease, many of the fitness apps depend on technology that users can wear, such that they never need to take it off, if they so choose.

4. *The promise of the driverless car.* Automakers including Toyota, Lexus, and Audi announced collaborations with innovators from companies such as Google and Apple in their ongoing effort to devise a car that can drive itself. Others were slightly less ambitious, such as the impending dashboard-mounted weather and music apps from GM. These models also plan to include 4G LTE hotspots within the cars themselves. In a combined effort, Honda, Hyundai, Audi, and GM are working with the chip manufacturer Nvidia and engineers from Google (along with input from the National Highway Traffic Safety Administration) to develop industry standards to define the rules for linked cars and their in-vehicle mobile apps.

Automakers, such as Toyota, are collaborating with companies including Apple and Google to create a self-driving car.

new channel of access, which makes customers more loyal and more likely to spend more with a particular retailer. Walgreens' applications and Web Pickup service allow customers to order prescriptions or review their prescription history, check the in-store inventories, and print photos. As Social and Mobile Marketing 5.2 summarizes, ever more new and exciting technologies seem poised to enter the consumer market.

Economic Situation

Marketers monitor the general economic situation, both in their home country and abroad, because it affects the way consumers buy merchandise and spend money. Some major factors that influence the state of an economy include the rate of inflation, foreign currency exchange rates, and interest rates.

Inflation refers to the persistent increase in the prices of goods and services. Increasing prices cause the purchasing power of the dollar to decline; in other words, the dollar buys less than it used to.

In a similar fashion, foreign currency fluctuations can influence consumer spending. For instance, in the summer of 2002 the euro was valued at slightly less than US$1. By 2013, it was worth $1.27 but only after it had risen to an all-time high of $1.60 in 2008.[37] As the euro becomes more expensive compared with the dollar, merchandise made in Europe and other countries tied to the euro becomes more costly to Americans, whereas products made in the United States cost less for European consumers. In general, the start of the decade of the 2010s has exhibited relatively weak consumer spending overall. Whether in Europe or the United States, consumers exhibit signs of uncertainty and a lack of confidence, leading them to hold off on many purchases.[38]

Interest rates represent the cost of borrowing money. When customers borrow money from a bank, they agree to pay back the loan, plus the interest that accrues. The interest, in effect, is the cost to the customers or the fee the bank charges those customers for borrowing the money. Likewise, if a customer opens a savings account at a bank, he or she will earn interest on the amount saved, which means the interest becomes the fee the consumer gets for loaning the money to the bank. If the interest rate goes up, consumers have an incentive to save more because they earn more for loaning the bank their money; when interest rates go down, however, consumers generally borrow more.

How do these three important economic factors—inflation, foreign currency fluctuations, and interest rates—affect firms' ability to market goods and services? Shifts in the three economic factors make marketing easier for some and harder for others. For instance, when inflation increases, consumers probably don't buy less food, but they may shift their expenditures from expensive steaks to less expensive hamburgers. Grocery stores and inexpensive restaurants win, but expensive restaurants lose. Consumers also buy less discretionary merchandise, though off-price and discount retailers often gain ground at the expense of their full-price competitors. Similarly, the sales of expensive jewelry, fancy cars, and extravagant vacations decrease, but the sale of low-cost luxuries, such as personal care products and home entertainment, tends to increase.

Political/Regulatory Environment

The political/regulatory environment comprises political parties, government organizations, and legislation and laws. Organizations must fully understand and comply with any legislation regarding fair competition, consumer protection, or industry-specific regulation. Since the turn of the century, the government has enacted laws that promote both fair trade and competition by prohibiting the formation of monopolies or alliances that would damage a competitive marketplace, fostering fair pricing practices for all suppliers and consumers.

The government enacts laws focused on ensuring that companies compete fairly with one another. Although enacted in the early part of the 20th century, they remain the backbone of U.S. legislation protecting competition in commerce. These laws include the 1890 Sherman Antitrust Act that prohibits monopolies

Tourists from other countries flock to the United States to shop because the value of the dollar is low compared to their own currency.

and other activities that would restrain trade or competition and makes fair trade within a free market a national goal; the 1914 Clayton Act that supports the Sherman Act by prohibiting the combination of two or more competing corporations through pooling ownership of stock and restricting pricing policies such as price discrimination, exclusive dealing, and tying clauses to different buyers; and the 1936 Robison-Patman Act that specifically outlaws price discrimination toward wholesalers, retailers, or other producers and requires sellers to make ancillary services or allowances available to all buyers on proportionately equal terms. These laws have been specifically used to increase competition, such as the deregulation of the telephone and energy industries, in which massive conglomerates such as Ma Bell, the nickname for AT&T, were broken into smaller, competing companies.

Legislation has also been enacted to protect consumers in a variety of ways. First, regulations require marketers to abstain from false or misleading advertising practices that might mislead consumers, such as claims that a medication can cure a disease when in fact it causes other health risks. Second, manufacturers are required to refrain from using any harmful or hazardous materials (e.g., lead in toys) that might place a consumer at risk. Third, organizations must adhere to fair and reasonable business practices when they communicate with consumers. For example, they must employ reasonable debt collection methods and disclose any finance charges, and they are limited with regard to their telemarketing and e-mail solicitation activities. A summary of the most significant legislation affecting marketing interests appears in Exhibit 5.5.

EXHIBIT 5.5 Consumer Protection Legislation

Year	Law	Description
1906	Federal Food and Drug Act	Created the Food and Drug Administration (FDA); prohibited the manufacture or sale of adulterated or fraudulently labeled food and drug products.
1914	Federal Trade Commission	Established the Federal Trade Commission (FTC) to regulate unfair competitive practices and practices that deceive or are unfair to consumers.
1966	Fair Packaging and Labeling Act	Regulates packaging and labeling of consumer goods; requires manufacturers to state the contents of the package, who made it, and the amounts contained within.
1966	Child Protection Act	Prohibits the sale of harmful toys and components to children; sets the standard for child-resistant packaging.
1967	Federal Cigarette Labeling and Advertising Act	Requires cigarette packages to display this warning: "Warning: The Surgeon General Has Determined That Cigarette Smoking Is Dangerous to Your Health."
1972	Consumer Product Safety Act	Created the Consumer Product Safety Commission (CPSC), which has the authority to regulate safety standards for consumer products.
1990	Children's Television Act	Limits the number of commercials shown during children's programming.
1990	Nutrition Labeling and Education Act	Requires food manufacturers to display nutritional contents on product labels.
1995	Telemarketing Sales Rule	Regulates fraudulent activities conducted over the telephone. Violators are subject to fines and actions enforced by the FTC.
2003	Controlling the Assault of Non-Solicited Pornography and Marketing Act of 2003 (CAN-SPAM Act)	Prohibits misleading commercial e-mail, particularly misleading subject and from lines.
2003	Amendment to the Telemarketing Sales Rule	Establishes a National Do Not Call Registry, requiring telemarketers to abstain from calling consumers who opt to be placed on the list.
2003	Do Not Spam Law	Laws created to reduce spam or unwarranted e-mails.
2010	Financial Reform Law	Created the Consumer Financial Protection Bureau whose aim is to enforce appropriate consumer-oriented regulations on a number of financial firms, such as banks, mortgage businesses, and payday and student lenders. It also set up the Financial Services Oversight Council to act as an early warning system.

Responding to the Environment

As the examples throughout this chapter show, many companies engage in tactics and marketing strategies that attempt to respond to multiple developments in the wider environment. For example, responding to pressures from the Federal Communications Commission (FCC; political and regulatory environment), the economic status of consumers (economic situation), increasing access to faster broadband capabilities (technological advances), and calls for greater social responsibility (social trends), 14 cable companies agreed to provide low-cost Internet access to impoverished families.[39] This remarkable agreement allows the cable companies to promote their social responsibility. But it also ensures that families whose children are eligible for free lunch programs can gain access to the services, opportunities, and options available only online. In a constantly changing marketing environment, the marketers that succeed are the ones that respond quickly, accurately, and sensitively to their consumers.

CHECK YOURSELF

1. What are the six key macroenvironmental factors?
2. Differentiate between country culture and regional culture.
3. What are some important social trends shaping consumer values and shopping behavior?

Reviewing Learning Objectives

 LO1 Outline how customers, the company, competitors, and corporate partners affect marketing strategy.

Everything a firm does should revolve around the customer; without the customer, nothing gets sold. Firms must discover their customers' wants and needs and then be able to provide a valuable product or service that will satisfy those wants or needs. If there were only one firm and many customers, a marketer's life would be a piece of cake. But because this situation rarely occurs, firms must monitor their competitors to discover how they might be appealing to their customers. Without monitoring competitors, a firm's customers might soon belong to its competitors. Though life certainly would be easier without competitors, it would be difficult, if not impossible, without corporate partners. Good marketing firms or departments work closely with suppliers, marketing research firms, consultants, and transportation firms to coordinate the extensive process of discovering what customers want and finally getting it to them when and where they want it. Each of these activities—discovering customer needs, studying competitors' actions,

and working with corporate partners—helps add value to firms' products and services.

 LO2 Explain why marketers must consider their macroenvironment when they make decisions.

What are the chances that a fast-food hamburger restaurant would be successful in a predominantly Hindu neighborhood? Not good. Marketers must be sensitive to such cultural issues to be successful, and they must also consider customer demographics—age, income, market size, education, gender, and ethnicity—to identify specific customer target groups. In any society, major social trends influence the way people live. In no other time in history has technology moved so rapidly and had such a pervasive influence on the way we live. Not only do marketers help identify and develop technologies for practical, everyday uses, but technological advances help marketers provide consumers with more products and services more quickly and efficiently. The general state of the economy influences how people spend their discretionary income. When the economy is healthy, marketing success comes relatively easily. But when the economy gets bumpy, only well-honed marketing skills can yield long-term successes. Naturally, all firms must abide by the law, and many legal issues affect marketing directly. These laws pertain to competitive practices and protecting consumers from unfair or dangerous products.

LO3 **Describe the differences among the various generational cohorts.**

Generational cohorts are groups of consumers of the same generation. They are likely to have similar purchase and consumption behaviors due to their shared experiences and stages of life. The four main types include Gen Z (born

2001–2014), Gen Y (born 1977–2000), Gen X (1965–1976), and Baby Boomers (1946–1964). Each of these segments exhibits different consumption patterns, attitudes toward the world, and preferences with regard to marketing efforts.

LO4 **Identify various social trends that impact marketing.**

Social trends have a tremendous impact on what consumers purchase and consume. Understanding these trends—health and wellness, green marketing, and privacy issues—can help marketers serve their customers better.

Key Terms

■ILEARNSMART·

- Baby Boomers, 151
- country culture, 149
- culture, 149
- demographics, 150
- Digital Native, 151
- economic situation, 160
- foreign currency fluctuations, 160

- Generation X (Gen X), 151
- Generation Y (Gen Y), 151
- Generation Z (Gen Z), 151
- generational cohort, 150
- green marketing, 157
- greenwashing, 158
- inflation, 160
- interest rates, 160

- macroenvironmental factors, 149
- Millennials, 151
- political/regulatory environment, 160
- regional culture, 149
- technological advances, 158

Marketing Applications

1. Assume you are going to open a new store selling fitness products. Describe it. Who are your competitors? What would you do to monitor your competitors' actions? Who are your customers? What are you going to do to appeal to them? What are your social responsibilities, and how will you meet them?

2. How do you approach buying a computer differently than your parents would? What about buying an outfit to wear to a party? How can firms use their knowledge of different age or generational cohorts to market their products and services better?

3. How can firms use customer demographics like income, market size, education, and ethnicity to market to their customers better?

4. Identify some of the ethnicity changes in the United States. Describe how they might affect the marketing practices of (a) a radio station in Texas,

(b) food retailers in cities, and (c) a home furnishing store in New York City.

5. Identify some recent technological innovations in the marketplace and describe how they have affected consumers' everyday activities.

6. Why should a T-shirt shop in the United States care about the value of the Hong Kong dollar?

7. Time-poor consumers have adopted various approaches to "buy" themselves more time, such as (a) voluntarily simplifying their complex lives, (b) using new technologies for greater empowerment and control, (c) using their time productively when traveling or commuting, and (d) multitasking. Identify and describe some products and services that consumers use to implement each of these strategies.

8. Identify a company that you believe does a particularly good job of marketing to different cultural groups. Justify your answer.

Quiz Yourself

1. Yuri is considering a new promotional campaign in which he will compare his products to those of his competitors. Before initiating the promotional campaign, Yuri will likely assess his competitors' strengths, weaknesses, and:
    a. likely reaction to Yuri's promotional activities.
    b. demographics.
    c. just-in-time processes.
    d. satisfaction quotient as perceived by customers.
    e. ethical values.

2. Marketers have learned that culture influences _____ consumers buy.
    a. what
    b. how
    c. where
    d. when
    e. all of the above

    (Answers to these two questions can be found on page 651.)

Net Savvy

1. Seventh Generation is the leading brand of non-toxic, environmentally safe household products in the United States. Visit its website (http://www.seventhgeneration.com) and review the philosophy behind the business. Next, review the site to identify the products the company offers. Briefly summarize some of the consumer trends you think are reflected. Describe the ways in which Seventh Generation's products address the wants and needs of its customers.

2. Visit The Cool Hunter (http://www.thecoolhunter.net) and identify examples that would provide marketers insights regarding social trends.

3. Visit and explore the website of your favorite breakfast cereal. Identify the demographics of its target customer. Evaluate the effectiveness of its marketing strategy.

Chapter Case Study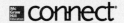

A NEXT-GENERATION CLEANSER[40]

Taking an Iroquois directive—"In our every deliberation, we must consider the impact of our decisions on the next seven generations"—the consumer product company Seventh Generation has applied a distinctly modern sensibility to derive a long-term approach to the marketing environment. Although its mission statement might be focused on future generations, its efforts to appeal to current consumers are always responsive to their immediate demands.

Seventh Generation dominates the environmentally friendly cleaning products market in the United States.

From its start in Vermont in 1988, Seventh Generation has grown to become a national brand with over $200 million in revenues.[41] Its growth has been sparked largely by consumer desires to buy more sustainable, environmentally safe green products. Approximately 71 percent of consumers in a recent survey indicated that they thought it was important to buy green offerings (up from 66 percent in 2008), and consumer demand for products in a wide range of categories continues to grow.[42]

But even as more categories appear to offer promising green opportunities for marketers, the primary purchase area continues to be groceries and household products—exactly the space that Seventh Generation dominates. As it has gained brand recognition and trust, it also has proactively altered its market. That is, Seventh Generation does not simply wait for customers to request options. It creates entirely new categories.

With a new line of detergents, Seventh Generation began promoting the idea that perhaps chemical brighteners—common to virtually all commercially available detergents, even those that avoid dyes or fragrances—are not necessary. The company took care not to suggest these chemicals were dangerous. It just says they're unnecessary, and for consumers interested in environmental concerns, that may be enough.

Previously, household magazines such as *Good Housekeeping* or *Real Simple* might have ranked the best detergent, the best dishwashing soap, and the best surface cleaner. But the entry of companies such as Seventh Generation has created new categories: best green detergent, best green dishwashing soap, and best green cleaner. Seventh Generation products consistently emerge victorious in these new category contests.[43]

In addition, to maintain its brand recognition, it uses extensive multimedia marketing initiatives. In print ads, it highlights the environmentally friendly contents of its laundry detergent. It provides free samples to active bloggers, along with blacklights so these consumers can test their own clothes to see the residues left by other detergents. Dozens have posted the results of their own in-home experiments.[44]

Yet its products also cost more, which offers a significant challenge in the very price-competitive cleaning products market. Even as many consumer product companies increasingly tout their down-market brands, Seventh Generation introduced a 4× concentrated laundry detergent that costs significantly more. The new derivation avoids all volatile organic compounds and relies on enzymes to get clothes clean.[45]

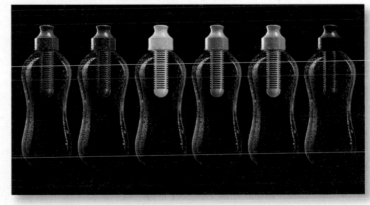

In 2013, Seventh Generation spent a significant sum to acquire bobble, a company that produces reusable, self-filtering water bottles. Because many consumers worry about their environmentally unfriendly consumption of plastic water bottles, but also are not willing to trust unfiltered tap water, the new product provides an effective solution. With this move, Seventh Generation also appears poised to "extend our influence and spread our practices more broadly by acquiring innovative brands in the sustainability space," in the words of the company CEO.[46]

To appeal to its environmentally conscious customers, Seventh Generation is incorporating reusable, self-filtering water bottles into it's products.

Questions

1. What consumer trends does Seventh Generation respond to most effectively?

2. Which consumer trends might it be missing?

Endnotes

1. Stephanie Rosenbloom, "A Hotel Room with 140 Characters," *The New York Times,* October 3, 2013, http://www.nytimes.com.

2. Thomas Cook Group, "Thomas Cook Launches Innovative Digital Hotel Concept," press release, October 31, 2013, http://www.thomascookgroup.com/thomas-cook-launches-innovative-digital-hotel-concept-sunconnect-october-2013/.

3. Stephanie Rosenbloom, "Now Checking In: Pampered Pets," *The New York Times,* September 18, 2013, http://www.nytimes.com.

4. Julie Weed, "At Hotels, New Ideas Mix with the Tried and True," *The New York Times,* July 22, 2013, http://www.nytimes.com.

5. Peter F. Drucker, *The Essential Drucker* (New York: Harper-Collins, 2001).

6. "Corning Announces Third-Quarter Results," *Corning News Release,* October 24, 2012, http://www.corning.com.

7. Maureen Morrison, "Pearle Vision Set to Unveil Brand Reboot," *Advertising Age,* April 22, 2013.

8. Linda Doell, "In Razor vs. Razor, neither Gillette nor Schick Gains Edge with Ad Watchdog," March 17, 2011, http://www.dailyfinance.com.

9. http://www.nau.com; Chris Dannen, "Wanted: The Light, Recycled Trench," *Fast Company,* November 19, 2010, http://www.fastcompany.com; Polly Labarre, "Leap of Faith," *Fast Company,* June 2007.

10. Del I. Hawkins and David L. Mothersbaugh, *Consumer Behavior: Building Marketing Strategy,* 11e (Burr Ridge, IL: McGraw-Hill /Irwin, 2009); Philip Cateora and John Graham, *International Marketing,* 16e (Burr Ridge, IL: McGraw-Hill/Irwin, 2012).

11. http://popvssoda.com/.

12. http://www.drpepper.com.

13. "Corporate Responsibility," http://info.cvscaremark.com.

14. Geoffrey E. Meredith, Charles D. Schewe, and Janice Karlovich, *Defining Markets, Defining Moments: America's 7 Generational Cohorts, Their Shared Experiences, and Why Businesses Should Care* (New York: Wiley, 2002).

15. "Consumers of Tomorrow: Insights and Observations about Generation Z," Grail Research, June 2010.

16. Suzy Menkes, "Marketing to the Millennials," *The New York Times,* March 2, 2010; Pamela Paul, "Getting Inside Gen Y," *American Demographics* 23, no. 9; Sharon Jayson, "A Detailed Look at the Millennials," *USA Today,* February 23, 2010.

17. http://www.familiesusa.org; http://www.bls.gov; U.S. Bureau of the Census, "Income, Poverty, and Health Insurance Coverage in the United States, 2010," http://www.census.gov.

18. Dave Gilson and Carolyn Perot, "It's the Inequality, Stupid," *Mother Jones* (March–April 2011), http://motherjones.com; Organisation for Economic Co-operation and Development, "Growing Unequal? Income Distribution and Poverty in OECD Countries," 2008, http://www.oecd.org.

19. http://www.Hammacher.com.

20. http://www.census.gov; http://www.infoplease.com.

21. http://www.familiesusa.org; http://www.bls.gov; U.S. Bureau of the Census, "Income, Poverty, and Health Insurance Coverage in the United States, 2010," http://www.census.gov.

22. Richard Thaler, "Breadwinning Wives and Nervous Husbands," *The New York Times,* June 1, 2013, http://www.nytimes.com.

23. Tom Pirovano, "U.S. Demographics Are Changing . . . Are Your Marketing Plans Ready?" *NielsenWire,* March 10, 2010, http://blog.nielsen.com; "Cents and Sensibility: Why Marketing to Multicultural Consumers Requires a Subtle Touch," *Knowledge@Wharton,* March 10, 2010, http://www.wharton.universia.net; "Ethnic Consumers Hold $282 Billion in Purchasing Power," February 24, 2009, http://news.newamericamedia.org.

24. Jeffrey S. Passel and D'Vera Cohn, "U.S. Population Projections: 2005–2050," Pew Research Center, http://pewhispanic.org.

25. Joel Kotkin, "The Changing Demographics of America," *Smithsonian magazine* (August 2010), http://www.smithsonianmag.com.

26. Julie Jargon, "Pizza Chain Seeks Slice of Bicultural Pie," *The Wall Street Journal,* December 30, 2010, http://online.wsj.com.

27. Todd Wasserman, "Report: Shifting African American Population," *Adweek,* January 12, 2010, http://www.adweek.com; U.S. Bureau of the Census, "Annual Social and Economic Supplement to the Current Population Survey," http://www.census.gov.

28. Nielsen, "The State of the African-American Consumer," September 2011, p. 5.

29. Centers for Disease Control and Prevention, "National Diabetes Fact Sheet, 2011," http://www.cdc.gov.

30. "Guidelines for Marketing Food to Kids Proposed," CSPI, press release, January 5, 2005.

31. Yoga Buzz, "Yoga Biz Thrives Despite Economy," October 24, 2011, http://blogs.yogajournal.com.

32. Catherine Clifford, "Yoga: The Booming Business of Zen," *CNNMoney,* October 18, 2011, http://money.cnn.com.

33. This definition of green marketing draws on work by Jacquelyn A. Ottman, *Green Marketing: Opportunity for Innovation* (Chicago: NTC Publishing, 1997).

34. http://www.sunchips.com/healthier_planet.shtml.

35. Elizabeth A. Harris et al., "A Sneaky Path into Target Customers' Wallets," *The New York Times,* January 17, 2014, http://www.nytimes.com.

36. John Bussey, "Taming the Spies of Web Advertising," *The Wall Street Journal,* August 8, 2013.

37. http://www.irs.gov/.

38. Paul Hannon, "Euro-Zone Consumer Spending Slows," *The Wall Street Journal,* December 4, 2013, http://www.online.wsj.com.

39. Brendan Greeley, "Providing Internet Access to the Poor," *Bloomberg Businessweek,* November 17, 2011, http://www.businessweek.com.

40. http://www.seventhgeneration.com.

41. Serena Ng, "Seventh Generation Picks Up Bobble Brand," *The Wall Street Journal,* May 30, 2013, http://online.wsj.com.

42. "71% of Consumers Think Green When Purchasing," *Environmental Leader,* April 3, 2013; "Seventh Gen, Whole Foods Top Green Brands Ranking," *Environmental Leader,* June 10, 2011, http://www.environmentalleader.com.

43. "The Best Cleaning Products," *Real Simple,* http://www.realsimple.com.

44. Andrew Adam Newman, "Seventh Generation Highlights Its Chemical-Free Detergent," *The New York Times,* December 29, 2010, http://www.nytimes.com/2010/12/30/business/media/30adco.html; "Seventh Generation Promotes Eco-Friendly

Detergents through Multichannel Marketing Initiative," December 30, 2010, http://www.ricg.com.

45. Dan D'Ambrosio, "Seventh Generation Looks to Buck Trend in Concentrated Laundry Detergent Market," *Burlington Free Press*, October 13, 2011.

46. "Seventh Generation Acquires bobble for Undisclosed Sum," press release, May 31, 2013, http://seventhgeneration. mwnewsroom.com/press-releases/seventh-generation-acquires-bobble-for-undisclosed-1022443.

i. Bonnie Fuller, "Baby-Boomer Marketers Are Misreading Millennials' Media Behavior," *Advertising Age*, May 13, 2013; Chingching Chang, "Dual System Model Comparisons of Print Advertisements and e-Store Product Pages: The Influence of Dominant Pictures on Decision Making," working paper (under review at *Journal of Advertising*).

ii. Image source, http://www.iprospect.com/digital-affluent-male; text sources, Natasha Singer, "E-Tailer Customization: Convenient or Creepy?" *The New York Times*, June 23, 2012; "Who Makes the Call at the Mall, Men or Women?" *The Wall Street Journal*, April 23, 2011; Tom Ryan, " 'His' and 'Her' Grocery Aisles," *Retail Wire*, June 6, 2011; Susan Reda, "Guess What? Men Shop, Too!" *Stores*, April 2010; Miguel Bustillo and Mary Ellen Lloyd, "Best Buy Tests New Appeals to Women," *The Wall Street Journal*, June 16, 2010.

iii. Robert Brown and Ruth Washton, "Latino Consumers: Demographic Patterns and Spending Trends among Hispanic Americans," 8th ed., Rockville, MD: Packaged Facts, January 2011.

iv. E. J. Schultz, "The Next Big Weapon for Supermarkets—the Dietician," *Advertising Age*, April 15, 2013, http://www.adage.com.

v. Emily Steel, "Nestlé Takes a Beating on Social-Media Sites," *The Wall Street Journal*, March 29, 2010, http://www.online.wsj.com; Jerry Lynch, "Achieving a Sustainable Palm Oil Commitment," *Taste of General Mills*, December 7, 2012, http://www.blog.generalmills.com; "Haagen-Dazs and General Mills to Help Smallholder Vanilla Farmers Increase Yields and Improve Sustainability Practices in Madagascar," *MarketWatch*, press release, February 20, 2013; "General Mills Joins U.S. Food Waste Challenge as Founding Partner," *The Wall Street Journal*, June 4, 2013, http://online.wsj.com; "General Mills Reports Progress on Global Responsibility Efforts," *The New York Times*, April 30, 2013, http://markets.on.nytimes.com.

vi. Jeanine Poggi, "The Top Three Trends at CES This Year, according to LiquidThread's Brent Poer," *Advertising Age*, January 8, 2014; Jeanine Poggi, "The Top CES Trends—as Seen by Tech Geek and GroupM Chairman-CEO Irwin Gotlieb," *Advertising Age*, January 10, 2014.

Credits

UNDERSTANDING THE MARKETPLACE

The three chapters in Section Two, Understanding the Marketplace, focus on three levels of marketing: to individual consumers; from business to business; and on the global playing field. Chapter 6, Consumer Behavior, discusses why individual consumers purchase products and services. The consumer decision process is highlighted. Chapter 7, Business-to-Business Marketing, explores the whys and hows of business-to-business buying. Finally, Chapter 8, Global Marketing, focuses on global markets. Thus, the three chapters in Section Two move from creating value for the individual consumer, to creating value for the firm or business, to creating value on the global level.

CHAPTER 6

CONSUMER BEHAVIOR

LEARNING OBJECTIVES

LO1 Articulate the steps in the consumer buying process.

LO2 Describe the difference between functional and psychological needs.

LO3 Describe factors that affect information search.

LO4 Discuss postpurchase outcomes.

LO5 List the factors that affect the consumer decision process.

LO6 Describe how involvement influences the consumer decision process.

In Chapter 1 we described the added value provided by the latest generation of smart devices, from Google Glass to the Nike Fit band. Our focus was on the remarkable strides made with regard to technology and innovation that have allowed users to track their exercise times, sleep patterns, and food intake,[1] or carry the Internet around with them at all times, mounted in the corner of their vision.[2] As we also noted, Google Glass has so appealed to consumers that they have competed to pay around $1,500, just to be able to be among the first to try out the new technological gadget.

What makes people shell out so much to try a virtually untested technology? What keeps others from giving it a go? And why are so many companies introducing some version of wearable technology, despite some warnings that the trend will never take off among regular consumers? The answers to these questions all revolve around consumer behavior, that is, the "dynamic interaction of affect and cognition, behavior, and the environment by which human beings conduct the exchange aspects of their lives."[3]

For wearable technology, the boom appears likely because consumers seek to behave in ways that add value to their lives. Thus they seek to fulfill needs that they recognize, enjoy themselves, impress others, and so forth. When a skier realizes that it would be helpful to be able to track altitude at each moment of a run, without having to pull a smartphone or other device out of an inner pocket, a need arises. The Recon ski goggles meet this need because they put lots of data within the skier's line of vision automatically, without having to pause the run, and without exposing any fingers to the elements.[4]

Samsung's Galaxy Gear similarly makes data more accessible but slightly less intrusively by providing a watch that syncs with people's smartphones. Rather than needing an extra hand to check the weather, users can simply glance down at their wrists. In addition, this innovation piggybacks off an existing product, namely, wristwatches, so people already are familiar with the notion of having an information tool encircling their wrists, making this version seem far less foreign. Consumers can feel more confident and perceive less risk, and are therefore more likely to purchase it.[5]

Google is partnering with the vision care insurance company VSP to enable users to add their prescription to their Google Glass, and even cover the costs for those who purchase the associated insurance plan.[6] Because the majority of people in the United States wear prescription glasses,[7] Google Glass ultimately might be more popular if people could integrate their prescription into it.

Noting the potential health care implications of wearable technology, including wrist bands that help people track their fitness goals, Google is also going a step further with its proposed contact lenses. Rather than providing information, these wearable forms of technology would serve to monitor the glucose levels in people's natural tears, enabling diabetics to keep constant track of their critical numbers without any blood or finger pricking.[8]

Samsung's smart watches sync with its smartphones.

Ultimately, the success of wearable technology depends on how consumers perceive it and therefore how they behave toward it. If wearable gadgets fulfill enough needs of consumers without creating too many risks or demanding too much cost, we are all likely to be sporting funny-looking glasses, watches, and other gear soon. If instead the prices and threat of looking absurd are too much for people to bear, wearable tech might just fizzle in the market.

We are all consumers, and we take this status for granted. But we are also complex and irrational creatures who cannot always explain our own choices and actions. This inability makes the vitally important job of marketing managers even more difficult, in that they must be able to explain consumers' behavior to give marketers as clear an understanding of their customers as possible.

To understand consumer behavior, we must ask *why* people buy goods or services. Using principles and theories from sociology and psychology, marketers have been able to decipher many consumer choices and develop basic strategies for dealing with consumers' behavior. Generally, people buy one product or service instead of another because they perceive it to be the better value for them; that is, the ratio of benefits to costs is higher for a particular product or service than for any other.

However, benefits can be subtle and less than rationally assessed, as we shall see. Consider Katie Smith, who is thinking of buying a new outfit for a job interview. She requires something fashionable but professional looking and doesn't want to spend a lot of money. In making the decision about where she should buy the outfit, Katie asks herself:

- Which alternative gives me the best overall value—the most appropriate, yet fashionable outfit at the lowest price?
- Which alternative is the best investment—the outfit that I can get the most use of?

Because Katie might have several reasons to choose a particular store or outfit, it is critical for companies such as Banana Republic or Macy's to key in on the specific benefits that are most important to her. Other factors that might influence Katie go beyond her conscious awareness, which means that the retailers need to be even more well versed in her decision process than she is.[9] Only then can they create a marketing mix that will satisfy Katie.

In this chapter, we explore the process that consumers go through when they buy products and services. Then we discuss the psychological, social, and situational factors that influence this consumer decision process. Throughout the chapter, we emphasize what firms can do to influence consumers to purchase their products and services.

THE CONSUMER DECISION PROCESS

The consumer decision process model represents the steps that consumers go through before, during, and after making purchases.[10] Because marketers often find it difficult to determine how consumers make their purchasing decisions, it is useful for us to break down the process into a series of steps and examine each individually, as in Exhibit 6.1.

Need Recognition

The consumer decision process begins when consumers recognize they have an unsatisfied need, and they would like to go from their actual, needy state to a different, desired state. The greater the discrepancy between these two states, the greater the need recognition will be. For example, your stomach tells you that you are hungry, and you would rather not have that particular feeling. If you are only a little hungry, you may pass it off and decide to eat later. But if your stomach is growling and you cannot concentrate, the *need*—the difference between your actual (hungry) state and your desired (not hungry) state—is greater and you'll want to eat immediately to get to your desired state. Furthermore, your hunger conceivably could be satisfied by a nice healthy salad, but what you really want is a bowl of ice cream. *Wants* are goods or services that are not necessarily needed but are desired.[11] Regardless of the level of your hunger, your desire for ice cream will never be satisfied by any type of salad. Consumer needs like these can be classified as functional, psychological, or both.[12]

Functional Needs Functional needs pertain to the performance of a product or service. For years, BMW has made functionally superior motorcycles. BMW's K1600 model has an inline six-cylinder motor, something previously available only in BMW automobiles, combined with a stiff aluminum frame. Thus it offers remarkable power on a lightweight bike, enabling it to outperform both the best luxury touring bikes in terms of comfort and serious sporty motorcycles in terms of speed.

Psychological Needs Psychological needs pertain to the personal gratification consumers associate with a product and/or service.[13] Purses, for instance, provide a functional need—to transport wallets and other personal items and keep them organized and safe. So why would anyone pay more than $5,000 for a purse that does not perform these tasks any better than a $100 purse? Because they seek to satisfy psychological needs. Each

EXHIBIT 6.1 The Consumer Decision Process

Need recognition

↓

Information search

↓

Alternative evaluation

↓

Purchase

↓

Post-purchase

What needs does a BMW K1600 satisfy?

LO1 Articulate the steps in the consumer buying process.

LO2 Describe the difference between functional and psychological needs.

Do Lana Marks bags, like this one carried by Bingbing Li, satisfy psychological or functional needs?

year, Lana Marks produces a single Cleopatra clutch purse valued at $250,000. The purse might be embellished, such as one version that featured more than 1,500 black and white diamonds, 18-carat gold, and alligator skin. The company permits one star each year to bring its purse to the Oscars; recent winners of this informal contest were Charlize Theron and Helen Mirren.[14] Even though these bags are not known for being particularly practical, strong demand for Lana Marks bags persists among women who love exciting (and expensive) purses.

These examples highlight that most goods and services seek to satisfy both functional and psychological needs, albeit to different degrees. Whereas the functional characteristics of a BMW K1600 are its main selling point, it also maintains a fashionable appeal for bikers and comes in several colors to match buyers' aesthetic preferences. Lana Marks purses satisfy psychological needs that overshadow the functional needs, though they still ultimately serve the function of carrying personal items.

Consider another, perhaps slightly more realistic, example for everyday consumers: You can get a $15 haircut at Supercuts or spend $125 at John Barrett's Salon in New York City.[15] Are the two haircuts objectively different? The answer might vary depending on which you believe represents a good haircut and a good value: One person might value getting a really good deal; another might enjoy the extra attention and amenities associated with an upscale, well-known salon. Successful marketing requires determining the correct balance of functional and psychological needs that best appeals to the firm's target markets.

Search for Information

The second step, after a consumer recognizes a need, is to search for information about the various options that exist to satisfy that need. The length and intensity of the search are based on the degree of perceived risk associated with purchasing the product or service. If the way your hair is cut is important to your appearance and self-image, you may engage in an involved search for the right salon

You can get a $15 haircut at Supercuts (left) or at John Barrett's Salon in New York City for $125 (right). From which service provider will you get the best value?

and stylist. Alternatively, an athlete looking for a short buzz cut might go to the closest, most convenient, and cheapest barber shop. Regardless of the required search level, there are two key types of information search: internal and external.

Internal Search for Information In an *internal search for information*, the buyer examines his or her own memory and knowledge about the product or service, gathered through past experiences. For example, every time Katie wants to eat salad for lunch, she and her friends go to Sweet Tomatoes, but if she's craving dessert, she heads straight to The Cheesecake Factory. In making these choices, she relies on her memory of past experiences when she has eaten at these restaurant chains.

External Search for Information In an *external search for information*, the buyer seeks information outside his or her personal knowledge base to help make the buying decision. Consumers might fill in their personal knowledge gaps by talking with friends, family, or a salesperson. They can also scour commercial media for unsponsored and (it is hoped) unbiased information, such as that available through *Consumer Reports*, or peruse sponsored media such as magazines, television, or radio. Perhaps the most common sources of external information these days are online search engines, such as Google and Bing. But to be effective, those search engines also must ensure that consumers' searches lead them to the most informative or helpful sites, as Ethical and Societal Dilemma 6.1 notes.

The Internet provides information in various ways.[16] For example, while watching an episode of Fox's *Glee*, Katie saw the character Marley wearing a fantastic outfit that included a flare dress and silver pendant. She pulled her laptop over, went to WornOnTv.net, and found the focal episode, which in turn told her where to purchase the items she loved. The pendant was designed by Baroni and available for $119, and the dress cost $48.[17] But Katie is also a savvy shopper, so when she searched for "Baroni Expressive Pendant" on Bing, she found that she could get it at a lower price from another retailer. Satisfied with that purchase, she began flipping through a magazine and saw Reese Witherspoon wearing a pair of adorable jeans. This time she navigated directly to TrueFit.com, which featured those very jeans, designed by 7 for All Mankind, on its home page.[18] Katie entered her measurements and style preferences, and the website returned recommendations of jeans that would be a good fit for her.

Katie liked the picture of Reese Witherspoon in jeans that she found in a magazine so much that she navigated to TrueFit.com and purchased them.

All these examples are external searches for information. Katie used the television show's dedicated site to find a style she liked; she referred to a magazine for additional style tips; and she found jeans that would be a perfect fit for her using the web. All these events took place without Katie ever leaving her home to go to the store or try on dozens of pairs of pants.

Factors Affecting Consumers' Search Processes It is important for marketers to understand the many factors that affect consumers' search processes. Among them are the following three factors.

 LO3 Describe factors that affect information search.

The Perceived Benefits versus Perceived Costs of Search Is it worth the time and effort to search for information about a product or service? For instance, most families spend a lot of time researching the housing market in their preferred area before they make a purchase, because homes are a very expensive and important purchase with significant safety and enjoyment implications. They likely spend

Ethical & Societal Dilemma **6.1** | Penalizing Negative SEO[i]

Companies that seek to get their websites featured prominently on search engines such as Google and Bing turn to well-known search engine optimization (SEO) techniques. The techniques vary in their cost, effectiveness, and ethicality. It's one thing to pay a fee to Google to achieve a top-five ranking in the search results. It's another thing completely to try to game the system or, even worse, create fake, poor-quality links to competitors, such that their sites fall in the rankings.

Such negative SEO seems to be on the rise, in two main forms. First, some companies work to increase the number of links their websites show by setting up "dummy" sites that link only to their main website. These links are often spurious. For example, a consumer searching for information about a particular city might find an apparent informational page. However, every time that page mentions the word *hotel*, it leads to a single company's hotel booking page. Second, competitors might build poor-quality links. Although the increase in the number of links would increase search visibility, the resulting connections would be bloated, unhelpful, and uninformative. Consumers quickly would learn to avoid the site.

In response to these concerns, Google has cracked down, punishing sites that feature any of these questionable tactics. Expedia recently saw a massive drop of approximately 25 percent in its web visibility after Google imposed penalties on it, causing its stock value to drop by 4.3 percent in a single day. The source of the poor links on Expedia's site is unclear—whether its marketing department got careless or competitors sought to damage it. But for Google, the source does not matter much.

Nor is Expedia the only example. A lyric site, RapGenius, acknowledged that it had engaged in some questionable tactics too, though it alleged essentially that everyone else was doing it already. Halifax Bank, owned by the renowned Lloyd's of London, also suffered penalties and a substantial drop in its search engine visibility.

The increasing prevalence and notoriety of these punishments create significant questions for consumers. Can they really trust the results they uncover when they type a search term into a search engine? Are the first few entries really the best links? Because consumers overwhelmingly choose from among the results that appear in the first page of a search engine query, companies continue to seek ways to improve their rankings. But if Google, Bing, or any other search engine wants to keep customers coming back, it needs to prevent any tactics that ultimately leave the customer unsatisfied and uninformed.

Expedia.com's SEO visibility dropped significantly when Google imposed a penalty for poor links on its site.

much less time researching which inexpensive dollhouse to buy for the youngest member of the family.[19]

The Locus of Control   People who have an internal locus of control believe they have some control over the outcomes of their actions, in which case they generally engage in more search activities. With an external locus of control, consumers

Social & Mobile Marketing 6.1   The Future of Health Is Mobile[ii]

A host of new applications and mobile links make it easier than ever for consumers to maintain their own health and well-being with just a few clicks. Whether the condition is chronic or new, these health-related offerings seek to make it easier for health care consumers to understand their options, consider solutions, and recognize when to seek immediate medical care. They also facilitate providers' efforts to stay up to date with the latest treatments and advances. Consider a few examples:

- An award-winning app mySugr turns the tedious task of glucose monitoring into a game for diabetics. They earn points for each data entry they make that helps them tame a monster named Diabetes. The app enables users to record their food consumption and take snapshots of what they have eaten, provides immediate data analyses, produces a summary report that users can send their doctors, and maintains the data in a central location.

- Doctor Mole allows people to take a selfie (i.e., self-portrait) of any suspicious skin growth. Using augmented reality technology, the app applies the well-established criteria for assessing the risk associated with each mole (i.e., asymmetry, borders, color, diameter). Users can determine whether they have a potentially cancerous malignancy or just a new freckle.

- With BurnMed, users draw on a displayed image of a body to indicate the extent of the burn suffered, whether by themselves, a friend, or a patient. This app seeks to target both laypeople and medical practitioners. In a lay setting, users can determine the seriousness of a burn they might have suffered at home. In a medical practice, emergency staff can quickly determine the appropriate treatment when faced with a crisis such as a tanker explosion that burns hundreds of victims.

- The vCath training tool is expressly for medical students who need to learn to insert neurosurgical catheters. In patients this step is critical and risky because students have little leeway for practicing their technique. The app

enables them to do so virtually, as many times as they wish, before confronting any patients.

Along with these dedicated apps, various hospitals and doctors are experimenting with software that reminds patients to take their medicine or when their next appointments are. By encouraging positive behaviors, these technology advances should lead to greater consumer health and happiness as well as benefits for society as a whole.

Smartphone apps empower consumers to take control of their health in exciting new ways.

believe that fate or other external factors control all outcomes. In that case, they believe it doesn't matter how much information they gather; if they make a wise decision, it isn't to their credit, and if they make a poor one, it isn't their fault. People who do a lot of research before purchasing individual stocks have an internal locus of control; those who purchase mutual funds are more likely to believe that they can't predict the market and probably have an external locus of control. These beliefs have widespread effects. For example, when people believe that they can choose their own consumption goals (internal locus of control), they work harder to achieve them than if those goals feel imposed upon them (external locus of control).[20] Social and Mobile Marketing 6.1 discusses how consumers are gaining a greater internal locus of control over their health by using smartphone apps.

Actual or Perceived Risk Five types of risk associated with purchase decisions can delay or discourage a purchase: performance, financial, social, physiological, and psychological. The higher the risk, the more likely the consumer is to engage in an extended search.

Performance risk involves the perceived danger inherent in a poorly performing product or service. An example of performance risk is the possibility that Katie Smith's new interview outfit is prone to shrinking when dry cleaned.

Financial risk is risk associated with a monetary outlay and includes the initial cost of the purchase, as well as the costs of using the item or service.[21] Katie is concerned not only that her new outfit will provide her with the professional appearance she is seeking, but also that the cost of dry cleaning will not be exorbitant. Retailers recognize buying professional apparel can be a financial burden and therefore offer guarantees that the products they sell will perform as expected. Their suppliers are also well aware that dry cleaning is expensive and can limit the life of the garment, so many offer easy-to-care-for washable fabrics.

Social risk involves the fears that consumers suffer when they worry others might not regard their purchases positively. When buying a fashionable outfit, consumers like Katie consider what their friends would like. Alternatively, because this job interview is so important, Katie might make a conscious effort to assert a distinctive identity or make a statement by buying a unique, more stylish, and possibly more expensive outfit than her friends would typically buy. She also hopes to impress her prospective boss, rather than her pals, with her choice.

Physiological risk could also be called safety risk. Whereas performance risk involves what might happen if a product does not perform as expected, physiological (or safety) risk refers to the fear of an actual harm should the product not perform properly. Although physiological risk is typically not an issue with apparel, it can be an important issue when buying other products, such as a car. External agencies and government bodies publish safety ratings for cars to help assuage this risk. Consumers compare the safety records of their various choices because they recognize the real danger to their well-being if the automobile they purchase fails to perform a basic task, such as stopping when the driver steps on the brakes or protecting the passengers in the cabin even if the car flips.

Finally, psychological risks are those risks associated with the way people will feel if the product or service does not convey the right image. Katie Smith, thinking of her outfit purchase, read several fashion magazines and sought her friends' opinions because she wanted people to think she looked great in the outfit, and she wanted to get the job!

Recent research suggests that psychological risks might help explain why consumers often think that "bigger is better." In particular, this research helps explain why some enjoy buying large-sized menu items at restaurants. Especially when consumers feel powerless or more vulnerable, they equate larger sizes—whether in televisions, houses, or menu items—with improved status.[22]

Evaluation of Alternatives

Once a consumer has recognized a problem and explored the possible options, he or she must sift through the choices available and evaluate the alternatives. Alternative evaluation often occurs while the consumer is engaged in the process of information search. For example, Katie Smith would rule out various stores because she knows they won't carry the style she needs for the job interview. Once in the store, she would try on lots of outfits and eliminate those that do not fit, do not look good on her, or are not appropriate attire for the occasion. Consumers forgo

Ann Taylor is part of the <u>retrieval set</u> of stores available to women for business apparel, but Banana Republic is in the <u>evoked set</u> for young women looking for business apparel.

alternative evaluations altogether when buying habitual (convenience) products; you'll rarely catch a loyal Pepsi drinker buying Coca-Cola.

Attribute Sets Research has shown that a consumer's mind organizes and categorizes alternatives to aid his or her decision process. Universal sets include all possible choices for a product category, but because it would be unwieldy for a person to recall all possible alternatives for every purchase decision, marketers tend to focus on only a subset of choices. One important subset is retrieval sets, which are those brands or stores that can be readily brought forth from memory. Another is a consumer's evoked set, which comprises the alternative brands or stores that the consumer states he or she would consider when making a purchase decision. If a firm can get its brand or store into a consumer's evoked set, it has increased the likelihood of purchase and therefore reduced search time because the consumer will think specifically of that brand when considering choices.

Katie Smith knows that there are a lot of apparel stores (universal set). However, only some have the style that she is looking for, such as Macy's, Ann Taylor, The Gap, and Banana Republic (retrieval set). She recalls that Ann Taylor is where her mother shops and The Gap is a favorite of her younger sister. But she is sure that Banana Republic and Macy's carry business attire she would like, so only those stores are in her evoked set.

When consumers begin to evaluate different alternatives, they often base their evaluations on a set of important attributes or evaluative criteria. Evaluative criteria consist of salient, or important, attributes about a particular product. For example, when Katie is looking for her outfit, she might consider things like the selling price, fit, materials and construction quality, reputation of the brand, and the service support that the retailer offers. At times, however, it becomes difficult to evaluate different brands or stores because there are so many choices,[23] especially when those choices involve aspects of the garment that are difficult to evaluate, such as materials and construction quality.

Consumers use several shortcuts to simplify the potentially complicated decision process: determinant attributes and consumer decision rules. Determinant attributes are product or service features that are important to the buyer and on which competing brands or stores are perceived to differ.[24] Because many important and desirable criteria are equal among the various choices, consumers look for something special—a determinant attribute—to differentiate one brand or store from another. Determinant attributes may appear perfectly rational, such as health and nutrition claims offered by certain foods and beverages, or they may be more

Ethical & Societal Dilemma 6.2   Wearing the "Healthy" Label: Natural and Organic Foods[iii]

With competition for shelf space always at a premium, today's supermarket aisles are more crowded than ever. Much of the new competition comes from natural and organic foods, which comprised about 10 and 5 percent, respectively, of the more than $700 billion U.S. food industry in 2013.

For a consumer facing a dizzying array of choices, these natural foods offer a unique appeal: They promise to improve personal and planetary health. Organic and natural food companies claim that their foods are safer and more nutritious because they are produced with only natural ingredients.

Consumers generally believe that these claims mean the food contains no artificial or highly processed ingredients. Yet Snapple's "natural" bottled iced tea contains high-fructose corn syrup, a highly processed, and controversial, form of sugar. In California, most organic strawberry farmers use seeds and plants from nurseries that are not organic, including growers producing fruit for Driscoll Strawberry Associates, the largest berry distributor in the world. The farmers argue that once their plants bear fruit, they halt their use of chemical pesticides and herbicides, so the berries themselves are still organic. These companies thus might be contradicting

How healthy is Snapple?

consumer expectations, but they are not actually violating federal requirements.

The U.S. Department of Agriculture (USDA) regulates the production of organic foods. Products bearing the USDA Organic label must be grown using organic, not conventional, farming methods. That regulation means using natural fertilizers, such as manure or compost; beneficial insects or birds to control insects rather than chemical insecticides; and crop rotation or other manual methods to control weeds rather than chemical herbicides. Animals raised for meat production must be given organic feed and access to the outdoors rather than antibiotics, growth hormones, and other medications.

Yet the USDA's National Organic Program (NOP) regulations do not explicitly govern the production of seeds and planting stock. Advocates who want to see sustainable production methods used throughout the food-growing process have called on the USDA to outlaw the use of chemical fumigants, including methyl bromide, a widely used pesticide and soil sterilizer known to deplete the ozone layer. Furthermore, NOP regulations allow conventional agricultural stock to be used whenever organically grown seeds and plants are not commercially available.

Nor does the USDA regulate the production of foods labeled natural, except for meats and poultry, which must be minimally processed and free of artificial colors, flavors, sweeteners, preservatives, and ingredients. No such specifics govern other foods that choose to carry the natural label rather than an organic claim.

For the consumer, the organic and natural food experience is also about perception. Some shoppers may believe these foods deliver healthful benefits, but studies also reveal that simply identifying a grocery item as a healthy food option may affect their eating experience. Specifically, people may perceive health-oriented foods to neither satisfy their needs of curbing their appetite nor taste good. Students given snacks labeled health bars reported feeling hungry afterward and craving foods they enjoyed more. In another study, respondents widely perceived "that 'healthy' isn't going to meet enjoyment goals," which likely reflects consumers' assumption that healthy foods won't taste good.

subtle and psychologically based, such as the red soles on a pair of Christian Louboutin heels. Ethical and Societal Dilemma 6.2 highlights the use of determinant attributes describing food and beverages marketed as natural when in fact they are not.

Consumer Decision Rules Consumer decision rules are the set of criteria that consumers use consciously or subconsciously to quickly and efficiently select from among several alternatives. These rules are typically either compensatory or noncompensatory.

EXHIBIT 6.2	Compensatory Purchasing Multi-Attribute Model for Buying Cereal				
	Taste	Calories	Natural/Organic Claims	Price	Overall Score
Importance Weight	0.4	0.1	0.3	0.2	
Cheerios	10	8	6	8	8.2
Post	8	9	8	3	7.1
Kashi	6	8	10	5	7.2

Compensatory A compensatory decision rule assumes that the consumer, when evaluating alternatives, trades off one characteristic against another, such that good characteristics compensate for bad characteristics.[25] For instance, Hanna Jackson is looking to buy breakfast cereal and is considering several factors such as taste, calories, price, and natural/organic claims. But even if the cereal is priced a little higher than Hanna was planning to spend, a superb overall rating offsets, or compensates for, the higher price.

Although Hanna probably would not go through the formal process of making the purchasing decision based on the multi-attribute model described in Exhibit 6.2, this exhibit illustrates how a compensatory model would work.[26] Hanna assigns weights to the importance of each factor. These weights must add up to 1.0. So, for instance, taste is the most important, with a weight of 0.4, and calories are least important, with a weight of 0.1. She assigns weights to how well each of the cereals might perform, with 1 being very poor and 10 being very good. Hanna thinks Cheerios has the best taste, so she assigns it a 10. Then she multiplies each performance rating by its importance rating to get an overall score for each cereal. The rating for Cheerios in this example is the highest of the three cereals $[(0.4 \times 10) + (0.1 \times 8) + (0.3 \times 6) + (0.2 \times 8) = 8.2)]$. This multi-attributes model allows the trade-off between the various factors to be incorporated explicitly into a consumer's purchase decision.

Noncompensatory Sometimes, however, consumers use a noncompensatory decision rule in which they choose a product or service on the basis of one characteristic or one subset of a characteristic, regardless of the values of its other attributes.[27] So although Cheerios received the highest overall score of 8.2, Hanna might still pick Kashi because she is particularly sensitive to claims of natural or organic contents, and this brand earned the highest score on this attribute (i.e., a 10). Once a consumer has considered the possible alternatives and evaluated the pros and cons of each, he or she can move toward a purchase decision.

Gilt.com encourages customers to buy now by offering a limited number of items for a short time period.

Purchase and Consumption

After evaluating the alternatives, customers are ready to buy. However, they don't always patronize the store or purchase the brand or item on which they had originally decided. It may not be available at the retail store, for example. Retailers therefore turn to the **conversion rate** to measure how well they have converted purchase intentions into purchases. One method of measuring the conversion rate is the number of real or virtual abandoned carts in the retailer's store or website.

Retailers use various tactics to increase the chances that customers will convert their positive evaluations into purchases. They can reduce the number of abandoned carts by making it easier to purchase merchandise. Most important, they should have plenty of stock on hand of the merchandise that customers want. They can also reduce the actual wait time to buy merchandise by opening more checkout lanes and placing them conveniently inside the store. To reduce perceived wait times, they might install digital displays to entertain customers waiting in line.[28]

For different types of companies, the conversion rate also refers to rentals (e.g., Netflix) or to outright purchases (e.g., haute couture), though some of these lines appear to be blurring as consumers seek new ways to access the items they want. At Rent the Runway, fashion- and budget-conscious shoppers gain temporary possession of the latest fashions from big names, including Badgley Mischka, Kate Spade, and Vera Wang. As if they were dealing with movies on DVDs, members rent haute couture dresses, handbags, jewelry, and even wedding gowns; pay anywhere between $50 and $400 for their chosen items; receive the glam wear in the mail within a few days; and then return the items after their fabulous affair has ended.[29] At the same time, Warner Bros. is working on a new idea to get movie renters to start buying more of its offerings. It purchased Flixster, the movie buff website, and initiated UltraViolet, a movie storage service that enables viewers to purchase a movie once and then access it on any of their connected devices (e.g., computer, tablet, smartphone, web-ready television).[30]

But conversion rates still tend to be lower for consumers using an Internet channel because they are able to examine and store products in their online shopping bag and still delay their purchase decision. To encourage customers to make purchase decisions, Zappos.com and Overstock.com create a sense of time-related pressure by telling customers an item may be about to go out of stock when they place the product in their online shopping bag. Other sites, such as Gilt, offer items for specified 36-hour periods or until sold out, and Neiman Marcus hosts online-only sales that are just two hours long. Many retailers send reminder e-mails to visitors about items in carts they have abandoned.[31]

LO4 Discuss postpurchase outcomes.

Postpurchase

The final step of the consumer decision process is postpurchase behavior. Marketers are particularly interested in postpurchase behavior because it entails actual rather than potential customers. Satisfied customers, whom marketers hope to create, become loyal, purchase again, and spread positive word of mouth, so they are quite important. There are three possible postpurchase outcomes, as illustrated in Exhibit 6.3: customer satisfaction, postpurchase cognitive dissonance, and customer loyalty (or disloyalty).

Customer Satisfaction Setting unrealistically high consumer expectations of the product through advertising, personal selling, or other types of promotion may lead to higher initial sales, but it eventually will result in dissatisfaction if the product fails to achieve high performance expectations. (For a related discussion about communication gaps, see Chapter 13.) This failure can lead to dissatisfied customers and the potential for negative word of mouth.[32] Setting customer expectations too low is an equally dangerous strategy. Many retailers fail to put their best foot forward. For instance, no matter how good the merchandise and service may be, if a store is not clean and appealing from the entrance, customers are not likely to enter.

Marketers can take several steps to ensure postpurchase satisfaction:

- Build realistic expectations, not too high and not too low.

- Demonstrate correct product use—improper usage can cause dissatisfaction.

- Stand behind the product or service by providing money-back guarantees and warranties.

- Encourage customer feedback, which cuts down on negative word of mouth and helps marketers adjust their offerings.

- Periodically make contact with customers and thank them for their support. This contact reminds customers that the marketer cares about their business and wants them to be satisfied. It also provides an opportunity to correct any problems. Customers appreciate human contact, though it is more expensive for marketers than e-mail or postal mail contacts.

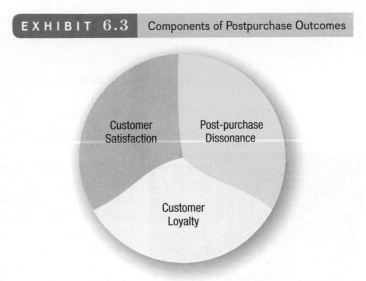

EXHIBIT 6.3   Components of Postpurchase Outcomes

Customer Satisfaction

Post-purchase Dissonance

Customer Loyalty

Postpurchase Cognitive Dissonance Postpurchase cognitive dissonance is an internal conflict that arises from an inconsistency between two beliefs or between beliefs and behavior. For example, you might have buyer's remorse after purchasing an expensive television because you question whether this high-priced version offers appreciably better quality than a set of similar size but at a lower price—or whether you need a television at all, considering your ability to stream content through your computer. Postpurchase cognitive dissonance generally occurs when a consumer questions the appropriateness of a purchase after his or her decision has been made.

Postpurchase cognitive dissonance is especially likely for products that are expensive, are infrequently purchased, do not work as intended, and are associated with high levels of risk. Marketers direct efforts at consumers after the purchase is made to address this issue.[33] General Electric sends a letter to purchasers of its appliances, positively reinforcing the message that the customer made a wise decision by mentioning the high quality that went into the product's design and production. Some clothing manufacturers include a tag on their garments to offer the reassurance that because of their special manufacturing process, perhaps designed to provide a soft, vintage appearance, there may be variations in color that have no effect on the quality of the item. After a pang of dissonance, satisfaction may then set in.

Let's check back in with our friend Katie to recognize these effects. When Katie purchased her interview outfit at Macy's, she tried it on for some of her friends. Her boyfriend said he loved it, but several of her girlfriends seemed less impressed. Katie thought it made her look more mature. Because of these mixed signals, some dissonance resulted and manifested itself as an uncomfortable, unsettled feeling. To reduce the dissonance, Katie could:

- Take back the outfit.
- Pay attention to positive information, such as looking up ads and articles about this particular designer.
- Seek more positive feedback from friends.
- Seek negative information about outfits made by designers not selected.

Stores collect customer information for their CRM programs from their loyalty cards.

Customer Loyalty In the postpurchase stage of the decision-making process, marketers attempt to solidify a loyal relationship with their customers. They want customers to be satisfied with their purchase and buy from the same company again. Loyal customers will buy only certain brands and shop at certain stores, and they include no other firms in their evoked set. As we explained in Chapter 2, such customers are therefore very valuable to firms, and marketers have designed customer relationship management (CRM) programs specifically to acquire and retain them.

Undesirable Consumer Behavior Although firms want satisfied, loyal customers, sometimes they fail to attain them. Passive consumers are those who don't repeat purchase or recommend the product to others. More serious and potentially damaging, however, is negative consumer behavior, such as negative word of mouth and rumors.

Negative word of mouth occurs when consumers spread negative information about a product, service, or store to others. When customers' expectations are met or even exceeded, they often don't tell anyone about it. But when consumers believe that they have been treated unfairly in some way, they usually want to complain, often to many people. The Internet has provided an effective method of spreading negative word of mouth to millions of people instantaneously through personal blogs, Twitter, and corporate websites. In turn, some firms rely on listening software offered by companies like Salesforce.com (as we discussed in Chapter 3), then respond to negative word of mouth through customer service representatives—whether online, on the phone, or in stores—who have the authority to handle complaints. Many companies also allow customers to post comments and complaints to proprietary social media sites.

For example, Whirlpool set up Facebook pages for its appliance brands Maytag, KitchenAid, and Whirlpool. Customers may share their thoughts on these sites without fear that their negative feedback will be deleted from the site. Whirlpool believes that it should keep the bad comments to open up discussions and emphasize the proactive measures the company is taking to remedy service or product failures.[34] If a customer believes that positive action will be taken as a result of the complaint, he or she is less likely to complain to family and friends or through the Internet. (A detailed example of word of mouth appears in Chapter 13.)

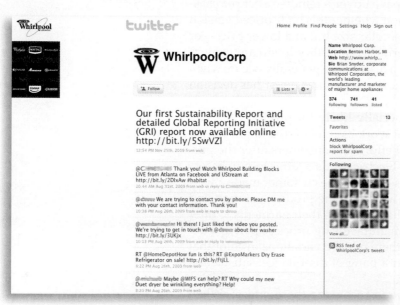

Whirlpool posts both good and bad comments on Twitter. It believes that posting negative comments opens up discussions and emphasizes the proactive measures the company is taking to remedy service or product failures.

CHECK YOURSELF

1. Name the five stages in the consumer decision process.
2. What is the difference between a need and a want?
3. Distinguish between functional and psychological needs.
4. What are the various types of perceived risk?
5. What are the differences between compensatory and noncompensatory decision rules?
6. How do firms enhance postpurchase satisfaction and reduce cognitive dissonance?

FACTORS INFLUENCING THE CONSUMER DECISION PROCESS

LO5 List the factors that affect the consumer decision process.

The consumer decision process can be influenced by several factors, as illustrated in Exhibit 6.4. First are the elements of the marketing mix, which we discuss throughout this book. Second are psychological factors, which are influences internal to the customer, such as motives, attitudes, perception, and learning. Third, social factors, such as family, reference groups, and culture, also influence the decision process. Fourth, there are situational factors, such as the specific purchase situation, a particular shopping situation, or temporal state (the time of day), that affect the decision process.

Every decision people make as consumers will take them through some form of the consumer decision process. But, like life itself, this process does not exist in a vacuum.

Psychological Factors

Although marketers can influence purchase decisions, a host of psychological factors affect the way people receive marketers' messages. Among them are motives, attitudes, perception, learning, and lifestyle. In this section, we examine how such psychological factors can influence the consumer decision process.[35]

Motives In Chapter 1 we argued that marketing is all about satisfying customer needs and wants. When a need, such as thirst, or a want, such as for a Diet Pepsi, is not satisfied, it motivates us, or drives us, to get satisfaction. So, a *motive* is a need or want that is strong enough to cause the person to seek satisfaction.

People have several types of motives. One of the best-known paradigms for explaining these motive types was developed by Abraham Maslow more than 30 years ago, called Maslow's hierarchy of needs.[36] Maslow categorized five groups

EXHIBIT 6.4 Factors Affecting the Consumer Decision Process

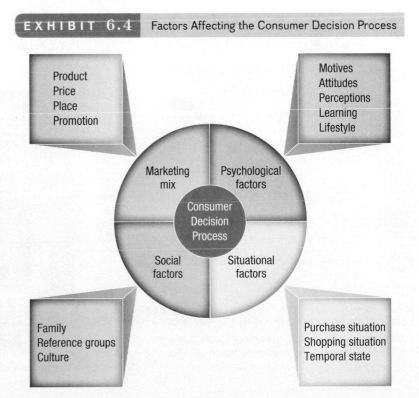

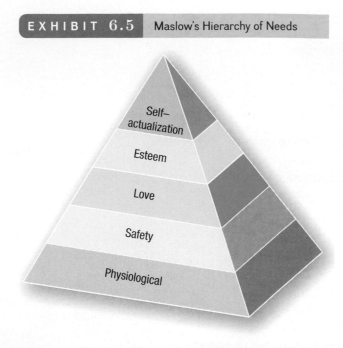

of needs, namely, physiological (e.g., food, water, shelter), safety (e.g., secure employment, health), love (e.g., friendship, family), esteem (e.g., confidence, respect), and self-actualization (people engage in personal growth activities and attempt to meet their intellectual, aesthetic, creative, and other such needs). The pyramid in Exhibit 6.5 illustrates the theoretical progression of those needs.

Physiological needs deal with the basic biological necessities of life—food, drink, rest, and shelter. Although for most people in developed countries these basic needs are generally met, there are those in both developed and less developed countries who are less fortunate. However, everyone remains concerned with meeting these basic needs.[37] Marketers seize every opportunity to convert these needs into wants by reminding us to eat at Taco Bell, drink milk, sleep on a Beautyrest mattress, and stay at a Marriott.

Safety needs pertain to protection and physical well-being. The marketplace is full of products and services that are designed to make you safer, such as airbags in cars and burglar alarms in homes, or healthier, such as vitamins and organic meats and vegetables.

Love needs relate to our interactions with others. Haircuts and makeup make you look more attractive, and deodorants prevent odor. Greeting cards help you express your feelings toward others.

Esteem needs allow people to satisfy their inner desires. Yoga, meditation, health clubs, and many books appeal to people's desires to grow or maintain a happy, satisfied outlook on life.

Finally, **self-actualization** occurs when you feel completely satisfied with your life and how you live. You don't care what others think. You drive a Ford Fusion because it suits the person you are, not

In this ad, Taco Bell satisfies the physiological need of food, while letting the consumer know that healthy eating can also be delicious.

Ads for fire protection satisfy safety needs.

because some celebrity endorses it or because you want others to think better of you.

Which of these needs applies when a consumer purchases a magazine? Magazines such as *Men's Health,* for instance, help satisfy physiological needs like how to eat healthy and exercise, but also esteem needs like how to be happy with one's life.[38] Magazines such as *Family Circle* provide tips on how to make the home a safer place to live, and magazines such as *Weddings* help satisfy love and belonging needs because they provide instructions on how to prepare gracious invitations for friends and family, for example. Many of these magazines fulfill several needs simultaneously, of course. Good marketers add value to their products or services by nudging people up the needs hierarchy and offering information on as many of the pyramid of needs as they can.

Yoga satisfies esteem needs by helping people satisfy their inner needs.

Attitude We have attitudes about almost everything. For instance, we like this class, but we don't like the instructor. We like where we live, but we don't like the weather. An attitude is a person's enduring evaluation of his or her feelings about and behavioral tendencies toward an object or idea. Attitudes are learned and long lasting, and they might develop over a long period of time, though they can also abruptly change. You might like your instructor for much of the semester—until she returns your first exam. The one thing attitudes have in common for everyone is their ability to influence our decisions and actions.

An attitude consists of three components. The cognitive component reflects a person's belief system, or what we believe to be true; the affective component involves emotions,[39] or what we feel about the issue at hand, including our like or dislike of something; and the behavioral component pertains to the actions we undertake based on what we know and feel. For example, Matt and Lisa Martinez see a poster for the latest *Avengers* movie. The ad lists quotes from different movie critics who call it a great and exciting film. Matt and Lisa therefore come to believe that the critics must be correct and that the new *Avengers* movie will be a good movie (cognitive component). Later they catch an interview with Robert Downey Jr., who talks about making the movie and his enjoyment playing Tony Stark (Ironman). Therefore, Matt and Lisa start to believe the movie will be fun and engaging because they appreciate action adventures and have enjoyed previous Marvel films (affective component). After weighing their various options—which include various other movies, other entertainment options such as attending a concert instead, or just staying home—Matt and Lisa decide to go see the movie (behavioral component).

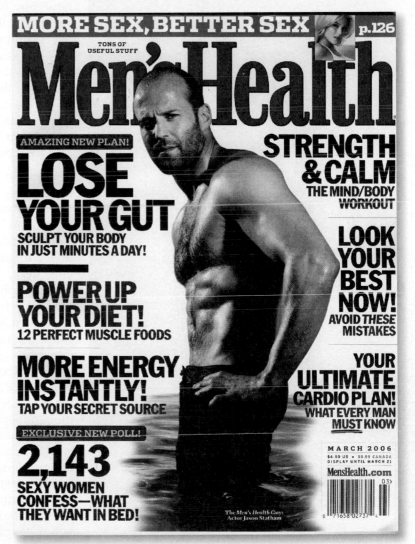

Which category of Maslow's hierarchy of needs does this magazine satisfy?

Ideally, agreement exists among these three components. But when there is incongruence among the three—if Matt and Lisa read positive reviews and like action films but do not find Robert Downey Jr. an appealing actor—cognitive dissonance might occur. Matt and Lisa might decide their reviews and their liking of action films will outweigh their dislike of Robert Downey Jr. and go see the movie. If they then find the movie unenjoyable because he is a primary star, they may feel foolish for having wasted their money.

Such dissonance is a terrible feeling that people try to avoid, often by convincing themselves that the decision was a good one in some way.[40] In this example, Matt and Lisa might focus on the special effects and the romantic elements of the movie while mentally glossing over the parts that featured the actor they did not enjoy. In this way, they can convince themselves that the parts they liked were good enough to counterbalance the part they didn't like, and thus, they make their moviegoing experience a positive event overall.

Although attitudes are pervasive and usually slow to change, the important fact from a marketer's point of view is that they can be influenced and perhaps changed through persuasive communications and personal experience. Marketing communication—through salepeople, advertisements, free samples, or other such methods—can attempt to change what people believe to be true about a product or service (cognitive) or how they feel toward it (affective). If the marketer is successful, the cognitive and affective components work in concert to affect behavior. Continuing with our example, suppose that prior to viewing the movie ad, Matt and Lisa thought that the new *Fast & Furious* movie would be the next one they would go see, but they had heard such good things about *Avengers*. The ad positively influenced the cognitive component of their attitude toward *Avengers,* making it consistent with their affective component.

Perception Another psychological factor, perception, is the process by which we select, organize, and interpret information to form a meaningful picture of the world. Perception in marketing influences our acquisition and consumption of goods and services through our tendency to assign meaning to such things as color, symbols, taste, and packaging. Culture, tradition, and our overall upbringing determine our perception of the world. For instance, Lisa Martinez has always wanted an apartment in the Back Bay neighborhood of Boston because her favorite aunt had one, and they had a great time visiting for Thanksgiving one year. However, from his past experiences Matt has a different perception. Matt thinks Back Bay apartments are small, expensive, and impractical for a couple thinking about having children—though they would be convenient for single people who work in downtown Boston. The city of Boston has worked hard in recent years to overcome the long-standing negative perceptual bias that Matt and many others hold by working with developers to create larger, modern, and more affordable apartments and using promotion to reposition the perception of apartments in the Back Bay for young couples.[41]

Learning Learning refers to a change in a person's thought process or behavior that arises from experience

Based on positive reviews (cognitive component) and positive feelings (affective component), many movie watchers will go see the latest Avengers *movie (behavioral component) and come away with a positive attitude.*

and takes place throughout the consumer decision process. After Katie Smith recognized that she needed an outfit for her job interview, she started looking for ads and searching for reviews and articles on the Internet. She learned from each new piece of information, so her thoughts about the look she wanted in an outfit were different from those before she had read anything. She liked what she learned about the clothing line from Macy's. She learned from her search, and it became part of her memory to be used in the future, possibly so she could recommend the store to her friends.

Learning affects both attitudes and perceptions. Throughout the buying process, Katie's attitudes shifted. The cognitive component came into play for her when she learned Macy's had one of the most extensive collections of career apparel. Once she was in the store and tried on some outfits, she realized how much she liked the way she looked and felt in them, which involved the affective component. Then she made her purchase, which involved the behavioral component. Each time she was exposed to information about the store or the outfits, she learned something different that affected her perception. Before she tried them on, Katie hadn't realized how easy it would be to find exactly what she was looking for; thus, her perception of Macy's selection of career clothing changed through learning.

Lifestyle Lifestyle refers to the way consumers spend their time and money to live. For many consumers, the question of whether the product or service fits with their actual lifestyle (which may be fairly sedentary) or their perceived lifestyle (which might be outdoorsy) is an important one. Some of the many consumers sporting North Face jackets certainly need the high-tech, cold weather gear because they are planning their next hike up Mount Rainier and want to be sure they have sufficient protection against the elements. Others, however, simply like the image that the jacket conveys—the image that they might be leaving for their own mountain-climbing expedition any day now—even if the closest they have come has been shoveling their driveway.

A person's perceptions and ability to learn are affected by their social experiences, which we discuss next.

Social Factors

The consumer decision process is influenced from within by psychological factors but also by the external, social environment, which consists of the customer's family, reference groups, and culture.[42] (Recall Exhibit 6.4.)

Family Many purchase decisions are made about products or services that the entire family will consume or use. Thus, firms must consider how families make purchase decisions and understand how various family members might influence these decisions.

When families make purchase decisions, they often consider the needs of all the family members. In choosing a restaurant, for example, all the family members may participate in the decision making. In other situations, however, different members of the family may take on the purchasing role. For instance, the husband and teenage child may look through car magazines and *Consumer Reports* to search

Children influence parents' purchasing decisions.

for information about a new car. But once they arrive at the dealership, the husband and wife, not the child, decide which model and color to buy, and the wife negotiates the final deal.[43]

Children and adolescents play an increasingly important role in family buying decisions. Kids in the United States spend over $208 billion a year on personal items such as snacks, soft drinks, entertainment, and apparel. They directly influence the purchase of another $300 billion worth of items such as food, snacks, beverages, toys, health and beauty aids, clothing, accessories, gifts, and school supplies. Their indirect influence on family spending is even higher—$600 billion for items such as recreation, vacations, technology, and the family car.[44] Even grandparents contribute to the economic impact of children in the United States. It is estimated that grandparents spend $10 billion on purchases for grandchildren.[45]

Influencing a group that holds this much spending power is vitally important. Traditional food retailers are already caught in a squeeze between Walmart, which lures low-end customers, and specialty retailers like Whole Foods, which targets the high end. Knowing how children influence food buying decisions is a strategic opportunity for traditional supermarkets and their suppliers to exploit. Currently, the age cohorts referred to as Gen Xers and Millennials (remember from Chapter 5 that these groups were born anywhere between 1965 and 2000 tend to shop at Target, Kmart, and Walmart and spend more at those stores than other generational groups.[46] Getting these groups to prefer one store, chain, or product over another can make a difference in the bottom line as well as in the chances for survival in a difficult marketplace.

Reference Groups A reference group is one or more persons whom an individual uses as a basis for comparison regarding beliefs, feelings, and behaviors. A consumer might have various reference groups, including family, friends, coworkers, or famous people the consumer would like to emulate. These reference groups affect buying decisions by (1) offering information, (2) providing rewards for specific purchasing behaviors, and (3) enhancing a consumer's self-image.[47]

Reference groups provide information to consumers directly through conversation or indirectly through observation. For example, Katie received valuable information from a friend about where she should shop for her interview outfit. On another occasion, she heard a favorite cousin who is a fashionista praising the virtues of shopping at Macy's, which solidified her decision to go there.

Some reference groups also influence behaviors by rewarding behavior that meets with their approval or chastising behavior that doesn't. For example, smokers are often criticized or even ostracized by their friends and made to smoke outside or in restricted areas. Research also suggests that consumers who feel ostracized tend to make riskier purchase decisions.[48] Thus ostracizing smokers may make them smoke more or engage in even riskier behaviors.

Consumers can identify and affiliate with reference groups to create, enhance, or maintain their self-image. Customers who want to be seen as earthy might buy Birkenstock sandals, whereas those wanting to be seen as high fashion might buy Lana Marks bags. If they purchase a gift for someone else and that gift conflicts with their self-image, they also seek to reestablish their preferred affiliation quickly by purchasing something more in line with their identity.[49]

With the increasing popularity of blogs, more and more people are getting recommendations for products from their favorite bloggers. When you follow a blog about kittens, you might notice that the author posts a scathing review of a particular cat tree or strongly recommends a product that encourages kittens to use their litter boxes. Because this blogger offers insights you appreciate, you go out to buy the litter box product but avoid adding that cat tree to your

What reference group is evoked by these Birkenstock sandals?

Bloggers can influence their readers to buy or not buy certain products or services.

shopping cart. In realizing the vast influence of this reference group, companies today offer prominent bloggers free products and sometimes even pay them to write positive reviews.[50]

Culture We defined culture in Chapter 5 as the shared meanings, beliefs, morals, values, and customs of a group of people. As the basis of the social factors that affect your buying decisions, the culture or cultures in which you participate are not markedly different from your reference groups. That is, your cultural group might be as small as your reference group at school or as large as the country in which you live or the religion to which you belong. Like reference groups, cultures influence consumer behavior. For instance, the culture at Katie's college is rather fashion conscious. This influences, to some extent, the way she spends, how she dresses, and where she shops.

Situational Factors

Psychological and social factors typically influence the consumer decision process the same way each time. For example, your motivation to quench your thirst usually drives you to drink a Coke or a Pepsi, and your reference group at the workplace coerces you to wear appropriate attire. But sometimes situational factors, or factors specific to the situation, override or at least influence psychological and social issues. These situational factors are related to the purchase and shopping situation as well as to temporal states.[51]

Purchase Situation Customers may be predisposed to purchase certain products or services because of some underlying psychological trait or social factor, but these factors may change in certain purchase situations. For instance, Samantha Crumb considers herself a thrifty, cautious shopper—someone who likes to get a good deal. But her best friend is getting married, and she wants to buy the couple a silver tray. If the tray were for herself, she would probably go to Crate & Barrel or possibly even Walmart. But because it is for her best friend, she went to Tiffany & Co. Why? To purchase something fitting for the special occasion of a wedding.

Shopping Situation Consumers might be ready to purchase a product or service but be completely derailed once they arrive in the store. Marketers use several

Superior Service 6.1   Doing Everything Right—H-E-B Supermarkets[iv]

When it comes to consumer behavior, the research is clear: If they want to succeed, companies selling to consumers need to attract consumers' attention, affection, and commitment; put them in a great mood, perhaps by offering them something for nothing; and help people make their decisions easily and in a way that causes them to feel smart and informed. It may be clear, but few companies are applying these lessons as effectively as a regional grocery store chain in Texas, H-E-B.

First, H-E-B gets its regional customers excited and entranced by playing on their shared identity of being from Texas. This option might be less effective in other regions with a weaker sense of identity, but in Texas, the idea that H-E-B is just like its consumers garners it substantial attention and affection. Then once it has people in its stores, it gets them to engage and commit to actually buying by adding tear-off coupons to its displays. Rather than just seeing a sale sign, customers must undertake the action of tearing off a coupon. This action is not particularly strenuous of course, but the simple move increases the chances that shoppers will follow through on their already committed effort by completing the purchase.

Second, H-E-B sets up an appealing and enjoyable atmosphere that seeks to put shoppers in a better mood. In particular, a plethora of coupons give buyers an additional item for free after they purchase. People simply love things for free, so the constant reminder of how much they can get, seemingly at no cost, enhances their moods. As if that were not enough, H-E-B also gives away lots of free samples. In addition to food samples, to keep shoppers' blood sugar levels up it specializes in wine samples. Because alcohol releases dopamine in people's brains, just a small sip of a nice Zinfandel can leave shoppers in a better mood.

Third, the entire operation seeks to make it easier for consumers to buy the products they want and feel pleased with

Fabio Viviani, Top Chefs fan favorite, cooks up Italian meatballs at H-E-B.

their purchases. H-E-B has avoided loyalty cards and instead simply offers all consumers in the store the same deals on the same items. Thus, shoppers do not need to remember to bring their store coupons or stick their loyalty cards in their wallets before they leave for their grocery run. The fresh food displays also offer obvious highlights of their freshness: a constant smell of rotisserie chicken near the deli display, a guacamole prepping station featuring chefs carving out the avocados right in front of shoppers, and sushi chefs working in the center of the store.

As a result, even though H-E-B remains a regional chain, with limited name recognition outside Texas, its ranking on a recent "consumer delight index" placed it on par with such well-known customer favorites as Trader Joe's and Whole Foods.

techniques to influence consumers at this choice stage of the decision process, as Superior Service 6.1 describes using one example.[52]

Store Atmosphere Some retailers and service providers have developed unique images that are based at least in part on their internal environment, also known as their atmospherics.[53] Research has shown that, if used in concert with other aspects of a retailer's strategy, music, scent, lighting, and even color can positively influence the decision process.[54] Restaurants such as Outback Steakhouse and The Cheesecake® Factory have developed internal environments that are not only pleasant but also consistent with their food and service.

Some Wegmans and Whole Foods stores have built bars and restaurants inside their stores, where customers can stop and relax, have a glass of wine or a bite to eat, but still get their shopping done for the week. Whole Foods has cutting-edge culinary centers that offer cooking classes in several of its stores. Other grocery store chains are following suit; the Brewers Yard Kroger in Ohio has a band play in the store on Friday nights. Still other grocery stores offer flat-screen televisions, comfortable chairs, free Wi-Fi hotspots, in-store cooking classes, or wine-tasting events to create interactive atmospheres that will appeal to customers.[55]

The Cheesecake Factory has developed atmospherics that are not only pleasant, but consistent with its image, menu, and service.

Salespeople Well-trained sales personnel can influence the sale at the point of purchase by educating consumers about product attributes, pointing out the advantages of one item over another, and encouraging multiple purchases. Each Apple store features a simple layout that enables shoppers to play with the latest gadgets, though the real key to success is the salespeople. Apple keeps its product lines relatively minimal so salepeople can become familiar with every product in the store. For more technical questions, Apple Geniuses are available and consultations can be scheduled.[56] A training manual recently leaked online shows that the company takes nothing for granted when training its employees, such that it uses role-playing scenarios, lists banned words, and specifies exactly how to communicate with agitated customers. Although technical expertise is a must, Apple also looks for salespeople with "magnetic personalities" and trains them in a five-point selling technique: **a**pproach customers warmly, **p**robe politely to assess their needs, **p**resent solutions the customer can do today, **l**isten and resolve worries the customer may still have, **e**nd by giving the customer a warm goodbye and invite them back.[57] What's that spell?

Crowding Customers can feel crowded because there are too many people, too much merchandise, or lines that are too long. If there are too many people in a store, some people become distracted and may even leave.[58] Others have difficulty purchasing if the merchandise is packed too closely together. This issue is a particular problem for shoppers with disabilities.

In-Store Demonstrations The taste and smell of new food items may attract people to try something they normally wouldn't. Similarly, some fashion retailers offer trunk shows, during which their vendors show their whole line of merchandise on a certain day. During these well-advertised events, customers are often enticed to purchase that day because they get special assistance from the salespeople and can order merchandise that the retailer otherwise does not carry.

In-store demonstrations, such as this one in an Albertson's grocery store, attract consumers to try and buy.

Promotions Retailers employ various promotional vehicles to influence customers once they have arrived in the store. An unadvertised price promotion can alter a person's preconceived buying plan. Multi-item discounts, such as "buy 1, get 1 free" sales, are popular means to get people to buy more than they normally would.[59] Because many people regard clipping coupons from the newspaper as too much trouble, some stores make coupons available in

Social & Mobile Marketing 6.2   Ensuring Mobile Dominance through In-Store Promotions[v]

Some consumers rely on websites to reach their favorite retailers. Others like to head to the stores themselves to check out the options. Still others want a mobile app that enables them to shop quickly and on the go. And increasingly, today's customers demand that retailers offer them all of these options, consistently and constantly, so that they can pick and choose the channel they want to use at any specific time.

This demand is the impetus for the latest developments in the marketing strategy of Sephora, the specialized beauty product retailer. Although it has long maintained a good reputation for its interactive website, the company remains in constant pursuit of a strategy that enables it to reach all its customers through the most channels at the most frequent times. It integrates these efforts with its constantly evolving loyalty program, in an effort to become nearly irresistible to beauty product consumers.

Users of the most recent version of its mobile app, Sephora to Go, can engage in any activities they would pursue in stores. The close alignment across these channels

Sephora engages its customers in the store with its mobile app, Sephora to Go.

provides a seamless experience. In addition, the app encourages customers to sign up for the loyalty program and create a Beauty Insider account. Once they have done so, they gain a mobile version of their loyalty card. They can check their loyalty points at any time, as well as redeem them however they wish. Downloadable bar codes also are available, which can be scanned in stores.

Simultaneously, Sephora's in-store signage encourages shoppers to sign up for the loyalty program and create a Beauty Insider account. That is, both channels issue similar calls to action. Moreover, the in-store signs encourage brick-and-mortar shoppers to take advantage of the benefits they can gain from interacting with the retailer, either online or through mobile apps.

As the company recognizes, "The majority of Sephora's clients are cross-channel shoppers," so it wants consumers to go ahead and use their phones while in the stores. In return, Sephora has enjoyed a 150 percent increase in the amount of mobile shopping its customers undertake.

the store, on the Internet, or on their cell phones. Another form of promotion is offering a free gift with the purchase of a good or service. This type of promotion is particularly popular with cosmetics, and Sephora has worked hard to integrate various elements of its shopping situation to encourage purchase, as Social and Mobile Marketing 6.2 shows.

Packaging It is difficult to make a product stand out in the crowd when it competes for shelf space with several other brands.[60] Customers spend just a few seconds standing in front of products as they decide whether to buy them.[61] This problem is particularly difficult for consumer packaged goods, such as groceries and health and beauty products. Marketers therefore spend millions of dollars designing and updating their packages to be more appealing and eye catching. This is why Pringles keeps packaging its chips in tubes that differ greatly from the formless bags farther down the aisle. But not all product packaging can, or should, remain the same, the way Pringles has. Doublemint Gum undertook its first packaging redesign nearly a century after its 1914 product launch. The move was designed to help the chewing gum appeal to a younger audience, even while it maintained its loyal base of older consumers. Another aging brand, Kraft's Macaroni & Cheese, similarly redesigned its packaging, which it launched originally in 1937.[62]

Temporal State Our state of mind at any particular time can alter our preconceived notions of what we are going to purchase. For instance, some people are morning people, whereas others function better at night. Therefore, a purchase situation may have different appeal levels depending on the time of day and the type of person the consumer is. Mood swings can alter consumer behavior.[63] Suppose Samantha received a parking ticket just prior to shopping at Tiffany & Co. It is likely that she would be less receptive to the salesperson's influence than if she came into the store in a good mood. Her bad mood might even cause her to have a less positive postpurchase feeling about the store. Because retailers cannot affect what happens outside the store very much, they should do everything possible to make sure their customers have a positive shopping experience once they are in the store.

The factors that affect the consumer decision process—the marketing mix, psychological factors, social factors, and situational factors—are all affected by the level of consumer involvement, the subject of the next section.

CHECK YOURSELF

1. What are some examples of specific needs suggested by Maslow's hierarchy of needs?

2. Which social factors likely have the most influence on (a) the purchase of a new outfit for a job interview and (b) the choice of a college to attend?

3. List some of the tactics stores can use to influence consumers' decision processes.

INVOLVEMENT AND CONSUMER BUYING DECISIONS

LO6 Describe how involvement influences the consumer decision process.

Consumers make two types of buying decisions depending on their level of involvement: extended problem solving or limited problem solving (which includes impulse purchases and habitual decision making). **Involvement** is the consumer's degree of interest in the product or service.[64] Consumers may have different levels of involvement for the same type of product. One consumer behavior theory, the elaboration likelihood model illustrated in Exhibit 6.6, proposes that high- and low-involvement consumers process different aspects of a message or advertisement.

EXHIBIT 6.6   Elaboration Likelihood Model

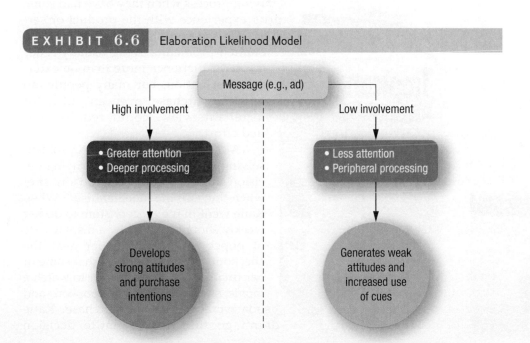

If both types of consumers viewed ads for career clothing, the high-involvement consumer (e.g., Katie, who is researching buying an outfit for a job interview) will scrutinize all the information provided (price, fabric quality, construction) and process the key elements of the message more deeply. As an involved consumer, Katie likely ends up judging the ad as truthful and forming a favorable impression of the product, or else she regards the message as superficial and develops negative product impressions (i.e., her research suggests the product is not as good as it is being portrayed).

In contrast, a low-involvement consumer will likely process the same advertisement in a less thorough manner. Such a consumer might pay less attention to the key elements of the message (price, fabric quality, construction) and focus on heuristic elements such as brand name (Macy's I·N·C) or the presence of a celebrity endorser. The impressions of the low-involvement consumer are likely to be more superficial.

Extended Problem Solving

The buying process begins when consumers recognize that they have an unsatisfied need. Katie Smith recognized her need to buy a new outfit for a job interview. She sought information by asking for advice from her friends, reading fashion magazines, and conducting research online. She visited several stores to determine which had the best options for her. Finally, after considerable time and effort analyzing her alternatives, Katie purchased an outfit at Macy's. This process is an example of extended problem solving, which is common when the customer perceives that the purchase decision entails a lot of risk. The potential risks associated with Katie's decision to buy the outfit include financial (did I pay too much?) and social (will my potential employer and friends think I look professional?) risks. To reduce her perceived risk, Katie spent a lot of effort searching for information before she actually made her purchase.

Limited Problem Solving

Limited problem solving occurs during a purchase decision that calls for, at most, a moderate amount of effort and time. Customers engage in this type of buying process when they have had some prior experience with the product or service and the perceived risk is moderate. Limited problem solving usually relies on past experience more than on external information. For many people, an apparel purchase, even an outfit for a job interview, could require limited effort.

A common type of limited problem solving is impulse buying, a buying decision made by customers on the spot when they see the merchandise.[65] When Katie went to the grocery store to do her weekly shopping, she saw a display case of popcorn and Dr Pepper near the checkout counter. Knowing that some of her friends were coming over to watch a movie, she stocked up. The popcorn and soda were an impulse purchase. Katie didn't go through the entire decision

What type of buying decision does each of these products represent?

process; instead, she recognized her need and jumped directly to purchase without spending any time searching for additional information or evaluating alternatives. The grocery store facilitated this impulse purchase by providing easily accessible cues (i.e., by offering the popcorn and soda in a prominent display, at a great location in the store, and at a reasonable price).

Some purchases require even less thought. Habitual decision making describes a purchase decision process in which consumers engage in little conscious effort. On her way home from the grocery store, for example, Katie drove past an In-N-Out Burger and swung into the drive-through for a cheeseburger and Diet Coke. She did not ponder the potential benefits of going to Wendy's instead for lunch. Rather, she simply reacted to the cue provided by the sign and engaged in habitual decision making. Marketers strive to attract and maintain habitual purchasers by creating strong brands and store loyalty (see Chapters 11 and 12) because these customers don't even consider alternative brands or stores.

Picking up a hamburger at a drive-through fast-food restaurant like In-N-Out Burger requires little thought. It is a habitual decision.

CHECK YOURSELF

1. How do low- versus high-involvement consumers process the information in an advertisement?
2. What is the difference between extended versus limited problem solving?

Reviewing Learning Objectives
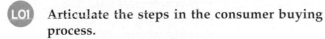

LO1 **Articulate the steps in the consumer buying process.**

The consumer buying process consists of five main steps: First, during need recognition, consumers simply realize they have an unsatisfied need or want that they hope to address. Second, they begin to search for information to determine how to satisfy that need. Third, during the alternative evaluation stage, they assess the various options available to them to determine which is the best for their purposes. Fourth, the purchase stage involves obtaining and using the product. Finally, consumers enter the postpurchase stage, during which they determine whether they are satisfied or dissatisfied with their choice.

LO2 **Describe the difference between functional and psychological needs.**

Functional needs pertain to the performance of a product or service. Psychological needs pertain to the personal gratification consumers associate with a product and/or service.

LO3 **Describe factors that affect information search.**

The information search that people undertake varies depending on both external and internal factors. Among the former, the type of product or service dictates whether people can make an easy, quick decision or instead must undertake significant research to find the best purchase option. A person's perceptions of the benefits versus the costs of the search also determine how much effort they undertake. These perceptions often relate closely to their perception of the risk involved in their purchase. Finally, people's locus of control, whether external or internal, strongly influences their information search actions.

LO4 **Discuss postpurchase outcomes.**

Marketers hope that after their purchase, consumers are satisfied and pleased with their purchase, which can lead to customer loyalty, a positive postpurchase outcome. However, consumers also may suffer postpurchase dissonance, or buyer's remorse.

LO5 **List the factors that affect the consumer decision process.**

The elements of the marketing mix (product, place, promotion, and price) have significant effects, of course. In addition, social factors, such as family and culture, influence not only what a consumer buys but also how a consumer goes about making a purchase decision. The psychological factors that influence purchase decisions include motives attitudes, perceptions, learning, and lifestyle. Finally, the specific factors that mark the purchase situation, like the store setting or even the time of day, can alter people's decision process.

LO6 **Describe how involvement influences the consumer decision process.**

More involved consumers, who are more interested or invested in the product or service they are considering, tend to engage in extended problem solving. They gather lots of information, scrutinize it carefully, and then make their decisions with caution, to minimize any risk they may confront. In contrast, less involved consumers often engage in limited problem solving, undertake impulse purchases, or rely on habit to make their purchase decisions.

Key Terms

■**LEARNSMART**

Marketing Applications

1. Does buying Kashi cereal satisfy a consumer's functional or psychological need? How might this information help a Kashi brand manager better promote the product?

2. When consumers buy a new notebook computer, what sort of information search (internal versus external) would they conduct? If you were a marketing manager for Sony, how would you use this information?

3. Explain the factors that affect the amount of time and effort that a consumer might take when choosing an oral surgeon to get his or her wisdom teeth removed. How would your answer change if the consumer were looking for a dentist to get a cleaning? How should the office manager for a dental practice use this information?

4. When evaluating different alternatives for a Saturday night outing at a fine restaurant, explain the difference between the universal set, the retrieval set, and the evoked set. From which set of alternatives will the consumer most likely choose the restaurant?

5. What can retailers do to make sure they have satisfied customers after the sale is complete?

6. Tazo makes a blend of exotic green teas, spearmint, and rare herbs into a tea called Zen. Using Maslow's hierarchy of needs, explain which need(s) is (are) being fulfilled by this tea.

7. You recently were invited to a formal event at the home of the president of your university. You decide such an event warrants a completely new outfit. Describe three social factors that might influence your purchase decision.

8. Trek has designed a new off-road bicycle designed to stand up to the rugged conditions of trail riding. Develop a theme for an advertising strategy that covers all three components of attitude.

9. What can a marketer do to positively influence a situation in which a consumer is ready to buy but has not yet done so?

10. You were recently hired by a multichannel retailer that promotes itself as an American firm selling only American-made goods. The products featured in advertising and in catalogs tell stories of the firms that produced the goods in the United States. The sales response to the firm's Made in America position has been incredible because it resonates with its customers' values. As a result, growth has been impressive. One day while speaking to a vendor, you find out a shipment of merchandise will be delayed because the product is coming from overseas and is late. A few days later you hear a similar story. As it turns out, the firm just barely earns the Made in the USA label. Though technically the products meet a standard to be classified as American made, you worry that the firm is not being truthful to its customers. You decide to write a letter to the VP of marketing detailing your concerns. What would you put in the letter?

Quiz Yourself

1. The consumer decision process model represents:
   a. the concept of habitual decision making.
   b. the retrieval of an evoked set based on physiological needs.
   c. the steps that consumers go through before, during, and after making purchases.
   d. the shift from an internal to an external locus of control.
   e. the types of decisions all consumers must make.

2. A key to successful marketing is determining how to meet the correct balance of _____ needs that best appeals to the firm's target markets.
   a. functional and social
   b. postpurchase and prepurchase
   c. safety and situational
   d. psychological and physiological
   e. functional and psychological

(Answers to these two questions are provided on page 651.)

Toolkit

Jill is trying to decide, once and for all, which soft drink company is her favorite. She has created a chart to help her decide. She has rated Coca-Cola, PepsiCola, and Jones Soda in terms of price, taste, variety, and packaging. She has also assessed how important each of these four attributes is in terms of her evaluations. Please use the toolkit provided in your instructor's Connect course to determine which cola Jill will choose using a compensatory model. Which cola would she choose using a noncompensatory model? If you were Jill, which model would you use, the compensatory or the noncompensatory? Why?

Net Savvy

1. Visit the Shopkick site (http://www.shopkick.com) and describe the benefits it offers consumers. How are these offers likely to influence consumers' behavior? Click on Download tab. What kinds of need appeals does this company make to encourage shoppers to join?

2. Customers use a variety of methods to provide feedback to companies about their experiences. Planetfeedback.com was developed as one such venue. Visit its website (http://www.planetfeedback.com) and identify the types of feedback that customers can provide. Look over the feedback for Verizon by typing "Verizon" in the company search space. Summarize some of the most recent comments. What is the ratio of positive to negative comments about Verizon during the last year or so? Describe the effect these comments might have on customer perceptions of Verizon.

3. Different companies emphasize different aspects of attitude in making decisions. Explore the Microsoft (http://www.microsoftstore.com) and Apple (store.apple.com) stores online. Discuss the primary attitude components that they are targeting and how the two stores differ.

4. Companies often emphasize either the functional or psychological needs their products fulfill. Go to *Car and Driver*'s website (http://www.caranddriver.com) and identify a luxury car company that emphasizes functional needs and one that emphasizes psychological needs.

Chapter Case Study

THE DIET BATTLE—WEIGHT WATCHERS, JENNY CRAIG, AND SLIM-FAST[66]

Want to lose weight? For about 71 million Americans and approximately 73 percent of all U.S. women, the answer is yes,[67] and for weight-loss companies, that's the right answer. The weight-loss industry, worth over $60 billion,[68] is growing steadily because lifestyles and food choices keep working against people's desire to lose weight. Many Americans spend their days sitting in front of a computer and their evenings sitting in front of a television. Restaurant meals, prepared foods, and high-fat, high-sugar snacks have replaced home-cooked meals, whole grains, and fresh produce. Exercise is limited to clicking a mouse or turning an ignition key. These habits are fattening (both literally and figuratively) the profits for the weight-loss industry, as well as expanding belt sizes. By the time we factor in diet pills, specially packaged weight-loss meals and snacks, diet programs, and the whole range of products and services promising bathing-suit bodies, we've got a highly lucrative market.

Three recognized diet aid behemoths, Weight Watchers, Jenny Craig, and Slim-Fast, share a substantial piece of the pie. These companies stress their flexibility and ability to accommodate a wide range of lifestyles. They also showcase success stories.[69] But they approach dieting differently in their quest for new members.

The Big Three

Founded in 1963, Weight Watchers International now boasts groups in more than 30 countries worldwide. The program teaches portion control and the basics of good nutrition, allowing members to select their own foods. A point system, based on nutritional value, encourages members to select healthy foods, exercise appropriately, and control portions.[70] Dieters record meals and snacks in a paper or electronic journal. Although members can follow the Weight Watchers regimen without support, the company notes that the most successful members are those who weigh in at weekly group sessions and attend meetings. Weight Watchers members can prepare their own food, dine out, or purchase Weight Watchers-prepared or -endorsed dinners, snacks, and desserts at most grocery stores. To further support dieters in making healthy food choices, Weight Watchers increased the number of points for fat content and reduced them for fiber.

Rated the top weight-loss program by Consumer Reports Health in 2011, Jenny Craig promises a unique and comprehensive plan for food, body, and mind.[71] Members eat meals and snacks prepared and packaged by Jenny Craig, supplemented by fresh fruits and vegetables. Jenny Craig's offerings provide portion control and accommodate busy schedules by reducing meal prep time. Members meet weekly on a one-on-one basis with a personal counselor and are encouraged to develop an exercise program. Like Weight Watchers, Jenny Craig offers customized programs for men and teenagers and for those who prefer to lose weight on their own rather than travel to a center. Jenny Craig lapped Weight Watchers and other diet programs in the Consumer Reports Health ranking because of members' success in weight loss, the duration of time they remained committed to the program, and the nutritional value of the foods.[72]

To entice men into its program, Jenny Craig uses Jason Alexander, the actor who played George Costanza on the TV series Seinfeld, *as a spokesperson, pictured here with another Jenny Craig spokesperson, Valerie Bertanelli, teenage TV star from the late 70s of* One Day at a Time *and* Touched by an Angel.

Slim-Fast, which ranked second in the Consumer Reports Health ratings, offers dieters a combination of three small and healthy snacks, two meal-replacement shakes, and one 500-calorie meal daily.[73] By eating six small meals daily, dieters maintain steady glucose levels, and the plan ensures adequate intakes of carbohydrates, protein, and fiber.[74]

Other diet programs abound, but even when people lose weight on these regimens, the losses tend to be temporary because the diets are based on unsustainable eating patterns, such as eliminating major food groups (e.g., no carbohydrates). Two of the big diet companies also offer social reinforcement and flexibility, which appears to help people remain committed to their weight-loss programs.

Defining the Difference

Perhaps the most significant difference among Jenny Craig, Slim-Fast, and Weight Watchers is the amount of effort required. Jenny Craig dieters don't have to think about what they eat; everything is prepared for them. Dieters on the Weight Watchers plan must learn how to make the right choices from among the foods that surround them in their daily lives. Slim-Fast combines both ease and education, but it provides fewer choices for controlled meals than Jenny Craig does. Each program competes heavily for members, particularly in the early months of the year, when Americans return to the scales after indulging for the holidays.

The diet giants are locked in another battle as well, this one targeted at men.[75] Although a completely different program isn't necessary—both genders need to cut calories and increase exercise to lose weight—marketing specifically to men has the power to bring in new members.

While the Weight Watchers programs are identical for men and women, the men's website is tailored to their interests and concerns, focusing more on working out and less on the eating plan. The men's site also mentions the link between obesity and erectile dysfunction, implying that a man's sex life might improve if he loses weight.

Jenny Craig's men's program also is very similar to its women's program, but tweaked to accommodate differences in food cravings and issues with portion control. Men on this program, Jenny Craig promises, can still have a beer and fries once in a while. To further entice men to its program, Jenny Craig uses Jason Alexander, the actor who played George Costanza on the television series *Seinfeld*, as a spokesperson.

The Slim-Fast program tends to appeal to men because they like to lose weight on their own rather than participating in group meetings.[76] The company has used male celebrities, including a former New York mayor, to sell its products.

Technology Support for Dieters

Dieters have a variety of electronic devices to help track food consumption and exercise. Using any Internet-ready device, Weight Watchers members can check points values for foods, including meals at popular restaurants, and add snacks or meals to their daily journal. Similar services and applications for fitness training are available via cell phone applications. Using a camera-equipped cell phone, for example, dieters can photograph a meal and send the picture to a registered dietitian, who replies with recommendations for modifying portions or food choices. Theoretically this approach is more honest than keeping a food diary, because dieters may be tempted not to record full amounts. These services require additional fees though.

Questions

1. Trace how you might go through the steps in the consumer decision process if you were thinking of going on a diet and using any of these diet programs.

2. How have Weight Watchers, Slim-Fast, and Jenny Craig created value?

3. Identify the determinant attributes that set the Weight Watchers, Slim-Fast, and Jenny Craig programs apart. Use those attributes to develop a compensatory purchasing model similar to the one in Exhibit 6.2.

4. How can Weight Watchers, Slim-Fast, and Jenny Craig increase the probability of customer satisfaction?

5. Which factors examined in this chapter might have the most impact on consumers' propensity to go on a diet and choose one of these diet programs?

Endnotes

1. David Pogue, "2 Wristbands Keep Tabs on Fitness," *The New York Times*, November 14, 2012, http://www.nytimes.com.

2. Clare Cain Miller, "New Apps Arrive on Google Glass," *The New York Times*, May 16, 2013, http://bits.blogs.nytimes.com/2013/05/16/new-apps-arrive-on-google-glass/; Daniel J. Simons and Christopher F. Chabris, "Is Google Glass Dangerous?" *The New York Times*, May 24, 2013, http://www.nytimes.com.

3. American Marketing Association, "Consumer Behavior," http://www.marketingpower.com/_layouts/Dictionary.aspx.

4. Bill Wasik, "Why Wearable Tech Will Be as Big as the Smartphone," *Wired*, December 17, 2013, http://www.wired.com.

5. Ewan Spence, "2014 Will Be the Year of Wearable Technology," *Forbes*, November 2, 2013, http://www.forbes.com.

6. Claire Cain Miller, "Google Glass to Be Covered by Vision Care Insurer VSP," *The New York Times,* January 28, 2014, http://www.nytimes.com.

7. http://www.statisticbrain.com/corrective-lenses-statistics/.

8. Hayley Tsukayama, "Google's Smart Contact Lens: What It Does and How It Works," *The Washington Post,* January 17, 2014, http://www.washingtonpost.com.

9. For example, when trying on a dress, Katie might be influenced by the way that same dress looks on a salesperson in the store. See Darren W. Dahl, Jennifer J. Argo, and Andrea C. Morales, "Social Information in the Retail Environment: The Importance of Consumption Alignment, Referent Identity, and Self-Esteem," *Journal of Consumer Research* 38, no. 5 (February 2012), pp. 860–71.

10. For a detailed discussion of customer behavior, see Michael R. Solomon, *Consumer Behavior: Buying, Having, and Being,* 11th ed. (Upper Saddle River, NJ: Pearson Prentice Hall, 2014).

11. Martin R. Lautman and Koen Pauwels, "Metrics That Matter: Identifying the Importance of Consumer Wants and Needs," *Journal of Advertising Research* 49, no. 3 (2009), 339–59.

12. Liz C. Wang et al., "Can a Retail Web Site Be Social?" *Journal of Marketing* 71, no. 3 (2007), pp. 143–57; Barry Babin, William Darden, and Mitch Griffin, "Work and/or Fun: Measuring Hedonic and Utilitarian Shopping Value," *Journal of Consumer Research* 20 (March 1994), pp. 644–56.

13. Jing Xu and Norbert Schwarz, "Do We Really Need a Reason to Indulge?" *Journal of Marketing Research* 46, no. 1 (February 2009), pp. 25–36.

14. "Lana Marks Cleopatra Bag," *Lord Glamour,* February 8, 2014, http://www.lordglamour.com/; Lopa Mohanty, "10 Most Expensive Handbag Brands in the World," *Fashion Lady,* May 31, 2013, http://www.fashionlady.in/; "Celebrities," *Lana Marks,* http://www.lanamarks.com/.

15. http://www.johnbarett.com.

16. Peng Huang, Nicholas H. Lurie, and Sabyasachi Mitra, "Searching for Experience on the Web: An Empirical Examination of Consumer Behavior for Search and Experience Goods," *Journal of Marketing* 73, no. 2 (March 2009), pp. 55–69.

17. http://www.nordstrom.com; http://www.baronidesigns.com.

18. http://www.truefit.com.

19. Lan Luo, Brian T. Ratchford, and Botao Yang, "Why We Do What We Do: A Model of Activity Consumption," *Journal of Marketing Research* 50 (February 2013), pp. 24–43.

20. Ying Zhang et al., "Been There, Done That: The Impact of Effort Investment on Goal Value and Consumer Motivation," *Journal of Consumer Research* 38, no. 1 (June 2011), pp. 78–93.

21. Debabrata Talukdar, "Cost of Being Poor: Retail Price and Consumer Price Search Differences across Inner-City and Suburban Neighborhoods," *Journal of Consumer Research* 35, no. 3 (October 2008), pp. 457–71.

22. David Dubois, Derek D. Rucker, and Adam D. Galinsky, "Super Size Me: Product Size as a Signal of Status," *Journal of Consumer Research* 38, no. 6 (April 2012), pp. 1047–62.

23. Benjamin Scheibehenne, Rainer Greifeneder, and Peter M. Todd, "Can There Ever Be Too Many Options? A Meta-Analytic Review of Choice Overload," *Journal of Consumer Research* 37, no. 3 (October 2010), pp. 409–45.

24. The term *determinance* was first coined by James Myers and Mark Alpert nearly three decades ago; http://www.sawtooth-software.com.

25. http://www.sawtoothsoftware.com.

26. Julie R. Irwin and Rebecca Walker Naylor, "Ethical Decisions and Response Mode Compatibility: Weighting of Ethical Attributes in Consideration Sets Formed by Excluding versus Including Product Alternatives," *Journal of Marketing Research* 46, no. 2 (April 2009), pp. 234–46; Richard Lutz, "Changing Brand Attitudes through Modification of Cognitive Structure," *Journal of Consumer Research* 1, no. 1 (1975), pp. 125–36.

27. Caroline Goukens, Siegfried Dewitte, and Luk Warlop, "Me, Myself, and My Choices: The Influence of Private Self-Awareness on Choice," *Journal of Marketing Research* 46, no. 5 (October 2009), pp. 682–92.

28. Ruby Roy Dholakia and Miao Zhao, "Retail Web Site Interactivity: How Does It Influence Customer Satisfaction and Behavioral Intentions?" *International Journal of Retail & Distribution Management* 37 (2009), pp. 821–38.

29. "30 Under 30 2011: Where Are They Now?" http://www.inc.com; http://www.renttherunway.com.

30. Brooks Barnes, "A Bid to Get Film Lovers Not to Rent," *The New York Times,* November 11, 2011, http://www.nytimes.com; "Where to Get," *UltraViolet,* http://www.uvu.com.

31. Claire Cain Miller, "Closing the Deal at the Virtual Checkout Counter," *The New York Times,* October 12, 2009.

32. "Beware of Dissatisfied Consumers: They Like to Blab," *Knowledge@Wharton,* March, 8, 2006, based on the "Retail Customer Dissatisfaction Study 2006" conducted by the Jay H. Baker Retailing Initiative at Wharton and The Verde Group.

33. Goutam Challagalla, R. Venkatesh, and Ajay K. Kohli, "Proactive Postsales Service: When and Why Does It Pay Off?" *Journal of Marketing* 73, no. 2 (March 2009), pp. 70–87.

34. Randall Stross, "Consumer Complaints Made Easy. Maybe Too Easy," *The New York Times,* May 28, 2011, http://www.nytimes.com.

35. For a more extensive discussion on these factors, see Banwari Mittal, *Consumer Behavior* (Cincinnati, OH: Open Mentis, 2008); Peter and Olson, *Consumer Behavior and Marketing Strategy.*

36. A. H. Maslow, *Motivation and Personality* (New York: Harper & Row, 1970).

37. Kelly D. Martin and Ronald Paul Hill, "Life Satisfaction, Self-Determination, and Consumption Adequacy at the Bottom of the Pyramid," *Journal of Consumer Research* 38, no. 6 (April 2012), pp. 1155–68; Hazel Rose Markus and Barry Schwartz, "Does Choice Mean Freedom and Well-Being?" *Journal of Consumer Research* 37, no. 2 (August 2010), pp. 344–55.

38. Stacy Wood, "The Comfort Food Fallacy: Avoiding Old Favorites in Times of Change," *Journal of Consumer Research* 36, no. 6 (April 2010), pp. 950–63; Stacey Finkelstein and Ayelet Fishbach, "When Healthy Food Makes You Hungry," *Journal of Consumer Research* 37, no. 3 (October 2010), pp. 357–67.

39. For recent research on the link between emotions and consumer behavior, see the "Emotions and Consumer Behavior" special issue of *Journal of Consumer Research* 40 (February 2014).

40. Leonard Lee, On Amir, and Dan Ariely, "In Search of Homo Economicus: Cognitive Noise and the Role of Emotion in Preference Consistency," *Journal of Consumer Research* 36, no. 2 (2009), pp. 173–87; Anish Nagpal and Parthasarathy Krishnamurthy, "Attribute Conflict in Consumer Decision Making: The Role of Task Compatibility," *Journal of Consumer Research* 34, no. 5 (February 2008), pp. 696–705.

41. http://www.bostonbackbay.com/.

42. For more discussion on these factors, see Mittal, *Consumer Behavior;* Peter and Olson, *Consumer Behavior and Marketing Strategy;* Michael Levy, Barton A. Weitz, and Dhruv Grewal, *Retailing Management,* 9th ed. (Burr Ridge, IL: Irwin/McGraw-Hill, 2013), Chapter 4; and the "Social Influence and Consumer Behavior" special issue of *Journal of Consumer Research* 40 (August 2013).

43. Juliano Laran, "Goal Management in Sequential Choices: Consumer Choices for Others Are More Indulgent than Personal Choices," *Journal of Consumer Research* 37, no. 2 (August 2010), pp. 304–14.

44. "Teenage Consumer Spending Statistics," *Statisticsbrain.com,* September 8, 2012, http://www.statisticsbrain.com; "Retailers Must Understand Modern Family Buying Decisions,"

45. Glenn Ruffenach, "How Much Are Your Grandkids Really Costing You?" *The Wall Street Journal,* August 1, 2011, http://online.wsj.com.

46. Todd Hale, "Mining the U.S. Generation Gaps," *Nielsen Wire,* March 4, 2010, http://blog.nielsen.com.

47. Gokcen Coskuner-Balli and Craig J. Thompson, "The Status Costs of Subordinate Cultural Capital: At-Home Fathers' Collective Pursuit of Cultural Legitimacy through Capitalizing Consumption Practices," *Journal of Consumer Research* 40 (June 2013), pp. 19–41.

48. Rod Duclos, Echo Wen Wan, and Yuwei Jiang, "Show Me the Honey! Effects of Social Exclusion on Financial Risk-Taking," *Journal of Consumer Research,* 40 (June 2013), pp. 122–35.

49. Morgan K. Ward and Susan Bronziarczyk, "It's Not Me, It's You: How Gift Giving Creates Giver Identity Threat as a Function of Social Closeness," *Journal of Consumer Research* 38, no. 1 (June 2011), pp. 164–81.

50. Carol Bryant, "The Truth about Paid Product Reviews and Disclosure," *Blog Paws,* September 5, 2013, http://www.blogpaws.com; see sites that recruit bloggers to do paid reviews: http://www.sponsoredreviews.com, http://www.payperpost.com, http://www.reviewme.com.

51. For an expanded discussion on these factors, see Mittal, *Consumer Behavior;* Peter and Olson, *Consumer Behavior and Marketing Strategy.* For some interesting experiments involving consumers' physical positioning and its effects on behavior, see Jeffrey S. Larson and Darron M. Billeter, "Consumer Behavior in 'Equilibrium': How Experiencing Physical Balance Increases Compromise Choice," *Journal of Marketing Research* 50 (August 2013), pp. 535–47.

52. Tracey S. Dagger and Peter J. Danaher, "Comparing the Effect of Store Remodeling on New and Existing Customers," *Journal of Marketing* (forthcoming). doi: http://dx.doi.org/10.1509/jm.13.0272.

53. The concept of atmospherics was introduced by Philip Kotler, "Atmosphere as a Marketing Tool," *Journal of Retailing* 49 (Winter 1973), pp. 48–64.

54. Sylvie Morin, Laurette Dubé, and Jean-Charles Chebat, "The Role of Pleasant Music in Servicescapes: A Test of the Dual Model of Environmental Perception," *Journal of Retailing* 83, no. 1 (2007), pp. 115–30.

55. http://www.wegmans.com; http://wholefoodsmarket.com/stores/cooking-classes/; Tracy Turner, "New Hangout Supermarket," *Columbus Dispatch,* March 20, 2011.

56. Tim Bajarin, "6 Reasons Apple Is So Successful," *Time,* May 7, 2012, http://techland.time.com.

57. Carmine Gallo, "Apple's Secret Employee Training Manual Reinvents Customer Service in Seven Ways," *Forbes,* August 30, 2012.

58. Ahreum Maeng, Robin J. Tanner, and Dilip Soman, "Conservative When Crowded: Social Crowding and Consumer Choice," *Journal of Marketing Research* 50 (December 2013), pp. 739–52; Alexander Chernev and Ryan Hamilton, "Assortment Size and Option Attractiveness in Consumer Choice among Retailers," *Journal of Marketing Research* 46, no. 3 (June 2009), pp. 410–20; Marc-Andre Kamel, Nick Greenspan, and Rudolf Pritzl, "Standardization Is Efficient but Localization Helps Shops to Stand Out," *The Wall Street Journal,* January 21, 2009.

59. Jeffrey Trachtenberg, "Publishers Bundle E-Books to Boost Sales, Promote Authors," *The Wall Street Journal,* February 11, 2011.

60. Pierre Chandon et al., "Does In-Store Marketing Work? Effects of the Number and Position of Shelf Facings on Brand Attention and Evaluation at the Point of Purchase," *Journal of Marketing* 73, no. 6 (November 2009), pp. 1–17.

61. Kirk Henderson and Kusum Ailawadi, "Shopper Marketing: Six Lessons for Retail from Six Years of Mobile Eye Tracking Research," *Review of Marketing Research* 12 (2014).

62. Christine Birkner, "Thinking Outside of the Box," *Marketing News,* March 30, 2011.

63. Dan King and Chris Janiszewski, "Affect-Gating," *Journal of Consumer Research* 38, no. 4 (December 2011), pp. 697–711.

64. Mittal, *Consumer Behavior;* Peter and Olson, *Consumer Behavior and Marketing Strategy.*

65. Yuping Liu-Thompkins and Leona Tam, "Not All Repeat Customers Are the Same: Designing Effective Cross-Selling Promotion on the Basis of Attitudinal Loyalty and Habit," *Journal of Marketing* 77 (September 2013), pp. 21–36; Karen M. Stilley, J. Jeffrey Inman, and Kirk L. Wakefield, "Planning to Make Unplanned Purchases? The Role of In-Store Slack in Budget Deviation," *Journal of Consumer Research* 37, no. 2 (2010), pp. 264–78; doi: 10.1086/651567.

66. This case was written by Kate Woodworth in conjunction with Dhruv Grewal and Michael Levy as the basis of class discussion rather than to illustrate either effective or ineffective marketing practices.

67. Lydia Saad, "To Lose Weight, Americans Rely More on Dieting than Exercise," Gallup, November 28, 2011, http://www.gallup.com/poll/150986/lose-weight-americans-rely-dieting-exercise.aspx; Vauhini Vara, "New Gadgets Aim to Help Users Watch Their Weight," *The Wall Street Journal,* May 12, 2005.

68. "U.S. Weight Loss Market Worth $60.9 Billion," May 9, 2011, http://www.prweb.com/releases/2011/5/prweb8393658.htm.

69. E. J. Schultz, "Why You Won't See Mariah Carey in Jenny Craig Ads Anymore," *Advertising Age,* August 12, 2013.

70. All About: Weight Loss and Diet Plans, http://www.aa-lose-weight-loss-diet-plans.com/diet-comparison/weight-watchers-jenny-craig.html.

71. Chris Moran, "Jenny Craig Beats Out Weight Watchers for Top Spot in Consumer Reports Health Ratings," May 10, 2011, http://consumerist.com/2011/05/jenny-craig-beats-out-weight-watchers-for-top-spot-in-consumer-reports-health-ratings.html; http://jennycraig.com/programs/.

72. Jennifer Fermino, "Jenny Craig Is Top Heavy Hitter," *New York Post,* May 10, 2011, http://www.nypost.com/p/news/national/craig_is_top_heavy_hitter_Le5SprctcoGlp93YLL55XJ.

73. http://www.slim-fast.com/plan/.

74. Maura Shenker, "Men's Slim-Fast Diet Health," Livestrong.com, July 20, 2011, http://www.livestrong.com/article/497109-mens-slim-fast-diet-health/.

75. Dave McGinn, "The Changing Face of Male Weight Loss," *The Globe and Mail,* December 23, 2010, http://www.theglobeandmail.com/life/health/the-changing-face-of-male-weight-loss/article1446724/; Jennifer LaRue Huget, "Weight Watchers and Jenny Craig Offer Programs for Men Who Want to Shed Pounds," *The Washington Post,* March 25, 2010; All About: Weight Loss and Diet Plans; Moran, "Jenny Craig Beats Out Weight Watchers for Top Spot"; Fermino, "Jenny Craig Is Top Heavy Hitter."

76. http://www.bestdietforme.com/top60dietreviews/SlimFast.htm.

i. Alistair Barr, "Was Expedia Targeted by 'Negative SEO' Campaign?" *USA Today,* January 22, 2014, http://www.usatoday.com; Joshua Steimle, "Expedia, Negative SEO, and

Google Penalties," *Forbes,* January 31, 2014, http://www.forbes.com; Denis Pinsky, "Understanding Negative SEO and Your Saboteur Within," *Forbes,* February 11, 2014, http://www.forbes.com; "Expedia Shares Fall with Online Search Visibility," *Seattle Times,* January 21, 2014, http://www.seattletimes.com.

ii. Bianca Banova, "The Future of Mobile Technology in Medicine: Innovative Medical Apps," *MedCity News,* April 24, 2013, http://medcitynews.com; William Cook, "Is That Little Mole a Big Problem?" *Daily Mail,* October 3, 2012, http://www.dailymail.co.uk; "mySugr App, Award-Winning iPhone App That Gamifies Blood Sugar Monitoring for People with Diabetes, Launches in US," *The Wall Street Journal,* June 6, 2013, press release, http://online.wsj.com; Mike H, " 'Diabetes Monster' App Actually Motivates!" *Diabetes Mine,* June 19, 2013, http://www.diabetesmine.com.

iii. Ronnie Cummins, "ORCA to Attack 'Natural' Products Labeling Fraud," *Organic Consumers Association,* March 7, 2013, http://www.organicconsumers.org; Ashby Jones, "Is Your Dinner 'All Natural' ?" *The Wall Street Journal,* September 20, 2011; "Diet and Nutrition Report," *Consumer Reports,* February 2009, http://www.consumerreports.org; Rachel Gross, "Farmers Seek to Raise Standards for Berries," *The New York Times,* September 23, 2011, http://www.nytimes.com; Mayo Clinic Staff, "Organic Foods: Are They Safer? More Nutritious?" http://www.mayoclinic.com; Natural and Organic Foods Backgrounder, Food Marketing Institute, http://www.fmi.org; Stacey R. Finkelstein and Ayelet Fishbach, "When Healthy Food Makes You Hungry," *Journal of Consumer Research* 37, no. 3 (October 2010), pp. 357–67.

iv. Roger Dooley, "The Smartest Supermarket You Never Heard Of," *Forbes,* January 28, 2014, http://www.forbes.com.

v. Lauren Johnson, "Sephora Magnifies Mobile Ambitions via In-Store Signage, Updated App," *Mobile Commerce Daily,* August 23, 2013.

Credits

CHAPTER 7

BUSINESS-TO-BUSINESS MARKETING

LEARNING OBJECTIVES

LO1 Describe the ways in which business-to-business (B2B) firms segment their markets.

LO2 List the steps in the B2B buying process.

LO3 Identify the roles within the buying center.

LO4 Describe the different types of organizational cultures.

LO5 Detail different buying situations.

Manufacturing in the United States is entering a totally new era, and no one company exemplifies the shift better than General Electric (GE). Already the largest U.S. manufacturing firm, GE also is seeking to become the most prolific user of innovative 3D printing. If it succeeds, it seems likely to change virtually every business-to-business (B2B) relationship we find today.

In traditional B2B exchanges, one company, such as a manufacturer, needs to work with another company to

obtain the raw materials it needs. So for example, to build parts for the airplane engines it sells, GE would turn to suppliers of titanium, grinding services, and tool manufacturers to provide the necessary materials. Then it would fabricate all the parts of the engine together and sell it to another company, such as an airline.

With its recent purchase of an existing 3D printing company, though, GE is signaling that it aims to cover all—or at least most—of these supply chain steps itself.[1] The 3D printing technology is additive: It builds parts (or toys or virtually anything else) by layering thin sheets of material, in programmed shapes, on top of one another. There is no grinding or removal of any material required, which substantially reduces waste. The promise of 3D printing suggests that someday, GE even could innovate its own processes, such as by printing out the sophisticated tools it might need to install all the various engine parts, which it also has printed.[2]

Thus far, GE uses 3D printing in about 10 percent of its manufacturing efforts, but it hopes to progressively increase this percentage over time. Within two decades, half of all its production is likely to rely, in some way, on its own in-house 3D printing facilities.[3] But at the moment, the actual printers themselves remain out of reach for most companies; even GE does not plan on building its own printers. Furthermore, the materials required for 3D printing, such as high-tech plastics and composites, are more expensive than traditional raw materials.[4]

So, do 3D printers, used throughout supply chains, represent the end of the traditional B2B relationships that GE has enjoyed in the past? Not quite. The printers themselves remain expensive and technologically advanced, and manufacturers relying on 3D printers need assistance with them. Furthermore, the capacity of existing printers is not sufficient for GE or any other major manufacturer to use them exclusively. For example, to produce enough airplane engine nozzles to fulfill the orders it currently has in hand, GE would need to maintain about 70 high-capacity 3D printers.[5] Even with its recent purchase of a dedicated 3D printer company, it has access to less than half that amount.

Business-to-business (B2B) marketing refers to the process of buying and selling goods or services to be used in the production of other goods and services for consumption by the buying organization and/or resale by wholesalers and retailers. Therefore, a typical B2B marketing transaction involves manufacturers (e.g., GE, Levi's, Siemens, IBM, Ford) selling to wholesalers that, in turn, sell products to retailers. B2B transactions can also involve service firms (e.g., UPS, Oracle, Accenture) that market their services to other businesses but not to the ultimate consumer (e.g., you). The distinction between a B2B and a business-to-consumer (B2C) transaction is not the product or service itself; rather, it is the ultimate user of that product or service. Another key distinction is that B2B transactions tend to be more complex and involve multiple members of both the buying organization (e.g., buyers, marketing team, product developers) and the selling organization (e.g., sellers, R&D support team), whereas B2C often entails a simple transaction between the retailer and the individual consumer.

The demand for B2B sales is often derived from B2C sales in the same supply chain. More specifically, **derived demand** reflects the link between consumers' demand for a company's output and the company's purchase of necessary inputs to manufacture or assemble that particular output. For example, if more customers want to purchase staplers (a B2C transaction), a company that produces them must purchase more metal from its supplier to make additional staplers (a B2B transaction).

Similar to organizations that sell directly to final consumers in B2C transactions, B2B firms focus on serving specific types of customer markets by creating value for those customers. Recognizing the growing demand for ever-increasing smartphone connectivity in cars, both Apple with its CarPlay and Google with its Android-based Open Automotive Alliance are making deals to integrate their OSS into cars. Ferrari, Audi, Mercedes-Benz, and Volvo each have announced they will begin offering CarPlay in some of their models as early as 2014; Google, on the other hand, has deals with Honda, Hyundai, and General Motors.[6]

Apple CarPlay integrates with dashboard of numerous cars.

Also like B2C firms, many B2B companies find it productive to focus their efforts on key industries or market segments. Although the average large corporation has over 175 social media accounts, small-business owners often struggle to maintain a single social media account on each of the major networks.[7] Enter the B2B firm Constant Contact. This firm provides a centralized dashboard for small businesses to manage their social media accounts, as well as templates for posts and help on creating social media campaigns. Constant Contact could target businesses of any size, but instead it has become one of the leaders in small-business social media management by narrowing its efforts on this key market segment.[8]

In this chapter, we look at the different types of B2B markets and examine the B2B buying process, with an eye toward how it differs from the B2C buying process we discussed in Chapter 6. Several factors influence the B2B buying process, and we discuss these as well.

B2B MARKETS

The most visible types of B2B transactions are those in which manufacturers and service providers sell to other businesses. However, resellers, institutions, and governments also may be involved in B2B transactions. Therefore, in the next sections we describe each of these B2B organizations (see Exhibit 7.1).

LO1 Describe the ways in which business-to-business (B2B) firms segment their markets.

Manufacturers and Service Providers

Manufacturers buy raw materials, components, and parts that allow them to make and market their own goods and ancillary services. For example, the German-based

EXHIBIT 7.1 B2B Markets

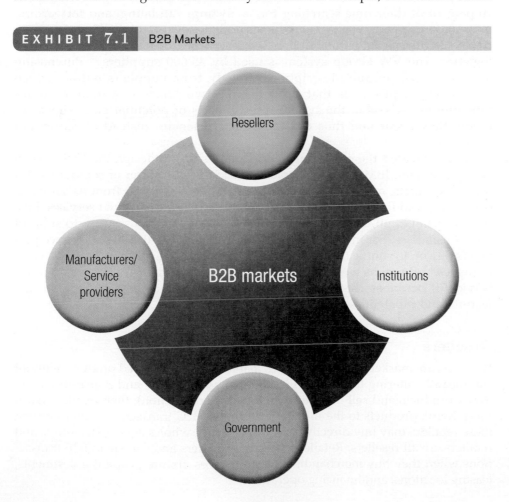

German-based Volkswagen Group, the largest auto manufacturer in Europe, owns and distributes numerous brands.

Volkswagen Group, the largest auto manufacturer in Europe, owns and distributes the Audi, Bentley, Bugatti, Lamborghini, Seat, Skoda, Scania VW, and VW Commercial Vehicles brands.[9] Whereas formerly purchasing agents spent 70 percent of their time searching for, analyzing, validating, and forwarding information about parts and components, today they can use VWSupplyGroup.com to communicate with suppliers for all transactions, from procurement to logistics. The VW Group system is used by 45,600 suppliers.[10] Purchasing agents receive product descriptions directly from suppliers online, which means search processes that used to take two hours now require about nine minutes. Users of the system receive alerts of potential parts shortages before they occur and thus can focus on efficiencies instead of redundant paperwork.

IBM provided the consulting services necessary to design the Volkswagen Group's system. IBM, which was once a major manufacturer of computers and related products, now generates over 90 percent of its profits from its software, consulting, and financing businesses—all of which are considered services. Like Volkswagen Group, it requires a host of B2B products and services to support these businesses. For instance, the airlines that IBM consultants and service providers rely on to shuttle them around the globe also use a mix of products such as airplanes and fuel as well as consulting, legal, and other services. As Superior Service 7.1 describes, IBM is constantly working to ensure that it can provide the features and capabilities its business customers need.

Resellers

Resellers are marketing intermediaries that resell manufactured products without significantly altering their form. For instance, wholesalers and distributors buy Xerox products and sell them to retailers (B2B transaction), then retailers resell those Xerox products to the ultimate consumer (B2C transaction). Alternatively, these retailers may buy directly from Xerox. Thus, wholesalers, distributors, and retailers are all resellers. Retailers represent resellers and engage in B2B transactions when they buy merchandise for their stores, fixtures, capital investments, leasing locations, and financing operations.

Superior Service 7.1 | Clouding over Computing Power[i]

As their computing power and security demands escalate, few businesses want to maintain their own hardware and servers anymore. Instead, they look to the cloud, where they seek to purchase more computing power, provided at a faster speed, with lower costs.

In response, traditional mainframe providers such as IBM are moving to expand their presence in the cloud. In particular, IBM has devoted billions of dollars to enhancing its cloud capabilities. First, it purchased a cloud company called SoftLayer for $2 billion to add that firm's 13 cloud computing centers to IBM's own 12 data centers. Second, it announced recently that it would allocate an additional $1.2 billion to expanding its cloud computing centers worldwide.

The services provided by these cloud centers will include not just power and data storage but also access to some of IBM's proprietary software and related products. Perhaps most famously, for some of the best IBM clients it will offer access to Watson, IBM's famous *Jeopardy*-winning computer.

The Singaporean bank DBS Group Holdings plans to use Watson to provide up-to-date insights and lessons to its financial planners, who in turn will share that information with high-net-worth clients. With Watson analyzing the massive amounts of financial data available in nearly real time, DBS hopes to improve the customized advising services it provides to wealthy clients, who then may agree to do more of their investing with the bank. To gain this access, DBS will pay around $12 million over three years. It also agreed to share its own data, contributing and updating Watson's knowledge stores constantly.

Watson's contribution to this shift in emphasis is so notable that IBM has decided to establish a separate "Watson unit." Rather than separating employees responsible for software, hardware, and services, this division will bring together approximately 2,000 employees to address all topics related to Watson. Furthermore, the division has a budget of approximately $100 million to use to fund venture projects that develop apps based on its technology platform.

How did IBM's Watson do on Jeopardy?

Institutions

Institutions, such as hospitals, educational organizations, and religious organizations, also purchase all kinds of goods and services. A public school system might have a $40 million annual budget for textbooks alone, which gives it significant buying power and enables it to take advantage of bulk discounts. However, if each school makes its own purchasing decisions, the system as a whole cannot leverage its combined buying power. Public institutions also engage in B2B relationships to fulfill their needs for capital construction, equipment, supplies, food, and janitorial services.

The U.S. government spends over $5 billion a year on aerospace and defense for everything from nuts and bolts to this F-14 Tomcat jetfighter.

Government

In most countries, the central government is one of the largest purchasers of goods and services. For example, the U.S. federal government spends about $3.7 trillion annually on procuring goods and services.[11] If you add in the amount state and local governments spend, these numbers reach staggering proportions. Specifically, with its estimated outlay of over $526.6 billion for fiscal year 2014, the Pentagon represents a spending force to be reckoned with,[12] especially when it comes to aerospace and defense (A&D) manufacturers, some of the Pentagon's greatest suppliers of products.

Across these various B2B markets, purchasing methods might vary with the range of options being pursued. As Social and Mobile Marketing 7.1 highlights, iPads are playing increasing roles in educational institutions and businesses, which suggests that institutions need to start making purchasing decisions about them too.

CHECK YOURSELF

1. What are the various B2B markets?

L02 List the steps in the B2B buying process.

THE BUSINESS-TO-BUSINESS BUYING PROCESS

As noted in the previous section, the B2B buying process is unique (Exhibit 7.2): It both parallels the B2C process and differs in several ways. Both start with need recognition, but the information search and alternative evaluation steps are more formal and structured in the B2B process. Typically, B2B buyers specify their needs in writing and ask potential suppliers to submit formal proposals, whereas B2C buying decisions are usually made by individuals or families and do not need formal proposals. Thus, for an individual to buy a tablet computer, all that is required is a trip to the store or a few minutes online and perhaps some preliminary research about iPads versus competitors.

For a school to buy thousands of tablet computers, however, it must complete requisition forms, accept bids from manufacturers, and obtain approval for the expenditure. The final decision rests with a committee, as is the case for most B2B buying decisions, which often demand a great deal of consideration.

EXHIBIT 7.2   Business-to-Business Buying Process

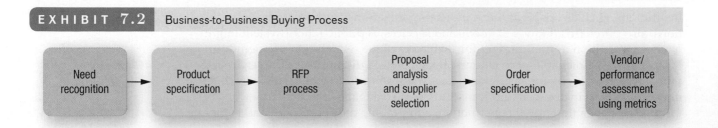

Need recognition → Product specification → RFP process → Proposal analysis and supplier selection → Order specification → Vendor/performance assessment using metrics

Social & Mobile Marketing 7.1 · iPads Go to Work[ii]

Since their introduction, iPads have rocketed into widespread use for gaming, online access, music, videos, and e-mail. Tech-savvy business executives and educators also have noted some advantages of these devices that could make them useful at work, as well as at play. Tablet computers weigh less and cost less than laptop computers. Uploaded e-books can be more up to date and are less expensive than physical textbooks. And in both the classroom and the workplace, the use of iPads extends the enthusiastic adoption of technology that is already occurring naturally in social contexts.

These devices, educators have learned, go beyond delivery of course materials by saving additional funds for schools and increasing the value for students. Students can watch videos or tutorials, take notes, or use interactive programs that demonstrate particular skills. They can scroll effortlessly through documents or between texts to reach a section relevant to the current class discussion. Part-time and distance students can communicate more readily with their classmates, potentially enhancing collaboration and team-based learning. Visual learners, children with autism spectrum disorders or learning disabilities, and students who have grown up using electronic devices in various facets of their lives all can benefit from the interactive nature of iPads. And all students benefit from developing comfort with technology, a vital skill set in tomorrow's workforce.

The iPad is finding fans in the workplace as well. Executives, staff members, and clients at companies as diverse as Wells Fargo Bank, the business management software developer SAP, and Daimler's Mercedes-Benz have adopted the device. Airplane pilots have begun replacing paper binders full of flight manuals, navigation charts, and other materials with iPads. Siemens Energy has equipped some of its wind turbine service technicians with iPads so that they have convenient access to manuals, checklists, and cameras, even from atop a

80 percent of Fortune 100 companies are either using the iPad or have launched pilot projects to try it.

300-foot tower. iPad's manufacturer Apple claims that 80 percent of *Fortune* 100 companies are either using the device or have launched pilot projects to try it.

Whether in the classroom or in the workplace, iPads are not without their disadvantages. Schools may save money in textbook costs but will need funding for repairs and wireless infrastructure. Tablets may enhance learning, but they cannot replace teachers or peer-to-peer interactions. Academic and business users find that the virtual keyboard is challenging for composing longer text, sharing applications is burdensome, and multitasking is impossible. Some companies are put off by iPad security breaches; others reject Apple's traditional focus on the consumer market, often at the expense of business sales. Despite these challenges, the iPad has gained a strong foothold in both the classroom and the workplace.

Finally, in B2C buying situations customers evaluate their purchase decision and sometimes experience postpurchase cognitive dissonance. But formal performance evaluations of the vendor and the products sold generally do not occur, as they do in the B2B setting. Let's examine all six stages in the context of a university buying tablets for its incoming first-year students to use as resources.

Stage 1: Need Recognition

In the first stage of the B2B buying process, the buying organization recognizes, through either internal or external sources, that it has an unfilled need. Hypothetical University wants to ensure its students are well educated and able to participate in a technologically connected workforce. It also seeks to grant them affordable access to required educational resources, from textbooks to library access to administrative tasks. The administration of the university also has reviewed research suggesting that portable devices, including tablet computers,

The first step in the B2B decision process is to recognize that the universities need to purchase 1,200 tablets.

can enhance students' in-class learning because they can directly and constantly interact with the materials and take notes in conjunction with the lecture and text, rather than only hearing information or seeing it on a whiteboard. The tablets also support innovative learning methodologies, such as the uses of interactive clickers in lecture-based courses. Using this information, the university has determined it will issue a table to each of the 1,200 students entering as its next graduating class.

Stage 2: Product Specification

After recognizing the need and considering alternative solutions, including laptop computers, the university wrote a list of potential specifications that vendors might use to develop their proposals. The school's specifications include screen size, battery life, processor speed, how the device connects to the Internet, and delivery date. In addition, the board of directors of the university has requested that a bundle of educational apps be preloaded on the tablets, that all other apps be removed, and that each tablet come equipped with a screen protector, power cord, cover, stand, keyboard, and headphones. The school hopes to obtain a four-year service contract that includes replacement within 24 hours for any tablets that are returned to the vendor for servicing.

Stage 3: RFP Process

The **request for proposals (RFP)** is a common process through which organizations invite alternative vendors or suppliers to bid on supplying their required components or specifications. The purchasing company may simply post its RFP needs on its website or work through various B2B web portals or inform their preferred vendors directly. Because the university does not have a preferred vendor for tablets yet, it issues an RFP and invites various tablet suppliers, technology companies, and other interested parties to bid on the contract.

Smaller companies may lack the ability to attract broad attention to their requests, so they might turn to a **web portal**, an Internet site whose purpose is to be a major starting point for users when they connect to the web. Although there are general portals such as Yahoo! or MSN, B2B partners connect to specialized or niche portals to participate in online information exchanges and transactions. These exchanges help streamline procurement or distribution processes. Portals can provide tremendous cost savings because they eliminate periodic negotiations and routine paperwork, and they offer the means to form a supply chain that can respond quickly to the buyer's needs.

Small to medium-sized companies looking for skilled service workers also can use portals such as Guru.com, started to help freelance professionals connect with companies that need their services, whether those services entail graphic design and cartooning or finance and accounting advice. Currently, nearly 1 million professionals list their offerings on this service-oriented professional exchange, and more than 30,000 companies regularly visit the site to post work orders. Guru.com thus provides value to both companies and freelancers by offering not only a site for finding each other but also dispute resolution, escrow for payments, and a means to rate freelancer quality.[13]

Stage 4: Proposal Analysis, Vendor Negotiation, and Selection

The buying organization, in conjunction with its critical decision makers, evaluates all the proposals it receives in response to its RFP. Hypothetical University reviews all proposals it receives, together with the board of directors, representatives from the teachers' union, and members of the student government. Many firms narrow the process to a few suppliers, often those with which they have existing relationships, and discuss key terms of the sale, such as price, quality, delivery, and financing. The university likely considers the bid by the company that installed computers in its library, assuming that provider performed well. Some firms have a policy that requires them to negotiate with several suppliers, particularly if the product or service represents a critical component or aspect of the business. This policy keeps suppliers on their toes; they know that the buying firm can always shift a greater portion of its business to an alternative supplier if it offers better terms.

The university evaluates proposals on the basis of the amount of experience the vendor has with tablet computers and similar technology products, because it wants to make sure that its investment is reliable in the short term and flexible enough to accommodate new apps or updates. In addition, the school wants to be sure the technology will remain relevant in the longer term and not become obsolete. The vendor's ability to meet its specifications also is important because if the processor is too slow, students are unlikely to make use of the devices. The vendor's financial position provides an important indication of whether the vendor will be able to stay in business.

Stage 5: Order Specification

In the fifth stage, the firm places its order with its preferred supplier (or suppliers). The order includes a detailed description of the goods, prices, delivery dates, and, in some cases, penalties for noncompliance. The supplier then sends an acknowledgment that it has received the order and fills it by the specified date. In the case of the school's tablets, the terms are clearly laid out regarding when and how the vendor is expected to perform any preventive maintenance, who the contact person is for any problems with delivery or the tablets themselves, and under what circumstances the vendor will be expected to provide a replacement for a malfunctioning tablet. Issues such as maintenance and replacement are important, because the university does not plan to keep any inventory of extra tablets on hand.

Stage 6: Vendor Performance Assessment Using Metrics

Just as in the consumer buying process, firms analyze their vendors' performance so they can make decisions about their future purchases. The difference is that in a B2B setting, this analysis is typically more formal and objective. Let's consider how Hypothetical University might evaluate the tablet vendor's performance, as in Exhibit 7.3, using the following metrics: delivery (based on promised delivery date), quality, customer service, and issue resolution.

1. The buying team develops a list of issues that it believes are important to consider in the vendor evaluation.

2. To determine the importance of each issue (column 1), the buying team assigns an importance score to each (column 2). The more important the issue, the higher its score, but the importance scores must add up to 1. In this case, the buying team believes that customer service and quality are most important, whereas the issue resolution and delivery are comparatively less important.

3. In the third column, the buying team assigns numbers that reflect its judgments about how well the vendor performs. Using a five-point scale, where 1 equals poor performance and 5 equals excellent performance, the

EXHIBIT 7.3	Evaluating a Vendor's Performance		
(1) Key Issues	(2) Importance Score	(3) Vendor's Performance	(4) Importance × Performance (2) × (3)
Customer Service	0.40	5	2.0
Issue Resolution	0.20	4	0.8
Delivery	0.10	5	0.5
Quality	0.30	3	0.9
Total	1.0		4.2

university decides that the tablet vendor performs quite well on all issues except product quality.

4. To calculate an overall performance score in the fourth column, the team combines the importance of each issue and the vendor's performance scores by multiplying them. Because the tablet vendor performed well on the most important issues, when we add the importance/performance scores in column 4, we find that the overall evaluation is pretty good—4.2 on a five-point scale.

CHECK YOURSELF

1. Identify the stages in the B2B buying process.
2. How do you perform a vendor analysis?

Identify the roles within the buying center.

THE BUYING CENTER

In most large organizations, several people are responsible for buying decisions. These buying center participants can range from employees who have a formal role in purchasing decisions (i.e., the purchasing or procurement department) to members of the design team that is specifying the particular equipment or raw material needed for employees who will be using a new machine that is being ordered. All these employees are likely to play different roles in the buying process, which vendors must understand and adapt to in their marketing and sales efforts.

We can categorize six buying roles within a typical buying center (see Exhibit 7.4). One or more people may take on a certain role, or one person may take on more than one of the following roles: (1) "initiator, the person who first suggests buying the particular product or service; (2) influencer, the person whose views influence other members of the buying center in making the final decision; (3) decider, the person who ultimately determines any part of or the entire buying decision—whether to buy, what to buy, how to buy, or where to buy; (4) buyer, the person who handles the paperwork of the actual purchase; (5) user, the person who consumes or uses the product or service; and (6) gatekeeper, the

| EXHIBIT 7.4 | Buying Center Roles |

person who controls information or access, or both, to decision makers and influencers."[14]

To illustrate how a buying center operates, consider purchases made by a hospital. Where do hospitals obtain their X-ray machines, syringes, and bedpans? Why are some medical procedures covered in whole or in part by insurance, whereas others are not? Why might your doctor recommend one type of allergy medication instead of another?

The Initiator—Your Doctor When you seek treatment from your physician, he or she initiates the buying process by determining the products and services that will best address and treat your illness or injury. For example, say that you fell backward off your snowboard and, in trying to catch yourself, you shattered your elbow. You require surgery to mend the affected area, which includes the insertion of several screws to hold the bones in place. Your doctor promptly notifies the hospital to schedule a time for the procedure and specifies the brand of screws she wants on hand for your surgery.

The Influencer—The Medical Device Supplier, the Pharmacy For years your doctor has been using ElbowMed screws, a slightly higher-priced screw. Her first introduction to ElbowMed screws came from the company's sales representative, who visited her office to demonstrate how ElbowMed screws were far superior to those of its competition. Your doctor recognized ElbowMed as a good value. Armed with empirical data and

From an ethical perspective, what information should pharmaceutical sales representatives provide to doctors?

case studies, ElbowMed's sales rep effectively influenced your doctor's decision to use that screw.

The Decider—The Hospital Even though your doctor requested ElbowMed screws, the hospital ultimately is responsible for deciding whether to buy ElbowMed screws. The hospital supplies the operating room, instrumentation, and surgical supplies, and, therefore, the hospital administrators must weigh a variety of factors to determine whether the ElbowMed screw is not only best for the patients but also involves a cost that is reimbursable by various insurance providers.

The Buyer The actual buyer of the screw will likely be the hospital's materials manager, who is charged with buying and maintaining inventory for the hospital in the most cost-effective manner. Whereas ElbowMed screws are specific to your type of procedure, other items, such as gauze and sutures, may be purchased through a group purchasing organization (GPO), which obtains better prices through volume buying.

The User—The Patient Ultimately, the buying process for this procedure will be greatly affected by the user, namely you, and your broken elbow. If you are uncomfortable with the procedure or have read about alternative procedures that you prefer, you may decide that ElbowMed screws are not the best treatment.

The Gatekeeper—The Insurance Company Your insurer may believe that ElbowMed screws are too expensive and that other screws deliver equally effective results and therefore refuse to reimburse the hospital in full or in part for the use of the screws.

In the end, the final purchase decision must take into consideration every buying center participant. Ethical and Societal Dilemma 7.1 examines the unethical, illegal, but also international practice of influencing the influencers through expensive gifts and payments.

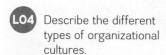 **LO4** Describe the different types of organizational cultures.

Organizational Culture

A firm's organizational culture reflects the set of values, traditions, and customs that guide its employees' behavior. The firm's culture often comprises a set of unspoken guidelines that employees share with one another through various work situations. For example, Walmart buyers are not allowed to accept even the smallest gift from a vendor, not even a cup of coffee. This rule highlights its overall corporate culture: It is a low-cost operator whose buyers must base their decisions only on the products' and vendors' merits.

At GE, the culture aims to ensure that members and partners regard B2B as a source of innovation, not a "boring-to-boring" proposition. Rather than lament the relatively less glamorous process of B2B processes, GE has "decided we are geeky and we are proud of it."[15] To promote its offerings, the company thus focuses on how it innovates in B2B settings, and it brings this attitude into its purchasing decisions.

As these examples show, organizational culture can have a profound influence on purchasing decisions. Corporate buying center cultures can be divided into four general types: autocratic, democratic, consultative, and consensus (as illustrated in Exhibit 7.5). Knowing which buying center culture is prevalent in a given organization helps the seller decide how to approach that particular client, how and to whom to deliver pertinent information, and to whom to make sales presentations.

In an autocratic buying center, even though there may be multiple participants, one person makes the decision alone, whereas the majority rules in a

Ethical & Societal Dilemma 7.1   Is It Business or Bribery?[iii]

In some parts of the world, accepting money, offering expensive gifts, or distributing payments to government and business officials to influence business decisions is considered an acceptable business practice. In other nations, these practices are unethical and illegal. As the world moves to a more global economy, pressure is mounting to level the playing field by eliminating bribery. Yet companies that have traditionally relied on business bribery argue that criminalizing this activity will negatively affect their ability to compete. How do executives doing business on an international scale respond when a behavior that could earn them a lucrative contract in one country could earn them jail time in another?

Whenever businesses cooperate with one another or companies intersect with governments, the opportunity exists for bribery. An extravagant gift or economic incentive may mean one contractor lands a lucrative contract. A private exchange of money between an executive and a public official may result in the official driving a new car while the executive's company bypasses a restriction that could hinder its growth. These types of interactions occur behind closed doors and between two people, yet they can have significant repercussions, including unsafe infrastructure, bridges, and buildings, if they occur in the context of large business transactions. Increasingly, players in the world's economies thus are pushing for an end to foreign bribery.

One tactic they are using is a public report by Transparency International that compares corruption rates of countries and industries. This investigation reveals unexpected trends, such as evidence that bribes passing from one business to another are almost as common as bribes slipped to public officials. By highlighting those business sectors or countries perceived as the worst offenders, the Bribery Index also aims to bring about change, whether through embarrassment or economic repercussions that result when companies refuse to do business in corrupt economies. Finally, this report highlights suggestions for reducing corruption and incentives for improvement.

As summarized in the graph below, the Transparency International Bribery Index reveals that all the world's 28 largest economies engage in bribery; China and Russia emerged as

Although in some parts of the world bribes are part of doing business, in the U.S. they are unethical and illegal.

those most likely to be using money and gifts to influence decisions. Both countries have recently begun enforcing legal repercussions for companies and individuals that engage in international business bribery. For example, when reports surfaced that representatives of GlaxoSmithKline (GSK) had bribed doctors, medical practices, and hospitals to prescribe only GSK drugs, China's news media and central government reacted with anger. Calling the drug company a "criminal godfather," Chinese authorities encouraged consumers to boycott its products. A **boycott** is when a group refuses to deal commercially with an organization to protest against its policies. As a result, GSK's business revenues fell by two-thirds in China.

The Transparency International report also highlights positive results of reduced corruption: A business survey conducted in Europe found that two-thirds of respondents believe that a company with a reputation for ethical behavior enjoys a commercial advantage. Findings such as these, along with improved transparency added to business practices, international anticorruption standards, monitoring and enforcement of anticorruption business policies and laws, and empowerment of whistle-blowers, may also help reduce international bribery rates.

Perceived corruption levels by country and companies' propensity to bribe

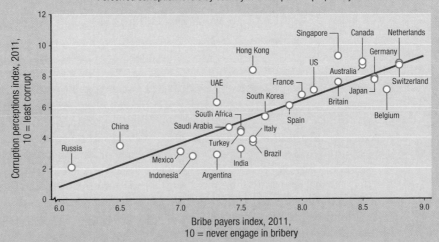

Source: © *The Economist* newspaper Limited, London (Jan 2014).

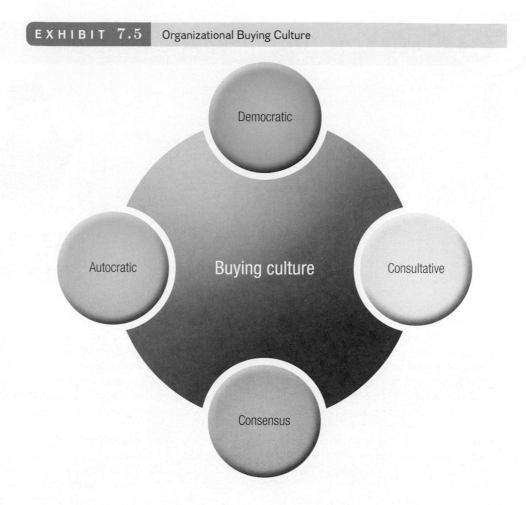

EXHIBIT 7.5   Organizational Buying Culture

democratic buying center. Consultative buying centers use one person to make a decision but solicit input from others before doing so. Finally, in a consensus buying center, all members of the team must reach a collective agreement that they can support a particular purchase.[16]

Cultures act like living, breathing entities that change and grow, just as organizations do. Even within some companies, culture may vary by geography, by division, or by functional department. Whether you are a member of the buying center or a supplier trying to sell to it, it is extremely important to understand its culture and the roles of the key players in the buying process. Not knowing the roles of the key players could waste a lot of time and even alienate the real decision maker.

Building B2B Relationships

In B2B contexts there are a multitude of ways to enhance relationships, and these methods seem to be advancing and evolving by the minute.[17] For example, blogs and social media can build awareness, provide search engine results, educate potential and existing clients about products or services, and warm up a seemingly cold corporate culture. An expert who offers advice and knowledge about products increases brand awareness, and a blog is a great medium for this information. Web analytics, such as traffic on the website and the number of comments, can offer tangible evaluations, but a better measure is how often the blog gets mentioned elsewhere, the media attention it receives, and the interaction, involvement, intimacy, and influence that it promotes.

Social & Mobile Marketing 7.2 — Making the Most of LinkedIn[iv]

Business-to-business (B2B) marketing may seem relatively impersonal, but even in formalized, standardized buying situations personal relationships count. Social media, with a bit of a tweak, play a key role in this setting, just as they do in consumer contexts. Perhaps the best example is LinkedIn, the social media site for business professionals. Launched in 2003, the site has been attracting roughly 1 million members weekly. Its worldwide membership surpassed the 200 million mark. The site is available in over 19 languages and more than 200 countries, which means that it can help B2B interactions overcome geographical boundaries.

In particular, LinkedIn can boast that executives from all the *Fortune* 500 companies have memberships on its site. Accordingly, its promise for networking, whether individually or for the company, is virtually unsurpassed. Such networking entails several key groups:

- *Customers and prospective customers.* LinkedIn allows a firm or its representatives to introduce themselves to possible buyers, using a credible and easily accessible format. The Q&A option on LinkedIn pages also allows customers to ask questions and suppliers to demonstrate their expertise.

- *Investors.* The LinkedIn page offers tangible evidence of the firm's existence and its promise, which is critical information for outsiders who might be willing to invest in its development.

- *Suppliers.* By starting their own group on LinkedIn, B2B buyers might better identify which suppliers in the market are best matched with their needs and most interested in providing the resources they need.

- *Employees and prospective employees.* LinkedIn is a great source for finding employees who are diligent,

LinkedIn is perhaps the best social media site for networking with business professionals.

professional, interested, and qualified. Furthermore, if a firm retains its links to former employees, it can gain a good source of referrals—assuming those employees left on good terms.

- *Analysts.* The job of an analyst is to find detailed information about a company and then recommend it, or not, to the market. LinkedIn gives firms a means to provide that information in a credible but still firm-controlled context.

The site also provides sophisticated analytics for keeping track of all these networking opportunities. Users can see who visited their pages, which descriptions they viewed, and even compare their LinkedIn performance against competitors' pages.

The LinkedIn.com social network is mainly used for professional networking in the B2B marketplace (see Social and Mobile Marketing 7.2). Twitter, the microblogging site, is also valuable for B2B marketers because they can communicate with other businesses as often as they want. Companies such as HootSuite make it easier for companies using Twitter to manage their followers, update their posts, track analytics, and even schedule tweets, just as they would to manage a traditional marketing campaign.[18]

The majority of B2B marketers use white papers for their marketing efforts, and the majority of B2B buyers regularly read them prior to making a purchase.[19] When executives confront an unfulfilled business need, they normally turn to white papers. Their B2B partner may have a technologically advanced solution, but buyers have to understand the solution before they can consider a purchase. A good white paper provides information about the industry and its challenges in an educational context, rather than a promotional sense, to avoid seeming like simply propaganda. That is, the goal of white papers is to provide valuable information that a businessperson can easily understand and that will help the company address its problems with new solutions.

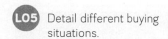

LO5 Detail different buying situations.

THE BUYING SITUATION

The type of buying situation also affects the B2B decision process. Most B2B buying situations can be categorized into three types: new buys, modified rebuys, and straight rebuys (see Exhibit 7.6). To illustrate the nuances among these three buying situations, consider how colleges and universities develop relationships with some of their suppliers. Most universities negotiate with sports apparel manufacturers, such as Nike, Reebok, and New Balance, to establish purchasing agreements for their sports teams. Those with successful sports teams have been very successful in managing these relationships, to the benefit of both the team and the company.[20] Large universities that win national championships, such as the University of Alabama or University of Southern California (USC), can solicit sponsorships in exchange for free athletic equipment, whereas less popular teams or smaller schools typically must accept an upfront sponsorship and then agree to buy from that vendor for a specified period of time. In exchange for this sponsorship, the vendors gain the right to sell apparel with the university logo and require the school's team to purchase only their equipment. Many apparel companies make a significant portion of their revenue through sponsorship deals that grant them the right to sell apparel with popular university logos.

In a new buy situation, a customer purchases a good or service for the first time,[21] which means the buying decision is likely to be quite involved because the buyer or the buying organization does not have any experience with the item. In the B2B context, the buying center is likely to proceed through all six steps in the buying process and involve many people in the buying decision. Typical new buys might range from capital equipment to components that the firm previously

---

EXHIBIT 7.6   Buying Situations

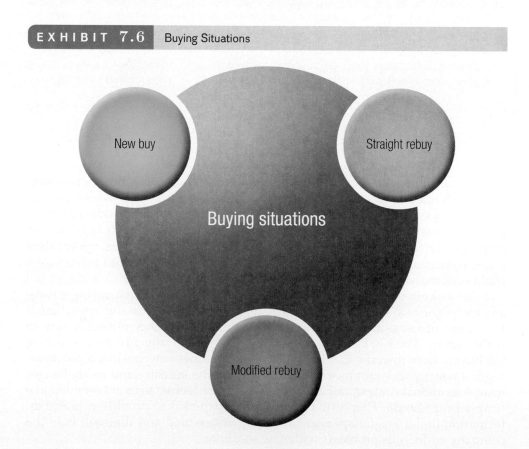

Schools like the University of Alabama negotiate with sports apparel manufacturers, such as Nike, to get free athletic equipment. The manufacturers, in turn, get to sell apparel with the university logo.

made itself but now has decided to purchase instead. For example, a small college might need to decide which apparel company to approach for a sponsorship. For smaller colleges, finding a company that will sponsor multiple sports teams—such as women's soccer as well as men's basketball—is a priority, though it also must balance other considerations, such as the length of the contract. Some vendors offer perks to attract new buyers; New Balance offers teams that sign up for long-term contracts custom fittings for their players' shoes. Each season, a sales team from New Balance visits the school and custom fits each player to achieve the best fit possible.

With another sort of example, Adding Value 7.1 highlights how HubSpot helps buyers become more informed about products before engaging in the B2B buying process.

Another example of a new buy occurs in the fashion industry, where runway shows offer wholesale buyers an opportunity to inspect new lines of clothing and place orders. Designer sales often occur during private meetings with buyers, both before and after runway shows. Buyers meet with the designers, discuss the line, and observe a model wearing the clothing. The buyer's challenge then is to determine which items will sell best in the retail stores he or she represents while trying to imagine what the item will look like in regular, as opposed to model, sizes. Buyers must also negotiate purchases for orders that may not be delivered for as much as six months. Buyers can suggest modifications to make the clothing more or less expensive or more comfortable for their customers. Buyers and designers recognize the significant value of this relationship, which occasionally prompts buyers to purchase a few items from a designer, even if those items do not exactly fit the store's core customers' tastes. Doing so ensures that the buyer will have access to the designer's collection for the next season.[22]

In a modified rebuy, the buyer has purchased a similar product in the past but has decided to change some specifications, such as the desired price, quality level, customer service level, options, and so forth. Current vendors are likely to have an advantage in acquiring the sale in a modified rebuy situation as long as the reason for the modification is not dissatisfaction with the vendor or its

Adding Value 7.1   Getting Out the Message with Inbound Marketing[v]

Search engines, company web pages, social media sites, and the blogosphere have transformed the way businesses learn about and shop for products and services. Unlike a decade ago, when a prospective customer had little knowledge of a vendor's products at first contact, today's customers have searched the Internet using relevant keywords and reviewed company websites by the time they speak with a vendor. As a result, they are well informed and seriously interested in a purchase, adding new efficiency to B2B transactions. But this development works only if companies have the marketing savvy to use today's technology to their advantage.

Two entrepreneurs noticed that small companies and start-ups without the skills to use these tools effectively get lost in the noise, even if prospective customers are searching for vendors in their niche. Furthermore, companies that enlist marketing firms are disadvantaged if those firms rely solely on traditional best practices, such as print advertising, telemarketing, and trade shows. To help these businesses, the two launched a software marketing program, HubSpot, designed to help companies transform their marketing approach. The idea was to abandon intrusive outbound marketing, which people are increasingly able to screen out, and replace it with inbound marketing. Inbound marketing, defined as any marketing tactic that relies on earning customer interest rather than buying it, is built on the understanding that Facebook, Twitter, online user reviews, smartphones, blogs, and websites are the true force behind the way comsumers in today's marketplace actually learn and shop.

HubSpot's software contains easy-to-use tools that help companies get noticed, convert website visitors to customers, and analyze the effectiveness of marketing efforts across channels. Among the tools in the first category, for example, is a keyword grader that helps companies create content and a list of relevant keywords to improve search engine odds and ranking. Using the lead conversion tools, marketers without technical skills can create landing pages with customizable lead capture forms, auto-response e-mails, and thank-you pages. These tools can also be used to send customized e-mails to new leads on a self-selected schedule. The marketing analytics tools allow HubSpot's customers to track competitors, evaluate the impact of a blog, and compare the effectiveness of all marketing channels to provide important insight into the behaviors of customers and the value of each channel to the bottom line.

HubSpot's approach has been successful for both the founders and their customers. The company, launched in June 2006, reached 3,500 customers in four years and is the second-fastest-growing software-as-a-service (SAS) company in history.

One customer, the nonprofit National Institute for Fitness and Sport (NIFS), wanted to increase its visibility with corporate and retirement fitness centers. After experiencing difficulty driving traffic to the company website—and after an expensive marketing company campaign proved ineffective—NIFS turned to HubSpot. The results were increases in traffic and leads by more than 200 percent and an increase in social media traffic of 16 percent. According to NIFS's director of media, the fitness company "picked up a number of requests for proposals from businesses that never would have paid attention to us initially because we were able to raise where we sit in the search engines."

Companies such as HubSpot are taking advantage of changes that have already occurred in the marketplace to reduce costs and improve the effectiveness of marketing. As technology evolves and more business and individual shoppers use online information to make their purchasing decisions, businesses will have to adapt their marketing strategies to encompass new technologies and new shopping behaviors.

HubSpot helps its customers get noticed on the Internet.

products. The Ohio State University's sports department might ask adidas to modify the specifications for its basketball shoes after noticing some improvements made to the adidas shoes used by the University of Michigan.

Straight rebuys occur when the buyer or buying organization simply buys additional units of products that had previously been purchased. Many B2B purchases are likely to fall in the straight rebuy category. For example, sports teams need to repurchase a tremendous amount of equipment that is not covered by apparel sponsorships, such as tape for athletes' ankles or weights for the weight room. The purchase of bottled water also typically involves a straight rebuy from an existing supplier.

These varied types of buying situations call for very different marketing and selling strategies. The most complex and difficult is the new buy because it requires the buying organization to make changes in its current practices and purchases. As a result, several members of the buying center will likely become involved, and the level of their involvement will be more intense than in the case of modified and straight rebuys. In new buying situations, buying center members also typically spend more time at each stage of the B2B buying process, similar to the extended decision-making process that consumers use in the B2C process. In comparison, in modified rebuys the buyers spend less time at each stage of the B2B buying process, similar to limited decision making in the B2C process (see Chapter 6).

In straight rebuys, however, the buyer is often the only member of the buying center involved in the process. Like a consumer's habitual purchase, straight rebuys often enable the buyer to recognize the firm's need and go directly to the fifth step in the B2B buying process, skipping the product specification, RFP process, and proposal analysis and supplier selection steps.

Over the course of a B2B relationship, the type of buying process also can change. The buying process for restaurants appears poised to undergo a significant transformation, because of the potential merger between Sysco and US Foods, the two largest food distributors in the United States. Restaurants that once considered their purchases of hamburger meat a straight rebuy might find that they need to reconsider the process. Because the merger would create a single, dominant food supplier, the new company will gain much more power over pricing. In turn, restaurants might need to enter into a modified rebuy (e.g., purchase lower quality hamburger to cut costs).

Thus, in various ways B2B marketing both differs from and mirrors the consumer behavior (B2C) process we detailed in Chapter 6. The differences in the six stages of the buying process make sense in view of the many unique factors that come into play. The constitution of the buying center (initiator, influencer, decider, buyer, user, and gatekeeper), the culture of the purchasing firm (autocratic, democratic, consultative, or consensus), and the context of the buying situation (new buy, modified rebuy, straight rebuy) all influence the B2B buying process in various ways, which means that sellers must be constantly aware of these factors if they want to be successful in their sales attempts. Finally, just as it has done seemingly everywhere we look, the Internet has radically changed some elements of the B2B world, increasing the frequency of both private electronic exchanges and auctions.

CHECK YOURSELF

1. What factors affect the B2B buying process?
2. What are the six buying roles?
3. What is the difference between new buy, rebuy, and modified rebuy?

Reviewing Learning Objectives

 Describe the ways in which business-to-business (B2B) firms segment their markets.

All firms want to divide the market into groups of customers with different needs, wants, or characteristics who therefore might appreciate products or services geared especially toward them. On a broad level, B2B firms divide the market into four types: manufacturers or service providers, resellers, institutions, and government. Manufacturers and service providers purchase materials to make their products and components and offer expertise to help run their businesses, such as computer and telephone systems. Resellers are primarily wholesalers, distributors, or retailers that sell the unchanged products. Institutions include nonprofit organizations such as hospitals, schools, or churches. Finally, governments purchase all types of goods and services, but in the United States, defense is among the largest expenditures.

 List the steps in the B2B buying process.

Similar to the B2C buying process, the B2B process consists of several stages: need recognition; product specification; the RFP process; proposal analysis, vendor negotiation, and selection; order specification; and vendor performance assessment using metrics. The B2B process tends to be more formalized and structured than the customer buying process.

 Identify the roles within the buying center.

The initiator first suggests the purchase. The influencer affects important people's perceptions and final decisions. The decider ultimately determines at least some of the buying decision—whether, what, how, or where to buy. The buyer handles the details of the actual purchase. The user consumes or employs the product or service. The gatekeeper controls information and access to decision makers and influencers. In B2B situations, it is likely that several people, organized into a buying center, will be involved in making the purchase decision. The vendor must understand the relationships among the participants of the buying center to be effective. A firm's organizational culture can also influence the decision process. For instance, if a firm is trying to sell to a young, high-tech computer component manufacturer, it might be well advised to send salespeople who are fluent in technology-speak and can easily relate to the customer.

 Describe the different types of organizational cultures.

Firm culture consists of unspoken guidelines that employees share through various work situations. They generally can be classified as autocratic, such that one person makes most decisions; democratic, where the majority rules; consultative, in which one person makes decisions based on the input of others; or consensus, which requires all members of the team to reach collective agreement.

 Detail different buying situations.

The buying process depends to a great extent on the situation. If a firm is purchasing a product or service for the first time (i.e., new buy), the process is much more involved than if it is engaging in a straight rebuy of the same item again. A modified rebuy falls somewhere in the middle, such that the buyer wants essentially the same thing but with slightly different terms or features.

Key Terms   ▦ILEARNSMART·

- autocratic buying center, 218
- boycott, 219
- business-to-business (B2B) marketing, 208
- buyer, 216
- buying center, 216
- consensus buying center, 220
- consultative buying center, 220
- decider, 216
- democratic buying center, 220
- derived demand, 208
- distributor, 210
- gatekeeper, 216
- influencer, 216
- initiator, 216

Marketing Applications

1. Provide an example of each of the four types of B2B organizations.

2. What are the major differences between the consumer buying process discussed in Chapter 6 and the B2B buying process discussed in this chapter? Use buying a desktop for personal use versus buying more than 100 desktops for a firm to illustrate the key points.

3. Assume you have written this textbook and are going to attempt to sell it to your school. Identify the six members of the buying center. What role would each play in the decision process? Rank them in terms of how much influence they would have on the decision, with 1 being most influential and 6 being least influential. Will this ranking be different in other situations?

4. Now provide an example of the three types of buying situations that the bookstore at your school might face when buying textbooks.

5. Finally discuss for which types of products it would do a straight rebuy and for which it would pursue a modified rebuy.

6. Mazda is trying to assess the performance of two manufacturers that could supply music systems for its vehicles. Using the information in the table below, determine which manufacturer Mazda should use.

Performance Evaluation of Brands			
Issues	Importance Weights	Manufacturer A's Performance	Manufacturer B's Performance
Sound	0.4	5	3
Cost	0.3	2	4
Delivery time	0.1	2	2
Brand cachet	0.2	5	1
Total	1		

7. Describe the organizational culture at your school or job. How would knowledge of this particular organization's culture help a B2B salesperson sell products or services to the organization?

8. You have just started to work in the purchasing office of a major pharmaceutical firm. The purchasing manager has asked you to assist in writing an RFP for a major purchase. The manager gives you a sheet detailing the specifications for the RFP. While reading the specifications, you realize that they have been written to be extremely favorable to one bidder. How should you handle this situation?

Quiz Yourself

1. Compared to the B2C process, the information search and alternative evaluation steps in the B2B process are:
   a. decentralized.
   b. less focused on customer value creation.
   c. identical.
   d. more formal and structured.
   e. based on derived supply analysis.

2. After need recognition and product specification, many firms using the B2B buying process:
   a. identify contract specifications.
   b. issue a request for proposals from invited suppliers.
   c. proceed to proposal analysis.
   d. enter vendor negotiation and selection.
   e. revise their need recognition analysis.

(Answers to these two questions can be found on page 651.)

Toolkit

B2B VENDOR ANALYSIS

Help David evaluate two software vendors. He has created a chart to help him decide which one to pick. He has rated the two vendors on brand strength, timeliness of deliveries, product quality, and ease of ordering. His firm is generally most interested in quality and then in timeliness. Reputation is somewhat important. The ease of ordering is least important. Please use the toolkit provided in your instructor's Connect course to evaluate the two software vendors.

Net Savvy

1. Ballymaloe Country Relish is an Irish delicacy, sold in fine food stores throughout Ireland. For consumers outside Ireland, it also lists various sellers in different countries. Visit ballymaloe-countryrelish.ie and click on "Find Us Near You" to find the most convenient source for you personally. Why does Ballymaloe offer such information and direct links to other retailers? What benefits does doing so provide the relish maker, the retailer, and customers?

2. Siemens worked with the custom motorcycle manufacturer Orange County Chopper to build the Smart Chopper—the first electric motorcycle. Visit http://www.usa.siemens.com/smartchopper/ to learn about the specifications and details of this new form of chopper. How is Siemens using this innovation to improve its relationships with its business customers? What other outcomes might this services provider expect from its efforts?

Chapter Case Study

LEVI STRAUSS, COTTON FARMERS, AND INTERNATIONAL PRODUCTION

Most people have multiple pairs of jeans, relying on them as a staple of their wardrobes. But few consumers really consider what has gone into each pair as they get dressed in the morning. Questions such as where they were made, how much material they contain, or the impact they have on the environment are less significant for most consumers. But for businesses such as Levi Strauss & Co., they are critical to the company's long-term survival and success.[23]

Levi's is a major consumer of cotton: A single pair of its 501 jeans uses nearly two pounds of cotton, and the vast majority of all Levi's products are made with cotton. Cotton needs water to grow, and jeans continue to require water throughout their life cycle, whether as part of the stone-wash softening process or in the laundry. By the time a pair of jeans bought today has reached the end of its life cycle, it will have used more than 900 gallons of water.[24]

A decade ago, this water consumption was of less concern. But changes in rainfall patterns caused by global climate change are directly tying Levi's future to water: Less water means less moisture for cotton crops, and less cotton means Levi's will either have to incorporate more synthetics into its clothing—a significant change to its brand—or pay more for scarce raw materials. If the company pays more, the increased prices may be passed along to customers, possibly resulting in Levi's loyalists moving to other brands. A third alternative, reducing the cost of other garment materials such as buttons and zippers, affects both the brand and quality standards, though it can help control the end cost charged to consumers.

Levi's works with its suppliers to implement sustainable water use in the production of its jeans.

To address these challenges, Levi's is working with suppliers to implement more sustainable water use and other environmental practices as well as more responsible practices with regard to workers throughout its supply chain. These partnerships are challenging to instigate and oversee because cotton is raised in more than 100 countries and grown primarily on small, family-owned farms.[25] Levi's began more than 20 years ago by creating a Terms of Engagement code of conduct that spells out what the company requires from its business partners in terms of social, ethical, legal, and environmental practices and employment standards. The agreement covers such issues as working ages, health and safety, and child labor, as well as wages, benefits, and disciplinary practices.[26]

The company has also partnered with other large consumers of cotton, including H&M, IKEA, Marks & Spencer, and adidas; environmental organizations such as the World Wildlife Federation; and the Better Cotton Initiative, a cotton industry association, to study growing practices that reduce water and pesticide use.[27] In one such study, conducted on a farm in India, cotton plants using a new drip irrigation system were taller and bore more flowers than those using traditional methods. The drip system reduced water use by about 70 percent and shortened the duration of electricity use for the system from three days to three hours. It also distributed fertilizer more evenly. Levi Strauss, IKEA, and adidas thus agreed to set aggressive goals for increasing the amount of this better cotton in their products. In addition, Levi Strauss has introduced a line of stone-washed denim that does not use water.

Another initiative aims to reorient the goals of the entire supply chain to produce more durable clothing options, rather than fast fashion. With input from Bangladeshi factory owners and cotton farmers from Pakistan, Levi Strauss has developed a Wellthread line of clothing that promises to last far longer than most other apparel items. By addressing the needs of its B2B partners, Levi Strauss hopes "to weave responsibility into every stage of design, manufacturing and usage, from the cotton fields to the factories to the market and beyond."[28]

In conjunction with other members of the apparel industry and outdoor-wear makers such as Target, Nike, Patagonia, and REI, Levi's has adopted a software tool, the Eco Index, that helps clothing manufacturers determine the environmental and human impact of their products.[29] These efforts go beyond water use to include every step of the garment's life cycle—from raw material production to disposal—and help companies make the most responsible decisions when sourcing and distributing their wares.

Questions

1. In pursuing more sustainable production, what steps of the B2B buying process will Levi Strauss need to revisit? Which are likely to become less important? More important?

2. For this pursuit to be successful, what type of organizational culture should Levi's foster?

Endnotes

1. "GE Is So Stoked about 3D Printing, They're Using It to Make Parts for Jet Engines," *The Economist*, November 24, 2013.

2. Beth McKenna, "3D Printing in the Aerospace Industry: How General Electric and United Technologies Are Using This Technology," *The Motley Fool*, February 28, 2014, http://www.fool.com.

3. "GE Says 3D Printing Will 'Touch' 50% of Manufacturing," *Investors Business Daily*, October 7, 2013.

4. Clint Boultin, "Printing Out Barbies and Ford Cylinders," *The Wall Street Journal*, June 5, 2013, http://online.wsj.com.

5. Tim Catts, "GE Turns to 3D Printers for Plane Parts," *Bloomberg Businessweek*, November 27, 2013, http://www.businessweek.com.

6. Samuel Gibs, "Battle for the Car: Will Google, Apple, or Microsoft Dominate?" *The Guardian*, March 6, 2014, http://www.theguardian.com.

7. Corey Eridon, "The Average Large Company Has 178 Social Media Accounts," *Hub Spot*, January 10, 2012, http://blog.hubspot.com.

8. http://www.constantcontact.com.

9. http://www.volkswagenag.com.

10. http://www.vwgroupsupply.com.

11. "Budget of the United States Government: Fiscal Year 2014," Executive Office of the United States: Office of Management and Budget.

12. Ibid.

13. http://www.guru.com.

14. These definitions are provided by http://www.marketingpower.com (the American Marketing Association's website). We have bolded the key terms.

15. E. J. Schultz, "GE Tells the Secret of Making Geeky Cool," *Advertising Age*, October 5, 2013, http://adage.com.

16. http://www.goer.state.ny.us.

17. Philip Letts, "Why Do B2B Firms Still Not 'Get' the Internet?" *Real Business*, March 13, 2014, http://realbusiness.co.uk; Amber Mac, "5 (Relatively Simple) Steps to B2B Social Media Success," *Fast Company*, February 14, 2014, http://www.fastcompany.com.

18. http://www.hootsuite.com.

19. Tracey Peden, "The Use of White Papers in Today's B2B Market," *Marketing Resources Blog*, May 28, 2013, http://blog.ubmcanon.com/bid/285080/.

20. Michael Krause, "How Does Oregon Football Keep Winning? Is It the Uniforms?" *Grantland*, August 30, 2011, http://www.grantland.com.

21. Fabiana Ferreira et al., "The Transition from Products to Solutions: External Business Model Fit and Dynamics," *Industrial Marketing Management* 42, no. 7 (2013), pp. 1093–1101; Mark W. Johnston and Greg W. Marshall, *Contemporary Selling: Building Relationships, Creating Value* (: Routledge, 2013); Barton A. Weitz, Stephen B. Castleberry, and John F. Tanner, *Selling Building Partnerships*, 6th ed. (Burr Ridge, IL: McGraw-Hill /Irwin, 2005), p. 93.

22. Maggie Hira, "How Does a Fashion Buyer Spend a Workday?" http://www.ehow.com; U.S. Department of Labor, http://www.bls.gov.

23. Leslie Kaufman, "Stone Washed Blue Jeans (Minus the Wash)," *The New York Times*, November 1, 2011, http://www.nytimes.com.

24. Ibid.

25. "Cotton/Raw Materials," http://www.levistrauss.com.

26. "Worker Rights," http://www.levistrauss.com.

27. "Sustainability," http://www.levistrauss.com/sustainability/.

28. Marc Gunther, "Levi Strauss Seeks to Slow Down Fast Fashion with Sustainable Practices," *The Guardian*, November 6, 2013, http://www.theguardian.com.

29. Christina Binkley, "How Green Are Your Jeans?" *The Wall Street Journal*, October 2010, http://wsjclassroom.com.

i. Quentin Harvey, "IBM Plans Big Spending for the Cloud," *The New York Times*, January 17, 2014, http://www.nytimes.com; Alex Barinka, "IBM's Watson to Help Rich DBS Clients with 'Jeopardy' Smarts," *Bloomberg Technology*, January 8, 2014, http://www.bloomberg.com/.

ii. Stephanie Reitz, "Many US Schools Adding iPads, Trimming Textbooks," *Yahoo Finance*, September 3, 2011, http://finance.yahoo.com; "Do iPads in Schools Change Behavior?" February 22, 2011, http://www.ipadinschools.com; Nick Wingfield, "Once Wary, Apple Warms Up to Business Market," *The New York Times*, November 15, 2011, http://www.nytimes.com; Rachel

King, "Apple Woos Businesses Despite Security Worries," *Bloomberg Businessweek*, July 7, 2010, http://www.msnbc. msn.com; Dawn Kawamoto, "iPad 2 Launch Adds Muscle to Apple's Invasion of Corporate America," *Daily Finance*, March 10, 2011, http://www.dailyfinance.com; Leander Kahney, "iPad May Replace Computers and Textbooks in Schools, Experts Predict," *Cult of Mac*, http://www. cultofmac.com.

iii.   Sean Silverthorne, "Business Ethics: Pay the Bribe?" *CBS Money Watch*, http://www.cbsnews.com; Stephen H. Unger, "Ethical Aspects of Bribing People in Other Countries," http://www1.cs.columbia.edu; Transparency International, "Bribe Payers Index 2011," http: //bpi.transparency.org/; "International Back Scratching," *The Economist*, November 2, 2011,

http://www.economist.com; Julia Kollewe, "GlaxoSmithKline's Boss's 2013 Bonus Doubled, Despite Scandal in China," *The Guardian*, February 27, 2014, http://www.thegudardian.com; Ernst and Young, "European Fraud Survey 2011: Recovery, Regulation and Integrity," http://www.ey.com.

iv.   LinkedIn Press Center, "About Us," http://press.linkedin.com; Heidi Cohen, "5 LinkedIn Business Goals," March 25, 2011, http://heidicohen.com; Maria Tabaka, "How to Launch a LinkedIn Company Page," *Inc.*, April 17, 2011, http://www.inc.com.

v.   http://www.hubspot.com; http://www.hubspot.com/customer-case-studies/; "Should Your Startup Be Hubspotting?" *Tech Cocktail*, May 6, 2013, http://www.tech.co; "2013 State of Inbound Marketing," *HubSpot*, May 2013, http://www.stateofinboundmarketing.com.

Credits

CHAPTER 8

GLOBAL MARKETING

LEARNING OBJECTIVES

LO1 Describe the components of a country market assessment.

LO2 Understand the marketing opportunities in BRIC countries.

LO3 Identify the various market entry strategies.

LO4 Highlight the similarities and differences between a domestic marketing strategy and a global marketing strategy.

Reviewing the tumultuous history and modern operations of Coca-Cola in India is like taking a quick survey of global marketing issues. From early failures to notable impacts on local regulations to joint efforts to growth efforts, the story of how this global brand has sought to make its mark in this developing nation is instructive.

When Coke first thought to move into India in the 1970s, it confronted a critical cultural difference between its home base and this foreign market. India was officially closed to foreign investment at the time, which meant that to enter, Coke would have to find an equal, Indian partner. Such a joint venture partnership would have required it to share its famously protected, secret formula

for making its carbonated beverage. It was totally unwilling to do so, thus it left for more than 20 years.

But as many developing nations have, India liberalized its economy, opening it to more foreign investments and offering more opportunities for foreign companies to enter. Accordingly, Coca-Cola came back in the mid-1990s,[1] but only a few years after its primary rival Pepsi had established a strong base there. To ensure its competitiveness and expand its coverage of the Indian consumer market, Coke bought four local soda brands from the Indian company Parle, so that it gained about 60 percent of the market, far outpacing Pepsi's 30 percent. Yet Coke itself is not the most popular carbonated drink. That distinction belongs to Thums Up, one of the Indian brands Coca-Cola purchased.[2]

Thus, Coke still faces some critical problems in the Indian market. In particular, people just don't drink that much Coke. Whereas the average global consumer drinks 92 bottles of Coke each year, the average

How the World Buys Its Coke
2011 per capita consumption of 8-ounce servings of Coke beverages in select countries

U.S. 403
Mexico 728
France 149
Russia 73
India 12
China 38
Brazil 230
South Africa 247

Source: Coca-Cola

Coke is a top global brand. However, its typical customer in India only buys 12 bottles per year, compared to 728 in Mexico, making India a country with enormous growth potential.

Indian consumer drinks only 12 of them (in Brazil, the average consumer drinks around 290 bottles each year).[3] But Coke believes it cannot just ignore this massive and growing consumer market, because it offers one of the few remaining parts of the world that offers such excellent growth opportunities.

Noting this potential, and in its efforts to "stay ahead of the curve," Coke plans to invest approximately $5 billion in India alone in the next few years.[4] The investment will go to increasing its bottling capacity, building the brand, and expanding its distribution. Brand building efforts might be especially necessary, considering the

water controversies that continue to plague Coca-Cola. Various groups have accused the company of using too much groundwater in its bottling operations, creating an ethical and societal backlash, protests, government fines, and even threats to demolish some of the most controversial plants.

However, with its investments in India and other developing nations, Coca-Cola is taking a very optimistic position: It plans to double its volumes sold and revenues by 2020. That's a pretty tall order for a fizzy drink that already ranks among the top global brands.

Increasing globalization affects not only massive U.S. corporations that actively search out new markets but also small and medium-sized businesses that increasingly depend on goods produced globally to deliver their products and services. Few people think about how globalization affects their daily lives, but take a minute to read the labels on the clothing you are wearing right now. Chances are that most of the items, even if they carry U.S. brand names, were manufactured in another part of the world.

In the United States, the market has evolved from a system of regional marketplaces to national markets to geographically regional markets (e.g., Canada and the United States together) to international markets and finally to global markets. Globalization refers to the processes by which goods, services, capital, people, information, and ideas flow across national borders. Global markets are the result of several fundamental changes such as reductions or eliminations of trade barriers by country governments, the decreasing concerns of distance and time with regard to moving products and ideas across countries, the standardization of laws across borders, and globally integrated production processes.[5]

Each of these fundamental changes has paved the way for marketing to flourish in other countries. The elimination of trade barriers and other governmental actions, for instance, allows goods and ideas to move quickly and efficiently around the world, which in turn facilitates the quick delivery of goods to better meet the needs of global consumers.

As a consequence, consumers have easy access to global products and services. When we walk into a toy store we expect to find Lego brand toys from Denmark. In the local sporting goods store we anticipate finding running shoes made in China by the German firm, adidas. In the grocery store we demand out-of-season produce such as blueberries from Chile in January. Or consider how a $12 digital camera for your keychain, made in Taiwan, could be produced, transported halfway around the world, and sold for so little money at your local Target. These are the questions we will be examining in this chapter.

We begin by looking at how firms assess the potential of a given market, with particular attention to the BRIC countries (Brazil, Russia, India, and China). Next we examine how firms make decisions to go global and choose how and what they will sell globally. Then we explore how to build the marketing mix for global products.

These 25-foot-tall replicas of the New York skyline are made completely out of Legos and have been on display at the Times Square Toys"R"Us in New York City. How do Legos get from their manufacturer in Denmark to toy stores in the United States?

ASSESSING GLOBAL MARKETS

 Describe the components of a country market assessment.

Because different countries, with their different stages of globalization, offer marketers a variety of opportunities, firms must assess the viability of various potential market entries. As illustrated in Exhibit 8.1, we examine four sets of criteria necessary to assess a country's market: economic analysis, infrastructure and technological analysis, government actions or inactions, and sociocultural analysis. Information about these four areas offers marketers a more complete picture of a country's potential as a market for products and services.

Economic Analysis Using Metrics

The greater the wealth of people in a country, generally, the better the opportunity a firm will have in that particular country. A firm conducting an economic analysis of a country market must look at three major economic factors using well-established metrics: the general economic environment, the market size and population growth rate, and real income.

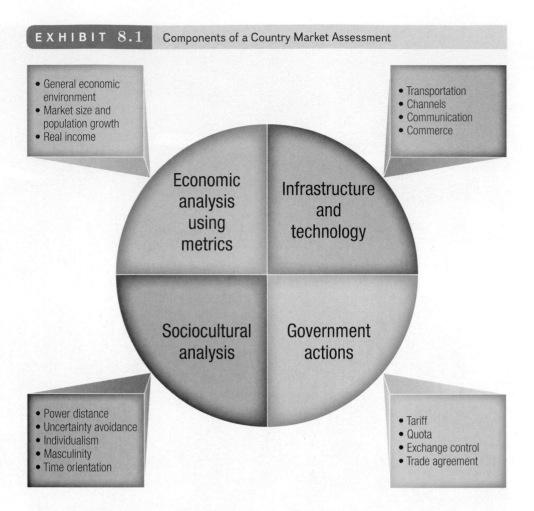

EXHIBIT 8.1   Components of a Country Market Assessment

- General economic environment
- Market size and population growth
- Real income

- Transportation
- Channels
- Communication
- Commerce

- Power distance
- Uncertainty avoidance
- Individualism
- Masculinity
- Time orientation

- Tariff
- Quota
- Exchange control
- Trade agreement

Economic analysis using metrics

Infrastructure and technology

Sociocultural analysis

Government actions

Evaluating the General Economic Environment In general, healthy economies provide better opportunities for global marketing expansions, and there are several ways a firm can use metrics to measure the relative health of a particular country's economy. Each way offers a slightly different view, and some may be more useful for some products and services than for others.

To determine the market potential for its particular product or service, a firm should use as many metrics as it can obtain. One metric is the relative level of imports and exports. The United States, for example, suffers a trade deficit, which means that the country imports more goods than it exports.[6] For U.S. marketers this deficit can signal the potential for greater competition at home from foreign producers. Firms would prefer to manufacture in a country that has a trade surplus, or a higher level of exports than imports, because it signals a greater opportunity to export products to more markets.

The most common way to gauge the size and market potential of an economy, and therefore the potential the country has for global marketing, is to use standardized metrics of output. Gross domestic product (GDP), the most widely used of these metrics, is defined as the market value of the goods and services produced by a country in a year. Gross national income (GNI) consists of GDP plus the net income earned from investments abroad (minus any payments made to nonresidents who contribute to the domestic economy). In other words, U.S. firms that invest or maintain operations abroad count their income from those operations in the GNI but not the GDP.[7]

Another frequently used metric of an overall economy is the purchasing power parity (PPP), a theory that states that if the exchange rates of two countries are in equilibrium, a product purchased in one will cost the same in the other, if

EXHIBIT 8.2	Big Mac Index

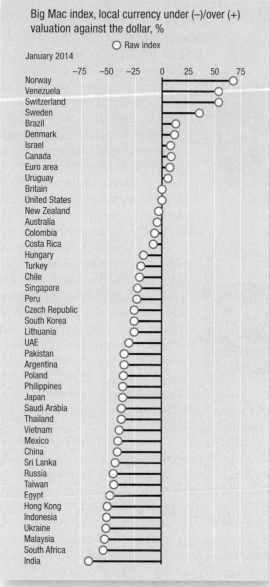

Big Mac index, local currency under (–)/over (+) valuation against the dollar, %

○ Raw index

January 2014

Source: © The Economist newspaper Limited, London (Jan 2014).

expressed in the same currency.[8] A novel metric that employs PPP to assess the relative economic buying power among nations is *The Economist*'s Big Mac Index, which suggests that exchange rates should adjust to equalize the cost of a basket of goods and services, wherever it is bought around the world. Using McDonald's Big Mac as the market basket, Exhibit 8.2 shows that the cheapest burger is in India, where it costs $1.54, compared with an average American price of $4.62. In Brazil, the same burger costs $5.25. This index thus implies that the Indian rupee is 67 percent undervalued, whereas the Brazilian real is about 13 percent overvalued, in comparison with the U.S. dollar.[9]

These various metrics help marketers understand the relative wealth of a particular country, though they may not give a full picture of the economic health of a country because they are based solely on material output. Nor is a weak dollar always a bad thing. For U.S. exporters, a weak dollar means greater demand for their products in foreign countries because they can sell at a lower price.[10]

"Minute Maid Pulpy Super Milky" combines fruit juice, milk powder, whey protein, and coconut bits for the Chinese market.

Although an understanding of the macroeconomic environment is crucial for managers facing a market entry decision, of equal importance is the understanding of economic metrics of market size and population growth rate.

Evaluating Market Size and Population Growth Rate

Global population has been growing dramatically since the turn of the 20th century at least. From a marketing perspective, however, growth has never been equally dispersed. Today, less developed nations by and large are experiencing rapid population growth, while many developed countries are experiencing either zero or negative population growth. The countries with the highest purchasing power today may become less attractive in the future for many products and services because of stagnated growth. And the BRIC countries are likely to be the source of most market growth.

In response, consumer goods companies are paying close attention to the strong demand in BRIC nations. Procter & Gamble (P&G), which enjoys a strong advantage in the Chinese market, also is expanding aggressively into India and Brazil and encountering stiff competition. In Brazil oral care is a highly competitive market, with Colgate and P&G competing. In India, big-name Western firms are competing for market share of laundry products.[11]

Another aspect related to market size and population growth pertains to the distribution of the population within a particular region; namely, is the population located primarily in rural or urban areas? This distinction determines where and how products and services can be delivered. Long supply chains, in which goods pass through many hands, are often necessary to reach rural populations in less developed countries and therefore add to the products' cost. India's 1.2 billion people live overwhelmingly in rural areas, although the population is moving toward urban areas to meet the demands of the growing industrial and service centers located in major cities such as Bangalore and New Delhi. This population shift, perhaps not surprisingly, is accompanied by rapid growth in the middle class. Furthermore, relatively careful banking policies and minimal dependence on exports have helped protect India from the global financial crisis. The business impacts of these combined trends of increasing urbanization, a growing middle class, a degree of protectionism by the central government, and a youthful populace make India an absolutely enormous market for consumer goods.

Evaluating Real Income

Firms can make adjustments to an existing product or change the price to meet the unique needs of a particular country market. Such shifts are particularly common for low-priced consumer goods. In settings in which consumers earn very low wages, the market is known as the "bottom of the pyramid." That is, there is a large, impoverished population that still wants and needs consumer goods but cannot pay the prices that the fewer, wealthier consumers in developed nations can. Thus P&G developed a single-use shampoo packet for consumers who cannot afford an entire bottle at one time. To increase consumption of Coca-Cola in rural India, the company lowered its price to the equivalent of about 10 cents per bottle; Cadbury International introduced Dairy Milk Shots for the equivalent of about 4 cents.[12] Textbook publishers sell paperback versions of U.S. books for a fraction of their U.S. price to countries where students would not otherwise be able to afford a text.

But pricing adjustments aren't only for inexpensive products. Fashion and jewelry manufacturers also make downward adjustments to their prices in countries where the incomes of their target markets cannot support higher prices. Nor is price the only factor that companies adjust to appeal to lower income markets. Haier sells washing machines that also have the capacity to wash vegetables to Chinese consumers who confront limited access to resources, such as water and electricity.[13]

Even as multinationals battle for dominance in emerging economies, local marketers are becoming increasingly price competitive in selling their wares. Local marketers already have strong familiarity with their markets, existing distribution channels, and good name recognition. These smaller firms can often exhibit greater flexibility in their pricing to hold on to market share. They also might be able to find a market niche that remained hidden to international firms. In Macau, for example, big international brands have built massive luxury casinos for the gambling public. But a local casino brand offers very low minimum buy-in amounts, so that lower-income gamblers have a place to go.[14] The best outcome for everyone involved is not just a higher share of an existing market but rather the ongoing development of the market for everyone.[15]

For the Chinese market, Haier sells washing machines that can wash both clothes and vegetables.

Analyzing Infrastructure and Technological Capabilities

The next component of any market assessment is an infrastructure and technological analysis. Infrastructure is defined as the basic facilities, services, and installations needed for a community or society to function, such as transportation and communications systems, water and power lines, and public institutions such as schools, post offices, and prisons.

Marketers are especially concerned with four key elements of a country's infrastructure: transportation, distribution channels, communications, and commerce. First, there must be a system to transport goods throughout the various markets and to consumers in geographically dispersed marketplaces—trains, roads, refrigeration. Second, distribution channels must exist to deliver products in a timely manner and at a reasonable cost. Third, the communications system, particularly media access, must be sufficiently developed to allow consumers to find information about the products and services available in the marketplace. Fourth, the commercial infrastructure, which consists of the legal, banking, and regulatory systems, allows markets to function. In the next section, we focus on how issues pertaining to the political and legal structures of a country can affect the risk that marketers face in operating in a given country.

Analyzing Governmental Actions

Governmental actions, as well as the actions of nongovernmental political groups, can significantly influence firms' ability to sell goods and services because they often result in laws or other regulations that either promote the growth of the global market or close off the country and inhibit growth. Some of the effects are difficult to predict in advance, as Ethical and Societal Dilemma 8.1 describes.

Tariffs A tariff, also called a duty, is a tax levied on a good imported into a country. In most cases, tariffs are intended to make imported goods more expensive and thus less competitive with domestic products, which in turn protects domestic industries from foreign competition. In other cases, tariffs might be imposed to penalize another country for trade practices that the home country views as unfair. For example, when the U.S. government determined the prices of solar panels

Ethical & Societal Dilemma 8.1   How Chinese Regulations Change Car-Buying Practices[i]

As the Scottish poet Robert Burns wrote, "The best laid schemes of mice and men/Go often awry." That is, we might have the best intentions to produce beneficial outcomes, but sometimes those plans have a way of leading to the opposite effect. It's a truth that consumer behavior researchers and marketers know only too well.

Consider, for example, the case of China and its latest attempt to limit automobile induced air pollution. The expansion of China's middle class has created a vast new population of consumers who can now afford cars. The nation's roads, especially in urban centers such as Shanghai, Guangzhou, Guiyang, and Beijing, have become clogged with vehicles. Pollution levels also have reached critical proportions. And China has moved into the top spot in terms of consumer car purchases, with some estimates suggesting that Chinese consumers will buy 30 million vehicles annually by 2020.

In response to these concerns, Chinese government officials have begun testing a licensing regulation that requires people to enter a lottery for a limited number of car registration tags. Without the license plate, drivers would face severe penalties. Thus, officials hoped to halt the growth in this sector and thereby limit pollution and congestion on the roads. Instead, consumers have taken the threat that the regulations would spread as a great reason to buy a new car immediately. If they might not be able to next year, they had better snag a car right now! In cities in which the regulations are already in place, the lucky license lottery winners also are buying bigger (i.e., more polluting), more expensive vehicles. As one consumer noted, "Would you want to put a 100,000 yuan plate on a 50,000 yuan car?" Because these consumers already are spending more than they might have planned, just to have the chance to enter the lottery for a license, they feel more justified spending more on the car itself. Average prices paid per car thus have leapt up approximately 88 percent in just two years.

These trends are great news for foreign luxury carmakers like Audi and Mercedes-Benz, whose sales in China have jumped. It is not so great for Chinese carmakers, which have long provided the lower-end, functional vehicles that China's population previously demanded. It also might not be great news for the environment, which was not at all what authorities planned when they implemented these regulations. The best-laid schemes, indeed.

imported from China were artificially low due to illegal subsidies, it imposed a tariff to help domestic firms compete.[16]

Quotas A quota designates a minimum or maximum quantity of a product that may be brought into a country during a specified time period. The United States, for instance, has committed to allowing at least 1.23 million tons of sugar to be imported (the quota) without a tariff because the country generally consumes more than it produces.[17] It then monitors consumption closely to protect domestic sugar farmers. If demand exceeds supply, it increases the quota, but the level depends on annual consumption and production rates.[18]

Tariffs and quotas can have fundamental and potentially devastating impacts on a firm's ability to sell products in another country. Tariffs artificially raise prices and therefore lower demand, and quotas reduce the availability of imported merchandise. Conversely, tariffs and quotas benefit domestically made products because they reduce foreign competition.

Exchange Control Exchange control refers to the regulation of a country's currency exchange rate, the measure of how much one currency is worth in relation to another.[19] A designated agency in each country, often the central bank, sets the rules for currency exchange, though in the United States the Federal Reserve sets the currency exchange rates. In recent years the value of the U.S. dollar has changed significantly compared with other important world currencies. When the dollar falls, it has a twofold effect on U.S. firms' ability to conduct global business. For firms that depend on imports of finished products, raw materials that they fabricate into other products, or services from other countries, the cost of doing business goes up dramatically. At the same time, buyers in other countries find the costs of U.S. goods and services much lower than they were before.

Trade Agreements Marketers must consider the trade agreements to which a particular country is a signatory or the trading bloc to which it belongs. A trade

Currency fluctuations enhance or impede tourists.

agreement is an intergovernmental agreement designed to manage and promote trade activities for a specific region, and a trading bloc consists of those countries that have signed the particular trade agreement.[20] Some major trade agreements cover two-thirds of the world's international trade: the European Union (EU), the North American Free Trade Agreement (NAFTA), Central America Free Trade Agreement (CAFTA), Mercosur, and the Association of Southeast Asian Nations (ASEAN).[21] These trade agreements are summarized in Exhibit 8.3. The EU represents the highest level of integration across individual nations, whereas the other agreements vary in their integration levels.

Analyzing Sociocultural Factors

Understanding another country's culture is crucial to the success of any global marketing initiative. Culture, or the shared meanings, beliefs, morals, values, and customs of a group of people, exists on two levels: visible artifacts (e.g., behavior,

EXHIBIT 8.3	Trade Agreements
Name	**Countries**
European Union	There are 28 member countries of the EU: Austria, Belgium, Bulgaria, Croatia, Cyprus, Czech Republic, Denmark, Estonia, Finland, France, Germany, Greece, Hungary, Ireland, Italy, Latvia, Lithuania, Luxembourg, Malta, Netherlands, Poland, Portugal, Romania, Slovakia, Slovenia, Spain, Sweden, and the United Kingdom. There are five official candidate countries to join the EU: Macedonia, Serbia, Turkey, Iceland, and Montenegro.
NAFTA	United States, Canada, and Mexico.
CAFTA	United States, Costa Rica, the Dominican Republic, El Salvador, Guatemala, Honduras, and Nicaragua.
Mercosur	Full members: Argentina, Brazil, Paraguay, Uruguay, and Venezuela.
ASEAN	Brunei Darussalam, Cambodia, Indonesia, Laos, Malaysia, Myanmar, Philippines, Singapore, Thailand, and Vietnam.

Source: Information about EU members is from http://europa.eu/about-eu/countries/.

France is the only place on the globe IKEA is not open on Sundays. Notice times for "Dimanche," the French word for Sunday, is absent from the store hours sign.

dress, symbols, physical settings, ceremonies) and underlying values (thought processes, beliefs, and assumptions).[22] Visible artifacts are easy to recognize, but businesses often find it more difficult to understand the underlying values of a culture and appropriately adapt their marketing strategies to them.[23]

For example, IKEA stores across the globe are open seven days a week—except in France. French law prevents retailers from selling on Sundays, and when IKEA tried to challenge the law by keeping one of its stores open, it provoked a lawsuit from a French workers' union. Although IKEA would love to sell over the whole weekend, leaving Sunday as a day of relaxation constitutes a fundamental foundation of French culture. But there is hope for IKEA— the recent slow economic growth and high unemployment of the country is putting pressure on the government to allow retailers to open on Sundays.[24]

For the Swiss, a similar prohibition against Sunday retailing may soon fall to the wayside. If stores remain closed, Switzerland will continue to lose tourism revenues because most foreign visitors, who tend to visit on the weekend, are accustomed to shopping on Sundays. Opening retail stores on Sundays could mean increased consumption and wages for workers who work more hours as well as employment for more people. But the loss of a day traditionally designated for family time and relaxation might be something the country cannot abide.[25] There may be no completely right answer to this dilemma, but global marketers clearly must be aware of the regulations and cultural norms of the countries they enter.

One important cultural classification scheme that firms can use is Geert Hofstede's cultural dimensions concept, which sheds more light on these underlying values. Hofstede initially proposed that cultures differed on four dimensions, but he has added two more dimensions in recent years.[26] Despite some arguments for using other models,[27] Hofstede's cultural dimensions offer a foundation for most research into culture:

1. **Power distance:** willingness to accept social inequality as natural.
2. **Uncertainty avoidance:** the extent to which the society relies on orderliness, consistency, structure, and formalized procedures to address situations that arise in daily life.
3. **Individualism:** perceived obligation to and dependence on groups.
4. **Masculinity:** the extent to which dominant values are male oriented. A lower masculinity ranking indicates that men and women are treated equally in all aspects of society; a higher masculinity ranking suggests that men dominate in positions of power.
5. **Time orientation:** short- versus long-term orientation. A country that tends to have a long-term orientation values long-term commitments and is willing to accept a longer time horizon for, say, the success of a new product introduction.
6. **Indulgence:** the extent to which society allows for the gratification of fun and enjoyment needs or else suppresses and regulates such pursuits.[28]

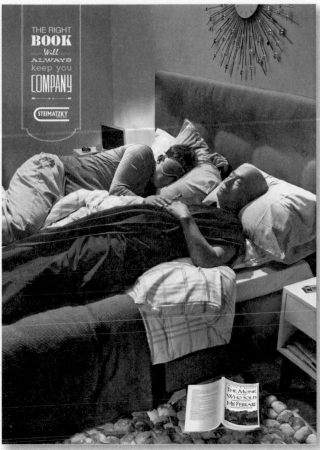

Ads from Steimatzky, the oldest and largest bookstore chain in Israel, illustrate marketing along one of Hofstede's cultural dimensions: one is highly feminine (left) and the other masculine (right).

To illustrate two of the six dimensions, consider the data and graph in Exhibit 8.4. Power distance is on the vertical axis and individualism is on the horizontal axis. Several Latin American countries, including Brazil, cluster high on power distance but low on individualism; the United States, Australia, Canada, and the United Kingdom, in contrast, cluster high on individualism but low on power distance. Using this information, firms should expect that if they design a marketing campaign that stresses equality and individualism, it will be well accepted in English-speaking countries, all other factors being equal, but not be as well received in Latin American countries.

We also find that China scores very high on its time orientation but low in individualism; India has medium to high levels on all five dimensions; and Russia posts notably high uncertainty avoidance and power distance scores. Hofstede is careful to warn that these scores are informative only in a comparative sense, but marketers clearly can use them to design strategies for the varied, promising, BRIC growth markets.[29]

> **EXHIBIT 8.4** Country Clusters

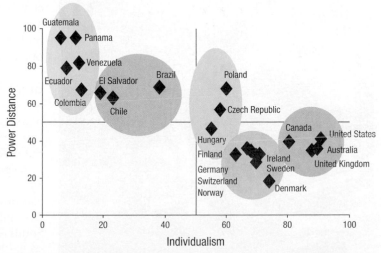

Sources: Geert Hofstede, Gert Jan Hofstede, and Michael Minkov, *Cultures and Organizations, Software of the Mind,* Third Revised Edition, McGraw-Hill 2010, ISBN: 0-07-166418-1. ©Geert Hofstede B.V. quoted with permission.

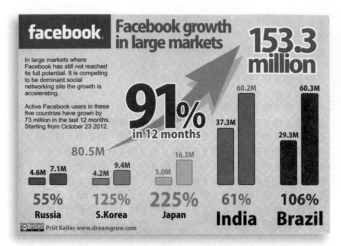

 Priit Kallas www.dreamgrow.com

Facebook and the use of social media marketing are growing phenomena worldwide.

Source: http://www.dreamgrow.com/social-media-trends-2013-1-5-billionpeople-using-facebook/.

Another means of classifying cultures distinguishes them according to the importance of verbal communication.[30] In the United States and most European countries, business relationships are governed by what is said and written down, often through formal contracts. In countries such as China and South Korea, however, most relationships rely on nonverbal cues, so that the situation or context means much more than mere words. For instance, business relationships in China often are formalized by just a handshake, and trust and honor are often more important than legal arrangements.

Overall, culture affects every aspect of consumer behavior: why people buy; who is in charge of buying decisions; and how, when, and where people shop. After marketing managers have completed the four parts of the market assessment, they are better able to make informed decisions about whether a particular country possesses the necessary characteristics to be considered a potential market for the firm's products and services.

In the next section, we detail the market entry decision process, beginning with a discussion of the various ways firms might enter a new global market.

LO2 Understand the marketing opportunities in BRIC countries.

The Appeal of the BRIC Countries

Changes in technology, especially communications, have been a driving force for growth in global markets for decades. The telegraph, radio, television, computer, and Internet have increasingly connected distant parts of the world. Today, communication is instantaneous. Sounds and images from across the globe are delivered to televisions, radios, and computers in real time, which enables receivers in all parts of the world to observe how others live, work, and play.

Like other countries in which McDonald's thrives, Brazil has a strong and growing middle class.

Perhaps the greatest change facing the global community in recent years has been the growth and expansion of four countries that together have come to be known as the BRIC countries: Brazil, Russia, India, and China. Some commentators suggest adding South Africa, to make BRICS, because of that nation's remarkable transformation into a functioning democracy.[31] The inspiring changes to South Africa suggest its increasing promise as a market, but its relatively smaller size leads us to focus on the four BRIC nations, with seemingly the greatest potential for growth, here. Let's examine each in turn.

Brazil[32] Long a regional powerhouse, Brazil's ability to weather, and even thrive, during the most recent economic storm has transformed it into a global contender. Currently, Brazil is the world's seventh largest economy, but predicted growth rates indicate it will move into the fifth spot within a few years. This growth has been aided by a large, literate population and the impositions of social programs that have allowed more than half of the 201 million Brazilians to enter the middle class. This large South American democracy welcomes foreign investors.

Russia[33] The relations between the United States and Russia are a little more complicated than for Brazil. Since the fall of the former Soviet Union, Russia has

In which of the BRIC countries does each of these classic structures reside?

undergone multiple upturns and downturns in its economy. However, its overall growth prospects appear promising, especially as a consumer market. Long denied access to consumer goods, the well-educated population of 143 million exhibits strong demand for U.S. products and brands. In particular, the number of Russian Internet users, presently at 67 million, is growing at a rate of approximately 14 percent annually, and is already Europe's largest Internet market.[34] The country also is negotiating to enter the World Trade Organization (WTO) to improve trade relations with other countries. Russia still faces an aging population and low birthrates. If these trends persist, Russia's population could decline by one-third in the next half century. At the same time, corruption is widespread, creating ethical dilemmas for firms trying to market their goods and services.

India[35] With more than 1.2 billion people, or approximately 15 percent of the world's population, together with expanding middle and upper classes, India is one of the world's fastest-growing markets. With a median age of 26.7 years, India has one of the youngest populations in the world. Its young inhabitants increasingly are adopting global attitudes while living in growing urban centers and shopping at large malls. The well-educated, modern generation is largely fluent in English, and the highly skilled workforce holds great attraction for firms that hope to expand using local talent, especially in technical fields.

India's retail environment is still dominated by millions of small stores and lacks modern supply chain management facilities and systems.[36] Recent changes by the Indian government, however, have the potential to significantly modernize the retail landscape, as the description in our opening vignette suggested. For example, foreign retailers that carry multiple brands, like Walmart, are now allowed to own up to 51 percent of joint ventures in India, and retailers that carry only their own brand, like Nike, can now own 100 percent of their Indian businesses.

China[37] For most of the 20th century, China experienced foreign occupation, civil unrest, major famine, and a strict one-party Communist regime. However, since 1978, China's leadership, while maintaining communist political ideals, has embraced market-oriented economic development, which has led to startlingly rapid gains. For many Chinese, recent developments have dramatically improved their living standards and their levels of personal freedom. Increasing liberalization in the economy has prompted a large increase in China's gross domestic product (GDP); it is now the second-largest economy and the third-largest market for U.S. exports. It makes an excellent target for consumer goods, assuming they can be produced at the right price.

Yet the country continues to suffer from drastically unequal economic distribution, which has led to a significant migrant workforce that subsists on part-time, low-paying jobs. These workers were hit hard by the global financial crisis, which reduced demand for Chinese exports for the first time in years. Furthermore, actual growth of the 1.3 billion-strong Chinese population slowed as a result of government population controls that limit each family to one child. Although China's median age is slightly younger than that of the United States currently, at 36.3 years, the extended application of the one-child policy means that China is one of the most rapidly aging countries in the world. The central government,

The retail landscape in India is changing. Consumers, particularly young ones, are attracted to large modern malls.

Relaxed Indian governmental restrictions now allow foreign retailers that carry their own brand, like Levi's, to own 100 percent of their Indian businesses.

Social & Mobile Marketing 8.1

The Growth of Social Networking—Brazil's Free Market versus China's Restrictions[ii]

By Facebook CEO Mark Zuckerberg's own admission, Facebook grew exponentially for years without a strategic plan for international growth. As the company has matured, however, Facebook has refocused its attention on global markets. Two countries offer a short course on how that attention must shift with the specific global target.

In Brazil, Facebook already has 65 million members, making the South American nation the second-largest market, behind the United States. It also ranks among the top markets for YouTube, Google, and Twitter. Part of the explanation for this great growth is Brazil's status as one of the most rapidly developing economies in the world. As people gain economic security, they have more resources to spend on social networking gadgets, as well as more leisure time to play with them.

But it also has to do with the culture. Brazil is known for the open, friendly attitudes of its people. For these "hyper-social" consumers, new ways to connect with friends and loved ones represent an important form of need fulfillment. International companies can enter freely, function according to a relatively well-established legal structure, and enjoy a pretty strong infrastructure as well.

In contrast, when companies confront the inherent openness of social networking with China's strict censorship rules, significant challenges arise. Successful entry by social and mobile marketers into China requires a particular blend of timing, skill, cultural understanding, and political savvy. These factors may not be quite in alignment for Facebook. The timing may be wrong because China's autocratic leaders have enforced greater controls on social networking and blogging recently. Nor do Facebook executives appear to have a full grasp of the political and cultural nuances of business in China, despite a good track record of respecting local cultural values, such as when it agreed to block content about Nazism in Germany or drawings of Muhammad in Pakistan. And even if Facebook were to navigate these challenges safely, China has a strong, enduring preference for companies owned and run by its own people.

Censorship issues are highly complex. For instance, how would Facebook respond to retaliation against users who criticize the government? For Google, whose mission statement simply advises "Don't Be Evil," such questions became all too pertinent when hackers in China gained access to the e-mail accounts of prominent human rights activists. When Western companies have cooperated with the Chinese government, some operations have led to the imprisonment of online activists.

In Brazil, the question is how many users the company can encourage to enjoy all the fun of Facebook. In China, a post on Facebook can lead to jail time. Thus, it becomes a question of basic human rights.

CEO Mark Zuckerberg (center) claims that Facebook will employ diplomacy in China, but censorship issues are highly complex.

concerned about these effects, appears to be reconsidering the policy, but its implications are likely to persist for several generations.

Even as vast numbers of U.S. companies actively target the massive Chinese market or explore options for entering it, as Social and Mobile Marketing 8.1 highlights, some challenges remain.

CHECK YOURSELF

1. What metrics can help analyze the economic environment of a country?
2. What types of governmental actions should we be concerned about as we evaluate a country?
3. What are some important cultural dimensions?
4. Why are each of the BRIC countries viewed as potential candidates for global expansion?

Control

Direct investment
Joint venture
Strategic alliance
Franchising
Export

Risk

L03 Identify the various market entry strategies.

CHOOSING A GLOBAL ENTRY STRATEGY

When a firm has concluded its assessment analysis of the most viable markets for its products and services, it must then conduct an internal assessment of its capabilities. As we discussed in Chapter 2, this analysis includes an assessment of the firm's access to capital, the current markets it serves, its manufacturing capacity, its proprietary assets, and the commitment of its management to the proposed strategy. These factors ultimately contribute to the success or failure of a market expansion strategy, whether at home or in a foreign market. After these internal market assessments, it is time for the firm to choose its entry strategy.

A firm can choose from many approaches when it decides to enter a new market, which vary according to the level of risk the firm is willing to take. Many firms actually follow a progression in which they begin with less risky strategies to enter their first foreign markets and move to increasingly risky strategies as they gain confidence in their abilities and more control over their operations, as illustrated in Exhibit 8.5. We examine these different approaches that marketers take when entering global markets, beginning with the least risky.

Exporting

Exporting means producing goods in one country and selling them in another. This entry strategy requires the least financial risk but also allows for only a limited return to the exporting firm. Global expansion often begins when a firm receives an order for its product or service from another country, in which case it faces little risk because it has no investment in people, capital equipment, buildings, or infrastructure.[38] By the same token, it is difficult to achieve economies of scale when everything has to be shipped internationally. The Swiss watchmaker Rolex sells relatively small numbers of expensive watches all over the world. Because its transportation

Rolex exports its watches to countries all over the world from its factory in Switzerland.

KFC and Pizza Hut are successful global franchisors.

costs are relatively small compared with the cost of the watches, the best way for it to service any market is to export from Switzerland.

Franchising

Franchising is a contractual agreement between a firm, the franchisor, and another firm or individual, the franchisee. A franchising contract allows the franchisee to operate a business—a retail product or service firm or a B2B provider—using the name and business format developed and supported by the franchisor. Many of the best-known retailers in the United States are also successful global franchisors, including McDonald's, Pizza Hut, Starbucks, Domino's Pizza, KFC, and Holiday Inn, all of which have found that global franchising entails lower risks and requires less investment than does opening units owned wholly by the firm. However, when it engages in franchising, the firm has limited control over the market operations in the foreign country, its potential profit is reduced because it must be split with the franchisee, and, once the franchise is established, there is always the threat that the franchisee will break away and operate as a competitor under a different name.

Strategic Alliance

Strategic alliances refer to collaborative relationships between independent firms, though the partnering firms do not create an equity partnership; that is, they do not invest in one another. Therefore, when Cisco Systems Inc. of San Jose, California, and Tata Consultancy Services of Mumbai, India, entered into their strategic alliance, they both continued to develop market-ready infrastructure and network solutions for customers, but they relied on each other to provide the training and skills that one or the other might have lacked. At the same time, Cisco maintains alliances with various other companies, including Microsoft, Nokia, IBM, and Accenture.

Joint Venture

A joint venture is formed when a firm entering a market pools its resources with those of a local firm. As a consequence, ownership, control, and profits are shared.

Adding Value 8.1   Tata Starbucks and the Indian Coffee Culture[iii]

Starbucks traditionally has relied on a franchising model to expand internationally. But when it came to India, the coffee chain took another approach. It allied with Tata Group, another huge, international name, to create the Tata Starbucks Limited joint venture. The two conglomerates are equal partners in the venture—which celebrated its first anniversary not with champagne but by releasing a new coffee blend: India Estates, comprised of only Indian-sourced coffee.

Since its initial launch with one store in October 2012, the joint venture has grown exponentially. Its store count reached 25 within a year, with stores in Delhi, Pune, and Mumbai. It also promises frequent new openings, including greater spread throughout the nation and localized offerings. For example, when the first store opened in Bangalore, in southern India, it offered more food options containing specific local flavors.

But it remains an international joint venture, and some marketing appeals span virtually every culture. Thus in autumn, Salted Caramel Mochas rolled out in India, just as they have done throughout the world for the past several years.

Starbucks is growing by leaps and bounds in India.

In addition to sharing financial burdens, a local partner offers the foreign entrant greater understanding of the market and access to resources such as vendors and real estate.

Some countries require joint ownership of firms entering their domestic markets, as is the case with the new regulations affecting multi-line retailers entering India, though many of these restrictions have loosened as a result of WTO negotiations and ever-increasing globalization pressures. Problems with this entry approach can arise when the partners disagree or if the government places restrictions on the firm's ability to move its profits out of the foreign country and back to its home country.

Yet joint ventures also can provide highly promising insights and benefits for all the partners, as Adding Value 8.1 suggests.

Lenovo actively promotes its products in Brazil.

Direct Investment

Direct investment requires a firm to maintain 100 percent ownership of its plants, operation facilities, and offices in a foreign country, often through the formation of wholly owned subsidiaries. This entry strategy requires the highest level of investment and exposes the firm to significant risks, including the loss of its operating and/or initial investments. A dramatic economic downturn caused by a natural disaster, war, political instability, or changes in the country's laws can increase a foreign entrant's risk considerably. Many firms believe that in certain markets, these potential risks are outweighed by the high potential returns. With this strategy, none of the potential profits must be shared with other firms. In addition to the high potential returns, direct investment offers the firm complete control over its operations in the foreign country.

Although we often tend to think of direct investment flowing from more to less developed economies, the dynamic international market means that sometimes it goes the other way. The computer maker Lenovo started in China but has since expanded its operations. In addition to purchasing IBM's PC division and Motorola's handset business unit, it established parallel headquarters in both Beijing and North Carolina. When it entered Brazil, it quickly established separate manufacturing plants, to keep its costs low.[39]

As we noted, each of these entry strategies entails different levels of risk and rewards for the foreign entrant. But even after a firm has determined how much risk it is willing to take, and therefore how it will enter a new global market, it still must establish its marketing strategy, as we discuss in the next section.

CHECK YOURSELF

1. Which entry strategy has the least risk and why?
2. Which entry strategy has the most risk and why?

LO4 Highlight the similarities and differences between a domestic marketing strategy and a global marketing strategy.

CHOOSING A GLOBAL MARKETING STRATEGY

Just like any other marketing strategy, a global marketing strategy includes two components: determining the target markets to pursue and developing a marketing mix that will sustain a competitive advantage over time. In this section, we examine marketing strategy as it relates specifically to global markets.

Target Market: Segmentation, Targeting, and Positioning

Global segmentation, targeting, and positioning (STP) are more complicated than domestic STP for several reasons. First, firms considering a global expansion have much more difficulty understanding the cultural nuances of other countries. Second, subcultures within each country also must be considered. Third, consumers often view products and their role as consumers differently in different countries.[40] A product, service, or even a retailer often must be positioned differently in different markets.

Even when an STP strategy appears successful, companies must continually monitor economic and social trends to protect their position within the market and adjust products and marketing strategies to meet the changing needs of global markets. In this sense, global marketing is no different from local or national marketing.

Segments and target markets can and should be defined by more than just geography. For example, when Yahoo! determines its segmentation and positioning strategies, it relies on research into a segment familiar throughout the world: moms. By working with a global market research firm, Yahoo! investigates how moms in Russia, Colombia, China, the United States, Mexico, India, the United Kingdom, Argentina, and France understand and use social media and other modern technologies. This study of global moms also aims to determine how digital technology affects family interactions, such as mealtimes, special occasions, and scheduling.[41] Looking on with great interest is the global product brand Procter & Gamble, which has run a global "Proud Sponsor of Moms" campaign during each recent iteration of the Olympic Games.[42]

Procter & Gamble targeted moms on a global basis with its "Proud Sponsor of Moms" campaign, which ran during the 2012 Summer Olympics.

Adding Value 8.2 | Ponying Up the Latest Ford Mustang[iv]

When the 2015 model of the classic American muscle car hits the streets, it won't only be on Route 66. Instead, Ford's latest iteration of its iconic car will be introduced simultaneously in six global cities, spanning four continents. The worldwide move aims to both acknowledge the car's 50-year history and expand its appeal to a broader market in the future.

In keeping with its tradition, the redesign retains most of the visual features that consumers have come to associate with the Mustang: blunt-nosed and stylish, with a substantial grille and a profile low to the ground. Despite some buzz that Ford would completely redesign the look (and apparently there was some debate about doing so inside the company), ultimately it chose to keep things visually similar.

In contrast, another recent version of a storied muscle car, the Chevy Camaro, broke with its historical look to adopt a more angular profile. This change seems popular. In the head-to-head-to-head competition among the Mustang, the Camaro, and the Dodge Charger, the Camaro seems to be pulling out ahead. Not only is the Camaro tops in sales among pony cars, but it also attracts a greater percentage of female drivers and a younger demographic than either of the other two options.

Ford's response is to introduce the newest Mustang as a global car, not just an American one. Along with its simultaneous grand release events in far-flung places such as Shanghai, Barcelona, and Sydney, Ford has undertaken a social media blitz, mostly targeting Mustang fan clubs and car groups worldwide. Even if it predicts that international sales will be responsible for only about 10 percent of revenues, Ford hopes the Mustang will serve as a sort of "ambassador," opening parking spaces and garages to other Ford models.

Chevrolet redesigned its classic Camaro (a 1969 version is pictured on the left) to have a more angular profile (right), making it popular with female and younger car buyers.

When any firm identifies its positioning within the market, it then must decide how to implement its marketing strategies using the marketing mix. Just as firms adjust their products and services to meet the needs of national target markets, they must alter their marketing mix to serve the needs of global markets.

Global Product or Service Strategies There are three potential global product strategies: (1) sell the same product or service in both the home country market and the host country; (2) sell a product or service similar to that sold in the home country but include minor adaptations; and (3) sell totally new products or services. The strategy a firm chooses depends on the needs of the target market. The level of economic development, as well as differences in product and technical standards, helps determine the need for and level of product adaptation. Cultural differences such as food preferences, language, and religion also play a role in product strategy planning.

Same Product or Service The most typical method of introducing a product outside the home country is to sell the same product or service in other countries. Ford Motor Co., for example, envisions a world car that will sell everywhere, as we discuss in Adding Value 8.2. However, in reverse innovation, companies

Campbell's research found that Russians eat a lot of soup, and they want timesaving preparation help. So it developed broths to enable cooks to prepare soups with their own flair.

Pringles sometimes changes flavors to reflect local tastes and demand, for example, these paprika-flavored chips sold in Italy and Germany.

initially develop products for niche or underdeveloped markets and then expand them into their original or home markets. For example, General Electric realized that adapting medical diagnostic equipment that had been developed in the United States to sell it in India was ineffective. Few Indian medical providers had sufficient resources to pay $20,000 for the massive machinery. Therefore, GE undertook innovation specific to the Indian market to develop a battery-operated, portable EKG (electrocardiogram) machine for $500. Then it realized that the small, affordable machines would appeal as well to U.S. emergency medical personnel in the field and therefore globalized its offer.[43]

Similar Product or Service with Minor Adaptations Campbell Soup discovered that even though Russia and China are two of the largest markets for soup in the world, cooks in those countries have unique demands. Chinese consumers drink 320 billion bowls of soup each year, and Russian buyers consume 32 billion servings, compared with only 14 billion bowls of soup served in the United States. However, Chinese cooks generally refuse to resort to canned soup; the average Chinese consumer eats soup five times each week, but he or she also takes great pride in preparing it personally with fresh ingredients. In contrast, Russian consumers, though they demand very high quality in their soups, had grown tired of spending hours preparing their homemade broths. To identify opportunities in these markets, Campbell sent teams of social anthropologists to study how Chinese and Russian cooks prepare and consume soup. When it faced further hurdles, it entered into a joint venture with the Swire soup company in China. But its efforts in Russia never panned out, forcing Campbell to withdraw after around four years. That is, even with extensive, devoted efforts by an industry giant, global marketing remains a challenge.[44]

Referred to as glocalization, some firms also standardize their products globally but use different promotional campaigns to sell them. The original Pringles potato chip product remains the same globally, as do the images and themes of the promotional campaign, with limited language adaptations for the local markets, although English is used whenever possible. However, the company changes Pringles' flavors in different countries, including paprika-flavored chips sold in Italy and Germany.[45]

Totally New Product or Service The level of economic development and cultural tastes also affects global product strategy because it relates directly to consumer behavior. For example, although you are likely to know Heinz for its tomato ketchup, as you traveled the globe you would find they sell many unique products in different companies. If you taste the ketchup in the Philippines, you'll be surprised to find its made with bananas instead of tomatoes (and sold under Heinz's Jufran label). In many East Asian countries Heinz competes by selling soy sauce. The size of the package varies by country as well. Whereas in the United States big bottles of condiments are sold, in poorer countries, such as Indonesia, condiments (e.g., soy sauce) are sold in single-serve packets for a few pennies.[46]

Global Pricing Strategies Determining the selling price in the global marketplace is an extremely difficult task.[47] Many countries still have rules governing the competitive marketplace, including those that affect pricing. For example, in parts of Europe, including Belgium, Italy, Spain, Greece, and France, sales are allowed only twice a year, in January and June or July. In most European countries retailers can't sell below cost, and in others they can't advertise reduced prices in advance of sales or discount items until they have been on the shelves more than a month. For firms such as Walmart and other discounters, these restrictions threaten their core competitive positioning as the lowest-cost provider in the market. Other issues, such as tariffs, quotas, antidumping laws, and currency exchange policies, can also affect pricing decisions.[48]

Competitive factors influence global pricing in the same way they do home country pricing, but because a firm's products or services may not have the same positioning in the global marketplace as they do in their home country, market prices must be adjusted to reflect the local pricing structure. Spain's fashion retailer Zara, for instance, is relatively inexpensive in the EU but is priced about 40 percent higher in the United States, putting it right in the middle of its moderately priced competition.[49] Zara is dedicated to keeping production in Spain, but it also must get its fashions to the United States quickly, so it incurs additional transportation expenses, which it passes on to its North American customers. Finally, as we discussed previously in this chapter, currency fluctuations affect global pricing strategies.

Global Distribution Strategies Global distribution networks form complex value chains that involve middlemen, exporters, importers, and different transportation systems. These additional middlemen typically add cost and ultimately increase the final selling price of a product. As a result of these cost factors, constant pressure exists to simplify distribution channels wherever possible.

The number of firms with which the seller needs to deal to get its merchandise to the consumer determines the complexity of a channel. In most developing countries, manufacturers must go through many types of distribution channels to get their products to end users, who often lack adequate transportation to shop at

Zara attracts fast fashion customers by offering great prices.

Superior Service 8.1   Getting Online Purchases to Chinese Consumers

E-commerce in China is just plain booming. Shoppers spread throughout China's vast landscape have limited access to traditional shopping sites but vastly increasing access to smartphones.[v] Thus they check with e-retailers such as Taobao or Alibaba to find virtually anything they want, then have it delivered to their doors.[vi]

Some of the most successful sites are those that provide a wide range of options, all in one place. As long as they can provide the chosen items, consumers keep flocking to these sites. That service provision can be tough, though, especially on special occasions such as Singles' Day. This recently created holiday falls on November 11 (the numerical form, 11/11, with its four 1s, signifies loneliness) and has sparked a retail revolution; on the most recent holiday, 402 million different shoppers visited one of Alibaba's linked sites to shop. That's more than one-third of China's total population. The vast numbers of consumers purchased $5.75 billion worth of goods, which far outpaced any previous single-day sales total, anywhere in the world. (For example, in the United States the most recent Cyber Monday prompted sales of just over $2 billion.)[vii]

Such vast numbers of orders demand reconsideration of the logistics in place. Alibaba added new servers to handle all the visitors. Western firms, such as Nike, Procter & Gamble, and adidas, also rejoiced at their ability to reach more rural and remote Chinese consumers, considering the difficulties they have had building brick-and-mortar outlets to reach people spread across the huge nation.

But the big players are not the only beneficiaries of this service demand. Urban dwellers, expressing their concerns about the potential for food contamination, seek out produce grown without pesticides. But those items are available only in rural locations, where farms are maintained using traditional methods. To facilitate access to the vegetables grown hundreds of miles away, regional websites take orders for dried radishes and bamboo shoots or local honey. Although many of the farmers are illiterate, local government authorities organize the websites, ordering policies, and shipping, to enable farmers to make a better living as well as to help consumers gain access healthy, natural foods.[viii]

central shopping areas or large malls. Therefore, consumers shop near their homes at small, family-owned retail outlets. To reach these small retail outlets, most of which are located far from major rail stations or roads, marketers have devised a variety of creative solutions. Unilever's strategy in India is a prime example of how a global company can adapt its distribution network to fit local conditions. Unilever trained 45,000 Indian women to serve as distributors, who in turn extended Unilever's reach to nearly 100,000 villages and their 3 million residents all across India. The program generates $250 million each year just in villages that otherwise would be too costly to serve.[50] For examples of other creative distribution strategies, consider Superior Service 8.1.

Global Communication Strategies The major challenge in developing a global communication strategy is identifying the elements that need to be adapted to be effective in the global marketplace. For instance, literacy levels vary dramatically across the globe. Consider again the BRIC nations: In India, approximately 38 percent of the adult population is illiterate (and for Indian women, the illiteracy rate surpasses 50 percent), compared with 10 percent in Brazil, less than 5 percent in China, and less than 1 percent in Russia.[51] Media availability also varies widely; some countries offer only state-controlled media. Advertising regulations differ too. In an attempt at standardization, the EU recently recommended common guidelines for its member countries regarding advertising to children and is currently initiating a multiphase ban on junk food advertising.[52]

Differences in language, customs, and culture also complicate marketers' ability to communicate with customers in various countries. Language can be particularly vexing for advertisers. For example, in the United Kingdom a thong is only a sandal, whereas in the United States it can also be an undergarment. To avoid the potential embarrassment that language confusion can cause, firms spend millions of dollars to develop brand names that have no preexisting meaning in any known language, such as Accenture (a management consulting firm) or Avaya (a subsidiary of Lucent Technologies, formerly Bell Labs).

Within many countries there are multiple variants on a language or more than one language. For example, China has three main languages; the written forms produce meaning through the characters used but the spoken forms depend on tone and pronunciation. Some firms choose names that sound similar to their English-language names, such as Nike, whose Chinese brand name is pronounced *nai-ke*. Others focus on the meanings of the characters, such that Citibank is known as *hui-qi-yinhang*, which means "star-spangled banner bank." Still other firms, such as Mercedes-Benz, have adapted their names for each language: *peng-zee* in Cantonese for Hong Kong, *peng-chi* in Mandarin for Taiwan, and *ben-chi* in Mandarin for mainland China. Naming is a constant challenge in China, especially to avoid the threat that a brand name evokes unwanted connotations, such as when Microsoft realized that the sound of its search engine name, Bing, meant "virus" in China—not the best image for an online company![53]

Noting the growth of luxury consumption, the *New York Times* began offering the option for luxury brands to purchase their own pages on its online version for China, with appropriate translations and links to dedicated sites. Because the site uses a simplified, traditional version of the Chinese language, it is accessible to all readers. The luxury brand advertisers—including Ferragamo, Cartier, and Bloomingdale's—then choose the content of the links. Whereas Cartier sends readers who click to its dedicated Cartier China site, Bloomingdale's provides a listing of its top 10 brands for the week, in English.[54]

Even with all these differences, many products and services serve the same needs and wants globally with little or no adaptation in their form or message. Firms with global appeal can run global advertising campaigns and simply translate the wording in the advertisements and product labeling.

Other products require a more localized approach because of cultural and religious differences. In a classic advertisement for Longines watches, a woman's bare arm and hand appear, with a watch on her wrist. The advertisement was considered too risqué for Muslim countries, where women's bare arms are never displayed in public, but the company simply changed the advertisement to show a gloved arm and hand wearing the same watch.

Even among English speakers, there can be significant differences in the effectiveness of advertising campaigns. Take the popular "What Happens in Vegas Stays in Vegas" advertising campaign, which has been very successful and spawned numerous copycat slogans in the United States. Essentially, the U.S. mass

Nike's Chinese brand name is pronounced "nai ke," which is very similar to the English pronunciation, and means "Enduring and Persevering."

market thought the provocative campaign pushed the envelope, but just far enough to be entertaining. However, when the Las Vegas tourism group extended its advertising to the United Kingdom, it found that the ad campaign was not nearly as effective. After conducting focus groups, the group found that British consumers did not find the advertisements edgy enough for their more irreverent British tastes. In response, the advertising agency began studying British slang and phrases to find ways to make the campaign even sexier and more provocative.[55]

CHECK YOURSELF

1. What are the components of a global marketing strategy?
2. What are the three global product strategies?

Reviewing Learning Objectives

 Describe the components of a country market assessment.

First, firms must assess the general economic environment. For instance, countries with a trade surplus, strong domestic and national products, growing populations, and income growth generally are relatively more favorable prospects. Second, firms should assess a country's infrastructure. To be successful in a particular country, the firm must have access to adequate transportation, distribution channels, and communications. Third, firms must determine whether the proposed country has a political and legal environment that favors business. Fourth, firms should be cognizant of the cultural and sociological differences between their home and host countries and adapt to those differences to ensure successful business relationships.

 Understand the marketing opportunities in BRIC countries.

Technology, particularly in the communication field, has facilitated the growth of global markets. Firms can communicate with their suppliers and customers instantaneously, easily take advantage of production efficiencies in other countries, and bring together parts and finished goods from all over the globe. Four countries that provide tremendous marketing opportunities are the BRIC nations— Brazil, Russia, India, and China. These countries have large populations that are increasingly interested in the latest goods and services.

 Identify the various market entry strategies.

Firms have several options for entering a new country, each with a different level of risk and involvement. Direct investment is the riskiest but potentially the most lucrative. Firms that engage in a joint venture with other firms already operating in the host country share the risk and obtain knowledge about the market and how to do business there. A strategic alliance is similar to a joint venture, but the relationship is not as formal. A less risky method of entering a new market is franchising, in which, as in domestic franchise agreements, the franchisor allows the franchisee to operate a business using its name and strategy in return for a fee. The least risky method of entering another country is simply exporting.

 Highlight the similarities and differences between a domestic marketing strategy and a global marketing strategy.

The essence of a global marketing strategy is no different from that of a domestic strategy. The firm starts by identifying its target markets, chooses specific markets to pursue, and crafts a strategy to meet the needs of those markets. However, additional issues make global expansion more problematic. For instance, should the product or service be altered to fit the new market better? Does the firm need to change the way it prices its products in different countries? What is the best way to get the product or service to the new customers? How should the firm publicize its product or service offering in various countries?

Key Terms

- direct investment, 251
- duty, 239
- exchange control, 240
- exchange rate, 240
- exporting, 248
- franchisee, 249
- franchising, 249
- franchisor, 249
- globalization, 234

- glocalization, 254
- gross domestic product (GDP), 236
- gross national income (GNI), 236
- infrastructure, 239
- joint venture, 249
- purchasing power parity (PPP), 236

- quota, 240
- reverse innovation, 253
- strategic alliance, 249
- tariff, 239
- trade agreements, 240
- trade deficit, 236
- trade surplus, 236
- trading bloc, 240

Marketing Applications

1. What is globalization? Why is it important for marketers to understand what globalization entails?

2. Moots is a high-end bicycle manufacturer located in Steamboat Springs, Colorado. Assume the company is considering entering the Brazilian, Chinese, and Indian markets. When conducting its market assessment, what economic factors should Moots consider to make its decision? Which market do you expect will be more lucrative for Moots? Why?

3. Now consider the political, economic, and legal systems of China, India, and Brazil. Explain why you think one country might be more hospitable to Moots than the others.

4. Colgate sells its products in many countries throughout the world. How would you expect its market position to differ in various countries, compared with that in the United States? Consider

various areas across the globe in formulating your answer.

5. CITGO, the petroleum company owned by the Venezuelan government, sells its products throughout the world. Do you anticipate that its market positioning and advertising differ in different countries? Why or why not?

6. What are the benefits of being able to offer a globally standardized product? What types of products easily lend themselves to global standardization?

7. What are some examples of companies that use a glocalization strategy?

8. Choose a firm that currently manufactures and sells its products or services only in the United States. Choose and defend a global entry strategy for the firm.

Quiz Yourself

1. The shift of population from rural to urban areas in countries such as India helps global marketers by:
   a. decreasing pollution.
   b. simplifying the supply chain needed to make goods and services available.
   c. increasing the human development index.
   d. decreasing competition for intellectual capital.
   e. increasing nonmaterial GDP output.

2. Marketers sometimes use Hofstede's cultural dimensions to design marketing campaigns:
   a. with low individualism symbolism when confronted with a time-oriented culture.

   b. using uncertainty avoidance to reduce power distance.
   c. with significant power distance.
   d. consistent with underlying cultural values in a country.
   e. with more consistent time orientation.

   (Answers to these two questions can be found on page 652.)

Net Savvy

1. For many small businesses, the idea of entering a foreign market is intimidating. The U.S. government and most state governments now offer assistance designed specifically for small-business owners. Visit the website of the Massachusetts Export Center at http://www.mass.gov/export/ and examine the types of services it provides. Click on the Export Statistics link. To what five countries did Massachusetts export the most? Are you surprised?

2. Nike is a global brand, yet it alters its promotions to meet local tastes. Go to http://store.nike.com/gb/en_gb/ and explore the UK site. Now go to the U.S. site. How are these websites different?

Chapter Case Study

THE GLOBALIZATION OF THE MOST UBIQUITOUS OF AMERICAN CUISINES—THE HAMBURGER

McDonald's France: I am loving it.

From the Maharaja Mac in India to the Prosperity Burger prepared especially for the Chinese New Year celebrations, McDonald's has built a global fast-food empire under its golden arches. Only 31 percent of McDonald's revenue now comes from sales in the United States, and most of its international growth has come from the surging economies of Brazil, Russia, China, and India.[56] A pioneer in overseas franchising, McDonald's has spared no effort in its attempts to penetrate foreign markets. In China, it plans to open one new outlet daily to meet its immediate goal of 2,000 stores.[57] In Brazil, it created Latin America's first environmentally certified fast-food restaurant. A vast market defined by stark cultural differences, India has required a more modest approach that would allow McDonald's to develop its real estate and supply infrastructure, train its local workforce and management at its famed Hamburger University, and adjust the menu for vegetarian customers.[58] The McAloo Tikki Burger has been a great success, and the company has started opening more McCafe storefronts.[59]

But McDonald's growth strategy relies on more than just added locations. In crowded cities, with real estate prices too high to build drive-through restaurants, the company has hired droves of motorbike drivers to bring Big Macs to customers. This nimble delivery approach is now a mainstay in cities from Beijing to Kuwait City. Online ordering will be next, though the challenge will be to reduce the cost of call centers to support this new distribution model.[60] In addition, McDonald's keeps looking for new mobile innovations, such as mobile ordering or payment options, to keep up with consumer demand.[61]

Fast-food restaurants enjoy some segment-specific benefits as they pursue such international expansion. Unlike retail brands, such as Walmart or Carrefour, restaurants pose less perceived competitive threats. Local eateries can exist side-by-side with a McDonald's, in a way that a mom-and-pop grocer cannot survive if an international hypermarket moves in next door.[62]

But even considering the massive growth in rapidly transitioning economies, Europe still generates the bulk of foreign sales for McDonald's. In France, for example, "MacDo" restaurants attract crowds that line up outside for a bite of lunch. But lunch might mean something a little different in this case: French McDonald's offer menus that feature Camembert cheese on the burgers, Heineken, and a McBaguette. Once, the secret to McDonald's success was "lockstep" consistency, the fact that a meal in Memphis tasted the same as it did in Moscow or Madrid. But the novelty of the American hamburger stand has worn off in the new millennium, and with it McDonald's ability to export American culture as its staple commodity. A cheeseburger, fries, and Coke don't register the same level of excitement when the café next door and the bistro down the block are also serving burgers. More and more, the key to McDonald's future appears to be found in the DNA of the places it inhabits. And with it, suddenly the fast-food giant that to many represents the globalization of taste suddenly finds itself in a very unlikely position: as a defender of local cuisine."[63]

McDonald's is successful in Israel because of its kosher offerings.

The kosher burger has been a hit in Israel, and Indian consumers seem to appreciate the opening of McDonald's first vegetarian restaurant. However, most new growth comes from Russia, where the company has 245 locations and controls 70 percent of the booming fast-food business. Even as fast-food competitors face potential market saturation in the United States, Russian demand for quick burgers appears to be insatiable.[64] Driving this Russian appetite has been the growth of a newly affluent middle class, with money to spend to dine out. Infrastructure development in Russia also has been a boon as cities open malls with food courts, highways are constructed with drive-through locations, and specialty suppliers of frozen food and packaging have appeared.

In the early years of Russian expansion, few private businesses existed to supply all the ingredients McDonald's needed to produce Big Macs and fries. The company solved the problem by building an enormous food processing plant outside Moscow. But it also worked to cultivate relationships with local Russian vendors and contractors to which it eventually could outsource its supply chain. Today, a grower who began selling cucumbers to McDonald's in 1990 has become the Pickle King of Russia, dominating the processed foods market.[65]

Questions

1. Which sociocultural factors have informed McDonald's global expansion?

2. Describe some of the global distribution strategies that McDonald's uses or might consider using to spread throughout the world.

3. Define the likely global STP strategy for McDonald's. In what ways does it need to vary its STP? In which target markets can it rely on a consistent positioning? Which consumers should it target in each national market?

Endnotes

1. Coca-Cola India, "Company History," http://www.coca-colaindia.com.

2. Ratna Bhushan, "Coca-Cola Plans Aggressive Ad Campaign in 2014 to Be India's Favourite Soft Drink," *Economic Times*, January 1, 2014, http://articles.economictimes.indiatimes.com.

3. Nikhil Gulati and Rumman Ahmed, "India Has 1.2 Billion People, but Not Enough Drink Coke," *The Wall Street Journal*, July 13, 2012, http://online.wsj.com.

4. Ibid.

5. Pierre-Richard Agenor, *Does Globalization Hurt the Poor?* (Washington, DC: World Bank, 2002); "Globalization: Threat or Opportunity," International Monetary Fund, http://www.imf.org.

6. For example, the deficit for the month of December 2013 was $57.6 million. See http://www.census.gov.

7. http://www.acdi-cida.gc.ca.

8. http://siteresources.worldbank.org/DATASTATISTICS/Resources/GNIPC.pdf; Arthur O'Sullivan, Steven Sheffrin, and Steve Perez, *Macroeconomics: Principles and Tools,* 8th ed. (Upper Saddle River, NJ: Prentice Hall, 2013).

9. *The Economist,* "The Big Mac Index," January 23, 2014, http://www.economist.com/content/big-mac-index.

10. Justin Dove, "Taking Advantage of Dollar Weakness," *Investor U,* July 28, 2011, http://www.investmentu.com.

11. Jack Neff, "Emerging-Market Growth War Pits Global Brand Giants against Scrappy Local Rivals," *Advertising Age,* June 13, 2011, http://adage.com.

12. "Coca-Cola Tackles Rural Indian Market" (video), *The Wall Street Journal,* May 3, 2010.

13. Melissa Ip, "Bottom of the Pyramid—a Decade of Observations," *Social Enterprise Buzz,* January 21, 2013, http://www.socialenterprisebuzz.com.

14. Kate O'Keeffe, "The Cheapest, Richest Casino in Macau," *The Wall Street Journal,* February 5, 2014.

15. Neff, "Emerging-Market Growth War."

16. Wayne Ma, "China Levies 6.5% Tariff on U.S. on U.S. Solar-Panel Materials," *The Wall Street Journal,* September 18, 2013, http://www.online.wsj.com.

17. Leslie Josephs, "U.S. Increases Sugar Quota for Second Time," *The Wall Street Journal,* June 23, 2011, http://online.wsj.com.

18. Leslie Josephs, "U.S. Unlikely to Raise Sugar-Import Quota," *The Wall Street Journal,* February 19, 2013, http://online.wsj.com.

19. "Exchange Rate," http://en.wikipedia.org/wiki/Exchange_rate.

20. http://ucatlas.ucsc.edu.

21. http://www.unescap.org.

22. Johny Johansson, *Global Marketing,* 5th ed. (New York: McGraw-Hill/Irwin, 2008).

23. Philip R. Cateora, Mary C. Gilly, and John L. Graham, *International Marketing,* 15th ed. (New York: McGraw-Hill, 2011); Danielle Medina Walker and Thomas Walker, *Doing Business Internationally: The Guide to Cross-Cultural Success,* 2nd ed. (Princeton, NJ: Trade Management Corporation, 2003).

24. Nicola Clark, "French Signal Flexibility on Sunday Closings," *The New York Times,* September 30, 2013, http://www.nytimes.com; 2014 IKEA French Store Hours, such as: http://www.ikeafans.com/directory/ikea-rennes-pac-153.html; Devorah Lauter, "IKEA Fined for Sunday Opening in France," *Forbes,* April 6, 2008.

25. Peter Siegenthaler, "Store Opening Hours: A Regular Vote Topic," *Swissinfo.ch,* June 18, 2012, http://www.swissinfo.ch/.

26. For a website dedicated to Hofstede's research, see http://www.geert-hofstede.com/.

27. Rosalie L. Tung and Alain Verbeke, eds., "Beyond Hofstede and GLOBE: Improving the Quality of Cross-Cultural Research," *Journal of International Business Studies* 41 (Special Issue, 2010).

28. Note that the time orientation and indulgence dimensions are relatively more recent additions to the categorization. See Geert Hofstede, "Dimensions of National Cultures," http://www.geerthofstede.eu/dimensions-of-national-cultures.

29. http://geert-hofstede.com/countries.html.

30. James W. Carey, *Communication as Culture,* rev. ed. (New York: Routledge, 2009).

31. *The Economist,* "Why Is South Africa Included in the BRICS?" March 29, 2013, http://www.economist.com/blogs/economist-explains/.

32. "Brazil," U.S. Department of State, http://www.state.gov; CIA, *The CIA World Factbook,* https://www.cia.gov/library/publications/the-world-factbook/.

33. "Russia," U.S. Department of State, http://www.state.gov; CIA, *The CIA World Factbook,* https://www.cia.gov.

34. Robin Wauters, "Already Europe's Largest Internet Market and Still Growing Astoundingly Fast: Russia by the Numbers," *The Next Web,* April 20, 2012, http://www.thenextweb.com.

35. "India," U.S. Department of State, http://www.state.gov; CIA, *The CIA World Factbook,* https://www.cia.gov.

36. Megha Bahree, "India Unlocks Door for Global Retailers," *The Wall Street Journal,* November 25, 2011.

37. U.S. Department of State, "China," http://www.state.gov; CIA, *The CIA World Factbook* https://www.cia.gov.

38. Lance Eliot Brouthers et al., "Key Factors for Successful Export Performance for Small Firms," *Journal of International Marketing* 17, no. 3 (2009), pp. 21–38; "Selling Overseas," November 12, 2009, http://www.entrepreneur.com.

39. Juro Osawa and Lorraine Luk, "How Lenovo Built a Tech Giant," *The Wall Street Journal,* January 30, 2014, http://online.wsj.com; Juro Osawa and Yun-Hee Kim, "PC Firm Lenovo Hunts for Brazil Acquisitions," *The Wall Street Journal,* May 28, 2012, http://online.wsj.com.

40. Philip R. Cateora, Mary C. Gilly, and John L. Graham, *International Marketing,* 14th ed. (New York: McGraw-Hill, 2009).

41. Jack Neff, "Yahoo Ramps Up Global Study of Moms and Technology," *Advertising Age,* November 17, 2011, http://adage.com.

42. http://www.pgeverydaysolutions.ca/thankyoumom/helping-moms.jsp.

43. Natalie Zmuda, "P&G, Levi's, GE Innovate by Thinking in Reverse," *Advertising Age,* June 13, 2011, http://adage.com.

44. Julie Jargon, "Can M'm, M'm Good Translate?" *The Wall Street Journal,* July 9, 2007, p. A16; Brad Dorfman and Martinne Geller, "Campbell Soup in Joint Venture to Expand in China," *Reuters,* January 12, 2011, http://www.reuters.com; Julie Jargon, "Campbell Soup to Exit Russia," *The Wall Street Journal,* June 29, 2011, http://online.wsj.com.

45. http://www.pringles.it/.

46. Bill Johnson, "The CEO of Heinz on Powering Growth in Emerging Markets," *Harvard Business Review,* October 2011.

47. Silvia Fabiana et al., eds., *Pricing Decisions in the Euro Era: How Firms Set Prices and Why* (Oxford: Oxford University Press, 2007); Cateora et al., *International Marketing.*

48. Fabiana et al., *Pricing Decisions;* Amanda J. Broderick, Gordon E. Greenley, and Rene Dentiste Mueller, "The Behavioural Homogeneity Evaluation Framework: Multi-Level Evaluations of Consumer Involvement in International Segmentation," *Journal of International Business Studies* 38 (2007), pp. 746–63; Terry Clark, Masaaki Kotabe, and Dan Rajaratnam, "Exchange Rate Pass-Through and International Pricing Strategy: A Conceptual Framework and Research Propositions," *Journal of International Business Studies* 30, no. 2 (1999), pp. 249–68.

49. Sarah Morris, "How Zara Clothes Turned Galacia into a Retail Hotspot," *Reuters,* October 31, 2011, http://www.reuters.com.

50. "India: Creating Rural Entrepreneurs," http://www.unilever.com.

51. CIA, *The CIA World Factbook,* https://www.cia.gov/library/publications/the-world-factbook/fields/2103.html.

52. Jess Halliday, "Industry Prepares to Fight Junk Food Ad Watershed," *Food and Drink Europe.com,* January 3, 2008, http://www.foodanddrinkeurope.com.

53. Michael Wines, "Picking Brand Names in Asia Is a Business Itself," *Advertising Age,* November 11, 2011, http://www.nytimes.com; Brand Channel, http://www.brandchannel.com.

54. Rachel Lamb, "Cartier, Ferragamo Ramp Up Global Marketing through New York Times China," *Luxury Daily,* June 29, 2012, http://www.luxurydaily.com/.

55. Joan Voight, "How to Customize Your U.S. Branding Effort to Work around the World," *Adweek,* September 3, 2008.

56. "McDonald's Sees Strong Revenue on Global Demand," Associated Press, December 8, 2011, http://www.msnbc.msn.com; Annie Gasparro, "Yum Splits India into Separate Division, Names New International CEO," *The Wall Street Journal,* November 23, 2011, http://online.wsj.com.

57. "McDonald's China Plans to Open a New Store Every Day in Four Years," *The Huffington Post,* September 28, 2011, http://www.huffingtonpost.com.

58. "McDonald's Best Practices," http://bestpractices.mcdonalds.com; Gasparro, "Yum Splits India into Separate Division."

59. Neha Thirani Bagri, "A Growing Taste for U.S. Fast Food in India," *The New York Times,* January 8, 2014, http://india.blogs.nytimes.com/.

60. Julie Jargon, "For Food Delivery, China Calls McDonald's," *The Wall Street Journal,* December 12, 2011, http://online.wsj.com.

61. Nat Rudarakanchana, "McDonald's (MCD) Going Mobile, Expanding in China and Three Other Takeaways from Last Scheduled Consumer Presentation of Uninspiring 2013," *International Business Times,* September 11, 2013, http://www.ibtimes.com.

62. Bagri, "A Growing Taste for U.S. Fast Food in India."

63. Matt Goulding, "Why the French Secretly Love the Golden Arches," *Slate,* August 2013, http://www.slate.com.

64. "McDonald's Sees Strong Revenue"; Ravi Krishnani, "McDonald's in Russia: Defeated Communism with a 'Happy' Meal," *Business Today,* http://www.businesstoday-eg.com; McDonald's Europe Virtual Press Office, press brief, http://www.mcdpressoffice.eu.

65. Andrew E. Kramer, "Russia's Evolution, Seen through Golden Arches," *The New York Times,* February 2, 2010, http://www.nytimes.com.

i. Rose Yu and Colum Murphy, "In China, Air Pollution Rules Spur Big Car Purchases," *The Wall Street Journal,* August 7, 2013, http://online.wsj.com.

ii. Jason Kincaid, "Mark Zuckerberg on Facebook's Strategy for China (and His Wardrobe)," *Tech Crunch,* October 16, 2010, http://techcrunch.com; Loretta Chao, "Brazil: The Social Media Capital of the Universe," *The Wall Street Journal,* February 4, 2013, http://online.wsj.com; Normandy Madden, "What Will Facebook Find If It Ventures into China?" *Advertising Age Global,* June 13, 2011, http://adage.com; Chloe Albanesius, "Human Rights Group Slams Facebook over China Strategy," *PCMag.com,* June 3, 2011, http://www.pcmag.com.

iii. Anil Urs and K. Giriprakash, "Tata Starbucks CEO: Our Business in India Continues to Exceed Expectations," *Hindu Business Line,* November 27, 2013, http://www.thehindubusinessline.com; Starbucks, "Starbucks Celebrates Its First Year in India with Launch of India Estates Blend," October 21, 2013, http://news.starbucks.com.

iv. Mike Ramsay, "Ford to Take Mustang Sports Car Global," *The New York Times,* December 4, 2013; "With 2015 Mustang, Ford Puts American Icon on Global Path," *Advertising Age,* December 5, 2013.

v. Christina Larson, "How to Reach China's Avid Shoppers," *Bloomberg Businessweek,* February 13, 2014, http://www.businessweek.com/articles/.

vi. Christina Larson, "The Secret of Taobao's Success," *Bloomberg Businessweek,* February 18, 2014, http://www.businessweek.com/articles/.

vii. Shanshan Wang and Eric Pfanner, "China's One-Day Shopping Spree Sets Record for Online Sales," *The New York Times,* November 11, 2013, http://www.nytimes.com.

viii. Christina Larson, "E-Commerce Gives a Lift to China's Rural Farmers," *Bloomberg Businessweek,* February 13, 2014, http://www.businessweek.com/articles/.

Credits

TARGETING THE MARKETPLACE

Section Three, Targeting the Marketplace, contains two chapters. Chapter 9 focuses on segmentation, targeting, and positioning. In this chapter, we examine how firms segment the marketplace, then pick a target market, and finally position their goods/services in line with their customers' needs and wants. Chapter 10 on marketing research identifies the various tools, techniques, and metrics that marketers use to uncover customers' needs and wants and to ensure that they create goods and services that provide value to their target markets.

CHAPTER 9

SEGMENTATION, TARGETING, AND POSITIONING

Imagine that you had access to 30 million pieces of daily information about how viewers pause, rewind, or fast-forward the shows they watch. Next imagine that you attracted around 4 million customer ratings each day. What if you could also glean information about when, where, and how viewers conducted their approximately 3 million daily searches for entertainment? For one, you might be exhausted: That's a lot of data. But for another, you would know precisely who was watching what, when, and through what channels, which would give you a great

HOUSE of CARDS

NETFLIX ORIGINAL

deal of information about what else those audiences would want to watch.[1]

You would also be Netflix, the movie rental company that has quickly and readily become one of the most popular and successful streaming content providers. Through careful analysis of its millions of viewers and how they watched shows, it realized that they liked the actor Kevin Spacey, the director David Fincher, and a British political thriller called *House of Cards*. Putting those three elements together meant that Netflix could produce a show that was nearly guaranteed to appeal to a wide range of viewers.

But even as it recognized the widespread appeal of the show, Netflix made sure to target advertisements for it to each specific segment. That is, fans of Spacey's, viewing *The Usual Suspects* one more time on Netflix saw advertisements for *House of Cards* that featured his powerful character. Female subscribers who had given top ratings to movies starring strong female leads instead

got a preview of Robin Wright and her powerful lead role. For serious cinemaphiles, the marketing centered on Fincher's risk-taking and daring oeuvre.

Part of the reason Netflix was able to establish such clear appeals for different segments of customers stemmed from the categorization it already had in place. To help recommend movies to its customers, Netflix has created approximately 79,000 categories of movie types—not just "New Releases" but also "Witty Romantic Independent Comedies," "Dark Thrillers Based on Books," or "Understated Movies."

The results of Netflix's careful data analysis and precise targeting are impressive—especially for a company that just a few short years ago seemed to be offering things customers most certainly did not want. For example, its efforts to separate its DVD-by-mail service from its streaming videos prompted customers to complain bitterly. The company's CEO Reed Hastings ultimately admitted fault and begged forgiveness, but it was a notable stumble, and one he vowed not to make again.

Through remarkably precise and careful assessments, Netflix instead is the source for nearly 30 percent of the streaming done by American households during peak hours. That is, of everyone in the country streaming content of any kind, approximately one in every three is watching something on Netflix.[2]

But Netflix also knows that its adult consumers can be fickle.. When faced with something they don't like, adults just switch to another entertainment offering. Children, in contrast, have fewer options and less room to switch. Hence, Netflix's original content also features an offering developed in cooperation with DreamWorks Animation to target youthful audiences explicitly.

The *Turbo: F.A.S.T.* television series will run, following the release of an animated film about the same character (a snail who gains super speed after being exposed to a freak accident). The deal also comes after another agreement between DreamWorks and Netflix, in which Netflix purchased the rights to show some of DreamWorks' most well-known titles. Around the same time, it also inked an agreement with Disney to access its library—including its recently acquired set of Lucas-Film movies.[3]

By appealing to children and their families, Netflix believes it can achieve new levels of customer loyalty. The children themselves are unlikely to switch because Netflix offers them easy access through their parents' iPads or their Wii consoles. Furthermore, few parents are willing to incur their children's wrath by canceling their Netflix subscription, when Netflix offers those children some of their favorite shows and movies.

In Chapter 1, we learned that marketing is about satisfying consumers' wants and needs. Chapter 2 noted how companies analyze their markets to determine the different kinds of products and services people want. But it is not sufficient just to produce such an offering. Firms must also position their offerings in the minds of customers in their target market in such a way that these consumers understand why the thing the company is providing meets their needs better than other, competitive offerings.

This process requires a marketing plan, as we discussed in Chapter 2. You should recall that the third step of this plan is to identify and evaluate opportunities by performing an STP (segmentation, targeting, and positioning) analysis. This chapter focuses on that very analysis.

LO1 Outline the different methods of segmenting a market.

THE SEGMENTATION, TARGETING, AND POSITIONING PROCESS

In this chapter, we discuss how a firm conducts a market segmentation or STP analysis (see Exhibit 9.1). We first outline a firm's overall strategy and objectives, methods of segmenting the market, and which segments are worth pursuing. Then we discuss how to choose a target market or markets by evaluating each segment's attractiveness and, on the basis of this evaluation, choose which segment or segments to pursue. Finally, we describe how a firm develops its positioning strategy.

Although the STP process in Exhibit 9.1 implies that the decision making is linear, this need not be the case. For instance, a firm could start with a strategy but then modify it as it gathers more information about various segments' attractiveness.

Step 1: Establish the Overall Strategy or Objectives

The first step in the segmentation process is to articulate the vision or objectives of the company's marketing strategy clearly. The segmentation strategy must be consistent with and derived from the firm's mission and objectives as well as

EXHIBIT 9.1 The Segmentation, Targeting, and Positioning Process

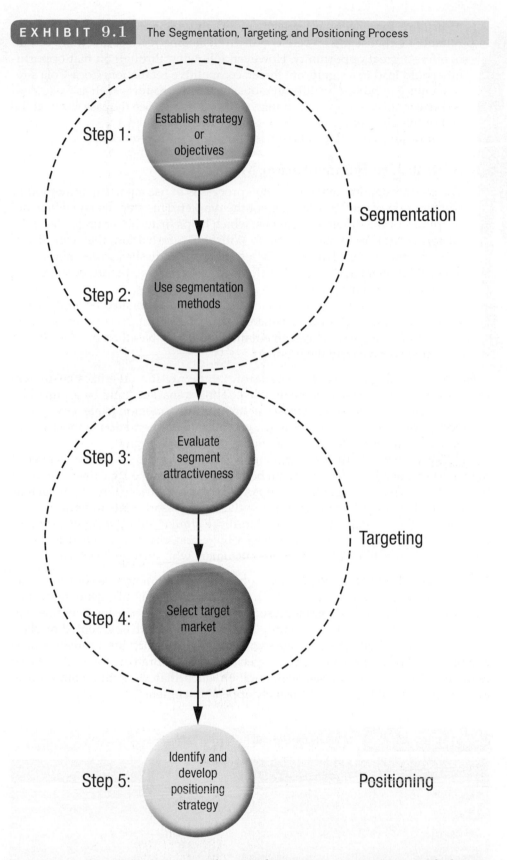

its current situation—its strengths, weaknesses, opportunities, and threats (SWOT). Coca-Cola's objective, for instance, is to increase sales in a mature industry. The company knows its strengths are its brand name and its ability to place new products on retailers' shelves, but its primary weakness is that it may not have

Coke Zero targets health-conscious men.

a product line for newer market segments. Identifying this potentially large and profitable market segment, before many of its mainstream competitors can do so, offers a great opportunity. However, following through on that opportunity could lead to a significant threat: competitive retaliation. Coca-Cola's recent choice to pursue health-conscious men with products such as Coke Zero is consistent with its overall strategy and objectives. (See the case study at the end of this chapter for more discussion of Coke's strategy.)

Now let's take a look at methods for segmenting a market.

Step 2: Use Segmentation Methods

The second step in the segmentation process is to use a particular method or combination of methods to segment the market. This step also develops descriptions of the different segments, which helps firms better understand the customer profiles in each segment. With this information, they can distinguish customer similarities within a segment and dissimilarities across segments. Marketers use geographic, demographic, psychographic, benefits, and behavioral segmentation methods, as Exhibit 9.2 details.

Soft drink marketers, for instance, divide the carbonated beverage landscape into caffeinated or decaffeinated, regular (with sugar) or diet, and cola versus something else. This segmentation method is based on the *benefits* that consumers derive from the products.

Geographic Segmentation Geographic segmentation organizes customers into groups on the basis of where they live. Thus, a market could be grouped by country, region (northeast, southeast), or areas within a region (state, city, neighborhoods, zip codes). Not surprisingly, geographic segmentation is most useful for companies whose products satisfy needs that vary by region.

Firms can provide the same basic goods or services to all segments even if they market globally or nationally, but better marketers make adjustments to meet the needs of smaller geographic groups.[4] A national grocery store chain such as Safeway or Kroger runs similar stores with similar assortments in various locations across the United States. But within those similar stores, a significant percentage of the assortment of goods will vary by region, city, or even neighborhood, depending on the different needs of the customers who surround each location.

Demographic Segmentation Demographic segmentation groups consumers according to easily measured, objective characteristics such as age, gender, income, and education. These variables represent the most common means to define segments because they are easy to identify and demographically segmented markets are easy to reach. Kellogg's uses age segmentation for its breakfast cereals: Cocoa Krispies and Fruit Loops are for kids; Special K and All-Bran are for adults. It also tends to adopt a gender-based segmentation, such that marketing communications about Special K almost exclusively appeal to women.

EXHIBIT 9.2	Methods for Describing Market Segments
Segmentation Method	**Sample Segments**
Geographic	Continent: North America, Asia, Europe, Africa Within the United States: Pacific, mountain, central, south, mid-Atlantic, northeast
Demographic	Age, gender, income
Psychographic	Lifestyle, self-concept, self-values
Benefits	Convenience, economy, prestige
Behavioral	Occasion, loyalty

Denizen jeans by Levi's are made exclusively for Target. What segmentation method is Target using?

Gender plays a very important role in how most firms market products and services.[5] For instance, TV viewing habits vary significantly between men and women. Men tend to channel surf—switching quickly from channel to channel—and watch prime-time shows that are action oriented and feature physically attractive cast members. Women, in contrast, tend to view shows to which they can personally relate through the situational plot or characters and those recommended by friends. Print media are similar: A company such as Proactiv, which seeks to appeal to both men and women worried about the condition of their skin, therefore carefully considers the gender-based appeal of different magazines when it purchases advertising space.

However, demographics may not be useful for defining the target segments for other companies. They are poor predictors of the users of activewear, such as jogging suits and athletic shoes. At one time, firms such as Nike assumed that activewear would be purchased exclusively by young, active people, but the health and fitness trend has led people of all ages to buy such merchandise. Even relatively inactive consumers of all ages, incomes, and education find activewear more comfortable than traditional street clothes.

Rethinking some stereotypical ideas about who is buying thus has become a relatively common trend among firms that once thought their target market was well defined. As Social and Mobile Marketing 9.1 shows, even some of the most well-known companies in the world must continually reconsider the true identity of their prime targets.

Psychographic Segmentation Of the various methods for segmenting, or breaking down, the market, psychographics is the one that delves into how consumers actually describe themselves. Usually marketers determine (through demographics, buying patterns, or usage) into which segment an individual consumer falls. Psychographics studies how people self-select, as it were, based on the characteristics of how they choose to occupy their time (behavior) and what underlying

Social & Mobile Marketing 9.1   Is Facebook Over?[i]

According to a recent study funded by the European Union, the terms that UK teens (16–18 years of age) use to describe Facebook include *embarrassing, old,* and *dead and buried.* These are not exactly the sorts of images that a company that revolutionized social media prefers to embrace. So what has led Facebook, once the social media home base of teens, to become the last place they want to be seen?

Most analyses suggest the main problem was its growing popularity—and more specifically, its growing popularity among their parents' generation. As mom, dads, aunts, uncles, and even grandparents joined the network, teens quickly became less willing to share quite so much. Humor sites collect various awkward moments when a teenager rails against an unfair parent on Facebook, only to have that parent respond with deeply embarrassing accounts of the teen's behavior or the imposition of a new punishment.

Beyond these direct contacts, teens tend to assume that anything their parents like cannot be cool for them as well. If their grandmother posts pictures of her vacation to Facebook, seemingly by definition the site cannot be cool anymore.

As challenging as these trends are for Facebook, it could always rebrand itself as the social media location for middle-aged users who want to share their thoughts about their children or grandchildren. The larger question is where teens will go next to get their social media fix. The growing popularity of Snapchat implies that teens might begin preferring temporary, ephemeral sharing, possibly in reaction to the lessons learned when Facebook posts remain accessible to employers and school administrators. Moreover, teens seemingly use various sites for different purposes: Twitter for wide broadcasts, Instagram for visual sharing, WhatsApp for more personal interactions.

The variety suggests a gap in the market, waiting for some innovative entrepreneur to devise the next big thing, a site that teens consider cool and compelling—until their parents find it and ruin it too, of course.

Have you used WhatsApp to do real time messaging?

psychological reasons determine those choices.[6] For example, a person might have a strong need for inclusion or belonging, which motivates him or her to seek out activities that involve others, which in turn influences the products he or she buys to fit in with the group. Determining psychographics involves knowing and understanding three components: self-values, self-concept, and lifestyles.

Self-values are goals for life, not just the goals one wants to accomplish in a day. They are the overriding desires that drive how a person lives his or her life. Examples might be the need for self-respect, self-fulfillment, or a specific sense of belonging. This motivation causes people to develop self-images of how they want to be and then images of a way of life that will help them arrive at these ultimate goals. From a marketing point of view, self-values help determine the benefits the target market may be looking for from a product. The underlying, fundamental, personal need that pushes a person to seek out certain products or brands stems from his or her desire to fulfill a self-value.

People's self-image, or self-concept, is the image people ideally have of themselves.[7] A person who has a goal to belong may see, or want to see, himself as a fun-loving, gregarious type whom people wish to be around. Marketers often make use of this particular self-concept through communications that show their products being used by groups of laughing people who are having a good time. The connection emerges between the group fun and the product being shown and connotes a lifestyle that many consumers seek.

Such tactics need to balance the ideal with the realistic. Advertisements for men's underwear tend to feature salacious shots of incredibly cut men, usually with shaved chests. But in making this appeal to women who might purchase briefs, boxers, and T-shirts for their husbands or partners, underwear marketers forgot about men as their underlying target market. And these male shoppers have long felt uncomfortable in stores, reaching for a box featuring a nearly naked man. Rather than being aspirational, the models had become so outside the norm that they seemed like a cruel taunt. Thus a recent advertising campaign by the men's underwear brand 2(x)ist features a handsome but not "perfect" model, wearing a robe that covers most of his body. The Mack Wheldon brand offers up another handsome but slightly goofy model, who trips while trying to take off his pants to reveal his underwear.[8]

Marketers like Benetton want their ads to appeal to people's self-concepts: "I'm like them (or I want to be like them), so I should buy their products."

Using lifestyle segmentation, Harley-Davidson has four main target markets: On the left is its core segment consisting of men older than 35 years. On the right are women older than 35 years.

Lifestyles, the third component of people's psychographic makeup, are the way we live.[9] If values provide an end goal and self-concept is the way one sees oneself in the context of that goal, lifestyles are how we live our lives to achieve goals.

One of the most storied lifestyles in American legend is the Harley way of life. The open road, wind in your hair, rebelling against conventions—the image nearly always depicted men like Dennis Hopper in *Easy Rider*. But the notions of freedom, rebellion, and standing out from a crowd vastly appeal to all sorts of people. In response, Harley-Davidson has shifted its STP methods to define four main target markets: core (men older than 35 years), young adults (both genders, 18–34 years), women (older than 35 years), and diverse (men and women, African American and Hispanic, older than 35 years).[10]

For women, for example, it encourages lifestyle events such as Garage Parties, women's-only social gatherings hosted in the evenings at dealerships to teach women the basics of motorcycling. The company publication *We Ride* focuses solely on female Hogs, and the HD-1 Customization website offers a separate process for women to build their cycles to match their build, power preferences, and color desires.[11]

The most widely used tool to support such psychographic segmentation efforts is the Value and Lifestyle Survey (VALS), owned and operated by Strategic Business Insights (SBI).[12] Consumers can be classified into the eight segments shown in Exhibit 9.3 based on their answers to the questionnaire (http://www.strategicbusinessinsights.com/vals/presurvey.shtml). The vertical dimension of the VALS framework indicates level of resources, including income, education, health, energy level, and degree of innovativeness. The upper segments have more resources and are more innovative than those on the bottom.

The horizontal dimension shows the segments' primary psychological motivation for buying. Consumers buy products and services because of their primary motivations—that is, how they see themselves in the world and how that self-image governs their activities. The three primary motivations of U.S. consumers are ideals, achievement, and self-expression. People who are primarily motivated by ideals are guided by knowledge and principles. Those who are motivated by achievement look for products and services that demonstrate success to their peers. Consumers who are primarily motivated by self-expression desire social or physical activity, variety, and risk.

VALS also enables firms to identify target segments and their underlying motivations. It shows correlations between psychology and lifestyle choices. For instance, a European luxury automobile manufacturer used VALS to identify online, mobile applications that would appeal to affluent, early-adopter consumers within the next five years.[13] The VALS analysis enabled the company to prioritize the most promising applications to develop. In another case, VALS was used to help a medical center identify customers most interested and able to afford cosmetic surgery. Based on the underlying motivations of its target customers, the center and its ad agency developed an ad campaign so successful that it had to be pulled early to avoid overbooking at the surgical center.

Firms are finding that psychographic segmentation schemes like VALS are often more useful for predicting consumer behavior than are demographics. This is because people who share demographics often have very different psychological traits. Take, for example, Jack and John, both 30-year-old, married college graduates. Demographically they are the same, but Jack is risk-averse and John is a risk

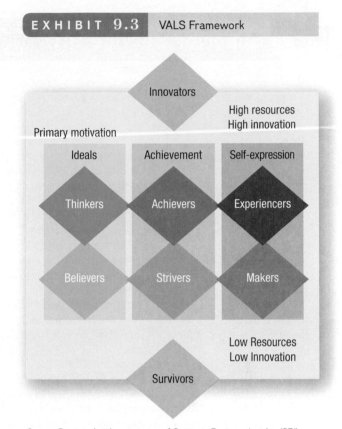

EXHIBIT 9.3 VALS Framework

Source: Reprinted with permission of Strategic Business Insights (SBI); www.strategicbusinessinsights.com/VALS.

It is just as easy to identify Thinkers (left) as it is Makers (right). A person is given the VALS questionnaire, and the VALS program at SRIC-BI runs the answers through the computer for scoring to determine the VALS type.

Superior Service 9.1　Just How Friendly Do Customers Want the Skies to Be?[ii]

Airline companies already collect most of the data that other sellers are desperate to access. Because of the security regulations surrounding modern travel, they know every customer's birthdate, identification number, and address. By simply tracking what customers do with the company, they can also readily learn vast behavioral information, such as where the passenger tends to travel, at what times of day, and in which seasons, as well as what the flier likes to drink and how much luggage he or she tends to bring along.

It's a vast treasure-trove of customer data. But until recently, airlines have done very little with this information, in terms of marketing to customers. That gap appears to be shrinking, though, as airlines recognize that they have a captive audience, stuck for several hours with no means to escape while they proffer their sales pitch. For example, Allegiant Air takes to the intercom system on flights to Las Vegas to tout tickets to fabulous shows, rental cars, and helicopter tours. In the first six months of 2013, it sold $21 million worth of such products.

Other airlines are focused more on selling their own products and upgrades. JetBlue plans to equip flight attendants with handheld devices so that it can engage in better inventory planning and determine exactly how much of which beverages to stock on each flight. United Airlines hopes to use its collected data to identify and target the passengers who are most likely to grab the opportunity to upgrade to an economy-plus or first-class ticket when they arrive at the airport.

But a captive audience also can quickly start to feel captured, instead of captivated. Because airlines gather so much personal information, and passengers have no means to opt

To improve customer service, JetBlue plans to equip flight attendants with handheld devices to improve inventory for beverages.

out of providing it, overly intrusive uses of these data quickly seem creepy. A flier entering the cabin and hearing the flight attendant welcome her by name might feel as if the company is stalking her. But another passenger who receives a vegetarian meal because the airline recognizes the pattern of his meal choices in the past might greatly appreciate the convenience. The challenge of finding the right balance is perhaps best summarized by one passenger's comment on a customer survey conducted by Quantas: "I do want you to know how I like my cappuccino, but I don't want you to know my dog's name."

---

taker. Jack is socially conscious and John is focused on himself. Lumping Jack and John together as a target does not make sense because the ways they think and act are totally different.

There are limitations to using psychographic segmentation, however. Psychographics are more expensive as a means to identify potential customers. With demographics, a firm like Nike can easily identify its customers as, say, men or women and then direct its marketing strategies to each group differently. The problem is that not all men are alike, as we saw with Jack and John. Women are not all alike either! To identify VALS Thinkers or Makers, companies use the VALS questionnaire in surveys or focus groups. Then VALS provides segment descriptions, linkages with consumer product and media data, communication styles, and zip code locations.[14]

Benefit Segmentation Benefit segmentation groups consumers on the basis of the benefits they derive from products or services. Because marketing is all about satisfying consumers' needs and wants, dividing the market into segments whose needs and wants are best satisfied by the product benefits can be a very powerful tool.[15] It is effective and relatively easy to portray a product's or service's benefits in the firm's communication strategies. Superior Service 9.1 outlines which benefits modern travelers want from airlines—and which ones they don't.

Hollywood in particular is a constant and effective practitioner of benefit segmentation. Although all movies may seem to provide the same service—entertainment for a couple of hours—film producers know that people visit the theater or rent films to obtain a vast variety of benefits, and market them accordingly. Need a laugh? Try the latest comedy from Adam Sandler or Melissa McCarthy. Want to cry and then feel warm and fuzzy? Go see *Trouble with the Curve,* starring Clint Eastwood, Amy Adams, and Justin Timberlake, for by the time you leave the theater, you are likely to feel quite happy: The lead characters will have faced obstacles, overcome them, and ultimately found love.

Behavioral Segmentation
Behavioral segmentation divides customers into groups on the basis of how they use the product or service. Some common behavioral measures include occasion and loyalty.

Occasion Behavioral segmentation based on when a product or service is purchased or consumed is called occasion segmentation. Men's Wearhouse uses this type of segmentation to develop its merchandise selection and its promotions. Sometimes men need a suit for their everyday work, but other suits are expressly for special occasions such as a prom or a wedding. Snack food companies such as Frito-Lay also make and promote snacks for various occasions—individual servings of potato chips for a snack on the run but 16-ounce bags for parties.

Loyalty Firms have long known that it pays to retain loyal customers. Loyal customers are those who feel so strongly that the firm can meet their relevant needs best that any competitors are virtually excluded from their consideration; that is, these customers buy almost exclusively from the firm. These loyal customers are the most profitable in the long term.[16] In light of the high cost of finding new customers and the profitability of loyal customers, today's companies are using loyalty segmentation and investing in retention and loyalty initiatives to retain their most profitable customers. From simple, "buy 10 sandwiches, get the 11th free" punchcards offered by local restaurants to the elaborate travel-linked programs run by hotel and airline affiliates, such loyalty segmentation approaches are ubiquitous. They also might be illegal in some implementations, as Ethical and Societal Dilemma 9.1 explains.

Using Multiple Segmentation Methods
Although all segmentation methods are useful, each has its unique advantages and disadvantages. For example, segmenting by demographics and geography is easy because information about who the customers are and where they are located is readily available, but these characteristics don't help marketers determine their customers' needs.

What emotions are evoked by the movie Trouble with the Curve *and its stars?*

Restaurants offer loyalty programs because it is less expensive to retain customers than to attract new ones.

Loyalty programs are so widespread, spanning so many industries, that they may seem unquestionable. But recent hearings held by the U.S. Congress Commerce Committee created some challenging questions, especially for the data warehouses that help companies target their ideal markets.

Part of the impetus for this questioning is the increased insights that marketers gain about their customers using technologically advanced data gathering methods. Especially when consumers opt in to a loyalty program, they grant data brokers access to vast amounts of information about them. These brokers, including Experian, Acxiom, and Epsilon, earn their revenues by gathering and warehousing these massive amounts of consumer data, and then selling selected slices to companies that want to target a particular audience.

The chair of the hearings, Democratic Senator John Rockefeller of West Virginia, voiced concerns that the practices of the data brokers were shrouded in secrecy, such that there was insufficient oversight of how they collected and used information about consumers. But his challenges also extended to some central tactics embraced by marketers.

By segmenting populations by gender, race, ethnicity, and income, Rockefeller asserted, data gatherers were inherently discriminatory. Predatory lenders who identify a population of lower income, less educated consumers might target them unfairly, such as by promising loans but only at very high interest rates. A list of people suffering from a genetic disease might attract the attention of unethical peddlers of "miracle cures." Because so much personal data is now available online, oversight of the uses of the data becomes even more difficult.

Rockefeller also objected to the defining feature of loyalty programs, namely, the provision of benefits to customers that the provider deems "better." Using the example of airlines, the hearing noted that in the aftermath of a cancellation, airlines often give priority to their best customers to help them find another route to their destination. Such practices in turn make the industry more frustrating and less serviceable for occasional or infrequent fliers. Overall, then, the harms to the broader society might outweigh the benefits to the individual or the firm.

Or perhaps the problem is merely unethical implementation, and the segmentation and targeting that Rockefeller decries is merely part of doing business.

Knowing what benefits customers are seeking or how the product or service fits a particular lifestyle is important for designing an overall marketing strategy, but such segmentation schemes present a problem for marketers attempting to identify specifically which customers are seeking these benefits. Thus, firms often employ a combination of segmentation methods, using demographics and geography to identify and target marketing communications to their customers, then using benefits or lifestyles to design the product or service and the substance of the marketing message.

One very popular mixture of segmentation schemes is geodemographic segmentation. Based on the adage "birds of a feather flock together," geodemographic segmentation uses a combination of geographic, demographic, and lifestyle characteristics to classify consumers. Consumers in the same neighborhoods tend to buy the same types of cars, appliances, and apparel and shop at the same types of retailers. Two of the most widely used tools for geodemographic segmentation are Potential Rating Index by Zip Market (PRIZM), developed by Nielsen Claritas (http://www.mybestsegments.com), and ESRI's (http://www.esri.com) Tapestry. Using detailed demographic data and information about the consumption and media habits of people who live in each U.S. block tract (zip code + 4), PRIZM can identify 66 geodemographic segments or neighborhoods. Each block group then can be analyzed and sorted by more than 60 characteristics, including income, home value, occupation, education, household type, age, and several key lifestyle variables. The information in Exhibit 9.4 describes two PRIZM clusters.

Geodemographic segmentation can be particularly useful for retailers because customers typically patronize stores close to their neighborhood. Thus, retailers can use geodemographic segmentation to tailor each store's assortment to the preferences of the local community. If a toy store discovers that one of its stores is surrounded by Big Sky Families, it might adjust its offering to include

EXHIBIT 9.4	PRIZM Clusters	
Segment Name	Bohemian Mix	Big Sky Families
Segment Number	16	33
Demographics Traits:		
Urbanicity:	Urban	Rural
Median household income:	$55,229	$54,449
Age ranges:	<55	<55
Presence of kids:	Family mix	HH w/kids
Homeownership:	Renters	Mostly owners
Employment levels:	White collar, Mix	Blue collar, Service, Mix
Education levels:	College grad	Some college
Ethnic diversity:	White, Black, Asian, Hispanic, Mix	White
Lifestyle Traits:		
	Shop at Express, 3mo	Own horse
	Own/lease new Volkswagen	Buy children's clothes, 6mos
	Go Snowboarding, 1yr	Own satellite dish
Food & Drink:		
	Drink Corona Extra beer, 1wk	Use baby foods, 1wk
	Buy from Au Bon Pain, 1mo	Buy from family restaurant, child decides, 6mo
	Buy from Dunkin Donuts, 1mo	Buy from Hardee's, 1mo
Media Usage:		
	Read *The New Yorker*, last issue	Read *Hunting*, last issue
	Visit Internet Movie Database (imdb.com), 1mo	Visit nascar.com, 1mo
	Write a blog online, 1mo	Watch The Disney Channel, 1wk

Source: The Nielsen Company.

less expensive toys. This kind of segmentation is also useful for finding new locations; retailers identify their best locations and determine what types of people live in the area surrounding those stores, according to the geodemographic clusters. They can then find other potential locations where similar segments reside.

CHECK YOURSELF

1. What are the various segmentation methods?

Step 3: Evaluate Segment Attractiveness

The third step in the segmentation process involves evaluating the attractiveness of the various segments. To undertake this evaluation, marketers first must determine whether the segment is worth pursuing, using several descriptive

 Describe how firms determine whether a segment is attractive and therefore worth pursuing.

EXHIBIT 9.5   Evaluation of Segment Attractiveness

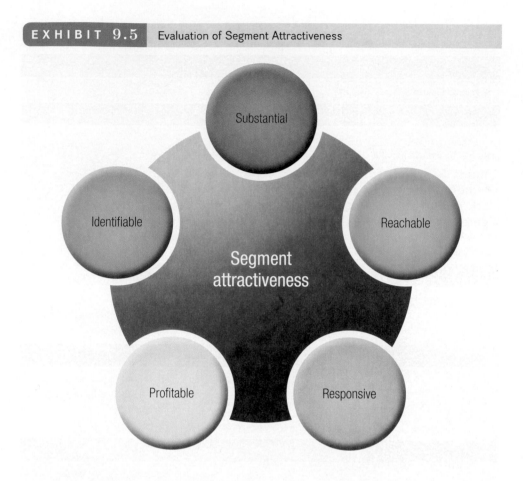

criteria: Is the segment identifiable, substantial, reachable, responsive, and profitable (see Exhibit 9.5)?

Identifiable Firms must be able to identify who is within their market to be able to design products or services to meet their needs. It is equally important to ensure that the segments are distinct from one another, because too much overlap between segments means that distinct marketing strategies aren't necessary to meet segment members' needs. Thus, people who follow the men's fashion blog *An Affordable Wardrobe* tend to be distinct from people who follow the women's fashion blog *Fabsugar*.

Substantial Once the firm has identified its potential target markets, it needs to measure their sizes. If a market is too small or its buying power insignificant, it won't generate sufficient profits or be able to support the marketing mix activities. As China's economy started growing, there were not enough middle-class car buyers to push foreign automakers to design an entry-level vehicle. It was only after that number reached substantial numbers that it became worthwhile for them to market to these identified consumers.

Reachable The best product or service cannot have any impact, no matter how identifiable or substantial the target market is, if that market cannot be reached (or accessed) through persuasive communications and product distribution. The consumer must know the product or service exists, understand what it can do for him or her, and recognize how to buy it. If Victoria's Secret fails to tell women that it is offering some less luxurious, more affordable options, shoppers will just walk right past the store and buy basic bras from the Macy's store in the same mall.

Responsive For a segmentation strategy to be successful, the customers in the segment must react similarly and positively to the firm's offering. If, through the firm's distinctive competencies, it cannot provide products or services to that segment, it should not target it. For instance, the Cadillac division of General Motors (GM) has introduced a line of cars to the large and very lucrative luxury car segment. People in this market typically purchase Porsches, BMWs, Audis, and Lexuses. In contrast, GM has been somewhat successful competing for the middle-priced family-oriented car and light truck segments. Thus, even though the luxury car segment meets all the other criteria for a successful segment, GM took a big risk in attempting to pursue this market.

If you are looking for a luxury SUV, General Motors hopes you will choose a Cadillac.

Profitable Marketers must also focus their assessments on the potential profitability of each segment, both current and future. Some key factors to keep in mind in this analysis include market growth (current size and expected growth rate), market competitiveness (number of competitors, entry barriers, product substitutes), and market access (ease of developing or accessing distribution channels and brand familiarity). Some straightforward calculations can help illustrate the profitability of a segment:

$$\text{Segment profitability} = (\text{Segment size} \times \text{Segment adoption percentage} \times \text{Purchase behavior} \times \text{Profit margin percentage}) - \text{Fixed costs}$$

where

Segment size = Number of people in the segment

Segment adoption percentage = Percentage of customers in the segment who are likely to adopt the product/service

Purchase behavior = Purchase price × number of times the customer would buy the product/service in a year

Profit margin percentage = (Selling price − variable costs) ÷ selling price

Fixed costs = Advertising expenditure, rent, utilities, insurance, and administrative salaries for managers

To illustrate how a business might determine a segment's profitability, consider Camillo's start-up lawn service. He is trying to determine whether to target homeowners or businesses in a small midwestern town. Exhibit 9.6 estimates the

EXHIBIT 9.6   Profitability of Two Market Segments for Camillo's Lawn Service

	Homeowners	Businesses
Segment size	75,000	1,000
Segment adoption percentage	1%	20%
Purchase behavior Purchase price Frequency of purchase	$100 12 times	$500 20 times
Profit margin percentage	60%	80%
Fixed costs	$400,000	$1,000,000
Segment profit	$140,000	$600,000

Adding Value 9.1   Are Baby Boomers Too Old for TV? Some Networks Seem to Think So[iv]

The western mystery show *Longmire*, aired on the A&E cable network, had a lot going for it. It was based on a series of bestselling books, featured an appealing hero, and attracted an average of 5.6 million viewers per show—quite a substantial number for a basic cable channel. And yet A&E canceled the show, refusing to renew it for a fourth season, citing as one of its reasons that its primary audience, which had a median age of 60 years, simply did not reflect its target market of 18- to 45-year-old viewers.

The 18–45-year demographic is famously appealing to television networks, because this age group appeals most to advertisers. Thus virtually every network, whatever its general theme or concept, aims to attract viewers whose ages fall within this three-decade range. To do so, they often pursue shows that offer edgy, controversial, or exciting content.

Longmire had none of those traits. A relatively straightforward procedural, its titular main character was a traditional hero, rather than a tormented antihero. As the show's executive producer readily noted, "This is not a cynical show." Possibly as a result, it was very popular among older audiences, who enjoyed the linear narrative and appealingly clever lead detective.

Such audiences may find themselves with less and less to watch though, because *Longmire* is not the only show A&E cancelled despite its high ratings among older viewers. It also gave the ax to *The Glades*, another option that viewers older than 60 years tended to tune in to watch. Nor is

A&E canceled its successful western show, Longmire, *because its primary audience was too old.*

A&E the only network to avoid targeting a Baby Boomer audience; even when its show *Harry's Law* garnered strong ratings among this cohort, NBC canceled it after just a couple of seasons.

Without generalizing too broadly about older viewers, they appear less interested in unscripted or reality shows, which may leave them out of luck. The latter are far less expensive to produce than scripted dramas and thus continue to spread across networks, including A&E, which hosts the reality show *Duck Dynasty*.

profitability of the two segments. The homeowner segment is much larger than the business segment, but there are already several lawn services with established customers. There is much less competition in the business segment. So, the segment adoption rate for the homeowner segment is only 1 percent, compared with 20 percent for the business segment. Camillo can charge a much higher price to businesses, and they use lawn services more frequently. The profit margin for the business segment is higher as well because Camillo can use large equipment to cut the grass and therefore save on variable labor costs. However, the fixed costs for purchasing and maintaining the large equipment are much higher for the business segment. Furthermore, he needs to spend more money obtaining and maintaining the business customers, whereas he would use less expensive door-to-door flyers to reach household customers. On the basis of these informed predictions, Camillo decides the business segment is more profitable for his lawn service.

This analysis provides an estimate of the profitability of two segments at one point in time. It is also useful to evaluate the profitability of a segment over the lifetime of one of its typical customers. To address such issues, marketers consider factors such as how long the customer will remain loyal to the firm, the defection rate (percentage of customers who switch on a yearly basis), the costs of replacing lost customers (advertising, promotion), whether customers will buy more or more expensive merchandise in the future, and other such factors.

Now that we've evaluated each segment's attractiveness (Step 3), we can select the target markets to pursue (Step 4).

Step 4: Select a Target Market

The fourth step in the STP process is to select a target market. The key factor likely to affect this decision is the marketer's ability to pursue such an opportunity or target segment. Thus, as we mentioned in Chapter 2, a firm assesses both the attractiveness of the target market (opportunities and threats based on the SWOT analysis and the profitability of the segment) and its own competencies (strengths and weaknesses based on the SWOT analysis) very carefully.

Determining how to select target markets is not always straightforward, especially when the firms consider certain markets to be too old to be worthwhile as Adding Value 9.1 on the opposite page explains.

Exhibit 9.7 illustrates several targeting strategies, which we discuss in more detail next.

Undifferentiated Targeting Strategy, or Mass Marketing When everyone might be considered a potential user of its product, a firm uses an undifferentiated targeting strategy. (See Exhibit 9.7.) Clearly, such a targeting strategy focuses on the similarities in needs of the customers as opposed to the differences. If the product or service is perceived to provide similar benefits to most consumers, there simply is little need to develop separate strategies for different groups.

Although not a common strategy in today's complex marketplace, an undifferentiated strategy is used for many basic commodities such as salt or sugar. However, even those firms that offer salt and sugar now are trying to differentiate

LO3 Articulate the differences among targeting strategies: undifferentiated, differentiated, concentrated, or micromarketing.

EXHIBIT 9.7   Targeting Strategies

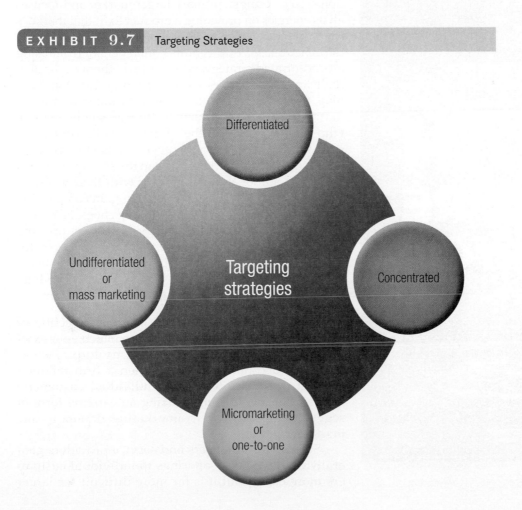

Conde Nast has more than 20 niche magazines focused on different aspects of life.

their products. Similarly, everyone with a car needs gasoline. Yet gasoline companies have vigorously moved from an undifferentiated strategy to a differentiated one by targeting their offerings to low-, medium-, and high-octane gasoline users.

Differentiated Targeting Strategy Firms using a **differentiated targeting strategy** target several market segments with a different offering for each (again see Exhibit 9.2). Condé Nast has more than 20 niche magazines focused on different aspects of life—from *Vogue* for fashionistas to *Bon Appetit* for foodies to *GQ* for fashion-conscious men to *The New Yorker* for literature lovers to *Golf Digest* for those who walk the links.

Firms embrace differentiated targeting because it helps them obtain a bigger share of the market and increase the market for their products overall. Readers of *Golf Digest* probably are unlike readers of *Architectural Digest* in their interests, as well as in their demographics, such as gender, age, and income. Providing products or services that appeal to multiple segments helps diversify the business and therefore lowers the company's (in this case, Condé Nast's) overall risk. Even if one magazine suffers a circulation decline, the impact on the firm's profitability can be offset by revenue from another publication that continues to do well. But a differentiated strategy is likely to be more costly for the firm.

Which segment is being targeted?

Concentrated Targeting Strategy When an organization selects a single, primary target market and focuses all its energies on providing a product to fit that market's needs, it is using a **concentrated targeting strategy**. Entrepreneurial start-up ventures often benefit from using a concentrated strategy, which allows them to employ their limited resources more efficiently. Newton Running, for instance, has concentrated its targeting strategy to runners—but not all runners. It focuses only on those who prefer to land on their forefeet while running, a style that recently has been suggested as more natural, efficient, and less injury-prone than the style encouraged by more traditional running shoes with their heel-first construction and substantial cushioning. In comparison, though it also is known for its running shoes, Nike uses a differentiated targeting strategy (recall the opening vignette about Nike in Chapter 2). It makes shoes for segments that include basketball and football players and skateboarders as well as fashion-conscious white-collar workers with its subsidiary brand Cole Haan.

Micromarketing[17] Take a look at your collection of belts. Have you ever had one made to match your exact specifications? (If you're interested, try http://www.leathergoodsconnection.com.) When a firm tailors a product or service to suit an individual customer's wants or needs, it is undertaking an extreme form of segmentation called **micromarketing** or **one-to-one marketing**.

Such small producers and service providers generally can tailor their offerings to individual customers more easily. But it is far more difficult for larger

Superior Service 9.2   With or without You: Specified Service[v]

With the effective use of technology, a customer service exchange can occur without any human interaction. This promise and the development of automated customer service offers benefits and harms, to both consumers and service providers.

For customers, the do-it-yourself component of customer self-service is convenient and appealing. Consumers can visit kiosks, websites, or chat rooms to find quick solutions to mundane problems.

For the service providers, greater technology means lower costs because they can hire fewer workers to respond to customer complaints and questions. In addition, they can provide more consistent service, no longer depending on the inherently variable human component.

Yet technology cannot solve advanced customer service problems or provide empathy to consumers in the midst of a service crisis. When consumers need the complex problem-solving skills that only a human can provide, the limitations of technology-based responses are frustrating. By the time they reach a human customer service representation, their expectations have jumped exponentially: They want perfect, expert assistance. Thus firms must give them more professional, highly trained service representatives. The increased expectations also enhance opportunities for service failures, to the detriment of the firm.

Zappos.com seems to have found a good balance that meets the specific needs of each individual customer who contacts the site. It uses automated technology to handle approximately 75 percent of its customer service transactions. But it also prides itself on hiring and training the best employees available to handle customer service. The other 25 percent of calls that go to a human respondent constitute powerful and influential customer service interactions. By effectively navigating these customer service issues, Zappos has built remarkable brand loyalty and a strong reputation as a customer service leader.

Zappos has a great balance between the convenience of a technology-based service and the heart found in the personal touch.

companies to achieve this degree of segmentation. Major players such as Dell (computers) and Lands' End (shirts) tried to capitalize on Internet technologies to offer custom products. Lands' End let customers choose from a variety of options in the fabric, type of collar, sleeve, shape, and based on the customer's specific measurements—but it halted this service when it could not manage to achieve profitable sales. Dell allowed customers to choose the size, color, and speed of their laptops, though it has backed off its promotions and limits the choice of software included. These adjustments demonstrate the difficulty of micromarketing; Superior Service 9.2 suggests a way to make it work.

The Internet clearly helps facilitate such a segmentation strategy. Companies can cater to very small segments, sometimes as small as one customer at a time, relatively efficiently and inexpensively (e.g., mortgage and insurance sites provide personalized quotes). An Internet-based company can offer one-to-one service more inexpensively than can other venues, such as retail stores or telephone-based businesses. For example, frequent fliers of American Airlines can check prices and choose special services online at a fraction of the cost that the company would incur for a phone consultation with a ticket agent.

The Internet also simplifies customer identification, in ways that are constantly changing, as we discussed in the opening vignette for Chapter 4. Cookies, or small text files a website stores in a visitor's browser, provide a unique identification of each potential customer who visits and details how the customer has searched the site. In turn, advertisers using retargeting technologies can link their advertisements to the browsing history of any individual user. For example, Twitter's Tailored Audiences service helps corporate clients advertise their products to any Twitter subscriber who has shown any interest in the brand through her or his online activities.[18]

Marketers also can ask visitors to fill out an online registration form. Using such information, the company can make a variety of recommendations to customers. Amazon.com is renowned for the algorithms it uses to provide recommendations for related products to customers as they browse the site, which match customer profiles to those of other customers. The marketing strategy therefore is customized in real time, using known and accurate data about the customer. Staples offers merchandise at different prices in different parts of the country—simply by asking customers to enter their zip codes.

Customers can even do the work themselves, both to create items for themselves and to find the perfect gifts for others.[19] Mars Chocolate North America's MY M&M's Brand site (http://www.mymms.com) lets customers customize their own M&M's Chocolate Candies with personalized greetings, including messages for birthday parties, sporting events, graduations, and weddings—as well as wedding proposals! Both online and in stores, Build-A-Bear lets young (or not so young) customers design their very own stuffed furry friend with unique clothes, accessories, sounds, and the name printed on its birth certificate.

www.mymms.com allows customers to customize their candy.

Some consumers appreciate such custom-made goods and services because they are made especially for them, which means they'll meet the person's needs exactly. If a tailor measures you first and then sews a suit that fits your shoulders, hips, and leg length exactly, it probably will fit better than an off-the-rack suit that you pick up at a department store. But such products and services are typically more expensive than ready-made offerings and often take longer to obtain. You can purchase a dress shirt in your size at Macy's and wear it out of the store. Ordering a tailored shirt from an online site that allows you to enter in your measurements might take five to six weeks to receive delivery. And if you visited an old-fashioned tailor, the processes of measuring you, ordering the material, and sewing the pants might take several months—at a much higher cost.

Build-A-Bear lets customers design their own stuffed furry friend with unique clothes, accessories, sounds, and the name printed on its birth certificate.

Step 5: Identify and Develop Positioning Strategy

LO4 Determine the value proposition.

The last step in developing a market segmentation strategy is positioning. Market positioning involves a process of defining the marketing mix variables so that target customers have a clear, distinctive, desirable understanding of what the product does or represents in comparison with competing products.

The positioning strategy can help communicate the firm's or the product's value proposition, which communicates the customer benefits to be received from a product or service and thereby provides reasons for wanting to purchase it.

To visualize the value proposition, examine the Circles for a Successful Value Proposition framework in Exhibit 9.8A.[20] The first circle represents the customer needs and wants, the second circle represents the benefits that the company provides (i.e., its capabilities), and the final circle represents the benefits provided by competitors. The best situation is if a firm's product or service offering overlaps with customer needs and wants but suffers no overlap with competitors' offerings (Exhibit 9.8A). The shaded portion reflects the value proposition, or the intersection of what the customer needs and wants with what the firm can offer. Unfortunately, even if the situation depicted in Exhibit 9.8A existed, the product or service then would be successful, so it likely would not be sustainable because competitors would attempt to copy the important product or service attributes and therefore begin to encroach on the firm's value proposition. Maintaining a unique value proposition can be sustained in the long term only in monopoly situations or possibly monopolistic competition situations.

In Exhibit 9.8B, the intersection of customer needs, the benefits provided by our focal firm, and the benefits provided by a competing firm reveal seven specific spaces where a product or service might be located. Let's look at each one in turn, using the offerings of the airline industry as hypothetical examples to understand each space.

EXHIBIT 9.8   Circles for a Successful Value Proposition

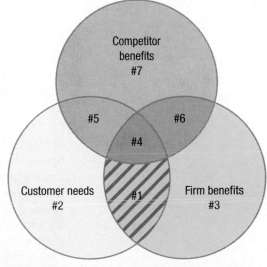

A. No overlap with competition

- Competitive offering
- Customer needs and wants
- Company offering
- The value proposition

B. Determining the value proposition

- Competitor benefits #7
- #5
- #6
- #4
- Customer needs #2
- #1
- Firm benefits #3

#1: Firm's value proposition.
#2: Customer's unmet needs (marketing opportunity).
#3: Firm's benefits that are not required—educate customer or redesign product.
#4: Key benefits that both the firm and competitor provide that customers require—
    carefully monitor performance relative to competitor on these benefits.
#5: Competitor's value proposition—monitor and imitate if needed.
#6: Benefits both firms provide that customers do not appear to need.
#7: Competitor benefits that are not required.

Space 1. Representing the firm's value proposition, this space reveals which customer needs are effectively met by the benefits that the firm provides but not by the benefits provided by competitors. That is, there is no overlap between competitors. When airline customers prefer a cattle-call approach to seating, which allows them to choose their own seats on the plane as long as they get an early check-in, they turn to Southwest, and Southwest alone, for their flights.

Space 2. These customer needs are unmet. It represents an important marketing opportunity in that the firm could create new products or augment existing services to satisfy these needs better. A direct route between two cities that currently are not connected by any airline represents a prime example of such a space.

Space 3. Customers express little need or desire for these company benefits. The firm thus has several options. It might educate customers about the importance and benefits that it provides with this space, to encourage customers to develop a sense of their need. Alternatively, it could reengineer its approach to stop providing these unwanted benefits, which likely would enable it to save money. For example, when airlines realized that passengers cared little about the appearance of a piece of lettuce underneath the in-flight sandwiches they were served, they saved millions of dollars they had previously spent on unwanted produce.

Space 4. These needs are being met by the benefits of the firm as well as by competitors. Many customers make frequent trips between major cities, like New York and Washington, DC, and many airlines offer multiple direct flights each day between these hubs. Each firm therefore works to compete effectively, such as by offering convenient flight times or striving to increase its on-time rates to make it easier for customers to compare firms on these specific features.

Space 5. This space constitutes the competitor's value proposition: the needs of customers that are met by benefits a competitor provides but not by the benefits provided by our focal firm. For example, only a few airlines host separate lounges for their best customers; a lower-cost airline cannot compete in this space. However, if more and more customers start to make demands for these benefits, the focal firm needs to monitor developments carefully and match some benefits if possible.

Space 6. Although both the focal firm and its competitors provide these benefits, they somehow are not meeting customer needs. The stringent security screening requirements aim to increase passenger safety, but they also represent a significant inconvenience that many fliers associate with airlines rather than federal regulators. Expending significant efforts to educate customers by the focal firm about these needs would also benefit competitors, so they likely are lower in the priority list of spending.

Space 7. Finally, some competitor benefits are either undesired or unnecessary among customers. Similar to Space 3, the competitor could invest money to educate customers about the importance of these benefits and highlight their needs through advertising and promotional campaigns. If so, the focal firm should recognize that this need is moving to Space 5. Alternatively, the competitor could reengineer its products to eliminate these benefits, in which case it requires no response from the focal firm.

Regardless of their existing space, firms must constantly and closely monitor their competitors' offerings. If competitors offer features that the firm does not, it is important to determine their importance to customers. Important attributes should be considered for inclusion in the firm's offering—or else they will provide a unique value proposition for competitors.

EXHIBIT 9.9	Value Proposition Statement Key Elements	
	Gatorade	7-Up
Target market:	To athletes around the world	To non-cola consumers
Offering name or brand:	Gatorade	7-Up
Product/service category or concept:	is the sports drink	is a non-caffeinated soft drink
Unique point of difference/ benefits:	representing the heart, hustle, and soul of athleticism and gives the fuel for working muscles, fluid for hydration, and electrolytes to help replace what is lost in sweat before, during, and after activity to get the most out of your body.	that is light, refreshing, lemon-lime flavored and has a crisp, bubbly, and clean taste.

In Exhibit 9.9, we highlight the elements of developing and communicating a firm's value proposition. The main value proposition components are:

1. Target market
2. Offering name or brand
3. Product/service category or concept
4. Unique point of difference/benefits

Let's focus on a couple of well-known products, Gatorade and 7-Up, and their potential value propositions (brackets are added to separate the value proposition components):

- **Gatorade:**[21] To [athletes around the world] [Gatorade] is the [sports drink] that [represents the heart, hustle, and soul of athleticism and gives the fuel for working muscles, fluid for hydration, and electrolytes to help replace what is lost in sweat before, during, and after activity to get the most out of your body].

- **7UP:**[22] To [non-cola consumers] [7-Up] is a [non-caffeinated soft drink] that [is light, refreshing, lemon-lime flavored, and has a crisp, bubbly, and clean taste].

What are the value propositions for Gatorade and 7UP?

L05 Define positioning, and describe how firms do it.

Positioning Methods

Firms position products and services based on different methods such as the value proposition, salient attributes, symbols, and competition. Thus, firms position their products and services according to value and salient attributes. Value is a popular positioning method because the relationship of price to quality is among the most important considerations for consumers when they make a purchase decision.

Remember that value does not necessarily mean low priced. For Louis Vuitton, appealing to its target market means making its offerings even more rare and expensive. Much of its recent revenues have come from lower margin products, such as perfume, so it introduced a new ultra-luxury line to appeal to its target market of the wealthiest customers. New offerings include clothing made of vicuna wool or lotus fibers—that is, extremely rare and difficult to harvest materials.[23] Other brands promote an idea of luxury being valuable because it lasts for generations, as exemplified by Patek Phillipe, Hermès, and Chanel.

Another common positioning strategy focuses on the product attributes that are most important to the target market. With its all-wheel-drive Quattro, Audi has positioned itself on performance and handling. Targeting a different market, Subaru positions its all-wheel drive slightly differently, instead focusing on safety and handling.

A well-known symbol can also be used as a positioning tool. What comes to mind when you think of Colonel Sanders, the Jolly Green Giant, the Gerber Baby, or Tony the Tiger? Or consider the Texaco star, the Nike swoosh, or the Ralph Lauren polo player. These symbols are so strong and well known that they create a position for the brand that distinguishes it from its competition. Many such symbols are registered trademarks that are legally protected by the companies that developed them.

Firms can choose to position their products or services against a specific competitor or an entire product/service classification. For instance, although most luggage companies focus on building lightweight and functional designs, Saddleback Leather focuses on rugged durability and a classic look. Offering a 100-year guarantee on its products, the owner Dave positions his bags as something "your grandkids will fight over." This craftsmanship comes at a cost—its suitcases sell for more than $1,000.

Marketers must be careful, however, that they don't position their product too closely to their competition. If, for instance, their package or logo looks too much like a competitor's, they might be opening themselves up to a trademark infringement

French retailer Hermès is positioned as a luxury brand, which makes its customers less price-sensitive for its products like this handmade Birkin bag which retails for $9,000.

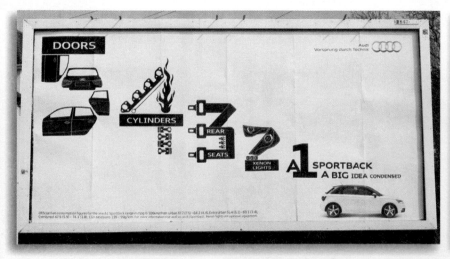

Audi has positioned itself as an uncompromising high performance car.

How does Saddleback Leather position itself?

lawsuit. Many private-label and store brands have been challenged for using packaging that appears confusingly similar to that of the national brand leaders in a category. Similarly, McDonald's sues anyone who uses the *Mc* prefix, including McSleep Inns and McDental Services, even though in the latter case there was little possibility that consumers would believe the fast-food restaurant company would branch out into dental services.

Positioning Using Perceptual Mapping

Now that we have identified the various methods by which firms position their products and services, we discuss the actual steps they go through to establish that position. When developing a positioning strategy, firms go through six important steps. But before you read about these steps, examine Exhibit 9.10 (Charts A–D), a hypothetical perceptual map of the soft drink industry. A perceptual map displays, in two or more dimensions, the position of products or brands in the consumer's mind. We have chosen two dimensions for illustrative purposes: sweet versus light taste (vertical) and less natural versus healthy (horizontal). Also, though this industry is quite complex, we have simplified the diagram to include only a few players in the market. The position of each brand is denoted by a small circle, and the numbered circles denote consumers' ideal points—where a particular market segment's ideal product would lie on the map. The larger the numbered circle, the larger the market size.

To derive a perceptual map such as shown in Exhibit 9.10, marketers follow six steps.

1. **Determine consumers' perceptions and evaluations of the product or service in relation to competitors'.** Marketers determine their brand's position by asking consumers a series of questions about their and competitors' products. For instance, they might ask how the consumer uses the existing product or services, what items the consumer regards as alternative sources to satisfy his or her needs, what the person likes or dislikes about the brand in relation to competitors, and what might make that person choose one brand over another. Exhibit 9.10A depicts the six products using two dimensions (light taste–sweet taste; and less natural–healthy).

2. **Identify the market's ideal points and size.** On a perceptual map, marketers can represent the size of current and potential markets. For

Gatorade and Powerade are positioned similarly and compete with each other for customers who seek healthy sweet drinks.

EXHIBIT 9.10A   Perceptual Maps

Chart A

Sweet taste

○ Pepsi   ○ Powerade

✛ Gatorade

Less natural   Healthy

○ Propel Fitness Water
○ Bottled water

Light taste

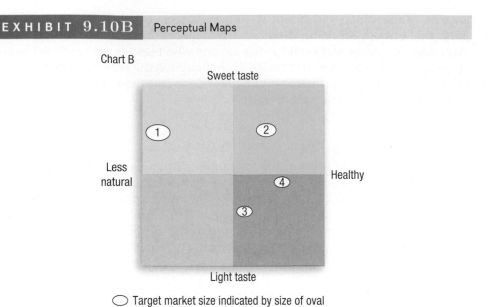

EXHIBIT 9.10B Perceptual Maps

Chart B

○ Target market size indicated by size of oval

example, Exhibit 9.10B uses differently sized ovals that correspond to the market size. Ideal point 1 represents the largest market, so if the firm does not already have a product positioned close to this point, it should consider an introduction. Point 3 is the smallest market, so there are relatively few customers who want a healthy, light-tasting drink. This is not to suggest that this market should be ignored; however, the company might want to consider a niche, rather than mass, market strategy for this group of consumers.

3. **Identify competitors' positions.** When the firm understands how its customers view its brand relative to competitors', it must study how those same competitors position themselves. For instance, Powerade positions itself closely to Gatorade, which means they appear next to each other on the perceptual map and appeal to target market 2 (see Exhibit 9.10C). They are also often found next to each other on store shelves, are similarly priced, and are viewed by customers as sports drinks. Gatorade also knows that its sports drink is perceived to be more like Powerade than like its own Propel Fitness Water (located near target market 3) or Coke (target market 1).

4. **Determine consumer preferences.** The firm knows what the consumer thinks of the products or services in the marketplace and their positions relative to

EXHIBIT 9.10C Perceptual Maps

Chart C

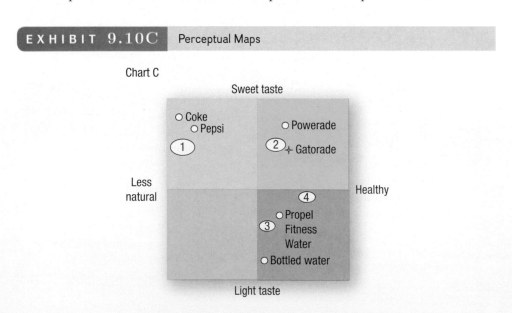

Gatorade uses athletes to compete for target markets in Exhibit 9.10.

one another. Now it must find out what the consumer really wants, that is, determine the ideal product or service that appeals to each market. For example, a huge market exists for traditional Gatorade, and that market is shared by Powerade. Gatorade also recognizes a market, depicted as the ideal product for segment 4 on the perceptual map, of consumers who would prefer a less sweet, less calorie-laden drink that offers the same rejuvenating properties as Gatorade. Currently, no product is adequately serving market 4.

5. **Select the position.** Continuing with the Gatorade example, the company has some choices to appeal to the "less sweet sports drink" target market 4. It could develop a new product to meet the needs of market 4 (see Exhibit 9.10D, option 1). Alternatively, it could adjust or reposition its marketing approach— its product and promotion—to sell original Gatorade to market 4 (option 2). Finally, it could ignore what target market 4 really wants and hope that consumers will be attracted to the original Gatorade because it is closer to their ideal product than anything else on the market.

6. **Monitor the positioning strategy.** Markets are not stagnant. Consumers' tastes shift, and competitors react to those shifts. Attempting to maintain the same

EXHIBIT 9.10D   Perceptual Maps

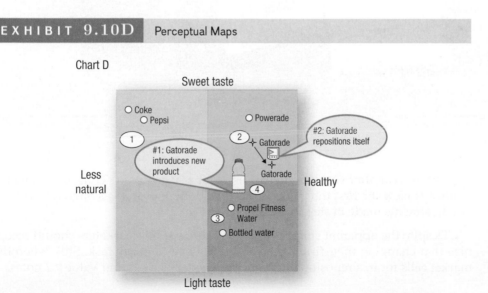

Adding Value 9.2   Fit as Fashion: The Repositioning of *Self* Magazine[vi]

At one time, fitness and fashion seemed like separate trends. Some people liked to read about how to tone their arms; others followed the hottest color trends. But in its research, *Self* magazine has determined that Millennial women are interested in both. In response, it has repositioned itself, moving from a sole focus on fitness issues to encompass more fashion and lifestyle features.

Among the changes being instituted, *Self* now includes an "It's a Thing" feature to highlight the latest trends; fashion coverage through its "You Look Awesome in That" section; and an advice column for readers who have found themselves in embarrassing situations that leave them begging, "Just Shoot Me." Rather than sweat-inducing workouts, the central theme is fun, with a healthy respect for fitness—such as an article outlining how to count the combined calories in bar snacks and drinks during an evening out.

To reflect its updated approach, *Self* adjusted its layout and formatting too. Larger font sizes emphasize the catchy article titles, and the pages use more white space. Such moves attempt to appeal to readers who have grown accustomed to short, snappy summaries of content—often through their extensive use of Twitter. The formatting guidelines also apply across the magazine's various access channels, including not just the print edition but also the website and its mobile app, Self Plus.

In its efforts to promote this repositioning, *Self* is licensing its brand to a fitness product line featuring popular tools such as kettleballs and yoga mats. It may extend the licenses to foods as well. Furthermore, it promoted the premiere of *Safe Harbor,* a movie starring Julianne Hough, in the same month that the young actor appeared on the magazine's first redesigned cover.

By increasing its appeal to this target market of 18- to 30-year-old female readers, *Self* also hopes to enhance its appeal to the advertisers that seek to catch these consumers' eyes. Advertising revenue and the number of ad pages purchased have decreased for *Self,* as well as for its existing competitors in the fitness market (*Shape, Women's Health*). To reverse the trend, *Self* is trying to become more things to more readers.

Self magexine is repositioning itself beyond fitness to include fashion and lifestyle features.

position year after year can spell disaster for any company. Thus, firms must always view the first three steps of the positioning process as ongoing, with adjustments made in step four as necessary.

Despite the apparent simplicity of this presentation, marketers should recognize that changing their firm's positioning is never an easy task. Still, when the market calls for it, a repositioning is often necessary, as Adding Value 9.2 notes.

Reviewing Learning Objectives

 Outline the different methods of segmenting a market.

There is really no one "best" method to segment a market. Firms choose from various methods on the basis of the type of product/service they offer and their goals for the segmentation strategy. For instance, if the firm wants to identify its customers easily, demographic or geographic segmentation likely will work best. But if it is trying to dig deeper into why customers might buy its offering, then psychographic, geodemographic, benefits, or behavioral segmentation (occasion and loyalty) work best. Typically, a combination of several segmentation methods is most effective.

 Describe how firms determine whether a segment is attractive and therefore worth pursuing.

Marketers use several criteria to assess a segment's attractiveness. First, the customer should be identifiable—companies must know what types of people are in the market so they can direct their efforts appropriately. Second, the market must be substantial enough to be worth pursuing. If relatively few people appear in a segment, it is probably not cost-effective to direct special marketing mix efforts toward them. Third, the market must be reachable—the firm must be able to reach the segment through effective communications and distribution. Fourth, the firm must be responsive to the needs of customers in a segment. It must be able to deliver a product or service that the segment will embrace. Finally, the segment must be profitable, both in the near term and over the lifetime of the customer.

 Articulate the differences among targeting strategies: undifferentiated, differentiated, concentrated, or micromarketing.

Firms use a targeting strategy after they have identified its segments. An undifferentiated strategy uses no targeting at all and works only for products or services that most consumers consider to be commodities. The difference between a differentiated and a concentrated strategy is that the differentiated approach targets multiple segments, whereas the concentrated targets only one. Larger firms with multiple product/service offerings generally use a differentiated strategy; smaller firms or those with a limited product/service offering often use a concentrated strategy. Firms that employ a micromarketing or one-to-one marketing strategy tailor their product/service offering to each customer—that is, it is custom-made. In the past, micromarketing was reserved primarily for artisans, tailors, or other craftspeople who would make items exactly as the customer wanted. Recently, however, larger manufacturers and retailers have begun experimenting with custom-made merchandise as well. Service providers, in contrast, are largely accustomed to customizing their offering.

 Determine the value proposition.

A firm's value proposition communicates the customer benefits to be received from a product or service and thereby provides reasons for wanting to purchase it. It consists of the attributes of a product or service that are desired by the target market, but not available from competitors. Firms could attempt to offer attributes that are important to its customers, whether or not they are offered by competitors. For attributes that are not important to its customers, it should either educate its customers about the importance of those attributes, deemphasize them, or not offer those product or service attributes.

 Define positioning, and describe how firms do it.

Positioning is the P in the STP (segmentation, targeting, and positioning) process. It refers to how customers think about a product, service, or brand in the market relative to competitors'

offerings. Firms position their products and services according to several criteria. Some focus on their offering's value—customers get a lot for what the product or service costs. Others determine the most important attributes for customers and position their offering on the basis of those attributes. Symbols can also be used for positioning, though few products or services are associated with symbols that are compelling enough to drive people to buy. Finally, one of the most common positioning methods relies on the favorable comparison of the firm's offering with the products or services marketed by competitors. When developing a positioning strategy and a perceptual map, firms go through six steps. First, they determine consumers' perceptions and evaluations of the product or service in relation to competitors. Second, they identify the market's ideal points and market sizes for those products or services. Third, they identify competitors' positions. Fourth, they determine consumer preferences. Fifth, they select the position. Finally, they monitor the positioning strategy.

Key Terms   ▪∣LEARNSMART·

- behavioral segmentation, 277
- benefit segmentation, 276
- concentrated targeting strategy, 284
- cookie, 286
- demographic segmentation, 270
- differentiated targeting strategy, 284
- geodemographic segmentation, 278
- geographic segmentation, 270
- ideal point, 291
- lifestyle, 274
- loyalty segmentation, 277
- market positioning, 287
- micromarketing, 284
- occasion segmentation, 277
- one-to-one marketing, 284
- perceptual map, 291
- psychographics, 271
- psychographic segmentation, 271
- self-concept, 273
- self-values, 273
- undifferentiated targeting strategy (mass marketing), 283
- value, 290
- Value and Lifestyle Survey (VALS), 274
- value proposition, 287

Marketing Applications

1. What segmentation methods would you suggest for a small entrepreneur starting her own business selling gourmet chocolates? Justify why you would recommend those methods.

2. You have been asked to identify various segments in the market and then a potential targeting strategy. Describe the segments for a pet supply store, and then justify the best targeting strategy to use.

3. What types of products would you use demographic segmentation for? How about psychographic segmentation? Explain how these products differ.

4. You have been asked to evaluate the attractiveness of a group of identified potential market segments. What criteria will you use to evaluate those segments? Why are these appropriate criteria?

5. A small-business owner is trying to evaluate the profitability of different segments. What are the key factors you would recommend she consider? Over what period of time would you recommend she evaluate?

6. Think about the various soft drinks that you know (e.g., Coca-Cola, Pepsi, 7-Up, Gatorade, Powerade). How do those various brands position themselves in the market?

7. Put yourself in the position of an entrepreneur who is developing a new product to introduce into the market. Briefly describe the product. Then, develop the segmentation, targeting, and positioning strategy for marketing the new product. Be sure to discuss (a) the overall strategy, (b) characteristics of the target market, (c) why that target market is attractive, and (d) the positioning strategy. Provide justifications for your decisions.

8. Think of a specific company or organization that uses various types of promotional material to market its offerings. The web, magazine ads, newspaper ads, catalogs, newspaper inserts, direct-mail pieces, and flyers might all be sources for a variety of promotional materials. Locate two or three promotional pieces for the company and use them as a basis to analyze the segments being targeted. Describe the methods used for segmenting the

market reflected in these materials, and describe characteristics of the target market according to the materials. Be sure to include a copy of all the materials used in the analysis.

9. You have been hired recently by a large bank in its credit card marketing division. The bank has relationships with a large number of colleges and prints a wide variety of credit cards featuring college logos, images, and the like. You have been asked to oversee the implementation of a new program targeting first-year college students at the schools with which the bank has a relationship. The bank has already purchased the names and home addresses of the incoming class. You have been told that no credit checks will be required for these cards as long as the student is over 18 years of age. The bank plans a first day of school marketing blitz that includes free hats, T-shirts, and book promotions, as well as free pizza, if the students simply fill out an application. Do you think it is a good idea to target this program to these new students?

Quiz Yourself

1. Four frequently used targeting strategies are micromarketing, undifferentiated, differentiated, and _____.
   a. geographic
   b. benefit-based
   c. economic
   d. global
   e. concentrated

2. Television advertising has recently expanded to include "mini-ads," which are short ads lasting 5 to 10 seconds. These ads are most useful in advertising to men, since men are more likely than women to channel surf during commercial breaks. This type of advertising will be more useful to marketers engaged in _____ segmentation.
   a. demographic
   b. psychographic
   c. behavioral
   d. benefit
   e. geographic

(Answers to these two questions can be found on page 651.)

Toolkit

MARKET POSITION MAP ANALYSIS

Assume you are a brand manager for a major manufacturer. You have identified a number of market segments and are trying to understand how its products are positioned relative to other manufacturers'. Please use the toolkit provided in your instructor's Connect course to conduct a market position analysis.

Net Savvy

1. Go to the Nielsen Claritas website (http://www. claritas.com/MyBestSegments/Default.jsp?ID =20&menuOption=ziplookup&pageName=ZIP% 2BCode%2BLookup). Enter your zip code to learn which segments are the top five in your zip code. Follow the links for each of the five most common PRIZM segments to obtain a segment description. Write up a summary of your results. Discuss the extent to which you believe these are accurate descriptions of the main segments of people who reside in your zip code.

2. Go to the VALS website (http://www.strategic-businessinsights.com/vals/presurvey.shtml), and click on the link to complete the VALS survey. After you submit your responses, a screen will display your primary and secondary VALS types. Click on the colored names of each segment to get additional information about them, and print out your results. Assess the extent to which these results reflect your lifestyle, and identify which characteristics accurately reflect your interests and activities and which do not.

Chapter Case Study   ▣ connect

COCA-COLA

Back in 1886, an Atlanta pharmacist created a caramel-colored liquid and brought it down the street to Jacobs' Pharmacy, where it was mixed with carbonated water and sold for five cents a glass.[24] The beverage caught on, and sales took off from the initial average of nine drinks a day,[25] to today's total of 1.7 billion Coke-owned beverages consumed daily. The success spawned bottling plants, six-pack cartons, international distribution—and imitators. For example, Pepsi followed in 1902 and today is a $29 billion conglomerate with vast holdings.[26]

Both companies spent decades marketing a single brand, Coke or Pepsi. But over the course of the 20th century, they both expanded their product lines by introducing drink alternatives such as Fanta, Sprite, TAB, Fresca, and Diet Coke (Coca-Cola), along with Diet Pepsi and Mountain Dew. The relatively simple segmentation that these offerings suggested has since grown increasingly complex and sophisticated, especially as the competitors have expanded their international sales into hundreds of diverse country markets. Although they face a number of smaller competitors, the primary focus in this mature market is to take customers away from its main rival, or else find a way to encourage existing customers to drink more cola—both challenging tasks. For Coca-Cola, the best solution is to pursue extensive product development for new and different market segments.[27]

Market Segmentation Strategy

In a tightening, competitive consumer market, Coke has developed unique products for various specific market segments. Because these unique products appeal to specific groups, Coke has been able to increase its sales without cannibalizing the sales of its other products. In addition to the products already mentioned, for example, the company launched caffeine-free versions of both Coke and Diet Coke to appeal to cola drinkers who wanted to cut back on their caffeine intake but preferred colas to lemon-lime-flavored drinks. By introducing these decaffeinated versions of traditional sodas, Coca-Cola increased the number of sodas it sold each day, without hurting sales, because the consumers targeted by these products already had been avoiding or minimizing cola consumption to reduce their caffeine intake.

Dieters Segment

As more Americans expressed concerns about their weight, Coca-Cola began by introducing Diet Coke, which became the number one selling diet soft drink in the United States within a year of hitting shelves. In 1986, Diet Cherry Coke joined the brand, followed by Diet Coke with Lemon. Diet Coke with Vanilla and Diet Coke with Lime followed quickly, along with Diet Black Cherry Vanilla Coke. Then new trends in the market led diet-conscious consumers to pay more attention to their overall health, not just calorie content. Thus the company introduced Diet Coke Plus—the familiar version of the beverage but with added vitamins and minerals. Coca-Cola Life has appeared only in Argentina and Chile so far; the reduced-calorie "sparkling beverage" promises natural sweeteners.[28]

"Real Men" Segment

Women hoping to drop a dress size may turn to diet sodas, but "real men" don't want to be caught with a "girly" diet drink. Coca-Cola had a response for them too: the high-profile launch of Coke Zero, which consistently avoided the dreaded word *diet*.[29] The successful introduction instead has relied on advertising featuring

Coca-Cola introduced Diet Coke Plus to appeal to a segment of cola drinkers that wants some added nutrients like vitamins B6 and B12.

such masculine images as James Bond to target men through its packaging, promotions, and image. By appealing to men between the ages of 18 and 34 years who wanted to drink a low-calorie cola but would prefer not to be seen buying or sipping Diet Coke, Coca-Cola increased its sales of Coke-branded products by one-third.[30]

The DIY Segment

Soda fountain sales have remained an important part of Coke's business since the company's inception. To boost its cola sales in restaurants, Coke combined the soda fountain concept with the do-it-yourself (DIY) trend to offer customers up to 104 individualized flavor choices in a new machine.[31] The Freestyle machine was created by the designers of Ferrari race cars. Size-controlled shots of concentrated flavors get released into carbonated water midstream, so the drink is mixed in the air; special technology keeps one consumer's beverage from picking up the flavors from the last drink poured. The Freestyle also allows moms to have a Diet Coke with Lime, while dads sip their Coke Zero with Lime and the kids select between a Caffeine-Free Vanilla Coke or a Caffeine-Free Diet Cherry Vanilla Coke.

Marketing Value to Segments

A successful new product introduction needs to combine an innovative product with a marketing campaign that communicates the value of that new product to the targeted segment. The Coke Zero launch provides a perfect illustration of this point. Coca-Cola designed a campaign supported by advertisements on television and radio, in print, on outdoor billboards, and online, as well as widespread sampling programs and opportunities.[32] Television commercials for Coke Zero show male athletes like Pittsburgh Steeler Troy Polamalu in a remake of the popular "Mean Joe Greene" commercial.[33] Others play on jokes about gender roles and modern relationships by promising that Coke Zero is like enjoying the benefits of having a "girlfriend without the drama." The ongoing media strategy has been to expose as many men as possible to the new product, with a significant bulk of the media budget spent on outdoor advertising.

Results of Coca-Cola's Segmentation Efforts

By using gender to segment the diet cola market, Coca-Cola was able to customize the advertising for Coca-Cola Zero to appeal to men, whereas Diet Coke ads could concentrate on women. In turn, Coke gained closer connections for its different products with each product's targeted market segment, and Coke Zero became one of the most successful launches in the company's long history.[34] The Freestyle dispenser began in only a few test markets, but in stores in which it was available, the machine bumped up beverage sales by 10 percent at a time when fountain sales on the whole were slipping. In response, several national restaurant chains, including Five Guys and Burger King, decided to roll out Freestyle machines in all their franchises.[35]

Through its efforts to identify and target such specific market segments, Coca-Cola has grown its stable of consumer brands, at least 16 of which earn billions in revenues.[36] Coca-Cola remains the most valuable brand, but Diet Coke and Coca-Cola Zero are not weak siblings: They have joined it as billion-dollar products in their own right.

Questions

1. Which types of segmentation strategies does Coca-Cola use to categorize the cola beverage market?
2. Are these types effective in this market? Provide support for your answer.

Endnotes

1. David Carr, "Giving Viewers What They Want," *The New York Times*, February 24, 2013, http://www.nytimes.com.

2. Ken Auletta, "Outside the Box," *The New Yorker*, February 3, 2014.

3. "Dreamworks Animation to Create Netflix's First Original Kids' Show," *Advertising Age*, February 12, 2013.

4. James Agarwal, Naresh K. Malhotra, and Ruth N. Bolton, "A Cross-National and Cross-Cultural Approach to Global Market Segmentation: An Application Using Consumers' Perceived Service Quality," *Journal of International Marketing* 18, no. 3 (September 2010), pp. 18–40.

5. Bill Carter, "ABC Viewers Tilt Female for a Network Light on Sports," *The New York Times*, December 17, 2013, http://www.nytimes.com; Alex Sood, "The Lost Boys Found: Marketing to Men through Games," *Fast Company*, March 10, 2011, http://www.fastcompany.com; Jeanine Poggi, "Men's Shopping Shrines," *Forbes*, September 30, 2008, http://www.forbes.com.

6. Michael R. Solomon, *Consumer Behavior*, 10th ed. (Upper Saddle River, NJ: Prentice Hall, 2012).

7. Rosellina Ferraro, Amna Kirmani, and Ted Matherly, "Look at Me! Look at Me! Conspicuous Brand Usage, Self-Brand Connection, and Dilution," *Journal of Marketing Research* 50, no. 4 (2013), pp. 477–88; Keith Wilcox and Andrew T. Stephen, "Are Close Friends the Enemy? Online Social Networks, Self-Esteem, and Self-Control," *Journal of Consumer Research* 40, no. 1 (2013), pp. 90–103.

8. Eric Wilson, "Less Ab, More Flab," *The New York Times*, May 22, 2013.

9. Michael R. Solomon, *Consumer Behavior: Buying, Having, and Being*, 10th ed. (Upper Saddle River, NJ: Prentice Hall, 2012).

10. James M. Hagerty, "Harley, with Macho Intact, Tries to Court More Women," *The Wall Street Journal*, October 31, 2011, http://online.wsj.com; Harley-Davidson, "Global Customer Focus," http://investor.harley-davidson.com.

11. Harley-Davidson, "Women Riders," http://www.harley-davidson.com.

12. http://www.strategicbusinessinsights.com/vals/store/USconsumers/intro.shtml.

13. http://www.strategicbusinessinsights.com/vals/applications/apps-pos.shtml.

14. "Segmentation and Targeting," http://www.kellogg.northwestern.edu; Carson J. Sandy, Samuel D. Gosling, and John Durant, "Predicting Consumer Behavior and Media Preferences: The Comparative Validity of Personality Traits and Demographic Variables," *Psychology & Marketing* 30, no. 11 (2013), pp. 937–49.

15. For an interesting take on this issue, see Joseph Jaffe, *Flip the Funnel* (Hoboken, NJ: Wiley, 2010).

16. V. Kumar, Ilaria Dalla Pozza, and Jaishankar Ganesh, "Revisiting the Satisfaction–Loyalty Relationship: Empirical Generalizations and Directions for Future Research," *Journal of Retailing* 89, no. 3 (2013), pp. 246–62; Irit Nitzan and Barak Libai, "Social Effects on Customer Retention," *Journal of Marketing* 75, no. 6 (November 2011), pp. 24–38.

17. Thorsten Blecker, *Mass Customization: Challenges and Solutions* (New York: Springer, 2006).

18. Jessica Guynn, "Social Networks Showing Users More Targeted Ads," *Los Angeles Times*, December 10, 2013, http://www.latimes.com.

19. C. Page Moreau, Leff Bonney, and Kelly B. Herd, "It's the Thought (and the Effort) That Counts: How Customizing for Others Differs from Customizing for Oneself," *Journal of Marketing* 75, no. 5 (September 2011), pp. 120–33.

20. This circular depiction of the value proposition is based on work by John Bers (Vanderbilt University) and adaptation and development of circles of success by Ronald Goodstein (Georgetown University).

21. http://www.gatorade.com/frequently_asked_questions/default.aspx.

22. http://www.drpeppersnapplegroup.com/brands/7up/.

23. Kyle Stock, "Louis Vuitton Shops for Even Richer Customers," *Bloomberg Businessweek*, September 25, 2013, http://www.businessweek.com.

24. http://heritage.coca-cola.com/.

25. "Our Company," http://www.thecoca-colacompany.com/.

26. "The Pepsi Cola Story," http://www.pepsiusa.com/.

27. Betsy McKay, "Zero Is Coke's New Hero," *The Wall Street Journal*, April 17, 2007.

28. James B. Stewart, "For Coke, Challenge Is Staying Relevant," *The New York Times*, February 28, 2014.

29. Kate Fitzgerald, "Coke Zero," *Advertising Age*, November 12, 2007.

30. "Products," http://www.thecoca-colacompany.com/.

31. "Company and Coca-Cola Highlights," http://www.thecoca-colacompany.com; Valerie Bauerlein, "Coke Goes High-Tech to Mix Its Sodas," *The Wall Street Journal*, May 10, 2010, http://online.wsj.com.

32. Ibid.

33. Various press releases, http://www.thecoca-colacompany.com.

34. Ibid.

35. "Five Guys Becomes Largest Chain to Roll Out Coca-Cola Freestyle Nationwide," September 30, 2011, http://www.thecoca-colacompany.com; "Burger King Restaurants to Launch Coca-Cola Freestyle Across the U.S.," December 6, 2011, http://www.thecoca-colacompany.com.

36. "Coca-Cola at a Glance," http://www.coca-colacompany.com/our-company/infographic-coca-cola-at-a-glance.

i. Chris Matyszczyk, "For Teens, Facebook Is 'Dead and Buried,'" *CNET*, December 27, 2013, http://news.cnet.com.

ii. Jack Nicas, "How Airlines Mine Personal Data In-Flight," *The Wall Street Journal*, November 8, 2013, http://www.online.wsj.com.

iii. Kate Kaye, "Rockefeller to Marketing Data Giants: You're on Notice," *Advertising Age*, December 18, 2013; Kate Kaye, "7 Reasons This Senior Senator Hates Your Loyalty Program," *Advertising Age*, December 20, 2013.

iv. Joe Flint, "Why TV Hit 'Longmire' Got Cancelled: Fans Too Old," *The Wall Street Journal*, September 11, 2014, http://online.wsj.com.

v. Keith Wilcox and Sangyoung Song, "Discrepant Fluency in Self-Customization," *Journal of Marketing Research* 48, no. 4 (August 2011), pp. 729–40; Doug Stephens, "The Declining Need for and Escalating Value of Human Service," *Retail Prophet*, September 26, 2011.

vi. Tanzina Vega, "Self Magazine Refocuses for a Younger Audience," *The New York Times*, February 10, 2013.

Credits

MARKETING RESEARCH

LO1 Identify the five steps in the marketing research process.

LO2 Describe the various secondary data sources.

LO3 Describe the various primary data collection techniques.

LO4 Summarize the differences between secondary data and primary data.

LO5 Examine the circumstances in which collecting information on consumers is ethical.

When we discussed Disney as an example of a stellar customer service provider in Chapter 2, we noted how it personalizes the experience for every visitor to the Magic Kingdom, Epcot, Hollywood, or any other park. To offer such remarkable personalization and service, Disney needs information: about who customers are, what they like, where they are going, and so on. That means that as good as Disney is at customer service, it may be even better at marketing research.

It has long engaged in observational research, by watching how people move through its parks. Such research helped it determine just how far apart each trash can should be, for example, to ensure that anytime a visitor was ready to throw away a wrapper or used cup, he or she had a ready receptacle in which to toss it.

Disney also combines the data it collects from guests at its hotels, information provided when people buy theme park tickets online, and other such purchasing details. Thus it can determine how many families are staying, but also

how many couples are using Disney for their honeymoon. In turn, it can distribute its attractions according to its target market: plenty of rides for kids, as well as romantic sites for couples to enjoy the weather and their time alone.

A more recent initiative takes Disney to the cutting edge of market research. Its massive new system, spanning all its parks and hotel properties, relies on a wristband, called My Magic+. The wristband represents hotel guests' room key and credit card, so simply by swiping it they can access their rooms or charge their poolside lunch to their room account. For day visitors to the parks, the bands enable them to check in for rides, make dinner reservations, or purchase souvenirs, charged to a linked credit card. If visitors download the My Disney Experience app before coming, they can also link their online choices with the My Magic+ bracelet to make sure they can rendezvous with Goofy at the time and place most convenient for them.[1]

These are the benefits the wristbands offer for customers. For Disney, they offer remarkable access to real-world data about how visitors and guests actually make purchase decisions. By tracking the timing of their ride choices, Disney learns when and where it needs to increase staffing, to ensure a smooth traffic flow. It can determine if the restaurant nearest its biggest roller coaster should be stocking more soup. Even inventory decisions are informed by far more detailed information, such as whether customers seem to prefer picking up a princess dress near Cinderella's castle or somewhere else in the park.

On a more personalized level, willing park visitors with a Magic band might agree to receive notifications about when they should hurry over to a popular ride, because the lines are relatively short. Such communications would not only appeal to customers but also could help Disney even out its ride capacity better. In this sense, Disney happily reported that soon after the introduction of the new system, it was able to accommodate approximately 3,000 more visitors during the holiday season than it had the previous year.[2]

Disney has started marketing the bands themselves as souvenirs—a collectible that people can take home to remember their visit, but also potentially a way for Disney to keep track of them. Such access has, perhaps not surprisingly, created some backlash among privacy experts and some consumers. Especially because so much of Disney's target market consists of children, these ethical questions are salient. Should a massive corporation have access to a child's name, favorite princess, and birthdate, for example?

Marketing research is a prerequisite of successful decision making. It consists of a set of techniques and principles for systematically collecting, recording, analyzing, and interpreting data that can aid decision makers involved in marketing goods, services, or ideas. When marketing managers attempt to develop their strategies, marketing research can provide valuable information that will help them make segmentation, positioning, product, place, price, and promotion decisions.

Firms invest billions of dollars in marketing research every year. The largest U.S.-based marketing research firm, the Nielsen Company, earns annual worldwide revenues of over $5 billion.[3] Why do marketers find this research valuable? First, it helps reduce some of the uncertainty under which they currently operate. Successful managers know when research might help their decision making and then take appropriate steps to acquire the information they need. Second, marketing research provides a crucial link between firms and their environments, which enables them to be customer oriented because they build their strategies by using customer input and continual feedback. Third, by constantly monitoring their competitors, firms can anticipate and respond quickly to competitive moves.

If you think market research is applicable only to corporate ventures though, think again. Nonprofit organizations and governments also use research to serve their constituencies better. The political sector has been slicing and dicing the voting public for decades to determine relevant messages for different demographics. Politicians desperately want to understand who makes up the voting public to determine how to reach them. But not only do they want to know your political views, they also want to understand your media habits, such as what magazines you subscribe to, so they can target you more effectively.

To do so, they rely on the five-step marketing research process we outline in this chapter. We also discuss some of the ethical implications of using the information that these databases can collect.

THE MARKETING RESEARCH PROCESS

EXHIBIT 10.1 The Marketing Research Process

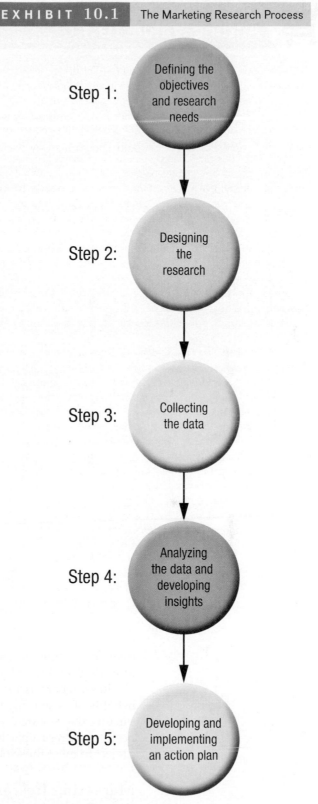

Step 1: Defining the objectives and research needs

Step 2: Designing the research

Step 3: Collecting the data

Step 4: Analyzing the data and developing insights

Step 5: Developing and implementing an action plan

Managers consider several factors before embarking on a marketing research project. First, will the research be useful; will it provide insights beyond what the managers already know and reduce uncertainty associated with the project? Second, is top management committed to the project and willing to abide by the results of the research? Related to both of these questions is the value of the research. Marketing research can be very expensive, and if the results won't be useful or management does not abide by the findings, it represents a waste of money. Third, should the marketing research project be small or large? A project might involve a simple analysis of data that the firm already has, or it could be an in-depth assessment that costs hundreds of thousands of dollars and takes months to complete.

The marketing research process itself consists of five steps (see Exhibit 10.1). Although we present the stages of the marketing research process in a step-by-step progression, of course research does not always, or even usually, happen that way. Researchers go back and forth from one step to another as the need arises. For example, marketers may establish a specific research objective, which they follow with data collection and preliminary analysis. If they uncover new information during the collection step or if the findings of the analysis spotlight new research needs, they might redefine their objectives and begin again from a new starting point. Another important requirement before embarking on a research project is to plan the entire project in advance. By planning the entire research process prior to starting the project, researchers can avoid unnecessary alterations to the research plan as they move through the process.

Marketing Research Process Step 1: Defining the Objectives and Research Needs

Because research is both expensive and time-consuming, it is important to establish in advance exactly what problem needs to be solved. For example, as Adding Value 10.1 outlines, McDonald's is considering ways to address a deeply troubling concern, namely, breakfast service that ends before noon. In general, though, marketers must clearly define the objectives of their marketing research project.

Consider a scenario: McDonald's wants a better understanding of its customers' experience. It also needs to understand how customers view the experience at Wendy's, a main competitor. Finally, McDonald's hopes to gain some insight into how it should set a price for and market its latest combo meal of a hamburger, fries, and drink. Any one of these questions could initiate a research project. The complexity of the project that the company eventually undertakes

 Identify the five steps in the marketing research process.

Adding Value 10.1   A Key Motivation for Waking Teens Early on Weekends Disappears—McDonald's Hints at Breakfast All Day[i]

Once upon a time, McDonald's did not offer any breakfast: no pancakes, no links, no nothing. Then in 1973 it introduced the Egg McMuffin, and today it generates almost a quarter of its revenues from its breakfast offerings,. But since that introduction, there has been one persistent problem suffered by night owls and morning laggards: Breakfast stops at 10:30 a.m. sharp. After this time, hungry diners must select a burger or wrap to wake them up, because no restaurants allow them to purchase traditional morning fare.

All that may be about to change. McDonald's has started testing, in limited regions, a "Breakfast After Midnight" menu in some of its 24-hour restaurants. This expansion has been relatively secretive, in that customers have to be in the local store at 2:00 a.m. to learn whether they can get their fix of egg, cheese, sausage, and biscuit. Some reports suggest the test markets appear already in Texas, Delaware, and Illinois (the site of McDonald's corporate headquarters). In addition, some overseas stores already have the all-day breakfast in place.

For late-morning risers everywhere else, the real excitement came when McDonald's CEO Don Thompson acknowledged, on a national news segment, that expanding the breakfast menu to make it available all day was a real possibility. The demand is clearly there, in that observers have identified breakfast as the biggest potential growth category for the brand, as well as its competitors.

The challenge is capacity. According to one franchise owner, because McDonald's continues to ask employees to use toasters and griddles to prepare its fast-food offerings—rather than faster options such as microwaves—selling both breakfast and dinner items simultaneously would strain the preparation capabilities of stores. Furthermore, McDonald's has already expanded its menu into other categories, such as wraps and salads. Perhaps adding another entire category of items would overly tax the busy employees.

McDonald's has started testing a "Breakfast After Midnight" menu in some of its 24-hour restaurants to provide its customers what they want, when they want it.

But for young adults rolling out of bed at noon on a Saturday, such arguments likely have little weight. Ultimately, McDonald's may be forced to provide what its customers want, exactly when and where they want it.

depends on how much time and resources it has available, as well as the amount of in-depth knowledge it needs.

Researchers assess the value of a project through a careful comparison of the benefits of answering some of their questions and the costs associated with conducting the research. When researchers have determined what information they need to address a particular problem or issue, the next step is to design a research project to meet those objectives.

Marketing Research Process
Step 2: Designing the Research

The second step in the marketing research project involves design. In this step, researchers identify the type of data needed and determine the research necessary to collect them. Recall that the objectives of the project drive the type of data needed, as outlined in Step 1.

Let's look at how this second step works, using the McDonald's customer experience. McDonald's needs to ask its customers about their McDonald's

experience. However, because people don't always tell the whole truth in surveys, the company also may want to observe customers to see how they actually enter the stores, interact with employees, and consume the product. The project's design might begin with available data, such as information that shows many customers arrive at 10:45 asking for breakfast or that people with children often come into the restaurants at lunchtime and order Happy Meals. Then McDonald's marketing researchers can start to ask customers specific questions about their McDonald's experience.

If McDonald's were to do research to better understand its customers' experience, it would study both the McDonald's experience and that of its major competitors, like Wendy's.

Marketing Research Process Step 3: Collecting the Data

Data collection begins only after the research design process. Based on the design of the project, data can be collected from secondary or primary data sources. **Secondary data** are pieces of information that have been collected prior to the start of the focal research project. Secondary data include both external and internal data sources. **Primary data**, in contrast, are those data collected to address specific research needs. Some common primary data collection methods include focus groups, in-depth interviews, and surveys.

For our hypothetical fast-food scenario, McDonald's may decide to get relevant secondary data from external providers such as National Purchase Diary Panel and Nielsen. The data might include the prices of different ingredients, sales figures, growth or decline in the category, and advertising and promotional spending. McDonald's is likely to gather pertinent data about sales from its franchisees. However, it also wants competitor data, overall food consumption data, and other information about the quick-service restaurant category, which it likely obtains from appropriate syndicated data providers. Based on the data, it might decide to follow up with some primary data using a survey.

No company can ask every customer his or her opinions or observe every customer, so researchers must choose a group of customers who represent

McDonald's assesses its customers' market experience by examining available data and then asks customers about their experience with products such as Value Meals.

the customers of interest, or a sample, and then generalize their opinions to describe all customers with the same characteristics. They may choose the sample participants at random to represent the entire customer market. Or they may choose to select the sample on the basis of some characteristic, such as their age, so they can research how seniors experience buying Value Meals.

Marketing researchers use various methods of asking questions to measure the issues they are tackling. In our hypothetical McDonald's scenario, assume the research team has developed a questionnaire (see Exhibit 10.2), using a few different types of questions. Section A measures the customer's experience in McDonald's,

EXHIBIT 10.2	A Hypothetical Fast-Food Survey

Please Evaluate Your Experience at McDonald's

A. McDonald's	Strongly Disagree 1	Disagree 2	Neither Agree or Disagree 3	Agree 4	Strongly Agree 5
McDonald's food tastes good	❑	❑	❑	☑	❑
McDonald's is clean	❑	❑	❑	☑	❑
McDonald's has low prices	❑	❑	❑	☑	❑

B. Wendy's	Strongly Disagree 1	Disagree 2	Neither Agree or Disagree 3	Agree 4	Strongly Agree 5
Wendy's food tastes good	❑	❑	❑	☑	❑
Wendy's is clean	❑	❑	❑	☑	❑
Wendy's has low prices	❑	❑	❑	☑	❑

C. McDonald's

	Never	1–2 times	3–4 times	More than 5 times
In the last month, how many times have you been to McDonald's? In the last month, how often did you order breakfast items at McDonald's?	❑	❑	❑	☑
If McDonald's offered breakfast items all the time, how often would you order them outside of normal breakfast times in a typical month?	❑	❑	❑	❑
On average, how much do you spend each visit at McDonald's?	$_____			
What is your favorite item at McDonald's?	_____			

D. Please tell us about yourself

	under 16	17–24	25–35	36+
What is your age?	❑	❑	❑	❑
What is your gender?	Male ❑	Female ❑		

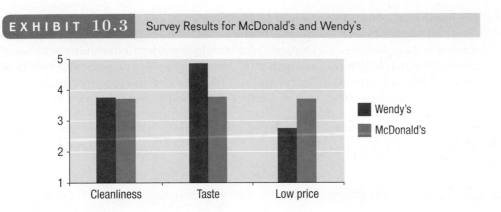

EXHIBIT 10.3 Survey Results for McDonald's and Wendy's

Wendy's

McDonald's

Cleanliness   Taste   Low price

Section B measures the customer's experience in Wendy's, Section C measures the customer's habits at McDonald's, and Section D measures customer demographics.[4]

Marketing Research Process Step 4: Analyzing the Data and Developing Insights

The next step in the marketing research process—analyzing and interpreting the data—should be both thorough and methodical. To generate meaningful information, researchers analyze and make use of the collected data. In this context, data can be defined as raw numbers or other factual information that, on their own, have limited value to marketers. However, when the data are interpreted, they become information, which results from organizing, analyzing, and interpreting data and putting them into a form that is useful to marketing decision makers. For example, a checkout scanner in the grocery store collects sales data about individual consumer purchases. Not until those data are categorized and examined do they provide information about which products and services were purchased together or how an in-store promotional activity translated into sales.

For the McDonald's example, we can summarize the results of the survey (from Exhibit 10.2) in Exhibit 10.3. Both McDonald's and Wendy's scored the same on the cleanliness of their restaurants, but McDonald's had lower prices, whereas Wendy's food tasted better. McDonald's may want to improve the taste of its food, but without raising prices too much, to compete more effectively with Wendy's.

Marketing Research Process Step 5: Developing and Implementing an Action Plan

In the final phase in the marketing research process, the analyst prepares the results and presents them to the appropriate decision makers, who undertake appropriate marketing strategies. A typical marketing research presentation includes an executive summary, the body of the report (which discusses the research objectives, methodology used, and detailed findings), the conclusions, the limitations, and appropriate supplemental tables, figures, and appendixes.[5]

In the McDonald's hypothetical scenario, according to the research findings, the company is doing fine in terms of cleanliness (comparable to its competitors) and is perceived to have lower prices, but the taste of its food could be improved. It also found that of those customers that purchased breakfast items relatively frequently (at least three times per month), 35 percent would go for breakfast outside the normal breakfast times frequently. Also, of those that never ordered breakfast items, 25 percent would order breakfast items outside the normal breakfast times occasionally (at least once a month.) Using this analysis and the related insights gained, McDonald's might consider hiring some gourmet chefs as consultants to improve the menu and offerings, and offer breakfast items

McDonald's marketing research will show how to better compete against Wendy's.

24/7 on a trial basis.[6] It then could highlight its efforts to improve the taste of the food and add desired offerings (e.g., breakfast items) through marketing communications and promotions. McDonald's also should consider undertaking additional pricing research to determine whether its lower prices enhance sales and profits or whether it could increase its prices and still compete effectively with Wendy's.

Now let's take a closer look at sources of secondary and primary data.

CHECK YOURSELF

1. What are the steps in the marketing research process?
2. What is the difference between data and information?

LO2 Describe the various secondary data sources.

SECONDARY DATA

A marketing research project often begins with a review of the relevant secondary data. Secondary data might come from free or very inexpensive external sources such as census data, information from trade associations, and reports published in magazines. Although readily accessible, these inexpensive sources may not be specific or timely enough to solve the marketer's research needs and objectives. Firms also can purchase more specific or applicable secondary data from specialized research firms. Finally, secondary sources can be accessed through internal sources, including the company's sales invoices, customer lists, and other reports generated by the company itself.

In political settings, such secondary data can be critical for candidates running for office. Both major political parties thus have developed proprietary databases that contain vast information about voters, broken down by demographic and geographic information. Before a local politician, canvasser, or poll taker even knocks on doors in a neighborhood, he or she likely knows which houses are inhabited by retirees, who has a subscription to the *Wall Street Journal* or *New York Times,* for whom the residents said they voted in the last election, or whether they served in the military. All these traits can give hints about the voters' likely concerns, which a good politician can address immediately upon knocking on the door. Such research also can dictate tactics for designing broader campaign materials or to zero in on very specific issues. Social media campaigns are a growing mechanism used to interact with potential voters in a more timely manner than more traditional methods. Monitoring tweets after a major address by a candidate, for instance, would provide instant feedback and direction for future communications.

Secondary data is useful to politicians so they know who they are talking to before they knock on their door.

Inexpensive External Secondary Data

Some sources of external secondary data can be quickly accessed at a relatively low cost. The U.S. Bureau of the Census (http://www.census.gov), for example, provides data about businesses by county and zip code. If you wanted to open a new location of a business you are already operating, these data might help you determine the size of your potential market.

Often, however, inexpensive data sources are not adequate to meet researchers' needs. Because the data initially were acquired for some purpose other than the research question at hand, they may not be completely relevant or timely. The U.S. census is a great source of demographic data about a particular market area, and it can be easily accessed at a low cost. However, the data are collected only at the beginning of every decade, so they quickly become outdated. If an entrepreneur wanted to open a retail flooring store in 2016, for example, the data would already be six years old, and the housing market likely would be stronger than it was in 2010. Researchers must also pay careful attention to how other sources of inexpensive secondary data were collected. Despite the great deal of data available on the Internet, easy access does not ensure that the data are trustworthy.

Syndicated External Secondary Data

Although the secondary data described previously are either free or inexpensively obtained, marketers can purchase external secondary data called syndicated data, which are available for a fee from commercial research firms such as IRI, the National Purchase Diary Panel, and Nielsen. Exhibit 10.4 contains information about various firms that provide syndicated data.

EXHIBIT 10.4   Syndicated Data Providers and Some of Their Services

Name	Services Provided
Nielsen (http://www.nielsen.com)	With its *Market Measurement Services*, the company tracks the sales of consumer packaged goods, gathered at the point of sale in retail stores of all types and sizes.
IRI (http://www.iriworldwide.com)	*InfoScan* store tracking provides detailed information about sales, share, distribution, pricing, and promotion across a wide variety of retail channels and accounts.
J.D. Power and Associates (http://www.jdpower.com)	Widely known for its automotive ratings, it produces quality and customer satisfaction research for a variety of industries.
Mediamark Research Inc. (http://www.mediamark.com)	Supplies multimedia audience research pertaining to media and marketing planning for advertised brands.
National Purchase Diary Panel (http://www.npd.com)	Based on detailed records consumers keep about their purchases (i.e., a diary), it provides information about product movement and consumer behavior in a variety of industries.
NOP World (http://www.nopworld.com)	The *mKids US* research study tracks mobile telephone ownership and usage, brand affinities, and entertainment habits of American youth between 12 and 19 years of age.
Research and Markets (http://www.researchandmarkets.com)	Promotes itself as a one-stop shop for market research and data from most leading publishers, consultants, and analysts.
Roper Center for Public Opinion Research (http://www.ropercenter.uconn.edu)	The *General Social Survey* is one of the nation's longest running surveys of social, cultural, and political indicators.
Simmons Market Research Bureau (http://www.smrb.com)	Reports on the products American consumers buy, the brands they prefer, and their lifestyles, attitudes, and media preferences.
Yankelovich (http://www.yankelovich.com)	The *MONITOR* tracks consumer attitudes, values, and lifestyles shaping the American marketplace.

Social & Mobile Marketing 10.1

Nielsen Seeks to Track Viewership, regardless of the Media People Use to Watch[ii]

As television viewers have changed their practices—such that more and more people catch the latest shows on their tablets or smartphones rather than home-based television screens—marketing researchers have unfortunately failed to keep up. For example, Nielsen, the most famous provider of ratings that reflect people's viewing patterns, maintained two separate measures: one for regular television and one for online viewing. It had no metric for views through other forms of streaming media.

That gap may be about to disappear, though. In the immediate future, Nielsen plans to introduce a Twitter-based measure that will assess the number of tweets about a show as a measure of popularity. Its initial metric suggests that every tweet represents about 50 people watching the show, regardless of where or how.

Then next year it plans to introduce a mobile-linked measurement system. With this proprietary method, Nielsen will enable the networks to issue their content through mobile applications that contain a preexisting link back to Nielsen's data collection methods. When a viewer downloads the app with the content, Nielsen knows it and can add that viewership to the show's and its network's ratings.

Such measures are critical for content providers, because ratings determine advertising sales and rates. A show or network with higher ratings attracts more potential advertisers and can charge them more. In recent months, when the traditional ratings formats showed that viewership was declining, advertisers grew concerned. At the same time, the networks protested loudly that the ratings were undercutting the extent of their true market by ignoring the people watching on their tablets.

Nielsen's moves seek to address those complaints, but they also have sparked some new concerns. In particular, insufficient evidence exists to confirm whether Twitter numbers are really a good representation of viewership. Without strong support for the link between tweets and the actual popularity of a show, the new measure might be meaningless. In addition, the mobile system is not slated to be ready for at least another year. Even when it appears, some observers suggest that it could be blocked by security features in Apple operating systems that prevent metering software from running simultaneously with other programs.

Thus marketing researchers face a problem without a ready solution. They know that consumers are moving away from their televisions, but they have no idea how to measure what they do after those viewers move.

Consumer packaged-goods firms that sell to wholesalers often lack the means to gather pertinent data directly from the retailers that sell their products to consumers, which makes syndicated data a valuable resource for them. Some syndicated data providers also offer information about shifting brand preferences and product usage in households, which they gather from scanner data, consumer panels—and several other cutting-edge methods, as detailed in Social and Mobile Marketing 10.1.

Scanner data are used in quantitative research obtained from scanner readings of Universal Product Code (UPC) labels at checkout counters. Whenever you go into your local grocery store, your purchases are rung up using scanner systems. The data from these purchases are likely to be acquired by leading marketing research firms, such as IRI or Nielsen, which use this information to help leading consumer packaged-goods firms (e.g., Kellogg's, Pepsi, Kraft) assess what is happening in the marketplace. For example, a firm can use scanner data to determine what would happen to its sales if it reduced the price of its least popular product by 10 percent in a given month. In the test market in which it lowers the price, do sales increase, decrease, or stay the same?

Pepsi and other consumer packaged-goods firms use scanner data that are obtained from scannner readings of UPC labels at checkout counters to help make marketing decsions.

Syndicated external secondary data are acquired from scanner data obtained from scanner readings of UPC codes at check-out counters (left) and from panel data collected from consumers that electronically record their purchases (right).

Panel data are information collected from a group of consumers, organized into panels, over time. Data collected from panelists often include their records of what they have purchased (i.e., secondary data) as well as their responses to survey questions that the client gives to the panel firm to ask the panelists (i.e., primary data). Secondary panel data thus might show that when Diet Pepsi is offered at a deep discount, 80 percent of usual Diet Coke consumers switch to Diet Pepsi. Primary panel data could give insights into what they think of each option. We discuss how marketing researchers use scanner and panel data to answer specific research questions further in the primary data section.

Overall, though, both panel and scanner data, as well as their more advanced iterations gathered through social media and online usage patterns, provide firms with a comprehensive picture of what consumers are buying or not buying. The key difference between scanner research and panel research is how the data are aggregated. Scanner research typically focuses on weekly consumption of a particular product at a given unit of analysis (e.g., individual store, chain, region); panel research focuses on the total weekly consumption by a particular person or household.

Internal Secondary Data

Internally, companies also generate a tremendous amount of secondary data from their day-to-day operations. One of the most valuable resources such firms have at their disposal is their rich cache of customer information and purchase history. However, it can be difficult to make sense of the millions and even billions of pieces of individual data, which are stored in large computer files called data warehouses. For this reason, firms find it necessary to use data mining techniques to extract valuable information from their databases.

Data mining uses a variety of statistical analysis tools to uncover previously unknown patterns in the data or relationships among variables. Some

Marketers use data mining techniques to determine what items people buy at the same time so they can be promoted and displayed together.

retailers try to customize their product and service offerings to match the needs of their customers. For instance, the UK grocer Tesco uses its loyalty card to collect massive amounts of information about its individual customers. Every time a loyalty card member buys something, the card is scanned and the store captures key purchase data specific to that member. But these specific data are basically useless until Tesco mines and analyzes them to identify three income groups: upscale, middle income, and less affluent. With this mined information, Tesco has been able to create appealing private-label product offerings for each group, according to their preferences, and began targeting promotions to each customer according to his or her income classification.

Data mining can also enable a home improvement retailer such as Lowe's to learn that 25 percent of the time its customers buy a garden hose, they also purchase a sprinkler. With such information, the retailer may decide to put the garden hoses next to the sprinklers in the store. Outside the retail realm, an investment firm might use statistical techniques to group clients according to their income, age, type of securities purchased, and prior investment experience. This categorization identifies different segments to which the firm can offer valuable packages that meet their specific needs. The firm also can tailor separate marketing programs to each of these segments.

By analyzing the enormous amount of information that it possesses about its customers, companies have developed statistical models that help identify when a customer is dissatisfied with his or her service. Once the company identifies an unhappy customer, it can follow up and proactively address that customer's issues. By mining customer data and information, the company also reduced its churn levels. Churn is the number of participants who discontinue use of a service, divided by the average number of total participants. With this knowledge, the company can focus on what it does best. Overall, firms hope to use data mining to generate customer-based analytics that they can apply to their strategic decision making and thereby make good customers better and better customers their best. Firms can also use this information to assess the profitability of their customers by determining the customer lifetime value (CLV). We offer more details of calculating CLV in Appendix 10A.

Big Data The field of marketing research has seen enormous changes in the last few years because of (1) the increase in the amounts of data to which retailers, service providers, and manufacturers have access; (2) their ability to collect these data from transactions, customer relationship management (CMR) systems, websites, and social media platforms that firms increasingly use to engage with their customers;[7] (3) the ease of collecting and storing these data; (4) the computing ability readily available to manipulate data in real time; and (5) access to in-house or available software to convert the data into valuable decision-making insights using analytic dashboards.

To specify this explosion of data, which firms have access to but cannot handle using conventional data management and data mining software, the term big data has arisen in the popular media. Leading firms already are converting their big data into customer insights, such as Amazon, Netflix, Google, Nordstrom, Kroger, Tesco, Macy's, American Express, and Walmart—though this list also keeps growing.[8]

Amazon may be the poster child for big data. Any Amazon shopper is familiar with its recommendation engine, which notes what the consumer is purchasing, analyzes purchase patterns by similar customers, and suggests other items the customer might enjoy, as well as what other people who bought the focal item also added to their shopping carts.[9] With more than 200 million active customers and billions of pieces of shopping data,[10] Amazon certainly qualifies as a big data user; its item-to-item collaborative filtering helps it determine which relevant products to suggest, generating almost one-third of its sales.[11]

UK grocery retailer Tesco processes its data at a rate of approximately 100 customer baskets per second, to cover its 6 million daily transactions.[12] Furthermore, each purchased product can feature up to 45 data attributes: Is it Tesco's own brand, an ethnic recipe, exotic (e.g., star fruit) or basic (e.g., apple), and so on? On the basis of the attributes of the items customers purchase, Tesco filters them to define who they are, who else lives in their household, and what hobbies they have, then provides specific incentives that match these characteristics.[13]

To enable these efforts, firms such as SAP, Splunk, and GoodData offer a host of software solutions to help firms better integrate their data, visualize them, and then move from data to real-time insights.[14] The suite of options previously were available only to the largest firms, but with costs falling they are now more accessible to smaller firms.

The big data explosion also stems from the growth of online and social media. In response, Google, Facebook, and Twitter all provide analytic dashboards designed to help their customers understand their own web traffic. In particular, Google has developed tremendous marketing analytical capabilities that it makes available to partner firms. Google helps firms attract customer traffic to their sites through the use of more relevant keywords, the purchase of Google AdWords, and better conversion methods.[15] Using Google Analytics, Puma has gained insights into which online content and products most engaged its web visitors, while also defining where these visitors lived. With these visitor behavioral data in hand, Puma has revised its website to be more dynamic (http://www.Puma.Com) and has created unique identifies for its various product categories (e.g., PUMA Golf), targeting them in accordance with the home region of the visitor.[16]

As Superior Service 10.1 explains, sometimes the "internal" data can be gathered by a partner firm too, providing deeper insights than an individual firm can derive.

CHECK YOURSELF

1. What is the difference between internal and external secondary research?

Superior Service 10.1

Google Analytics Promises Movie Studios the Ability to Predict Performance, Weeks Prior to Opening[iii]

When a lot of movie watchers search for the trailer for a film in the month before the movie opens, it promises a bigger opening weekend. Such a claim might seem somewhat self-evident, but Google has announced that it has the means to quantify this effect and thereby help movie studios predict their profits, up to a month prior to the opening day.

More precisely, Google asserts that search volume for the movie title (combined with a few other metrics, such as the season and whether the movie is a franchise) offers a 94 percent accurate prediction of box office performance.

Other proprietary information that Google can use to predict success includes the volume of clicks on search ads. If, for example, one movie prompted 20,000 more paid clicks than another film, it will bring in approximately $7.5 million more in revenues during its opening weekend. Furthermore, the search effects are not limited to Google; YouTube searches reveal similar predictive information. From its analysis, Google recommends that studios need to go beyond just a one-week window, because studying the search and click trends for a month increases the accuracy and power of its predictions significantly.

Moving beyond the implications for opening weekend, Google asserts that weekday searches in the weeks leading up to the release offer better predictors of continued revenues. That is, if a film fan searches for a movie title on a Tuesday, she or he is more likely to hold off on seeing the movie, rather than rushing out during opening weekend. On a related note, Google notes that nearly half of all moviegoers choose the film they will see that night on the same day. Thus, studios need to maintain a marketing presence far past opening day, to be sure to catch the laggard customers' attention.

But unless the movie is a big name, an anticipated release, or a franchise, most people have no idea of what is coming to their local Cineplex. Instead, during weeks without a major movie release, Google notes that consumers undertake more generic searches to gather information about what new movies might be available. On average, these film buffs consider 13 sources of information before they select a specific film to watch.

Google analytics are increasingly used to predict the success of movies.

PRIMARY DATA COLLECTION TECHNIQUES

LO3 Describe the various primary data collection techniques.

In many cases, the information researchers need is available only through primary data or data collected to address specific research needs. Depending on the nature of the research problem, the primary data collection method can employ a *qualitative* or a *quantitative* research method.

As its name implies, qualitative research is used to understand the phenomenon of interest through broad, open-ended responses. It provides initial information that helps the researcher more clearly formulate the research objectives. Qualitative research is more informal than quantitative research methods and includes observation, following social media sites, in-depth interviews, and focus groups (see Exhibit 10.5, left side).

Once the firm has gained insights from doing qualitative research, it is likely to engage in quantitative research, which are structured responses that can be statistically tested. Quantitative research provides information needed to confirm insights and hypotheses generated via qualitative research or secondary data. It also helps managers pursue appropriate courses of action. Formal studies such as specific experiments, scanner and panel data, or some combination of these are quantitative in nature (see Exhibit 10.5, right side). We now examine each of these primary data collection techniques in order.

Observation Observation entails examining purchase and consumption behaviors through personal or video camera scrutiny, or by tracking their movements electronically as they move through a store. For example, researchers might observe customers while they shop or when they go about their daily lives, during which processes they use a variety of products. Observation can last for a very brief period of time (e.g., two hours watching teenagers shop for clothing in the mall), or it may take days or weeks (e.g., researchers live with families to observe their use of products). When consumers are unable to articulate their experiences, observation research becomes particularly useful; how else could researchers determine which educational toys babies choose to play with or confirm details of the buying process that consumers might not be able to recall accurately?

Although traditionally firms might videotape customers' movements, Microsoft's Kinect sensors are providing a less intrusive option. Discretely embedded in aisles of retail stores, the sensors provide three-dimensional spatial recognition. Thus retailers and their suppliers can unobtrusively track the amount of time people spend in front of a shelf, which products they touch or pick up, the products they return to shelves, and finally what they add to their carts purchase.[17] The data gathered can be used to improve store layouts because they can identify causes of slow-selling merchandise, such as poor shelf placement. By studying customers' movements, marketers can also learn where customers pause or move quickly or where there is congestion. This information

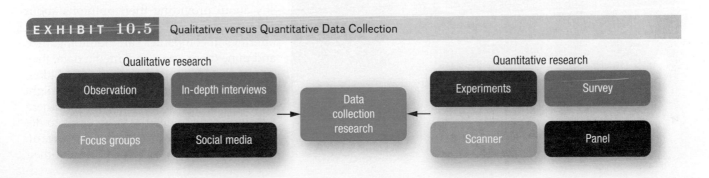

EXHIBIT 10.5 Qualitative versus Quantitative Data Collection

Qualitative research

Observation · In-depth interviews · Focus groups · Social media

→ Data collection research ←

Quantitative research

Experiments · Survey · Scanner · Panel

Using Microsoft Kinect sensors, firms like Shopperception create heatmaps of shopper interactions with the products (touches, pickups, and returns). The red represents the hot zones where shoppers touch the most, yellow less, and blue not at all.

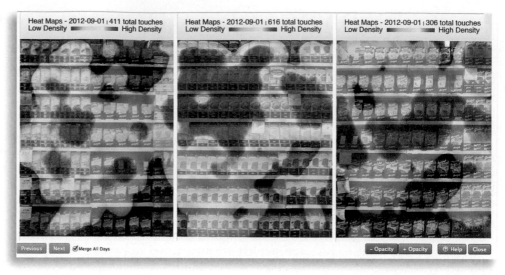

can help them decide if the layout and merchandise placement is operating as expected, such as whether new or promoted merchandise is getting the attention it deserves.

Observation may be the best method, and sometimes the only way, to determine how consumers might use a product, and therefore be useful for designing and marketing them. By watching women wash their hair in a rural town in China, Procter & Gamble recognized the fallacy of its assumption that the poorest consumers were interested only in functionality of a product—how to get hair clean. One woman struggled to find ways to wash her long hair effectively, even in the face of severe water shortages, rather than cut off what she considered the source of her beauty. Based on its research, P&G has added value by selling Rejoice shampoo inexpensively ($1.50) to a market that was using alternative options such as laundry detergent. Other observations pushed P&G to develop a more skin-sensitive laundry detergent after noting how many people in developing markets wash their clothes by hand.[18] These insights might be helpful, both for the company that gathers them and for consumers who ultimately benefit from better products.

By watching women in rural China wash their hair, Procter & Gamble learned that even their poorest customers wanted beautiful hair, but it has to be packaged affordably.

Social Media

Social media sites are a booming source of data for marketers. Marketers have realized that social media can provide valuable information that could aid their marketing research and strategy endeavors. In particular, contributors to social media sites rarely are shy about providing their opinions about the firm's own products or its competitors' offerings. If companies can monitor, gather, and mine these vast social media data, they can learn a lot about their customers' likes, dislikes, and preferences. They then might cross-reference such social media commentary with consumers' past purchases to derive a better sense of what they want. Customers also appear keen to submit their opinions about their friends' purchases, interests, polls, and blogs.

Blogs in particular represent valuable sources of marketing research insights. Marketers are paying attention to online reviews about everything from restaurants to running shoes to recycling. *The Truth About Cars* blog is known for its unflinchingly objective reviews of various makes and models as well as discussions about the industry as a whole, marketing tactics, and global competition,

among other topics.[19] Analyzing the content of this blog, and others like it, provides an excellent source of ideas and information for auto industry executives. Another creative use of social media for market research involves building online communities for companies. When it considered the launch of its South Beach product line, Kraft hired Communispace to create a virtual community (an online network of people who communicate about specific topics) of target consumers: 150 women who wanted to lose weight and 150 health and wellness opinion leaders. The participants openly shared their frustrations and difficulties managing their weight because the community environment prompted them to sense that everyone else on the site struggled with similar issues and concerns. By monitoring the community, Kraft learned that it would need to educate consumers about the South Beach Diet and offer products that could address cravings throughout the day, not just at mealtimes. Six months after the line's introduction, Kraft had earned profits of $100 million.[20]

When Kraft considered the launch of its South Beach product line, it created a virtual community of women who wanted to lose weight and "health and wellness" opinion leaders.

Noting these various opportunities and marketing research sources online, many companies—including Ford Motor Co., PepsiCo, Coca-Cola, and Southwest Airlines—have added heads of social media to their management teams. These managers take responsibility for scanning the web for blogs, postings, tweets, or Facebook posts in which customers mention their experience with a brand. By staying abreast of this continuous stream of information, companies can gather the most up-to-date news about their company, products, and services as well as their competitors. These social media searches allow companies to learn about customers' perceptions and resolve customer complaints they may never have heard about through other channels.

The data gathered through the searches also undergo careful analyses: Are customer sentiments generally positive, negative, or neutral? What sort of intensity or interest levels do they imply? How many customers are talking about the firm's products, and how many focus instead on competitors'? This data analysis is understandably challenging, considering the amount of data available online. However, monitoring consumer sentiments has grown easier with the development of social media monitoring platforms.

Using a technique known as sentiment mining, firms collect consumer comments about companies and their products on social media sites such as Facebook, Twitter, and online blogs. The data are then analyzed to distill customer attitudes toward and preferences for products and advertising campaigns. Scouring millions of sites by combining automated online search tools with text analysis techniques, sentiment mining yields qualitative data that provide new insight into what consumers really think. Companies plugged into this real-time information can become more nimble, allowing for quick changes in a product rollout or a new advertising campaign.[21]

In-Depth Interviews

In an in-depth interview, trained researchers ask questions and listen to and record the answers, and then pose additional questions to clarify or expand on a particular issue. For instance, in addition to simply watching teenagers shop for apparel, interviewers might stop them one at a time in the mall to ask them a few

Although relatively expensive, in-depth interviews can reveal information that would be difficult to obtain with other methods.

questions, such as: "We noticed that you went into and came out of Abercrombie & Fitch very quickly without buying anything. Why was that?" If the subject responds that no one had bothered to wait on her, the interviewer might ask a follow-up question like, "Oh? Has that happened to you before?" or "Do you expect more sales assistance there?"

In-depth interviews provide insights that help managers better understand the nature of their industry as well as important trends and consumer preferences, which can be invaluable for developing marketing strategies. Specifically, they can establish a historical context for the phenomenon of interest, particularly when they include industry experts or experienced consumers. They also can communicate how people really feel about a product or service at the individual level. Finally, marketers can use the results of in-depth interviews to develop surveys.

In-depth interviews are, however, relatively expensive and time-consuming. The interview cost depends on the length of the interaction and the characteristics of the people included in the sample. If the sample must feature medical doctors, for example, the costs of getting sufficient interviews will be much higher than the costs associated with intercepting teenagers in a mall.

Focus Group Interviews

In focus group interviews, a small group of persons (usually 8 to 12) come together for an intensive discussion about a particular topic. Using an unstructured method of inquiry, a trained moderator guides the conversation, according to a predetermined, general outline of topics of interest. Researchers usually record the interactions by videotape or audiotape so they can carefully comb through the interviews later to catch any patterns of verbal or nonverbal responses. In particular, focus groups gather qualitative data about initial reactions to a new or existing product or service, opinions about different competitive offerings, or reactions to marketing stimuli, like a new ad campaign or point-of-purchase display materials.[22]

To obtain new information to help it continue its innovative success derived from its introduction of low-sodium choices, Campbell Soup conducted extensive focus groups with female shoppers who indicated they would buy ready-to-eat soups. The groups clearly revealed the women's top priorities: a nutritious soup that contained the ingredients they would use if they made soup. They wanted, for example, white meat chicken, fresh vegetables, and sea salt. In addition, focus group participants were equally clear about what they did *not* want, like high fructose corn syrup, MSG, and other stuff whose names they could not even pronounce.[23]

The growth of online technology, as well as computer and video capabilities, have provided tremendous benefits for focus group research, which now often takes place online. Online focus group firms offer a secure site as a platform for companies to listen in on focus groups and even interact with consumers, without anyone having to travel. The client company not only saves costs but also gains access to a broader range of potential customers who live in various neighborhoods, states, or even countries.

CHECK YOURSELF

1. What are the types of qualitative research?

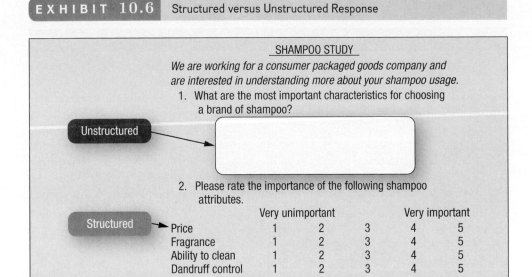

| EXHIBIT 10.6 | Structured versus Unstructured Response |

SHAMPOO STUDY

*We are working for a consumer packaged goods company and
are interested in understanding more about your shampoo usage.*

1. What are the most important characteristics for choosing
   a brand of shampoo?

Unstructured

2. Please rate the importance of the following shampoo
   attributes.

Structured

	Very unimportant				Very important
Price	1	2	3	4	5
Fragrance	1	2	3	4	5
Ability to clean	1	2	3	4	5
Dandruff control	1	2	3	4	5

Survey Research

Arguably the most popular type of quantitative primary collection method is a survey—a systematic means of collecting information from people using a questionnaire. A questionnaire is a document that features a set of questions designed to gather information from respondents and thereby accomplish the researchers' objectives. Individual questions on a questionnaire can be either unstructured or structured. Unstructured questions are open ended and allow respondents to answer in their own words. An unstructured question like "What are the most important characteristics for choosing a brand of shampoo?" yields an unstructured response. However, the same question could be posed to respondents in a structured format by providing a fixed set of response categories, such as price, fragrance, ability to clean, or dandruff control, and then asking respondents to rate the importance of each. Structured questions are closed-ended questions for which a discrete set of response alternatives, or specific answers, is provided for respondents to evaluate (see Exhibit 10.6).

Developing a questionnaire is part art and part science. The questions must be carefully designed to address the specific set of research questions. Moreover, for a questionnaire to produce meaningful results, its questions cannot be misleading in any fashion (e.g., open to multiple interpretations), and they must address only one issue at a time. They also must be worded in vocabulary that will be familiar and comfortable to those being surveyed. The questions should be sequenced appropriately: general questions first, more specific questions next, and demographic questions at the end. Finally, the layout and appearance of the questionnaire must be professional and easy to follow, with appropriate instructions in suitable places. For some tips on what *not* to do when designing a questionnaire, see Exhibit 10.7.[24]

Similar to focus groups, marketing surveys can be conducted either online or offline, but online marketing surveys offer researchers the chance to develop a database quickly with many responses, whereas offline marketing surveys provide a more direct approach that includes interactions with the target market. Web surveys have steadily grown as a percentage of all quantitative surveys. Online surveys have a lot to offer marketers with tight deadlines and small budgets.[25]

In particular, the response rates for online surveys are relatively high. Typical response rates run from 1 to 2 percent for

Survey research uses questionnaires to collect primary data. Questions can be either unstructured or structured.

EXHIBIT 10.7	What Not to Do When Designing a Questionnaire	
Issue	Good Question	Bad Question
Avoid questions the respondent cannot easily or accurately answer.	When was the last time you went to the grocery store?	How much money did you spend on groceries last month?
Avoid sensitive questions unless they are absolutely necessary.	Do you take vitamins?	Do you dye your gray hair?
Avoid double-barreled questions, which refer to more than one issue with only one set of responses.	1. Do you like to shop for clothing? 2. Do you like to shop for food?	Do you like to shop for clothing and food?
Avoid leading questions, which steer respondents to a particular response, irrespective of their true beliefs.	Please rate how safe you believe a BMW is on a scale of 1 to 10, with 1 being not safe and 10 being very safe.	BMW is the safest car on the road, right?
Avoid one-sided questions that present only one side of the issue.	To what extent do you believe fast food contributes to adult obesity using a five-point scale? 1: Does not contribute, 5: Main cause	Fast food is responsible for adult obesity. Agree/Disagree

Source: Adapted from A. Parasuraman, Dhruv Grewal, and R. Krishnan, *Marketing Research,* 2nd ed. (Boston: Houghton Mifflin, 2007), Ch. 10.

mail and 10 to 15 percent for phone surveys. For online surveys, in contrast, the response rate can reach 30 to 35 percent or even higher in business-to-business research. It also is inexpensive. Costs likely will continue to fall as users become more familiar with the online survey process. Results are processed and received quickly. Reports and summaries can be developed in real time and delivered directly to managers in simple, easy-to-digest reports, complete with color, graphics, and charts. Traditional phone or mail surveys require laborious data collection, tabulation, summary, and distribution before anyone can grasp their results.

Diverse online survey software, such as Qualtrics, SurveyMonkey, and Zoomerang, make it very easy to draft an online survey using questions from existing survey libraries. A survey link can be sent easily in an e-mail to potential respondents or panelists as well as posted on specific sites that are likely to attract the target audience or people who are willing to perform online work (e.g., Amazon's Mechanical Turk Site).

Panel- and Scanner-Based Research

As discussed previously, panel and scanner research can be either secondary or primary. In this section, we consider the use of a panel to collect primary data. Walmart's UK subsidiary Asda uses an 18,000-customer panel, which it calls Pulse of the Nation, to help determine which products to carry. Asda sends e-mails to each participant with product images and descriptions of potential new products. The customers' responses indicate whether they think each product should be carried in stores. As an incentive to participate, Asda enters respondents automatically in a drawing for free prizes.[26]

Experimental Research

Experimental research (an experiment) is a type of quantitative research that systematically manipulates

Walmart's U.K. subsidiary Asda uses an 18,000-customer panel, which it calls "Pulse of the Nation," to help determine which products to carry.

EXHIBIT 10.8	Hypothetical Pricing Experiment for McDonald's				
	1	2	3	4	5
Market	Unit Price	Market Demand at Price (in Units)	Total Revenue (Col. 1 × Col. 2)	Total Cost of Units Sold ($300,000 Fixed Cost + $2.00 Variable Cost)	Total Profits (Col. 3 ÷ Col. 4)
1	$4	200,000	$800,000	700,000	$100,000
2	5	150,000	750,000	600,000	150,000
3	6	100,000	600,000	500,000	100,000
4	7	50,000	350,000	400,000	(50,000)

one or more variables to determine which variables have a causal effect on other variables. For example, in our earlier scenario, one thing the hypothetical McDonald's research team was trying to determine was the most profitable price for a new menu combo item (hamburger, fries, and drink). Assume that the fixed cost of developing the item is $300,000 and the variable cost, which is primarily composed of the cost of the food itself, is $2. McDonald's puts the item on the menu at four prices in four markets. (See Exhibit 10.8.) In general, the more expensive the item, the less it will sell. But by running this experiment, the restaurant chain determines that the most profitable price is the second least expensive ($5). These findings suggest some people may have believed the most expensive item ($7) was too expensive, so they refused to buy it. The least expensive item ($4) sold fairly well, but McDonald's did not make as much money on each item sold. In this experiment, the changes in price likely caused the changes in quantities sold and therefore affected the restaurant's profitability.

Firms are also actively using experimental techniques on Facebook. Once a firm has created its Facebook page, it can devise advertisements and rely on Facebook's targeting options to deliver those ads to the most appropriate customer segments. To make sure the communication is just right, companies can experiment with alternative versions and identify which advertisement is most effective. State Bicycle Co., a manufacturer in Arizona, needed to determine what other interests its customers had, as well as who its main competitors were. Therefore, it tested a range of ads, targeting customers who searched for different bands (e.g., did more Arcade Fire or Passion Pit fans click their link?) and other bicycle manufacturers. With this information, it devised new contests and offerings on its own homepage to attract more of the visitors who were likely to buy.[27] Facebook tries to help its corporate clients

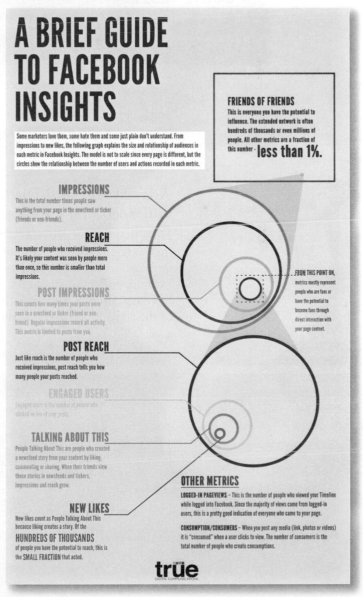

Facebook analytics help firms increase customer engagement.
Source: truedigital.com

Using an experiment, McDonald's would test the price of new menu items to determine which is the most profitable.

enhance their own customers' engagement and influence through a variety of options: check-ins, asking for customer comments, sharing information with friends, and so on.[28] It measures all these forms of data, contributing even further to the information businesses have about their page visitors.

LO4 Summarize the differences between secondary data and primary data.

Advantages and Disadvantages of Primary and Secondary Research

Now that we have discussed the various secondary and primary data collection methods, think back over our discussion and ask yourself what seem to be the best applications of each and when you would want to go to secondary sources or use primary collection methods. We can see that both primary data and secondary data have certain inherent and distinct advantages and disadvantages. For a summary of the advantages and disadvantages of each type of research, see Exhibit 10.9.

EXHIBIT 10.9   Advantages and Disadvantages of Secondary and Primary Data

Type	Examples	Advantages	Disadvantages
Secondary research	❑ Census data ❑ Sales invoices ❑ Internet information ❑ Books ❑ Journal articles ❑ Syndicated data	❑ Saves time in collecting data because they are readily available ❑ Free or inexpensive (except for syndicated data)	❑ May not be precisely relevant to information needs ❑ Information may not be timely ❑ Sources may not be original, and therefore usefulness is an issue ❑ Methodologies for collecting data may not be appropriate ❑ Data sources may be biased
Primary research	❑ Observed consumer behavior ❑ Focus group interviews ❑ Surveys ❑ Experiments	❑ Specific to the immediate data needs and topic at hand ❑ Offers behavioral insights generally not available from secondary research	❑ Costly ❑ Time consuming ❑ Requires more sophisticated training and experience to design study and collect data

CHECK YOURSELF

1. What are the types of quantitative research?
2. What are the advantages and disadvantages of primary and secondary research?

THE ETHICS OF USING CUSTOMER INFORMATION

 Examine the circumstances in which collecting information on consumers is ethical.

As we noted in Chapter 4, upholding strong business ethics requires more than a token nod to ethics in the mission statement. A strong ethical orientation must be an integral part of a firm's marketing strategy and decision making. It is particularly important for marketers to adhere to ethical practices when conducting marketing research. The American Marketing Association provides three guidelines for conducting marketing research: (1) It prohibits selling or fund-raising under the guise of conducting research, (2) it supports maintaining research integrity by avoiding misrepresentation or the omission of pertinent research data, and (3) it encourages the fair treatment of clients and suppliers.[29] Numerous codes of conduct written by various marketing research societies all reinforce the duty of researchers to respect the rights of the subjects in the course of their research. The bottom line: Marketing research should be used only to produce unbiased, factual information.

As technology continues to advance, the potential threats to consumers' personal information grow in number and intensity. Ethical and Societal Dilemma 10.1 discusses an interesting example of how retailers are using mannequins with hidden cameras to monitor shoppers. Marketing researchers must be vigilant to avoid abusing their access to these data. Security breaches at some of the United States' largest retailers, banks, credit-reporting services, and peer-to-peer networks have shown just how easily stored data can be abused.[30] From charitable giving to medical records to Internet tracking, consumers are more anxious than ever about preserving their fundamental right to privacy. They also demand increasing control over the information that has been collected about them.

Many firms voluntarily notify their customers that any information provided to them will be kept confidential and not given or sold to any other firm. As more firms adopt advanced marketing research technology, such as neuromarketing and facial recognition software, they also are working to ensure they receive permission from consumers. For example, Coca-Cola's neuromarketing experiments will record participants' faces as they watch advertisements or prototypes, then assess how their eyes moved, when they smiled or frowned, and so on—but only after those participants have agreed to be recorded.[31]

In contrast, consumers have little control over facial recognition software that allows companies to detect demographic information based on their appearances. For example, digital billboards embedded with such software can identify passersby and then display ads targeted to them based on their age, gender, and attention level.[32] The resulting communication is precisely targeted, which should make the advertisement more interesting to the consumer walking by—though it also could lead to embarrassing encounters. Imagine, for example, a teenager with skin problems having a billboard loudly broadcast an acne product ad as he walks by!

Several organizations, including the Center for Democracy & Technology (CDT) and the Electronic Privacy Information Center (EPIC), have emerged as watchdogs over data mining of consumer information. In addition, national and state governments in the United States play a part in protecting privacy. Companies are legally

Ethical & Societal Dilemma 10.1   Oh, Say, Can You See? The Implications of Mannequins That Capture Shoppers' Demographic Data[iv]

The basic elements of a new data gathering tool develop-ment for retailers are not in any real contention. By spending about $5,000 to purchase an EyeSee mannequin from a pro-vider called Almax, retailers gain not only a place to display clothing but also a discreet recording tool that indicates the genders, ages, and ethnicities of the customers who walk by the display.

Rather more controversial are the discussions about the implications of this innovation. On one side, consumer privacy advocates complain that the mannequins obtain information about shoppers without their permission. Although Almax as-serts that the technology embedded in the displays does not actually record the information, these commentators worry that the mannequins could be used to survey shoppers solely for the benefit of the retailer. Because the mannequins do not look any different from regular mannequins, shoppers have no way of knowing whether someone (or something) is watching them as they walk through the store. Furthermore, consumers have no control over what retailers do with the aggregated data.

On the other side, retailers note that because the manne-quins do not record, their use is no different from that of a closed-circuit system. Furthermore, some commentators argue that consumers should have no expectation of privacy in public spaces. Certainly, a staffer could similarly mark down people's ages, races, and genders as they walk through the shop doors. The electronic form simply does this work better and more accurately.

In implementing the new technology, one retailer recognized the predominance of Asian shoppers after about 4:00 p.m., so it hired more Chinese-speaking staffers to put on the floor to assist them. Another retailer realized that a lot of children were walking through its stores, so it added an entirely new children's clothing line to its offerings. Buoyed by its early suc-cesses, Almax also plans to add a function that would capture shoppers' conversations as they pass by the mannequins.

Current legislation allows retailers to maintain cameras and record customers for security purposes as long as they post warnings that customers might be recorded. However, the use of the mannequins is clearly for marketing purposes, not security. And most retailers seem to prefer to keep their usage of the new technology under wraps. Almax has not

Eye See mannequins do not record, nor store, any image, so the privacy of the customer is protected.

officially released the names of any of its clients—perhaps somewhat ironically, citing their need for privacy.

From your perspective as a consumer, do you believe that mannequins that record your movements, image, and possibly conversations in a store invade your privacy? If so, would you avoid stores that use this technology?

required to disclose their privacy practices to customers on an annual basis.[33] As the U.S. federal government has failed to enact comprehensive privacy laws for the In-ternet, several states are starting to consideration legislation. While this may be good for the consumer, companies will have to deal with adherence to a complex patchwork of different privacy regulations across the country, making business on the Internet harder to conduct.[34]

On Facebook, facial detection software applied to photographs eliminates the need for users to continue to tag the same people multiple times. It also stores all users' biometric data. **Biometric data** include one or more physical traits such as facial characteristics, iris scans, or fingerprints. Facebook users can turn off the facial detection function, but their biometric data are still collected. In Germany,

New and Improved... Labeling!
Campbell Soup used biometrics to analyze consumers' response to their label and changed the packaging to reflect their preferences revealed by the study.

New label

Old shelf label

CLASSIC FAVORITES

Cream of Potato

Campbell's
CONDENSED SOUP

CREAM of POTATO

Campbell's.
CONDENSED SOUP

Source: the company

The different varieties of soup were color-coded to help consumers distinguish them more easily.

Steam was added because people indicated they felt more emotionally engaged if the soup looked warm.

The spoon was removed. People thought it was unnecessary and had little emotional response to it.

The bowl was updated.

Eyetrack studies showed when the logo was placed at the top it drew too much attention and the red background also made all the labels look too similar.

Campbell's redesigned its cans based on information it obtained through neuro-marketing studies.

Source: Campbell Soup Company

with its strict privacy laws, regulators have demanded that Facebook stop collecting any biometric data.

Going even deeper than using biometric data, *neuromarketing* claims the ability to read consumers' minds using wireless electroencephalogram (EEG) scanners that measure the involuntary brain waves that occur when they view a product, advertisement, or brand images.[35] Such insights would be invaluable for marketers to discover what truly appeals to consumers. For example, based on results of a series of neuromarketing studies, Campbell's has recently changed its soup labels by shrinking the logo and emphasizing the soup to increase customers' emotional responses to the cans.[36] But as anyone who has ever seen a science fiction movie can imagine, the potential for abuses of such tools are immense. And a key question remains: Do any consumers want marketers reading their brain waves and marketing goods and services to them in a manner that bypasses their conscious thoughts? One firm, NeuroFocus, used neuromarketing techniques with several global firms to garner customer information that would be difficult, if not impossible, to obtain using more traditional research methods.

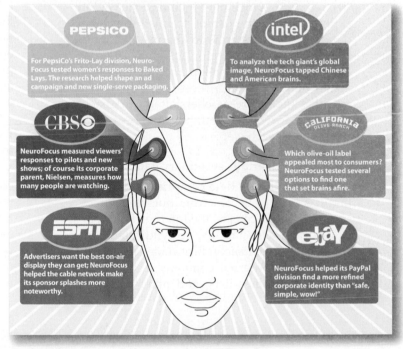

PEPSICO For PepsiCo's Frito-Lay division, Neuro-Focus tested women's responses to Baked Lays. The research helped shape an ad campaign and new single-serve packaging.

intel To analyze the tech giant's global image, NeuroFocus tapped Chinese and American brains.

CBS NeuroFocus measured viewers' responses to pilots and new shows; of course its corporate parent, Nielsen, measures how many people are watching.

CALIFORNIA OLIVE RANCH Which olive-oil label appealed most to consumers? NeuroFocus tested several options to find one that set brains afire.

ESPN Advertisers want the best on-air display they can get; NeuroFocus helped the cable network make its sponsor splashes more noteworthy.

ebay NeuroFocus helped its PayPal division find a more refined corporate identity than "safe, simple, wow!"

Findings from neuromarketing studies by NeuroFocus.

CHECK YOURSELF

1. Under what circumstances is it ethical to use consumer information in marketing research?
2. What challenges do technological advances pose for the ethics of marketing research?

Reviewing Learning Objectives

 Identify the five steps in the marketing research process.

The first step is to define objectives and research needs, which sounds so simple that managers often gloss over it. But this step is crucial to the success of any research project because, quite basically, the research must answer those questions that are important for making decisions. In the second step, designing the research project, researchers identify the type of data that are needed, whether primary or secondary, on the basis of the objectives of the project from Step 1, and then determine the type of research that enables them to collect those data. The third step involves deciding on the data collection process and collecting the data. The process usually starts with qualitative research methods such as observation, in-depth interviews, or focus groups. The information gleaned from the qualitative research is then used in quantitative research, which may include a survey, an experiment, or the use of scanner and panel data. The fourth step is to analyze and interpret the data and develop insights. The fifth and final step is to develop and implement an action plan. Although these steps appear to progress linearly, researchers often work backward and forward throughout the process as they learn at each step.

 Describe the various secondary data sources.

External secondary data comprise information that has been collected from outside sources, such as the U.S. census, the Internet, books, articles, trade associations, or syndicated data services. Internal secondary data can also be derived from internal company records such as sales, customer lists, and other company reports and are analyzed using data mining and big data software.

 Describe the various primary data collection techniques.

Primary data are collected to address specific research needs. Techniques used for primary qualitative research include observation, social media, in-depth interviews, and focus groups. Techniques used for primary quantitative research include surveys (both offline and online), scanner, panel, and experiments.

 Summarize the differences between secondary data and primary data.

Compared with primary research, secondary research is quicker, easier, and generally less expensive. However, if you are using secondary data using big data, then the investment in programs supporting secondary data can be expensive. However, because secondary research is collected for reasons other than those pertaining to the specific problem at hand, the information may be dated, biased, or simply not specific enough to answer the research questions. Primary research, in contrast, can be designed to answer very specific questions, but it also tends to be more expensive and time-consuming.

 Examine the circumstances in which collecting information on consumers is ethical.

Marketing researchers should gain permission to collect information on consumers, and it should be for the sole purpose of conducting marketing research endeavors. Information should not be collected under the guise of marketing research when the intent is to sell products or to fundraise. In addition, marketers must take responsibility for protecting any information they collect.

Key Terms

LEARNSMART

- big data, 315
- biometric data, 326
- churn, 314
- customer lifetime value (CLV), 335
- data, 309
- data mining, 313
- data warehouses, 313
- experiment, 322
- experimental research, 322
- focus group interview, 320
- in-depth interview, 319
- information, 309
- marketing research, 304
- observation, 317
- panel data, 313
- primary data, 307
- qualitative research, 317

Marketing Applications

1. A large hardware store collects data about what its customers buy and stores these data in a data warehouse. If you were the store's buyer for lawn equipment, what would you want to know from the data warehouse that would help you be a more successful buyer?

2. Identify a nonprofit organization that might use marketing research, and describe one example of a meaningful research project that it might conduct. Discuss the steps it should undertake in this project.

3. Marketing researchers do not always go through the steps in the marketing research process in sequential order. Provide an example of a research project that might not follow this sequence.

4. A sunglasses retailer is trying to determine if there is a significant market for its merchandise in a specific mall location where it is considering opening a store. It has an active Facebook page where customers routinely visit to get coupons, and comment on the latest sunglasses offered. How can this retailer use Facebook and Facebook Insights to decide if it should open the new store?

5. A consumer packaged-goods company (e.g., Pepsi) has just developed a new beverage. The company needs to estimate the demand for such a new product. What sources of syndicated data could it explore?

6. A bank manager notices that by the time customers get to the teller, they seem irritated and impatient. She wants to investigate the problem further, so she hires you to design a research project to figure out what is bothering the customers. The bank wants three studies: (a) several focus groups of their customers, (b) observation using a hidden camera, and (c) an online survey of 500 customers. Which studies are qualitative, and which are quantitative?

7. Best Buy has an extensive loyalty program, Best Buy Reward Zone, that allows it to track its customers' purchasing habits over time. How can Best Buy use these big data to improve sales?

8. Suppose your university wants to modify its course scheduling procedures to better serve students. What are some secondary sources of information that might be used to conduct research into this topic? Describe how these sources might be used. Describe a method you could use to gather primary research data about the topic. Would you recommend a specific order in obtaining each of these types of data? Explain your answer.

9. Manuel is planning to launch a new gourmet taco truck and is trying to decide where he should park his truck and what features and prices would entice consumers. He sends a request for proposal to four marketing research vendors, and three respond, as described in the table below. Which vendor should Manuel use? Explain your rationale for picking this vendor over the others.

Vendor A	Vendor B	Vendor C
The vendor that Manuel has used in the past estimates it can get the job done for $200,000 and in two months. The vendor plans to do a telephone-based survey analysis and use secondary data from the U.S. Census.	Manuel's key competitor has used this vendor, which claims that it can get the job done for $150,000 and in one month. This vendor plans to do a telephone-based survey analysis and use secondary data. During a discussion pertaining to its price and time estimates, the vendor indicates it will draw on insights it has learned from a recent report prepared for one of Manuel's competitors.	This well-known vendor has recently started to focus on the restaurant industry. It quotes a price of $180,000 and a time of one month. The vendor plans to conduct a web-based survey analysis and use secondary data.

Quiz Yourself

1. Walmart is known for its efficient logistical systems. Every time consumers buy something, that purchase is recorded and sent to company headquarters, where it is used to generate reorders to vendors. In addition, customers' billions of purchases are analyzed using data mining techniques to uncover _____.

   a. the impact of income tax laws

   b. patterns of consumers' purchasing behavior

   c. the relationship between primary and secondary data

   d. new ideas for human resources management

   e. competitors' pricing strategies

2. Just as marketers create value by meeting the needs and wants of consumers, marketing researchers create value if _____.

   a. the research is expensive

   b. all participants like the research design

   c. the research does not cost too much

   d. the results will be used in making management decisions

   e. the research is finished quickly

   (Answers to these two questions can be found on pages 651–652.)

Net Savvy

1. Go to the website for the marketing research company Kantar (http://www.kantar.com). Click on "Company News," and then click on one of the recent press releases. What types of research does Kantar conduct, and what types of insights does it develop for its clients?

2. The epinions.com website (http://www.epinions.com) is a clearinghouse for consumer reviews about different products and services. Think of a particular business with which you are familiar, and then review the ratings and comments for that business on the epinions website. Discuss the extent to which this site might be useful to a marketer for that company who needs to gather market research about the company and its competitors. Identify the type of research this process involves—secondary or primary.

Chapter Case Study

AUTOTRADER.COM: HOW RESEARCH SEPARATES FACT FROM FICTION

Imagine you are responsible for making next year's media buys for a large automobile dealership. You have your choice among traditional media, like television and newspaper advertising, and Internet-based channels, like social networking sites and automotive sites. How do you decide which types of advertising are most likely to build sales? How can you determine if an approach that works for a dealership in one city will work in another?

The online automobile dealer AutoTrader.com recognizes that convincing car dealers, associations, and manufacturers to advertise on its site requires proof that their media dollars will be well spent. To provide that proof, it offers the numbers that it collects from its website, which show that it hosts more than 3 million vehicle listings from 40,000 dealers and 250,000 private owners and more than 4 million qualified buyers each month.[37] But these basic quantitative details cannot prove that advertising on the site actually leads to sales. To accomplish that goal, AutoTrader.com also conducts market research to help dealers understand how people shop for cars and how the site can deliver those customers as an integral part of the car-shopping process.[38]

Many media buyers assume that the most accurate measure of the success of an online advertisement is click-through rates, that is, the number of clicks on an ad, divided by the number of times the ad gets shown. Although this measure indicates

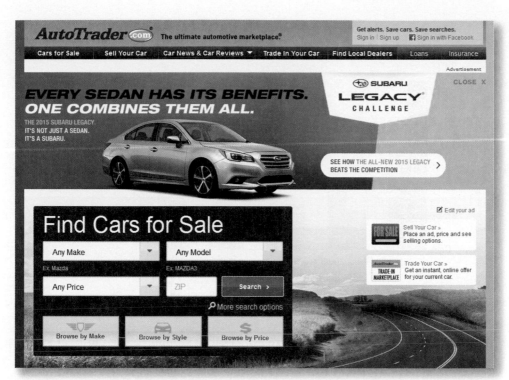

Buying or selling a car? Check out AutoTrader.com.

how many times an advertisement is viewed, it does not provide a reliable metric for the ad's impact on customer behavior, especially when it comes to making the final purchase decision. Car dealers also hold their own beliefs about their customers' behavior, which may be inaccurate but still determine their advertising choices. Therefore, to attract advertising dollars, AutoTrader.com needed to provide hard data, coming directly from the source—that is, the dealers and customers themselves.

The marketing research performed by AutoTrader.com mainly serves to demonstrate the value of the Internet for selling vehicles.[39] In a survey of recent car buyers, the company found that 71 percent of respondents consulted the Internet to facilitate their new or used car purchase. Most of these buyers reported that the Internet was the single most influential source behind their ultimate purchase choice, that it was the most helpful source of information, and that social media sites played only a small role in their final decision. The study also helped quantify other metrics surrounding car shopping behavior, such as the average length of time consumers spend shopping for a car and how much of that time involves Internet browsing versus visiting dealerships. The result—that buyers spend more than half their shopping time online—helped substantiate the value of advertising on AutoTrader.com. This finding was strengthened by further data showing that independent sites like AutoTrader were used more frequently than dealer or manufacturer sites.

Going even a step further, AutoTrader.com sought to connect advertising on its site to dealership visits, which represent the main goal of advertising on AutoTrader.com by car dealers. Marketing researchers first determined what dealers believed about their customers' behavior, using surveys. Then they gathered information from customers as they left dealerships, to find out the truth. To ensure accuracy and applicability, these researchers solicited customers of dealerships located in diverse markets, selling a variety brands, and operating as both franchises and independently. The results debunked a lot of conventional wisdom (see Exhibit 10.10). For example, newspaper advertising was less effective than dealers had imagined, but Internet advertising played a more significant role in driving walk-in traffic.

While this information might be true based on an average across national dealerships, some dealers believed it was not the case at their particular business. To help convince these skeptics, AutoTrader.com launched hundreds of mini–research studies, including phone interviews with car buyers from individual

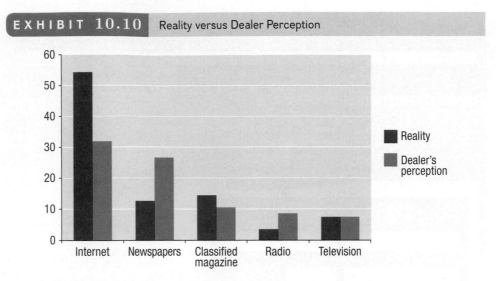

EXHIBIT 10.10   Reality versus Dealer Perception

Source: Adapted from: Joe Richard, "How AutoTrader.com. Uses Primary Research to Clarify the Car-Shopping Process," *Quirk's Marketing Research Review*, July 2011, p. 36, http://www.quirks.com/articles/2011/20110704.aspx.

stores. The results that emerged were remarkably similar to the national study, though some differences reflected geographic locations of the dealership.

Armed with this research, you are now confident that you understand the behavior of car buyers well enough to make your media buy. But can you be completely sure that marketing research accurately predicts customer behavior? Probably not, because human behavior depends on a vast array of factors, many of which cannot be measured. But marketing research can help you ensure that your advertising dollars are spent wisely and in ways that seem most likely to increase sales.

Questions

1.   What are the objectives of AutoTrader.com's marketing research? How have its research projects contributed to the firm's ability to meet these objectives?

2.   What methods has AutoTrader.com used to collect data about the effectiveness of dealer advertisements displayed on its site?

Endnotes

1. Brooks Barnes, "At Disney Parks, a Bracelet Meant to Build Loyalty (and Sales)," *The New York Times,* January 7, 2013, http://www.nytimes.com.

2. Christopher Palmeri, "Disney Bets $1 Billion on Technology to Track Theme-Park Visitors," *Bloomberg Businessweek,* March 7, 2014, http://www.businessweek.com.

3. Jack Honomichl, "The 2013 Honomichl Global Top 25 Report," August 25, 2013.

4. Detailed illustrations of scales are provided in two books: Gordon C. Bruner, *Marketing Scales Handbook: A Compilation of Multi-Item Measures,* vol. 7 (Carbondale, IL: GCBII Productions, Fort Worth, TX: 2013); William O. Bearden, Richard G. Netemeyer, and Kelly L. Haws, *Handbook of Marketing Scales: Multi-Item Measures for Marketing and Consumer Behavior Research* (Thousand Oaks, CA: Sage, 2011).

5. For a more thorough discussion of effective written reports, see A. Parasuraman, Dhruv Grewal, and R. Krishnan, *Marketing Research,* 2nd ed. (Boston: Houghton Mifflin, 2007), Ch. 16.

6. John Cloud, "McDonald's Chef: The Most Influential Cook in America?" *Time,* February 22, 2010, http://www.time.com.

7. Jeff Kelly, "Big Data: Hadoop, Business, Analytics, and Beyond," *Wikibon,* February 5, 2014, http://wikibon.org.

8. Rachel Wolfson, "Retailers Using Big Data: The Secret Behind Amazon and Nordstrom's Success," *Big Data News,* December 11, 2014, http://www.bigdatanews.com.

9. "How Amazon Is Leveraging Big Data," *BigData Startups,* http://www.bigdata-startups.com/BigData-startup/amazon-leveraging-big-data/.

10. Amazon, http://www.amazon.com.

11. Wolfson, "Retailers Using Big Data."

12. "Tesco Doubles Customer Rewards in Further Boost to Clubcard," press release, August 14, 2009.

13. Jenny Davey, "Every Little Bit of Data Helps Tesco Rule Retail," *TimesOnline.com,* October 4, 2009.

14. Quentin Hardy, "Big Data Picks Up the Pace," *The New York Times,* March 5, 2014, http://bits.blogs.nytimes.com.

15. Google, "Analytic Guide," http://www.google.com.

16. Google, "Puma Kicks Up Order Rate 7% with Insights from Google Analytics and Viget," case study, 2013.

17. "In Retail Stores, Research Tool Uses Kinect to Track Shoppers' Behavior," *Retail*, December 29, 2011, http://www.springwise.com.

18. Jennifer Reingold, "Can P&G Make Money in a Place Where People Earn $2 Per Day?" *CNN Money*, January 6, 2011, http://features.blogs.fortune.cnn.com.

19. http://www.thetruthaboutcars.com/.

20. "Client Story: Kraft," http://www.communispace.com.

21. Rachael King, "Sentiment Analysis Gives Companies Insight into Consumer Opinion," *Bloomberg Businessweek*, March 1, 2011, http://www.businessweek.com.

22. Richard A. Krueger and Mary Anne Casey, *Focus Groups: A Practical Guide for Applied Research* (Thousand Oaks, CA: Sage, 2009).

23. http://www.campbellsoup.com.

24. Adapted from Parasuraman et al., *Marketing Research*, Ch. 10.

25. Floyd J. Fowler, *Survey Research Methods* (Thousand Oaks, CA: Sage, 2009); Don A. Dillman, Glenn Phelps, Robert Tortora, Karen Swift, Julie Kohrell, Jodi Berck, and Benjamin L. Messer, "Response Rate and Measurement Differences in Mixed-Mode Surveys Using Mail, Telephone, Interactive Voice Response (IVR) and the Internet," *Social Science Research* 38 (March 2009), pp. 1–18.

26. https://pulse.asda.com; "Asda Wins Vision Critical's European Insight Community Award," press release, *Research*, September 30, 2013, http://www.research-live.com/news/.

27. Facebook, "State Bicycle Co.: Building a Strong Customer Base," case study, https://www.facebook.com/advertising/success-stories/state-bicycle.

28. Facebook, https://www.facebook.com/business/a/online-sales.

29. http://www.marketingpower.com/AboutAMA/Pages/Statement%20of%20Ethics.aspx; http://www.helleniccomserve.com.

30. Federal Trade Commission, "Widespread Data Breaches Uncovered by FTC Probe: FTC Warns of Improper Release of Sensitive Consumer Data on P2P File-Sharing Networks," February 22, 2010, http://www.ftc.gov.

31. Roger Dooley, "Neuromarketing: for Coke, It's the Real Thing," *Forbes*, March 7, 2013, http://www.forbes.com.

32. Natasha Singer, "Face Recognition Makes the Leap from Sci-Fi," *The New York Times*, November 12, 2011.

33. Cecilia Kang, "Library of Congress Plan for Twitter: A Big, Permanent Retweet," *The Washington Post*, April 16, 2010; http://www.cdt.org; Mark Penn, "Did Google Violate Privacy Laws?" http://www.politicallyillustrated.com, April 2, 2010; Lona M. Farr, "Whose Files Are They Anyway? Privacy Issues for the Fundraising Profession," *International Journal of Non-profit and Voluntary Sector Marketing* 7, no. 4 (November 2002), p. 361.

34. Somini Sengupta, "No U.S. Action, So States Move on Privacy Law," *The New York Times*, October 30, 2013, http://www.nytimes.com.

35. MP Mueller, "The Secret of Neuromarketing: Go for the Pain," *The New York Times*, August 7, 2012, http://www.nytimes.com.

36. Ilan Brat, "The Emotional Quotient of Soup Shopping," *The Wall Street Journal*, February 17, 2010, http://online.wsj.com.

37. http://www.autotrader.com.

38. Joe Richards, "How AutoTrader.com Uses Primary Research to Clarify the Car-Shopping Process," *Quirk's Marketing Research Review* (July 2011), p. 36, http://www.quirks.com.

39. Bruce Giffin and Joe Richards, "The Role of the Internet in the New and Used Vehicle Purchase Process," *Polk View*, February 2011, http://www.industryrelations.autotrader.com.

i. Ashley Lutz, "McDonald's Comes Even Closer to Offering a 24-Hour Breakfast," *Business Insider*, June 6, 2013; Robert Lara, "The True Steamy Story of the Egg McMuffin Hockey Puck Breakfast Turns 40," Adweek.com, August 9, 2013.

ii. Amol Sharma and Suzanne Vranica, "Nielsen to Add Data for Mobile TV Viewing," *The Wall Street Journal*, September 19, 2013.

iii. Kirsten Acuna, "Google Says It Can Predict Which Films Will Be Huge Box Office Hits," *Business Insider*, June 6, 2013.

iv. Andrew Roberts, "In Some Stores, the Mannequins Are Watching You," *Bloomberg Businessweek*, December 6, 2012, http://www.businessweek.com; Amar Toor, "EyeSee Mannequin Silently Collects Customer Data for Overzealous Retailers," *The Verge*, November 20, 2012, http://www.theverge.com; Joanna Stern, "Department Store Mannequins Are Watching You. No, Really," *ABC News*, November 26, 2012, http://abcnews.go.com.

Credits

USING SECONDARY DATA TO ASSESS CUSTOMER LIFETIME VALUE (CLV)

This appendix examines how secondary data from customer transactions can help determine the value of a customer over time. Specifically, **customer lifetime value** (CLV) refers to the expected financial contribution from a particular customer to the firm's profits over the course of their entire relationship.[1]

To estimate CLV, firms use past behaviors to forecast future purchases, the gross margin from these purchases, and the costs associated with servicing the customers. Some costs associated with maintaining customer relationships include communicating with customers through advertising, personal selling, or other promotional vehicles to acquire their business initially and then retain them over time.

Measures of customer lifetime value typically apply to a group or segment of customers and use available secondary data. A basic formula for CLV, with the assumption that revenues and profits arrive at the start of the year, is as follows:[2]

$$CLV = \frac{\sum_{t=1}^{T} [\text{profit at t} \times \text{retention rate}^{t-1}]}{(1 + i)^{t-1}} - \text{acquisition costs}$$

To implement this CLV formula, we must answer the following questions:

1. How many years (t) can we expect to do business with a customer? The total number of years is denoted by T.

2. What can we expect the annual profits to be from an individual customer or an average

customer? These profits are based on sales minus the costs of merchandise and the costs of serving and retaining the customer.

3. What is the retention rate, that is, the average percentage of customers who continue to purchase from the firm from one time period to another? A 90 percent retention rate means that if we have 100 customers in the first year, we will have 90 at the beginning of the second year.

4. What is the discount rate (i)? The discount rate is based on the idea that a dollar is worth less in the future than it is today, so the company can use it to adjust future profits and determine a customer's value today for the customer's purchases in the future. For example, if the discount rate is 10 percent, $100 in profits at the beginning of year 2 are worth only $90.91 (100/(1 + .1)) at the beginning of year 1.

Consider Gregory Missoni, a fairly new client of Very Clean Cleaners who switched from his other dry cleaner because Very Clean sent him $100 worth of coupons in a direct mailing.

● ● ●

Greg just picked up his $200 shirt from Very Clean and found that the dry cleaner had broken a brown button and replaced it with a white button. When he complained, the clerk acted as if it were no big deal. Greg explained to the clerk that it was a very expensive shirt that deserved more careful handling, then asked to speak with the manager. At this point, how important is it for the manager to make sure Greg is satisfied, so that he will continue to bring his dry cleaning to Very Clean Cleaners? To answer this question, the manager uses the following information:

■ It cost Very Clean $100 to acquire Greg as a customer. Thus, the acquisition cost is $100.

■ Very Clean expects Greg to remain a client for 5 years (time horizon T = 5 years).

■ Very Clean expects to make a $1,000 profit each year from Greg's dry cleaning.

■ On average, 10 percent of customers defect to another cleaner each year. Therefore, the expected retention rate is 90 percent.

■ The discount rate is 10 percent per year (i in this illustration). For simplicity, Very Clean assumes all profits are accrued at the beginning of the year.

Very Clean Cleaners should consider a customer's lifetime value to determine its service levels.

Applying the formula, such that CLV equals the profits from years 1–5, less the acquisition costs, we obtain:

$$CLV = \frac{\$1,000 \times (.90)^0}{(1 + .1)^0} + \frac{\$1,000 \times (.90)^1}{(1 + .1)^1} + \frac{\$1,000 \times (.90)^2}{(1 + .1)^2}$$
$$\text{Year 1} \qquad\qquad \text{Year 2} \qquad\qquad \text{Year 3}$$

$$\frac{\$1,000 \times (.90)^3}{(1 + .1)^3} + \frac{\$1,000 \times (.90)^4}{(1 + .1)^4} - \$100$$
$$\text{Year 4} \qquad\qquad \text{Year 5}$$

Or

$$CLV = \$1,000 + \$818.2 + \$669.4 + \$547.7 + \$448.1 - \$100 = \$3,383.40$$

Let's see how the formula works. The expected profit from Greg is $1,000 per year. Very Clean assumes profits accrue at the beginning of the year, so the profits for the first year equal $1,000; they are not affected by the retention rate or the discount rate.

However, the retention and discount rates have effects on the profits for the subsequent time periods. In the second year, the retention rate, which Very Clean determined was 90 percent (i.e., 90 percent of customers continue to do business with it) modifies profits, such that expected profits in the second year equal $1,000 × 90% = $900. Moreover, the discount rate is applied such that the profits received in the second year are worth less than if they had been received in the first year. Therefore, the $900 received at the beginning of the second year must be divided by 1.1, which is equivalent to $818.20.

Using similar calculations for the third year, the expected profits adjusted for retention are $1,000 × .9 × .9 = $810. The discount rate then reduces the profit to $810 ÷ $1.1^2 = $669.40 in today's dollars. (Note that the discount rate is squared because it refers to two years in the future.) After calculating the adjusted and discounted profits for the fourth and fifth years in similar fashion, we realize the sum of estimated discounted profits for five years is $3,483.40. However, we still must subtract the $100 spent to acquire Greg, which provides a CLV of $3,383.40.

According to this analysis, it would be a good idea for the manager to take a long-term perspective when evaluating how to respond to Greg's complaint about his button. Greg cannot be viewed as a $2.50 customer, as he would be if Very Clean determined his value based on the cost of laundering his shirt, nor should he be viewed as a $200 customer, based on the cost of the shirt. He actually is worth a lot more than that.

For illustrative purposes, we have simplified the CLV calculations in this example. We assumed that the average profits remain constant at $1,000. But firms usually expect profits to grow over time or else grow, level off, and then perhaps decline. Retention costs, such as special promotions used to keep Greg coming back, also do not appear in our illustration, though such additional costs would reduce annual profits and CLV. Finally, we assume a five-year time horizon; the CLV obviously would differ for longer or shorter periods. For an infinite time horizon, with first period payments upfront, the formula becomes fairly simple:[3]

$$CLV = profits \times \left[1 + \frac{\text{retention rate}}{(\$1 + \text{discount rate} + \text{retention rate})}\right]$$
$$- \text{ acquisition costs}$$

$$= \$1,000 \times \left[1 + \frac{.9}{(1 + .1 - .9)}\right] - \$100$$

$$= \$1,000 \times (1 + 4.5) - \$100$$

$$= \$5,500 - \$100 = \$5,400$$

This illustration thus explains how firms can use secondary data to calculate CLV; it further demonstrates the importance of knowing a customer's lifetime value when executing marketing tactics and strategies.

Endnotes

1. V. Kumar, A. Petersen and R. P. Leone, "How Valuable Is Word of Mouth?" *Harvard Business Review,* October 2007, pp. 139–46; V. Kumar and M. George, "Measuring and Maximizing Customer Equity: A Critical Analysis," *Journal of the Academy of Marketing Science* 35, no. 2 (June 2007), pp. 157–71; V. Kumar, D. Shah, and R. Venkatesan, "Managing Retailer Profitability: One Customer at a Time!" *Journal of Retailing* 82, no. 4 (October 2006), pp. 277–294; V. Kumar, "Profitable Relationships," *Marketing Research: A Magazine of Management and Applications* 18, no. 3 (Fall 2006), pp. 41–46; V. Kumar, "Customer

Lifetime Value: A Databased Approach," *Journal of Relationship Marketing* 5, no. 2/3 (2006), pp. 7–35; S. Gupta, D. Hanssens, B. Hardie, W. Kahn, V. Kumar, N. Lin, N. Ravishanker, and S. Sriram, "Modeling Customer Lifetime Value," *Journal of Service Research* 9 (November 2006), pp. 139–55; V. Kumar, R. Venkatesan, and W. Reinartz, "Knowing What to Sell, When and to Whom," *Harvard Business Review*, March, 2006, pp. 131–37; W. Reinartz, J. Thomas, and V. Kumar, "Balancing Acquisition and Retention Resources to Maximize Profitability," *Journal of Marketing* 69 (January 2005), pp. 63–79; R. Venkatesan and V. Kumar, "A Customer Lifetime Value Framework for Customer Selection and Resource Allocation Strategy," *Journal of Marketing* 68 (October 2004), pp. 106–25; V. Kumar and J. A. Petersen, "Maximizing ROI or Profitability: Is One Better Than the Other," *Marketing Research: A Magazine of Management and Applications* 16, no. 3 (Fall 2004), pp. 28–34; V. Kumar, G. Ramani, and T. Bohling, "Customer Lifetime Value Approaches and Best Practice Applications," *Journal of Interactive Marketing* 18, no. 3 (Summer 2004), pp. 60–72; J. Thomas, Werner Reinartz, and V. Kumar, "Getting the Most Out of All Your Customers," *Harvard Business Review* (July–August 2004), pp. 116–23; Werner Reinartz and V. Kumar, "The Impact of Customer Relationship Characteristics on Profitable Lifetime Duration," *Journal of Marketing* 67 (January 2003), pp. 77–99; W. Reinartz and V. Kumar, "The Mismanagement of Customer Loyalty," *Harvard Business Review* (July 2002), pp. 86–97; W. Reinartz and V. Kumar, "On the Profitability of Long Lifetime Customers: An Empirical Investigation and Implications for Marketing," *Journal of Marketing* 64 (October 2000), pp. 17–32.

2. We have made some minor adjustments to the formula suggested by Gupta et al., "Modeling Customer Lifetime Value."

3. S. Gupta and D. R. Lehmann, *Managing Customers as Investments* (Philadelphia, PA: Wharton School Publishing, 2005); Gupta et al., "Modeling Customer Lifetime Value."

VALUE CREATION

Section Four devotes three chapters to how marketing contributes to value creation. Chapter 11 and Chapter 12 explore strategies and tactics in the development and management of successful products and their brands. Although many of the concepts involved in developing and managing services are similar to those of physical brands, Chapter 13 addresses the unique challenges of the marketing of services.

PRODUCT, BRANDING, AND PACKAGING DECISIONS

To convey its brand of unconscious cool and radical adventure, Red Bull embraces daredevil stunts but also seeks to avoid making it look as if it is trying too hard to promote itself in so doing. Thus its branding operations walk a delicate line: Make a name for the brand but without appearing to do so.

Consider the Red Bull Stratos project. Over a period of approximately five years, Red Bull bankrolled the experimental development of a flight suit that would enable daredevil and skydiver Felix Baumgartner to free fall from 24 miles up, break the sound barrier, and still survive his jump from space.[1] More than 70 technicians, physicians, and scientists worked for years on the project, ultimately allowing Baumgartner to jump successfully in October 2012.

A camera mounted on his helmet recorded the entire experience, including the early moments, when he spun out of control in the thin stratosphere, until nearly five minutes later, when he landed. Approximately 8 million people watched the jump live. Then the video, along with associated footage of the efforts to prepare for the jump, began to enjoy its really massive viral popularity. People wowed at the sight of a man flying through space, literally. They shared links, and mainstream media reported on both the event and the footage.

Despite this popularity, Red Bull purposefully chose not to enter the Stratos marketing communication in any award competitions for best advertising, noting, "Our approach towards communications is that we don't really talk about ourselves too much. Rather, we focus on what we do—the events we create and produce and the athletes we support—versus who we are. With this guiding principle, we do not submit for awards very often."[2]

Rather, the company has continually sought to reinforce its image as a cutting-edge, danger-seeking, boundary-pushing entity. The data gathered through the Stratos project are being made available to pilots and astronauts who might need to bail out of a disabled aircraft. The newly designed space suit also revealed that it could protect the human body against the extreme conditions in the stratosphere. The medical director of the project, who previously was in charge of ensuring the health of NASA's space shuttle crews, noted, "We're pushing the technical envelope" with regard to space jumps.

Pushing the envelope is just what Red Bull wants its brand to be known for doing. By sponsoring events such as the space jump or even its annual Flugtag competition, Red Bull brands itself as fun, a little crazy, and ready for anything. But by letting the events speak largely for themselves, rather than promoting its participation in a traditional sense, it also maintains an image of slightly detached cool. It hopes that consumers who would like to think of themselves the same way will find this branding deeply compelling.

As a key element of a firm's marketing mix (the four Ps), product strategies are central to the creation of value for the consumer. A product is anything that is of value to a consumer and can be offered through a voluntary marketing exchange. In addition to goods, such as soft drinks, or services, such as a stay in a hotel, products might be places (e.g., Six Flags theme parks), ideas (e.g., stop smoking), organizations (e.g., MADD), people (e.g., Oprah Winfrey), or communities (e.g., Facebook) that create value for consumers in their respective competitive marketing arenas.

This chapter begins with a discussion of the complexity and types of products. Next we examine how firms adjust their product lines to meet and respond to changing market conditions. Then we turn our attention to branding—why are brands valuable to the firm, and what are the different branding strategies firms use? We also never want to underestimate the value of a product's package and label. These elements should send a strong message from the shelf: Buy me! The final section of this chapter examines packaging and labeling issues.

 **LO1** Describe the components of a product.

COMPLEXITY AND TYPES OF PRODUCTS

Complexity of Products

There is more to a product than its physical characteristics or its basic service function. Marketers involved with the development, design, and sale of products think of them in an interrelated fashion, as depicted in Exhibit 11.1. At the center is the

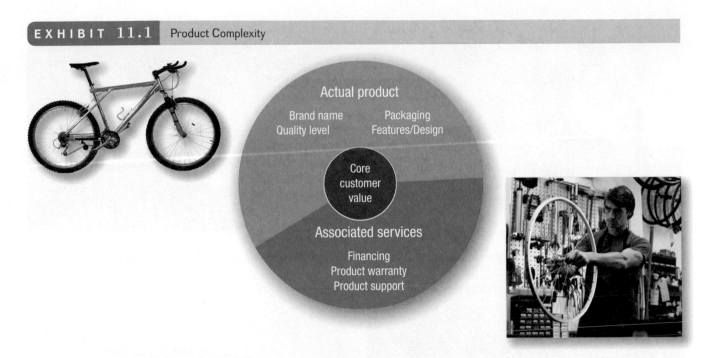

EXHIBIT 11.1   Product Complexity

Actual product

Brand name   Packaging
Quality level   Features/Design

Core
customer
value

Associated services

Financing
Product warranty
Product support

core customer value, which defines the basic problem-solving benefits that consumers are seeking. When Mars manufactures M&M's, Snickers, and other confectionary products, or when Trek designs bicycles, each company's core question is, what are customers looking for? With Mars, is it a sweet, great tasting snack, or is it an energy boost? With Trek, is the bike being used for basic green transportation (a cruiser), or is it for speed and excitement (a road, hybrid, or mountain bike)?

Marketers convert core customer value into an actual product. Attributes such as the brand name, features/design, quality level, and packaging are important, but the level of their importance varies, depending on the product. The Trek Madone 7 Series, for instance, is positioned as "see how fastest feels."[3] It features a carbon frame that is light, stiff, and comfortable; an advanced shifting system; and other high-tech features. Not only is it beautiful to look at, but customers can choose from three fits—pro, performance, and touring.

The associated services in Exhibit 11.1, also referred to as the augmented product, include the nonphysical aspects of the product, such as product warranties, financing, product support, and after-sale service. The amount of associated services also varies with the product. The associated services for a package of M&M's may include only a customer complaint line, which means they are relatively less important than the associated services for a Trek bicycle. The frame of the Madone 7 Series bicycle is guaranteed for the lifetime of the original owner. Trek sells its bikes only in shops that have the expertise to service them properly. Every possible consumer question is answered on Trek's comprehensive website. Trek even has a financing program that allows customers to purchase a new bike on credit.

When developing or changing a product, marketers start with the core customer value to determine what their potential customers are seeking. Then they make the actual physical product and add associated services to round out the offering.

Types of Products

 Identify the types of consumer products.

Marketers consider the types of products they are designing and selling because these types affect how they will promote, price, and distribute their products. There are two primary categories of products and services that reflect who buys them: consumers or businesses. Chapter 7 discussed products for businesses. Here we discuss consumer products.

A medical professional is a specialty service. Apparel is a shopping product. Soda is a convenience product. Insurance is an unsought service.

Consumer products are products and services used by people for their personal use. Marketers further classify consumer products by the way they are used and how they are purchased.

Specialty Products/Services Specialty products/services are those for which customers express such a strong preference that they will expend considerable effort to search for the best suppliers. Road bike enthusiasts, like those interested in the Trek Madone 7 Series, devote lots of time and effort to selecting just the right one. Other examples might include luxury cars, legal or medical professionals, or designer apparel.

Shopping Products/Services Shopping products/services are products or services for which consumers will spend a fair amount of time comparing alternatives, such as furniture, apparel, fragrances, appliances, and travel alternatives. When people need new sneakers, for instance, they often go from store to store shopping—trying shoes on, comparing alternatives, and chatting with salespeople.

Convenience Products/Services Convenience products/services are those products or services for which the consumer is not willing to expend any effort to evaluate prior to purchase. They are frequently purchased commodity items, usually bought with very little thought, such as common beverages, bread, or soap.

Unsought Products/Services Unsought products/services are products or services that consumers either do not normally think of buying or do not know about. Because of their very nature, these products/services require lots of marketing effort and various forms of promotion. When new-to-the-world products are first introduced, they are unsought products. Do you have cold hands and don't know what to do about it? You must not have heard yet of HeatMax HotHands Hand Warmers, air-activated packets that provide warmth for up to 10 hours. Do you have an internship in a less developed country and your regular insurance cannot give you the coverage you may need in case of an emergency? You now can turn to a Medex insurance policy.

> ## CHECK YOURSELF
>
> 1. Explain the three components of a product.
> 2. What are the four types of consumer products?

PRODUCT MIX AND PRODUCT LINE DECISIONS

 **LO3** Explain the difference between a product mix's breadth and a product line's depth.

The complete set of all products and services offered by a firm is called its **product mix**. An abbreviated version of BMW's product mix appears in Exhibit 11.2. The product mix typically consists of various **product lines**, which are groups of associated items that consumers tend to use together or think of as part of a group of similar products or services. BMW's product lines (brands) include BMW, cars targeted at middle-aged professionals; the MINI, cars targeted to the young adult market; Rolls-Royce, cars targeted at the ultra-wealthy market; and BMW Motorrad, its motorcycle line.

The product mix reflects the breadth and depth of the company's product lines. A firm's product mix **breadth** represents a count of the number of product lines offered by the firm; BMW has four, as indicated by the four columns in Exhibit 11.2. Product line **depth**, in contrast, equals the number of products within a product line. Within BMW's Rolls-Royce brand, for example, it offers Phantom, Wraith, and Ghost models.

However, adding unlimited numbers of new products can have adverse consequences. Too much breadth in the product mix becomes costly to maintain, and too many brands may weaken the firm's reputation.[4] With more products and product lines, the firm must keep track of trends and developments in various industries, which might tax its resources. For example, when it realized just how dynamic and changing the global PC market had become, Sony made the strategic choice to sell off, or divest itself of, any PC business. In so doing, it gained more flexibility and could assign more resources and attention to its smartphone and tablet product lines.[5]

E X H I B I T 11.2	Abbreviated List of BMW Product Mix		

Product Lines			
BMW	**MINI**	**Rolls-Royce**	**Motorrad**
2 Series	Clubman	Ghost	C Series
3 Series	Convertible	Phantom	F Series
4 Series	Countryman	Wraith	G Series
5 Series	Coupe		K Series
6 Series	Hardtop		R Series
7 Series	John Cooper Works		S Series
X Series	Paceman		
Z4 Series	Roadster		
M Series			
BMW i			
Hybrid			

BMW's MINI product line targets young adults.

So why do firms change their product mix's breadth or depth?[6]

Increase Depth Firms might add items to address changing consumer preferences or to preempt competitors while boosting sales (see the addition of product A4 in Exhibit 11.3). At Taco Bell, the addition of new varieties of its Doritos Locos Tacos enable it to appeal better to consumers who enjoy spicy foods or love Cool Ranch flavor. The tacos still contain the same ingredients, but the availability of 123 different Doritos flavors significantly increases the product line's depth.[7] Social and Mobile Marketing 11.1 describes another extension in a product market, as Axe expands its fragrance product line to create a version for women.

EXHIBIT 11.3   Changes to a Product Mix

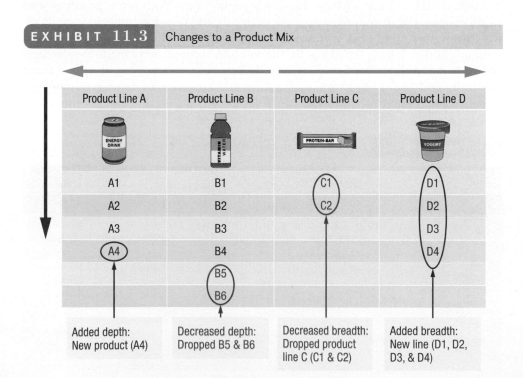

Social & Mobile Marketing 11.1   Axe Brand's Anarchy Fragrance and Graphic Novel[i]

Axe body spray already owned 75 percent of the men's fragrance market, so when its owner, Unilever, wanted to grow the brand, it needed to expand its product depth. Thus came Axe Anarchy, a scent offered in both male and female versions, to exploit the promise of irresistible sexuality that has proven successful so far.

In a decade's worth of controversial Axe commercials, average guys drew very attractive women to them simply by spraying themselves with the scent. The Anarchy message is even edgier. As the name suggests, the product promises the notion of sexual energy that goes slightly out of control. An early commercial depicts a chaotic series of events, including a car pileup, in which a man and a woman remain oblivious to the havoc but gravitate toward each other until they are just inches apart. "Unleash the chaos," the screen recommends, as the video cuts to shots of the two actors spraying themselves. "New Axe Anarchy for him and for her."

Noting its youthful target market, Unilever also wanted to ensure that the advertising medium for Anarchy fit the brand extension, so the company unleashed an interactive digital campaign in the form of an online graphic novel. The serialized, comic book fantasy about the chaotic exploits of the Anarchy Girls would evolve in real time, in response to viewer input. The author and *X-Men* creator Scott Lobdell was hired to create the narrative in collaboration with any of the 2.3 million fans who registered on YouTube, Facebook, Twitter, and Axe's other social channels to help shape the story.

The marketing subtext was clear: Break the narrative and break through sexually, which seemed to offer a potent message for young women. But some observers remain unconvinced that Axe's bold, crowd-sourced digital venture will help the brand make the crossover into the women's body spray market. Could graphic novels, with their traditionally young male audience, really connect with young women? Do the Anarchy Girls—with their revealing clothing and unrealistic bodies—really empower, or do they just objectify women? Would Axe's explosive brand expansion strategy actually alienate the very audience that built its body spray brand—that is, average-guy male teens trying to attract a special girl? Would advertising to girls make Axe lose credibility among boys?

To promote the Axe Anarchy fragrance to young men and women, Unilever created a comic book fantasy about "Anarchy Girls," available in real time on YouTube and other social media.

To increase product line breadth, a firm may add a new line of jam products to complement their bread line.

Decrease Depth From time to time, it is also necessary to delete products within a product line to realign the firm's resources (see the deletion of products B5 and B6 in Exhibit 11.3). The decision is never taken lightly. Generally, substantial investments have been made to develop and manufacture the products. Yet firms often must prune their product lines to eliminate unprofitable or low margin items and refocus their marketing efforts on their more profitable items. Procter & Gamble (P&G) introduced Tide Basic as an extension of its Tide line—probably the best-known detergent brand and a product that enjoys a reputation as an innovative, high-end brand. Tide Basic was priced 20 percent cheaper than regular Tide, but P&G deleted the extension less than a year after introducing it, worried that an inexpensive, less effective version simply undermined its brand rather than offering an appealing alternative.[8]

Decrease Breadth Sometimes it is necessary to delete entire product lines to address changing market conditions or meet internal strategic priorities (e.g., deleting product line C in Exhibit 11.3). Thus, the firm drops its line of bread and focuses its attention on its dairy products—milk and cheese (product lines A and B).

Increase Breadth Firms often add new product lines to capture new or evolving markets and increase sales (e.g., product line D in Exhibit 11.3). The firm adds a whole new line of jam products. Jam is a complementary product to its bread line.

CHECK YOURSELF

1. What is the difference between product mix breadth and product line depth?
2. Why change product mix breadth?
3. Why change product line depth?

BRANDING

Using its new slogan, "I will," Under Armour features Canelo Alvarez, boxing's welterweight World Champion, wearing its digital performance monitoring system.

A company lives or dies based on brand awareness. Consumers cannot buy products that they don't know exist. Even if the overall brand name is familiar, it won't help sales of individual products un less consumers know what products are available under that name. Sports fans have long been familiar with the rallying cry for Under Armour and its line of athletic gear: "Protect this house." But when the company chose to refresh its tagline, it undertook a massive ad campaign to introduce its new slogan, "I will." In addition to extensive online and outdoor advertising, Under Armour intensified its branding efforts during the NBA All-Star Weekend, when television ads flooded the airwaves, promising new technology introductions and working to expand its appeal to both male and female sportswear consumers.[9]

Branding also provides a way for a firm to differentiate its product offerings from those of its competitors. Both Snapple and Tropicana make and

I WILL.

CANELO
ALVAREZ

EXHIBIT 11.4	What Makes a Brand?
Brand Element	**Description**
Brand name	The spoken component of branding, it can describe the product or service characteristics and/or be composed of words invented or derived from colloquial or contemporary language. Examples include Comfort Inn (suggests product characteristics), Apple (no association with the product), or Zillow.com (invented term).
URLs (uniform resource locators) or domain names	Locations of pages on the Internet, which often substitute for the firm's name, such as Toyota (http://www.toyota.com).
Logos and symbols	Visual branding elements that stand for corporate names or trademarks. Symbols are logos without words. Examples include the McDonald's arch.
Characters	Brand symbols that could be human, animal, or animated. Examples include the Energizer Bunny and Rice Krispies' Snap, Crackle and Pop.
Slogans	Short phrases used to describe the brand or persuade consumers about some characteristics of the brand. Examples include State Farm's "Like A Good Neighbor" and Dunkin' Donuts' "America Runs On Dunkin'."
Jingles/Sounds	Audio messages about the brand that are composed of words or distinctive music. An example is Intel's four-note sound signature that accompanies the Intel Inside slogan.

Source: Adapted from Kevin Lane Keller, *Strategic Brand Management*, 4th ed. (Upper Saddle River, NJ: Prentice Hall, 2012).

sell fruit drinks, yet consumers may choose one over the other because of the associations that the brands invoke. As we discuss in more detail subsequently, brand names, logos, symbols, characters, slogans, jingles, and even distinctive packages constitute the various brand elements firms use,[10] which they usually choose to be easy for consumers to recognize and remember. Most consumers know the Nike swoosh and would recognize it even if the word *Nike* did not appear on the product or in an advertisement. Exhibit 11.4 summarizes some of these brand elements.

LO4 Identify the advantages that brands provide firms and consumers.

Value of Branding for the Customer

Brands add value to merchandise and services, for both consumers and sellers, beyond physical and functional characteristics or the pure act of performing the service.[11] Let's examine some ways in which brands add value for both customers and the firm.

Brands Facilitate Purchases Brands are often easily recognized by consumers, and because they signify a certain quality level and contain familiar attributes, brands help consumers make quick decisions, especially about their purchases.[12] The cola market is a particularly strong example of this benefit. Some people think cola is cola, such that one brand is not too different from another. But branding has made it easy for Pepsi drinkers to find the familiar logo on the store shelf and more likely that they simply buy one of Pepsi's other products, should they decide to switch to a diet soda or a flavored version. From promotions, past purchases, or information from friends and family, they recognize the offering before they even read any text on the label, and they likely possess a perception of the brand's level of quality, how it tastes, whether it

Characters like Rice Krispies' Snap, Crackle, and Pop help build a brand.

is a good value, and, most important, whether they like it and want to buy it. Brands enable customers to differentiate one firm or product from another. Without branding, how could we easily tell the difference between Coca-Cola and Pepsi before tasting them?

Brands Establish Loyalty Over time and with continued use, consumers learn to trust certain brands. They know, for example, that they wouldn't consider switching brands and, in some cases, feel a strong affinity to certain brands. Amazon.com has a loyal following because its reputation for service prompts customers to turn to it first. A customer whose $500 PlayStation3 was apparently stolen during delivery received another PlayStation3, without even having to pay additional shipping costs. Amazon lost $500, plus shipping, on a mistake that was not its fault, but it also gained a reputation for service with this customer, who would not only buy more electronics from Amazon but also tell everyone he could think of about this extraordinary example of customer service and choose Amazon's brand extension into the Kindle offerings before similar options provided by other brands.[13]

Brands Protect from Competition and Price Competition Strong brands are somewhat protected from competition from other firms and price competition. Because such brands are more established in the market and have a more loyal customer base, neither competitive pressures on price nor retail-level competition is as threatening to the firm. Lacoste is widely known for its cotton knit shirts. Although many similar brands are available and some retailers offer their own brands, Lacoste is perceived to be of superior quality, garners a certain status among its users, and therefore can command a premium price.

Lacoste has a superior-quality image that helps protect it from competition and enables it to command relatively high prices.

Brands Are Assets For firms, brands are also assets that can be legally protected through trademarks and copyrights and thus constitute a unique form of ownership. Firms sometimes have to fight to ensure their brand names are not being used, directly or indirectly, by others. In the 1950s, Princess Marcella Borghese, the descendant of ancient Roman rulers, as well as a pope—started a line of eponymous high-end cosmetics; in the mid-1970s, she entered into an agreement with Revlon, which purchased the rights to "the words and phrases "Borghese," "Marcella Borghese," and "Princess Marcella Borghese." Revlon has since sold that license and the associated trademarks, and Borghese Inc. now functions as an independent manufacturer of cosmetics and related products. But Princess Marcella was not the last Borghese, and her son and his family continue to use their family name. They also learned the cosmetics business too, so they sell a line of personal care products through HSN and offer a parallel product line of pet products under the brand name The Royal Treatment. Publicity surrounding these brands inevitably features the names of the founders, so the current owners of Borghese Inc. (who are not members of the family) worry about trademark infringement—especially when Princess Marcella's grandson Lorenzo became a popular media superstar by starring on the reality series *The Bachelor*. Borghese Inc.'s CEO issued a warning letter to Lorenzo, reminding him that he was not allowed to imply that he was connected in any way with the company, regardless of his name. The family insists it is not trying to infringe on the company's trademark, but also that it has no plans to give up its noble name or its efforts to build its own businesses.[14]

| EXHIBIT 11.5 | The World's 10 Most Valuable Brands |

2013 Rank	2012 Rank	Brand	Country	Sector	Brand Value (in $ Billions)
1	2	Apple	United States	Technology	$98.3
2	4	Google	United States	Technology	93.2
3	1	Coca-Cola	United States	Beverages	79.2
4	3	IBM	United States	Business Services	78.8
5	5	Microsoft	United States	Technology	59.5
6	6	GE	United States	Diversified	46.9
7	7	McDonald's	United States	Restaurants	41.9
8	9	Samsung	South Korea	Technology	39.6
9	8	Intel	United States	Technology	37.3
10	10	Toyota	Japan	Automotive	35.3

Source: From Interbrand.com, http://www.interbrand.com/best_global_brands.aspx.

Brands Affect Market Value Having well-known brands can have a direct impact on the company's bottom line. The value of a company is its overall monetary worth, comprising a vast number of assets. When the brand loses value, it also threatens other assets. For RadioShack, once the first destination for consumers seeking a Walkman or boom box, the loss of brand value as it has struggled to maintain relevance as a provider of modern, cutting-edge technology, has pushed it to close approximately 500 stores and pursue an aggressive strategy to rebrand and gain back some of the value.[15]

The value of a brand can be defined as the earning potential of that brand over the next 12 months.[16] The world's 10 most valuable brands for 2013 appear in Exhibit 11.5.

 LO5 Explain the various components of brand equity.

Apple is the most valuable brand in the world.

Brand Equity for the Owner

The value of a brand translates into brand equity, or the set of assets and liabilities linked to a brand that add to or subtract from the value provided by the product or service.[17] Like the physical possessions of a firm, brands are assets a firm can build, manage, and harness over time to increase its revenue, profitability, and overall value. For example, firms spend millions of dollars on promotion, advertising, and other marketing efforts throughout a brand's life cycle. Marketing expenditures allocated carefully can result in greater brand recognition, awareness, perceived value, and consumer loyalty for the brand, which all enhance the brand's overall equity. Such benefits can be particularly strong if the brand markets itself ethically, as Ethical and Societal Dilemma 11.1 notes.

How do we know how good a brand is, or how much equity it has? Experts look at four

Ethical & Societal Dilemma 11.1   (Not) Marketing Sugary Drinks to Kids[ii]

Obesity rates are often highest in the nations and regions that drink the most soda. The sugary, high-calorie versions of popular carbonated beverage brands in turn have been widely blamed for the growing rates of obesity, especially among children. Those complaints also are growing as brands expand outside the United States and potentially threaten the long-term health of kids across the globe.

Even as it strongly maintains that sodas are not the main culprit in rising obesity rates, Coca-Cola has acknowledged its own limited responsibility and therefore vowed not to advertise in settings in which children make up more than 35 percent of the anticipated audience (previously, it set this standard at 50 percent). Thus Coke ads have disappeared from cartoon networks and youth-oriented shows, children's magazines, and so forth.

In addition to its commitment not to advertise directly to children younger than 12 years of age, Coke has invested in initiatives to promote more physical activity and to encourage consumers to consider lower calorie alternatives, whether Diet Coke or Minute Maid juices (which Coca-Cola also owns). Beyond advertising, Coke's new product development efforts are largely focused on identifying and integrating natural low-calorie sweeteners. In some countries, its packaging also will feature more prominent information about calorie contents.

Yet critics point out that even as Coke promises to stop targeting children, it has confirmed that it has no plans to stop relying on its popular polar bear advertisements during the holiday season, nor will it eliminate images of children enjoying Coke in its ads. Thus while Coca-Cola might be working to reduce the amount of marketing children might see during their favorite programs, it certainly does not plan to stop appealing to young consumers altogether.

Should Coca-Cola and other consumer packaged goods companies be allowed to advertise to children?

aspects of a brand to determine its equity: brand awareness, perceived value, brand associations, and brand loyalty.

Brand Awareness Brand awareness measures how many consumers in a market are familiar with the brand and what it stands for and have an opinion about it. The more aware or familiar they are, the easier their decision-making process is, which improves the chances of purchase. Familiarity matters most for products that are bought without much thought, such as soap or chewing gum, but brand awareness is also critical for infrequently purchased items or those the consumer has never purchased before. If the consumer recognizes the brand, it probably has attributes that make it valuable.[18] For those who have never purchased a Toyota, the simple awareness that it exists can help facilitate a purchase. Marketers create brand awareness through repeated exposures of the various brand elements (brand name, logo, symbol, character, packaging, or slogan) in the firm's communications to consumers through advertising, publicity, or other methods (see Chapters 18–20).

Certain brands gain such predominance in a particular product market over time that they become synonymous with the product itself; that is, the brand name starts being used as the generic product category. Examples include Kleenex tissues, Clorox bleach, Band-Aid adhesive bandages, and the Google search engine. Companies must be vigilant in protecting their brand names because if they are used so generically, over time the brand itself can lose its trademark status. For competitors, this trend similarly is destructive: If everyone with an upset stomach asks for Pepto-Bismol and never considers any alternatives, brands such as Activia suffer smaller chances of making it into customers shopping baskets. To counteract such concerns, Activia uses well-known celebrities such as Shakira in its advertisements, to make sure it is recognizable and prominent.[19]

Perceived Value The perceived value of a brand is the relationship between a product's or service's benefits and its cost. Customers usually determine the offering's value in relationship to that of its close competitors. If they believe a less expensive brand is about the same quality as a premium brand, the perceived value of that cheaper choice is high. Merchandise sold by Target and Kohl's is not always perceived to be the highest quality, nor is the apparel the most fashion-forward. But not every customer needs to

These brands are so strong that they have become synonymous with the product itself.

show up at school looking like they came from a fashion show runway. At the same time, these retailers hire high-fashion designers to create reasonably priced lines to feature in their stores—as Target did with Jason Wu and Prabal Gurung to create well-designed pieces at Target-level prices.

Brand Associations Brand associations reflect the mental and emotional links that consumers make between a brand and its key product attributes, such as a logo and its color, slogan, or famous personality. These brand associations often result from a firm's advertising and promotional efforts. Toyota's hybrid car, the Prius, is known for being economical, a good value, stylish, and good for the environment. But firms also attempt to create specific associations with positive consumer emotions such as fun, friendship, good feelings, family gatherings, and parties. Jingles can establish particularly strong associations, especially when

Target teamed up with high-fashion designer Jason Wu to create reasonably priced, yet very fashionable apparel.

Friskies cat food is associated with its famous "spokesperson," Grumpy Cat.

they are catchy and get stuck in consumers' heads. State Farm Insurance continues to rely on the jingle that Barry Manilow wrote for it in the 1970s: In modern advertisements, young customers in trouble sing the phrase "like a good neighbor, State Farm is there," and an agent magically appears on scene.[20]

Because of his vast viral popularity, Grumpy Cat (real name: Tardar Sauce) has been approached by several brands that seek to be associated with him, to benefit from his entertaining, satirical, and hip image. The feline's naturally unhappy looking mouth now appears across Friskies' product line. Mashable featured Grumpy Cat in its tent at South by Southwest, and a bidding process led to the promise of an upcoming Grumpy Cat movie.[21]

Brand Loyalty Brand loyalty occurs when a consumer buys the same brand's product or service repeatedly over time rather than buy from multiple suppliers within the same category.[22] Therefore, brand-loyal customers are an important source of value for firms. First, firms such as airlines, hotels, long-distance telephone providers, credit card companies, and retailers reward loyal consumers with loyalty or customer relationship management (CRM) programs, such as points customers can redeem for extra discounts or free services, advance notice of sale items, and invitations to special events sponsored by the company. Second, the marketing costs of reaching loyal consumers are much lower because the firm does not have to spend money on advertising and promotion campaigns to attract these customers. Loyal consumers simply do not need persuasion or an extra push to buy the firm's brands. Third, loyal customers tend to praise the virtues of their favorite products, retailers, or services to others. This positive word of mouth reaches potential customers and reinforces the perceived value of current customers, all at no cost to the firm. Fourth, a high level of brand loyalty insulates the firm from competition because, as we noted in Chapter 2, brand-loyal customers do not switch to competitors' brands, even when provided with a variety of incentives.

Brand loyalty is not always easy to achieve though. In most cases, it requires substantially better quality or a distinctive promise. For example, lifetime satisfaction guarantees are expensive to maintain. They mean that any customer, at any time, can come back to the company to complain about some feature they find unappealing, even if the item had been purchased decades before. They are accordingly quite rare. But for the companies that offer them, such as The North Face, Craftsman, and Darn Tough socks, unconditional guarantees evoke tremendous loyalty. Even if customers never need to replace one of these products, knowing that the company is willing to offer the guarantee makes them more likely to purchase a related item from the same brand.[23]

> **CHECK YOURSELF**
>
> 1. How do brands create value for the customer and the firm?
> 2. What are the components of brand equity?

BRANDING STRATEGIES

LO6 Determine the various types of branding strategies used by firms.

Firms institute a variety of brand-related strategies to create and manage key brand assets, such as the decision to own the brands, establishing a branding policy, extending the brand name to other products and markets, cooperatively using the brand name with that of another firm, and licensing the brand to other firms.

Brand Ownership

Brands can be owned by any firm in the supply chain, whether manufacturers, wholesalers, or retailers. There are two basic brand ownership strategies: manufacturer brands and retailer/store brands, as Exhibit 11.6 shows. Additionally, the brands can be marketed using a common/family name or as individual brands.

Manufacturer Brands Manufacturer brands, also known as national brands, are owned and managed by the manufacturer. Some famous manufacturer brands are Nike, Coca-Cola, Kitchen Aid, and Sony. With these brands, the manufacturer develops the merchandise, produces it to ensure consistent quality, and invests in a marketing program to establish an appealing brand image. The majority of the brands marketed in the United States are manufacturer brands, and manufacturing firms spend millions of dollars each year to promote their brands. By owning their brands, manufacturers retain more control over their marketing strategy, are able to choose the appropriate market segments and positioning for the brand, and can build the brand and thereby create their own brand equity.

EXHIBIT 11.6 Who Owns the Brand?

Who Owns the Brand?		Manufacturer/National Brand	Retailer/Store Brand
Commom Name or Not?	Family Brands	Kellogg's family line 	Kroger's line 
	Individual Brands	Kellogg's individual brand 	Kroger's individual brand 

Retailer/Store Brands Retailer/store brands, also called private-label brands, are products developed by retailers. In some cases, retailers manufacture their own products, whereas in other cases they develop the design and specifications for their retailer/store brands and then contract with manufacturers to produce those products. Some national brand manufacturers work with retailers to develop a special version of their standard merchandise offering to be sold exclusively by the retailer.

In the past, sales of store brands were limited. But in recent years, as the size of retail firms has increased through growth and consolidation, more retailers have the scale economies to develop private-label merchandise and use this merchandise to establish a distinctive identity. In addition, manufacturers are more willing to accommodate the needs of retailers and develop co-brands for them.[24] At Stop & Shop, 40 percent of sales in some stores come from store brand options.[25] Both Costco and Trader Joe's have based their brand identities around their store brands.

Naming Brands and Product Lines

Although there is no simple way to decide how to name a brand or a product line, the more the products vary in their usage or performance, the more likely it is that the firm should use individual brands. For example, General Motors uses several individual brands (Cadillac, Chevrolet, and GMC), each catering to very different target markets and meeting different needs. Hyundai, on the other hand, uses only one brand since usage and level of performance are relatively homogeneous.

Family Brands A firm can use its own corporate name to brand all its product lines and products, so Kellogg's incorporates the company name into the brand name of Kellogg's Rice Krispies (refer to Exhibit 11.2). When all products are sold under one family brand, the individual brands benefit from the overall brand awareness associated with the family name. Kellogg's uses its family brand name prominently on its cereal brands (e.g., Kellogg's Special K, Kellogg's Froot Loops, Kellogg's Rice Krispies).

Individual Brands A firm can use individual brand names for each of its products. For example, while Kellogg's makes good use of the family branding strategy, it also allows other products, such as Morningstar Farms, Famous Amos cookies, Keebler cookies, and Cheez-Its (Exhibit 11.2), to keep individual identities not readily seen as being under the Kellogg's umbrella.[26]

Kellogg's uses a family branding strategy in which several product lines are sold under one name.

Kellogg's also uses an individual branding strategy since Keebler, Cheez-It, Morningstar, and Famous Amos are all marketed using separate names.

Brand and Line Extensions[27]

A **brand extension** refers to the use of the same brand name in a different product line. It is an increase in the product mix's breadth.[28] The dental hygiene market, for instance, is full of brand extensions; Colgate and Crest sell toothpaste, toothbrushes, and other dental hygiene products, even though their original product line was just toothpaste. A **line extension** is the use of the same brand name within the same product line and represents an increase in a product line's depth.

There are several advantages to using the same brand name for new products. First, because the brand name is already well established, the firm can spend less in developing consumer brand awareness and brand associations for the new product.[29] Kellogg's has branched out from the cereal company it once was. Its strategy of branding the corporate name into the product name has allowed it to introduce new products quicker and more easily. Kellogg's Eggo Syrup was a natural extension to its product line of breakfast foods.

Second, if either the original brand or the brand extension has strong consumer acceptance, that perception will carry over to the other product. Consumers who had not used the Neutrogena brand before trying the brand extension, Neutrogena Wave power cleanser, might be encouraged to try Neutrogena's core product line of cleansers and moisturizing lotions, especially if their experience with the Wave has been positive.[30]

Third, when brand extensions are used for complementary products, a synergy exists between the two products that can increase overall sales. For example, Frito-Lay markets both chips and dips under its Frito-Lay and Tostitos brand names. When people buy the chips, they tend to buy the dips as well.

Not all brand extensions are successful, however. Some can dilute brand equity.[31] **Brand dilution** occurs when the brand extension adversely affects consumer perceptions about the attributes the core brand is believed to hold.[32] Here are some examples of unsuccessful brand extensions:[33]

- Cheetos Lip Balm was based on the idea that if you like Cheetos, you would want to wipe it all over your lips.

- Lifesavers Soda did well in prelaunch taste tests but didn't in subsequent sales.

- Colgate Kitchen Entrees were microwavable frozen dinner entrees that shared the name with the famous toothpaste.

- Bic thought that since people wanted their disposable lighters and razors, they would also want disposable underwear. They were wrong.

LO7 Distinguish between brand extension and line extension.

Using a brand extension strategy, Frito-Lay markets both chips and dips under its Frito-Lay and Tostitos brand names.

Lifesavers unsuccessfully attempted a brand extension strategy with its line of soda.

To prevent the potentially negative consequences of brand extensions, firms consider the following:

- Marketers should evaluate the fit between the product class of the core brand and that of the extension.[34] If the fit between the product categories is high, consumers will consider the extension credible, and the brand association will be stronger for the extension. Thus, when Starbucks introduced its line of instant coffee, VIA, it made sense to its customers.

- Firms should evaluate consumer perceptions of the attributes of the core brand and seek out similar attributes for the extension because brand-specific associations are very important for extensions.[35] For example, if HP printers were associated with reliability, performance, and value, consumers would expect the same brand-specific attributes in other products that carried the HP brand name.

- Firms should refrain from extending the brand name to too many products and product categories to avoid diluting the brand and damaging brand equity. Donald Trump has been quite successful lending his name to various property, television lines, and Macy's clothing but was unsuccessful with extending himself to branding steaks.

- Firms should consider whether the brand extension will be distanced from the core brand, especially if the firm wants to use some but not all of the existing brand associations. Marriott has budget, midtier, and luxury hotels. Its luxury hotels, including the Ritz-Carlton, Edition, and Renaissance, do not use the name Marriott at all.[36]

Co-branding

Co-branding is the practice of marketing two or more brands together on the same package, promotion, or store. Co-branding can enhance consumers' perceptions of product quality by signaling unobservable product quality through links between the firm's brand and a well-known quality brand. For example, Yum Brands frequently combines two or more of its restaurant chains, including A&W, KFC, Long John Silver's, Pizza Hut, and Taco Bell, into one store space. This co-branding strategy is designed to appeal to diverse market segments and extend the hours in which each restaurant attracts customers. Yet co-branding also creates risks, especially when the customers of each of the brands turn out to be vastly different. For example, the Burger King and Häagen-Dazs co-branding strategy failed because the customer profiles for each brand were too different.[37] Co-branding may also fail when there are disputes or conflicts of interest between the co-brands.

Brand Licensing

Brand licensing is a contractual arrangement between firms whereby one firm allows another to use its brand name, logo, symbols, and/or characters in exchange for a negotiated fee.[38] Brand licensing is common for toys, apparel, accessories, and entertainment products, such as video games. The firm that provides the right to use its brand (licensor) obtains revenues through royalty payments from the firm that has obtained the right to use the brand (licensee). These royalty payments may take the form of an upfront, lump-sum licensing fee or be based on the dollar value of sales of the licensed merchandise.

One very popular form of licensing is the use of characters created in books and other media. Such entertainment licensing has generated tremendous revenues for movie studios. Disney, for instance, flooded retail stores with products based on its *Frozen* movie. *Star Wars* memorabilia has continued to be successful

The NBA licenses products like these bobblehead figures of Dallas Mavericks and San Antonio Spurs players to a manufacturer in exchange for a negotiated fee.

since the first film was released in the 1970s. A long-standing staple of licensing has been major league sports teams that play in the NBA, NFL, or NHL as well as various collegiate sports teams.

Licensing is an effective form of attracting visibility for the brand and thereby building brand equity while also generating additional revenue. There are, however, some risks associated with it. For the licensor, the major risk is the dilution of its brand equity through overexposure of the brand, especially if the brand name and characters are used inappropriately.[39]

Brand Repositioning

Brand repositioning or rebranding refers to a strategy in which marketers change a brand's focus to target new markets or realign the brand's core emphasis with changing market preferences.[40] Although repositioning can improve the brand's fit with its target segment or boost the vitality of old brands, it is not without costs and risks. Firms often need to spend tremendous amounts of money to make tangible changes to the product and packages as well as intangible changes to the brand's image through various forms of promotion, as Adding Value 11.1 details. These costs may not be recovered if the repositioned brand and messages are not credible to consumers or if the firm has mistaken a fad for a long-term market trend. Examples of recent rebranding efforts that have provoked consumers' disdain include Olive Garden, The Gap, and Tropicana.[41]

CHECK YOURSELF

1. What are the differences between manufacturer and private-label brands?
2. What is co-branding?
3. What is the difference between brand extension and line extension?
4. What is brand repositioning?

Adding Value 11.1 | The Global Appeal and Rebranding Efforts of American Airlines[iii]

For more than 40 years, American Airlines had used the same logo: a pair of capital *A*s, one red and one blue, surrounding the silhouette of a diving eagle. When the airline purchased 550 new planes, made from a new composite material, it had to change the look of the finish, so it decided to change its look altogether, including a new logo, new designs for the plane interiors, a new website, and new kiosk interfaces in terminals.

The most visible element thus far is the new logo, which removes the double *A* and offers a more abstract version of an eagle. The abstract image is oriented more horizontally, rather than vertically downward. On the new planes, this eagle logo will appear near the front, as if pointing the direction for the flight. Furthermore, the tails of each airplane will feature another abstract image, evocative of the U.S. flag with blue and red stripes (but no stars).

The abstraction of the images reflects American Airlines' goals for the rebranding, namely, to emphasize the "American spirit" without evoking negative images of the United States in global markets. Futurebrand, the agency that American Airlines hired to assist it with its efforts, polled consumers around the world to identify positive traits they associated with the United States. The effort sought to determine not just how people view American but also how they view America in a global age.

The results highlighted images of progress, technology, and entertainment, but they also cautioned against any implication of attack or aggression. Therefore the downward diving eagle needed to go because it was likely to be interpreted as attacking. A direct representation of the U.S. flag might have been perceived as jingoistic, whereas the abstracted version simply provides a more neutral identifying hint.

In eliminating a widely familiar logo, along with its well-known letter typeface, American Airlines clearly is taking a risk that it will lose brand recognition among customers who unconsciously seek the same look they have always seen at the airport. But in a global economy, a company with an American identity, in all senses of the term, needs to take care to emphasize the positives while avoiding more controversial elements.

American Airlines' new logo is an abstract version of an eagle. The tails of each plane feature an abstraction of the U.S. flag.

LO8 Indicate the advantages of a product's packaging and labeling strategy.

PACKAGING

Packaging is an important brand element with more tangible or physical benefits than other brand elements. Packages come in different types and offer a variety of benefits to consumers, manufacturers, and retailers. The primary package is the one the consumer uses, such as the toothpaste tube. From the primary package, consumers typically seek convenience in terms of storage, use, and consumption.

The secondary package is the wrapper or exterior carton that contains the primary package and provides the UPC label used by retail scanners. Consumers can use the secondary package to find additional product information that may not be available on the primary package. Like primary packages, secondary packages add consumer value by facilitating the convenience of carrying, using, and storing the product.

Whether primary or secondary, packaging plays several key roles: It attracts the consumers' attention. It enables products to stand out from their competitors. It offers a promotional tool (e.g., "NEW" and "IMPROVED" promises on labels). Finally, it allows for the same product to appeal to different markets with different sizes, such that convenience stores stock little packages that travelers can buy at the last minute, whereas Costco sells extra large versions of products.

Firms occasionally change or update their packaging as a subtle way of repositioning the product. A change can be used to attract a new target market and/or appear more up-to-date to its current market. For instance, the Morton Salt umbrella girl has significantly changed since it was first introduced in 1914, but the slogan "when it rains it pours" endures today. Changes also can make consumers feel like they are receiving something tangible in return for paying higher prices, even when the product itself remains untouched. Whether true or not, consumers see new packaging and tend to think that the "new" product may be worth trying. In honor of its 100th birthday, Morton has redesigned the packaging of over 100 individual items to give a clean, modern feel.[42]

Some packaging changes are designed to make the product more recognizable, such as Daisy Brand's redesign of its cottage cheese containers. Known for using no more than four ingredients in any of its cottage cheese products, the redesign has taken a simple, Spartan look and paired it with blue lids. The color blue of the lid varies by the fat content of the cottage cheese. Combining a simple container and varying colored lids, Daisy Brand expects its new containers will grab consumers' attention in the dairy case and increase sales.[43]

An interesting recent development in packaging is a move to "sustainable packaging." Sustainable packaging is product packaging that is ecologically responsible. Leaders in this area of innovation include Coca-Cola, Microsoft, Waste Management, Aveda, and Zappos. These firms host a sustainable packaging conference that brings together more than 250 firms to discuss new methods to produce environmentally responsible packaging that is also cost effective. Ideas from this conference include returnable packaging, use of 3D printing, and flexible packaging. They have also set up a website with information on future conferences, and information for the industry at http://www.sustainability-in-packaging.com.[44]

Sometimes sustainable packaging changes (or any change for that matter) can backfire, though, such as when PepsiCo replaced its Sun Chips bags with new 100 percent compostable bags. While the bags would save a tremendous amount of waste in landfills, they were also extremely noisy and crinkly. Customers balked and Sun Chips lost market share. Facebook pages like "SORRY BUT I CAN'T HEAR YOU OVER THIS SUN CHIPS BAG" got more than 49,000 likes. Having committed to sustainable packaging it would be near impossible for Pepsi to revert to its old-style packages. Suffering criticism and loss of sales, the company developed a newer, quieter bag that customers liked a great deal more.[45]

Retailers' and manufacturers' priorities for secondary packaging often differ from those of their customers. They want convenience in terms of displaying and selling the product. In addition, secondary packages are often packed into larger cartons, pallets, or containers to facilitate shipment and storage from the manufacturer to the retailer. These shipping packages benefit the manufacturer and the retailer, in that they protect the shipment during transit; aid in loading, unloading, and storage; and allow cost efficiencies due to the larger order and shipment sizes. But sometimes retailers and manufacturers give in to popular demand, as when L'eggs rereleased its iconic egg packaging for sheer energy pantyhose.[46]

Packaging can also be used in a far subtler way, namely, to help suppliers save costs. When the costs of producing a product rise significantly, manufacturers are faced with either raising prices, something customers don't usually like, or reducing the amount of product sold in a package. Chobani reduced the size of its Greek yogurt containers from 6 ounces to 5.3 ounces without changing the price. Although there was a time when customers might not have noticed this 12 percent decrease,

Morton Salt changed its packaging to celebrate its 100th anniversary.

Daisy Brand simplified its cottage cheese containers and added colored lids to make them more recognizable.

Ethical & Societal Dilemma 11.2   Calories 0, Vitamins 0: How Much Information Can Water Labels Provide?[iv]

Water, water everywhere. Especially in developed countries, consumers everywhere can simply turn on the tap, and there it is. And yet firms have been successful in packaging this almost free, natural resource, creating some cachet for it, and selling it.

Bottled water enjoyed double-digit growth, year to year, as U.S. consumers doubled the amount they drank from 13.4 to 29.3 gallons per year. The popularity and growth of the industry has attracted attention, though. Bottled and tap water companies operate under different regulations. Yet many observers and government agencies argue the rules should be the same, with water bottle labeling subject to regulations as detailed as those that the tap water companies experience.

Bottled water, as a food product, currently is regulated by the Food and Drug Administration (FDA), so it lists nutrition information and ingredients on the labels (i.e., 0 percent of most nutrients; contents: water). In contrast, municipal water is controlled by the Environmental Protection Agency (EPA), which has more authority to enforce quality standards. The result may be misinformed consumers, many of whom believe bottled water is

Would more comprehensive labels on bottled water change your water consumption behavior?

safer and healthier than tap water. And yet according to the U.S. Government Accounting Office (GAO), the FDA lacks the authority to require water bottlers to use certified water quality tests or report those test results. Also, the existing requirements to ensure safe bottled water, both state and federal, are less comprehensive than the rules about safeguarding tap water.

Even without such regulations, consumers may be changing their attitudes. The bottled water industry recently has experienced flat growth. The cause may be the economic downturn, which has forced consumers to cut costs wherever possible. Environmental concerns may be another factor since bottled water creates significant waste. Perhaps better labeling of products will mean even less ambiguity about the value of bottled versus tap water, which could offer opportunities for differentiation among bottled water brands that adopt different bottling and labeling methods.

Would more comprehensive labels on bottled water change your water consumption behavior? Is bottled water better than tap water? Is buying bottled water an ecologically sound purchase decision?

L'eggs pantyhose packaging forgoes retailer and manufacturer convenience for its iconic egg shape.

today consumers are very aware that everything from cleansing tissues to ice cream containers are shrinking. Today's customers are more empowered as well, as the Chobani example shows. As soon as these newer, smaller packages hit store shelves, customers took to Twitter and Facebook and immediately began complaining about the change, further raising awareness of the packaging change.[47]

Product Labeling

Labels on products and packages provide information the consumer needs for his or her purchase decision and consumption of the product. In that they identify the product and brand, labels are also an important element of branding and can be used for promotion. The information required on them must comply with general and industry-specific laws and regulations, including the constituents or ingredients contained in the product, where the product was made, directions for use, and/or safety precautions.

Many labeling requirements stem from various laws, including the Federal Trade Commission Act of 1914, the Fair Packaging and Labeling Act of 1967, and the Nutrition Labeling Act of 1990. Several federal agencies, industry groups, and consumer watchdogs carefully monitor product labels. The Food and Drug Administration is the primary federal agency that reviews food and package labels and ensures that the claims made by the manufacturer are true. Ethical and Societal Dilemma 11.2 illustrates the problems associated with the different regulations that apply to various edible products as well as some associated labeling concerns.

A product label is much more than just a sticker on the package; it is a communication tool. Many of the elements on the label are required by laws and regulations (i.e., ingredients, fat content, sodium content, serving size, calories), but other elements remain within the control of the manufacturer. How manufacturers use labels to communicate the benefits of their products to consumers varies by the product. Many products highlight specific ingredients, vitamin content or nutrient content (e.g., iron), and country of origin. This focus signals to consumers that the product offers these benefits. The importance of the label as a communication tool should not be underestimated.

Reviewing Learning Objectives

LO1 Describe the components of a product.

The product itself is important, but so are its associated services, such as support or financing. Other elements combine to produce the core customer value of a product: the brand name, quality level, packaging, and additional features.

LO2 Identify the types of consumer products.

These products tend to be classified into four groups: specialty, shopping, convenience, and unsought products. Each classification involves a different purchase situation and consumer goal.

LO3 Explain the difference between a product mix's breadth and a product line's depth.

Breadth, or variety, entails the number of product lines that a company offers. Depth involves the number of categories within one specific product line.

LO4 Identify the advantages that brands provide firms and consumers.

Brands play important roles in enabling people to make purchase decisions more easily and encouraging customer loyalty. For firms specifically, they also constitute valuable assets and improve a company's bottom line and help protect against competition.

LO5 Explain the various components of brand equity.

Brand equity summarizes the value that a brand adds, or subtracts, from the offering's value. It comprises brand awareness, or how many consumers in the market are familiar with the brand; brand associations, which are the links consumers make between the brand and its image; and brand loyalty, which occurs when a consumer will only buy that brand's offer. Brand equity also encompasses the concept of perceived value, which is a subjective measure that consumers develop to assess the costs of obtaining the brand.

LO6 Determine the various types of branding strategies used by firms.

Firms use a variety of strategies to manage their brands. First, they decide whether to offer manufacturer and/or private-label brands. Second, they have a choice of using an overall family brand or a collection of product line or individual brands. Third, to reach new markets or extend their current market, they can extend their current brands to new products. Fourth, firms can co-brand with another brand to create sales and profit synergies for both. Fifth, firms with strong brands have the opportunity to license their brands to other firms. Finally, as the marketplace changes, it is often necessary to reposition a brand.

LO7 Distinguish between brand extension and line extension.

Whereas a brand extension uses the same brand name for a new product that gets introduced into new or the same markets, a line extension is simply an increase of an existing product line by the brand.

LO8 Indicate the advantages of a product's packaging and labeling strategy.

Similar to brands, packaging and labels help sell the product and facilitate its use. The primary package holds the product, and its label provides product information. The secondary package provides additional consumer information on its label and facilitates transportation and storage for both retailers and their customers. Labels have become increasingly important to consumers because they supply important safety, nutritional, and product usage information.

Key Terms

■LEARNSMART

- actual product, 343
- associated services, 343
- augmented product, 343
- brand association, 353
- brand awareness, 352
- brand dilution, 357
- brand equity, 351
- brand extension, 357
- brand licensing, 358
- brand loyalty, 354
- brand repositioning (rebranding), 359
- breadth, 345

- co-branding, 358
- consumer product, 344
- convenience products/ services, 344
- core customer value, 343
- depth, 345
- family brands, 356
- individual brands, 356
- line extension, 357
- manufacturer brands (national brands), 355
- perceived value, 353
- primary package, 360

- private-label brands, 356
- product, 342
- product line, 345
- product mix, 345
- retailer/store brands, 356
- secondary package, 360
- shopping products/ services, 344
- specialty products/ services, 344
- unsought products/ services, 344

Marketing Applications

1. L.L.Bean guarantees that its products will last forever. What features of a pair of pants from L.L.Bean would be part of the actual product and which would be part of the associated services?

2. Classify each of the following products into either convenience, shopping, specialty, or unsought goods: toothpaste, life insurance, Sharp TV, Eggo waffles, lettuce, Coach handbag, adidas soccer cleats, furniture.

3. Study the following two product mixes. For Product Mix 1: A, B, C and D are the lines; and for Product Mix 2: X, Y and Z are the lines.

A	B	C	D		X	Y	Z
a1	b1	c1	d1		x1	y1	z1
a2	b2	c2	d2		x2	y2	z2
a3	b3	c2			x3	y3	ze
					x4	y4	

| Product Mix 1 | Product Mix 2 |

Which mix has more *breadth* and why? Which mix is *deeper* and why?

4. Suppose you are the coffee buyer at Kroger's. There is a strong corporate initiative to increase store label merchandise. Discuss the advantages and disadvantages of offering private-label coffee.

5. Identify a specific brand that has developed a high level of brand equity. What specific aspects of that brand establish its brand equity?

6. Are you loyal to any brands? If so, pick one and explain why you believe you are loyal, beyond that you simply like the brand. If not, pick a brand that you like and explain how you would feel and act differently toward the brand if you were loyal to it.

7. Sears owns several store brands, including DieHard, Kenmore, and Craftsman. Each brand features many models that may appeal to various customer groups. Wouldn't it be easier to just identify them all as Sears? Justify your answer.

8. Do you think all edible items sold in a grocery store should have an ingredient and nutrition label? Consider the perspectives of consumers, the manufacturer, and the store.

9. You are the brand manager for a firm that makes herbs, spices, and other food additives. You have had complaints from some of your retail outlets that they are finding empty bottles of pure vanilla extract stashed around the store. Apparently, due to the high (35 percent) alcohol content of pure vanilla extract, people are grabbing the cute little bottles, having a drink, and getting rid of the evidence. Anecdotal evidence from store employees indicates that the majority of the imbibers are teenagers. The cost of placing a tamperproof cap on the extract is a relatively insignificant percentage of the purchase price, but will make it more difficult to open, particularly for older customers. Also, there has been a significant rise in sales to retailers as a result of the vanilla bean "addicts." What should you do?

Quiz Yourself

1. One key feature of the value of a brand is that _____.
   a. it often protects the firm from competition and price competition
   b. it no longer needs to be supported by advertising and promotion
   c. if it becomes a generic name, the brand is worth even more
   d. it cannot be successfully imitated by a retailer's own brand
   e. competitors will typically abandon a sector altogether rather than compete

2. It is almost impossible to watch a sporting event on television without seeing Nike's "swoosh" check mark, which is Nike's _____.
   a. name
   b. symbol
   c. design
   d. term
   e. theme

   (Answers to these questions can be found on page 652.)

Net Savvy

1. Visit Mac Cosmetic's website (http://www.maccosmetics.com). Identify and briefly describe the depth and the breadth of its product lines.

2. Go to BMW's website (http://www.bmwusa.com) and identify a few recently introduced brand extensions to the marketplace. Discuss whether you believe the brand extension examples you provided will benefit or harm the firm.

Chapter Case Study

OPRAH WINFREY, A BRAND UNTO HERSELF

A cultural icon who rose from poverty to become one of the world's most influential entrepreneurs, Oprah Winfrey is many things to many people. Certainly she is an entertainer who comes across as women's most intimate friend and advocate. Winfrey also has inspired and coached an audience of millions on how to "live your best life." But perhaps most of all, Oprah Winfrey is a marketer and the savvy leader of a media empire that has extended her brand worldwide.

Starting with her immensely successful TV program, *The Oprah Winfrey Show*, Winfrey expanded her personal brand through a range of other vehicles, which in any other context would be known as product lines. These lines include her production companies, Harpo Films, Harpo Radio, Harpo Print and Harpo Studios; *O, The Oprah Magazine*; Oprah.com, her website, which profiles all her ventures;

When you think of Oprah Winfrey, think big: Harpo Productions, Inc.; O, The Oprah Magazine; O at Home Magazine; Harpo Films; and the Oxygen television network; not to mention her philanthropic work with the Oprah Winfrey Foundation.

Oprah's Book Club, which some have credited with saving the publishing industry; multiple TV and radio spin-offs; and OWN, the Oprah Winfrey Network, also called her "next chapter."[48] Each element functions as a division of Harpo Productions, her multimedia entertainment company.

Building on Oprah's own compelling story of personal triumph, the Winfrey brand offers multitudes of fans not only an example of self-improvement but also authentic proof, from Winfrey's own life, that anyone can control his or her own destiny. Over the years, Winfrey has chronicled her childhood of poverty and sexual abuse, struggles to control her weight, and the difficulties of being a powerful woman in a highly competitive industry. The revealing details have only strengthened the connection with her viewers, who adore her. The message is compelling and authentic: If I can do it, you can, too.

Viewers believe her. That trust gives Winfrey tremendous influence, and it also translates into a flair for helping other brands connect with her audience. An inveterate shopper, she likes to showcase the products she loves. Her endorsements, offered without compensation, can make little-known products into superstars overnight. The month following her episode featuring aromatherapy slippers called Foot Cozys, manufacturer DreamTimes sold 20,000 pairs, up from its usual monthly volume of 3,000. Marketing experts say the Oprah brand, built on the credo of self-improvement and living well, now ranks with the towering brands of Coca-Cola and the Marlboro Man, leaving one observer to admit, "I'm hard-pressed to think of a stronger brand than Oprah."[49] That means that the Oprah brand has been enormously profitable, making Winfrey the wealthiest of America's 400 richest self-made women, with a combined worth of $2.7 billion.[50]

Winfrey began building her public persona long before she gained any national recognition, starting as a local news anchor in Nashville and then a talk-show host in Baltimore. With her move to Chicago in 1984, Winfrey gained increasing attention when her morning program, *AM Chicago*, surpassed the ratings achieved by the then–talk show king Phil Donahue. By 1986, her program was rebranded as *The Oprah Winfrey Show*, and its host was gaining a reputation for offering confessional, straight talk, like a "group therapy session."[51]

Her daily program reigned supreme among talk shows for 25 years, drawing 12 million U.S. viewers at its peak, with more than 4,500 episodes and 30,000 guests. The messages of confronting life's difficult realities and taking time for self-care remained central in brand extensions, including syndicated spin-offs such as *Dr. Phil* and *Rachael Ray*. Newer shows, usually featuring Winfrey's favored celebrity life coaches, have also increased her brand recognition. On his shows, Dr. Mehmet Oz provides insights into living a "longer, more vibrant life." *In the Bedroom with Dr. Laura Berman* counsels women about how to juggle the pressures of home and work and still feel sexy.[52]

Other extensions focus on different areas. Winfrey has continued to promote her brand and ethos of personal growth in her monthly magazine *O, The Oprah Magazine*, which features Winfrey on every cover and has a circulation of about 2.4 million, making it the 18th largest in terms of circulation in the United States.[53] Movies produced by Harpo Films also have brought some of the country's most respected actors together with scripts arising from acclaimed books, such as *Tuesdays with Morrie*, featuring Jack Lemmon and based on the best-selling novel by Detroit sportswriter Mitch Albom; *Their Eyes Were Watching God*, based on the Zora Neale Hurston novel and starring Halle Berry; *Beloved*, a film based on Toni

Morrison's Pulitzer Prize–winning novel, directed by Jonathan Demme and co-starring Winfrey and Danny Glover; and *The Great Debaters*, which received a Golden Globe nomination and co-starred Denzel Washington and Forest Whitaker. Winfrey also provided backing for the release of *Precious*, an Oscar-winning film based on a novel by Sapphire. Each new introduction celebrated the preservation of human dignity against terrible odds—disabling disease, crippling poverty and abuse, racism.

The latest venture—launching her own cable television network—took Winfrey into new territory, with lots of challenges, though still aligned with her brand's promise of controlling one's own destiny. It's not her first risky move: Buoyed by the terrific success of *The Oprah Winfrey Show*, in the late 1980s, Winfrey bolted from both King World Productions, which syndicated the show, and ABC, which produced it. Taking total control through Harpo Productions gave her complete ownership of the brand and syndication fees, estimated at $100 million. That move established the cornerstone of her empire.

But the initial launch of OWN was rocky, and for its first two years the network struggled to earn profits. Early reviews criticized Winfrey for taking the fun out of her programming.[54] *Oprah's Lifeclass*, the flagship show and latest incarnation of Winfrey's personal brand, came off like a series of lectures, preaching that "you are responsible for changing your life and making it better."[55] More recently, the network has sought to balance such uplifting but boring messages with American viewers' appetite for gossip. Its reality series *Lindsay* documents the efforts of the young actor and frequent news item Lindsay Lohan to get her life in order.[56]

Just a few months after the launch of OWN, Winfrey shuffled her leadership structure and took the top post herself. As always, she was determined to take control of her brand and her company. She would do what she had always exhorted others to do: Live her best life through her own brand.

Questions

1. Visit the company website (http://www.oprah.com) and identify and describe the different product lines that it markets.

2. How would you describe its product line breadth?

3. Review the different product categories in each of the company's product lines. Which has the greatest depth? Which has the least?

4. How has the company positioned its brand? How does it go about communicating its position?

Endnotes

1. John Tierney, "24 Miles, 4 Minutes, and 834 M.P.H., All in One Jump," *The New York Times*, October 14, 2012, http://www.nytimes.com.

2. Ann-Christine Diaz, "Notably Missing at Cannes? Red Bull 'Stratos,'" *Creativity*, June 25, 2013, http://creativity-online.com.

3. http://www.trekbikes.com.

4. Sharon Ng, "Cultural Orientation and Brand Dilution: Impact of Motivation Level and Extension Typicality," *Journal of Marketing Research* 47, no. 1 (February 2010), pp. 186–98.

5. Sam Byford, "Sony Quits the PC Business to Focus on Mobile," *The Verge*, February 6, 2014, http://www.theverge.com.

6. Michael A. Wiles, Neil A. Morgan, and Lopo L. Rego, "The Effect of Brand Acquisition and Disposal on Stock Returns," *Journal of Marketing* 76, no. 1 (2012), pp. 38–58.

7. Austin Carr, "Deep Inside Taco Bell's Doritos Locos Tacos," *Fast Company*, May 1, 2013, http://www.fastcompany.com.

8. Ellen Byron, "Tide Turns 'Basic' for P&G in Slump," *The Wall Street Journal*, August 6, 2009; Barry Silverstein, "P&G Scrubs Out Tide Basic," *BrandChannel*, June 6, 2010, http://www.brandchannel.com.

9. Natalie Zmuda, "Under Armour Unveils Anthem to Kick Off Its Biggest Global Ad Push," *Advertising Age*, February 12, 2013.

10. Kevin Lane Keller, *Strategic Brand Management: Building, Measuring, and Managing Brand Equity,* 4th ed. (Upper Saddle River, NJ: Prentice Hall, 2012); David A. Aaker, *Building Strong Brands* (New York: Simon & Schuster, 2012).

11. This discussion of the advantages of strong brands is adapted from Keller, *Strategic Brand Management.*

12. Kevin Lane Keller and Donald R. Lehmann, "Assessing Long-Term Brand Potential," *Journal of Brand Management* 17 (2009), pp. 6–17.

13. Evan Carmichael, "Obsess over Your Customers—Jeff Bezos," http://www.youngentrepreneur.com, April 7, 2009; http://www.amazon.com/New-Rules-Marketing-PR-Podcasting/dp/0470113456.

14. Christine Haughney, "Borghese v. Borghese: Battle for a Royal Name," *The New York Times,* June 15, 2013, http://www.nytimes.com.

15. Rob Walker, "How RadioShack Plans to Rescue Itself from Irrelevance," *Yahoo Tech,* February 12, 2014, https://www.yahoo.com.

16. http://www.interbrand.com. The net present value of the earnings over the next 12 months is used to calculate the value.

17. David Aaker, *Brand Portfolio Strategy: Creating Relevance, Differentiation, Energy, Leverage, and Clarity* (New York: Free Press, 2004); David A. Aaker, *Managing Brand Equity* (New York: Free Press, 1991).

18. Rong Huang and Emine Sarigöllü, "How Brand Awareness Relates to Market Outcome, Brand Equity, and the Marketing Mix," *Journal of Business Research* 65, no. 1 (2012), pp. 92–99; Lopo L. Rego, Matthew T. Billett, and Neil A. Morgan, "Consumer-Based Brand Equity and Firm Risk," *Harvard Business Review* 73, no. 6 (November 2009), pp. 47–60; Natalie Mizik and Robert Jacobson, "Valuing Branded Businesses," *Harvard Business Review* 73, no. 6 (November 2009), pp. 137–53.

19. David Kiefaber, "Activia Shows That Inside Shakira's Famous Stomach Are . . . More Shakiras!," *Adweek,* March 18, 2014, http://www.adweek.com.

20. Tim Nudd, "Zoinks! State Farm Saves Scooby-Doo and the Gang in Groovy Animated Spot," *Adweek,* October 29, 2013, http://www.adweek.com.

21. Katherine Rosman, "Grumpy Cat Has an Agent, and Now a Movie Deal," *The New York Times,* May 31, 2013, http://www.nytimes.com.

22. http://www.marketingpower.com/_layouts/Dictionary.aspx?dLetter=B.

23. Robert Klara, "For Some Retail Brands, Lifetime Guarantees Never Went Out of Fashion," *Adweek,* March 17, 2014, http://www.adweek.com.

24. Lien Lamey, Barbara Deleersnyder, Marnik G. Dekimpe, and Jan-Benedict E. M. Steenkamp, "How Business Cycles Contribute to Private-Label Success: Evidence from the United States and Europe," *Journal of Marketing* 71 (January 2007), pp. 1–15; PLMA (2009), http://www.plmainternational.com.

25. Stephanie Strom, "Groceries Are Cleaning Up in Store Brand Aisles," *The New York Times,* October 2, 2013, http://www.nytimes.com.

26. "Kellogg's 2010 Annual Report," http://annualreport2010.kelloggcompany.com.

27. The distinction between brand and line extensions is clarified in Barry Silverstein, "Brand Extensions: Risks and Rewards," Brandchannel.com, January 5, 2009.

28. See Alokparna Basu Monga and Deborah Roedder John, "What Makes Brands Elastic? The Influence of Brand Concept and Styles of Thinking on Brand Extension Evaluation," *Journal of Marketing* 74, no. 3 (May 2010), pp. 80–92; Thorsen Hennig-Thurau, Mark B. Houson, and Torsten Heitjans, "Conceptualizing and Measuring the Monetary Value of Brand Extensions: The Case of Motion Pictures," *Journal of Marketing* 73, no. 6

(November 2009), pp. 167–83; Rajeev Batra, Peter Lenk, and Michel Wedel, "Brand Extension Strategy Planning: Empirical Estimation of Brand–Category Personality Fit and Atypicality," *Journal of Marketing Research* 47, no. 2 (April 2010), pp. 335–47.

29. David Aaker, *Aaker on Branding: 20 Principles That Drive Success* (Morgan James, 2014); Aaker, *Building Strong Brands.*

30. http://www.neutrogena.com; Vanitha Swaminathan, Richard J. Fox, and Srinivas K. Reddy, "The Impact of Brand Extension Introduction on Choice," *Journal of Marketing* 65, no. 3 (2001), pp. 1–15.

31. Rosellina Ferraro, Amna Kirmani, and Ted Matherly, "Look at Me! Look at Me! Conspicuous Brand Usage, Self-Brand Connection, and Dilution," *Journal of Marketing Research* 50, no. 4 (August 2013), pp. 477–88; Sanjay Sood and Kevin Lane Keller, "The Effects of Brand Name Structure on Brand Extension Evaluations and Parent Brand Dilution," *Journal of Marketing Research* 49, no. 3 (June 2012), pp. 373–82.

32. Ferraro et al. "Look at Me!"; Sharon Ng, "Cultural Orientation and Brand Dilution: Impact of Motivation Level and Extension Typicality," *Journal of Marketing Research* 47, no. 1 (February 2010), pp. 186–98.

33. Mario Marsicano, "Cheetos Lip Balm & More Bizarre Brand Extensions," *The Wall Street Journal,* July 15, 2009.

34. Susan Spiggle, Hang T. Nguyen, and Mary Caravella. "More Than Fit: Brand Extension Authenticity," *Journal of Marketing Research* 49, no. 6 (2012), pp. 967–83; Franziska Völckner et al., "The Role of Parent Brand Quality for Service Brand Extension Success," *Journal of Service Research* 13, no. 4 (2010), pp. 379–96.

35. Guoqun Fu, Jiali Ding, and Riliang Qu, "Ownership Effects in Consumers' Brand Extension Evaluations," *Journal of Brand Management* 16 (2009), pp. 221–33; Christoph Burmann, Sabrina Zeplin, and Nicola Riley, "Key Determinants of Internal Brand Management Success: An Exploratory Empirical Analysis," *Journal of Brand Management* 16 (2009), pp. 264–84.

36. http://www.marriott.com/corporateinfo/glance.mi.

37. Aaker, *Building Strong Brands.*

38. Keller, *Strategic Brand Management.*

39. Ibid.

40. Mukesh Kumar Mishra and Dibyendu Choudhury, "The Effect of Repositioning on Brand Personality: An Empirical Study on BlackBerry Mobile Phones," *IUP Journal of Brand Management* 10, no. 2 (2013); Pascale G. Quester and Nathalie Fleck, "Club Med: Coping with Corporate Brand Evolution," *Journal of Product & Brand Management* 19, no. 2 (2010), pp. 94–102.

41. Maureen Morrison and Natalie Zmuda, "When Good Logos Go Bad," *Advertising Age,* March 17, 2014, http://adage.com.

42. "Morton Salt Girl Birthday Brings Brand Refresh," *Packaging World,* March 12, 2014, http://www.packworld.com.

43. "Daisy Updates Cottage Cheese Pack," *Packaging World,* March 13, 2014, http://www.packworld.com.

44. "Microsoft, Waste Management, The Coca-Cola Company and More at Sustainability in Packaging 2014," *Sustainability in Packaging,* January 6, 2014.

45. Leslie Brokaw, "Pepsi's Biodegradable Backlash: The Snack Bag That Was Too Noisy," *Green Biz,* March 18, 2014, http://www.greenbiz.com.

46. "Iconic L'eggs Sheer Energy Egg Package Returns," *Packaging World,* March 6, 2014, http://www.packworld.com.

47. Kate Little, "Chobani Yogurt Is Latest Victim in Shrinking Grocery Case," *CNBC,* January 4, 2014, http://www.cnbc.com.

48. Susan Berfield, "Brand Oprah Has Some Marketing Lessons," *Bloomberg Businessweek*, May 19, 2011, http://www.businessweek.com.

49. Ibid.

50. Clare O'Connor, "Forbes 400: Meet America's Richest Women (and Not Just Oprah and Meg)," *Forbes*, September 22, 2011, http://www.forbes.com.

51. Sara Krulwich, "Oprah Winfrey," *The New York Times*, May 25, 2011, http://topics.nytimes.com.

52. "The Dr. Oz Show," Oprah Radio, June 3, 2011, http://www.oprah.com; "The Dr. Laura Berman Show," Oprah Radio, June 1, 2011, http://www.oprah.com.

53. "eCirc for Consumer Magazines," *Alliance for Audited Media*, June 30, 2013.

54. Alessandra Stanley, "Among the Lectures, a Bit of Shtick," *The New York Times*, October 14, 2011, http://www.nytimes.com.

55. *Oprah's Lifeclass*, Oprah.com, http://www.oprah.com.

56. Tierney Sneed, " 'Lindsay' Just as Much about Oprah's Recovery as Lindsay Lohan's," *U.S. News & World Report*, March 5, 2014, http://www.usnews.com.

i. http://www.axeanarchy.axe.us/novel; Andrew Adam Newman, "Axe Adds Fragrance for Women to Its Lineup," *The New York Times*, January 8, 2012, http://www.nytimes.com; Dianna Dilworth, "Axe Campaign Has Fans Collaboratively Write Graphic Novel Online," *Direct Marketing News*, January 10, 2012, http://www.dmnews.com; Todd Wasserman, "Axe Launches Fragrance with a Graphic Novel on YouTube," *Mashable Business*, January 10, 2012, http://mashable.com.

ii. Tiffany Hsu, "Coca-Cola Anti-Obesity Promises Include No Advertising to Kids," *Los Angeles Times*, May 8, 2013, http://articles.latimes.com; Mike Esterl and Paul Ziobro, "Coke to Limit Ads to Kids, Push Diet Drinks," *The Wall Street Journal*, http://online.wsj.com.

iii. Mark Wilson, "American Airlines Rebrands Itself, and America Along with It," *Fast Company*, January 22, 2012.

iv. U.S. Government Accounting Office, "Bottled Water: FDA Safety and Consumer Protections Are Often Less Stringent Than Comparable EPA Protections for Tap Water," July 8, 2009; Associated Press, "Stricter Labeling Urged for Bottled Water," *The Wall Street Journal*, July 8, 2008.

Credits

CHAPTER 12

DEVELOPING NEW PRODUCTS

LEARNING OBJECTIVES

LO1 Identify the reasons firms create new products.

LO2 Describe the different groups of adopters articulated by the diffusion of innovation theory.

LO3 Describe the various stages involved in developing a new product or service.

LO4 Explain the product life cycle.

In Chapter 7, we discussed how 3D printing is changing the interactions between businesses in business-to-business markets. But those are secondary effects, in a way. The most prominent and talked about revolution brought about by 3D printing and the increasing availability of 3D printers pertains to the innovative new products that companies and individual consumers might create with them.

In some cases, the products are not radical innovations but rather new versions of existing products. Our discussion of General Electric's uses of the technology described how it was seeking cost benefits and supply chain flexibility by printing out airplane parts, rather than purchasing them from other, traditional manufacturers. The examples in various popular media similarly seek a better production method: On *Grey's Anatomy*, the doctors printed a new, more flexible heart valve for an infant in distress. In *The Big Bang Theory*, the nerds used the advanced technology to print personalized bobble heads of themselves. Thus the production process is new, but the end product serves the same purpose.

In real life, similar examples abound. For regular consumers who pay hundreds of dollars to install a

3D printer on their desk, the goal is frequently the production of fun or artful or useful household items: toys for the kids, a sculpted bowl, or plastic forks and knives. For the construction and preservation crew on *This Old House*, 3D printing enabled them to build a model of a historic property, to better guide their careful renovations and avoid damage to the ancient framework.

In the fashion industry, 3D printing created a corset and wings worn by models in the latest Victoria's Secret Fashion Show.[1] The massive wings represented a creative innovation; had they been produced with traditional methods, their weight would never have allowed the slight model to carry them down the runway. Fashion designers in various realms are investigating how they can adapt the technology to enable consumers to order and purchase clothing with exactly tailored fit. The production process also becomes notably faster, which constitutes a significant appeal in the rapidly changing world of fashion, where getting to market first is usually a notable benefit. The printers even enable clothing manufacturers to experiment with new combinations of materials.

As more companies and consumers seek out the printers, their prices have dropped precipitously. The technology keeps improving, and the machines seem poised to take off, such that some prognosticators claim that 3D printers will become as ubiquitous as regular ink printers in people's homes.[2] Other observers question whether they will really follow a traditional diffusion throughout the market.[3] Citing reasons such as the continued sophistication of the process, these critics argue that 3D printers have not yet become easy enough to use for an everyday consumer to adopt. In addition, different printers would be needed to print items out of different materials. If a house-hold wanted to print a wooden frame for the family portrait, plastic bumpers to protect the walls from the corners of the picture, and nickel nails to hang it, they would need three separate printers, for example.

A separate question involves what happens if an art lover, rather than hanging a family portrait, programs a 3D printer to reproduce a famous sculpture or trademarked item. If it is possible for parents to print out new LEGO sets, identical to those they might buy in the store, are they engaging in theft or trademark infringement?[4]

Maybe the biggest controversy—and the greatest promise—comes about when we consider one more possibility for 3D printing: food. The Chef Jet printer can take extrusions of edible items and print them out in various shapes, colors, and sizes. Some applications seem less likely to work; diners cannot get a steak from a printer. Furthermore, people who worry about artificial-seeming foods might never warm up to the idea. But the printers can combine multiple vegetables together into a single paste, enabling parents to sneak broccoli and kale to their kids by adding in another flavor and printing it in the shape of a train or cool toy.[5] And though important, for most consumers that's not even the best idea. The best notion is the one in which they can get chocolate, in the flavor, density, and amount they want, even if the chocolate craving hits at 3:00 a.m. and without ever leaving their homes.[6]

Few three-letter words are more exciting than *new*. It brings forth an image of freshness, adventure, and excitement. Yet *new* also is a complex term when it comes to market offerings because it might mean adding something new to an existing product, introducing a flavor never offered before, or relying on different packaging that provides added value. But the most exhilarating type of new product is something never seen before. Thousands of patent applications pursue this elusive prize: a successful and truly innovative new product.

Imagine living 200 years ago: You cook meals on a stove fueled by coal or wood; you write out homework by hand (if you are lucky enough to attend school) and by candlelight. To get to school, you hike along unpaved roads to reach a small, cold, basic classroom with just a few classmates who listen to a lecture from a teacher writing on a blackboard.

Today, you finish your homework on a laptop computer with word processing software that appears to have a mind of its own and can correct your spelling automatically. Your climate-controlled room has ample electric light. While you work on your laptop, you also talk with a friend using the hands-free headset of your wireless phone. As you drive to school in your car, you pick up fast food from a convenient drive-through window while browsing and listening to your personal selection of songs playing through your car speakers, connected wirelessly to your iPad. Your friend calls to discuss a slight change to the homework, so you pull over to grab your iPhone, make the necessary change to your assignment, and e-mail it from your smartphone to your professor. When you arrive at school, you sit in a 200-person classroom, where you can plug in your laptop, take notes on your iPad, or digitally record the lecture. The professor adds notes on the day's PowerPoint presentations using her tablet computer. You have already down-loaded the PowerPoint presentations and add similar notes through your own laptop. After class, to complete your planning for a last-minute party, you send out a Facebook invitation to your friends and ask for responses to get a head count. You then text your roommate, telling her to get food and drinks for the right number of people, which she orders through an online grocer that will deliver later in the day.

Our lives are defined by the many new products and services developed through scientific and technological advances and by the added features included in products that we have always used. In this second chapter dealing with the first P in the marketing mix (product), we continue our discussion from the preceding chapter and explore how companies add value to product and service offerings through innovation. We also look at how firms develop new products and services on their own. We conclude the chapter with an examination of how new products and services get adopted by the market and how firms can change their marketing mix as the product or service moves through its life cycle.

WHY DO FIRMS CREATE NEW PRODUCTS?

 LO1 Identify the reasons firms create new products.

New market offerings provide value to both firms and customers. But the degree to which they do so depends on how new they really are. When we say a "new product/service," we don't necessarily mean that the market offer has never existed before. Completely new-to-the-market products represent fewer than 10 percent of all new product introductions each year. It is more useful to think of the degree of newness or innovativeness on a continuum from truly new-to-the-world—as WiFi was a few years ago—to slightly repositioned, such as when Kraft's Capri Sun brand of ready-to-drink beverages were repackaged in a bigger pouch to appeal to teens.

Kraft's Capri Sun has gotten bigger.

Regardless of where on the continuum a new product lies, firms have to innovate. Innovation refers to the process by which ideas are trans-formed into new offerings, including products, services, processes, and branding concepts that will help firms grow. Without innovation and its resulting new products and services, firms would have only two choices: continue to market current products to current customers or take the same product to an-other market with similar customers.

Although innovation strategies may not always work in the short run—some estimates indicate that only about 3 percent of new products actually succeed—various overriding and long-term reasons compel firms to continue introducing new products and services, as the following sections describe.

Changing Customer Needs

When they add products, services, and processes to their offerings, firms can cre-ate and deliver value more effectively by satisfying the changing needs of their

Moving? Rent Frogbox reusable plastic boxes and spare the landfills.

current and new customers or by keeping customers from getting bored with the current product or service offering. Sometimes companies can identify problems and develop products or services that customers never knew they needed. For example, moving can be stressful; among other things, having to buy, build, and dispose of moving boxes is a hassle, expensive, and not very good for the environment. Canadian firm Frogbox rents out reusable plastic moving boxes. It delivers them to the customer and picks them up at the new address when they are finished. The boxes stack neatly inside each other and don't require assembly, eliminating the time-consuming task of building and breaking down boxes. The firm is called Frogbox because it donates 1 percent of sales to frog habitat restoration.[7] Adding to its sustainability efforts, it uses solar energy to power its website and waste-generated biodiesel to fuel its trucks.

In other cases, customers enter new stages in their lives that intensify their demand for such innovations. Technology advances are obvious examples: Waterproof phone cases were rarely a necessity until people started carrying their smartphones everywhere, including near the kitchen sink, into the bathroom, and poolside. For parents of infants, the market is relatively stable, in the sense that most products have been around for years. But Huggies also recognized that parents of toddlers often struggled to get their wriggly babies to stay still for diaper changes, so it introduced Little Movers Slip-Ons, to help make the change a fun game rather than a frustrating struggle. The per diaper price is about 16 cents more than a regular diaper, but Huggies also knows that if it can appeal to the relatively loyal parent segment (approximately 55 percent of whom nearly always buy their preferred brand), its innovation can help it maintain market share.[8]

Huggies Little Movers Slip-On diapers are designed to make life easier for parents.

Market Saturation

The longer a product exists in the marketplace, the more likely it is that the market will become saturated. Without new products or services, the value of the firm will ultimately decline.[9] Imagine, for example, if car companies simply assumed and expected that people would keep their cars until they stopped running. If that were the case, there would be no need to come up with new and innovative models; companies could just stick with the models that sell well. But few consumers actually keep the same car until it stops running. Even those who want to stay with the same make and model often want something new, just to add some variety to their lives. Therefore, car companies revamp their models every year, whether with new features like advanced GPS or a more powerful

Adding Value 12.1 Carmakers Look for an Edge, above and under the Hood[i]

The competition and new partnerships generated by the global car market have yielded a wealth of new product approaches, both above and below the hood, as automakers strive to meet an international aesthetic while also responding to near-universal demand for more fuel-efficient cars. In particular, U.S. carmakers can no longer simply appeal to American tastes, with tailfins, boxy SUVs, and little concern about fuel economy. Car design must meet the demands of drivers overseas. General Motors recently introduced a new concept car, the Chevrolet Tru 140S, an "affordable exotic" model that gets 40 miles per gallon. Another Chevrolet concept, Code 130R, takes elements from the BMW 1 Series, the 1960s Ford Anglia from Europe, and Japanese subcompact car models.

While crafting new looks, GM also is looking for designs that will survive shifting trends. The Cadillac ATS sedan, which aims to compete with the BMW 3 Series, is not nearly as distinctive as classic Cadillac models from the past. But its understated style may enable the ATS to age more gracefully and require fewer, less frequent redesigns. Ford hired European designers to come up with many of its most successful recent models, including the Focus and the Fiesta. These small, quick, sporty cars appeal to the worldwide market. Chrysler's new owner Fiat has added Italian elements to make the U.S. brand appear more global in its design.

Automakers also are relying heavily on new engineering to meet global demand. Tighter fuel-efficiency standards and shifting buyer preferences are forcing carmakers to develop lighter, smaller-cylinder cars, more electrics and hybrids, and new turbocharged engines that couple with electric motors. Even luxury cars are becoming lighter. Mercedes-Benz has spent seven years developing the aluminum body of its new SL 550, which is 308 pounds lighter than the previous model yet still offers unparalleled torsion resistance.

Smaller engines are getting a second look too: For the first time in 20 years, Cadillac is offering a four-cylinder engine to

The 2015 Cadillac ATS is less distinctive than earlier models. As a result its understated style may require fewer redesigns.

deliver fuel efficiency in its ATS. The appeal of these smaller, powerful engines is vast. Ford's new Fusion Hybrid couples a new, lighter lithium ion battery with a lighter four-cylinder engine to deliver six more miles per gallon in fuel efficiency. Plug-in hybrids are entering the market, including Ford's Fusion Energi, which competes with the Chevy Volt and models influenced by Toyota's Prius.

While redesigning its cars for more European tastes, Fiat-owned Chrysler has revived some of the engineering that made its Dodge Dart compact so efficient. And GM has used its globally successful small-car platform as the basis for both its Chevrolet Sonic subcompact and the Buick Encore crossover. With design oriented to global tastes and engineering focused on a newer, more efficient bottom line, automakers worldwide are hoping drivers will like what they see.

---

engine or by redesigning the entire look of the vehicle. The firms sustain their growth by getting consumers excited by the new looks and new features, prompting many car buyers to exchange their old vehicle years before its functional life is over. Adding Value 12.1 notes some other innovations that carmakers are trying.

Saturated markets can also offer opportunities for a company that is willing to adopt a new process or mentality. At one point in time, mass marketers would not even consider entering a market that they believed would not earn at least $50 million. But General Mills is looking to niche markets for its future growth. Whereas only 1 percent of the U.S. population suffers from celiac disease—a condition that damages the digestive system when sufferers ingest gluten—a much higher percentage of U.S. consumers say they want to reduce or eliminate gluten, a wheat protein, from their diet. As awareness increases, those percentages are growing, such that the U.S. market could be broadly

General Mills provides a number of gluten-free options at http://www.chex.com/Recipes/GlutenFree.aspx.

worth up to $10 billion.[10] General Mills has created more than 300 gluten-free products, including both variations on its regular offerings, like Chex cereals, and brand-new concepts, such as gluten-free desserts and pancake mixes.[11]

Managing Risk through Diversity

Through innovation, firms often create a broader portfolio of products, which help them diversify their risk and enhance firm value better than a single product can.[12] If some products in a portfolio perform poorly, others may do well. Firms with multiple products can better withstand external shocks, including changes in consumer preferences or intensive competitive activity. For this reason, firms such as 3M demand that a specific percentage of their sales each year must come from new products introduced within the previous few years. In the cookie aisle, Keebler offers many variations of its basic product, cookies, including Animals, Chips Deluxe, E.L. Fudge, Gripz, Sandies, Vanilla Wafers, and Vienna Fingers. This diversification enables Keebler to enjoy more consistent performance than it would with just one kind of cookie.

Fashion Cycles

In industries that rely on fashion trends and experience short product life cycles—including apparel, arts, books, and software markets—most sales come from new products. For example, a motion picture generates most of its theater, DVD, and cable TV revenues within a year of its release. If the same selection of books were always for sale, with no new titles, there would be no reason to buy more. Consumers of computer software and video games demand new offers because once they have beaten the game,

The Keebler line's risk is lessened by offering many variations of its basic product, cookies.

Video games like Call of Duty Advanced Warfare are "fashionable" because consumers demand new versions. Once they have "beat" the game, they want to be challenged with a new experience.

To generate sales, apparel fashion designers produce entirely new product selections a few times per year.

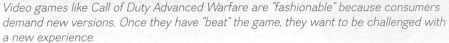

they want to be challenged by another game or experience the most recent version, as the remarkable sales of successive versions of the Call of Duty game exemplify.[13] In the case of apparel, fashion designers produce entirely new product selections a few times per year.

Improving Business Relationships

New products do not always target end consumers; sometimes they function to improve relationships with suppliers. For example, Kraft, the maker of Capri Sun, found that its lemonade flavor was selling poorly. Through a little market research, it realized that the reason was the placement of the packages in pallets. Because it was placed at the bottom of the stack in pallets, lemonade was the last flavor retailers would sell. By changing and innovating its pallet, Kraft offered chimney stacks for each flavor, enabling the retail stockers to reach whichever flavor they needed easily. Sales of Capri Sun's lemonade improved by 162 percent.[14]

Even if they succeed in innovating and creating new products, new-to-the-world products are not adopted by everyone at the same time. Rather, they diffuse or spread through a population in a process known as *diffusion of innovation*.

CHECK YOURSELF

1. What are the reasons firms innovate?

DIFFUSION OF INNOVATION

 LO2 Describe the different groups of adopters articulated by the diffusion of innovation theory.

The process by which the use of an innovation—whether a product, a service, or a process—spreads throughout a market group, over time and across various categories of adopters, is referred to as diffusion of innovation.[15] The theory surrounding diffusion of innovation helps marketers understand the rate at which consumers are likely to adopt a new product or service. It also gives them a means to identify potential markets for their new products or services and predict their potential sales, even before they introduce the innovations.[16]

Truly new product introductions, that is, new-to-the-world products that create new markets, can add tremendous value to firms. These new products, also called pioneers or breakthroughs, establish a completely new market or radically change both the rules of competition and consumer preferences in a market.[17] The Apple iPod is a pioneer product. Not only did it change the way people listen to music, but it also created an entirely new industry devoted to accessories such as cases, ear buds, docking stations, and speakers. Although Apple offers many of these accessories itself, other companies have jumped on the bandwagon, ensuring that you can strap your iPod to your arm while on the move or insert it into the base of a desk lamp equipped with speakers to get music and light from your desk. And don't forget: The iPod also launched perhaps the most notable other recent pioneer, the iPhone, along with the innovative iTunes service, the iPod Touch, and even the iPad.[18]

Apple has released several pioneer products in recent years, including the iPhone.

Pioneers have the advantage of being first movers; as the first to create the market or product category, they become readily recognizable to consumers and thus establish a commanding and early market share lead. Studies also have found that market pioneers can command a greater market share over a longer time period than later entrants can.[19]

Yet not all pioneers succeed. In many cases, imitators capitalize on the weaknesses of pioneers and subsequently gain advantage in the market. Because pioneering products and brands face the uphill task of establishing the market alone, they pave the way for followers, who can spend less marketing effort creating demand for the product line and focus directly on creating demand for their specific brand. Also, because the pioneer is the first product in the market, it often has a less sophisticated design and may be priced relatively higher, leaving room for better and lower-priced competitive products.

An important question to ask is, Why is the failure rate for new products so high? One of the main reasons is the failure to assess the market properly by neglecting to do appropriate product testing, targeting the wrong segment, and/or poor positioning.[20]

K-Cup Packs were a pioneer coffee delivery method that created a new coffee market.

EXHIBIT 12.1	Illustrative Product Failures	
Product	**Concept**	**Why It Failed**
New Coke	In response to growing market pressure, Coca-Cola launched a reformulated version of its classic cola in 1985 that was so hated it was pulled from shelves three months later.	Coke underestimated the consumers' affinity to the original formulation and their unwillingness to change.
Sony Betamax	In 1975, Sony bet big on the Betamax, one of the first ever mass-produced home video recording systems.	Unfortunately, the next year, JVC launched the VHS player, ensuring a format war similar to the Blu-ray and HD-DVD format wars of 2006.
Harley-Davidson Perfume	After being successful with lighters and T-shirts bearing the Harley logo, Harley-Davidson branched out into its own line of perfumes associated with the motorcycle lifestyle.	Although lighters and T-shirts may resonate with the Harley image, customers were not as attracted to smelling like a motorcycle.
Bic Underwear	Bic is well known for its disposable products: pens, lighters, and razors. Capitalizing on its ability to cross product categories, Bic began producing underwear.	The concept of buying underwear from a company well known for disposable pens was confusing and off-putting to consumers.
Bottled Water for Pets	Trying to capitalize on the pet pampering craze, makers of *Thirsty Cat!* and *Thirsty Dog!* launched a line of bottled water for cats and dogs. No longer did owners need to give their pet tap water; instead they could give them a daily pet drink in flavors such as Crispy Beef, Tangy Fish, and Grilled Chicken.	Although people do indeed desire to pamper their pets, the idea of purchasing bottled water for them never caught on. The associations generated by their flavors, such as tangy fish-tasting water, probably did not help either.
Frito-Lay Lemonade	To Frito-Lay, lemonade seemed like a reasonable enough brand extension. After all, the high salt content of corn chips often leads consumers to search out something to quench their thirst.	Associating a salty snack with a supposed thirst quencher did not go over well.
Kellogg's Breakfast Mates	Capitalizing on the convenience market, Kellogg's Breakfast Mates launched a line of cereal products in 1998 that came with cereal, spoon, and milk.	Sometimes a good idea is poorly executed. The milk was usually warm because it did not require refrigeration and the product was not child-friendly, making its appeal very limited.
Apple Newton	Launched in 1993 with a price tag of more than $700, the Apple Newton was one of the first PDAs, which then led the way for the Palm Pilot, BlackBerry, and iPad.	The Newton concept was ahead of its time. Unfortunately due to its bulky size and ridicule by comedians, the Newton lasted only until 1998.
Colgate Kitchen Entrees	Colgate launched a line of frozen dinners. Apparently the idea was that consumers would enjoy eating a Colgate meal and then using Colgate on their toothbrush afterward.	The association of toothpaste with a chicken stir-fry was something customers did not find appetizing.
Clairol's Touch of Yogurt Shampoo	Clairol marketed a shampoo with a touch of yogurt to improve hair quality.	Consumers were not enticed with the idea of washing their hair with yogurt, something Clairol should have known after its Look of Buttermilk failed in test markets a few years earlier.

Source: DailyFinance.com, "Top 25 Biggest Product Flops of All Time," http://www.dailyfinance.com/photos/top-25-biggest-product-flops-of-all-time/3662621.

Firms may also overextend their abilities or competencies by venturing into products or services that are inconsistent with their brand image and/or value proposition. We discuss some infamous product failures in Exhibit 12.1.

As the diffusion of innovation curve in Exhibit 12.2 shows, the number of users of an innovative product or service spreads through the population over a period of time and generally follows a bell-shaped curve. A few people buy the product or service at first, then more buy, and finally fewer people buy as the degree of the diffusion slows. These purchasers can be divided into five groups according to how soon they buy the product after it has been introduced.

Innovators

Innovators are those buyers who want to be the first on the block to have the new product or service. These buyers enjoy taking risks and are regarded as highly

Clairol's Touch of Yogurt Shampoo failed because consumers didn't like the idea of washing their hair with yogurt.

Users of Gillette's Fusion Proglide are early adopters.

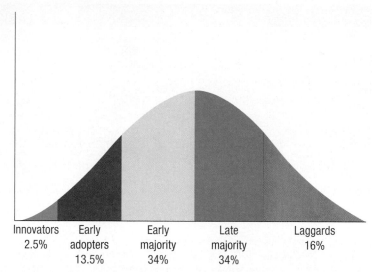

EXHIBIT 12.2	Diffusion of Innovation Curve

| Innovators 2.5% | Early adopters 13.5% | Early majority 34% | Late majority 34% | Laggards 16% |

Time of adoption of the innovation

Source: Adapted from Everett M. Rodgers, *Diffusion of Innovation* (New York: Free Press, 1983).

knowledgeable. You probably know someone who is an innovator—or perhaps you are one for a particular product or service category. For example, the person who stood in line overnight to be sure to get a ticket for the very first showing of the latest superhero movie is an innovator in that context. Those consumers who already have 3D printers at their homes are likely innovators too. Firms that invest in the latest technology, either to use in their products or services or to make the firm more efficient, also are considered innovators. Typically, innovators keep themselves very well informed about the product category by subscribing to trade and specialty magazines, talking to other experts, visiting product-specific blogs and forums that describe the coolest new products,[21] and attending product-related forums, seminars, and special events. Yet innovators represent only about 2.5 percent of the total market for any new product or service.

These innovators are crucial to the success of any new product or service, though, because they help the product gain market acceptance. Through talking about and spreading positive word of mouth about the new product, they prove instrumental in bringing in the next adopter category, known as early adopters.[22]

Early Adopters

The second subgroup that begins to use a product or service innovation is early adopters. They generally don't like to take as much risk as innovators do but instead wait and purchase the product after careful review. Thus, this market waits for the first reviews of the latest movie before purchasing a ticket, though they likely still go a week or two after it opens. They do not stand in line to grab the first Samsung 4K televisions; only after reading the innovators' complaints and praises do they decide whether the new technology is worth the cost.[23] But most of them go ahead and purchase because early adopters tend to enjoy novelty and often are regarded as the opinion leaders for particular product categories.

This group, which represents about 13.5 percent of all buyers in the market, spreads the word. As a result, early adopters are crucial for bringing the other three buyer categories to the market. If the early adopter group is relatively small, the number of people who ultimately adopt the innovation likely will also be small.

Early Majority

The early majority, which represents approximately 34 percent of the population, is crucial because few new products and services can be profitable until this large group buys them. If the group never becomes large enough, the product or service typically fails.

The early majority group differs in many ways from buyers in the first two stages. Its members don't like to take as much risk and therefore tend to wait until the bugs are worked out of a particular product or service. This group probably rents the latest *Hunger Games* movie during the first week it comes out on video. Thus, early majority members experience little risk because all the reviews are in, and their costs are lower because they're renting the movie instead of going to the theater. When early majority customers enter the market, the number of competitors in the marketplace usually also has reached its peak, so these buyers have many price and quality choices.

Late Majority

At 34 percent of the market, the late majority is the next group of buyers to enter a new product market. When they do, the product has achieved its full market potential. Perhaps these movie watchers wait until the newest movie is easy to find at Red Box or put it low on their Netflix queue, to be delivered after the other consumers interested in watching it have already seen it. By the time the late majority enters the market, sales tend to level off or may be in decline.

Laggards

Laggards make up roughly 16 percent of the market. These consumers like to avoid change and rely on traditional products until they are no longer available. In some cases, laggards may never adopt a certain product or service. When the sequel to *Hunger Games*, *Catching Fire*, eventually shows up on their regular television networks, they are likely to go ahead and watch it.

Using the Diffusion of Innovation Theory

Using the diffusion of innovation theory, firms can predict which types of customers will buy their new product or service immediately after its introduction as well as later as the product is more and more accepted by the market. With this knowledge, the firm can develop effective promotion, pricing, and other marketing strategies to push acceptance among each customer group. Let's consider an example of some everyday products that nearly all of us use at some point.

Although it is not as flashy as Google Glass or the latest iPhone, everyone uses cleaning supplies. Oftentimes the innovators who adopt new cleaning products are the ones who are the most fanatical about cleaning.

Early majority members would probably rent the latest Hunger Games *movie rather than see it in theaters when it first comes out. They can assess the movie from its reviews, and the cost of a rental is lower than at the theater. Overall these consumers experience little risk.*

Consumers who are fixated on cleaning will spend substantial amounts for the most technologically advanced machines, like this Dyson Ball Vacuum.

Firms conduct in-depth research into how people clean their homes to identify such segments. This research finds that some people are so obsessive about cleaning that they spend nearly 20 hours every week doing it, while others are so reluctant that they avoid cleaning as much as they can; their average weekly cleaning time is about 2.5 hours.[24] Their options with regard to the products to purchase to assist them in their cleaning tasks are vast, from scrubbers to sprays to vacuums to dusters. Thus, in the vacuum cleaner market, manufacturers recognize that the segment of consumers who will spend substantial amounts for the most technologically advanced, powerful, easy-to-maneuver machines, such as the latest Dyson model, are likely to be the segment of consumers that is most fixated on cleaning.[25] But another segment just wants some basic suction to get the grit out of their rugs.

Relative Advantage If a product or service is perceived to be better than substitutes, then the diffusion will be relatively quick. As advertising for Swiffer products emphasizes, its mops and dusters promise to make cleaning faster, easier, and more efficient. In featuring real families, it seeks to highlight the relative advantage for all types of cleaners. Older people who might once have gotten on their hands and knees to scrub the floor can now rely on the design of the cleaning pads on the end of the mop to get the job done. Their children, who have never been very good at cleaning, can swipe a few surfaces and get the house looking clean before their parents visit. And a man who has lost an arm to cancer can still help his family keep the house clean, because the duster does not require him to use a spray or climb a ladder to dust the ceiling fan.[26]

Electrolux revolutionizes the vacuum market with a bagless vacuum cleaner.

Compatibility A diffusion process may be faster or slower, depending on various consumer features, including international cultural differences. Electrolux's latest bagless vacuums offer a key innovation: They solve the age-old problem of how to empty the chamber without having a cloud of particles fly out by compacting the dirt into a "pellet." To make the product more compatible with the needs of people in different cultures, it is made in various sizes. The U.S. version offers a carpet nozzle with a motor, to deal with the dirt accumulated in Americans' larger, often carpeted homes. Because in many Asian "megacities" consumers live in tiny apartments, Electrolux has introduced a smaller version that is also very quiet.[27]

Observability When products are easily observed, their benefits or uses are easily communicated to others, which enhances the diffusion process. To demonstrate to consumers why they should spend $400 on a blender, Blendtec launched an extensive YouTube campaign titled "Will It Blend?" to demonstrate the effectiveness of the blender. In each video, a spokesperson in a white lab coat blends a different product in the Blendtec—from iPads to baseballs to Justin Bieber's autobiography—and gives visible proof to consumers of the quality of the product. The humor and innovativeness of this product demonstration has caused these videos to go viral, with over 230 million views and 700,000 subscribers.[28] Yet some cleaning products face a serious challenge in making their innovations widely observable because few consumers spend a lot of time talking about the products that are of a more personal nature, such as what they use to clean their toilets. Even a great product might diffuse more slowly if people feel uncomfortable talking about what they perceive to be involved in their personal care.

Complexity and Trialability Products that are relatively less complex are also relatively easy to try. These products will generally diffuse more quickly and lead to greater/faster adoption than those that are not so easy to try. In the cleaning products range, it is far easier to pick up a new spray cleaner at the grocery store to try at home than it is to assess and test a new vacuum. In response, manufacturers seek ways to help people conduct trials. For example, Dyson's displays in national retailers such as Bed, Bath, & Beyond often include floor space that allows shoppers to run the machine, to see how well the roller ball works or watch it pick up dirt.

The diffusion of innovation theory thus comes into play in the immediate and long-term aftermath of a new product or service introduction. But before the introduction, firms must actually develop those new offerings. In the next section, we detail the process by which most firms develop new products and services and how they introduce them into the market.

CHECK YOURSELF

1. What are the five groups on the diffusion of innovation curve?
2. What factors enhance the diffusion of a good or service?

HOW FIRMS DEVELOP NEW PRODUCTS

LO3 Describe the various stages involved in developing a new product or service.

The new product development process begins with the generation of new product ideas and culminates in the launch of a new product and the evaluation of its success. The stages of the new product development process, along with the important objectives of each stage, are summarized in Exhibit 12.3.

Idea Generation

To generate ideas for new products, a firm can use its own internal research and development (R&D) efforts, collaborate with other firms and institutions, license technology from research-intensive firms, brainstorm, research competitors' products and services, and/or conduct consumer research; see Exhibit 12.4. Firms that

EXHIBIT 12.3 The Product Development Process

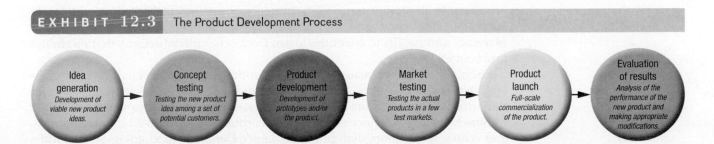

Idea generation
Development of viable new product ideas.

Concept testing
Testing the new product idea among a set of potential customers.

Product development
Development of prototypes and/or the product.

Market testing
Testing the actual products in a few test markets.

Product launch
Full-scale commercialization of the product.

Evaluation of results
Analysis of the performance of the new product and making appropriate modifications.

EXHIBIT 12.4   Sources of New Product Ideas

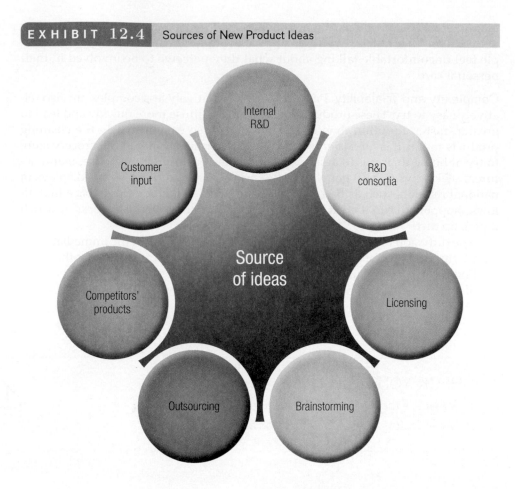

want to be pioneers rely more extensively on R&D efforts, whereas those that tend to adopt a follower strategy are more likely to scan the market for ideas. Let's look at each of these idea sources.

Internal Research and Development Many firms have their own R&D departments, in which scientists work to solve complex problems and develop new ideas. Historically, firms such as IBM in the computer industry, Black and Decker in the consumer goods industry, 3M in the industrial goods industry, and Merck and Pfizer in the pharmaceuticals industry have relied on R&D development efforts for their new products. In other industries, such as software, music, and motion pictures, product development efforts also tend to come from internal ideas and R&D financial investments.

The product development costs for these firms are quite high, and the resulting new product or service has a good chance of being a technological or market breakthrough. Firms expect such products to generate enough revenue and profits to make the costs of R&D worthwhile. R&D investments generally are considered continuous investments, so firms may lose money on a few new products. In the long run, though, these firms are betting that a few extremely successful new products, often known as blockbusters, can generate enough revenues and profits to cover the losses from other introductions that might not fare so well.

Some global firms also are taking an approach called reverse innovation, as we discussed in Chapter 7. They turn to subsidiaries in less developed markets for new product ideas. From its Shanghai research center, Coca-Cola developed Minute Maid Pulpy, a juice drink that the corporation has moved into 19 countries and is now worth more than $1 billion. Levi's Denizen brand got its start in India

From where do you think the idea for a waterproof tablet from Fujitsu was derived? Internal R&R, R&D consortia, licensing, brainstorming, outsourcing, competitor's products, customer input, or a combination?

and China, where the company worked on ideas for producing more affordable jeans. In the U.S. market, Denizen jeans sell for about half the cost of a pair of regular Levi's and are available exclusively at Target.[29]

R&D Consortia In recent years, more and more firms have been joining consortia, or groups of other firms and institutions, possibly including government and educational institutions, to explore new ideas or obtain solutions for developing new products. Here, the R&D investments come from the group as a whole, and the participating firms and institutions share the results.

In many cases, the consortia involve pharmaceutical or high-tech members, whose research costs can run into the millions—too much for a single company to bear. The National Institutes of Health (NIH) sponsors medical foundations to conduct research to treat rare diseases. The research is then disseminated to the medical community, thus encouraging the development of drugs and therapies more quickly and at a lower cost than would be possible if the research were privately funded. The U.S. cable industry has initiated its CableLabs–Energy Lab consortium to find ways to improve the energy efficiency of cable set-top boxes and develop more advanced cable services, such as better sleep settings, to promote other forms of energy conservation.[30]

Licensing For many other scientific and technological products, firms buy the rights to use the technology or ideas from other research-intensive firms through a licensing agreement. This approach saves the high costs of in-house R&D, but it means that the firm is banking on a solution that already exists but has not been marketed. Some of the largest recent licensing deals in the pharmaceutical industry are for potential weight-loss solutions. In separate deals, one worth $1.4 billion and another worth $1.1 billion, two big pharmaceutical firms licensed the marketing rights for new products developed by small biotechnology firms to combat obesity.[31] Yet neither drug had received FDA approval at the time of the deals!

Brainstorming Firms often engage in brainstorming sessions during which a group works together to generate ideas. One of the key characteristics of a brainstorming session is that no idea can be immediately accepted or rejected. The moderator of the session may channel participants' attention to specific product

Balance Body partnered with IDEO to develop a less-intimidating, more-user-friendly reformer to be used with Pilates.

features and attributes, performance expectations, or packaging. Only at the end of the session do the members vote on the best ideas or combinations of ideas. Those ideas that receive the most votes are carried forward to the next stage of the product development process.

Outsourcing In some cases, companies have trouble moving through these steps alone, which prompts them to turn to outside firms such as IDEO, a design firm based in Palo Alto, California. IDEO offers not new products but rather a stellar service that helps clients generate new product and service ideas in industries such as health care, toys, and computers. IDEO employs anthropologists, graphic designers, engineers, and psychologists whose special skills help foster creativity and innovation. As exercise is becoming more and more popular, companies are looking for ways to capitalize on the beginner's market. Balanced Body is a company that makes and sells reformers to be used with Pilates. A reformer is a device that helps Pilates participants develop good alignment, core strength, and flexibility. When Balanced Body did research and found that people starting Pilates found the reformers that were currently on the market to be too intimidating, it partnered with IDEO to develop a reformer that had better user experience while maintaining the high level of functionality its products engender.[32] In an eight-week period, IDEO created a redesigned model with fewer wheels while improving functionality and adjustability of the product and reducing the cost of the machine.

Competitors' Products A new product entry by a competitor may trigger a market opportunity for a firm, which can use reverse engineering to understand the competitor's product and then bring an improved version to market. Reverse engineering involves taking apart a product, analyzing it, and creating an improved product that does not infringe on the competitor's patents, if any exist. This copycat approach to new product development is widespread and practiced by even the most research-intensive firms. Copycat consumer goods show up in apparel, grocery and drugstore products as well

Social & Mobile Marketing 12.1 — When Microsoft Plays Catch-Up[ii]

Microsoft is one of the most innovative companies of all time. After revolutionizing the home computer industry, it set out to be a leader in the information technology home entertainment fields. It seems like not a year ever goes by without something new from the brainchild of Bill Gates.

But one area in which Microsoft has been behind the curve is the search engine market. Google, with its nearly 70 percent market share and massive name recognition, does not appear to be in any real danger from competitors, including Microsoft's Bing.com. But Bing already has outpaced Yahoo.com for the remainder of the market, and its market share has been growing, slowly but surely. Perhaps most important, it is distinguishing itself by providing more frequent updates and feature additions than the other search engines. Consumers benefit overall because Bing is forcing competitors to improve their offering to keep pace with Microsoft or prevent it from stealing market share from them.

Its efforts have paid off somewhat: Bing now attracts an approximately 18 percent market share among U.S. users, whereas Yahoo! accounts for only about 10 percent. Google maintains a remarkably high share, though that level has decreased in recent years. Despite these seeming successes, the costs of its copycat efforts have meant that the division responsible for Bing lost $2.56 billion in one recent fiscal year.

To differentiate itself better, Bing is being promoted as a decision engine rather than a search engine. It integrates Foursquare, a location-based phone application, into Bing

Microsoft's Bing competes with Google in the search engine market.

Maps results. Users can focus on a particular area, such as South Boston, which means Bing can act like an integrative day planner and list the best things to do in that area. It is working on developing a desktop application, and Bing links seamlessly with Facebook to show users which search outcome their friends like best. Despite Microsoft's problems developing search engines, Bing suggests it intends to stay aggressive in this market.

---

as in technologically more complex products such as automobiles and computers, as Social and Mobile Marketing 12.1 notes.

Customer Input Listening to the customer in both B2B and B2C markets is essential for successful idea generation.[33] Because customers for B2B products are relatively few, firms can follow their use of products closely and solicit suggestions and ideas to improve those products either by using a formal approach, such as focus groups, interviews, or surveys, or through more informal discussions. The firm's design and development team then works on these suggestions, sometimes in consultation with the customer. This joint effort between the selling firm and the customer significantly increases the probability that the customer eventually will buy the new product.

Customer input in B2C markets comes from a variety of sources, though increasingly through social media. By monitoring online feedback, whether requested by the firm or provided voluntarily in customer reviews, companies can get better ideas about new products or necessary changes to existing ones. The recent introduction of Green Giant snack chips provides a good example of using inputs from various types of partners. General Mills (which owns the Green Giant brand) heard a pitch for a new vegetable-based snack chip from its supplier Shearer's Chips. The chip manufacturer developed 10 options for its business customer, General Mills. Then General Mills solicited input from its end consumers to find out which flavors they might like best. Online reviews suggested the need for a much zestier version of the roasted vegetable tortilla chips, which ultimately appeared on store shelves.[34]

In some cases, consumers may not expressly demand a new product, even though their behavior demonstrates their desire for it. For example, Home Depot conducted

By listening to consumers' input, the Big Gripper bucket was designed to make it easier to handle.

some in-home research with consumers to see where they might have unexpressed needs. Although they never mentioned their need, the researchers realized that women engaged in heavy-duty gardening tasks wound up struggling with the bulky, heavy buckets they were using to transport dirt and fertilizer to different areas of the yard. In partnership with a design firm, it thus developed the Big Gripper bucket with a more ergonomic handle, a secondary grip on the side (to make it easier to tip the bucket), and another grip on the bottom. In this case, Home Depot has improved on a product that has not changed notably in decades, by observing how people use it.[35]

Another particularly successful customer input approach is to analyze lead users, those innovative product users who modify existing products according to their own ideas to suit their specific needs.[36] If lead users customize a firm's products, other customers might wish to do so as well. Thus, studying lead users helps the firm understand general market trends that might be just on the horizon. Manufacturers and retailers of fashion products often spot new trends by noticing how innovative trendsetters have altered their clothing and shoes. Designers of high-fashion jeans distress their products in different ways depending on signals they pick up on the street. One season jeans appear with whiskers, the next season they have holes, the next, paint spots.

At the end of the idea-generation stage, the firm should have several ideas that it can take forward to the next stage: concept testing.

Concept Testing

Ideas with potential are developed further into concepts, which in this context refer to brief written descriptions of the product; its technology, working principles, and forms; and what customer needs it would satisfy.[37] A concept might also include visual images of what the product would look like.

Concept testing refers to the process in which a concept statement is presented to potential buyers or users to obtain their reactions. These reactions enable the developer to estimate the sales value of the product or service concept, possibly make changes to enhance its sales value, and determine whether the idea is worth further development.[38] If the concept fails to meet customers' expectations, it is doubtful it would succeed if it were to be produced and marketed. Because concept testing occurs very early in the new product introduction process, even before a real product has been made, it helps the firm avoid the costs of unnecessary product development.

The concept for an electric scooter might be written as follows:

> The product is a lightweight electric scooter that can be easily folded and taken with you inside a building or on public transportation. The scooter weighs 25 pounds. It travels at speeds of up to 15 miles per hour and can go about 12 miles on a single charge. The scooter can be recharged in about two hours from a standard electric outlet. The scooter is easy to ride and has simple controls—just an accelerator button and a brake. It sells for $299.[39]

Concept testing progresses along the research techniques described in Chapter 10. The firm likely starts with qualitative research, such as in-depth interviews or focus groups, to test the concept, after which it can undertake quantitative research through Internet or mall-intercept surveys. Video clips on the Internet might show a virtual prototype and the way it works so that potential customers can evaluate the product or service. In a mall-intercept survey, an interviewer would provide a description of the concept to the respondent and then ask several questions to obtain his or her feedback.

The most important question pertains to the respondent's purchase intentions if the product or service were made available. Marketers also should ask whether

Innovative customers called lead users are especially influential in the fashion industry because designers frequently change their designs based on trends they see on the street.

the product would satisfy a need that other products currently are not meeting. Depending on the type of product or service, researchers might also ask about the expected frequency of purchase, how much customers would buy, whether they would buy it for themselves or as a gift, when they would buy, and whether the price information (if provided) indicates a good value. In addition, marketers usually collect some information about the customers so they can analyze which consumer segments are likely to be most interested in the product.

Some concepts never make it past the concept testing stage, particularly if respondents seem uninterested. Those that do receive high evaluations from potential consumers, however, move on to the next step, product development.

Product Development

Product development or product design entails a process of balancing various engineering, manufacturing, marketing, and economic considerations to develop a product's form and features or a service's features. An engineering team develops a product prototype that is based on research findings from the previous concept testing step as well as their own knowledge about materials and technology. A prototype is the first physical form or service description of a new product, still in rough or tentative form, which has the same properties as a new product but is produced through different manufacturing processes—sometimes even crafted individually.[40]

Product prototypes are usually tested through alpha and beta testing. In alpha testing, the firm attempts to determine whether the product will perform according to its design and whether it satisfies the need for which it was intended.[41] Rather than use potential consumers, alpha tests occur in the firm's R&D department. For instance, Ben & Jerry's Ice Cream alpha tests all its proposed new flavors on its own (lucky) employees at its corporate headquarters in Vermont.

Many people, consumer groups, and governmental agencies are concerned when alpha testing involves tests on animals, particularly when it comes to pharmaceuticals and cosmetics.

Is Ben & Jerry's Ice Cream doing alpha or beta testing?

Ethical & Societal Dilemma 12.1   Should Firms Test on Animals?[iii]

Product testing on animals has been a primary issue for animal rights activists for years. As public opposition to animal testing increases, so do many companies' declarations that they do not test products on animals. However, such statements can be misleading because even though the whole product may not have been tested on animals, the individual ingredients may have been. To help clarify any confusion, companies can apply to the Coalition for Consumer Information on Cosmetics (CCIC), a national group formed by eight animal welfare group members such as the United States Humane Association and the Doris Day Animal League, and be certified as cruelty free. They then can purchase the trademarked Leaping Bunny Logo from CCIC for use on their labels.

One of the founding principles of The Body Shop, and one that has resonated well with its customers, is that its products are free of animal testing. Another major cosmetics manufacturer, Procter & Gamble, has eliminated animal testing on more than 80 percent of its products. It uses a combination of in vitro testing, computer modeling, and historical data to determine the safety of new products and ingredients. These methods are more expensive than more traditional methods, but P&G claims that the results are better. If performed correctly, new chemicals can either be dropped from consideration or pushed forward in as little as three days compared to the six months previously required for animal testing.

However, animal welfare groups continue to push P&G and other firms to stop the use of animal testing altogether. People for the Ethical Treatment of Animals (PETA) publicly cites companies it accuses of engaging in animal testing and other activities considered to be inhumane and praises those that do not. PETA's efforts have caused firms like Hugo Boss, H&M, and Liz Claiborne to stop buying their wool from Australia because some Australian sheep farmers shear their sheep's wool in inhumane ways.

The European Union has passed a ban on animal testing altogether. Beginning in 2009 and finalized in 2013, any cosmetic tested on animals, even in other parts of the world, cannot be sold in the European Union. However, the cosmetics industry is worried that this ban will not only affect their companies' sales but also their customers' ability to find the products they want. The EU cosmetics industry successfully

Activists of the People for the Ethical Treatment of Animals (PETA) participate in a protest against animal slaughter near a mall where Hermes—the French luxury goods company—has a store in Jakarta, Indonesia. PETA demanded Hermes stop selling exotic animal skin products and released gruesome videos of reptiles being skinned alive in Indonesia.

lobbied for an extension on certain areas of toxicity testing to provide more time to find alternatives. The cosmetics industry believes it will be difficult to find alternative testing methods in time, and if it cannot, it will have fewer ingredients to make the products consumers want.

In contrast, China requires animal testing on cosmetics products before they may be sold in that nation. To avoid the risk that Chinese authorities will test their products, some companies choose not to enter the market. However, such a stance might not be viable in the long term, as the already massive Chinese market—especially for cosmetics—grows.

The issues involved in animal testing are complex. At the broadest level, should firms be allowed to develop products that customers want, even if there is some potential harm to the environment or to those animals that share the environment with humans? More specifically, should firms be allowed to test products on animals, even when those products are not specifically designed to improve the health and well-being of their human users? Does the testing that is performed endanger the lives or health of the animals?

Ethical and Societal Dilemma 12.1 discusses these concerns in the United States, the European Union, and China.

In contrast, beta testing uses potential consumers, who examine the product prototype in a real-use setting to determine its functionality, performance, potential problems, and other issues specific to its use. The firm might develop several prototype products that it gives to users, then survey those users to determine whether the product worked as intended and identify any issues that need resolution.

The advent of the Internet has made recruiting beta testers easier than ever. Through sites such as OnlineBeta (http://www.onlinebeta.com), everyday people can sign up to become beta testers for products from companies such as Dell, Kodak, and TomTom. To further automate the beta testing process, YouEye is developing eye tracking technology that works with an individual's webcam. Instead of needing to spend thousands of dollars on eye tracking equipment and having customers come into labs, firms will be able to utilize everyday webcams to track not only what a person attends to on a computer screen, but also his or her emotional reactions to these products.[42]

Market Testing

The firm has developed its new product or service and tested the prototypes. Now it must test the market for the new product with a trial batch of products. These tests can take two forms: premarket testing and test marketing.

Premarket Tests Firms conduct premarket tests before they actually bring a product or service to market to determine how many customers will try and then continue to use the product or service according to a small group of potential consumers. One popular proprietary premarket test version is called Nielsen BASES. During the test, potential customers are exposed to the marketing mix variables, such as the advertising, then surveyed and given a sample of the product to try.[43] After some period of time, during which the potential customers try the product, they are surveyed about whether they would buy/use the product again. This second survey provides an estimation of the probability of a consumer's repeat purchase. From these data, the firm generates a sales estimate for the new product that enables it to decide whether to introduce the product, abandon it, redesign it before introduction, or revise the marketing plan. An early evaluation of this sort—that is, before the product is introduced to the whole market—saves marketers the costs of a nationwide launch if the product fails.

Sometimes firms simulate a product or service introduction, in which case potential customers view the advertising of various currently available products or services along with advertising for the new product or service. They receive money to buy the product or service from a simulated environment, such as a mock web page or store, and respond to a survey after they make their purchases. This test can determine the effectiveness of a firm's advertising as well as the expected trial rates for the new product.

Test Marketing A method of determining the success potential of a new product, test marketing introduces the offering to a limited geographical area (usually a few cities) prior to a national launch. Test marketing is a strong predictor of product success because the firm can study actual purchase behavior, which is more reliable than a simulated test. A test marketing effort uses all the elements of the marketing mix: It includes promotions such as advertising and coupons, just as if the product were being introduced nationally, and the product appears in targeted retail outlets, with appropriate pricing. On the basis of the results of the test marketing, the firm can estimate demand for the entire market.

Test marketing costs more and takes longer than premarket tests, which may provide an advantage to competitors that could get a similar or better product to market first without test marketing. For this reason, some firms might launch new products without extensive consumer testing and rely instead on intuition, instincts, and guts.[44]

Product Launch

If the market testing returns with positive results, the firm is ready to introduce the product to the entire market. This most critical step in the new product introduction requires tremendous financial resources and extensive coordination of all aspects of the marketing mix. For any firm, if the new product launch is a failure, it may be difficult for the product—and perhaps the firm—to recover. For example, though the number of 3D movie theaters continues to grow, ticket sales for

Is the 3D experience worth the price?

these offerings first leveled off and now have started to decline. The introduction of the new technology was popular enough that sellers invested heavily in building more than 15,000 3D screens, and Hollywood promised a wider range of 3D film options. But if—as appears to be the case—moviegoers have decided that the realistic, three-dimensional images are not worth the higher ticket price, such investments might be painful for both movie studios and movie theaters.[45]

So what does a product launch involve? First, on the basis of the research it has gathered on consumer perceptions, the tests it has conducted, and competitive considerations, the firm confirms its target market (or markets) and decides how the product will be positioned. Then the firm finalizes the remaining marketing mix variables for the new product, including the marketing budget for the first year.[46]

Promotion The test results help the firm determine an appropriate integrated marketing communications strategy.[47] Promotion for new products is required at each link in the supply chain. If the products are not sold and stocked by retailers, no amount of promotion to consumers will sell the products. Trade promotions, which are promotions to wholesalers or retailers to get them to purchase the new products, often combine introductory price promotions, special events, and personal selling. Introductory price promotions are limited-duration, lower-than-normal prices designed to provide retailers with an incentive to try the products. Manufacturers may run a special event in the form of a special display in a grocery aisle, an introductory celebration, or a party in conjunction with an interesting event like the Academy Awards.

Another outlet for exposing buyers to new products is a trade show, which is a temporary concentration of manufacturers that provides retailers the opportunity to view what is available and new in the marketplace. The fashion world's equivalent to trade shows are fashion weeks in which fashion manufacturers meet with retailers and have elaborate runway shows to introduce their new products. Finally, as in many B2B sales situations, personal selling may be the most efficient way to get retailers to purchase their products.

Manufacturers also use promotion to generate demand for new products with consumers. If manufacturers can create demand for the products among consumers, they will go to retailers asking for it (pull demand; see Chapter 19), further inducing retailers to carry the products. These promotions are often coupled with short-term price reductions, coupons, or rebates. Sometimes manufacturers promote new products in advance of the product launch to create excitement with potential customers as well as to measure the likely demand so they have appropriate supply available. Automobile and motorcycle manufacturers, for instance, advertise their new products months before they are available on the dealers' floors.

For products that are somewhat complex or conceptually new, marketers may need to provide for more consumer education about the product's benefits than they would for simpler and more familiar products. The quantum dot technology that is being developed to improve the LCD screens on televisions, computers, and mobile phones is not something that most consumers understand. But marketers can encourage their adoption by highlighting the clearly evident appeal of energy efficiency, longer battery life, and more vibrant color offered by the innovative technology.[48] In addition, technical support staff, such as Apple's Geniuses, often must be trained to answer customer questions that may arise immediately after the launch of a new technical innovation.

Place   The manufacturer coordinates the delivery and storage of the new products with its retailers to ensure that it is available for sale when the customer wants it, at the stores the customer is expecting to find it, and in sufficient quantities to meet demand. Manufacturers work with their retailers on decisions such as:

- Should the merchandise be stored at retailers' distribution centers or distributed directly to stores?
- What initial and fill-in quantities should be shipped?
- Should the manufacturer be involved in reordering decisions?
- Should the merchandise be individually packaged so it is easy to display in the stores?
- Should price stickers be affixed on the merchandise at the factory or at the store?
- Should the manufacturer be involved in the maintenance of the merchandise once in the store?

Price   Like the promotion of new products, setting prices is a supply chain–wide decision. Manufacturers must decide at what price they would like products to sell to consumers on the basis of the factors discussed in Chapter 14. They often encourage retailers to sell at a specified price known as the manufacturer's suggested retail price (MSRP). Although retailers often don't abide by the MSRP, manufacturers can withhold benefits such as paying for all or part of a promotion or even refusing to deliver merchandise to noncomplying retailers. It is sometimes easier to start with a higher MSRP and then over time lower it than it is to introduce the new product at a low price and then try to raise the price.

When setting the MSRP, manufacturers also consider the price at which the new products are sold to the retailers. The retailers not only need to make a profit on each sale, but they may also receive a slotting allowance from the manufacturer, which is a fee paid simply to get new products into stores or to gain more or better shelf space for their products.

Timing   The timing of the launch may be important, depending on the product.[49] Hollywood studios typically release movies targeted toward general audiences (i.e., those rated G or PG) during the summer when children are out of school. New automobile models traditionally are released for sale during September, and fashion products are launched just before the season of the year for which they are intended.

Evaluation of Results

After the product has been launched, marketers must undertake a critical post-launch review to determine whether the product and its launch were a success or failure and what additional resources or changes to the marketing mix are needed, if any. Many firms use panel data to improve the probability of success during the test marketing phase of a new product introduction. The consumer panel data are collected by panelists scanning in their receipts using a home scanning device. This information is used to measure individual household first-time trials and repeat purchases. Through such data, market demand can be estimated, so the firm can figure out how best to adjust its marketing mix. Some products never make it out of the introduction stage, especially those that seem almost laughable in retrospect. Bottled water for pets? Harley-Davidson perfume?[50]

For those products that do move on, firms can measure the success of a new product by three interrelated factors: (1) its satisfaction of technical requirements, such as performance; (2) customer acceptance; and (3) its satisfaction of the firm's financial requirements, such as sales and profits.[51] If the product is not performing sufficiently well, poor customer acceptance will result, which in turn leads to poor financial performance.

The new product development process, when followed rationally and sequentially, helps avoid such domino-type failures. The product life cycle, discussed in the next section, helps marketers manage their products' marketing mix during and after introduction.

CHECK YOURSELF

1. What are the steps in the new product development process?
2. Identify different sources of new product ideas.

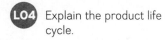 **LO4** Explain the product life cycle.

THE PRODUCT LIFE CYCLE

The **product life cycle** defines the stages that products move through as they enter, get established in, and ultimately leave the marketplace. It thereby offers marketers a starting point for their strategy planning. The stages of the life cycle often reflect marketplace trends, such as the healthy lifestyle trend that today places organic and green product categories in their growth stages. Exhibit 12.5 illustrates

EXHIBIT 12.5   Product Life Cycle

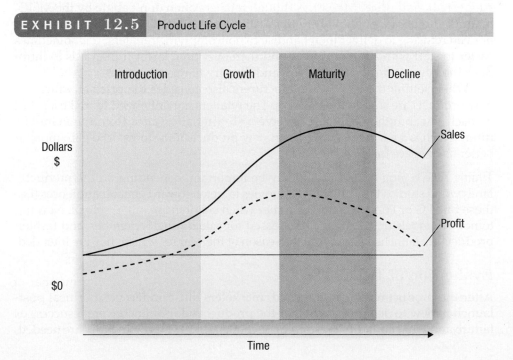

EXHIBIT 12.6	Characteristics of Different Stages of the Product Life Cycle			
	Introduction	Growth	Maturity	Decline
Sales	Low	Rising	Peak	Declining
Profits	Negative or low	Rapidly rising	Peak to declining	Declining
Typical consumers	Innovators	Early adopters and early majority	Late majority	Laggards
Competitors (number of firms and products)	One or few	Few but increasing	High number of competitors and competitive products	Low number of competitors and products

a typical product life cycle, including the industry sales and profits over time. In their life cycles, products pass through four stages: introduction, growth, maturity, and decline. When the product category first launches, its products initiate the introduction stage. In the growth stage, the product gains acceptance, demand and sales increase, and more competitors emerge in the product category. In the maturity stage, industry sales reach their peak, so firms try to rejuvenate their products by adding new features or repositioning them. If these efforts succeed, the product achieves new life.[52] If not, it goes into decline and eventually exits the market.

Not every product follows the same life cycle curve. Many products, such as home appliances, stay in the maturity stage for a very long time. Manufacturers may add features to dishwashers and washing machines, but the mature product category remains essentially the same and seems unlikely to enter the decline stage unless some innovative, superior solution comes along to replace them.

The product life cycle offers a useful tool for managers to analyze the types of strategies that may be required over the life of their products. Even the strategic emphasis of a firm and its marketing mix (four Ps) strategies can be adapted from insights about the characteristics of each stage of the cycle, as we summarize in Exhibit 12.6.

Let's look at each of these stages in depth.

Introduction Stage

The introduction stage for a new, innovative product or service usually starts with a single firm, and innovators are the ones to try the new offering. Some new-to-the-world products and services that defined their own product category and industry include the telephone (invented by Alexander Graham Bell in 1876), the transistor semiconductor (Bell Laboratories in 1947), the Walkman portable cassette player (Sony in 1979), the Internet browser (Netscape in 1994), personal digital assistant (Palm in 1996), iTunes (Apple in 2001), Facebook (2004), Blu-ray (Sony in 2006), iPad (Apple in 2010), and smartwatches (Pebble In 2013). Sensing the viability and commercialization possibilities of some market-creating new product, other firms soon enter the market with similar or improved products at lower prices. The same pattern holds for less innovative products such as apparel, music, and even a new soft drink flavor. The introduction stage is characterized by initial losses to the firm due to its high start-up costs and low levels of sales revenue as the product begins to take off. If the product is successful, firms may start seeing profits toward the end of this stage.

Growth Stage

The growth stage of the product life cycle is marked by a growing number of product adopters, rapid growth in industry sales, and increases in both the number of competitors and the number of available product versions.[53] The market becomes more segmented and consumer preferences more varied, which increases the potential for new markets or new uses of the product or service.[54]

Also during the growth stage, firms attempt to reach new consumers by studying their preferences and producing different product variations—varied colors, styles, or features—which enable them to segment the market more precisely. The goal of this segmentation is to ride the rising sales trend and firmly establish the firm's brand, so as not to be outdone by competitors. For example, many food manufacturers are working hard to become the first brand that consumers think of when they consider organic products. Del Monte was the first of the major canned vegetable sellers to go organic. The cans feature bold "organic" banners across the front and promise that no pesticides were used to produce the food items. Even though Del Monte products have been around for over 100 years, in this growth category, the company is a newer entrant in the organic market, so it must work to establish its distinctive appeal.[55]

As firms ride the crest of increasing industry sales, profits in the growth stage also rise because of the economies of scale associated with manufacturing and marketing costs, especially promotion and advertising. At the same time, firms that have not yet established a stronghold in the market, even in narrow segments, may decide to exit in what is referred to as an industry shakeout.

Maturity Stage

The maturity stage of the product life cycle is characterized by the adoption of the product by the late majority and intense competition for market share among firms. Marketing costs (e.g., promotion, distribution) increase as these firms vigorously defend their market share against competitors. They also face intense competition on price as the average price of the product falls substantially compared with the shifts during the previous two stages of the life cycle. Lower prices and increased marketing costs begin to erode the profit margins for many firms. In the later phases of the maturity stage, the market has become quite saturated, and practically all potential customers for the product have already adopted the product. Such saturated markets are prevalent in developed countries.

In the United States, most consumer packaged goods found in grocery and discount stores are already in the maturity stage. For example, in the well-established hair care product market, consumer goods companies constantly search for innovations to set themselves apart and extend the time in which they maintain their position in the maturity stage. Observing the popularity of new skin care products, hair care manufacturers have integrated similar product benefits to their products. These companies have introduced antiaging shampoos and conditioners, prewash hair masks, serums, and multiple-step solutions that go beyond the old mantra of wash, rinse, and repeat.[56]

Firms pursue various strategies during this stage to increase their customer base and/or defend their market share. Other tactics include entry into new markets and market segments and developing new products.

Entry into New Markets or Market Segments Because a market is saturated, firms may attempt to enter new geographical markets, including international markets (as we discussed in Chapter 8), that may be less saturated. For example, pharmaceutical companies are realizing that they need to turn to BRIC countries for

Recognizing that shampoo is a mature product category, Alterna and other manufacturers have introduced anti-aging hair products.

continued growth in the coming years. While the U.S. and European markets are fairly saturated, it is predicted that BRIC countries will go from representing 5 percent of the total pharmaceutical market in 2005 to 30 percent by 2016.[57]

However, even in mature markets, firms may be able to find new market segments. Apple is well known for releasing new versions of its iPhone and iPad yearly and development cycles are getting even shorter. Although people still get excited over these new products, they are also beginning to suffer from "device exhaustion" in which they are becoming progressively less likely to continue to upgrade their phones and tablets. As a result, it is predicted by 2015 the smartphone and tablet market will be mature.[58] Although the market may be maturing, for many people these new versions are prohibitively expensive, even when signing a two-year contract. To expand to these lower-income market segments, Apple doesn't get rid of its older devices when a new one comes along. Instead, it reduces the price on the older versions that are cheaper to produce. As a result, it is able to reach customers that would never be able to afford the latest iPhone model.

Development of New Products Despite market saturation, firms continually introduce new products with improved features or find new uses for existing products because they need constant innovation and product proliferation to defend market share from intense competition. Firms continually introduce new products to ensure that they are able to retain or grow their respective market shares. Hallmark, which has been the hallmark name for greeting cards for a long time, is trying a variety of innovations. They include customizable greeting cards, plates, and interactive storybooks that can be personalized for various recipients, as well as greeting applications that are available for both iPod and iPad users.[59]

To reach new market segments Apple reduces the price of older versions of its products when new ones are released.

Decline Stage

Firms with products in the decline stage either position themselves for a niche segment of diehard consumers or those with special needs or they completely exit the market. The few laggards who have not yet tried the product or service enter the market at this stage. Take vinyl long-playing records (LPs) for example. In an age of Internet-downloaded music files, it may seem surprising that vinyl records are still made and sold. Sales of vinyl LPs had long been declining, but they have

Hallmark's "Life Is a Special Occasion" campaign moves beyond the idea that cards are only for holidays or birthdays. It encourages consumers to connect with loved ones all the time.

enjoyed a resurgence in just the past few years as diehard music lovers demand the unique sound of a vinyl record rather than the digital sound of CDs and music files. Still, the 5.5 million LPs sold in the United States per year pales in comparison with the 1.26 billion digital downloads.[60] The grooves in vinyl records create sound waves that are similar to those of a live performance, however, which means they provide a more authentic sound, which in turn means nightclub DJs, discerning music listeners, and collectors will always prefer them.[61]

Aiding this continued demand is the fact that there are simply too many albums of music from the predigital era that are available only on vinyl. It may take many years, maybe even decades, for all the music from earlier generations to be digitized. Until that time, turntable equipment manufacturers, small record-pressing companies such as Music Connection in Manhattan, and new and emerging record companies, such as Premier Crue Music, continue to have a market that demands their LPs.[62]

The Shape of the Product Life Cycle Curve

In theory, the product life cycle curve is bell shaped with regard to sales and profits. In reality, however, each product or service category has its own individual shape; some move more rapidly through their product life cycles than others, depending on how different the category is from offerings currently in the market and how valuable it is to the consumer. New products and services that consumers accept very quickly have higher consumer adoption rates very early in their product life cycles and move faster across the various stages.

For example, Blu-ray players and Blu-rays moved much faster than DVDs across the life cycle curve and have already reached the maturity stage, likely because consumers who already owned DVDs were accustomed to playing prerecorded movies and TV shows. It also was easy to switch DVD customers to Blu-ray technology because DVDs played on Blu-ray players, and Blu-rays had better video and audio quality than DVDs. With the advent of 4K televisions that offer resolutions four times higher than current 1080p HD TVs, it is likely we may see another fast adoption of a new video format, such as 4K Blu-ray.

Strategies Based on Product Life Cycle: Some Caveats

Although the product life cycle concept provides a starting point for managers to think about the strategy they want to implement during each stage of the life cycle of a product, this tool must be used with care. The most challenging part of applying the product life cycle concept is that managers do not know exactly what shape each product's life cycle will take, so there is no way to know precisely what stage a product is in. If, for example, a product experiences several seasons of declining sales, a manager may decide that it has moved from the growth stage to decline and stop promoting the product. As a result, of course, sales decline further. The manager then believes he or she made the right decision because the product continues to follow a predetermined life cycle. But what if the original sales decline was due to a poor strategy or increased competition—issues that could have been addressed with positive marketing support? In this case, the product life cycle decision became a self-fulfilling prophecy, and a growth product was doomed to an unnecessary decline.[63] Fortunately, new research, based on the history of dozens of consumer products, suggests that the product life cycle concept is indeed a valid idea, and new analytical tools now provide rules for detecting the key turning points in the cycle.[64]

DVD customers quickly switched to Blu-rays because of the enhanced picture and sound quality.

Reviewing Learning Objectives

 Identify the reasons firms create new products.

Firms need to innovate to respond to changing customer needs, prevent declines in sales from market saturation, diversify their risk, and respond to short product life cycles, especially in industries such as fashion, apparel, arts, books, and software markets, where most sales come from new products. Finally, innovations can help firms improve their business relationships with suppliers.

 Describe the different groups of adopters articulated by the diffusion of innovation theory.

The diffusion of innovation theory can help firms predict which types of customers will buy their products or services immediately upon introduction, as well as later as they gain more acceptance in the market. Innovators are those buyers who want to be the first to have the new product or service. Early adopters do not take as much risk as innovators but instead wait and purchase the product after careful review. The members of the early majority don't like to take risks and therefore tend to wait until "the bugs" have been worked out of a particular product or service. The late majority are buyers who purchase the product after it has achieved its full market potential. Finally, laggards like to avoid change and rely on traditional products until they are no longer available. Laggards may never adopt a certain product or service.

 Describe the various stages involved in developing a new product or service.

When firms develop new products, they go through several steps. First, they generate ideas for the product or service using several alternative techniques, such as internal research and development, R&D consortia, licensing, brainstorming, tracking competitors' products or services, or working with customers. Second, firms test their concepts by either describing the idea of the new product or service to potential customers or showing them images of what the product would look like. Third, the design process entails determining what the product or service will actually include and provide. Fourth, firms test market their designs. Fifth, if everything goes well in the test market, the product is launched. Sixth, firms must evaluate the new product or service to determine its success.

 Explain the product life cycle.

The product life cycle helps firms make marketing mix decisions on the basis of the product's stage in its life cycle. In the introduction stage, companies attempt to gain a strong foothold in the market quickly by appealing to innovators. During the growth stage, the objective is to establish the brand firmly. When the product reaches the maturity stage, firms compete intensely for market share, and many potential customers already own the product or use the service. Eventually, most products enter the decline phase, during which firms withdraw marketing support and eventually phase out the product. Knowing where a product or service is in its life cycle helps managers determine its specific strategy at any given point in time.

Key Terms   ⊒∎LEARNSMART·

- alpha testing, 389
- beta testing, 390
- concept, 388
- concept testing, 388
- decline stage, 395
- diffusion of innovation, 378
- early adopters, 380
- early majority, 381
- first movers, 378
- growth stage, 395
- innovation, 373

- innovators, 379
- introduction stage, 395
- introductory price promotion, 392
- laggards, 381
- late majority, 381
- lead users, 388
- manufacturer's suggested retail price (MSRP), 393
- maturity stage, 395
- pioneers (breakthroughs), 378

- premarket test, 391
- product design, 389
- product development, 389
- product life cycle, 394
- prototype, 389
- reverse engineering, 386
- slotting allowance, 393
- test marketing, 391
- trade promotion, 392
- trade show, 392

Marketing Applications

1. Some people think that a product should be considered "new" only if it is completely new to the market and has never existed before. Describe or give examples of other types of new products.

2. Android Wear is a new category of wearable computing devices that link to android smartphones. How quickly do you think this product will diffuse among the U.S. population? Describe the types of people that you expect will be in each of the diffusion of innovation stages.

3. What are the advantages and disadvantages for companies that are the first to introduce products that create new markets?

4. Identify and describe the ways that companies generate new product ideas. Which of these ways involve the customer? How can firms assess the value of the ideas that customers generate?

5. Describe an example of a new product or service that is targeted at the college student market. Using the concept testing discussion in the chapter, describe how you would conduct a concept test for this product or service.

6. Using the same product or service you used in question 5, use the diffusion of innovation theory to assess how quickly it will diffuse based on its relative advantage, compatibility, observability, complexity, and trialability.

7. How does the Internet help companies gain customer input on their existing and new products?

8. Nature's Path is about to introduce a type of granola and is in the market testing phase of the new product development process. Describe two ways that Nature's Path might conduct initial market testing prior to launching this new product.

9. As a brand manager at Kimberly Clark, you are responsible for marketing its newest Huggies slip-on diaper. How would slotting allowances and trade promotions help promote your product?

10. In what stage of the product life cycle is the PlayStation 4 video game console? Is Sony's marketing strategy—its four Ps—consistent with the product's stage in its life cycle? Explain.

11. You have recently been hired by a cosmetics company in the product development group. The firm's brand is a top-selling, high-end line of cosmetics. The head of the development team has just presented research that shows that "tween" girls, aged 11 to 15, are very interested in cosmetics and have the money to spend. The decision is made to create a line of tween cosmetics based on the existing adult line. As the product moves through development you begin to notice that the team seems to lean toward a very edgy and sexual theme for the line, including naming the various lines "envy," "desire," "prowess," and "fatal attraction." You begin to wonder, is this concept too much for girls in the targeted age group?

Quiz Yourself

1. The diffusion of innovation theory is useful to marketers in helping them _____ .
   a. adjust to the performance life cycle
   b. avoid the cost of concept testing
   c. predict which types of customers will buy their product immediately and later
   d. predict how long it will take for a new product to gain market acceptance
   e. forecast sales for a new product

2. Inkjet personal computer printers were a big improvement over the dot matrix printers they replaced. Inkjet printers gained rapid acceptance in the marketplace primarily because of their _____ .
   a. relative advantage
   b. compatibility
   c. observability
   d. complexity
   e. trialability

   (Answers to these two questions can be found on page 652.)

Net Savvy

1. Go to http://www.quirky.com and read about how Quirky develops new products. How is this different than traditional new product development?

2. The automotive industry is constantly adding new and different products and technologies to their cars—both above and under the hood. Conduct an Internet or library database search and discuss two innovative new automotive technologies that are changing the industry.

Chapter Case Study

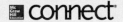

IS THE GLASS HALF FULL? THE LAUNCH OF GOOGLE GLASS

From its very start, Google has embraced the idea of innovation actively. The founders began their company with the (at the time) totally innovative concept of an online search engine. Then they instituted the "20 percent" rule, according to which all employees had to spend at least one workday per week on creative, off-the-wall project ideas. With such a foundation, Google's record of innovation is naturally impressive, from Google Maps to Street View to driverless cars, from the Android operating system to Chromebooks. But the innovation getting the most attention these days is, of course, Google Glass.

Although the device has yet to be widely introduced, it seems as if everyone knows what Google Glass is already—and has an opinion about its efficacy, appeal, and look. The wearable product allows users to surf the Internet and gather information simply by looking up and to the right. They can swipe their finger over a sensor behind their ears to pull up a Google map and navigate, take pictures, or initiate the embedded Bluetooth technology to make a call.[65]

The initial rollout of Google Glass was limited, purposefully, by a couple of factors. First, Google set the price very high, at around US$1,500. That meant that only the most dedicated tech geeks, and those with plenty of disposable income, would be the ones first sporting the headband-like devices. Second, Google required people to register for the chance to receive a set.[66] Even if thousands wanted to spend the money, Google allowed only a select few to receive them at any one time.

This slow, measured rollout provided several benefits for Google. Because it sought to minimize the supply available, Google created a perception that Glass was extremely popular and stirred up excitement in potential customers. The press buzz and word of mouth spread remarkably far and quickly. Furthermore, it identified a ready-made segment of beta testers. By making sure that those who used the early versions of Google Glass were really interested in it, Google knew that the feedback they provided was more likely to be insightful and related to the underlying technology. Thus it did not have to filter out, initially, complaints about it being too hard to use from people without much technological savvy or other reviews that seemed less important to the developers.

But as Google quickly learned, anytime you give people access to a new device, their feedback is going to include some unexpected elements. Google assumed most comments would be about technology improvements. Instead, much of the information it gleaned involved the look of the device and the alternative uses it could support. For example, although there was never

Google Glass is one of the latest of many significant Google innovations.

any danger that Google Glass would become a high-fashion option, people sought to make them at least a little more attractive. The solution was an easy one: offer Google Glass in several colors, so that fashionable folks could coordinate with their phones, purses, or favorite hues.

In terms of the functions for which people actually use Google Glass, the innovator's predictions again were just a little inaccurate. Google anticipated that Glass would resonate most with busy business professionals who found the act of taking their smartphones out of their pockets too inefficient. But it learned quickly that even these professional segments used Glass in far more casual manners. In one example, a pet lover explained that it was far easier to take funny cat videos when both hands were free to tempt the feline with a toy.[67]

Along with this feedback, Google noted some surprise at the diversity of people interested in Glass. As Leila Takayama, a researcher with Google, explained, "We were expecting the people to be extremely tech savvy—to kind of look like us Googlers. But what we actually saw were people who were much more diverse. They were people who were just sort of curious."[68] This surprising finding actually bodes very well for Google Glass, because the next step for Google seemingly must be to expand the target market beyond the early adopter segment.

One means of doing so is by adding more functions. Google has entered into an agreement with a nationwide vision care insurer, which covers people who need corrective lenses and allows them to add those lenses to the Google Glass device at a subsidized price.[69] Thus the market expands to a health care setting, in which Glass is not just a fun technology tool but a means for people to see better while also gaining access to the search benefits inherent to the innovation. Moreover, Google is actively encouraging app developers to expand their related offerings, to make sure Glass users have access to a vast range of relevant games, tools, and uses. A recent addition is a music capability, such that users can tell Google Glass to play music they have loaded into their Google Play accounts.[70]

Moreover, the Internet is filled with predictions of how far the price of Google Glass will drop. One analyst predicts a price cut to $600 relatively soon, followed by a further reduction.[71] Most estimates suggest that ultimately it will settle in the range of $300 or so.[72] Noting that approximately 10,000 users have been willing to pay $1,500 for the devices, these price predictions also argue that at $350, Google could have nearly 70,000 adopters within just a few years. And it seemingly will need them: Google has admitted that it plans for Google Glass to account for 3 percent of its total revenue by 2015.[73]

To achieve that result, Google also needs to address the potential threat associated with its competitors and their alternative versions of wearable smart technology. For example, Apple has reportedly been working with Corning Glass, which has developed a shatter-resistant, bendable glass it calls Willow Glass. Noting that such a product could easily bend around a person's wrist, prognosticators are anticipating the announcement of an Apple smartwatch any day. Their predictions have received some support from Apple's hiring trends, in that its watch division has grown substantially. Perhaps even more worrisome for Google, though, Apple recently filed a patent for an overeye technology device that would send information directly to the wearer's retina.[74]

But all these competitors might have another problem in their efforts to diffuse their wearable technologies globally, to the point that they become ubiquitous. Whether due to privacy concerns or simply because they consider the technology "creepy," some consumers appear to be rejecting the innovations out of hand. Without any legal framework in place, Glass wearers conceivably could record others without their permission or add face recognition software that identifies passersby. Several casinos have banned the devices, and privacy experts worry about the potential abuses in private-seeming locations in public places, such as restrooms and changing rooms.[75]

As Google notes, Glass might not be the best option for spies. A light on the device illuminates anytime it is recording or taking pictures, and the wearer must be directly facing anything she or he wants to record. The company also points to similar concerns about cameras integrated into cell phones—a function that people barely worry about anymore.

Still, it's enough of a problem that Google released an official guide on how not to be rude or creepy. Its suggestions include making sure that users ask for permission before recording anyone and taking off the device before entering a restroom. Google also takes the time to explain that "Standing alone in the corner of a room staring at people while recording them through Glass is not going to win you any friends."[76]

Questions

1. At what stage of its product life cycle is Google Glass?

2. What was the go-to-market strategy for Google Glass, and how successful has it been thus far?

3. How is the product diffusing? At what stage is it in the diffusion curve? Explain your answer.

4. Using the diffusion of innovation theory, assess how quickly Google Glass will diffuse based on its relative advantage, compatibility, observability, complexity, and trialability.

Endnotes

1. Steven Kurutz, "Taking Fashion to a New Dimension: With 3-D Printing, Clothing That Leaves Out the Sewing Machine," *The New York Times*, December 13, 2013, http://www.nytimes.com.

2. Beth McKenna, "3D Printing in the Aerospace Industry: How General Electric and United Technologies Are Using This Technology," *The Motley Fool*, February 28, 2014, http://www.fool.com.

3. Tim Laseter and Jeremy Hutchison-Krupat, "A Skeptic's Guide to 3D Printing," *strategy + business*, November 26, 2013, http://www.strategy-business.com.

4. Phyllis Korkki, "Beyond 3-D Printers' Magic, Possible Legal Wrangling," *The New York Times*, November 23, 2013, http://www.nytimes.com.

5. A. J. Jacobs, "Dinner Is Printed," *The New York Times*, September 21, 2013, http://www.nytimes.com.

6. Tess Stynes, "Hershey Envisions a 3-D Printer for Chocolate," *The Wall Street Journal*, January 16, 2014, http://online.wsj.com.

7. "Doing the Right Thing," http://www.frogbox.com/therightthing.php.

8. Andrew Adam Newman, "Making the Diaper Change Easier for the Changer," *The New York Times*, July 28, 2011, http://www.nytimes.com; "The Huggies Brand Encourages Parents to Showcase Their Active Babies," *The New York Times*, January 19, 2012, http: //markets.on.nytimes.com.

9. Koen Pauwels, Jorge Silva-Risso, Shuba Srinivasan, and Dominique M. Hanssens, "New Products, Sales Promotions, and Firm Value: The Case of the Automobile Industry," *Journal of Marketing* 68, no. 4 (2008), p. 142.

10. Elaine Watson, "What's the Size of the US Gluten-Free Prize? $490m, $5bn, or $10bn?" *Food Navigator USA*, February 17, 2014, http://www.foodnavigator-usa.com.

11. http://www.bettycrocker.com/products/gluten-free-products; Keith O'Brien, "Should We All Go Gluten-Free?" *The New York Times*, November 25, 2011, http://www.nytimes.com.

12. Kalpesh Kaushik Desai and Kevin Lane Keller, "The Effects of Ingredient Branding Strategies on Host Brand Extendibility," *Journal of Marketing* 66, no. 1 (2002), pp. 73–93.

13. Erik Kain, " 'Madden NFL 25' Sales Down over Last Year, First Week Still Tops 1M Units," *Forbes*, September 5, 2013, http://www.forbes.com.

14. http://www.ideo.com/work/featured/kraft.

15. http://www.marketingpower.com/_layouts/Dictionary.aspx?dLetter=D.

16. Michael J. Barone and Robert D. Jewell, "The Innovator's License: A Latitude to Deviate from Category Norms," *Journal of Marketing* 77 (January 2013), pp. 120–34; Barak Libai, Eitan Muller, and Renana Peres, "The Diffusion of Services," *Journal of Marketing Research* 46 (April 2009), pp. 163–75; Yvonne van Everdingen, Dennis Fok, and Stefan Stremersch, "Modeling Global Spillover of New Product Takeoff," *Journal of Marketing Research* 46 (October 2009), pp. 637–52.

17. Stanley F. Slater, Jakki J Mohr, and Sanjit Sengupta, "Radical Product Innovation Capability: Literature Review, Synthesis, and Illustrative Research Propositions," *Journal of Product Innovation Management* (forthcoming); Rosabeth Moss Kanter, *SuperCorp: How Vanguard Companies Create Innovation, Profits, Growth, and Social Good* (New York: Crown Business, 2009); Rajesh K. Chandy, Jaideep C. Prabhu, and Kersi D. Antia, "What Will the Future Bring? Dominance, Technology Expectations, and Radical Innovation," *Journal of Marketing* 67, no. 3 (2003), pp. 1–18; Harald J. van Heerde, Carl F. Mela, and Puneet Manchanda, "The Dynamic Effect of Innovation on Market Structure," *Journal of Marketing Research* 41, no. 2 (2004), pp. 166–83.

18. http://www.apple.com; Clayton M. Christensen and Michael E. Raynor, *The Innovator's Solution* (Boston: Harvard Business School Press, 2003).

19. Rajan Varadarajan, Manjit S. Yadav, and Venkatesh Shankar, "First-Mover Advantage in the Internet-Enabled Market Environment," in *Handbook of Strategic e-Business*

Management (Heidelberg: Springer, 2014), pp. 157–85; James L. Oakley, Adam Duhachek, Subramanian Balachander, and S. Sriram, "Order of Entry and the Moderating Role of Comparison Brands in Brand Extension Evaluation," *Journal of Consumer Research* 34, no. 5 (2008), pp. 706–12; Fernando F. Suarez and Gianvito Lanzolla, "Considerations for a Stronger First Mover Advantage Theory," *Academy of Management Review* 33, no. 1 (2008), pp. 269–70; Ralitza Nikolaeva, "The Dynamic Nature of Survival Determinants in E-commerce," *Journal of the Academy of Marketing Science* 35, no. 4 (2007), pp. 560–71.

20. "Top 10 Reasons for New Product Failure," *The Marketing Fray,* January 7, 2010, http://www.marketingfray.com.

21. http://smashinghub.com/10-coolest-upcoming-gadgets-of-2011.htm.

22. Barak Libai, Eitan Muller, and Renana Peres, "Decomposing the Value of Word-of-Mouth Seeding Programs: Acceleration versus Expansion," *Journal of Marketing Research* 50, no. 2 (2013), pp. 161–76; Jacob Goldenberg, Sangman Han, Donald R. Lehmann, and Jae Weon Hong, "The Role of Hubs in the Adoption Process," *Journal of Marketing* 73 (March 2009), pp. 1–13.

23. Chris Gaylord, "Future Is Fuzzy for 4K, Ultra-High-Definition TVs," *The Christian Science Monitor,* February 26, 2014, http://www.csmonitor.com.

24. Ellen Byron, "The Cleanest House of All," *The Wall Street Journal,* March 20, 2013, http://online.wsj.com.

25. Carol Matlack, "Electrolux's Holy Trinity for Hit Products," *Bloomberg Businessweek,* October 31, 2013, http://www.businessweek.com.

26. Gabriel Beltrone, "Most Inclusive Ad Ever? Swiffer Spot Stars Interracial Family, and Dad's an Amputee," *Adweek,* January 21, 2014, http://www.adweek.com.

27. Matlack, "Electrolux's Holy Trinity for Hit Products."

28. https://www.youtube.com/user/Blendtec.

29. Natalie Zmuda, "P&G, Levi's, GE Innovate by Thinking in Reverse," *Advertising Age,* June 13, 2011, http://adage.com; "Minute Maid Pulpy Joins Growing List of Billion Dollar Brands for the Coca-Cola Company," press release, February 1, 2011, http://www.thecoca-colacompany.com.

30. Rajani Baburajan, "U.S. Cable Industry Launches CableLabs—Energy Lab within Its R&D Consortium," *Green Technology World,* November 21, 2011, http://green.tmcnet.com.

31. Stefan Stremersch and Walter Van Dyck, "Marketing of the Life Sciences: A New Framework and Research Agenda for a Nascent Field," *Journal of Marketing* 73 (July 2009), pp. 4–30; Brady Huggett, John Hodgson, and Riku Lähteenmäki, "Public Biotech 2010—The Numbers," *Nature Biotechnology* 29 (2011), pp. 585–91, http://www.nature.com.

32. "Pilates Allegra 2 Reformer for Balanced Body," IDEO Case Study, 2011.

33. Dominik Mahr, Annouk Lievens, and Vera Blazevic, "The Value of Customer Cocreated Knowledge during the Innovation Process," *Journal of Product Innovation Management* (2013); Pilar Carbonell, Ana I. Rodríguez-Escudero, and Devashish Pujari, "Customer Involvement in New Service Development: An Examination of Antecedents and Outcomes," *Journal of Product Innovation Management* 26 (September 2009), pp. 536–50; Glen L. Urban and John R. Hauser, " 'Listening In' to Find and Explore New Combinations of Customer Needs," *Journal of Marketing* 68, no. 2 (2004), p. 72.

34. Jeff Bellairs, "Innovation and Collaboration Swiftly Launch Green Giant Snack Chips," *Taste of General Mills,* June 19, 2013, http://www.blog.generalmills.com.

35. Josephy Flaherty, "How Home Depot Copied Apple to Build an Ingenious New Bucket," *Wired,* December 31, 2013, http://www.wired.com.

36. Michael Nir, *Agile Project Management* (New York: CreateSpace, 2013); Jim Highsmith, *Agile Product Management: Creating Innovative Products* (Boston, Addison-Wesley, 2009); http://www.betterproductdesign.net; Eric von Hippel, *The Sources of Innovation* (New York: Oxford University Press, 1988); Eric von Hippel, "Successful Industrial Products from Consumers' Ideas," *Journal of Marketing* 42, no. 1 (1978), pp. 39–49.

37. Karl T. Ulrich and Steven D. Eppinger, *Product Design and Development,* 5th ed. (Boston: Irwin/McGraw-Hill, 2011).

38. http://www.marketingpower.com.

39. Ulrich and Eppinger, *Product Design and Development.*

40. Min Zhao, Steven Hoeffler, and Darren W. Dahl, "The Role of Imagination-Focused Visualization on New Product Evaluation," *Journal of Marketing Research* 46 (February 2009), pp. 46–55; http://www.marketingpower.com.

41. Ulrich and Eppinger, *Product Design and Development.*

42. Frederic Lardinois, "YouEye Raises $3M for Its Webcam-Based Usability Testing Service with Emotion Recognition," *Tech Crunch,* May 7, 2013, http://www.techcrunch.com.

43. http://en-us.nielsen.com/tab/product_families/nielsen _bases.

44. Gernot H. Gessinger, *Materials and Innovative Product Development: From Concept to Market* (Oxford: Elsevier, 2009).

45. Michael Cieply, "New Challenge for Filmmakers: Adding Dimension to 3-D Movies," *The New York Times,* August 11, 2013, http://www.nytimes.com.

46. Product Development Management Association, *The PDMA Handbook of New Product Development,* 3rd ed., Kenneth B. Kahn, ed. (New York: Wiley, 2012).

47. Bulent Menguc, Seigyoung Auh, and Aypar Uslu, "Customer Knowledge Creation Capability and Performance in Sales Teams," *Journal of the Academy of Marketing Science* 41, no. 1 (2013), pp. 19–39; Christian Homburg, Jan Wieske, and Torsten Bornemann, "Implementing the Marketing Concept at the Employee–Customer Interface: The Role of Customer Need Knowledge," *Journal of Marketing* 73 (July 2009), pp. 64–81; Torsten Bornemann, Ashwin W. Joshi, and Sanjay Sharma, "Customer Knowledge Development: Antecedents and Impact on New Product Performance," *Journal of Marketing* 68, no. 4 (2004), p. 47.

48. Katherine Bourzac, "Colorful Quantum Dot Displays Coming to Market," *Technology Review,* http://www.technologyreview.com.

49. Jan Hendrik Fisch and Jan-Michael Ross, "Timing Product Replacements under Uncertainty—the Importance of Material–Price Fluctuations for the Success of Products That Are Based on New Materials," *Journal of Product Innovation Management* (2014); Yuhong Wu, Sridhar Balasubramanian, and Vijay Mahajan, "When Is a Preannounced New Product Likely to Be Delayed?" *Journal of Marketing* 68, no. 2 (2004), p. 101.

50. http://www.walletpop.com/specials/top-25-biggest-product-flops-of-all-time.

51. http://www.pdma.org/.

52. Theodore Levitt, *Marketing Imagination* (New York: Free Press, 1986).

53. Donald R. Lehmann and Russell S. Winer, *Analysis for Marketing Planning,* 7th ed. (Burr Ridge IL: McGraw-Hill/Irwin, 2008).

54. Ibid.; Glen L. Urban and John R. Hauser, *Design and Marketing of New Products,* 2nd ed. (Upper Saddle River, NJ: Prentice Hall, 1993), pp. 120–21.

55. http://www.organicearthday.org/DelMonteFoods.htm; http://www.delmonte.com/Products/.

56. Euromonitor International, "A Revival in Hair Care Innovation," August 12, 2013, http://blog.euromonitor.com.

57. "Winning in Emerging Markets to Drive Growth in the Life Sciences Industry," *Accenture,* 2013, http://www.accenture.com; Eric D. Beinhocker, Diana Farrell, and Adil S. Zainulbhai,

"Tracking the Growth of India's Middle Class," *McKinsey Quarterly* (August 2007).

58. Wallace Witkowski, "iPhones and Other Portables Suffering from 'Device Exhaustion,' Analyst Says," *The Wall Street Journal*, August 20, 2013, http://blogs.marketwatch.com.

59. Natalie Zmuda and Jennifer Rooney, "Hallmark Breaks Out of Special Occasion Mold," *Advertising Age*, July 6, 2011, http://adage.com.

60. Alan Kozzin, "Weaned on CDs, They're Reaching for Vinyl," *The New York Times*, June 9, 2013, http://www.nytimes.com; Ed Christman, "Digital Music Sales Decrease for First Time in 2013," *BillboardBiz*, January 3, 2014, http://www.billboard.com.

61. Yvonne Zipp, "As Vinyl Records Get Back in the Groove, Kalamazoo Record Stores See Sales Climb," *MLive*, January 15, 2012, http://www.mlive.com.

62. Steven Levenstein, "Sony's New USB Turntable Sparks Vinyl Revival," March 14, 2008, http://www.inventospot.com; http://www.electronichouse.com; Roy Bragg, "LP Vinyl Records Are Making a Comeback in Audiophile Circles," *Knight Ridder Tribune Business News*, January 3, 2004 (ProQuest Document ID: 521358371); Susan Adams, "You, the Record Mogul," *Forbes*, October 27, 2003, p. 256ff.

63. Goutam Challagalla, R. Venkatesh, and Ajay Kohli, "Proactive Postsales Service: When and Why Does It Pay Off?" *Journal of Marketing* 73 (March 2009), pp. 70–87; Kevin J. Clancy and Peter C. Krieg, "Product Life Cycle: A Dangerous Idea," *Brandweek*, March 1, 2004, p. 26; Nariman K. Dhalla and Sonia Yuseph, "Forget the Product Life-Cycle Concept," *Harvard Business Review* (January/February 1976), p. 102ff.

64. Jan R. Landwehr, Daniel Wentzel, and Andreas Herrmann, "Product Design for the Long Run: Consumer Responses to Typical and Atypical Designs at Different Stages of Exposure," *Journal of Marketing* 77, no. 5 (2013), pp. 92–107; Peter Golder and Gerard Tellis, "Cascades, Diffusion, and Turning Points in the Product Life Cycle," MSI Report No. 03-120, 2003.

65. David Pogue, "Google Glass and the Future of Technology," *The New York Times*, September 12, 2012, http://pogue.blogs.nytimes.com.

66. http://www.google.com/glass/start/how-to-get-one/.

67. David Zax, "Google Glass's Unexpected Lessons in Product Launching," *Fast Company*, February 3, 2014, http://www.fastcompany.com.

68. Ibid.

69. Claire Cain Miller, "Google Glass to Be Covered by Vision Care Insurere VSP," *The New York Times*, January 28, 2014, http://www.nytimes.com.

70. Ben Sisario, "Google Glass Will Expand Its Features into Music," *The New York Times*, November 12, 2013, http://www.nytimes.com.

71. Tony Danova, "BI Intelligence Forecast: Google Glass Will Become a Mainstream Product and Sell Millions by 2016," *Business Insider*, December 31, 2013, http://www.businessinsider.com.

72. Kevin C. Tofel, "Why Google Glass Costs $1500 Now and Will Likely Be Around $299 Later," *Gigaom*, August 8, 2013, http://gigaom.com; Liz Gannes, "Google Glass Could Be $3-Billion-a-Year Business, Says Analyst," *All Things Digital*, September 4, 2013, http://allthingsd.com.

73. Nick Bilton, "Disruptions: Where Apple and Dick Tracy May Converge," *The New York Times*, February 10, 2013.

74. Ibid.; Farhad Manjoo, "The Great Tech War of 2012," *Fast Company*, October 19, 2011, http://www.fastcompany.com.

75. Amir Efrati and Geoffrey A. Fowler, "Google Glass Is Watching—Now What?" *The Wall Street Journal*, May 17, 2013, http://online.wsj.com.

76. Nick Bilton, "Google Offers a Guide to Not Being a 'Creepy' Google Glass Owner," *The New York Times*, February 19, 2014, http://bits.blogs.nytimes.com.

i. Phil Patton, "Out of the Melting Pot and into a Global Market," *The New York Times*, January 13, 2012, http://www.nytimes.com; Paul Stenquist, "A Buffet of Canny Tweaks in Hot Pursuit of Mileage," *The New York Times*, January 13, 2012, http://www.nytimes.com; "Ford to Take Mustang Sports Car Global," *The New York Times*, December 4, 2013, http://www.nytimes.com; "With 2015 Mustang, Ford Puts American Icon on Global Path," *Advertising Age*, December 5, 2013, http://adage.com.

ii. Jack Adams, "US Search Engine Market Share Figures Steady in February," *Clickthrough*, March 21, 2014, http://www.clickthrough-marketing.com; Steve Lohr, "Can Microsoft Make You 'Bing'?" *The New York Times*, July 30, 2011, http://www.nytimes.com; Renay San Miguel, "Bing's New Bells and Whistles Could Leave Searchers' Heads Ringing," *TechNewsWorld*, March 29, 2010; Jared Newman, "How Microsoft Plans to Beat Google with Bing," *PCWorld*, August 1, 2011, http://www.pcworld.com.

iii. The Humane Society, "Cosmetic and Product Testing," http://www.humanesociety.org; The Body Shop, "Saying No to Animal Testing," http://www.thebodyshop.com; Procter & Gamble, "Animal Welfare and Alternatives," http://www.pg.com; http://www.peta.org; http://ec.europa.eu/consumers/sectors/cosmetics/animal-testing/index_en.htm.

Credits

CHAPTER 13

SERVICES: THE INTANGIBLE PRODUCT

LEARNING OBJECTIVES

LO1 Describe how the marketing of services differs from the marketing of products.

LO2 Discuss the four gaps in the Service Gaps Model.

LO3 Examine the five service quality dimensions.

LO4 Explain the zone of tolerance.

LO5 Identify three service recovery strategies.

There are so many funny and entertaining uses for Twitter that it might be hard to imagine how it helps businesses, marketers, and consumers. Hard to imagine, that is, until we consider some of the growing list of examples of how Twitter transforms service into a dynamic, responsive, active practice to keep customers happy.

Whether they sell traditional products, such as Samsung's televisions, or services, such as Seamless's food delivery, companies are recognizing the need to attend carefully to Twitter to appeal and respond to the people buying what they have to offer. As we have noted several times in this text already, the rise of social media means that consumer complaints and questions spread far wider, and more quickly, than they have in the past. Thus when a blogger for a communications consultancy found that the Samsung television he bought the day before the Super Bowl was not working

correctly, he immediately posted his complaint on Twitter. In addition to sharing the information with all his friends and followers, he alerted Samsung to the problem. The company maintains a constant presence on Twitter and other social media, looking for concerns and problems it can resolve.

Within an hour of the post (which took place, recall, on Super Bowl Sunday), a Samsung customer service representative had contacted him through Twitter, promised a follow-up service call within 24 hours, and then maintained contact to ensure the replacement part that the television needed was delivered and installed on time. In the blogger's own words, "I am not overstating it to say that . . . in a couple of hours of work, [the customer service] team saved a $1,000 sale."[1]

Notable in this example was how quickly the company responded, which is essential for effective customer service. Especially on social media, customers want a rapid response; their expectations of what a fast response means have shifted. At one time, cable service providers were famous (and not in a good way) for their casual attitude in responding to com-

plaints. But with more customers ready to drop cable altogether, Comcast has expanded its Twitter presence, so that it can answer technical support issues quickly. The employees responsible for monitoring and responding to tweeted complaints also are technical specialists, so that they know what to do when a person's wireless router seems to have stopped working, for example.[2]

But as companies get better about responding through social media, customers become even more demanding.[3] Accordingly, service providers such as Seamless, a food delivery service from the United Kingdom, makes sure that employees are monitoring Twitter at all hours of the day.[4] It may seem as if people would be unlikely to order Thai food at 9:00 a.m., but if they are, they want the service to be available and responsive to them. Despite these strong examples of the benefits of Twitter-based service, some evidence suggests that up to 70 percent of all service providers fail to maintain a Twitter handle to facilitate connections with their customers or monitor tweets for mentions of their name at all.[5]

Such a failure seems incomprehensible for good marketers. Twitter not only enables others to provide superior service but also is a service provider itself. The service it entails mostly involves facilitating connections among friends and followers. But for customers annoyed with the service failures of other companies, it also offers a place to vent their frustration. For companies that are paying attention, the Twitter platform gives them a public forum to demonstrate that they have heard and acknowledged those complaints.[6] In many cases, simply being heard can be enough to turn a raging, angry complainer into a docile and happy consumer.

Specialized services like personal training are thriving.

Whereas a service is any intangible offering that involves a deed, performance, or effort that cannot be physically possessed,[7] customer service specifically refers to human or mechanical activities firms undertake to help satisfy their customers' needs and wants. By providing good customer service, firms add value to their products.

Exhibit 13.1 illustrates the continuum from a pure service to a pure good. Most offerings, like those of Samsung, lie somewhere in the middle and include some service and some good (i.e., a hybrid of the two). Even those firms that are engaged primarily in selling a good, such as an apparel store, typically view service as a method to maintain a sustainable competitive advantage. This chapter moves on to take an inclusive view of services as anything from pure service businesses, such as Twitter, to a business that uses service as a differentiating tool to help it sell physical goods.

Economies of developed countries such as of the United States have become increasingly dependent on services. Services account for 76 percent of the U.S. gross domestic product (GDP), a much higher percentage than they did 50, 20, or even 10 years ago. In turn, the current list of *Fortune* 500 companies contains more service companies and fewer manufacturers than in previous decades.[8] This dependence and the growth of service-oriented economies in developed countries have emerged for several reasons.

First, it is generally less expensive for firms to manufacture their products in less developed countries. Even if the goods are finished in the United States, some of their components

EXHIBIT 13.1 The Service–Product Continuum

| Doctor | Hotel | Dry cleaners | Restaurant | Apparel specialty store | Grocery store |

Service dominant ⟶ Product dominant

likely were produced elsewhere. In turn, the proportion of service production to goods production in the United States, and other similar economies, has steadily increased over time.

Second, people place a high value on convenience and leisure. For instance, household maintenance activities, which many people performed themselves in the past, have become more popular and quite specialized. Food preparation, lawn maintenance, house cleaning, pet grooming, laundry and dry cleaning, hair care, and automobile maintenance are all often performed by specialists.

Third, as the world has become more complicated, people are demanding more specialized services—everything from plumbers to personal trainers, from massage therapists to tax preparation specialists, from lawyers to travel and leisure specialists and even to health care providers. The aging population in particular has increased the need for health care specialists, including doctors, nurses, and caregivers in assisted living facilities and nursing homes, and many of those consumers want their specialists to provide personalized, dedicated services.

SERVICES MARKETING DIFFERS FROM PRODUCT MARKETING

LO1 Describe how the marketing of services differs from the marketing of products.

The marketing of services differs from product marketing because of the four fundamental differences involved in services: Services are intangible, inseparable, heterogeneous, and perishable.[9] (See Exhibit 13.2.) This section examines these differences and discusses how they affect marketing strategies.

EXHIBIT 13.2   Core Differences between Services and Goods

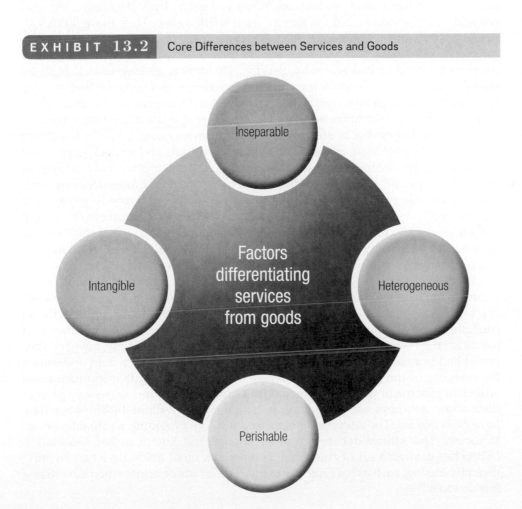

Intangible

As the title of this chapter implies, the most fundamental difference between a product and a service is that services are intangible—they cannot be touched, tasted, or seen like a pure product can. When you get a physical examination, you see and hear the doctor, but the service itself is intangible. This intangibility can prove highly challenging to marketers. For instance, it makes it difficult to convey the benefits of services—try describing whether the experience of visiting your dentist was good or bad and why. Service providers (e.g., physicians, dentists) therefore offer cues to help their customers experience and perceive their service more positively, such as a waiting room stocked with television sets, beverages, and comfortable chairs to create an atmosphere that appeals to the target market.

A service that cannot be shown directly to potential customers also is difficult to promote. Marketers must creatively employ symbols and images to promote and sell services, as Six Flags does in using its advertising to evoke images of happy families and friends enjoying a roller coaster ride. Professional medical services provide appropriate images of personnel doing their jobs in white coats surrounded by high-tech equipment. Educational institutions promote the quality of their services by touting their famous faculty and alumni as well as their accreditations. They also often use images of happy students sitting spellbound in front of a fascinating professor or going on to lucrative careers of their own.

Because of the intangibility of services, the images that marketers use must reinforce the benefit or value that a service provides. Professional service providers, such as doctors, lawyers, accountants, and consultants, depend heavily on consumers' perceptions of their integrity and trustworthiness, but they also need to market their offerings using promotional campaigns. At one time, lawyers were prohibited from advertising because such marketing seemingly would undermine the integrity of the profession. The repeal of those laws resulted in much more advertising, some of which may go too far. Critics point to the aggressive promotions some attorneys use to prey on potential clients' vulnerabilities after they have been injured. The lawyers claim instead they are providing a valuable service to society. This ethical debate continues, though the American Bar Association (ABA) has drafted a set of rules that its members must abide by when creating their advertising, such as banning any use of pop-up ads or actors when advertising law services.[10]

Adding Value 13.1 Carbonite's Secure Online Backup[i]

The prospect of losing data haunts virtually every computer user. And for good reason, especially among business users: The Federal Emergency Management Agency says 40 to 60 percent of small businesses fail to reopen after they suffer a severe data disruption. To address their fears of data loss or contamination, some users rely on external hard drives or disk storage. But that means they have to remember to perform the backup, and these options do not provide protection against a fire or other emergencies that destroy that hard drive along with the computer.

Online backups involve backing up the data on remote servers. This provides a more secure, less user-dependent alternative. Carbonite was one of the first entrants into this market. It provides simple, affordable, unlimited online backup for individual home users as well as small and medium businesses. With these target markets, Carbonite has kept its service, price, and customer support well within the reach of users. The basic yearly rate for a home customer is $59 per computer; a business pays $269 a year to cover all company computers.

Carbonite software runs invisibly on both Macs and PCs, performing backups automatically. With customers in more than 100 countries, the company has backed up more than 100 billion files and recovered nearly 10 billion of them in the past few years. For portable, digital access, the company offers free mobile applications for BlackBerry, iPad, iPhone, and Android devices. In addition, it has expanded its capabilities as it has grown, such that it now helps clients in medical professions ensure the security of patients' information, in line with existing privacy regulations (e.g., the Health Insurance Portability and Accountability Act [HIPAA]).

To live up to its promise of hassle-free service, the company also offers free support by telephone, e-mail, and online live chat. It answers customer inquiries on its Twitter and Facebook sites, which then provide transparent proof of its handling of customer complaints. As for security, Carbonite's system is comparable to the safeguards used by major banks, credit card companies, and online retailers. All files are encrypted with two layers of technology, stored on enterprise-grade servers to protect against mechanical disk failure, and kept in state-of-the-art data centers guarded 24 hours a day,

Carbonite backs up computer data on remote servers.

365 days a year. Personnel must pass through biometric scans and electronic pin coding to enter.

Carbonite thus has firmly established its market position by delivering a reliable, secure, easy-to-use service, combined with reasonable pricing and easily accessible technical support. As the shift to cloud computing intensifies, the company's main advantage may be its focus on staying abreast of user needs and expectations so it can keep all its customers happy.

For lawyers, the challenge of advertising services creates an ethical dilemma. But some other services have found excellent ways to make their offerings more tangible to their customers, as Adding Value 13.1 notes.

Inseparable Production and Consumption

Unlike a pair of jeans that may have been made six months prior to their purchase, halfway around the world, services are produced and consumed at the same time; that is, service and consumption are inseparable. When getting a haircut, the customer is not only present but also may participate in the service process.

Furthermore, the interaction with the service provider may have an important impact on the customer's perception of the service outcome. If the hairstylist appears to be having fun while cutting hair, it may affect the experience positively.

Because the service is inseparable from its consumption, customers rarely have the opportunity to try the service before they purchase it. And after the service has been performed, it can't be returned. Imagine telling your hairstylist that you want to have the hair around your ears trimmed as a test before doing the entire head. Because the purchase risk in these scenarios can be relatively high, service firms sometimes provide extended warranties and 100 percent satisfaction guarantees. The Choice Hotels chain, for instance, states: "When you choose to stay at a Comfort Inn, Comfort Suites, Quality, Clarion, or Sleep Inn hotel, we are committed to making you feel understood, welcome, and important."[11]

Heterogeneous

The more humans are needed to provide a service, the more likely there is to be **heterogeneity** or variability in the service's quality. A hairstylist may give bad haircuts in the morning because he or she went out the night before. Yet that stylist still may offer a better service than the undertrained stylist working in the next station over. A restaurant, which offers a mixture of services and products, generally can control its food quality but not the variability in food preparation or delivery. If a consumer has a problem with a product, it can be replaced, redone, destroyed, or, if it is already in the supply chain, recalled. In many cases, the problem can even be fixed before the product gets into consumers' hands. But an inferior service can't be recalled; by the time the firm recognizes a problem, the damage has been done.

Marketers also can use the variable nature of services to their advantage. A micromarketing segmentation strategy can customize a service to meet customers' needs exactly (see Chapter 9). Exercise facilities might generally provide the same weights, machines, and mats, but at Planet Fitness, customers know that the gym explicitly seeks to offer a laidback, less intense setting. Planet Fitness actively avoids targeting hardcore gym rats with its service offering. Instead, local storefronts offer pizza nights and bowls of free Tootsie Rolls, varying the details to match the needs and preferences of their local members. Thus each gym seeks to live up to the chain's overall promise to make going to exercise a pleasant experience, rather than an intimidation festival.[12]

In an alternative approach, some service providers tackle the variability issue by replacing people with machines. For simple transactions such as getting cash, using an automated teller machine (ATM) is usually quicker and more convenient—and less variable—than waiting in line for a bank teller. Many retailers have installed kiosks with broadband Internet access in their stores. In addition to offering customers the opportunity to order merchandise not available in the store, kiosks can provide routine customer service, freeing employees to deal with more demanding customer requests and problems and reducing service variability. For example, customers can use kiosks to locate merchandise in the store and determine whether specific products, brands, and sizes are available. Kiosks can also be used to automate existing store services, such as gift registry management, rain checks, film drop-off, credit applications, and preordering service for bakeries and delicatessens.

Planet Fitness's service offerings are customized to their customer's needs.

Since services are perishable, service providers like ski areas offer less expensive tickets at night to stimulate demand.

Perishable

Services are perishable in that they cannot be stored for use in the future. You can't stockpile your membership at Planet Fitness like you could a six-pack of V8 juice, for instance. The perishability of services provides both challenges and opportunities to marketers in terms of the critical task of matching demand and supply. As long as the demand for and supply of the service match closely, there is no problem, but unfortunately, this perfect matching rarely occurs. A ski area, for instance, can be open as long as there is snow, even at night, but demand peaks on weekends and holidays, so ski areas often offer less expensive tickets during off-peak periods to stimulate demand. Airlines, cruise ships, movie theaters, and restaurants confront similar challenges and attack them in similar ways.

Certainly, providing great service is not easy, and it requires a diligent effort to analyze the service process piece by piece. In the next section, we examine what is known as the Gaps Model, which is designed to highlight those areas where customers believe they are getting less or poorer service than they should (the gaps) and how these gaps can be closed.

CHECK YOURSELF

1. What are the four marketing elements that distinguish services from products?
2. Why can't we separate firms into just service or just product sellers?

PROVIDING GREAT SERVICE: THE GAPS MODEL

L02 Discuss the four gaps in the Service Gaps Model.

Customers have certain expectations about how a service should be delivered. When the delivery of that service fails to meet those expectations, a service gap results. The Service Gaps Model (Exhibit 13.3) is designed to encourage the

EXHIBIT 13.3   Gaps Model for Improving Retail Service Quality

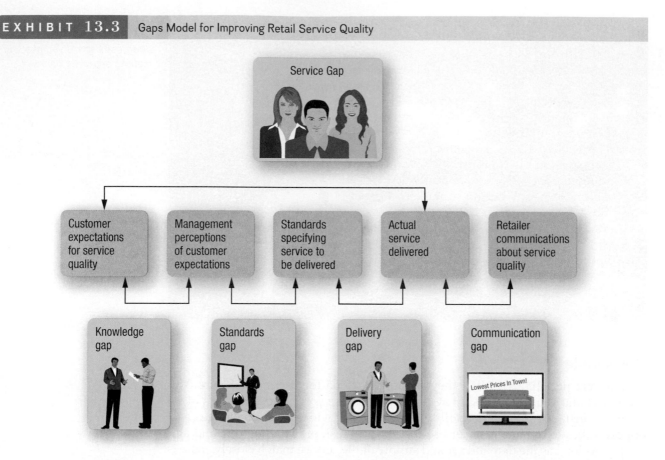

Sources: Adapted from Valarie Zeithaml, A. Parasuraman, and Leonard Berry, *Delivering Quality Customer Service* (New York: The Free Press, 1990); and Valarie Zeithaml, Leonard Berry, and A. Parasuraman, "Communication and Control Processes in the Delivery of Service Quality," *Journal of Marketing* 52, no. 2 (April 1988), pp. 35–48.

systematic examination of all aspects of the service delivery process and prescribes the steps needed to develop an optimal service strategy.[13]

As Exhibit 13.3 shows, there are four service gaps:

1. The knowledge gap reflects the difference between customers' expectations and the firm's perception of those customer expectations. Firms can close this gap by determining what customers really want by doing research using marketing metrics such as service quality and the zone of tolerance (discussed later).

2. The standards gap pertains to the difference between the firm's perceptions of customers' expectations and the service standards it sets. By setting appropriate service standards, training employees to meet and exceed those standards, and measuring service performance, firms can attempt to close this gap.

3. The delivery gap is the difference between the firm's service standards and the actual service it provides to customers. This gap can be closed by getting employees to meet or exceed service standards when the service is being delivered by empowering service providers, providing support and incentives, and using technology where appropriate.[14]

4. The communication gap refers to the difference between the actual service provided to customers and the service that the firm's promotion program promises. If firms are more realistic about the services they can provide and at the same time manage customer expectations effectively, they generally can close this gap.

As we discuss the four gaps subsequently, we will apply them to the experience that Marcia Kessler had with a motel in Maine. She saw an ad for a package weekend that quoted a very reasonable daily rate and listed the free amenities available at Green Valley Motel: free babysitting services, a piano bar with a nightly singer, a free Continental breakfast, a heated swimming pool, and newly decorated rooms. When she booked the room, Marcia discovered that the price advertised was not available during the weekend, and a three-day minimum stay was required. Because of the nice amenities, however, she went ahead. After checking in with a very unpleasant person at the front desk, Marcia and her husband found that their room appeared circa-1950 and had not been cleaned. When she complained, all she got was attitude from the assistant manager. Resigned to the fact that they were slated to spend the weekend, she decided to go for a swim. Unfortunately, the water was heated by Booth Bay and stood at around 50 degrees. No one was using the babysitting services because there were few young children at the resort. It turns out the piano bar singer was the second cousin of the owner, and he couldn't carry a tune, let alone play the piano very well. The Continental breakfast must have come all the way from the Continent, because everything was stale and tasteless. Marcia couldn't wait to get home.

What service gaps did Marcia experience while on vacation at the motel in Maine?

The Knowledge Gap: Understanding Customer Expectations

An important early step in providing good service is knowing what the customer wants. It doesn't pay to invest in services that don't improve customer satisfaction. To reduce the knowledge gap, firms must understand customers' expectations. To understand those expectations, firms undertake customer research and increase the interaction and communication between managers and employees.

Customers' expectations are based on their knowledge and experiences.[15] Marcia's expectations were that her room at the motel in Maine would be ready when she got there, the swimming pool would be heated, the singer would be able to sing, and the breakfast would be fresh. Not a lot to expect, but in this extreme example, the Green Valley Motel was suffering a severe knowledge gap, perhaps based on its assumption that being on the ocean in Maine was enough. If the resort never understood her expectations, it is unlikely it would ever be able to meet them.

Expectations vary according to the type of service. Marcia's expectations might have been higher, for instance, if she were staying at a Ritz-Carlton rather than the Green Valley Motel. At the Ritz, she might have expected employees to know her by name, be aware of her dietary preferences, and to have placed fresh fruit of her choice and fresh-cut flowers in her room before she arrived. At the Green Valley Motel, she expected easy check-in/checkout, easy access to a major highway, a clean room with a comfortable bed, and a TV, at a bare minimum.

People's expectations also vary depending on the situation. If she had been traveling on business, the Green Valley Motel might have been fine (had the room at least been clean and modern), but if she were celebrating her 10th wedding anniversary, she probably would prefer the Ritz. Thus, the service provider needs to not only know and understand the expectations of the customers in its target market but also have some idea of the occasions of service usage.

Samsung provided an example of excellent service in our chapter opener. To make sure it was prepared to handle complaints effectively through Twitter, when the company first initiated its handle, it did not post anything for 90 days. Instead, it read everything that customers tweeted about it during those three months, to ensure it knew what issues were common and how people wanted them resolved. JetBlue similarly tracks complaints; it quickly learned to schedule more customer

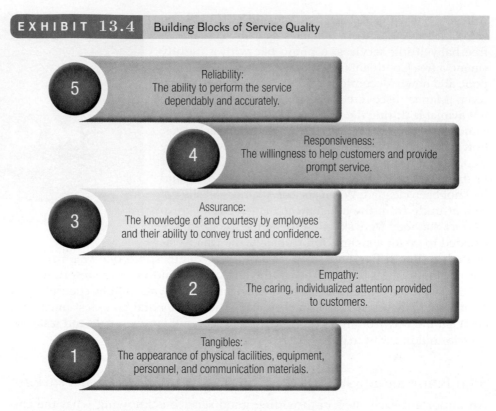

EXHIBIT 13.4   Building Blocks of Service Quality

5 — Reliability:
The ability to perform the service dependably and accurately.

4 — Responsiveness:
The willingness to help customers and provide prompt service.

3 — Assurance:
The knowledge of and courtesy by employees and their ability to convey trust and confidence.

2 — Empathy:
The caring, individualized attention provided to customers.

1 — Tangibles:
The appearance of physical facilities, equipment, personnel, and communication materials.

service representatives to work when severe weather threatens to delay many flights and frustrate more passengers.[16]

LO3 Examine the five service quality dimensions.

Evaluating Service Quality Using Well-Established Marketing Metrics To meet or exceed customers' expectations, marketers must determine what those expectations are. Yet because of their intangibility, the service quality, or customers' perceptions of how well a service meets or exceeds their expectations, often is difficult for customers to evaluate.[17] Customers generally use five distinct service dimensions to determine overall service quality: reliability, responsiveness, assurance, empathy, and tangibles (see Exhibit 13.4). Adding Value 13.2 describes how the Broadmoor Hotel maintains its five-star rating by focusing on these five service characteristics.

If you were to apply the five service dimensions to your own decision-making process, for instance, when you selected a college—which provides you the service of education—you might find results like those in Exhibit 13.5.

EXHIBIT 13.5   Collegiate Service Dimensions

	University A	University B
Reliability	Offers sound curriculum with extensive placement services and internships.	Curriculum covers all the basics but important courses are not always available. Career placement is haphazard at best.
Responsiveness	Slow to respond to application. Very structured visitation policy. Rather inflexible with regard to personal inquiries or additional meetings.	Quick response during application process. Open visitation policy. Offers variety of campus resources to help with decision making.
Assurance	Staff seems very confident in reputation and services.	Informal staff who convey enthusiasm for institution.
Empathy	Seems to process student body as a whole rather than according to individual needs or concerns.	Very interested in providing a unique experience for each student.
Tangibles	Very traditional campus with old-world look and feel. Facilities are manicured. Dorm rooms are large, but bathrooms are a little old.	New campus with modern architecture. Campus is less manicured. Dorm rooms are spacious with newer bathrooms.

Adding Value 13.2 — The Broadmoor Manages Service Quality for a Five-Star Rating[ii]

Established in 1891 as a gambling casino and transformed into a grand resort in 1918, the Broadmoor, in Colorado Springs, Colorado, is one of the world's premier resorts. It has received a record 50 consecutive years of five-star ratings from the *Forbes Travel Guide*. Perry Goodbar, former vice president of sales and marketing for the Broadmoor, emphasizes, "It's the people who truly make this place special. Exceptional service quality begins with exceptional people." Some aspects of its service quality are as follows:

Reliability Every new Broadmoor employee, before ever encountering a customer, attends a two-and-a-half-day orientation session and receives an employee handbook. Making and keeping promises to customers is a central part of this orientation. Employees are trained always to give an estimated time for service, whether it be room service, laundry service, or simply how long it will take to be seated at one of the resort's restaurants. When an employee makes a promise, he or she keeps that promise. Employees are trained to never guess if they don't know the answer to a question. Inaccurate information only frustrates customers. When an employee is unable to answer a question accurately, he or she immediately contacts someone who can.

Assurance The Broadmoor conveys trust by empowering its employees. An example of an employee empowerment policy is the service recovery program. If a guest problem arises, employees are given discretionary resources to rectify the problem or present the customer with something special to help mollify them. For example, if a meal is delivered and there's a mistake in the order or how it was prepared, a server can offer the guest a free item such as a dessert or, if the service was well below expectations, simply take care of the bill. Managers then review each situation to understand the nature of the problem and help prevent it from occurring again.

Tangibles One of the greatest challenges for the Broadmoor in recent years has been updating rooms built in the early part of the 20th century to meet the needs of 21st-century visitors. To accomplish this, it spent millions in improvements, renovating rooms, and adding a new outdoor pool complex.

Empathy One approach used to demonstrate empathy is personalizing communications. Employees are instructed to always address a guest by name, if possible. To accomplish this, employees are trained to listen and observe carefully to determine a guest's name. Subtle sources for this information include convention name tags, luggage ID tags, credit cards, or checks. In addition, all phones within the Broadmoor display a guest's room number and name on a screen.

Responsiveness Every employee is instructed to follow the HEART model of taking care of problems. First, employees must "Hear what a guest has to say." Second, they must "Empathize with them" and then "Apologize for the situation." Fourth, they must "Respond to the guest's needs" by "Taking action and following up."

The Broadmoor in Colorado Springs, Colorado, is known for exceptional service quality.

If your expectations include an individualized experience at a state-of-the-art institution, perhaps University B is a better alternative for you. But if you are relying heavily on academic performance and career placement from your university experience, then University A might be a better choice in terms of the five service dimensions. If a strong culture and tradition are important to you, University A offers this type of environment. What your expectations are has a lot to do with your perception of how your university falls within these service dimensions.

Marketing research (see Chapter 10) provides a means to better understand consumers' service expectations and their perceptions of service quality. This research can be extensive and expensive, or it can be integrated into a firm's everyday interactions with customers. Today, most service firms have developed voice-of-customer programs and employ ongoing marketing research to assess how well they are meeting their customers' expectations. A systematic voice-of-customer (VOC) program collects customer inputs and integrates them into managerial decisions.

LO4 Explain the zone of tolerance.

An important marketing metric to evaluate how well firms perform on the five service quality dimensions (again see Exhibit 13.4) is the zone of tolerance, which refers to the area between customers' expectations regarding their desired service and the minimum level of acceptable service—that is, the difference between what the customer really wants and what he or she will accept before going elsewhere. To define the zone of tolerance, firms ask a series of questions about each service quality dimension that relate to

- The desired and expected level of service for each dimension, from low to high.
- Customers' perceptions of how well the focal service performs and how well a competitive service performs, from low to high.
- The importance of each service quality dimension.

Exhibit 13.6 illustrates the results of such an analysis for Lou's Local Diner, a family-owned restaurant. The rankings on the left are based on a nine-point scale, on which 1 is low and 9 is high. The length of each box illustrates the zone of

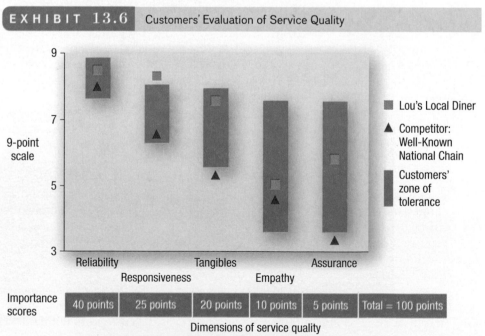

EXHIBIT 13.6   Customers' Evaluation of Service Quality

Note: The scale ranges from a 9 indicating very high service quality on a given service quality dimension to a 1 indicating very low service quality.

tolerance for each service quality dimension. For instance, according to the short length of the reliability box, customers expect a fairly high level of reliability (top of the box) and will accept only a fairly high level of reliability (bottom of the box). On the other end of the scale, customers expect a high level of assurance (top of the box) but will also accept a fairly low level (bottom of the box). This difference is to be expected because the customers also were asked to assign an important score to the five service quality dimensions so that the total equals 100 percent (see bottom of Exhibit 13.6). Looking at the average importance score, we conclude that reliability is relatively important to these customers but assurance is not. So customers have a fairly narrow zone of tolerance for service dimensions that are fairly important to them and a wider range of tolerance for those service dimensions that are less important. Also note that Lou's Local Diner always rates higher than its primary competitor, Well-Known National Chain, on each dimension.

Lou's Local Diner always rates higher than its primary competitor, Well-Known National Chain, on each service quality dimension.

Further note that Well-Known National Chain scores below the zone of tolerance on the tangibles dimension, meaning that customers are not willing to accept the way the restaurant looks and smells. Lou's Local Diner, in contrast, performs above the zone of tolerance on the responsiveness dimension—maybe even too well. Lou's may wish to conduct further research to verify which responsiveness aspects it is performing so well, and then consider toning those aspects down. For example, being responsive to customers' desires to have a diner that serves breakfast 24 hours a day can be expensive and may not add any further value to Lou's Diner, because customers would accept more limited times.

A very straightforward and inexpensive method of collecting consumers' perceptions of service quality is to gather them at the time of the sale. Service providers can ask customers how they liked the service—though customers often are reticent to provide negative feedback directly to the person who provided the service—or distribute a simple questionnaire. Regardless of how information is collected, companies must take care not to lose it, which can happen if there is no effective mechanism for filtering it up to the key decision makers. Furthermore, in some cases, customers cannot effectively evaluate the service until several days or weeks later. Automobile dealers, for instance, often call their customers a week after they perform a service such as an oil change to assess their service quality.

Another excellent method for assessing customers' expectations is making effective use of customer complaint behavior. Even if complaints are handled effectively to solve customers' problems, the essence of the complaint is too often lost on managers. For instance, an airline established a policy that customer service reps could not discuss any issues involving fees to travel agents with customers. So when a customer calls to complain about these fees, the representative just changes the subject, and management therefore never finds out about the complaint.[18]

Even firms with the best formal research mechanisms in place must put managers on the frontlines occasionally to interact directly with the customers. The late Sam Walton, founder of Walmart, participated in and advocated this strategy, which is known as "management by walking around."[19] Unless the managers who make the service quality decisions know what their service providers are facing on a day-to-day basis, and unless they can talk directly to the customers with whom those service providers interact, any customer service program they create will not be as good as it could be.

The Standards Gap: Setting Service Standards

Getting back to the Green Valley Motel in Maine for a moment, suppose because of a number of complaints or because business was falling off, it set out to determine customers' service expectations and gained a pretty good idea of them. The next step would be to set its service standards accordingly and develop systems to meet the customers' service expectations. How, for instance, can it make sure that every room is cleaned and ready by an optimum time of day in the eyes of the customers, or that the breakfast is checked for freshness and quality every day? To consistently deliver service that meets customers' expectations, firms must set specific, measurable goals. For instance, for the Green Valley Motel, the most efficient process might have been to start cleaning rooms at 8:00 a.m. and finish by 5:00 p.m. But many guests want to sleep late, and new arrivals want to get into their room as soon as they arrive, often before 5:00. So a customer-oriented standard would mandate that the rooms get cleaned between 10:00 a.m. and 2:00 p.m.

Service providers generally want to do a good job as long as they know what is expected of them. Motel employees should be shown, for instance, exactly how managers expect them to clean a room and what specific tasks they are responsible for performing. In general, more employees will buy into a quality-oriented process if they are involved in setting the goals. For instance, suppose an important employee of the motel objects to disposable plastic cups and suggests actual drinking glasses in the rooms would be classier as well as more ecological. There might be a cost–benefit trade-off to consider here, but if management listens to her and makes the change in this case, it should likely make the employee all the more committed to other tasks involved in cleaning and preparing rooms.

Service providers, like this room service delivery person at a hotel, generally want to do a good job, but they need to be trained to know what exactly a good job entails.

The employees must be thoroughly trained not only to complete their specific tasks but also how to treat guests, and the manager needs to set an example of high service standards, which will permeate throughout the organization. The kind of attitude Marcia got, for instance, when she registered a complaint with the assistant manager at the Green Valley is not a recipe for generating repeat customers and should not be tolerated. For frontline service employees under stress, however, pleasant interactions with customers do not always come naturally. Although people can be taught specific tasks related to their jobs, this is not easily extended to interpersonal relations. But it is simply not enough to tell employees to be nice or do what customers want. A quality goal should be specific, such as: Greet every customer/guest you encounter with "Good morning/afternoon/evening, Sir or Ma'am." Try to greet customers by name.

The Delivery Gap: Delivering Service Quality

The delivery gap is where the rubber meets the road, where the customer directly interacts with the service provider. Even if there are adequate standards in place, the employees are well trained, and management is committed to meeting or exceeding customers' service expectations, there can still be delivery gaps. It could very well have been that Marcia experienced several delivery gaps at the Green Valley Motel. It could have been that the unclean room, the assistant manager's attitude, the unheated swimming pool, the poor piano bar singer, or the stale food resulted from unforeseen or unusual circumstances. Although some of these issues such as an unclean room or the attitude

Marcia encountered should have been avoided, it is possible that the motel had a power outage resulting in the unheated swimming pool, the regular piano bar singer was ill, and the breakfast was stale because of a missed delivery. The maid could not vacuum the room because of the lack of power, and the assistant manager felt assaulted on all sides by these problems. But the result was a lost customer. Even if there are no other gaps, a delivery gap always results in a service failure.

Delivery gaps can be reduced when employees are empowered to spontaneously act in the customers' and the firm's best interests when problems or crises are experienced. Such empowerment might have saved the day for Marcia and the Green Valley. Empowerment means employees are supported in their efforts to do their jobs effectively.[20]

Empowering Service Providers In the service context, empowerment means allowing employees to make decisions about how service is provided to customers. When frontline employees are authorized to make decisions to help their customers, service quality generally improves. Empowerment becomes more important when the service is more individualized. Nordstrom provides an overall objective—satisfy customer needs—and then encourages employees to do whatever is necessary to achieve the objective. For example, a Nordstrom shoe sales associate decided to break up two pairs of shoes, one a size 10 and the other a size 10½, to sell a hard-to-fit customer. Although the other two shoes were unsalable and therefore it made for an unprofitable sale, the customer purchased five other pairs that day and became a loyal Nordstrom customer as a result. Empowering service providers with only a rule like "Use your best judgment" (as Nordstrom does) might cause chaos. At Nordstrom, department managers avoid abuses by coaching and training salespeople to understand what "Use your best judgment" specifically means.

Support and Incentives for Employees To ensure that service is delivered properly, management needs to support the service providers in several ways and give them incentives. This is basic. A service provider's job can often be difficult, especially when customers are unpleasant or less than reasonable. But the service provider cannot be rude or offensive just because the customer is. The old cliché "Service with a smile" remains the best approach, but for this to work, employees must feel supported.

First, managers and coworkers should provide emotional support to service providers by demonstrating a concern for their well-being and standing behind their decisions. Because it can be very disconcerting when a server is abused by a customer who believes her food was improperly prepared, for instance, restaurant managers must be supportive and help the employee get through his or her emotional reaction to the berating experienced.[21] Such support can extend to empowering the server to rectify the situation by giving the customer new food and a free dessert, in which case the manager must understand the server's decision, not punish him for giving away too much.

Second, service providers require instrumental support—the systems and equipment to deliver the service properly. Many retailers provide state-of-the-art instrumental support for their service providers. In-store kiosks help sales associates provide more detailed and complete product information and enable them to make sales of merchandise that is either not carried in the store or is temporarily out of stock.

Third, the support that managers provide must be consistent and coherent throughout the organization. Patients expect physicians to provide great patient care using state-of-the-art procedures and medications, but because they are tied to managed-care systems (health maintenance organizations [HMOs]), many doctors must squeeze more people into their office hours and prescribe less optimal,

Social & Mobile Marketing 13.1   Linking American Express Members to Purchases[iii]

Even when online retailers offer great merchandise, the customer service they offer can be a deciding factor in their success. But relating to customers also can be highly variable. How do you mobilize an entire company to speak with one voice and meet various customers' needs, so that the service provision consistently meets, or exceeds, customers' service standards?

For American Express, the solution is to make it easy for its members to connect with the offers they want most from a wide variety of merchants. To start, American Express made it possible for cardholders to load special offers from various sellers onto their credit card accounts by using specific hashtags when they link with American Express's Twitter account. For example, if someone was looking for a new Sony television, she could visit American Express, post "#sony," and gain access to any special deals the company might have on offer for cardholders that week.

Then American Express expanded these delivery options, such that with the specific, special hashtags it had provided to cardholders, customers could make purchases from partners such as Amazon and Microsoft.

Beyond just product purchases, in a partnership with the travel website TripAdvisor, American Express enabled its members to link their credit cards to their travel profiles. Once they booked a trip, members received special offers for

American Express facilitates a conversation between its members and its merchants by providing special offers on Twitter.

local hotels, car rental agencies, and so on. Of course, they could purchase these add-on options readily because their credit card already was linked to the site.

---

less expensive courses of treatment. These conflicting goals can be very frustrating to patients.

Finally, a key part of any customer service program is providing rewards to employees for their excellent service. Numerous firms have developed a service reputation by ensuring that their employees are themselves recognized for recognizing the value the firm places on customer service. Travelocity, for example, features employees who champion the customer service experience in a weekly e-mail. Believing that engaged employees are the key to customer satisfaction, it works to create an atmosphere that reinforces the commitment to customers by encouraging employees to nominate colleagues who exemplify its commitment to customers. Through constant feedback about who is serving the customer best, as well as smaller events such as monthly lunches with the CEO for selected employees, Travelocity creates a business environment that recognizes and rewards customer service.[22] The results for Travelocity have been a wealth of awards, such as a top ranking on the Customer Online Respect Survey and a designation as the World's Leading Travel Internet Site for several consecutive years.[23]

Use of Technology As our chapter opener confirmed, technology can be employed to reduce delivery gaps. Technology has become an increasingly important facilitator of the delivery of services. Using technology to facilitate service delivery can provide many benefits, such as access to a wider variety of services, a greater degree of control by the customer over the services, and the ability to obtain information. Social and Mobile Marketing 13.1 describes one such option. The

Which store has better customer service: the one with self-checkout (left), or the store offering a face-to-face interaction with the customer? It depends on whom you ask.

use of technology also improves the service provider's efficiency and reduces servicing costs; in some cases, it can lead to a competitive advantage over less service-oriented competitors.[24]

Technological advances that help close the delivery gap are expanding. Salons and cosmetics counters use kiosks to show customers how they would look with different beauty products and various hair colors. Stores enable customers to scan price tags and then have a kiosk recommend complementary items. Touchscreen terminals at tables in restaurants, from Uno Chicago Grill to Applebee's to Chili's, let customers order food and play games from the comfort of their own table.[25] The technological delivery of services can cause problems though. Some customers either do not embrace the idea of replacing a human with a machine for business interactions or have problems using the technology. In other cases, the technology may not perform adequately, such as ATMs that run out of money or are out of order. Supermarket self-checkout devices are too challenging for some customers.

The Communications Gap: Communicating the Service Promise

Poor communication between marketers and their customers can result in a mismatch between an ad campaign's or a salesperson's promises and the service the firm can actually offer. Although firms have difficulty controlling service quality because it can vary from day to day and provider to provider, they have nearly constant control over how they communicate their service package to their customers. This control involves a significant responsibility, as Ethical and Societal Dilemma 13.1 notes.

If a firm promises more than it can deliver, customers' expectations won't be met. An advertisement may lure a customer into a service situation once, but if the service doesn't deliver on the promise, the customer will never return. Dissatisfied customers also are likely to tell others about the underperforming service, using word of mouth or, increasingly, the Internet, which has become an important channel for dissatisfied customers to vent their frustrations.

Ethical & Societal Dilemma 13.1   Fake Reviews[iv]

Yelp, TripAdvisor, and Amazon have all made user ratings and reviews a familiar—and even essential—part of the online toolbox for shoppers and other consumers. From the consumer's perspective, what better preparation could there be for a major purchase than to see what other, objective customers have to say about the product or service under consideration?

For retailers and service professionals, online reviews offer a huge benefit too. For some companies, especially small service providers that cannot afford much marketing, online reviews function as a low-cost form of advertising. A business seeking to meet or exceed customer expectations receives valuable, candid feedback from customers, which it can use to measure how well it is meeting customer expectations. Some firms even use this feedback in their formal marketing research process to improve company operations.

Online reviews like this one from Yelp benefit consumers, retailers, and service providers as long as the reviews are written by unbiased customers.

From this straightforward perspective, honest reviews are the most valuable resource that exists in review sites. But such straightforwardness is not enough for companies that provide poor service and attract reviews befitting their abilities. Rather than improving their service, many of these companies engage in the unethical practice of writing fake reviews themselves, hiring dedicated companies to flood sites with positive fake reviews, or bribing customers to pad their comments with positive assertions. Considering this unethical practice just another example—though in a modern form—of false advertising, state and federal regulators are taking action to ensure that such deceptive advertising does not pay. Moreover, as customers get wise to these moves, companies that fake their reviews often get caught.

VIP Deals, an online retailer that sells leather cases for digital tablets on Amazon, invited its customers to post reviews—and promised that if those reviews were positive, the customer would receive a complete refund. Within weeks, nearly all of the company's 355 online reviews gave the VIP Deals leather case four or five stars. But Amazon guidelines prohibit compensation for customer reviews, and the VIP Deals page soon disappeared.

A leather case for your iPad is one thing. Accurate, truthful information takes on paramount importance for a service like plastic surgery. But Lifestyle Lift seemed to disregard customers' expectations that they could receive truthful information. When unhappy customers started posting too many negative comments on its website, the company launched a coverup, rather than investigating the complaints to help its physicians and staff address the problems. On bogus websites, fictitious posters gave high praise to the company while also asserting that previously posted complaints had been phony. The state of New York soon filed suit and prompted a $300,000 settlement from Lifestyle Lift. New York's attorney general also has announced that his office will be pursuing such false advertisers more actively in the future, doling out stringent penalties as it finds them.

Crowd-sourced online opinions of consumers have become a major source of information about products and services (recall our discussion of crowd-sourcing in Chapter 11). When that information is authentic, it serves consumers and companies both. But when companies manipulate online reviews, it seems as if all of society is harmed. What—if anything—should be done about it?

The communications gap can be reduced by managing customer expectations and by promising only what you can deliver, or possibly even a little less.[26] Suppose you need an operation, and the surgeon explains, "You'll be out of the hospital in five days and back to your normal routine in a month." You have the surgery and feel well enough to leave the hospital three days later. Two weeks after that, you're playing tennis again. Clearly, you will tend to think your surgeon is a genius. However, regardless of the operation's success, if you had to stay in the hospital for 10 days and it took you two months to recover, you would undoubtedly be upset.

A relatively easy way to manage customer expectations is to coordinate how the expectation is created and the way the service is provided. Expectations typically are created through promotions, advertising, or personal selling. Delivery is another function altogether. If a salesperson promises a client that an order can be delivered in one day, and that delivery actually takes a week, the client will be disappointed. However, if the salesperson coordinates the order with those responsible for the service delivery, the client's expectations likely will be met.

Customer expectations can be managed when the service is delivered. Recorded messages tell customers who have phoned a company with a query how many minutes they will have to wait before the next operator is available. Sellers automatically inform online customers of any items that are out of stock. Whether online or in a store, retailers can warn their customers to shop early during a sale because supplies of the sale item are limited. People are generally reasonable when they are warned that some aspect of the service may be below their expectations. They just don't like surprises!

Service Quality and Customer Satisfaction and Loyalty

Good service quality leads to satisfied and loyal customers. As we discussed in Chapter 6, customers inevitably wind up their purchase decision process by undertaking a postpurchase evaluation. This evaluation after the purchase may produce three outcomes: satisfaction, dissonance, and loyalty (see again Exhibit 6.3 in Chapter 6). Dissonance may just be a passing emotion that is overcome; we will discuss recovery from an actual service failure in the next section. Satisfaction, on the other hand, often leads to loyalty.

Assuming that none of the service gaps that we have discussed occur, or at least are not too wide, customers should be more or less satisfied. Surveys of customers that ask them to identify the retailer that provides the best customer service thus often show some consistency. A service provider that does a good job one year is likely to keep customers satisfied the next year too. Some of the best service providers year after year include Amazon, Zappos, L.L.Bean, and Nordstrom.

If a firm not only minimizes but eliminates any service gaps, customers are likely to exhibit significant loyalty to that firm—which is what Amazon hopes to achieve with its Amazon Prime service, as Superior Service 13.1 describes. Customers want to continue receiving such superior service and have no desire to go elsewhere for the offerings it provides them.

Nordstrom consistently is ranked at the top of customer satisfaction surveys.

Superior Service 13.1   Priming the Pump to Let Loyalty Flow[v]

When Amazon first introduced its Prime service, its goal was to build customer loyalty. For $79 per year, membership guaranteed unlimited two-day shipping on all products purchased on the site. The innovation was an immediate success. Millions of Amazon's customers signed up, and they were less likely to purchase from anywhere else.

The program played directly on their consumer psychology: Customers realize that they earn more from the program when they use it more, at no extra cost to them. For example, 10 products purchased on Amazon with two-day shipping likely pay for the $79 membership. If they go on to buy 100 or 1,000 products, still for just $79, customers feel like they have put one over on the company. In a sense, they have. Amazon has demonstrated its willingness to lose significant profits to develop its program and build unparalleled customer loyalty.

Over time, Amazon added many new features to Prime, and the cost remained the same for nearly a decade. But ultimately, noting estimates that it lost approximately $11 per Prime customer each year, Amazon realized that the service was dampening its profits due to its higher operating expenses. Accordingly, at the start of 2014 it announced the price of Prime memberships would increase to $99 per year. Despite negative reactions from existing Prime members who hate the idea of paying $20 more for their benefits, Amazon believes the move ultimately will be profitable because it continues to add to the services it offers.

For example, Amazon offers a book-lending service for Prime customers who own the Kindle Fire, such that they may read one free e-book each month. Furthermore, Prime members gain free access to approximately 40,000 movies and television programs through Amazon's streaming services. As Amazon adds more products to its retail site, customers also might find the Prime service even more valuable because they can get their groceries shipped for free, not just their reading entertainment. That is, though some existing members may drop Prime, rebelling against the price increase, others continue to find the service highly valuable.

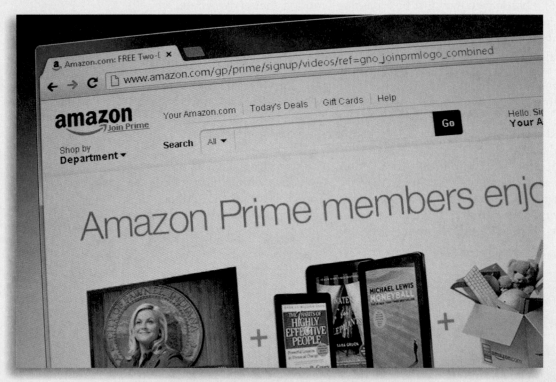

Is Amazon Prime worth $99 a year?

CHECK YOURSELF

1. Explain the four service gaps identified by the Service Gaps Model.
2. List at least two ways to overcome each of the four service gaps.

SERVICE RECOVERY

LO5 Identify three service recovery strategies.

Despite a firm's best efforts, sometimes service providers fail to meet customer expectations. When this happens, the best course of action is to attempt to make amends with the customer and learn from the experience. Of course, it is best to avoid a service failure altogether, but when a failure does occur, the firm has a unique opportunity to demonstrate its customer commitment. Effective service recovery efforts can significantly increase customer satisfaction, purchase intentions, and positive word of mouth, though customers' post-recovery satisfaction levels usually fall lower than their satisfaction level prior to the service failure.

Remember the Green Valley Motel in Maine? It could have made amends with Marcia Kessler after its service failures if it had taken some relatively simple, immediate steps: The assistant manager could have apologized for his bad behavior and quickly upgraded her to a suite and/or given her a free night's lodging for a future stay. The motel could also have given her a free lunch or dinner to make up for the bad breakfast. Alternatively, the assistant manager could have asked Marcia how he could resolve the situation and worked with her to come up with an equitable solution. None of these actions would have cost the motel much money.

Had it used the customer lifetime value approach we described in Chapter 10, the motel would have realized that by not taking action, it lost Marcia as a customer forever. Over the next few years, she could have been responsible for several thousand dollars in sales. Instead, Marcia is now likely to spread negative word of mouth about the motel to her friends, family, and through online review sites, such as Yelp.com, because of its failure to recover. Effective service recovery thus demands (1) listening to the customers and involving them in the service recovery, (2) providing a fair solution, and (3) resolving the problem quickly.[27]

Listening to the Customers and Involving Them in the Service Recovery

Firms often don't find out about service failures until a customer complains. Whether the firm has a formal complaint department or the complaint is offered directly to the service provider, the customer must have the opportunity to air the complaint completely, and the firm must listen carefully to what he or she is saying.

Customers can become very emotional about a service failure, whether the failure is serious (a botched surgical operation) or minor (the wrong change at a restaurant). In many cases, the customer may just want to be heard, and the service provider should give the customer all the time he or she needs to get it out. The very process of describing a perceived wrong to a sympathetic listener or the Twitterverse is therapeutic in and of itself. Service providers therefore should welcome the opportunity to be that sympathetic ear, listen carefully, and appear (and actually be) eager to rectify the situation to ensure it doesn't happen again.[28]

When the company and the customer work together, the outcome is often better than either could achieve on their own. This co-creation logic applies especially well to service recovery. A service failure is a negative experience, but when customers participate in its resolution, it results in a more positive outcome than simply listening to their complaint and providing a preapproved set of potential solutions that may satisfy them.

Suppose, for instance, that when you arrived at the airport in San Francisco, your flight had been overbooked and you were bumped. Of course, good customer service required the ticket agent to listen to your frustration and help provide a fair solution. But the most obvious potential solution from the airline's perspective might not have been the best solution for you. It might have been inclined to put you on the next available flight, which would be a red-eye that left at midnight and got you to New York at 6:30 a.m. But if you don't sleep well on planes and you have an important business meeting the next afternoon, the best solution from your perspective would be to have the airline put you up in an air-port hotel so you can get a good night's sleep and then put you on an early morn-ing flight that would get you to New York in time for your meeting, well-rested and ready to go. Thus, by working closely with you to understand your needs, the ticket agent would be able to co-create a great solution to the service failure.

Finding a Fair Solution

Most people realize that mistakes happen. But when they happen, customers want to be treated fairly, whether that means *distributive* or *procedural* fairness.[29] Their perception of what "fair" means is based on their previous experience with other firms, how they have seen other customers treated, material they have read, and stories recounted by their friends.

Distributive Fairness Distributive fairness pertains to a customer's perception of the benefits he or she received compared with the costs (inconvenience or loss). Customers want to be compensated a fair amount for a perceived loss that re-sulted from a service failure. If, for instance, a person arrives at the airport gate and finds her flight is overbooked, she may believe that taking the next flight that day and receiving a travel voucher is adequate compensation for the inconve-nience. But if no flights are available until the next day, the traveler may require additional compensation, such as overnight accommodations, meals, and a round-trip ticket to be used at a later date.[30]

The key to distributive fairness, of course, is listening carefully to the cus-tomer. One customer, traveling on vacation, may be satisfied with a travel voucher, whereas another may need to get to the destination on time because of a business appointment. Regardless of how the problem is solved, customers typically want tangible restitution—in this case, to get to their destination—not just an apology. If providing tangible restitution isn't possible, the next best thing is to assure the customer that steps are being taken to prevent the failure from recurring.

Procedural Fairness With regard to complaints, procedural fairness refers to the perceived fairness of the process used to resolve them. Customers want efficient complaint procedures over whose outcomes they have some influence. Customers tend to believe they have been treated fairly if the service providers follow specific company guidelines. Nevertheless, rigid adherence to rules can have deleterious effects. Have you ever returned an item to a store, even a very inexpensive item, and been told that the return needed a manager's approval? The process likely took several minutes and irritated everyone in the checkout line. Furthermore, most managers' cursory inspection of the item or the situation would not catch a fraudulent return. In a case like this, the procedure the company uses to handle a return probably overshadows any potential positive outcomes. Therefore, as we noted previously, service providers should be empowered with some procedural flexibility to solve customer complaints.

A no-questions-asked return policy has been offered as a customer service by many retailers such as L.L.Bean. But because of its high cost as a result of custom-ers abusing the policy, many retailers such as Bean's competitor, REI, have modi-fied their return policies.[31] Some large retailers now limit their returns to 90 days, considered a reasonable amount of time for customers to return an item. Others will only grant a store credit based on the lowest selling price for the item if the customer doesn't have a receipt. In addition, for some consumer electronics prod-ucts that have been opened, customers must pay a 15 percent restocking fee.

Resolving Problems Quickly

The longer it takes to resolve a service failure, the more irritated the customer will become and the more people he or she is likely to tell about the problem. To re-solve service failures quickly, firms need clear policies, adequate training for their employees, and empowered employees. Health insurance companies, for instance, have made a concerted effort in recent years to avoid service failures that occur because customers' insurance claims have not been handled quickly or to the customers' satisfaction. As we noted in the chapter opener, the speed of social media connections puts increasing pressure on providers to resolve any failures immediately—literally within hours, in many cases.

CHECK YOURSELF

1. Why is service recovery so important to companies?
2. What can companies do to recover from a service failure?

Reviewing Learning Objectives

LO1 **Describe how the marketing of services differs from the marketing of products.**

Unlike products, services are intangible, inseparable, variable, and perishable. They cannot be seen or touched, which makes it difficult to describe their benefits or promote them. Service providers therefore enhance service delivery with tangible attributes, like a nice atmosphere or price benefits. Services get produced and consumed at the same time, so marketers must work quickly, and they are more variable than products, though service providers attempt to reduce this variability as much as possible. Finally, because consumers cannot stockpile perishable services, marketers often provide incentives to stagger demand.

LO2 **Discuss the four gaps in the Service Gaps Model.**

The knowledge gap reflects the difference between customers' expectations and the firm's perception of those customer expectations. Firms need to match customer expectations with actual service through research. The standards gap is the difference between the firm's perceptions of customers' expectations and the service standards it sets. Appropriate service standards and measurements of service performance help close this gap. The delivery gap is the difference between the firm's service standards and the actual service it provides to customers. Closing this gap requires adequate training and empowerment of employees. The communication gap refers to the difference between the actual service provided to customers and the service that the firm's promotion program promises. Firms close the communications gap by managing

customer expectations and promising only what they can deliver.

LO3 **Examine the five service quality dimensions.**

First, reliability refers to whether the provider consistently provides an expected level of service. Second, responsiveness means that the provider notes consumers' desires and requests and then addresses them. Third, assurance reflects the service provider's own confidence in its abilities. Fourth, empathy entails the provider's recognition and understanding of consumer needs. Finally, tangibles are the elements that go along with the service, such as the magazines in a doctor's waiting room.

LO4 **Explain the zone of tolerance.**

The area between customers' desired service and the minimum level of service they will accept is the zone of tolerance. It is the difference between what the customer really wants and what he or she will accept before going elsewhere. Firms can assess their customers' zone of tolerance by determining the desired and expected level of service for each service dimension, their perceptions of how well the focal service performs and how well a competitive service performs, and the importance of each service quality dimension.

LO5 **Identify three service recovery strategies.**

In a best-case scenario, the service never fails. But some failures are inevitable and require the firm to make amends to the customer by (1) listening carefully and involving the customer in the service recovery; (2) finding a fair solution to the problem that compensates the customer for the failure and follows procedures the customer believes are fair; and (3) resolving the problem quickly.

Key Terms

- communication gap, 414
- customer service, 408
- delivery gap, 414
- distributive fairness, 428
- emotional support, 421
- empowerment, 421
- heterogeneity, 412

- inseparable, 411
- instrumental support, 421
- intangible, 410
- knowledge gap, 414
- perishable, 413
- procedural fairness, 428

- service, 408
- service gap, 413
- service quality, 416
- standards gap, 414
- voice-of-customer (VOC) program, 418
- zone of tolerance, 418

Marketing Applications

1. Those companies from which you purchase products and services are not pure sellers of services, nor are they pure sellers of products. What services does an Apple store provide? What goods does a hairstylist provide?

2. You have been sitting in the waiting room of your mechanic's shop for more than an hour. With the knowledge that products are different from services, develop a list of the things the shop manager could do to improve the overall service delivery. Consider how the shop might overcome problems associated with the tangibility, separability, heterogeneity, and perishability of services.

3. You have conducted a zone of tolerance analysis for your local pizza restaurant. You find that the lengths of the reliability and responsiveness boxes are much greater than those of the other three service quality dimensions. You also find that the restaurant is positioned above the zone box on reliability but below the box on responsiveness. What should you tell the manager to do?

4. Assume you were hired by the local grocery store to help assess their service quality. How would you go about undertaking this project?

5. What should a restaurant server do who is faced with an irate customer who has received undercooked food after a long wait? How can he or she avoid a service failure by being empowered? What should the server do?

6. What types of support and incentives could your university provide advisers to help make them more attentive to students' needs?

7. What mobile apps do you use that help facilitate your transactions with a specific retailer or service provider? Would you rather use the apps or engage in a face-to-face relationship with a person? How, if at all, would your parents' answer to these two questions differ?

8. A local health club is running a promotional campaign that promises you can lose an inch a month off your waist if you join the club and follow its program. How might this claim cause a communications gap? What should the club do to avoid a service failure?

9. Suppose the health club didn't listen to your advice and ran the promotional campaign as is. A new member has come in to complain that not only did he not lose inches off his waist, he actually gained weight. How should the health club manager proceed?

10. You are hired by a career consulting firm that promises to market new graduates to high-paying employers. The firm provides potential clients with an impressive list of employers. It charges the clients a fee, and then a separate finder's fee if the client gets a position. The firm aggressively markets its services and has a large client base. You learn that the firm simply takes submitted résumés and posts them to a variety of online job search engines. The firm never actually contacts any firms on its clients' behalf. The CEO, himself a recent college grad, tells you that the firm never promises to actually contact potential employers, only that it has access to employers and will distribute clients' résumés. What do you think of the career consulting firm's practices?

Quiz Yourself

1. When marketers say that services are _____, they are referring to the fact that services cannot be touched, tasted, or seen like a pure product can.
    a. intangible
    b. inseparable
    c. variable
    d. perishable
    e. replenishable

2. Cheryl will only let Martiné cut her hair. She has tried other hairstylists, but she knows from experience that Martiné cuts her hair well every time. For Cheryl, _____ is the most important of the five service quality dimensions.
    a. assurance
    b. reliability
    c. tangibles
    d. responsiveness
    e. empathy

    (Answers to these two questions can be found on page 652.)

Toolkit

SERVICES ZONE OF TOLERANCE

Please use the Toolkit provided in your instructor's Connect course to assess the zone of tolerance for several service providers.

Net Savvy

1. What services does Zipcar (www.zipcar.com) offer? Go to Zipcar's website and click on "for everybody." Evaluate how quick it is to reserve a car in a major city or at a university that has a dedicated Zipcar car pickup/dropoff location.

2. Go to Zappos's website, http://www.zappos.com and examine its customer service offerings. Next, go to Reseller Ratings, http://www.resellerratings.com and look up Zappos. Based on these reviews, does Zappos have a service gap? If so, how can the company close it?

Chapter Case Study   ▣ connect

ZIPCAR: DELIVERING ONLY AS MUCH DRIVING AS YOU WANT

Historically, the expectation that your car would be waiting for you at the curb every morning was hard-wired into many Americans, especially those who experienced the growth of the auto industry. But that expectation has disappeared for many city dwellers, frustrated by the soaring costs and parking pressures that confront them with each trip around the crowded block. For them, Zipcar, the world's leading car-sharing company,[32] offers the pleasure of driving without the hassles of ownership.

The Cambridge, Massachusetts–based company rents self-service vehicles by the hour or day to urban residents who prefer to pay for just as much driving as they absolutely need. Car sharing eliminates issues related to parking shortages; overnight parking restrictions; or soaring gas, insurance, and tax bills. That promise resonates well with consumer expectations on many fronts, especially among Zipcar's primary urban customers, the large segments of college students who also enjoy the service, and even suburbanites who work in the city.

Yet as Zipcar CEO Scott Griffith realizes, the company's biggest growth obstacle is Americans' inability to envision life without a car.[33] To push an attitude shift, Zipcar makes the car-sharing experience as easy as possible, with just four simple steps:

1. Join the network.
2. Reserve your car online or from your smartphone.
3. Unlock the car with your Zipcard.
4. Drive away.

Today the car-sharing network has more than 740,000 members and tens of thousands of vehicles located in 34 metropolitan areas and hundreds of college campuses throughout the United States, Canada, Spain, and Britain.[34] With so many locations, the company could bring convenient car sharing to a far larger market; it estimates that 10 million residents, business commuters, and university students now live or work just a short walk away from an available Zipcar.[35]

Zipcar is banking on more than shifting attitudes. Emerging trends due to the economic downturn and changing buying habits have helped spur growth. On average, automobiles consume 19 percent of household incomes,[36] yet many cars stand idle for 90 percent of each day. Drivers seeking a less expensive and less wasteful alternative thus might save up to 70 percent on their transportation costs because an annual Zipcar membership costs just $42, and the average member spends $428 a year.[37]

Zipcar's service model fits in with the emergence of on-demand, pay-per-use options, such as Netflix for movies, iTunes for music, and e-readers for books.[38] Moreover, the popularity of mobile shopping and the growing expectation that they can order anything, anywhere, anytime from their smartphones have made urban young adults and college students two of Zipcar's most fervent member groups. For these "Zipsters," ordering up a set of wheels on the go is far more appealing than being saddled with car payments.

A strong urban public transportation system also helps make car sharing more attractive. That's why Zipcar started off in high-density urban areas such as Boston, New York, and Washington, DC, with their great public transportation systems already in place. Wherever subways and buses work, car sharing can extend the transit system's reach. By locating cars near transit route endpoints, travelers gain an easy extension on subway or bus schedules to their final destinations. Zipcar

Zipcars are for people who don't need a car all the time, like urbanites and college students.

even offers members an overnight option, for grabbing a car in the evening and returning it the next morning.

Finally, the logic of car sharing works well in settings marked by increased urbanization. According to the United Nations, cities will contain 59 percent of the world's population by 2030.[39] Many of these areas already face congestion, space demands, and environmental threats from crowding too many gas-driven vehicles into a small, population-dense space. Griffith estimates that every Zipcar would replace 15 to 20 personal cars.[40] Thus some cities work with Zipcar to identify and secure parking spaces close to subway stops and rail stations. New York and Chicago also rent Zipcars for municipal workers so they can shuttle more efficiently across city locations during their workday. Zipcar also provides fleet management services to local, state, and federal agencies.

Car sharing could translate into a $10 billion market globally.[41] Cities in Europe and Asia are well primed for car sharing, by virtue of their strong rail systems, heavy reliance on public transit, and widespread adoption of mobile and wireless technologies. A deal with Spain's largest car-sharing company, Avancar, represents the first venture in Zipcar's planned global expansion.[42]

Such growth requires strong logistics, and Zipcar is backed by a corps of fleet managers and vehicle coordinators who track, schedule, and oversee vehicle maintenance; proprietary hardware and software technology that helps it communicate with drivers and track vehicles; and a large fleet that includes hybrid vehicles for fuel efficiency, as well as minivans to appeal to families who want to take a trip to the beach. Zipcar estimates that it processes 2.6 million reservations per year, and its reservation system has almost never failed.[43] Struggling to keep up with such demands also led Zipcar to enter into a merger with Avis, the international car rental company.[44]

These behind-the-scenes moves aim to make Zipcar's service simple, convenient, and reliable. But failures are inevitable, as one customer's experience showed. The customer went to pick up his designated vehicle at the time and place reserved for him, but he discovered no car there. The Zipcar representative told him that it might be out, being serviced or cleaned, or it could have been delayed by another driver running late. But such excuses did little to alleviate the frustration of being stuck with no transportation.

Learning of his predicament, Zipcar tried but was unable to find another car in close proximity. Therefore, it quickly authorized the customer to take a taxi and promised to reimburse him up to $100. Although the "free ride" did not altogether mitigate the stress and inconvenience of the service failure, Zipcar's response showed him that the company was committed to doing right by him, even if that meant sending business to a competitor, the taxi company.

The considerable dimensions of a global car-sharing market are already emerging. Zipcar's 10-year experience and first-mover status in the market positions it well to compete. But the race to dominate is sure to intensify, and some members have expressed dismay that it would align with a traditional car rental company, when its appeal was largely that it offered an alternative to traditional car rentals.[45] Whether Zipcar can maintain its space in this market depends mostly on its ability to meet its own standards for customer service—simplicity, convenience, and reliability—consistently and effectively.

Questions

1. Using the building blocks (five dimensions) of service quality (see Exhibit 13.4), evaluate Zipcar.

2. Compare Zipcar's service quality performance with that of the most recent car rental service (e.g., Avis, Hertz) that you may have used.

3. How well has Zipcar handled service failure situations? What could it do to improve recovery efforts?

Endnotes

1. Chuck Hemann, "Social Customer Service: How Samsung Support Saved a Sale," *Common Sense*, February 11, 2013, http://blog.wcgworld.com.

2. Rachel Sprung, "4 Examples of Excellent Twitter Customer Service," *Social Media Examiner*, August 1, 2013, http://www.socialmediaexaminer.com.

3. Knowledge@Wharton, "The Ignored Side of Social Media: Customer Service," *Knowledge@Wharton*, January 2, 2014, http://knowledge.wharton.upenn.edu/article/ignored-side-social-media-customer-service/.

4. Sprung, "4 Examples of Excellent Twitter Customer Service."

5. Knowledge@Wharton, "The Ignored Side of Social Media."

6. Jessica Reed, "Twitter and Customer Service: Maximizing Responsiveness in 140 Characters," *Social Media Today*, April 11, 2013, http://socialmediatoday.com.

7. Valarie A. Zeithaml, Mary Jo Bitner, and Dwayne D. Gremler, *Services Marketing: Integrating Customer Focus across the Firm*, 6th ed. (Burr Ridge, IL: McGraw-Hill/Irwin, 2012).

8. Bureau of Economic Analysis, news release, January 27, 2012, http://www.bea.gov; "Fortune 500," *CNNMoney*, May 23, 2011, http://money.cnn.com.

9. Zeithaml et al., *Services Marketing*.

10. "Center for Professional Responsibility," http://www.abanet.org.

11. Choice Hotels, "Special Guest Policies," http://www.choicehotels.com.

12. Andrew Adam Newman, "A Gym for People Who Don't Like Gyms," *The New York Times*, January 2, 2013, http://www.nytimes.com.

13. The discussion of the Gaps Model and its implications draws heavily from Michael Levy, Barton A. Weitz, and Dhruv Grewal, *Retailing Management*, 9th ed. (Burr Ridge, IL: Irwin/McGraw-Hill, 2013); it is also based on the classic work of Zeithaml, Parasuraman, and Berry, *Delivering Quality Service*; Valerie Zeithaml, Leonard Berry, and A. Parasuraman, "Communication and Control Processes in the Delivery of Service Quality," *Journal of Marketing* 52, no. 2 (April 1988), pp. 35–48.

14. Zhen Zhu, Cheryl Nakata, K. Sivakumar, and Dhruv Grewal, "Fix It or Leave It? Customer Recovery from Self-Service Technology Failures," *Journal of Retailing* 89, no. 1 (2013), pp. 15–29.

15. Velitchka D. Kaltcheva, Robert D. Winsor, and A. Parasuraman, "Do Customer Relationships Mitigate or Amplify Failure Responses?" *Journal of Business Research* 66, no. 4 (2013), pp. 525–32; Ruth N. Bolton, Anders Gustafsson, Janet McColl-Kennedy, Nancy J. Sirianni, and K. Tse David, "Small Details That Make Big Differences: A Radical Approach to Consumption Experience as a Firm's Differentiating Strategy," *Journal of Service Management* 25, no. 2 (2014), pp. 253–74; Lance A. Bettencourt, Stephen W. Brown, and Nancy J. Sirianni, "The Secret to True Service Innovation," *Business Horizons* 56, no. 1 (2013), pp. 13–22.

16. Reed, "Twitter and Customer Service."

17. Zeithaml et al., *Services Marketing*.

18. Janelle Barlow, "A Complaint Is a Gift Corner," http://www.tmius.com.

19. Michael Bergdahl, *The Retail Revolution: How Wal-Mart Created a Brave New World of Business* (New York: Metropolitan Books, 2009); Michael Bergdahl, *The 10 Rules of Sam Walton: Success Secrets for Remarkable Results* (Hoboken, NJ: Wiley, 2006).

20. Steven W. Rayburn, "Improving Service Employee Work Affect: The Transformative Potential of Work Design," *Journal of Services Marketing* 28, no. 1 (2014), pp. 71–81; Zhu et al., "Fix It or Leave It?"; Ying Hong, Hui Liao, Jia Hu, and Kaifeng Jiang, "Missing Link in the Service Profit Chain: A Meta-Analytic Review of the Antecedents, Consequences, and Moderators of Service Climate," *Journal of Applied Psychology* 98, no. 2 (2013), p. 237.

21. Jason Colquitt, Jeffery LePine, and Michael Wesson, *Organizational Behavior: Improving Performance and Commitment in the Workplace*, 3rd ed. (Burr Ridge, IL: McGraw-Hill, 2012); Felicitas M. Morhart, Walter Herzog, and Torsten Tomczak, "Brand-Specific Leadership: Turning Employees into Brand Champions," *Journal of Marketing* 73 (September 2009), pp. 122–42.

22. Marguerite Darlington, "The History and Future of Mobile's Role in Fashion," *FashionablyMarketing.me*, November 22, 2011.

23. "Travelocity," http://www.sabre-holdings.com/ourBrands/travelocity.html; "Awards," http://svc.travelocity.com.

24. Suzanne C. Makarem, Susan M. Mudambi, and Jeffrey S. Podoshen, "Satisfaction in Technology-Enabled Service Encounters," *Journal of Services Marketing* 23, no. 1 (2009).

25. Sarah Nassauer, "Chili's to Install Tabletop Computer Screens," *The Wall Street Journal*, September 15, 2013, http://online.wsj.com; Alicia Kelso, "Uno Chicago Grill Engages Customers with Tabletop Technology," *Pizza Marketplace*, October 29, 2013, http://www.pizzamarketplace.com; Jeff Morganteen, "CEO: 100,000 Tablets Coming to Applebee's in 2014," *CNBC*, December 10, 2013, http://www.cnbc.com.

26. Anita Whiting and Naveen Donthu, "Closing the Gap between Perceived and Actual Waiting Times in a Call Center: Results from a Field Study," *Journal of Services Marketing* 23, no. 5 (2009), pp. 279–328.

27. Zhu et al., "Fix It or Leave It?"; María Leticia Santos-Vijande, Ana María Díaz-Martín, Leticia Suárez-Álvarez, and Ana Belén del Río-Lanza, "An Integrated Service Recovery System (ISRS): Influence on Knowledge-Intensive Business Services Performance," *European Journal of Marketing* 47, no. 5/6 (2013), pp. 934–63.

28. Christian Grönroos and Päivi Voima, "Critical Service Logic: Making Sense of Value Creation and Co-creation," *Journal of the Academy of Marketing Science* 41, no. 2 (2013), pp. 133–50; Anne L. Roggeveen, Michael Tsiros, and Dhruv Grewal, "Understanding the Co-Creation Effect: When Does Collaborating with Customers Provide a Lift to Service Recovery?" *Journal of the Academy of Marketing Science* 40, no. 6 (2012), pp. 771–90.

29. Kaltcheva et al., "Do Customer Relationships Mitigate or Amplify Failure Responses?"; Yany Grégoire, Thomas M. Tripp, and Renaud Legoux, "When Customer Love Turns into Lasting Hate: The Effects of Relationship Strength and Time on Customer Revenge and Avoidance," *Journal of Marketing* 73 (November 2009), pp. 18–32.

30. Roggeveen, Tsiros, and Grewal, "Understanding the Co-Creation Effect."

31. Amy Martinez, "REI Now Limiting Returns to One Year," *Seattle Times*, June 3, 2013.

32. http://www.zipcar.com.

33. April Kilcrease, "A Conversation with Zipcar's CEO Scott Griffith," GigaOM, December 5, 2011, http://gigaom.com.

34. http://www.zipcar.com.

35. United States Securities and Exchange Commission, "Zipcar S-1 Filing," June 1, 2010, http://sec.gov/.

36. Kilcrease, "A Conversation with Zipcar's CEO Scott Griffith."

37. United States Securities and Exchange Commission, "Zipcar S-1 Filing"; JP Morgan SMid Cap Conference, December 11, 2011.

38. Tina Rosenberg, "It's Not Just Nice to Share, It's the Future," *The New York Times*, June 5, 2013, http://www.nytimes.com.

39. United States Securities and Exchange Commission, "Zipcar S-1 Filing."

40. Kilcrease, "A Conversation with Zipcar's CEO Scott Griffith."

41. Ibid.

42. United States Securities and Exchange Commission, "Zipcar S-1 Filing."

43. Ibid.

44. Brad Tuttle, "Does Selling Out to Avis Represent Success for Zipcar? Failure? Something Else?" *Time*, January 3, 2013, http://business.time.com.

45. Ibid.

i. Ramon Ray, "Carbonite Offers Data Peace of Mind: A Solid Solution for Small Biz," *Business Insider*, January 24, 2012, http://www.businessinsider.com; David Huber, "Carbonite Inc. (CARB) Online Backup Service," IRA.com, January 26, 2011, http://www.ira.com; "Carbonite Gains from HIPAA Regulations," *Zacks*, March 24, 2014, http://www.zacks.com; "Pricing," http://www.carbonite.com; Eric A. Taub, "Storing Your Files inside the Cloud," *The New York Times*, March 2, 2011, http://www.nytimes.com.

ii. http://www.forbestravelguide.com/five-star-spas.htm; Allison Scott, "New Renovations Add to the Guest and Meeting Experience," http://www.release-news.com; http://www.broadmoor.com.

iii. Chanelle Bessette, "Social Media Superstars 2014," *CNN*, January 16, 2014, http://money.cnn.com.

iv. David Streitfield, "For $2 a Star, an Online Retailer Gets 5-Star Product Reviews," *The New York Times*, January 26, 2012, http://www.nytimes.com; David Streitfield, "Faking It to Make It: A Beautiful Try," *The New York Times*, January 27, 2012, http://bits.blogs.nytimes.com; David Streitfield, "Give Yourself 5 Stars? Online, It Might Cost You," *The New York Times*, September 22, 2013, http://www.nytimes.com.

v. Stu Woo, "Amazon 'Primes' Pump for Loyalty," *The Wall Street Journal*, November 14, 2011, http://online.wsj.com; Stu Woo and John Letzing, "Amazon's Spending Habit Hurts Profit," *The Wall Street Journal*, February 1, 2012, http://online.wsj.com; David Streitfield, "Complaints as Amazon Raises the Cost of Prime," *The New York Times*, March 13, 2014, http://www.nytimes.com.

Credits

VALUE CAPTURE

CHAPTER 14
Pricing Concepts for Establishing Value

CHAPTER 15
Strategic Pricing Methods

Section Five contains two chapters on pricing dedicated to value capture. Chapter 14 examines the importance of setting the right price, the relationship between price and quantity sold, break-even analysis, the impact of price wars, and how the Internet has changed the way people shop. Chapter 15 looks specifically at how to set prices.

CHAPTER 14

PRICING CONCEPTS FOR ESTABLISHING VALUE

- **LO1** List the four pricing orientations.
- **LO2** Explain the relationship between price and quantity sold.
- **LO3** Explain price elasticity.
- **LO4** Describe how to calculate a product's break-even point.
- **LO5** Indicate the four types of price competitive levels.

Pricing is a key part of the value proposition for any purchase. After all, among the other definitions we have used in this book, value reflects the relationship between benefits and costs. When the economy sours, and consumer income drops, no sticker prices can escape sharp scrutiny, especially in the supermarket. For example, shoppers on tight budgets still need to buy cleaning supplies, but when they do so, they tend to be much more sensitive to the prices for the various detergents their household needs.

In such price sensitive and highly competitive markets, companies must be creative in finding ways to balance profits and consumers. Procter & Gamble (P&G) had long floated high above its competitors in the sea of laundry detergents, with its Tide brand enjoying 38 percent share of the laundry soap market in North America.[1] However, a wave of lower-priced competitors crashed onto P&G when consumers began looking more actively for better deals. Thrifty shoppers began turning from their trusty Tide brand to cheaper alternatives, such as Arm & Hammer detergent, made by Church & Dwight, Co.

Not a company to rest on its laurels, P&G pursued several strategic responses to the challenge. For consumers interested in convenience, it introduced, developed, and expanded on the concept of laundry detergent pods—single-use packs that eliminate the mess and the need for measuring associated with liquids or powders. Although this option has expanded the breadth of Tide's product lines, and established an approximately $1 billion market for P&G, the pods create higher per-wash costs for consumers.[2]

Therefore, for consumers determined to use cheaper detergents, it also has developed and introduced Tide Simply Clean & Fresh, a liquid detergent that retails for about

35 percent less than the $12 price of a 100-ounce bottle of regular Tide.[3] In an effort to reduce the risk of sales cannibalization of its premium, higher-priced products, P&G makes sure that Simply Clean never appears for sale alongside other Tide brands, nor does it sport the easily recognizable orange Tide-branded container. In stores, Simply Clean is placed alongside its competitor brand on store shelves, despite its higher price point. The primary target markets are consumers from hardworking households, many of whom work in tough, odor-generating jobs and environments. With this approach, P&G can ensure that it never turns its back on its flagship brand.

However, to offset the lower profit margins earned on Tide Simply Clean, P&G also needs to increase margins on premium Tide detergents, including Tide Plus, which contain extra ingredients (e.g., color-safe bleach). In the consumer-goods industry a popular pricing method allows brands to raise their prices in a way that remains largely hidden to consumers, unless they do a lot of extra research. Specifically, the brand increases wholesale prices while also reducing the size of the containers; what was formerly a 100-ounce bottle of detergent becomes a 92-ounce bottle, and the previously 50-ounce

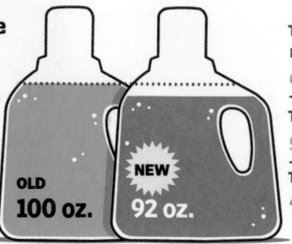

Less for More

Procter & Gamble is cutting the number of loads but not the price on some of its premium Tide detergents, compensating for its new low-cost version.

Note: Pricing is determined by individual retailers. Each 100 oz. bottle recently cost $11.99 at a New York City Target store.

OLD 100 oz.

NEW 92 oz.

TIDE PLUS FEBREZE

LOADS   PRICE PER LOAD:

60 | 48 | ▲ **25%**

TIDE PLUS BLEACH ALTERNATIVE

52 | 48 | ▲ **9%**

TIDE PLUS DOWNY

48 | 48 | **Unchanged**

Source: analyst reports, company documents
The Wall Street Journal

Source: Serena Ng, "At P&G, New Tide Comes In, Old Price Goes Up," *The Wall Street Journal,* February 10, 2014, http://wsj.online.com.

bottle contains only 46 ounces. The retail price remains the same; the package looks practically identical. Few consumers check the actual volume of such commonly purchased products, so they likely never realize that their detergent is costing them more per ounce.

Although P&G's product portfolio is broad, including various detergent brands such as Gain, Era, and Cheer, it has chosen to focus where consumers are most invested, namely, in its Tide products. In trying to ensure Tide's market share advantage, P&G has shown its willingness to adjust its regular pricing strategies, develop new products with varying profit margins, and reduce bottle sizes while maintaining the same retail price. In essence, Procter & Gamble is keeping an eye on the way the tides are turning in the laundry detergent market.

Although knowing how consumers arrive at their perceptions of value is critical to developing successful pricing strategies, sellers also must consider other factors—which is why developing a good pricing strategy is such a formidable challenge to all firms. Do it right, and the rewards to the firm will be substantial. Do it wrong, and failure will be swift and severe. But even if a pricing strategy is implemented well, consumers, economic conditions, markets, competitors, government regulations, and even a firm's own products change constantly—and that means that a good pricing strategy today may not remain an effective pricing strategy tomorrow.

So much rides on marketers setting the right price that we take two chapters to explain the role of price in the marketing mix. First, in this chapter we explain what "price" is as a marketing concept, why it is important, how marketers set pricing objectives, and how various factors influence price setting. In the next chapter, we extend this foundation by focusing on specific pricing strategies that capitalize on capturing value.

Imagine that a consumer realizes that to save money on a particular item, she will have to drive an additional 20 miles. She may determine that her time and travel costs are not worth the savings, so even though the price tag is higher at a nearby store, she judges the overall cost of buying the product there to be lower. To include aspects of price such as this, we may define price as the overall sacrifice a consumer is willing to make to acquire a specific product or service. This sacrifice necessarily includes the money that must be paid to the seller to acquire the item, but it also may involve other sacrifices, whether nonmonetary, like the value of the time necessary to acquire the product or service, or monetary, like travel costs, taxes, shipping costs, and so forth, all of which the buyer must give up to take possession of the product.[4] It's useful to think of overall price like this to see how the narrower sense of purchase price fits in.

Because price is the only element of the marketing mix that does not generate costs, but instead generates revenue, it is important in its own right. Every other element in the marketing mix may be perfect, but with the wrong price, sales and thus revenue will not accrue. Research has consistently shown that consumers usually rank price as one of the most important factors in their purchase decisions.[5]

Knowing that price is so critical to success, why don't managers put greater emphasis on it as a strategic decision variable? Price is the most challenging of the four Ps to manage, partly because it is often the least understood. Historically, managers have treated price as an afterthought to their marketing strategy, setting prices according to what competitors were charging or, worse yet, adding up their costs and tacking a desired profit on to set the sales price. Prices rarely changed except in response to radical shifts in market conditions. Even today pricing decisions are often relegated to standard rules of thumb that fail to reflect our current understanding of the role of price in the marketing mix.

Price is a particularly powerful indicator of quality when consumers are less knowledgeable about the product category—a lesson brought home by the movie (based on the book of the same name) *Moneyball*. As the character played by Jonah Hill argues convincingly to Brad Pitt's character, baseball teams often overpay for young, untested talent or big name players, because they don't know how else to set an accurate price.[6]

In summary, marketers should view pricing decisions as a strategic opportunity to create value rather than as an afterthought to the rest of the marketing mix. Let us now turn to the five basic components of pricing strategies.

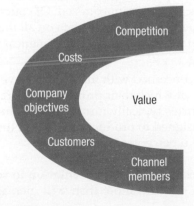

Demonstrating that price is often used to judge quality, in the movie Moneyball, *Jonah Hill explains to Brad Pitt's character that baseball teams often overpay for young, untested talent or big name players, because they don't know how else to gauge an appropriate salary.*

THE FIVE Cs OF PRICING

Successful pricing strategies are built around the five critical components (the five Cs) of pricing found in Exhibit 14.1. We examine these components in some detail because each makes a significant contribution to formulating good pricing policies.[7] To start, the first step is to develop the company's pricing objectives.

EXHIBIT 14.1 The 5 Cs of Pricing

Competition

Costs

Company objectives

Value

Customers

Channel members

EXHIBIT 14.2	Company Objectives and Pricing Strategy Implications
Company Objective	**Examples of Pricing Strategy Implications**
Profit-oriented	Institute a companywide policy that all products must provide for at least an 18 percent profit margin to reach a particular profit goal for the firm.
Sales-oriented	Set prices very low to generate new sales and take sales away from competitors, even if profits suffer.
Competitor-oriented	To discourage more competitors from entering the market, set prices very low.
Customer-oriented	Target a market segment of consumers who highly value a particular product benefit and set prices relatively high (referred to as premium pricing).

Company Objectives

By now, you know that different firms embrace very different goals. These goals should spill down to the pricing strategy, such that the pricing of a company's products and services should support and allow the firm to reach its overall goals. For example, a firm with a primary goal of very high sales growth will likely have a different pricing strategy than a firm with the goal of being a quality leader.

Each firm then embraces objectives that seem to fit with where management thinks the firm needs to go to be successful, in whatever way it defines success. These specific objectives usually reflect how the firm intends to grow. Do managers want it to grow by increasing profits, increasing sales, decreasing competition, or building customer satisfaction?

Company objectives are not as simple as they might first appear. They often can be expressed in slightly different forms that mean very different things. Exhibit 14.2 introduces some common company objectives and corresponding examples of their implications for pricing strategies. These objectives are not always mutually exclusive, because a firm may embrace two or more noncompeting objectives.

LO1 List the four pricing orientations.

Profit Orientation Even though all company methods and objectives may ultimately be oriented toward making a profit, firms implement a profit orientation specifically by focusing on target profit pricing, maximizing profits, or target return pricing.

- Firms usually implement target profit pricing when they have a particular profit goal as their overriding concern. To meet this targeted profit objective, firms use price to stimulate a certain level of sales at a certain profit per unit.

- The maximizing profits strategy relies primarily on economic theory. If a firm can accurately specify a mathematical model that captures all the factors required to explain and predict sales and profits, it should be able to identify the price at which its profits are maximized. Of course, the problem with this approach is that actually gathering the data on all these relevant factors and somehow coming up with an accurate mathematical model is an extremely difficult undertaking.

- Other firms are less concerned with the absolute level of profits and more interested in the rate at which their profits are generated relative to their investments. These firms typically turn to target return pricing and employ pricing strategies designed to produce a specific return on their investment, usually expressed as a percentage of sales.

Sales Orientation Firms using a sales orientation to set prices believe that increasing sales will help the firm more than will increasing profits. Tide might adopt such an orientation selectively, when it introduces new products that it wants to establish in the market. A new health club might focus on unit sales, dollar sales, or market share and therefore be willing to set a lower membership fee and accept less profit at first to focus on and generate more unit sales. In contrast, a high-end jewelry store might focus on dollar sales and maintain higher prices. The jewelry store relies on its prestige image, as well as the image of its suppliers, to provoke sales. Even though it sells fewer units, it can still generate high dollar sales levels.

Some firms may be more concerned about their overall market share than about dollar sales per se (though these often go hand in hand), because they believe that market share better reflects their success relative to the market conditions than do sales alone. A firm may set low prices to discourage new firms from entering the market, encourage current firms to leave the market, and/or take market share away from competitors—all to gain overall market share. For example, though Apple has sold more than 10 billion songs since the introduction of its iTunes service, it wants to keep increasing its market share, especially as competitors such as Amazon.com make inroads in this arena. Therefore, instead of 99 cents per song—the fixed pricing structure it previously maintained—Apple sets three price tiers (69 cents, 99 cents, and $1.29) for its songs, according to their popularity and recency. The songs that are the most popular cost the most, but by charging less for less popular songs, Apple aims to increase its sales per customer.[8]

P&G increases sales by introducing new Tide products.

Yet adopting a market share objective does not always imply setting low prices. Rarely is the lowest-price offering the dominant brand in a given market. Heinz ketchup, Philadelphia cream cheese, Crest toothpaste, and Nike athletic shoes have all dominated their markets, yet all are premium-priced brands. On the services side, IBM claims market dominance in human resource outsourcing, but again, it is certainly not the lowest-price competitor.[9] **Premium pricing** means the firm deliberately prices a product above the prices set for competing products to capture those customers who always shop for the best or for whom price does not matter. Thus, companies can gain market share by offering a high-quality product at a price that is perceived to be fair by its target market as long as they use effective communication and distribution methods to generate high value perceptions among consumers. Although the concept of value is not overtly expressed in sales-oriented strategies, it is at least implicit because, for sales to increase, consumers must see greater value.

Competitor Orientation When firms take a **competitor orientation**, they strategize according to the premise that they should measure themselves primarily against their competition. Some firms focus on **competitive parity**, which means they set prices that are similar to those of their major competitors. Another competitor-oriented strategy, **status quo pricing**, changes prices only to meet those of the competition. For example, when Delta increases its average fares, American Airlines and United often follow with similar increases; if Delta

Philadelphia brand cream cheese dominates its market and is a premium-priced brand.

Can you tell the difference between the $8,500 and the $320 speakers?

rescinds that increase, its competitors tend to drop their fares too.[10] Value is only implicitly considered in competitor-oriented strategies, but in the sense that competitors may be using value as part of their pricing strategies, copying their strategy might provide value.

Customer Orientation A customer orientation is when a firm sets its pricing strategy based on how it can add value to its products or services. When CarMax promises a "no-haggle" pricing structure, it exhibits a customer orientation because it provides additional value to potential used car buyers by making the process simple and easy.[11]

Firms may offer very high-priced, "state-of-the-art" products or services in full anticipation of limited sales. These offerings are designed to enhance the company's reputation and image and thereby increase the company's value in the minds of consumers. Paradigm, a Canadian speaker manufacturer, produces what many audiophiles consider a high-value product, yet offers speakers priced as low as $320 per pair. However, Paradigm also offers a very high-end speaker for $8,500 per pair. Although few people will spend $8,500 on a pair of speakers, this "statement" speaker communicates what the company is capable of and can increase the image of the firm and the rest of its products—even that $320 pair of speakers. Setting prices with a close eye to how consumers develop their perceptions of value can often be the most effective pricing strategy, especially if it is supported by consistent advertising and distribution strategies.

After a company has a good grasp on its overall objectives, it must implement pricing strategies that enable it to achieve those objectives. As the second step in this process, the firm should look toward consumer demand to lay the foundation for its pricing strategy.

CHECK YOURSELF

1. What are the five Cs of pricing?
2. Identify the four types of company objectives.

Customers

When firms have developed their company objectives, they turn to understanding consumers' reactions to different prices. The second C of the five Cs of pricing focuses on the customers. Customers want value, and as you likely recall, price is half of the value equation.

To determine how firms account for consumers' preferences when they develop pricing strategies, we must first lay a foundation of traditional economic theory that helps explain how prices are related to demand (consumers' desire for products) and how managers can incorporate this knowledge into their pricing strategies.[12] But first read through Adding Value 14.1, which considers how Apple has leveraged consumers' love for its offerings into a sophisticated pricing strategy.

 Explain the relationship between price and quantity sold.

Demand Curves and Pricing A demand curve shows how many units of a product or service consumers will demand during a specific period of time at different prices. Although we call them "curves," demand curves can be either straight or

Adding Value **14.1** Apple Prices in the Premium Price Segment[i]

For years, Apple had a strong reputation for offering high quality at high prices. The first iPhone cost nearly $500—way more than most other phones, but well worth it for Apple aficionados. Mac computers also cost more, but they offered great quality, advanced technology, and better protection from viruses and malware.

Today, though, Apple actually undercuts many of its competitors. Although Apple products still appear in the premium price category and continue to offer significant quality, the iPad Air (at $485) costs less than a comparable Surface Pro from Microsoft ($620). The 11-inch MacBook Air is $899; Samsung's entry into the ultrathin notebook category, the Series 9, instead runs $1,249. Obviously, there are cheaper computers available, but when it comes to matching offerings, Apple is often the least expensive entrant in the premium market.

It is able to do so largely because of its increasing popularity. As more and more consumers adopt Apple products, its increasing scale has enabled the company to buy more supplies for less. For example, it had the resources to enter into a five-year $1.25 billion deal that gave Apple first dibs on flash memory chips, which are critical for iPods and similar devices. With the supply going first to Apple, its competitors have had to scramble to find and bid for the remaining chips on the market, which has pushed their costs higher. But rather than

Although Apple products are considered to be in the premium price category, it continues to price below competition.

increase the prices of its consumer products, Apple has chosen to pass on its supply chain efficiencies to customers in the form of lower prices. With this customer-oriented strategy, it should increase its market share even further, leading to a virtuous cycle that may be hard for any competitors to break.

---

curved, as Exhibit 14.3 shows. Of course, any demand curve relating demand to price assumes that everything else remains unchanged. For the sake of expediency, marketers creating a demand curve assume that the firm will not increase its expenditures on advertising and that the economy will not change in any significant way.

Exhibit 14.3 illustrates a classic downward-sloping demand curve for teeth whitening kits. As price increases, demand for the product or service decreases. In this case, consumers will buy more as the price decreases. As we noted in

EXHIBIT 14.3 Demand Curve for Teeth Whitening Kits

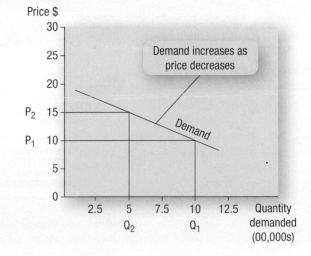

Adding Value 14.1, Apple expects increasing purchases with lower prices. We can expect a demand curve similar to this one for many, if not most, products and services.

The horizontal axis in Exhibit 14.3 measures the quantity demanded for the teeth whitening kits in units and plots it against the various price possibilities indicated on the vertical axis. Each point on the demand curve then represents the quantity demanded at a specific price. So, in this instance, if the price of a kit is $10 per unit ($P_1$), the demand is 1,000,000 units (Q_1), but if the price were set at $15 ($P_2$), the demand would be only 500,000 units (Q_2). The firm will sell far more teeth whitening kits at $10 each than at $15 each. Why? Because of the greater value this price point offers.

Knowing the demand curve for a product or service enables a firm to examine different prices in terms of the resulting demand and relative to its overall objective. In our preceding example, the retailer will generate a total of $10,000,000 in sales at the $10 price ($10 × 1,000,000 units) and $7,500,000 in sales at the $15 price ($15 × 500,000 units). In this case, given only the two choices of $10 or $15, the $10 price is preferable as long as the firm wants to maximize its sales in terms of dollars and units. But what about a firm that is more interested in profit? To calculate profit, it must consider its costs, which we cover in the next section.

But not all products or services follow the downward-sloping demand curve for all levels of price depicted in Exhibit 14.3. Consider **prestige products or services**, which consumers purchase for their status rather than their functionality. The higher the price, the greater the status associated with it and the greater the exclusivity because fewer people can afford to purchase it. German automaker Porsche is known for making fabulous and fast sports cars. Its entry-level car, the Boxster, was introduced in 1997 with a starting price of about $40,000.[13] In 2013, the starting price of the newly designed Boxster was over $51,000.[14] But with options, the sportier Boxster S could run over $100,000.[15] Remember, this is the entry-level model!

With prestige products or services, a higher price may lead to a greater quantity sold, but only up to a certain point. The price demonstrates just how rare,

exclusive, and prestigious the product is. When customers value the increase in prestige more than the price differential between the prestige product and other products, the prestige product attains the greater value overall.

However, prestige products can also run into pricing difficulties. The Fender Telecaster and Stratocaster guitars are absolute necessities for any self-respecting guitar hero, but for students just learning or hobbyists, the price of owning a Fender "axe" was simply too much. In response, Fender introduced a separate, budget-priced line of similar guitars under a different brand name, so as not to dilute the prestige of the Fender name. The Squier line, made in Japan with automated manufacturing and less expensive parts, offers a look similar to the famous Fender guitars and performance just a notch below the originals. Today, an American-made Vintage Hot Rod '57 Fender Stratocaster lists for $1,700, more than 14 times as much as a Squier Bullet Strat model that retails for around $120.[16]

Exhibit 14.4 illustrates a demand curve for a hypothetical prestige service, a Caribbean cruise. As the graph indicates, when the price increases from $1,000 ($P_1$) to $5,000 ($P_2$), the quantity demanded actually increases from 200,000 (Q_1) to 500,000 (Q_2) units. However, when the price increases to $8,000 ($P_3$), the demand then decreases to 300,000 (Q_3) units.

Although the firm likely will earn more profit selling 300,000 cruises at $8,000 each than 500,000 cruises at $5,000 each, we do not know for sure until we bring costs into the picture. However, we do know that more consumers are willing to book the cruise as the price increases initially from $1,000 to $5,000 and that more consumers will choose an alternative vacation as the price increases further from $5,000 to $8,000.

We must consider this notion of consumers' sensitivity to price changes in greater depth.

Price Elasticity of Demand Although we now know something about how consumers react to different price levels, we still need to determine how consumers respond to actual changes in price. These responses vary depending on the product or service. For example, consumers are generally

Singer Avril Lavigne uses a Fender guitar.

L03 Explain price elasticity.

EXHIBIT 14.4   Demand Curve for Caribbean Cruise

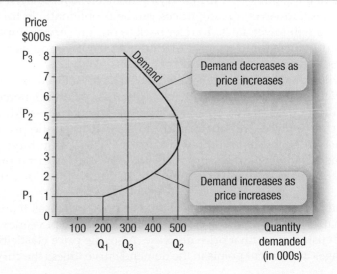

Based on Exhibit 14.4, price increases do not affect sales significantly up to a certain point. But after that point, sales decrease because consumers believe it is no longer a good value.

less sensitive to price increases for necessary items, like milk, because they have to purchase the items even if the price climbs. When the price of milk goes up, demand does not fall significantly because people still need to buy milk. However, if the price of T-bone steaks rises beyond a certain point, people will buy less because they can turn to the many substitutes for this cut of meat. Marketers need to know how consumers will respond to a price increase (or decrease) for a specific product or brand so they can determine whether it makes sense for them to raise or lower prices.

Price elasticity of demand measures how changes in a price affect the quantity of the product demanded. Specifically, it is the ratio of the percentage change in quantity demanded to the percentage change in price. We can calculate it with the following formula:

$$\text{Price elasticity of demand} = \frac{\text{\% Change in quantity demanded}}{\text{\% Change in price}}$$

The demand curve provides the information we need to calculate the price elasticity of demand. For instance, what is the price elasticity of demand if we increase the price of our teeth whitening kit from $10 to $15?

$$\text{\% Change in quantity demanded} = \frac{(1{,}000{,}000 - 500{,}000)}{1{,}000{,}000} = 50\%, \text{ and}$$

$$\text{\% Change in price} = \frac{(\$10 - \$15)}{10} = -50\%, \text{ so}$$

$$\text{Price elasticity of demand} = \frac{50\%}{-50\%} = -1.$$

Thus, the price elasticity of demand for our teeth whitening kit is −1.

In general, the market for a product or service is price sensitive (or **elastic**) when the price elasticity is less than −1, that is, when a 1 percent decrease in price produces more than a 1 percent increase in the quantity sold. In an elastic scenario, relatively small changes in price will generate fairly large changes in the quantity demanded, so if a firm is trying to increase its sales, it can do so by lowering prices. However, raising prices can be problematic in this context because doing so will lower sales. To refer back to our grocery examples, a retailer can significantly increase its sales of filet mignon by lowering its price, because filets are elastic.

The market for a product is generally viewed as price insensitive (or **inelastic**) when its price elasticity is greater than −1, that is, when a 1 percent decrease in price results in less than a 1 percent increase in quantity sold. Generally, if a firm must raise prices, it is helpful to do so with inelastic products or services because in such a market, fewer customers will stop buying or reduce their purchases. However, if the products are inelastic, lowering prices will not appreciably increase demand; customers just don't notice or care about the lower price.

Consumers are generally more sensitive to price increases than to price decreases.[17] That is, it is easier to lose current customers with a price increase than it is to gain new customers with a price decrease. Also, the price elasticity of demand usually changes at different points in the demand curve unless the curve is actually a straight line, as in Exhibit 14.3. For instance, a prestige product or service, like our Caribbean cruise example in Exhibit 14.4, enjoys a highly inelastic demand curve up to a certain point, so price increases do not affect sales significantly. But when the price reaches that certain point, consumers start turning to other alternatives, because the value of the cruise has finally been reduced by the extremely high price.

Ideally, firms could maximize their profits if they charged each customer as much as the customer was willing to pay. For instance, if a wealthy, price insensitive customer wants to buy a new car, a Ford dealer would like to price a particular car at $40,000, but then price the same car at $35,000 to a more price sensitive customer. Such a practice is legal when retailers sell to consumers such as in an eBay auction, but is permitted only under certain circumstances in B2B settings.[18]

Although charging different prices to different customers is legal and widely used in some retail sectors, such as automobile

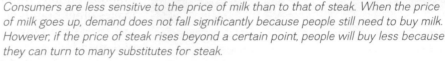

Consumers are less sensitive to the price of milk than to that of steak. When the price of milk goes up, demand does not fall significantly because people still need to buy milk. However, if the price of steak rises beyond a certain point, people will buy less because they can turn to many substitutes for steak.

and antique dealers, it has not been very practical in most retail stores until recently. Retailers have increased their use of dynamic pricing techniques due to the information that is available from point-of-sale data collected on the Internet purchases and in stores. Dynamic pricing, also known as individualized pricing refers to the process of charging different prices for goods or services based on the type of customer, time of the day, week, or even season, and level of demand. Retailers may also charge customers different prices based on their loyalty status derived from their CRM systems (i.e., platinum customers receive lower prices than silver ones). Early adopters of dynamic pricing techniques were service retailers, such as airlines, hotels, cruises lines, and so on. It is quite common for passengers on the same plane to have paid different fares depending on when they bought their ticket. The ease of using dynamic pricing when selling merchandise on the Internet is much greater than in a store because only one person sees the price.

Factors Influencing Price Elasticity of Demand We have illustrated how price elasticity of demand varies across different products and at different points along a demand curve, as well as how it can change over time. What causes these differences in the price elasticity of demand? We discuss a few of the more important factors next.

Income Effect The income effect refers to the change in the quantity of a product demanded by consumers due to a change in their income. Generally, as people's income increases, their spending behavior changes: They tend to shift their demand from lower-priced products to higher-priced alternatives. That is, consumers buy hamburger when they're stretching their money but steak when they're flush. Similarly, they may increase the quantity they purchase and splurge on a five-star hotel during their six-day Las Vegas trip rather than

If there are many close substitues for a product, customers will be sensitive to small price changes, and the product will be highly elastic. If, for instance, Skippy raises its price, many customers will switch to another brand.

three-star lodging over a weekend visit. Conversely, when incomes drop, consumers turn to less expensive alternatives or purchase less.

Substitution Effect The substitution effect refers to consumers' ability to substitute other products for the focal brand. The greater the availability of substitute products, the higher the price elasticity of demand for any given product will be. For example, there are many close substitutes in the laundry detergent category. If Tide raises its prices, many consumers will turn to competing brands (e.g., Arm & Hammer Detergent), because they are more sensitive to price increases when they can easily find lower-priced substitutes. Extremely brand-loyal consumers, however, are willing to pay a higher price, up to a point, because in their minds, Tide still offers a better value than the competing brands, and they believe the other brands are not adequate substitutes.

Keep in mind that marketing plays a critical role in making consumers brand loyal. And because of this brand loyalty and the lack of what consumers judge to be adequate substitutes, the price elasticity of demand for some brands is very low. For example, Polo/Ralph Lauren sells millions of its classic polo shirts at $85, while shirts of equal quality but without the polo player logo sell for much less. Getting consumers to believe that a particular brand is unique, different, or extraordinary in some way makes other brands seem less substitutable, which in turn increases brand loyalty and decreases the price elasticity of demand.

Cross-Price Elasticity Cross-price elasticity is the percentage change in the quantity of Product A demanded compared with the percentage change in price in Product B. If Product A's price increased, Product B could either increase or decrease, depending on the situation and whether the products are complementary or substitutes. We refer to products like Blu-ray discs and Blu-ray players as complementary products, which are products whose demands are positively related, such that they rise or fall together. In other words, a percentage increase in the quantity demanded for Product A results in a percentage increase in the quantity demanded for Product B.[19] However, when the price for Blu-ray players dropped, the demand for DVD players went down, so DVD players and Blu-ray players are substitute products because changes in their demand are negatively related. That is, a percentage increase in the quantity demanded for Product A results in a percentage decrease in the quantity demanded for Product B.[20] In addition, on the Internet, shopping bots like TheFind.com and Bizrate.com have made it much easier for people to shop for substitutable products like consumer electronics, which likely has affected the price elasticity of demand for such products.[21]

The way a product or service is marketed to customers can have a profound effect on its price elasticity. Superior Service 14.1 describes how good marketing by Universal Theme Parks in the form of greater customer convenience can make customers less sensitive to price. Prior to this point, we have focused on how changes in prices affect how much customers buy. Clearly, knowing how prices affect sales is important, but it cannot give us the whole picture. To know how profitable a pricing strategy will be, we must also consider the third C, costs.

Superior Service 14.1 | The Increasing Costs of Play: New Offers and Pricing by Disney and Universal Theme Parks[ii]

The price to get into Disneyland, in Anaheim, California, has increased by $5, to $92 ($86 for children). The price to get into Disney World, in Orlando, Florida, already was $95 ($89 for children). At Universal Studios Hollywood, a one-day pass is $80. But instead of just raising its prices to match Disney, Universal has introduced a new pricing plan that offers greater access to those willing to pay more—quite a lot more.

The VIP service at Universal allows park visitors to bypass every line in the park, after having their car parked by a valet. They get free breakfast and lunch in a luxury lounge, serving scallops and short ribs, for example. Then they can access the backlots, while toting their free gift bags with mints, hand sanitizer, and a poncho to wear on water rides. All this, at a cost of $299 per ticket. For those who don't worry about their breath or eating fancy meals, a $149 option instead offers just line-jumping privileges.

Universal Theme Parks offer premium service offerings at a premium price.

Even as it introduced this new service, Universal noted that it had no plans to expand its primary offering. That is, it did not plan to open any new rides or attractions this year. Its parks pulled in approximately 20 million people in 2012, which represented a nearly 20 percent increase over the year before. And according to some of these visitors, without a VIP option, they simply would not attend, because they hate dealing with the crowds.

Such benefits raise some questions about the economic stratification Universal is promoting, such that only the wealthy get to enjoy all the perks. For Disney, concerns about damage to its "magical" image have halted it from classifying different price points for tickets. Yet as a recent controversy—in which wealthy families hired people with disabilities to join their trips so that they could skip lines—showed, demand for such special treatment exists.

Even though theme parks are enjoying record attendance and revenue levels, they keep looking for ways to increase their appeal. New rides and attractions are expensive, and in many cases, they seem out of date pretty quickly. In this case, the magic may be in the pricing.

CHECK YOURSELF

1. What is the difference between elastic demand and inelastic demand?
2. What are the factors influencing price elasticity?

Costs

To make effective pricing decisions, firms must understand their cost structures so they can determine the degree to which their products or services will be profitable at different prices. In general, prices should *not* be based on costs, because consumers make purchase decisions based on their perceived value; they care little about the firm's costs to produce and sell a product or deliver a service. Although companies incur many different types of costs as a natural part of doing business, there are two primary cost categories: variable and fixed.

Variable Costs Variable costs are those costs, primarily labor and materials, that vary with production volume. As a firm produces more or less of a good or service, the total variable costs increase or decrease at the same time. Because each unit of the product produced incurs the same cost, marketers generally express variable costs on a per-unit basis. Consider a bakery like Entenmann's: The majority of the variable costs are the cost of the ingredients, primarily flour. Each time Entenmann's makes a loaf of bread, it incurs the cost of the ingredients.

In the service industry, variable costs are far more complex. A hotel, for instance, incurs certain variable costs each time it rents a room, including the costs associated with the labor and supplies necessary to clean and restock the room. Note that the hotel does not incur these costs if the room is not booked. Suppose that a particular hotel calculates its total variable costs to be $10 per room; each time it rents a room, it incurs another $10 in variable costs. If the hotel rents out 100 rooms on a given night, the total variable cost is $1,000 ($10 per room × 100 rooms).

In either case, however, variable costs tend to change depending on the quantity produced. If Entenmann's makes 100,000 loaves of bread in a month, it would have to pay a higher price for ingredients on a per pound basis than if it were producing a million loaves. Similarly, a very large hotel will be able to get a lower per unit price on most, if not all, the supplies it needs to service the room because it purchases such a large volume. However, as the hotel company continues to grow, it may be forced to add more benefits for its employees or increase wages to attract and keep long-term employees. Such changes will increase its overall variable labor costs and affect the total variable cost of cleaning a room. Thus, though not always the case, variable costs per unit may go up or down (for all units) with significant changes in volume.

Fixed Costs Fixed costs are those costs that remain essentially at the same level, regardless of any changes in the volume of production. Typically, these costs include items such as rent, utilities, insurance, administrative salaries (for executives and higher-level managers), and the depreciation of the physical plant and equipment. Across reasonable fluctuations in production volume, these costs remain stable; whether Entenmann's makes 100,000 loaves or a million, the rent it pays for the bakery remains unchanged.

Total Cost Finally, the total cost is simply the sum of the variable and fixed costs. For example, in one year, our hypothetical hotel incurred $100,000 in fixed costs. We also know that because the hotel booked 10,000 room nights, its total variable cost is $100,000 (10,000 room nights × $10 per room). Thus, its total cost is $200,000.

Next, we illustrate how to use these costs in simple analyses that can inform managerial decision making about setting prices.

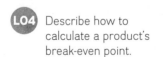

Describe how to calculate a product's break-even point.

Break-Even Analysis and Decision Making

A useful technique that enables managers to examine the relationships among cost, price, revenue, and profit over different levels of production and sales is called break-even analysis. Central to this analysis is the determination of the break-even point, or the point at which the number of units sold generates just enough revenue to equal the total costs. At this point, profits are zero. Although profit, which represents the difference between the total cost and the total revenue (Total revenue or sales = Selling price of each unit sold × Number of units sold), can indicate how much money the firm is making or losing at a single period of time, it cannot tell managers how many units a firm must produce and sell before it stops losing money and at least breaks even, which is what the break-even point does.

How do we determine the break-even point? Exhibit 14.5 presents the various cost and revenue information we have discussed in a graphic format. The graph contains three curves (recall that even though they are straight, we still call them curves): fixed costs, total costs, and total revenue. The vertical axis measures the revenue or costs in dollars, and the horizontal axis measures the quantity of units sold. The fixed cost curve will always appear as a horizontal line straight across the graph, because fixed costs do not change over different levels of volume.

The total cost curve starts where the fixed cost curve intersects the vertical axis at $100,000. When volume is equal to zero (no units are produced or sold), the fixed costs of operating the business remain and cannot be avoided. Thus, the lowest point the total costs can ever reach is equal to the total fixed costs. Beyond that point, the total cost curve increases by the amount of variable costs for each additional unit, which we calculate by multiplying the variable cost per unit by the number of units, or quantity.

Finally, the total revenue curve increases by the price of each additional unit sold. To calculate it, we multiply the price per unit by the number of units sold. The formulas for these calculations are as follows:

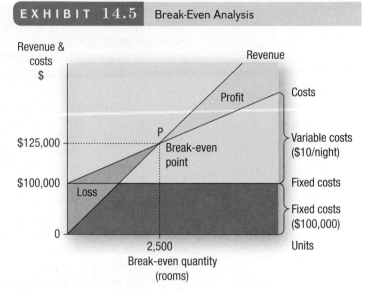

EXHIBIT 14.5 Break-Even Analysis

$$\text{Total variable costs} = \text{Variable cost per unit} \times \text{Quantity}$$

$$\text{Total costs} = \text{Fixed costs} + \text{Total variable costs}$$

$$\text{Total revenue} = \text{Price} \times \text{Quantity}$$

We again use the hotel example to illustrate these relationships. Recall that the fixed costs are $100,000 and the variable costs are $10 per room rented. If the rooms rent for $50 per night, how many rooms must the hotel rent over the course of a year to break even? If we study the graph carefully, we find the break-even point at 2,500, which means that the hotel must rent 2,500 rooms before its revenues equal its costs. If it rents fewer rooms, it loses money (the red area); if it rents more, it makes a profit (the green area). To determine the break-even point in units mathematically, we must introduce one more variable, the **contribution per unit**, which is the price less the variable cost per unit.

In this case,

$$\text{Contribution per unit} = \$50 - \$10 = \$40$$

Therefore, the break-even point becomes

$$\text{Break-even point (units)} = \frac{\text{Fixed costs}}{\text{Contributions per unit}}$$

That is,

$$\text{Break-even point (units)} = \frac{\$100,000}{\$40} = 2,500 \text{ room nights}$$

When the hotel has crossed the break-even point of 2,500 rooms, it will start earning profit at the same rate of the contribution per unit. So if the hotel rents 4,000 rooms—1,500 rooms more than the break-even point—its profit will be $60,000 (1,500 rooms × $40 contribution per unit).

$$\text{Profit} = (\text{Contribution per unit} \times \text{Quantity}) - \text{Fixed costs}$$

$$\text{Profit} = (\$40 \times 4,000) - \$100,000 = \$60,000$$

Or an alternative formula would be:

$$\text{Profit} = (\text{Price} \times \text{Quantity}) - (\text{Fixed costs} + (\text{Variable costs} \times \text{Quantity}))$$

$$\text{Profit} = (\$50 \times 4,000) - (\$100,000 + (\$10 \times 4,000))$$

$$\text{Profit} = \$200,000 - (\$100,000 + \$40,000) = \$60,000$$

Let's extend this simple break-even analysis to show how many units a firm must produce and sell to achieve a target profit. Say the hotel wanted to make $200,000 in profit each year. How many rooms would it have to rent at the current price? In this instance, we need only add the targeted profit to the fixed costs to determine that number:

$$\text{Break-even point (units)} = \frac{\text{(Fixed costs + Target profit)}}{\text{Contributions per unit}}$$

or

$$7,500 \text{ rooms} = \frac{(\$100,000 + \$200,000)}{\$40}$$

Although a break-even analysis cannot actually help managers set prices, it does help them assess their pricing strategies, because it clarifies the conditions in which different prices may make a product or service profitable. It becomes an even more powerful tool when performed on a range of possible prices for comparative purposes. For example, the hotel management could analyze various prices, not just $50, to determine how many hotel rooms it would have to rent at what price to make a $200,000 profit.

Naturally, however, there are limitations to a break-even analysis. First, it is unlikely that a hotel has one specific price that it charges for each and every room, so the price it would use in its break-even analysis probably represents an "average" price that attempts to account for these variances. Second, prices often get reduced as quantity increases, because the costs decrease, so firms must perform several break-even analyses at different quantities. Third, a break-even analysis cannot indicate for sure how many rooms will be rented or, in the case of products, how many units will sell at a given price. It only tells the firm what its costs, revenues, and profitability will be given a set price and an assumed quantity. To determine how many units the firm actually will sell, it must bring in the demand estimates we discussed previously.

Markup and Target Return Pricing

In many situations, the manufacturer may want to achieve a standard markup—let's say 10 percent of cost. In our example of the teeth whitening kit, let's assume:

Variable costs per unit are:	$8.00
Fixed costs are:	$1,000,000.00
Expected sales are:	1,000,000 units

The teeth whitening kit manufacturer would like to calculate the price at which it would make a 10 percent markup.

In a hotel, the cost of the physical structure, including the lobby, is fixed—it is incurred even if no rooms are rented. The costs of washing the towels and sheets are variable—the more rooms that are rented, the more the costs.

The formula for calculating a target return price based on a markup on cost is:

Target return price = (Variable costs + (Fixed costs ÷ Expected Unit sales))
× (1 + Target return % [expressed as a decimal])

In this example, this would result in the firm charging $9.90.

Target return price = ($8.00 + ($1,000,000.00 ÷ 1,000,000.00)) × (1 + 0.10)
Target return price = $9.00 × 1.1 = $9.90

CHECK YOURSELF

1. What is the difference between fixed costs and variable costs?
2. How does one calculate the break-even point in units?

Competition

LO5 Indicate the four types of price competitive levels.

Because the fourth C, competition, has a profound impact on pricing strategies, we use this section to focus on its effect, as well as on how competitors react to certain pricing strategies. There are four levels of competition—monopoly, oligopolistic competition, monopolistic competition, and pure competition—and each has its own set of pricing challenges and opportunities (see Exhibit 14.6).

In a monopoly, one firm provides the product or service in a particular industry, which results in less price competition. For example, there is often only one provider of power in each region of the country: Florida Power and Light in most of Florida, NStar in most of Massachusetts, and so forth. Power companies operate more efficiently when there is one service provider, so the government regulates the pricing of utility monopolies to prevent them from raising prices uncontrollably.

EXHIBIT 14.6 | Four Levels of Competition: Can you match each photo to its respective type of competition?

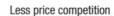

Less price competition | More price competition

| Monopoly
One firm controls
the market | Oligopoly
A handful of firms
control the market | Fewer firms |

| Monopolistic competition
Many firms selling
differentiated products
at different prices | Pure competition
Many firms selling
commodities for the
same prices | Many firms |

A monopoly that restricts competition by controlling an industry can be deemed illegal and broken apart by the government.

When a market is characterized by oligopolistic competition, only a few firms dominate. Firms typically change their prices in reaction to competition to avoid upsetting an otherwise stable competitive environment. Examples of oligopolistic markets include the soft drink market and commercial airline travel. Sometimes reactions to prices in oligopolistic markets can result in a price war, which occurs when two or more firms compete primarily by lowering their prices. Firm A lowers its prices; Firm B responds by meeting or beating Firm A's new price. Firm A then responds with another new price, and so on. In some cases though, these tactics result in predatory pricing, when a firm sets a very low price for one or more of its products with the intent to drive its competition out of business. Predatory pricing is illegal in the United States.

Monopolistic competition occurs when there are many firms competing for customers in a given market but their products are differentiated. When so many firms compete, product differentiation rather than strict price competition tends to appeal to consumers. This is the most common form of competition. Hundreds of firms make wristwatches, thus the market is highly differentiated. Timex sells a durable watch that tells time and has a stopwatch and a sporty design. Swatch watches have more style than Timex watches, but if you are looking for style, fashion designers such as Armani have their own wristwatches. Timepiece aficionados may opt for high-quality watches such as Patek Philippe or Vacheron Constantin. Depending on the features, style, and quality, companies compete for very different market segments. By differentiating their products using various attributes, prices, and brands, they create unique value propositions in the minds of their customers.

With pure competition, a large number of sellers offer standardized products or commodities that consumers perceive as substitutable, such as grains, gold, meat, spices, or minerals. In such markets, price usually is set according to the laws of supply and demand. For example, wheat is wheat, so it does not matter to a commercial bakery whose wheat it buys. However, the secret to pricing success in a pure competition market is not necessarily to offer the lowest price, because doing so might create a price war and erode profits. Instead, some firms have brilliantly decommoditized their products. For example, most people feel that all chickens purchased in a grocery are the same. But companies like Tyson have branded their chickens to move into a monopolistically competitive market.

When a commodity can be differentiated somehow, even if simply by a sticker or logo, there is an opportunity for consumers to identify it as distinct from the rest, and in this case, firms can at least partially extricate their product from a pure competitive market.

CHECK YOURSELF

1.   What are the four different types of competitive environments?

Channel Members

Channel members—manufacturers, wholesalers, and retailers—have different perspectives when it comes to pricing strategies. Consider a manufacturer that is focused on increasing the image and reputation of its brand but working with a retailer that is primarily concerned with increasing its sales. The manufacturer may desire to keep prices higher to convey a better image, whereas the retailer wants lower prices and will accept lower profits to move the product, regardless of consumers' impressions of the brand. Unless channel members carefully communicate their pricing goals and select channel partners that agree with them, conflict will surely arise.

Channels can be very difficult to manage, and distribution outside normal channels does occur. A gray market employs irregular but not necessarily illegal methods; generally, it legally circumvents authorized channels of distribution to sell goods at prices lower than those intended by the manufacturer.[22] Many manufacturers of consumer electronics therefore require retailers to sign an agreement that demands certain activities (and prohibits others) before they may become authorized dealers. But if a retailer has too many high-definition televisions in stock, it may sell them at just above its own cost to an unauthorized discount dealer. This move places the merchandise in the market at prices far below what authorized dealers can charge, and in the long term, it may tarnish the image of the manufacturer if the discount dealer fails to provide sufficient return policies, support, service, and so forth.

To discourage this type of gray market distribution, many manufacturers have resorted to large disclaimers on their websites, packaging, and other communications to warn consumers that the manufacturer's product warranty becomes null and void unless the item has been purchased from an authorized dealer.

Reviewing Learning Objectives

LO1 List the four pricing orientations.

A profit-oriented pricing strategy focuses on maximizing, or at least reaching, a target profit for the company. A sales orientation instead sets prices with the goal of increasing sales levels. With a competitor-oriented pricing strategy, a firm sets its prices according to what its competitors do. Finally, a customer-oriented strategy determines consumers' perceptions of value and prices accordingly.

LO2 Explain the relationship between price and quantity sold.

Generally, when prices go up, quantity sold goes down. Sometimes, however—particularly with prestige products and services—demand actually increases with price.

LO3 Explain price elasticity.

Changes in price generally affect demand; price elasticity measures the extent of this effect. It is based on the percentage change in quantity divided by the percentage change in price. Depending on the resulting value, a market offering can be identified as elastic, such that the market is very price sensitive, or inelastic, in which case the market cares little about the price.

LO4 Describe how to calculate a product's break-even point.

Because the break-even point occurs when the units sold generate just enough profit to cover the total costs of producing those units, it requires knowledge of the fixed cost, total cost, and total revenue curves. When these curves intersect, the marketer has found the break-even point.

LO5 Indicate the four types of price competitive levels.

In a monopoly setting, one firm controls the market and sets the price. In an oligopolistic competitive market, a few firms dominate and tend to set prices according to a competitor-oriented strategy. Monopolistic competition occurs when there are many firms competing for customers in a given market but their products are differentiated. Finally, pure competition means that consumers likely regard the products offered by different companies as basic substitutes, so the firms must work hard to achieve the lowest price point, limited by the laws of supply and demand.

Key Terms

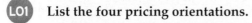

- break-even analysis, 452
- break-even point, 452
- competitive parity, 443
- competitor orientation, 443
- complementary products, 450
- contribution per unit, 453
- cross-price elasticity, 450
- customer orientation, 444
- demand curve, 444

Marketing Applications

1. You and your two roommates are starting a pet grooming service to help put yourselves through college. There are two other well-established pet services in your area. Should you set your price higher or lower than that of the competition? Justify your answer.

2. One roommate believes the most important objective in setting prices for the new pet grooming business is to generate a large profit while keeping an eye on your competitors' prices; the other roommate believes it is important to maximize sales and set prices according to what your customers expect to pay. Who is right and why?

3. Assume you have decided to buy an advertisement in the local newspaper to publicize your new pet grooming service. The cost of the ad is $1,000. You have decided to charge $40 for a dog grooming, and your variable costs are $20 for each dog. How many dogs do you have to groom to break even on the cost of the ad? What is your break-even point if you charge $60 per dog?

4. The local newspaper ad isn't helping much, so you decide to post your services on an auction site, where customers can bid for your services. What should the starting price of the auction be?

5. Is there a difference between a $5,900 Loro Piana vicuña sweater and a $150 cashmere sweater from L.L.Bean? Have you ever purchased a higher-priced product or service because you thought the quality was better than that of a similar, lower-priced product or service? What was the product or service? Do you believe you made a rational choice?

6. A soft drink manufacturer opened a new manufacturing plant in the Midwest. The total fixed costs are $100 million. It plans to sell soft drinks for $6.00 for a package of 10 12-ounce cans to retailers. Its variable costs for the ingredients are $4.00 per package. Calculate the break-even volume. What would happen to the break-even point if the fixed costs decreased to $50 million, or the variable costs decreased to $3.00 due to declines in commodity costs. What would the break-even be if the firm wanted to make $20 million?

7. On your weekly grocery shopping trip, you notice that the price of spaghetti has gone up 50 cents a pound. How will this price increase affect the demand for spaghetti sauce, rice, and Parmesan cheese? Explain your answer in terms of the price elasticity of demand.

8. How do pricing strategies vary across markets that are characterized by monopolistic, oligopolistic, monopolistic competition, and pure competition?

9. Suppose you are in the market for a new Sharp LCD television. You see one advertised at a locally owned store for $300 less than it costs at HHGregg. The salesperson at the local store tells you that the television came from another retailer in the next state that had too many units of that model. Explain who benefits and who is harmed from such a gray market transaction: you, Sharp, HHGregg, the local store?

10. Has the Internet helped lower the price of some types of merchandise? Justify your answer.

11. Imagine that a pharmaceutical company has just developed a cure to a major fatal disease. Because the firm is the only one even close to a cure for this disease, price is inelastic, meaning it could virtually charge any price and people would pay. Discuss the ethical implications of choosing a price.

Quiz Yourself

1. Marketers can deliver high value through high or low prices, depending on _____.
    a. profit contribution per unit
    b. the bundle of benefits the product or service delivers
    c. monopolistic competition
    d. target return pricing that is greater than variable cost per unit
    e. the income effect

2. Ferrari and Lamborghini are manufacturers of very expensive automobiles. Their limited edition cars often sell for $300,000 or more. For most consumers, these are prestige products, and demand is likely to be _____.
    a. cross-price elastic
    b. price inelastic
    c. price elastic
    d. status quo elastic
    e. derived demand inelastic

(Answers to these two questions can be found on page 652.)

Toolkit

BREAK-EVEN ANALYSIS

A shoe manufacturer has recently opened a new manufacturing plant in Asia. The total fixed costs are $50 million. It plans to sell the shoes to retailers for $50, and its variable costs (material and labor) are $25 per pair. Calculate the break-even volume. Now see what would happen to the break-even point if the fixed costs increased to $60 million due to the purchase of new equipment, or the variable costs decreased to $20 due to a new quantity discount provided by the supplier. Please use the toolkit provided in your instructor's Connect course to experiment with changes in fixed cost, variable cost, and selling price to see what happens to break-even volume.

Net Savvy

1. Several different pricing models can be found on the Internet. Each model appeals to different customer groups. Go to www.eBay.com and try to buy this book. What pricing options and prices are available? Do you believe that everyone will choose the least expensive option? Why or why not? Now go to www.Amazon.com. Is there more than one price available for this book? If so, what are those prices? Are different versions available? If you had to buy another copy of this book, where would you buy it, and why would you buy it there?

2. Prices can vary, depending on the market being served and the novelty of the products. Shapeways allows anyone to upload a design and get it 3D printed. The best designs then are available to other customers to have printed in a variety of materials. Go to https://www.youtube.com/v/qJuTM0Y7U1k and learn more about Shapeways. Then go to its website, www.shapeways.com, and search for "Inception" and click on the design by the user roessnakhan. Note the difference in prices of the item to be printed in plastic versus metal. Now go to Amazon and search for "Inception Totem" and note the prices for a similar metal totem. How does the price of the item vary between Shapeways and Amazon? What would account for these differences in price? Why would a consumer purchase the product from Shapeways instead of Amazon? How is Shapeways communicating value?

Chapter Case Study   connect

PLANET FITNESS: PRICING FOR SUCCESS[23]

How does going completely against the grain of a typical fitness club strategy lead to success? That's the question that Planet Fitness appears uniquely positioned to answer. Most health clubs provide members with vast and seemingly valuable

EXHIBIT 14.7	Membership Costs of Planet Fitness and Competition in New York City	
Gym	Monthly Cost	Up-Front Cost
24 Hour Fitness	$44.99	$99.77
Bally Total Fitness	$29.99	$88.98
LA Fitness	$12.95/wk	$25.90
Planet Fitness	$10.00	$29.00
Snap Fitness	$39.99	$ 0.00

extra amenities, such as child care, juice bars and protein supplements, on-staff professional trainers, and a broad range of fitness classes.[24] But many customers find the prices too high because they see little value in some of these amenities. Further reducing the value of traditional gym memberships, many consumers regard the social aspects unpleasant and offputting—whether that means observing others with nearly perfect bodies posturing in the mirror or listening to grunting exercisers huff with every lift.

While its competitors target upscale fitness buffs working on their six-pack abs, Planet Fitness successfully pursues an entirely different market: those who do not really enjoy going to the gym but know they need to do so to stay healthy. These exercisers are unlikely to hit the gym five or six times a week, making conventional gym memberships, which demand yearly contracts and fees of $49 to $95 per month, appear more expensive on a per-visit basis. Planet Fitness's formula is different: At $10 a month, the membership offers good value, even if customers get to the club only a couple of times each week.[25]

In combination with its low price point, Planet Fitness promises a clean, friendly, laid-back workout environment featuring brand-name cardiovascular and strength equipment. Although it does not have the high-end amenities its competitors promise (e.g., pools, juice bars), the clubs maintain the key elements its members want: brand-name equipment, unlimited fitness training, flat-screen televisions, and large locker rooms. Its customers know from its advertising that they can expect a nonintimidating workout environment, or as Planet Fitness promises, "No gymtimidation. No lunks. Just $10 a month."[26] With its foundation in the idea that simple is better,[27] Planet Fitness has become the fastest-growing full-sized fitness club in the United States. Exhibit 14.7 compares the prices of several major gyms.

For those who want a little more, Planet Fitness also offers a premium PF BlackCard membership for $19.99 a month, which promises access to nearly all the clubs in the Planet Fitness chain, unlimited guest privileges, use of tanning and massage chairs, and half-priced drinks.[28]

In addition to these in-club benefits, Planet Fitness's growth has been reinforced by its effective location strategy and marketing efforts that focus on attracting new customers. The low-cost monthly membership makes it easy to draw new members. Because most members come in only a couple of times each week, Planet Fitness also enjoys operating efficiencies and economies of scale, achieved by welcoming a high volume of members on any one day.[29]

Planet Fitness treats customers like real people. What kind of fitness club offers members pizza on the first Monday of every month, bagels on the first Tuesday, and Tootsie Rolls on a regular basis?[30] The kind of gym that plans to expand to 1,000 locations in 2015, with an eventual goal of more than 2,000, and that attracts more than 5 million members and systemwide sales approaching $700 million.[31]

Questions

1. What benefits do customers receive in return for the sacrifice they make when buying a membership at Planet Fitness?

2. How does this benefit–sacrifice ratio give Planet Fitness a competitive advantage in its industry?

3. Given its price strategy, why is it essential for Planet Fitness to continually attract new members? Do its high-end pricing competitors face the same need? Why or why not?

Endnotes

1. Serena Ng, "At P&G, New Tide Comes In, Old Price Goes Up," *The Wall Street Journal*, February 10, 2014, http://wsj.online.com.

2. Dale Buss, "P&G Looks to Wring More Value out of Tide Brand with Lower-Priced Detergent," *BrandChannel*, September 4, 2013, http://www.brandchannel.com.

3. Ng, "At P&G, New Tide Comes In."

4. R. Suri and M. V. Thakor, " 'Made in Country' versus 'Made in County': Effects of Local Manufacturing Origins on Price Perceptions," *Psychology & Marketing* 30, no. 2 (2013), pp. 121–32; R. Suri, K. B. Monroe, and U. Koc, "Math Anxiety and Its Effects on Consumers' Preference for Price Promotion Formats," *Journal of the Academy of Marketing Science* 41, no. 3 (2013), pp. 271–82; Kent B. Monroe, *Pricing: Making Profitable Decisions*, 3rd ed. (New York: McGraw-Hill, 2003); Dhruv Grewal, Kent B. Monroe, and R. Krishnan, "The Effects of Price Comparison Advertising on Buyers' Perceptions of Acquisition Value and Transaction Value," *Journal of Marketing* 62 (April 1998), pp. 46–60.

5. Jennifer Frighetto, "U.S. Consumers Place More Importance on Price and Value," ACNielsen, October 28, 2008.

6. *Moneyball*, directed by Bennett Miller (2011; Sony Pictures). See also Michael Lewis, *Moneyball* (New York: Norton, 2004).

7. Dhruv Grewal et al., "Evolving Pricing Practices: The Role of New Business Models," *Journal of Product & Brand Management* 20, no. 7 (2011), pp. 510–13; Bang-Ning Hwang et al., "An Effective Pricing Framework in a Competitive Industry: Management Processes and Implementation Guidelines," *Journal of Revenue and Pricing Management* (November 2009); Robert J. Dolan, "Note on Marketing Strategy," Harvard Business School Background Note (November 2000), pp. 1–17.

8. Ethan Smith and Yukari Iwatani Kane, "Apples Changes Tune on Music Pricing," *The Wall Street Journal*, January 7, 2009.

9. "IBM Market Share Leader in Human Resources (HR) Business Transformation Outsourcing, Enterprise Sector," press release.

10. Rebecca Heslin, "Virgin America Joins Airline Fare Sale Stampede," *USA Today*, January 6, 2010; "Delta Rescinds Fare Increase on Some of Its U.S. Routes," *Salt Lake City News*, September 11, 2007.

11. http://www.carmax.com/enus/car-dealer/default.html.

12. Nick Wingfield, "Apple's Lower Prices Are All Part of the Plan," *The New York Times*, October 24, 2011, http://www.nytimes.com.

13. http://auto.howstuffworks.com/porsche-boxster-history.htm.

14. http://www.motortrend.com/new_cars/12/porsche/sports_car/pricing/.

15. http://jalopnik.com/2013-porsche-boxster-s-the-jalopnik-review-558339290.

16. Fender Electric Guitars, http://www.fender.com.

17. Monroe, *Pricing: Making Profitable Decisions*.

18. This type of B2B price discrimination is illegal under the Robinson-Patman Act of 1936. B2B sellers are allowed to charge different prices for merchandise of the same "grade and quality" if (1) the price difference is justified by different costs in manufacture, sale, or delivery (e.g., volume discounts); or (2) the price concession was given in good faith to meet a competitor's price. See http://www.ftc.gov/tips-advice/competition-guidance/guide-antitrust-laws/price-discrimination-robinson-patman.

19. http://www.marketingpower.com/_layouts/Dictionary.aspx?dLetter=C.

20. http://www.marketingpower.com/_layouts/Dictionary.aspx?dLetter=S.

21. Joan Lindsey-Mullikin and Dhruv Grewal, "Market Price Variation: The Availability of Internet Market Information," *Journal of the Academy of Marketing Science* 34, no. 2 (2006), pp. 236–43.

22. *Merriam-Webster's Dictionary of Law*, 1996.

23. This case was written by Jeanne L. Munger (University of Southern Maine) in conjunction with the textbook authors Dhruv Grewal and Michael Levy, as a basis for class discussion rather than to illustrate effective or ineffective marketing practices.

24. "Planet Fitness Continues Successful Growth with Puerto Rico Expansion," press release, http://www.marketwatch.com/story/.

25. http://www.planetfitness.com/.

26. Andrew Adam Newman, "A Gym for People Who Don't Like Gyms," *The New York Times*, January 3, 2013, http://www.nytimes.com.

27. Judith Ohikuare, "The Secret of Planet Fitness's Success," *Inc.*, February 2013, http://www.inc.com/magazine/.

28. "Planet Fitness Continues Successful Growth."

29. Beth Kowitt, "The Southwest Airlines of the Gym Business," *Fortune*, November 21, 2013, http://features.blogs.fortune.cnn.com/.

30. Newman, "A Gym for People."

31. Kowitt, "The Southwest Airlines."

i. Nick Wingfield, "Apple's Lower Prices Are All Part of the Plan," *The New York Times*, October 24, 2011, http://www.nytimes.com.

ii. Brooks Barnes, "At Theme Parks, a V.I.P. Ticket to Ride," *The New York Times*, June 9, 2013; "Ticket to Disneyland: Now $92," *The Wall Street Journal*, June 3, 2013; https://www.universalorlando.com/Theme-Park-Tickets/Vip-Experience.aspx.

Credits

CHAPTER 15

STRATEGIC PRICING METHODS

LEARNING OBJECTIVES

LO1 Identify three methods that firms use to set their prices.

LO2 Describe the difference between an everyday low price (EDLP) strategy and a high/low strategy.

LO3 Explain the difference between a price skimming and a market penetration pricing strategy.

LO4 Identify tactics used to reduce prices to consumers.

LO5 Identify tactics used to reduce prices to businesses.

LO6 List the pricing practices that are illegal or unethical.

Setting the right price helps a firm meet its strategic goals, such as launching a new product, bringing in new customers, and providing opportunities to increase its share of customers' wallet.[1] Success largely depends on offering the right price for the right product that the firm's targeted customer segment is interested in purchasing. For example, every year, right around September, consumers confront a pricing shift for an unexpected commodity: chicken wings. In the fall, as the U.S. football season gets started, demand for the appetizers keeps growing, until it hits a peak during the week of the Super Bowl. The supply of the product is relatively limited though—a chicken can have only two wings—which means prices for the snacks jump.

The market, in addition to maintaining its annual tradition of dipping wings in sauce on Sunday afternoons, recently experienced another bump from a new source.

new MIGHTY WINGS®

McDonald's announced plans to introduce chicken wings for a limited time, between September and November. It also released projections that it would sell approximately 250 million orders. Even before the McDonald's Mighty Wings appeared on any menus, prices jumped, based mainly on predictions.

Of course, in anticipation of its menu addition, McDonald's also started stockpiling its inventory of wings.

It did so in grand fashion, purchasing approximately 50 million pounds of wings, which left other wing joints struggling to find supply of wings and chicken producers searching for buyers for the other parts of their chickens. Accordingly, the price changes have been dramatic in the wholesale market, up from approximately $0.90 per pound to just over $2.00. The McDonald's effect is not limited to wings, either. Since the fast-food giant added apples to its menu, this perishable market has seen substantial price increases. The impact is logical: When McDonald's started buying apples, it immediately became one of the largest apple purchasers in the world.

Prices for chicken breast meat continue to rise too, for two related reasons. First, McDonald's has expanded its use of this cut meat in menu items such as wraps. Second, when the prices for wings go up, chicken farmers raise the price of breast meat too, because it would be inefficient to raise chickens to sell only the wings. Analysts suggest that, unlike apples, wings will be temporary guests on the McDonald's menu board, not permanent residents. The company's influence on the wing market was so intense that it ran the risk of pricing itself right out of its supply!

And indeed, the plan did not work out quite as the Golden Arches had hoped. The wings themselves were relatively spicy, so consumers accustomed to the simple tastes of McDonald's burgers and fries never flocked to the new menu offering. At prices of higher than $1.00 per wing, they also did not offer a compelling financial reason to buy. Fast food fans could get far more food for the same amount of money by simply glancing down the Dollar Menu.

As a result, McDonald's was left with approximately 20 percent of its supply in its warehouses—that is, about 10 million pounds of frozen, unsold wings. To avoid overwhelming inventory holding costs, McDonald's needs to get those wings to consumers, so it promises that the Mighty Wings will rise again. The product is still the same though: slightly too spicy wings, available in franchise outlets. If it hopes to convince people to consume them, McDonald's likely needs to lower the price significantly. Such a promotion ($0.60 per wing) promises lower prices on the wings for a limited time, in the hope to sell out of all the remaining supply.

For franchise owners, the idea of cutting prices on wings is less than appealing. For most franchisees, sales at discounted prices mean reductions in their profits. That is, they still pay McDonald's the same amount to receive inventory, but they earn less from selling those products at the mandated discount price. Furthermore, the question remains whether consumers will find the promotional price compelling enough. If the wings really are too spicy for most people's palettes, it is unlikely that they would eat them at virtually any price. If the wings were originally too expensive, will the promotional price (approximately a 19 percent price reduction) now drive traffic?

Coming up with the "right" price is never easy, as this opening example shows. How can a firm determine what consumers are willing to pay and what they can charge? To answer such questions, we examine various pricing strategies and tactics in this chapter. We focus on specific considerations for setting pricing strategies, then discuss several pricing strategies. We also examine the implications of various pricing tactics for both consumers and businesses, as well as some of the more important legal and ethical issues associated with pricing.

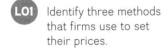 **LO1** Identify three methods that firms use to set their prices.

CONSIDERATIONS FOR SETTING PRICE STRATEGIES

Firms embrace different objectives, face different market conditions, and operate in different manners. Thus, they employ unique pricing strategies that seem best for the particular set of circumstances in which they find themselves. Even a single firm needs different strategies across its products and services and over time as market conditions change. The choice of a pricing strategy thus is specific to the product/service and target market. Although firms tend to rely on

EXHIBIT 15.1   Pricing Strategies

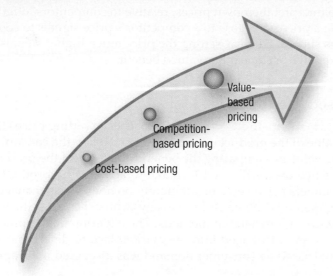

similar strategies when they can, each product or service requires its own specific strategy, because no two are ever exactly the same in terms of the marketing mix. Three different methods that can help develop pricing strategies—cost based, Competition based, and value based—are discussed in this section (see Exhibit 15.1).

Cost-Based Methods

As their name implies, cost-based pricing methods determine the final price to charge by starting with the cost. Relevant costs (e.g., fixed, variable, overhead) and a profit are added. Then this total amount is divided by the total demand to arrive at a cost-plus price. For example, assume the fixed costs to produce an item are $200,000, the variable costs add up to $100,000, and the estimated number of units to be produced is 30,000. Then,

$$(100{,}000 + 200{,}000) \div 30{,}000 = \$10$$

which is the total allocated cost per unit when 30,000 units are produced. If the desired markup is 20 percent, we multiply $10 by 1.20 (i.e., by 100 + 20 = 120 percent) to attain the cost-plus price for this item: $12. This sales price represents a cost-plus-percentage markup.

Cost-based methods do not recognize the role that consumers or competitors' prices play in the marketplace, though. Although they are relatively simple, compared with other methods used to set prices, cost-based pricing requires that all costs be identified and calculated on a per-unit basis. Moreover, the process assumes that these costs will not vary much for different levels of production. If they do, the price might need to be raised or lowered according to the production level. Thus, with cost-based pricing, prices are usually set on the basis of estimates of average costs.

Competition-Based Methods

Recall from Chapter 14 that some firms set prices according to their competitors' prices. But even if they do not have a strict competitor orientation, most firms still know that consumers compare the prices of their products with the different product/price combinations that competitors offer. Thus, using a competition-based pricing method, they may set their prices to reflect the way they want consumers to interpret their own prices, relative to competitors' offerings. For example, setting a price very close to a competitor's price signals to consumers that the product is similar, whereas setting the price much higher signals greater features, better quality, or some other valued benefit.

Value-Based Methods

Value-based pricing methods include approaches to setting prices that focus on the overall value of the product offering as perceived by the consumer. Consumers determine value by comparing the benefits they expect the product to deliver with the sacrifice they will need to make to acquire the product. Of course, different consumers perceive value differently. So how does a manager use value-based pricing methods? We consider two key approaches here: the improvement value and the cost of ownership methods. The experimental approach in which different prices are introduced into the marketplace to determine which is the most profitable based on consumer demand was discussed in Chapter 10.

Improvement Value Method With the first method, the manager must estimate the improvement value of a new product or service. This improvement value represents an estimate of how much more (or less) consumers are willing to pay for a product relative to other comparable products. For example, suppose a major telecommunications company has developed a new cell phone. Using any of a host of research methods—such as consumer surveys—the manager could get customers to assess the new product relative to an existing product and provide an estimate of how much better it is, or its improvement value.

Exhibit 15.2 illustrates how to calculate the improvement value. Consumers evaluate how much better (or worse) the new cell phone is than an existing product on five dimensions: clarity, range, security, battery life, and ease of use. According to the respondents to the survey, the new cell phone has 20 percent more clarity than the comparison phone. These consumers also weight the importance of the five attributes by allocating 100 points among them to indicate their relative importance; for the clarity dimension, this weighting is 0.40. When the manager multiplies the improvement weight by the relative importance percentage, clarity (20 × 0.40) emerges with a weighted factor of 8 percent. The marketer repeats the process for each benefit and sums the weighted factors to arrive at an approximation of the improvement value of the new product from customers' point of view. In this illustration, the improvement value is equal to 21 percent, so if the other cell phone costs $100, the firm should be able to charge customers a value-based price as high as $121 ($100 × 1.21).

EXHIBIT 15.2	Improvement Value		
Incremental Benefits	**Improved Value**	**Benefit Weight**	**Weighted Factor**
Clarity	20%	0.40	8%
Range	40%	0.20	8%
Security	10%	0.10	1%
Battery life	5%	0.20	1%
Ease of use	30%	0.10	3%
Overall		1.00	21%

One way to determine the price of a new product, like a new cell phone model, is to determine the improvement value from the customers' perspective.

Cost of Ownership Method Another value-based method for setting prices determines the total cost of owning the product over its useful life. Using the cost of ownership method, consumers may be willing to pay more for a particular product because, over its entire lifetime, it will eventually cost less to own than a cheaper alternative.[2]

Consider, for example, that an energy-efficient fluorescent lightbulb costs $3 and is expected to last 6,000 hours. Alternatively, a conventional lightbulb costs $1 but its average life is only 1,500 hours. The fluorescent bulb is expected to last four times longer than a conventional bulb, but it costs three times as much. Using the cost of ownership method, and considering the cost per hour, the fluorescent bulb manufacturer could charge $4 for each bulb, if it wanted to be equivalent to the cost of the conventional bulb. But research also has indicated that many consumers are reluctant to spend $4 for a bulb when they have been used to getting them for $1, so the manufacturer chose to charge only $3.

Implementing Value-Based Pricing Methods Although value-based pricing methods can be quite effective, they also necessitate a great deal of consumer research to be implemented successfully. Sellers must know how consumers in different market segments will attach value to the benefits delivered by their products, as Adding Value 15.1 describes. They also must account for changes in consumer attitudes, because the way customers perceive value today may not be the way they perceive it tomorrow.

CHECK YOURSELF

1. What are the three different considerations for setting prices?
2. How can you use value-based methods for setting prices?

Adding Value **15.1**   Value at a Premium Price: Moving Consumers Away from a View of Cheap as Valuable[i]

Value, as we know, is the relationship of benefits to costs, or what consumers get for what they give. But in consumer situations, value pricing and value options often imply the cheapest offerings. A value menu seems to mean really low prices, rather than referring to the benefits that the menu items provide to consumers. But this common misunderstanding may be changing.

As the slow economic recovery continues to plod along, marketers cannot simply keep their fingers crossed and hope that eventually buyers will be willing to pay more for their products. Instead, as Procter & Gamble has profitably learned with its Tide Pods, as discussed in the opener in Chapter 14, they need to offer more value, which will prompt consumers to pay more because they are getting more. The added convenience of the single-use pods, together with the detergent's effective cleaning technology and the brand's high-quality image, have convinced household laundry buyers to pay more per wash—and be happy about their choice.

To provide more value options to its customers, Wendy's has expanded its pricing options. If a fast-food patron wants a smaller item on a particular visit, he or she can purchase from the 99-cent menu. But if he or she is much hungrier or in the mood for a fresher option, this consumer can jump up to a $1.99 menu item. Each option provides value, but the value is perceived differently by different people and in different situations. In a sense, these moves mimic the trends in dollar stores, which quickly realized that limiting themselves to only $1 options also limited the depth of their offerings and made them less appealing to consumers, who sought a great deal, not just a way to get rid of all their single dollar bills.

Ford has enjoyed higher revenues from adding its Sync hands-free communication technology. Approximately 50 percent of Ford buyers cite the technology as a primary reason for their purchase choice. The associated price increase for this feature is reportedly around $4,000—not cheap, but apparently perceived to be a good value by many. Marketers can charge more and increase profits by providing more benefits, when they are perceived to add value to consumers in some meaningful way. For modern marketers, this lesson may seem basic, but it is also one that they need to be reminded of regularly.

Adding value doesn't necessarily mean a low price. Ford added value with its Sync hands-free communication technology. It is not cheap, but perceived to be a good value by its customers.

Adding Value 15.2   Walmart Offers Low-Priced Organic Foods[ii]

One word can strike fear into the heart of any small retailer: Walmart! Because it enjoys massive economies of scale, Walmart's entry into a market can cause tremors for even other large retailers, because somehow it always manages to underprice everyone else with the everyday low pricing (EDLP) strategy for which it has become famous. Long a consumer-goods giant, the Arkansas-based behemoth also has turned its massively successful EDLP practices to the grocery industry, where it quickly became the country's largest grocer as well.

Not satisfied with being just the largest grocer, Walmart aims to gain a substantial share of the lucrative organic food market. In true Walmart fashion, it intends to do so using its well-known, EDLP strategies. Organic products typically feature premium prices, but at Walmart, "there will be no premium for the customer to purchase organic products," according to the executive vice president of grocery at Walmart U.S. "They will be able to purchase organic at non-organic prices." In-house research indicated that consumers would overwhelmingly purchase organic products if they cost less, so Walmart responded.

But how can Walmart be the only retailer to offer organic products at nonorganic prices? The plan is to collaborate with WildOats to deliver organic items through an atypical "bigger is better" mentality. That is, organic foods typically come from small farms, which send their products out to be processed at facilities that simultaneously process conventional foods. The switches from organic to conventional processing and back again require a great deal of labor, which increases costs and thus prices. Because of their economies of scale, Walmart and WildOats can work with larger farms and processing plants that cater only to organic food production, saving time, labor, and money—by a margin of as much as 20 to 30 percent.

As promising as this model sounds, Walmart also is hedging its bets, introducing the WildOats organic line in only about

Consistent with its EDLP strategy, Walmart is offering organic products at non-organic prices.

half its nationwide stores. Because the premise for the offer requires high-quality organic products at nonorganic prices, company executives want to be certain they can stock shelves to meet demand and not be caught short if any suppliers confront production difficulties in the short term. As is also its habit, Walmart is thinking long term and locking its suppliers into agreements that will enable it to meet the enormous requirements associated with its lofty organic goals.

In the near future, though, it is likely you can visit your local Walmart to grab not just a DVD, diapers, and oil for your car but also the ingredients for a gourmet organic meal. That's one-stop shopping at its finest.

PRICING STRATEGIES

In this section, we discuss a number of commonly used price strategies: everyday low pricing, high/low pricing, and new product strategies.[3]

Everyday Low Pricing (EDLP)

With an **everyday low pricing (EDLP)** strategy, companies stress the continuity of their retail prices at a level somewhere between the regular, nonsale price and the deep-discount sale prices their competitors may offer.[4] By reducing consumers' search costs, EDLP adds value; consumers can spend less of their valuable time comparing prices, including sale prices, at different stores. With its EDLP strategy, Walmart communicates to consumers that, for any given group of often-purchased items, its prices will tend to be lower than those of any other company in that market. This claim does not necessarily mean that every item that consumers may purchase will be priced lower at Walmart than anywhere else—in fact, some competitive retailers will offer lower prices on some items. However, for an average purchase, Walmart's prices tend to be lower overall. Adding Value 15.2 describes Walmart's foray into organic produce using its EDLP strategy.

 LO2 Describe the difference between an everyday low pricing (EDLP) strategy and a high/low strategy.

A high/low pricing strategy relies on the promotion of sales, during which prices are temporarily reduced to encourage purchases.

LO3 Explain the difference between a price skimming and a market penetration pricing strategy.

The reference prices for these pants are both $24.99. It provides potential customers with an idea of the "regular price" before it was put on sale.

High/Low Pricing

An alternative to EDLP is a high/low pricing strategy, which relies on the promotion of sales, during which prices are temporarily reduced to encourage purchases. A high/low strategy is appealing because it attracts two distinct market segments: those who are not price sensitive and are willing to pay the "high" price and more price sensitive customers who wait for the "low" sale price. High/low sellers can also create excitement and attract customers through the "get them while they last" atmosphere that occurs during a sale.

Sellers using a high/low pricing strategy often communicate their strategy through the creative use of a reference price, which is the price against which buyers compare the actual selling price of the product and that facilitates their evaluation process. The seller labels the reference price as the "regular price" or an "original price." When consumers view the "sale price" and compare it with the provided reference price, their perceptions of the value of the deal will likely increase.[5]

In the advertisement on this page, Sears has provided a reference price, in smaller print and labeled "Reg.," to indicate that $24.99 is the regular price of Lee jeans. In addition, the advertisement highlights the current "sale" price of $21.99. Thus, the reference price suggests to consumers that they are getting a good deal and will save money. However, as Ethical and Societal Dilemma 15.1 notes, sometimes the veracity of such a reference price is open to challenge.

New Product Pricing Strategies

Developing pricing strategies for new products is one of the most challenging tasks a manager can undertake. When the new product is similar to what already appears on the market, this job is somewhat easier, because the product's approximate value has already been established and the value-based methods described earlier in this chapter can be employed. But when the new product is truly innovative, or what we call "new to the world," determining consumers' perceptions of its value and pricing it accordingly become far more difficult.

Two distinct new product pricing strategies are discussed next: market penetration pricing and price skimming.

Market Penetration Pricing Firms using a market penetration strategy set the initial price low for the introduction of the new product or service. Their objective is to build sales, market share, and profits quickly. The low market penetration price is an incentive to purchase the product immediately. Firms using a market penetration strategy expect the unit cost to drop significantly as the accumulated volume sold increases, an effect known as the experience curve effect. With this effect, as sales continue to grow, the costs continue to drop.

Ethical & Societal Dilemma 15.1   Is It Really 45 Percent Off?[iii]

For the truly fashionable—or at least those who consider themselves as members of that group—the trade-off between luxury and affordability can be a tricky one. You want the newest, hottest fashion, but trying to keep up can be exhausting on your wallet. What's a maven to do?

Private sale online sites such as Gilt, RueLaLa, and HauteLook promise a solution. They host limited-time sales of products from high-end fashion brands. A sale starts at a specified time and lasts for 48 hours, or until the sale is sold out. So, if you must have the Nova Armored Baby Beaton handbag from Burberry, you can have it for 45 percent off the list price, or $877 instead of $1,595, as long as you are on Hautelook.com when the sale starts. Brick-and-mortar retailers are following suit with "flash sales," such as when Banana Republic offers 40 percent of its full-priced sweaters but only between 11:00 a.m. and 2:00 p.m. on specific days.

But is it really 40 or 45 percent off, and 45 percent off what? A reference price like $1,595 gives consumers a cue as to what that specific handbag should be worth. Research shows that the greater the difference between a suggested retail and a sale price, the greater the perceived value. When customers see Sears offering a refrigerator for $1,300 off its original price, that huge number is nearly impossible to ignore. The better the deal, the more consumers will be attracted to buy. But if the retailer inflates the suggested or original price, the percentage discount and dollars off seem much better than they actually are.

When the private sale sites have been caught inflating the suggested retail prices to show a greater percentage discount, they generally claim that the original prices they list are accurate and come from the manufacturer. Any errors, they argue, are because the manufacturer gave them the wrong price, or else it might be due to employee error. For example, if the suggested retail price of the Burberry bag was actually only $1,100 instead of $1,595, then the bag was discounted only 20 percent. A customer in the heat of the moment may

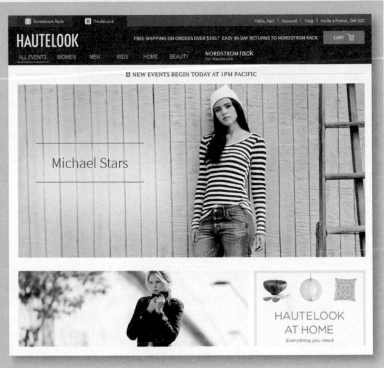

What does a 45 percent off sale on private online sales sites like HauteLook really mean? Is it as good a deal as it appears?

buy the bag because it is reported to be 45 percent off; were it only 20 percent off, she might not have purchased.

In some cases, the complicated coupon, discount, and flash pricing offers make it nearly impossible to determine the extent of the deal without a calculator. Because consumers rarely have the time or energy to calculate exactly what kind of discount they are getting, retailers can play on their excitement when it seems like a great deal.

Should private sale sites and in-store retailers be required to substantiate their reference prices? Which price should they use as the reference price? Is it their responsibility if the manufacturer gives them the wrong pricing information? Do you think they are intentionally misleading their customers?

In addition to offering the potential to build sales, market share, and profits, penetration pricing discourages competitors from entering the market because the profit margin is relatively low. Furthermore, if the costs to produce the product drop because of the accumulated volume, competitors that enter the market later will face higher unit costs, at least until their volume catches up with the early entrant.

A penetration strategy has its drawbacks. First, the firm must have the capacity to satisfy a rapid rise in demand—or at least be able to add that capacity quickly. Second, low price does not signal high quality. Of course, a price below their expectations decreases the risk for consumers to purchase the product and test its quality for themselves. Third, firms should avoid a penetration pricing strategy if some segments of the market are willing to pay more for the product; otherwise, the firm is just "leaving money on the table."

Price skimming is often used for high demand video games like Mario Kart because fans will pay a higher price to be one of the first to own the newest version.

Price Skimming In many markets, and particularly for new and innovative products or services, innovators and early adopters (see Chapter 12) are willing to pay a higher price to obtain the new product or service. This strategy, known as price skimming, appeals to these segments of consumers who are willing to pay the premium price to have the innovation first. This tactic is particularly common in technology markets, where sellers know that customers of the hottest and coolest products will wait in line for hours, desperate to be the first to own the newest version. These innovators are willing to pay the very highest prices to obtain brand-new examples of technology advances, with exciting product enhancements. However, after this high-price market segment becomes saturated and sales begin to slow down, companies generally lower the price to capture (or skim) the next most price sensitive market segment, which is willing to pay a somewhat lower price. For most companies, the price dropping process can continue until the demand for the product has been satisfied, even at the lowest price points.

The spread of new media for movies illustrates a price skimming strategy. As with VCRs in the 1970s and DVD players in the 1990s, consumers were slow to embrace the new, more expensive Blu-ray discs. But enough early adopters purchased the Blu-ray discs that manufacturers continued to refine Blu-ray players to penetrate wider target markets. Consumers are buying the devices at a faster pace than the earlier movie-playing devices. One obvious reason for this sales growth is that prices for high-quality Blu-ray players have dropped below $80,[6] a steep drop from the $300-plus that retailers charged for debut models.[7]

For price skimming to work though, the product or service must be perceived as breaking new ground in some way, offering consumers new benefits currently unavailable in alternative products. When they believe it will work, firms use skimming strategies for a variety of reasons. Some may start by pricing relatively high to signal high quality to the market. Others may decide to price high at first to limit demand, which gives them time to build their production capacities. Similarly, some firms employ a skimming strategy to try to quickly earn back some of the high research and development investments they made for the new product. Finally, firms employ skimming strategies to test consumers' price sensitivity. A firm that prices too high can always lower the price (recall our discussion in Chapter 12 of Amazon's price decreases for the original Kindle), but if the price is initially set too low, it is almost impossible to raise it without significant consumer resistance.

Furthermore, for a skimming pricing strategy to be successful, competitors cannot be able to enter the market easily; otherwise, price competition will likely force lower prices and undermine the whole strategy. Competitors might be prevented from entering the market through patent protections, their inability to copy the innovation (because it is complex to manufacture, its raw materials are hard to get, or the product relies on proprietary technology), or the high costs of entry.

Skimming strategies also face a significant potential drawback in the relatively high unit costs associated with producing small volumes of products. Therefore, firms must consider the trade-off between earning a higher price and suffering higher production costs. Finally, firms using a skimming strategy for new products must face the consequences of ultimately having to lower the price as demand wanes. Margins suffer, and customers who purchased the product or service at the higher initial price may become irritated when the price falls.

PRICING TACTICS

 LO4 Identify tactics used to reduce prices to consumers.

It is important to distinguish clearly between pricing strategies and pricing tactics. A **pricing strategy** is a long-term approach to setting prices broadly in an integrative effort (across all the firm's products) based on the five Cs (company objectives, costs, customers, competition, and channel members) of pricing discussed in Chapter 14. **Pricing tactics**, in contrast, offer short-term methods to focus on select components of the five Cs. Generally, a pricing tactic represents either a short-term response to a competitive threat (e.g., lowering price temporarily to meet a competitor's price reduction) or a broadly accepted method of calculating a final price for the customer that is short term in nature. We separate our discussion of pricing tactics into those directed at end consumers and those aimed at intermediaries in a business-to-business (B2B) setting.

Pricing Tactics Aimed at Consumers

When firms sell their products and services directly to consumers, rather than to other businesses, the pricing tactics they use naturally differ. Some of the tactics aimed directly at consumers—such as markdowns, quantity discounts, seasonal discounts, coupons, rebates, leasing, price bundling, leader pricing, and price lining—continue to be important factors.

Markdowns Markdowns are the reductions retailers take on the initial selling price of the product or service.[8] An integral component of the high/low pricing strategy we described previously, markdowns enable retailers to get rid of slow-moving or obsolete merchandise, sell seasonal items after the appropriate season, and match competitors' prices on specific merchandise. Retailers must get rid of merchandise that isn't selling, because holding on to such items hurts the retailer's image and ties up money in inventory that could be used more productively elsewhere. Retailers also use markdowns to promote merchandise and increase sales. Particularly when used in conjunction with promotions, markdowns can increase traffic into the store or onto their websites, which many retailers view as half the battle. Once customers are in the store or on their websites, retailers always hope they will purchase other products at regular prices.

Quantity Discounts for Consumers The most common implementation of a quantity discount at the consumer level is the **size discount**. Take, for example, three sizes of General Mills' popular cereal Cheerios: 10-, 14-, and 18-ounce boxes are priced at approximately $2.99, $3.99, and $4.49, respectively. The larger the quantity, the less the cost per ounce, which means the manufacturer is providing a quantity discount. The goal of this tactic is to encourage

Customers get a size discount for buying larger sizes. With Cheerios, the larger the box, the less it costs per ounce.

consumers to purchase larger quantities each time they buy. In turn, these consumers are less likely to switch brands and often tend to consume more of the product, depending on the product usage characteristics. Typically, buying a larger package of toilet tissue does not mean consumers will use it faster, but buying a larger box of cereal may encourage them to eat more of it or eat it more often.[9]

Seasonal Discounts Seasonal discounts are price reductions offered on products and services to stimulate demand during off-peak seasons. You can find hotel rooms, ski lift tickets, snowmobiles, lawn mowers, barbeque grills, vacation packages, flights to certain destinations, and Christmas cards at discounts during their "off" seasons. Some consumers even plan their buying around these discounts, determined to spend the day after Christmas stocking up on discounted wrapping paper and bows for the following year.

Coupons Coupons offer a discount on the price of specific items when they're purchased. Coupons are issued by manufacturers and retailers in newspapers, on products, on the shelf, at the cash register, over the Internet, and through the mail.[10] Retailers use coupons because they can induce customers to try products for the first time, convert those first-time users to regular users, encourage large purchases, increase usage, and protect market share against competition. However, the impact of coupons on profitability is questionable.

Coupon promotions, like all temporary promotions, may be stealing sales from a future period without any net increase in sales. For instance, if a supermarket runs a coupon promotion on sugar, households may buy a large quantity of sugar and stockpile it for future use. Thus, unless the coupon is used mostly by new buyers, the net impact on sales is negligible, and there will be a negative impact on profits due to the amount of the redeemed coupons and cost of the coupon redemption procedures.

Coupons also may annoy, alienate, and confuse consumers and therefore do little to increase store loyalty. Customers see an ad for a supermarket with a headline reading "Double Coupons" but don't realize there might be conditions, such as a minimum purchase required, or that it may only apply to certain manufacturers.

Recognizing these problems, some retailers have reduced coupon usage and cut the number of days in which customers can redeem coupons. Other retailers, like CVS, are making coupons more attractive to loyal customers by customizing their content to be in line with their unique needs. For instance, if a customer typically spends a small amount during each shopping trip, the customer will receive coupons that encourage larger purchases, such as "buy one, get one free." If another customer spends a lot each time she shops, but shops sporadically, that customer will get coupons that expire relatively quickly. Unique coupons will also encourage customers to try new brands within categories that they normally purchase, or products that complement their usual purchases, such as shampoo to customers that purchase hair color.[11]

Internet sites provide customers with instant coupons. For instance, a customer might go to a Walmart and find the latest Lego video game for $29.99. A scan of the bar code on his cell phone to ShopSavvy.com might find the same item at a Target a mile away for $19.99. Another scan to MyCoupons.com provides a coupon for $10.00, thus saving the customer $20.00 in a matter of minutes.

Coupons offer a discount on the price of specific items when they're purchased.

Rebates Rebates provide another form of discounts for consumers off the final selling price. In this case, however, the manufacturer, instead of the retailer, issues the refund as a portion of the purchase price returned to the buyer in the form of cash. Rebates can be even more frustrating than coupons for consumers, but the idea is similar. Whereas a coupon provides instant savings when presented, a rebate promises savings, usually mailed to the consumer at some later date, only if the consumer carefully follows the rules. The "hassle factor" for rebates thus is higher than for coupons. The consumer must first buy the item during a specified time period, then mail in the required documentation—which usually includes the original sales receipt—and finally wait four to six weeks (or more!) for a check to arrive.

Manufacturers generally like rebates because as much as 90 percent of consumers never bother to redeem them. Manufacturers also embrace this form of price reduction because it lets them offer price cuts to consumers directly. With a traditional wholesale price cut from its vendors, retailers can keep the price on the shelf the same and pocket the difference. Rebates can also be rolled out and shut off quickly. That allows manufacturers to fine-tune inventories or respond quickly to competitors without actually cutting prices. Finally, because buyers are required to fill out forms with names, addresses, and other data, rebates become a great way for vendors to build a customer data warehouse. From the retailer's perspective, rebates are more advantageous than coupons since they increase demand in the same way coupons may, but the retailer has no handling costs.

Leasing For some products, discounts, coupons, and rebates may not be sufficient to bring the price to within consumers' reach. With a lease, consumers pay a fee to purchase the right to use a product for a specific amount of time. They never own the product, they are just renting it. Leasing products opens up new, less price sensitive, target markets. Some consumers also like leases because they get tired of the product before its useful life is over, and they don't have to worry about selling it, trading it, or throwing it away. Car companies have used leasing options for years to appeal to consumers who plan to keep their cars only for a few years and will want to trade in for a new model sooner rather than later. Other industries are recognizing that what works for Toyotas and Chevy trucks also works for gowns, handbags, art, and luxury cars.

Price Bundling When you signed up for your high-speed Internet connection, did you also get cable TV and telephone? If so, you probably pay less than if you were to get the three services separately. This practice of selling more than one product for a single, lower price is called price bundling.[12] Firms bundle products or services together to encourage customers to stock up so they won't purchase competing brands, to encourage trial of a new product, or to provide an incentive to purchase a less desirable product or service to obtain a more desirable one in the same bundle.

Leader Pricing Leader pricing is a tactic that attempts to build store traffic by aggressively pricing and advertising a regularly purchased item, often priced at or just above the store's cost. The rationale behind this tactic argues that, while in the store to get the great deal on, say, milk, the consumer will also probably pick up other items, which sell at a higher margin. The higher margins and profits on these other items then will more than cover the lower markup on the milk. Imagine the marketing potential of various combinations of products; the store uses leader pricing on cocktail sauce, which gives employees the perfect opportunity to ask, "How about a pound of fresh shrimp to go with the cocktail sauce you're purchasing?" Leader pricing can be illegal under some circumstances though, as discussed subsequently in this chapter.

Stores like Aldi use a pricing tactic called leader pricing to build store traffic aggressively, pricing and advertising regularly purchased items often at or just above the store's cost.

EXHIBIT 15.3	Business-to-Business Pricing Tactics
Tactic	**Description**
Seasonal discounts	An additional reduction offered as an incentive to retailers to order merchandise in advance of the normal buying season.
Cash discounts	An additional reduction that reduces the invoice cost if the buyer pays the invoice prior to the end of the discount period.
Allowances	Advertising or slotting allowances (additional price reductions) offered in return for specific behaviors. Advertising allowances are offered to retailers if they agree to feature the manufacturer's product in their advertising and promotional efforts. Slotting allowances are offered to get new products into stores or to gain more or better shelf space.
Quantity discounts	Providing a reduced price according to the amount purchased.
Uniform delivered versus zone pricing	Uniform delivered price: shipper charges one rate, no matter where the buyer is located. Zone price: different prices depending on the geographical delivery area.

Price Lining When marketers establish a price floor and a price ceiling for an entire line of similar products and then set a few other price points in between to represent distinct differences in quality, the practice is called price lining. Imagine that you need a new dress shirt because you have an important job interview. You go to brooksbrothers.com and find similar looking shirts for $92 (non-iron), $185 (Egyptian cotton), and $278 (luxury). Which are you going to buy? Are you going to risk the success of the interview by purchasing the least expensive shirt? Probably not. Will the interviewee be able to tell the difference between the $135 classic cotton and the $295 Sea Island cotton shirt? Probably not. You will probably purchase the middle-quality shirt because you don't want to look cheap, but you really can't afford the highest-priced shirt.[13]

Business Pricing Tactics and Discounts

L05 Identify tactics used to reduce prices to businesses.

The pricing tactics employed in B2B settings differ significantly from those used in consumer markets. Among the most prominent are seasonal and cash discounts, allowances, quantity discounts, and uniform delivered versus zone pricing. (See Exhibit 15.3.)

Seasonal Discounts A seasonal discount is an additional reduction offered as an incentive to retailers to order merchandise in advance of the normal buying season. For instance, Lennox may offer its air conditioner dealers an additional seasonal discount if they place their orders and receive delivery before April 1, prior to the warm months when air conditioner sales are highest. If it can ship earlier in the season, Lennox can plan its production schedules more easily and lessen its finished goods inventory. Its dealers, however, must weigh the benefits of a larger profit because of the discount versus the extra cost of carrying the inventory for a longer period of time.

Cash Discounts A cash discount reduces the invoice cost if the buyer pays the invoice prior to the end of the discount period. Typically, it is expressed in the form of a percentage, such as "3/10, n/30," or "3%, 10 days, net 30," which means the buyer can take a 3 percent discount on the total amount of the invoice if the bill is paid within 10 days of the invoice date; otherwise the full, or net, amount is due within 30 days. Why do B2B sellers offer cash discounts to customers? By encouraging early payment, they benefit from the time value of money. Getting money earlier rather than later enables the firm to either invest the money to earn a return on it or avoid borrowing money and paying interest on it. In both instances, the firm is better off financially.

Allowances Another pricing tactic that lowers the final cost to channel members is allowances, such as advertising or slotting allowances, offered in return for specific behaviors. An **advertising allowance** offers a price reduction to channel members if they agree to feature the manufacturer's product in their advertising and promotional efforts. Advertising allowances are legal as long they are available to all customers and not structured in such a way that they consistently and obviously favor one or a few buyers over others. **Slotting allowances** are fees paid to retailers simply to get new products into stores or to gain more or better shelf space for their products. Some argue that slotting allowances are unethical because they put small manufacturers that cannot readily afford allowances at a competitive disadvantage. Demanding large slotting allowances could be considered a form of bribery—"paying off" the retailer to get preferential treatment.

Quantity Discounts A **quantity discount** provides a reduced price according to the amount purchased. The more the buyer purchases, the higher the discount and, of course, the greater the value.

A **cumulative quantity discount** uses the amount purchased over a specified time period and usually involves several transactions. This type of discount particularly encourages resellers to maintain their current supplier because the cost to switch must include the loss of the discount. Recall that we noted that automobile dealers must buy the products they hope to sell to consumers from the manufacturer. They often attempt to meet a quota or a sales goal for a specific time period, such as a quarter or a year, because if they meet those quotas, they earn discounts on all the cars they purchased from the manufacturer, in the form of a cumulative quantity discount. For this very reason, you will often find good deals on cars at the end of a quarter or fiscal year. If the dealership can just sell a few more cars to meet its quota, the cumulative quantity discount earned can be substantial, so taking a few hundred dollars less on those last few cars is well worth the opportunity to receive a check worth many times the amount of the losses.

A **noncumulative quantity discount**, though still a quantity discount, is based only on the amount purchased in a single order. It therefore provides the buyer with an incentive to purchase more merchandise immediately. Such larger, less frequent orders can save manufacturers order processing, sales, and transportation expenses. For example, a retail store might get a 40 percent discount off the manufacturer's suggested retail price for placing a $500 order; a 50 percent discount for an order of $501 to $4,999; and a 60 percent discount for an order of greater than $5,000.

Uniform Delivered versus Zone Pricing These pricing tactics are specific to shipping, which represents a major cost for many manufacturers. With a **uniform delivered pricing** tactic, the shipper charges one rate, no matter where the buyer is located, which makes things very simple for both the seller and the buyer. **Zone pricing**, however, sets different prices depending on a geographical division of the delivery areas. For example, a manufacturer based in New York City might divide the United States into seven different zones and use different shipping rates for each zone to reflect the average shipping cost for customers located therein. This way, each customer in a zone is charged the same cost for shipping. Zone pricing can be advantageous to the shipper because it reflects the actual shipping charges more closely than uniform delivered pricing can.

CHECK YOURSELF

1. What are some consumer-oriented pricing tactics?
2. What are some B2B-oriented pricing tactics?

L06 List the pricing practices that are illegal or unethical.

LEGAL AND ETHICAL ASPECTS OF PRICING

With so many different pricing strategies and tactics, it is no wonder that unscrupulous firms find ample opportunity to engage in pricing practices that can hurt consumers. We now take a look at some of the legal and ethical implications of pricing.

Prices tend to fluctuate naturally and respond to varying market conditions. Thus, though we rarely see firms attempting to control the market in terms of product quality or advertising, they often engage in pricing practices that can unfairly reduce competition or harm consumers directly through fraud and deception. A host of laws and regulations at both the federal and state levels attempt to prevent unfair pricing practices, but some are poorly enforced, and others are difficult to prove.

U.K.-based Tesco wasn't allowed to make the claim that is "Britains's Biggest Discounter" because it was considered to be misleading. Such a claim would probably be considered to be puffery in the U.S., and therefore allowed.

Deceptive or Illegal Price Advertising

Although it is always illegal and unethical to lie in advertising, a certain amount of "puffery" is typically allowed (see Chapter 19).[14] But price advertisements should never deceive consumers to the point of causing harm. For example, a local car dealer's advertising that it had the "best deals in town" would likely be considered puffery. In contrast, advertising "the lowest prices, guaranteed" makes a very specific claim and, if not true, can be considered deceptive.

Deceptive Reference Prices Previously, we introduced reference prices, which create reference points for the buyer against which to compare the selling price. If the reference price is bona fide, the advertisement is informative. If the reference price has been inflated or is just plain fictitious, however, the advertisement is deceptive and may cause harm to consumers. But it is not easy to determine whether a reference price is bona fide. What standard should be used? If an advertisement specifies a "regular price," just what qualifies as regular? How many units must the store sell at this price for it to be a bona fide regular price—half the stock? A few? Just one? Finally, what if the store offers the item for sale at the regular price but customers do not buy any? Can it still be considered a regular price? In general, if a seller is going to label a price as a regular price, the Better Business Bureau suggests that at least 50 percent of the sales have occurred at that price.[15]

Loss Leader Pricing As we discussed previously, leader pricing is a legitimate attempt to build store traffic by pricing a regularly purchased item aggressively but still above the store's cost. Loss leader pricing takes this tactic one step further by lowering the price *below* the store's cost. No doubt you have seen "buy one, get one free" offers at grocery and discount stores. Unless the markup for the item is 100 percent of the cost, these sales obviously do not generate enough revenue from the sale of one unit to cover the store's cost for both units, which means it

Is this a legitimate sale, or is the retailer using deceptive reference prices?

has essentially priced the total for both items below cost, unless the manufacturer is absorbing the cost of the promotion to generate volume. In some states, this form of pricing is illegal.

Bait and Switch Another form of deceptive price advertising occurs when sellers advertise items for a very low price without the intent to really sell any. This bait-and-switch tactic is a deceptive practice because the store lures customers in with a very low price on an item (the bait), only to aggressively pressure these customers into purchasing a higher-priced model (the switch) by disparaging the low-priced item, comparing it unfavorably with the higher-priced model, or professing an inadequate supply of the lower-priced item. Again, the laws against bait-and-switch practices are difficult to enforce because salespeople, simply as a function of their jobs, are always trying to get customers to trade up to a higher-priced model without necessarily deliberately baiting them. The key to proving deception centers on the intent of the seller, which is also difficult to prove.

Predatory Pricing

When a firm sets a very low price for one or more of its products with the intent to drive its competition out of business, it is using predatory pricing. Predatory pricing is illegal under both the Sherman Antitrust Act and the Federal Trade Commission Act because it constrains free trade and represents a form of unfair competition. It also tends to promote a concentrated market with a few dominant firms (an oligopoly).

But again, predation is difficult to prove. First, one must demonstrate intent, that is, that the firm intended to drive out its competition or prevent competitors from entering the market. Second, the complainant must prove that the firm charged prices lower than its average cost, an equally difficult task.

The issue of predatory pricing has arisen because of Google's dominance in the search engine market. Advertisers on Google bid on specific keywords; if they win the auction, their product appears first in the paid results section on the search engine. However, Google also includes a "quality handicap" and charges poor quality advertisers more. It claims this tactic ensures that users are more likely to find high-quality results from their searches. The algorithm it uses to define quality is confidential, but some experts allege that Google has manipulated the paid search results in such a way that it undermines competitors' offerings while promoting its own. It appears these claims may be true; in 2012 the Federal Trade Commission (FTC) found enough evidence for search results manipulation that it recommended the government sue Google, and in 2013 a European Commission came to similar conclusions.[16] The unresolved question is: because of Google's dominance in the search engine market, with its resulting ability to control prices, would its practice of charging more for its "quality handicap" be predatory?

Price Discrimination

There are many forms of price discrimination, but only some of them are considered illegal under the Clayton Act and the Robinson-Patman Act. When firms sell the same product to different resellers (wholesalers, distributors, or retailers) at different prices, it can be considered price discrimination; usually, larger firms receive lower prices.

We have already discussed the use of quantity discounts, which is a legitimate method of charging different prices to different customers on the basis of the quantity they purchase. The legality of this tactic stems from the assumption that it costs less to sell and service 1,000 units to one customer than 100 units to 10 customers. But quantity discounts must be available to all customers and not be structured in such a way that they consistently and obviously favor one or a few buyers over others.

Is this price discrimination illegal?

The Robinson-Patman Act does not apply to sales to end consumers, at which point many forms of price discrimination occur. For example, students and seniors often receive discounts on food and movie tickets, which is perfectly acceptable under federal law. Those engaged in online auctions like eBay are also practicing a legal form of price discrimination because sellers are selling the same item to different buyers at various prices. In addition, to deal ethically with the rising costs of health care, some hospitals offer a "sliding scale" based on income, such that lower-income patients receive discounts or even free medical care, especially for children.[17]

Price Fixing

Price fixing is the practice of colluding with other firms to control prices. Price fixing might be either horizontal or vertical. Whereas horizontal price fixing is clearly illegal under the Sherman Antitrust Act, vertical price fixing falls into a gray area.[18]

Horizontal price fixing occurs when competitors that produce and sell competing products or services collude, or work together, to control prices, effectively taking price out of the decision process for consumers. This practice clearly reduces competition and is illegal. Six South African airlines were accused of colluding to hike the price of fares for flights within the country during the World Cup.[19] The major tobacco companies also have been accused of colluding to fix the prices of cigarettes worldwide.[20] As a general rule of thumb, competing firms should refrain from discussing prices or terms and conditions of sale with competitors. If firms want to know competitors' prices, they can look at a competitor's advertisements, its websites, or its stores.

Vertical price fixing occurs when parties at different levels of the same marketing channel (e.g., manufacturers and retailers) agree to control the prices passed on to consumers. Manufacturers often encourage retailers to sell their merchandise at a specific price, known as the manufacturer's suggested retail price (MSRP). Manufacturers set MSRP prices to reduce retail price competition among retailers, stimulate retailers to provide complementary services, and support the manufacturer's merchandise. Manufacturers enforce MSRPs by withholding benefits such as cooperative advertising or even refusing to deliver merchandise to noncomplying retailers. The Supreme Court has ruled that the ability of a manufacturer to require retailers to sell merchandise at MSRP should be decided on a case-by-case basis, depending on the individual circumstances.[21]

According to Canada's Competition Bureau, some well-known candy producers have engaged in both types of price fixing, as outlined in Ethical and Societal Dilemma 15.2.

As these legal issues clearly demonstrate, pricing decisions involve many ethical considerations. In determining both their pricing strategies and their pricing tactics, marketers must always balance their goal of inducing customers, through price, to find value and the need to deal honestly and fairly with those same customers. Whether another business or an individual consumer, buyers can be influenced by a variety of pricing methods. It is up to marketers to determine which of these methods works best for the seller, the buyer, and the community.

CHECK YOURSELF

1. What common pricing practices are considered to be illegal or unethical?

Ethical & Societal Dilemma 15.2

Getting Your Chocolate Fix Might Be Getting More Expensive[iv]

According to Canada's official Competition Bureau, long-time rivals Mars (maker of such candies as M&M's, Snickers, and the Dove line of chocolates) and Nestlé (which produces Butterfinger and Crunch candies, among others) have collaborated with various independent wholesalers to bump up the prices of their chocolates to a fixed level.

In addition to the corporations themselves, the executives in charge of Nestlé Canada, Mars Canada, and ITWAL (a wholesale distributor) have been named individually in the prosecution. All three firms have expressed their determination to fight the charges.

Mars, maker of Snickers, and its competitor, Nestlé, have been accused of collaborating with independent wholesalers to bump up the prices of their chocolates to a fixed level.

Although Hershey's Canadian arm was initially included as another coconspirator in the scheme, its cooperation with authorities has allowed it to avoid direct prosecution. Even as it admits engaging in price fixing though, Hershey's claims that the events in question occurred under previous management, and that all such ethical issues have since been resolved. John Pacman, Canada's Interim Commissioner of Competition, appeared confident in the case, noting that "Price-fixing is a serious criminal offence and today's charges demonstrate the Competition Bureau's resolve to stop cartel activity in Canada."

Reviewing Learning Objectives

 LO1 **Identify three methods that firms use to set their prices.**

The various methods of setting prices have their advantages and disadvantages. The three primary methods are cost based, competition based, and value based. The cost-based techniques are quick and easy but fail to reflect the competitive environment or consumer demand. Although it is always advisable to be aware of what competitors are doing, using competition-based pricing should not occur in isolation without considering cost considerations and consumer reactions. Taking a value-based approach to pricing, whether the improvement value or the total cost of ownership approach, in conjunction with these other methods provides a nicely balanced method of setting prices.

LO2 **Describe the difference between an everyday low pricing (EDLP) strategy and a high/low strategy.**

An everyday low pricing strategy is maintained when a product's price stays relatively constant at a level that is slightly lower than the regular price from competitors using a high/low strategy, and is less frequently discounted. Customers enjoy an everyday low pricing strategy because they know that the price will always be the about the same and a

better price than the competition. High/low pricing strategy starts out with a product at one (higher) price, and then discounts the product. This strategy first attracts a less price sensitive customer that pays the regular price, and then a very price sensitive customer that pays the low price.

 LO3 **Explain the difference between a price skimming and a market penetration pricing strategy.**

When firms use a price skimming strategy, the product or service must be perceived as breaking new ground or customers will not pay more than what they pay for other products. Firms use price skimming to signal high quality, limit demand, recoup their investment quickly, and/or test people's price sensitivity. Moreover, it is easier to price high initially and then lower the price than vice versa. Market penetration, in contrast, helps firms build sales and market share quickly, which may discourage other firms from entering the market. Building demand quickly also typically results in lowered costs as the firm gains experience making the product or delivering the service.

 LO4 **Identify tactics used to reduce prices to consumers.**

Marketers use a variety of tactics to provide lower prices to consumers. The tactics include markdowns, quantity discounts, seasonal discounts, coupons, rebates, leasing, price bundling, leader pricing, and price lining. For example, leader pricing involves retailers pricing certain products or services at very low prices, with the hope that these same customers will also buy other, more profitable items.

 Identify tactics used to reduce prices to businesses.

Seasonal discounts give retailers an incentive to buy prior to the normal selling season, cash discounts prompt them to pay their invoices early, and allowances attempt to get retailers to advertise the manufacturer's product or stock a new product. In addition, quantity discounts can cause retailers to purchase a larger quantity over a specific period of time or with a particular order. Finally, zone pricing bases the cost of

shipping the merchandise on the distance between the retailer and the manufacturer—the farther away, the more it costs.

 List the pricing practices that are illegal or unethical.

There are almost as many ways to get into trouble by setting or changing a price as there are pricing strategies and tactics. Some common legal issues pertain to advertising deceptive prices. Specifically, if a firm compares a reduced price with a "regular" or reference price, it must actually have sold that product or service at the regular price. Bait and switch is another form of deceptive price advertising, where sellers advertise items for a very low price without the intent to really sell any at that price. Collusion among firms to fix prices is always illegal.

Key Terms   ▪LEARNSMART˙

- advertising allowance, 477
- bait and switch, 479
- cash discount, 476
- competition-based pricing method, 466
- cost-based pricing method, 465
- cost of ownership method, 467
- coupon, 474
- cumulative quantity discount, 477
- everyday low pricing (EDLP), 469
- experience curve effect, 470
- high/low pricing, 470
- horizontal price fixing, 480

- improvement value, 466
- leader pricing, 475
- lease, 475
- loss leader pricing, 478
- manufacturer's suggested retail price (MSRP), 480
- markdowns, 473
- market penetration strategy, 470
- noncumulative quantity discount, 477
- predatory pricing, 479
- price bundling, 475
- price discrimination, 479
- price fixing, 480

- price lining, 476
- price skimming, 472
- pricing strategy, 473
- pricing tactics, 473
- quantity discount, 477
- rebate, 475
- reference price, 470
- seasonal discount, 476
- size discount, 473
- slotting allowance, 477
- uniform delivered pricing, 477
- value-based pricing method, 466
- vertical price fixing, 480
- zone pricing, 477

Marketing Applications

1. Suppose you have been hired as the pricing manager for a drugstore chain that typically adds a fixed percentage onto the cost of each product to arrive at the retail price. Evaluate this technique. What would you do differently?

2. Some high-fashion retailers, notably H&M and Zara, sell what some call "disposable fashion"—apparel priced so reasonably low that it can be disposed of after just a few wearings. Here is your

dilemma: You have an important job interview and need a new suit. You can buy the suit at one of these stores for $129 or at Brooks Brothers for $500. Of course, the Brooks Brothers suit is of higher quality and will therefore last longer. How would you use the two value-based approaches described in this chapter to determine which suit to buy?

3. A phone manufacturer is determining a price for its product using a cost-based pricing strategy.

The fixed costs are $100,000, and the variable costs are $50,000. If 1,000 units are produced and the company wants to have a 30 percent markup, what is the price of the phone?

4. Identify two stores at which you shop, one of which uses everyday low pricing and another that uses a high/low pricing strategy. Do you believe that each store's chosen strategy is appropriate for the type of merchandise it sells and the market of customers to whom it is appealing? Justify your answer.

5. As the product manager for Whirlpool's line of washing machines, you are in charge of pricing new products. Your product team has developed a revolutionary new washing machine that relies on radically new technology and requires very little water to get clothes clean. This technology will likely be difficult for your competition to copy. Should you adopt a skimming or a penetration pricing strategy? Justify your answer.

6. What is the difference between a cumulative and a noncumulative quantity discount?

7. If you worked for a manufacturing firm located in Oregon and shipped merchandise all over the United States, which would be more advantageous, a zone or a uniform delivered pricing policy? Why? What if your firm were located in Kansas—would it make a difference?

8. Coupons and rebates benefit different distribution channel members. Which would you prefer if you were a manufacturer, a retailer, and a consumer? Why?

9. Suppose the president of your university got together with the presidents of all the universities in your athletic conference for lunch. They discussed what each university was going to charge for tuition the following year. Are they in violation of federal laws? Explain your answer.

10. Imagine that you are the newly hired brand manager for a restaurant that is about to open. Both the local newspaper and a gourmet food magazine recently ran articles about your new head chef, calling her one of the best young chefs in the country. In response to these positive reviews, the company wants to position its brand as a premium, gourmet restaurant. Your boss asks what price you should charge for the chef's signature filet mignon dish. Other restaurants in the area charge around $40 for their own filet offerings. What steps might you undertake to determine what the new price should be?

11. You have been hired by a regional supermarket chain as the candy and snack buyer. Your shelves are dominated by national firms, like Wrigley's and Nabisco. The chain imposes a substantial slotting fee to allow new items to be added to their stock selection. Management reasons that it costs a lot to add and delete items, and besides, these slotting fees are a good source of revenue. A small, minority-operated, local firm produces several potentially interesting snack crackers and a line of gummy candy, all with natural ingredients, added vitamins, reduced sugar, and a competitive price—and they also happen to taste great. You'd love to give the firm a chance, but its managers claim the slotting fee is too high. Should your firm charge slotting fees? Are slotting fees fair to the relevant shareholders—customers, stockholders, vendors?

Quiz Yourself

1. When the first hybrid automobiles became available on the market, manufacturers had only minimal production capacity. They used a price skimming strategy primarily to _____.
   a. recoup high research and development costs
   b. signal high quality
   c. limit demand
   d. penetrate a market
   e. test consumers' price sensitivity

2. It is important to Joanne to get value for her money, but she does not want to spend time comparison shopping. Joanne will likely respond to _____ pricing but not _____ pricing.
   a. high/low; everyday low
   b. premium; everyday low
   c. discount; vertical
   d. horizontal; flattening
   e. everyday low; high/low

(Answers to these two questions can be found on page 652.)

Net Savvy

1. Go to www.coupons.com. In which product categories does this website offer coupons? Choose a product from each category.
   - How effective are coupons for selling these types of products? Why?
   - Do any sellers offer rebates through this website? Why or why not?
   - What are the benefits to the seller of using Coupons.com instead of offering coupons in a newspaper?
   - How do you think coupons.com makes money? For example, consider what companies are advertising on the site. Do the same companies who advertise on their site offer coupons?

2. Visit the website for Bag, Borrow, or Steal (www.bagborroworsteal.com) and select handbags. Click on the "Handbags," then choose "Gucci," in the Designer category on the left column, and then "Sort by" Price. What is the difference between Gucci's highest and lowest priced bags? Notice that if a product says "Waitlist," it has already been borrowed, but if it says "Borrow," then it is available for you to borrow. Are the bags that are waitlisted the highest priced or the lowest priced? How would you determine the price it charges to rent a bag?

Chapter Case Study

PRICE WARS IN THE CELLULAR MARKET

Cell phone companies may already have all the available customers. Cellular subscriptions will top 7.3 billion worldwide by the end of 2014—which will be larger than the global population.[22] Currently in the United States there are 103.1 cell phones being used for every 100 people.[23] This means there are more cellular subscriptions than there are people in the United States. Examining how cell phone companies like Verizon Wireless, AT&T, Sprint, and T-Mobile grow once they've run out of potential customers provides a glimpse into the value of strategic pricing.

The Players

With 121.3 million subscribers,[24] Verizon leads the pack. In addition to cellular phone service, it offers broadband capability through its wireless network, which was the first to a offer broadband network in the United States. Verizon not only boasted the first wireless consumer 3G multimedia service, but today it also hosts the largest 4G LTE network. Furthermore, its international presence spreads over 200 countries and has the lowest monthly churn rates, losing only 1.26 percent of customers each month.[25]

AT&T traces its roots back to 1876 and Alexander Graham Bell's discovery of the telephone. Although it lags behind Verizon in number of subscribers (110.4 million), it earns more revenue. It also claims to have the fastest mobile broadband network. Moreover, AT&T promises the widest international wireless coverage that offers 99.999 percent reliability. With its Wi-Fi network, the company again claims to have the largest international coverage of any U.S. wireless carrier.[26]

Sprint holds third place with approximately 55 million customers. The company's most recent innovation is its leading development of the first wireless 4G service.[27] The company merged with Nextel to provide walkie-talkie service in 2004, but running separate networks through the 2G Nextel service and the 3G and 4G Sprint lines has been expensive. Sprint decommissioned its Nextel services as of June 30, 2013.[28] In 2014, Sprint partnered with streaming music provider Spotify to offer its customers access to exclusive music offerings and reduced rates on the service.[29]

T-Mobile USA is owned by Deutsch Telecom and was the subject of several acquisition attempts by competitors, including AT&T and Sprint, throughout 2011 and 2012. With 46.684 million subscribers, T-Mobile relies on its global partners to ensure worldwide coverage.[30] In addition it is a member of the Open Handset Alliance, a collaboration designed to develop the Android platform and provide innovative mobile services more quickly.[31]

Market Shares and Price Wars

As the cost of cell service has continued to decline, customers' bills have remained flat or decreased. Increasing prices is not an option for building revenue in this market. With no new customers to attract, the major phone companies have sought instead to increase their share of the market. Accomplishing that goal has meant competing ferociously to attract customers from competitors. But if the companies try to lure subscribers with reduced rates, they run the very real risk of causing harm to their economic bottom line. At the same time, the players cannot afford to sit on their hands and do nothing, especially as consumers give up their home phones, leading to contraction in the landline business.

The tactics the competitors use are constantly changing and often confusing to the customer.[32] For example, in 2014, Verizon launched its "Everything More" plans that allow families to have up to four lines, unlimited talk and text, and 10 GB of shareable data for $160 per month. A week later, AT&T introduced "Mobile Share Value Plans" that not only matched the $160 price and offerings of Verizon for four lines, but also allowed families to choose to use the same features across three lines for $145 per month or $130 across two lines. Additionally, as several analysts have pointed out, cell phone companies use extremely confusing pricing structures, which likely reduces the chances a customer will switch carriers.[33] The exception to this is T-Mobile, which has responded to these pricing tactics by offering simple to understand, no-contract wireless plans costing between $40 and $80 a month for single lines.[34]

Although it may seem as though everyone is using advanced data plans on smartphones and tablets, there remains a market for voice-only options as well. Verizon Wireless cut prices for its voice-only plans and offers a 700-minute-per-month plan for a single line as low as $30. Similarly, AT&T offers similar plans. For $40 per month, AT&T subscribers can get unlimited talk and text with a basic phone (nonsmartphone). T-Mobile's cheapest plan also includes unlimited talk and text and similarly costs $40 per month. With Sprint, you'll have to go prepaid (pay at the beginning of the month instead of the end), but you can get 500 minutes of voice with unlimited text for $35 per month.

The goal of cost cuts on voice plans, according to Verizon Wireless CEO Lowell McAdam, is to get customers enrolled in more expensive unlimited plans, especially for data. Capturing market share from competitors is also important, but it does not offer the same value in terms of generating revenue. Verizon Wireless, for example, gave up an estimated $540 million in voice revenue but experienced an estimated net gain of $90 million because of changes in data plan sales and because of the healthier margins associated with data plans.[35]

Networks account for only a piece of a wireless company's revenue stream. To access voice, text, or data services, customers need handsets, which are becoming increasingly more sophisticated. But here again, companies are cutting prices on handsets in an effort to attract market share. Suppliers of Apple devices sometimes sell the iPhones for $200 less than they have paid Apple for them, just to lure subscribers to their two-year plans.

The war is far from over, especially in such a rapidly changing, frequently innovating market. The rise in demand for high-speed 4G mobile broadband use has challenged overburdened networks, and cell phone companies are forced to invest in their networks to avoid service failures and customer complaints. If voice plan usage drops further, revenue from data plans may no longer provide the margins cell phone companies need. Some wireless providers may consolidate; others will fade away.

Questions

1. Who are the key players in this industry?
2. If a price war will reduce margins, as the case suggests, why would any company embrace this strategy?
3. On what other strategy elements could the wireless companies compete?
4. What pricing tactics could Verizon use to target consumer customers?
5. What pricing tactics could Verizon use to target business customers?

Endnotes

1. Venessa Wong, "Why Is Chicken More Expensive? Ask McDonald's," *Bloomberg Businessweek*, August 28, 2013; Maureen Morrison, "Why McDonald's Mighty Wings Failed to Take Flight," *Advertising Age*, December 20, 2013.

2. Thomas T. Nagle, John E. Hogan and Joseph Zale, *The Strategy and Tactics of Pricing: A Guide to Growing More Profitability*, 5th ed. (Upper Saddle River, NJ: Pearson, 2010).

3. R. Hamilton and A. Chernev, "Low Prices Are Just the Beginning: Price Image in Retail Management," *Journal of Marketing* 77, no. 6 (2013), pp. 1–20; Dinesh K. Gauri, Minakshi Trivedi, and Dhruv Grewal, "Understanding the Determinants of Retail Strategy: An Empirical Analysis," *Journal of Retailing* 84, no. 3 (2008), pp. 256–67.

4. Michael Levy, Barton A. Weitz, and Dhruv Grewal, *Retailing Management*, 9th ed. (Burr Ridge, IL: Irwin/McGraw-Hill, 2014).

5. Abhijit Biswas et al., "Consumer Evaluations of Sale Prices: Role of the Subtraction Principle," *Journal of Marketing* 77, no. 4 (2013), pp. 49–66.

6. http://www.amazon.com.

7. Eric A. Staub, "As Prices Fall, Blu-Ray Players Are Invited Home," *The New York Times*, December 13, 2009.

8. This section draws from Levy et al., *Retailing Management*.

9. Nailya Ordabayeva and Pierre Chandon, "Predicting and Managing Consumers' Package Size Impressions," *Journal of Marketing* 77, no. 5 (2013), pp. 123–37; Xiaoyan Deng and Raji Srinivasan, "When Do Transparent Packages Increase (or Decrease) Food Consumption?" *Journal of Marketing* 77, no. 4 (2013), pp. 104–17; Sha Yang and Priya Raghubir, "Can Bottles Speak Volumes? The Effect of Package Shape on How Much to Buy," *Journal of Retailing* 81, no. 4 (2005), pp. 269–81.

10. This section is adapted from Levy et al., *Retailing Management*.

11. Personal communication with Rob Price, VP of Retail Marketing, CVS, June 16, 2009.

12. Marco Bertini and Luc Wathieu, "Research Note: Attention Arousal through Price Partitioning," *Marketing Science* 27, no. 2 (2008), pp. 236–46; Rebecca W. Hamilton and Joydeep Srivastava, "When 2+2 Is Not the Same as 1+3: Variations in Price Sensitivity across Components of Partitioned Prices," *Journal of Marketing Research* 45, no. 4 (2008), pp. 450–61.

13. http://www.brooksbrothers.com.

14. Alison Jing Xu and Robert S. Wyer Jr., "Puffery in Advertisements: The Effects of Media Context, Communication Norms and Consumer Knowledge," *Journal of Consumer Research*, August 2010.

15. J. Lindsey-Mullikin and R. D. Petty, "Marketing Tactics Discouraging Price Search: Deception and Competition," *Journal of Business Research* 64, no. 1 (2011), pp. 67–73. doi: 10.1016/j.jbusres.2009.10.003.

16. Steve Lohr, "Drafting Antitrust Case, F.T.C. Raises Pressure on Google," *The New York Times*, October 12, 2012, http://www.nytimes.com; Claire Cain Miller, "Europeans Reach Deal with Google on Searches," *The New York Times*, April 14, 2013, http://www.nytimes.com.

17. Uwe E. Reinhardt, "Ending Hospital Price Discrimination against the Uninsured," *The New York Times*, January 8, 2010.

18. Daniel M. Garrett, Michelle Burtis, and Vandy Howell, "Economics of Antitrust: An Economic Analysis of Resale Price Maintenance," http://www.GlobalCompetitionReview.com, 2008; Stephen Labaton, "Century-Old Ban Lifted on Minimum Retail Pricing," *The New York Times*, June 29, 2007.

19. "South African Airlines to Be Investigated for Alleged World Cup Price-Fixing, Report DialAFlight," *Business Wire*, February 1, 2010.

20. Tom Bawden, "Bloody Nose for OFT in Row over Tobacco Price-Fixing," *The Independent (London)*, December 13, 2011, http://www.independent.co.uk; "The Marlboro Cartel," http://www.smokingate.com.

21. Garrett et al., "Economics of Antitrust"; Labaton, "Century-Old Ban Lifted."

22. Joshua Pramis, "Number of Mobile Phones to Exceed World Population by 2014," *Digital Trends*, February 28, 2013.

23. "Wireless Quick Facts," *CTIA The Wireless Association*, http://www.ctia.org (accessed May 5, 2014).

24. "Grading the Top U.S. Wireless Carriers in the Fourth Quarter of 2013," *FierceWireless*, March 12, 2014.

25. http://aboutus.verizonwireless.com; "Grading the Top U.S. Wireless Carriers."

26. http://www.att.com/gen/investor-relations?pid=5711; "Grading the Top U.S. Wireless Carriers."

27. http://www.sprint.com/about/; "Grading the Top U.S. Wireless Carriers."

28. Roger Cheng, "Sprint Gets the Nextel Monkey Off Its Back," *CNET*, February 8, 2012, http://news.cnet.com; http://newsroom.sprint.com.

29. http://newsroom.sprint.com.

30. "Grading the Top U.S. Wireless Carriers."

31. http://www.tmobile.com/Company/CompanyInfo.aspx?tp=Abt_Tab_CompanyOverview&tsp=Abt_Sub_History.

32. Adrian Covert, "Choosing the Cheapest Cell Phone Plan Is a Headache," *CNN Money*, February 4, 2014, http://money.cnn.com.

33. Jared Newman, "Which Wireless Plan Is Cheapest?" *Time*, February 14, 2014.

34. Roy Furchgott, "T-Mobile Unveils New Pricing Plan, Kind Of," *The New York Times*, March 26, 2013; Marguerite Reardon, "T-Mobile CEO: Stop the Bull**** with Carrier Plans," *CNET*, March 26, 2013.

35. Olga Kharif, "Verizon Wireless-AT&T 'Price War' May Boost Revenues," *Bloomberg Businessweek*, January 20, 2010.

i. Maureen Morrison and Matthew Creamer, "How P&G, Ford, and Wendy's Are Redefining Value," *Advertising Age*, April 22, 2013.

ii. Elizabeth A. Harris and Stephanie Strom, "Walmart to Sell Organic Food, Undercutting Big Brands," *The New York Times*, April 10, 2014, http://www.nytimes.com; Dan Charles, "Can Wal-Mart Really Make Organic Food Cheap for Everyone?" *NPR*, April 19, 2014, http://www.wbur.org/npr/; Steven Overly, "Wal-Mart Plans to Bring Its Compete-on-Price Approach to Organic Food: Here's How," *The Washington Post*, April 10, 2014, http://www.washingtonpost.com.

iii. Carl Bialik, Elizabeth Holmes, and Ray A. Smith, "Many Discounts, Few Deals," *The Wall Street Journal*, December 15, 2010, http://online.wsj.com; Vanessa O'Connell, "It's 50% Off . . . Well, Maybe 35%. How Good Are Deals on Members-Only Web Sites?" *The Wall Street Journal*, January 16, 2010; http://www.hautelook.com; http://www.gilt.com.

iv. "Chocolate Firms Nestle and Mars Accused of Price Fixing," *BBC News*, June 7, 2013.

Credits

VALUE DELIVERY: DESIGNING THE CHANNEL AND SUPPLY CHAIN

Section Six deals with the value delivery system. It is critical that merchandise is delivered in time to stores to meet customer demand. To achieve this, retailers have initiated many innovative programs with their vendors and developed sophisticated transportation and warehousing systems. We devote two chapters to value delivery. Chapter 16 takes a look at marketing channels and how to manage the supply chain, while Chapter 17 concentrates on retailing and omnichannel marketing.

SUPPLY CHAIN AND CHANNEL MANAGEMENT

Already well established as an efficient shipper of orders, Amazon continues to seek to do even better. Currently, Amazon receives an order, labels and packages it, loads it onto a delivery truck (run by UPS or the U.S. Postal Service, depending on the day and delivery details), and waits for confirmation that this third-party logistics provider has delivered the product directly to the customer's door. In this traditional process, the online retail giant seeks to improve by adding more warehouses that can provide more customers with overnight or same-day delivery.

But two more striking innovations instead aim to reinvent the supply chain completely, to benefit both customers and itself. First, Amazon recently applied for and received a patent for its "anticipatory shipping" system, which starts readying packages for delivery before the customer even adds the item to his or her virtual cart.[1] With anticipatory shipping, Amazon boxes and ships out products that it expects customers will want, according to their previous purchases, in the belief that they are likely to order them soon. To determine what to ship, Amazon uses information from customers' previous orders, product searches, shopping cart contents, and previous returns.

This innovation promises to be particularly beneficial for popular books, movies, and games, for which people clearly announce their desire to have the item in hand the very day it is released. If Amazon can get it to their homes on that same day, it might discourage customers from visiting physical retail locations, because their wait times would be even lower than brick-and-mortar stores can offer. In this sense, Amazon is using Big Data to predict demand and thus edge out its rivals. However, critics caution that when Amazon's algorithms are incorrect, the necessary returns could grow rapidly to become quite costly. In response, Amazon has suggested that it might simply convert any unwanted deliveries into gifts, thus building goodwill among customers who receive a desirable new order for no cost.

Second, Amazon has not limited its streamlining efforts to the retailer–customer link. Instead, it has created its Vendor Flex program, which seeks to lower overall transportation costs. Among the first partners in Amazon's Vendor Flex program is Procter & Gamble (P&G), which agreed to allow Amazon to build fulfillment centers within P&G's own warehouses. The cost savings accrue because the new system eliminates the costs of transporting P&G's products to Amazon's fulfillment centers.

Not everyone is excited about this innovative new partnership, though. Companies such as Target, which have enjoyed long-term relationships with P&G, are taking notice and taking action. After learning of the Vendor Flex program between Amazon and P&G, Target reacted by moving all P&G products from prominent end-cap positions in its stores to less prestigious and less visible locations. Target also stopped using P&G as its primary source of advice for planning merchandising strategies within each category.

In this chapter, we discuss the third P, *place,* which includes all activities required to get the right product to the right customer when that customer wants it.[2] Specifically, as we noted in Chapter 1, **marketing channel management**, which also has been called **supply chain management**, refers to a set of approaches and techniques firms employ to efficiently and effectively integrate their suppliers, manufacturers, warehouses, stores, and transportation intermediaries into a seamless operation in which merchandise is produced and distributed in the right quantities, to the right locations, and at the right time, as well as to minimize systemwide costs while satisfying the service levels their customers require.[3] Students of marketing often overlook or underestimate the importance of place in the marketing mix, simply because it happens behind the scenes. Yet marketing channel ·management adds value, say for Amazon's customers, because it gets the products to them efficiently, quickly, and at low cost.

LO1 Understand the importance of marketing channels and supply chain management.

THE IMPORTANCE OF MARKETING CHANNEL/SUPPLY CHAIN MANAGEMENT

So far in this book we have reviewed the methods companies use to conduct in-depth market research, gain insights into consumer and business behaviors, segment markets, select the best target markets, develop new products and services, and set prices that provide good value. But even if firms execute these activities flawlessly, unless they can secure the placement of products in appropriate outlets in sufficient quantities exactly when customers want them, they are likely to fail. Adding Value 16.1 examines how Goya Foods recognized it needed to do a better job at getting products into stores to satisfy customers' demands and what it did about it.

Convincing wholesalers and retailers to carry new products can be more difficult than you might think. **Wholesalers** are firms that buy products from manufacturers and resell them to retailers; retailers sell products directly to consumers. For example, PenAgain, a small California-based manufacturer of ergonomic pens and other writing instruments, wanted to put its offerings in Walmart stores, but first it had to get Walmart to buy what it was selling.[4] After a tough selling session, Walmart agreed to give PenAgain a one-month trial in 500 stores, but only if it lowered its costs. PenAgain thus moved production overseas. Walmart provided no marketing support though, and PenAgain was too small to afford traditional print or television advertising, so it developed a

Adding Value 16.1   The Beans May Be Slow Cooked, but the Delivery Is Quick[i]

As Goya Foods celebrated its 75th year in business, its top managers were dealing with some very serious growing pains. Selling a wide variety of Hispanic and Latin foods, the company had achieved a dominant market share, was the largest Hispanic-owned company in the United States, and had annual sales of around $1 billion. In specific local and regional markets, demand for its products was substantial—a great success that also came with a notable challenge.

That is, many of the markets that loved Goya products had slightly different preferences, reflecting the diversity of Hispanic consumers in the United States. People of Cuban heritage wanted items made somewhat differently than consumers whose families originated in Mexico, and so on. Thus, the number of unique inventory items or stock keeping units (SKUs) that Goya provided reached over 1,600. The supply chain network grew more complex. And in all the confusion, service levels, as measured by its in-stock availability, dropped. Quite simply, with all the complexity, buyers were spending too much time manually calculating and determining shipments and inventory levels, leaving them insufficient time or energy to think strategically. Making decisions without sophisticated analytics was not something that Goya could sustain anymore.

For Goya, the solution was to automate the transportation and inventory planning processes, using software that enabled it to keep track of demand, order fulfillment, and replenishment with minimal effort. By automating its ordering processes, Goya's buyers could work smarter. For

To satisfy its diverse market of Hispanic consumers, Goya expanded the number of unique inventory items it carried to 1,600. To keep service levels high, Goya implemented an automated transportation and inventory planning system.

example, making sure delivery trucks were more efficiently used resulted in millions of dollars in transportation savings. The new system also improved its in-stock availability to 98 percent, which resulted in a proportional increase in sales.

viral marketing program and produced displays to use in the stores. A viral marketing program is one that encourages people to pass along a marketing message to other potential consumers. To keep track of sales, it relied on Walmart's Internet-based Retail Link system, though it also hired a firm that sends representatives into stores to check out display placement and customer traffic. Finally, PenAgain agreed to adhere to strict packaging, labeling, and shipping requirements. And remember, for all this effort, its entry in stores was only a test, and a very expensive gamble! But if it could succeed in Walmart stores, PenAgain would be well on its way to prosperity.

In the simplified supply chain in Exhibit 16.1, manufacturers make products and sell them to retailers or wholesalers. The exhibit would be much more complicated if we had included the suppliers of materials to manufacturers and all the manufacturers, wholesalers, and stores in a typical marketing channel.

Exhibit 16.1 represents a typical flow of manufactured goods: Manufacturers ship to a wholesaler or to a retailer's distribution center (e.g., Manufacturer 1 and Manufacturer 3) or directly to stores (Manufacturer 2). In addition, many variations on this supply chain exist. Some retail chains, such as Home Depot or Costco, function as both retailers and wholesalers. They act as retailers when they sell to consumers directly and as wholesalers when they sell to other businesses such as building contractors or restaurant owners. When manufacturers such as Avon sell directly to consumers, they perform both production and retailing activities. When Dell sells computers to a university or business, it engages in a business-to-business

EXHIBIT 16.1   Simplified Supply Chain

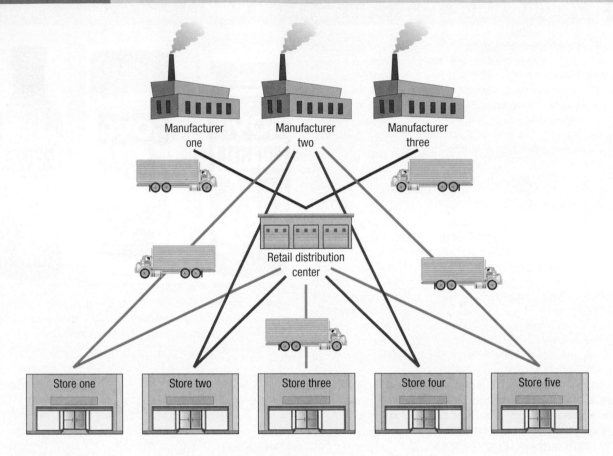

(B2B) transaction, but when it sells to students or employees individually, it is a B2C (business-to-consumer) operation.

Marketing Channels Add Value

Why do manufacturers use wholesalers or retailers? Don't these added channel members just cut into their profits? Wouldn't it be cheaper for consumers to buy directly from manufacturers? In a simple agrarian economy, the best supply chain likely does follow a direct route from manufacturer to consumer: The consumer goes to the farm and buys food directly from the farmer. Modern eat-local environmental campaigns suggest just such a process. But before the consumer can eat a fresh steak procured from a local farm, she needs to cook it. Assuming the consumer doesn't know how to make a stove and lacks the materials to do so, she must rely on a stove maker. The stove maker, which has the necessary knowledge, must buy raw materials and components from various suppliers, make the stove, and then make it available to the consumer. If the stove maker isn't located near the consumer, the stove must be transported to where the consumer has access to it. To make matters even more complicated, the consumer may want to view a choice of stoves, hear about all their features, and have the stove delivered and installed.

Each participant in the channel adds value.[5] The components manufacturer helps the stove manufacturer by supplying parts and materials. The stove maker turns the components into the stove. The transportation company gets the stove to the retailer. The retailer stores the stove until the customer wants it, educates the customer about product features, and delivers and installs the stove. At each step, the stove becomes more costly but also more valuable to the consumer.

How many companies are involved in making and getting a stove to your kitchen?

Marketing Channel Management Affects Other Aspects of Marketing

Every marketing decision is affected by and has an effect on marketing channels. When products are designed and manufactured, how and when the critical components reach the factory must be coordinated with production. The sales department must coordinate its delivery promises with the factory or distribution or fulfillment centers. A distribution center, a facility for the receipt, storage, and redistribution of goods to company stores, may be operated by retailers, manufacturers, or distribution specialists.[6] Similar to a distribution center, instead of shipping to stores, fulfillment centers are used to ship directly to customers. Furthermore, advertising and promotion must be coordinated with those departments that control inventory and transportation. There is no faster way to lose credibility with customers than to promise deliveries or run a promotion and then not have the merchandise when the customer expects it.

DESIGNING MARKETING CHANNELS

LO2 Understand the difference between direct and indirect marketing channels.

When a firm is just starting out or entering a new market, it doesn't typically have the option of designing the best marketing channel structure—that is, choosing from whom it buys or to whom it sells. A new sporting goods retailer may not have the option of carrying all the manufacturer lines it wants because other competing retailers in its market area might carry the same products. On the other side, a small specialty sporting goods apparel manufacturer may not be able to place its products in major stores like Sports Authority because its line is unproven, and the products might duplicate lines that the retailer already carries. Chapter 17 discusses how manufacturers choose their retailer partners in more depth.

Although there are thus various constraints on marketing channel partners with regard to the design of the best channel structure, all marketing channels take the form of a direct channel, an indirect channel, or some combination thereof.

Direct Marketing Channel

As shown in Exhibit 16.2, there are no intermediaries between the buyer and seller in a direct marketing channel. Typically, the seller is a manufacturer, such as when a carpentry business sells bookcases through its own store and online to individual consumers. The seller also can be an individual, such as when a knitter sells blankets and scarves at craft fairs, on Etsy, and through eBay. (Recall our discussion of consumer-to-consumer [C2C] transactions in Chapter 1.) When the buyer is another business, such as when Boeing sells planes to JetBlue, the marketing channel still is direct, but in this case, the transaction is a business-to-business one (see Chapter 7).

Indirect Marketing Channel

In indirect marketing channels, one or more intermediaries work with manufacturers to provide goods and services to customers. In some cases,

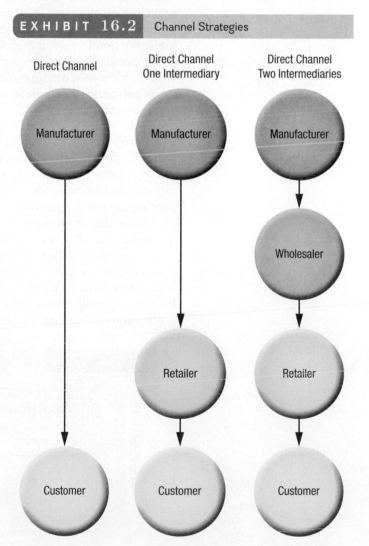

EXHIBIT 16.2 Channel Strategies

Direct Channel

Direct Channel One Intermediary

Direct Channel Two Intermediaries

Manufacturer

Manufacturer

Manufacturer

Wholesaler

Retailer

Retailer

Customer

Customer

Customer

only one intermediary might be involved. Automobile manufacturers such as Ford and General Motors often use indirect distribution, such that dealers act as retailers, as shown in the middle of Exhibit 16.2. The right side of Exhibit 16.2 reveals how wholesalers are more common when the company does not buy in sufficient quantities to make it cost effective for the manufacturer to deal directly with them—independent book sellers, wine merchants, or independent drug stores, for example. Wholesalers are also prevalent in less developed economies, in which large retailers are rare.

LO3 Describe how marketing channels are managed.

MANAGING THE MARKETING CHANNEL AND SUPPLY CHAIN

Marketing channels and supply chains comprise various buying entities, such as retailers and wholesalers; sellers, such as manufacturers or wholesalers; and facilitators of the exchange, such as transportation companies. Similar to interpersonal interactions, their relationships can range from close working partnerships to one-time arrangements. In almost all cases, though, interactions occur because the parties want something from each other: Home Depot wants hammers from Stanley Tool Company; Stanley wants an opportunity to sell its tools to the general public; both companies want UPS to deliver the merchandise.

Each member of the marketing channel also performs a specialized role. If one member believes that another has failed to do its job correctly or efficiently, it can replace that member. So, if Stanley isn't getting good service from UPS, it can switch to FedEx. If Home Depot believes its customers do not perceive Stanley tools as a good value, it may buy from another tool company. Home Depot even could decide to make its own tools or use its own trucks to pick up tools from Stanley. However, anytime a marketing channel member is replaced, the function it has performed remains, so someone needs to complete it.[7]

If a marketing channel is to run efficiently, the participating members must cooperate. Often, however, supply chain members have conflicting goals, and this may result in channel conflict (Exhibit 16.3). For instance, Stanley wants Home Depot to carry all its tools but not those of its competitors so that Stanley can maximize its sales. But Home Depot carries a mix of tool brands so it can maximize the sales in its tool category. When supply chain members that buy and sell to one another are not in agreement about their goals, roles, or rewards, vertical channel conflict or discord results.

Horizontal channel conflict can also occur when there is disagreement or discord among members at the same level in a marketing channel, such as two competing retailers or two competing manufacturers. As we mentioned in the opening vignette, Target experiences a conflict with Amazon because of its Vendor Flex program with Procter & Gamble (P&G). Amazon benefits from the program, which lowers its transportation costs, but Target believes that it gives its competitor an unfair advantage.

EXHIBIT 16.3   Vertical versus Horizontal Channel Conflict

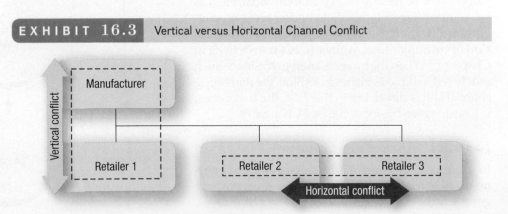

GOING BACK TO REGULAR TOOLS WOULD BE LIKE

GOING BACK TO BLACK AND WHITE TV.

FatMax XTREME
Introducing the next level of high-performance hand tools. Designed to get the job done faster, easier, better. Learn more at stanleytools.com/xtreme

STANLEY

The Home Depot and Stanley Tool Company have a mutually beneficial partnership. The Home Depot buys tools from Stanley because their customers find value in Stanley products. Stanley sells tools to Home Depot because they have established an excellent market for its products.

Avoiding vertical channel conflicts demands open, honest communication. Buyers and vendors all must understand what drives the other party's business, their roles in the relationship, each firm's strategies, and any problems that might arise over the course of the relationship. Amazon and P&G recognize that it is in their common interest to remain profitable business partners. Amazon's customers demand and expect to find P&G products on its website; P&G needs the sales generated through Amazon. Amazon cannot demand prices so low that P&G cannot make money, and P&G must be flexible enough to accommodate the needs of this important customer. With a common goal, both firms then have the incentive to cooperate because they know that by doing so, each will boost its sales.

Common goals also help sustain the relationship when expected benefits fail to arise. If one P&G shipment fails to reach the Amazon section of one of its fulfilment centers, due to an uncontrollable event such as a demand forecasting miscalculation, Amazon does not suddenly call off the whole arrangement. Instead, it recognizes the incident as a simple, isolated mistake and maintains the good working relationship, because Amazon knows that both it and P&G are committed to the same goals in the long run.

In this sense, their partnership exhibits both of the non–mutually exclusive ways that exist to manage a marketing channel or supply chain: Coordinate the channel using a vertical marketing system and develop strong relationships with marketing channel partners—topics we now examine.

Managing the Marketing Channel and Supply Chain through Vertical Marketing Systems

Although conflict is likely in any marketing channel, it is generally more pronounced when the channel members are independent entities. Marketing channels that are more closely aligned, whether by contract or ownership, share common goals and therefore are less prone to conflict.

In an independent or conventional marketing channel, several independent members—a manufacturer, a wholesaler, and a retailer—attempt to satisfy their own

Amazon and Procter & Gamble recognize that it is in their common interest to remain profitable business partners.

EXHIBIT 16.4   Independent versus Vertical Marketing Channels

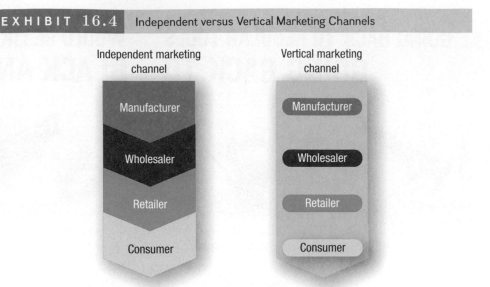

objectives and maximize their profits, often at the expense of the other members, as we portray in Exhibit 16.4 (left). None of the participants have any control over the others. Using our previous example, the first time Walmart purchases pens from PenAgain, both parties likely try to extract as much profit from the deal as possible. After the deal is consummated, neither party feels any responsibility to the other.

Over time, though, Walmart and PenAgain might develop a relationship marked by routinized, automatic transactions, such that Walmart's customers come to expect PenAgain products in stores, and PenAgain depends on Walmart to buy a good portion of its output. This scenario represents the first phase of a vertical marketing system, a marketing channel in which the members act as a unified system, as in Exhibit 16.4 (right). Three types of vertical marketing systems—administered, contractual, and corporate—reflect increasing phases of formalization and control. The more formal the vertical marketing system, the less likely conflict is to ensue.

Administered Vertical Marketing System The Walmart–PenAgain marketing channel relationship offers an example of an administered vertical marketing system: There is no common ownership or contractual relationships, but the dominant channel member controls or holds the balance of power. Because of its size and relative power, Walmart imposes controls on PenAgain. Power in a marketing channel exists when one firm has the means or ability to dictate the actions of another member at a different level of distribution (Exhibit 16.5). A retailer like Walmart exercises its power over suppliers in several ways. With its reward power, Walmart offers rewards, often a monetary incentive, if PenAgain will do what Walmart wants it to do. Coercive power arises when Walmart threatens to punish or punishes the other channel member for not undertaking certain tasks, such as if it were to delay payment to PenAgain for a late delivery. Walmart may also have referent power over PenAgain if the supplier desperately wants to be associated with Walmart, because being known as an important Walmart supplier enables PenAgain to attract other retailers' business. If Walmart exerts expertise power over PenAgain, it relies on its expertise with marketing pens. Because Walmart has vast information about the office supply and back-to-school markets, it can exert information power over PenAgain by providing or withholding such important market information. Finally, legitimate power is based on getting a channel member, such as PenAgain, to behave in a certain way because of a contractual agreement between the two firms. As Walmart deals with PenAgain and its other suppliers, it likely exerts multiple types of power to influence their

EXHIBIT 16.5 Bases of Power

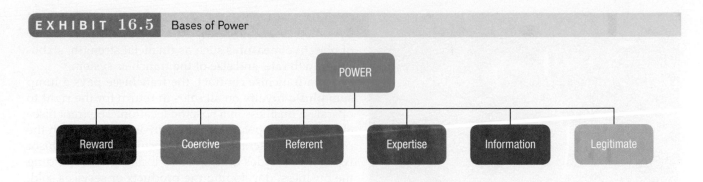

behaviors. If either party dislikes the way the relationship is going though, it can simply walk away.

Contractual Vertical Marketing System Over time, Walmart and PenAgain may formalize their relationship by entering into contracts that dictate various terms, such as how much Walmart will buy each month and at what price, as well as the penalties for late deliveries. In contractual vertical marketing systems like this, independent firms at different levels of the marketing channel join through contracts to obtain economies of scale and coordination and to reduce conflict.[8]

Franchising is the most common type of contractual vertical marketing system. Franchising is a contractual agreement between a franchisor and a franchisee that allows the franchisee to operate a retail outlet using a name and format developed and supported by the franchisor. Exhibit 16.6 lists the United States'

EXHIBIT 16.6 Top 10 Franchises for 2014

Rank	Franchise Name	Number of U.S. Outlets	Startup Costs
1	Anytime Fitness **Fitness Center**	2,425	$56.3K–353.9K
2	Hampton Hotels **Midprice Hotels**	1,942	$3.7M–13.52M
3	Subway **Subs, salads**	41,121	$85.69K–262.85K
4	Supercuts **Hair Salon**	2,324	$108.75K–203.6K
5	Jimmy John's Gourmet Sandwiches **Gourmet Sandwiches**	1,872	$300.5K–489.5K
6	7-Eleven Inc. **Convenience Stores**	50,944	$30.79K–1.63M
7	Servpro **Insurance/disaster restoration and cleaning**	1,614	$134.8K–183.44K
8	Denny's Inc. **Family Restaurant**	1,697	$1.17M–2.4M
9	Pizza Hut Inc. **Pizza, pasta, wings**	14,357	$297K–2.1M
10	Dunkin' Donuts **Coffee shop**	10,862	$294K–1.51M

Source: Entrepreneur's 2014 Franchise 500, www.entrepreneur.com.

Anytime Fitness was ranked the number one franchise by Entrepreneur *magazine in 2014.*

top franchise opportunities. These rankings, determined by *Entrepreneur* magazine, are created using a number of objective measures such as financial strength, stability, growth rate, and size of the franchise system.[9]

In a franchise contract, the franchisee pays a lump sum plus a royalty on all sales in return for the right to operate a business in a specific location. The franchisee also agrees to operate the outlet in accordance with the procedures prescribed by the franchisor. The franchisor typically provides assistance in locating and building the business, developing the products or services sold, management training, and advertising. To maintain the franchisee's reputation, the franchisor also makes sure that all outlets provide the same quality of services and products.

A franchise system combines the entrepreneurial advantages of owning a business with the efficiencies of vertical marketing systems that function under single ownership (i.e., a corporate system, as we discuss next). Franchisees are motivated to make their stores successful because they receive the profits after they pay the royalty to the franchisor. The franchisor is motivated to develop new products, services, and systems and to promote the franchise because it receives royalties on all sales. Advertising, product development, and system development are all done efficiently by the franchisor, with costs shared by all franchisees.

Corporate Vertical Marketing System In a corporate vertical marketing system, the parent company has complete control and can dictate the priorities and objectives of the marketing channel because it owns multiple segments of the channel, such as manufacturing plants, warehouse facilities, and retail outlets. By virtue of its ownership and resulting control, potential conflict among segments of the channel is lessened.

American Apparel, a clothing manufacturer based in Los Angeles, California, represents a corporate vertical marketing system because it manufactures its own products rather than having contractual relationships with other firms, and it operates its own retail stores selling T-shirts and other men's and women's sportswear. With this corporate ownership structure, it is able to bring fashion-sensitive items from the idea stage to market in a very short time.

Managing Marketing Channels and Supply Chains through Strategic Relationships

American Apparel represents a corporate vertical marketing system because it manufactures its own products and operates its own retail stores.

There is more to managing marketing channels and supply chains than simply exercising power over other members in an administered system or establishing a contractual or corporate vertical marketing system. There is also a human side.

In a conventional marketing channel, relationships between members reflect their arguments over the split of the profit pie: If one party gets ahead, the other party falls behind. Sometimes this type of transaction is acceptable if the parties have no interest in a long-term relationship. If Walmart believes that PenAgain's ergonomic pens are just a short-term fad, it may only be interested in purchasing once. In that case, it might seek to get the best one-time price it can, even if doing so means that PenAgain will make very little money and therefore might not want to sell to Walmart again.

More frequently, firms seek a strategic relationship, also called a partnering relationship, in which the marketing channel members are committed to maintaining the relationship over the long term and investing in opportunities that are mutually beneficial. In a conventional or administered marketing channel, there are significant incentives to establish a strategic relationship, even without contracts or ownership relationships. Both parties benefit because the size of the profit pie has increased, so both the buyer and the seller increase their sales and profits. These strategic relationships are created explicitly to uncover and exploit joint opportunities, so members depend on and trust each other heavily; share goals and agree on how to accomplish those goals; and are willing to take risks, share confidential information, and make significant investments for the sake of the relationship. Successful strategic relationships require mutual trust, open communication, common goals, interdependence, and credible commitments.

Mutual Trust Mutual trust holds a strategic relationship together. Trust is the belief that a partner is honest (i.e., reliable, stands by its word, sincere, fulfills obligations) and benevolent (i.e., concerned about the other party's welfare). When vendors and buyers trust each other, they are more willing to share relevant ideas, clarify goals and problems, and communicate efficiently. Information shared between the parties, such as inventory positions in stores, thus becomes increasingly comprehensive, accurate, and timely.

With trust, there's also less need for the supply chain members to constantly monitor and check up on each other's actions, because each believes the other won't take advantage, even if given the opportunity. Although it is important in all relationships, monitoring supply chain members becomes particularly pertinent when suppliers are located in less developed countries, where issues such as the use of child labor, poor working conditions, and below-subsistence wages have become a shared responsibility. Ethical and Societal Dilemma 16.1 highlights how Apple has both stumbled in this responsibility and changed its practices to improve its dedication to ethical choices.

Open Communication To share information, develop sales forecasts together, and coordinate deliveries, Walmart and its suppliers maintain open and honest communication. This maintenance may sound easy in principle, but some businesses don't tend to share information with their business partners. But open, honest communication is a key to developing successful relationships because supply chain members need to understand what is driving each other's business, their roles in the relationship, each firm's strategies, and any problems that arise over the course of the relationship.

Common Goals Supply chain members must have common goals for a successful relationship to develop. Shared goals give both members of the relationship an incentive to pool their strengths and abilities and exploit potential opportunities together. Such commonality also offers an assurance that the other partner won't do anything to hinder the achievement of those goals within the relationship.

Walmart and its suppliers recognize that it is in their common interest to be strategic partners. Walmart needs its suppliers to satisfy its customers, and those manufacturers recognize that if they can keep Walmart happy, they will have more than enough business for years to come. With common goals, both firms have an incentive to cooperate, because they know that by doing so, both can boost sales. If Walmart needs a special production run of pens to meet demand for back-to-school buyers, PenAgain will work to meet the challenge. If PenAgain has difficulty financing its inventory, it is in Walmart's best interest to help it, because they are committed to the same goals in the long run.

Ethical & Societal Dilemma 16.1   Do Customers Care More about the Newest iPhone or about Working Conditions in China?[ii]

An iPad user reading a recent issue of *The New York Times* on his or her tablet might have suffered a strange sense of guilt. The newspaper published reports of labor abuses that seemingly run rampant in the Chinese factories responsible for producing Apple's most popular products. These in-depth reports cataloged a long list of failures: the presence of child workers, more than 12-hour shifts, regular workweeks of longer than 60 hours, workers housed in tiny dormitories with approximately 20 people limited to three rooms, allegations of suicides, and lax safety standards that have led to fatal explosions.

The reports focus mostly on a Foxconn factory in Chengdu, in southwestern China, that manufactures iPhones and iPads. An explosion caused by insufficient ventilation of aluminum dust (created when the cases for the gadgets are polished) in May 2011 killed four workers. A similar explosion followed six months later at another factory. The ensuing investigations by *The New York Times* revealed multiple other violations of the code of conduct that Apple has established for its suppliers.

With this code of conduct, as well as the frequent audits it performs, Apple asserts that it is doing the best that it can to ensure its suppliers live up to reasonable standards and fair labor practices. An anonymous former Apple executive asserts, "There is a genuine, companywide commitment to the code of conduct." Yet abuses continue, as Apple's own corporate responsibility reports reveal. Audits show that several supply companies continue to engage in labor practices that violate the code, with few punishments or changes to the supply chain.

Part of the reason stems from Apple's need for secrecy—once it finds a supply partner that can manufacturer its high-tech gadgets, it wants to maintain that relationship to avoid any leakage of innovation information. So even if a supplier violates the code again and again, Apple is unlikely to switch.

Furthermore, Apple's focus on innovation means that it must work constantly to come up with new ideas and products, which it needs to produce quickly and in sufficient quantities to keep customers happy. This demanding supply chain leaves little room for flexibility. When Apple says it needs 1 million products, then its supplier is going to do whatever it takes to get those products ready in time. The code of conduct might ask that factory workers be limited to 60-hour workweeks, but in truth, Apple is asking the factories to keep running all day, every day, to make the order. In fact, an investigation by the Fair Labor Association in late 2013 found that while working conditions are improving, Foxconn facilities continue to require their workers to exceed the legal limits for overtime hours.

To keep its costs low, Apple also offers very slim profit margins to suppliers. In turn, these factories aim to reduce their own costs. Another Apple supplier thus began using a toxic chemical, instead of rubbing alcohol, to polish the screens of iPhones, because the chemical dries faster. But it exposes workers to the threat of paralysis and nerve damage.

The primary reason for these labor abuses may come only at the end of the supply chain—the consumer. A survey of Apple consumers showed that only 2 percent of them recognized labor issues as a concern. In a remarkably succinct summary of the challenge, another anonymous Apple executive asserted, "You can either manufacture in comfortable, worker-friendly factories, or you can reinvent the product every year, and make it better and faster and cheaper, which requires factories that seem harsh by American standards. And right now, customers care more about a new iPhone than working conditions in China."

Although Apple attempts to monitor its channel partners' behavior with regard to labor issues, sometimes abuses fall through the cracks.

Interdependence When supply chain members view their goals and ultimate success as intricately linked, they develop deeper long-term relationships. Interdependence between supply chain members that is based on mutual benefits is key to developing and sustaining the relationship.[10] Walmart's suppliers recognize that without Walmart, their sales would be significantly less. Although certainly the more powerful member of the supply chain, Walmart also recognizes that it can depend on these suppliers to be a dependable source of supply, thus enabling it to have a very efficient marketing channel.

Credible Commitments Successful relationships develop because both parties make credible commitments to, or tangible investments in, the relationship. These commitments go beyond just making the hollow statement, "I want to be your partner"; they involve spending money to improve the products or services provided to the customer and on information technology to improve supply chain efficiency.[11] As our chapter opener described, Amazon and P&G have worked closely to set up their Vendor Flex program, enabling Amazon to operate fulfillment centers within P&G's own warehouses and thereby lower transportation expenses.

Similar to many other elements of marketing, managing the marketing channel can seem like an easy task at first glance: Put the right merchandise in the right place at the right time. But the various elements and actors involved in a marketing channel create its unique and compelling complexities and require firms to work carefully to ensure they are achieving the most efficient and effective chain possible. We now turn our attention to how information and merchandise flow through marketing channels.

CHECK YOURSELF

1. What is the difference between an indirect and a direct marketing channel?

2. What are the differences among the three types of vertical marketing systems?

3. How do firms develop strong strategic partnerships with their marketing channel partners?

MAKING INFORMATION FLOW THROUGH MARKETING CHANNELS

 LO4 Describe the flow of information and merchandise in the marketing channel.

Information flows from the customer to stores, to and from distribution centers, possibly to and from wholesalers, to and from product manufacturers, and then on to the producers of any components and the suppliers of raw materials. To simplify our discussion—and because information flows are similar in other marketing channel links and B2B channels—we shorten the supply chain in this section to exclude wholesalers as well as the link from suppliers to manufacturers. Exhibit 16.7 illustrates the flow of information that starts when a customer buys a Sony HDTV at Best Buy. The flow follows these steps:

Flow 1 (Customer to Store): The sales associate at Best Buy scans the Universal Product Code (UPC) tag on the HDTV packaging, and the customer receives a receipt. The UPC tag is the black-and-white bar code found on most merchandise. It contains a 13-digit code that indicates the manufacturer of the item, a description of the item, information about special packaging, and special promotions.[12] In the future, RFID tags, discussed later in this chapter, may replace UPC tags.

Flow 2 (Store to Buyer): The point-of-sale (POS) terminal records the purchase information and electronically sends it to the buyer at Best Buy's corporate office. The sales information is incorporated into an inventory management system and used to monitor and analyze sales and decide to reorder more HDTVs, change a price, or plan a promotion. Buyers also send information to stores about overall sales for the chain, ways to display the merchandise, upcoming promotions, and so on.

Flow 3 (Buyer to Manufacturer): The purchase information from each Best Buy store is typically aggregated by the retailer as a whole, which creates an order for new merchandise and sends it to Sony. The buyer at Best Buy may

EXHIBIT 16.7   Information Flows

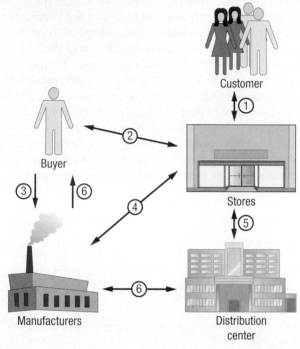

also communicate directly with Sony to get information and negotiate prices, shipping dates, promotional events, or other merchandise-related issues.

Flow 4 (Store to Manufacturer): In some situations, the sales transaction data are sent directly from the store to the manufacturer, and the manufacturer decides when to ship more merchandise to the distribution centers and the stores. In other situations, especially when merchandise is reordered frequently, the ordering process is done automatically, bypassing the buyers. By working together, the retailer and manufacturer can better satisfy customer needs.

Flow 5 (Store to Distribution Center): Stores also communicate with the Best Buy distribution center to coordinate deliveries and check inventory status. When the store inventory drops to a specified level, more HDTVs are shipped to the store, and the shipment information is sent to the Best Buy computer system.

Flow 6 (Manufacturer to Distribution Center and Buyer): When the manufacturer ships the HDTVs to the Best Buy distribution center, it sends an advanced shipping notice to the distribution centers. An advanced shipping notice (ASN) is an electronic document that the supplier sends the retailer in advance of a shipment to tell the retailer exactly what to expect in the shipment. The center then makes appointments for trucks to make the delivery at a specific time, date, and loading dock. When the shipment is received at the distribution center, the buyer is notified and authorizes payment to the vendor.

Data Warehouse

Purchase data collected at the point of sale (information flow 2 in Exhibit 16.7) goes into a huge database known as a data warehouse, similar to those described in Chapter 10. Using the data warehouse, the CEO can learn not only how the

The flow of information starts when the UPC tag is scanned at the point-of-purchase.

corporation is generally doing but also look at the data aggregated by quarter for a merchandise division, a region of the country, or the total corporation. A buyer may be more interested in a particular manufacturer in a certain store on a particular day. Analysts from various levels of the retail operation extract information from the data warehouse to make a plethora of marketing decisions about developing and replenishing merchandise assortments.

In some cases, manufacturers also have access to this data warehouse. They communicate with retailers by using electronic data interchange (EDI) and supply chain systems known as vendor-managed inventory.

In information flows 3, 4, and 6 in Exhibit 16.7, the retailer and manufacturer exchange business documents through EDI. Electronic data interchange (EDI) is the computer-to-computer exchange of business documents from a retailer to a vendor and back. In addition to sales data, purchase orders, invoices, and data about returned merchandise can be transmitted back and forth. With EDI, vendors can transmit information about on-hand inventory status, vendor promotions, and cost changes to the retailer, as well as information about purchase order changes, order status, retail prices, and transportation routings. Thus EDI enables channel members to communicate more quickly and with fewer errors than in the past, ensuring that merchandise moves from vendors to retailers more quickly.

Vendor-managed inventory (VMI) is an approach for improving marketing channel efficiency in which the manufacturer is responsible for maintaining the retailer's inventory levels in each of its stores.[13] By sharing the data in the retailer's data warehouse and communicating that information via EDI, the manufacturer automatically sends merchandise to the retailer's store or distribution or fulfillment center when the inventory at the store reaches a prespecified level.[14]

In ideal conditions, the manufacturer replenishes inventories in quantities that meet the retailer's immediate demand, reducing stockouts with minimal inventory. In addition to providing a better match between retail demand and supply, VMI can reduce the vendor's and the retailer's costs. Manufacturer salespeople no longer need to spend time generating orders on items that are already in the stores, and their role shifts to selling new items and maintaining relationships. Retail buyers and planners no longer need to monitor inventory levels and place orders.

CHECK YOURSELF

1. What are the marketing channel links associated with each information flow?
2. How do marketing channel members use data warehouses to make decisions?
3. What is EDI and how is it used?
4. Why do some marketing channels use VMI, while others do not?

MAKING MERCHANDISE FLOW THROUGH MARKETING CHANNELS

Exhibit 16.8 illustrates different types of merchandise flows:

1. Sony to Best Buy's distribution centers, or
2. Sony directly to stores.
3. If the merchandise goes through distribution centers, it is then shipped to stores,
4. and then to the customer.

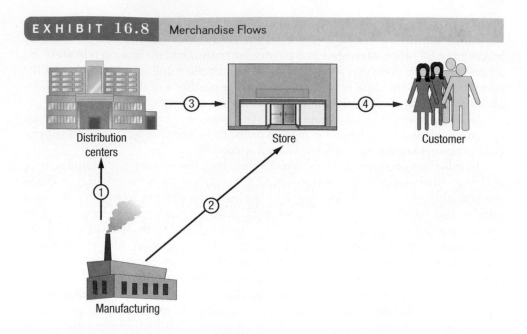

EXHIBIT 16.8   Merchandise Flows

Making merchandise flow involves first deciding whether the merchandise will go from the manufacturer to a retailer's distribution center or directly on to stores. Once in a distribution center, multiple activities take place before it is shipped on to a store.

Distribution Centers versus Direct Store Delivery

As indicated in Exhibit 16.8, manufacturers can ship merchandise directly to a retailer's stores—direct store delivery (flow 2)—or to their distribution centers (flow 1). Although manufacturers and retailers may collaborate, the ultimate decision is usually up to the retailer and depends on the characteristics of the merchandise and the nature of demand. To determine which distribution system—distribution centers or direct store delivery—is better, retailers consider the total cost associated with each alternative and the customer service criterion of having the right merchandise at the store when the customer wants to buy it.

There are several advantages to using a distribution center:

- More accurate sales forecasts are possible when retailers combine forecasts for many stores serviced by one distribution center rather than doing a forecast for each store. Consider a set of 50 Target stores, serviced by a single distribution center that each carries Michael Graves toasters. Each store normally stocks 5 units for a total of 250 units in the system. By carrying the item at each store, the retailer must develop individual forecasts, each with the possibility of errors that could result in either too much or too little merchandise. Alternatively, by delivering most of the inventory to a distribution center and feeding the stores merchandise as they need it, the effects of forecast errors for the individual stores are minimized, and less backup inventory is needed to prevent stockouts.

- Distribution centers enable the retailer to carry less merchandise in the individual stores, which results in lower inventory investments systemwide. If the stores get frequent deliveries from the distribution center, they need to carry relatively less extra merchandise as backup stock.

- It is easier to avoid running out of stock or having too much stock in any particular store because merchandise is ordered from the distribution center as needed.

- Retail store space is typically much more expensive than space at a distribution center, and distribution centers are better equipped than stores to prepare merchandise for sale. As a result, many retailers find it cost effective to store merchandise and get it ready for sale at a distribution center rather than in individual stores.

But distribution centers aren't appropriate for all retailers. If a retailer has only a few outlets, the expense of a distribution center is probably unwarranted. Also, if many outlets are concentrated in metropolitan areas, merchandise can be consolidated and delivered by the vendor directly to all the stores in one area economically. Direct store delivery gets merchandise to the stores faster and thus is used for perishable goods (meat and produce), items that help create the retailer's image of being the first to sell the latest product (e.g., video games), or fads. Finally, some manufacturers provide direct store delivery for retailers to ensure that their products are on the store's shelves, properly displayed, and fresh. For example, employees delivering Frito-Lay snacks directly to supermarkets replace products that have been on the shelf too long and are stale, replenish products that have been sold, and arrange products so they are neatly displayed.

Superior Service 16.1 explores how the two retail giants Amazon and Walmart are vying to win the same-day grocery delivery battle.

The Distribution (or Fulfillment) Center

The distribution center performs the following activities: management of inbound transportation; receiving and checking; storing, and cross-docking; getting merchandise floor ready; ticketing and marking; preparing to ship merchandise to store; and shipping merchandise to stores. Fulfillment centers perform the same functions, but because they deliver directly to customers, rather than to stores, they do not have to get merchandise floor ready. To illustrate these activities being undertaken in a distribution center, we'll continue our example of Sony HDTVs being shipped to a Best Buy distribution center.

Management of Inbound Transportation Traditionally, buyers focused their efforts, when working with vendors, on developing merchandise assortments, negotiating prices, and arranging joint promotions. Now, buyers and planners are much more involved in coordinating the physical flow of merchandise to stores. Planners are employees responsible for the financial planning and analysis of merchandise and its allocation to stores. The TV buyer has arranged for a truckload of HDTVs to be delivered to its Houston, Texas, distribution center on Monday between 1:00 and 3:00 p.m. The buyer also specifies how the merchandise should be placed on pallets for easy unloading.

The truck must arrive within the specified time because the distribution center has all of its 100 receiving docks allocated throughout the day, and much of the merchandise on this particular truck is going to be shipped to stores that evening. Unfortunately, the truck was delayed in a snowstorm. The dispatcher—the person who coordinates deliveries to the distribution center—reassigns the truck delivering the HDTVs to a Wednesday morning delivery slot and charges the firm several hundred dollars for missing its delivery time. Although many manufacturers pay transportation expenses, some retailers negotiate with their vendors to absorb this expense. These retailers believe they can lower their net merchandise cost and better control merchandise flow if they negotiate directly with trucking companies and consolidate shipments from many vendors.

Receiving and Checking Using UPC or RFID Receiving is the process of recording the receipt of merchandise as it arrives at a distribution center. Checking is the process of going through the goods upon receipt to make sure they arrived undamaged and that the merchandise ordered was the merchandise received.

Superior Service 16.1   Who Will Win the Same-Day Grocery Delivery War: Amazon or Walmart?[iii]

Amazon has more than 89 fulfillment centers, with more to come. The complex machinery and supply chain mechanisms allow Amazon to ship out products in less than 2.5 hours from the time a customer clicks "Place Your Order." Yet, fulfillment center teams are always working to develop innovative ways to cut the time down even further. In addition to warehouse speed, these centers excel in proximity. Amazon has spent billions building centers closer and closer to customers.

Now Amazon is expanding its grocery delivery business, AmazonFresh. Previously available only in Seattle, Amazon sees AmazonFresh as the future of shopping. Customers can get whatever they want, whenever they want, wherever they want, and as fast as they demand it. During a recent launch in Los Angeles, customers enjoyed free trials of PrimeFresh, the upgraded version of Amazon Prime, including

Walmart's Superama can profitably deliver groceries in Mexico, partly because the cost of doing so is much lower than in the United States.

free shipping of products and free delivery of groceries for orders over $35. In both Los Angeles and Seattle, Amazon maintains a fleet of Fresh trucks that deliver everything from full-course meals to chocolate from local merchants. As Amazon evolves into a same-day delivery service, its fleet could become yet another competitive advantage.

Yet AmazonFresh remains a challenge, mainly because of the differences associated with grocery products: It cannot ship milk the same way it ships diapers. Despite the tremendous logistical and economic hurdles to creating a same-day delivery service, Amazon hopes to expand its grocery customers and turn monthly customers to weekly or even twice weekly buyers.

In Mexico, Walmart has achieved the goal of same-day grocery delivery, where Superama, its high-end grocery chain, delivers groceries in as little as three hours. When Superama first began home delivery in 1993, managers would take orders by telephone or fax. As volume increased, it created a web page and then a mobile application that today accounts for approximately 20 percent of Superama's online orders. Such e-commerce has been a success, though Walmart also uses portable credit card terminals to limit customers' perceptions of the risk of typing in their card information online.

Much of this delivery success in Mexico is a result of the nation's densely populated urban areas. Demand is highest in Mexico City, which also accounts for much of Mexico's wealth. Due to traffic congestion and more dual-income families, demand for grocery deliveries is high; most of the deliveries are made by freelance drivers who get $1.50 per delivery using their own transportation, rather than relying on a fleet of Walmart-owned trucks.

Walmart is betting big on the Mexican market as a "detonator for growth" and seeks to triple the number of stores offering grocery delivery in Mexico within a year. Superama's target market is households with income of $3,000 a month, or 35 percent of the nation's population. As one of Walmart's largest foreign markets, Mexico contributes $27 billion (or 6 percent) to the retailer's annual sales. Superama also has helped Walmart dominate the market (92 percent share) for online grocery shopping in Mexico.

Thus two retail giants have staked their claims, relying on their distinct capabilities. Considering the delivery cost advantages in Mexico and Amazon's head start in the United States, can Walmart catch its Internet-only rival in the U.S. same-day grocery delivery market? And just as important, how much does it need to do so?

In the past, checking merchandise was a very labor-intensive and time-consuming process. Today, however, many distribution systems using EDI are designed to minimize, if not eliminate, these processes. The advance shipping notice (ASN) tells the distribution center what should be in each carton. A UPC label or radio frequency identification (RFID) tag on the shipping carton that identifies the carton's contents is scanned and automatically counted as it is being received and checked. Radio frequency identification (RFID) tags are tiny computer chips that automatically transmit to a special scanner all the information about a container's contents or individual products. Approximately as large as a pinhead, these RFID tags consist of an antenna and a chip that contains an electronic product code that stores far more information about a product than bar (UPC) codes can. The tags also act as passive tracking devices, signaling their presence over a radio frequency when they pass within a few yards of a special scanner. The tags have long been used in high-cost applications, such as automated highway toll systems and security identification badges. As the cost of the tags and implementation technology has decreased, their uses have become more prevalent in retail supply chain applications.

Walmart speeds merchandise from its distribution centers to stores.

Storing and Cross-Docking After the merchandise is received and checked, it is either stored or cross-docked. When merchandise is stored, the cartons are transported by a conveyor system and forklift trucks to racks that go from the distribution center's floor to its ceiling. Then, when the merchandise is needed in the stores, a forklift driver or a robot goes to the rack, picks up the carton, and places it on a conveyor system that routes the carton to the loading dock of a truck going to the store.

Using a cross-docking distribution center, merchandise cartons are prepackaged by the vendor for a specific store. The UPC or RFID labels on the carton indicate the store to which it is to be sent. The vendor also may affix price tags to each item in the carton. Because the merchandise is ready for sale, it is placed on a conveyor system that routes it from the unloading dock at which it was received to the loading dock for the truck going to the specific store—hence the name *cross-docked*. The cartons are routed on the conveyor system automatically by sensors that read the UPC or RFID label on the cartons. Cross-docked merchandise is in the distribution center only for a few hours before it is shipped to the stores.

Merchandise sales rate and degree of perishability or fashionability typically determine whether cartons are cross-docked or stored. For instance, because Sony's HDTVs sell so quickly, it is in Best Buy's interest not to store them in a distribution center. Similarly, cross-docking is preferable for fashion apparel or perishable meat or produce.

Getting Merchandise Floor-Ready For some merchandise, additional tasks are undertaken in the distribution center to make the merchandise floor-ready. Floor-ready merchandise is merchandise that is ready to be placed on the selling floor. Getting merchandise floor-ready entails ticketing, marking, and, in the case of some apparel, placing garments on hangers (or maybe attaching RFID chips). For the U.K.-based grocery chain Tesco, it is essential that products ship in ready-to-sell units so that it has little manipulation or sorting to do at the distribution center or in the stores. To move the store-ready merchandise it receives from suppliers quickly into the store, Tesco demands that products sit on roll cages rather than pallets. Then, store employees can easily wheel them onto the retail floor. The stores' backrooms only have two or three days' worth of backup inventory, and it is important to keep inventory levels low and receive lots of small, accurate deliveries from its suppliers—which also helps cut costs.[15]

Ticketing and marking refers to affixing price and identification labels to the merchandise. It is more efficient for a retailer to perform these activities at a distribution center than in its stores. In a distribution center, an area can be set aside and a process implemented to efficiently add labels and put apparel on hangers. Conversely, getting merchandise floor-ready in stores can block aisles and divert sales people's attention from their customers. An even better approach from the retailer's

Robots are often used to help prepare merchandise to be shipped to stores.

perspective is to get vendors to ship floor-ready merchandise, thus totally eliminating the expensive, time-consuming ticketing and marking process.

Preparing to Ship Merchandise to a Store At the beginning of the day, the computer system in the distribution center generates a list of items to be shipped to each store on that day. For each item, a pick ticket and shipping label is generated. The pick ticket is a document or display on a screen in a forklift truck indicating how much of each item to get from specific storage areas. The forklift driver goes to the storage area, picks up the number of cartons indicated on the pick ticket, places UPC shipping labels on the cartons that indicate the stores to which the items are to be shipped, and puts the cartons on the conveyor system, where they are automatically routed to the loading dock for the truck going to the stores. In some distribution and fulfillment centers, these functions are performed by robots.

Shipping Merchandise to Stores Shipping merchandise to stores from a distribution center has become increasingly complex. Most distribution centers run 50 to 100 outbound truck routes in one day. To handle this complex transportation problem, the centers use sophisticated routing and scheduling computer systems that consider the locations of the stores, road conditions, and transportation operating constraints to develop the most efficient routes possible. As a result, stores are provided with an accurate estimated time of arrival, and vehicle usage is maximized.

Inventory Management through Just-in-Time Inventory Systems

Marketing channel management offers the 21st century's answer to a host of distribution problems faced by firms. As recently as the early 1990s, even the most innovative firms needed 15 to 30 days—or even more—to fulfill an order from the warehouse to the customer. The typical order-to-delivery process had several steps: order creation, usually using a telephone, fax, or mail; order processing, using a manual system for credit authorization and assignment to a warehouse; and physical delivery. Things could, and often did, go wrong. Ordered goods were not available. Orders were lost or misplaced. Shipments were misdirected. These mistakes lengthened the time it took to get merchandise to customers and potentially made the entire process more expensive.

Faced with such predicaments, firms began stockpiling inventory at each level of the supply chain (retailers, wholesalers, and manufacturers), but keeping inventory where it is not needed becomes a huge and wasteful expense. If a manufacturer has a huge stock of items stuck in a warehouse, it not only is not earning profits by selling those items but also must pay to maintain and guard that warehouse.

Therefore, many firms, such as American Apparel, Zara, Mango, and Forever 21, have adopted a practice developed by Toyota in the 1950s (see the Zara case study at the end of this chapter). Just-in-time (JIT) inventory systems, also known as quick response (QR) systems in retailing, are inventory management systems that deliver less merchandise on a more frequent basis than traditional inventory systems. The firm gets the merchandise just in time for it to be used in

To reduce lead time, UPS works with adidas by providing it with special labeling, garments on hangers, and advanced shipping notices.

the manufacture of another product or for sale when the customer wants it. The benefits of a JIT system include reduced lead time (the amount of time between the recognition that an order needs to be placed and the arrival of the needed merchandise at the seller's store and is available for sale), increased product availability, and lower inventory investment.[16]

Reduced Lead Time By eliminating the need for paper transactions, the EDI in the JIT systems reduces lead time. Even better, the shorter lead times further reduce the need for inventory, because the shorter the lead time, the easier it is for the retailer to forecast its demand.

Increased Product Availability and Lower Inventory Investment In general, as a firm's ability to satisfy customer demand by having stock on hand increases, so does its inventory investment; that is, it needs to keep more backup inventory in stock. But with JIT, the ability to satisfy demand can actually increase while inventory decreases. Because a firm like American Apparel can make purchase commitments or produce merchandise closer to the time of sale, its own inventory investment is reduced. American Apparel needs less inventory because it's getting less merchandise in each order but receiving those shipments more often. Because firms using JIT order merchandise to cover shorter-term demand, their inventory is reduced even further.

The ability to satisfy customer demand by keeping merchandise in stock also increases in JIT systems as a result of the more frequent shipments. For instance, if an American Apparel store runs low on a medium-sized, red T-shirt, its JIT system ensures a shorter lead time than those of more traditional retailers. As a result, it is less likely that the American Apparel store will be out of stock for its customers before the next T-shirt shipment arrives.

Costs of a JIT System Although firms achieve great benefits from a JIT system, it is not without its costs. The distribution function becomes much more complicated with more frequent deliveries. With greater order frequency also come smaller orders, which are more expensive to transport and more difficult to coordinate. Therefore, JIT systems require a strong commitment by the firm and its vendors to cooperate, share data, and develop systems.

For more on JIT inventory systems, see the end-of-chapter case, "Zara Delivers Fast Fashion."

CHECK YOURSELF

1. How does merchandise flow through a typical marketing channel?
2. Why have just-in-time inventory systems become so popular?

Reviewing Learning Objectives

 Understand the importance of marketing channels and supply chain management.

Marketing channels allow companies to get their products in the appropriate outlets in sufficient quantities to meet consumer demand. To anticipate this demand, advertising and promotions must be coordinated with the departments that control inventory and transportation. Otherwise, customers would come in seeking a promotion and not find the product.

Without the members in a marketing channel, consumers would be forced to find raw materials, manufacture products, and somehow get them to where they could be used, all on their own. Thus, each marketing channel member adds value to the product by performing one or more of these functions. Marketing channel management also creates value for each firm in the chain and helps bind together many company functions, including manufacturing, inventory management, transportation, advertising, and marketing.

LO2 **Understand the difference between direct and indirect marketing channels.**

There are ways by which businesses get their goods to consumers. Using a direct marketing channel, a customer can purchase goods from the manufacturer without needing to go through a retailer or intermediary, generally online (e.g., Ascend speakers) or at company stores (e.g., Apple). More commonly, manufacturers choose to offer their goods to consumers through an intermediary, such as a retailer (e.g., Walmart), implementing an indirect marketing channel strategy.

 Describe how marketing channels are managed.

The more closely aligned the marketing channel members are with each other, the less likely there will be significant conflict. An administered marketing channel occurs when a dominant and powerful marketing channel member has control over the other members. In a contractual marketing channel (e.g., franchising), coordination and control are dictated by contractual relationships between members. Corporate marketing channels can operate relatively smoothly because one firm owns the various levels of the chains. Marketing channels also can be effectively managed through strong relationships developed with marketing channel partners. To create such relationships, the partners must trust each other, communicate openly, have compatible goals, realize there is benefit in being interdependent, and be willing to invest in each other's success.

 Describe the flow of information and merchandise in the marketing channel.

Information flow involves: flow 1 (customer to store), flow 2 (store to buyer), flow 3 (buyer to manufacturer), flow 4 (store to manufacturer), flow 5 (store to distribution center), and flow 6 (manufacturer to distribution center and buyer). Merchandise flow involves flow 1 (manufacturer to retailer distribution centers), flow 2 (manufacturer directly to stores), flow 3 (distribution centers to stores, when shipped first to distribution centers), and flow 4 (retailer to customer).

Key Terms

 LEARNSMART

- administered vertical marketing system, 498
- advanced shipping notice (ASN), 504

- checking, 507
- coercive power, 498
- contractual vertical marketing system, 499

- corporate vertical marketing system, 500
- cross-docking distribution center, 509

Marketing Applications

1. Describe marketing channel management by identifying the major activities that it involves. Identify several ways that marketing channel management adds value to a company's offerings, with regard to both consumers and business partners.

2. In what ways can the flow of information be managed in the supply chain? How can the ready flow of information increase a firm's operating efficiencies?

3. Describe how B2B transactions might employ EDI to process purchase information. Considering the information discussed in Chapter 7 about B2B buying situations, determine which buying situation (new task, modified rebuy, or straight rebuy) would most likely align with the use of EDI technology. Justify your answer.

4. What are the differences between the use of a traditional distribution center and one that relies on cross-docking? Discuss the extent to which one is more efficient than the other, being sure to detail your reasoning.

5. Discuss the advantages to a retailer like Macy's of expending the time and effort to get merchandise floor-ready at either the point of manufacture or in the distribution center rather than having retail store staff members do it in the stores. Provide the logic behind your answer.

6. A just-in-time (JIT) inventory system appears to be an important success factor for retailers like American Apparel and Forever 21. Choose a local retailer and examine the advantages and disadvantages of its use of a JIT system. Do you believe it should use JIT? Why?

7. Give an example of a retailer that participates in an independent (conventional) supply chain and one involved in a vertical marketing system. Discuss the advantages and disadvantages of each.

8. For each of the following consumer products, identify the type of vertical marketing system used, and justify your answer: (a) Bertolli pasta sold through grocery stores, (b) Krispy Kreme donuts sold through franchises, and (c) www.polo.com by Ralph Lauren.

9. Why might a big company like Dell want to develop strategic partnerships with locally owned computer stores? Describe what Dell would have to do to maintain such relationships.

10. You are hired as an assistant brand manager for a popular consumer product. One day in an emergency meeting, the brand manager informs the group that there is a problem with one of the suppliers and that he has decided to send you over to the manufacturing facilities to investigate the problem. When you arrive at the plant, you learn that a key supplier has become increasingly unreliable in terms of quality and delivery. You ask the plant manager why the plant doesn't switch suppliers, because it is becoming a major problem for your brand. He informs you that the troubled supplier is his cousin, whose wife has been very ill, and he just can't switch right now. What course of action should you take?

Quiz Yourself

1. Which of the following is NOT one of the activities carried on in a distribution center?
   a. Coordinating inbound transportation
   b. Receiving, checking, storing, and cross-docking
   c. Distributing paychecks and paystubs for retail employees
   d. Getting merchandise floor ready
   e. Coordinating outbound transportation

2. When Cynthia's Boutique receives dresses, they already have price tags and are on hangers. Cynthia's Boutique receives _____ merchandise.
   a. floor-ready
   b. repurposed
   c. just-in-time
   d. quick response
   e. horizontal channel

   (Answers to these two questions can be found on page 652.)

Net Savvy

1. Zappos.com, an online shoe seller, has received praise for its stellar supply chain management. Go to http://about.zappos.com/zappos-story/fulfillment-facility, read the "In the Beginning," "Looking Ahead," and "Customer Testimonial" sections, and see how a shoe ultimately reaches the customer. How does its fulfillment center enable Zappos to adhere to its marketing communications message and provide excellent customer service?

2. The case study for this chapter examines how Zara International, a division of Inditex, successfully manages its supply chain. Visit Inditex's website (http://www.inditex.com) and go to "Sustainability," then review the company's commitment to sustainable management, particularly the section that pertains to its Suppliers and the Code of Conduct for its suppliers. Considering the discussion in this chapter about strategic relationships, how does Inditex address the factors necessary for mutually beneficial partnerships, according to its code of conduct?

Chapter Case Study

ZARA DELIVERS FAST FASHION[17]

In the fast fashion retail business strategy, supply chain management processes serve to introduce fashionable merchandise rapidly, such that stores can respond immediately to customer demand for merchandise. This was pioneered by Zara, a global specialty apparel chain located in La Coruna, Spain, but it also has been adopted by other retailers, including American Apparel, H&M (headquartered in Sweden), TopShop (UK), and Forever 21 (United States).

The approach is particularly effective for specialty apparel retailers that target fashion-conscious consumers who simply must have the latest looks—but they want to do so on a very limited budget. These shoppers load up on new fast fashions every few weeks, instead of purchasing a few higher-priced basics every few months.

To fit with such short cycles and meet customers' demands, the fast fashion process starts with the receipt of timely information from store managers. At Zara, store managers always have their reporting devices literally in hand. These hand-held devices, which are linked directly to the company's corporate office in Spain, enable daily reports on what customers are buying (or not) and what they are asking for but not finding.

Zara's competitive advantage in specialty apparel retailing is based on its efficient supply chain that delivers fashionable merchandise to its stores frequently.

For example, customers might want a purple version of a pink shirt that they see on the shop floor. Managers immediately pass the information on to the designers in Spain. Those designers then communicate electronically with the factory that produces fabric for shirts. This factory starts up its automated equipment, which is run by assemblers who live in close proximity to the factory. (The undyed fabric comes from Asia, where Zara finds inexpensive sources, and then bulk fabric ships to Spain and Portugal to be manufactured into apparel.) The robots in the company's 23 highly automated factories start cutting out shirts and mixing purple dye. For final construction, a network of 300 or so small assemblers, located near the factories in Galicia, Spain, and northern Portugal, take responsibility for making the final product. Finally, to ensure timely delivery, the shirts get shipped by truck to stores in Europe and by air express to stores in the rest of the world.

The Benefits of Fast Fashion for Zara

Zara's main advantage over its competitors, such as The Gap and H&M, has resulted from its highly responsive and tightly organized supply chain. Unlike these competitors, Zara selects factory locations that are in close geographic proximity to the company's headquarters in Spain. Although this approach increases labor costs, compared with outsourced production in lower-cost countries in Asia, it also improves communication, reduces shipping costs and time, and reduces the time before new fashions appear in stores. It also gives Zara the flexibility to modify its operations in one supply chain function to expedite processes in another, such as pricing or tagging. It might hang merchandise on racks in the warehouse so that store employees can move apparel directly from delivery to the sales floor. And it can do all this because it maintains complete control over the entire process.

Furthermore, instead of shipping new products a few times a season, as many of its competitors do, Zara makes deliveries to every one of its stores every few days. The purple shirts would be in stores in two weeks—compared with the several months it would take for most department stores and other specialty apparel stores to accomplish the same feat. Because its fast fashion system also ensures shorter lead times, it's less likely that any Zara store will be out of stock before the next sweater shipment arrives. Limiting the stock in stores even can create a sense of scarcity among its customers. If they don't buy now, the item might not be available next time they visit the store. By producing and shipping in these small quantities, Zara can quickly recover from its (rare) fashion faux pas.

Finally, the efficiency of its supply chain means Zara rarely has to discount merchandise that is not selling. At Zara, the number of items that end up marked down is about half the industry average. Even with these results, Zara still manages to introduce around 10,000 new designs and 40,000 new SKUs each year.

Moving Too Fast? The Negative Effects of Fast Fashion

Despite some strong signals of success—including annual growth rates of approximately 20 percent in terms of sales and number of stores—Zara started to outgrow its own strategy. By their very nature, fashion trends change rapidly and constantly, and so must the merchandise on Zara's shop floors. Faced with disappointed customers, some sales managers ordered extra quantities of hot items, to avoid stockouts. Even with this attempt to circumvent the replenishment system, some stores still suffered from stockouts, because they received fewer units than they had ordered when overall demand exceeded inventory levels. For some items, Zara even confronted perhaps the most frustrating scenario in a supply chain: Inventory sat unused, eating up storage costs, at one location, even as another store desperately pleaded for the same inventory to meet its customers' demand.

As noted among the benefits, the company launches as many as 10,000 new styles annually, with a range of colors and sizes, resulting in hundreds of thousands of SKUs in the system. If we add in replenishment orders, which are received twice weekly, Zara's average shipping total reached nearly 2.5 million items per week, all coming from the company's distribution center. Its legendary supply chain efficiency thus was in danger of a clogged artery.

In response, Zara has adopted some new mathematical processes that turn human experience and mountains of data into actionable information. These models factor in store managers' unique requests for merchandise replenishments, together with historical trends in the sales of the same item. Merchandise display practices have been altered, such as removing all sizes of a garment from the sales floor if a popular size is not available. This practice helps reduce customer frustration, in that they never see an item that might not be available in their size. It also diminishes shipping; if the medium size is unavailable, the small and large sizes do not get shipped either. Instead, these remaining sizes head toward the stores that still have all sizes in stock, so they can be available to customers there.

Growth, costs, market demand, and technology advances all can push retail executives to rethink their business processes. But truly savvy managers search for ways to optimize operations, even when business is running smoothly. As Zara learned, current approaches will not necessarily work tomorrow. As the founder of Zara's corporate owner Inditex told the company's first deputy chair and CEO, "Once a month, come here thinking that we are near bankruptcy. You will find a lot of things to change."[18]

Questions

1. How does an individual firm like Zara manage a supply chain? How does it get new products from design to store so quickly?

2. What are some of the ways that Zara's supply chain management system has helped create value for its customers? Provide specific examples.

3. What challenges did Zara's focus on supply chain efficiency create? Are all such systems destined to suffer such "growing pains"?

Endnotes

1. Greg Besinger, "Amazon Wants to Ship Your Package Before You Buy It," *The Wall Street Journal*, January 17, 2014, http://wsjonline.com.

2. This chapter draws from Michael Levy, Barton A. Weitz, and Dhruv Grewal, *Retailing Management*, 9th ed. (Burr Ridge, IL: McGraw-Hill/Irwin, 2012).

3. Ibid.

4. Based on Barton A. Weitz, "PenAgain Sells to Walmart," in Michael Levy and Barton A. Weitz, *Retailing Management*, 8th ed. (Burr Ridge, IL: McGraw-Hill/Irwin, 2012), pp. 564–65; http://www.Penagain.com; Gwendolyn Bounds, "The Long Road to Walmart," *The Wall Street Journal*, September 19, 2005, p. R1; Gwendolyn Bounds, "One Mount to Make It," *The Wall Street Journal*, May 30, 2006, p. B1.

5. Terry L. Esper et al., "Demand and Supply Integration: A Conceptual Framework of Value Creation through Knowledge Management," *Journal of the Academy of Marketing Science* 38, no. 1 (2010), pp. 5–18.

6. See http://www.marketingpower.com/_layouts/Dictionary.aspx.

7. George E. Stigler, "The Division of Labor Is Limited by the Extent of the Market," *Journal of Political Economy* 59, no. 3 (1951), pp. 185–93.

8. http://www.marketingpower.com/live/mg-dictionary.

9. "Entrepreneur's 2014 Franchise 500," http://www.entrepreneur.com.

10. Lisa Scheer, Fred Miao, and Jason Garrett, "The Effects of Supplier Capabilities on Industrial Customers' Loyalty: The Role of Dependence," *Journal of the Academy of Marketing Science* 38, no. 1 (2010), pp. 90–104; Robert W. Palmatier, Rajiv Dant, and Dhruv Grewal, "A Longitudinal Analysis of Theoretical Perspectives of Interorganizational Relationship Performance," *Journal of Marketing* 71 (October 2007), pp. 172–94; Robert W. Palmatier et al., "A Meta-Analysis on the Antecedents and Consequences of Relationship Marketing Mediators: Insight into Key Moderators," *Journal of Marketing* 70 (October 2006), pp. 136–53.

11. Donna Davis and Susan Golicic, "Gaining Comparative Advantage in Supply Chain Relationships: The Mediating Role of Market-Oriented IT Competence," *Journal of the Academy of Marketing Science* 38, no. 1 (2010), pp. 56–70; Beth Davis-Sramek, Richard Germain, and Karthik Iyer, "Supply Chain Technology: The Role of Environment in Predicting Performance," *Journal of the Academy of Marketing Science* 38, no. 1 (2010), pp. 42–55; Erin Anderson and Barton Weitz, "The Use of Pledges to Build and Sustain Commitment in Distribution Channels," *Journal of Marketing Research* 29 (February 1992), pp. 18–34.

12. http://www.marketingpower.com/_layouts/Dictionary.aspx.

13. http:// http://www.vendormanagedinventory.com.

14. G. P. Kiesmüller and R. A. C. M. Broekmeulen, "The Benefit of VMI Strategies in a Stochastic Multi-Product Serial Two Echelon System," *Computers and Operations Research* 37, no. 2 (2010), pp. 406–16; Dong-Ping Song and John Dinwoodie, "Quantifying the Effectiveness of VMI and Integrated Inventory Management in a Supply Chain with Uncertain Lead-Times and Uncertain Demands," *Production Planning & Control* 19, no. 6 (2008), pp. 590–600; S. P. Nachiappan, A. Gunasekaran, and N. Jawahar, "Knowledge Management System for Operating Parameters in Two-Echelon VMI Supply Chains," *International Journal of Production Research* 45, no. 11 (2007), pp. 2479–505; Andres Angulo, Heather Nachtmann, and Matthew A. Waller, "Supply Chain Information Sharing in a Vendor Managed Inventory Partnership," *Journal of Business Logistics* 25 (2004), pp. 101–20.

15. Kevin Scarpati, "Tesco Big Price Drop Helped by Supply Chain Management," *Supply Chain Digital*, September 23, 2011, http://www.supplychaindigital.com; Michael Garry, "Supply Chain Systems Seen Boosting Tesco's U.S. Stores," *Supermarket News* 55, no. 43 (2007).

16. André Luís Shiguemoto and Vinícius Amaral Armentano, "A Tabu Search Procedure for Coordinating Production, Inventory and Distribution Routing Problems," *International Transactions in Operational Research* 17, no. 2 (2009), pp. 179–95; Ayse Akbalik et al., "Exact Methods and a Heuristic for the Optimization of an Integrated Replenishment-Storage Planning Problem," *International Transactions in Operational Research* 15, no. 2 (March 2008), pp. 195–214.

17. Vertica Bhardwaj and Ann Fairhurst, "Fast Fashion: Response to Changes in the Fashion Industry," *International Review of Retail, Distribution and Consumer Research* 20 (February 2010), pp. 165–73; Felipe Caro et al., "Zara Uses Operations Research to Reengineer Its Global Distribution Process," *Interfaces* 40 (2010), pp. 71–84; Carmen Lopez and Ying Fan, "Case Study: Internationalisation of the Spanish Fashion Brand Zara," *Journal of Fashion Marketing and Management* 13, no. 2 (2009), pp. 279–96; Mark Mulligan, "Spanish Professor Who Uncovers the Detail in Retail; Constant Contact with Corporate Life Is a Valuable Teaching Tool," *Financial Times*, August 18, 2008, p. 12; "Combining Art with Science, Zara Competes with 'Fast Fashion,'" *SupplyChainBrain*, February 7, 2008.

18. Zeynep Ton, Elena Corsi, and Vincent Dessain, "Zara: Managing Stores for Fast Fashion," Harvard Business School Case, March 2011.

i. SCDigest, "Supply Chain News: Goya Foods Shows Path to Success for Mid-Market Companies from New Supply Chain Planning Tools," July 13, 2011, http://www.scdigest.com.

ii. Connie Guglielmo, "Apple's Supplier Labor Practices in China Scrutinized after Foxconn, Pegatron Reviews," *Forbes*, December 12, 2013, http://www.forbes.com; "Apple's Chinese Factories Improved Working Conditions," Associated Press, December 12, 2013; Charles Duhigg and David Barboza, "In China, Human Costs Are Built into an iPad," *The New York Times*, January 25, 2012, http://www.nytimes.com/; Melissa J. Anderson, "The Supply Chain Enters the Spotlight," *Evolved Employer*, February 14, 2012, http://www.evolvedemployer.com/.

iii. J.J. McCorvey, "AmazonFresh Is Jeff Bezos' Last Mile Quest for Total Retail Domination," *Fast Company*, August 5, 2013; Amy Guthrie and Shelly Banjo, "Mexico Delivers for Walmart," *The Wall Street Journal*, February 19, 2014.

Credits

CHAPTER 17

RETAILING AND OMNICHANNEL MARKETING

LEARNING OBJECTIVES

LO1 Discuss the four factors manufacturers should consider as they develop their strategy for working with retailers.

LO2 Outline the considerations associated with choosing retail partners.

LO3 List the three levels of distribution intensity.

LO4 Describe the various types of retailers.

LO5 Describe the components of a retail strategy.

LO6 Identify the benefits of stores.

LO7 Identify the benefits of omnichannel retailing.

LO8 Detail the challenges of omnichannel retailing.

When H&M opened its flagship Times Square store, it aimed to create not just the most exciting store in the fashionable chain's range of locations but also perhaps the most cutting-edge example of retail in the world. Consider some of the innovations and offerings the store provides to customers.

Before they even walk through the doors, customers can enjoy the display created by massive 30 × 200-foot LED screens over the entrance and morphing onto the sides of the building. For those who happen to be just passing by, the interactive window displays are nearly impossible to ignore, drawing attention and foot traffic. During the Super Bowl, for example, people could vote for which version of an underwear ad would appear on these screens: one with David Beckham fully clothed or one in which he appeared in only his eponymous brand of underwear.

Inside, the space is remarkably massive, even for Times Square, at approximately 42,000 square feet. Rents in this area of town average around $2,000 per square foot, so H&M needs to make a lot of sales. To cover all this ground, the retailer has more than 300 sales clerks on staff, and it stays open 16 hours per day (closing only between 1:00 and 9:00 a.m.), seven days a week. It also keeps 24 cash registers ringing, though there's no need for every customer to visit a cash register. The 44 dressing rooms also are equipped with iPads and individual checkout stations for people to "try and buy." At the very moment a customer tries on an outfit and realizes it works, he or she can also go ahead and buy it, without having to wait in line.

Then again, waiting in line might be fun, because the store features a wealth of entertaining distractions. On opening day, Lady Gaga offered a command performance. More regularly, light boxes display messages summarizing temporary deals or upcoming events. From the third-floor ceiling, trusses support mannequins, making it appear as if well-dressed bodies are flying above the shop floor. A glitter wall dresses the background behind the checkout stations, and a DJ booth keeps the music playing constantly and interactively.

Because H&M appeals largely to a youthful, technologically savvy target market that is eternally ready to share through social media, shoppers can show off their clothing options on an LED-recorded runway. The captured video is available to send to their personal e-mail address, upload to a social media site (with the hash tag "hmtimessquare"), and be broadcast throughout the store on the same day. Thus if a shopper is convinced that the latest offerings from Dividend, a trendy flannel and fatigue clothing line, look utterly fabulous on her, she can make sure all her friends, as well as hundreds of the other shoppers in the store, see her in them.[1]

Retailing sits at the end of the supply chain, where marketing meets the consumer. But there is far more to retailing than just manufacturing a product and making it available to customers. It is primarily the retailer's responsibility to make sure that these customers' expectations are fulfilled.

Retailing is defined as the set of business activities that add value to products and services sold to consumers for their personal or family use. Our definition includes products bought at stores, through catalogs, and over the Internet, as well as services such as fast-food restaurants, airlines, and hotels. Some retailers claim they sell at wholesale prices, but if they sell to customers for their personal use, they are still retailers, regardless of their prices. Wholesalers (see Chapter 16) buy products from manufacturers and resell them to retailers or industrial or business users.

Retailing today is changing, both in the United States and around the world. Manufacturers no longer rule many supply chains, as they once did. Retailers such as Walmart (U.S. food retailer), Tesco (UK-based food retailer), Costco (U.S. warehouse club), Carrefour (French hypermarket), Kroger (U.S. grocery chain), Schwarz (German conglomerate), Metro (German retail conglomerate), Home Depot (U.S. home improvement), Aldi Enkauf (German discount food retailer), Target (U.S. food retailer), and Walgreens (U.S. drugstore)[2]—the largest retailers in the world—dictate to their suppliers what should be made, how it should be configured, when it should be delivered, and, to some extent, what it should cost. These retailers are clearly in the driver's seat.

LO1 Discuss the four factors manufacturers should consider as they develop their strategy for working with retailers.

This chapter extends Chapter 16's discussion of supply chain management by examining why and how manufacturers use retailers. The manufacturer's strategy depends on its overall market power and how consistent a new product or product line is with current offerings. Consider the following scenarios:

- Scenario 1: Cosmetics conglomerate Estée Lauder's subsidiary brand M·A·C is introducing a new line of mascara.

- Scenario 2: Coach, well known for its women's handbags, has introduced a line of men's leather goods, apparel, gifts, shoes, and other accessories—products not previously in its assortment.

- Scenario 3: Eva, a young entrepreneur, is launching a new line of environmentally friendly (green) cosmetics.

Each of these scenarios is different and requires the manufacturer to consider alternatives for reaching its target markets through retailers.

M·A·C will use different criteria for placing products in retail stores than either Coach for Men or Eva's green cosmetics.

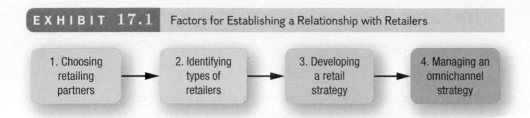

EXHIBIT 17.1 Factors for Establishing a Relationship with Retailers

| 1. Choosing retailing partners | → | 2. Identifying types of retailers | → | 3. Developing a retail strategy | → | 4. Managing an omnichannel strategy |

Exhibit 17.1 illustrates four factors manufacturers consider to establish their strategy for working with retailers.[3] In choosing retail partners, the first factor, manufacturers assess how likely it is for certain retailers to carry their products. Manufacturers also consider where their target customers expect to find the products, because those are exactly the stores in which they want to place their products. The overall size and level of sophistication of the manufacturer will determine how many of the marketing channel functions it performs and how many it will hand off to other channel members. Finally, the type and availability of the product and the image the manufacturer wishes to portray will determine how many retailers within a geographic region will carry the products.

For the second factor, manufacturers identify the types of retailers that would be appropriate to carry their products. Although the choice is often obvious—such as a supermarket for fresh produce—manufacturers may have a choice of retailer types for some products.

As we discussed in Chapter 16, a hallmark of a strong marketing channel is one in which manufacturers and retailers coordinate their efforts. In the third factor, manufacturers and retailers therefore develop their strategy by implementing the four Ps.

Finally, many retailers and some manufacturers use an omnichannel or multichannel strategy, which involves selling in more than one channel (e.g., store, catalog, and Internet). The fourth factor therefore consists of examining the circumstances in which sellers may prefer to adopt a particular strategy. Although these factors are listed consecutively, manufacturers may consider them all simultaneously or in a different order.

CHOOSING RETAILING PARTNERS

LO2 Outline the considerations associated with choosing retail partners.

Imagine, as a consumer, trying to buy a new leather jacket without being able to visit a retailer or buy online. You would have to figure out exactly what size, color, and style of jacket you wanted. Then you would need to contact various manufacturers, whether in person, by phone, or over the Internet, and order the jacket. If the jacket fit you reasonably well but not perfectly, you still might need to take it to a tailor to have the sleeves shortened. You wouldn't find this approach to shopping very convenient.

Manufacturers like Coach use retailers such as Macy's to undertake partnerships that create value by pulling together all the actions necessary for the greatest possible customer convenience and satisfaction. The store offers a broad selection of purses, leather jackets, scarves, and other accessories that its buyers have carefully chosen in advance. Customers can see, touch, feel, and try on any item while in the store. They can buy one scarf or leather jacket at a time or buy an outfit that works together. Finally, the store provides a salesperson to help customers coordinate their outfits and a tailor to make the whole thing fit perfectly.

Coach partners with retailers to help conveniently deliver its products to satisfied customers.

When choosing retail partners, manufacturers look at the basic channel structure, where their target customers expect to find the products, channel member characteristics, and distribution intensity.

Channel Structure

The level of difficulty a manufacturer experiences in getting retailers to purchase its products is determined by the degree to which the channel is vertically integrated, as described in Chapter 16; the degree to which the manufacturer has a strong brand or is otherwise desirable in the market; and the relative power of the manufacturer and retailer.

Scenario 1 represents a corporate vertical marketing system. Because M-A-C is made by Estée Lauder and operates its own stores, when the new mascara line is introduced, the stores receive the new line automatically with no decision on the part of the retailer. In contrast, Revlon would have a much more difficult time getting CVS to buy a new mascara line because these supply chain partners are not vertically integrated.

When an established firm such as Coach enters a new market with men's leather goods, apparel, gifts, shoes, and other accessories, as is the case in Scenario 2, it cannot place the products with any retailer. It must determine where its customers would expect to find these products and then use its established relationships with women's handbag buyers, the power of its brand, and its overall reputation to leverage its position in this new product area.

Eva (Scenario 3) would have an even more difficult time convincing a retailer to buy and sell her green cosmetics line because she lacks power in the marketplace—she is small, and her brand is unknown. She would have trouble getting buyers to see her, let alone consider her line. She might face relatively high slotting allowances just to get space on retailers' shelves. But like Coach in Scenario 2, Eva should consider where the end customer expects to find her products, as well as some important retailer characteristics.

Customer Expectations

Retailers should also know customer preferences regarding manufacturers. Manufacturers, in contrast, need to know where their target market customers expect to find their products and those of their competitors. As we see in the hypothetical example in Exhibit 17.2, Coach currently sells handbags at stores such as Dillard's,

EXHIBIT 17.2   Coach and Cole Haan Distribution

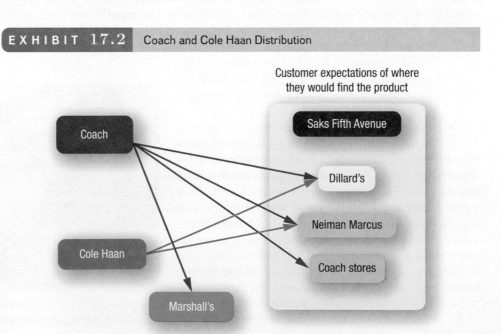

Neiman Marcus, and Marshalls as well as in its own stores (orange arrows). Its competitor Cole Haan sells at Dillard's and Neiman Marcus (green arrows). A survey of male Coach customers shows that they would expect to find its products at Saks Fifth Avenue, Dillard's, Neiman Marcus, and its own stores (blue box). On the basis of this information, Coach decides to try selling at Saks Fifth Avenue but to stop selling at Marshalls to better meet customers' expectations.

Customers generally expect to find certain products at some stores but not at others. For example, Estée Lauder would not choose to sell to CVS or Dollar General because its customers would not expect to shop at those stores for high-end cosmetics such as Estée Lauder's. Instead, CVS might carry less expensive cosmetic brands, such as Revlon and Maybelline, and bargain closeouts probably appear at Dollar General. But male Coach customers definitely expect to find the brand's clothing offerings at major department stores and at Coach stores.

Channel Member Characteristics

Several factors pertaining to the channel members themselves help determine the channel structure. Generally, the larger and more sophisticated the channel member, the less likely that it will use supply chain intermediaries. Eva will probably use a group of independent salespeople to help sell her line of green cosmetics, whereas a large manufacturer such as Estée Lauder will use its own sales force that already has existing relationships in the industry. In the same way, an independent grocery store might buy merchandise from a wholesaler, but Walmart, the world's largest grocer, only buys directly from the manufacturer. Larger firms often find that by performing the channel functions themselves, they can gain more control, be more efficient, and save money.

Distribution Intensity

When setting up distribution for the first time, as is the case with Eva's green cosmetics (Scenario 3), or introducing a new product line, as is the case with Coach for men (Scenario 2), firms decide the appropriate level of distribution intensity—the number of channel members to use at each level of the marketing channel. Distribution intensity commonly is divided into three levels: intensive, exclusive, and selective.

Intensive Distribution An intensive distribution strategy is designed to place products in as many outlets as possible. Most consumer packaged goods companies, such as Pepsi, Procter & Gamble, Kraft, and other nationally branded products found in grocery and discount stores, strive for and often achieve intensive distribution. Pepsi wants its product available everywhere—grocery stores, convenience stores, restaurants, and vending machines. The more exposure the products get, the more they sell.

Exclusive Distribution Manufacturers also might use an exclusive distribution policy by granting exclusive geographic territories to one or very few retail customers so no other retailers in the territory can sell a particular brand. Exclusive distribution can benefit manufacturers by assuring them that the most appropriate retailers represent their products. Luxury goods firms such as Coach limit distribution to a few select, higher-end retailers in each region. The company believes that selling its products to full-line discount stores or off-price retailers would weaken its image.

When supply is limited or a firm is just starting out, providing an exclusive territory to one retailer or retail chain helps ensure enough inventory to provide the

Most consumer packaged goods companies, such as Pepsi (top), strive for intensive distribution—they want to be everywhere. But cosmetics firms such as Estee Lauder (bottom) use an exclusive distribution strategy by limiting their distribution to a few select higher-end retailers in each region.

LO3 List the three levels of distribution intensity.

buying public an adequate selection. By granting exclusive territories, Eva guarantees her retailers will have an adequate supply of her green cosmetics. This guarantee gives these retailers a strong incentive to market her products. The retailers that Eva uses know there will be no competing retailers to cut prices, so their profit margins are protected. This knowledge gives them an incentive to carry more inventory and use extra advertising, personal selling, and sales promotions.

Selective Distribution Between the intensive and exclusive distribution strategies lies selective distribution, which relies on a few selected retail customers in a territory to sell products. Like exclusive distribution, selective distribution helps a seller maintain a particular image and control the flow of merchandise into an area. These advantages make this approach attractive to many shopping goods manufacturers. Recall that shopping goods are those products for which consumers are willing to spend time comparing alternatives, such as most apparel items, home items like branded pots and pans or sheets and towels, branded hardware and tools, and consumer electronics. Retailers still have a strong incentive to sell the products but not to the same extent as if they had an exclusive territory.

As we noted in Chapter 16, like any large complicated system, a marketing channel is difficult to manage. Whether the balance of power rests with large retailers such as Walmart or with large manufacturers such as Procter & Gamble, channel members benefit by working together to develop and implement their channel strategy. In the next section, we explore the different types of retailers with an eye toward which would be most appropriate for each of our scenarios: M-A-C Cosmetics, Coach's products for men, and Eva's new line of environmentally friendly cosmetics.

CHECK YOURSELF

1. What issues should manufacturers consider when choosing retail partners?
2. What are the differences among intensive, exclusive, and selective levels of distribution intensity?

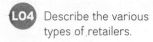 **LO4** Describe the various types of retailers.

IDENTIFY TYPES OF RETAILERS

At first glance, identifying the types of retailers that Coach and Eva may wish to pursue when attempting to place their new lines seems straightforward. But the choice is not always easy. Manufacturers need to understand the general characteristics of different types of retailers to determine the best channels for their product. The characteristics of a retailer that are important to a food manufacturer may be quite different from those considered valuable by a cosmetics manufacturer. In the next few sections, we examine the various types of retailers, identify some major players, and discuss some of the issues facing each type (Exhibit 17.3).

Food Retailers

The food retailing landscape is changing dramatically. Twenty years ago, consumers purchased food primarily at conventional supermarkets. Now conventional supermarkets account for only slightly more than 60 percent of food sales (not including restaurants).[4] Not only do full-line discount stores like Walmart and Target now offer a full assortment of grocery items in their superstores, but traditional supermarkets also are carrying more nonfood items. Many supermarkets offer pharmacies, health care clinics, banks, and cafés.

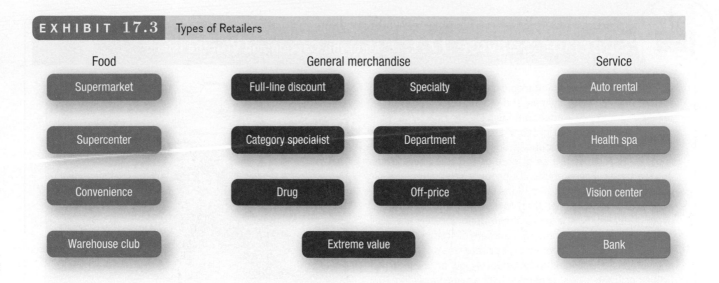

EXHIBIT 17.3 Types of Retailers

Food	General merchandise		Service
Supermarket	Full-line discount	Specialty	Auto rental
Supercenter	Category specialist	Department	Health spa
Convenience	Drug	Off-price	Vision center
Warehouse club	Extreme value		Bank

The world's largest food retailer, Walmart, attains more than $443 billion in sales of supermarket-type merchandise. On this measure, it is followed by Carrefour (France), Tesco (United Kingdom), Metro Group (Germany), Schwartz Group (Germany), and Kroger (United States).[5] In North America specifically, the largest supermarket chains in order are Walmart, Kroger, Costco, Target, Safeway, Supervalu, Loblaw, Publix, and Ahold US.[6]

Supermarkets

A conventional supermarket is a large, self-service retail food store offering groceries, meat, and produce, as well as some nonfood items such as health and beauty aids and general merchandise.[7] Perishables including meat, produce, baked goods, and dairy products account for 30 percent of supermarket sales and typically have higher margins than packaged goods.[8]

Whereas conventional supermarkets carry about 30,000 SKUs, limited-assortment supermarkets, or extreme-value food retailers, stock only about 1,500 SKUs.[9] The two largest limited-assortment supermarket chains in the United States are Save-A-Lot and ALDI. Rather than carrying 20 brands of laundry detergent, limited-assortment supermarkets offer one or two brands and sizes, one of which is a store brand. By trimming costs, limited-assortment supermarkets can offer merchandise at prices 40 percent lower than those at conventional supermarkets.[10]

Although conventional supermarkets still sell the majority of food merchandise, they are under substantial competitive pressure on multiple sides: from supercenters, warehouse clubs, extreme-value retailers, convenience stores, and even drug stores.[11] All these types of retailers have increased the amount of space they devote to consumables.

To compete successfully against intrusions by other food retailing formats, conventional supermarkets are differentiating their offerings by (1) emphasizing fresh perishables, (2) targeting green and ethnic consumers, (3) providing better value with private-label merchandise, and (4) providing a better shopping experience. One excellent example of these efforts comes in the form of a stellar grocer, Trader Joe's, as Superior Service 17.1 explains.

Supercenters Supercenters are large stores (185,000 square feet) that combine a supermarket with a full-line discount store. Walmart operates more than 3,000 supercenters in the United States,[12] accounting for the vast majority of

Superior Service 17.1   Meet the Captain and Visit the Island[i]

The employees are wearing tropical shirts, the product labels feature puns and silly rhymes, and the manager goes by "Captain." But dismissing Trader Joe's as a joke is a bad idea, especially if you're another grocery store chain that wants to appeal to discerning shoppers. Just ask Whole Foods. The roots of its success are as diverse as the customers Trader Joe's attracts. For example, its product lines offer organic, gourmet, and multicultural options (and sometimes combinations of all three), rather than focusing on any one type of product appeal. Furthermore, those options rarely are available anywhere else, because 80 percent of Trader Joe's product assortment consists of its own private labels. The plentiful, unique options also tend to be relatively low priced—likely an artifact of Trader Joe's ownership by the same family that runs the low-priced ALDI chain.

With these product and price offerings, rather than being all things to everyone, Trader Joe's is a little something for anyone. Full, stock-up shopping trips still require another grocer, but for a little something special and tasty, Trader Joe's provides a compelling alternative. Accordingly, it attracts a diverse fan base, approximately equally split between households that earn more than $100,000 annually and those that average closer to $25,000. Still, many of the customers at Trader Joe's exhibit some appealing similarities for retailers, including high levels of education, a health emphasis, and a high level of comfort with technological innovations.

In these traits, Trader Joe's customers are remarkably similar to those who shop at Whole Foods, despite the vast differences in the price positions the two chains take. Whole

If you don't think shopping for groceries is fun, try Trader Joe's.

Foods' CEO even has admitted that the company views Trader Joe's as its primary competitor and that its own "365" private label represents a direct response to the offerings on hand at Trader Joe's. Yet its unique positioning sets Trader Joe's apart from other grocers in consumers' minds; it also helps it stand alone when it comes to some pertinent measures of success. Namely, in the grocery industry, the average rate of sales per square foot is $521. Whole Foods, with its high-end, pricey, trendy image, nearly doubles that rate, with sales per square foot of $973. And Trader Joe's, with its small, island-themed stores? It achieves an utterly astounding $1723 per square foot on average.

Warehouse clubs have expanded their assortment of the electronics category, and are known for great prices.

total supercenter sales—far outpacing its competitors Meijer, SuperTarget (Target), Fred Meyer (Kroger Co.), and Super Kmart Center (Sears Holding). By offering broad assortments of grocery and general merchandise products under one roof, supercenters provide a one-stop shopping convenience to customers.

Warehouse Clubs   Warehouse clubs are large retailers (100,000 to 150,000 square feet) that offer a limited and irregular assortment of food and general merchandise, little service, and low prices to the general public and small businesses. The largest warehouse club chains are Costco, Sam's Club (Walmart), and BJ's Wholesale Club (operating only on the U.S. East Coast). Customers are attracted to these stores because they can stock up on large packs of basics like paper towels, mega-sized packaged groceries such as a quart of ketchup, best-selling books and CDs, fresh meat and produce, and an unpredictable assortment of upscale merchandise and services (e.g., jewelry, electronics, and home decor) at lower prices than are available at other retail stores. Typically, members pay an annual fee of around $50, which amounts to significant additional income for the chains.

Although both Coach for Men and Eva's products could be sold in warehouse clubs, these retailers probably are not the best choices. Both product lines will have an upscale image, which is inconsistent with any warehouse club. If, however, either firm has overstock merchandise as a result of overestimating demand or underestimating returned merchandise from retailers, warehouse clubs are a potential outlet.

Convenience Stores Convenience stores provide a limited variety and assortment of merchandise at a convenient location in 3,000- to 5,000-square-foot stores with speedy checkout. They are the modern version of the neighborhood mom-and-pop grocery or general store. Convenience stores enable consumers to make purchases quickly without having to search through a large store and wait in a lengthy checkout line. Convenience store assortments are limited in terms of depth and breadth, and they charge higher prices than supermarkets. Milk, eggs, and bread once represented the majority of their sales, but now most sales come from gasoline and cigarettes.

Convenience stores also face increased competition from other retail formats. In response to these competitive pressures, convenience stores are taking steps to decrease their dependency on gasoline sales by offering fresh food and healthy fast food, tailoring assortments to local markets, and making their stores even more convenient to shop. Finally, convenience stores are adding new services, such as financial service kiosks that give customers the opportunity to cash checks, pay bills, and buy prepaid telephone minutes, theater tickets, and gift cards.

In addition to convenience, Seven-Eleven is a trendy place for young consumers in Indonesia to hang out.

General Merchandise Retailers

The major types of general merchandise retailers are department stores, full-line discount stores, specialty stores, category specialists, home improvement centers, off-price retailers, and extreme-value retailers.

Department Stores Department stores are retailers that carry a broad variety and deep assortment, offer customer services, and organize their stores into distinct departments for displaying merchandise. The largest department store chains in the United States include Sears, Macy's, Kohl's, JCPenney, and Nordstrom.[13] Department stores would be an excellent retail channel for Coach for Men and Eva's new lines.

To compete and gain better traction among younger consumers, who generally favor smaller specialty stores,[14] many department stores are increasing the amount of exclusive and private-label merchandise they sell. For example, Jennifer Lopez has a clothing line at Kohl's, and Ralph Lauren has a line of casual apparel exclusively at JCPenney called American Living. Customers looking for exclusive dinnerware collections can go to Macy's and get the Rachel Bilson line, or else find the Kardashian Kollection at Sears.[15] Macy's has also developed its own brands available exclusively at its stores, including Alfani (women's fashion) and the Hotel Collection (luxury fabrics).

Department stores like Macy's carry a broad variety and deep assortment, offer customer services, and organize their stores into distinct departments for displaying merchandise.

Full-Line Discount Stores Full-line discount stores are retailers that offer a broad variety of merchandise, limited service, and low prices. The largest full-line discount store chains are Walmart, Target, and Kmart (Sears Holding).

Although full-line discount stores typically might carry men's leather goods, accessories, and cosmetics, they are not good options for Coach for Men or Eva's new green cosmetics line. Customers do not expect higher-end products in full-line discount stores. Rather, they are looking for value prices on these items and are willing to compromise on quality or cachet.

Walmart accounts for approximately two-thirds of full-line discount store retail sales in the United States.[16] Target has experienced considerable growth because its stores offer fashionable merchandise at low prices in a pleasant shopping environment. The retailer has developed an image of cheap chic by offering limited-edition exclusive apparel and cosmetic lines.

Specialty Stores Specialty stores concentrate on a limited number of complementary merchandise categories targeted toward very specific market segments by offering deep but narrow assortments and sales associate expertise. Although such shops are familiar in brick-and-mortar forms, more retailers also are expanding their online specialty profile as well.

Estée Lauder's M-A-C line of cosmetics sells in the company's own retail specialty stores as well as in some department stores. Certain specialty stores would be excellent outlets for the new lines by Coach for Men and Eva. Customers likely expect to find Coach for Men leather goods and accessories in men's apparel or leather stores. Eva's line of green cosmetics would fit nicely in a cosmetics specialty store such as Sephora.

Drugstores Drugstores are specialty stores that concentrate on pharmaceuticals and health and personal grooming merchandise. Prescription pharmaceuticals represent almost 70 percent of drugstore sales. The largest drugstore chains in the United States are CVS, Walgreens, and Rite Aid.[17]

Drugstores face competition from pharmacies in discount stores and from pressure to reduce health care costs. In response, the major drugstore chains are offering a wider assortment of merchandise, including more frequently purchased food items, as well as new services, such as the convenience of drive-through windows for picking up prescriptions, in-store medical clinics, and even makeovers and spa treatments.[18] CVS is particularly adept at garnering loyal customers as Adding Value 17.1 recognizes.

Although Estée Lauder's new line would not be consistent with the merchandise found in drugstores, Eva's green cosmetics may be a welcome addition. Some drugstores have recognized consumer demand for green products, even though Eva's cosmetics may be priced higher than its competitors. Eva must decide whether her high-end products will suffer a tarnished image if she sells them in drugstores or whether drugstores could be a good channel for increasing her brand awareness.

Category Specialists Category specialists are big-box retailers or category killers that offer a narrow but deep assortment of merchandise. Most category specialists use a predominantly self-service approach, but they offer assistance to customers in some areas of the stores. For example, the office supply store Staples has a warehouse atmosphere with cartons of copy paper stacked on pallets, plus equipment in boxes on shelves. But in some departments, such as computers, electronics, and other high-tech products, salespeople staff the display area to answer questions and make suggestions.

Estee Lauder's M-A-C cosmetic lines sell in specialty stores such as Sephora.

Adding Value 17.1   CVS Devises Ways to Keep Its Customers Coming Back[ii]

CVS is working hard to develop more strategic personalization efforts with its ExtraCare customers. CVS will offer tailored versions of its weekly print circulars to ExtraCare loyalty program customers. This initiative, myWeeklyAd, will use data gathered from CVS ExtraCare members' previous purchases. Users of the my-WeeklyAd service will also be able to build digital shopping lists tailored to the store that they most often frequent; the list will even tell them in what aisle they can find certain products. The service also gives customers customized coupons and offers.

Like many retailers, CVS relies heavily on the distribution of circulars to drive traffic and increase sales. Today's technologies allow CVS to reach more customers at a less expensive rate, as well as make shopping easier for customers. CVS believes that the myWeeklyAd service will provide customers with increased convenience and create a more personalized shopping experience.

What's your deal?," an ad campaign created by CVS/pharmacy, is designed to help ExtraCare members understand the benefits of myWeekly Ad, a personalized circular tailored to each customer.

CVS has also created a "What's Your Deal?" campaign to showcase the individualized attention that customers get. This ad features a mother of two children receiving deals on pain relievers and cleaning wipes, while a lovelorn man might receive deals for mints, candy, and hair gel.

However, some critics argue that making personalized recommendations to consumers can sometimes be intrusive and turn some customers off. Some Internet bloggers have also created memes imitating how some Extra-Care members' receipts can extend up to five or six feet with all of the coupons. For many customers, that is just too much.

By offering a complete assortment in a category at somewhat lower prices than their competition, category specialists can kill a category of merchandise for other retailers, which is why they are frequently called category killers. Using their category dominance, these retailers exploit their buying power to negotiate low prices.

Extreme-Value Retailers   Extreme-value retailers are small, full-line discount stores that offer a limited merchandise assortment at very low prices. The largest extreme-value retailers are Dollar General and Family Dollar Stores.

Like limited assortment food retailers, extreme-value retailers reduce costs and maintain low prices by buying opportunistically from manufacturers with excess merchandise, offering a limited assortment, and operating in low-rent locations. They offer a broad but shallow assortment of household goods, health and beauty aids, and groceries.

Many value retailers target low-income consumers, whose shopping behavior differs from that of typical discount store or warehouse club customers. Although these consumers might demand well-known national brands, they often cannot afford to buy large-sized packages. So vendors such as Procter & Gamble often create special, smaller packages for extreme-value retailers, often using the reverse innovation approaches we discussed in Chapter 8. Also, higher-income consumers are increasingly patronizing these stores for the thrill of the hunt.

Dollar General is one of the United States' largest extreme value retailers. It has small full-line discount stores that offer a limited assortment at very low prices.

Off-price retailers like Big Lots offer an inconsistent assortment of brand name merchandise at a significant discount from the manufacturer's suggested retail price (MSRP).

Some shoppers regard the extreme-value retailers as an opportunity to find some hidden treasure among the household staples.

Extreme-value retailers would not be an obvious consumer choice for Coach for Men or Eva's new lines, because these stores are not consistent with the brands' image. But if these manufacturers find themselves in an overstock situation, they could use these retailers to reduce inventory. For the same reason, they might use off-price retailers.

Off-Price Retailers Off-price retailers offer an inconsistent assortment of brand name merchandise at a significant discount from the manufacturer's suggested retail price (MSRP). In today's market, these off-price retailers may be brick-and-mortar stores, online outlets, or a combination of both. America's largest off-price retail chains are TJX Companies (which operates TJMaxx, Marshalls, Winners [Canada], HomeGoods, AJWright, and HomeSense [Canada]), Ross Stores, Burlington Coat Factory, Big Lots Inc., Overstock.com, and Bluefly.com.

To be able to sell at prices 20 to 60 percent lower than the MSRP,[19] most merchandise is bought opportunistically from manufacturers or other retailers with excess inventory at the end of the season. Therefore, customers cannot be confident that the same merchandise or even type of merchandise will be available each time they visit a store or website. The discounts off-price retailers receive from manufacturers reflect what they do not do as well: They do not ask suppliers to help them pay for advertising, make them take back unsold merchandise, charge them for markdowns, or ask them to delay payments.

Service Retailers

The retail firms discussed in the previous sections sell products to consumers.[20] However, service retailers, or firms that primarily sell services rather than merchandise, are a large and growing part of the retail industry. Consider a typical Saturday: After a bagel and cup of coffee at a nearby Peet's Coffee and Tea, you go to the Laundromat to wash and dry your clothes, drop off a suit at a dry cleaner, have a prescription filled at a CVS drugstore, and make your way to Jiffy Lube to

Service retailers, like this night club, sell services rather than merchandise.

Superior Service 17.2 Giving New Meaning to Going Mobile: Restaurateurs Move from Storefronts to Trucks[iii]

The success of fast food in the United States resulted from the growth of the car culture—people in cars loved to grab a burger, some fries, and a shake and then keep on driving down the road. But several restaurants are flipping this traditional model, in which customers drove to the restaurant, by taking their food to customers in food trucks.

The explosive popularity of food trucks has created multiple effects, especially in urban locations and on campuses that now host food truck rallies but also engage in vigorous debates about where the trucks can locate. For food retailers, these new options also create a new form of competition. Why would college students undergo the chore of driving to a restaurant if a food truck is parked right next to their dorm, for example? As a representative of the National Restaurant Association noted, "When you think of consumer needs for convenience, food trucks are a natural evolution of the growth of the off-premises market."

Accordingly, chains such as White Castle have begun experimenting with expanding into this mobile supply channel. Beginning with just a couple of trucks, White Castle will make its mobile food supply available for events and weddings.

As it tests various locations, the long-standing chain will add more CraveMobiles, which it plans to keep open 24/7.

In addition to making it easier to access their products (and eliminating the type of quest made infamous by Harold and Kumar), the food trucks give White Castle and other chains—including Wendy's, Taco Bell, and Applebee's, among others—an optimal environment for testing out new recipes and menu additions prior to adding them to their brick-and-mortar stores throughout the country.

This added sales channel is not limited to fast-food or quick-service restaurants. Consumer packaged-goods companies such as Stouffer's are jumping on the bandwagon too. Several branded food trucks have already begun rolling through the United States, handing out samples of its macaroni and cheese. Although this food truck version has clear marketing benefits, it also seeks to benefit communities. The Stouffer's trucks mainly will locate at or near charitable events, whether during benefit concerts or in locations where people could use a little comfort food. In the aftermath of Hurricane Sandy, the Mac 'n Cheese truck provided victims in New York with a welcome sight and a warm meal.

Restaurant chains, such as White Castle, now offer food trucks.

have your car's oil changed. In a hurry, you drive through a Burger King so you can eat lunch quickly and be on time for your haircut at Supercuts. By midafternoon, you're ready for a workout at your health club. After stopping at home for a change of clothes, you're off to dinner, a movie, and dancing with a friend. Finally, you end your day with a café latte at Starbucks, having interacted with 10 service retailers during the day.

There are a wide variety of service retailers, along with some national companies that provide these services. These companies are retailers because they sell goods and services to consumers. However, some are not just retailers. For example, airlines, banks, hotels, and insurance and express mail companies sell their services to businesses as well as consumers. Superior Service 17.2 highlights how restaurateurs are selling exciting food offerings out of trucks.

Organizations such as banks, hospitals, health spas, legal clinics, entertainment firms, and universities that offer services to consumers traditionally have not considered themselves retailers. Yet due to increased competition, these organizations are adopting retailing principles to attract customers and satisfy their needs.

Several trends suggest considerable future growth in services retailing. For example, the aging population will increase demand for health care services. Younger people are also spending more time and money on health and fitness. Busy parents in two-income families are willing to pay to have their homes cleaned, lawns maintained, clothes washed and pressed, and meals prepared so they can spend more time with their families.

Now that we've explored the types of stores, we can examine how manufacturers and retailers coordinate their retail strategy using the four Ps.

CHECK YOURSELF

1. What strategies distinguish the different types of food retailers?
2. What strategies distinguish the different types of general merchandise retailers?
3. Are organizations that provide services to consumers retailers?

LO5 Describe the components of a retail strategy.

DEVELOPING A RETAIL STRATEGY USING THE FOUR PS

Like other marketers, retailers perform important functions that increase the value of the products and services they sell to consumers. We now examine these functions, classified into the four Ps: product, price, promotion, and place.

Product

A typical grocery store carries 30,000 to 40,000 items; a regional department store might carry as many as 100,000. Providing the right mix of merchandise and services that satisfies the needs of the target market is one of retailers' most fundamental activities. Offering assortments gives customers a choice. To reduce transportation costs and handling, manufacturers typically ship cases of merchandise, such as cartons of mascara or boxes of leather jackets, to retailers. Because customers generally do not want or need to buy more than one of the same item, retailers break up the cases and sell customers the smaller quantities they desire. Adding Value 17.2 highlights how Home Depot is providing customers better access to more products both in the store and online.

Manufacturers don't like to store inventory because their factories and warehouses are typically not available or attractive shopping venues. Consumers don't want to purchase more than they need because storage consumes space. Neither group likes keeping inventory that isn't being used because doing so ties up money that could be used for something else. Retailers thus provide, in addition to other values to both manufacturers and customers, a storage function, though many retailers are beginning to push their suppliers to hold the inventory until they need it. (Recall our discussion of JIT inventory systems in Chapter 16.)

It is difficult for retailers to distinguish themselves from their competitors through the merchandise they carry because competitors can purchase and sell many of the same popular brands. Thus, many retailers have developed private-label brands (also called store brands), which are products developed and marketed by a retailer and available only from that retailer. For example, if you want a Giani Bernini leather handbag, you have to go to Macy's.

Retailers often work together with their suppliers to develop an exclusive brand. An exclusive brand is a brand that is developed by a national brand vendor, often in conjunction with a retailer, and is sold exclusively by the retailer. So, for example, cosmetics powerhouse Estée Lauder sells two brands of cosmetics and skin care products—American Beauty and Flirt—exclusively at Kohl's. The products are priced between mass-market brands such as CoverGirl or Maybelline (sold mainly in drugstores, discount stores, and supermarkets) and

Material Girl is a Macy's exclusive brand developed by Madonna and her daughter Lourdes Leon.

Adding Value 17.2 — Home Depot—Providing Customers Better Access to Products[iv]

By paying attention to what shoppers actually are buying in their stores, many big-box retailers that previously sought to stock a focused product assortment are shifting their inventories to feature more seemingly mismatched items. Shoppers at Home Depot wanted charcoal to go along with the new grills they had just bought, and laundry detergent to use with their new washer/dryer combos, so the home improvement store has expanded its offerings of such consumer goods. Other examples may seem even less convergent though. Staples now stocks coffee pods, because office employees and home-based workers rely on their single-serving machines for a caffeine boost. But it also provides personal deodorant and shaving cream. By stocking such items, Staples hopes that people popping in for toner will also appreciate the convenience of purchasing some basic necessities in the same store, rather than visiting another retailer to gather such items.

Additionally, as customers continue to grow more comfortable with online buying, Home Depot is increasing its investment in its e-commerce operations. This provides customers access to more than 600,000 items, whereas the largest store can carry only 35,000 products. It also allows customers to enjoy in-home delivery of bulky products such as sinks or patio sets, rather than having to find a way to lug the heavy items home on their own. It also has set predictions for what it believes will be the fastest movers online: quick purchases such as light bulbs and extension cords, combined with big, heavy items such as appliances.

With their online efforts, Home Depot also hopes to appeal to its business customers. Online ordering would enable a contractor to put together an e-commerce order for the project it has scheduled for the next day, then stop by the store to pick up the entire supply on the way to the project site. Such options are not without challenges though.

Why does Home Depot's internet site carry more than 600,000 items, while its largest stores carry only 35,000?

Lauder's higher-end brands (sold primarily in more fashion-forward department stores such as Macy's and Dillard's).

Exclusive brands offer a double benefit: They are available at only one retailer, and they provide name recognition similar to that of a national brand. The disadvantage of exclusive brands, from the manufacturer's perspective, is that they can be sold by only one retailer, and therefore, the manufacturer's market is limited. From the retailer's perspective, the disadvantage is that it has to share its profits with the national brand manufacturer, whereas with a private-label brand, it does not.

Given the price of a Coach bag, would you expect to find it in Saks Fifth Avenue or JCPenney?

Price

Price helps define the value of both the merchandise and the service, and the general price range of a particular store helps define its image. Although both Saks Fifth Avenue and JCPenney are department stores, their images could not be more different. Thus, when Coach considers which of these firms is most appropriate for its new line for men, it must keep in mind customers' perceived images of these retailers' price–quality relationship. The company does not, for instance, want to attempt to sell its new line at JCPenney if it is positioning the line with a relatively high price.

Price must always be aligned with the other elements of a retailer's strategy: product, promotion, and place. A customer would not expect to pay $600 for a Coach for Men briefcase at a JCPenney store, but she might question the briefcase's quality if its price is significantly less than $600 at Neiman Marcus. As we discovered in Chapters 14 and 15, there is much more to pricing than simply adding a markup onto a product's cost. Manufacturers must consider at what price they will sell the product to retailers so that both the manufacturer and the retailer can make a reasonable profit. At the same time, both the manufacturer and the retailer are concerned about what the customer is willing and expecting to pay.

Promotion

Retailers and manufacturers know that good promotion, both within the retail environments and in the media, can mean the difference between flat sales and a growing consumer base. Advertising in traditional media such as newspapers, magazines, and television continues to be important to get customers into stores. Increasingly, electronic communications are being used for promotions as well. Some traditional approaches, such as direct mail, are being reevaluated by retailers, but many are still finding value in sending catalogs to customers and selected mailing lists. Companies also offer real-time promotions on their websites. For example, CVS.com contains in-store and online coupons that customers can use immediately on the website or print to use in the store. Coupons.com offers coupons that customers can use immediately for many grocery store items. Customers can follow this vendor on Twitter@Coupons to find even more savings opportunities.

Technology is thus expanding the ways in which retailers can reach customers with their promotional message. For example, customers can access a retailer's Internet site using a variety of devices, ranging from a computer to a mobile phone. Due to the rapid growth of domestic and international broadband access through mobile devices, retailers are investing in mobile commerce (M-commerce)— product and service purchases through mobile devices. However, the typical retailer's website is not designed to accommodate a mobile device's small screen and slower download speeds. Various firms, including Sephora, therefore have developed special sites for users to access through mobile devices. In addition, Sephora and other retailers have created specialized applications that enable mobile device users to shop or obtain more merchandise information.

A coordinated effort between the manufacturer and retailer helps guarantee that the customer receives a cohesive message and that both entities maintain their image. For example, Coach for Men might work with its most important retailers to develop advertising and point-of-sale signs. It may even help defray the costs of

Consumers can access retailers' coupons from their mobile devices.

advertising by paying all or a portion of the advertising's production and media costs, an agreement called cooperative (co-op) advertising.

Store credit cards and gift cards are subtler forms of promotion that also facilitate shopping. Retailers might offer pricing promotions—such as coupons, rebates, and in-store or online discounts, or perhaps buy-one-get-one-free offers—to attract consumers and stimulate sales. These promotions play a very important role in driving traffic to retail locations, increasing average purchase size, and creating opportunities for repeat purchases. But retail promotions also are valuable to customers; they inform customers about what is new and available and how much it costs.

Another type of promotion occurs inside the store, where retailers use displays and signs, placed at the point of purchase (POP) or in strategic areas such as the end of aisles, to inform customers and stimulate purchases of the featured products.

In addition to traditional forms of promotion, many retailers are devoting more resources to their overall retail environment as a means to promote and showcase what the store has to offer. These promotions may take the form of recognizable approaches, such as in-store and window displays, or they may be entirely new experiences designed to help retailers draw customers and add value to the shopping experience. Bass Pro Shops Outdoor World in Lawrenceville, Georgia, offers a 30,000-gallon aquarium stocked with fish for casting demonstrations, an indoor archery range, and a 43-foot climbing wall. These features enhance customers' visual experiences, provide them with educational information, and enhance the store's sales potential by enabling customers to try before they buy. In addition to adding fun to the shopping experience, these activities help offset the current drop in brick-and-mortar customers engendered by online shopping.

A variety of factors influence whether customers will actually buy once they are in the store. Some of these factors are quite subtle. Consumers' perceptions of value and their subsequent patronage are heavily influenced by their perceptions of the store's look and feel. Music, color, scent, aisle size, lighting, the availability of seating, and crowding can also significantly affect the overall shopping experience.[21] Therefore, the extent to which stores offer a more pleasant shopping experience fosters a better mood, resulting in greater spending.

Consider the funky C. Wonder emporium for example. This 7,000-square-foot store is divided into various nooks, each with its own personality or feel, including English Town House, Vail Cabin, Palm Springs Modern, and Hollywood

The customer experience is enhanced at C. Wonder by displaying merchandise in a variety of nooks with different personalities, having electronically enhanced fitting rooms, and using microchips embedded in the sales tags so customers can checkout anywhere in the store.

Regency. The separate sectors help customers navigate through the vast amount of merchandise available. To grant them control over their experience, C. Wonder's fitting rooms also come equipped with control panels, such that people trying on items can adjust the type and volume of music played, as well as the lighting, to suit their preferences.[22]

Personal selling and customer service representatives are also part of the overall promotional package. Retailers must provide services that make it easier to buy and use products, and retail associates—whether in the store, on the phone, or on the Internet—provide customers with information about product characteristics and availability. These individuals can also facilitate the sale of products or services that consumers perceive as complicated, risky, or expensive, such as an air conditioning unit, a computer, or a diamond ring. Manufacturers can play an important role in preparing retail sales and service associates to sell their products. Eva thus could conduct seminars or webinars about how to use and sell her new line of green cosmetics and supply printed educational materials to sales associates. Last but not least, sales reps handle the sales transactions.

In some retail firms, salesperson and customer service functions are being augmented, or even replaced, by technology in the form of in-store kiosks, the Internet, or self-checkout lanes. At C. Wonder, microchips embedded in the sales tags of every item help the sales staff keep track of where the merchandise is in the store. They also can check out customers anywhere in the store using handheld registers, which eliminates the need for customers to head to the checkout counter before they leave.[23]

Traditionally, retailers treated all their customers the same. Today, the most successful retailers concentrate on providing more value to their best customers. The knowledge retailers gain from their store personnel, the Internet browsing and buying activities of customers, and the data they collect on customer shopping habits can be used in customer relationship management (CRM). Using this information, retailers may modify product, price, and/or promotion to attempt to increase their share of wallet—the percentage of the customer's purchases made from that particular retailer. For instance, omnichannel retailers use consumer information collected from the customers' Internet browsing and buying behavior to send dedicated e-mails to customers promoting specific products or services. Retailers also may offer special discounts to good customers to help them become even more loyal.

Place

Retailers already have realized that convenience is a key ingredient to success, and an important aspect of this success is convenient locations.[24] As the old cliché claims, the three most important things in retailing are location, location, location. Many customers choose stores on the basis of where they are located, which makes great locations a competitive advantage that few rivals can duplicate. For instance, once Starbucks saturates a market by opening in the best locations, Peet's will have difficulty breaking into that same market—where would it put its stores?

In pursuit of better and better locations, retailers are experimenting with different options to reach their target markets. Walgreens has free-standing stores, unconnected to other retailers, so the stores can offer a drive-up window for customers to pick up their prescriptions. Walmart, Staples, and others are opening smaller stores in urban locations to serve those markets better.

To make their locations more convenient, Walgreens has some free-standing stores, not connected to other retailers, so the stores can offer a drive-up window for customers to pick up their prescriptions.

BENEFITS OF STORES FOR CONSUMERS

LO6 Identify the benefits of stores.

In this section, we explore the relative advantages of the most traditional retail channels, the brick-and-mortar stores, from consumers' perspective. In the following section, we examine how the addition of the Internet channel has added value to retailers' ability to satisfy their customers' needs.

Browsing Shoppers often have only a general sense of what they want (e.g., a sweater, something for dinner, a gift) but don't know the specific item they want. They go to a store to see what is available before making their final decision about what to buy. Although some consumers surf the web and look through catalogs for ideas, many still prefer browsing in stores. Some also employ both approaches, getting a sense of what's available through catalogs or the Internet and then going to the store to try on apparel or view the actual object.

Touching and Feeling Products Perhaps the greatest benefit offered by stores is the opportunity for customers to use all five of their senses—touch, smell, taste, vision, and hearing—to examine products.

Personal Service Sales associates have the capability to provide meaningful, personalized information. Salespeople can be particularly helpful when purchasing a complicated product, like consumer electronics, or something the customer doesn't know much about, like raw Japanese selvedge denim jeans.

Cash and Credit Payment Stores are the only channel that accepts cash payments. Some customers prefer to pay with cash because it is easy, resolves the transaction immediately, and does not result in potential interest payments. And, of course, some people don't have a credit card. Some customers also prefer to use their credit card or debit card in person rather than send the payment information electronically via the Internet.

Entertainment and Social Experience In-store shopping can be a stimulating experience for some people, providing a break in their daily routine and enabling them to interact with friends.

Immediate Gratification Stores have the advantage of allowing customers to get the merchandise immediately after paying for it.

Risk Reduction When customers purchase merchandise in stores, the physical presence of the store reduces their perceived risk of buying and increases their confidence that any problems with the merchandise will be corrected.

At LegoLand in Minneapolis' Mall of America, customers can browse, touch, and feel the product, enjoy personal service, be entertained, and interact with others.

BENEFITS OF THE INTERNET AND OMNICHANNEL RETAILING

LO7 Identify the benefits of omnichannel retailing.

In the previous section, we detailed the relative benefits of stores from the consumers' perspective. In this section, we examine how the addition of the Internet channel to traditional store-based retailers has improved their ability to serve their customers and build a competitive advantage in several ways.

First, the addition of an Internet channel has the potential to offer a greater selection of products. Second, an Internet channel enables retailers to provide customers with more personalized information about products and services. Third, it offers sellers the unique opportunity to collect information about consumer shopping behavior—information that they can use to improve the shopping experience across all channels. Fourth, the Internet channel allows sellers to enter new markets economically.

Deeper and Broader Selection

One benefit of adding the Internet channel is the vast number of alternatives retailers can make available to consumers without crowding their aisles or increasing their square footage. Stores and catalogs are limited by their size. By shopping on the Internet, consumers can easily visit and select merchandise from a broader array of retailers. Individual retailers' websites typically offer deeper assortments of merchandise (more colors, brands, and sizes) than are available in stores or catalogs. This expanded offering enables them to satisfy consumer demand for less popular styles, colors, or sizes. Many retailers also offer a broader assortment (more categories) on their websites. Staples.com, for instance, offers soft drinks and cleaning supplies, which are not available in stores, so that its business customers will view it as a one-stop shop.

Personalization

Another benefit of adding the Internet channel is the ability to personalize promotions and services economically, including heightened service or individualized offerings.

Personalized Customer Service Traditional Internet channel approaches for responding to customer questions—such as FAQ (frequently asked questions) pages and offering an 800 number or e-mail address to ask questions—often do not provide the timely information customers are seeking. To improve customer service from an electronic channel, many firms offer live online chats, so that customers can click a button at any time and participate in an instant messaging conversation with a customer service representative. This technology also enables firms to send a proactive chat invitation at specific times to visitors to the site. Virgin Airlines programs its chat windows to appear at the moment a customer chooses a flight, because its goal is to upsell these willing buyers to a more expensive fare.[25] Other online retailers use metrics such as the amount of time spent on the site or number of repeat visits to determine which customers will receive an invitation to chat.

Personalized Offering The interactive nature of the Internet also provides an opportunity for retailers to personalize their offerings for each of their customers, based on customers' behavior. Just as a well-trained salesperson would make recommendations to customers prior to checkout, an interactive web page can make suggestions to the shopper about items that he or she might like to see based on previous purchases, what other customers who purchased the same item purchased, or common web viewing behavior.

Some omnichannel retailers are able to personalize promotions and Internet home pages on the basis of several attributes tied to the shopper's current or previous web sessions, such as the time of day, time zone as determined by a computer's Internet address, and assumed gender.[26] However, some consumers worry about this ability to collect information about purchase histories, personal information, and search behavior on the Internet. How will this information be used in the future? Will it be sold to other firms, or will the consumer receive unwanted promotional materials online or in the mail?

Expand Market Presence

The market for customers who shop in stores is typically limited to consumers living in proximity to those stores. The market for catalogs is limited by the high cost of printing and mailing them and increasing consumer interest in environmentally friendly practices. By adding the Internet channel, retailers can expand their market without having to build new stores or incur the high cost of additional catalogs. Adding an Internet channel is particularly attractive to retailers with strong brand names but limited locations and distribution. For example, retailers such as Nordstrom, REI, IKEA, and L.L.Bean are widely known for offering unique, high-quality merchandise. If these retailers only had a store, customers would have to travel vast distances to buy the merchandise they carry.

EFFECTIVE OMNICHANNEL RETAILING

Detail the challenges of omnichannel retailing.

Consumers desire a seamless experience when interacting with omnichannel retailers. They want to be recognized by a retailer, whether they interact with a sales associate, the retailer's website, or the retailer's call center by telephone. Customers want to buy a product through the retailer's Internet or catalog channels and pick it up or return it to a local store; find out if a product offered on the Internet channel is available at a local store; and, when unable to find a product in a store, determine if it is available for home delivery through the retailer's Internet channel.

However, providing this seamless experience for customers is not easy for retailers. Because each of the channels is somewhat different, a critical decision facing omnichannel retailers is the degree to which they should or are able to integrate the operations of the channels.[27] To determine how much integration is best, each retailer must address issues such as integrated CRM, brand image, pricing, and the supply chain.

Integrated CRM

Effective omnichannel operations require an integrated CRM (customer relationship management) system with a centralized customer data warehouse that houses a complete history of each customer's interaction with the retailer, regardless of whether the sale occurred in a store, on the Internet, or on the telephone.[28] This information storehouse allows retailers to efficiently handle complaints, expedite returns, target future promotions, and provide a seamless experience for customers when they interact with the retailer through multiple channels.

Brand Image

Retailers need to provide a consistent brand image across all channels. For example, Patagonia reinforces its image of selling high-quality, environmentally friendly sports equipment in its stores, catalogs, and website. Each of these channels emphasizes function, not fashion, in the descriptions of Patagonia's products. Patagonia's position about taking care of the environment is communicated by carefully lighting its stores and using recycled polyester and organic, rather than pesticide-intensive cotton, in many of its clothes.

Pricing

Pricing represents another difficult decision for an omnichannel retailer. Customers expect pricing consistency for the same SKU across channels (excluding shipping charges and sales tax). However, in some cases, retailers need to adjust their pricing strategy because of the competition they face in different channels. For example, Barnes & Noble offers lower prices through its Internet channel (www.bn.com) than in its stores to compete effectively against Amazon.com.

Retailers with stores in multiple markets often set different prices for the same merchandise to compete better with local stores. Customers generally are not aware of these price differences because they are only exposed to the prices in

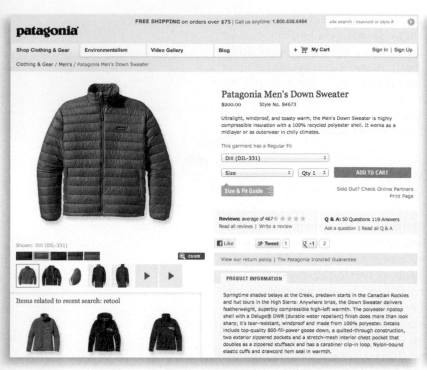

Multichannel retailers like Patagonia sell on the Internet (left), in catalogs (right), and in stores (bottom).

their local markets. However, omnichannel retailers may have difficulties sustaining these regional price differences when customers can easily check prices on the Internet.

Supply Chain

Omnichannel retailers struggle to provide an integrated shopping experience across all their channels because unique skills and resources are needed to manage each channel.[29] For example, store-based retail chains operate and manage many stores, each requiring the management of inventory and people. With Internet and catalog operations, inventory and telephone salespeople instead are typically centralized in one or two locations. Also, retail distribution centers (DCs) supporting a store channel are designed to ship many cartons of merchandise to stores. In contrast, the DCs supporting a catalog and Internet channel are designed to ship a few items to individual customers. The difference in shipping orientation for the two types of operations requires a completely different type of distribution center.

Due to these operational differences, many store-based retailers have a separate organization to manage their Internet and catalog operations. But as the omnichannel operation matures, retailers tend to integrate all operations under one organization. Both Walmart and JCPenney initially had separate organizations for their Internet channel but subsequently integrated them with stores and catalogs.

CHECK YOURSELF

1. What are the components of a retail strategy?

2. What are the advantages of traditional stores versus Internet-only stores?

3. What challenges do retailers face when marketing their products through multiple channels?

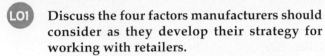

Reviewing Learning Objectives

LO1 Discuss the four factors manufacturers should consider as they develop their strategy for working with retailers.

When they initiate the decision process for choosing retail partners, manufacturers determine how likely it is that certain retailers would carry their products and whether target customers expect to find their products for sale at those retail locations. Next, manufacturers need to identify types of retailers that would be appropriate locations for their products. After identifying likely and appropriate retailers, manufacturers work with their retailer partners to develop a strategy that comprises the four Ps. Finally, manufacturers, again with their retail partners, must determine which elements of an omnichannel strategy will be effective.

LO2 Outline the considerations associated with choosing retail partners.

Manufacturers often start by noting the basic channel structure, which includes the level of vertical integration, the relative strength of the retailer and the manufacturer, and the strength of the brand. They also consider where their target customers expect to find products, which depends largely on the retailer's image. Channel member characteristics also are important inputs, as is the level of distribution intensity.

LO3 List the three levels of distribution intensity.

Intensive distribution intensity means the product is available virtually everywhere, in as many places as will agree to carry it. In an exclusive distribution intensity strategy, the manufacturer allows only one retailer (or retail chain) in each area to sell its products. Selective distribution is the middle ground option; several retailers carry the products, but not all of them.

LO4 Describe the various types of retailers.

Retailers generally fall into one of three categories: food retailers, general merchandise retailers, or service retailers. Each of the categories consists of various formats, including supermarkets, supercenters, warehouse clubs, convenience stores, department stores, discount stores, specialty retailers, drugstores, category specialists, extreme-value retailers, and off-price stores. Although service retailers primarily sell services, if they sell to consumers, they are still retailers. Service retailers span the gambit from universities to automobile oil change shops.

LO5 Describe the components of a retail strategy.

To develop a coordinated strategy—which represents a key goal for an effective channel partnership between retailers and manufacturers—both retailers and manufacturers need to consider all of the four Ps in conjunction: product, place, promotion, and price.

LO6 Identify the benefits of stores.

Because consumers often have just a general idea of what they want to purchase, stores' main benefits come from giving shoppers a place to browse. They can touch and feel products, obtain personal services, pay using cash or credit, engage in an entertaining and social experience, receive instant gratification, and reduce their sense of risk.

LO7 Identify the benefits of omnichannel retailing.

The various types of retail channels—stores, catalogs, and the Internet—all offer their own benefits and limitations, including those related to availability, convenience, and safety, among others. If a retailer adopts an omnichannel strategy, it can exploit the benefits and mitigate the limitations of each channel and help expand its overall market presence. Furthermore, an omnichannel strategy offers the chance to gain a greater share of customers' wallets and more insight into their buying behaviors.

LO8 Detail the challenges of omnichannel retailing.

To function in multiple channels, retailers must organize their operations carefully to ensure an integrated customer experience. In particular, they have to have an integrated CRM system, and determine how to maintain a consistent brand image across the various channels, whether to charge the same or different prices, and how best to deliver merchandise to multiple channels.

Key Terms

⊞LEARNSMART

- big-box retailer, 528
- category killer, 528
- category specialist, 528
- convenience store, 527
- conventional supermarket, 525
- cooperative (co-op) advertising, 535
- department store, 527
- distribution intensity, 523
- drugstore, 528
- exclusive brand, 532
- exclusive distribution, 523

- extreme-value food retailer, 525
- extreme-value retailer, 529
- full-line discount store, 528
- intensive distribution, 523
- limited-assortment supermarket, 525
- mobile commerce (M-commerce), 534
- off-price retailer, 530
- omnichannel or multichannel strategy, 521

- online chat, 538
- private-label or store brand, 532
- retailing, 520
- selective distribution, 524
- service retailer, 530
- share of wallet, 536
- specialty store, 528
- supercenter, 525
- warehouse club, 526

Marketing Applications

1. Does Reebok pursue an intensive, an exclusive, or a selective distribution intensity strategy? Would you suggest any changes to this strategy?

2. Why don't traditional department stores have the same strong appeal to younger American consumers that they once enjoyed during their heyday in the last half of the 20th century? Discuss which types of retailers are now competing with department stores.

3. Assume that adidas, the shoe manufacturer, has decided to sell expensive wristwatches for men and women. What factors should it consider when developing its strategy for choosing retail partners?

4. Some argue that retailers can be eliminated from the distribution channel because they only add costs to the final product without creating any value-added services in the process. Do you agree with this perspective? Are consumers likely to make most purchases directly from manufacturers in the near future? Provide justification for your answers.

5. Assume you have been given some money but told that it must be invested in a retailer's stock. In which type of retailer would you choose to invest? Which specific retailer? Provide a rationale for your answers.

6. Provide examples of how manufacturers work with retailers to jointly plan and implement the four Ps.

7. Why have so many brick-and-mortar retailers adopted an omnichannel strategy?

8. You can purchase apparel at a discount store, specialty store, category specialist, off-price retailer, department store, or Internet-only store. From which of these types of stores do you shop? Explain why you prefer one type store over another.

9. Should Tana (a young entrepreneur), launching a new line of environmentally friendly (green) cosmetics, sell through a physical store, catalog, or Internet? Explain two key benefits of each channel for her business.

10. Search the Internet for a product you want to buy. Are there differences in the prices, shipping charges, or return policies among the different retailers offering the product? From which retailer would you buy? Explain the criteria you would use to make the decision.

11. Name a retailer from which you have received personalized service, product, or promotion offerings online. What form of personalization did you receive? Did the personalization influence your purchase decision? Explain why or why not.

Quiz Yourself

1. Retailing is where marketing _____.
   a. is replaced by personal selling
   b. meets the consumer
   c. meets corporate management
   d. sells itself to the corporation
   e. conducts all of its transactions

2. If you were a marketer for a clothing manufacturer and you wanted to improve revenues from merchandise with minor construction errors, production overruns, and returns, you would be attracted to using _____.
   a. department stores
   b. specialty stores
   c. category specialists
   d. off-price retailers
   e. supercenters

   (Answers to these two questions can be found on page 652.)

Net Savvy

1. How do JCrew.com and Gap.com provide value to their customers beyond the physical products they sell? Why would a customer purchase online instead of going to the store? Under what circumstances would the customer prefer a store-based experience?

2. Select a familiar omnichannel retailer. Evaluate its website in terms of how well it provides value to its customers. Do you believe that offering multiple selling channels to customers enhances their shopping experience? How does it help the retailer? Explain your answer.

Chapter Case Study

TARGET AND ITS NEW GENERATION OF PARTNERSHIPS

Minneapolis-based Target has been an innovator in structuring retail partnerships that offer customers something special: fashion-forward housewares and apparel at prices they can afford. In addition to its Target.com website, the company operates 1,683 stores in 48 states, which includes 239 SuperTarget stores, along with 37 distribution centers nationally and a separate headquartered location in India.[30] Apparel and accessories account for approximately 20 percent of Target's annual sales.

Similar to rivals Walmart and Kmart, Target offers the vast breadth of a full-line discount store, featuring everything from cosmetics to baby clothes, housewares to electronics. But Target also has uniquely positioned itself through a series of exclusive partnerships with top designers, such as Zac Posen, Missoni, and Altuzarra, who have collaborated with the retailer to offer limited-edition, distinctive products. Although other retailers also have developed relationships with designers to create exclusive brands—such as Keds for Kate Spade New York and Derek Lam for DesigNation at Kohl's—these competitors have struggled to maintain their lower prices.[31]

Thus, though it is not alone in partnering with designers, Target appears to be the best practitioner of this strategy. The company launched its first retail partnership in 1999 with renowned architect Michael Graves, whose teakettles and toasters were hailed for having brought the word "design" back to the housewares category.[32] Since then, the company has worked with more than 80 design partners who have generally welcomed the chance to reach a mass market with their exclusive labels.[33]

Most of the partnerships have been limited to a specific time, which also has built a sense of urgency and exclusivity around the offers. Target's holiday offerings featured a number of designer labels: Harajuku Mini kids' clothing from designer Gwen Stefani; hats from Albertus Swanepoel; and a jewelry line featuring designs by Dana Kellin. Whether time-limited or longer term, such partnerships have consistently offered high-profile labels at moderate prices, helping the retailer boost its bottom line.

Target's collaboration with Missoni made the biggest splash though. The fashion world was stunned when the Italian fashion house agreed to create a collection for Target. The big American retail store is the diametric opposite of the high-end shops that have typically carried Missoni's expensive knitwear and apparel. Target's announcement through Facebook, other social media sites, and a Manhattan pop-up shop for fashion editors, celebrities, and other Missoni clientele helped stoke public excitement.

Of course, such excitement can cause problems as well. Target's website crashed just moments after the Missoni launch, as customers clicked in droves to buy up the designer duds.[34] Although the site remained up when Jason Wu (the designer of Michelle Obama's famous inaugural gown) released his line, many stores reported nearly immediate stockouts. Customers in a Miami store watched in shock and dismay as one couple swooped in and purchased the entire selection that was on the retail floor.[35]

Now Target has created a new model for retail partnership as a way to offer its shoppers something different. Through a store-inside-a-store initiative that it has dubbed The Shops at Target, the retailer is partnering directly with small specialty shops and boutiques to offer their limited-edition merchandise, from dog biscuits to vintage furniture, at prices ranging from $1.99 to $159.99.

The store-within-a-store, with dedicated space branded by the designer, has already proven a successful strategy elsewhere. Macy's has Ralph Lauren boutiques; Bloomingdale's has Chanel boutiques. JCPenney, a close Target competitor, also hosts Sephora boutiques, MNG by Mango, and other designer brands.[36]

The Shops at Target collaboration is being rolled out as a series of six-week partnerships. For its first round, the retailer chose five independently owned specialty shops—The Candy Store; the Cos Bar cosmetic shop; Polka Dog Bakery; the Privet House home accessories shop; and The Webster, a high-end Miami clothing store—all getting their first crack at a national market through Target's nearly 1,800 locations, not to mention its website. Target plans to repeat the program subsequently with new sets of boutiques, but the initial group alone will add nearly 400 new and exclusive products to Target's online and store inventories.[37]

In a separate but parallel development, Target has also announced that Apple will open 25 small retail shops at Target locations around the country.[38] This isn't a first for Apple; it already has some ministores at Best Buy locations. So what's the special appeal? Target already sells both iPads and iPods, but the expanded in-store venture can introduce Apple products to new groups of customers, including those who might not be looking for electronics.[39] Full-blown shops for Apple products, with their own décor and personality, should encourage Target shoppers to test out the products. Furthermore, of the vast number of people who enter Target stores every day, many of them will stumble on an Apple shop and be unable to resist playing around with the appealing, fun products. Whether they buy on that shopping trip or on another visit back to Target, Apple thus is likely to expand its sales.

Target shoppers thus have come to expect a steady stream of exclusive new designer brands, along with the constant possibility of finding something unique, even unpredictable, in the next aisle over. Now the big merchandiser is hoping to keep that excitement going with its new specialty-shop partnerships. But just as it was introducing that new retail model, Target was also forced to announce disappointing sales figures and declining profits.[40] The question going forward will be whether Target—the store loyal customers have dubbed "Tarzhay" for its supply of "cheap chic"—can keep its steady customers coming back, while attracting more shoppers with new rounds of boutique surprises.

Questions

1. Assess the role of consumer expectations in Target's success as a major discount retailer.
2. What differentiates Target's new retail partnership model from its longstanding partnerships with top designers? What are the relative strengths of each?

3. What explains Target's ability to attract top designers and high-end specialty shops as retail partners?

4. Given that Apple has long operated its own retail locations, how do you explain its interest in partnering with Target?

5. Using the factors for choosing retail partners outlined in the chapter, do you believe that Eva's line of green cosmetics should attempt to get placement in Target?

6. Develop a strategy for Target to promote Eva's line of green cosmetics as part of its new specialty shop partnership program.

Endnotes

1. Susannah Edelbaum, "LED Screens, Interactive Windows, a High-Tech H&M, Oh My!" *The High Low*, November 12, 2013, http://thehighlow.com; Sharon Edelson, "H&M Opening High-Tech Flagship in Times Square," *Women's Wear Daily*, November 12, 2013; Ruth La Ferla, "Lady Gaga Drops In at H&M and the Crowd Goes . . . Well, You Know," *The New York Times*, November 15, 2013, http://www.nytimes.com; Joel Landau, "David Beckham Appears at H&M Store in Times Square," *New York Daily News*, February 1, 2014, http://www.nydailynews.com/.

2. "2011 Global 250 Retailers," *Stores Magazine*, January 2012, http://www.stores.org/STORES%20Magazine%20January%20 2014/global-powers-retailing-top-250.

3. This chapter draws heavily from Michael Levy, Barton A. Weitz, and Dhruv Grewal, *Retailing Management*, 9th ed. (Burr Ridge, IL: McGraw-Hill/Irwin, 2015).

4. "Sales of Food at Home by Type of Outlet Table," *USDA Economic Research Service*, 2010, http://www.ers.usda.gov/datafiles/Food_ Expenditures/Food_Expenditures/2010table14_percent.xls.

5. "Top 25 Global Food Retailers 2012," *Supermarket News*, 2012, http://supermarketnews.com/top-25-global-food-retailers-2012/.

6. "Top 75 Retailers & Wholesalers 2012," *Supermarket News*, 2012, http://supermarketnews.com/top-75-retailers-wholesalers-2012.

7. "Conventional Supermarket," *TermWiki*, http://en.termwiki.com/ EN:conventional_supermarket (accessed September 6, 2012).

8. "The Fresh Perspective Industry Newsletter," *Perishables Group*, December 2011, http://www.perishablesgroup.com/dnn/ LinkClick.aspx?fileticket=CZXbD9yso5g%3D&tabid=4162.

9. "Low-End Grocery Stores Carve Out Niche," *Contact Center Solutions Industry News*, October 13, 2007, http://www.tmcnet. com/usubmit/2007/10/13/3012485.htm.

10. Ibid.

11. Emily Bryson York, "Stuck in the Middle, Big Grocers Make Changes," *Chicago Tribune*, January 6, 2011.

12. "Walmart Supercenters," http://walmartstores.com.

13. https://www.deloitte.com/assets/Dcom-Global/Local%20Assets/ Documents/Consumer%20Business/dtt_CBT_GPRetailing2012. pdf.

14. Karen Talley, "Department Stores Are in Good Position after 1Q Resurgence," *Dow Jones Newswires*, May 16, 2011.

15. Stephanie Clifford, "To Stand Out, Retailers Flock to Exclusive Lines," *The New York Times*, February 14, 2011; Amy Verner, "How Department Stores Can Stay Relevant (and Chic)," *Globe and Mail* (Toronto), April 21, 2012.

16. "Walmart Annual Report," http://walmartstores.com; Sandra M. Jones, "Wal-Mart Making Little Plans," *Chicago Tribune*, May 14, 2011.

17. Russell Redman, "Industry Outlook: Drug Chains Lifted by Improved Economy," *Chain Drug Review*, May 2, 2011, http://www. chaindrugreview.com.

18. Katherine Rosman, "Aspirin, Q-Tips and a New You," *The Wall Street Journal*, March 25, 2010; Sandra M. Jones, "Walgreens Plans Makeover in More Stores," *Chicago Tribune*, March 24, 2010.

19. http://www.wikinvest.com/industry/Off-price_Retail.

20. This section draws from Levy et al., *Retailing Management*, Chapter 2.

21. Nancy M. Pucinelli et al., "The Value of Knowing What Customers Really Want: Interpersonal Accuracy as an Environmental Cue," working paper (2012); Nancy Puccinelli et al., "Customer Experience Management in Retailing: Understanding the Buying Process," *Journal of Retailing* 85 (2009), pp. 15–30.

22. Patricia Marx, "C. Wonder," *The New Yorker*, November 21, 2011, p. 34.

23. Ibid.

24. Kathleen Seiders et al., "SERVCON: A Multidimensional Scale for Measuring Perceptions of Service Convenience," *Journal of the Academy of Marketing Science* 35, no. 1 (2007), pp. 144–56; Leonard Berry, Kathleen Seiders, and Dhruv Grewal, "Understanding Service Convenience," *Journal of Marketing* 66, no. 3 (July 2002).

25. Sherice Jacobs, "3 Ways Live Chat Software Can Improve Your Conversion Rates," *The Daily Egg*, July 23, 2013, http://blog. crazyegg.com.

26. "Sponsored Supplement: Expanding the Reach of Personalization," *Internet Retailer*, March 2010.

27. Christian Homburg, Josef Vollmayr, and Alexander Hahn, "Firm Value Creation through Major Channel Expansions: Evidence from an Event Study in the United States, Germany, and China," *Journal of Marketing*, 2014, http://dx.doi.org/10.1509/ jm.12.0179.

28. Hongshuang (Alice) Li and P. K. Kannan, "Attributing Conversions in a Multichannel Online Marketing Environment: An Empirical Model and a Field Experiment," *Journal of Marketing Research* 51 (February 2014), pp. 40–56.

29. Jie Zhang et al., "Crafting Integrated Multichannel Retailing Strategies," *Journal of Interactive Marketing*, 2010.

30. Target.com, "Corporate Overview," http://pressroom.target.com.

31. Jessica Wohl, "Target Hopes Exclusive Designer Deals Boost Sales," *Reuters*, August 2, 2011; Greg Petro, "Retailer/Designer Collaborations—The Missing Link," *Forbes*, February 28, 2013, www.forbes.com.

32. Mary Catherine O'Connor, "Target Shoppers: Say Goodbye to Michael Graves' Budget-Friendly Design," *smartplanet,* February 16, 2012, http://www.smartplanet.com.

33. Target.com, "Target Unveils New Design Partnership Program," January 13, 2012, http://pressroom.target.com.

34. Emanualla Grinberg, "'Missoni for Target' Line Crashes Site," *CNN.com,* September 13, 2011, http://articles.cnn.com.

35. "Jason Wu for Target Apparel Sells Out in Hours," *ABCNews. com,* February 6, 2012, http://abcnews.go.com.

36. Stephanie Clifford, "In a Test, Target Plans to Add an Apple 'Store' Inside 25 Stores," *The New York Times,* January 12, 2101, http://www.nytimes.com.

37. Ibid.; Target.com, "Target Unveils New Design Partnership Program."

38. Samantha Murphy, "Apple Mini-Stores Coming to Target," *The Wall Street Journal,* January 13, 2012, http://mashable.com.

39. Ibid.; Clifford, "In a Test."

40. Ibid.

i. Elaine Watson, "Quirky, Cult-Like, Aspirational, but Affordable: The Rise and Rise of Trader Joe's," *The Packaged Facts,* April 15, 2014.

ii. Stuart Elliott, "For CVS Regulars, Ads Tailored Just for Them," *The New York Times,* October 10, 2013.

iii. Cary Stemle, "Has the Food Truck Bubble Burst?" *QSR News,* May 1, 2013, http://www.qsrweb.com; Dale Buss, "White Castle Joins CPG, QSR Brands on Food Truck Bandwagon," *BrandChannel,* June 21, 2013, http://www.brandchannel.com; Venessa Wong, "White Castle Slides into Food-Truck Trend," *Bloomberg Businessweek,* June 12, 2013, http://www.businessweek.com.

iv. Shelly Banjo and Serena Ng, "Home Depot: The Place to Go for Toilet Paper?" *The Wall Street Journal,* June 6, 2014; Shelly Banjo, "Home Depot Lumbers into E-Commerce," *The Wall Street Journal,* April 16, 2014.

Credits

VALUE COMMUNICATION

In Section Seven we explore value communication. Today, value communication methods are more complex because of new technologies that have added e-mail, blogs, Internet, and podcasts to the advertising mix that once utilized only radio, television, newspapers, and magazines to relay messages to consumers. Chapter 18 introduces the breadth of integrated marketing communications. Chapter 19 discusses advertising, public relations, and sales promotions. The text concludes with a discussion of personal selling in Chapter 20.

CHAPTER 18

INTEGRATED MARKETING COMMUNICATIONS

The incredible expansion of the Internet and online tools has radically changed the manner in which marketers communicate with customers. More and more, companies spread their messages over all sorts of media—television, print, radio, e-mail, Internet, and so on. To really stand out then, a company may need to go further than ever.

To achieve success in a market, companies invariably must communicate the value of their offerings in diverse, well-rounded ways. When companies promote their brands through multiple channels, they stand a better chance of reaching their customers. Coordination across these platforms is the key to effective omnichannel (or multichannel) marketing communications. But it is difficult

限りある地球資源を大切にしましょう

to ensure brand consistency when radio, television, online, and print ads each require different types of elements, unique voices, and varying styles. In addition, firms need to integrate their marketing communications even further by incorporating new opportunities to reach customers through social media sites, such as Facebook and Twitter.

Even well-known brands need to consider these issues. It might seem, for example, that Coca-Cola is such a well-defined brand that its communications would be automatically consistent across marketing channels. But as sales of its iconic Coke and Diet Coke brands have suffered some stagnation in recent years—likely attributable to increasing emphases on healthy lifestyles and concerns about artificial sweeteners and too much sugar in our diets[1]—this assumption has required some rethinking. The amount of sugar in one 12-ounce can of Coke exceeds the total recommended daily amount for an adult consumer,[2] which suggests that Coca-Cola needs to find a new way to appeal to buyers. In particular, for Millennials—young consumers who "expect unlimited

choice, personalized and delivered through multiple channels at maximum speed"—Coca-Cola has adopted a multi-pronged communication strategy.[3]

For example, the very shape of a Coke bottle represents a form of communication, leading Coca-Cola to enhance its reliance on packaging as a means to appeal to consumers. In Australia, an experiment with personalized packaging still clearly evoked the brand, through the shape and coloring, but used the most popular teen names in the country, such as Mike, Suzy, and Dave. Thus, any Suzy picking up a drink could have her own personalized beverage, boasting her name. In Japan, the personalized packaging was a little different: In a partnership with Sony, Coca-Cola promised each customer a free song download with each purchase that was customized to their birth year. A consumer born in 1990 would receive a different song than someone born in 1999, leading each buyer to sense a personal link to the brand.[4]

Along with these packaging innovations, Coca-Cola is experimenting with new product innovations, which it markets in various ways. To encourage expanded uses of its Freestyle machines, for example (see Social and Mobile Marketing 18.1 on page 556), it has developed an app that saves users' preferences and favored soda blends. Thus it emphasizes its personalization ability through mobile communications as well.

Along with these personalized forms of communication, Coca-Cola aims for a consistent message that it can specify as needed. A recent example, "Live Positively," provides Coca-Cola with a framework for discussing all its brands, including those that refer to noncarbonated beverages such as Powerade, Minute Maid juices, and Dasani water. In this framework, the company seeks to establish that Coke, Diet Coke, and other beverages are all elements of a healthy lifestyle, such that none of them requires complete abstinence, nor should any of them be the only thing a person drinks all day. This healthy lifestyle approach also is evident in Coca-Cola's consistent sponsorships of sports events, such as the FIFA World Cup.

For this event, it has developed an integrated campaign titled "The World's Cup" that includes several short documentary films under the heading "Where Will Happiness Strike Next?"; an official anthem; a massive photomosaic of fans' pictures and messages, combined in the "Happiness Flag"; and a digital film for release on television titled "One World, One Game."[5]

Even as it reportedly mulls new acquisitions of tea, coffee, and other beverage brands, Coca-Cola promises to focus most of its advertising communications on its flagship Coke brand, including an increase of $1 billion in its global advertising budget in coming years.[6] As the boundaries of advertising shift to include digital and social media, the integration of multiple marketing channels is crucial for catching customers wherever they are: through apps on their mobile devices, in front of the television, typing on their home computer, or on the go. The challenge persists, even for a marketing giant like Coca-Cola.

As this description of Coca-Cola's marketing campaigns attests, each element of an integrated marketing communications (IMC) strategy must have a well-defined purpose and support and extend the message delivered by all the other elements.

Throughout this book, we have focused our attention on how firms create value by developing products and services. However, consumers are not likely to come flocking to new products and services unless they are aware of them. Therefore, marketers must consider how to communicate the value of a product and/or service—or more specifically, the value proposition—to the target market. A firm must develop a communication strategy to demonstrate the value of its product. We begin our discussion by examining what IMC is, how it has developed, and how it contributes to value creation.

Integrated marketing communications (IMC) represents the promotion P of the four Ps. It encompasses a variety of communication disciplines—advertising, personal selling, sales promotion, public relations, direct marketing, and online marketing including social media—in combination to provide clarity, consistency, and maximum communicative impact.[7] Instead of consisting of separated marketing communications elements with no unified control, IMC programs regard each of the firm's marketing communications elements as part of a whole, each of which offers a different means to connect with the target audience. This integration of elements provides the firm with the best means to reach the target audience with the desired message, and it enhances the value story by offering a clear and consistent message.

There are three elements in any IMC strategy: the consumer, the channels through which the message is communicated, and the evaluation of the results of the communication. This chapter is organized around these three elements. In the first section, the focus is on consumers, so we examine how consumers receive communications, whether via media or other methods, as well as how the delivery of that communication affects a message's form and contents. The second

EXHIBIT 18.1 The Communication Process

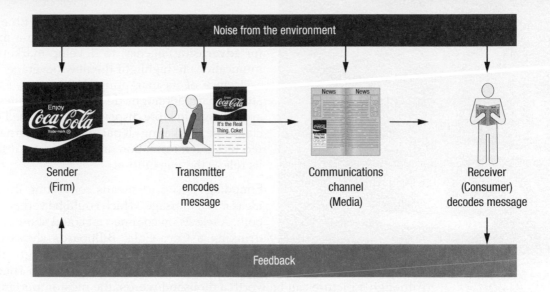

section examines the various communication channels that make up the components of IMC and how each is used in an overall IMC strategy. The third section considers how the level of complexity in IMC strategies leads marketers to design new ways to measure the results of IMC campaigns.

COMMUNICATING WITH CONSUMERS

As the number of communication media has increased, the task of understanding how best to reach target consumers has become far more complex. In this section, we examine a model that describes how communications go from the firm to the consumer and the factors that affect the way the consumer perceives the message. Then we look at how marketing communications influence consumers—from making them aware that a product or service exists to moving them to buy.

 LO1 Identify the components of the communication process.

To make customers aware of Coke's Freestyle vending machines, it works with retailers such as Dairy Queen to send messages.

The Communication Process

Exhibit 18.1 illustrates the communication process. Let's first define each component and then discuss how they interact.

The Sender The message originates from the sender, who must be clearly identified to the intended audience. As our opening vignette revealed, Coca-Cola has introduced new options in its packaging and products, which it must communicate to consumers. For its Freestyle vending machines, for example, Coca-Cola works with retailers and other outlets that host Freestyle, such as Dairy Queen, Burger King, Kroger, Five Guys Burgers, or Kmart, to send messages about its new machines. To highlight the free song downloads, it partners with Sony. In other cases, Coca-Cola works independently to send out various types of messages through different channels that highlight its familiar red-and-white

To appeal to a broad audience, Coca-Cola has successfully placed its products on American Idol, *featuring judges Keith Urban, Jennifer Lopez, and Harry Connick Jr.*

color scheme, images of happy consumers, or its iconic bottle shape.

The Transmitter The sender works with a creative department, whether in-house or from a marketing (or advertising) agency, to develop marketing communications to highlight the new beverage. With the assistance of its marketing department, Coca-Cola and its partners might develop its websites, mobile apps, flyers, in-store displays, and televised commercials. The marketing department or external agency receives the information and transforms it for use in its role as the transmitter.

Encoding Encoding means converting the sender's ideas into a message, which could be verbal, visual, or both. A television commercial could show consumers drinking a Coca-Cola. Billboards showcasing the well-designed machines might highlight their pictures with a message asking, "Have You Tried It Yet?" Although a picture can be worth a thousand words, the most important facet of encoding is not what is sent but rather what is received. Consumers must receive information that makes them want to try the new machine and to continue to buy from it for the innovation to be successful.

The Communication Channel The communication channel is the medium—print, broadcast, the Internet, and so forth—that carries the message. Coca-Cola could transmit through television, radio, and various print advertisements, but it also realizes that the media chosen must be appropriate to connect itself (the sender) with its desired recipients. If the company believes its target market is broad, Coca-Cola might advertise or place its products on popular television shows such as *The Big Bang Theory* and *American Idol*.

The Receiver The receiver is the person who reads, hears, or sees and processes the information contained in the message and/or advertisement. The sender, of course, hopes that the person receiving it will be the one for whom it was originally intended. Coca-Cola wants its message received and decoded properly by a broad population, including teens, young adults, and families. Decoding refers to the process by which the receiver interprets the sender's message.

Noise Noise is any interference that stems from competing messages, a lack of clarity in the message, or a flaw in the medium. It poses a problem for all communication channels. Coca-Cola may choose to advertise in newspapers that its target market doesn't read, which means the rate at which the message is received by those to whom it has relevance has been slowed considerably. As we have already defined, encoding is what the sender intends to say, and decoding is what the receiver hears. If there is a difference between them, it is probably due to noise.

Feedback Loop The feedback loop allows the receiver to communicate with the sender and thereby informs the sender whether the message was received and decoded properly. Feedback can take many forms: a customer's purchase of the item, a complaint or compliment, the redemption of a coupon or rebate, a tweet about the product on Twitter, and so forth.

How Consumers Perceive Communication

The actual communication process is not as simple as the model in Exhibit 18.1 implies. Each receiver may interpret the sender's message differently, and senders often adjust their message according to the medium used and the receivers' level of knowledge about the product or service.

Receivers Decode Messages Differently

Each receiver decodes a message in his or her own way, which is not necessarily the way the sender intended. Different people shown the same message will often take radically different meanings from it. For example, what does the image on the right convey to you?

If you are a user of this brand, it may convey satisfaction. If you recently went on a diet and gave up your soda, it may convey dismay or a sense of loss. If you have chosen to be a nonuser, it may convey some disgust. If you are a recently terminated employee, it may convey anger. The sender has little, if any, control over what meaning any individual receiver will take from the message.

Senders Adjust Messages According to the Medium and Receivers' Traits

Different media communicate in varied ways, so marketers make adjustments to their messages and media depending on whether they want to communicate with suppliers, shareholders, customers, or the general public, as well as the specific segments of those groups.[8] In a recent marketing campaign, Jeep solicited the talents of celebrities that were likely to appeal to various consumer segments, to ensure appropriate perceptions across the board, as Adding Value 18.1 explains.

For example, the high-technology firm Analtech sells thin layer chromatography plates to companies that need equipment to determine the ingredients of samples of virtually anything. It is not a particularly easy product to explain and sell to laypeople, particularly since some purchasers might not have a science degree. Therefore, in addition to traditional marketing through trade shows and scientific conferences, Analtech developed a Monty Python–inspired YouTube video (http://www.ichromatography.com/adventuresofana.html) that features a witch that overcomes threats to drown her by proving that the ink in the king's decree is actually from the sheriff's pen. It also highlights points in *CSI* episodes when the television detectives rely on its products. With these more broadly popular appeals, Analtech ensures its messages reach and can be received accurately by a wider audience, with less noise than might occur through more scientific appeals.

Consumers will perceive this giant billboard differently depending on their level of knowledge and attitude toward the brand.

The AIDA Model

L02 Explain the four steps in the AIDA model.

Clearly, IMC is not a straightforward process. After being exposed to marketing communications, consumers go through several steps before actually buying or taking some other action. There is not always a direct link between a particular form of marketing communications and a consumer's purchase.

Adding Value 18.1　Blurring the Lines: How Characters—Both Fictional and Real—Drive Jeep Cherokees[i]

The distinction between scripted shows and reality offerings on television continues to grow increasingly porous. Actors famous for playing characters show off their actual selves on reality shows. In the meantime, people who first gained fame as a "Real Housewife" or "Survivor" leverage their notoriety into acting careers. In case the lines were not wavy enough, recent marketing moves by the Chrysler group includes advertising in the identity mix as well.

Buoyed by the success of the product placement of the Dodge Challenger and Charger lines in the Syfy Network's show (and related video game) *Defiance*, Chrysler moved quickly to develop a series of television advertisements to reflect "The Cherokee Effect." In these spots, aired on the range of NBCUniversal channels, familiar faces from popular shows appear driving the SUVs and describing how they achieve adventure in their vehicles.

The first four spots star a range of types of celebrities: Sarah Hyland is the young actress who plays the character Haley on *Modern Family* (which is now in syndication on the NBCUniversal-owned USA Network). Terrence Jenkins presents entertainment news on the E! network. Kyle Richards is a real housewife of Beverly Hills. Former NBA player Baron Davis presents his own style and interviews others to demonstrate *How I Rock It*. Thus the range of stars is diverse not just in their ages, genders, and races but also in their routes to fame: acting, entertainment news host, reality television star, athlete.

This diversity is purposeful, in that the SUV category appeals to a relatively broad target market. Thus a sports fan might enjoy the Baron Davis spot most, whereas a younger consumer of sitcoms likely will follow Sarah Hyland's experience more closely. Yet across the spots, the focus is consistently on the notion that the driving and experiences in the Jeep model they drive are real and accurate depictions of how they live. Each spokesperson provided input to the content of his or her commercial, to help ensure that the dialogue sounds real instead of scripted.

Furthermore, each celebrity's Jeep adventure comes available in two versions: a 30-second spot that will air on the same NBCUniversal network on which the celebrity's show airs, and an extended, 2-minute version available through the relevant website. Thus for example, to see Kyle Richards's longer drive, viewers can click onto bravo.com, and for more on Terrence Jenkins's Cherokee experience, they can visit E!'s website.

To create effective IMC programs, marketers must understand how marketing communications work. Generally, marketing communications move consumers stepwise through a series of mental stages, for which there are several models. The most common is the **AIDA model** (Exhibit 18.2),[9] which suggests that **A**wareness leads to **I**nterest, which leads to **D**esire, which leads to **A**ction. At each stage, the consumer makes judgments about whether to take the next step in the process.

EXHIBIT 18.2　The AIDA Model

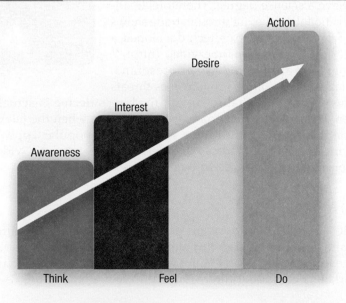

Customers actually have three types of responses, so the AIDA model is also known as the think, feel, do model. In making a purchase decision, consumers go through each of the AIDA steps to some degree, but the steps may not always follow the AIDA order. For instance, during an impulse purchase, a consumer may feel and do before he or she thinks.

Awareness Even the best marketing communications can be wasted if the sender doesn't gain the attention of the consumer first. Brand awareness refers to a potential customer's ability to recognize or recall that the brand name is a particular type of retailer or product/service. Thus, brand awareness is the strength of the link between the brand name and the type of merchandise or service in the minds of customers.

Coca-Cola already has excellent brand awareness and thus might not have to focus as much effort on this step when it wants to introduce a new flavor or its Freestyle machines. Social and Mobile Marketing 18.1 highlights how Google used these Freestyle machines to allow customers to send a Coke across the world.

There are several awareness metrics, including aided recall and top-of-mind awareness. Aided recall is when consumers indicate they know the brand when the name is presented to them. Top-of-mind awareness, the highest level of awareness, occurs when consumers mention a specific brand name first when they are asked about a product or service. For example, Harley-Davidson has top-of-mind awareness if a consumer responds "Harley" when asked about American-made motorcycles. High top-of-mind awareness means that the brand probably enters the evoked set of brands (see Chapter 6) when customers decide to shop for that particular product or service. Manufacturers, retailers, and service providers build top-of-mind awareness by having memorable names; repeatedly exposing their name to customers through advertising, locations, and sponsorships; and using memorable symbols.

As an excellent example of the last method, imagine two smaller circles, sitting on opposite sides atop a larger circle. Did you see Mickey Mouse ears? Did you think of Disney? In addition, the company has moved on to images brighter than circles to ensure that its name comes easily to the front of young consumers' minds. Whether individual acts such as Austin Mahone, Selena Gomez, or Demi Lovato or groups such as the R5, Lemonade Mouth, and Allstar Weekend, Disney starts off its stars with Disney Channel shows, records them on the Disney-owned Hollywood Record label, plays the songs in heavy rotation on Radio Disney and Disney movie soundtracks, organizes concert tours with Disney-owned Buena Vista Concerts, and sells tie-in merchandise throughout Disney stores. Each of these marketing elements reminds the various segments of the target market about both the brand (e.g., One Direction) and its owner, Disney. With this omnichannel approach, Disney gets the same product into more markets than would be possible with a more conservative approach—further building top-of-mind awareness for both Disney and its stars.[10]

Interest Once the consumer is aware that the company or product exists, communication must work to increase his or her interest level. It isn't enough to let people know that the product exists; consumers must be persuaded that it is a product worth investigating. Because Stouffer's was suffering from a reputation of offering poor quality meal options, it reoriented its marketing campaigns to focus on its "real food" ingredients that led to meals good enough to make even a teenager put down her phone to join her family at dinnertime.[11] Thus, the ads' messages include attributes that are of interest to the target audience—in this case, parents who want to sit down to a nice dinner with their children. Disney increases interest in an upcoming tour or record by including a mention, whether casual or not, in the stars' television shows. Because the primary target market for the tour is also probably watching the show, the message is received by the correct recipient.

Social & Mobile Marketing 18.1

Making the Old New by Turning a Classic Campaign into a Mobile Event[ii]

I'd like to teach the world to sing

In perfect harmony.

I'd like to buy the world a Coke

And keep it company.

Even if you weren't alive in 1971, when Coca-Cola's famous Hilltop ad premiered, you likely can sing along to its theme song. This enduring familiarity reflects the success of the original ad campaign, which is a significant part of the reason that Google is remixing the notion, both literally and figuratively, in its latest marketing communications.

The utopian ideal behind the Hilltop advertisement and song was that everyone across the world could get along, if only given the chance to share a Coke. Google's advertising seeks to put that theory to the test by establishing a mobile app that allows people to buy a drink for someone on the other side of the Earth. A user in New York purchases the Coke, and then a specially designed vending machine in Buenos Aires, Argentina, or Cape Town, South Africa, distributes the can to a surprised buyer. In addition, the machine records the recipient's reaction and allows him or her to send a thank-you note, if he or she chooses. After receiving the video of the reaction, the Coke-sender has an option to post it to social media sites to demonstrate the connection made.

Although the program might seem to be advertising for Coca-Cola (and certainly it creates communication about Coke), it is actually a campaign by and for Google, "to show what our technology was capable of, not talk about it," as Google's product marketing manager put it.

The campaign, which Google calls Project Re:Brief, also is not limited to Coke. Google also has put a modern spin on Alka-Seltzer's classic 1972 "I can't believe I ate the whole thing" advertisement as well as two ads from the 1960s: Volvo's "Drive it like you hate it" and Avis car rental's "We try harder." In the revised Volvo commercial, Google links the car's driver to Google Maps, showing where he has gone as his car approaches 3 million miles on its odometer. The Alka-Seltzer update shows videos of the overeater throughout the day, using links to Google's YouTube service.

The Re:Brief ads thus marry nostalgia with modern conveniences—a combination that Google would love to exploit in all its communications.

Google's Project Re:Brief campaign marries classic advertising from companies like Coca-Cola, Volvo, Alka-Seltzer, and Avis, with Google's state-of-the art technology.

Desire After the firm has piqued the interest of its target market, the goal of subsequent IMC messages should move the consumer from "I like it" to "I want it." If Lucy Hale appears on *Good Morning America* (on ABC, which is owned by Disney) and talks about her upcoming album and how great it is going to be, the viewing audience is all the more likely to demand access—in this case, probably parents who hope to score points with their adolescent children by buying the latest single or reserving seats to an upcoming tour. Stouffer's aims to enhance consumers' desire through its food truck initiatives, which offers free samples of various frozen entrees, dressed up with extra ingredients to show families how delicious a frozen dinner can be with just a few extra steps.[12]

Action The ultimate goal of any form of marketing communications is to drive the receiver to action. Thus Stouffer's likely hands out coupons for its products from its food trucks, to help push customers to make the purchase during their next trip to the grocery store. As long as the message has caught consumers' attention and made them interested enough to consider the product as a means to satisfy a specific desire of theirs, they likely will act on that interest by either searching for the product or making a purchase. If young consumers watch the Disney Channel's show *Shake It Up* or visit Disney's Fashion Studio website to see what the stars are wearing, they might in turn beg their parents to make an actual purchase of Bella Thorne and Zendaya's most recent "Shake It Up" album.

The Lagged Effect Sometimes consumers don't act immediately after receiving a form of marketing communications because of the lagged effect—a delayed response to a marketing communications campaign. It generally takes several exposures to an ad before a consumer fully processes its message.[13] In turn, measuring the effect of a current campaign becomes more difficult because of the possible lagged response to a previous one. For example, Toyota's "Prius Goes Plural" campaign promotes its addition of a family-sized (Prius v) and urban version (Prius c) of its popular hybrid car model. The campaign demands consumer participation by challenging the viewing public to come up with a plural form of the word *Prius* (e.g., Prii, Prien, Priuses), as touted in online banner and television ads,

When Zendaya (left) and Bella Thorne (right) appear on Shake It Up, *demand for their albums increase.*

Toyota's Prius Goes Plural campaign promotes its addition of a family-sized (Prius v) and urban version (Prius c) to its popular hybrid car model.

virtual polling booths, and videos. But the Prius v was not slated for release until six months after the campaign started, and the lag time for the Prius c was even longer. Thus the company might never know for sure whether exposure to this form of marketing communications actually led consumers to check out or purchase the new vehicles.[14]

Now that we've examined various aspects of the communication process, let's look at how specific media are used in an IMC program.

CHECK YOURSELF

1. What are the different steps in the communication process?
2. What is the AIDA model?

ELEMENTS OF AN INTEGRATED MARKETING COMMUNICATIONS STRATEGY

For any communications campaign to succeed, the firm must deliver the right message to the right audience through the right media, with the ultimate goal of profiting from long-term customer relationships rather than just short-term transactions. Reaching the right audience is becoming more difficult, however, as the media environment grows more complicated.

No single channel is necessarily better than another channel; the goal of IMC is to use them in conjunction so that the sum exceeds the total of the individual channels. However, advances in technology have led to a variety of new and traditional media options for consumers, all of which vie for consumers' attention. Print media have also grown and become more specialized. This proliferation of media has led many firms to shift their promotional dollars from advertising to direct marketing, website development, product placements, and other forms of promotion in search of the best way to deliver messages to their target audiences.

 LO3 Describe the various integrative communication channels.

We now examine the individual elements of IMC and the way each contributes to a successful IMC campaign (see Exhibit 18.3). The elements can be viewed on two axes: passive and interactive (from the consumer's perspective) and offline and online. Some elements (e.g., advertising, sales promotion, public relations, personal selling, direct and online marketing) are discussed in far more detail in subsequent chapters, so we discuss them only briefly here.

Note that as the marketer's repertoire of IMC elements has expanded, so too have the ways in which marketers can communicate with their customers. So, for instance, direct marketing appears in all four boxes. Firms have expanded their use of these traditional media (e.g., advertising, public relations, and sales promotions) from pure offline approaches to a combination of offline and online.

Advertising

Perhaps the most visible of the IMC components, advertising entails the placement of announcements and persuasive messages in time or space purchased in any of the mass media by business firms, nonprofit organizations, government agencies, and individuals who seek to inform and/or persuade members of a

EXHIBIT 18.3   Elements of an IMC Strategy

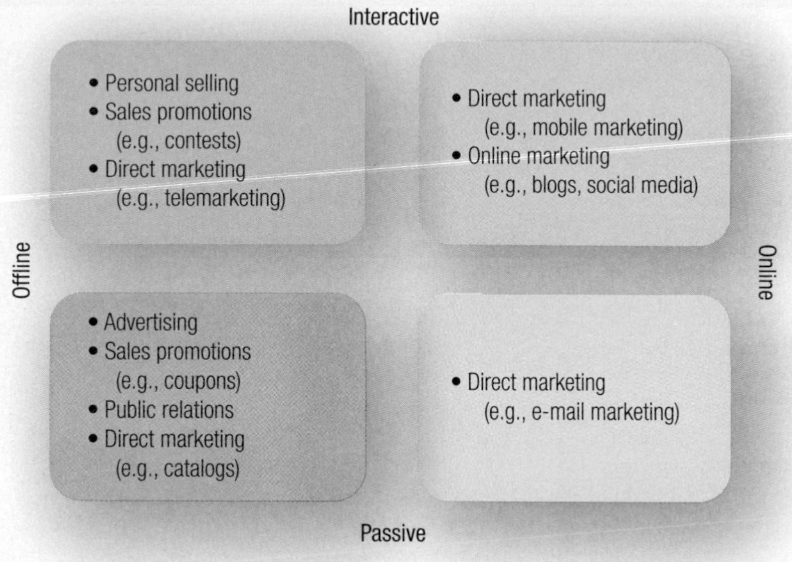

Interactive

- Personal selling
- Sales promotions
  (e.g., contests)
- Direct marketing
  (e.g., telemarketing)

- Direct marketing
  (e.g., mobile marketing)
- Online marketing
  (e.g., blogs, social media)

Offline

Online

- Advertising
- Sales promotions
  (e.g., coupons)
- Public relations
- Direct marketing
  (e.g., catalogs)

- Direct marketing
  (e.g., e-mail marketing)

Passive

particular target market or audience about their products, services, organizations, or ideas.[15] In Chapter 19, we discuss the purpose of advertising and its various types, but for now, we note that advertising is extremely effective for creating awareness of a product or service and generating interest. Mass advertising can entice consumers into a conversation with marketers, though it does not necessarily require much action by consumers, which places it on the passive end of the spectrum. Traditionally, advertising has been passive and offline (e.g., television, magazines, newspapers; see Exhibit 18.3), though recently there has been a growth in online advertising and interactive features. Advertising thus must break through the clutter of other messages to reach its intended audience. To do so, many advertisers rely on certain images; Ethical and Societal Dilemma 18.1 notes the conflict when advertisers use underweight models in ads they aim at teenaged consumers.

Public Relations

Public relations (PR) is the organizational function that manages the firm's communications to achieve a variety of objectives, including building and maintaining a positive image, handling or heading off unfavorable stories or events, and maintaining positive relationships with the media. Like advertising, this tactic is relatively passive in that customers do not have to take any action to receive it. Public relations activities support the other promotional efforts by the firm by generating free media attention, as we discuss further in Chapter 19.

Sales Promotions

Sales promotions are special incentives or excitement-building programs that encourage the purchase of a product or service, such as coupons, rebates, contests, free samples, and point-of-purchase (POP) displays. Marketers typically design these incentives for use in conjunction with other advertising or personal selling programs. Many sales promotions, such as free samples or POP displays, are designed to build short-term sales. Others, such as contests and sweepstakes, have become integral components of firms' CRM programs as a means to build customer loyalty. We discuss such sales promotions in more detail in Chapter 19.

Ethical & Societal Dilemma **18.1**   Too Skinny[iii]

The objective of an integrated marketing communications (IMC) campaign is to build profits by encouraging consumers to purchase more products. But what happens if the campaign leads to harmful behaviors? Companies could claim that shoppers have a choice about the goods they purchase or assert that marketing only influences brand decisions. But sometimes marketing directed at younger consumers complicates that reasoning, because few children or teens can separate unhealthy body images from the popular fashion looks that surround them.

Advertising models have always tended to be thin, but they have become increasingly so in the past decade. The tragic deaths of Ana Carolina Reston and Isabelle Caro—two very thin models suffering from anorexia—led some fashion industry leaders to call for a change. That was nearly a decade ago, and still underage and dangerously thin young girls continue to find work as fashion advertising models. The designers and clothing companies continue to hire girls as young as 14 years of age to walk the runway—a clear child-labor law violation according to critics. Even worse, it continues to reinforce the notion that to be beautiful, women and girls need to starve themselves.

These concerns apply not only to the teenaged girls targeted by such ads but also to the models themselves—young girls who are working long hours, subjected to harsh criticisms and widespread rejection. Most child development research suggests that children younger than 16 years are ill-prepared to deal with such scenarios.

In the United Kingdom, the Advertising Standards Authority (ASA) has banned some ads outright for being "socially irresponsible." An ad run by Drop Dead, a British clothing line, prompted the watchdog agency to condemn the brand's image: a shockingly thin model who sends dangerously inappropriate style signals to teenage girls. In its statement, the ASA complained that the young model's "hip, rib and collar bones were highly visible" and noted that she had visible (and unnatural) "hollows in her thighs." Under such pressures, some UK companies have begun to respond. The fashion brand Topshop removed an ad from its website after advocates complained that the featured model was dangerously gaunt and thus a negative influence on young shoppers.

In the United States, the Council of Fashion Designers of America (CFDA) also has denounced the hiring of underage models, yet violations continue. Recently, it called on designers and modeling agencies to require identification from models, showing that they were at least 16 years old. It also began educating industry members to recognize early signs of eating disorders, called for the provision of healthy snacks backstage, and banned the use of models under 18 years at

Promoting products using ultra-thin models sends dangerously inappropriate style signals to teenage girls.

fittings or photo shows held after midnight. Despite widespread skepticism that the industry can regulate itself, the National Eating Disorders Association has applauded the CFDA guidelines.

Change appears to be coming, but slowly still. Designers such as Tommy Hilfiger and Tory Burch complain that the models who apply with them continue to appear young and thin. "I still see some girls coming in who are really emaciated," Burch said. "It's still a problem." Those concerned about the ultra-thin style promoted by fashion advertising for young girls will be watching, but changing the tone of this communication is more challenging than just checking IDs and offering up a snack.

Personal Selling

Personal selling is the two-way flow of communication between a buyer and a seller that is designed to influence the buyer's purchase decision. Personal selling can take place in various settings: face-to-face, video teleconferencing, on the telephone, or over the Internet. Although consumers don't often interact with professional sales people, personal selling represents an important component of many IMC programs, especially in business-to-business (B2B) settings.

The cost of communicating directly with a potential customer is quite high compared with other forms of promotion, but it is simply the best and most efficient way to sell certain products and services. Customers can buy many products and services without the help of a salesperson, but salespeople simplify the buying process by providing information and services that save customers time and effort. In many cases, sales representatives add significant value, which makes the added expense of employing them worthwhile. We devote Chapter 20 to personal selling and sales management.

Direct Marketing

The component of IMC that has received the greatest increase in aggregate spending recently is direct marketing, or marketing that communicates directly with target customers to generate a response or transaction.[16] Direct marketing contains a variety of traditional and new forms of marketing communications initiatives. Traditional direct marketing includes mail and catalogs sent through the mail; direct marketing also includes e-mail and mobile marketing.

Internet-based technologies have had a profound effect on direct marketing initiatives. E-mail, for instance, can be directed to a specific consumer. Firms use e-mail to inform customers of new merchandise and special promotions, confirm the receipt of an order, and indicate when an order has been shipped. Currently available technologies also mean handheld devices can function as a payment medium: Just tap your cell phone, and the transaction occurs in much the same way it occurs with a credit card.[17]

The increased use of customer databases has enabled marketers to identify and track consumers over time and across purchase situations, which has contributed to the rapid growth of direct marketing. Marketers have been able to build these databases, thanks to consumers' increased use of credit and debit cards, store-specific credit and loyalty cards, and online shopping, all of which require the buyer to give the seller personal information that becomes part of its database. Because firms understand customers' purchases better when they possess such information, they can more easily focus their direct marketing efforts appropriately. Ethical and Societal Dilemma 18.2 details how companies are targeting consumers with promotions based on their purchasing behavior and how the government has reacted to curb potential abuse.

Direct marketing retailers try to target their customers carefully so they will be more receptive to their messages. Omaha Steaks, for example, sends e-mail coupons for items that customers have purchased previously, mails slick pictures of gourmet steaks and meal packages to addresses that have received orders in the past, and calls customers personally during likely gift-giving occasions, such as the holidays, to offer to repeat a previous gift order. These different forms of direct marketing demonstrate how this IMC format can vary on both the interactivity and online/offline dimensions of the matrix.

Mobile marketing is marketing through wireless handheld devices, such as cellular telephones.[18] Smartphones have become far more than tools to place calls; they offer a kind of mobile computer with the ability to obtain sports scores, weather, music, videos, and text messages as well as purchase merchandise. Marketing success rests on integrating marketing communications with fun, useful apps that are

Ethical & Societal Dilemma 18.2   The Consumer Privacy Bill of Rights[iv]

Whereas once companies bought ads on websites related to the product being promoted (e.g., a healthy drink on the GNC website), more targeted advertising now pursues a particular customer rather than all visitors to a particular site. Based on web browsing activity and past purchases, a firm such as Target can, for instance, determine with some degree of accuracy who among its customers is pregnant. It can then entice those women or their husbands to visit Target or Target.com and buy baby-related products, using promotions and coupons geared directly to them. But how would these customers react if they were to receive these promotions knowing that Target should have no idea that they were pregnant? Even worse, what would be the reaction if a targeted promotion was sent to the home of an unwed teenage mother whose father was unaware of the pregnancy?

Because of the changing ways in which firms are using data collected from their customers, the Consumer Privacy Bill of Rights was passed, so that consumers can more easily choose not to be tracked. In particular, consumers now have the following rights:

- **Individual Control** Consumers can control what personal data companies collect and how it is used.

- **Transparency** Consumers should be able to easily find and understand the privacy practices of companies.

- **Context** Companies that collect and use personal data will do so in ways consistent with how consumers provided the data.

- **Security** The use of personal data will not put consumers at risk.

- **Access and Accuracy** Companies should make efforts to make sure that personal data is accurate and provide access to consumers to correct data that is inaccurate.

- **Focused Collection** The collection of consumers' personal data will be limited and restricted by the context of how it was supplied in the first place.

- **Accountability** Companies are responsible to establish systems, train employees, and limit the access of third parties to consumers' personal data. They are responsible both to consumers and enforcement authorities to ensure that this takes place.

Are consumers' personal privacy rights being unjustly invaded by firms that provide them with targeted promotions based on their browsing habits? Or are the marketing firms engaged in these activities just providing them with helpful information that may make their buying decisions more pleasant and efficient?

consistent with these consumer attitudes toward mobile devices. In response, firms are steadily improving customers' potential experience with their mobile interface. Exhibit 18.4 highlights five successful mobile marketing campaigns.

Online Marketing

We now examine several electronic media vehicles: websites, blogs, and social media.

Websites Firms have increased their emphasis on communicating with customers through their websites. They use their websites to build their brand image and educate customers about their products or services as well as where they can be purchased. Retailers and some manufacturers sell merchandise directly to consumers over the Internet. For example, in addition to selling merchandise, Office Depot's website hosts a Business Resource Center for its business customers that provides advice, product knowledge, and connections to networking contacts in other businesses. It also provides forms that businesses can use to comply with Occupational Safety and Health Act (OSHA) requirements, check job applicant records, estimate cash flow, and develop a sexual harassment policy; posts workshops for running a business; and summarizes local and national business news. By providing this information, Office Depot reinforces its image as an essential source of products, services, and information for small businesses.

Many firms operate websites devoted to community building. These sites offer an opportunity for customers with similar interests to learn about products and services that support their hobbies and share information with others. Visitors can also post questions seeking information and/or comments about issues, products, and services. Many firms, especially retailers (e.g., Amazon), encourage customers to post reviews of products they have bought or used and even have visitors to their websites rate the

EXHIBIT 18.4	Illustrative Mobile Marketing Campaigns
Company	**Campaign**
Fiat 2014 500L launch campaign	To celebrate the launch of the four-door Fiat 500L, the company created dynamic ads that included photo galleries and 360-degree views of the car. Once the customer engages the ad (by swiping a car across the screen), she can change the color of the car, watch videos, and find a local dealer. Fiat reports an 80 percent engagement rate with the campaign.
Ford "Are You Human?"	Ford recognized that most people hate CAPTCHA verifications. To make a fun alternative and drive brand awareness, Ford created a human verification task that requires a person to drag a Ford Fiesta across a map of the United States along a dotted line. The system was used by more than 3,200 websites.
JetBlue Voice-activated ads	Although most mobile campaigns emphasize touch and rich media, such as videos, Jet Blue decided to get consumers' attention in another way—voice. Customers had the opportunity to play a "Learn to Speak Pigeon" game by speaking into the microphone of the phone.
McDonald's Social mobile ads	After embedding ads for McDonald's in social media apps such as Twitter and Facebook, the company created a campaign in which its new "McDonald's Mighty Wings" were stolen. Customers could look at the seven potential culprits, including NFL quarterbacks Joe Flacco and Colin Kaepernick, via the mobile ads. The ad then directed customers to the nearest McDonald's to try the Mighty Wings.
Pinkberry "How Close Are You?"	Pinkberry created a mobile campaign that used customers' GPS to identify the nearest store and included it in ads within the Pandora music app. Customers were told Pinkberry is only X miles away, and when they clicked on the ad they were given a $1 off coupon.

Source: Adapted from Lauren Johnson, "Top 10 Mobile Advertising Campaigns of 2013," *Mobile Marketer,* December 24, 2013, http://www.mobilemarketer.com.

quality of the reviews. Research has shown that these online product reviews increase customer loyalty and provide a competitive advantage for sites that offer them.[19]

Blogs A blog (weblog) contains periodic posts on a common web page. A well-received blog can communicate trends, announce special events, create positive word of mouth, connect customers by forming a community, allow the company to respond directly to customers' comments, and develop a long-term relationship with the company. By its very nature, a blog is supposed to be transparent and contain authors' honest observations, which can help customers determine their trust and loyalty levels. Nowadays, blogs are becoming more interactive as the communication between bloggers and customers has increased. In addition, blogs can be linked to other social media such as microblog Twitter. See Chapter 3 for greater discussion.

Social Media The term social media refers to media content distributed through social interactions (see Chapter 3). The three most popular facilitators of social media are YouTube, Facebook, and Twitter. In these online sites, consumers review, communicate about, and aggregate information about products, prices, and promotions. These social media also allow users to interact

To increase customer loyalty and provide a competitive advantage, firms like Amazon encourage customers to post reviews of products or services they have bought or used.

among themselves (e.g., form a community) as well as provide other like-minded consumers (i.e., members of their community) and marketers their thoughts and evaluations about a firm's products or services. Thus, social media help facilitate the consumer decision process (Chapter 6) by encouraging need recognition, information search, alternative evaluation, purchase, and postpurchase reviews.

CHECK YOURSELF

1. What are the different elements of an IMC program?

PLANNING FOR AND MEASURING IMC SUCCESS

We begin by examining how marketers set strategic goals before implementing any IMC campaign. After they have established those goals, marketers can set the budget for the campaign and choose the marketing metrics they will use to evaluate whether it has achieved its strategic objectives.

Goals

As with any strategic undertaking, firms need to understand the outcome they hope to achieve before they begin. These goals can be short-term, such as generating

Southwest Airlines' "Grab Your Bag. It's On!" campaign's goal is to encourage travelers to fly despite tough economic conditions.

Columbia Sportswear Company's Greater Outdoors campaign's goal is to showcase Columbia's technical innovation ability and overcome perceptions of inferior products.

EXHIBIT 18.5	Illustrative Marketing Goals and Related Campaigns			
Company and Campaign	**Goals**	**Target Market**	**Media Used**	**Outcome**
ASICS "Sound Mind, Sound Body"	Branch out beyond serious runner market segment and target casual runners.	Even split males and females, aged 30–49	Television and print ads, online advertising	12% increase in market share
Columbia Sportswear Company "Greater Outdoors"	Showcase Columbia's technical innovation ability and overcome perceptions of inferior products.	60% males, aged 20–59	Print ads, mobile media, social media, videos, online advertising	1% increase in sales, and +2-point brand awareness increase compared with previous year
GAP "Ready for Holiday Cheer"	Capture consumers' attention and get them to shop in the store during the holiday season.	Even split males and females, aged 20–39	Print inserts, television ads, special website, social media, customizable videos	Kelly Awards Best Inset Winner, sales turned from a 12% decline in the previous year to a 1% increase
Southwest Airlines "Grab Your Bag. It's On!"	Encourage travelers to fly despite tough economic conditions.	Even split males and females, all ages	Television, radio, print, and in-airport ads	Contributed $99 million in profits
BMW "Diesel Reinvented"	Overcome the negative image of diesel that most consumers have.	Three segments: idea class, enthusiasts, and environmentally conscious	Print ads, videos	+1,463% year-to-year sales increase

Source Adapted from: http://www.magazine.org/advertising/case_studies/.

inquiries, increasing awareness, and prompting trial. Or they can be long-term in nature, such as increasing sales, market share, and customer loyalty. Some other goals are outlined in Exhibit 18.5.

Such goals, both short- and long-term, should be explicitly defined and measured. They also might change over time, as Superior Service 18.1 describes. Regardless of their measure or changes, though, goals constitute part of the overall promotional plan, which is usually a subsection of the firm's marketing plan. Another part of the promotional plan is the budget.

Setting and Allocating the IMC Budget

Firms use a variety of methods to plan their marketing communications budgets. Because all the methods of setting a promotional budget have both advantages and disadvantages, no one method should be used in isolation.[20]

The objective-and-task method determines the budget required to undertake specific tasks to accomplish communication objectives. To use this method, marketers first establish a set of communication objectives, then determine which media best reach the target market and how much it will cost to run the number and types of communications necessary to achieve the objectives. This process—set objectives, choose media, and determine costs—must be repeated for each product

LO4 Explain the methods used to allocate the integrated marketing communications (IMC) budget.

Superior Service 18.1 Changing Priceline by Killing Captain Kirk—and Then Bringing Him Back[v]

When Priceline, the online travel service, started offering a new fixed-price discount, in addition to its longstanding "name your own price" discounts, the company basically had to change the subject. That meant killing the messenger: the over-the-top actor William Shatner. His mouthy, dramatic "The Negotiator" character had personified Priceline's negotiated discount approach for more than a decade.

As a global leader in online travel services, Priceline offers online reservations for airline tickets, hotel rooms, rental cars, vacation packages, and cruises. It serves consumers in more than 140 countries, with services available in 41 languages. The company has long offered travelers a way to negotiate low-price discounts, but it also needed to expand its offer, and redefine its goals, to become known for offering fixed-price options for same-day reservations.

Although it was rapidly becoming the fastest-growing part of its hotel business, Priceline also wanted to alert more customers to its new fixed-price Tonight-Only Deals service. To get that new message through, Priceline decided it needed a new approach, especially in its television advertising. According to Priceline's chief marketing officer, Shatner's bawdy parody of a tough guy "negotiator" had so dominated the company's commercial image that it might make it tough for viewers to pick up on Priceline's new, same-day fixed-pricing. "One of the challenges we face is that Bill is so awesome and so closely associated with Priceline that we needed to grab back consumers' attention," he said.

So Priceline had Shatner rush travelers off a bus as it hit a bend in the road, then teetered at the edge of a cliff. Without their vehicle, these riders would need a place to stay the night, so Shatner hands them his mobile phone—just as the bus pitches over into the abyss and crashes in flames. ("It's what he would have wanted," protests one survivor who has taken the time to book a room rather than mourn the lost Negotiator.)

To make its fixed-price discount deals even more accessible to its highly mobile customer base, Priceline developed free apps for Apple's iPad, iPhone, and iPod Touch, as well as for Android devices. A Tonight-Only Deals app is part of its free Hotel Negotiator application. Noting the easier, faster, hipper approach to booking rooms, Priceline then bridged the

To appeal to a younger audience, Priceline replaced longtime tough guy "negotiator" William Shatner with Kaley Cuoco of The Big Bang Theory.

generational gap in 2013 by hiring actress Kaley Cuoco of *The Big Bang Theory* to play the Negotiator's daughter, schooled in the art of modern negotiation and never without her mobile phone.

or service. The sum of all the individual communication plan budgets becomes the firm's total marketing communications budget. In addition to the objective-and-task method, various rule-of-thumb methods can be used to set budgets (see Exhibit 18.6).

These rule-of-thumb methods use prior sales and communication activities to determine the present communication budget. Although they are easy to implement, they have various limitations, as noted in Exhibit 18.6. Clearly, budgeting is not a simple process. It may take several rounds of negotiations among the various managers, who are each competing for resources for their own areas of responsibility, to devise a final IMC budget.

EXHIBIT 18.6	Rule-of-Thumb Methods	
Method	**Definition**	**Limitations**
Competitive parity	The communication budget is set so that the firm's share of communication expenses equals its share of the market.	Does not allow firms to exploit the unique opportunities or problems they confront in a market. If all competitors use this method to set communication budgets, their market shares will stay approximately the same over time.
Percentage-of-sales	The communication budget is a fixed percentage of forecasted sales.	Assumes the same percentage used in the past, or by competitors, is still appropriate for the firm. Does not take into account new plans (e.g., to introduce a new line of products in the current year).
Available budget	Marketers forecast their sales and expenses, excluding communication, during the budgeting period. The difference between the forecast sales and expenses plus desired profit is reserved for the communication budget. That is, the communication budget is the money available after operating costs and profits have been budgeted.	Assumes communication expenses do not stimulate sales and profit.

Measuring Success Using Marketing Metrics

Once a firm has decided how to set its budget for marketing communications and its campaigns have been developed and implemented, it reaches the point that it must measure the success of the campaigns, using various marketing metrics.[21] Each step in the IMC process can be measured to determine how effective it has been in motivating consumers to move to the next step in the buying process. However, recall that the lagged effect influences and complicates marketers' evaluations of a promotion's effectiveness, as well as the best way to allocate marketing communications budgets. Because of the cumulative effect of marketing communications, it may take several exposures before consumers are moved to buy, so firms cannot expect too much too soon. They must invest in the marketing communications campaign, with the idea that it may not reach its full potential for some time. In the same way, if firms cut marketing communications expenditures, it may take time before they experience a decrease in sales.

Traditional Media When measuring IMC success, the firm should examine when and how often consumers have been exposed to various marketing communications. Specifically, the firm uses measures of frequency and reach to gauge consumers' exposure to marketing communications. For most products and situations, a single exposure to a communication is hardly enough to generate the desired response. Therefore, marketers measure the frequency of exposure—how often the audience is exposed to a communication within a specified period of time. The other measure used to measure consumers' exposure to marketing communications is reach, which describes the percentage of the target population exposed to a specific marketing communication, such as an advertisement, at least once.[22] Marketing communications managers usually state their media objectives in terms of gross rating points (GRP), which represent reach multiplied by frequency (GRP = Reach × Frequency).

L05 Identify marketing metrics used to measure IMC success.

When calculating the gross rating points (GRP) of America's Next Top Model, the advertiser would multiply the reach times the frequency.

This GRP measure can refer to print, radio, or television, but any comparisons require a single medium. Suppose that Kenneth Cole places seven advertisements in *Vogue* magazine, which reaches 50 percent of the fashion-forward target segment. The total GRP generated by these seven magazine advertisements is 50 reach × 7 advertisements = 350 GRP. Now suppose Kenneth Cole includes 15 television ads as part of the same campaign, run during the program *America's Next Top Model*, which has a rating (reach) of 9.2. The total GRP generated by these 15 advertisements is 138 (9.2 × 15 = 138). However, advertisements typically appear in more than one television program. So, if Kenneth Cole also advertises 12 times during *The Voice*, which earns a rating of 1.8, its GRP would be 1.8 × 12 = 21.6, and the total GRP for both programs would be 138 + 21.6 = 159.6.

Web-Based Media Taken together, firms are spending over $130 billion annually on online advertising, which includes paid search, display ads, e-mail, and sponsorships.[23] As shown in the graph on the left, while the percentage increase of digital ad spending to total spending is slowing somewhat (red line), the absolute level of spending (bar chart) and relative share of digital ad spending to total spending continues to increase (blue line). Although GRP is an adequate measure for television and radio advertisements, assessing the effectiveness of any web-based communication efforts in an IMC campaign generally requires web tracking software, which measures how much time viewers spend on particular web pages, the number of pages they view, how many times users click banner ads, which website they came from, and so on. All these performance metrics can

Digital Ad Spending Worldwide, 2010-2016
billions, % change and % of total media ad spending

Year	Digital ad spending	% change	% share
2010	$72.37	17.5%	15.2%
2011	$87.27	20.6%	17.7%
2012	$102.83	19.8%	17.8%
2013	$118.40	21.7%	15.1%
2014	$134.65	23.4%	13.7%
2015	$149.18	24.8%	10.8%
2016	$163.04	25.9%	9.3%

■ Digital ad spending   ■ % change   ■ % share

Note: Includes advertising that appears on desktop and laptop computers as well as mobile phones and tablets, and includes all the various formats of advertising on those platforms; excludes SMS, MMS and P2P messaging-based advertising

Source: eMarketer.com, December 2012.

be easily measured and assessed using a variety of software, including Google Analytics.

Facebook also helps companies see who has been visiting their fan pages, what those people are doing on the fan pages, and who is clicking their advertisements.[24] By keeping track of who is visiting their fan pages, marketers can better customize the material on their pages by getting to know the people visiting.

Planning, Implementing, and Evaluating IMC Programs—an Illustration of Google Advertising

Imagine a hypothetical upscale sneaker store in New York City, called Transit, that is modeled after vintage New York City subway trains. Transit's target market is young, well-educated, hip men and women aged 17 to 34 years. The owner's experience indicates the importance of personal selling for this market because these consumers (1) make large purchases and (2) seek considerable information before making a decision. Thus, Jay Oliver, the owner, spends part of his communication budget on training his sales associates. Oliver has realized his communication budget is considerably less than that of other sneaker stores in the area. He has therefore decided to concentrate his limited budget on a specific segment and use electronic media exclusively in his IMC program.

The IMC program Oliver has developed emphasizes his store's distinctive image and uses his website, social shopping, and some interesting community building techniques. Social shopping is the use of the Internet to communicate about product preferences with other shoppers. For instance, he has an extensive customer database as part of his CRM system from which he draws information for matching new merchandise with his customers' past purchase behaviors and little personal nuggets of information that he or other sales associates have collected on the customers. He then e-mails specific customers information about new products that he believes they will be interested in. He also encourages customers to use blogs hosted on his website. Customers chat about the hot new sneakers, club events, and races. He does everything with a strong sense of style.

To reach new customers, he is using search engine marketing (SEM). In particular, he is using Google AdWords, a search engine marketing tool offered by Google that allows advertisers to show up in the Sponsored Links section of the search results page based on the keywords potential customers use (see the sponsored link section in the right-hand column of the preceding Google screen grab).

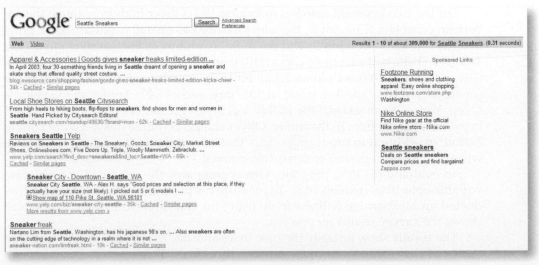

Advertisers pay Google to show up in the Sponsored Link section in the right-hand column of this screen grab based on the keywords customers use in their searches.

EXHIBIT 18.7	ROMI Assessment					
(1) Keyword	(2) Clicks	(3) Marketing Expenditure	(4) Sales	(5) Gross Margin = Sales × Gross Margin% = Sales × 50%	(6) Gross Margin ($) (Col. 5) − Marketing Expenditure (Col. 3)	(7) ROMI = (Col. 6/Col. 3) × 100
Sneaker store	110	$10/day	$70/day	$35/day	$25	250%
New York City sneakers	40	$25/day	$80/day	$40/day	$15	60%

The cost of the sneakers is 50 percent of the sale price.

He likes this option because of Google's efforts to rank pages fairly, a topic covered in more detail in Ethical and Societal Dilemma 6.1 on page 176.

Oliver must determine the best keywords to use for his sponsored link advertising program. Some potential customers might search using the keywords "sneakers," "sneakers in New York City," "athletic shoes," or other such versions. Using Google AdWords, Oliver can assess the effectiveness of his advertising expenditures by measuring the reach, relevance, and return on investment for each of the keywords that potential customers used during their Internet searches.

To estimate reach, Oliver uses the number of impressions (the number of times the ad appears in front of the user) and the click-through rate (CTR). To calculate CTR, he divides the number of times a user clicks an ad by the number of impressions.[25] For example, if a sponsored link was delivered 100 times and 10 people clicked on it, then the number of impressions is 100, the number of clicks is 10, and the CTR would be 10 percent.

The relevance of the ad describes how useful an ad message is to the consumer doing the search. Google provides a measure of relevance through its AdWords system using a quality score. The quality score looks at a variety of factors to measure how relevant a keyword is to an ad's text and to a user's search query. In general, a high-quality score means that a keyword will trigger ads in a higher position and at a lower cost-per click.[26] In a search for "sneaker store," the Transit ad showed up fourth, suggesting high relevance.

Using the following formula, Oliver also can determine an ad's return on marketing investment (ROI):

$$\text{ROMI} = \frac{\text{Gross Margin-Marketing Expenditure}}{\text{Marketing Expenditure}} \times 100$$

For the two keyword searches in Exhibit 18.7, Oliver finds how much the advertising cost him (Column 3), the sales produced as a result (Column 4), the gross margin in dollars (Column 5), and the ROMI (Column 7). For "sneaker store," the Transit website had a lot more clicks (110) than the clicks received from "New York City sneakers" (40) (see Column 2, Exhibit 18.7). Even though the sales were lower for the keywords "sneaker store" at $35/day, versus $40/day for the keywords "New York City sneakers," the ROMI was much greater for the "sneaker store" keyword combination. In the future, Oliver should continue this keyword combination, in addition to producing others that are similar to it, in the hope that he will attain an even greater return on investment.

To evaluate his IMC program, Oliver compares the results of the program with his objectives (Exhibit 18.8). To measure his program's effectiveness, he conducted an inexpensive online survey using the questions in Exhibit 18.8, which shows the survey results for one year.

The results show a steady increase in awareness, knowledge of the store, and choice of the store as a primary source of sneakers. This research provides evidence that the IMC program was conveying the intended message to the target audience.

EXHIBIT 18.8	Program Effectiveness Results			
Communication Objective	Question	Before Campaign	Six Months After	One Year After
Awareness (% mentioning store)	What stores sell sneakers?	38%	46%	52%
Knowledge (% giving outstanding rating for sales assistance)	Which stores would you rate outstanding on the following characteristics?	9	17	24
Attitude (% first choice)	On your next shopping trip for sneakers, which store would you visit first?	13	15	19
Visit (% visited store)	Which of the following stores have you been to?	8	15	19

CHECK YOURSELF

1. Why is the objective-and-task method of setting an IMC budget better than the rule-of-thumb methods?
2. How do firms use GRP to evaluate the effectiveness of traditional media?
3. How would a firm evaluate the effectiveness of its Google advertising?

Reviewing Learning Objectives

LO1 Identify the components of the communication process.

The communication process begins with a sender, which provides the message to a transmitter that develops or encodes the message for transmission through a communication channel. When a recipient receives the message, it may have been altered by noise in the environment. To find out, the sender needs to receive some form of feedback from the recipient.

LO2 Explain the four steps in the AIDA model.

Awareness is the first "thinking" step, during which the consumer simply recognizes a brand or product. During the interest step, the consumer starts to "feel" and become intrigued enough to explore the product or brand. This interest then leads to another feeling, namely, desire for the marketed item. Finally, to be successful, marketing communication must prompt an action: a purchase, a commitment, a recommendation, or whatever else the company is trying to get consumers to do.

LO3 Describe the various integrative communication channels.

Advertising has long been the primary channel for marketing communication and is still a constant presence, but other media channels have become more and more prominent. For example, direct marketing media options, particularly online options, have increased in recent years. Outbound direct marketing telephone calls have declined, but Internet-based technologies like e-mail and m-commerce have increased. Public relations also has become increasingly important as other media forms become more expensive and as consumers grow more skeptical of commercial messages. With regard to new and electronic media, the wealth of recent options include websites, corporate blogs, and social media such as YouTube, Facebook, and Twitter.

Explain the methods used to allocate the integrated marketing communications (IMC) budget.

Various rule-of-thumb methods rely on prior sales and communication activities to determine the best allocation. For example, the competitive parity method sets the budget so that the share of communication expenses equals the firm's share of the market. The percentage-of-sales method, just as it sounds, uses a fixed percentage of sales as the amount of the budget. In contrast, the objective-and-task method establishes specific communication objectives, identifies which media can best attain those objectives, and then determines the related costs to expend.

 Identify marketing metrics used to measure IMC success.

Marketers rely on a mix of traditional and nontraditional measures to determine IMC success. Because potential customers generally need to be exposed to IMC messages several times before they will buy, firms estimate the degree to which customers are exposed to a message by multiplying frequency (the number of times an audience is exposed to a message) by reach (the percentage of the target population exposed to a specific marketing communication). Measuring Internet IMC effectiveness requires different measures, such as click-through tracking that measures how many times users click on banner advertising on websites.

Key Terms

- advertising, 558
- AIDA model, 554
- aided recall, 555
- blog (weblog), 563
- brand awareness, 555
- click-through rate (CTR), 570
- communication channel, 552
- decoding, 552
- direct marketing, 561
- encoding, 552
- feedback loop, 552
- frequency, 567
- gross rating points (GRP), 567

- impressions, 570
- integrated marketing communications (IMC), 550
- lagged effect, 557
- mobile marketing, 561
- noise, 552
- objective-and-task method, 565
- personal selling, 561
- public relations (PR), 559
- reach, 567
- receiver, 552
- relevance, 570

- return on investment (ROI), 570
- rule-of-thumb methods, 566
- sales promotion, 559
- search engine marketing (SEM), 569
- sender, 551
- social media, 563
- social shopping, 569
- top-of-mind awareness, 555
- transmitter, 552
- web tracking software, 568

Marketing Applications

1. Assume that the contemporary apparel company Juicy Couture has embarked on a new IMC strategy. It has chosen to advertise on TV during the *NBC Nightly News* and in print in *Time* magazine. The message is designed to announce new styles for the season and uses a 17-year-old woman as the model. Evaluate this strategy, and if appropriate propose an alternative.

2. Using the steps in the AIDA model, explain why a potential consumer in question 1 who views Juicy Couture's advertising may not be ready to go out and purchase a new pair of jeans.

3. Suppose a snack company introduces a new product called SumSeeds—sunflower seeds with energy boosters like caffeine, taurine, lysine, and ginseng. How would you expect this product's IMC program to differ from that for regular sunflower seeds sold as snacks?

4. It's holiday time, and you've decided to purchase a box of chocolates for the person of your choice. Evaluate how Godiva's advertising, personal selling, public relations, and electronic media might influence your purchase decision. How might the relative importance of each of these

IMC elements be different if your parents were making the purchase?

5. Suppose you saw your instructor for this course being interviewed on TV about the impact of a big storm on an upcoming holiday's sales. Is this interview part of your college's IMC program? If so, do you believe it benefits the college? How?

6. A retail store places an ad in the local newspaper for yoga wear. The sales of the featured items increase significantly for the next two weeks. Sales in the rest of the sportswear department go up as well. What do you think are the short- and long-term objectives of the ad? Justify your answer.

7. As an intern for Coca-Cola, you have been asked to help with developing an IMC budget. The objective of the IMC strategy is to raise Diet Coke's market share by 2 percent in the United States in the next 18 months. Your manager explains, "It's real simple; just increase the budget 2 percent over last year's." Evaluate your manager's strategy.

8. You were sitting in the school cafeteria yesterday, and a young man from your marketing class, whom you don't know well, asked if he could sit down. He then started telling you about this very cool new Google app, "WordLens," that allows you to translate signs into different languages in real time using the camera on your smartphone. Although you recognize the merit in the product, you later find out that he works for Google. Do you believe his action constitutes an ethical IMC strategy? How will it affect your attitude toward Google and the potential that you will purchase the product?

Quiz Yourself

1. The basic goal of integrated marketing communications is to _____.
   a. communicate the value proposition to the target market
   b. create desire
   c. manipulate consumers
   d. outspend competitors
   e. tell the world about your company

2. Most manufacturing and retailing marketers worry constantly about whether or not their IMC efforts are paying off. They assess various forms of _____ to determine what is working and what is not.
   a. noise
   b. pretesting
   c. precoding
   d. encoding
   e. feedback

(Answers to these two questions can be found on page 652.)

Toolkit

RETURN ON MARKETING EXPENDITURES

Suppose Jay Oliver (marketing manager of Transit sneaker store) is considering two search engine marketing (SEM) options to reach out to new customers to market Transit. In particular, he is using Google AdWords, a search engine marketing tool offered by Google that allows firms to show up in searches based on the keywords potential customers use. Transit is targeting young adults aged 17 to 28. The sneaker market is about $500,000,000 sales annually, and the target market is about 35 percent of that. Their gross margins are 20 percent. Oliver estimates that Transit will capture a 2 percent market share of the target market with a $500,000 advertising and keyword budget (option 1) and a 3 percent market share with a $1,000,000 advertising and keyword budget (option 2). Which marketing plan produces the higher ROI for the year? Please use the toolkit provided in your instructor's Connect course to assess the ROI of the two options.

Net Savvy

1. Visit http://thephelpsagency.com and click on the "Work" tab at the top. Compare the IMC for the different companies. What were the goals of the integrated marketing campaign? Which IMC components were used in that particular campaign? How do those components contribute to the success of the IMC campaign in achieving its stated goals?

Chapter Case Study

HOW INTEGRATED IS VOLVO'S IMC STRATEGY?

For consumers, Volvo means one thing. For businesses that rely on the automotive manufacturer for their delivery trucks and large-capacity vehicles, it means something else. In turn, the company faces the challenge of communicating about its offers to a wide variety of audiences, promising different solutions to different needs while still maintaining a consistent positioning.

A long-running joke once held that a truthful advertising campaign for Volvo's cars would read, "We're boxy, but we're safe." That is, the company tended to ignore stylish designs or fashionable add-ons in its single-minded focus on making the safest automobiles on the road. The business-to-business (B2B) side of the company similarly designed and marketed itself as technically superior. In both consumer and business markets, Volvo made relatively straightforward promises of safety and effectiveness that, while not particularly exciting, seemed consistent.

However, consistency is not enough in the modern, cut-throat competition for automotive sales. In response, Volvo has undergone several renewed attempts at communicating and positioning itself as something exciting, mainly because it is so dependable.

For example, in B2B markets, Volvo began issuing a series of award-winning marketing films designed to demonstrate just how precise the engineering is on its trucks. Through recent innovations, Volvo's designers and engineers have enhanced the maneuverability, sensitivity, and driving precision of the big rigs that it sells worldwide. To reveal the sensitivity of Volvo Dynamic Steering on the FMX truck line, it filmed "The Hamster Stunt," in which a hamster named Charlie runs on a hamster track built into the steering wheel and thereby determines the direction of the massive semitrailer vehicle.[27]

In "The Technician," a live engineer who worked on designing the truck series agrees to be buried in dirt up to his neck. His head protrudes 275 millimeters (11 inches) out of the ground, which is enough for the truck, with its 300-mm (12-inch) clearance to the undercarriage, to literally drive over him.

The steadiness and ease of handling the trucks is a significant benefit, especially for long-haul truckers. Therefore, Volvo used two different films to highlight this promise: In "The Ballerina Stunt," a woman dressed in a tutu walks a tightrope strung between two moving trucks. Not to be outdone by a ballerina, the martial arts expert and actor Jean-Claude Van Damme holds himself in the splits between the windows of two trucks while they drive—in reverse in this case.[28] As Volvo has been quick to assure viewers, there are no special effects or computer graphics in any of these shots. The 53-year-old action star really did do the splits, and the trucks truly were moving in reverse.

Each of the short films is available exclusively on YouTube, where they have attracted more than 100 million views. In addition, traditional news media reported widely on the campaign, especially after the spots started earning awards in marketing competitions such as the "best in show" winner of The One Show advertising event. Not only did people who viewed the films start following Volvo more readily on YouTube, Twitter, and Facebook, but they also left YouTube to visit Volvo's own branded site. According to the company's calculations, unique buyer visits to the Volvo trucks website increased from around 175,000 to 300,000 per month in the aftermath of the campaign.[29]

But few regular consumers worry about whether their station wagons or sedans can hold Van Damme in a splits. Instead, they want a strong, reliable car that offers some sense of luxury. Volvo is a relatively higher-priced brand, which means that it regards its main competitors as other luxury car brands, including Mercedes-Benz, Audi, BMW, and Lexus. Even as it competes with them, though, Volvo recognizes and seeks to build on its distinctiveness, in that it has never been primarily about "looking good."

Accordingly, its consumer marketing focuses on how the benefits of driving a Volvo are unique from those associated with driving other luxury brands. The theme is consistent across several marketing channels. For example, one comparative television spot shows a perfectly coiffed, stylish female driver of a Mercedes SUV checking her makeup in her rearview mirror. The shot pans to the car in the next lane—a Volvo, of course—in which the female driver also is checking her rearview mirror. But in this case, she is checking on and making funny faces at two children in the backseat, who giggle in response. The tagline—"Volvos aren't for everyone, and we kinda like it that way," gives buyers and potential buyers a means to distinguish themselves from a stereotype of conspicuous consumption.[30]

The linked Facebook element of this same campaign features a small dog in a purse, with the tagline, "If your dog has a wardrobe, the Volvo S60 probably isn't for you." On billboards and outdoor media in the greater Los Angeles area, Volvo also promises that its S60 is "100% real. Can't say that about everything around here." Although this ad ran mainly in Southern California, Volvo also has moved to consolidate its communications globally, such as by working with a single global marketing firm and strongly encouraging collaboration between its U.S. and European in-house marketing teams.[31]

The campaigns are thus a little cheeky and funny, while also promising a distinct benefit to consumers who prefer not to appear ostentatious or flashy. To coincide with these advertising campaigns, Volvo also has introduced some new, updated, slightly sportier models. In these categories, it recognizes that it competes most directly with Audi, which similarly seeks a "new luxury" positioning, rather than the "old luxury" widely associated with BMW or Mercedes. In this head-to-head competition, Volvo made a daring promise: For any consumer who test drove both its S60 and the Audi A4, then purchased the A4, Volvo would pay the first month's car payment.[32]

Even as Volvo has undergone changes in ownership and some fluctuations in its share of both B2B and consumer markets, it has maintained a sense of uniqueness and distinction. Its goal in its marketing communications, across the board, is to make sure that identity—or "what the brand is all about"[33]—is clear to all its customers in all its markets and across all channels of communication.

Questions

1. Which IMC components do Volvo's business and consumer advertising efforts use? How are they integrated?
2. What step(s) in the AIDA process do each of these marketing communications attempt to achieve?

Endnotes

1. Mike Esterl, "Coke Sticks to Its Strategy While Soda Sales Slide," *The Wall Street Journal,* April 9, 2014, http://online.wsj.com.

2. Ibid.

3. Avi Dan, "Just How Does Coca-Cola Reinvent Itself in a Changed World?" *Forbes,* October 7, 2013, http://www.forbes.com.

4. Ibid.

5. Coca-Cola, "2014 FIFA World Cup," http://www.coca-colacompany.com/fifa-world-cup/; Lara O'Reilly, "Coke Holds Back Marketing Spend as It Prepares for World Cup Splurge," *Marketing Week,* April 15, 2014, http://www.marketingweek.co.uk.

6. Esterl, "Coke Sticks to Its Strategy."

7. Terence Shimp and J. Craig Andrews, *Advertising Promotion and Other Aspects of Integrated Marketing Communications* (Boston: Cengage Learning, 2013).

8. Ibid.

9. E. K. Strong, *The Psychology of Selling* (New York: McGraw-Hill, 1925).

10. Disney, "Music," http://music.disney.com; Phil Gallo, "Disney Music Tops Interscope in Album Market Share, Enters the EDM Fray," *Billboard,* May 10, 2014, http://www.billboard.com.

11. Andrew Adam Newman, "Trying to Bolster the Image of Frozen Meals as Sales Lag," *The New York Times,* April 23, 2014, http://www.nytimes.com.

12. Ibid.

13. John Philip Jones, "What Makes Advertising Work?" *The Economic Times,* July 24, 2002.

14. http://popsop.com/wp-content/uploads/toyota_prius_plural_02.jpg; http://www.youtube.com/watch?v=nUor4gdFoyg&feature=player_embedded#!; http://www.saatchi.com/news /archive/prius_goes_plural_through_new_integrated_campaign.

15. American Marketing Association, "Advertising," *Dictionary of Marketing Terms,* https://www.ama.org/resources/Pages/Dictionary.

16. Teri Evans, "Firms Hold Fast to Snail Mail Marketing," *The Wall Street Journal,* January 12, 2010, http://online.wsj.com; George E. Belch and Michael A. Belch, *Advertising and Promotion: An Integrated Marketing Communications Perspective* (New York: McGraw-Hill, 2007).

17. Rebecca Lieb, "Q&A: Cindy Krum Cuts through the Mobile Marketing Alphabet Soup of NFC and RFID," http://econsultancy.com, March 16, 2010.

18. Akihisa Fujita, "Mobile Marketing in Japan: The Acceleration of Integrated Marketing Communications," *Journal of Integrated Marketing Communications* (2008), pp. 41–46; Mobile update, http://www.businessinsider.com; http://www.informationweek.com; http://www.nearbynow.com (accessed May 26, 2010).

19. Yubo Chen, Scott Fay, and Qi Wang, "The Role of Marketing in Social Media: How Online Consumer Reviews Evolve," *Journal of Interactive Marketing* 25, no. 2 (May 2011), pp. 85–94.

20. This section draws from Michael Levy, Barton A. Weitz, and Dhruv Grewal, *Retailing Management,* 9th ed. (Burr Ridge, IL: McGraw-Hill /Irwin, 2015).

21. Megan Halscheid, Micheline Sabatté, and Sejal Sura, "Beyond the Last Click: Measuring ROI and Consumer Engagement with Clickstream Analysis," *Journal of Integrated Marketing Communications,* 2009, pp. 43–50; Vikram Mahidhar and Christine Cutten, "Navigating the Marketing Measurement Maze," *Journal of Integrated Marketing Communications,* 2007, pp. 41–46.

22. http://www.riger.com.

23. Robert Hof, "Digital Ad Spending Tops $100 Billion in 2012," *Forbes,* January 9, 2013, http://www.forbes.com.

24. "Facebook Pages: Insights for Your Facebook Page," http://www.facebook.com.

25. "Marketing and Advertising Using Google," Google 2007.

26. http://publishing2.com.

27. Nathan Velayudhan, "Volvo Trucks Videos—from Hamsters to Van Damme," *Auto Express,* November 18, 2013, http://www.autoexpress.co.uk.

28. Ibid.

29. Volvo Trucks Global, "Volvo Trucks Campaign Receives One of the Advertising World's Most Prestigious Awards," November 5, 2013, http://www.volvotrucks.com/trucks/global.

30. Dale Buss, "Unapologetically, Volvo Aims Its New Campaign at True Believers," *Forbes,* April 15, 2013, http://www.forbes.com.

31. Alexandra Bruell, "Volvo Consolidates Global Media with Mindshare," *Advertising Age,* February 24, 2014, http://adage.com.

32. Ibid.

33. Ibid.

i. Stuart Elliot, "Recalling TV's Golden Age, Stars Pitch Products Tied to Their Shows," *The New York Times,* December 4, 2013.

ii. Todd Wasserman, "How Coke Spread Happiness (and Cokes) via Mobile," *Mashable.com,* August 7, 2012, http://mashable.com; Stuart Elliot, "Google Remixes Old Campaigns, Adding Dash of Digital Tools," *The New York Times,* March 8, 2012, http://www.nytimes.com.

iii. Eric Wilson, "Checking Models' IDs at the Door," *The New York Times,* February 8, 2012, http://www.nytimes.com; David Gianastasio, "Fashion Site Nixes Photo of Freakishly Thin-Looking Model," *Adweek,* July 13, 2011, http://www.adweek.com; Ellie Krupnick, "Drop Dead Ads Banned by ASA for Too-Skinny Model," *The Huffington Post,* November 10, 2011, http://www.huffingtonpost.com.

iv. Emily Steel, "How Marketers Hone Their Aim Online," *The Wall Street Journal,* June 19, 2007; Charles Duhigg, "How Companies Learn Your Secrets," *The New York Times,* February 16, 2012; George Anderson, "White House, Web Giants Address Consumer Privacy Online," *Retail Wire,* February 24, 2012.

v. David Vinjamuri, "Priceline Just Killed William Shatner—or Did They?" *Forbes,* February 3, 2012, http://www.forbes.com; Dennis Schaal, "Priceline Unveils New Ad Campaign with Shatner and Kareem," *tnooz,* February 14, 2011, http://www.tnooz.com; Rich Tomaselli, "Priceline Kills the Messenger Because Ads Worked Too Well," *Advertising Age,* January 30, 2010, http://adage.com; "Priceline.com to Webcast 4th Quarter 2011 Financial Results on February 27th," *The New York Times,* January 30, 2012, http://markets.on.nytimes.com; "Priceline Shocker: The Negotiator's Secret Daughter Revealed!" YouTube, January 8, 2013, http://www.youtube.com/watch?v=EDSnjfxu_lg; Lynn Elber, "Kaley Cuoco Joins Shatner in Priceline Ad Campaign," Associated Press, January 9, 2013, http://bigstory.ap.com.

Credits

CHAPTER 19

ADVERTISING, PUBLIC RELATIONS, AND SALES PROMOTIONS

LEARNING OBJECTIVES

LO1 Describe the steps in designing and executing an advertising campaign.

LO2 Identify three objectives of advertising.

LO3 Describe the different ways that advertisers appeal to consumers.

LO4 Identify the various types of media.

LO5 Identify agencies that regulate advertising.

LO6 Describe the elements of a public relations toolkit.

LO7 Identify the various types of sales promotions.

When it comes down to it, what is the point of advertising? Generally we think that its goal is to get someone—normally, the person receiving the ad—to do something, and that "something" is nearly always a purchase. But as advertising grows more creative, innovative, and varied, the action induced by such communications might remain several steps away from purchasing.

Consider the advertising plan exhibited by the fast-food chain Chipotle Mexican Grill. Once McDonald's held a large ownership share of the company, but Chipotle has been on its own for nearly a decade—a status many consumers have not realized.[1] The quickly growing chain distinguishes itself with its mission statement, "Food with Integrity," which it interprets as "our commitment to finding the very best ingredients, raised with respect for the animals, the environment, and the farmers."[2] Thus it seeks to get across a message about its own identity, but also about the importance of sustainable farming and foods produced more naturally. To do so, Chipotle has adopted a marketing plan that spans a range of media. In animated YouTube films, two artful spots feature characters that reject a factory model of food production by embracing farm-fresh vegetables and meats. Only at the very end of each spot does the name Chipotle even appear. The focus is more on the message

than on the brand, which may be why consumers are so willing to interact with and share that message. The spots both feature music by popular musicians, namely, Fiona Apple and Willie Nelson (covering a Coldplay track). The animation is sophisticated and of high quality. And in each case, the protagonist—a farmer or a scarecrow—rejects a model in which pigs, cows, and chickens are artificially fattened by chemicals and kept in cages, in preference for a free-range approach.[3] Expanding on this idea, Chipotle proposed and produced a series of 30-minute films for Hulu titled *Farmed and Dangerous*. These scripted, live-action comedies mention Chipotle only once and are presented alongside every other series offered by Hulu, with no signal that they are advertising. Ads for various products instead appear within the shows themselves. In the satiric show content, the horrors of industrial agriculture are the focus, including the dastardly deeds of an evil scientist seeking to develop eight-winged chickens.[4]

Such fearful depictions of inhumane treatment and unnatural food production lead viewers readily to value-based judgments—namely, that it would be better to eat food produced ethically. From this broad perception, Chipotle hopes that ultimately consumers will more readily include it in their consideration set as a company that reflects such values.

Once they do, Chipotle reinforces its status as something more than just a burrito outlet. In its "Cultivating Thought" initiative, Chipotle agreed to inscribe its disposable cups with "Two-Minute Thoughts" written by renowned authors and public figures. The writers range from the comedians Bill Hader and Sarah Silverman to the Nobel Laureate Toni Morrison to the social scientists Steven Pinker and Malcolm Gladwell. By providing these short texts on its cups, Chipotle guarantees that lone diners have somewhere to put their eyes while they eat; it also gives consumers access to some deep thoughts, written by some very smart people.[5]

As these elements of Chipotle's advertising strategy reveal, advertising does far more than encourage consumers to buy stuff. It can make them laugh, prompt them to think about their consumption, encourage them to embrace a particular set of values, and lead them to read challenging texts. And if all that communication comes together just right, it also can sell quite a lot of guacamole.

Advertising is a paid form of communication delivered through media from an identifiable source about an organization, product, service, or idea designed to persuade the receiver to take some action now or in the future.[6] This definition provides some important distinctions between advertising and other forms of promotion, which we discussed in the previous chapter. First, advertising is not free; someone has paid, with money, trade, or other means, to get the message shown. Second, advertising must be carried by some medium—television, radio, print, the web, T-shirts, sidewalks, and so on. Third, legally, the source of the message must be known or knowable. Fourth, advertising represents a persuasive form of communication, designed to get the consumer to take some action. That desired action can range from "free-range chickens are better" to "buy a Chipotle burrito."

Advertising encompasses an enormous industry and clearly is the most visible form of marketing communications—so much so that many people think of marketing and advertising as synonymous. Global advertising expenditures are almost $500 billion, and almost half that amount is spent in the United States. Although expenditures dropped somewhat during the global downturn, advertising remains virtually everywhere, and predictions are that it will continue to grow.[7]

Yet how many of the advertisements you were exposed to yesterday do you remember today? Probably not more than three or four. As you learned in Chapter 6, perception is a highly selective process. Consumers simply screen out messages that are not relevant to them. When you notice an advertisement, you may not react to it. Even if you react to it, you may not remember it later. Even if you remember the ad, you may not remember the brand or sponsor—or worse yet from the advertiser's point of view, you may remember it as an advertisement for another brand.[8]

To get you to remember their ad and the brand, advertisers must first get your attention. As we discussed in Chapter 18, the increasing number of communication channels and changes in consumers' media usage have made the job of advertisers far more difficult.[9] As our opening example about Chipotle's varied and innovative ads demonstrated, advertisers continually endeavor to use creativity and various media to reach their target markets.

As a consumer, you are exposed only to the end product—the finished advertisement. But many actions must take place before you actually get to see an ad, as the Toolkit available online for this chapter will show you. In this chapter, we examine the ingredients of a successful advertising campaign from identifying a target audience to creating the actual ad to assessing performance. Although our discussion is generally confined to advertising, much of the process for developing an advertising campaign is applicable to the IMC media vehicles discussed in Chapter 18. We conclude with some regulatory and ethical issues for advertising, then move on to public relations and sales promotions, and their use.

 LO1 Describe the steps in designing and executing an advertising campaign.

Designing and carrying out a successful advertising program requires much planning and effort. Exhibit 19.1 shows the key steps in the process, each of which

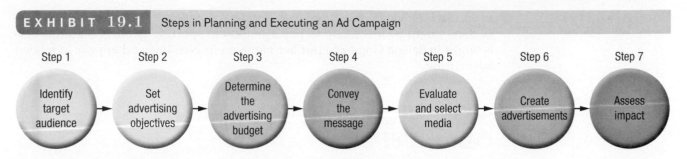

EXHIBIT 19.1   Steps in Planning and Executing an Ad Campaign

Step 1	Step 2	Step 3	Step 4	Step 5	Step 6	Step 7
Identify target audience	Set advertising objectives	Determine the advertising budget	Convey the message	Evaluate and select media	Create advertisements	Assess impact

helps ensure that the intended message reaches the right audience and has the desired effect. Let's examine each of these steps.

STEP 1: IDENTIFY TARGET AUDIENCE

The success of an advertising program depends on how well the advertiser can identify its target audience. Firms conduct research to identify their target audience, then use the information they gain to set the tone for the advertising program and help them select the media they will use to deliver the message to that audience.

During this research, firms must keep in mind that their target audience may or may not be the same as current users of the product. For example, adidas knows that FIFA fans likely are at least familiar with its offerings, even if they do not currently purchase sports gear from adidas. Thus some advertisements feature the international football (or soccer) stars Zinedine Zidane and Lionel Messi,

adidas uses different ads to appeal to different target markets. Jozy Altidore (left) appeals to soccer fans, while Selena Gomez (right) attracts teenaged pop music fans.

to encourage them to buy more of the brand's products.[10] But teenaged pop music fans might be less likely to pay attention to sporting goods. So adidas also brought in Selena Gomez to put her name on its Neo line and appear in related advertising.[11]

STEP 2: SET ADVERTISING OBJECTIVES

Advertising campaign objectives are derived from the overall objectives of the marketing program and clarify the specific goals that the ads are designed to accomplish. Generally, these objectives appear in the advertising plan, a subsection of the firm's overall marketing plan that explicitly analyzes the marketing and advertising situation, identifies the objectives of the advertising campaign, clarifies a specific strategy for accomplishing those objectives, and indicates how the firm can determine whether the campaign was successful.[12] An advertising plan is crucial because it will later serve as the yardstick against which advertising success or failure is measured.

Generally, in advertising to consumers, the objective is a pull strategy in which the goal is to get consumers to pull the product into the marketing channel by demanding it. Push strategies also exist and are designed to increase demand by focusing on wholesalers, retailers, or salespeople. These campaigns attempt to motivate the seller to highlight the product, rather than the products of competitors, and thereby push the product to consumers. In this chapter, we focus on pull strategies. Push strategies are examined in Chapters 16, 17, and 20.

All advertising campaigns aim to achieve certain objectives: to inform, persuade, and remind customers. Another way of looking at advertising objectives is to examine an ad's focus. Is the ad designed to stimulate demand for a particular product or service or more broadly for the institution in general? Also, ads can be used to stimulate demand for a product category or an entire industry, or for a specific brand, firm, or item. We first look at the broad overall objectives: to inform, persuade, and remind. Then we examine advertising objectives based on the focus of the ad: product versus institutional.

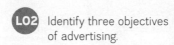 Identify three objectives of advertising.

Informative Advertising

Informative advertising is a communication used to create and build brand awareness, with the ultimate goal of moving the consumer through the buying cycle to a purchase. Such advertising helps determine some important early stages of a product's life cycle (see Chapter 12), particularly when consumers have little information about the specific product or type of product. Retailers often use informative advertising to tell their customers about an upcoming sales event or the arrival of new merchandise.

Persuasive Advertising

When a product has gained a certain level of brand awareness, firms use persuasive advertising to motivate consumers to take action. Persuasive advertising generally occurs in the growth and early maturity stages of the product life cycle, when competition is most intense, and attempts to accelerate the market's acceptance of the product. In later stages of the product life cycle, persuasive advertising may be used to reposition an established brand by persuading consumers to change their existing perceptions of the advertised product. Firms such as Lancôme often use persuasive advertising to convince consumers to take action—switch brands,[13] try a new product, or even continue to buy the advertised product.

Reminder Advertising

Finally, reminder advertising is a communication used to remind or prompt repurchases, especially for products that have gained market acceptance and are in the maturity stage of their life cycle. Such advertising certainly appears in traditional media, such as television or print commercials, but it also encompasses other forms of advertising. For example, if you decide to buy tissue paper, do you carefully consider all the options, comparing their sizes, prices, and performance, or do you just grab the first thing you see on the shelf? When your grocery store places a display of Kleenex facial tissues on the end of the paper products aisle, it relies on your top-of-the-mind awareness of the Kleenex brand, which the manufacturer has achieved through advertising. That is, Kleenex tissue paper maintains a prominent place in people's memories and triggers their response, without them

Lancome's persuasive ads attempt to motivate consumers to take action: try the product, switch brands, or continue to buy the product.

This ad is designed to remind consumers that when they need tissues, don't think too hard. Just pick up a box of Kleenex.

having to put any thought into it. The advertising and the end cap display thus prompt you, and many other consumers, to respond by buying a package, just the response Kleenex hoped to attain.

Focus of Advertisements

An ad campaign's objectives determine each specific ad's focus. The ad can be product focused, might have an institutional focus, or could have a public service focus. Product-focused advertisements inform, persuade, or remind consumers about a specific product or service. The Pepsi Max ad shown here is designed to generate sales for Pepsi Max.

Institutional advertisements inform, persuade, or remind consumers about issues related to places, politics, or an industry. Perhaps the best-known institutional advertising campaign is the long-running "Got Milk?" campaign to encourage milk consumption by appealing to consumers' needs to affiliate with the milk-mustached celebrities shown in the ads.[14] The ads highlight the beneficial properties of milk for building strong bones, which involves a more informative appeal, combined with a mild emotional fear appeal in its assertion that failing to drink milk can lead to medical problems. Its Spanish-language ad campaign, "Toma Leche," similarly touts milk as a wonder tonic that fights cavities, sleeplessness, and bone loss. A recent campaign, as exemplified in the ad with Rebecca Romjin and her babies, even promises that drinking milk helps families stay together.[15]

A specific category of institutional advertising is public service advertising (PSA). PSAs focus on public welfare; generally they are sponsored by nonprofit institutions,

This product-focused advertisement is designed to inform, persuade, or remind consumers about Pepsi Max.

civic groups, religious organizations, trade associations, or political groups.[16] Like product and institutionally focused advertising, PSAs also inform, persuade, or remind consumers, but the focus is for the betterment of society. As such, PSAs represent a form of social marketing, defined as the application of marketing principles to a social issue to bring about attitudinal and behavioral change among the general public or a specific population segment.

For the National Aeronautics and Space Administration (NASA), the goal is to help Americans to recognize the value of the organization and the science it sponsors—even without the grandiose missions that once marked NASA's development. Instead, the science it continues to support leads to advancements that benefit society at large. Thus Stephen Colbert highlights the promise of new vaccines developed on the International Space Station (and holds out hope for new high-tech ice cream flavors); Mary J. Blige touts her collaboration with NASA to encourage girls to pursue careers in science; and Dwayne "The Rock" Johnson promises that the coolest thing about NASA's spin-off technologies are the ways they can help people on Earth perform better.[17]

Because PSAs are a special class of advertising, under Federal Communications Commission (FCC) rules, broadcasters must devote a specific amount of free airtime to them. Also, since they often are designed by top advertising agencies for nonprofit clients, PSAs usually are quite creative and stylistically appealing. For example, what is your reaction to the truth public service

The Got Milk institutional advertising campaign is used to encourage milk consumption by appealing to consumers' needs to affiliate with milk-mustached celebrities like actor Taye Diggs.

antismoking campaign summarized in Ethical and Societal Dilemma 19.1?

Regardless of whether the advertising campaign's objective is to inform, persuade, or remind, with a focus on a particular product or the institution in general, each campaign's objectives must be specific and measurable. For a brand awareness campaign, for example, the objective might be to increase brand awareness among the target market by 50 percent within six months. Another campaign's goal may be to persuade 10 percent of a competitor's customers to switch to the

Mary J. Blige appears with NASA space shuttle astronaut Leland Melvin to encourage young women to expand their career choices by studying science, technology, engineering and mathematics (STEM).

Ethical & Societal Dilemma 19.1   Getting to the Truth[i]

Smoking is the single biggest preventable cause of death in the world; someone dies from tobacco use every eight seconds. Smoking causes cancers of the lung, throat, and mouth; it also leads to high blood pressure, heart problems, and lung diseases other than cancer. Yet worldwide, one in five teens between the ages of 13 and 15 years smokes, and many of those smokers will reach for their cigarettes for another 15 to 20 years. What can marketers do to help people avoid or quit this hazardous habit?

As part of the historic tobacco settlement between various states' attorneys general and the tobacco industry, the American Legacy Foundation receives over a billion dollars to educate the public about the dangers of smoking. The foundation uses this money to fund the "truth" campaign, the largest national young antismoking campaign and the only campaign not controlled by the tobacco industry. The campaign's goal is to tell the truth about the tobacco industry, including

The American Legacy Foundation produces anti-smoking ads like this one designed to tell the truth about the tobacco industry, including health effects, marketing strategies, and manufacturing practices.

health effects, marketing strategies, and manufacturing practices. Focused primarily on youths between the ages of 12 and 17 years, the campaign presents facts and allows teens to make their own decisions rather than telling them what they should or should not do.

The campaign had a direct impact on smoking, accelerating the decline in teen smoking during its first two years. Seven years after "truth" was launched, research showed that teens exposed to the campaign had a more accurate perception of the number of their peers who smoke. Considering how much most teens want to fit in with their peers, changing perceptions can help reduce the number of young people who pick up a cigarette.

To reach them, "truth" uses videos online and in cinemas as well as social media, website games, television integration,

radio advertising, and live tours. It has employed scare tactics, such as a pile of body bags piled up in front of Philip Morris headquarters. But it also relies on humor, animation, murals at the SXSW music festival, and Broadway-style song and dance routines to communicate the message.

But is humor the right way to communicate about a subject that kills millions of people each year? Is a pile of body bags an effective way to reach young smokers, who don't believe nicotine-related diseases will happen to them? Is this kind of messaging, which tobacco companies claim is abusive to them and their employees, appropriate or fair? How would you feel if you worked for a tobacco company? How would you feel about tobacco advertising if someone in your family had emphysema from smoking?

advertised brand. Once the advertising campaign's objectives are set, the firm sets the advertising budget.

STEP 3: DETERMINE THE ADVERTISING BUDGET

The various budgeting methods for marketing communications (Chapter 18) also apply to budgeting for advertising. First, firms must consider the role that advertising plays in their attempt to meet their overall promotional objectives. Second, advertising expenditures vary over the course of the product life cycle. Third, the nature of the market and the product influence the size of advertising budgets. The nature of the market also determines the amount of money spent on advertising. For instance, less money is spent on advertising in B2B (business-to-business) marketing contexts than in B2C (business-to-consumer) markets. Personal selling, as we discuss in Chapter 20, likely is more important in B2B markets.

STEP 4: CONVEY THE MESSAGE

In this step, marketers determine what they want to convey about the product or service. First, the firm determines the key message it wants to communicate to the target audience. Second, the firm decides what appeal would most effectively convey the message. We present these decisions sequentially, but in reality, they must be considered simultaneously.

The Message

The message provides the target audience with reasons to respond in the desired way. A logical starting point for deciding on the advertising message is to tout the key benefits of the product or service. The message should communicate its problem-solving ability clearly and in a compelling fashion. In this context, advertisers must remember that products and services solve problems, whether real or perceived. That is, people are not looking for 1/4-inch drill bits; they are looking for 1/4-inch holes to hang a picture on the wall.[18] Because there are many ways to make a 1/4-inch hole, a firm like Black & Decker must convey to consumers that its drill bit is the best way to get that hole.

Another common strategy differentiates a product by establishing its unique benefits. This distinction forms the basis for the unique selling proposition (USP) or the value proposition (as discussed in Chapter 9), which is often the common theme or slogan in an advertising campaign. A good USP communicates the unique attributes of the product and thereby becomes a snapshot of the entire campaign. Some of the most famous USPs include the following:

Red Bull . . . Gives You Wings

Ford . . . Built Tough

Oreo . . . Milk's Favorite Cookie

TNT . . . We Know Drama

Kellogg's Corn Flakes Is The Original and Best Cereal

The New York Times . . . All The News That's Fit to Print

Trek . . . We Believe in Bikes

Vail . . . Like Nothing On Earth

Ford's USP sends a powerful message about the benefits of purchasing its vehicles.

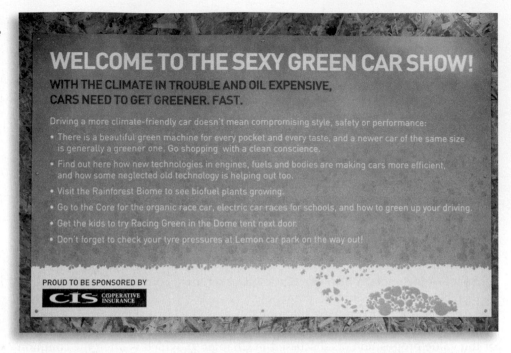

The selling proposition communicated by the advertising must be not only unique to the brand but also meaningful to the consumer. It furthermore must be sustainable over time, even with repetition.

The Appeal

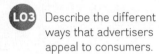

Describe the different ways that advertisers appeal to consumers.

Advertisers use different appeals to portray their products or services and persuade consumers to purchase them, though advertising tends to combine the types of appeals into two categories: informational and emotional.

Informational Appeals Informational appeals help consumers make purchase decisions by offering factual information that encourages consumers to evaluate the brand favorably on the basis of the key benefits it provides.[19] Thus, ads for the Sexy Green Car Show in Cornwall, UK, espouse multiple ways in which consumers can educate themselves and act in a more environmentally conscious manner when it comes to their automobiles. This appeal is well suited to this type of product: By informing consumers about a potential source of its competitive advantage, including tangible features and images of science, the advertising copy directly delivers an informational, persuasive message.

Emotional Appeals An emotional appeal aims to satisfy consumers' emotional desires rather than their utilitarian needs. These appeals therefore focus on feelings about the self.[20] The key to a successful emotional appeal is the use of emotion to create a bond between the consumer and the brand. Exhibit 19.2 shows firms and examples of the most common types of emotional appeals: fear, safety, humor, happiness, love (or sex),[21] comfort, and nostalgia.[22]

Which emotional appeal is Chevrolet using with its new slogan?

EXHIBIT 19.2   Emotional Appeals in Advertising

Emotional Appeal	Company	Example
Fear/Safety	ADT Security	"Breaking into Your Apartment Is Easier than You Think"
Humor	Best Buy	"Game On, Santa"
Happiness	Tropicana	"Awake to Alive"
Love/sex	Axe Body Spray	"Unleash the Chaos"
Comfort	Kleenex	"Softness Worth Sharing"
Nostalgia	Chevrolet	"Find New Roads"

STEP 5: EVALUATE AND SELECT MEDIA

The content of an advertisement is tied closely to the characteristics of the media that firms select to carry the message and vice versa. Media planning refers to the process of evaluating and selecting the media mix—the combination of the media used and the frequency of advertising in each medium—that will deliver a clear, consistent, compelling message to the intended audience.[23] For example, Macy's may determine that a heavy dose of television, radio, print, and billboards is appropriate for the holiday selling season between Thanksgiving and the end of the year.

Because the media buy, the actual purchase of airtime or print pages, is generally the largest expense in the advertising budget, marketers must make their decisions carefully. Television advertising is by far the most expensive. To characterize these various types of media, we use a dichotomy: mass and niche media.

Mass and Niche Media

Mass media channels include outdoor/billboards, newspapers, magazines, radio, and television and are ideal for reaching large numbers of anonymous audience members. Niche media channels are more focused and generally used to reach narrower segments, often with unique demographic characteristics or interests. Specialty television channels (e.g., Home and Garden TV) and specialty magazines such as *Skateboarder* or *Cosmo Girl* all provide examples of niche media. The Internet provides an opportunity to appeal to the masses through ads on the home page of Internet sites such as www.comcast.net or www.yahoo.com or more niched opportunities such as an American Express business card on *The Wall Street Journal* site (wsjonline.com).

 LO4 Identify the various types of media.

Choosing the Right Medium

For each class of media, each alternative has specific characteristics that make it suitable for meeting specific objectives (see Exhibit 19.3).[24] For example, consumers use different media for different purposes, to which advertisers should match their messages. Television is used primarily for escapism and entertainment, so most television advertising relies on a mix of visual and auditory techniques.

Communication media also vary in their ability to reach the desired audience. For instance, radio is a good medium for products such as grocery purchases or fast food because many consumers decide what to purchase either on the way to

EXHIBIT 19.3	Types of Media Available for Advertising	
Medium	**Advantages**	**Disadvantages**
Television	Wide reach; incorporates sound and video.	High cost; several channel and program options; may increase awareness of competitors' products.
Radio	Relatively inexpensive; can be selectively targeted; wide reach.	No video, which limits presentation; consumers give less focused attention than TV. Exposure periods are short.
Magazines	Very targeted; subscribers pass along to others.	Relatively inflexible; takes some time for the magazine to be available.
Newspapers	Flexible; timely; able to localize.	Can be expensive in some markets; advertisements have short life span.
Internet/mobile	Can be linked to detailed content; highly flexible and interactive; allows for specific targeting.	Becoming cluttered; the ad may be blocked by software on the computer.
Outdoor/billboard	Relatively inexpensive; offers opportunities for repeat exposure.	Is not easily targeted; has placement problems in some markets; exposure time is very short.
Direct marketing	Is highly targeted; allows for personalization.	Cost can vary depending on type of direct marketing used; traditional media, like mail, will be more expensive than newer media.

the store or while in the store. Because many people listen to the radio in their cars, it becomes a highly effective means to reach consumers at a crucial point in their decision process. Twitter offers several options for advertisers to enhance their reach, as Social and Mobile Marketing 19.1 explains. As we discussed in Chapter 18, each medium also varies in its reach and frequency. Advertisers can determine how effective their media mix has been in reaching their target audience by calculating the total GRP (Reach × Frequency) of the advertising schedule, which we discuss next.

Determining the Advertising Schedule

Another important decision for the media planner is the advertising schedule, which specifies the timing and duration of advertising. There are three types of schedules:

- A continuous schedule runs steadily throughout the year and therefore is suited to products and services that are consumed continually at relatively steady rates and that require a steady level of persuasive and/or reminder advertising. For example, Procter & Gamble advertises its Tide brand of laundry detergent continuously.

- Flighting refers to an advertising schedule implemented in spurts, with periods of heavy advertising followed by periods of no advertising. This pattern generally functions for products whose demand fluctuates, such as suntan lotion, which manufacturers may advertise heavily in the months leading up to and during the summer.

- Pulsing combines the continuous and flighting schedules by maintaining a base level of advertising but increasing advertising intensity during certain periods. For example, airlines, hotels, and car rental companies might continuously advertise to ensure brand awareness but might increase the advertising in spikes during certain low demand periods.

Social & Mobile Marketing 19.1

Simplicity as a Strength and as a Weakness: Twitter's Advertising Formats and Future Plans[ii]

The overall strategy embraced by Twitter seems to follow the KISS principle: Keep it simple, stupid! The microblogging service provider is defined by the simplicity of the communication it enables, and its advertising strategy has matched that simplicity—at least thus far.

Twitter sells advertising in three formats, and three formats only. Unlike popular social media competitors such as Facebook, it does not collect detailed demographic information, so it lacks the ability to target advertising on an individual level. Instead, Twitter allows advertisers to

1. Pay to appear at the top of a list of suggested accounts that users can follow.

2. Buy a "trending" ranking, such that the firm's name or product appears to be particularly popular among users. This option is clearly labeled as advertising, but it also exploits Twitter's popular "trending topics" summary of the top 10 newsworthy events or celebrities or topics

that users are searching Twitter to find at that very moment.

3. Insert a promoted tweet. These tweets appear in the user's feed, alongside tweets by others whom the user expressly seeks to follow. They also can be personalized to some extent, in that they reflect search terms entered by the user (e.g., a search for "cool tech" returns, before any other content, an advertisement from Verizon Wireless, touting its latest smartphone deal).

Twitter is preparing for its initial public offering. In this process, it is taking a few steps that suggest it might be adding a bit more complexity to its advertising strategy. Twitter recently purchased MoPub, a company that specializes in inserting marketing messages into mobile applications through an auction mechanism. Other predictions indicate that Twitter will seek to diversify its market by building a global presence.

STEP 6: CREATE ADVERTISEMENTS

After the advertiser has decided on the message, type of ad, and appeal, its attention shifts to the actual creation of the advertisement. During this step, the message and appeal are translated creatively into words, pictures, colors, and/or music. Often, the execution style for the ad will dictate the type of medium used to deliver the message. To demonstrate an image, advertisers can use television and magazines. To promote price, they can use newspapers and radio. To appeal to specific target markets, they can use some of the electronic media vehicles described in Chapter 18. When using multiple media to deliver the same message, however, they must maintain consistency across the execution styles—that is, integrated marketing—so that the different executions deliver a consistent and compelling message to the target audience.

How do advertisers go about creating advertisements? They simultaneously consider the objectives of the ad, the targeted customer segment(s), the product or service's value proposition or the unique selling proposition, and how the ad will be coordinated with other IMC elements.

They then go about creating an ad or the ad campaign. Using the print ad for Duluth Trading Company shown on the next page as an example, the first component that the reader generally notices is the visual, and as such it should be eye-catching. The picture of the shipyard welder denotes tough masculinity. Although it is not always possible to meet all possible objectives with the visual, other important purposes are to identify the subject of the ad, show the product being used and its unique features, create a favorable impression of the product or advertiser, and arouse the readers' interest in the headline, which is generally noticed second.[25]

The headline is the large type in an ad that is designed to draw attention. In the Duluth Trading Company ad, the headline "Last Pants Standing" works with the visual to connote toughness and durability. But the subhead, a smaller headline, provides more information about the pants it is selling; specifically, it is the fire hose workpants. Headlines and subheads should be short and use simple words; and include the primary product or service benefits, the name of the brand, and an interest-provoking idea. They should ideally contain an action verb and give enough information for learning even if only the headline is read.

The body copy represents the main text portion of the ad. It is used to build on the interest generated by the visual and headlines, explains in more depth what the headline and subheads introduced, arouses desire for the product, and provides enough information to move the target consumer to action. In this case, the body copy, "The only pants tough enough for shipyard welder, Mike L," is short but powerful.

Finally, the ad typically has a number of brand elements that identify the sponsor of the ad, typically through a logo (Duluth Trading Company) and a unique selling proposition (not found in this ad). The advertiser must convey its message using compelling visuals, headlines, body copy, and identifying brand elements.

Although creativity plays a major role in the execution stage, advertisers must remain careful not to let their creativity overshadow the message. Whatever the execution style, the advertisement must be able to attract the audience's attention, provide a reason for the audience to spend its time viewing the advertisement, and accomplish what it set out to do. In the end, the execution style must match the medium and objectives.

Automobile manufacturers and dealers are among the most active advertisers and use very different messages in their advertising campaigns. Consider, for instance, two well-known car companies that recently introduced new four-door sedan models, each with very different advertising campaigns.

- **Chevrolet Malibu.** Another entry into the hybrid market, the Malibu employs a battery pack and offers good gas mileage. It is also positioned as a family sedan, though the most recent revamping reduced the size of the backseat. Likely advertising outlets include family-oriented magazines and television spots.

- **Ford Fusion.** With a focus on fuel economy, ads for the new Fusion promise its availability with both a hybrid and a conventional engine. Furthermore, it emphasizes Ford's SYNC technology which uses voice recognition to make phone calls, find and play music, and get directions. With these appeals, Ford is focusing largely on social media to get young consumers, who tend to care about technology and environmental concerns, attached to the new model.[26]

Ads for the new Ford Fusion emphasize fuel economy as well as interesting technology that it hopes will appeal to young consumers.

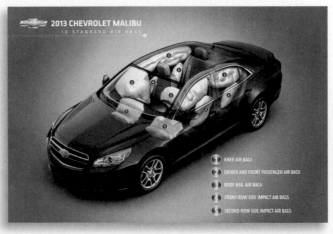

Although the Chevy Malibu offers a fuel-efficient hybrid model, it is positioned as a family sedan.

Ethical & Societal Dilemma 19.2

When Makeup Companies Really Do Make Up Models' Faces[iii]

Is Julia Roberts really that good looking? Of course, she's beautiful, but the portrayal of her face in advertising has, more likely than not, been given a Photoshop fix. Airbrushing may be as old as advertising, but improved technology makes the changes nearly imperceptible—can you tell the difference between the normal thickness of an eyelash and the version that Taylor Swift sported in a CoverGirl NatureLuxe Mousse Mascara ad? Ultimately, the National Advertising Division of the Council of Better Business Bureaus ruled the ad was misleading, prompting the brand to pull the ad.

But in other cases, cosmetics and fashion companies claim that fixing elements of appearance is both ubiquitous and expected by consumers. They assert they are not misleading anyone but rather creating a perfect image for their brand. So is it wrong for cosmetic companies to retouch ads, brushing away wrinkles and skin imperfections digitally?

The UK Advertising Standards Agency considers touching up photos in ads to be wrong. That oversight agency banned two ads by L'Oréal recently, charging that they were misleading. One ad featured Julia Roberts promoting Teint Miracle, a new Lancome skin product that, according to the company, provides "luminosity to the skin." The other featured the model Christy Turlington, promoting a cosmetic concealer called Eraser that promises to hide wrinkles and skin discoloration. Although the company protested that the ads did not exaggerate their product effectiveness, the UK Advertising Standards Agency was not convinced.

When selling cosmetics, is it ethical to touch up photos of models and celebrities like Julia Roberts to make them even more beautiful?

Do consumers want realistic images and measured promises, or do they accept and even prefer exaggerated claims and unrealistic images of beauty?

At times, though, even when advertisers think they have done their best to appeal to consumers, their actions can backfire, as Ethical and Societal Dilemma 19.2 describes.

STEP 7: ASSESS IMPACT USING MARKETING METRICS

The effectiveness of an advertising campaign must be assessed before, during, and after the campaign has run. Pretesting refers to assessments performed before an ad campaign is implemented to ensure that the various elements are working in an integrated fashion and doing what they are intended to do.[27] Tracking includes monitoring key indicators, such as daily or weekly sales volume, while the advertisement is running to shed light on any problems with the message or the medium. Posttesting is the evaluation of the campaign's impact after it is has been implemented. At this last stage, advertisers assess the sales and/or communication impact of the advertisement or campaign.

Measuring sales impact can be especially challenging because of the many influences other than advertising on consumers' choices, purchase behavior, and attitudes. These influences include the level of competitors' advertising, economic

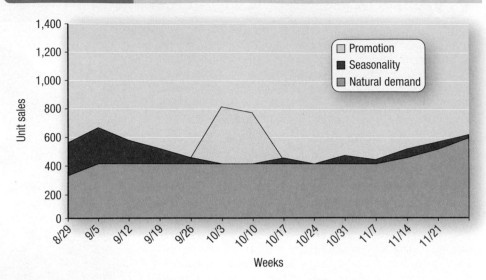

EXHIBIT 19.4 Hypothetical Sales History for Red Bull in a Grocery Store Chain

Sales volume is a good indicator of advertising effectiveness for frequently purchased consumer goods in the maturity stage of the product life cycle, such as Red Bull energy drink.

conditions in the target market, sociocultural changes, in-store merchandise availability and even the weather, all of which can influence consumer purchasing behavior. For instance, the sales resulting from even the best ads can be foiled by a lack of merchandise in the stores or a blizzard. Advertisers must try to identify these influences and isolate those of the particular advertising campaign.

For frequently purchased consumer goods in the maturity stage of the product life cycle such as soda, sales volume offers a good indicator of advertising effectiveness. Because their sales are relatively stable, and if we assume that the other elements of the marketing mix and the environment have not changed, we can attribute changes in sales volume to changes in advertising. Exhibit 19.4 illustrates a hypothetical sales history for Red Bull in a grocery store chain. Using a statistical technique called time-series analysis, sales data from the past is used to forecast the future. The data in Exhibit 19.4 can be decomposed into its basic trend (green), the seasonal influences (red), and the lift or additional sales caused by the advertising (orange). In this case, the lift caused by the advertising campaign is substantial.

For other types of goods in other stages of the product life cycle, sales data offer but one of the many indicators that marketers need to examine to determine advertising effectiveness. For instance, in high-growth markets, sales growth alone can be misleading because the market as a whole is growing. In such a situation, marketers measure sales relative to those of competitors to determine their relative market share. Firms find creative ways to identify advertising effectiveness. For example, digital cable allows them to present a specific advertisement to certain neighborhoods and then track sales by local or regional retailers.

CHECK YOURSELF

1. What are the steps involved in planning an ad campaign?
2. What is the difference between informational, persuasive, and reminder advertising?
3. What are the pros and cons of the different media types?
4. How can the effectiveness of advertising be evaluated?

REGULATORY AND ETHICAL ISSUES IN ADVERTISING

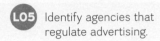

LO5 Identify agencies that regulate advertising.

In the United States, the regulation of advertising involves a complex mix of formal laws and informal restrictions designed to protect consumers from deceptive practices.[28] Many federal and state laws, as well as a wide range of self-regulatory agencies and agreements, affect advertising (Exhibit 19.5). The primary federal agencies that regulate advertising activities are the Federal Trade Commission (FTC), Federal Communications Commission (FCC), and Food and Drug Administration (FDA). In addition to these agencies, others, such as the Bureau of Alcohol, Tobacco, Firearms, and Explosives and the U.S. Postal Service, regulate advertising to some degree.

The FTC is the primary enforcement agency for most mass media advertising, although occasionally it cooperates with other agencies to investigate and enforce regulations on particular advertising practices. In one recent case, the FTC charged Pure Green Coffee, a Florida company, with false advertising and misrepresentation in its efforts to sell green coffee beans as a weight-loss aid. The company not only promised more benefits of the coffee beans than have been proven but also created fake websites designed to look like news outlets, and used logos from *The Dr. Oz Show* to imply that the popular television personality endorsed the product.[29]

Many product categories fall under self-regulatory restrictions or guidelines. For example, advertising to children is regulated primarily through self-regulatory mechanisms designed by the National Association of Broadcasters and the Better Business Bureau's Children's Advertising Review Unit. The only formal regulation of children's advertising appears in the Children's Television Act of 1990, which limits the amount of advertising broadcast during children's viewing hours.[30]

Recently, to make matters even more complicated for advertisers, state attorney general offices have begun to inquire into various advertising practices and assert their authority to regulate advertising in their states. The European Union also has increased its regulation of advertising for member nations. Many of these state and European regulations are more restrictive than existing U.S. federal requirements.

The line between what is legal and illegal is more difficult to discern when it comes to puffery, which is the legal exaggeration of praise, stopping just short of deception, lavished on a product. When Match.com claims that it leads to "better first dates," it's puffery because *better* is a subjective measure. But if it

EXHIBIT 19.5	Federal Agencies That Regulate Advertising	
Federal Agency	**General Purpose**	**Specific Jurisdiction**
Federal Trade Commission (FTC) (1914)	Enforces federal consumer protection laws.	Enforces truth in advertising laws; defines deceptive and unfair advertising practices.
Federal Communications Commission (FCC) (1934)	Regulates interstate and international communications by radio, television, wire, satellite, and cable.	Enforces restrictions on broadcasting material that promotes lotteries (with some exceptions); cigarettes, little cigars, or smokeless tobacco products; or that perpetuates a fraud. Also enforces laws that prohibit or limit obscene, indecent, or profane language.
Food and Drug Administration (1930)	Regulates food, dietary supplements, drugs, cosmetics, medical devices (including radiation-emitting devices such as cell phones), biologics (biological issues), and blood products.	Regulates package labeling and inserts, definition of terms such as *light* and *organic*, and required disclosure statements (warning labels, dosage requirements, etc.).

Is this ad an example of puffery or deception?

claims it produces "more second dates," it must be able to back up its numerical, quantitative assertion. Even cartoon bears must follow the rules: Charmin's animated spokescharacters need to be drawn with a few pieces of toilet paper on their rears, instead of none, to ensure that Charmin's claims extend only to leaving less toilet paper behind than other brands (puffery), not eliminating the problem altogether (deception).[31]

How do the courts determine what makes an ad deceptive, rather than simply puffery? The FTC's position is that it "will not pursue cases involving obviously exaggerated or puffing representations, i.e., those that ordinary consumers do not take seriously."[32] In general, the less specific the claim, the less likely it is considered to be deceptive. In the end, puffery is acceptable as long as consumers know that the firm is stretching the truth through exaggeration.[33]

PUBLIC RELATIONS

As you may recall from Chapter 18, **public relations (PR)** involves managing communications and relationships to achieve various objectives, such as building and maintaining a positive image of the firm, handling or heading off unfavorable stories or events, and maintaining positive relationships with the media. In many cases, public relations activities support other promotional efforts by generating free media attention and general goodwill.

Prada garnered positive public relations when Lupita Nyong'o wore its gown to the Academy Awards.

Designers, for example, vie to have celebrities, especially those nominated for awards, wear their fashions on the red carpet. Their brands offer intangible benefits, not just functional benefits. Events such as the Oscars, with its 35 million annual viewers, provide an unparalleled opportunity to showcase the emotional benefits of the brand and make others want to be a part of it. Thus, the celebrities whom designers pursue and offer their items to are those who will sell the most or provide the best iconic images. Lupita Nyong'o's great popularity during the recent awards season meant that she could wear Ralph Lauren to the Golden Globes, then switch to Prada for the Academy Awards, and garner press for both design firms.[34] The placement of designer apparel at media events benefits both the designer and the celebrity. And neither happens by accident. Public relations people on both sides help orchestrate the events to get the maximum benefit for both parties.

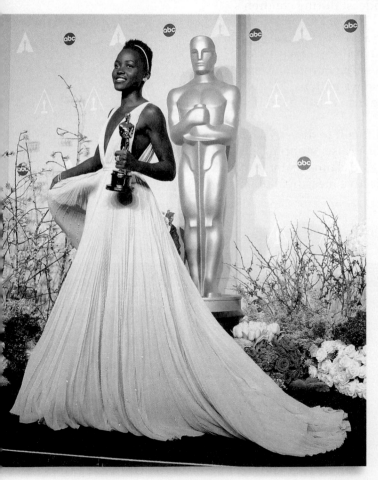

Good PR has always been an important success factor. Yet in recent years, the importance of PR has grown as the costs of other forms of marketing communications have increased. At the same time, the influence of PR has become more powerful as consumers have become increasingly skeptical of marketing claims made in other media.[35] In many instances, consumers view media coverage generated through PR as more credible and objective than any other aspects of an IMC program because the firm does not buy the space in print media or time on radio or television.

Chili's restaurants partners with St. Jude's Children's Research Hospital in a cause-related marketing campaign. Among other chili-related fund raising initiatives, customers can make a digital pepper and give a donation, and then share the pepper with friends via Facebook, Twitter, or Instagram.

Certainly the Chili's restaurant chain conducts plenty of media buys in traditional advertising spaces. But it also has partnered with St. Jude's Children's Research Hospital in one of the most successful examples of cause-related marketing (i.e., commercial activity in which businesses and charities form a partnership to market an image, product, or service for their mutual benefit)[36] in history. For several years, the restaurant has offered customers the opportunity to purchase a paper icon—in the shape of a chili, natch—that they may color and hang on restaurant walls. The cause marketing campaign runs in September, which is also National Childhood Cancer Awareness Month. On the last Monday of the month, the restaurant puts its money where its mouth is and donates all its profits on sales during the day to St. Jude. In addition to the relatively common Create-a-Chili paper icons, employees of the restaurants make and sell customized T-shirts and wristbands. Making peppers out of paper is not the only way people can donate to St. Jude. Chili's now has a website, http://morehope.chilis.com, that allows customers to make a digital pepper (and give a donation) and then share the pepper with friends via Facebook, Twitter, or Instagram. Civic-minded consumers can also buy St. Jude–branded Chili's gift cards on this site.[37]

Part of Red Bull's PR toolkit is its event sponsorship of a cliff diving event.

Another very popular PR tool is event sponsorship. Event sponsorship occurs when corporations support various activities (financially or otherwise), usually in the cultural or sports and entertainment sectors. Red Bull is a frequent sponsor of various kinds of sports events, such as Red Bull Air Race and numerous extreme sports events (e.g., cliff diving). Some of them are big name events; the titles of most college football playoff games now include the name of their sponsors (e.g., the Allstate Sugar Bowl). Others are slightly less famous; for example, Rollerblade USA, the maker of Rollerblade in-line skates, sponsors Skate-In-School, a program it developed with the National Association for Sport and Physical Education (NAPSE) to promote the inclusion of rollerblading in physical education curricula.

EXHIBIT 19.6	Elements of a Public Relations Toolkit
PR Element	**Function**
Publications: Brochures, special-purpose single-issue publications such as books	Inform various constituencies about the activities of the organization and highlight specific areas of expertise.
Video and audio: Programs, public service announcements	Highlight the organization or support cause-related marketing efforts.
Annual reports	Give required financial performance data and inform investors and others about the unique activities of the organization.
Media relations: Press kits, news releases, speeches, event sponsorships	Generate news coverage of the organization's activities or products/services.
Electronic media: Websites, e-mail campaigns	Websites can contain all the previously mentioned toolbox elements while e-mail directs PR efforts to specific target groups.

LO6 Describe the elements of a public relations toolkit.

Firms often distribute a PR toolkit to communicate with various audiences. Some toolkit elements are designed to inform specific groups directly, whereas others are created to generate media attention and disseminate information. We describe the various elements of a PR toolkit in Exhibit 19.6.

CHECK YOURSELF

1. Why do companies use public relations as part of their IMC strategy?
2. What are the elements of a public relations toolkit?

LO7 Identify the various types of sales promotions.

SALES PROMOTION

Advertising rarely provides the only means to communicate with target customers. As we discussed in Chapter 18, a natural link appears between advertising and sales promotion. **Sales promotions** are special incentives or excitement-building programs that encourage consumers to purchase a particular product or service, typically used in conjunction with other advertising or personal selling programs. Many sales promotions, like free samples or point-of-purchase (POP) displays, attempt to build short-term sales, whereas others, such as loyalty programs, contests, and sweepstakes, have become integral components of firms' long-term customer relationship management (CRM) programs, which they use to build customer loyalty.

We present these sales promotion tools next. The tools of any sales promotion can be focused on any channel member—wholesalers, retailers, or end-user consumers. Just as we delineated for advertising, when sales promotions are targeted at channel members, the marketer is employing a push strategy; when it targets consumers themselves, it is using a pull strategy. Some sales promotion tools can be used with either a push or pull strategy. We now consider each of the tools and how they are used.

Types of Sales Promotion

Coupons Coupons offer a discount on the price of specific items when they're purchased. Coupons are issued by manufacturers and retailers in newspapers, on products, on the shelf, at the cash register, over the Internet, and through the mail to stimulate demand. Some retailers have linked their coupons directly to their loyalty programs. The drugstore chain CVS tracks customers' purchases when they use their ExtraCare loyalty card and gives them coupons that are tailored just for them and their unique needs.[38] If a customer typically spends a small amount during each shopping trip, he or she might receive coupons to encourage larger purchases, such as buy one, get one free.

Internet sites also provide customers with instant coupons of their choosing. Imagine a customer who visits her local Walmart and finds a Hot Wheels video game for $29.99. By scanning the bar code using her cell phone, she connects to ShopSavvy.com and finds that the same item at a Target store a mile away is only $19.99. Another scan and a connection to MyCoupons.com provides her with a $10 coupon—which means she's saved $20 in a matter of minutes and just a few clicks.

Some coupons, whether printed from the Internet or sent to mobile phones, also contain information about the customer who uses it.[39] The bar code may identify the customer, his or her Internet address, Facebook page information, and even the search terms the customer used to find the coupon in the first place. These new breeds of coupons may look standard, but they offer up a startling amount of data, which promises benefits for advertisers who want to target their marketing more closely. Traditionally, coupons had low redemption rates and were therefore a relatively inexpensive sales promotion tool, but using customer data to create more targeted promotions has resulted in higher redemption rates, increasing their expense.

This sales promotion deal for Payless ShoeSource is a short-term price promotion that encourages customers to buy a second pair of shoes at one-half off.

Deals A deal refers generally to a type of short-term price reduction that can take several forms, such as a featured price, a price lower than the regular price; a certain percentage more free offer contained in larger packaging; or a buy one, get one free offer as shown in the Payless ad above. Another form of a deal involves a special financing arrangement, such as reduced percentage interest rates or extended repayment terms. Deals encourage customers to try a product because they lower the risk for consumers by reducing the cost of the good.

But deals can also alter perceptions of value—a short-term price reduction may signal a different price–quality relationship than would be ideal from the manufacturer's perspective. In addition, as Old Spice learned, offering too many deals can offset likely gains. Its popular Old Spice Guy campaign attracted consumer attention through funny television commercials and interactive online campaigns, and sales of Old Spice jumped. But the company offered so many buy one, get one free deals at the same time that the potential profit impact of the great ads was essentially eliminated by the costs of the deals.[40]

Premiums A premium offers an item for free or at a bargain price to reward some type of behavior, such as buying, sampling, or testing. These rewards build goodwill among consumers, who often perceive high value in them. Premiums can be distributed in a variety of ways: They can be included in the product packaging, such as the toys inside cereal boxes; placed visibly on the package, such as a coupon for free milk on a box of Cheerios; handed out in the store; or delivered in the mail, such as the free perfume offers Victoria's Secret mails to customers. Furthermore, premiums can be very effective if they are consistent with the brand's message and image and highly desirable to the target market. However, finding a premium that meets these criteria at a reasonable cost can be a serious challenge.

Contests A contest refers to a brand-sponsored competition that requires some form of skill or effort. ESPN's website hosts a page devoted just to sports-related contests: Get Me to the World Cup sponsored by Sony or Player of the Month presented by Kia.[41] For the Get Me to the World Cup contest, each participant must create and upload a short video demonstrating why he or she should be the one picked to attend the international event. For those who need some help sparking their creativity, ESPN provides some sample videos—including one by Kobe Bryant.

Sweepstakes A form of sales promotion that offers prizes based on a chance drawing of entrants' names, sweepstakes do not require the entrant to complete a task other than buying a ticket or filling out a form. For example, fans who purchased movie tickets to see *Dolphin Tale* from the Fandango website were automatically entered into a sweepstakes for a family vacation to St. Petersburg, Florida, where the movie's star Winter—a dolphin fitted with a prosthetic tail—lives. Considering its success, the promotion is likely to be repeated for the sequel, *Dolphin Tale 2*. Often the key benefit of sweepstakes is that they encourage current consumers to consume more if the sweepstakes form appears inside the packaging or with the product. Many states, however, specify that no purchase can be required to enter sweepstakes.

Samples Sampling offers potential customers the opportunity to try a product or service before they make a buying decision. Distributing samples is one of the most costly sales promotion tools but also one of the most effective. Quick-service restaurants and grocery stores frequently use sampling. For instance, Starbucks provides samples of new products to customers. Costco uses so many samples that customers can have an entire meal. Sometimes trial-sized samples come in the mail or are distributed in stores.

Loyalty Programs As part of a sales promotion program, loyalty programs are specifically designed to retain customers by offering premiums or other incentives to customers who make multiple purchases over time. Well-designed loyalty programs encourage consumers to increase their engagement and purchases from a given firm. Such sales promotions are growing increasingly popular and are tied to long-term CRM systems. (Loyalty programs are examined in Chapters 2 and 3.) These programs need to be carefully managed because they can be quite costly.

Point-of-Purchase Displays Point-of-purchase (POP) displays are merchandise displays located at the point of purchase, such as at the checkout counter in a supermarket. Retailers have long recognized that the most valuable real estate in the store is at the POP since they increase product visibility and encourage trial. Customers see products such as a magazine or a candy bar while they are waiting to pay for their purchases and impulsively purchase them. In the Internet version of a POP display, shoppers are stimulated by special merchandise, price reductions, or complementary products that Internet retailers feature on the checkout screen.

Rebates Rebates are a particular type of price reduction in which a portion of the purchase price is returned by the seller to the buyer in the form of cash. Many products, such as consumer electronics, offer significant mail-in rebates that may lower the price of the item significantly. Some companies enjoy the added exposure when they appear on consumer websites like PriceGrabber.com and Nextag.com, where products are sorted by the price, with links to the retailer's website. The firms garner considerable value from rebates because they attract consumers and therefore stimulate sales, but they may not have to pay off all the rebates offered.

Product Placement When marketers use product placement, they pay to have their product included in nontraditional situations, such as in a scene in a movie or television program.[42] By doing so, they increase the visibility of their products. Product placement may be subtly placed, such as when American Idol judges are seen drinking Coca-Cola. On CBS's *The Big Bang Theory,* not only do scenes regularly show the characters working and eating there, but Sheldon also asserts his need to get "access to the Cheesecake Factory walk-in freezer." Although many firms would embrace product placement in hit shows and movies and are willing to pay for it, for Apple, the challenge is a little less stringent. U.S. film and television directors seem to love its sleek white laptops, ear-budded iPods, and ubiquitous iPhones. Thus more than one-third of all top-grossing films at the U.S. box office—129 of 374 movies—have included Apple-branded products in the past decade. Recent appearances include both popular offerings and critically acclaimed broadcasts, from Phil's desperate efforts to score an iPad on *Modern Family* to more nefarious uses depicted in *House of Cards*.[43] Apple is also unique in that it claims it does not pay for product placement, nor does it comment on film appearances. An analytics firm that estimates the dollar value of product placements has reported that Apple's five-minute screen time in *Mission Impossible* alone was worth more than $23 million.[44] Apple seemingly can earn those returns without paying for the placements, but not all companies are so lucky.

Using Sales Promotion Tools

Marketers must be careful in their use of sales promotions, especially those that focus on lowering prices. Depending on the item, consumers may stock up when items are offered at a lower price, which simply shifts sales from the future to now and thereby leads to short-run benefits at the expense of long-term sales stability. For instance, using sales promotions such as coupons to stimulate sales of household cleaning supplies may cause consumers to stockpile the products and decrease demand for those products in the future. But a similar promotion used with a perishable product such as Dannon yogurt should increase its demand at the expense of competitors like Yoplait.

Many firms are also realizing the value of cross-promoting, when two or more firms join to reach a specific target market. To achieve a successful cross-promotion, the two products must appeal to the same target market and together create value for consumers. J.Crew has teamed up with several famous brands, including Havaianas, Barbour, Timex, New Balance, Ray-Ban and Speedo, to offer well-known brands in the J.Crew stores and website.[45]

The goal of any sales promotion is to create value for both the consumers and the firm. By understanding the needs of its customers, as well as how best to entice them to purchase or consume a particular product or service, a firm can develop promotional messages and events that are of interest to and achieve the desired response from those customers. Traditionally, the role of sales promotion has been to generate short-term results, whereas the goal of advertising was to generate long-term results. As this chapter demonstrates, though, both sales promotion and advertising can generate both long- and short-term effects. The effective combination of both types of activities leads to impressive results for the firm and the consumers.

CHECK YOURSELF

1. What are various forms of sales promotions?
2. What factors should a firm consider when evaluating a sales promotion?

Reviewing Learning Objectives

 Describe the steps in designing and executing an advertising campaign.

Firms (1) identify their target market, (2) set advertising objectives, (3) set the advertising budget, (4) depict their product or service, (5) evaluate and select the media, (6) create the ad, and (7) assess the impact of the ad.

 Identify three objectives of advertising.

All advertising campaigns are designed to inform, persuade, or remind customers. Informative advertising is communication used to create and build brand awareness. Persuasive advertising is communication used to motivate consumers to take action. Finally, reminder advertising is communication used to remind or prompt repurchases.

LO3 Describe the different ways that advertisers appeal to consumers.

Advertising appeals are either informational or emotional. Informational appeals influence purchase decisions with factual information and strong arguments built around relevant key benefits that encourage consumers to evaluate the brand favorably. Emotional appeals indicate how the product satisfies emotional desires rather than utilitarian needs.

LO4 Identify the various types of media.

Firms can use mass media channels like newspapers or television to reach large numbers of anonymous audience members. Niche media, such as cable television and specialty magazines, are generally used to reach narrower segments with unique demographic characteristics or interests. When choosing media, firms must match their objectives to that channel. Also, certain media are better at reaching a particular target audience than others.

LO5 Identify agencies that regulate advertising.

Advertising is regulated by a plethora of federal and state agencies. The most important federal agencies are the FTC, which protects consumers against general deceptive advertising; the FCC, which has jurisdiction over radio, television, wire, satellite, and cable and covers issues regarding the use of tobacco products and objectionable language; and the FDA, which regulates food, dietary supplements, drugs, cosmetics, and medical devices.

LO6 Describe the elements of a public relations toolkit.

A variety of elements compose a firm's public relations toolkit. They include publications, video and audio programs, public service announcements, annual reports, media kits (e.g., press kits), news releases, and electronic media (e.g., websites).

LO7 Identify the various types of sales promotions.

Sales promotions are special incentives or excitement-building programs that encourage purchase and include coupons, deals, premiums, contests, sweepstakes, samples, POP displays, rebates, and product placement. They either push sales through the channel, as is the case with contests directed toward retail salespeople, or pull sales through the channel, as coupons and rebates do.

Key Terms

 LEARNSMART

- advertising, 580
- advertising plan, 582
- advertising schedule, 590
- body copy, 592
- brand elements, 592
- cause-related marketing, 597
- contest, 599
- continuous schedule, 590
- coupon, 598
- cross-promoting, 601
- deal, 599
- emotional appeal, 588
- event sponsorship, 597
- flighting, 590
- headline, 591
- informational appeal, 588
- informative advertising, 582

- institutional advertisement, 584
- lift, 594
- loyalty program, 600
- mass media, 589
- media buy, 589
- media mix, 589
- media planning, 589
- niche media, 589
- persuasive advertising, 582
- point-of-purchase (POP) display, 600
- posttesting, 593
- premium, 599
- pretesting, 593
- product placement, 600
- product-focused advertisement, 584

- public relations (PR), 596
- public service advertising (PSA), 584
- puffery, 595
- pull strategy, 582
- pulsing, 590
- push strategy, 582
- rebate, 600
- reminder advertising, 583
- sales promotion, 598
- sampling, 600
- social marketing, 585
- subhead, 591
- sweepstakes, 600
- tracking, 593
- unique selling proposition (USP), 587

Marketing Applications

1. What are the objectives of the Chipotle ad (page 579)? Does the ad have more than one objective? Explain your answer.

2. Using the same ad, explain what kind of appeal it uses.

3. Verizon spends millions of dollars each year on advertising for many different purposes. Provide an example of how it might design an informative ad, a persuasive ad, and a reminder ad.

4. Name a current advertising slogan you believe is particularly effective for developing a unique selling proposition.

5. Bernard's, a local furniture company, target markets to college students with apartments and households of young people purchasing their first furniture items. If you worked for Bernard's, what type of media would you use for your advertising campaign? Justify your answer.

6. Should Bernard's use continuous, pulsing, or flighting for its advertising schedule? Why?

7. Suppose Porsche is introducing a new line of light trucks and has already created the advertising campaign. How would you assess the effectiveness of the campaign?

8. Suppose now that Porsche is planning a sales promotion campaign to augment its advertising campaign for the new line of light trucks. Which push and pull sales promotion tools do you believe would be most effective? Why?

9. Consider all the diet products that are currently advertised on television today, including weight-loss supplements, weight-loss programs, and fitness equipment. Do you believe that some of these ads overstate what the product or service can actually do? Do you think any of these ads are actually deceptive or puffery?

10. You are invited to your six-year-old niece's birthday party and bring her the new superhero doll being advertised on television. She's thrilled when she unwraps the gift but is in tears a short time later because her new doll is broken. She explains that on TV, the doll flies and does karate kicks, but when she tried to play with the doll this way, it broke. You decide to call the manufacturer, and a representative tells you he is sorry your niece is so upset but that the ad clearly states the doll does not fly. The next time you see the televised ad, you notice very small print at the bottom that states the doll does not fly. You decide to write a letter to the FTC about this practice. What information should you include in your letter?

Quiz Yourself

1. After the advertiser has decided on the message, type of ad, and appeal, its attention now shifts to _____ .
   a. logistical support
   b. new product development
   c. advertising assessment
   d. determination of why they should advertise
   e. creation of the advertisement

2. Unlike advertising, public relations _____ .
   a. supports promotional efforts by generating "free" media attention
   b. accounts for a greater increase in marketing spending
   c. converts mass media advertising into direct marketing
   d. is considered a human resource function
   e. should not be considered as part of the marketing area

(Answers to these two questions can be found on page 652.)

Toolkit

MAKE AN ADVERTISEMENT

Suppose you have been hired to develop a new ad for a product or service to target the college student market. The ad will appear in college student newspapers around the world. Please use the toolkit provided in your instructor's Connect course to develop the ad.

Net Savvy

1. Go to the website for the Children's Advertising Review Unit (CARU), one of the major self-regulatory bodies for children's advertising, at http://www.asrcreviews.org. Click on "CARU" and then "About Us—CARU" and examine the activities of CARU. How does this form of regulation complement the more formal regulation of federal and state agencies? Now look under the "Press Releases" link. Choose one of the press releases and discuss what action CARU took against the identified company or group. What was the main issue in the case?

2. *PR Newswire* attempts to provide information for "professional communicators." Visit its website at http://www.prnewswire.com and click on the "PR Newswire Services" link to explore the services it has to offer. What would you consider this organization's primary purpose? To whom does *PR Newswire* address the advertising appeals on its website?

Chapter Case Study

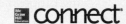

MAKING MASTERCARD PRICELESS

How do you pay for books, clothing, groceries, or travel? For many consumers, the answer is MasterCard, which has more than 200 million cards in circulation.[46] Yet despite the credit card's popularity, it lags behind its major competitor, Visa, by nearly 100 million cards. It is also outstripped by American Express for both monthly and annual purchases and spending volume. Because MasterCard's primary function is to process transactions between each customer's bank and each merchant's bank, the company must appeal to two customer bases to build market share: the merchants who accept MasterCard for payment and the purchasers who use the card. These audiences are closely related, which implies that a single campaign can target both, likely even for an extended period. However, even the most successful campaigns can grow stale.

In 1997, MasterCard International and the advertising agency McCann Erickson Worldwide launched the emotion-based "Priceless" campaign, which celebrated life's most precious moments with the tagline, "There are some things money can't buy. For everything else, there's MasterCard."[47] The campaign was hugely successful, saving MasterCard from disaster, even in direct competition with the more widely accepted Visa card.[48] However, as consumer values and needs changed and the marketplace evolved, MasterCard faced a new challenge: how to retain customer loyalty and brand identification while reinvigorating its advertising. The solution was the "Priceless Cities" campaign.

Expanding Services to Meet Market Demand

In 1966, a group of California banks created a member-owned association called the Interbank Card Association. This association grew its services, changing its name to MasterCard in 1979 to reflect a commitment to international growth.[49] As it reached new markets across the globe, MasterCard also focused on technology innovation to help make economic transactions faster, more convenient, and more secure. The company acquired interest in the international credit card EuroCard (known today as Europay International), as well as Cirrus, a worldwide interbank network that links MasterCard, Maestro, and Diner's Club credit, debit, and prepaid cards to an international network of ATMs. The company also added fraud/risk management providers to its network of services.

Today MasterCard's technology platform can handle more than 160 million transactions every hour with a 99.9 percent reliability rate,[50] and the company has issued a contactless, or smart, card that communicates with terminals via radio waves. This payment method does not require a signature and can be a card or key fob that is tapped rather than swiped; it also appears as a smartphone app. To provide even more value to customers, the company has added sophisticated consulting and information services that help merchants gain insight into consumer spending, according to their transaction data and in-depth analyses.[51] These efforts have dovetailed with changes in consumer behavior as shoppers have begun relying more on electronic payment options and less on paper-based currency. In 2006, the company transitioned to a new corporate governance and ownership structure and began trading on the New York Stock Exchange.

"Priceless" Revisited

MasterCard began its "Priceless" campaign by identifying its target audience, which in this case focused on consumers. Hoping to persuade shoppers to keep their MasterCard at the top of their wallets, the campaign stressed the relationship between the card and experiences, as opposed to possessions. In early television ads, the narration linked the price of beauty parlor visits and new outfits to the "priceless" expression on an ex-boyfriend's face at a reunion, to create positive self-assessment feelings.[52] In another, the cost of tickets, refreshments, and souvenirs at a game was tied to the "priceless" opportunity for meaningful conversation between father and son, to invoke both happiness and love.[53] The "Priceless" campaign included various promotions and competitions, in addition to these television spots.

In 2004, "Priceless" print ads took a new tack, weaving well-known retailers into the ads, together with MasterCard's theme. These retailers—which represented another of MasterCard's target audiences—received value from the prominent placement of their names and product images in the ads. Messaging moved from the general to the specific; an ad showing a teenaged rock band playing in a garage that might once have said, "extra-long extension cord, $11; moving them out of the living room: priceless," was modified to indicate that the extension cord was from Radio Shack. The result was a form of symbiotic marketing in which well-known brand names helped attract consumer attention to MasterCard ads, and each brand appeared to be endorsing the other.[54]

Magic Moments, "Priceless Cities"

In July 2011, MasterCard launched an expanded campaign, called "Priceless Cities." This campaign, kicked off initially in New York, offers cardholders special experiences in major cities that can be shared with family and friends.[55] Designed to provide busy consumers with memorable opportunities in the realms of sports, music, entertainment, shopping, travel, arts, culture, and dining out, the campaign touted early opening times at the toy store FAO Schwartz, a safari sleepover at the Bronx Zoo, prime tickets to a Yankees game with an ex-Yankee, and VIP dining experiences designed by a famed chef.[56] The idea, says MasterCard's chief marketing officer, is to transform consumers' perception of the card from simply part of a priceless moment to being the force that enables such experiences. In a shaky economy, when most competitors focus on deals and discounts, the MasterCard campaign attracts attention by appealing to emotions rather than wallets and stressing unforgettable experiences rather than cost savings. The campaign forges an additional bond with card users, because it places MasterCard at the center of these memorable social activities.

The ads run in more than 100 countries and air in more than 50 languages and the overall campaign uses print, radio, transit, outdoor advertising, and television. It also includes digital platforms to drive home its message, including a new section of the MasterCard website created specifically for the campaign, as well as social media channels such as Facebook and Twitter. Cardholders register at the site to access special offers; World Elite MasterCard holders get preferred access to the events, as well as special offers.

Marketers must continuously evaluate their campaigns and update them to ensure they are effectively communicating with their customers. New channels like social marketing can change shopping behaviors, creating opportunities that must be considered as part of any marketing strategy. As MasterCard has shown, even the best ideas need new infusions and innovations to keep appealing to their targets.

Questions

1. Why was the original "Priceless" campaign such a success?
2. Why has MasterCard started to use "Priceless" more actively in its messaging?

Endnotes

1. Noam Cohen, "Chipotle Blurs Lines with Satirical Series about Industrial Farming," *The New York Times,* January 27, 2014, http://www.nytimes.com.

2. Chipotle, "What Is Food with Integrity?" http://www.chipotle.com/en-us/fwi/fwi.aspx.

3. Stuart Elliot, "Chipotle Returns to Animation to Support Sustainable Farming," *The New York Times,* September 16, 2013.

4. Cohen, "Chipotle Blurs Lines."

5. Kristina Monllos, "Eating Alone? Chipotle Cups Now Come with Original Writing from Literary Giants," *Adweek,* May 15, 2014, http://www.adweek.com.

6. George E. Belch and Michael A. Belch, *Advertising and Promotion: An Integrated Marketing Communications Perspective* (New York: McGraw-Hill, 2007); Jef I. Richards and Catherine M. Curran, "Oracles on 'Advertising': Searching for a Definition," *Journal of Advertising* 31, no. 2 (Summer 2002), pp. 63–77.

7. Alexandra Bruell, "ZenithOptimedia Forecasts Slow, Steady Growth in Global Ad Spend," *Advertising Age,* March 12, 2012, http://www.adage.com.

8. Dan Zigmond et al., "Measuring Advertising Quality on Television: Deriving Meaningful Metrics from Audience Retention Data," *Journal of Advertising Research* 49, no. 4 (December 2009), pp. 419–28; Robert G. Heath, Agnes C. Nairn, and Paul A. Bottomley, "How Effective Is Creativity? Emotive Content in TV Advertising Does Not Increase Attention," *Journal of Advertising Research* 49, no. 4 (December 2009), pp. 450–63; Raymond R. Burke and Thomas K. Srull, "Competitive Interference and Consumer Memory for Advertising," *Journal of Consumer Research* 15 (June 1988), pp. 55–68; Kevin Lane Keller, "Memory Factors in Advertising: The Effect of Advertising Retrieval Cues on Brand Evaluation," *Journal of Consumer Research* 14 (December 1987), pp. 316–33.

9. Markus Pfeiffer and Markus Zinnbauer, "Can Old Media Enhance New Media? How Traditional Advertising Pays Off for an Online Social Network," *Journal of Advertising Research* 50, no. 1 (2010), pp. 42–49; Terry Daugherty, Matthew Eastin, and Laura Bright, "Exploring Consumer Motivations for Creating User-Generated Content," *Journal of Interactive Advertising* 8, no. 2 (2008); Anthony Bianco, "The Vanishing Mass Market," *BusinessWeek,* July 12, 2004, pp. 61–68.

10. Brendan Greeley, "World Cup Shootout: Can Nike Beat adidas at Soccer?" *Bloomberg Businessweek,* May 15, 2014, http://www.businessweek.com.

11. adidas, "Neo," http://www.adidas.com/us/content/selenagomez.

12. William F. Arens, Michael F. Weigold, and Christian Arens, *Contemporary Advertising,* 12th ed. (New York: McGraw-Hill, 2008).

13. Tulin Erdem, Michael Keane, and Baohong Sun, "The Impact of Advertising on Consumer Price Sensitivity in Experience Goods Markets," *Quantitative Marketing and Economics* 6 (June 2008), pp. 139–76; Xiaojing Yang and Robert E. Smith, "Beyond Attention Effects: Modeling the Persuasive and Emotional Effects of Advertising Creativity," *Marketing Science* 28 (September/October 2009), pp. 935–49; Matthew Shum, "Does Advertising Overcome Brand Loyalty? Evidence from the Breakfast Cereal Market," *Journal of Economics and Management Strategy* 13, no. 2 (2004), pp. 77–85.

14. "Got Milk?," http://www.gotmilk.com.

15. Elaine Wong, "Rebecca Romjin Makes Milk Run," *Brandweek,* January 13, 2010.

16. http://www.marketingpower.com/_layouts/Dictionary.aspx?dLetter=P.

17. NASA, "PSAs," http://www.nasa.gov/content/nasas-public-service-announcements-psas/#.U4ihAig4k08.

18. Theodore Levitt, *The Marketing Imagination* (New York: Free Press, 1986).

19. Belch and Belch, *Advertising and Promotion.*

20. Katherine White and John Peloza, "Self-Benefit versus Other-Benefit Marketing Appeals: Their Effectiveness in Generating Charitable Support," *Journal of Marketing* 73 (July 2009), pp. 109–24.

21. Darren W. Dahl, Jaideep Sengupta, and Kathleen D. Vohs, "Sex in Advertising: Gender Differences and the Role of Relationship Commitment," *Journal of Consumer Research* 36, no. 2 (2009), pp. 215–31; Jaideep Sengupta and Darren W. Dahl, "Gender-Related Reactions to Gratuitous Sex Appeals in Advertising," *Journal of Consumer Psychology* 18, no. 1 (2008), pp. 62–78.

22. Jack Loftus, "ADT Ad Campaign Scares Homeowners into Buying ADT Security," *Gizmodo,* http://gizmodo.com; Jack Neff, "What the Stylish Garbage Can Is Wearing," *Advertising Age,* November 3, 2011, http://adage.com; Natalie Zmuda, "Best Buy Ups Holiday Spending, Introduces 'Game On, Santa' Campaign," *Advertising Age,* November 17, 2011, http://adage.com; Andrew Adam Newman, "Axe Adds Fragrance for Women to Its Lineup," *The New York Times,* January 8, 2012, http://www.nytimes.com.

23. *AMA Dictionary,* http://www.marketingpower.com/_layouts /Dictionary.aspx?dLetter=M.

24. Some illustrative articles look at the effectiveness of given media: H. Risselada, P. C. Verhoef, and T. H. Bijmolt, "Dynamic Effects of Social Influence and Direct Marketing on the Adoption of High-Technology Products," *Journal of Marketing* 78, no. 4 (2014); Robert Heath, "Emotional Engagement: How Television Builds Big Brands at Low Attention," *Journal of Advertising Research* 49, no. 1 (March 2009), pp. 62–73; Lex van Meurs and Mandy Aristoff, "Split-Second Recognition: What Makes Outdoor Advertising Work?" *Journal of Advertising Research* 49, no. 1 (March 2009), pp. 82–92.

25. William F. Arens, David H. Schaefer, and Michael F. Weigold, *Advertising, M-Series* (Burr Ridge: Irwin/McGraw-Hill, 2012).

26. Stephen Williams, "New Sedans Aim to Break Out of the Pack," *Advertising Age*, February 20, 2012, http://adage.com.

27. Dean M. Krugman et al., *Advertising: Its Role in Modern Marketing* (New York: Dryden Press, 1994), pp. 221–26.

28. Herbert Jack Rotfeld and Charles R. Taylor, "The Need for Interdisciplinary Research of Advertising Regulation: A Roadmap for Avoiding Confusion and Errors," *Journal of Advertising*, Winter 2009.

29. "FTC Charges Green Coffee Bean Sellers with Deceiving Consumers through Fake News Sites and Bogus Weight Loss Claims," May 19, 2014, http://www.ftc.gov/news-events/press-releases.

30. Debra Harker, Michael Harker, and Robert Burns, "Tackling Obesity: Developing a Research Agenda for Advertising Researchers," *Journal of Current Issues & Research in Advertising* 29, no. 2 (2007), pp. 39–51; N. Kapoor and D. P. S. Verma, "Children's Understanding of TV Advertisements: Influence of Age, Sex and Parents," *Vision* 9, no. 1 (2005), pp. 21–36; Catharine M. Curran and Jef I. Richards, "The Regulation of Children's Advertising in the U.S.," *International Journal of Advertising and Marketing to Children* 2, no. 2 (2002).

31. Irina Slutsky, "Nine Things You Can't Do in Advertising If You Want to Stay on the Right Side of the Law," *Advertising Age*, March 7, 2011, http://adage.com.

32. Bob Hunt, "Truth in Your Advertising: Avoid Puffery?" *Realty Times*, June 20, 2007.

33. Ibid.

34. Blue Carreon, "The 2014 Oscars Best Dressed List," *Forbes*, March 2, 2014, http://www.forbes.com.

35. Diego Rinallo and Suman Basuroy, "Does Advertising Spending Influence Media Coverage of the Advertiser?" *Journal of Marketing* 73 (November 2009), pp. 33–46; Carl Obermiller and Eric R. Spangenberg, "On the Origin and Distinctness of Skepticism toward Advertising," *Marketing Letters* 11, no. 4 (2000), p. 311.

36. Jackie Huba, "A Just Cause Creating Emotional Connections with Customers," http://www.inc.com.

37. http://morehope.chilis.com; http://causerelatedmarketing.blogspot.com/2008/03/how-chilis-used-cause-related-marketing.html.

38. Personal communication with Rob Price, VP of Retail Marketing, CVS, June 16, 2009; Carol Angrisani, "CVS Moves to Personalization," *SN: Supermarket News* 56, no. 2 (March 24, 2008), p. 29.

39. Stephanie Clifford, "Web Coupons Know Lots about You, and They Tell," *The New York Times*, April 16, 2010.

40. Jack Neff, "Old Spice Is Killing It on YouTube Again, but Sales Are Down Double-Digits," *Advertising Age*, August 4, 2011, http://adage.com.

41. http://sports.espn.go.com/espn/contests/index.

42. Eva A. van Reijmersdal, Peter C. Neijens, and Edith G. Smit, "A New Branch of Advertising: Reviewing Factors That Influence Reactions to Product Placement," *Journal of Advertising Research* 49, no. 4 (December 2009), pp. 429–49; Pamela Mills Homer, "Product Placement: The Impact of Placement Type and Repetition on Attitude," *Journal of Advertising*, Fall 2009.

43. Abe Sauer, "Beats and Apple: A Match Made in Product Placement Heaven," *Brandchannel.com*, May 28, 2014, http://www.brandchannel.com; Abe Sauer, "The Envelope, Please: The 2014 Brandcameo Product Placement Awards," *Brandchannel.com*, February 27, 2014, http://www.brandchannel.com; Abe Sauer, "Announcing the 2012 Brandcameo Product Placement Award Winners," *Brandchannel.com*, February 13, 2012, http://www.brandchannel.com.

44. Abe Sauer, "The Envelope, Please."

45. http://www.jcrew.com.

46. http://www.cardhub.com/edu/market-share-by-credit-card-network/.

47. http://www.youtube.com/watch?v=3dcxQ2dvqmc.

48. http://marketingpractice.blogspot.com/2006/11/mastercard-priceless.html.

49. http://www.mastercard.com/us/company/en/docs/Corporate-Overview_FINAL.pdf.

50. https://www.mastercard.com/us/company/en/docs/Corporate-Overview_FINAL.pdf.

51. http://www.mastercardadvisors.com/.

52. http://www.youtube.com/watch?v=3dcxQ2dvqmc.

53. http://www.youtube.com/watch?v=Q_6stXKGuHo.

54. Stuart Elliott, "MasterCard Revamps Print Ads," *The New York Times*, August 11, 2004.

55. Stuart Elliott, "MasterCard Brings 'Priceless' to a Pricey Place," *The New York Times*, July 7, 2011; http://www.creditcardeducation.com/news/mastercard-offers-priceless-city-experiences.html.

56. http://newsroom.mastercard.com/press-releases/priceless-new-york-gives-mastercard-cardholders-privileged-access-to-the-citys-preeminent-experiences/.

i. truth, "Facts," http://www.thetruth.com/facts/; Alina Tugend, "Cigarette Makers Take Anti-Smoking Ads Personally," *The New York Times*, October 27, 2002.

ii. Vindu Goel, "For Twitter, Key to Revenue Is No Longer Ad Simplicity," *The New York Times*, September 16, 2013, http://www.nytimes.com.

iii. David Kiefaber, "Taylor Swift's CoverGirl Ad Is Pulled over Bogus Eyelashes," *Adweek*, December 23, 2011, http://www.adweek.com; David Gianastasio, "Turlington Ads: So Photoshopped They're Misleading?" *Adweek*, July 28, 2011, http://www.adweek.com; Tanzina Vega, "British Authority Bans Two Ads by L'Oréal," *The New York Times*, July 27, 2011, http://mediadecoder.blogs.nytimes.com.

Credits

CHAPTER 20

PERSONAL SELLING AND SALES MANAGEMENT

LEARNING OBJECTIVES

LO1 Describe the value added of personal selling.

LO2 Define the steps in the personal selling process.

LO3 Describe the key functions involved in managing a sales force.

LO4 Describe the ethical and legal issues in personal selling.

The Boeing Company is one of the largest manufacturers of airplanes in the world;[1] following an industry consolidation in the mid-1990s, it is actually one of two members of an industrywide duopoly (Airbus is the other).[2] The long production and R&D lead times in this sector, combined with very high prices per unit, have led to a fierce rivalry between Boeing and Airbus.

For many years, Boeing ranked second in terms of market share, leading to some challenging managerial and strategic concerns during the 2000s. A series of CEOs were dismissed for various reasons, leaving Boeing's reputation in question. Although strong in the defense sector, Boeing continued to cede market share to Airbus in the commercial airline segment, largely due to the introduction of the innovative, exciting Airbus 330. Finally, Boeing was in the midst of divesting a large percentage of its manufacturing facilities, in an attempt to move to an outsourcing model.[3]

The competitive landscape thus forced Boeing to make a strategic move if it hoped to survive. Headed by Michael Bair and three other top Boeing executives, the firm decided

to develop a new line of jet planes, designated 787 "Dream-liners." The 787 could fly internationally but would carry fewer passengers than traditional international airplanes. With this innovation, Boeing positioned itself to capture a "blue ocean" market, in which it could potentially support around 400 new international routes that attracted too little demand for larger planes but might be profitable for airlines that flew the new 787. Furthermore, because cost savings represented a key deciding factor for its business customers (i.e., the airlines), Boeing designed the plane with new composite materials that reduced fuel costs by 20 percent.[4]

To meet the related design requirements, not only was the cutting-edge plane model made almost entirely of composite parts, but these parts also allowed each plane to be "snapped together" in as little as three days. But the complexity of the design forced Boeing to outsource more than 70 percent of its production, using an unprec-edented "global systems integrator" strategy in this busi-ness-to-business market. Whereas once Boeing controlled the majority of production, now it was trusting the manu-facturing quality of its expensive, complex products to partners in the supply chain.

Unfortunately, its trust was misplaced. The new man-ufacturing approach saved time and money, but the

Dreamliner has continued to be awash in production and design issues. In 2013, fires caused by short circuits in the new lithium ion batteries that Boeing included in its planes caused the entire global fleet of 787s to be grounded for three months. Despite clearance to fly again, the U.S. National Transportation Safety Board con-tinued to express concern about the safety of the 140 Dreamliners currently in flight worldwide.[5]

How does a company that sells jets for prices ranging from $76 million to $360 million respond to a crisis like this?[6] Boeing relied on its world-class salespeople, such as John Wojick. Empowered by Boeing, Wojick offered greater flexibility in delivery times, as well as heavy discounts, to his business customers. He also noted the need to engage in tough conversations with his customers, during which he was required to communicate truthfully about what Boeing knows, and does not know, about the failures.[7]

The personal selling approach adopted by Wojick and his colleagues has helped stem the damage for Boe-ing. Within four months of taking over as global head of sales, Wojick landed a contract for 150 planes (at a value of nearly $15 billion). As a result, Boeing was able to over-take Airbus as the top ranking airline manufacturer, in terms of orders and deliveries.[8]

Just like advertising, which we discussed in Chapter 19, personal selling is so important to integrated marketing communications that it deserves its own chapter. Almost everyone is engaged in some form of selling. On a personal level, you sell your ideas or opinions to your friends, family, employers, and professors. Even if you have no interest in personal selling as a career, a strong grounding in the topic will help you in numerous career choices. Consider, for instance, Harry Turk, a very successful labor attorney. He worked his way through college selling sweaters to fraternities across the country. Although he loved his part-time job, Harry decided to become an attorney. When asked whether he misses selling, he said, "I use my selling skills every day. I have to sell new clients on the idea that I'm the best attorney for the job. I have to sell my partners on my legal point of view. I even use selling skills when I'm talking to a judge or jury."

LO1 Describe the value added of personal selling.

THE SCOPE AND NATURE OF PERSONAL SELLING

Personal selling is the two-way flow of communication between a buyer or buyers and a seller, designed to influence the buyer's purchase decision. Personal selling can take place in various situations: face-to-face, via video teleconferencing, on the telephone, or over the Internet, for example. More than 14 million people are employed in sales positions in the United States,[9] including those involved in business-to-business (B2B) transactions—like manufacturer's representatives selling to retailers or other businesses—and those completing business-to-consumer (B2C) transactions, such as retail salespeople, real estate agents, and insurance agents. Salespeople are referred to in many ways: sales representatives or reps, account executives, agents. And as Harry Turk found, most professions rely on personal selling to some degree.

Salespeople don't always get the best coverage in popular media. In Arthur Miller's famous play *Death of a Salesman,* the main character Willie Loman leads a pathetic existence and suffers from the loneliness inherent in being a traveling salesman.[10] The characters in David Mamet's play *Glengarry Glen Ross* portray salespeople as crude, ruthless, and of questionable character. Unfortunately, these powerful Pulitzer Prize–winning pieces of literature weigh heavily on our collective consciousness and often overshadow the millions of hardworking professional salespeople who have fulfilling and rewarding careers and who add value to their firm and provide value for their customers.

Personal Selling as a Career

Personal or professional selling can be a satisfying career for several reasons. First, many people love the lifestyle. Salespeople are typically out on their own. Although they occasionally work with their managers and other colleagues, salespeople tend to be responsible for planning their own day. This flexibility translates into an easier balance between work and family than many office-bound jobs can offer. Many salespeople now can rely on virtual offices, which enable them to communicate from anywhere and at any time with their colleagues and customers. Because salespeople are evaluated primarily on the results they produce, as long as they meet and exceed their goals, they experience little day-to-day supervision. You might find a salesperson at the gym in the middle of the day, when few other people are there, because no one keeps track of the length of his or her lunch break.

Second, the variety of the job often attracts people to sales. Every day is different, bringing different clients and customers, often in a variety of places. Their issues and problems and the solutions to those problems all differ and require creativity.[11] Third, professional selling and sales management can be a very lucrative career. Sales is among the highest-paying careers for college graduates, and compensation often includes perks, such as the use of a company car or bonuses for high performance. A top performer can have a total compensation package of over $150,000; even starting salespeople can make well over $50,000. Although the monetary compensation can be significant, the satisfaction of being involved in interesting, challenging, and creative work is rewarding in and of itself.

Fourth, because salespeople are the frontline emissaries for their firm, they are very visible to management. Furthermore, their performance is fairly straightforward to measure, which means that high-performing salespeople who aspire to management positions are in a good position to be promoted.

The Value Added by Personal Selling

The benefits for salespeople mean that they are expensive for firms. Experts estimate that the average cost of a single B2B sales call is about $600.[12] So why include them in the marketing channel at all? In response to this question, some firms have turned to the Internet and technology to lower the costs of personal selling. (See Social and Mobile Marketing 20.1.) Other firms, especially retailers, have made the decision not to use a sales force and thus require customers to perform the sales function on their own. But the firms that continue to use personal selling as part of their integrated marketing communications program recognize the value that it adds to their product or service mix. That is, personal selling is worth more than it costs. Personal selling adds value by educating customers and providing advice, saving the customer time, making things easier for customers, and building long-term strategic relationships with customers.[13]

Many salespeople now can rely on virtual offices, which enable them to communicate via the Internet with colleagues and customers.

Salespeople Provide Information and Advice Imagine how difficult it would be to buy a custom suit, a house, or a car without the help of a salesperson. UPS wouldn't dream of investing in a new fleet of airplanes without the benefit of Boeing's selling team. Boeing's sales team can provide UPS with the technical aspects of the aircraft as well as the economic justification for the purchase. If you need formalwear for your friend's upcoming wedding or a school dance, you might find it helpful to solicit the input of a retail sales associate, who can tell you what colors are hot this season, how to tie a bowtie, how each garment tends to fit, what the latest fashions are in formalwear, and how long your dress should be for a function that starts at 6:00 p.m. Certainly you could figure out most of this information on your own, but most customers find value in and are willing to pay for the education and advice that salespeople provide.

Salespeople Save Time and Simplify Buying Time is money! Customers perceive value in time and labor savings. In many grocery and drugstore chains, salespeople employed by the vendor that supplies the merchandise straighten stock, set up displays, assess inventory levels, and write orders. In some

Salespeople provide information and advice.

Social & Mobile Marketing 20.1   Personal Selling Goes Virtual[i]

Rising fuel costs, increasing staff productivity, cutbacks in airline service, minimizing carbon footprints, reducing corporate expenditure—these are just some of the reasons for meetings to go virtual. Foremost among them is that the technology has matured to the point that conversing in cyberspace frequently makes more sense than meeting in the same room. Accordingly, sales personnel infrequently need to meet potential customers face-to-face, because they instead rely on GoToMeeting, WebEx, or Skype to get to know their clients. Such telepresence technologies strongly influence firms' bottom lines, by enabling them to transition from expensive field sales staff to less costly inside sales representatives.

In its most advanced forms, telepresence goes far beyond Skype though. It relies on three screens that display life-sized images of conference attendees, plus an additional screen for shared work. Resolution on the screens exceeds that of high-definition televisions. Images can be magnified, allowing attendees to view minute product details from across the globe. These systems, which also feature custom lighting and acoustics, cost as much as $350,000. For corporations such as Cisco, which has more than 200 telepresence rooms, the investment still represents a savings over travel costs. It isn't alone: The management consulting and technology service firm Accenture estimates its teleconferencing rooms save millions of dollars each year, as well as saving its staff the wear and tear of travel.

Other collaborative technologies involve less financial outlay. Web-meeting services, for example, allow companies to conduct online training, edit documents collaboratively, demonstrate applications, give training or sales presentations, poll attendees, chat online, conduct question-and-answer sessions, and provide technical support. As long as participants have a computer with a web browser and an Internet connection, they can use collaborative tools such as wikis or voice-over-Internet protocol (VoIP) technology.

Such technologies also help small companies go global. Lisa Kirschner, president of a Chicago-based marketing and graphic design firm, had a hot lead in Italy. But she lacked the resources to meet in person and felt brainstorming via e-mail would be too cumbersome. Taking the risk of investing in web conferencing, which was unheard of in her industry, she ultimately secured clients in Italy, Japan, and Britain. The technology has earned her $100,000—one-eighth of her total annual revenue.

In parallel, new technologies that enable virtual conferences have led to reductions in business travel and slumps in the conference business. For example, Expos2 digitizes conferences, such that attendees begin with a screen showing the convention center layout. From there they can follow links to exhibits, programs, and live presentations with interactive functionality. Digital meeting technology aims not simply to replace face-to-face meetings or travel but rather to provide an alternative for companies that must optimize their travel budgets. Still, closing a deal is more likely during an in-person meeting, and business travel to other countries provides important insights into communities and cultures. All transactions benefit from a personal touch. But web-based and videoconferencing technology appear likely to keep influencing the ways companies do business.

Salespeople no longer have to meet face to face with their customers to make the sale.

A salesperson's product knowledge and ability to facilitate the sale can make buying a car easy and possibly even enjoyable.

cases, such as bakeries or soft drink sales, salespeople and truck drivers even bring in the merchandise and stock the shelves. These are all tasks that retail employees would otherwise have to do. To appeal to end customers, manufacturers might send salespeople into stores to provide cooking demonstrations or free samples in the case of grocery stores, or trunk or made-to-measure shows in the case of apparel or shoe retailers. In this case, the vendor increases convenience for both its immediate customer (the retailer) and the end consumer.

Salespeople Build Relationships As we discussed in Chapter 16, building strong marketing channel relationships is a critical success factor. Who in the organization is better equipped to manage this relationship than the salesperson, the front-line emissary for the firm? The most successful salespeople are those who build strong relationships with their customers—a rule that holds across all sorts of sales. That is, whether you are selling yourself as a job candidate, a product produced by your company, or a concept to a client, your sale is not successful if it leads to just a one-time transaction. Instead, good salespeople of all stripes consistently take a long-term perspective.

Building on the relationship concept introduced in Chapter 16, relationship selling refers to a sales philosophy and process that emphasizes a commitment to maintaining the relationship over the long term and investing in opportunities that are mutually beneficial to all parties.[14] Relationship-oriented salespeople work with their customers to find mutually beneficial solutions to their wants and needs. As we described in Chapter 7, colleges often negotiate long-term agreements with apparel companies to supply their sports teams. Similarly, a Lenovo sales team might be working with your university to provide you with the computer support and security you need during the years you spend working on the school's network.

THE PERSONAL SELLING PROCESS

LO2 Define the steps in the personal selling process.

Although selling may appear a rather straightforward process, successful salespeople must follow several steps. Depending on the sales situation and the buyer's readiness to purchase, the salesperson may not use every step, and the time required for each step varies with the situation. For example, if a customer goes

EXHIBIT 20.1   The Personal Selling Process

Generate and qualify leads

↓

Preapproach

↓

Sales presentation and overcoming reservations

↓

Closing the sale

↓

Follow-up

into The Gap already prepared to purchase some chinos, the selling process will be fairly quick. But if Lenovo is attempting to sell personal computers for the first time to your university, the process may take several months. With this in mind, let's examine each step of the selling process (Exhibit 20.1).

Step 1: Generate and Qualify Leads

The first step in the selling process is to generate a list of potential customers (leads) and assess their potential (qualify). Salespeople who already have an established relationship with a customer will skip this step, and it is not used extensively in retail settings. In B2B situations, however, it is important to work continually to find new and potentially profitable customers.

Salespeople can generate and qualify leads in a variety of ways.[15] They might discover potential leads by talking to current customers, doing research on the Internet, or networking at events such as trade shows, industry conferences, or chamber of commerce meetings. Salespeople can also generate leads through cold calls and social media.

The Internet, and sites like LinkedIn and Twitter in particular, have been a boon for generating and qualifying leads. Prior to its explosion, it was cumbersome to perform research on products, customers, or competitors. Salespeople would rely on a research staff for this information, and it could take weeks for the research to be completed and sent through the mail. Today, salespeople connect with potential customers through Twitter and LinkedIn. Salespeople curate blogs to draw in customers and generate leads, a process known as inbound marketing. While these are all important tools, they are unlikely to replace cold calling anytime soon as many customers still cannot be reached via social media.[16]

Trade shows also offer an excellent forum for finding leads. These major events are attended by buyers who choose to be exposed to products and services offered by potential suppliers in an industry. Consumer electronics buyers always make sure that they attend the annual International Consumer Electronics Show (CES) in Las Vegas, the world's largest trade show for consumer technology (http://www.cesweb.org). The most recent show was attended by 155,000 people (including more than 34,000 international attendees), such as vendors, developers, and suppliers of consumer-technology hardware, content, technology delivery systems, and related products and services.[17] Nearly 3,100 vendor exhibits took up 1.861 million net square feet of exhibit space, showcasing the very latest products and services. Vendors often use CES to introduce new products, including the first camcorder (1981), high-definition television (HDTV, 1998), and Internet protocol television (IP TV, 2005). At the 2014 CES conference more than 3,000 exhibitors showed off tens of thousands of new products.[18] In addition to providing an opportunity

Trade shows, like the International Consumer Eletronics Show in Las Vegas, are an excellent way to generate and qualify leads.

Adding Value 20.1 — College Athletics Turn to the Pros for Sales Help[ii]

Not that long ago, a few billboards and word of mouth were enough to sell out tickets for a college game. Demand for tickets to college basketball and football games was so high that many schools added seats as fast as they could and still had to turn fans away. But a dip in the economy, increased demands on leisure time, rising gas prices, and better television technology have combined to diminish ticket sales, leaving colleges with empty seats and a diminishing revenue stream, even as they face other budget constraints. In response, some athletic programs are outsourcing ticket sales to commission-driven experts, in the hopes of bringing fans back to the bleachers.

Ticket marketing companies catering to colleges use the model adopted by professional sports organizations: Sales staff work for commissions and make as many as 100 calls a day to students, alumni, faculty, and anyone else connected to the university. As these callers chat about the team, the school, or college athletics, they listen for clues to customers' personalities and needs, then adjust their sales strategy accordingly. The commission structure ensures the strong motivation of the sales force, which benefits the schools because every ticket sold promises additional potential income in the form of concessions. Furthermore, filled stadiums significantly improve the public perception of the team, team spirit, and the likelihood of national publicity.

Some ticketing companies also provide related services to help generate revenue. Callers versed in the specifics of the college's athletics program might request donations for athletic scholarships or sport-related programming. Sport marketers with contacts in the world of professional athletics can help schools pull together appropriate fundraising events. They provide research and insights, coordinate print production for programs and signage, assist with challenging media situations, help build sales of apparel and merchandise, and even rent seat cushions for homecoming games. Sophisticated software programs link ticketing, fundraising, and marketing functions to help track interactions, increase ticket sales, and improve the college's brand.

Other athletic departments prefer to hire and manage their own ticket sales staff. This approach gives the school greater control over its brand. It also avoids privacy concerns about sharing university databases with an external seller, which may be too aggressive for the school's educational environment, or running afoul of complex NCAA rules. However, internal sales might not be as effective, considering the competing priorities that confront the athletic department, the limited experience of the sales staff, the prohibitions on commission-based incentives for university employees, and ineffective channels of communication.

---

for retail buyers to see the latest products, the CES conference program features prominent speakers from the technology sector.[19]

Cold calls are a method of prospecting in which salespeople telephone or go to see potential customers without appointments.[20] Telemarketing is similar to a cold call, but it always occurs over the telephone. Sometimes professional telemarketing firms, rather than the firm's salespeople, make such calls. Adding Value 20.1 examines how colleges use it to boost attendance at sports events.

However, cold calls and telemarketing have become less popular over time, primarily because their success rate is fairly low. During cold calls, the salesperson is not able to establish the potential customer's specific needs because the receiver of the call is not expecting it, and therefore may not be willing to participate in it. Accordingly, these methods can be very expensive. Second, both federal and state governments are regulating the activities of telemarketers. Federal rules prohibit telemarketing to consumers whose names appear on the national Do-Not-Call list, which is maintained by the Federal Trade Commission. Even for

Telemarketing is a type of cold call in which salespeople generate or qualify leads on the telephone.

those consumers whose names are not on the list, the rules prohibit calling before 8:00 a.m. or after 9:00 p.m. (in the consumer's time zone) or after the consumer has told the telemarketer not to call. Federal rules also prohibit unsolicited fax messages, calls, or messages to cell phones.

After salespeople generate leads, they must qualify those leads by determining whether it is worthwhile to pursue them and attempt to turn them into customers. In B2B settings, the costs of preparing and making a presentation are so substantial that the seller must assess a lead's potential. Salespeople consider, for example, whether the potential customer's needs pertain to a product or a service. They should assess whether the lead has the financial resources to pay for the product or service.[21] Clients looking to sell multimillion-dollar properties want real estate agents to qualify potential buyers first. Therefore, the sales agents might create a password-protected website that features floor plans and inside views for the shopping convenience of interested buyers. But to obtain the password, the customer must be prequalified as someone who could actually afford to buy the property. Such qualifications save both the agent and the seller the trouble of showing properties to curious people who could never actually afford to buy.

In a retail setting, though, qualifying potential customers is both dangerous and potentially illegal. Retail salespeople should never judge a book by its cover and assume that a person in the store doesn't fit the store's image or cannot afford to purchase there. Such actions can quickly rise to the level of unethical and illegal discrimination, as recently alleged by several African American shoppers against such well-known retail names as Macy's and Barneys.[22] Although not illegal, imagine the frustration you might feel if you visit an upscale jewelry store to purchase an engagement ring, only to be snubbed because you are dressed in your everyday, casual school clothes.

Step 2: Preapproach and the Use of CRM Systems

The **preapproach** occurs prior to meeting the customer for the first time and extends the qualification of leads procedure described in Step 1. Although the salesperson has learned about the customer during the qualification stage, in this step, he or she must conduct additional research and develop plans for meeting with the customer. Suppose, for example, a management consulting firm wants to sell a bank a new system for finding checking account errors. The consulting firm's salesperson should first find out everything possible about the bank: How many checks does it process? What system is the bank using now? What are the benefits of the consultant's proposed system compared with the competition? The answers to these questions provide the basis for establishing value for the customer.

Salespeople input customer information into their tablets to develop a customer database for CRM systems.

In the past, this customer information, if it was available at all, was typically included in a manual system that each individual salesperson kept, using a notebook or a series of cards. Today, salespeople often can access all this information immediately and conveniently from their firm's customer relationship management (CRM) system.

In most cases, these CRM systems have several components. There is a customer database or data warehouse. Whether the salesperson is working for a retail store or manages a selling team for an aerospace contractor, he or she can record transaction information, customer contact information, customer preferences, and market segment information about the customer. Once the data have been analyzed and CRM programs developed, salespeople can help implement the programs. Superior Service 20.1 describes the success of the most popular CRM system today, Salesforce.com.

Having done the additional research, the salesperson establishes goals for meeting with the customer. It is important that he or she knows ahead of

Superior Service 20.1   Selling in the Cloud: The Growth and Success of Salesforce.com[iii]

At one time, CRM systems were the exclusive domain of wealthy companies. With costs running into hundreds of thousands of dollars, CRM systems represented a massive investment in both money and the time required to establish them. Each system needed its own servers and support from vendors to ensure its maintenance and consistent functioning.

This scenario clearly represented an opportunity for a company that could offer easier, less expensive, leaner services. Enter Salesforce.com. Instead of complete, onsite CRM solutions, it promised to host all computing and data storage on its own servers, in the cloud. Clients did not need to find massive funds to purchase the system, because Salesforce.com initiated the first CRM-related software-as-a-service (SaaS) model. That is, client firms did not buy any software but instead paid Salesforce.com a subscription fee that varied according to the number of licenses they needed. Each user license cost approximately $65 a month, representing a substantial cost savings compared with full CRM systems. Moreover, because the software was in the cloud, salespeople could access their customer data anywhere, through their smartphones or tablets, rather than having to return to the office to link into an in-house system.

And Salesforce.com didn't stop there. To build the most comprehensive service possible, the company created an entire section on its website that enabled clients to build and trade apps that would integrate with and extend the functionality of its system. To add value to its platform, it also has acquired dozens of firms that have developed innovative CRM technology. In recognition of its innovative, aggressive efforts, *Forbes* named Salesforce.com as one of the most innovative companies in practice today.

The move to a SaaS, cloud-based CRM model in turn opened doors for vast segments of companies that never would have been able to purchase a full system. For several years, Salesforce.com thus has enjoyed a leading position in the CRM service market, in terms of total revenue, revenue growth, and market share growth, including revenues that surpassed $20 billion and a 13.7 percent adjusted gross revenue. As Salesforce.com's president and vice chair Keith Block asserts, "Salesforce.com's CRM market share leadership is a reflection of the consistent innovation we deliver to our customers."

Salesforce.com offers its clients CRM solutions at a price most businesses can afford.

time exactly what should be accomplished. For instance, the consulting firm's salesperson cannot expect to get a purchase commitment from the bank after just the first visit. But a demonstration of the system and a short presentation about how the system would benefit the customer would be appropriate. It is often a good idea to practice the presentation prior to the meeting, using a technique known as role playing, in which the salesperson acts out a simulated buying situation while a colleague or manager acts as the buyer. Afterward, the practice sales presentation can be critiqued and adjustments can be made.

Step 3: Sales Presentation and Overcoming Reservations

The Presentation Once all the background information has been obtained and the objectives for the meeting are set, the salesperson is ready for a person-to-person meeting. Let's continue with our bank example. During the first part of the meeting, the salesperson needs to get to know the customer, get his or her attention, and create interest in the presentation to follow. The beginning of the presentation may be the most important part of the entire selling process, because it is when the salesperson establishes exactly where the customer is in his or her buying process (Exhibit 20.2). (For a refresher on the B2B buying process, see Chapter 7.)

Suppose, for instance, that the bank is in the first stage of the buying process: need recognition. It would not be prudent for the salesperson to discuss the pros and cons of different potential suppliers, because doing so would assume that the customer already had reached Step 4 (of the B2B buying process), proposal analysis and customer selection. By asking a series of questions though, the salesperson can assess the bank's need for the product or service and adapt or customize the presentation to match the customer's need and stage in the decision process.[23]

Asking questions is only half the battle; carefully listening to the answers is equally important. Some salespeople, particularly inexperienced ones, believe that to be in control, they must do all the talking. Yet it is impossible to really understand where the customer stands without listening carefully. What if the chief operating officer (COO) says, "It seems kind of expensive"? If the salesperson isn't listening carefully, he or she won't pick up on the subtle nuances of what the customer is really thinking. In this case, it probably means the COO doesn't see the value in the offering.

When the salesperson has gotten a good feel for where the customer stands, he or she can apply that knowledge to help the customer solve its problem or satisfy its need. The salesperson might begin by explaining the features or characteristics of the system that will reduce checking account errors. It may not be obvious, solely on the basis of these features, that the system adds value beyond the bank's current practices. Using the answers to some of the questions the salesperson posed earlier in the meeting, he or she can clarify the product's advantages over current or past practices, as well as the overall benefits of adopting the new system. The salesperson might explain, for instance, that the bank can expect a 20 percent improvement in checking account errors and that, because of the size of the bank and number of checks it processes per year, this improvement would represent $2 million in annual savings. Because the system costs $150,000 per year and will take only three weeks to integrate into the current system, it will add significant and almost immediate value.

It is important to ask questions at the beginning of a sales presentation to establish where the customer is in his or her buying process.

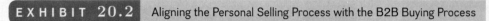

EXHIBIT 20.2   Aligning the Personal Selling Process with the B2B Buying Process

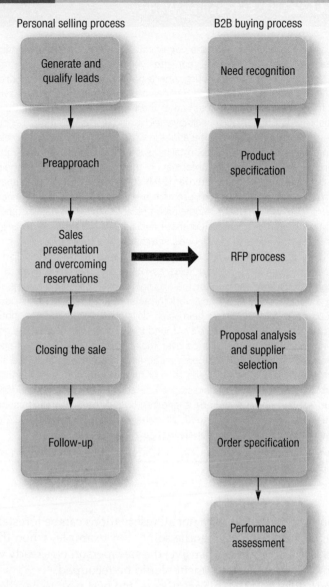

As this hypothetical example hints, personal selling often relies on an old-fashioned skill: storytelling. Even if they use advanced technologies and Internet-based communication media, salespeople must communicate their messages and sales pitches in ways that resonate with their audience of potential customers. As research in neuroscience continues to affirm, virtually everyone uses at least some level of emotional reaction in determining their choices. To appeal to customers, salespeople thus need to tell a story that engages people's imaginations.[24]

Handling Reservations An integral part of the sales presentation is handling reservations or objections that the buyer might have about the product or service. Although reservations can arise during each stage of the selling process, they are very likely to occur during the sales presentation. Customers may raise reservations pertaining to a variety of issues, but they usually relate in some way to value, such as that the price is too high for the level of quality or service.

Good salespeople know the types of reservations buyers are likely to raise. They may know, for instance, that their service is slower than competitors' or that

Superior Service 20.2 | Soft Selling Works[iv]

Ever feel as though a salesperson is trying not to tap her foot or roll his eyes while you decide what flavor ice cream you want? Or ever had a sales associate eagerly assure you an outfit looks great on you, when the mirror tells you differently? If so, those salespeople are making a significant mistake. By focusing on a single transaction, they could be losing repeat customers. Soft selling, or acting as a knowledgeable consultant to help customers solve a problem, is far more likely to result in a completed sale in the present and more business in the future.

The soft sell, also known as consultative or customer-centric sales, involves creating and maintaining a pleasant environment, interacting pleasantly with customers, providing useful information about products, helping customers reach a decision, and selling a product or service that the sales associate believes in. The concept isn't new: In the days of small neighborhood stores, employees greeted shoppers by name, knew their preferences and personalities, and helped customers track down products, even if it meant calling a competitor (remember *Miracle on 34th Street?*). But a focus on profits instead introduced the hard sell, characterized by pressure and hype. Over time, hard selling backfired, driving customers to more pleasant environments for their purchases. Now savvy retailers, returning to the original approach, are building profits, even in the midst of a challenging economy.

Yoforia's frozen yogurt stores provide a good example of soft sales of soft serve. Servers greet customers warmly, suggest samples to help with flavor decisions, and describe what makes the yogurt healthy. The result has significant sales increases year after year. Soft selling has even made it to the Girl Scouts, where parents helping their children hawk Thin Mints and Samoas are making sign-up sheets available in public spaces rather than tracking coworkers to their cubicles.

Consultative selling also works well for larger purchases, and even in situations in which months or years may elapse before a transaction takes place. The idea is to provide prospects with quality information that helps them solve their problems— delivered over lunch or via webinar, blog, white paper, or e-mail. It needn't promote a particular product or service. Rather, the focus should be on reliable content that consumers can use to make a purchase decision. Apple stores have online screenings of new models and the Genius Bar for free technical help.

Training sales associates in consultative selling requires subtlety. Sales associates at The Container Stores are selected for their ability to solve problems and relate to customers. They work for salary and not for commissions. Servers at Yoforia gain sales skills through one-on-one interactions with the store's cofounder Jun Kim, who stresses a good customer experience over making sales. The key to a positive experience is constant communication with customers to determine their needs, then using that information to identify appropriate choices and provide advice. Additional products or services should be suggested only if the customer has indicated a potential need. Ultimately, the goal of soft sales is to keep a customer for life, not just a single transaction.

---

their selection is limited. Although not all reservations can be forestalled, effective salespeople can anticipate and handle some. For example, when the bank COO said the check service seemed expensive, the salesperson was ready with information about how quickly the investment would be recouped.

As in other aspects of the selling process, the best way to handle reservations is to relax and listen, then ask questions to clarify any reservations.[25] For example, the salesperson could respond to the COO's reservation by asking, "How much do you think the bank is losing through checking account errors?" Her answer might open up a conversation about the positive trends in a cost–benefit analysis. Such questions are usually more effective than trying to prove the customer's reservation is not valid, because the latter approach implies the salesperson isn't really listening and could lead to an argument—the last thing a customer usually wants.

Step 4: Closing the Sale

Closing the sale means obtaining a commitment from the customer to make a purchase. Without a successful close, the salesperson goes away emptyhanded, so many salespeople find this part of the sales process very stressful. Although losing a sale is never pleasant, salespeople who are involved in a relationship with their customers must view any specific sales presentation as part of the progression toward ultimately making the sale or building the relationship. An unsuccessful close on one day may just be a means of laying the groundwork for a successful close during the next meeting. Superior Service 20.2 examines the art of soft selling.

Although we have presented the selling process as a series of steps, closing the sale rarely follows so neatly. However, good salespeople listen carefully to what potential customers say and pay attention to their body language. By reading these signals, they can achieve an earlier close. Suppose that our hypothetical bank, instead of being in the first step of the buying process, were in the final step of negotiation and selection. An astute salesperson would pick up on these signals and ask for the sale.

Step 5: Follow-Up

> "It ain't over till it's over."
> —Yogi Berra[26]

With relationship selling, it is never really over, even after the sale is closed. The attitudes customers develop after the sale become the basis for how they purchase in the future. The follow-up therefore offers a prime opportunity for a salesperson to solidify the customer relationship through great service quality. Let's apply the five service quality dimensions we discussed in Chapter 13 to understand the follow-up:[27]

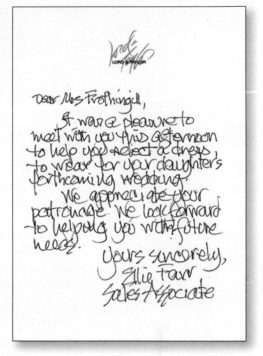

A postsale follow-up letter, call, or e-mail is the first step in initiating a new order and sustaining the relationship.

- **Reliability.** The salesperson and the supporting organization must deliver the right product or service on time.

- **Responsiveness.** The salesperson and support group must be ready to deal quickly with any issue, question, or problem that may arise.

- **Assurance.** Customers must be assured through adequate guarantees that their purchase will perform as expected.

- **Empathy.** The salesperson and support group must have a good understanding of the problems and issues faced by their customers. Otherwise, they cannot give them what they want.

- **Tangibles.** Because tangibles reflect the physical characteristics of the seller's business, such as its website, marketing communications, and delivery materials, their influence is subtler than that of the other four service quality dimensions. That doesn't mean it is any less important. Retail customers are generally more pleased with a purchase if it is carefully wrapped in nice paper instead of being haphazardly thrown into a crumpled plastic bag. The tangibles offer a signal that the product is of high quality, even though the packaging has nothing to do with the product's actual performance.

When customers' expectations are not met, they often complain—about deliveries, the billing amount or process, the product's performance, or after-sale services such as installation or training (recall the Gaps Model from Chapter 13). Effectively handling complaints is critical to the future of the relationship. As we noted in Chapter 13, the best way to handle complaints is to listen to the customer, provide a fair solution to the problem, and resolve the problem quickly.

The best way to nip a postsale problem in the bud is to check with the customer right after he or she takes possession of the product or immediately after the service has been completed. This speed demonstrates responsiveness and empathy. It also shows the customer that the salesperson and the firm care about customer satisfaction. Finally, a postsale follow-up call, e-mail, or letter takes the salesperson back to the first step in the sales process for initiating a new order and sustaining the relationship.

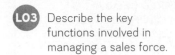

CHECK YOURSELF

1. Why is personal selling important to an IMC strategy?
2. What are the steps in the personal selling process?

LO3 Describe the key functions involved in managing a sales force.

MANAGING THE SALES FORCE

Like any business activity involving people, the sales force requires management. Sales management involves the planning, direction, and control of personal selling activities, including recruiting, selecting, training, motivating, compensating, and evaluating, as they apply to the sales force.

Managing a sales force is a rewarding yet complicated undertaking. In this section, we examine how sales forces can be structured, some of the most important issues in recruiting and selecting salespeople, sales training issues, ways to compensate salespeople, and finally how to supervise and evaluate salespeople.

Sales Force Structure

Imagine the daunting task of putting together a sales force from scratch. Will you hire your own salespeople, or should they be manufacturer's representatives? What will each salesperson's primary duties be: order takers, order getters, sales support? Finally, will they work together in teams? In this section, we examine each of these issues.

Company Sales Force or Manufacturer's Representative
A company sales force comprises people who are employees of the selling company. Independent agents, also known as manufacturer's representatives, or reps, are salespeople who sell a manufacturer's products on an extended contract basis but are not employees of the manufacturer. They are compensated by commissions and do not take ownership or physical possession of the merchandise.

Manufacturer's representatives are useful for smaller firms or firms expanding into new markets, because such companies can achieve instant and extensive sales coverage without having to pay full-time personnel. Good sales representatives have many established contacts and can sell multiple products from noncompeting manufacturers during the same sales call. Also, the use of manufacturer's reps facilitates flexibility; it is much easier to replace a rep than an employee and much easier to expand or contract coverage in a market with a sales rep than with a company sales force.

Company sales forces are more typically used for established product lines. Because the salespeople are company employees, the manufacturer has more control over what they do. If, for example, the manufacturer's strategy is to provide extensive customer service, the sales manager can specify exactly what actions a company sales force must take. In contrast, because manufacturer's reps are paid on a commission basis, it is difficult to persuade them to take any action that doesn't directly lead to sales.

Salesperson Duties
Although the life of a professional salesperson is highly varied, salespeople generally play three important roles: order getting, order taking, and sales support.

Order Getting
An order getter is a salesperson whose primary responsibilities are identifying potential customers and engaging those customers in discussions to attempt to make a sale. An order getter is also responsible for following up to ensure that the customer is satisfied and to build the relationship. In B2B settings, order getters are primarily involved in new buy and modified new buy situations (see Chapter 7). As a result, they require extensive sales and product knowledge

training. The Coca-Cola salesperson who goes to Safeway's headquarters to sell a special promotion of Vanilla Coke is an order getter.

Order Taking An order taker is a salesperson whose primary responsibility is to process routine orders, reorders, or rebuys for products. Colgate employs order takers around the globe who go into stores and distribution centers that already carry Colgate products to check inventory, set up displays, write new orders, and make sure everything is going smoothly.

Sales Support Sales support personnel enhance and help with the overall selling effort. For example, if a Best Buy customer begins to experience computer problems, the company has a Geek Squad door-to-door service as well as support in the store. Those employees who respond to the customer's technical questions and repair the computer serve to support the overall sales process.

Order takers process routine orders, reorders, or rebuys for products.

Combination Duties Although some salespeople's primary function may be order getting, order taking, or sales support, others fill a combination of roles. For instance, a computer salesperson at Staples may spend an hour with a customer educating him or her about the pros and cons of various systems and then make the sale. The next customer might simply need a specific printer cartridge. A third customer might bring in a computer and seek advice about an operating system problem. The salesperson was first an order getter, next an order taker, and finally a sales support person.

Some firms use selling teams that combine sales specialists whose primary duties are order getting, order taking, or sales support but who work together to service important accounts. As companies become larger and products more complicated, it is nearly impossible for one person to perform all the necessary sales functions.

Recruiting and Selecting Salespeople

When the firm has determined how the sales force will be structured, it must find and hire salespeople. Although superficially this task may sound as easy as posting the job opening on the Internet or running an ad in a newspaper, it must be performed carefully, because firms don't want to hire the wrong person. Salespeople are very expensive to train. Among other creative hiring tactics, Zappo's famously considers finding the right people so important that it will pay them to leave after a few weeks if they are not a good fit.[28]

In their critical efforts to find the right person for the job though, companies must take care to avoid biased practices, such that they would hire on the basis of stereotypes instead of qualifications. For most people, the picture of someone selling Avon products likely involves a middle-aged woman, namely, the "Avon Lady." But sales revenues for these products continue to provide salespeople a successful living, prompting plenty of women and men to try their hand at selling Avon.[29] Hiring based on misplaced assumptions about gender or other categories can be damaging to the company, as well as discriminatory.

The most important activity in the recruiting process is to determine exactly what the salesperson will be doing and what personal traits and abilities a person should have to do the job well. For instance, the Coca-Cola order getter who goes to Safeway to pitch a new product will typically need significant sales experience, coupled with great communication and analytical skills. Coke's order takers need to be reliable and able to get along with lots of different types of people in the stores, from managers to customers.

Many firms give candidates personality tests, but they stress different personality attributes, depending on the requisite traits for the position and the personality characteristics of their most successful salespeople.[30] For instance, impatience is often a positive characteristic for sales because it creates a sense of urgency to

Is P90X creator Tony Horton a born salesperson or was he made into one?

close the sale. But for very large, complicated sales targeting large institutions, like the bank in our previous example, an impatient salesperson may irritate the decision makers and kill the deal.

When recruiting salespeople, it helps to possess certain personal traits. What are those personal traits? Managers and sales experts generally agree on the following:[31]

- *Personality.* Good salespeople are friendly, sociable, and, in general, like being around people. Customers won't buy from someone they don't like.

- *Optimism.* Good salespeople tend to look at the bright side of things. Optimism also may help them be resilient—the third trait.

- *Resilience.* Good salespeople don't easily take no for an answer. They keep coming back until they get a yes.

- *Self-motivation.* As we have already mentioned, salespeople have lots of freedom to spend their days the way they believe will be most productive. But if the salespeople are not self-motivated to get the job done, it probably won't get done.

- *Empathy.* Empathy is one of the five dimensions of service quality discussed previously in this chapter and in Chapter 13. Good salespeople must care about their customers, their issues, and their problems.

Sales Training

Even people who possess all these personal traits need training. All salespeople benefit from training about selling and negotiation techniques, product and service knowledge, technologies used in the selling process, time and territory management, and company policies and procedures.

Firms use varied delivery methods to train their salespeople, depending on the topic of the training, what type of salesperson is being trained, and the cost versus the value of the training. For instance, an on-the-job training program is excellent for communicating selling and negotiation skills, because managers can observe the sales trainees in real selling situations and provide instant feedback. They can also engage in role-playing exercises in which the salesperson acts out a simulated buying situation and the manager critiques the salesperson's performance.

A much less expensive, but for some purposes equally valuable, training method is the Internet. Online training programs have revolutionized the way training happens in many firms. Firms can provide new product and service knowledge, spread the word about changes in company policies and procedures, and share selling tips in a user-friendly environment that salespeople can access anytime and anywhere. Distance learning sales training programs through teleconferencing enable a group of salespeople to participate with their instructor or manager in a virtual classroom. And testing can occur online as well. Online sales training may never

Technology has changed the lives of salespeople and sales training. Companies can conduct distance learning and training through videoconferencing.

replace the one-on-one interaction of on-the-job training for advanced selling skills, but it is quite effective and efficient for many other aspects of the sales training task.[32]

Motivating and Compensating Salespeople

An important goal for any effective sales manager is to get to know his or her salespeople and determine what motivates them to be effective. Some salespeople prize their freedom and like to be left alone; others want attention and are more productive when they receive accolades for a job well done. Still others are motivated primarily by monetary compensation. Great sales managers determine how best to motivate each of their salespeople according to what is most important to each individual. Although sales managers can emphasize different motivating factors, except in the smallest companies, the methods used to compensate salespeople must be fairly standardized and can be divided into two categories: financial and nonfinancial.

Financial Rewards Salespeople's compensation usually has several components. Most salespeople receive at least part of their compensation as a salary, a fixed sum of money paid at regular intervals. Another common financial incentive is a commission, which is money paid as a percentage of the sales volume or profitability. A bonus is a payment made at management's discretion when the salesperson attains certain goals. Bonuses usually are given only periodically, such as at the end of the year. A sales contest is a short-term incentive designed to elicit a specific response from the sales force. Prizes might be cash or other types of financial incentives. For instance, Volkswagen may give a free trip to Germany for the salesperson who sells the most Touaregs.

The bulk of any compensation package is made up of salary, commission, or a combination of the two. The advantage of a salary plan is that salespeople know exactly what they will be paid, and sales managers have more control. Salaried salespeople can be directed to spend a certain percentage of their time handling customer service issues. Under a commission system, however, salespeople have only one objective—make the sale! Thus, a commission system provides the most incentive for the sales force to sell.

Volkswagen may give a free trip to Germany for the salesperson who sells the most Touaregs.

Mary Kay gives high-performing salespeople an award that has both high symbolic value and material value—a pink Cadillac.

Nonfinancial Rewards As we have noted, good salespeople are self-motivated. They want to do a good job and make the sale because it makes them feel good. But this good feeling also can be accentuated by recognition from peers and management. For instance, the internal monthly magazine at the cosmetics firm Mary Kay provides an outlet for not only selling advice but also companywide recognition of individual salespeople's accomplishments.[33]

Nonfinancial rewards should have high symbolic value, as plaques, pens, or rings do. Free trips or days off are also effective rewards. More important than what the reward is, however, is the way it is operationalized. For instance, an award should be given at a sales meeting and publicized in the company newsletter. It should also be done in good taste, because if the award is perceived as tacky, no one will take it seriously.[34] Mary Kay recognizes salespeople's success with unusually large rewards that have both high symbolic and high material value. More than 100,000 independent beauty consultants and sales directors have earned the use of one of the famous pink Cadillacs, but it is also possible to gain rewards and recognition such as a set of faux pearl earrings within the first week of becoming a consultant.

Evaluating Salespeople by Using Marketing Metrics Salespeople's evaluation process must be tied to their reward structure. If salespeople do well, they should receive their rewards in the same way that if you do well on your exams and assignments in a class, you should earn a good grade. However, salespeople should be evaluated and rewarded for only those activities and outcomes that fall under their control. If Macy's makes a unilateral decision to put Diesel jeans in all its stores, after a negotiation with Diesel's corporate headquarters in Italy, the Diesel sales representatives responsible for individual Macy's stores should not receive credit for making the sale, nor should they get all the windfall commission that would ensue from the added sales.

Considering this guiding principle—evaluate and reward salespeople for what they do and not for what they don't do—how should sales managers evaluate salespeople? The answer is never easy because measures must be tied to performance, and there are many ways to measure performance in a complex job such as selling. For example, evaluating performance on the basis of monthly sales alone fails to consider how profitable the sales were, whether any progress was made to build new business that will be realized sometime in the future, or the level of customer service the salesperson provided. Because the sales job is multifaceted with many contributing success factors, sales managers should use multiple measures.[35]

In business practice, salesperson evaluation measures can be objective or subjective. Sales, profits, and the number of orders represent examples of objective measures. Although each is somewhat useful to managers, such measures do not provide an adequate perspective for a thorough evaluation because there is no means of comparison with other salespeople. For instance, suppose salesperson A generated $1 million last year, but salesperson B generated $1.5 million. Should salesperson B automatically receive a significantly higher evaluation? Now consider that salesperson B's territory has twice as much potential as salesperson A's. Knowing this, we might suppose that salesperson A has actually done a better job. For this reason, firms use ratios such as profit per customer, orders per call, sales per hour, or expenses compared to sales as their objective measures.

Whereas objective measures are quantitative, subjective measures seek to assess salespeople's behavior: what they do and how well they do it. By their very nature, subjective measures reflect one person's opinion about another's performance. Thus, subjective evaluations can be biased and should be used cautiously and only in conjunction with multiple objective measures.

CHECK YOURSELF

1. What do sales managers need to do to manage their sales force successfully?
2. What is the difference between monetary and nonmonetary incentives?

ETHICAL AND LEGAL ISSUES IN PERSONAL SELLING

 LO4 Describe the ethical and legal issues in personal selling.

Although ethical and legal issues permeate all aspects of marketing, they are particularly important for personal selling. Unlike advertising and other communications with customers, which are planned and executed on a corporate level, personal selling involves a one-to-one, and often face-to-face, encounter with the customer. Therefore, sellers' actions are not only highly visible to customers but also to other stakeholders, such as the communities in which they work.

Ethical and legal issues arise in three main areas. First, there is the relationship between the sales manager and the sales force. Second, in some situations, an inconsistency might exist between corporate policy and the salesperson's ethical comfort zone. Third, both ethical and legal issues can arise when the salesperson interacts with the customer, especially if that salesperson or the selling firm collects significant information about the customer. To maintain trustworthy customer relationships, companies must take care that they respect customer privacy and respect the information comfort zone—that is, the amount of information a customer feels comfortable providing.[36]

The Sales Manager and the Sales Force

Like any manager, a sales manager must treat people fairly and equally in everything he or she does. With regard to the sales force, this fairness must include hiring, promotion, supervision, training, assigning duties and quotas, compensation and incentives, and firing.[37] Federal laws cover many of these issues. For instance, equal employment opportunity laws make it unlawful to discriminate against a person in hiring, promotion, or firing because of race, religion, nationality, sex, or age.

The Sales Force and Corporate Policy

Sometimes salespeople face a conflict between what they believe represents ethical selling and what their company asks them to do to make a sale. Suppose an insurance agent, whose compensation is based on commission, sells a homeowner's policy to a family that has just moved to New Orleans, an area prone to flooding as a result of hurricanes.

Salespeople must live within their own ethical comfort zone. Should insurance salespeople disclose inadequate hurricane coverage and risk not making the sale?

Ethical & Societal Dilemma 20.1   When Realtors Become Reality Stars[v]

Reality television has spread to nearly every facet of life, and real estate is no exception. On shows such as *Million Dollar Listing, House Hunters, Property Virgins, Selling New York,* and *Designed to Sell,* viewers can watch as homeowners try to sell their properties and potential buyers search for their perfect home. Helping them every step of the way are real estate professionals, some of whom have gained notoriety as reality television stars themselves.

The *Million Dollar Listing* series, with versions in New York and Los Angeles, has made household names out of agents such as Ryan Serhant and Josh Altman. The handsome young realtors not only broker massive real estate deals but also share stories about their personal lives and allow cameras to catch them in the shower, in at least one memorable episode. As Altman recognized, "Nobody wants to see the guy who just sells houses every week. They want to see that drama between the realtors." As a result, some of the featured realtors have developed such an extensive fan base that they have hired publicists, managers, and drivers, as well as assistants whose sole job is to respond to contacts from fans.

The depictions of real estate transactions clearly make for great television. Consumers enjoy the voyeuristic glimpse into other people's financial affairs and living conditions, especially when those conditions include multimillion-dollar homes. The *Million Dollar Listing* episodes each average around 1.25 million viewers, leading networks such as Bravo and HGTV to keep adding new versions and twists to their lineups of real estate reality television shows.

But according to some observers, the shows create a destructive and potentially dangerous impression of what real estate transactions involve and what the responsibilities of professional realtors are. The agents often are presented in less than flattering light, which could be damaging for their reputation. For example, one cast member on *The Real Housewives of Orange County* left the show mainly because she believed that participating in bickering and being subjected to wine thrown on her ultimately would be too professionally embarrassing to be healthy for her business.

Agencies that prohibit their brokers from appearing on such shows also note that discretion and clients' privacy are central goals for realtors—aspects that rarely are prioritized on reality television. Furthermore, if the agent becomes the star, the broker might come to overshadow the agency's brand, as well as the sale itself.

The shows also present a condensed, highly edited version of the real estate process, naturally. Sales of big properties (and even smaller ones) take months to complete, and much of the activity involves paperwork, e-mailing, and research. None of these elements are particularly compelling in video, so the shows tend to exclude them and focus more on loud negotiations, flashy open houses, or snarky interactions.

Yet for many of the star realtors, these potentially negative effects fade away in the face of the massive marketing bump they receive from their notoriety. Bravo asserts that every broker who has appeared on one of its shows has enjoyed increased business through the association. The well-known agents agree: One indicated that his business had jumped by 20 percent, and another noted that he moved from selling midrange condos to dealing in luxury estates, which earned him $200 million in commissions in a single recent year.

Even though the policy covers hurricane damage, it does not cover water damage from hurricanes. If the salesperson discloses the inadequate coverage, the sale might be lost because additional flood insurance is very expensive. What should the salesperson do? Salespeople must live within their own ethical comfort zone. If this, or any other situation, is morally repugnant to the salesperson, he or she must question the choice to be associated with such a company.[38]

Salespeople also can be held accountable for illegal actions sanctioned by the employer. If the homeowner asks if the home is above the floodplain or whether water damage from flooding is covered by the policy, and it is company policy to intentionally mislead potential customers, both the salesperson and the insurance dealership could be susceptible to legal action.

The Salesperson and the Customer

As the frontline emissaries for a firm, salespeople have a duty to be ethically and legally correct in all their dealings with their customers. Not only is it the right thing to do, it simply means good business. Long-term relationships can deteriorate quickly if customers believe that they have not been treated in an ethically proper manner. Unfortunately, salespeople sometimes get mixed signals from their managers or simply do not know when their behaviors might be considered unethical or illegal. Formal guidelines can help, but it is also important to integrate these guidelines into training programs in which salespeople can discuss various issues that arise in the field with their peers and managers.[39] Most important, however, is for sales managers to lead by example. If managers are known to cut ethical corners in their dealings with customers, it shouldn't surprise them when their salespeople do the same. Ethical and Societal Dilemma 20.1 considers the ethical issues that realtors face.

CHECK YOURSELF

1. What are three areas of personal selling in which ethical and legal issues are more likely to arise?

Reviewing Learning Objectives

LO1 Describe the value added of personal selling.

Although the cost of an average B2B sales call is expensive, many firms believe they couldn't do business without their sales forces. Customers can buy many products and services without the help of a salesperson, but in many other cases, it is worth the extra cost built into the price of a product to be educated about the product or get valuable advice. Salespeople can also simplify the buying process and therefore save the customer time and hassle.

LO2 Define the steps in the personal selling process.

Although we discuss selling in terms of steps, it truly represents a process, and the time spent in each step varies according to the situation. In the first step, the salesperson generates a list of viable customers. During the second step, the preapproach, the salesperson gathers information about the customer and prepares for the presentation. The third step, the sales presentation, consists of a personal meeting between the salesperson and the customer. Through discussion and by asking questions, the salesperson learns where the customer is in the buying process and tailors the discussion around what the firm's product or service can do to meet that customer's needs. During the fourth step, the close, the salesperson asks for the order. Finally, during the follow-up, the salesperson and support staff solidify the long-term relationship by making sure the customer is satisfied with the purchase and addressing any complaints. The follow-up therefore sets the stage for the next purchase.

LO3 Describe the key functions involved in managing a sales force.

The first task of a sales manager, assuming a firm is starting a sales force from scratch, is to determine whether to use a company sales force or manufacturer's representatives. Then sales managers must determine what the primary selling responsibilities will be—order getter, order taker, or sales support. The sales manager recruits and selects salespeople, but because there are all sorts of sales jobs, he or she must determine what it takes to be successful and then go after people with those attributes. In the next step, training, firms can choose between on-the-job and online training. Sales managers are also responsible for motivating and compensating salespeople. Most salespeople appreciate a balance of financial and nonfinancial rewards for doing a good job. Finally, sales managers are responsible for evaluating their salespeople. Normally, salespeople should be evaluated on a combination of objective measures, such as sales per hour, and subjective measures, such as how friendly they appear to customers.

LO4 Describe the ethical and legal issues in personal selling.

Ethical and legal issues arise in three areas in personal selling. First, ethical and legal issues could arise based on how the sales manager interacts with the sales force. Second, there might be inconsistencies between corporate policy and the salesperson's ethical comfort zone. Finally, ethical and legal issues can arise as the salesperson interacts with customers.

Key Terms

- bonus, 625
- closing the sale, 620
- cold call, 615
- commission, 625
- company sales force, 622
- inbound marketing, 614
- independent agent, 622
- lead, 614

- manufacturer's representative (rep), 622
- order getter, 622
- order taker, 623
- personal selling, 610
- preapproach, 616
- qualify, 614
- relationship selling, 613

- role playing, 618
- salary, 625
- sales contest, 625
- sales management, 622
- sales support personnel, 623
- selling team, 623
- telemarketing, 615
- trade show, 614

Marketing Applications

1. How has your perception of what it would be like to have a career in sales changed since you read this chapter?

2. "Salespeople just make products cost more." Do you agree or disagree with this statement? Discuss why you've taken that position.

3. Choose an industry or a specific company that you would like to work for as a salesperson. How would you generate and qualify leads?

4. Why is it important for salespeople to be good listeners? To be good at asking questions?

5. Suppose you are a salesperson at a high-end jewelry store. What can you do to ensure that your customers are satisfied? Now imagine you are the store manager of the same store; what can you do in your position to guarantee customers remain happy with the service they receive?

6. Imagine that a time machine has transported you back to 1961. How was a day in the life of a salesperson selling appliances such as washing machines different in 1961 than it is now?

7. What are some of the potentially ethically troubling and illegal situations facing professional salespeople, and how should they deal with them?

8. Why would Gillette use a company sales force, while a small independent manufacturer of organic shaving cream uses manufacturer's representatives?

9. Similar to the way a sales manager evaluates a salesperson, your instructors evaluate your performance to assign you a grade. Choose one of your classes and analyze the advantages and disadvantages of the objective and subjective bases used to evaluate your performance.

10. A customer has the following reservations. How do you respond?
    a. "I really like all the things this copier does, but I don't think it's going to be very reliable. With all those features, something's got to go wrong."
    b. "Your price for this printer is higher than the price I saw advertised on the Internet."

11. Imagine that you have just been hired by the school newspaper to sell ad space. You are asked what you think would be a "fair" compensation package for you. Using the information from the chapter, make a list of all the elements that should be included in your compensation package. How would this compensation package change over time and with continued performance?

12. You have taken a summer job in the windows and doors department of a large home improvement store. During sales training, you learn about the products, how to best address customers' needs, and how to sell the customer the best product to fit their needs regardless of price point. One day your manager informs you that you are to recommend Smith Windows to every window customer. Smith Windows are more expensive and don't really provide superior benefit except in limited circumstances. The manager is insistent that you recommend Smith. Not knowing what else to do, you recommend Smith Windows to customers who would have been better served by lower-cost windows. The manager rewards you with a sales award. Later the manager tells you that he received an all-expenses-paid cruise for his family from Smith Windows. What, if anything, should you do with this information?

Quiz Yourself

1. Tana went to Gap ready to buy a new blouse, but was not sure which color or style she wanted. The sales representative, sensing Tana's buying mode, began with the _____ stage of the selling process.
   a. generate leads
   b. preapproach
   c. closing the sale
   d. follow-up
   e. sales presentation

2. The beginning of the sales presentation may be the most important part of the selling process, because this is where the salesperson establishes _____.
   a. whether the customer is in the buying process
   b. how much time has been allocated for the presentation
   c. which of the alternative products to demonstrate
   d. whether to quote a full price or discount price
   e. which type of follow-up will be needed

(Answers to these two questions can be found on page 652.)

Net Savvy

1. Go to Salesforce.com's YouTube channel at http://www.youtube.com/user/salesforce. Watch a few of the short videos and discuss how the tools described would help you as a salesperson.

2. To learn more about careers in sales, go to http://www.bls.gov/oco/, the website for the Bureau of Labor Statistics. This site contains a wealth of information about careers in all fields. Click on "Sales." Choose any of the sales fields listed, and explore that career field. What experience is necessary to be hired for that job? What is the median salary? What do earners in the highest 10 percent of performance earn? Is job growth anticipated in that field?

Chapter Case Study

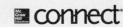

ALTA DATA SOLUTIONS: MAKING THE SALE[40]

When Vicki Nguyen reached her office, she had a message from Mike Smith, the regional sales manager, to meet him in his office regarding the Burtell Inc. order. Vicki Nguyen is a senior sales associate for Alta Data Solutions Inc., a firm that markets software and hardware designed for data storage. The Burtell order represents a multimillion-dollar contract for Alta Data Solutions and would help Burtell boost its productivity levels and revenue for the region. To prepare for the meeting, Nguyen reviews her sales call report notes on the Burtell account.

Alta Data Solutions

Alta Data Solutions provides software and hardware solutions to large firms and has an established track record for delivering an exceptional standard of quality and high levels of customer service. This excellent reputation allows Alta Data Solutions to charge a substantial premium, ranging from 10 to 20 percent above the market leader.

The data storage software services market has been dominated for two decades by this market leader. Alta Data Solutions holds the second position in the marketplace, with a considerably lower but growing market share. Only one other competitor, an aggressive, small, low-price player, holds a significant market share; this provider has made inroads into the market in the past several years through its aggressive sales tactics.

Alta Data Solutions has just built a new facility and hired 50 new software programmers. Therefore, the company must generate new business to meet its higher financial goals; even more important in the short run, it must keep the new programmers working on interesting projects to retain them.

Burtell Inc.

Burtell Inc. is a division of a major U.S.-based consumer products firm. Its purchasing department negotiates contracts for software services and coordinates the interface among a variety of members from different departments. The business environment for consumer products has become highly competitive in recent years, leading to tight budgets and higher levels of scrutiny of the value added by vendors. Competition is fierce, as large numbers of end-user customers are considering vendors that provide the most data analysis with their products.

Burtell Inc. has been consistently buying software development services from the market leader since 1991 and is generally satisfied with its service. A recent change in corporate leadership, however, has increased concerns about its overreliance on one vendor for a particular service. Also, because of the difficult economic climate, the company is concerned about the cost of software services and whether it is necessary to provide such a high service level.

Vicki Nguyen's Call Report

A call report is like a diary of sales calls made to a particular client. The notes in Vicki Nguyen's Burtell file pertaining to the current negotiations began on June 4:

> June 4: I contacted Bethany O'Meara, chief purchasing officer at Burtell, to introduce myself to her and get a sense of what their future software needs might be. She told me that the slowed business climate had caused Burtell to institute a program for increased efficiency in operations and that they would be looking to negotiate a new contract for software solutions. She gave me some insights into the technological aspects of their needs.

> June 18: Met with Jon Aaronson, head of R&D, to explain our productivity-enhancing solutions. Went into considerable depth explaining how Alta could service their needs and learned what they were looking for in a provider. I went over some specific product specification issues, but Jon did not seem impressed. But he did ask for a price and told me that the final decision rested with Brad Alexander, the chief financial officer.

> July 2: Presented to Bethany O'Meara and Jon Aaronson. They first asked about the price. I gave them a quote of $10 million. They suggested that other services were much cheaper. I explained that our price reflected the latest technology and that the price differential was an investment that could pay for itself several times over through faster communication speeds. I also emphasized our reputation for high-quality customer service. While the presentation appeared to meet their software needs, they did not seem impressed with the overall value. I also sent a copy of the presentation in report form to Brad Alexander and attempted to get an appointment to see him.

July 9: Contacted Jon Aaronson by phone. He told me that we were in contention with three other firms and the debate was heated. He stated that the other firms were also touting their state-of-the-art technology. Discussed a lower price of $7 million. Also encouraged him to visit Alta Data Solutions headquarters to meet with the product manager who oversaw the product development efforts and would manage the implementation of the product. He wasn't interested in making the two-day trip even though it would spotlight our core competencies.

July 15: Received a conference call from Brad Alexander and Jon Aaronson to discuss the price. Brad said the price was still too high and that he could not depreciate that amount over the life of the software and meet target levels of efficiency. He wanted a final quote by August 6.

What are the key points Vicki Nguyen should make in her presentation?

The Final Pitch

Vicki Nguyen prepared for her meeting with Mike Smith, Alta's regional sales manager, by going over her notes and market data about the competitors. Smith's voicemail had said they'd be meeting to put together their best possible proposal.

Questions

Help Vicki Nguyen prepare her sales presentation.

1. Who should be at the presentation?
2. How should she start the meeting?
3. What are the key points she should make in her presentation?
4. What reservations should she expect? How should she handle them?

Endnotes

1. Sam Howe, "The Tale of Boeing's High-Risk Flight into the Jet Age," *Seattle Times*, October 2, 2010.
2. "Airlines Industry Profile: United States," *Datamonitor*, October 2010, pp. 13–14.
3. Suresh Kotha et al., "Boeing 787: The Dreamliner," *Harvard Business School Case #9-305-101*, June 21, 2005.
4. Ibid.
5. Clive Irving, "NTSB Doesn't Think the Boeing 787 Dreamliner Is Safe Enough to Fly," *The Daily Best*, May 28, 2014.
6. http://www.boeing.com/boeing/commercial/prices/.
7. Jon Ostrower, "Boeing's Top Salesman Works to Rebuild Customer Trust, Fend Off Airbus," *The Wall Street Journal*, October 8, 2013, http://online.wsj.com.
8. Ibid.
9. Bureau of Labor Statistics, http://www.bls.gov.
10. This section draws from Mark W. Johnston and Greg W. Marshall, *Relationship Selling*, 3rd ed. (Burr Ridge, IL: Irwin/McGraw-Hill, 2009); Mark W. Johnston and Greg W. Marshall, *Relationship Selling and Sales Management*, 2nd ed. (Burr Ridge, IL: Irwin/McGraw-Hill, 2007).
11. Geoffrey James, "Selling Gets Complex," *Strategy+Business*, August 27, 2009; Dale Carnegie, *How to Win Friends and Influence People* (New York: Pocket, 1990); Neil Rackham, *SPIN Selling* (New York: McGraw-Hill, 1988).
12. http://4dsales.com/the-cost-of-a-sales-call/.
13. Bill Stinnett, *Think Like Your Customer* (Burr Ridge, IL: McGraw-Hill, 2004).
14. Pam Baker, "Best Sales Practices: Build Lasting Relationships," *CRM Buyer*, January 27, 2009.
15. Mark W. Johnston and Greg W. Marshall, *Relationship Selling*, 2nd ed. (Burr Ridge, IL: Irwin/McGraw-Hill, 2008).
16. S. Anhtony Iannarino, "The Last Word on Cold Calling versus Social Media," *The Sales Blog*, April 21, 2014, http://www.thesalesblog.com; Justin Fishaw, "Has LinkedIn Replaced Cold Calling?" *SocialMediaToday*, August 21, 2013, http://www.socialmediatoday.com; Ken Krogue, "Cold Calling Is Dead, Thanks to LinkedIn," *Forbes*, August 9, 2013, http://www.forbes.com.
17. Mark Ward, "CES 2014: What Does the Show Mean to Las Vegas?" *BBC News*, January 9, 2014, http://www.bbc.com.
18. Pete Pachal, "Mashable's Best Tech of CES 2014," *Mashable*, January 7, 2014, http://www.mashable.com.
19. "2012 CES Grows, Excites, and Catalyzes," January 13, 2012, http://www.cesweb.org.

20. Christine Comaford, "Sales Stuck? Try Sticking to a Script," *BusinessWeek,* April 4, 2008.

21. Christine Comaford-Lynch, "A Bad Lead Is Worse Than No Lead at All," *BusinessWeek,* March 26, 2008.

22. J. David Goodman, "Profiling Complaints by Black Shoppers Followed Changes to Stores' Security Policies," *The New York Times,* October 29, 2013, http://www.nytimes.com.

23. Barton A. Weitz, Harish Sujan, and Mita Sujan, "Knowledge, Motivation, and Adaptive Behavior: A Framework for Improving Selling Effectiveness," *Journal of Marketing,* October 1986, pp. 174–91.

24. Dennis Nishi, "To Persuade People, Tell Them a Story," *The Wall Street Journal,* November 9, 2013, http://online.wsj.com.

25. Robert Keller, "Handling Objections in Today's Tough Environment," *SMM,* March 30, 2009.

26. http://www.quotedb.com/quotes/1303.

27. Mark W. Johnston and Greg W. Marshall, *Churchill/Ford/Walker's Sales Force Management,* 9th ed. (Burr Ridge, IL: McGraw-Hill /Irwin, 2009).

28. Adam Auriemma, "Zappos Zaps Its Job Postings," *The Wall Street Journal,* May 26, 2014, http://online.wsj.com.

29. Lynn Huber, "Can Men Sell Avon?" *Online Beauty Biz,* May 25, 2014, http://www.onlinebeautybiz.com; Sadie Whitelocks, "I'm an Avon Laddie! Salesman, 21, Is Part of the New Breed of Men Muscling in on Door-to-Door Trade," *DailyMail,* December 14, 2011, http://www.dailymail.co.uk.

30. Susan Greco, "Personality Testing for Sales Recruits," *INC.,* March 1, 2009.

31. Ned Smith, "10 Traits of Successful Salespeople," *Business News Daily,* March 20, 2013, http://www.businessnewsdaily.com; Steven W. Martin, "Seven Personality Traits of Top Salespeople," *Harvard Business Review,* June 27, 2011, http://blogs.hbr.org; Julie Chang, "Born to Sell?" *Sales and Marketing Management,* July 2003, p. 36.

32. Felicia G. Lassk et al., "The Future of Sales Training: Challenges and Related Research Questions," *Journal of Personal Selling and Sales Management* 32, no 1 (2012), pp. 141–54.

33. "Mary Kay: Where's the Money?" http://www.marykay.com; http://www.Marykay.com/lsoulier; "Mary Kay Museum," http://www.addisontexas.net.

34. Johnston and Marshall, *Relationship Selling and Sales Management.*

35. For a discussion of common measures used to evaluate salespeople, see Johnston and Marshall, *Churchill/Ford/Walker's Sales Force Management.*

36. David H. Holtzman, "Big Business Knows Us Too Well," *BusinessWeek,* June 22, 2007.

37. Johnston and Marshall, *Churchill/Ford/Walker's Sales Force Management.*

38. Nicolas McClaren, "The Personal Selling and Sales Management Ethics Research: Managerial Implications and Research Directions from a Comprehensive Review of the Empirical Literature," *Journal of Business Ethics* 112, no. 1 (January 2013), pp. 101–25; Sean R. Valentine and Connie R. Bateman, "The Impact of Ethical Ideologies, Moral Intensity, and Social Context on Sales-Based Ethical Reasoning," *Journal of Business Ethics* 102, no. 1 (August 2011), pp. 155–68.

39. Casey Donoho and Timothy Heinze, "The Personal Selling Ethics Scale: Revisions and Expansions for Teaching Sales Ethics," *Journal of Marketing Education* 33, no. 1 (April 2011), pp. 107–22.

40. This case was written by Jeanne Munger in conjunction with the textbook authors Dhruv Grewal and Michael Levy as the basis of class discussion rather than to illustrate either effective or ineffective marketing practice. For a discussion of common measures used to evaluate salespeople, see Johnston and Marshall, *Churchill/Ford/Walker's Sales Force Management.*

i. Jeff Green, "Sales Moves Beyond Face-to-Face Deals, onto the Web," *Bloomberg Businessweek,* January 10, 2013, http://www.businessweek.com; Al Jury, "The Golden Ratio of Virtual Meetings to Face-to-Face," June 19, 2011, http://virtualteamsblog.com; Joe Sharkey, "On the Road—New Meetings Industry Arises after Boom and Bust," *The New York Times,* February 1, 2010; Brad Grimes, "Have Web, Don't Travel," http://pcworld.about.com; "Brainstorming Online," *BusinessWeek,* Fall 2005, http://www.businessweek.com.

ii. Steve Berkowitz, "Marketers Reshape How College Teams Sell Tickets," *USA Today,* August 5, 2011, http://www.usatoday.com; "Accelerating the Trend toward Outsourcing Athletic Event Ticket Sales, Two More Universities Partner with IMG College," press release, May 31, 2011, http://www.imgworld.com; IMG College, http://www.imgcollege.com.

iii. "Salesforce.com Named #1 CRM Software Provider in Gartner's Worldwide CRM Market Share Report for Second Consecutive Year," *The Wall Street Journal,* April 29, 2014, http://online.wsj.com; Victoria Barret, "Why Salesforce.com Ranks #1 on Forbes' Most Innovative List," *Forbes,* September 5, 2012, http://www.forbes.com; Mi Ji et al., "Salesforce.com: Creating a Blue Ocean in the B2B Space," *INSEAD Case# INS255,* 2013.

iv. Jeremy Quittner, "The Art of the Soft Sell," *BWSSmallBiz–Sales,* October 9, 2009; Rachel Emma Silverman, "Selling Girl Scout Cookies at the Office," *The Wall Street Journal,* February 6, 2009; "B2B Sales Pitching: Why Soft Selling Works," http://bx.businessweek.com/how-to-market-your-small-business/view?url5http%3A%2F%2Fblog.verticalresponse.com%2-Fverticalresponse_blog%2F2010%2F04%2Fb2b-sales-pitch-educational-selling-vs-the-hard-sell.html.

v. Candace Jackson, "A Real Estate Star Is Born," *The Wall Street Journal,* August 1, 2013.

Credits

actual product The physical attributes of a product including the brand name, features/design, quality level, and packaging.

administered vertical marketing system A *supply chain* system in which there is no common ownership and no contractual relationships, but the dominant channel member controls the channel relationship.

ad-supported apps Apps that are free to download, but place ads on the screen when using the program to generate revenue.

advanced shipping notice (ASN) An electronic document that the supplier sends the retailer in advance of a shipment to tell the retailer exactly what to expect in the shipment.

advertising A paid form of communication from an identifiable source, delivered through a communication channel, and designed to persuade the receiver to take some action, now or in the future.

advertising allowance Tactic of offering a price reduction to channel members if they agree to feature the manufacturer's product in their advertising and promotional efforts.

advertising plan A section of the firm's overall marketing plan that explicitly outlines the objectives of the advertising campaign, how the campaign might accomplish those objectives, and how the firm can determine whether the campaign was successful.

advertising schedule The specification of the timing and duration of advertising.

affective component A component of *attitude* that reflects what a person feels about the issue at hand—his or her like or dislike of something.

AIDA model A common model of the series of mental stages through which consumers move as a result of marketing communications: *A*wareness leads to *I*nterests, which lead to *D*esire, which leads to *A*ction.

aided recall Occurs when consumers recognize a name (e.g., of a brand) that has been presented to them.

alpha testing An attempt by the firm to determine whether a product will perform according to its design and whether it satisfies the need for which it was intended; occurs in the firm's research and development (R&D) department.

associated services (also called augmented product) The non-physical attributes of the product including product warranties, financing, product support, and after-sale service.

attitude A person's enduring evaluation of his or her feelings about and behavioral tendencies toward an object or idea; consists of three components: *cognitive, affective,* and *behavioral.*

augmented product See *associated services.*

autocratic buying center A buying center in which one person makes the decision alone, though there may be multiple participants.

B2B See *business-to-business marketing.*

B2C See *business-to-consumer marketing.*

Baby Boomers Generational cohort of people born after World War II, between 1946 and 1964.

bait and switch A deceptive practice of luring customers into the store with a very low advertised price on an item (the bait), only to aggressively pressure them into purchasing a higher-priced model (the switch) by disparaging the low-priced item, comparing it unfavorably with the higher-priced model, or professing an inadequate supply of the lower-priced item.

behavioral component A component of *attitude* that comprises the actions a person takes with regard to the issue at hand.

behavioral segmentation A segmentation method that divides customers into groups based on how they use the product or service. Some common behavioral measures include occasion and loyalty.

benefit segmentation The grouping of consumers on the basis of the benefits they derive from products or services.

beta testing Having potential consumers examine a product prototype in a real-use setting to determine its functionality, performance, potential problems, and other issues specific to its use.

big box retailer Discount stores that offer a narrow but deep assortment of merchandise; see also *category killer.*

big data Data sets that are too large and complex to analyze with conventional data management and data mining software.

biometric data Digital scanning of the physiological or behavioral characteristics of individuals as a means of identification.

blog (weblog) A web page that contains periodic posts; corporate blogs are a new form of marketing communications.

body copy The main text portion of an ad.

bonus A payment made at management's discretion when the salesperson attains certain goals; usually given only periodically, such as at the end of the year.

bounce rate The percentage of times a visitor leaves the website almost immediately, such as after viewing only one page.

boycott A group's refusal to deal commercially with some organization to protest against its policies.

brand The name, term, design, symbol, or any other features that identify one seller's good or service as distinct from those of other sellers.

brand association The mental links that consumers make between a brand and its key product attributes; can involve a logo, slogan, or famous personality.

brand awareness Measures how many consumers in a market are familiar with the brand and what it stands for; created through repeated exposures of the various brand elements (brand name, logo, symbol, character, packaging, or slogan) in the firm's communications to consumers.

brand dilution Occurs when a brand extension adversely affects consumer perceptions about the attributes the core brand is believed to hold.

brand elements Characteristics that identify the sponsor of a specific ad.

brand equity The set of assets and liabilities linked to a brand that add to or subtract from the value provided by the product or service.

brand extension The use of the same brand name for new products being introduced to the same or new markets.

branding In an advertisement, the portion that identifies the sponsor of the ad.

brand licensing A contractual arrangement between firms, whereby one firm allows another to use its brand name, logo, symbols, or characters in exchange for a negotiated fee.

brand loyalty Occurs when a consumer buys the same brand's product or service repeatedly over time rather than buying from multiple suppliers within the same category.

brand repositioning (rebranding) A strategy in which marketers change a brand's focus to target new markets or realign the brand's core emphasis with changing market preferences.

breadth Number of product lines offered by a firm; also known as variety.

break-even analysis Technique used to examine the relationships among cost, price, revenue, and profit over different levels of production and sales to determine the *break-even point*.

break-even point The point at which the number of units sold generates just enough revenue to equal the total costs; at this point, profits are zero.

breakthroughs See *pioneers*.

bricks-and-mortar store A traditional, physical store.

business ethics Refers to a branch of ethical study that examines ethical rules and principles within a commercial context, the various moral or ethical problems that might arise in a business setting, and any special duties or obligations that apply to persons engaged in commerce.

business-to-business (B2B) marketing The process of buying and selling goods or services to be used in the production of other goods and services, for consumption by the buying organization, or for resale by wholesalers and retailers.

business-to-consumer (B2C) marketing The process in which businesses sell to consumers.

buyer The buying center participant who handles the paperwork of the actual purchase.

buying center The group of people typically responsible for the buying decisions in large organizations.

C2C See *consumer-to-consumer marketing*.

cannibalization Customers who formerly made purchases through one retail channel switch to a different retail channel without increasing the overall sales to the retailer.

cash discount Tactic of offering a reduction in the invoice cost if the buyer pays the invoice prior to the end of the discount period.

category depth The number of stock keeping units (SKUs) within a category.

category killer A specialist that offers an extensive assortment in a particular category, so overwhelming the category that other retailers have difficulty competing.

category specialist A retailer that offers a narrow variety but a deep assortment of merchandise.

cause-related marketing Commercial activity in which businesses and charities form a partnership to market an image, a product, or a service for their mutual benefit; a type of promotional campaign.

channel conflict When members of a marketing channel are in disagreement or discord. Channel conflict can occur between members of the same marketing channel (see also *vertical channel conflict* or *vertical supply chain conflict*) or between members at the same level of a marketing channel (see also *horizontal channel conflict* or *horizontal supply chain conflict*).

checking The process of going through the goods upon receipt to ensure they arrived undamaged and that the merchandise ordered was the merchandise received.

churn The number of consumers who stop using a product or service, divided by the average number of consumers of that product or service.

click path Shows how users proceed through the information on a website—not unlike how grocery stores try to track the way shoppers move through their aisles.

click-through rate (CTR) The number of times a user clicks on an online ad divided by the number of impressions.

close-out retailers Stores that offer an inconsistent assortment of low priced, brand name merchandise.

closing the sale Obtaining a commitment from the customer to make a purchase.

co-branding The practice of marketing two or more brands together, on the same package or promotion.

coercive power Threatening or punishing the other channel member for not undertaking certain tasks. Delaying payment for late delivery would be an example.

cognitive component A component of *attitude* that reflects what a person believes to be true.

cold calls A method of prospecting in which salespeople telephone or go to see potential customers without appointments.

commission Compensation or financial incentive for salespeople based on a fixed percentage of their sales.

communication channel The medium—print, broadcast, the Internet—that carries the message.

communication gap A type of *service gap*; refers to the difference between the actual service provided to customers and the service that the firm's promotion program promises.

company sales force Comprised of people who are employees of the selling company and are engaged in the selling process.

compensatory decision rule At work when the consumer is evaluating alternatives and trades off one characteristic against another, such that good characteristics compensate for bad ones.

competitive intelligence (CI) Used by firms to collect and synthesize information about their position with respect to their rivals; enables companies to anticipate market developments rather than merely react to them.

competitive parity A firm's strategy of setting prices that are similar to those of major competitors.

competition-based pricing method An approach that attempts to reflect how the firm wants consumers to interpret its products relative to the competitors' offerings; for example, setting a price close to a competitor's price signals to consumers that the product is similar, whereas setting the price much higher signals greater features, better quality, or some other valued benefit.

competitor orientation A company objective based on the premise that the firm should measure itself primarily against its competition.

complementary products Products whose demand curves are positively related, such that they rise or fall together; a percentage increase in demand for one results in a percentage increase in demand for the other.

concentrated targeting strategy A marketing strategy of selecting a single, primary target market and focusing all energies on providing a product to fit that market's needs.

concepts Brief written descriptions of a product or service; its technology, working principles, and forms; and what customer needs it would satisfy.

concept testing The process in which a concept statement that describes a product or a service is presented to potential buyers or users to obtain their reactions.

consensus buying center A buying center in which all members of the team must reach a collective agreement that they can support a particular purchase.

consultative buying center A buying center in which one person makes the decision but he or she solicits input from others before doing so.

consumer decision rules The set of criteria that consumers use consciously or subconsciously to quickly and efficiently select from among several alternatives.

consumer product Products and services used by people for their personal use.

consumer-to-consumer (C2C) marketing The process in which consumers sell to other consumers.

contest A brand-sponsored competition that requires some form of skill or effort.

continuous advertising schedule Runs steadily throughout the year and therefore is suited to products and services that are consumed continually at relatively steady rates and that require a steady level of persuasive or reminder advertising.

contractual vertical marketing system A system in which independent firms at different levels of the supply chain join together through contracts to obtain economies of scale and coordination and to reduce conflict.

contribution per unit Equals the price less the variable cost per unit. Variable used to determine the break-even point in units.

control phase The part of the strategic marketing planning process when managers evaluate the performance of the marketing strategy and take any necessary corrective actions.

convenience products/services Those for which the consumer is not willing to spend any effort to evaluate prior to purchase.

convenience store Type of retailer that provides a limited number of items at a convenient location in a small store with speedy checkout.

conventional supermarket Type of retailer that offers groceries, meat, and produce with limited sales of nonfood items, such as health and beauty aids and general merchandise, in a self-service format.

conversion rates Percentage of consumers who buy a product after viewing it.

cookie Computer program, installed on hard drives, that provides identifying information.

cooperative (co-op) advertising An agreement between a manufacturer and retailer in which the manufacturer agrees to defray some advertising costs.

core customer value The basic problem-solving benefits that consumers are seeking.

corporate blog A website created by a company and often used to educate customers.

corporate social responsibility (CSR) Refers to the voluntary actions taken by a company to address the ethical, social, and environmental impacts of its business operations and the concerns of its stakeholders.

corporate vertical marketing system A system in which the parent company has complete control and can dictate the priorities and objectives of the supply chain; it may own facilities such as manufacturing plants, warehouse facilities, retail outlets, and design studios.

cost-based pricing A pricing strategy that involves first determining the costs of producing or providing a product and then adding a fixed amount above that total to arrive at the selling price.

cost-based pricing method An approach that determines the final price to charge by starting with the cost, without recognizing the role that consumers or competitors' prices play in the marketplace.

cost of ownership method A value-based method for setting prices that determines the total cost of owning the product over its useful life.

country culture Entails easy-to-spot visible nuances that are particular to a country, such as dress, symbols, ceremonies, language, colors, and food preferences, and subtler aspects, which are trickier to identify.

coupon Provides a stated discount to consumers on the final selling price of a specific item; the retailer handles the discount.

cross-docking distribution center A distribution center to which vendors ship merchandise prepackaged and ready for sale. The merchandise goes to a staging area rather than into storage. When all the merchandise going to a particular store has arrived in the staging area, it is loaded onto a truck, and away it goes. Thus, merchandise goes from the receiving dock to the shipping dock—cross dock.

cross-price elasticity The percentage change in demand for product A that occurs in response to a percentage change in price of product B; see also *complementary products*.

cross-promoting Efforts of two or more firms joining together to reach a specific target market.

cross-shopping The pattern of buying both premium and low-priced merchandise or patronizing both expensive, status-oriented retailers and price-oriented retailers.

culture The set of values, guiding beliefs, understandings, and ways of doing things shared by members of a society; exists on two levels: visible artifacts (e.g., behavior, dress, symbols, physical settings, ceremonies) and underlying values (thought processes, beliefs, and assumptions).

cumulative quantity discount Pricing tactic that offers a discount based on the amount purchased over a specified period and usually involves several transactions; encourages resellers to maintain their current supplier because the cost to switch must include the loss of the discount.

customer excellence Involves a focus on retaining loyal customers and excellent customer service.

customer lifetime value The expected financial contribution from a particular customer to the firm's profits over the course of their entire relationship.

customer orientation A company objective based on the premise that the firm should measure itself primarily according to whether it meets its customers' needs.

customer relationship management (CRM) A business philosophy and set of strategies, programs, and systems that focus on identifying and building loyalty among the firm's most valued customers.

customer service Specifically refers to human or mechanical activities firms undertake to help satisfy their customers' needs and wants.

data Raw numbers or facts.

data mining The use of a variety of statistical analysis tools to uncover previously unknown patterns in the data stored in databases or relationships among variables.

data warehouses Large computer files that store millions and even billions of pieces of individual data.

deal A type of short-term price reduction that can take several forms, such as a "featured price," a price lower than the regular price; a "buy one, get one free" offer; or a certain percentage "more free" offer contained in larger packaging; can involve a special financing arrangement, such as reduced percentage interest rates or extended repayment terms.

deceptive advertising A representation, omission, act, or practice in an advertisement that is likely to mislead consumers acting reasonably under the circumstances.

decider The buying center participant who ultimately determines any part of or the entire buying decision—whether to buy, what to buy, how to buy, or where to buy.

decline stage Stage of the product life cycle when sales decline and the product eventually exits the market.

decoding The process by which the receiver interprets the sender's message.

delivery gap A type of *service gap;* the difference between the firm's service standards and the actual service it provides to customers.

demand curve Shows how many units of a product or service consumers will demand during a specific period at different prices.

democratic buying center A buying center in which the majority rules in making decisions.

demographics Information about the characteristics of human populations and segments, especially those used to identify consumer markets such as by age, gender, income, and education.

demographic segmentation The grouping of consumers according to easily measured, objective characteristics such as age, gender, income, and education.

department store A retailer that carries many different types of merchandise (broad variety) and lots of items within each type (deep assortment); offers some customer services; and is organized into separate departments to display its merchandise.

depth The number of categories within a product line.

derived demand The linkage between consumers' demand for a company's output and its purchase of necessary inputs to manufacture or assemble that particular output.

determinant attributes Product or service features that are important to the buyer and on which competing brands or stores are perceived to differ.

differentiated targeting strategy A strategy through which a firm targets several market segments with a different offering for each.

diffusion of innovation The process by which the use of an innovation, whether a product or a service, spreads throughout a market group over time and over various categories of adopters.

Digital Natives See *Generation Z.*

direct investment When a firm maintains 100 percent ownership of its plants, operation facilities, and offices in a foreign country, often through the formation of wholly owned subsidiaries.

direct marketing Sales and promotional techniques that deliver promotional materials individually.

direct marketing channel The manufacturer sells directly to the buyer.

dispatcher The person who coordinates deliveries to distribution centers.

distribution center A facility for the receipt, storage, and redistribution of goods to company stores or customers; may be operated by retailers, manufacturers, or distribution specialists.

distribution intensity The number of supply chain members to use at each level of the supply chain.

distributive fairness Pertains to a customer's perception of the benefits he or she received compared with the costs (inconvenience or loss) that resulted from a service failure.

distributor A type of reseller or marketing intermediary that resells manufactured products without significantly altering their form. Distributors often buy from manufacturers and sell to other businesses like retailers in a B2B transaction.

diversification strategy A growth strategy whereby a firm introduces a new product or service to a market segment that it does not currently serve.

drugstore A specialty store that concentrates on health and personal grooming merchandise, though pharmaceuticals may represent more than 60 percent of its sales.

dumping The practice of selling a good in a foreign market at a price that is lower than its domestic price or below its cost.

duty See *tariff.*

dynamic pricing Refers to the process of charging different prices for goods or services based on the type of customer, time of the day, week, or even season, and level of demand.

early adopters The second group of consumers in the diffusion of innovation model, after *innovators,* to use a product or service innovation; generally don't like to take as much risk as innovators but instead wait and purchase the product after careful review.

early majority A group of consumers in the diffusion of innovation model that represents approximately 34 percent of the population; members don't like to take much risk and therefore tend to wait until bugs are worked out of a particular product or service; few new products and services can be profitable until this large group buys them.

economic situation Macroeconomic factor that affects the way consumers buy merchandise and spend money, both in a marketer's home country and abroad; see also *inflation, foreign currency fluctuations,* and *interest rates.*

elastic Refers to a market for a product or service that is price sensitive; that is, relatively small changes in price will generate fairly large changes in the quantity demanded.

electronic data interchange (EDI) The computer-to-computer exchange of business documents from a retailer to a vendor and back.

emotional appeal Aims to satisfy consumers' emotional desires rather than their utilitarian needs.

emotional support Concern for others' well-being and support of their decisions in a job setting.

employment marketing Marketing programs to attract applicants to the hiring firm.

empowerment In context of service delivery, means allowing employees to make decisions about how service is provided to customers.

encoding The process of converting the sender's ideas into a message, which could be verbal, visual, or both.

English auction A type of auction in which goods and services are simply sold to the highest bidder.

entrepreneur A person who organizes, operates, and assumes the risk of a new business venture.

environmental concerns Include, but are not limited to, the excessive use of natural resources and energy, refuse from manufacturing processes, excess trash created by consumer goods packages, and hard-to-dispose-of products like tires, cell phones, and computer monitors.

esteem needs Needs that enable people to fulfill inner desires.

ethical climate The set of values within a marketing firm, or in the marketing division of any firm, that guide decision making and behavior.

evaluative criteria Consist of a set of salient, or important, attributes about a particular product.

event sponsorship Popular PR tool; occurs when corporations support various activities (financially or otherwise), usually in the cultural or sports and entertainment sectors.

everyday low pricing (EDLP) A strategy companies use to emphasize the continuity of their retail prices at a level somewhere between the regular, nonsale price and the deep-discount sale prices their competitors may offer.

evoked set Comprises the alternative brands or stores that the consumer states he or she would consider when making a purchase decision.

exchange The trade of things of value between the buyer and the seller so that each is better off as a result.

exchange control Refers to the regulation of a country's currency *exchange rate*.

exchange rate The measure of how much one currency is worth in relation to another.

exclusive brand Developed by national brand vendor and retailer and sold only by that retailer.

exclusive distribution Strategy in which only selected retailers can sell a manufacturer's brand.

exclusive geographic territories Territories granted to one or very few retail customers by a manufacturer using an exclusive distribution strategy; no other customers can sell a particular brand in these territories.

experience curve effect Refers to the drop in unit cost as the accumulated volume sold increases; as sales continue to grow, the costs continue to drop, allowing even further reductions in the price.

experiment See *experimental research*.

experimental research (experiment) A type of conclusive and quantitative research that systematically manipulates one or more variables to determine which variables have a causal effect on another variable.

expertise power When a channel member uses its expertise as leverage to influence the actions of another channel member.

exporting Producing goods in one country and selling them in another.

extended problem solving A purchase decision process during which the consumer devotes considerable time and effort to analyzing alternatives; often occurs when the consumer perceives that the purchase decision entails a lot of risk.

external locus of control Refers to when consumers believe that fate or other external factors control all outcomes.

external search for information Occurs when the buyer seeks information outside his or her personal knowledge base to help make the buying decision.

external secondary data Data collected from sources outside of the firm.

extreme-value food retailer See *limited-assortment supermarkets*.

extreme-value retailer A general merchandise discount store found in lower-income urban or rural areas.

factory outlets Outlet stores owned by manufacturers.

family brand A firm's own corporate name used to brand its product lines and products.

feedback loop Allows the receiver to communicate with the sender and thereby informs the sender whether the message was received and decoded properly.

financial risk Risk associated with a monetary outlay; includes the initial cost of the purchase, as well as the costs of using the item or service.

first movers Product pioneers that are the first to create a market or product category, making them readily recognizable to consumers and thus establishing a commanding and early market share lead.

fixed costs Those costs that remain essentially at the same level, regardless of any changes in the volume of production.

flighting (advertising schedule) An advertising schedule implemented in spurts, with periods of heavy advertising followed by periods of no advertising.

floor-ready merchandise Merchandise that is ready to be placed on the selling floor immediately.

focus group interview A research technique in which a small group of persons (usually 8 to 12) comes together for an intensive discussion about a particular topic, with the conversation guided by a trained moderator using an unstructured method of inquiry.

foreign currency fluctuations Changes in the value of a country's currency relative to the currency of another country; can influence consumer spending.

franchisee See *franchising*.

franchising A contractual agreement between a *franchisor* and a *franchisee* that allows the franchisee to operate a business using a name and format developed and supported by the franchisor.

franchisor See *franchising*.

freemium apps Apps that are free to download, but include in-app purchases (see also *in-app purchases*).

frequency Measure of how often the audience is exposed to a communication within a specified period of time.

fulfillment center Warehouse facilities used to ship merchandise directly to customers.

full-line discount stores Retailers that offer low prices, limited service, and a broad variety of merchandise.

functional needs Pertain to the performance of a product or service.

gatekeeper The buying center participant who controls information or access to decision makers and influencers.

General Agreement on Tariffs and Trade (GATT) Organization established to lower trade barriers, such as high tariffs on imported goods and restrictions on the number and types of imported products that inhibited the free flow of goods across borders.

generational cohort A group of people of the same generation—typically have similar purchase behaviors because they have shared experiences and are in the same stage of life.

Generation X (Gen X) Generational cohort of people born between 1965 and 1976.

Generation Y (Gen Y) Generational cohort of people born between 1977 and 2000; biggest cohort since the original postwar baby boom. Also called *Millennials*.

Generation Z (Gen Z) Generational cohort of people born between 2001 and 2014. Also known as *Digital Natives* because people in this group were born into a world that already was full of electronic gadgets and digital technologies, such as the Internet and social networks.

generic (house) brand No-frills products offered at a low price without any branding information.

geodemographic segmentation The grouping of consumers on the basis of a combination of geographic, demographic, and lifestyle characteristics.

geographic segmentation The grouping of consumers on the basis of where they live.

globalization Refers to the processes by which goods, services, capital, people, information, and ideas flow across national borders.

globalization of production Also known as *offshoring*; refers to manufacturers' procurement of goods and services from around the globe to take advantage of national differences in the cost and quality of various factors of production (e.g., labor, energy, land, capital).

global labor issues Includes concerns about working conditions and wages paid to factory workers in developing countries.

glocalization The process of firms standardizing their products globally, but using different promotional campaigns to sell them.

goods Items that can be physically touched.

gray market Employs irregular but not necessarily illegal methods; generally, it legally circumvents authorized channels of distribution to sell goods at prices lower than those intended by the manufacturer.

green marketing Involves a strategic effort by firms to supply customers with environmentally friendly merchandise.

green product An ecologically safe product that may be recyclable, biodegradable, more energy-efficient, and/or have better pollution controls.

greenwashing Exploiting a consumer by disingenuously marketing products or services as environmentally friendly, with the goal of gaining public approval and sales.

gross domestic product (GDP) Defined as the market value of the goods and services produced by a country in a year; the most widely used standardized measure of output.

gross national income (GNI) Consists of GDP plus the net income earned from investments abroad (minus any payments made to nonresidents who contribute to the domestic economy).

gross rating points (GRP) Measure used for various media advertising—print, radio, or television; *GRP = Reach × Frequency*.

growth stage Stage of the product life cycle when the product gains acceptance, demand and sales increase, and competitors emerge in the product category.

habitual decision making A purchase decision process in which consumers engage with little conscious effort.

headline In an advertisement, large type designed to draw attention.

heterogeneity As it refers to the differences between the marketing of products and services, the delivery of services is more variable.

high/low pricing A *pricing* strategy that relies on the promotion of sales, during which prices are temporarily reduced to encourage purchases.

hit A request for a file made by web browsers and search engines. Hits are commonly misinterpreted as a metric for website success; however, the number of hits typically is much larger than the number of people visiting a website.

home improvement center Category specialist that offers home improvement tools for contractors and do-it-yourselfers.

horizontal channel conflict A type of channel conflict in which members at the same level of a marketing channel, for example, two competing retailers or two competing manufacturers, are in disagreement or discord, such as when they are in a price war.

horizontal price fixing Occurs when competitors that produce and sell competing products collude, or work together, to control prices, effectively taking price out of the decision process for consumers.

horizontal supply chain conflict See *horizontal channel conflict.*

house brand See *private-label brands.*

ideal point The position at which a particular market segment's ideal product would lie on a *perceptual map.*

ideas Intellectual concepts—thoughts, opinions, and philosophies.

implementation phase The part of the strategic marketing planning process when marketing managers (1) identify and evaluate different opportunities by engaging in segmentation, targeting, and positioning (see also *segmentation, targeting, and positioning*) and (2) implement the marketing mix using the four Ps.

impressions The number of times an advertisement appears in front of the user.

improvement value Represents an estimate of how much more (or less) consumers are willing to pay for a product relative to other comparable products.

impulse buying A buying decision made by customers on the spot when they see the merchandise.

in-app purchases When a game or app prompts or allows customers to make small "micropurchases" to enhance an app or game.

inbound marketing Marketing activities that draw the attention of customers through blogs, Twitter, LinkedIn, and other online sources, rather than using more traditional activities that require having to go out to get customers' attention, such as making a sales call.

income effect Refers to the change in the quantity of a product demanded by consumers due to a change in their income.

independent agents Salespeople who sell a manufacturer's products on an extended contract basis but are not employees of the manufacturer; also known as *manufacturer's representatives* or *reps.*

independent (conventional) marketing channel A marketing channel in which several independent members—a manufacturer, a wholesaler, and a retailer—each attempts to satisfy its own objectives and maximize its profits, often at the expense of the other members.

independent (conventional) supply chain A loose coalition of several independently owned and operated supply chain members—a manufacturer, a wholesaler, and a retailer—all attempting to satisfy their own objectives and maximize their own profits, often at the expense of the other members.

in-depth interview An exploratory research technique in which trained researchers ask questions, listen to and record the answers, and then pose additional questions to clarify or expand on a particular issue.

indirect marketing channel When one or more intermediaries work with manufacturers to provide goods and services to customers.

individual brands The use of individual brand names for each of a firm's products.

individualized pricing See *dynamic pricing.*

inelastic Refers to a market for a product or service that is price insensitive; that is, relatively small changes in price will not generate large changes in the quantity demanded.

inflation Refers to the persistent increase in the prices of goods and services.

influencer The buying center participant whose views influence other members of the buying center in making the final decision.

information Organized, analyzed, interpreted data that offer value to marketers.

informational appeal Used in a promotion to help consumers make purchase decisions by offering factual information and strong arguments built around relevant issues that encourage them to evaluate the brand favorably on the basis of the key benefits it provides.

information power A type of marketing channel power within an administered vertical marketing system in which one party (e.g., the manufacturer) provides or withholds important information to influence the actions of another party (e.g., the retailer).

informative advertising Communication used to create and build brand awareness, with the ultimate goal of moving the consumer through the buying cycle to a purchase.

infrastructure The basic facilities, services, and installations needed for a community or society to function, such as transportation and communications systems, water and power lines, and public institutions like schools, post offices, and prisons.

initiator The buying center participant who first suggests buying the particular product or service.

innovation The process by which ideas are transformed into new products and services that will help firms grow.

innovators Those buyers who want to be the first to have the new product or service.

inseparable A characteristic of a service: it is produced and consumed at the same time; that is, service and consumption are inseparable.

institutional advertisement A type of advertisement that informs, persuades, or reminds consumers about issues related to places, politics, or an industry (e.g., Got Milk? ads).

instrumental support Providing the equipment or systems needed to perform a task in a job setting.

intangible A characteristic of a service; it cannot be touched, tasted, or seen like a pure product can.

integrated marketing communications (IMC) Represents the promotion dimension of the four Ps; encompasses a variety of communication disciplines—general advertising, personal selling, sales promotion, public relations, direct marketing, and electronic media—in combination to provide clarity, consistency, and maximum communicative impact.

intensive distribution A strategy designed to get products into as many outlets as possible.

interest rates These represent the cost of borrowing money.

internal locus of control Refers to when consumers believe they have some control over the outcomes of their actions, in which case they generally engage in more search activities.

internal search for information Occurs when the buyer examines his or her own memory and knowledge about the product or service, gathered through past experiences.

internal secondary data Data collected from a firm's own data taken from their day-to-day operations.

International Monetary Fund (IMF) Established with the original General Agreement on Tariffs and Trade (GATT); primary purpose is to promote international monetary cooperation and facilitate the expansion and growth of international trade.

introduction stage Stage of the product life cycle when innovators start buying the product.

introductory price promotion Short-term price discounts designed to encourage trial.

involvement Consumer's interest in a product or service.

irregulars Merchandise with minor construction errors.

joint venture Formed when a firm entering a new market pools its resources with those of a local firm to form a new company in which ownership, control, and profits are shared.

just-in-time (JIT) inventory systems Inventory management systems designed to deliver less merchandise on a more frequent basis than traditional inventory systems; the firm gets the merchandise "just in time" for it to be used in the manufacture of another product, in the case of parts or components, or for sale when the customer wants it, in the case of consumer goods; also known as *quick response (QR) inventory systems* in retailing.

keyword analysis An evaluation of what keywords people use to search on the Internet for their products and services.

knowledge gap A type of *service gap;* reflects the difference between customers' *expectations* and the firm's perception of those expectations.

laggards Consumers who like to avoid change and rely on traditional products until they are no longer available.

lagged effect A delayed response to a marketing communication campaign.

late majority The last group of buyers to enter a new product market; when they do, the product has achieved its full market potential.

lead time The amount of time between the recognition that an order needs to be placed and the arrival of the needed merchandise at the seller's store, ready for sale.

lead users Innovative product users who modify existing products according to their own ideas to suit their specific needs.

leader pricing Consumer pricing tactic that attempts to build store traffic by aggressively pricing and advertising a regularly purchased item, often priced at or just above the store's cost.

leads A list of potential customers.

learning Refers to a change in a person's thought process or behavior that arises from experience and takes place throughout the consumer decision process.

lease A written agreement under which the owner of an item or property allows its use for a specified period of time in exchange for a fee.

legitimate power A type of marketing channel power that occurs if the channel member exerting the power has a contractual agreement with the other channel member that requires the other channel member to behave in a certain way. This type of power occurs in an administered vertical marketing system.

licensed brand An agreement allows one brand to use another's name, image, and/or logo for a fee.

lifestyles A component of *psychographics;* refers to the way a person lives his or her life to achieve goals.

lift Additional sales caused by advertising.

limited-assortment supermarkets Retailers that offer only one or two brands or sizes of most products (usually including a store brand) and attempt to achieve great efficiency to lower costs and prices.

limited problem solving Occurs during a purchase decision that calls for, at most, a moderate amount of effort and time.

line extension The use of the same brand name within the same product line and represents an increase in a product line's depth.

locational excellence A method of achieving excellence by having a strong physical location and/or Internet presence.

locational privacy A person's ability to move normally in public spaces with the expectation that his or her location will not be recorded for subsequent use.

logistics management The integration of two or more activities for the purpose of planning, implementing, and controlling the efficient flow of raw materials, in-process inventory, and finished goods from the point of origin to the point of consumption.

loss leader pricing Loss leader pricing takes the tactic of *leader pricing* one step further by lowering the price below the store's cost.

love needs Needs expressed through interactions with others.

loyalty program Specifically designed to retain customers by offering premiums or other incentives to customers who make multiple purchases over time.

loyalty segmentation Strategy of investing in loyalty initiatives to retain the firm's most profitable customers.

macroenvironmental factors Aspects of the external environment that affect a company's business, such as the culture, demographics, social trends, technological advances, economic situation, and political/regulatory environment.

manufacturer brands (national brands) Brands owned and managed by the manufacturer.

manufacturer's representatives (reps) See *independent agents.*

manufacturer's suggested retail price (MSRP) The price that manufacturers suggest retailers use to sell their merchandise.

markdowns Reductions retailers take on the initial selling price of the product or service.

market development strategy A growth strategy that employs the existing marketing offering to reach new market segments, whether domestic or international.

market growth rate The annual rate of growth of the specific market in which the product competes.

market penetration strategy A growth strategy that employs the existing marketing mix and focuses the firm's efforts on existing customers.

market positioning Involves the process of defining the marketing mix variables so that target customers have a clear, distinctive, desirable understanding of what the product does or represents in comparison with competing products.

market segment A group of consumers who respond similarly to a firm's marketing efforts.

market segmentation The process of dividing the market into groups of customers with different needs, wants, or characteristics—who therefore might appreciate products or services geared especially for them.

market share Percentage of a market accounted for by a specific entity.

marketing An organizational function and a set of processes for creating, *capturing,* communicating, and delivering value to customers and for managing customer relationships in ways that benefit the organization and its stakeholders.

marketing channel The set of institutions that transfer the ownership of and move goods from the point of production to the point of consumption; consists of all the institutions and marketing activities in the marketing process.

marketing channel management Also called supply chain management, refers to a set of approaches and techniques firms employ to efficiently and effectively integrate their suppliers.

marketing ethics Refers to those ethical problems that are specific to the domain of marketing.

marketing information system (MkIS) A set of procedures and methods that apply to the regular, planned collection, analysis, and presentation of information that then may be used in marketing decisions.

marketing mix (four Ps) Product, price, place, and promotion—the controllable set of activities that a firm uses to respond to the wants of its target markets.

marketing plan A written document composed of an analysis of the current marketing situation, opportunities and threats for the firm, marketing objectives and strategy specified in terms of the four Ps, action programs, and projected or pro forma income (and other financial) statements.

marketing research A set of techniques and principles for systematically collecting, recording, analyzing, and interpreting data that can aid decision makers involved in marketing goods, services, or ideas.

marketing strategy A firm's target market, marketing mix, and method of obtaining a sustainable competitive advantage.

Maslow's hierarchy of needs A paradigm for classifying people's motives. It argues that when lower-level, more basic needs (physiological and safety) are fulfilled, people turn to satisfying their higher-level human needs (social and personal); see also *physiological, safety, social,* and *personal needs.*

mass customization The practice of interacting on a one-to-one basis with many people to create custom-made products or services; providing one-to-one marketing to the masses.

mass media Channels that are ideal for reaching large numbers of anonymous audience members; include national newspapers, magazines, radio, and television.

maturity stage Stage of the product life cycle when industry sales reach their peak, so firms try to rejuvenate their products by adding new features or repositioning them.

maximizing profits A profit strategy that relies primarily on economic theory. If a firm can accurately specify a mathematical model that captures all the factors required to explain and predict sales and profits, it should be able to identify the price at which its profits are maximized.

M-commerce See *mobile commerce.*

media buy The actual purchase of airtime or print pages.

media mix The combination of the media used and the frequency of advertising in each medium.

media planning The process of evaluating and selecting the *media mix* that will deliver a clear, consistent, compelling message to the intended audience.

metric A measuring system that quantifies a trend, dynamic, or characteristic.

microblog Differs from a traditional blog in size. Consists of short sentences, short videos, or individual images. Twitter is an example of a microblog.

micromarketing An extreme form of segmentation that tailors a product or service to suit an individual customer's wants or needs; also called *one-to-one marketing.*

Millennials See *Generation Y.*

mission statement A broad description of a firm's objectives and the scope of activities it plans to undertake; attempts to answer two main questions: What type of business is it? What does it need to do to accomplish its goals and objectives?

mobile commerce (M-commerce) Communicating with or selling to consumers through wireless handheld devices such as cellular phones.

mobile marketing Marketing through wireless handheld devices.

modified rebuy Refers to when the buyer has purchased a similar product in the past but has decided to change some specifications, such as the desired price, quality level, customer service level, options, or so forth.

monopolistic competition Occurs when there are many firms that sell closely related but not homogeneous products; these products may be viewed as substitutes but are not perfect substitutes.

monopoly One firm provides the product or service in a particular industry.

motive A need or want that is strong enough to cause the person to seek satisfaction.

multi-attribute model A compensatory model of customer decision making based on the notion that customers see a product as a collection of attributes or characteristics. The model uses a weighted average score based on the importance of various attributes and performance on those issues.

multichannel retailers Retailers that sell merchandise in more than one retail channel (e.g., store, catalog, and Internet).

multichannel strategy See *omnichannel strategy.*

need recognition The beginning of the consumer decision process; occurs when consumers recognize they have an unsatisfied need and want to go from their actual, needy state to a different, desired state.

negative word of mouth Occurs when consumers spread negative information about a product, service, or store to others.

new buy In a B2B setting, a purchase of a good or service for the first time; the buying decision is likely to be quite involved because the buyer or the buying organization does not have any experience with the item.

niche media Channels that are focused and generally used to reach narrow segments, often with unique demographic characteristics or interests.

noise Any interference that stems from competing messages, a lack of clarity in the message, or a flaw in the medium; a problem for all communication channels.

noncompensatory decision rule At work when consumers choose a product or service on the basis of a subset of its characteristics, regardless of the values of its other attributes.

noncumulative quantity discount Pricing tactic that offers a discount based on only the amount purchased in a single order; provides the buyer with an incentive to purchase more merchandise immediately.

North American Industry Classification System (NAICS) codes U.S. Bureau of Census classification scheme that categorizes all firms into a hierarchical set of six-digit codes.

objective-and-task method An IMC budgeting method that determines the cost required to undertake specific tasks to accomplish communication objectives; process entails setting objectives, choosing media, and determining costs.

observation An exploratory research method that entails examining purchase and consumption behaviors through personal or video camera scrutiny.

occasion segmentation A type of behavioral segmentation based on when a product or service is purchased or consumed.

odd prices Prices that end in odd numbers, usually 9, such as $3.99.

off-price retailer A type of retailer that offers an inconsistent assortment of merchandise at relatively low prices.

offshoring See *globalization of production*.

oligopolistic competition Occurs when only a few firms dominate a market.

omnichannel (multichannel) strategy Selling in more than one channel (e.g., stores, Internet, catalog).

one-to-one marketing See *micromarketing*.

online chat Instant messaging or voice conversation with an online sales representative.

operational excellence Involves a firm's focus on efficient operations and excellent supply chain management.

opt in The option giving the consumer complete control over the collection and dissemination of his/her personal information, usually referred to in an Internet setting.

opt out The option whereby the consumer must actively choose to prevent personal information from being used or shared with third parties, usually referred to in an Internet setting.

order getter A salesperson whose primary responsibilities are identifying potential customers and engaging those customers in discussions to attempt to make a sale.

order taker A salesperson whose primary responsibility is to process routine orders or reorders or rebuys for products.

organizational culture Reflects the set of values, traditions, and customs that guide a firm's employees' behavior.

outlet stores Off-price retailers that often stock irregulars, out-of-season merchandise, or overstocks from the parent company.

own brands See *private-label brands*.

page view The number of times an Internet page gets viewed by any visitor.

paid apps Apps that charge the customer an up-front price to download the app ($0.99 is the most common), but offer full functionality once downloaded. Similar to the *freemium* mode.

paid apps with in-app purchases Apps that require the consumer to pay initially to download the app and then offer the ability to buy additional functionality.

panel data Information collected from a group of consumers.

panel research A type of quantitative research that involves collecting information from a group of consumers (the panel) over time; data collected may be from a survey or a record of purchases.

perceived value The relationship between a product's or service's benefits and its cost.

perception The process by which people select, organize, and interpret information to form a meaningful picture of the world.

perceptual map Displays, in two or more dimensions, the position of products or brands in the consumer's mind.

performance risk Involves the perceived danger inherent in a poorly performing product or service.

perishability A characteristic of a service: it cannot be stored for use in the future.

personal blog Website written by a person who receives no products or remuneration for his or her efforts.

personal selling The two-way flow of communication between a buyer and a seller that is designed to influence the buyer's purchase decision.

persuasive advertising Communication used to motivate consumers to take action.

physiological needs Those relating to the basic biological necessities of life: food, drink, rest, and shelter.

physiological risk The fear of an actual harm should a product not perform properly.

pick ticket A document or display on a screen in a forklift truck indicating how much of each item to get from specific storage areas.

pioneers New product introductions that establish a completely new market or radically change both the rules of competition and consumer preferences in a market; also called *breakthroughs*.

planners In a retailing context, employees who are responsible for the financial planning and analysis of merchandise, and its allocation to stores.

planning phase The part of the strategic marketing planning process when marketing executives, in conjunction with other top managers (1) define the mission or vision of the business and (2) evaluate the situation by assessing how various players, both in and outside the organization, affect the firm's potential for success.

point-of-purchase (POP) display A merchandise display located at the point of purchase, such as at the checkout counter in a grocery store.

political/regulatory environment Comprises political parties, government organizations, and legislation and laws.

pop-up stores Temporary storefronts that exist for only a limited time and generally focus on a new product or a limited group of products offered by a retailer, manufacturer, or service provider; give consumers a chance to interact with the brand and build brand awareness, but are not designed primarily to sell the product.

postpurchase cognitive dissonance The psychologically uncomfortable state produced by an inconsistency between beliefs and behaviors that in turn evokes a motivation to reduce the dissonance; buyers' remorse.

posttesting The evaluation of an IMC campaign's impact after it has been implemented.

power A situation that occurs in a marketing channel in which one member has the means or ability to have control over the actions of another member in a channel at a different level of distribution, such as if a retailer has power or control over a supplier.

preapproach In the personal selling process, occurs prior to meeting the customer for the first time and extends the qualification of leads procedure; in this step, the salesperson conducts additional research and develops plans for meeting with the customer.

predatory pricing A firm's practice of setting a very low price for one or more of its products with the intent to drive its competition out of business; illegal under both the Sherman Antitrust Act and the Federal Trade Commission Act.

premarket test Conducted before a product or service is brought to market to determine how many customers will try and then continue to use it.

premium An item offered for free or at a bargain price to reward some type of behavior, such as buying, sampling, or testing.

premium pricing A competitor-based pricing method by which the firm deliberately prices a product above the prices set for competing products to capture those consumers who always shop for the best or for whom price does not matter.

prestige products or services Those that consumers purchase for status rather than functionality.

pretesting Assessments performed before an ad campaign is implemented to ensure that the various elements are working in an integrated fashion and doing what they are intended to do.

price The overall sacrifice a consumer is willing to make—money, time, energy—to acquire a specific product or service.

price bundling Consumer pricing tactic of selling more than one product for a single, lower price than what the items would cost sold separately; can be used to sell slow-moving items, to encourage customers to stock up so they won't purchase competing brands, to encourage trial of a new product, or to provide an incentive to purchase a less desirable product or service to obtain a more desirable one in the same bundle.

price discrimination The practice of selling the same product to different resellers (wholesalers, distributors, or retailers) or to the ultimate consumer at different prices; some, but not all, forms of price discrimination are illegal.

price elasticity of demand Measures how changes in a price affect the quantity of the product demanded; specifically, the ratio of the percentage change in quantity demanded to the percentage change in price.

price fixing The practice of colluding with other firms to control prices.

price lining Consumer market pricing tactic of establishing a price floor and a price ceiling for an entire line of similar products and then setting a few other price points in between to represent distinct differences in quality.

price skimming A strategy of selling a new product or service at a high price that *innovators* and *early adopters* are willing to pay in order to obtain it; after the high-price market segment becomes saturated and sales begin to slow down, the firm generally lowers the price to capture (or skim) the next most price sensitive segment.

price war Occurs when two or more firms compete primarily by lowering their prices.

pricing strategy A long-term approach to setting prices for the firms' products.

pricing tactics Short-term methods, in contrast to long-term pricing strategies, used to focus on company objectives, costs, customers, competition, or channel members; can be responses to competitive threats (e.g., lowering price temporarily to meet a competitor's price reduction) or broadly accepted methods of calculating a final price for the customer that is short term in nature.

primary data Data collected to address specific research needs.

primary demand advertising Ads designed to generate demand for the product category or an entire industry.

primary package The packaging the consumer uses, such as the toothpaste tube, from which he or she typically seeks convenience in terms of storage, use, and consumption.

private-label brands Brands developed and marketed by a retailer and available only from that retailer; also called *store brands*.

procedural fairness Refers to the customer's perception of the fairness of the process used to resolve complaints about service.

product Anything that is of value to a consumer and can be offered through a voluntary marketing exchange.

product category An assortment of items that the customer sees as reasonable substitutes for one another.

product design See *product development*.

product development Also called *product design;* entails a process of balancing various engineering, manufacturing, marketing, and economic considerations to develop a product's form and features or a service's features.

product development strategy A growth strategy that offers a new product or service to a firm's current target market.

product excellence Involves a focus on achieving high-quality products; effective branding and positioning is key.

product life cycle Defines the stages that new products move through as they enter, get established in, and ultimately leave the marketplace and thereby offers marketers a starting point for their strategy planning.

product lines Groups of associated items, such as those that consumers use together or think of as part of a group of similar products.

product mix The complete set of all products offered by a firm.

product placement Inclusion of a product in nontraditional situations, such as in a scene in a movie or television program.

product-focused advertisements Used to inform, persuade, or remind consumers about a specific product or service.

professional blog Website written by a person who reviews and gives recommendations on products and services.

profit orientation A company objective that can be implemented by focusing on *target profit pricing, maximizing profits,* or *target return pricing.*

projective technique A type of qualitative research in which subjects are provided a scenario and asked to express their thoughts and feelings about it.

prototype The first physical form or service description of a new product, still in rough or tentative form, that has the same properties as a new product but is produced through different manufacturing processes, sometimes even crafted individually.

psychographic segmentation A method of segmenting customers based on how they spend their time and money, what activities they pursue, and their attitudes and opinions about the world in which they live.

psychographics Used in segmentation; delves into how consumers describe themselves; allows people to describe themselves using those characteristics that help them choose how they occupy their time (behavior) and what underlying psychological reasons determine those choices.

psychological needs Pertain to the personal gratification consumers associate with a product or service.

psychological risk Associated with the way people will feel if the product or service does not convey the right image.

public relations (PR) The organizational function that manages the firm's communications to achieve a variety of objectives, including building and maintaining a positive image, handling or heading off unfavorable stories or events, and maintaining positive relationships with the media.

public service advertising (PSA) Advertising that focuses on public welfare and generally is sponsored by nonprofit institutions, civic groups, religious organizations, trade associations, or political groups; a form of *social marketing.*

puffery The legal exaggeration of praise, stopping just short of deception, lavished on a product.

pull supply chain Strategy in which orders for merchandise are generated at the store level on the basis of demand data captured by point-of-sales terminals.

pulsing (advertising schedule) Combines the continuous and flighting schedules by maintaining a base level of advertising but increasing advertising intensity during certain periods.

purchasing power parity (PPP) A theory that states that if the exchange rates of two countries are in equilibrium, a product purchased in one will cost the same in the other, expressed in the same currency.

pure competition Occurs when different companies sell commodity products that consumers perceive as substitutable; price usually is set according to the laws of supply and demand.

push strategy Designed to increase demand by motivating sellers—wholesalers, distributors, or salespeople—to highlight the product, rather than the products of competitors, and thereby push the product onto consumers.

push supply chain Strategy in which merchandise is allocated to stores on the basis of historical demand, the inventory position at the distribution center, and the stores' needs.

qualify (leads) The process of assessing the potential of sales leads.

qualitative research Informal research methods, including observation, following social media sites, in-depth interviews, focus groups, and projective techniques.

quantitative research Structured responses that can be statistically tested to confirm insights and hypotheses generated via qualitative research or secondary data.

quantity discount Pricing tactic of offering a reduced price according to the amount purchased; the more the buyer purchases, the higher the discount and, of course, the greater the value.

questionnaire A form that features a set of questions designed to gather information from respondents and thereby accomplish the researchers' objectives; questions can be either unstructured or structured.

quick response (QR) inventory system An inventory management system used in retailing; merchandise is received just in time for sale when the customer wants it; see also *just-in-time (JIT) inventory systems.*

quota Designates the maximum quantity of a product that may be brought into a country during a specified time period.

radio frequency identification (RFID) tags Tiny computer chips that automatically transmit to a special scanner all the information about a container's contents or individual products.

reach Measure of consumers' exposure to marketing communications; the percentage of the target population exposed to a specific marketing communication, such as an advertisement, at least once.

rebate A consumer discount in which a portion of the purchase price is returned to the buyer in cash; the manufacturer, not the retailer, issues the refund.

receiver The person who reads, hears, or sees and processes the information contained in the message or advertisement.

receiving The process of recording the receipt of merchandise as it arrives at a distribution center or store.

recession A temporary depression in economic activity or prosperity.

reference group One or more persons whom an individual uses as a basis for comparison regarding beliefs, feelings, and behaviors.

reference price The price against which buyers compare the actual selling price of the product and that facilitates their evaluation process.

referent power A type of marketing channel power that occurs if one channel member wants to be associated with another channel member. The channel member with whom the others wish to be associated has the power and can get them to do what they want.

regional culture The influence of the area within a country in which people live.

related diversification A growth strategy whereby the current target market and/or marketing mix shares something in common with the new opportunity.

relational orientation A method of building a relationship with customers based on the philosophy that buyers and sellers should develop a long-term relationship.

relationship selling A sales philosophy and process that emphasizes a commitment to maintaining the relationship over the long term and investing in opportunities that are mutually beneficial to all parties.

relative market share A measure of the product's strength in a particular market, defined as the sales of the focal product divided by the sales achieved by the largest firm in the industry.

relevance In the context of search engine marketing (SEM), it is a metric used to determine how useful an advertisement is to the consumer.

reminder advertising Communication used to remind consumers of a product or to prompt repurchases, especially for products that have gained market acceptance and are in the maturity stage of their life cycle.

reps See *independent agents*.

request for proposals (RFP) A process through which buying organizations invite alternative suppliers to bid on supplying their required components.

resellers Marketing intermediaries that resell manufactured products without significantly altering their form.

reserve price The price in an auction that is the minimum amount at which a seller will sell an item.

retailer/store brands Products developed by retailers. Also called *private-label brands*.

retailing The set of business activities that add value to products and services sold to consumers for their personal or family use; includes products bought at stores, through catalogs, and over the Internet, as well as services like fast-food restaurants, airlines, and hotels.

retrieval set Includes those brands or stores that the consumer can readily bring forth from memory.

return on investment (ROI) The amount of profit divided by the value of the investment. In the case of an advertisement, the ROI is (Sales revenue generated by ad − Ad's cost) ÷ Ad's cost.

reverse auction The buyer provides specifications to a group of sellers, who then bid down the price until the buyer accepts a specific bid.

reverse engineering Involves taking apart a competitor's product, analyzing it, and creating an improved product that does not infringe on the competitor's patents, if any exist.

reverse innovation When companies initially develop products for niche or underdeveloped markets, and then expand them into their original or home markets.

reward power A type of marketing channel power that occurs when the channel member exerting the power offers rewards to gain power, often a monetary incentive, for getting another channel member to do what it wants it to do.

ritual consumption Refers to a pattern of behaviors tied to life events that affect what and how people consume.

role playing A good technique for practicing the sales presentation prior to meeting with a customer; the salesperson acts out a simulated buying situation while a colleague or manager acts as the buyer.

rule-of-thumb methods Budgeting methods that base the IMC budget on either the firm's share of the market in relation to competition, a fixed percentage of forecasted sales, or what is left after other operating costs and forecasted sales have been budgeted.

safety needs One of the needs in Maslow's hierarchy of needs; pertain to protection and physical well-being.

safety risk See *physiological risk*.

salary Compensation in the form of a fixed sum of money paid at regular intervals.

sales contest A short-term incentive designed to elicit a specific response from the sales force.

sales management Involves the planning, direction, and control of personal selling activities, including recruiting, selecting, training, motivating, compensating, and evaluating, as they apply to the sales force.

sales orientation A company objective based on the belief that increasing sales will help the firm more than will increasing profits.

sales promotions Special incentives or excitement-building programs that encourage the purchase of a product or service, such as coupons, rebates, contests, free samples, and point-of-purchase displays.

sales support personnel Employees who enhance and help with a firm's overall selling effort, such as by responding to the customer's technical questions or facilitating repairs.

sample A group of customers who represent the customers of interest in a research study.

sampling Offers potential customers the opportunity to try a product or service before they make a buying decision.

scanner data A type of syndicated external secondary data used in quantitative research that is obtained from scanner readings of UPC codes at check-out counters.

scanner research A type of quantitative research that uses data obtained from scanner readings of Universal Product Codes (UPCs) at checkout counters.

search engine marketing (SEM) A type of web advertising whereby companies pay for keywords that are used to catch consumers' attention while browsing a search engine.

seasonal discount Pricing tactic of offering an additional reduction as an incentive to retailers to order merchandise in advance of the normal buying season.

secondary data Pieces of information that have already been collected from other sources and usually are readily available.

secondary package The wrapper or exterior carton that contains the primary package and provides the UPC label used by retail scanners; can contain additional product information that may not be available on the primary package.

segmentation, targeting, and positioning (STP) Firms use these processes to identify and evaluate opportunities for increasing sales and profits.

selective demand Demand for a specific brand.

selective demand advertising Ads designed to generate demand for a specific brand, firm, or item.

selective distribution Lies between the intensive and exclusive distribution strategies; uses a few selected customers in a territory.

self-actualization When a person is completely satisfied with his or her life.

self-concept The image a person has of himself or herself; a component of *psychographics*.

self-values Goals for life, not just the goals one wants to accomplish in a day; a component of *psychographics* that refers to overriding desires that drive how a person lives his or her life.

selling teams Combinations of sales specialists whose primary duties are order getting, order taking, or sales support but who work together to service important accounts.

sender The firm from which an IMC message originates; the sender must be clearly identified to the intended audience.

sentiment analysis A technique that allows marketers to analyze data from social media sites to collect consumer comments about companies and their products.

sentiment mining Data gathered by evaluating customer comments posted through social media sites such as Facebook and Twitter.

service Any intangible offering that involves a deed, performance, or effort that cannot be physically possessed; intangible customer benefits that are produced by people or machines and cannot be separated from the producer.

service gap Results when a service fails to meet the expectations that customers have about how it should be delivered.

service quality Customers' perceptions of how well a service meets or exceeds their expectations.

service retailer A firm that primarily sells services rather than merchandise.

share of wallet The percentage of the customer's purchases made from a particular retailer.

shopping products/services Those for which consumers will spend time comparing alternatives, such as apparel, fragrances, and appliances.

showrooming Customers visit a store to touch, feel, and even discuss a product's features with a sales associate, and then purchase it online from another retailer at a lower price.

situational factors Factors affecting the consumer decision process; those that are specific to the situation that may override, or at least influence, psychological and social issues.

situation analysis Second step in a marketing plan; uses a SWOT analysis that assesses both the internal environment with regard to its **S**trengths and **W**eaknesses and the external environment in terms of its **O**pportunities and **T**hreats.

size discount The most common implementation of a quantity discount at the consumer level; the larger the quantity bought, the less the cost per unit (e.g., per ounce).

slotting allowances Fees firms pay to retailers simply to get new products into stores or to gain more or better shelf space for their products.

social marketing The content distributed through online and mobile technologies to facilitate interpersonal interactions.

social media Media content used for social interactions such as YouTube, Facebook, and Twitter.

social reach A metric used to determine to how many people a person influences (e.g., number of individuals in the person's social networks such as Facebook and LinkedIn).

social risk The fears that consumers suffer when they worry others might not regard their purchases positively.

social shopping Using the Internet to communicate about product preferences with other shoppers.

social shoppers Consumers who seek emotional connections through shopping.

specialty products/services Products or services toward which the customer shows a strong preference and for which he or she will expend considerable effort to search for the best suppliers.

specialty store A type of retailer that concentrates on a limited number of complementary merchandise categories in a relatively small store.

standards gap A type of *service gap*; pertains to the difference between the firm's perceptions of customers' expectations and the service standards it sets.

status quo pricing A competitor-oriented strategy in which a firm changes prices only to meet those of competition.

stock keeping units (SKUs) Individual items within each product category; the smallest unit available for inventory control.

store brands See *private-label brands*.

STP See *segmentation, targeting, and positioning*.

straight rebuy Refers to when the buyer or buying organization simply buys additional units of products that have previously been purchased.

strategic alliance A collaborative relationship between independent firms, though the partnering firms do not create an equity partnership; that is, they do not invest in one another.

strategic business unit (SBU) A division of the firm itself that can be managed and operated somewhat independently from other divisions and may have a different mission or objectives.

strategic (partnering) relationship A supply chain relationship that the members are committed to maintaining long term, investing in opportunities that are mutually beneficial; requires mutual trust, open communication, common goals, and credible commitments.

structured questions Closed-ended questions for which a discrete set of response alternatives, or specific answers, is provided for respondents to evaluate.

subhead An additional smaller headline in an ad that provides a great deal of information through the use of short and simple words.

substitute products Products for which changes in demand are negatively related; that is, a percentage increase in the quantity demanded for product A results in a percentage decrease in the quantity demanded for product B.

substitution effect Refers to consumers' ability to substitute other products for the focal brand, thus increasing the price elasticity of demand for the focal brand.

supercenter Large stores combining full-line discount stores with supermarkets in one place.

supply chain The group of firms that make and deliver a given set of goods and services.

supply chain management Refers to a set of approaches and techniques firms employ to efficiently and effectively integrate their suppliers, manufacturers, warehouses, stores, and transportation intermediaries into a seamless value chain in which merchandise is produced and distributed in the right quantities, to the right locations, and at the right time, as well as to minimize systemwide costs while satisfying the service levels their customers require.

survey A systematic means of collecting information from people that generally uses a *questionnaire*.

sustainable competitive advantage Something the firm can persistently do better than its competitors.

sweepstakes A form of sales promotion that offers prizes based on a chance drawing of entrants' names.

SWOT analysis A method of conducting a situation analysis within a marketing plan in which both the internal environment with regard to its **S**trengths and **W**eaknesses and the external environment in terms of its **O**pportunities and **T**hreats are examined.

syndicated data Data available for a fee from commercial research firms such as Information Resources Inc. (IRI), National Purchase Diary Panel, and ACNielsen.

target marketing/targeting The process of evaluating the attractiveness of various segments and then deciding which to pursue as a market.

target profit pricing A pricing strategy implemented by firms when they have a particular profit goal as their overriding concern; uses price to stimulate a certain level of sales at a certain profit per unit.

target return pricing A pricing strategy implemented by firms less concerned with the absolute level of profits and more interested in the rate at which their profits are generated relative to their investments; designed to produce a specific return on investment, usually expressed as a percentage of sales.

tariff A tax levied on a good imported into a country; also called a *duty*.

technological advances Macroenvironmental factor that has greatly contributed to the improvement of the value of both products and services in the past few decades.

telemarketing A method of prospecting in which salespeople telephone potential customers.

test marketing Introduces a new product or service to a limited geographic area (usually a few cities) prior to a national launch.

ticketing and marking Creating price and identification labels and placing them on the merchandise.

top-of-mind awareness A prominent place in people's memories that triggers a response without them having to put any thought into it.

total cost The sum of the *variable* and *fixed costs*.

tracking Includes monitoring key indicators, such as daily or weekly sales volume, while the advertisement is running to shed light on any problems with the message or the medium.

trade agreements Intergovernmental agreements designed to manage and promote trade activities for specific regions.

trade area The geographical area that contains the potential customers of a particular retailer or shopping center.

trade deficit Results when a country imports more goods than it exports.

trade promotion Advertising to wholesalers or retailers to get them to purchase new products, often through special pricing incentives.

trade shows Major events attended by buyers who choose to be exposed to products and services offered by potential suppliers in an industry.

trade surplus Occurs when a country has a higher level of exports than imports.

trading bloc Consists of those countries that have signed a particular trade agreement.

transactional orientation Regards the buyer-seller relationship as a series of individual transactions, so anything that happened before or after the transaction is of little importance.

transmitter An agent or intermediary with which the sender works to develop the marketing communications; for example, a firm's creative department or an advertising agency.

undifferentiated targeting strategy (mass marketing) A marketing strategy a firm can use if the product or service is perceived to provide the same benefits to everyone, with no need to develop separate strategies for different groups.

uniform delivered pricing The shipper charges one rate, no matter where the buyer is located.

unique selling proposition (USP) A strategy of differentiating a product by communicating its unique attributes; often becomes the common theme or slogan in the entire advertising campaign.

Universal Product Code (UPC) The black-and-white bar code found on most merchandise.

universal set Includes all possible choices for a product category.

unrelated diversification A growth strategy whereby a new business lacks any common elements with the present business.

unsought products/services Products or services consumers either do not normally think of buying or do not know about.

unstructured questions Open-ended questions that allow respondents to answer in their own words.

user The person who consumes or uses the product or service purchased by the buying center.

value Reflects the relationship of benefits to costs, or what the consumer *gets* for what he or she *gives*.

Value and Lifestyle Survey (VALS) A psychographic tool developed by SRI Consulting Business Intelligence; classifies consumers into eight segments: innovators, thinkers, believers, achievers, strivers, experiencers, makers, or survivors.

value-based pricing method An approach that focuses on the overall value of the product offering as perceived by consumers, who determine value by comparing the benefits they expect the product to deliver with the sacrifice they will need to make to acquire the product.

value cocreation Customers act as collaborators with a manufacturer or retailer to create the product or service.

value proposition The unique value that a product or service provides to its customers and how it is better than and different from those of competitors.

variability A characteristic of a service: its quality may vary because it is provided by humans.

variable costs Those costs, primarily labor and materials, that vary with production volume.

vendor-managed inventory (VMI) An approach for improving supply chain efficiency in which the manufacturer is responsible for maintaining the retailer's inventory levels in each of its stores.

vertical channel conflict A type of channel conflict in which members of the same marketing channel, for example, manufacturers, wholesalers, and retailers, are in disagreement or discord.

vertical marketing system A supply chain in which the members act as a unified system; there are three types: *administered, contractual,* and *corporate.*

vertical price fixing Occurs when parties at different levels of the same marketing channel (e.g., manufacturers and retailers) collude to control the prices passed on to consumers.

vertical supply chain conflict See *vertical channel conflict.*

viral marketing program A promotional strategy that encourages people to pass along a marketing message to other potential consumers.

virtual community Online networks of people who communicate about specific topics.

voice-of-customer (VOC) program An ongoing marketing research system that collects customer inputs and integrates them into managerial decisions.

warehouse clubs Large retailers with an irregular assortment, low service levels, and low prices that often require membership for shoppers.

web portal An Internet site whose purpose is to be a major starting point for users when they connect to the web.

web tracking software Used to assess how much time viewers spend on particular web pages and the number of pages they view.

wholesalers Those firms engaged in buying, taking title to, often storing, and physically handling goods in large quantities, then reselling the goods (usually in smaller quantities) to retailers or industrial or business users.

zone of tolerance The area between customers' expectations regarding their desired service and the minimum level of acceptable service—that is, the difference between what the customer really wants and what he or she will accept before going elsewhere.

zone pricing The shipper sets different prices depending on a geographic division of the delivery areas.

Quiz Yourself Answer Key

Chapter 1

1. Melanie works for a small computer software company. Her boss is constantly improving the company's products but neglects customers, billing, and promoting of the company. Her boss is probably stuck in the _____ era.

   Answer: (a) production-oriented

2. In delivering value, marketing firms attempt to find the most desirable balance between:

   Answer: (c) the need to provide benefits to customers and the desire to keep down costs

Chapter 2

1. Even when large discount retailers enter a market, a few small, local retailers survive and prosper. These small retailers have probably developed a(n) _____ that allows them to survive.

   Answer: (c) sustainable competitive advantage

2. Many of today's college graduates will make their livings providing goods and services to Baby Boomers, the large group of Americans born in the period after World War II. Baby Boomers are a _____ market segment.

   Answer: (e) demographic

Chapter 3

1. Suppose that Nike wanted to use Facebook to increase awareness of a new line of tennis shoes. Which of the following methods would allow Nike to specifically target Facebook users who have mentioned tennis in their profiles?

   Answer: (c) Placing a Facebook ad.

2. When a company that uses social media runs a contest online, it will measure its effectiveness in a variety of ways. One such measure is the conversion rate. The conversion rate for the contest promotion would be:

   Answer: (d) the percentage of visitors to the page describing the contest who entered the contest

Chapter 4

1. The Johnson & Johnson credo:

   Answer: (e) has guided the firm since it was written in the 1940s.

2. When making decisions, managers often have to decide between doing what is beneficial for them (and possibly the firm) in the short run, and doing what is right and beneficial for the firm and for society in the long run. To address this conflict, a firm must:

   Answer: (d) ensure that long-term goals are aligned with the short-term goals of each individual within the firm

Chapter 5

1. Yuri is considering a new promotional campaign in which he will compare his products to those of his competitors. Before initiating the promotional campaign, Yuri will likely assess his competitors' strengths, weaknesses, and:

   Answer: (a) likely reaction to Yuri's promotional activities.

2. Marketers have learned that culture influences _____ consumers buy.

   Answer: (e) all of the above

Chapter 6

1. The consumer decision process model represents:

   Answer: (c) the steps that consumers go through before, during, and after making purchases

2. A key to successful marketing is determining how to meet the correct balance of _____ needs that best appeals to the firm's target markets.

   Answer: (e) functional and psychological

Chapter 7

1. Compared to the B2C process, the information search and alternative evaluation steps in the B2B process are:

   Answer: (d) more formal and structured

2. After need recognition and product specification, many firms using the B2B buying process:

   Answer: (b) issue a request for proposals from invited suppliers.

Chapter 8

1. The shift of population from rural to urban areas in countries such as India helps global marketers by:

   Answer: (b) simplifying the supply chain needed to make goods and services available

2. Marketers sometimes use Hofstede's cultural dimensions to design marketing campaigns:

   Answer: (d) consistent with underlying cultural values in a country

Chapter 9

1. Four frequently used targeting strategies are micromarketing, undifferentiated, differentiated, and _____.

   Answer: (e) concentrated

2. Television advertising has recently expanded to include "mini-ads," which are short ads lasting 5 to 10 seconds. These ads are most useful in advertising to men, since men are more likely than women to channel surf during commercial breaks. This type of advertising will be more useful to marketers engaged in _____ segmentation.

   Answer: (a) demographic

Chapter 10

1. Walmart is known for its efficient logistical systems. Every time consumers buy something, that purchase is recorded and sent to company headquarters, where it is used to generate reorders to vendors. In addition, customers' billions of purchases are analyzed using data mining techniques to uncover _____.

   Answer: (b) patterns of consumers' purchasing behavior

2. Just as marketers create value by meeting the needs and wants of consumers, marketing researchers create value if _____.

Answer: (d) the results will be used in making management decisions

Chapter 11

1. One key feature of the value of a brand is that _____.

Answer: (a) it often protects the firm from competition and price competition

2. It is almost impossible to watch a sporting event on television without seeing Nike's "swoosh" check mark, which is Nike's _____.

Answer: (b) symbol

Chapter 12

1. The diffusion of innovation theory is useful to marketers in helping them _____.

Answer: (c) predict which types of customers will buy their product immediately and later

2. Inkjet personal computer printers were a big improvement over the dot matrix printers they replaced. Inkjet printers gained rapid acceptance in the marketplace primarily because of their _____.

Answer: (a) relative advantage

Chapter 13

1. When marketers say that services are _____, they are referring to the fact that services cannot be touched, tasted, or seen like a pure product can.

Answer: (a) intangible

2. Cheryl will only let Martiné cut her hair. She has tried other hairstylists, but she knows from experience that Martiné cuts her hair well every time. For Cheryl, _____ is the most important of the five service quality dimensions.

Answer: (b) reliability

Chapter 14

1. Marketers can deliver high value through high or low prices, depending on _____.

Answer: (b) the bundle of benefits the product or service delivers

2. Ferrari and Lamborghini are manufacturers of very expensive automobiles. Their limited edition cars often sell for $300,000 or more. For most consumers, these are prestige products, and demand is likely to be _____.

Answer: (b) price inelastic

Chapter 15

1. When the first hybrid automobiles became available on the market, manufacturers had only minimal production capacity. They used a price skimming strategy primarily to _____.

Answer: (c) limit demand

2. It is important to Joanne to get value for her money, but she does not want to spend time comparison shopping. Joanne will likely respond to _____ pricing but not _____ pricing.

Answer: (e) everyday low; high/low

Chapter 16

1. Which of the following is NOT one of the activities carried on in a distribution center?

Answer: (c) Distributing paychecks and paystubs for retail employees

2. When Cynthia's Boutique receives dresses, they already have price tags and are on hangers. Cynthia's Boutique receives _____ merchandise.

Answer: (a) floor-ready

Chapter 17

1. Retailing is where marketing _____.

Answer: (b) meets the consumer

2. If you were a marketer for a clothing manufacturer and you wanted to improve revenues from irregulars, production overruns, and returns, you would be attracted to using _____.

Answer: (d) off-price retailers

Chapter 18

1. The basic goal of integrated marketing communications is to _____.

Answer: (a) communicate the value proposition to the target market

2. Most manufacturing and retailing marketers worry constantly about whether or not their IMC efforts are paying off. They assess various forms of _____ to determine what is working and what is not.

Answer: (e) feedback

Chapter 19

1. After the advertiser has decided on the message, type of ad, and appeal, its attention now shifts to _____.

Answer: (e) creation of the advertisement

2. Unlike advertising, public relations _____.

Answer: (a) supports promotional efforts by generating "free" media attention

Chapter 20

1. Tana went to Gap ready to buy a new blouse, but was not sure which color or style she wanted. The sales representative, sensing Tana's buying mode, began with the _____ stage of the selling process.

Answer: (e) sales presentation

2. The beginning of the sales presentation may be the most important part of the selling process, because this is where the salesperson establishes _____.

Answer: (a) whether the customer is in the buying process

name index

company/product index

subject index